זוה"ר כעצם השמים לטוהר

ספר הזוהר

על התורה מאיש אלים קדוש הוא נורא
מאד התנא ר' שמעון בן יוחאי ז"ל עם
חדושים רבים : ובה : סתרי תורה :
ומדרש הנעלם : ותוספתא על קצת
פרשיות : והוספנו חדושים על זולתינו
גם על ספר בראשית כל חבור הרעיא
מהימנא : וחדושי הבהיר : ומדרש רות
מדרש חזית : ומאמר תא חזי : והיכלו'
ומורה מקום מהפסוקי : ובסוף הספר
תמצא לוח מפסוקי הפתיחות : ושאר
כל הפסוקים הנדרשים והנכפלים
בהזוהר : גדפס עם רב העיון

בקרימונה

קרית מלך רב : אדוננו המלך פיליפ'
ירה אמן : שנת כי לא יטש
י"י את עמו : ונסתיים
שנת השׁ"ך :

בבית יואן סוויקרזיו וסאנכונוסיטונו
ויכראלו כנראה בסוף ספר

ספר הזהר

The

ZOHAR

ספר הזהר

Pritzker Edition

VOLUME ONE

Translation and Commentary by
Daniel C. Matt

STANFORD UNIVERSITY PRESS
STANFORD, CALIFORNIA

The translation and publication of the Zohar *is made possible through the thoughtful and generous support of the Pritzker Family Philanthropic Fund.*

The administrative support to this project in its initial period by the Graduate Theological Union is gratefully acknowledged.

Stanford University Press
Stanford, California

© 2004 by Zohar Education Project, Inc.
All rights reserved.

For further information, including the Aramaic text of the *Zohar*, please visit www.sup.org/zohar

Library of Congress Cataloging-in-Publication Data

Zohar. English.
   The Zohar/translation and commentary by Daniel C. Matt.–
    Pritzker ed.
    v. cm.
   Text includes some words in Hebrew and Aramaic.
   Includes bibliographical references.
   ISBN 0-8047-4747-4
  1. Bible. O.T. Pentateuch–Commentaries–Early works to 1800.
2. Cabala–Early works to 1800. 3. Zohar. I. Matt, Daniel Chanan.
II. Title.
BM525.A52 M37 2003
296.1'62–dc22   2003014884

Original Printing 2004

Last figure below indicates year of this printing:
13   12   11   10   09   08

Printed in the United States of America
on acid-free, archival-quality paper.

Designed by Rob Ehle
Typeset by El Ot Pre Press & Computing Ltd., Tel Aviv,
in 10.5/14 Minion.

To Margot

Academic Committee

for the Translation of the Zohar

Contents

Diagram of the Ten Sefirot   xi

Foreword
MARGOT PRITZKER   xiii

Translator's Introduction
DANIEL C. MATT   xv

Acknowledgments   xxvi

Introduction
ARTHUR GREEN   xxxi

הקדמת ספר הזהר Haqdamat Sefer ha-Zohar   1

פרשת בראשית Parashat Be-Reshit
(Genesis 1:1–6:8)   107

פרשת נח Parashat Noaḥ
(Genesis 6:9–11:32)   339

Abbreviations   453

Transliteration of Hebrew and Aramaic   457

Glossary   459

Bibliography   463

Index of Sources   485

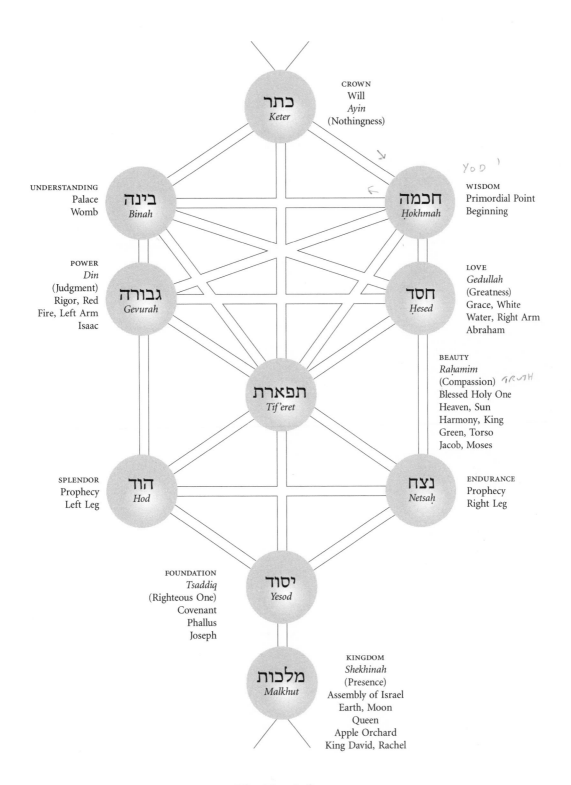

CROWN
Will
Ayin
(Nothingness)

YOD

UNDERSTANDING
Palace
Womb

WISDOM
Primordial Point
Beginning

POWER
Din
(Judgment)
Rigor, Red
Fire, Left Arm
Isaac

LOVE
Gedullah
(Greatness)
Grace, White
Water, Right Arm
Abraham

BEAUTY
Raḥamim
(Compassion)   TRUTH
Blessed Holy One
Heaven, Sun
Harmony, King
Green, Torso
Jacob, Moses

SPLENDOR
Prophecy
Left Leg

ENDURANCE
Prophecy
Right Leg

FOUNDATION
Tsaddiq
(Righteous One)
Covenant
Phallus
Joseph

KINGDOM
Shekhinah
(Presence)
Assembly of Israel
Earth, Moon
Queen
Apple Orchard
King David, Rachel

The Ten Sefirot

Foreword

SOME YEARS AGO, I began to study the Torah. As my facility with the text grew, I pursued the midrashic literature of the rabbis, and the interpretations of the classic medieval commentators. Eventually, I began to inquire about mystical commentaries on the Torah. I turned to the *Zohar,* seeking an English translation of its original Aramaic. I soon learned that previous translations not only were incomplete but also had been undertaken in the early twentieth century. Therefore, they did not reflect the enormous advances in scholarship since made by Gershom Scholem and his students. It was at this point that I realized how much I wanted to be able to study the *Zohar* from an English translation that would draw upon the research and scholarship of the past half-century. I determined to sponsor such a translation; the book you hold in your hands is the result.

By its nature and purpose, the *Zohar* is difficult to penetrate. For hundreds of years it was inaccessible to all but a few. Furthermore, after the Sabbatean episode of the seventeenth century, the Jewish community became concerned about the potency of mystical ideas; leaders were anything but eager to promulgate the *Zohar.* Even with the rise of Hasidism as a mystically based movement starting in the eighteenth century, the *Zohar* remained a closed book. Consequently, bringing the *Zohar* to the English-reading public was—and continues to be—a complex, challenging task.

The words that can express my appreciation to Daniel C. Matt are found on every page of his translation of the *Zohar.* His scholarship, his artistry, and his poetry speak for themselves. You, the reader, are in his debt.

The odyssey of the past nine years, which will continue for some years to come, has been shepherded through a tangle of legal and administrative steps with the able and devoted skill of Glen Miller.

Professor Arthur Green, who co-chairs the Academic Committee for the Translation of the *Zohar,* has been a thoughtful and faithful counselor from the inception of the project.

My husband Tom, while not a student of the *Zohar,* recognized the magnitude and the importance of this project. He has kept us ever vigilant and focused with his insightful questions and thoughts and his constant support.

From conception through gestation and finally to birth, this project would not have been realized without the wisdom, knowledge, and nurturing of Rabbi Yehiel Poupko. He is my teacher and my friend, and it is to him that this edition of the *Zohar* is dedicated.

It is with a sense of fulfillment and awe for Daniel Matt's remarkable accomplishment that my family and I now present the *Zohar* to the English-reading public, with the hope that the radiance that flows from this great work and from the Jewish mystical tradition will bring light to those who seek it.

Margot Pritzker

Translator's Introduction

DANIEL C. MATT

SEFER HA-ZOHAR (The Book of Radiance)[1] has amazed and overwhelmed readers ever since it emerged mysteriously in medieval Spain (Castile) toward the end of the thirteenth century. Written mostly in a unique Aramaic, this master-piece of Kabbalah exceeds the dimensions of a normal book; it is virtually a body of literature, comprising over twenty discrete sections. The bulk of the *Zohar* consists of a running commentary on the Torah, from Genesis through Deuteronomy. This translation begins and focuses there—in what are projected to be ten volumes; two subsequent volumes will cover other, shorter sections.[2]

Arthur Green's introduction to this volume traces the development of Kabbalah and discusses the historical and literary context of the *Zohar*, its style, the complex question of authorship, and the symbolism of the ten *sefirot* (various aspects of the divine Self). Here I wish to treat several topics directly related to this translation and commentary.

Establishing the Text of the Zohar

This edition reflects a newly constructed, precise text of the *Zohar*, based on original manuscripts. Why was the creation of such a text necessary? All previous translations of the *Zohar* are based on the standard printed editions, which nearly all derive from the Mantua edition (1558–60), supplemented by variant readings from the Cremona edition (1559–60). At first I intended to

---

1. The title derives from the word זהר (*zohar*) in Daniel 12:3: *The enlightened will shine like the* zohar, *radiance* [or: *splendor*], *of the sky.*

2. On the various sections of the *Zohar*, see Gershom Scholem, *Kabbalah*, 214–19; Isaiah Tishby, *Wisdom of the Zohar*, 1:1–7. All of these sections are written in Aramaic, except for *Midrash ha-Ne'lam*, which is written in Hebrew and Aramaic.

The following sections are scheduled to be translated as part of the running commentary on the Torah, as in the standard editions of the *Zohar*: *Raza de-Razin, Sava de-Mishpatim, Sifra di-Tsni'uta, Idra Rabba, Idra Zuta, Rav Metivta,* and *Yanuqa.* The two subsequent volumes will include *Midrash ha-Ne'lam, Matnitin, Tosefta, Sitrei Torah, Heikhalot, Sitrei Otiyyot,* "Vision of Ezekiel," *Qav ha-Middah,* and *Zohar* to Song of Songs. Two sections identified as imitations written by a later kabbalist, *Tiqqunei ha-Zohar* and *Ra'aya Meheimna,* are not planned to be included.

follow the same procedure, but upon examining many of the original manuscripts of the *Zohar* dating from the fourteenth through sixteenth centuries, I discovered a significant number of superior readings that had been rejected or revised by editors of the first printed editions.

Upon further examination, I noticed something more intriguing—a phenomenon familiar to scholars of medieval texts. Within the manuscripts themselves were signs of an editorial process: revision, reformulation, and emendation.[3] After careful analysis, I concluded that certain manuscripts of older lineage reflect an earlier version of the *Zohar*, which was then reworked in manuscripts of later lineage.[4]

I realized that I could no longer rely on the printed editions of the *Zohar*, since these obscured earlier versions. So I took it upon myself to reconstruct a new-ancient version of the Aramaic text based on the manuscripts, one which could serve as the foundation for this translation.

If I could have located a complete, reliable manuscript of the *Zohar*, this would have provided a starting point. Unfortunately no such manuscript exists anywhere in the world; in all likelihood it never did, since from the start the *Zohar* was circulated in sections or booklets. Probably no single complete *Book of the Zohar* existed until it was printed nearly three hundred years later in the sixteenth century, collated from various manuscripts.[5]

3. See Ernst Goldschmidt, *Medieval Texts and Their First Appearance in Print*; Malachi Beit-Arié, "Transmission of Texts by Scribes and Copyists: Unconscious and Critical Interferences"; Israel Ta-Shma, "The 'Open' Book in Medieval Hebrew Literature: The Problem of Authorized Editions"; Daniel Abrams, introduction to *Sefer ha-Bahir*, edited by idem, 8–14; idem, "Critical and Post-Critical Textual Scholarship of Jewish Mystical Literature."

4. Among the manuscripts reflecting an earlier version are the following: Cambridge, University Library, MS Add. 1023; Munich, Bayerische Staatsbibliothek, Cod. Hebr. 217; New York, Jewish Theological Seminary, MS 1761; Oxford, Bodleian Library, MS 1564; Paris, Bibliothèque nationale, heb. 779; Rome, Biblioteca Casanatense, MS 2971; Toronto, University of Toronto, MS Friedberg 5-015; Vatican, Biblioteca Apostolica, ebr. 206, 208. Manuscripts resembling (and perhaps underlying) the Mantua edition include: London, British Museum, MS 762; Paris, Bibliothèque nationale, heb. 781; Parma, Perreau 15/A.

A list of eighty-four *Zohar* manuscripts (assembled by a team working under Rivka Schatz-Uffenheimer) was published by Zvia Rubin in "Mif'al ha-Zohar: Mattarot ve-Hessegim," 172–73. Ronit Meroz of Tel Aviv University is conducting a systematic analysis of over six hundred extant manuscripts and fragments of the *Zohar*. In her extensive research she has identified numerous examples of editing and revision. While the discovery noted here of earlier and later versions of the *Zohar* is my own, I have benefited from discussions with her and wish to thank her for sharing her insights with me. See her article "Zoharic Narratives and Their Adaptations" and her other studies listed in the Bibliography.

For further information on the manuscripts of the *Zohar*, see Tishby, *Wisdom of the Zohar*, 1:99–101; Scholem, *Kabbalah*, 236–37; and the comments of Malachi Beit-Arié, cited by Ta-Shma, *Ha-Nigleh she-ba-Nistar*, 103–4.

5. See Abrams, "Eimatai Ḥubberah ha-Haqdamah le-Sefer ha-Zohar?"; idem, "Critical and Post-Critical Textual Scholarship of Jewish Mystical Literature," 61.

This situation left me with two choices. I could select the best manuscript for each individual Torah portion of the *Zohar* and produce a "diplomatic" text, an exact reproduction of the original. Or, I could fashion a critical text, selecting from a wide range of variants in different manuscripts.

After consulting with members of our Academic Committee for the Translation of the *Zohar,* I chose to compose a critical text, based on a selection and evaluation of the manuscript readings. The primary reason was simply that even for individual sections of the *Zohar* there is no one "best" manuscript: each has its own deficiencies and scribal errors. Back in the sixteenth century, the editors in Mantua and Cremona also fashioned critical texts, the former drawing on ten manuscripts, the latter on six.[6]

For the first two volumes of the translation, I identified approximately twenty reliable manuscripts, based on the criteria of provenance, age, lack of scribal errors, and legibility. The originals are preserved in the libraries of Oxford, Cambridge, London, Paris, Munich, Rome, the Vatican, Parma, Toronto, and the Jewish Theological Seminary, while microfilm copies are available in the Institute for Microfilmed Hebrew Manuscripts, in the Jewish National and University Library on the campus of the Hebrew University, Jerusalem.[7]

It is appropriate to describe more fully the methodology used in this scholarly undertaking. My research assistant meticulously combs through about half of these manuscripts and prepares a list of variant readings. For particularly difficult words or phrases, we check additional manuscripts. In addition to the manuscripts, my assistant lists variants from the Mantua and Cremona editions of the *Zohar,* as well as the edition used by Moses Cordovero in his sixteenth-century commentary, *Or Yaqar.*[8]

My procedure for establishing the Aramaic text is as follows. I begin with Reuven Margaliot's edition of *Sefer ha-Zohar,*[9] based on the Vilna edition, which in turn is based on the Mantua edition. This represents a relatively reliable starting point. In front of me I have the list of variants prepared by my research assistant, photocopies of the original manuscripts, and other witnesses referred to previously.[10] I peruse the variants line by line. Some of these are

6. See Tishby, *Wisdom of the Zohar,* 1:98. For an enlightening comparison of diplomatic and critical editing, see Chaim Milikowsky, "Further on Editing Rabbinic Texts."

7. See the list of *Zohar* manuscripts in the Bibliography, and above, note 4. Bound copies of nearly all of these manuscripts are housed in the Gershom Scholem Collection, Jewish National and University Library.

8. I also check readings in other sources including: Menaḥem Recanati, *Peirush al ha-Torah;* Joseph Angelet, *Livnat ha-Sappir;* Abraham Galante, in *Or ha-Ḥammah;* Shim'on Lavi, *Ketem Paz;* Abraham Azulai, *Or ha-Levanah;* Joseph Ḥamiẓ, ed., *Derekh Emet* (a list of emendations to the Mantua edition); Shalom Buzaglo, *Miqdash Melekh;* Yehudah Ashlag, *Peirush ha-Sullam;* and *Gershom Scholem's Annotated Zohar.* See the Bibliography.

9. *Sefer ha-Zohar,* ed. Reuven Margaliot.

10. See above, note 8.

simply scribal errors or glosses, but some represent what appear to be better readings. When I identify an apparently better reading, I check if it is shared and confirmed by several reliable manuscripts and witnesses. If it is, I consider substituting it for the printed text.

Over the centuries, *Sefer ha-Zohar* has been revised by countless scribes and editors who tried to smooth away the rough edges of the text by adding an explanatory phrase, correcting an apparent syntactical mistake, or taming a wild neologism by substituting a more familiar, bland term. Often, relying on the variants, I decide to remove these accumulated layers of revision, thereby restoring a more original text. I seek to recover the *Zohar*'s primal texture and cryptic flavor.

If the early manuscripts preserve unusual, striking wording that is revised or "corrected" by several later manuscripts and the printed editions, I tend to go with the older reading. Often, according to the more reliable manuscripts, a Zoharic rabbi creatively paraphrases a Talmudic saying. Some of the later manuscripts and the printed editions may then restore this saying to its exact Talmudic form. In such cases I emend the printed text in favor of the *Zohar*'s original formulation—original in both senses: older and creative. In the commentary I cite the Talmudic saying on which the paraphrase is based, so that readers can see the transition and trace the imaginative process.

I do not claim to be fully restoring "*the* original text of the *Zohar*." There may never have been any such thing, since the text probably emerged over many years, written and distributed piecemeal. However, through painstaking analysis of the variants, I am able to scrape away some seven hundred years of accretion and corruption, and at least approach that elusive, hypothetical original. This Aramaic text of the *Zohar*, the basis of my translation, is available for study and scholarly examination.[11]

Translation and Commentary

All translation is inherently inadequate, a well-intentioned betrayal. In the words of the second-century sage Rabbi Yehudah, "One who translates a verse literally is a liar; one who adds to it is a blasphemer."[12] Furthermore, the *Zohar* is notoriously obscure—perhaps the most difficult Jewish classic to translate. It was composed in Castile mostly in Aramaic, a language no longer spoken in medieval Spain.[13] The author(s) concocted a unique blend of Aramaic out of traditional sources, especially the Babylonian Talmud and *Targum Onqelos* (an

---

11. At the website of Stanford University Press: www.sup.org/zohar.

12. BT *Qiddushin* 49a.

13. On the *Zohar*'s Aramaic, see Scholem, *Kabbalah*, 226–29; Tishby, *Wisdom of the Zohar*, 1:64–68.

Aramaic translation of the Torah). This unparalleled neo-Aramaic is peppered with enigmatic expressions, puns, outlandish constructions, puzzling neologisms, solecisms, and traces of medieval Hebrew and Castilian.

The *Zohar*'s prose is poetic, overflowing with multiple connotations, composed in such a way that you often cannot pin down the precise meaning of a phrase. The language befits the subject matter, which is mysterious, elusive, and ineffable; words can merely suggest and hint. An unfathomable process may be stated, then immediately denied: "It split and did not split its aura."[14] Occasionally we encounter oxymorons, such as "new-ancient words," alluding to the dual nature of the *Zohar*'s secrets, recently composed yet ascribed to ancient sources.[15] The first impulse of divine emanation is described as בוצינא דקרדינותא (*botsina de-qardinuta*), "a spark of impenetrable darkness,"[16] so intensely bright that it cannot be seen.

Through the centuries, the potency of the *Zohar*'s language has mesmerized even those who could not plumb its secrets. While kabbalists delved deeply, the uninitiated chanted the lyrical Aramaic, often unaware of its literal meaning. In the words of an eighteenth-century mystic, "Even if one does not understand, the language is suited to the soul."[17]

No doubt it is risky to translate the *Zohar,* but it would be worse to leave these gems of wisdom buried in their ancient Aramaic vault. So I have plunged in, seeking to transmit some of the *Zohar*'s magic. The previous English translation (composed in the 1930s by Harry Sperling, Maurice Simon, and Paul Levertoff) reads smoothly but often misunderstands the text.[18] Its genteel prose is more a paraphrase than an accurate translation—avoiding unfamiliar terms, censoring erotic material, skipping difficult passages and even entire sections. The English flows too fluently compared to the original, subduing the unruly Aramaic, failing to render its untamed vibrancy. Moreover, since the translation is unaccompanied by a commentary, the symbolism remains impenetrable.

Despite its shortcomings, I have learned much from consulting this translation, along with others.[19] But my approach is significantly different. Though I wish to make the *Zohar* accessible, I also want to convey its strangeness,

---

14. *Zohar* 1:15a. Citations of the *Zohar* refer to the standard Aramaic pagination (based on the Mantua edition of 1558–60), which in *The Zohar: Pritzker Edition* is indicated in the running head on each page.

15. See Daniel Matt, "'New-Ancient Words': The Aura of Secrecy in the *Zohar*."

16. *Zohar* 1:15a.

17. Moses Ḥayyim Luzzatto, in his preface to *Qelaḥ Pitḥei Ḥokhmah,* cited by Tishby, *Wisdom of the Zohar,* 1:29.

18. This five-volume edition is entitled *The Zohar* (see Bibliography). Scholem remarks (*Kabbalah,* 241) that it "suffers from incomplete or erroneous understanding of many parts of the kabbalistic exposition."

19. I have also consulted four different Hebrew translations, by Yehudah Ashlag, Daniel Frisch, Yehudah Edri, and Yechiel Bar-Lev; Charles Mopsik's French translation, *Le Zohar;*

potency, and rich ambiguity. Here the commentary is essential. When the translation cannot adequately express a multifaceted phrase, I unfold the range of meaning in the commentary. When the translation is as cryptic as the original Aramaic, the commentary rescues the stranded reader.

My style of translation is literal yet poetic. I am convinced that a literal rendering of the *Zohar* is not only the most accurate but also the most colorful and zestful—the best way to transmit the lyrical energy of the Aramaic. Still, at times, the multivalent language invites a certain freedom of expression. Let me cite two related examples. In *Zohar* 1:83a, Rabbi Shim'on describes the night-time journey of the soul, soaring skyward from her sleeping body: "Flying, she encounters those קומרין טהירין (*qumrin tehirin*) of defilement."

What does this bizarre term mean? The Sperling-Simon translation renders it as "certain bright but unclean essences."[20] The English translation of Tishby's *Wisdom of the Zohar* reads: "the deceiving lights of uncleanness,"[21] while Tishby's original Hebrew translation reads a bit differently: קימורי נגוהות (*qimmurei negohot*)—roughly: "vaulted splendors"—though in his note he acknowledges that the meaning is "doubtful."[22] I render the sentence as follows: "Flying, she encounters those hooded, hunchbacked, dazzling demons of defilement." The accompanying commentary explains that these are malevolent forces who block the ascent of an unworthy soul. *Qumrin* derives via rabbinic usage from the Greek *qamara*, "arched cover," while *tehirin* is a cognate of the Aramaic *tihara*, meaning "brightness, noon." One class of demons is named *tiharei*, "noonday demons."

The virtuous soul who evades these demons reaches heaven and receives a divine message. According to another Zoharic passage (1:130a), while descending back to her sleeping earthbound body, the soul is assailed by חבילי טריקין (*havilei teriqin*). The Sperling-Simon translation renders this phrase as "malignant bands."[23] The English translation of Tishby's *Wisdom of the Zohar* reads: "ill-intentioned destructive powers."[24] I render it as "ravaging bands of truculent stingers." The commentary explains that *havilei* derives from either *hevel*, "band, group," or the verb *hvl*, "to injure, destroy." *Teriqin* derives from the root *trq*, "to sting, bite."

---

the Hebrew anthology by Fischel Lachower and Isaiah Tishby, *Mishnat ha-Zohar*, and its English version, *The Wisdom of the Zohar*, trans. David Goldstein; and the recent English translation edited by Michael Berg, *The Zohar by Rabbi Shimon bar Yochai*, which, however, is based not on the original Aramaic but on Ashlag's Hebrew translation. For details on all of these, see the Bibliography.

20. *The Zohar*, trans. Harry Sperling and Maurice Simon, 1:277.

21. Tishby, *Wisdom of the Zohar*, trans. Goldstein, 2:818.

22. Idem, *Mishnat ha-Zohar*, 2:134. He concludes by saying that the phrase may mean: "delusive lights."

23. *The Zohar*, trans. Sperling and Simon, 2:19.

24. Tishby, *Wisdom of the Zohar*, trans. Goldstein, 2:813.

Although the *Zohar*'s basic vocabulary is limited, its roots generate a rich variety of meanings. For example, the root תקן (*tqn*) spans the following range: "establish, institute, mend, restore, correct, perfect, prepare, arrange, array, adorn." The root סלק (*slq*) can mean: "rise, raise, culminate, attain, surpass, depart, disappear, die, remove, postpone, reserve, emit (fragrance)." In normal Aramaic and Hebrew, the specific verbal conjugation determines which meaning of the root applies, but the *Zohar* ignores or flouts rules of grammar—confusing the conjugations, playing with multiple meanings, often leaving the reader stumped and wondering.

Mysticism strives to penetrate a realm beyond distinctions, but this mystical masterpiece demands constant decision making, challenging the reader or translator to navigate between conflicting meanings and determine the appropriate one—or sometimes to discover how differing meanings pertain simultaneously. The frequent dilemmas of interpretation suggest that in exploring the *Zohar*, linguistic search and spiritual search go hand in hand.

Especially puzzling, though charming, are the neologisms strewn throughout the *Zohar*, intended to bewilder and astound the reader.[25] Some derive from rare Talmudic terms, which the author refashions by intentionally misspelling or by inverting letters; some derive from Greek, Latin, or Castilian; some appear to be pure inventions. These nonce words often contain the letters ט (*tet*), ס (*samekh*), פ (*pe*), ק (*qof*), and ר (*resh*) in various combinations: קוספיתא (*quspita*), קטפירא (*qatpira*), קירטא (*qirta*), קסירא (*qesira*), קוסטרא (*qustera*), טופסרא (*tufsera*). *Qustera* derives from the Latin word *castrum* (plural, *castra*), "fortress, castle." *Qatpira* and its variations mean several things, including "knot" (based on Aramaic קטרא [*qitra*]) and "waterskin."[26]

One newly coined noun, טיקלא (*tiqla*), is particularly versatile. In various contexts it can mean "scale, hollow of the hand, fist, potter's wheel, and water clock." This last sense refers to a device described in ancient and medieval scientific literature, which in the *Zohar* functions as an alarm clock, calibrated to wake kabbalists precisely at midnight for the ritual study of Torah.[27] A similar device was employed in Christian monasteries to rouse monks for their vigils. How appropriate to invent a word for an invention!

Often, by pondering the context, comparing Zoharic and rabbinic parallels, and scouring sundry dictionaries and lexicons, one can decipher or at least conjecture the meaning of these weird terms, but some remain as perplexing as originally intended.[28]

25. See Tishby, *Wisdom of the Zohar*, 1:66–67.

26. See Yehuda Liebes, *Peraqim be-Millon Sefer ha-Zohar*, 349–54.

27. See *Zohar* 1:92b and my commentary.

28. After wrestling with Zoharic neologisms for years, I no longer share Tishby's view (*Wisdom of the Zohar*, 1:66) that "only rarely is it possible to determine their meaning from the context, while for the most part it is difficult even to guess what the author had in

In translating biblical citations, I have consulted various translations but generally composed my own.[29] Sometimes, in quoting a verse, the *Zohar* intends a meaning different from that conveyed by any known translation. In such cases I usually translate the verse as the *Zohar* understands it and then explain the difference in the commentary.

The main purpose of the commentary is to clarify the dense symbolism and unique terminology. Here I seek to elicit the meaning of the text, drawing it forth from the *Zohar*'s own language without being heavy-handed—without ruining the subtlety and ambiguity of the original. Remember that the *Zohar* was not intended to be easily understood but rather to be deciphered. I want to allow and compel the reader to wrestle with the text. Over the centuries, the tendency has grown to overinterpret, with commentators often insisting on assigning sefirotic significance to nearly every image and metaphor. I have resisted this tendency, while still identifying sefirotic correspondences when they are called for. Often a phrase or passage implies more than one meaning; the reader is encouraged to ponder various possibilities.

To clarify the context, I cite sources and parallels from the Bible, rabbinic literature, and the *Zohar* itself, with occasional references to secondary literature. The aim is not to overwhelm the reader by citing everything conceivable, but rather to provide what is needed to make sense of this enigmatic work of art.[30]

In composing the commentary, I have drawn on numerous traditional and modern *Zohar* commentaries, especially those of Moses Cordovero, Shim'on Lavi, Ḥayyim Vital, Abraham Galante, Shalom Buzaglo, Yehudah Ashlag, Charles Mopsik, and Daniel Frisch.[31] Other valuable resources include the annotations of Reuven Margaliot (*Nitsotsei Zohar*) in his edition of the *Zohar*, Isaiah Tishby's monumental *Mishnat ha-Zohar* (The Wisdom of the *Zohar*), Gershom Scholem's *Annotated Zohar*, and Yehuda Liebes's eye-opening *Peraqim be-Millon Sefer ha-Zohar* (Sections of the *Zohar* Lexicon).

A glossary, bibliography, and an index of biblical and rabbinic citations are appended to each volume. A diagram of the ten *sefirot* appears on page xi of

---

mind." Still, I can appreciate the confession of David Goldstein (translator of *Wisdom of the Zohar*), who, after rendering several obscure lines directly from the Aramaic, writes (ibid., 106, n. 16): "The English translations given are purely hypothetical."

29. Translations I have consulted include the King James Version, New International Version, New Revised Standard Version, the *JPS Hebrew-English Tanakh*, Everett Fox's *The Five Books of Moses*, and Richard Elliott Friedman's *Commentary on the Torah with a New English Translation*.

30. I have tried to follow the sage advice of Samuel Sandmel, who years ago warned scholars about the dangers of "parallelomania." See his presidential address of that title delivered to the Society of Biblical Literature and Exegesis and published in *Journal of Biblical Literature* 81 (1962): 1–13.

31. See the Bibliography.

this volume. The standard Aramaic pagination of the *Zohar* is indicated in the running head on each page (e.g., 1:34b).

How to Read the Zohar

There is no single right way to read and proceed through the *Zohar*, but I can point out certain features and suggest several guidelines.

First of all, the *Zohar* is dynamic—full of surprises. Typically we find that "Rabbi Ḥiyya and Rabbi Yose were walking on the way," wandering through the hills of Galilee, sharing secrets of Torah—but also moving from one dimension to another, accompanied by *Shekhinah*, the Divine Presence Herself. Who knows whom they will encounter on the road? A child amazes them with wisdom, a beggar enriches them with precious teachings, a cantankerous old donkey-driver turns out to be a sage in disguise.

You are about to enter an enchanted realm. Still, although the *Zohar* sometimes reads like a mystical novel, remember that this is fundamentally a biblical commentary. It's helpful to have a Bible at hand to check the original context, to see how a particular verse becomes a springboard for the imagination. Every few pages we read: "Rabbi Ḥiyya opened," "Rabbi Yose opened," signifying that he is opening not only his exposition but also the verse: disclosing new layers of meaning, expanding the range of interpretation. The reader of the *Zohar* should be open, too—open to new ways of thinking and imagining. As the *Ḥavrayya* (Companions) continually exclaim, "Come and see!"

The *Zohar* is firmly rooted in tradition but thrives on discovery. "This verse has been discussed, but come and see!" "This verse has been established, but come and see!"[32] "Innovations of Torah are required here!"[33] Innovation emerges through scrutinizing the biblical text, so questioning becomes a supreme value. After Rabbi Ḥizkiyah asks Rabbi Abba a challenging question, we are told that "Rabbi Abba came and kissed him."[34] Why? Because, as one commentator notes here, "The question is half the answer; without a question, there is no reason for an answer."[35]

Even when the meaning of a verse is perfectly clear, the *Zohar* may question its structure, sometimes probing so deeply that the reader is stunned. To take an extreme example, come and see how Rabbi El'azar deals with the concluding verse in the story of the Garden of Eden, which could hardly be more explicit: *He drove out Adam.*[36] "We do not know who divorced whom: if the blessed

---

32. *Zohar* 1:56b, 112a, 136a, and frequently.

33. Ibid., 155b.

34. Ibid., 155a.

35. Abraham Galante, in *Or ha-Ḥammah*, ad loc. On questioning in the *Zohar*, see Matt, "New-Ancient Words," 198–99.

36. Genesis 3:24. Literally, *He drove out the human.*

Holy One divorced Adam, or not."[37] As the rabbi demonstrates by exegetical artifice, the mystical meaning is the shocking alternative lurking within that bland phrase, "or not": Adam *drove out,* divorced *Shekhinah,* splitting Her from Her divine partner, *Tif'eret,* and from himself. Once, as Adam, humanity was wedded to God. The original sin lies in losing intimacy with the divine, thereby constricting unbounded awareness. This loss follows inevitably from tasting the fruit of discursive knowledge; it is the price we pay for maturity and culture. The spiritual challenge is to search for that lost treasure—without renouncing the self or the world.

As you read, see how the *Ḥavrayya* coax new meaning out of a biblical verse, phrase, word—or even letter. Often, they rely on standard rabbinic techniques of interpretation, such as verbal analogy: "Here is written: [such-and-such a biblical expression], and there is written: [an identical (or nearly identical) expression]," implying a close link between the two expressions.

The hermeneutical leap may be long, far from the literal meaning, but sometimes a verse is read "hyperliterally," ignoring idiomatic usage in favor of a radically spiritual sense. For example, when God commands Abraham, לך לך (*Lekh lekha*), *Go forth, . . . to the land that I will show you* (Genesis 12:1), Rabbi El'azar insists on reading the words more literally than they were intended: *Lekh lekha, Go to yourself!*[38] Search deep within to discover your true self.

Another startling illustration is the *Zohar's* reading of the opening words of the Torah, traditionally rendered: *In the beginning God created.* Everyone assumes the verse describes the creation of the world, but for the *Zohar* it alludes to a more primal beginning: the emanation of the *sefirot* from *Ein Sof* ("Infinity"). How is this allusion discovered, or invented? By insisting on reading the Hebrew words in their precise order: בראשית ברא אלהים (*Bereshit bara Elohim*), construed now as *With beginning, It created Elohim*—that is, by means of *Ḥokhmah* (the *sefirah* of "Wisdom," known as *beginning*), *It* (ineffable *Ein Sof*) emanated *Binah* (the *sefirah* of "Understanding," known by the divine name *Elohim*).[39] *God,* it turns out, is the object of the verse, not the subject! The ultimate divine reality, *Ein Sof,* transcends and explodes our comfortable conception of "God." The *Zohar* dares us to confront this reality, as it transforms the familiar story of Creation into divine biography.

So, as you undertake this adventure, expect to be surprised—stay alert. The *Zohar's* teachings are profound and intense; one who hopes to enter and emerge in peace should be careful, persevering, simultaneously receptive and active. The message is not served to you on a platter; you must engage the text

---

37. *Zohar* 1:53b.
38. Ibid., 78a.
39. Ibid., 15a.

and join the search for meaning. Follow the words to what lies beyond and within; open the gates of imagination.

Above all, don't reduce everything you encounter in these pages to something you already know. Beware of trying to find "the essence" of a particular teaching. Although usually essence is the goal of mystical search, here essence is inadequate unless it stimulates you to explore ever deeper layers, to question your assumptions about tradition, God, and self. In the words of a Zoharic parable:

> There was a man who lived in the mountains. He knew nothing about those who lived in the city. He sowed wheat and ate the kernels raw. One day he entered the city. They offered him good bread. The man asked, "What's this for?"
>
> They replied, "It's bread, to eat!"
>
> He ate, and it tasted very good. He asked, "What's it made of?"
>
> They answered, "Wheat."
>
> Later they offered him thick loaves kneaded with oil. He tasted them, and asked, "And what are these made of?"
>
> They answered, "Wheat."
>
> Later they offered him royal pastry kneaded with honey and oil. He asked, "And what are these made of?"
>
> They answered, "Wheat."
>
> He said, "Surely I am the master of all of these, since I eat the essence of all of these: wheat!"
>
> Because of that view, he knew nothing of the delights of the world, which were lost on him. So it is with one who grasps the principle but is unaware of all those delectable delights deriving, diverging from that principle.[40]

xxv

---

40. *Zohar* 2:176a–b. The wheat and its products (kernels, bread, cake, and pastry) may symbolize four levels of meaning in Torah: simple, homiletical, allegorical, and mystical. See Matt, *The Essential Kabbalah,* 207.

TO THANK ALL the people who have helped me begin to plumb the *Zohar* would burst this book's binding. So here I will briefly trace my path and acknowledge some of those who have helped me along the way.

My father, of blessed memory, Rabbi Hershel Jonah Matt, taught me that God is real, and that by studying Torah you can experience *Shekhinah,* the Divine Presence. (I have sketched his life and assembled his writings in *Walking Humbly with God.*) My mother, Gustine, has always been a fountain of love and a source of strength; I am grateful for her deep wisdom.

I first ventured into *Sefer ha-Zohar* in 1970 during my junior year abroad at Hebrew University in Jerusalem. The thick volumes were simultaneously forbidding and alluring; deciphering the Aramaic text was a puzzle, a challenge, a quest. Soon I fell in love with the *Zohar,* captivated by its lush imagery and poetic magic. My teachers that year in Kabbalah included Joseph Dan, Efraim Gottlieb, and Rivka Schatz-Uffenheimer—and a kabbalist, Rav Toledano. I thank them all for guiding me into the orchard.

From Jerusalem I returned to Brandeis University, where I completed my undergraduate degree and then, after some European travel, plunged into graduate study in Jewish mysticism with Alexander Altmann, a superb *Wissenschaft* scholar and a gem of a man. He directed my doctoral dissertation, which consisted of a critical edition of *The Book of Mirrors,* a previously unpublished fourteenth-century Hebrew commentary on the Torah by David ben Judah he-Ḥasid. I chose to edit this text because it included the first extended translations of the *Zohar,* from Aramaic to Hebrew. I was encouraged to undertake this project by Gershom Scholem, while serving as his teaching assistant in the fall of 1975.

After I completed my dissertation, my friend Arthur Green invited me to compose an annotated translation of selections from the *Zohar* for the Paulist Press, as one volume in their *Classics of Western Spirituality.* Years earlier, Art had initiated me into the mystical thought of Hasidism, which stimulated me to uncover its roots in the *Zohar.* I am grateful for his insight and guidance over the years, and for demonstrating how to combine scholarship and spirituality.

For two decades, I taught Jewish mysticism in Berkeley at the Graduate Theological Union (GTU), a school where Jews, Christians, and Buddhists study side by side, stimulating one another. I learned much there from my colleagues and students; I want to thank, in particular, David Winston and David Biale for their friendship and for the depth of their learning.

I had been at the GTU for many years already when, one afternoon in September 1995, Art Green called me on the phone and told me about a woman from Chicago named Margot Pritzker. She had been studying the *Zohar* with Rabbi Yehiel Poupko, but the dated English translation they were reading had proved inadequate. Margot had decided to commission a new translation, said Art, and she was inviting me to undertake the task! I was astounded, and told my friend that I needed a few days to consider this.

The days turned into weeks, which turned into months, as I kept wrestling with the thrilling, terrifying offer. I decided to translate a short section of the *Zohar* to see how it felt, but I poured myself into the experiment so intensely, day after day, that I was left drained, exhausted, discouraged. How could I keep this up for years and years? I reluctantly resolved to decline the offer, but Art convinced me to at least meet this woman and her rabbi; so the following May, the four of us gathered at the O'Hare Hyatt. I expressed my hesitation to them, and told Margot that the project could take twelve to fifteen years—to which she responded, "You're not scaring me!" I was won over by her genuine desire to penetrate the *Zohar* and make it accessible to English readers. A year or so later, over Independence Day weekend 1997, the *Zohar* project formally began with a two-day conference outside Chicago attended by the leading academic scholars of Kabbalah. They were invited not just to participate in this conference but to constitute the Academic Committee for the Translation of the *Zohar,* which was intended to guide and support this translation. (The members of the committee are listed at the front of this volume.) Over the past six years, I have benefited immensely from their feedback and encouragement. I thank all of them, especially Moshe Idel, Yehuda Liebes, Ronit Meroz, and Elliot Wolfson. Time and again, Yehuda generously shared insights drawn from his vast, intimate knowledge of the *Zohar.* I smile, recalling the many times we wrestled over the mystifying Aramaic, deepening our understanding of the text and our friendship.

I spent the second year of the project (1998–99) at the Institute for Advanced Studies at the Hebrew University of Jerusalem on a program entitled "Studying the *Zohar,*" directed by Yehuda Liebes. Here seven fellows and seven other visiting scholars (all fourteen of us, members of the Academic Committee) engaged in research on various aspects of the text. Our weekly seminars were devoted to a close reading of *Zohar* passages—often those that I was currently translating. Here I presented a draft of my translation and benefited from the responses of my colleagues. I am grateful to all of them, as well as to the staff of the Institute, who provided an ideal setting for our research. When the yearlong program ended in June 1999, the institute graciously allowed me to retain an office for the following year as well.

In the summer of 2000, it was finally time to leave the tranquil environment of the institute. Fortunately, Rabbi David Hartman provided me with an office at the Shalom Hartman Institute across town, where I spent the following two years (2000–2002) in an atmosphere simultaneously peaceful and stimulating. David's enthusiasm for Torah energizes everyone around him, and I thank him for his support and encouragement, and for his healthy skepticism of mystical excess. I was enriched by my contact with many of the fellows at the Hartman Institute, especially Donniel Hartman (co-director), Daniel Abrams, Moshe Halbertal, Moshe Idel, Israel Knohl, Levi Lauer, Menachem Lorberbaum, Yair Lorberbaum, Israel Ta-Shma, and Shlomo Naeh. Shlomo was always generous in sharing with me his immense linguistic knowledge.

As described in the Translator's Introduction, I have based my English rendering on a critical text of the *Zohar*, which I have constructed by drawing on variant readings from a wide range of manuscripts. I could not have accomplished this task without my indefatigable research assistant, Barry Mark, who spent more than five years painstakingly preparing lists of these variants for the first two volumes of the translation. I thank him immensely for his years of devotion to this task. Recently, Merav Carmeli has followed in his footsteps, proving herself a worthy successor, and I am indebted to her as well.

Arthur Green has carefully read large portions of this translation and offered criticism and suggestions, for which I am truly grateful. As co-chair of the Academic Committee for the Translation of the *Zohar*, he has helped guide the project from its birth.

Numerous libraries offered valuable resources, especially the Gershom Scholem Collection and the Institute of Microfilmed Hebrew Manuscripts, both housed in the Jewish National and University Library, Jerusalem. I want to thank, in particular, Esther Liebes (head of the Scholem Collection) for her constant willingness to help, Benjamin Richler (director of the Institute of Microfilmed Hebrew Manuscripts) along with his staff, and Adam Verete for checking obscure references. Other libraries and collections that provided precious material include: Bayerische Staatsbibliothek, Munich; Biblioteca Apostolica, Vatican; Biblioteca Casanatense, Rome; Biblioteca Palatina, Parma; Bibliothèque nationale, Paris; the Bodleian Library, University of Oxford; the British Library; Cambridge University Library; the Flora Lamson Hewlett Library of the Graduate Theological Union; the Friedberg Collection, University of Toronto Library; the Guenzburg Collection of the Russian State Library, Moscow; and the Library of the Jewish Theological Seminary.

The team at Stanford University Press, led by Geoffrey Burn and Norris Pope, has been superb to work with and wondrously adept at generating the first, demanding volumes of this complex classic. In addition to Geoffrey and Norris, I want to thank Lowell Britson, Alan Harvey, Randy Hurst, David

Jackson, Patricia Myers, and especially Mariana Raykov and Rob Ehle. Rabbi David E. S. Stein's expert copyediting polished this *Book of Radiance*.

As I toiled and exulted over the *Zohar*, I have received sound advice and warm encouragement from my far-flung siblings: Rabbi Jonathan Matt (Israel), David Matt (Iowa), and Debbie Erdfarb (New Jersey).

My wife, Ḥana, and I have been delving together into the *Zohar* ever since we met, discovering and sharing its new-ancient meanings, gazing into each other's souls through its penetrating lens. Thank you for your compassionate wisdom and unfailing support. You bring to life the verse: *On her tongue, a Torah of love* (Proverbs 31:26). You help me understand the words of Rabbi El'azar (*Zohar* 1:141a): "Isaac embraced faith, seeing *Shekhinah* dwelling in his wife."

My angelic children, Michaella and Gavriel, have never lost their sense of wonder, and I thank them for arousing mine. May this translation touch you and open up new worlds!

Rabbi Yehiel Poupko, co-chair of the Academic Committee, has excited and inspired me ever since our first meeting seven years ago. Descended from a famous kabbalist, the *Shelah* (Isaiah Horowitz), he is intimately bound to the *Zohar* and has devoted himself to spreading its light. I thank him for conducting this project so deftly and passionately.

Glen Miller, vice president of Zohar Education Project, Inc., has vitalized this adventure through his vision and devotion. On a practical level, he has navigated the ark of *Zohar* through countless legal and administrative passageways. I am profoundly grateful.

Thomas J. Pritzker has generously supported and heartened all of us through this long process. I thank him deeply. And I wonder: Is there a correlation between Tom's passion for exploring caves to discover ancient Asian art and the fact that, according to tradition (see below, page 76), the *Zohar* was composed in a cave?

Margot, how can I express my gratitude to you? You have enabled me to devote myself to what I love—that is every scholar's dream. You have not only sponsored this immense project; you have participated, probing the translation and commentary, skillfully guiding the entire process. I hope that I have responded to your bold generosity by opening up the *Zohar* for you and for all those who, thanks to you, will be illumined by its rays. To you I dedicate this translation.

Finally, to the One beyond all names: Blessed are You for enlivening and sustaining me, and for bringing me to this moment.

D.C.M.

Introduction

I

THE ZOHAR IS the great medieval Jewish compendium of mysticism, myth, and esoteric teaching. It may be considered the highest expression of Jewish literary imagination in the Middle Ages. Surely it is one of the most important bodies of religious text of all times and places. It is also a lush garden of sacred eros, filled to overflowing with luxurious plantings of love between master and disciples, among the mystical companions themselves, between the souls of Israel and *Shekhinah*—God's lovely bride—but most of all between the male and female elements that together make up the Godhead. Revered and canonized by generations of faithful devotees, the *Zohar*'s secret universe serves as the basis of kabbalistic faith, both within the boundaries of Judaism and beyond it, down to our own day, which has seen a significant revival of interest in Kabbalah and its teachings.

The *Zohar* is a work of sacred fantasy. To say this about it is by no means to impugn the truth of its insights or the religious profundity of its teachings. The Middle Ages are filled with fantasy. Angels and demons, heavenly principalities, chambers of heaven and rungs within the soul, secret treasures of the spirit that could be seen only by the elect, esoteric domains without end—all of these were to be found in the writings of Jewish, Christian, and Islamic authors throughout medieval times. All of them partake of fantasy. It may be said that all theological elaborations, insofar as they are allowed to become pictorial, are fantasy. They depict realities that have not been seen except by the inner eye of those who describe them, or by their sacred sources.

In the case of Judaism, prohibitions derived from the second of the Ten Commandments forbade the depiction of such sacred realms in any medium other than that of words. Perhaps because of this, the literary imagination became extraordinarily rich. All those creative energies that might in other contexts have sought to reify sacred myth in painting, sculpture, manuscript illumination, or stained glass here had to focus on the word—especially on the timeless Jewish project of commentary and exegesis. In this sense the *Zohar* may be seen as the greatest work of medieval Jewish "iconography"—one that exists only in the words of the written page, thence to be distilled in the imagination of its devoted students.

Written in a lofty combination of Aramaic and Hebrew, the *Zohar* was first revealed to the world around the year 1300. Those who distributed it, orally and in small written fragments, claimed that it was an ancient text they had recently rediscovered, and that it had been composed in the circle of those described within its pages—Rabbi Shim'on son of Yoḥai and his disciples, who lived in the land of Israel during the second century of the Common Era. The obscurity of the *Zohar*'s origins combined with its unique language and its rich poetic imagination to lend to the work an aura of unfathomable mystery. While a few of the more critical spirits in each century doubted the *Zohar* and questioned its authority, the great majority of readers, and later of Jewry as a whole, believed in the *Zohar* and venerated it, considering it a holy revelation and a sacred scripture that was to be ranked alongside the Bible and the Talmud as a divinely inspired source of religious truth. Only in modern times, and largely for apologetic reasons, was the *Zohar* deleted from the canon of what was considered "mainstream" Judaism.

Translation of the *Zohar* into Western languages began as early as the fifteenth century, when passages were rendered into Latin for use by Christian devotees of esoteric lore in Renaissance Italy. In the twentieth century, various translations of the *Zohar*, or at least of most sections of it, appeared in German, French, and English. The previous standard English translation is that of Harry Sperling and Maurice Simon, published in 1931–34 by the Soncino Press.

The present translation and commentary by Daniel Matt reflect the high standards of *Zohar* scholarship that have been achieved in recent decades. These are the result of the new attention paid to Kabbalah in academic circles, largely thanks to the writings of Gershom Scholem (1897–1982) and the cadre of scholars he and his successors have trained within the Israeli universities. The first to bring Scholem's approach to kabbalistic studies to North American shores was Alexander Altmann (1906–1987) at Brandeis University, whose students include both the translator of these volumes and the author of this introduction. Further discussion of the translation and the principles under-lying it may be found in the Translator's Introduction.

The purpose of this introduction is to equip the reader to better appreciate the *Zohar* text. The translation before you is one that takes full cognizance of the poetic spirit in which the *Zohar* was composed and especially of the elevated tone achieved by its unique use of language. To appreciate these in the fullest sense, it must be said, the *Zohar* needs to be read, indeed studied, in the original. Like most of the kabbalistic tradition within which it stands, the *Zohar* is entranced with the mysteries of language, in both its oral and written forms. No translation could do justice to the *Zohar*'s rich and creative appropriation of the nuances of Hebrew and Aramaic speech, its startling transformation of countless biblical verses, and the frequent subtle rereadings of the Talmudic/midrashic legacy that together comprise much of the *Zohar*'s charm and genius. Nevertheless, a great deal can be gained through carefully reading and studying the *Zohar* in translation. For this to be possible, however, the reader needs to be initiated into the symbolic language in which the work was written.[1] Although the *Zohar*'s poesis often transcends the symbolic conventions, they are always present in the background of the writers' imagination. So too, it was assumed, would they be present in the mind of the reader. The *Zohar* was composed in the hope that it would be passed on and studied within circles of initiates, as indeed it was for many generations.

To appreciate the *Zohar*, you will also need to know something of the historical and literary context in which it appeared. The *Zohar* made use of a very wide selection of Jewish texts that preceded it, ranging from the Torah itself to legal, mystical, and philosophical works that were written just shortly before its appearance. It reflected on all of these and used them freely as inspiration for its own unique sort of innovative and sometimes even playful religious creativity. It is also much concerned with the Jews and their history: that recorded in Scripture, the present exile, and the dream of messianic redemption. These, too, form part of the background needed to understand the *Zohar*.

This introduction will begin by outlining the development of Kabbalah in the century leading up to the *Zohar*, considering also the use made in Kabbalah of prior Jewish sources. We will then turn to the *Zohar* itself, discussing in turn its style of thought and exegesis, its narrative modes, and the question of the *Zohar*'s appearance and authorship. Because this essay serves as an introduction to the entire *Zohar* text, we will not quote passages to exemplify the analysis offered. We hope that the reader will proceed from this introduction to a careful reading of the text and commentary, finding ample passages throughout the *Zohar* against which to test the claims offered in this brief introductory essay.

The "tall order" detailed in the preceding paragraphs requires a disclaimer. Monographs and learned articles have been written on each of the subjects just mentioned. Some of them have been the subject of entire books. This introduction does not seek to break new ground in most of them. It is rather a digest of what the writer considers to be the finest scholarship and deepest

---

1. A much expanded version of this introduction to the *Zohar* is to be found in my *Guide to the Zohar*, also available from Stanford University Press. There the symbolic language of Kabbalah (i.e., the sefirotic system) is more fully outlined and discussed. The most comprehensive introduction to the subject is the three-volume *Wisdom of the Zohar* by Isaiah Tishby, originally written in Hebrew. The English translation by David Goldstein offers a thorough historical analysis of many topics covered by the *Zohar*, followed by selected passages. Although the Hebrew version was published in 1949–61 and thus predates much of current *Zohar* scholarship, Tishby's work remains an invaluable source of knowledge.

insights regarding the *Zohar* that have been written since Scholem began the era of modern Kabbalah scholarship. While responsibility for any misunderstandings or omissions in this introduction are entirely my own, I wish to acknowledge fully that the insights contained within it are those of three or four generations of scholars who have labored hard as today's *meḥatstsedei ḥaqla*, "reapers in the field," of *Zohar* scholarship. Many of these are members of the Academic Committee for the Translation of the *Zohar*, and their names are listed at the front of this volume. I am grateful to each of them for their contributions to our collective efforts to understand even "a drop in the sea" of the *Zohar*'s profound secrets.

II

Jewish mysticism in the Middle Ages is a rereading of earlier Jewish tradition, including both the Bible and the corpus of rabbinic literature. It has to be understood in the context of the great project of medieval Jewry as a whole, the interpretation of a received, authoritative, and essentially complete body of normative Jewish teaching. This body of teaching, canonized in the Gaonic age (eighth–tenth centuries), nominally commanded the loyalty of all Jewry, with the exception of a Karaite minority. But the deeper attachment of Jews to this tradition had to be re-won constantly, especially in the face of both Christian and Muslim polemics against Judaism, ever the religious culture of a minority living in the shadow of one or the other of its giant offspring. Increasingly, various new intellectual currents that came into fashion among the Jews also occasioned a need for defense or reinterpretation of the tradition. These included Mut'azilite Philosophy, Neoplatonism, and Aristotelianism. The classic form for such reinterpretation of authoritative texts was the commentary, whether on one or more books of the Bible or on a part of the Talmudic legacy. Kabbalah, a new sort of mystical-esoteric exegesis first appearing in the twelfth century, may be seen as another medieval rereading of the received Jewish canon.

In order to understand the ways in which Kabbalah, and particularly the *Zohar*, finds its home within the earlier tradition, we need to distinguish five elements that are present in the legacy that medieval Jews had received from the Judaism of late antiquity or the Talmudic age. Although these five are not at all equal either in the amount of text devoted to them or in the degree of formal authority with which they are accredited, each was to play an important role in the new configuration of Judaism that Kabbalah represents.

First of the five is *aggadah*, the narrative tradition, contained in the Talmud and the various works of Midrash. Midrash is a hermeneutical term, renderable both as "inquiry" and "homiletics," indicating a way of delving into Scripture that tended toward fanciful and extended rereadings. Much of *aggadah* is legendary in content, expanding biblical history and recreating the biblical landscape in the setting of the rabbinic world. But *aggadah* also includes tales of the rabbis themselves and teachings of wisdom in many forms: maxims, parables, folk traditions, and so forth.

The kabbalists made great use of the midrashic/aggadic tradition, drawing on both its methods of interpretation and its contents. The hermeneutical assumptions of Midrash, including the legitimacy of juxtaposing verses from anywhere within Scripture without concern for dating or context, the rearranging of words or even occasional substitution of letters, use of numerology and abbreviation as ways to derive meaning, the endless glorification of biblical heroes and the tarring of villains—all of these and others were carried over from Midrash into Kabbalah. Indeed many of them were used by other sorts of medieval preachers as well. But the content of the aggadic worldview—with its mythic picture of God as Creator and divine Ruler who sees everywhere; who acts in history; who responds to prayer and human virtue, even suspending the laws of nature to rescue His beloved; who mourns with Israel the destruction of their shared Temple and suffers with them the pain of exile—all this too was faithfully carried over into the kabbalistic imagination. In fact the kabbalists were partial to the most highly anthropomorphic and mythic versions of rabbinic tradition, such as were contained in the eighth-century collection *Pirqei de-Rabbi Eli'ezer*. Here they stood in sharp contrast to the prior emerging intellectual trend of the Middle Ages: Jewish philosophy, which exercised a degree of critical skepticism with regard to the more fantastic claims of the *aggadah* and sought out, whenever possible, those more modest and somewhat naturalistic viewpoints that could be found among certain of the early rabbis.

xxxv

Second is the tradition of *halakhah*, the legal and normative body of Talmudic teaching, the chief subject of study for Jews throughout the era, and thus the main curriculum upon which most kabbalists themselves were educated. The early kabbalists lived fully within the bounds of *halakhah* and created a meaning system that justified its existence. While later Kabbalah (beginning in the early fourteenth century) contains some elements that are quite critical of *halakhah*, little of this trend is evident in the period before the *Zohar*. Some transmitters of Kabbalah—Rabbi Moses Naḥmanides (see below) is the great example—were also active in the realm of halakhic creativity, writing responsa and commentaries on Talmudic tractates. More common was a certain intellectual specialization, undoubtedly reflecting spiritual temperament, spawning kabbalists who lived faithfully within *halakhah* and whose writings show its patterning of their lives, but who devoted their literary efforts chiefly to the realm of mystical exegesis, including kabbalistic comments on the commandments or reflection on aspects of halakhic practice.

A third element of the rabbinic legacy is the liturgical tradition. While liturgical praxis was codified within *halakhah* and thus in some ways is a subset of it, the texts recited in worship—including a large corpus of liturgical poetry, or *piyyut*—constitute a literary genre of their own. Medieval writers, including the mystics of both Spain and Ashkenaz, were much concerned with establishing the precise proper wording of each prayer. The text of the prayer book had been mostly fixed by compendia dating from the tenth century; in the Middle Ages, however, it became the object of commentaries, many of which sought to find their authors' own theologies reflected in these venerated and widely known texts by the ancient rabbis. This is especially true of the kabbalists, who devoted much attention to the *kavvanah,* or inward meaning, of liturgical prayer.

The fourth strand of earlier tradition is that of Merkavah mysticism. *Merkavah* designates a form of visionary mystical praxis that reaches back into the Hellenistic era but was still alive as late as tenth-century Babylonia. Its roots lie close to Apocalyptic literature, except that here the voyager taken up into the heavens is usually offered a private encounter with the divine glory, one that does not involve metahistorical predications. Those who "went down into the *merkavah*" sought visions that took them before the throne of God, allowing them to travel through the divine "palaces" (*heikhalot*), realms replete with angels and, at the height of ecstasy, to participate in or even lead the angelic chorus. The term *merkavah* (chariot) links this tradition to the opening vision of the prophet Ezekiel, which was seen as the great paradigm for all such visionary experiences and accounts. It is also connected to the *qedushah* formula ("Holy, holy, holy is *YHVH* of hosts; the whole earth is filled with His glory!") of Isaiah 6, since it is this refrain that most Merkavah voyagers recount hearing the angels sing as they stand with them in the heavenly heights.

The Merkavah tradition was known to the medievals in two ways. Treatises by those who had practiced this form of mysticism, often preserved in fragmentary and inchoate form, were copied and brought from the Near East to western Europe, as we shall see below. But just as important were the references to Merkavah practice in the Talmudic literature itself, a fact that lent legitimacy to the fascination that latter-day mystics clearly felt for this material. Such great Talmudic sages as Rabbi Akiva and Rabban Yoḥanan son of Zakkai were associated with Merkavah traditions. Akiva, considered in some aggadic sources to be a sort of second Moses, is the subject of the most famous of all rabbinic accounts of such mystical voyages. He alone, unlike the other three of the "four who entered the orchard," was able to "enter in peace and leave in peace." While some modern scholars question the historicity of associating the early rabbinic sages with Merkavah praxis, in the Middle Ages the Talmudic sources were quite sufficient to sustain this link. It was the philosophic questioners of the Merkavah traditions, rather than their mystical supporters, who were hard-pressed to defend their views. Merkavah traditions also had considerable influence on the rabbinic liturgy, and this association too raised their esteem in medieval eyes.

The fifth and final element of this ancient legacy is the hardest to define, partly because it hangs on the thread of a slim body of text, but also because it contains elements that seem contradictory to one another. I refer to the speculative/magical tradition that reached medieval Jewry through the little book called *Sefer Yetsirah* and various other small texts, mostly magical in content, that are associated with it. *Sefer Yetsirah* has been shown to be a very ancient work, close in spirit to aspects of Greek esotericism that flourished in the late Hellenistic era. While the practice associated with this school of thought is magical/theurgic, even including the attempt to make a *golem*, its chief text contains the most abstract worldview to be found within the legacy of ancient Judaism. By contemplating the core meaning of both numbers and letters, it reaches toward a notion of cosmic unity that underlies diversity, of an abstract deity that serves as cosmic center, in whom (or perhaps better: "in which") all being is rooted. The magical praxis is thus a form of *imitatio dei*, man's attempt to reignite the creative spark by which the universe has emerged from within the Godhead. Here we have the roots of a theology more abstract than anything to be found in the *aggadah* or the Merkavah tradition, an essentially speculative and nonvisual mysticism.

Sefer Yetsirah was the subject of a wide variety of commentaries in the Middle Ages, rationalists as well as mystics claiming it as their own. In the twelfth century, the language and style of thought found in this work became central to the first generations of kabbalistic writing, as reflected by commentaries on it and by the penetration of its terminology into other works as well.

Kabbalah must be seen as a dynamic mix of these five elements, sometimes with one dominating, sometimes adding the mix of another. It was especially the first and last listed, the aggadic/mythic element and the abstract/speculative/magical tradition that seemed to vie for the leading role in forging the emerging kabbalistic way of thought.

Jewish esoteric traditions began to reach the small and isolated communities of western Europe (some of which dated back to Roman times) perhaps as early as the ninth or tenth century. How these ancient materials first came to Franco-German Jewry is lost in legend, but it is clear from manuscript evidence that much of the old Merkavah and magical literature was preserved among the earliest Ashkenazic Jews, along with their devotion to both *halakhah* and *aggadah*. These esoteric sources were studied especially by groups in the Rhineland, who added to them their own speculations on God, the cosmos, and the secrets of the Torah. Out of these circles there emerged in the late twelfth and early thirteenth centuries a movement known to history as *Hasidut Ashkenaz*, a pietistic revivalism based on small communities or brotherhoods of mystics who committed themselves to high standards of ascetic practice and contemplative devotion. These groups also played a key role in the preservation and further development of esoteric traditions.

It was in the area of southern France called Provence, culturally akin in the High Middle Ages to northern Spain, that a somewhat different sort of esoteric speculations began to emerge. These came to be called by the name Kabbalah, a term applied to this emerging school of mystical thought in the early thirteenth century. The word means "tradition"; its use in this context indicates that the kabbalists saw themselves as a conservative element within the Jewish religious community. Their secrets—so they claimed—were *qabbalah*, esoteric teachings received from ancient masters by means of faithful oral transmission from one generation to the next.

The Provençal Jewish community in the twelfth century was one of great cultural wealth, forming something of a bridge between the spiritual legacy of Jewish creativity in Spain of Muslim times and the rather separate world of Jewry in the Ashkenazic or Franco-Rhenish area. It is in this cultural realm that Kabbalah first appears, about the middle of the twelfth century. The origins of this spiritual and literary movement are obscure and still much debated. There are clearly elements of Near Eastern origin in the earliest Kabbalah, materials related to Merkavah and late midrashic texts that were present in the Holy Land in the ninth or tenth centuries. There are also strong influences of elements that were to appear in Rhineland Hasidism as well, indicating that at some early point these two movements had a common origin. But here in Provence, a new sort of religious discourse began to emerge in circles of mystics who combined knowledge of these various traditions. These groups, which may have been several generations in formation, are known to us as the editors of one of the strangest and most fascinating documents in the long history of Hebrew literature. This slim volume is known as *Sefer ha-Bahir*, awkwardly renderable as *The Book of Clarity*. We first find reference to it in Provençal works of the latter twelfth century, and from that time forward it has a continuous history as a major shaper of Jewish mystical ideas.

The *Bahir* takes the form of ancient rabbinic Midrash, expounding on biblical phrases, tying one verse of Scripture to another, and constructing units of its own thought around what it offers as scriptural exegesis. Like the old Midrash, it makes frequent use of parables, showing special fondness for those involving kings and their courts, in which God is repeatedly compared to "a king of flesh and blood." In form, then, the *Bahir* is quite traditional. But as soon as the reader opens its pages to look at the content, astonishment takes over. The text simply does not work as Midrash. Questions are asked and not answered, or answered in a way that only adds mystification. Images are proposed that in the midrashic context surely refer to God, and then suddenly things are said that make such a reading theologically impossible (The "King" turns out to have an older brother, for example). What sort of questions are these, and what sort of answers? The scholar is sometimes tempted to emend the text!

If one comes to the *Bahir*, on the other hand, bearing some familiarity with the methods of mystical teachers, particularly in the Orient, the text may seem less bizarre. Despite its title, the purpose of the book is precisely to mystify rather than to make anything "clear" in the ordinary sense. Here the way to clarity is to discover the mysterious. The reader is being taught to recognize how much there is that he doesn't know, how filled Scripture is with seemingly impenetrable secrets. "You think you know the meaning of this verse?" says the *Bahir* to its reader. "Here is an interpretation that will throw you on your ear and show you that you understand nothing of it at all." Everything in the Torah, be it a tale of Abraham, a poetic verse, or an obscure point of law, hints at a reality beyond that which you can obtain by the ordinary dialectics of either Talmudic or philosophical thinking.

As we read on in the *Bahir*, it becomes clear that the authors are not simply advocating obscurantism for its own sake. The text has in mind a notion, often expressed only vaguely, of a world that lies behind the many hints and mysteries of the scriptural word. To say it briefly, the *Bahir* and all kabbalists that follow it claim that the true subject of Scripture is God Himself, that revelation is essentially an act of divine self-disclosure. Because most people would not be able to bear the great light that comes with knowing God, the Torah reveals divinity in secret form. Scripture is strewn with hints as to the true nature of "that which is above" and the mysterious process within divinity that led to the creation of this world. Only in the exoteric, public sense is revelation primarily a matter of divine *will*, teaching the commandments Israel is to follow in order to live the good life. The inner, esoteric revelation is rather one of divine *truth*, a web of secrets pointing to the innermost nature of God's own self. That self is disclosed in the garb of a newly emergent symbolic language, one describing the inner life of the Deity around a series of image-clusters that will come to be called (in a term derived from *Sefer Yetsirah*) the ten *sefirot*.

The earliest documentary evidence of Kabbalah is found in two very different sorts of literary sources. The *Bahir* constitutes one of these. Alongside it there is a more theoretical or abstract series of kabbalistic writings. These appear first in the family and close circle of Rabbi Abraham ben David of Posquieres, a well-known Provençal Talmudic authority. His son, Rabbi Isaac the Blind (d. ca. 1235), and others linked to his study circle (including family members) evidence an ongoing tradition of kabbalistic praxis both in their brief commentaries on prayer and on *Sefer Yetsirah*, and in their written reflections on names of God. These treatises—quite laconic in style when compared with the mythic lushness of the *Bahir*—point to an already well-defined system of kabbalistic contemplation, suggesting that their appearance after 1150 may reflect a decision to reveal in writing that which had been previously kept secret, rather than an entirely new genre of religious creativity. The sort of rabbinic circles in which Kabbalah is first found are highly conservative; it is hard to imagine them inventing this new sort of religious language on their own. It seems more likely that they saw themselves as guardians and transmitters of a secret tradition, passed down to them from sources unknown, but in their eyes surely ancient.

The context for the publication of kabbalistic secrets is the great spiritual turmoil that divided Provençal Jewry in the second half of the twelfth century: the controversy over philosophy, and especially over the works of Rabbi Moses Maimonides (1135–1204). This conflict came to a head with the public burning of Maimonides' *Guide for the Perplexed* (by the Dominicans, but possibly with the tacit approval of anti-Maimonidean Jews) in 1232. The surrounding struggle engaged the intellectual life of the Provençal Jewish elite for several decades. As the era's great halakhic authority and codifier of Jewish law, Maimonides' name commanded tremendous respect. In many writings of the age, he is simply referred to as "the Rabbi." But his works raised not a few questions regarding his degree of theological orthodoxy. Did Maimonides go too far in his insistence that the Bible's ascription of emotions to God, as well as bodily attributes, was a form of anthropomorphism that needed to be explained away? Was it right that he derived so much of his wisdom from non-Jewish sources, the Greek and Islamic philosophical traditions? Was he correct in identifying the ancient rabbinic references to "The Account of the Chariot" and "The Account of Creation" with metaphysics and physics as the philosophers taught them? Did he have a right to dismiss certain old Jewish esoteric speculations as inauthentic nonsense? Still more painful in this law-centered culture: how could the rabbi have given legal status to his own Aristotelian philosophic views, seemingly insisting, in the opening section of his Code, that any Jew who did not share them was either an idolator or a naive fool?

But the heart of the Maimonidean controversy went deeper than all of these accusations, touching the very heart of the philosophical notion of the Godhead. Philosophy insisted on divine perfection—on the unchanging, all-knowing, all-capable quality of God. If perfect and unchanging, this God was necessarily self-sufficient and in no need of human actions of any sort. Why, then, would such a God care about performance of the commandments? How could a Torah centered on religious law, including so much of ritual performance, represent the embodiment of divine will? Maimonides taught that indeed God had no "need" for us to fulfill the commandments. The chief purpose of religious observance was educational, a God-given way of cultivating the mind to turn toward God. But once the lesson had been learned, some suspected, there would be those who would come to see the form itself as no longer needed. Moreover it was rumored that in some circles of wealthy Jewry in Muslim Spain, the abstractions of philosophy had begun to serve as an excuse for a more lax view of the commandments and the details of their observance.

Some rabbis of Provence were deeply loyal to a more literalist reading of the Talmudic and midrashic legacy, one that left little room for the radical rationalization of Judaism proposed by the philosophers. Others had been exposed to the esoteric traditions of the Rhineland and northern France, which stood in conflict with the new philosophy partly because they seemed to highlight—rather than minimize—the anthropomorphic passages in Scripture and tradition. The Franco-Rhenish tradition also had room for a strong magical component to religion. Ancient speculations on secret names of God and the angels still held currency in these circles. The power of using such names to affect the divine will, utter blasphemy in the eyes of the Maimonidean, was taken for granted in early Ashkenaz, as it had been centuries earlier throughout the Jewish world.

The secrets of Kabbalah were made public in this age as a way to combat the influence of Maimonidean rationalism. The freedom and implied disinterest in human affairs of the philosophers' God frightened the mystics into coming out of the deep esotericism that had until then restricted them to oral transmission of their teachings within closed conventicles of initiates. Their secrets were to serve as an alternative explanation of the Torah, one that saw Torah and its commandments not only as playing a vital role in the ongoing spiritual life of Israel, but also as having a cosmos-sustaining role in a view of the universe that made them absolutely essential. It is no accident that two of the key subjects discussed in these earliest kabbalistic speculations are the *kavvanot*, or secret meanings of prayer, and *ta'amei ha-mitsvot*, the reasons for the commandments. Both of these are interpreted in a way that insists on the cosmic effects of human actions. The special concentration on divine names played an essential part in early Kabbalah, setting in course a theme that was to be developed over many centuries of kabbalistic praxis.

The secret doctrines first taught in Provence were carried across the Pyrenees in the early thirteenth century, inspiring small circles of mystics in the adjacent district of Catalonia. One key center of this activity was the city of Gerona, well known as the home of two of the most important rabbinic figures of the age, Rabbi Moses ben Naḥman (called Naḥmanides) and Rabbi Jonah Gerondi (ca. 1200–1263). Naḥmanides, perhaps the most widely respected Jewish intellectual figure of the thirteenth century, is the most important personage associated with the early dissemination of kabbalistic secrets. He was a leading Talmudic commentator, scriptural interpreter, and legal authority. His Torah commentary includes numerous passages—most brief and intentionally obscure, but several lengthy and highly developed—where he speaks "in the way of truth," referring to secret kabbalistic traditions. Alongside Naḥmanides there emerged a somewhat separate circle of kabbalists including two very important teachers, Rabbi Ezra ben Solomon and Rabbi Azriel. These figures seem to have been more innovative than Naḥmanides in their kabbalistic exegesis and also more open to the Neoplatonic philosophy of Abraham Ibn Ezra and others that was gaining credence in their day. Naḥmanides was essentially conservative in his kabbalistic readings, insisting that he was only passing down what he had received from his teachers, and his view of philosophical thought in general was quite negative. Rabbi Ezra, the author of commentaries on the Song of Songs and some Talmudic *aggadot*, and his disciple Rabbi Azriel, who wrote a larger treatise on the *aggadot* as well as a widely quoted

XLI

commentary on the liturgy, combined the legacy of the *Bahir* with teachings received from Rabbi Isaac the Blind and his nephew Rabbi Asher ben David. They read Kabbalah in a Neoplatonic spirit, which is to say that they saw the *sefirot* as an ordered series of emanations, increasingly removed from an unknowable primal source.

This Catalonian kabbalistic tradition remained fairly close to the original purpose we have suggested for the publication of kabbalistic secrets. Naḥmanides' inclusion of openly kabbalistic references in his highly popular Torah commentary complemented his fierce polemical attacks in that same work on Maimonides' philosophical interpretation of the Torah. Jacob bar Sheshet, another key Gerona figure, also engaged in the battle against the rationalists. While neither Rabbi Azriel nor Rabbi Ezra of Gerona is known to have written anything outside the realm of Kabbalah, their writings reflect significant rabbinic learning and show them to belong to the same traditionalist and antiAristotelian circles. Neoplatonism, they found, was a philosophy more amenable to the needs of mystics, thus rediscovering in a Jewish context something that Christian mystics had come to know many centuries earlier.

Around the middle of the thirteenth century, a new center of kabbalistic activity became active in Castile, to the west of Catalonia. Soon the writings of this new group, out of which the *Zohar* was to emerge, overshadowed those of the earlier Catalonian circle with regard to both volume and originality of output. The Castilian kabbalists' writings were not characterized by the highly conservative rabbinic attitude that had been lent to Kabbalah by such figures as Rabbi Isaac the Blind and Naḥmanides. This circle had its roots more planted in the *Bahir* tradition than in that of the abstract language of early Provençal/Catalonian Kabbalah. Mythic imagery was richly developed in the writings of such figures as the brothers Rabbi Isaac and Rabbi Jacob ha-Kohen and their disciple Rabbi Moses of Burgos. Their writings show a special fascination with the "left side" of the divine emanation and the world of the demonic. Rabbi Isaac ha-Kohen developed a full-blown mythos in which the forces of evil were presented as near autonomous powers emanated in an act of purgation from the depths of divinity. Dependent upon both the divine and the human for their existence, they exist at the liminal outskirts of the sefirotic realm and the phenomenal universe, at the very borders of chaos and nonbeing. There they wait in ambush for the *Shekhinah* and the worlds that She creates and nurtures. Thus, to the world picture of divine sefirotic hierarchy and an emanated cosmos, the Castilians add a parallel but antithetical realm of the demonic, serving as the source of all that is destructive in the cosmos.

This conception of the "left-hand emanation" is founded on a set of suggestive aggadic statements and biblical verses. In particular, the Castilian kabbalists' imagination was sparked by Rabbi Abbahu's famous dictum: "The blessed Holy One created and destroyed worlds before He created these, saying: 'These please me. Those did not please me.'" Out of this and other fragments of aggadic thought, Rabbi Isaac spun an elaborate mythos in which the *sefirah Binah*, at the dawn of time, welled forth emanations of pure *din* (literally "judgment," but resulting in absolute forces of destruction, whose intensity doomed them to almost immediate annihilation). From the residue of these destructive forces rose a hierarchy of powers of unmitigated judgment. Possessing no creative potency of their own, these forces are ontologically dependent upon divinity and are energized by the power released by human transgression.

Because of their fascination with myths of the demonic realm, this group was characterized by Gershom Scholem as the "Gnostic Circle" of Castilian kabbalists. Their writings had great influence in the further development of kabbalistic thought. They are the most immediate predecessors of the circle of kabbalists represented in the *Zohar*. The mythic imagination of the *Zohar*, reaching to its greatest heights in depicting the realms of evil, has its roots in this setting. It is likely that Rabbi Moses de León, the central figure in both the writing and the circulation of the *Zohar*, saw himself as a disciple of these "Gnostic" kabbalists. Rabbi Todros Abulafia, a kabbalist who also served as an important political leader of Castilian Jewry, is another important link between these two groups. Although significant in their own day, the writings of the Gnostic circle were mostly forgotten by later generations of kabbalists and were not printed until Scholem himself retrieved them from rare surviving manuscripts.

There is another difference between Catalonian and Castilian circles that is especially important for understanding the *Zohar*'s place in the history of Kabbalah. The earliest kabbalists were fascinated with the origin of the sefirotic world, devoting much of their speculation to the highest *sefirot* and their relationship to that which lies beyond them. They were also deeply committed to the full unity of the sefirotic world, even to its circularity, so that the rising of all the *sefirot* to be united with the highest one was a frequently articulated goal of contemplation. Varied patterns of inner connection in the upper worlds were reflected in the *kavvanot* (mystical directions) of prayers and in understandings of ritual commandments, but the ultimate goal of all of these was the full restoration of the divine unity and the rise of all to the highest rung, designated as *maḥashavah* or *haskel* (contemplation, intellect). The situation was quite different in the Castilian writings. Here the emphasis was placed on the lower part of the sefirotic world, especially on the relationships between "right" and "left" and "male" and "female." The counterbalancing of demonic energies needed the strengthening of the right-hand power of divine love, and this could be awakened by human love of God and performance of the commandments. But as these writings developed, it was fascination with the sexual mysteries, reflected in the joining together of divine male and female, that overwhelmed all other symbolic interests. The uniting of the male sixth/ninth *sefirot* with the female tenth became the chief and in some places almost unique object of concern and way of explaining the religious life as a whole. This *mysterium coniunctionis* or *zivvuga qaddisha* lies at the very heart of Zoharic teaching.

In the divergence between these two tendencies within Kabbalah, we see mythic and abstractionist elements struggling within the emerging self-articulation of the mystical spirit. In raising all to the very heights of the sefirotic world, the Catalonians were voting for abstraction, a Kabbalah that led the mystic to experience a God not entirely removed from the rarified transpersonal deity of the Jewish philosophers. The Castilians may have incorporated some aspects of Gerona's Neoplatonism, but their spirit is entirely different. Perhaps influenced in part by renewed contact with more mythically-oriented Ashkenazic elements, and in part reflecting also the romantic troubadour ethos of the surrounding culture, they write in a spirit far from that of philosophy. Here we find a strong emphasis on the theurgic, quasi-magical effect of kabbalistic activity on the inner state of the Godhead, and its efficacy in bringing about divine unity and thus showering divine blessing upon the lower world. Their depictions of the upper universe are highly colorful, sometimes even earthy. The fascination with both the demonic and the sexual that characterizes their work lent to Kabbalah a dangerous and close-to-forbidden edge that undoubtedly served to make it more attractive, both in its own day and throughout later generations.[2]

The last quarter of the thirteenth century was a period of great creative expansion among the kabbalists of Castile. The sefirotic Kabbalah—as detailed in the works of such well-known figures as Moses de León, Todros Abulafia, Joseph Gikatilla, Isaac Ibn Sahula, Joseph ben Shalom Ashkenazi, Joseph Angelet, and Joseph of Hamadan, all dating from the period between 1280 and 1310—constitutes a considerable and highly varied body of writing, even leaving aside the *Zohar* itself. It was within this circle that fragments of a more poetic composition, written mostly in lofty and mysterious Aramaic rather than Hebrew, first began to circulate. These fragments, composed within one or two generations but edited over the course of the following century and a half, are known to the world as the *Zohar*.

2. The emergence of kabbalistic teaching is more complex and obscure than has been described in the preceding paragraphs. The relationship between Kabbalah and certain late forms of midrashic writing is still not entirely clear. The nature and degree of contact between early kabbalists and the German Hasidic circles, especially as reflected in the writings of Rabbi Eleazar of Worms (ca. 1165–ca. 1230), continues to puzzle scholars. The group of abstract mystical writings known as *Sifrei ha-Iyyun*, or *Books of Contemplation*, fits somewhere into this puzzle, but its precise date and relationship to other parts of the pre-Zoharic corpus is still debated by scholars. The sources of the highly distinctive school of "prophetic" or "ecstatic" Kabbalah taught by Rabbi Abraham Abulafia (1240–after 1292), while having little connection to the *Zohar*, also would require treatment in a full picture of the emergence of kabbalistic thought. But this very brief treatment of major schools and themes should suffice to set forth the context out of which the *Zohar* emerged.

III

Kabbalah represents a radical departure from any previously known version of Judaism, especially in the realm of theology. While kabbalists remained loyal followers of normative Jewish praxis as defined by *halakhah*, the theological meaning system that underlay their Judaism was reconstructed. The God of the kabbalists is not primarily the powerful, passionate Leader and Lover of His people found in the Hebrew Bible, not the wise Judge and loving Father of the rabbinic *aggadah*, nor the enthroned King of Merkavah visionaries. The kabbalists' God also differs sharply from the increasingly abstract notions of the deity created by Jewish philosophers in the Middle Ages, beginning in the tenth century with Saadia Gaon and culminating in the twelfth with Maimonides—whose work often stands in the background as the object of kabbalistic polemics. The image of God that first appears in *Sefer ha-Bahir*—to be elaborated by several generations of kabbalists until it achieved its highest poetic expression in the *Zohar*—is a God of multiple mythic potencies, obscure entities eluding precise definition but described through a remarkable web of images, parables, and scriptural allusions. Together these entities constitute the divine realm; "God" is the collective aggregate of these potencies and their inner relationship. The dynamic interplay among these forces is the essential myth of Kabbalah—the true inner meaning, as far as its devotees are concerned, both of the Torah and of human life itself.

In describing the God of the kabbalists as a figure of myth, we mean to say that the fragmented narratives and scriptural interpretations found in the *Bahir* and other early kabbalistic writings refer to a secret inner life of God, lifting the veil from the ancient Jewish insistence on monotheism and revealing a complex and multifaceted divine realm. In sharp contrast to the well-known ancient adage of Ben Sira ("Do not seek out what is too wondrous for you; do not inquire into that which is concealed from you"), these writings precisely seek to penetrate the inner divine world and to offer hints to the reader about the rich and complex life to be found there. Of course, outright polytheism (like that of the pagan Gnostic groups of late antiquity) is out of the question here at the heart of a medieval Jewry that defined itself through proud and devoted attachment to the faith in one God. What we seem to discover in the early Kabbalah are various stages of divine life, elements within the Godhead that interact with one another. In the *Bahir*, these potencies relate quite freely and mysteriously with one another; a fixed pattern of relationships is somehow vaguely in the background, but not clearly presented. In the century of development following the *Bahir*'s publication (1150–1250), the system comes to be quite firmly fixed. It is that pattern that lies behind the fanciful and multi-layered creativity of the *Zohar*.

What we are speaking of here is the realm of divine entities that are called *sefirot* by early kabbalistic sources. The term originates in *Sefer Yetsirah*, where it refers to the ten primal numbers which, along with the twenty-two letters of the Hebrew alphabet, comprise the "thirty-two wondrous paths of wisdom" or the essential structure of existence. For the kabbalist, it is these forces and the dynamic interplay among them that constitutes the inner life of the Godhead. To know God, a necessary condition of proper worship (on this point the kabbalists agree with the philosophers), one must understand the symbolic language of the *sefirot*. To be a kabbalist is to contemplate the flow of energy among the *sefirot* and reflect upon their ultimate unity.

The non-*Bahir* writings of early Kabbalah add an important new element to this picture. Here the term *Ein Sof* begins to appear as the hidden source from which the ten *sefirot* emerge. Originally part of an adverbial phrase meaning "endlessly," *Ein Sof* is used in this context in a nominal sense to designate "the Endless" or "that which is beyond all limits." *Ein Sof* refers to the endless and undefinable reservoir of divinity, the ultimate source out of which everything flows. *Ein Sof* is utterly transcendent in the sense that no words can describe it, no mind comprehend it. But it is also ever-present in the sense of the old rabbinic adage "He is the place of the world." To say that *Ein Sof* is "there" but not "here" would entirely falsify the notion. Nothing can ever exist outside of *Ein Sof*. It is thus not quite accurate to say that the *sefirot* "emerge" or "come out of" *Ein Sof*. Within the hidden reaches of infinity, in a way that of necessity eludes human comprehension, there stirs a primal desire, the slightest rippling in the stillness of cosmic solitude. That desire (not a change, the more philosophically-oriented kabbalist hastens to add, but an aspect of reality that has been there forever) draws the infinite well of energy called *Ein Sof* toward self-expression: a becoming manifest or a concretization that begins with the subtlest of steps, moves toward the emergence of "God" as divine persona, manifests its spectrum of energies in the "fullness" of the ten *sefirot*, and then spills over with plentitude to create all the "lower" worlds, including—as its very lowest manifestation—the material universe. The *sefirot* are thus a revelation, a rendering more accessible, of that which has existed in *Ein Sof* all along.

We are now ready to trace the pattern of the *sefirot* and the essential symbols associated with them. The description in the following paragraphs does not summarize any particular passage in a single kabbalistic text, but attempts to offer a summary understanding of the *sefirot* as they were portrayed in the emerging Castilian Kabbalah of the late thirteenth century. (See the Diagram of the Ten *Sefirot*, above, page xi.)

The highest *sefirah* represents the first stirrings of intent within *Ein Sof*, the arousal of desire to come forth into the varied life of being. There is no specific "content" to this *sefirah*; it is a desire or intentionality, an inner movement of the spirit, that potentially bears all content, but actually none. It is therefore often designated by the kabbalists as "Nothing." This is a stage of reality that lies between being wholly within the One and the first glimmer of separate existence. Most of the terms used to describe this rather vague realm are apophatic in nature, describing it negatively. "The air [or: ether] that cannot be grasped" is one favorite; "the hidden light" is another. The prime pictorial image assigned to it is that of the crown: *Keter*, the starting point of the cosmic process. Sometimes this rung of being is referred to as *Keter Elyon*, the Supreme Crown of God. This image is derived partly from a depiction of the ten *sefirot* in anthropic form, that is to say, in the image of a human being. Since this personification is of a royal personage, the highest manifestation of that emerging spiritual "body" will be the crown. But we should also recall that the more primary meaning of the word *keter* is "circle"; it is from this that the notion of the crown is derived. In *Sefer Yetsirah* we are told that the *sefirot* are a great circle, "their end embedded in their beginning, and their beginning in their end." The circularity of the *sefirot* will be important to us further along in our description.

Out of *Keter* emerges *Hokhmah*, the first and finest point of "real" existence. All things, souls, and moments of time that are ever to be, exist within a primal point, at once infinitesimally small and great beyond measure. (Like mystics everywhere, kabbalists love the language of paradox, a way of showing how inadequate words really are to describe this reality.) The move from *Keter* to *Hokhmah*, the first step in the primal process, is a transition from nothingness to being, from pure potential to the first point of real existence. The kabbalists are fond of describing it by their own reading of a verse from Job's Hymn to Wisdom: "Wisdom comes from Nothingness" (Job 28:12). All the variety of existence is contained within *Hokhmah*, ready to begin the journey forward.

But *Hokhmah*, meaning "wisdom," is also the primordial *teaching*, the inner mind of God, the Torah that exists prior to the birth of words and letters. As being exists here in this ultimately concentrated form, so too does truth or wisdom. The kabbalists are building on the ancient midrashic identification of Torah with primordial wisdom and the midrashic reading of "In the beginning" as "through Wisdom" God created the world. Here we begin to see their insistence that Creation and Revelation are twin processes, existence and language, the real and the nominal, emerging together from the hidden mind of God. As the primal point of existence, *Hokhmah* is symbolized by the letter *yod*, smallest of the letters, the first point from which all the other letters will be written. Here all of Torah, the text and the commentary added to it in every generation—indeed all of human wisdom—is contained within a single *yod*. This *yod* is the first letter of the name of God. The upper tip of the *yod* points toward *Keter*, itself designated by the *alef* or the divine name *Ehyeh*.

This journey from inner divine Nothingness toward the beginning of existence is one that inevitably arouses duality, even within the inner realms. As *Hokhmah* emerges, it brings forth its own mate, called *Binah*, "understanding" or "contemplation." *Hokhmah* is described as a point of light that seeks out a grand mirrored palace of reflection. The light seen back and forth in those countless mirrored surfaces is all one light, but infinitely transformed and magnified in the reflective process. *Hokhmah* and *Binah* are two that are inseparably linked to one another; either is inconceivable to us without the other. *Hokhmah* is too fine and subtle to be detected without its reflections or reverberations in *Binah*. The mirrored halls of *Binah* would be dark and unknowable without the light of *Hokhmah*. For this reason they are often treated by kabbalists as the primal pair, ancestral *Abba* and *Imma*, Father and Mother, deepest polarities of male and female within the divine (and human) Self. The point and the palace are also primal Male and Female, each transformed and fulfilled in their union with one another. The energy that radiates from the point of *Hokhmah* is described chiefly in metaphors of flowing light and water, verbal pictures used by the mystics to speak of these most abstract levels of the inner Mind. But images of sexual union are never far behind these; the flow of light is also the flow of seed that fills the womb of *Binah* and gives birth to all the further rungs within the ten-in-one divine structure, the seven "lower" *sefirot*.

This first triad of *sefirot* together constitutes the most primal and recondite level of the inner divine world. It is a reality that the kabbalist regularly claims is quite obscure and beyond human ken, although the many references to *kavvanah* reaching *Keter* and to the union of all the *sefirot* with their source undercut such assertions. But for most passages in the *Zohar*, *Binah* stands as the womb of existence, the jubilee in which all returns to its source, the object of *teshuvah* (turning, returning)—in short, the highest object of the religious quest to return to the source. Out of the womb of *Binah* flow the seven "lower" *sefirot*, constituting seven aspects of the divine persona. Together these comprise the God who is the subject of worship and the One whose image is reflected in each human soul. The divine Self, as conceived by Kabbalah, is an interplay of these seven forces or inner directions. So too is each human personality, God's image in the world. This "holy structure" of the inner life of God is called the "Mystery of Faith" by the *Zohar* and is refined in countless images by kabbalists through the ages. "God," in other words, is the first Being to emerge out of the divine womb, the primal "entity" to take shape as the endless energies of *Ein Sof* begin to coalesce.

These seven *sefirot*, taken collectively, are represented in the spatial domain by the six directions around a center (in the tradition of *Sefer Yetsirah*) and in the realm of time by the seven days of the week, culminating in the Sabbath. Under the influence of Neoplatonism, the kabbalists came to describe the *sefirot* as emerging in sequence. This sequence does not necessarily have to be one of time, as the *sefirot* comprise the inner life of *YHVH*, where time does not mean what it does to us. The sequence is rather one of an intrinsic logic, each stage a response to that which comes "before" it. The structure consists of two dialectical triads (sets of thesis, antithesis, and synthesis) and a final vehicle of reception that also energizes the entire system from "below," corresponding to *Keter* at the "upper" end.

First to manifest is *Ḥesed,* the grace or love of God. The emergence of God from hiding is an act filled with love, a promise of the endless showering of blessing and life on all beings, each of whose birth in a sense will continue this process of emerging from the One. This gift of love is beyond measure and without limit, the boundless compassion of *Keter* now transposed into a love for each specific form and creature that is ever to emerge. This channel of grace is the original divine *shefa,* the bounteous and unlimited love of God. But the divine wisdom also understands that love alone is not the way to bring forth "other" beings and to allow them their place. Judaism has always known God to embody judgment as well as love. The proper balance between these two, ever the struggle of the rabbis themselves (loving the people as well as the law), is a struggle that Jewish sources have long seen as existing in God as well. *Ḥesed* therefore emerges linked to its own opposite, described both as *Din,* the judgment of God, and *Gevurah,* the bastion of divine power. This is a force that measures and limits love, that controls the flow of *Ḥesed* in response to the needs, abilities, and deserts of those who are to receive it.

Ḥesed represents the God of love, calling forth the response of love in the human soul as well. *Gevurah* represents the God we humans fear, the One before whose power we stand in trembling. The kabbalists saw *Ḥesed* as the faith of Abraham, described by the prophet as "Abraham My lover" (Isaiah 41:8). Abraham, the first of God's true earthly followers, stands parallel to *Ḥesed,* the first quality to emerge within God. He is the man of love, the one who will leave all behind and follow God across the deserts, willing to offer everything, even to place his beloved son upon the altar, for love of God. *Gevurah,* on the other hand, is the God called "Fear of Isaac" (Genesis 31:42). This is the divine face Isaac sees when bound to that altar, confronting the God he believes is about to demand his life. Isaac's piety is of a different quality than his father's. Trembling obedience, rather than love, marks his path through life. In the *Zohar,* the "Fear of Isaac" is sometimes depicted as a God of terror.

The linking together of *Ḥesed* and *Gevurah* is an infinitely delicate balance. Too much love and there is no judgment, none of the moral demand that is so essential to the fabric of Judaism. But too much power or judgment is even worse. The kabbalists see this aspect of the divine and human self as fraught with danger, the very birthplace of evil. *Gevurah* represents the "left" side of the divine as the *sefirot* emerge in humanlike form. The *Zohar* speaks of a discontent that arises on this "left" side of God. *Gevurah* becomes impatient with *Ḥesed,* unwilling to see judgment set aside in the name of love. Rather than permitting love to flow in measured ways, *Gevurah* seeks for some cosmic moment to rule alone, to hold back the flow of love. In this "moment," divine power turns to rage or fury; out of it all the forces of evil are born, darkness emerging from the light of God, a shadow of the divine universe that continues to exist throughout history, sustained by the evil wrought by humans below. Here we have one of the most important moral lessons of Kabbalah. Judgment not tempered by love brings about evil; power obsessed with itself turns demonic. The force of evil is often referred to by the *Zohar* as *sitra aḥra*, the "other side," indicating that it represents a parallel emanation to that of the *sefirot*. But the origin of that demonic reality that both parallels and mocks the divine is not in some "other" distant force. The demonic is born of an imbalance within the divine, flowing ultimately from the same source as all else, the single source of being.

The proper balance of *Ḥesed* and *Gevurah* results in the sixth *sefirah*, the center of the sefirotic universe. This configuration represents the personal God of biblical and rabbinic tradition. This is God seated on the throne, the one to whom prayer is most centrally addressed. Poised between the "right" and "left" forces within divinity, the "blessed Holy One" is the key figure in a central column of *sefirot*, positioned directly below *Keter*, the divine that precedes all duality. The sixth *sefirah* is represented by the third patriarch, Jacob, also called Israel—the perfect integration of the forces of Abraham and Isaac, the God who unites and balances love and fear.

Nonpersonal designations for this sixth *sefirah* include *Tif'eret* (Beauty, Splendor), *Raḥamin* (Compassion), *mishpat* (balanced judgment), and *emet* (truth). The three consonants of *emet* represent the first, middle, and last letters of the alphabet. Truth is stretched forth across the whole of Being, joining the extremes of right and left, *Ḥesed* and *Gevurah*, into a single integrated personality. Thus is the sixth *sefirah* also described as the central "beam" in God's construction of the universe. Adopting a line from Moses' Tabernacle (Exodus 26:28), depicted by the rabbis as reflecting the cosmic structure, Jacob or the sixth *sefirah* is called "the central beam, reaching from one end unto the other."

In Jacob or *Tif'eret* we reach the synthesis that resolves the original tension between *Ḥesed* and *Gevurah*, the inner "right" and "left," love and judgment. The "blessed Holy One" as a personal God is also the uppermost manifestation called "Israel," thus serving as a model of idealized human personality. Each member of the house of Israel partakes of this Godhead, who may also be understood as a totemic representation of His people below. "Jacob" is in this sense the perfect human—a new Adam, according to the sages—the radiant-faced elder extending blessing through the world. This is also the God of *imitatio dei*. In balancing their own lives, the people of Israel imitate the God who stands at the center between right and left, balancing all the cosmic forces. That God knows them and sees Himself in them, meaning that the struggle to integrate love and judgment is not only the great human task, but also a reflection of the cosmic struggle. The inner structure of psychic life *is* the hidden structure of the universe; it is because of this that we can come to know God by the path of inward contemplation and true self-knowledge.

The key dialectical triad of *Ḥesed-Gevurah-Tif'eret* is followed on the kabbalistic chart by a second triad, that of the *sefirot Netsaḥ, Hod*, and *Yesod*, arranged in the same manner as those above them. Little that is new takes place on this level of divinity. These *sefirot* are essentially channels through which the higher energies pass on their way into the tenth *sefirah*, *Malkhut* or *Shekhinah*, the source of all life for the lower worlds. The only major function assigned to *Netsaḥ* and *Hod* in the kabbalistic sources is their serving as the sources of prophecy. Moses is the single human to rise to the level of *Tif'eret*, to become "bridegroom of the *Shekhinah*." Other mortals can experience the sefirotic universe only as reflected in the *Shekhinah*, the single portal though which they can enter. (This is the "formal" view of the kabbalists, though it is a position exceeded by a great many passages in the *Zohar* and elsewhere.) The prophets other than Moses occupy an intermediate position, receiving their visions and messages from the seventh and eighth *sefirot*, making prophecy a matter of participation in the inner sefirotic life of God.

The ninth *sefirah* represents the joining together of all the cosmic forces, the flow of all the energies above now united again in a single place. In this sense the ninth *sefirah* is parallel to the second: *Ḥokhmah* began the flow of these forces from a single point; now *Yesod* (Foundation), as the ninth is called, reassembles them and prepares to direct their flow once again. When gathered in *Yesod*, it becomes clear that the life animating the *sefirot*, often described in metaphors of either light or water, is chiefly to be seen as male sexual energy, specifically as semen. Following the Greek physician Galen, medieval medicine saw semen as originating in the brain (*Ḥokhmah*), flowing down through the spinal column (the central column, *Tif'eret*), into the testicles (*Netsaḥ* and *Hod*), and thence into the phallus (*Yesod*). The sefirotic process thus leads to the great union of the nine *sefirot* above, through *Yesod*, with the female *Shekhinah*. She becomes filled and impregnated with the fullness of divine energy and She in turn gives birth to the lower worlds, including both angelic beings and human souls.

The biblical personality associated with the ninth *sefirah* is Joseph, the only figure regularly described in rabbinic literature as *tsaddiq* or "righteous." He is given this epithet because he rejected the wiles of Potiphar's wife, making him a symbol of male chastity or sexual purity. The *sefirah* itself is thus often called *tsaddiq*, the place where God is represented as the embodiment of moral righteousness. So too is *Yesod* designated as *berit* or "covenant," again referring to sexual purity through the covenant of circumcision.

But there is more than one way to read these symbols. The ninth *sefirah* stands for male potency as well as sexual purity. The kabbalists resolutely insist that these are ideally identical and are not to be separated from one another. Of course sexual transgression and temptation were well known to them; the circle of the *Zohar* was quite extreme in its views on sexual sin—and on the great damage it could cause both to soul and cosmos. But the inner world of the *sefirot* was completely holy, a place where no sin abided. Here the flow of male energy represented only fruitfulness and blessing. The fulfillment of the entire sefirotic system, especially as seen in Castile, lay in the union of these two final *sefirot*. *Yesod* is, to be sure, the agent or lower manifestation of *Tif'eret*, the true bridegroom of the Song of Songs or the King who weds the *matronita*—*Shekhinah*—as the grand lady of the cosmos. But the fascination with the sexual aspect of this union is very strong, especially in the *Zohar*, and that leads to endless symbolic presentations of the union of *Yesod* and *Malkhut*, the feminine tenth *sefirah*.

By far the richest network of symbolic associations is that connected with the tenth and final *sefirah*. As *Malkhut* (Kingdom), it represents the realm over which the King (*Tif'eret*) has dominion, sustaining and protecting her as the true king takes responsibility for his kingdom. At the same time, it is this *sefirah* that is charged with the rule of the lower world; the blessed Holy One's *Malkhut* is the lower world's ruler. The biblical personage associated with *Malkhut* is David (somewhat surprisingly, given its usual femininity), the symbol of kingship. David is also the psalmist, ever crying out in longing for the blessings of God to flow from above. While *Malkhut* receives the flow of all the upper *sefirot* from *Yesod*, She has some special affinity for the left side. For this reason She is sometimes called "the gentle aspect of judgment," a mitigated version of *Gevurah*. Several *Zohar* passages, however, paint Her in portraits of seemingly ruthless vengeance in punishing the wicked. A most complicated picture of femininity appears in the *Zohar*, ranging from the most highly romanticized to the most frightening and bizarre.

The last *sefirah* is also called *Shekhinah*, an ancient rabbinic term for the indwelling divine presence. In the medieval Jewish imagination, this appellation for God had been transformed into a winged divine being, hovering over the community of Israel and protecting them from harm. The *Shekhinah* was also said to dwell in Israel's midst, to follow them into exile, and to participate in their suffering. In the latest phases of midrashic literature, there begins to appear a distinction between God and His *Shekhinah*, partly a reflection of medieval philosophical attempts to assign the biblical anthropomorphisms to a being less than the Creator. The kabbalists identify this *Shekhinah* as the spouse or divine consort of the blessed Holy One. She is the tenth *sefirah*, therefore a part of God included within the divine ten-in-one unity. But She is tragically exiled, distanced from Her divine Spouse. Sometimes She is seen to be either seduced or taken captive by the evil hosts of *sitra aḥra*; then God and the righteous below must join forces in order to liberate Her. The great drama of religious life, according to the kabbalists, is that of protecting *Shekhinah* from the forces of evil and joining Her to the holy Bridegroom who ever awaits Her. Here one can see how medieval Jews adapted the values of chivalry—the rescue of the maiden from the clutches of evil—to fit their own spiritual context.

As the female partner within the divine world, the tenth *sefirah* comes to be described by a host of symbols, derived both from the natural world and from the legacy of Judaism, that are classically associated with femininity. She is the moon, dark on her own but receiving and giving off the light of the sun. She is the sea, into whom all waters flow; the earth, longing to be fructified by the rain that falls from heaven. She is the heavenly Jerusalem, into whom the King will enter; She is the throne upon which He is seated, the Temple or Tabernacle, dwelling place of His glory. She is also *Keneset Yisra'el*, the embodied "Community [or: Assembly] of Israel" itself, identified with the Jewish people. The tenth *sefirah* is a passive/receptive female with regard to the *sefirot* above Her, receiving their energies and being fulfilled by their presence within Her. But She is ruler, source of life, and font of all blessing for the worlds below, including the human soul. The kabbalist sees himself as a devotee of the *Shekhinah*. She may never be worshiped separately from the divine unity. Indeed, this separation of *Shekhinah* from the forces above was the terrible sin of Adam that brought about exile from Eden. Yet it is only through Her that humans have access to the mysteries beyond. All prayer is channelled through Her, seeking to energize Her and raise Her up in order to effect the sefirotic unity. The primary function of the religious life, with all its duties and obligations, is to rouse the *Shekhinah* into a state of love.

All realms outside the divine proceed from *Shekhinah*. She is surrounded most immediately by a richly pictorialized host. Sometimes these surrounding beings are seen as angels; at others, they are the maidens who attend the Bride at Her marriage canopy. They inhabit and rule over variously described realms or "palaces" of light and joy. The *Zohar* devotes much attention to describing seven such palaces with names that include "Palace of Love," "Palace of the Sapphire Pavement" (alluding to the vision of God in Exodus 24:10), "Palace of Desire," and so forth. The "palaces" (*heikhalot*) of the Zoharic world are historically derived from the remains of the ancient Merkavah or Heikhalot mysticism, a tradition that was only dimly remembered by the *Zohar*'s day. In placing the *heikhalot* beneath the *Shekhinah*, the kabbalists mean to say that the visionary ascent of the Merkavah mystic was a somewhat lesser sort of religious experience than their own symbolic/contemplative ascent to the heights of the sefirotic universe, one that ascended with the *Shekhinah* as She reached into the highest realms. While the inner logic of the kabbalists' emanational thinking would seem to indicate that *all* beings, including the physical universe, flow forth from *Shekhinah*, the medieval abhorrence of associating God with corporeality complicates the picture, leaving Kabbalah with a complex and somewhat divided attitude toward the material world. The world in which we live, especially for the *Zohar*, is a thorough mingling of divine and demonic elements. Both the holy imprint of the ten *sefirot* and the frightening structure of multilayered *qelippot*, or demonic "shells," are to be found within it.

IV

The *Zohar* first made its appearance in Castile toward the end of the thirteenth century. Passages from it are included in works by Castilian and Catalonian kabbalists writing at about that time. In some cases these are presented as quotations, attributed to "Yerushalmi" (usually referring to the Jerusalem Talmud, but sometimes also to other work originating in the Holy Land) or to Midrash, particularly "the Midrash of Rabbi Shim'on son of Yoḥai." Some refer to it as an ancient work. In other cases, including passages in the writings of well-known Castilian kabbalist Moses de León and the Barcelona author Baḥya ben Asher, pieces identical to sections of the *Zohar* are simply absorbed within their writings and presented as their own. By the second decade of the fourteenth century, the *Zohar* is referred to (by the author of *Tiqqunei Zohar*) as a "prior" or completed document. Large portions of it are by then available to such authors as David ben Judah he-Ḥasid, who paraphrases and translates various sections, and the Italian kabbalist Menaḥem Recanati, who quotes copiously from the *Zohar* in his own commentary on the Torah. Recanati seems to be the first one to regularly refer to this group of sources by the term *Zohar*.

The question of the *Zohar*'s origins has puzzled its readers ever since its first appearance, and no simple and unequivocal statement as to the question of its authorship can be made even in our own day. There is no question that the work was composed in the decades immediately preceding its appearance. It responds to literary works and refers to historical events that place it in the years following 1270. The 1280s seem like the most likely decade for composition of the main body of the *Zohar*, probably preceded by the *Midrash ha-Ne'lam* and possibly certain other sections. Indeed it is quite possible that the *Zohar* was still an ongoing project when texts of it first appeared, and that parts of it were being written even a decade later. Because the question of the *Zohar*'s origins has been so hotly debated by readers and scholars over the centuries, it is important to offer a brief account here of the history of this discussion.

Debate about the *Zohar*'s origins began in the very decade of its appearance. Fragments of the *Zohar* were first distributed by Rabbi Moses de León, who claimed that they were copied from an ancient manuscript in his possession. This was a classic technique of pseudepigraphy, the attribution of esoteric teachings to the ancients, to give them the respectability associated with hoary tradition. While some naive souls seem to have believed quite literally in the antiquity of the text and the existence of such a manuscript, others, including some of De León's fellow kabbalists, joined with him in the pretense in order to heighten the prestige of these teachings. While they may have known that De León was the writer, and may even have participated in mystical conversations that were reflected in the emerging written text, they did believe that the *content* of the *Zohar*'s teachings was indeed ancient and authentic. They probably saw nothing wrong in the creation of a grand literary fiction that provided for these ancient-yet-new teachings an elevated literary setting, one worthy of their profound truth. There were, however, skeptics and opponents of the *Zohar* right from the beginning, who depicted the whole enterprise as one of literary forgery.

Fascinating evidence of this early controversy is found in an account written by the kabbalist Isaac of Acre, a wandering mystic who arrived in Castile in 1305. A manuscript version of Isaac's account was known to the sixteenth-century chronicler Abraham Zacuto and was included in his *Sefer Yuḥasin*. Isaac tells us that he had already heard of the *Zohar*, and came to Castile to learn more about it and specifically to investigate the question of the *Zohar*'s origins. He managed to meet De León shortly before the latter's death. De León assured him that the ancient manuscript was real, and offered to show it to him. By the time Isaac arrived at Avila, where De León had lived in the last years of his life, he had a chance only to meet the kabbalist's widow. She denied that the manuscript had ever existed, recounting that her husband had told her that he was claiming ancient origins for his own work for pecuniary advantage. Others, however, while agreeing that there was no ancient manuscript source, claimed that De León had written the *Zohar* "through the power of the Holy Name." (This might refer either to some sort of trancelike "automatic writing" or to a sense that he saw himself as a reincarnation of Rabbi Shim'on and—through the Name—had access to his teachings.) Various other players then enter the account in a series of claims and counterclaims, and the text breaks off just before a disciple of De León is able to present what seems like promising testimony in the *Zohar*'s behalf.

This account has been used by opponents of the *Zohar* and of Kabbalah in general in various attempts to dismiss the *Zohar* as a forgery and Moses de León as a charlatan. Most outspoken among these attempts is that of the nineteenth-century historian Heinrich Graetz, for whom the *Zohar* was the epitome of the most lowly, superstitious element within medieval Judaism. Graetz and others assumed that the wife was the one who spoke the truth, all other explanations serving to cover or justify the obvious chicanery of the author. Wanting to denigrate the *Zohar*—which did not fit the early modern Enlightenment idea of proper Judaism—Graetz did not consider the possibility that De León might have told his wife such things for reasons other than their being the simple truth. Sadly, her account may reflect the kabbalist's assumption of his wife's inability to appreciate his literary intentions. The claim that he did it for the sake of selling books has about it the air of an explanation to a spouse, offered in a dismissive context.

Modern *Zohar* scholarship begins with the young Gershom Scholem's attempts to refute Graetz. He set out in the late 1920s to show that the picture was more complex and that indeed there might be earlier layers to the *Zohar*.

Awed by the vastness of the *Zohar* corpus, he found it hard to believe that all of it could have been the work of a single author. But in a series of stunningly convincing essays Scholem reversed himself and came to the conclusion that the entire *Zohar* had indeed been written by De León. He supported this conclusion by careful analysis of the *Zohar's* language, its knowledge of the geography of the land of Israel, its relationship to philosophy and to earlier works of Kabbalah, and references to specific historical events or dates. Most convincing was Scholem's painstaking philological analysis. Scholem compared the *Zohar's* unique (and sometimes "mistaken") use of Aramaic linguistic forms to characteristic patterns of language to be found (uniquely, he claimed) in De León's Hebrew works. Here he believed he had found something of a literary fingerprint, making it finally clear that De León was the author. As to the magnitude of the work and its attribution to a single individual, Scholem was consoled by historical parallels, particularly that of Jakob Boehme, a seventeenth-century German shoemaker, originally illiterate, who had composed a vast corpus of writings under the force of mystical inspiration.

But the matter is by no means ended here. The fact that Scholem agreed with Graetz on the question of single authorship did not at all mean that he shared in his lowly opinion of the *Zohar* or its author. The parallel to Boehme in fact sounds rather like the writing "through the power of the Holy Name" that had been suggested to Isaac of Acre. Assuming that Moses de León did write the entire *Zohar*, the question became one of understanding *how* this might be the case. Two specific questions here come to the fore. One concerns the notable differences between the *Zohar's* various sections. Could one person have written the *Midrash ha-Ne'lam*, with its hesitant, incomplete usage of sefirotic symbolism; the *Idrot*, where that symbolism was incorporated and surpassed; and the obscure *Matnitin* and *Heikhalot*, along with the rich narrative and homilies of the main *Zohar* text? What can account for all these seeming variations in both literary style and symbolic content?

The other question has to do with the intriguing relationship between a single author and the many voices that speak forth from within the *Zohar's* pages. Is the community of mystics described here entirely a figment of the author's creative imagination? Is there not some real experience of religious community that is reflected in the *Zohar's* pages? Might it be possible, to take an extreme view, that each of the speakers represents an actual person, a member of the Castilian kabbalists' circle, here masked behind the name of an ancient rabbi? Or is there some other way in which the presence of multiple authors (or participants in the group's ongoing conversations) can be detected within the *Zohar's* pages?

Contemporary scholarship on the *Zohar* (especially the pioneering work of Yehuda Liebes and its development by Ronit Meroz) has parted company with Scholem on the question of single authorship. While it is tacitly accepted that De León did either write or edit long sections of the *Zohar*, including the main narrative (homiletical body) of the text, he is not thought to be the only writer involved. Multiple layers of literary creativity can be discerned within the text. It may be that the *Zohar* should be seen as the product of a *school* of mystical practitioners and writers, one that may have existed even before 1270 and continued into the early years of the fourteenth century. Certain texts, including the *Midrash ha-Ne'lam* (perhaps an earlier rescension of it than that which has survived?) belong to the oldest stratum of writing. Then the main part of the *Zohar*, including both the epic tale and teachings of Rabbi Shim'on and his disciples, was indeed composed in the decades claimed by Scholem. Work on the *Zohar* did not cease, however, with the turn of the fourteenth century or the passing of Moses de León. In fact, the author of the *Tiqqunei Zohar* and the *Ra'aya Meheimna*, seen by Scholem as "later" addenda to the *Zohar* corpus, may represent the third "generation" of this ongoing school. It would have been in his day, and perhaps with the cooperation of several editors, that the fragments of the *Zohar* as first circulated were linked together into the somewhat larger units found in the surviving fourteenth- and fifteenth-century manuscripts.

There is no single, utterly convincing piece of evidence that has led scholars to this revision of Scholem's view. It is rather a combination of factors stemming from close readings of the text and a body of scholarship on it that did not yet exist in Scholem's day. There is considerable evidence of what might be called "internal commentary" within the *Zohar* text. The "Secrets of the Torah" are an expansion of the brief and enigmatic *Matnitin*, as the *Idrot* comment and enlarge upon themes first developed in the *Sifra di-Tsni'uta*. In the *Zohar* narrative, whole or partial stories are told more than once—one version seemingly an expansion of an earlier rescension. The same is true of certain homilies, some of which are repeated in part or whole several times within the text. These expansions and repetitions could be explained as the developing project of a single author; however, when taken together with other factors (the differing sections of the *Zohar* and the multiple "voices" that speak within the text), they point more toward multiple or collective authorship. Historical evidence has shown that closed schools or societies (*havurot*) for various purposes were a common organizational form within Spanish Jewry. The image of Rabbi Shim'on and his followers, encountering a series of mysterious teachers in the course of their wanderings, looks rather like a description of a real such school, meeting various mystics from outside its ranks who were then accepted by the school's leader as legitimate teachers of secret Torah.

It is particularly intriguing to compare this fictionalized but historically real school of kabbalists to another that is rather more clearly described in documents available to us. In neighboring Catalonia, the kabbalistic school of Naḥmanides lasted—side by side with his halakhic school—for three generations. Naḥmanides' disciple Solomon ben Adret (ca. 1235–ca. 1310) carried his master's teachings forward to a group of disciples who then wrote multiple commentaries on the secret aspects of Naḥmanides' work. That circle was significantly more conservative in its views of kabbalistic creativity than was the Castilian group. But we could easily imagine a parallel school of Castilian kabbalists—beginning with the "Gnostics" of the mid-thirteenth century and extending forward over the same three generations—whose collective literary product, much freer and richer in imagination than the Naḥmanidean corpus, included the body of work finally edited into what later generations have come to know as the *Zohar*. It may indeed be that the competition between these two schools of mystical thought had some role in advancing the editing process that finally resulted in the *Zohar* as we know it in its printed version.

V

The *Zohar* was composed in the Castile of the late thirteenth century, a period that marked the near completion of the Reconquista and something of a golden age of enlightenment in the history of Christian Spain. As the wars of conquest ended, the monarchy was able to ground itself and establish central authority over the semi-independent and often unruly Spanish nobility. This included responsibility for protection of the Jews, who generally fared better at the hands of kings than at the arbitrary mercy of local rivals. Alfonso X (1252–1284) was known as *el Sabio* or "the Wise" because of his interest in the sciences—which he was willing to learn from Jews and Muslims when necessary—as well as history, literature, and art.

Jews retained a high degree of juridical and cultural autonomy, as well as freedom of religious practice, in the Castile of this period. They constituted a significant percentage of city and town dwellers, generally choosing to live in self-enclosed neighborhoods and communities. But Jews were seen by Christian society as barely tolerated outsiders, and they viewed themselves as humiliated and victimized exiles. As an emerging class of Christian burghers came to see the Jews as rivals, the economic opportunities afforded by the early Reconquista years were gradually eroded. Jews were required to wear distinguishing garb, synagogue building was restricted, and various burdens of extra taxation came to be an expected part of Jewish life.

Most significantly, Jews were under constant pressure to convert to Christianity in the atmosphere of a church triumphant with the glory of having vanquished the Moorish armies and standing on the verge of ending the "stain" of Islamic incursion into Christian Europe. Alfonso X commissioned translations of both the Qur'an and the Talmud into Castilian, partly out of scholarly interest but also as an aid to the ongoing missionary campaign. The success of the Reconquista itself was trumpeted as great testimony to the validity of Christian claims. The Christian supersessionist theology, beginning with the Church Fathers but growing in stridency through the Middle Ages, claimed tirelessly that Judaism after Christ was an empty shell, a formalist attachment to the past, lacking in true faith. This message was delivered regularly in polemical writings, in sermons that Jews were forced to hear, and in casual encounters between Jews and Christians. We should remember that Jews in Spain spoke the same language as their neighbors and lived with them in the same towns and cities. Their degree of isolation from their surroundings was significantly less than that of later Jews in eastern Europe, the lens through which all Jewish diaspora experience is often mistakenly viewed in our time.

In this context, the *Zohar* may be viewed as a grand defense of Judaism, a poetic demonstration of the truth and superiority of Jewish faith. Its authors knew a great deal about Christianity, mostly from observing it at close hand but also from reading certain Christian works, including the New Testament, which Dominicans and other eager seekers of converts were only too happy to place in the hands of literate and inquisitive Jews. The kabbalists' attitude toward the religion of their Christian neighbors is a complex one, and it also has come down to us through a veil of self-censorship. Jews writing in medieval Europe, especially those promulgating innovative religious teachings that were controversial even within the Jewish community, must have been well aware that their works would be read by Christian censors (often themselves Jewish apostates) who would make them pay dearly for outright insults to the Christian faith.

The *Zohar* is filled with disdain and sometimes even outright hatred for the gentile world. Continuing in the old midrashic tradition of repainting the subtle shadings of biblical narrative in moralistic black and white, the *Zohar* pours endless heaps of wrath and malediction on Israel's enemies. In the context of biblical commentary these are always such ancient figures as Esau, Pharaoh, Amalek, Balaam, and the mixed multitude of runaway slaves who left Egypt with Israel, a group treated by the *Zohar* with special venom. All of these were rather safe objects for attack, but it does not take much imagination to realize that the true address of this resentment was the oppressor in whose midst the authors lived. This becomes significantly clearer when we consider the *Zohar*'s comments on the religion of these ancient enemies. They are castigated repeatedly as worshipers of the demonic and practitioners of black magic, enemies of divine unity and therefore dangerous disturbers of the cosmic balance by which the world survives. Israel, and especially the kabbalistic "companions" who understand this situation, must do all they can to right the balance and save the *Shekhinah* from those dark forces and their vast network of accursed supporters on earth. As Moses had fought off the evil spells of Balaam—darkest of all magicians—in his day, so must the disciples of Rabbi Shim'on fight those evil forces that stand opposed to the dawning of the messianic light that is soon to come.

All of this is said, of course, without a single negative word about Christianity. But Rabbi Shim'on and his second-century companions lived in a time when the enemies of biblical Israel had long disappeared from the earth.

The same is even more true of the reader in medieval Christian Spain, who is being firmly admonished to join the battle against those who would strengthen the evil forces—wounding or capturing the *Shekhinah* and thus keeping the divine light from shining into this world. It does not require a great deal of imagination to understand who these worshipers of darkness must be. We must remember, of course, that this was also the era when the Christian image of the Jew as magician and devil-worshiper was becoming rampant. The *Zohar*'s unstated but clearly present view of Christianity as sorcery is a mirror reflection of the image of Judaism that was gaining acceptance, with much more dangerous consequences, throughout the Christian world.

But this is only one side of the picture. As people of deep faith and of great literary and aesthetic sensibility, the kabbalists also found themselves impressed by, and perhaps even attracted to, certain aspects of the Christian story and the religious lives of the large and powerful monastic communities that were so prominent in Christian Spain. The tale of Jesus and his faithful apostles, the passion narrative, and the struggles of the early Church were all powerful and attractive stories. Aspects of Christian theology—including both the complicated oneness of the trinitarian God and the passionate and ever present devotion to a quasi-divine female figure—made their mark on the kabbalistic imagination. The monastic orders, and especially their commitment to celibacy and poverty, must have been impressive to mystics whose own tradition did not make such demands on them, but who shared the medieval otherworldliness that would have highly esteemed such devotion.

The kabbalists were much disconcerted by the power of Christianity to attract Jewish converts, an enterprise that was given high priority particularly by the powerful Dominican order. Much that is to be found in the *Zohar* was intended to serve as a counterweight to the potential attractiveness of Christianity to Jews, and perhaps even to the kabbalists themselves. Of course this should not be seen as an exclusive way of reading the *Zohar*, a mystical work which was not composed chiefly as a polemical text. Nevertheless, the need to proudly assert Judaism's spirit in the face of triumphalist Christianity stands in the background of the *Zohar* and should not be ignored as we read it.

VI

The *Zohar*, as the contemporary reader of the original encounters it, is a three-volume work, constituting some sixteen hundred folio pages, ordered in the form of a commentary on the Torah. The first volume covers the *Zohar* on Genesis, the second volume is *Zohar* on Exodus, and the third volume completes the remaining three books of the Torah. The text is divided into homilies on the weekly Torah portions, taking the form of an ancient midrash. Within this form, however, are included long digressions and subsections of the *Zohar*, some of which have no relation to this midrashic structure and seem to be rather arbitrarily placed in one Torah portion or another.[3] An addition to the three volumes is *Zohar Ḥadash* (New *Zohar*), a collection of materials that were omitted from the earliest printed *Zohar* editions but were later culled from manuscript sources. Here we find addenda to the Torah portions but also partial commentaries on Ruth, Lamentations, and the Song of Songs. Another work usually considered part of the *Zohar* literature is *Tiqqunei Zohar*, a kabbalistic commentary on the opening verse of Genesis that explicates it in seventy ways. This work—along with the *Ra'aya Meheimna* or "Faithful Shepherd" passages published within the *Zohar* itself, mostly taking the form of a commentary on the commandments—is seen by modern scholars to be the work of a slightly later kabbalist, one who wrote perhaps in the opening decades of the fourteenth century and saw himself as continuing the *Zohar* tradition.

As stated, the main body of the *Zohar* takes the form of midrash: a collection of homiletical explications of the biblical text. The *Zohar* enters fully into the midrashic genre, even though that form of writing was considered antiquated in the time and place where the *Zohar* was composed. Its authors were especially learned in aggadah and used it ingeniously, often convincingly portraying themselves as ancient midrashic masters. But the anachronism of their style was intentional. The *Zohar* is an attempt to re-create a form of discourse that would have seemed appropriate to a work originating with its chief speakers, Rabbi Shim'on son of Yoḥai and those of his circle, who lived in the land of Israel eleven hundred years earlier. In fact, this medieval midrash is based on a thorough knowledge of the entire earlier Jewish tradition, including rabbinic, philosophical, and esoteric works. Its purpose, as will quickly become clear to the reader, goes far beyond that of the ancient midrashic model. The *Zohar* seeks nothing less than to place the kabbalistic tradition, as it had developed over the preceding centuries, into the mouths of these much-revered sages of antiquity and to use them as its mouthpiece for showing the reader that the entire Torah is alive with kabbalistic secrets and veiled references to the "mystery of faith" as the kabbalists taught it. In this sense, the *Zohar* may be seen as an attempt to create a new midrash or, as one scholar has put it, a renaissance of the midrashic art in the Middle Ages.

The old midrashic homilies were often preceded by a series of "Openings," introductory proems in which the homilist would demonstrate his skill, picking his way through a series of biblical associations eventually leading up to the subject at hand. The *Zohar* too uses such "Openings," but with a very different purpose in mind. Here the preacher wants to "open" the scriptural verse itself, remove its outer shell, and find its secret meaning. In this way, the verse itself may serve as an opening or a gateway into the "upper" world for the one

---

3. For a discussion of how these special sections of the *Zohar* have been handled in this translation, see the Translator's Introduction.

who reads it. This leads us closer to the real purpose of Zoharic exegesis. The *Zohar* wants to take the reader inside the divine life. It wants ever to retell the story of the flow of the *sefirot*, their longings and union, the arousal of love above and the way in which that arousal causes blessing to flow throughout the worlds. This is the essential story of Kabbalah, and the *Zohar* finds it in verse after verse, portion after portion, of the Torah text. But each retelling offers a new and often startlingly different perspective. The *Zohar* is ever enriching the kabbalistic narrative by means of retelling it from the vantage point of yet another hermeneutic insight. On each page yet another verse, word, or tale of the Torah is opened or "uncovered" to reveal new insight into the great story of the *Zohar*, that which it proffers as the truth of the Torah, of the cosmos, and of the reader's soul.

In the series of homilies by various speakers around a particular verse or moment in the scriptural text, the *Zohar* takes its readers through multiple layers of understanding, reaching from the surface layer of "plain" meaning into ever more profound revelations. A great love of language is revealed in this process; plays on words and subtle shadings of meaning often serve as ways to a total reconfiguration of the Scripture at hand. For this reason, the *Zohar*'s best readers, both traditional and modern, are those who share its endless fascination with the mystery of words, including both their aural and graphic (or "spoken" and "written") manifestations.

Other kabbalists contemporaneous with the *Zohar* were offering multileveled readings of Scripture as well. Rabbi Baḥya ben Asher of Barcelona immediately comes to mind. His Torah commentary, written in the 1290s, offers the best example of the fourfold interpretation of Scripture in its Jewish form: verse after verse is read first for its plain meaning, then according to "the way of Midrash," followed by "the way of intellect" or philosophical allegory, and finally "the way of Kabbalah." Rabbi Baḥya's work is in fact important as one of the earliest sources for quotations from the *Zohar*.

The *Zohar* offers no such neat classifications. Insights offered by a group of "companions" discussing a text may bounce back and forth from readings that could be (and sometimes indeed are) found in earlier midrashic works to ways of reading that belong wholly to the world of Kabbalah. Kabbalistic interpretations are sometimes so well "sewn" into the midrashic fabric that the reader is left wondering whether the kabbalistic referent might not indeed be the "real" meaning of a given biblical verse or rabbinic passage. In one well-known text, the *Zohar* refers to mystical interpretations as the "soul" of Torah, distinguished from the narrative that forms the outward "garments" and the legal derivations that serve as Torah's "body" (playing on the phrase *gufei Torah* ["bodies of Torah"], that in rabbinic parlance means "essential teachings"). That text also suggests a further level of readings, the "innermost soul" of Torah that will not be fully revealed until messianic times. But when encountering actual passages from the *Zohar*, it is not easy to determine just where their author stood in the process of undressing the textual bride. Here as almost everywhere, the poesis of the *Zohar* overflows the banks, thwarting any attempt at gradation or definition. It is mostly within the area of "soul" or kabbalistic readings that the assembled sages reveal layer after layer, showing that this level of reading itself is one that contains inexhaustible riches of the imagination. There is not a single mystical interpretation of a verse or passage that is *the* secret in the eyes of the *Zohar*. "Secret" (*sod* in Hebrew; *raza* in Aramaic) is rather a *method*, a way of reading that contains endless individual secrets within it.

The language of sefirotic symbolism offers the *Zohar* limitless opportunities for creative interpretations of Scripture. On the one hand, the *Zohar*'s speakers and authors exult in the newness and originality of this exegesis. Rabbi Shim'on and his disciples speak glowingly of *ḥiddushei Torah*, novellae in Torah interpretation, and their great value. God and the angels join in rejoicing over each new insight. But the *Zohar* also seeks to deny the newness of kabbalistic interpretation. Not only is the work itself allegedly an ancient one; the interpretive craft of the *Zohar* goes to a higher, deeper, and hence also more "ancient" level of the text. As the highest rung within the Godhead is sometimes called *Attiqa*, the elder or "ancient one," so does profound interpretation take Torah "back to its antiquity," to its original, pristine, highest state.

The *Zohar* stands within the long tradition of Jewish devotion to sacred study as a religious act. The faithful are commanded to "contemplate it day and night" (Joshua 1:8), traditionally taken to mean that the study and elaboration of Torah is ideally the full-time obligation of the entire community of male Israelites (women were exempted from the obligation to study, and only rarely were they offered more than a rudimentary education). This community viewed the Torah as an object of love, and an *eros* of Torah study is depicted in many passages in the rabbinic *aggadah*. Based on biblical images of feminine wisdom, Torah was described as the daughter and delight of God and as Israel's bride. Study of Torah, especially the elaboration of its law, was described by the sages as courtship and sometimes even as the shy, scholarly bridegroom's act of love, the consummation of this sacred marriage. The midrash on the Song of Songs, compiled in the sixth or seventh century, devotes a large part of its exegesis of that erotic text to discussing the revelation at Sinai and the delights of both God and the sages in the study of Torah.

The *Zohar* is well aware of these precedents and expands upon them in its own richer and even more daring version of *amor dei intellectualis*. The lush and well-watered gardens of the Song of Songs are the constant dwelling place of the *Zohar*, where frequent invocation of the Canticle is the order of the day. In the kabbalists' literary imagination, the gardens of eros in the Song, the *pardes* or "orchard" of mystical speculation itself, and the mystical Garden of Eden—into which God wanders each night "to take delight in the souls of the righteous"—have been thoroughly linked with one another. The description in

Genesis (2:10) of paradise—"a river goes forth from Eden to water the garden, whence it divides into four streams"—and certain key verses of the Canticle— "a spring amid the gardens, a well of living waters, flowing from Lebanon" (4:15) and others—are quoted endlessly to invoke the sense that to dwell in mystical exegesis is to sit in the shade of God's garden. Even more: the mystical exegete comes to understand that all of these gardens are but reflections of the true inner divine garden, the world of the *sefirot*, which *Sefer ha-Bahir* had already described as lush with trees, springs, and ponds of water.

The *Zohar* is devoted to the full range of religious obligations that the Torah places upon the community of Israel. The mysteries of the command-ments and the rhythms of the sacred year very much occupy its pages, even if we discount the somewhat later *Ra'aya Meheimna* (Faithful Shepherd) section, which is almost wholly devoted to the meaning of the commandments. Both prayer and the ancient Temple ritual, the classic Jewish forms of devotion, are given lofty kabbalistic interpretations, and the figure of the priest in particular is very central to the Zoharic imagination. Still, it is fair to say that the central religious act for the *Zohar* is the very one in which its heroes are engaged as described throughout its pages, and that is the act of study and interpretation of Torah. Again and again Rabbi Shim'on waxes eloquent in praise of those who study Torah, especially those who do so after midnight. They indeed take the place of the priests and Levites of old, "who stand in the house of the Lord by night." Those who awaken nightly to study the secrets of Torah become the earthly attendants of the divine bride, ushering Her into the chamber where She will unite at dawn with Her heavenly spouse. This somewhat modest depiction of the mystic devotee's role in the *hieros gamos* or sacred marriage rite that stands at the center of the kabbalistic imagination does not exclude a level of emotional/mystical reality in which the kabbalist himself is also the lover of that bride and a full participant in, rather than merely an attendant to, the act of union.

Torah in the *Zohar* is not conceived as a text, as an object, or as material, but as a living divine presence, engaged in a mutual relationship with the person who studies her. More than that, in the Zoharic consciousness Torah is compared to a beloved who carries on with her lovers a mutual and dynamic courtship. The *Zohar* on the portion *Mishpatim* contains, within the literary unit known as *Sava de-Mishpatim*, a description of a maiden in a palace. Here the way of the Torah's lover is compared to the way of a man with a maiden. Arousal within Torah is like an endless courting of the beloved: constant walking about the gates of her palace, an increasing passion to read her letters, the desire to see the beloved's face, to reveal her, and to be joined with her. The beloved in the nexus of this relationship is entirely active. She sends signals of her interest to her lover, she intensifies his passionate desire for her by games of revealing and hiding. She discloses secrets that stir his curiosity. She desires to be loved. The beloved is disclosed in an erotic progression before her lover out of a desire to reveal secrets that have been forever hidden within her. The relationship between Torah and her lover, like that of man and maiden in this parable, is dynamic, romantic, and erotic. This interpretive axiom of the work—according to which the relationship between student and that studied is not one of subject and object but of subject and subject, even an erotic relationship of lover and beloved—opens a great number of new possibilities.[4]

Seeing the act of Torah study as the most highly praised form of devotional activity places the *Zohar* squarely within the Talmudic tradition and at the same time provides a setting in which to go far beyond it. Here, unlike in the rabbinic sources, the *content* of the exegesis as well as the *process* is erotic in character. Formerly it was the ancient rabbis' intense devotion to the text and to the *process* of Torah study that had been so aptly described by the erotic metaphor. The laws derived in the course of this passionate immersion in the text were then celebrated as resulting from the embrace of Torah, even when they dealt with heave-offerings and tithes or ritual defilement and ablutions. (The Talmudic rabbi Akiva—the greatest hero of the rabbinic romance with the text—was inspired by his great love of Torah to derive "heaps and heaps of laws from the crowns on each of the letters." That indeed had been the genius of Rabbi Akiva's school of thought: *all* of Torah, even the seemingly most mundane, belonged to the great mystical moment of Sinai, the day when God gave Torah to Israel and proclaimed His love for her in the Song of Songs.) But the authors of the *Zohar* crave more than this. The *content* as well as the *process* has to reveal the great secret of unity, not merely the small secrets of one law or another. In the *Zohar*, the true subject matter that the kabbalist finds in every verse is the *hieros gamos* itself, the mystical union of the divine male and female—the eros that underlies and transforms Torah, making it into a symbolic textbook on the inner erotic life of God.

VII

But the *Zohar* is not only a book of Torah interpretation. It is also very much the story of a particular group of students of the Torah, a peripatetic band of disciples gathered around their master Rabbi Shim'on son of Yoḥai. In the main body of the *Zohar*, there appear nine such disciples: Rabbi El'azar (the son of Rabbi Shim'on), Rabbi Abba, Rabbi Yehudah, Rabbi Yitsḥak, Rabbi Ḥizkiyah, Rabbi Ḥiyya, Rabbi Yose, Rabbi Yeisa, and Rabbi Aḥa. A very significant part of the *Zohar* text is devoted to tales of their wanderings and adventures, proclamations of their great love for one another, accounts of their devotion to their master, and echoes of the great pleasure he takes in hearing their teachings. While on the road, wandering about from place to place in the

4. Melila Hellner-Eshed, "The Language of Mystical Experience in the Zohar: The Zohar through Its Own Eyes" (in Hebrew) (Ph.D. diss., Hebrew University, 2000), 19.

Holy Land, they encounter various other teachers in the form of mysterious elders, wondrous children, merchants, and donkey-drivers, all of whom are possessed of secrets that they share with this band of loving and faithful companions. Usually these mysterious figures know more than the wanderers had expected, and Rabbi Shim'on's disciples are often outshone in wisdom by these most unlikely figures. That too is part of the *Zohar's* story. A contemporary scholar notes that there are more than three hundred whole and partial stories of this sort contained within the *Zohar* text. In some places the narrative shifts from the earthly setting to one that takes place partly in heaven or "the Garden of Eden," in which the master is replaced by God Himself, who proclaims His pleasure at the innovations offered as the kabbalists engage in Torah.

These tales of Rabbi Shim'on and his disciples, wandering about the Galilee a thousand years before the *Zohar* was written, are clearly a work of fiction. But to say that is by no means to deny the possibility that a very real mystical brotherhood underlies the *Zohar* and shapes its spiritual character. Anyone who reads the *Zohar* over an extended period of time will come to see that the interface among the companions and the close relationship between the tales of their wanderings and the homilies they occasion are not the result of fictional imagination alone. Whoever wrote the work knew very well how fellow students respond to companionship and support and are inspired by one another's glowing rendition of a text. He (or they) has felt the warm glow of a master's praises and the shame of being shown up by a stranger in the face of one's peers. The *Zohar*—leaving aside for now the question of who actually penned the words—*reflects the experience* of a kabbalistic circle. It is one of a series of such circles of Jewish mystics, stretching back in time to Qumran, Jerusalem, Provence, and Gerona, and forward in history to Safed, Padua, Miedzybozh, Bratslav, and again to Jerusalem. The small circle of initiates gathered about a master is the way Kabbalah has always happened, and the *Zohar* is no exception. In fact, the collective experience of this group around Rabbi Shim'on son of Yoḥai as "recorded" in the *Zohar* forms the paradigm for all later Jewish mystical circles.

The group life reflected in the text is that of a band of living kabbalists, except that they occupied Castile of the thirteenth century rather than the land of Israel of the second. They lived in Toledo and Guadalajara rather than Tiberias and Sepphoris. Whether these real kabbalists wandered about in the Spanish countryside as their fictional counterparts did in the Holy Land is hard to know, but they certainly felt that the most proper setting for study of Torah was out of doors, especially in a garden or a grove of trees. Occasionally the companions in the *Zohar's* pages have conversations indoors, as when the disciples visit Rabbi Shim'on or they all travel to the home of Rabbi Pinḥas son of Ya'ir. Interestingly there is no house of study or synagogue that appears as a setting for any of their encounters. The *Zohar* very much prefers that they take place under the shade of a certain tree, at a spring of water, or at some similar place that might call to mind a verse from a psalm or the Song of Songs, with which a homily might then open.

The very frequent references in the text to the importance of secret Torah study at night raises the likelihood that this group of Spanish kabbalists shared for some time, as a regular, ritualized activity, a late-night session for the study of Kabbalah. If they were anything like their fictional counterparts, these sessions began after midnight and went until dawn, concluding with morning prayers. These nightly gatherings (of course there is no way to be certain whether or for how long they did take place on an actual level) were omitted on the Sabbath, when it was the companion's duty to be at home with his wife. They reached their annual climax on the eve of *Shavu'ot*, when the vigil was in preparation for a new receiving of the Torah. The intense climax of the *Zohar* narrative is the tale of two great and highly ritualized meetings of master and disciples in the *Idra*, a special chamber of assembly. In the first of these two assemblies, three of the companions die in the ecstasy of their mystical devotions. The second, the *Idra Zuta* or Lesser Assembly, records the death of Rabbi Shim'on himself and forms the grand conclusion of the *Zohar*.

Gershom Scholem once suggested that the *Zohar* takes the form of a "mystical novel." This suggestion is particularly intriguing because the *Zohar* appeared in Spain some three hundred years before Cervantes, who is often seen as the father of the modern novel. One may see the tales of Rabbi Shim'on and the companions as a sort of novel in formation, but it is clear that the form is quite rudimentary. When the *Zohar* wants to express an idea, it needs to slip back into the more familiar literary form of textual hermeneutics. The novelist in the classic post-Cervantes sense is one who can develop ideas or suggest complex thought patterns by means of character development and plot themselves, rather than by having the characters assemble and make a series of speeches to one another (though such moments are not entirely unknown in later fiction). It might be interesting to place the *Zohar* into the setting of such works as medieval troubadour romances, Chaucer's fourteenth-century *Canterbury Tales*, or the *Thousand and One Nights*. All of these are narrative cycles, frameworks of story into which smaller units (in these cases narrative, in the *Zohar*'s case homiletical) can be fitted. All of them, too, may be seen as precursors of the novel.

But the peregrinations of Rabbi Shim'on and his disciples are more than the "story" of the *Zohar*, whether fictional or masking a historical reality. In the *Zohar*, everything is indeed more than it appears to be. Master and disciples represent wandering Israel, both the ancient tribes in the wilderness on their way to the promised land, and the people of Israel in their present exile. While the ancient rabbis suggest to the would-be scholar to "exile yourself to a place of Torah," here exile or wandering is itself that place. The "place of Torah" is indeed wherever the companions happen to be, the home of the master or the grove of trees. Said in words that they might prefer, the "garden" of mystical conversation follows them wherever they wander, just as Miriam's movable well gave drink to Israel throughout their forty-year trek through the wilderness. The adventures of the companions show their participation in Israel's greatest suffering, that of exile.

Israel's historic exile, however, is itself symbolic, an earthly representation of a still greater exile, that of the *Shekhinah* from Her divine spouse. The nature and origin of this inner divine "exile" is one of the kabbalists' great mysteries. Some passages, both in the *Zohar* and in earlier sources, attribute it to the sin of Adam and Eve. In this sense, Kabbalah may be said to have a true sense of the "fall" or "original sin" of humans, much more so than the older rabbinic sources. The world as first created was a true Garden of Eden because the blessed Holy One and *Shekhinah* were "face-to-face," joined in constant embrace like that of the upper *sefirot Ḥokhmah* and *Binah*. Divine blessing thus coursed through the system without interruption, flowing through all of *Shekhinah*'s "hosts" and "palaces" into an idealized lower world as well. Only Adam and Eve's sin—sometimes depicted as that of separating *Shekhinah* from the upper *sefirot* to worship Her alone (symbolized by the separation of the Tree of Knowledge from its roots in the Tree of Life)—disturbed this initial harmony, which since the expulsion from Eden has been sporadic rather than constant, dependent upon the balance of human virtue and transgression.

But other passages express a somewhat darker vision of the exile within God. Here the very existence of the lower worlds is an after-effect of divine exile and would not have taken place without it. Some of these sources employ the old Platonic myth of androgyny, embedded in an ancient midrashic description of Adam and Eve, to explain the cosmic reality. Adam and Eve, according to the *aggadah*, were Siamese twins, conjoined back-to-back. This single being is that described in Genesis 1:27: "God created the human in His form; in the divine form He created him, male and female He created them." The forming of Eve from Adam's rib (or "side") in the following chapter is the separation of this pair, in which they are first turned face-to-face to one another, so that they might meet, see one another, and unite to propagate the species, fulfilling God's first command. The kabbalists claim that in this sense too humans are made in God's image: the *sefirot Tif'eret* and *Malkhut* were a single entity, back-to-back. They had to be "sawed" apart (a rather violent choice of verb) so that they might be properly united. Only through this union does the divine life begin to flow outward, giving life to worlds below. In order for our life to come about, in other words, God has to undergo a transformative act of great pain, one in which the divine becomes separated from itself, its future reunification to depend entirely upon the actions of these creatures below. Here exile and suffering are inherent in the cosmos, and the balm provided by human goodness is somewhat more superficial, an oasis of relief in the wandering that is indeed the necessary human and cosmic condition.

It is this exile that the kabbalists are acting out in their wanderings through the Galilee of their imagination. In this sense, it may indeed be said that the *Zohar* in its entirety is a symbolic work, not just a collection of symbolic interpretations of Scripture. The narratives themselves may be seen as the most profoundly symbolic and "kabbalistic" part of the *Zohar*'s *oeuvre*, not just a framework into which the homilies are woven.

VIII

Our discussion to this point leads us now to confront the question of the *Zohar* and religious/mystical experience. A first reading of the *Zohar* might give one the impression of a work that is more *mythical* than *mystical* in content; i.e., more involved with a narrative of cosmic origins and structures than it is with inner experience, the soul, or higher states of consciousness. But this view is partially misleading. To read the *Zohar* well is to fathom the experiential dimension of the entire text, including narrative, exegesis, cosmology, and all the rest. The kabbalist speaking in the sefirotic idiom is laying bare the inner-most structure of reality as he both understands and *experiences* it. That same structure is reflected in the cosmos, in Torah, and in the human (or more precisely: "Jewish") soul. The language of sefirotic symbolism provides a new lens through which to see Torah. But the power of that reading, especially as practiced in the circle of the *Zohar*, offers more than a hermeneutic. To open one's inner eyes to the new reality created by that pattern of thinking is to live within the realm of the *sefirot* themselves. The transformations of language and inner experience go hand in hand with one another; the breakthrough in consciousness to a higher realm of contemplative existence is conveyed through the vehicle of self-expression in sefirotic terms. Therefore to speak of the origins of the sefirotic universe, or to interpret the Torah text in terms of sefirotic symbols, is also to enter into those places within the soul. For the speakers within the *Zohar*, as for the ideal kabbalist in any time, to speak of the *sefirot* is not only to draw on a body of esoteric knowledge, but also to enter the inner universe where sefirotic language is the guide to measured experience.

    The authors of the *Zohar* do not generally feel the need to tell their readers that this is the case. In a work written for initiates, the link between the intellectual and experiential dimensions was taken for granted. It is primarily the frequent expressions of enthusiasm and ecstasy with which the text is dotted that serve to indicate how deeply and personally the sefirotic teachings were felt. The repeated refrain "Had I come into the world only to hear this, it would be sufficient!" and the kisses showered upon speakers by their grateful companions make it clear to any but the most obtuse of readers that in the pages of the *Zohar* we are witnessing the shared inner life of a vital mystical circle and not merely a series of exercises in biblical homiletics.

The sefirotic universe as a representation of inner religious experience may be described in more specific ways as well, though these are surely not exhaustive. The "descent" of the *sefirot*, beginning with *Keter*, is said to describe the emergence of God from hiddenness to revelation. Both the creation of the world and the giving of Torah are this-worldly extensions of that inner divine process. On a more realistic plane, however, so too is the mystic's own inner life. Sefirotic symbolism provides a language for describing the mystic's own return from an experience of absorption in the "nothingness" of God and gradual reintegration into the framework of full human personality, the re-emergence of conscious selfhood. It should be emphasized that the *Zohar* never makes such a claim. In general the kabbalists were loathe to speak too openly about the experiential aspects of their teaching. Especially when it came to the highest triad of the sefirotic world, to speak in terms that claimed direct experience was considered far beyond the bounds of propriety. But one who reads the kabbalists with an eye to comparative and phenomenological descriptions of mysticism cannot but suspect that such experience underlies the sources. The accounts of a mysterious energy that flows from undefined endlessness, through a primal arousal of will, into a single point that is the start of all being, and thence into the womb-palace where the self (divine or human) is born, sound familiarly like descriptions of the rebirth of personality that follows the contemplative mystical experience. Even though the *Zohar* depicts it chiefly as the original journey of God, we understand that the mystical life repeats that divine process. In fact, it is out of their own experience that the mystics know what they do of the original journey on which theirs is patterned. Perhaps one can go even a step further to claim that the constant movement within the sefirotic world, including both the flow of energy "downward" from *Keter* and the rising up of *Malkhut* and the lower worlds into the divine heights, represents the dynamic inner life of the mystic and the spiritual motion that ever animates his soul. It is these nuances of inner movement that constitute the "real" subject of a very large part of the *Zohar* and the world it creates. To most fully appreciate the *Zohar* as a mystical text is to understand these movements as reverberations within the mystic's soul of events as they transpire within the sefirotic cosmos that constitutes the divine reality.

When the *Zohar* does speak of mystical experience, it is largely through use of the term *devequt*, "attachment" or "cleaving" to God, and its Aramaic cognates. Ever since the early rabbinic discussions of Deuteronomy 4:4 ("You who cleave to YHVH your God are all alive today") and 10:20 ("Fear YHVH your God, cleave to Him and serve Him"), *devequt* has played a central role in the devotional life of pious Jews. But the *Zohar* is also quick to associate this term with its first biblical usage in Genesis 2:24, where man "cleaves to his wife and they become one flesh." Attachment to God, for the *Zohar*, is erotic attachment, whether referring to the kabbalist's own attachment to God by means of Torah, to *Shekhinah*'s link to the upper "male" *sefirot* as God's bride, or in the rare passages where Moses becomes the kabbalistic hero and himself weds *Shekhinah*, entering the Godhead in the male role. The contemplative and erotic aspects of attachment to God are just different ways of depicting the same reality, quite wholly inseparable from one another.

With the experience of human love and sexuality as its chief metaphor for intimacy, the *Zohar* depicts *devequt* as a temporary and fleeting experience. Scholars have debated for some time the question of whether true *unio mystica* is to be found in the *Zohar*. But this debate may itself hinge on the sexual analogy. Is there true loss of self or absorption within union to be attained in sexual climax? How does one begin to answer such a question without interviewing all of the world's great lovers? Whether or not the experience underlying countless passages in the *Zohar* can be described as "union" lies, I would submit, beyond our ken. But it is clear that there is no possibility offered of *permanent* bliss to those still attached to bodily existence; only in the world to come will the disembodied spirits of the righteous enjoy the endless delight of basking in the divine presence. Religious experience in this world is but a foretaste of that eternal joy.

As the *Zohar* seeks to develop a language for what we may call its *eros* of poetic creativity, exegesis of the Song of Songs plays a major role. The *Zohar* turns with great frequency, especially in its proems or homiletical "warm-ups," to that great font of sacred *eros*. The Song of Songs, a text in which *eros* in fact remains unconsummated, offers poetic language for every other aspect of the complete drama of courting, including even loss, separation, and longing. All of these come to the fore in the *Zohar's* frequent disquisitions on the Song, which is often most surprisingly linked to verses describing some aspect of the Tabernacle cult or another seemingly dry detail of biblical law. Those texts are utterly transformed by association with the Canticle. The Torah text as a whole, it may be said, is "washed over" in an eroticizing bath created by repeated juxtaposition of Torah texts with verses of the Song of Songs, poetically enriching the *eros* of sefirotic symbolization itself.

The *Zohar* learned from the Neoplatonist milieu within which it existed to speak of the flow of energy, usually described as light, from one cosmic realm to the next. The Neoplatonists tended to emphasize the diminution of that light as it reached "downward" toward the material plane. For the kabbalist, this constantly renewed pouring forth of divine presence could be felt, both in the daily renewal of nature and in the creative vigor of Torah interpretation. He sought to align himself with the cosmic flow, in order to receive its bounty, but also to act in such ways as to stimulate the flow itself. Images of both light and water abound in the *Zohar's* pages to describe the *shefa*, the endless flux of divine bounty that sustains the universe. In the context of the *Zohar*, it is clear that this fluid is also the divine seed, that which enters into *Shekhinah* and allows for the constant rebirth of life in the realms beneath Her.

Read this way, the *Zohar* is very much a mystical, often even an ecstatic, work, or at least one in which the ecstatic dimension is very highly developed. One of the strongest expressions of this reality is found in the *Zohar*'s powerful and poetic soliloquies around the word *zohar* itself, and on the verse (Daniel 12:3) from which the work's title is taken: "The enlightened shall shine like the radiance [*zohar*] of the sky, and those who lead multitudes to righteousness, like the stars, forever." *Zohar* represents a hidden radiance issuing forth from the highest sefirotic realms, a showering of sparks lighting up all that comes in its path. Its inspiration is surely the night sky, the wondrous event of shooting stars against the background of the Milky Way. But like all such images in mystical literature, the beacon of light or drop of divine seed is a pictorial representation of an event that takes place also within the mystic's heart, the inspiration that "sparks" this creative vision.

The inner event of this radiant presence is outwardly manifest in the shining gaze of the kabbalist's face. "The enlightened shall shine" is also understood in this rather literal way. Here, as frequently in the *Zohar*, there is an assimilation of the kabbalist to the biblical description of Moses as he emerged from the Tent of Meeting, his face glowing with the radiant presence of God. But the kabbalist is also Moses' brother Aaron, the ancient priest whose face shines with divine presence as he bestows the blessing of God's own countenance upon the children of Israel. "May the Lord cause His face to shine upon you" (Numbers 6:25) is seen as the Torah's personified way of calling forth the same light that the kabbalist as Neoplatonist perceives to be shining forth from one cosmic rung to another. He now seeks to become the earthly bearer of that light, transmitting it to his community of disciples and readers. This is the kabbalist (most often personified in the *Zohar* by Rabbi Shim'on son of Yoḥai) in the role of *tsaddiq*, conveyer of divine light.

A main purpose of the *Zohar* is to arouse within the reader a constant longing for such "enlightenment" or inspiration. The great religious creativity—and even the ecstatic deaths—of Rabbi Shim'on and his disciples are meant to induce in the reader a sense that he too, as an initiate into the *Zohar*'s secrets, may continue in this path. While no generation before the advent of messiah will fully equal that of Rabbi Shim'on, all those who come in his wake are encouraged to follow in his path. The *Zohar* is thus a highly evocative work, one that seeks to create and sustain a mood of ecstatic devotion. Certain familiar biblical verses, including the "garden" passages mentioned above, are used as awakeners—one might almost think of them as "bells"—to regularly restimulate awareness, rousing readers from their daily torpor and reminding them of the constant vital flow needed to quicken the cosmos. This reminder is meant to renew and refresh their participation in Israel's great collective task of rousing *Shekhinah*. She in turn awakens Her divine Lover to release the flow of light/water/seed, enveloping Her in His presence and renewing the universal flow of life.

The "Eden" (or "Lebanon") whence that flow is to come is an accessible if hidden rung within the divine and human self. It is not just an ancient and lost site of the biblical tale, nor is it only the "paradise" to which souls will ascend after death. Eden is the "upper world," a recondite and inward aspect of being that is mirrored in the "garden," the One who needs to be watered by that flow. We creatures of the "lower world," trees growing in the garden, need to trace back the course of that river to its source, linking the upper and lower worlds (*Binah* and *Shekhinah*, but also *Shekhinah* and "this" world, or *Shekhinah* and the soul), so that the flow will never cease.

Reflecting on these nature-evoking verses takes us back to the typically outdoor settings of the companions' conversations, which we have mentioned earlier. These settings represent the varied topography of the land of Israel as it existed in the authors' imagination, including deserts and vast, forbidding mountains as well as fertile oases and springs of water. The lush garden, especially as evoked in the Song of Songs, is a particularly characteristic setting to inspire such conversations. This may be connected to the much older designation of the "place" of mystical speculation as *pardes* or "orchard." But it is related also to the verses quoted here and to the series of connected gardens in which the kabbalist sees himself as dwelling. This world is a lower garden, needing constantly to be watered by sources from above, ultimately by the love and sustenance that is the gift of *Shekhinah*. But She too is a garden, nurtured by the river that comes forth from the hidden Eden, itself also a "garden" in some unknown, mysterious way. Somewhere between this world and *Shekhinah* stands the "Garden of Eden" that contains the souls of the righteous, both those who have completed their time on earth and those not yet born. It too is divided into "upper" and "lower" sections, described in various mythic ways.

All of these gardens are linked to one another. The kabbalist sitting and studying Torah with his companions in an earthly garden—physically in Castile, but imaginatively in the Holy Land—is aware that at the same moment the righteous in the Garden of Eden are also engaged in such study. Their garden is open from above, because it is taught that God Himself descends into that Garden to take delight in the souls of the righteous. All of these point still higher, toward the sefirotic gardens, and all these levels of the imagination fructify and enrich one another. The sweet aromas rising from these gardens also play a role in the descriptions of mystical intoxication frequently found in the *Zohar*'s pages.

IX

The unique genius that finds expression in the *Zohar* has everything to do with language. Its homiletical style builds upon midrashic sensitivity to the nuances of biblical language, and often seeks to go beyond it. Underlying every page of the *Zohar*'s reading of Torah is a rich "ear" for associative links and plays on words, a constant search for "hints" within the text that will allow for an opening to deeper levels of interpretation. This careful attention to the text is joined to the *Zohar*'s readiness to apply to it the symbolic language of the *sefirot* that we have discussed above. It is the interplay between these two factors, heightened midrashic sensitivity and the old/new grid of sefirotic symbols, that creates the unique and powerful poesis of the *Zohar*.

Another element that plays a key role in the powerful impression the *Zohar* has made on its readers throughout the generations is the sonorous and seemingly mysterious Aramaic in which it is written. All the sections of the *Zohar*, except for about half of *Midrash ha-Ne'lam*, are written in Aramaic rather than Hebrew. While scholars have devoted much attention to the unique grammatical and syntactical features of the *Zohar*'s Aramaic, few have tried to understand *why* it is that the *Zohar* is written in Aramaic and what meaning this surprising choice of language might have had for the work's authors.

Aramaic was the spoken language of Jews, both in the land of Israel and in Babylonia, from late biblical times (fourth–third century B.C.E.) until after the Islamic conquest and its replacement by Arabic (seventh century C.E.). The Talmud, in both its Babylonian and Palestinian versions, is composed mostly in Aramaic, as are portions of Midrash and other rabbinic writings. The Targum, existing in several versions, is the old Jewish translation of the Bible into Aramaic.

By the time the *Zohar* was written, Aramaic was a purely literary language for all but a tiny group of Jews in the mountains of Kurdistan. Knowledge of it elsewhere was purely passive, even among rabbinic scholars; only very rarely was a short treatise or poem still written in Aramaic. The choice to compose the *Zohar* in Aramaic gave to the work an archaic cast, and this immediately set the stage for its mysterious quality.

In Spain of the thirteenth century, unlike Palestine of the second, Aramaic was a mysterious and only vaguely understood language. Presenting secrets in Aramaic rather than Hebrew (a method that had been tried, in brief texts, before the *Zohar*) shrouded them in an obscuring veil, forcing a slower pace of reading upon those who delved into its pages. It also permitted a certain grandiloquence that might have seemed pretentious in the more familiar vehicle of medieval Hebrew. Images that might have been seen as trivial in Hebrew, especially if frequently repeated, maintained a certain mysterious grandeur when veiled by the obscurity of Aramaic dress.

The *Zohar*'s Aramaic made the text slightly, but not impossibly, more difficult for the educated Jewish reader in its day. This was probably the precise intent: to offer the reader a sense that he had come to a more profound, and therefore less penetrable, sort of teaching. With some extra effort, it would reveal to him the secret universe that the *Zohar* sought to share and pass on to its elite community of readers. Students of the *Zohar* come quickly to understand that the Aramaic of the *Zohar* is indeed a penetrable veil. The real difficulty in reading the text is that of mastering the symbolic language and the subtlety with which it was employed.

It may also be that the *Zohar*'s composition in Aramaic was not entirely a matter of conscious choice. Perhaps it was something that "happened," either in the author's psyche or in the community of mystics where Zoharic teachings were first shared orally. If there was a living community of kabbalists in Castile in the 1280s, meeting by night in courtyards and gardens to study the secrets of the Torah, in what language did they share those secrets with one another? How did the transition take place from discussing the Hebrew text of Torah in Castilian—their only spoken language—back into Hebrew or Aramaic, for transcription onto the written page? Could it be that the richly vocalic sound of Aramaic—where each noun ends in a vowel—better reflected the sounds of their own speech than did Hebrew? Were they themselves somehow "seduced" by the mysterious sound of Aramaic to follow it into the fantasy realm represented by the *Zohar*?

These speculations may also be applied to the written text itself, especially if we assume that Rabbi Moses de León is the author of large portions of the *Zohar*. Some twenty Hebrew treatises by De León have survived, and several of these have now been published. Compared to the *Zohar*, they are relatively dull and uninspired. While the doctrinal content is very much the same, they possess little of the poetic muse and freedom of expression that so characterize the *Zohar*. One has the impression that De León stepped into another world when writing the *Zohar*, and the transition from Hebrew to Aramaic was one of the ways he marked that portal. Working in this other, more dimly perceived language released his muse, as it were, giving him the freedom to soar to heights of imagination and literary excess that he would not have dared attempt in Hebrew. We might almost say that the use of Aramaic was some part of "the Holy Name" by which it was said that De León had written the *Zohar*.

The Aramaic of the *Zohar* is indeed a unique composite of dialects and features drawn from ancient literary sources. Details of Scholem's analysis of the *Zohar*'s language can be found in his writings and need not be repeated here. See also the Translator's Introduction to this volume for further discussion of linguistic questions that have direct bearing on the translation before you.

X

During the last two centuries of Jewish life in Spain, the *Zohar* continued to be copied and studied among small groups of devotees. It competed with two other schools of kabbalistic thought, the Catalonian and the Abulafian, for the attention of those few interested in mystical pursuits. Some kabbalists seem to have combined these various approaches, or else to have "migrated" in the course of their own quests from one school of mystical thought to another. Jewish rationalism was also very much alive in Spain through the fifteenth century, probably continuing to have a larger following than did Kabbalah. Manuscripts of the *Zohar* also reached Italy, the Byzantine lands of the eastern Mediterranean, and the Holy Land during this period.

It was after the expulsion of Spanish Jewry in 1492 that the influence of Kabbalah entered a period of rapid growth. Various explanations have been offered for this increased interest in the mystical tradition. Some have attributed it to the suffering and despair that visited this once-proud group of Jewish communities in the period between 1391 and 1492. The devastation of the age, so it is said, caused Jews to seek out deeper resources of consolation than those offered by the typically optimistic worldview of the philosophers. Others claim that the growth of Kabbalah came as a response of a different sort to the Spanish expulsion. Jews throughout the Mediterranean world, including many Spanish exiles, were shocked and disgraced by the high numbers of Spanish Jews who converted to Christianity in the course of the fifteenth century. Once again the blame was placed partly at the door of philosophy, the intellectual sophistication of Spanish Jewry having supposedly led to a laxity in religious observance and a relative indifference to the question of religious identity. Yet another view attributes the growth in Kabbalah's influence to the new home cultures in which former Iberian Jews found themselves. Ottoman Turkey, with its closed *millet* system—in which each faith community held fast to exclusive truth-claims and total denigration of all outside influences—was a hospitable environment for precisely the closed-minded Zoharic view of the outside world, rather than the Aristotelian quasi-universalism of the philosophers, which had served the needs of a very different age.

Whatever the reason (and a combination of the above factors is most likely), we begin to see new kabbalistic works written and old ones distributed and explicated in the early sixteenth century. The *Zohar* and other works of the Castilian tradition are especially prominent in this period. Perhaps typical is the figure of Rabbi Meir ibn Gabbai, a Turkish kabbalist who tells us that he was born in Spain in 1481 and left as a child among the exiles. Ibn Gabbai's magnum opus, *Avodat ha-Qodesh* (Venice, 1567), is a grand systematization of Kabbalah and a defense of it against philosophy. Typically of the sixteenth century, Ibn Gabbai knows a great many earlier texts and seeks to harmonize them with one another. But the great source of kabbalistic truth is the *Zohar*, which he quotes on virtually every page as "the Midrash of Rabbi Shim'on son of Yoḥai."

The kabbalistic conventicles of Safed, which flourished in the late sixteenth century, also accorded to the *Zohar* top place as the authoritative source of kabbalistic truth. Clearly, the choice of Safed as a place of settlement for Jews attached to the kabbalistic legacy had much to do with its proximity to Meron, the supposed burial place of Rabbi Shim'on son of Yoḥai. His tomb had been a site of pilgrimage for local Jews long earlier, but with the growth of the Safed community it became a truly important shrine. Both Rabbi Moses Cordovero

(1522–1570), who probably immigrated to Safed from elsewhere in the Ottoman realm, and Rabbi Isaac Luria (1534–1572), who came from Egypt, chose to live in Safed because of the nearness of holy graves and the possibility (described by Cordovero in his *Sefer Gerushin*) of achieving mystical knowledge through prostration upon them. Among the sacred dead of the Galilee, Rabbi Shim'on, now acclaimed as the undisputed author of the *Zohar*, took a central place. Luria specifically hoped to achieve a true understanding of passages in the *Zohar* by visiting what he believed to be the grave of its author.

The "return" of Kabbalah to the Galilean landscape of the *Zohar's* heroes fired the imagination of Jews throughout the Diaspora. Reports of the holy men of Safed, especially the mysterious figure of Luria, known as *ha-Ari ha-Qadosh* (the Holy Lion), were widely copied and printed in several versions. A vast literature of both kabbalistic writings and ethical or pietistic works influenced by Kabbalah poured forth from the printing presses of Venice, Constantinople, and Amsterdam—to be distributed throughout the Jewish world. It did not take long until the claim emerged that the soul of the *Ari* was in fact a reincarnation of that of Rabbi Shim'on son of Yoḥai.

It was in this period that the *Zohar* came to be considered not only an ancient and holy book, but a *canonical* text, bearing authority comparable to that of the Bible and the Talmud. The authority of the *Zohar* as the prime source of mystical truth had already been considered by fourteenth-century kabbalists, some of whom came to view its word as superior to that of Naḥmanides, for example, because of its allegedly greater antiquity. Naḥmanides was portrayed by these as a "modern" source, whose word could be set aside by a contrary quotation from the work of Rabbi Shim'on son of Yoḥai. But in the sixteenth century, it was said that Elijah himself had appeared to Rabbi Shim'on, and the *Zohar's* authority became that of heaven itself. Meir ibn Gabbai traced the kabbalistic tradition back to Sinai, claiming that Zoharic secrets were given to Moses along with the written Torah.

Canonical status, in the context of Judaism, bears with it halakhic authority as well as mystical prestige. If the *Zohar* contained the "true" meaning of both written and oral Torah, might it be used as a source of legal authority, especially in ritual and liturgical matters, as well? This question came up among halakhic scholars, especially in the few cases in which the *Zohar* seemed to contradict the majority opinion of rabbis deciding the law on the basis of Talmudic precedent and its formulation in responsa and codes. In fact, as scholars have shown, these cases mostly turn on local custom—the *Zohar* reflecting either Franco-German or old Spanish customs, while the *halakhah* had decided in favor of others. A classic example of such halakhic dispute involving the *Zohar* concerns the donning of *tefillin* on the intermediate weekdays of *Pesaḥ* and *Sukkot*. The *Zohar* expresses itself most strongly on the issue, considering the wearing of *tefillin* on those days an insult to the festival and a virtual sacrilege. Although the halakhic codes mostly tended otherwise, some halakhic authorities bowed to the *Zohar*, and the use of *tefillin* on those days was rejected throughout the Sephardic (and later Hasidic) communities.

Thanks to the influence of the Safed revival of mystical studies, Kabbalah became widely known among eastern European Jews in the seventeenth century. The works of Rabbi Isaiah Horowitz, a Prague kabbalist who later settled in Jerusalem, carried the teachings of Ibn Gabbai and Cordovero, among others, to preachers throughout the Ashkenazic communities. Here, too, the *Zohar* was very widely quoted. Prayer books with kabbalistic commentaries, including those by both Cordovero and Horowitz, brought kabbalistic thinking into the realm of actual synagogue practice. The highly mythical Kabbalah of Naftali Bacharach, seventeenth-century German author of *Emeq ha-Melekh* (Valley of the King), is primarily influenced by the language and imagery of the *Zohar*.

Another area of the growing canonicity of the *Zohar* is reflected in its use in liturgical contexts and its appearance in digests of daily religious practice. Various kabbalistic *Tiqqunim* or "Orders" were published throughout the seventeenth and eighteenth centuries. These include many collections of *Zohar* passages to be recited during the vigils of *Shavu'ot* and *Hosha'na Rabbah*, at the Sabbath table, and on various other occasions. It came to be understood in this period that oral recitation of the *Zohar* was efficacious even for those who did not understand its meaning. In the nineteenth century, vocalized editions of the *Zohar* were printed to allow for this situation, and to assure that the recitation would nevertheless be performed with some degree of accuracy. There were also various digests produced for daily study/recitation, especially in the eighteenth century. The most widespread of these was called *Ḥoq le-Yisra'el* (Cairo, 1740), including passages to be recited each day from the Torah, Prophets, Hagiographa, Mishnah, Talmud, *Zohar*, ethical guides, and legal digests. The *Ḥemdat Yamim*, an anonymous compendium of kabbalistic praxis (Izmir, 1731/32), prescribes readings from the *Zohar* for nearly every conceivable occasion in the Jewish liturgical year. In both of these compendia, we see the *Zohar* at the apex of its acceptance and integration into the daily regimen of Jewish spiritual life.

In the late seventeenth and early eighteenth centuries, the messianic movement around Sabbatai Tsevi (1626–1676) swept through the Jewish communities. In the more radical forms of Sabbateanism, the *Zohar* carried even greater weight as the authority of Talmudic law came to be questioned. The kabbalistic system of Nathan of Gaza (1643/4–1680), the great prophet of Sabbateanism, is based on the imagery of the *Zohar*; and devotion to the *Zohar* was touted loudly throughout the history of Sabbateanism. Some of the later Ashkenazic Sabbateans—followers of Jacob Frank—came to refer to themselves as "Zoharites," Jews who followed the authority of the *Zohar* while rejecting that of the Talmud and the rabbis. This, of course, would be a spurious claim had the authors of the *Zohar* been asked their opinion, since they had no intention of rebelling against Talmudic authority. But by this time (and in these circles), the *Zohar* was being read through the lenses of such radical inter-preters as the *Ra'aya Meheimna*, the fifteenth-century *Sefer ha-Qanah*, the anonymous work *Galei Razayya*, and the writings of Nathan of Gaza. When seen as the font of this literary tradition, the *Zohar* could be read as a very radical work indeed.

The decline of Sabbateanism in the mid-eighteenth century preceded by only a few decades the beginning of the Enlightenment era in western Europe and the admission of Jews into a more open and religiously tolerant society. As large numbers of Jews became eager supporters of what they could only see as emancipation, readings of Judaism that supported or fit this new situation became widespread. One feature of this emerging post-Enlightenment Judaism, whether in its Reform or Orthodox versions, was either an open rejection or a quiet setting aside of Kabbalah and the *Zohar* in particular. Scholem wrote an essay about several obscure nineteenth-century figures whom he designated as "The Last Kabbalists in Germany." We have already spoken of Heinrich Graetz's negative views of the *Zohar*, a position that was widely shared by his contemporaries. While there were a few scholars in the period of the *Wissenschaft des Judentums* (Adolph Jellinek of Vienna is the most notable) who studied the *Zohar*, it was mostly neglected by westernized Jews throughout the nineteenth and early twentieth centuries.

In eastern Europe, the situation was quite different. Hasidism, a popular religious revival based on Kabbalah, continued to revere the *Zohar* and believe in its antiquity. Several significant *Zohar* commentaries were written within Hasidic circles, and the authors of Hasidic works often referred to the *Zohar*. Rabbi Pinḥas of Korzec, an early Hasidic master, was said to have thanked God that he was born after the appearance of the *Zohar*, "for the *Zohar* kept me a Jew." Hasidic legend has it that when the *Zohar* was published by his sons, who owned the printing-works in Slawuta, they dipped the press in the *miqveh* (ritual bath) before printing each volume, so great was the holy task that was about to come before it! Hasidic masters, because of this legend, went out of their way to acquire copies of the Slawuta edition of the *Zohar* and to study from it. The great opponent of Hasidism, Rabbi Elijah (the "Gaon") of Vilna (1720–1797), was also a kabbalist, and a small group within the circle of his disciples continued the study of *Zohar* for several generations.

Among the Sephardic and Mizraḥi Jews, the reputation of the *Zohar* as a holy book was particularly strong. Jews in such far-flung communities as Morocco, Turkey, and Iraq studied it avidly. Simple Jews recited the *Zohar* much in the way that uneducated eastern European Jews recited the Psalms. Beginning in the eighteenth century, Jerusalem became known as a center of kabbalistic studies, and Jews from throughout these communities went there and studied works that emanated from that center. Outside of Europe, it was primarily the Lurianic Kabbalah that held sway, and the *Zohar*, while revered, was generally viewed through the Lurianic prism. Only as Enlightenment ideas began to spread in the early twentieth century, partly through the arrival of European Jews in the Colonial era, did the authority of the *Zohar* come into question.

The writings of Scholem, Tishby, and the scholars following in their wake have done much to make the *Zohar* intelligible to moderns and to renew interest in its study. Tishby's *Wisdom of the Zohar*, translating selected passages from Aramaic into Hebrew, was a highly successful attempt to make the *Zohar* more accessible to an educated Israeli readership. The interest aroused among scholars of religion by Scholem's highly readable and insightful essays, especially those first presented at the Eranos conferences, served to kindle great interest in Kabbalah within the broader scholarly community. This interest is maintained today thanks to the profound and sometimes provocative studies of Yehuda Liebes and Elliot Wolfson. The important writings of Moshe Idel continue to bring Kabbalah to the attention of the scholarly and intellectual world. The availability of English and other translations, including the selections in Tishby and anthologies by both Scholem and Matt, have also served the *Zohar* well in creating readerships outside of Israel. In more recent decades, this intellectual interest in Kabbalah has spread to wider circles, including many who are concerned with questions of symbolism, philosophy of language, and related issues.

At the same time, two other seemingly unrelated phenomena have come together to greatly increase the interest in *Zohar* studies at the turn of the twenty-first century. One is the broad interest throughout the Western world in works of mysticism and "spirituality." Our age has seen a great turn toward sources of wisdom neglected by two centuries of modernity, partly in hope of finding in them a truth that will serve as a source of guidance for the difficult and complex times in which we live. Recently, an interest in the *Zohar* and Kabbalah has emerged as part of this trend. As is true of all the other wisdoms examined in the course of this broad cultural phenomenon, the interest in Kabbalah includes both serious and trivial or "faddist" elements. This revival of Kabbalah is a complicated phenomenon within itself, containing expressions of great hunger for religious experience and personal growth, alongside the broader quest for wisdom.

This interest has come to be combined with a very different renewal of Kabbalah, primarily in Israel, after the 1967 and 1973 wars. It is manifest in the growth of kabbalistic *yeshivot* or academies, the publication of many new editions of kabbalistic works, and a campaign of public outreach intended to spread the teachings of Kabbalah more broadly. This new emphasis on Kabbalah is partly due to the reassertion of pride in the Sephardic and Mizraḥi heritage, where Kabbalah has an important place. It is also in part related to the difficult and trying times through which Israel has lived, resulting in both a resurgence of messianism and a turn to "practical Kabbalah"—a long-standing part of Near Eastern Judaism—as a source of protection against enemies and hope of victory over them. The Kabbalah taught in these circles is primarily of the Lurianic variety, as interpreted through a long chain of Jerusalem-based teachers. Some versions of what is proffered as "Kabbalah" today can only be described as highly debased versions of the original teachings. But the *Zohar*, even if reinterpreted in Lurianic terms, is revered throughout these circles as the primary font of kabbalistic truth, the ancient teaching of Rabbi Shim'on son of Yoḥai.

How this very complex interweaving of forces will affect the future of interest in Kabbalah is yet to be seen. It is certain, however, that the *Zohar* will continue to find a place in the hearts of new readers, some of whom will turn to the more authentic and profound aspects of its teachings. It is hoped that these readers will be helped and guided by the present translation and commentary.

THE ZOHAR

Haqdamat Sefer ha-Zohar

INTRODUCTION TO THE *ZOHAR*

R abbi Ḥizkiyah opened, "*Like a rose*[1] *among thorns, so is my beloved among the maidens* (Song of Songs 2:2). Who is *a rose*? Assembly of Israel.[2] For there is a rose, and then there is a rose! Just as a rose among thorns is colored red and white,[3] so Assembly of Israel includes judgment and compassion. Just as a rose has thirteen petals, so Assembly of Israel has thirteen qualities of compassion surrounding Her on every side.[4] Similarly, from the moment אלהים (*Elohim*),

1. *rose* שושנה (*Shoshanah*) probably means "lily" or "lotus" in Song of Songs, but here Rabbi Ḥizkiyah has in mind a rose.

See *Vayiqra Rabbah* 23:3; *Shir ha-Shirim Rabbah* on 2:2; *Zohar* 1:137a, 221a; 2:20a (*MhN*), 189b; 3:107a, 180b, 233b, 286b; Ezra of Gerona, *Peirush Shir ha-Shirim,* 489 (lily); Joseph ibn Akhnin, *Peirush Shir ha-Shirim,* 63–65 (rose); Moses de León, *Sefer ha-Rimmon,* 183–84; *Zohorei Ya'bets.*

A Ladino translation of the verse (*The Ladino Five Scrolls,* ed. Lazar, 4–5) reads: "Commo la roza entre los espinos, ansi mi conpañera entre las dueñas."

2. **Assembly of Israel** כנסת ישראל (*Keneset Yisra'el*). In rabbinic Hebrew, this phrase denotes the people of Israel. The midrash on the Song of Songs describes an allegorical love affair between the maiden (the earthly community of Israel) and her lover (the Holy One, blessed be He). See *Shir ha-Shirim Rabbah* on 2:1. In the *Zohar, Keneset Yisra'el* can refer to the earthly community but also (often primarily) to *Shekhinah,* the divine feminine counterpart of the people, the aspect of God most intimately connected with

them. The lovers in the Song of Songs are pictured as the divine couple: *Tif'eret* and *Shekhinah.*

3. **colored red and white** As is *Rosa gallica versicolor* (also known as *Rosa mundi*), one of the oldest of the striped roses, whose flowers are crimson splashed on a white background. The striping varies and occasionally flowers revert to the solid pink of their parent, *Rosa gallica.* The parent was introduced to Europe in the twelfth or thirteenth century by Crusaders returning from Palestine. Both parent and sport were famous for their aromatic and medicinal qualities. Elsewhere (2:20a–b) the *Zohar* alludes to the process of distilling oil from the petals of the flower to produce rose water, a popular remedy. During this process the color gradually changes from red to white.

4. **thirteen petals...thirteen qualities of compassion...** A rose blossom can have thirteen petals in its second tier. In rabbinic tradition, God's thirteen attributes of compassion are derived from Exodus 34:6–7. See BT *Rosh ha-Shanah* 17b. According to Kabbalah, these qualities originate in *Keter,* the

God, is mentioned, it generates thirteen words to surround Assembly of Israel and protect Her; then it is mentioned again.[5] Why again? To produce five sturdy leaves surrounding the rose.[6] These five are called Salvation;[7] they are five gates.[8] Concerning this mystery it is written: *I raise the cup of salvation* (Psalms 116:13). This is the cup of blessing, which should rest on five fingers—and no more[9]—like the rose, sitting on five sturdy leaves, paradigm of five fingers. This rose is the cup of blessing.

"From the second אלהים (*Elohim*) till the third, five words appear. From here on: light—created, concealed, contained in the covenant,[10] entering the rose, emitting seed into Her. This is the *tree bearing fruit with its seed in it* (Genesis 1:12).[11] That seed endures in the actual sign of covenant. Just as the image of the covenant is sown in forty-two couplings of that seed, so the engraved, explicit name[12] is sown in forty-two letters of the act of Creation."[13]

highest *sefirah,* the realm of total compassion untainted by judgment.

5. **אלהים (*Elohim*), *God,* is mentioned...** The divine name אלהים (*Elohim*), *God,* refers here to *Binah,* the Divine Mother. Between its first and second occurrences in the opening verses of Genesis there are thirteen words, which allude to the thirteen qualities of compassion originating in *Keter,* emanating from *Binah* and surrounding the rose of *Shekhinah.*

6. five sturdy leaves... The leaves of rose plants grow in clusters of five, nine, or thirteen leaves. And between the second and third occurrences of אלהים (*Elohim*) in Genesis are five words, alluding to five divine leaves: the five *sefirot* emanating from *Binah* and transmitting the flow to *Shekhinah.* These *sefirot* are *Hesed, Gevurah, Tif'eret* (including *Yesod*), *Netsah,* and *Hod.*

7. Salvation The flow of emanation saves the rose of *Shekhinah* from the demonic thorns surrounding Her.

8. five gates By which one enters the divine realm.

9. cup of blessing...on five fingers... According to the Talmud, the cup of wine is held in the right hand during the blessing after food. See BT *Berakhot* 51a: "One takes it with both hands and places it on the right hand." Cf. *Zohar* 1:156a (*ST*), 250a; 2:138b, 143b, 157b.

10. light—created, concealed... See BT *Ḥagigah* 12a: "Rabbi El'azar said, 'With the light created by the blessed Holy One on the first day, one could gaze and see from one end of the universe to the other. When the blessed Holy One foresaw the corrupt deeds of the generation of the Flood and the generation of the Dispersion [the generation of the Tower of Babel], He immediately hid it from them, as is written: *The light of the wicked is withheld* (Job 38:15). For whom did He hide it? For the righteous in the time to come.'"

Elsewhere, the Midrash links the hidden light with Psalms 97:11: *Light is sown for the righteous.* See *Tanḥuma, Shemini* 9; *Shemot Rabbah* 35:1; *Midrash Tehillim* 27:1.

Rabbi Ḥizkiyah now specifies *where* the primordial light was concealed: in the covenant, which is a name for the *sefirah* of *Yesod*—the divine phallus, site of the covenant of circumcision. *Yesod* is also known as Righteous. See *Zohar* 1:21a, 31b–32a, 45b; 2:35a, 148b–149a; 166b–167a, 230a.

11. *tree bearing fruit...* The tree symbolizes male divinity.

12. explicit name The Ineffable Name, YHVH. See *Devarim Rabbah* 3:8; *Midrash Tehillim* 114:9; *Zohar* 2:48a.

13. forty-two couplings...forty-two letters of the act of Creation The forty-two-letter name is mentioned in the name of

2

בראשית (Be-reshit), *In the beginning.*

Rabbi Shim'on opened, "*The blossoms have appeared on the earth, [the time of pruning has arrived; the voice of the turtledove is heard in our land]* (Song of Songs 2:12). *The blossoms* are the act of Creation, which *appeared on the earth.* When? On the third day, as is written: *The earth brought forth vegetation* (Genesis 1:12). Then they *appeared on the earth. The time of pruning has arrived*—the fourth day, on which *the pruning of tyrants* (Isaiah 25:5) took place.[14] מארת (Me'orot), *Lights,* spelled deficiently.[15] *The voice of the turtledove* is the fifth day, as is written: *Let the waters swarm* [*with a swarm of living creatures, and let birds fly above the earth, across the expanse of the sky*] (Genesis 1:20), generating offspring. *Is heard* is the sixth day, as is written: *Let us make a human being* (Genesis 1:26), who was destined to declare acting before hearing, for here is written: [1b] נעשה (Na'aseh), *Let us make, a human being,* and there is written: נעשה (Na'aseh), *We will do, and we will listen* (Exodus 24:7).[16] *In our land* is the Sabbath day, paradigm of the land of eternal life.[17]

3

Rav, though not recorded, in BT *Qiddushin* 71a. According to one later view, it consists of the first forty-two letters of the Torah, from the ב (*bet*) of בראשית (*Be-reshit*) through the ב (*bet*) of בהו (*bohu*), *void* (Genesis 1:2).

See *Tosafot, Ḥagigah* 11b, s.v. *ein doreshin; KP* 1:46c–d; Trachtenberg, *Jewish Magic and Superstition,* 94–95; cf. Maimonides, *Guide of the Perplexed,* 1:62. Cordovero (*OY*) describes how the name YHVH ("the engraved, explicit name") can be permuted into a forty-two-letter name; cf. *Zohar* 2:260a. In *Zohar* 1:9a, Moses' staff is described as "radiating the engraved name in every direction with the radiance of the wise who engraved the explicit name in forty-two colors." Cf. *Zohar* 1:15b, 30a; 2:130b, and 175b: "...the forty-two holy letters of the holy name, by which heaven and earth were created."

14. *pruning of tyrants...* זמיר (*Zemir*) is usually translated "singing of" in this verse, but Rabbi Shim'on understands it as "pruning of," i.e., the pruning of the demonic powers, the *tyrants* (*KP*; cf. *Zohar* 3:4b), or

the pruning of humans by the demonic tyrants (*OY*).

15. מארת (*Me'orot*), *Lights,* spelled deficiently In Genesis 1:14, the word מארת (*me'orot*) is written without *vavs,* the vowel letters. (Such variant spelling is common in the Torah and affects neither pronunciation nor the plain meaning of the words.) This deficient spelling implies that something was missing on the fourth day of Creation, a lack representing the potential for evil or "curse": מארה (*me'erah*).

See Proverbs 3:33; JT *Ta'anit* 4:4, 68b; *Pesiqta de-Rav Kahana* 5:1; *Soferim* 17:4; Rashi and *Minḥat Shai* on Genesis 1:14; *Zohar* 1:12a, 19b, 33b.

16. *We will do, and we will listen* Spoken by the people of Israel at Mount Sinai. With these words, Israel demonstrated true faith by committing themselves to fulfill and enact God's word even before hearing the details. See BT *Shabbat* 88a.

17. **paradigm of the land...** According to BT *Berakhot* 57b, the Sabbath is "a reflection of the world to come."

"*The blossoms* are the patriarchs, who entered the divine mind before Creation[18] and entered the world that is coming,[19] where they were treasured away. From there, they emerged secretly and were concealed within prophets of truth.[20] When Joseph was born, they were concealed within him.[21] When Joseph entered the Holy Land, he planted them there. Then they *appeared on earth,* were revealed there. When are they visible? When the rainbow is revealed in the world.[22] When the rainbow appears, they are revealed. Then, *the time of pruning has arrived,* time to excise the wicked from the world. Why are they spared? Because *the blossoms have appeared on the earth.* Had they not *appeared,* they would not remain in the world,[23] nor would the world endure. Who sustains the world, enabling the patriarchs to be revealed? The voice of children engaging in Torah.[24] For the sake of those children, the world is saved. Corresponding to them, *We will make you wreaths of gold* (Song of Songs 1:11).

18. **patriarchs, who entered...** See *Bereshit Rabbah* 1:4: "Six things preceded Creation.... The patriarchs arose in thought [i.e., were intended] to be created." In the Kabbalah, the patriarchs (Abraham, Isaac, and Jacob) represent the triad of *sefirot: Ḥesed, Gevurah,* and *Tif'eret.* Cf. *Zohar* 1:39b, 97a–b; 3:4b.

19. **the world that is coming** עלמא דאתי (*Alma de-atei*), the Aramaic equivalent of the rabbinic Hebrew העולם הבא (*ha-olam ha-ba*), "the world that is coming." This concept is often understood as referring to the hereafter and is usually translated as "the world to come." From another point of view, however, "the world that is coming" already exists, occupying another dimension. See *Tanḥuma, Vayiqra* 8: "The wise call it *ha-olam ha-ba* not because it does not exist now, but for us today in this world it is still to come." Cf. Maimonides, *Mishneh Torah, Hilkhot Teshuvah* 8:8; and Guttmann, *Philosophies of Judaism,* 37: "'The world to come' does not succeed 'this world' in time, but exists from eternity as a reality outside and above time, to which the soul ascends."

In Kabbalah "the world that is coming" often refers to *Binah,* the continuous source of emanation, who gives birth to the lower *sefirot.* See *Zohar* 3:290b (*IZ*): "the world that is coming, constantly coming, never ceasing."

Cf. *Bahir* 106 (160); Asher ben David, *Peirush Shelosh Esreh Middot,* in *Kabbalah* 2 (1997): 293; Moses de León, *Sheqel ha-Qodesh,* 26 (30); idem, *Sod Eser Sefirot,* 375; *Zohar* 1:83a, 92a.

20. **prophets of truth** The *sefirot* of *Netsaḥ* and *Hod,* the source of prophecy.

21. **Joseph...** Joseph symbolizes the *sefirah* of *Yesod,* the divine phallus, since he withstood the test of sexual temptation in Egypt (Genesis 39). The upper triad of *sefirot* (*Ḥesed, Gevurah,* and *Tif'eret*) flows into him, and when *Yesod* enters *Shekhinah* ("the Holy Land," "earth"), the sefirotic triad is planted there and revealed. Though Joseph never returned to the land of Israel, his bones did. See Joshua 24:32.

22. **When the rainbow is revealed...** The rainbow symbolizes both *Yesod* and *Shekhinah,* in whose union *Ḥesed, Gevurah,* and *Tif'eret* are revealed in their respective colors: white, red, and green.

23. **they would not remain...** The wicked would not remain.

24. **voice of children...** See BT *Shabbat* 119b: "Resh Lakish said in the name of Rabbi Yehudah the Prince, 'The world endures only for the sake of the breath of children in the house of study.'" Cf. *Zohar* 1:146b; 3:17b.

These are little children, youngsters, as is written: *Make two cherubim of gold* (Exodus 25:18)."[25]

בראשית (*Be-reshit*), *In the beginning.*

Rabbi El'azar opened, "*Lift your eyes on high and see: Who created these?* (Isaiah 40:26). *Lift your eyes on high.*

To which site? The site toward which all eyes gaze. Which is that? *Opening of the eyes.*[26] There you will discover that the concealed ancient one, susceptible to questioning, *created these.* Who is that? *Who.*[27] The one called End of Heaven above,[28] whose domain extends over everything. Since it can be questioned, yet remains concealed and unrevealed, it is called *Who.* Beyond, there is no question.[29]

---

25. *Make two cherubim...* In BT *Sukkah* 5b, Rabbi Abbahu interprets the word כרוב (*keruv*), "cherub," as כרביא (*ke-ravya*), "like a child." The plump childlike angels of Christian art derive either from this tradition or from the Greco-Roman *Erotes,* "loves." Here Rabbi Shim'on relates the golden cherubim to the golden wreaths of the Song of Songs, concluding that both images allude to children.

26. *Opening of the eyes* פתח עינים (*Petaḥ einayim*). The phrase originates in Genesis 38:14, where it means "the entrance to Einayim," a village where Tamar seduced her father-in-law, Judah. The midrash on Genesis (*Bereshit Rabbah* 85:7) discovers a deeper meaning: "Rabbi [Yehudah the Prince] said, 'We have searched through the entire Bible and have not found a place called *Petaḥ Einayim.* What is *Petaḥ Einayim?* This indicates that she [Tamar] gazed at the opening toward which all eyes gaze and said, 'May it be the divine will that I not leave this house empty.'" In the *Zohar,* this opening is identified with *Shekhinah,* gateway to the divine. See 3:71b–72a.

27. *Who* מי (*Mi*). *Binah,* the Divine Mother, is called *Who.* A spiritual seeker may inquire about Her, but such questions do not yield ordinary answers. The identity of the divine is discovered only in a realm beyond words. The mystical name *Who* becomes a focus of meditation, as question

turns into quest. See Shim'on Lavi, *KP,* 1:91a: "Concerning everything that cannot be grasped, its question constitutes its answer."

See *Zohar* 1:29b–30a, 45b, 85b–86a, 237b; 2:126b–127a, 138a, 139b, 226a, 231b.

28. **End of Heaven above** See Deuteronomy 4:32: *For ask now of primal days, which were before you: from the day that God created humankind on earth, and from one end of heaven to the other.* In BT *Ḥagigah* 11b, this verse is interpreted as imposing a limit on cosmological speculation: "You may inquire concerning *from one end of heaven to the other,* but you may not inquire concerning what is above, what is below, what came before, what will come after." See M *Ḥagigah* 2:1; *Bereshit Rabbah* 1:10.

These restrictions on cosmological speculation recall the Gnostic striving after "the knowledge of who we were, what we have become, where we were, where we have been thrown, where we hasten, from what we are redeemed, what birth is and what rebirth" (Clement of Alexandria, *Excerpts from Theodotus* 78:2). See *Zohar* 1:30a; Moses de León, *Sheqel ha-Qodesh,* 31; idem, *Sefer ha-Rimmon,* 20, 375; idem, *Sod Eser Sefirot Belimah,* 371.

29. **Beyond...** The realms beyond *Binah,* namely, *Ḥokhmah, Keter,* and *Ein Sof,* are so unknowable that no question concerning them can even be formulated.

5

"This end of heaven is called *Who*. There is another below, called *What*.[30] What distinguishes the two? The first, concealed one—called *Who*—can be questioned. Once a human being questions and searches,[31] contemplating and knowing rung after rung to the very last rung—once one reaches there: *What? What do you know? What have you contemplated? For what have you searched?* All is concealed, as before.

"Concerning this mystery it is written: *What can I take as a witness to you? What can I compare to you?* (Lamentations 2:13). When the holy Temple was destroyed, a voice cried out: '*What can I take as a witness to you? What can I compare to you?*' I take *What* as a witness to you. Every single day I have called witnesses against you, since days of old, as is written: *I call heaven and earth to witness against you this day* (Deuteronomy 30:19).[32] I compare you to *What*, precisely![33] I crowned you with holy crowns, gave you dominion over the world, as is written: *Is this the city that was called perfect crown of beauty, joy of all the earth?* (Lamentations 2:15). I called you *Jerusalem built up, a city bound together* (Psalms 122:3). Now, *What can I liken to you, [to console you]?* (Lamentations, ibid., 13).[34] Just as you sit desolate, so it is above, as it were. Just as now, the holy people do not enter you in holy array, so I swear to you that I Myself will not enter above until your inhabitants enter you below.[35] This is your consolation: I compare this rung to you completely.[36] But now that you are here, *your ruin is vast as the ocean* (ibid.).[37] Yet if you say you cannot endure or be healed, then *Who will heal you* (ibid.), really! That concealed, high rung in which all exists will heal you and raise you up.

6

30. **What** מה (*Mah*), a name for *Shekhinah*, last of the ten *sefirot*, daughter of *Binah*. See *Zohar* 2:127a. *Binah* and *Shekhinah* comprise the two ends of heaven, above and below *Tif'eret*, who is called Heaven.

31. **and searches** ומפשפש, *Umphashpesh*. Cr reads here: ומתפשט, *u-mitpashshet*, "and expands." See *Bahir* 134 (194); and Azriel of Gerona, *Peirush ha-Aggadot*, 39: "Thought expands (מתפשטת, *mitpashshetet*) and ascends to its source. When it reaches there, it is stopped and can ascend no further."

32. *I call heaven and earth...* Earth symbolizes *Shekhinah*.

33. **I compare you to *What*, precisely!** Israel resembles *Shekhinah* perfectly.

34. *What can I liken...* Again, Israel and *Shekhinah* (*What*) are compared.

35. **I Myself will not enter...** The blessed Holy One promises not to enter the heavenly Jerusalem, *Shekhinah*, until the earthly Jerusalem is restored. See *Tanḥuma, Pequdei* 1: "There is a Jerusalem above aligned with Jerusalem below. Out of His love for the one below, He fashioned another above.... He has sworn that His presence will not enter the heavenly Jerusalem until the earthly Jerusalem is rebuilt."

See Revelation 21:2; *Targum Yonatan*, Psalms 122:3; BT *Ta'anit* 5a; *Zohar* 1:80b (*ST*), 128b, 183b, 231a; 3:15b, 68b, 147b.

36. **this rung...** *Shekhinah*.

37. **But now that you are here, *your ruin is vast...*** Now that Israel has fallen to the low state of exile, her *ruin is vast as the ocean*, another name for *Shekhinah*, who shares Israel's exile.

"*Who* is End of Heaven above; *What* is End of Heaven below. Jacob inherited this, *running from end to end* (Exodus 26:28),[38] from first end, *Who*, to last end, *What*, for he stands in the middle. So, *Who created these*."

Rabbi Shim'on said, "El'azar, my son, cease your words,[39] so that the concealed mystery on high, unknown to any human, may be revealed."

Rabbi El'azar was silent.

Rabbi Shim'on wept and paused for a moment. Then he said, "El'azar, what is *these*?[40] If you answer, 'Stars and constellations,' they are always visible there[41] and were created by *What*, as is said: *By the word of YHVH the heavens were made* (Psalms 33:6).[42] As for things concealed, such would not be referred to as *these*, for that word indicates something revealed. This mystery was only revealed one day when I was at the seashore. Elijah[43] came and asked me, 'Rabbi, do you know the meaning of *Who created these*?' I answered, 'These are the heavens and their array, the work of the blessed Holy One. Human beings should contemplate them and bless Him, as is written: *When I behold Your heavens, the work of* [2a] *Your fingers, the moon and stars that You set in place, . . . YHVH our Lord, how majestic is Your name throughout the earth!* (Psalms 8:4, 10).

38. *running from end to end* A description of the central wooden beam of the Tabernacle in the desert. The *Zohar* applies this description to *Tif'eret*, the central *sefirah*, symbolized by Jacob, who spans the *sefirot* from *Binah* (*Who*) to *Shekhinah* (*What*). See *Zohar* 1:148b (*ST*).

39. **cease your words** פסוק מליך, *Pesoq millaikh*. The phrase could also be translated: "utter your words." See BT *Ḥagigah* 15a–b: פסוק לי פסוקך, *pesoq li pesuqekha*, "Recite for me your verse"; cf. *Zohar* 1:238b. "Cease" fits the context of our passage, but the ambiguity may be intentional, in which case a better rendering would be: "Complete your words," or "Cut your words."

40. *these* In the verse from Isaiah 40:26: *Lift up your eyes and see: Who created these?* Now that the mystical meaning of *Who* has been established, Rabbi Shim'on explores the meaning of *these*.

41. **they are always visible there** So why would the verse say, *Lift up your eyes and see*, implying that there is something new to see?

42. *By the word of YHVH . . .* The word *of YHVH* symbolizes *Shekhinah*, who conveys the divine essence. Thus the heavens were made by Her (also known as *What*), not by *Binah* (*Who*).

See *Zohar* 1:119b; 3:191a, 193b.

43. **Elijah** According to the Bible (2 Kings 11:12), the prophet Elijah did not die a normal death but was carried off to heaven in a chariot of fire. He became associated with the Messianic age (Malachi 3:23–24) and in rabbinic tradition is described as "still existing" (BT *Bava Batra* 121b) and revealing divine secrets to righteous humans (BT *Bava Metsi'a* 59b).

In Kabbalah mystical experiences are known as revelations of Elijah. See Scholem, *On the Kabbalah*, 19–21; *Zohar* 1:151a; 3:221a, 231a; *ZH* 59d. In *Zohar* 3:241b Elijah turns to Rabbi Shim'on for instruction! Elsewhere (*ZH* 63d, 70d, 73c [*ShS*]) Elijah encourages him to reveal the secrets and says (62c), "My words will be written by you."

"Elijah said to me, 'Rabbi, the word was concealed with the blessed Holy One, and He revealed it in the Academy on High.[44] Here it is:

'When Concealed of all Concealed[45] verged on being revealed, it produced at first a single point,[46] which ascended to become thought. Within, it drew all drawings, graved all engravings,[47] carving within the concealed holy lamp[48] a graving of one hidden design, holy of holies, a deep structure emerging from thought, called מי (Mi), Who, origin of structure.[49] Existent and non-existent, deep and hidden, called by no name but Who.

'Seeking to be revealed, to be named, it garbed itself in a splendid, radiant garment and created אלה (elleh), these.[50] אלה (Elleh) attained the name: these letters joined with those, culminating in the name אלהים (Elohim).[51] Until it created אלה (elleh), it did not attain the name אלהים (Elohim).[52] Based on this mystery, those who sinned with the Golden Calf said "אלה (Elleh), These, are your gods, O Israel!" (Exodus 32:8).[53] Just as מי (mi) is combined with אלה (elleh), so the name אלהים (Elohim) is constantly polysemous.[54] Through this mystery, the universe exists.'

"Then Elijah flew off; I did not see him. From him I discovered the word, whose mysterious secret I have demonstrated."

Rabbi El'azar and all the Companions came and bowed down in front of him. Weeping, they said, "If we have come into the world only to hear this, it is enough."[55]

8

44. **Academy on High** The Heavenly Academy, where souls of the righteous study Torah with God.

45. **Concealed of all Concealed** Ein Sof or Keter, the most hidden recesses of divinity.

46. **single point** The primordial point of Ḥokhmah ("Wisdom"), the first emanation.

47. **it drew all drawings...** The sefirot were prefigured within divine thought before they emerged in the process of emanation.

48. **concealed holy lamp** Ḥokhmah.

49. **graving of one hidden design...** Binah, the origin of the structure of the seven lower sefirot.

50. **created אלה (elleh), these** Binah emanated the seven lower sefirot, which are less hidden than Binah and therefore referred to as these.

51. **these letters joined... אלהים (Elohim)** The letters אלה (elleh) (these) joined with the letters מי (mi) (who) to form the divine name אלהים (Elohim). See Zohar 2:105a.

52. **Until it created...** Binah was not called אלהים (Elohim) until She emanated the seven lower sefirot.

53. **"אלה (Elleh), These, are your gods..."** Their sin was that they separated the lower, more concrete sefirot (אלה [elleh], these) from their mysterious source, Binah (מי [Mi], Who), and worshiped these alone.

54. **constantly polysemous** The name Elohim refers not only to Binah, but also to Gevurah and Shekhinah, as well as to angels and human judges. See Moses de León, Sefer ha-Mishqal, 42–43.

55. **"If we have come..."** Similar exclamations appear in rabbinic literature and often in the Zohar. See Pesiqta de-Rav Kahana 1:3; Shir ha-Shirim Rabbah on 3:11; Qohelet Rabbah on 6:2; Qohelet Zuta 5:17; BT Berakhot 16a, 24b; Shabbat 41a; Zohar 1:148b, 164b, 240a; 2:99a, 121b, 122a, 193b; 3:26a; KP 1:20d.

Rabbi Shim'on said, "So the heavens and their array were created by מה (*Mah*), *What*,[56] as is written: *When I behold Your heavens, the work of Your fingers, the moon and stars that You set in place,* . . . מה (*mah*), *how, majestic is Your name throughout the earth! Your splendor is celebrated above heaven* (Psalms 8:4, 1). *Above heaven*,[57] to attain the name. For it created a light for its light, one enclothed in the other, and it attained a high name. So, *In the beginning* אלהים (*Elohim*) *created* (Genesis 1:1), אלהים (*Elohim*) above.[58] For מה (*Mah*) was not so, is not composed until these letters—אלה (*elleh*)—are drawn from above to below and Mother lends Daughter Her garments, though not adorning Her with Her adornments.[59] When does She adorn Her fittingly? When all males appear before Her, as is written: [*All your males shall appear*] *before the Sovereign, YHVH* (Exodus 23:17).[60] This one is called Sovereign, as is said: *Behold, the ark of the covenant, Sovereign of all the earth* (Joshua 3:11).[61] Then the letter ה (*he*) departs and י (*yod*) enters, and She adorns Herself in masculine clothing in the presence of every male in Israel.[62] Other letters Israel draws from above to this site: אלה (*Elleh*), *These, I remember* (Psalms 42:5).[63] 'With my mouth I mentioned them, in my yearning I poured out my tears, drawing forth these letters. Then *I conduct them* from above *to the house of Elohim*, to be *Elohim*, like Him.'[64] With what? *With joyous shouts of praise, the festive throng.*"

9

56. מה (***Mah***), ***What*** Shekhinah.

57. ***Above heaven*** Heaven refers to *Tif'e-ret*, above which lies *Binah*.

58. ***In the beginning*** אלהים (***Elohim***) ***created*** . . . By emanating the lower *sefirot*, "a light for its light," *Binah* attained the name *Elohim*.

59. מה (***Mah***) ***was not so*** . . . *Shekhinah* does not emerge until *Binah* emanates the seven lower *sefirot*. Only then can *Binah*, the Divine Mother, lend Her garments, the lower *sefirot*, to Her daughter, *Shekhinah*.

60. ***All your males*** . . . All Israelite males are commanded to appear in God's Temple in Jerusalem three times a year on the pilgrimage festivals: *Pesaḥ* ("Passover"), *Sha-vu'ot* (Festival of "Weeks"), and *Sukkot* (Festival of "Booths"). Here the command implies that the masculine power of the *se-firot* must be drawn down to *Shekhinah*, the Sovereign. Through the ritual of pilgrimage, *Shekhinah* is adorned.

61. ***Behold, the ark*** . . . *Shekhinah* is *the ark* housing the *sefirah* of *Yesod*, the covenant.

See *Zohar* 1:33b, 59b, 228b; Moses de León, *Sheqel ha-Qodesh*, 75 (95).

62. **letter** ה (***he***) . . . The letter ה (*he*) signifies the feminine; the letter י (*yod*), the masculine. When the masculine powers of the *sefirot* reach *Shekhinah*, She is trans-formed from feminine to masculine, from מה (*Mah*) to מי (*Mi*). Then She rules the world.

63. אלה (***Elleh***), ***These, I remember*** The verse continues: *and pour out my soul: how I walked with the crowd, conducting them to the house of Elohim with joyous shouts of praise, the festive throng*. With the arrival of these letters, *Shekhinah* also attains the name of אלהים (*Elohim*): מי (*mi*) plus אלה (*elleh*). Here the verse describes both the earthly pilgrimage to the Temple and the divine procession of emanation to *Shekhinah*. The two meanings are linked because the human ritual below stimulates the *sefirot* above.

64. **to be *Elohim*, like Him** So *Shekhinah* will be *Elohim*, like *Binah*. On the masculine nature of *Binah*, see *Zohar* 1:5b, 17b, 96a; 2:127b; *ZḤ* 72b (*ShS*).

Rabbi El'azar said, "My silence assembled a temple above, a temple below.[65] Indeed, 'a word is worth one coin; silence, two.'[66] 'A word is worth one coin': what I said, the meaning I aroused. 'Silence, two': by holding my silence, two worlds were created, erected as one."

Rabbi Shim'on said, "From here on, the completion of the verse, as is written: *The one who brings forth their array by number* (Isaiah 40:26).[67] These are two rungs, each of which should be inscribed. One is *What*; the other, *Who*. This is above, that is below. The one above is inscribed by the words: *The one who brings forth their array by number,* the one who is known, beyond compare.[68] Similarly, 'The one who brings forth bread from the earth,'[69] the one who is known, the lower rung, and all is one.[70] *By number*: 600,000, standing together, generating forces according to their kind, beyond number.[71] *And calls them each by name,* both the 600,000 and their forces. What does this mean: *by name*? If you say they were called individually by name—not so, for then the verse should read *each by its name*. Rather, as long as this rung had not ascended and was still called מי (*Mi*), *Who*, it did not give birth nor bring forth what was hidden, each according to its kind, though all of them were hidden within. Once it *created* אלה (*elleh*), *these*, and attained its name, אלהים (*Elohim*), then by the power of this name, it yielded them perfectly. This is the meaning of *calls them each by name*: by its very name, it called forth each and every kind to exist perfectly. Similarly, *See, I have called by name Bezalel* (Exodus 31:2):[72] 'I mentioned My name so that Bezalel would attain perfect

10

65. **temple above...below** The temple above is *Binah*; the one below, *Shekhinah*. See BT *Sanhedrin* 99b: "Rav said, '[Whoever engages in Torah for its own sake,] it is as if he built the heavenly and earthly palaces.'"

On the heavenly and earthly temples, see *Mekhilta, Shirta* 10; JT *Berakhot* 4:5, 8c; *Tanḥuma, Vayaqhel* 7; *Pequdei* 1–3; *Shemot Rabbah* 33:4; *Midrash Tehillim* 30:1.

Rabbi El'azar's silence stimulated his father, Rabbi Shim'on, to reveal mysteries of two realms.

66. **a word is worth...** A proverb cited by Rav Dimi in BT *Megillah* 18a.

67. **completion of the verse...** The verse that Rabbi Shim'on and his son have been expounding continues: *Who brings forth their array by number and calls them each by name: because of His great might and vast power, not one is missing.*

68. **the one who is known, beyond compare** *Binah*. Rabbi Shim'on interprets the opening letter ה (*he*) of המוציא (*ha-motsi*), *who brings forth,* as a definite article ("the one who") rather than simply a relative pronoun ("who").

69. **'The one who brings forth bread...'** The traditional blessing over bread, derived from Psalms 104:14. Again, the ה (*he*) is interpreted as a definite article.

70. **the one who is known, the lower rung, and all is one** *Shekhinah* is modeled on *Binah*, shares Her name (*Elohim*), and is also known as *Earth*.

71. **600,000...beyond number** The number represents the six *sefirot* between *Binah* and *Shekhinah*, which generate innumerable offspring. See *Zohar* 1:21b–22a.

72. *See, I have called by name Bezalel* Referring to the chief artisan of the Tabernacle in the Sinai Desert.

existence.' *His great might* (Isaiah 40:26).[73] What is this? First of rungs, to which all desires ascend, ascending there [2b] secretly.[74] *And vast power*—mystery of the upper world,[75] which attained the name *Elohim,* as we have said. *Not one is missing*—not one of those 600,000 generated by the power of the name. Because *not one is missing,* whenever any of the Children of Israel died as punishment for their sins, the people were counted, and not even one of the 600,000 was lacking,[76] so that everything accorded with the paradigm: just as *not one is missing* above, so *not one is missing* below."

בראשית (*Be-reshit*), *In the beginning.*

Rav Hamnuna Sava said, "We find the letters backward:[77] ב (*Bet*) first, followed by ב (*bet*): בראשית (*Be-reshit*), *In the beginning,* followed by ברא (*bara*), *created.* Then א (*alef*) first, followed by א (*alef*): אלהים (*Elohim*), followed by את (*et*).

"The reason is: When the blessed Holy One wished to fashion the world, all the letters were hidden away.[78] For two thousand years before creating the world,[79] the blessed Holy One contemplated them and played with them. As He verged on creating the world, all the letters presented themselves before Him, from last to first.[80]

11

---

73. *His great might*   This is the continuation of the verse from Isaiah: *Because of His great might and vast power, not one is missing*; cited above, note 67.

74. **First of rungs...**   Either *Keter,* also known as *Ratson* ("Will, Desire"), or *Hokhmah,* the first *sefirah* that can be identified. See *Zohar* 2:231b.

75. **the upper world**   *Binah.*

76. **Children of Israel...600,000...** The total number of male Israelites above the age of twenty who left Egypt was approximately 600,000. See Exodus 12:37; Numbers 11:21. The precise total of the first census taken in the Sinai Desert was 603,550 (Exodus 38:26; Numbers 1:46; cf. Numbers 26:51; *Leqaḥ Tov,* Numbers 1:46). The 600,000 Israelites parallel the 600,000 divine forces.

See *Mekhilta, Baḥodesh* 3: "If even one of them had been missing [at Mount Sinai], they would not have been worthy of receiving [the Torah]." Cf. *Mekhilta de-Rasbhi,* on Exodus 19:11; *Devarim Rabbah* 7:8.

77. **We find the letters backward**   The first two words of the Torah begin with the second letter of the alphabet, ב (*bet*); the next two words of the Torah begin with the first letter, א (*alef*).

78. **hidden away**   Before Creation, the letters were concealed within the divine mind and arranged in reverse order.

79. **For two thousand years...**   See *Bereshit Rabbah* 8:2: "Rabbi Shim'on son of Lakish said, 'The Torah preceded the creation of the world by two thousand years.'"

80. **all the letters presented themselves before Him...**   A similar story appears in *Alfa Beita de-Rabbi Aqiva,* Version 2 (*Battei Midrashot,* 2:396–404); *Midrash Aseret ha-Dibberot* (*Beit ha-Midrash,* 1:62–63); *Midrash Shir ha-Shirim* (ed. L. Greenhut) 5:11; *Zohar* 1:205b; *ZH* 88c–d (*MhN, Rut*); *TZ, Haqdamah,* 16a. The *Zohar* draws primarily on *Alfa Beita de-Rabbi Aqiva.* See Michal Oron, in *Meḥqerei Yerushalayim be-Maḥashevet Yisra'el* 3 (1984): 97–109.

"The letter ת (*tav*) entered first of all. She said, 'Master of the worlds, may it please You to create the world by me, for I complete Your seal: אמת (*emet*), truth[81]—and You are called Truth.[82] It is fitting for the King of Truth to begin with a letter of truth and to create the world by me.'

"The blessed Holy One replied, 'You are seemly and worthy, but not deserving to initiate Creation, since you are destined to be marked on the foreheads of the faithful who fulfilled the Torah from א (*alef*) to ת (*tav*), and by your mark they will die.[83] Furthermore you are the seal of מות (*mavet*), death.[84] So you do not deserve to serve as the instrument of Creation.' She immediately departed.

"The letter ש (*shin*) came before Him. She said, 'Master of the worlds, may it please You to create the world by me, for by me You are named שדי (*Shaddai*), and it is fitting to create the world by a holy name.'

"He replied, 'You are seemly, you are good, and you are true, but since letters of deceit take you as their accomplice, I do not wish to create the world by you. For a lie cannot exist unless ק״ר (*qof-resh*) take you.'[85] So whoever wants to tell a lie will first lay a foundation of truth and then construct the lie.[86] For ש (*shin*) is a letter of truth, a true letter of the patriarchs, who were united in it;[87] ק״ר (*qof-resh*) are letters that appear on the evil side.[88] In order to survive, they entangle the letter ש (*shin*), forming קשר (*qesher*), conspiracy. Seeing this, she left His presence.

81. **Your seal:** אמת **(*emet*), truth** According to Rabbi Ḥanina (BT *Shabbat* 55a), God's seal is אמת (*emet*), "truth," the final letter of which is ת (*tav*).

82. **You are called Truth** See Jeremiah 10:10: יהוה (*YHVH*) *is the God of truth.*

83. **destined to be marked...** See Ezekiel 9:3–4: *He [*יהוה (*YHVH*)*] called to the man dressed in linen with the scribe's kit at his waist, and* יהוה (*YHVH*) *said to him, "Pass through the city, through Jerusalem, and put a mark [*תו (*tav*)*] on the foreheads of those who moan and groan over all the abominations being committed in it."* See Greenberg, *Ezekiel,* 177. In the old Hebrew script, the ת (*tav*) was shaped like an X, the simplest mark. Its purpose in Ezekiel was to distinguish the righteous from the rest of the population, but according to Rabbi Aḥa son of Rabbi Ḥanina (BT *Shabbat* 55a), even those marked were killed, since their silence in the face of the wicked implicated them.

84. **seal of** מות **(*mavet*), death** The word מות (*mavet*), "death," ends with the letter ת (*tav*).

85. **letters of deceit...** ק״ר **(*qof-resh*)...** The word שקר (*sheqer*), "lie," begins with ש (*shin*) and continues: קר (*qof, resh*). See BT *Shabbat* 104a; Judah ben Barzillai, *Peirush Sefer Yetsirah,* 146.

86. **whoever wants to tell a lie...** See Rashi on Numbers 13:27, who paraphrases BT *Sotah* 35a; *Zohar* 2:215b, 264a; 3:161a.

87. ש **(*shin*) is a letter of truth...** The three prongs of the ש (*shin*) stand for the three patriarchs: Abraham, Isaac, and Jacob, who symbolize the triad of *sefirot: Ḥesed, Gevurah,* and *Tif'eret.* See *Zohar* 1:25b (*TZ*); 2:204a.

88. **appear on the evil side** Perhaps because they stand for קליפה (*qelippah*), "husk," and רע (*ra*), "evil." See *Zohar* 2:180b; *ZḤ* 8c (*SO*).

12

"The letter צ (*tsadi*) entered. She said to Him, 'Master of the world, may it please You to create the world by me, for צדיקים (*tsaddiqim*), the righteous, are sealed by me, and You, who are called צדיק (*Tsaddiq*), Righteous, are signified by me, as is written: *For* יהוה (*YHVH*) *is* צדיק (*tsaddiq*)—*loving righteousness* (Psalms 11:7). It is fitting to create the world by me!'

"He replied, 'צ (*Tsadi*), you are צדיק (*tsaddiq*), but you should remain hidden—not so revealed—so as not to provide the world a pretext.' How so? She is נ (*nun*). י (*Yod*) from the name of the holy covenant comes and rides on her, is united with her.[89] This is the mystery: When the blessed Holy One created Adam, He created him with two faces.[90] So the י (*yod*) faces backward, like this: צ.[91] They were not turned face-to-face, like this: צ.[92] It looked upward like this: צ. It looked downward like this: צ.[93] The blessed Holy One said to her, 'Turn back, for I intend to split you and transfigure you face-to-face, but you will arise elsewhere.'[94] She left His presence and departed.

13

89. She is נ (*nun*)... The letter צ (*tsadi*) consists of a נ (*nun*) and a י (*yod*). See *Bahir* 42 (61); *Sefer ha-Temunah*, 2, 21a. The נ (*nun*) symbolizes *Shekhinah*, the feminine (נקבה [*neqevah*]). The י (*yod*) symbolizes *Yesod*, the divine phallus, who is called "covenant." The mark of the covenant of circumcision is pictured as the smallest of the Hebrew letters. In *Tanhuma, Tsav* 14, *Shemini* 8, this mark is identified with the י (*yod*) of the divine name שדי (*Shaddai*). A German Hasidic tradition identifies the mark with the *yod* of יהוה (*YHVH*).

See *Zohar* 1:13a, 56a, 95a–b; 2:36a, 216b; 3:142a (*IR*), 215b, 220a, 256a (*RM*); Wolfson, in *JQR* 78 (1987): 77–112; idem, *Circle in the Square*, 29–48. Liebes (*Studies*, 154–58) suggests that the צ (*tsadi*) alludes to Jesus.

90. two faces דו פרצופין (*Du partsufin*). See *Bereshit Rabbah* 8:1: "Rabbi Yirmeyah son of El'azar said, 'When the blessed Holy One created Adam, He created him androgynous, as is said: *Male and female He created them* (Genesis 1:27).' Rabbi Shemu'el son of Nahamani said, 'When the blessed Holy One created Adam, He created him with two faces. Then He sawed him and gave him two backs, one on this side and one on that.'"

See BT *Berakhot* 61a; *Eruvin* 18a; Plato, *Symposium* 189d–191d; *Zohar* 1:13b, 47a; 2:55a; 3:5a, 44b; Matt, *Zohar*, 217.

91. י (*yod*) faces backward... This reflects the Sephardic practice of writing the צ (*tsadi*). See Scholem; Friedman, *Tsidqat ha-Tsaddiq*, 41–55; Meshi-Zahav, *Qovets Sifrei Setam*, intro, 36; 8, 149–52, 239–40; Havlin, in *Alei Sefer* 12 (1986): 13–19; Ta-Shma, *Ha-Nigleh she-ba-Nistar*, 65, 139, nn. 163–66.

92. not turned face-to-face... Initially the union between the masculine and feminine aspects of God was back-to-back and thus incomplete. See *Zohar* 2:176b (*SdTs*); 3:292b (*IZ*); BT *Bava Batra* 99a. This incomplete union is symbolized by the configuration of the צ (*tsadi*). The צ (*tsadi*) must remain hidden so that this secret will not become widely known and "provide the world a pretext" to impugn the divine union.

93. It looked upward...downward... Trying to face its partner. See Tishby, *Wisdom of the Zohar*, 2:564.

94. you will arise elsewhere The י (*yod*) and the נ (*nun*) will face one another not here but in another letter: ט (*tet*). See *KP*.

"The letter פ (*pe*) entered. She said to Him, 'Master of the world, may it please You to create the world by me, for I signify פורקנא (*purqena*), the redemption, that You will someday bring to the world, also called פדות (*pedut*), deliverance. It is fitting to create the world by me!'

"He replied, 'You are seemly, but you signify hidden transgression, like a serpent striking, then tucking its head into its body:[95] so one who sins bows his head, stretching out his hands.'

"Similarly ע (*ayin*) stands for עון (*avon*), iniquity. Although she said, 'I imply ענוה (*anavah*), humility,' the blessed Holy One replied, 'I will not create the world by you.' She left His presence.

"The letter ס (*samekh*) entered. She said to Him, 'Master of [3a] the world, may it please You to create the world by me, for by me סמיכא (*semikha*), support, exists for those who fall, as is written: סומך יהוה (*Somekh YHVH*), *YHVH supports, all who fall* (Psalms 145:14).'

"He replied, 'So you are needed where you are; do not move! If you leave, what would happen to the fallen, who depend on you?' She immediately left His presence.

"The letter נ (*nun*) entered. She said to Him, 'Master of the world, may it please You to create the world by me, for by me You are called נורא (*Nora*), *Awesome, in praises* (Exodus 15:11). By me, the praise of the righteous is called נאוה (*navah*), *comely* (Psalms 33:1).'

"He replied, 'נ (*Nun*), return to your place, for because of you ס (*samekh*) returned to her place.[96] Depend on her.' She returned immediately, leaving His presence.

"The letter מ (*mem*) entered. She said to him, 'Master of the world, may it please You to create the world by me, for by me You are called מלך (*Melekh*), King.'

"He replied, 'Certainly so, but I will not create the world by you, since the world needs a king. Return to your place, you along with ל (*lamed*) and ך (*khaf*),[97] for the world should not be without a king.'

"At that moment the letter כ (*kaf*) descended from His throne of glory[98] and said, 'Master of the world, may it please You to create the world by me, for I am Your כבוד (*Kavod*), Glory.'

95. **hidden transgression...** The form of the letter פ (*pe*) resembles someone trying to hide his head. See *Zohar* 3:119b.

96. **because of you...** נ (*Nun*) stands for נופלים (*nofelim*), the "fallen."

97. ל (*lamed*) **and** ך (*khaf*) The other two letters in the word מלך (*melekh*), "king,"

which precede the letter מ (*mem*) in the alphabet.

98. **letter כ (*kaf*) descended...** The final ך (*khaf*) in the word מלך (*melekh*) was eliminated, but now the regular כ (*kaf*) approaches God.

"When כ (*kaf*) descended from the throne of glory, 200,000 worlds trembled, the throne trembled, and all the worlds verged on collapse. The blessed Holy One said to her, 'כ, כ (*Kaf, kaf*), what are you doing here? I will not create the world by you. Return to your place, for you imply כליה (*kelayah*), destruction—*a decree of destruction* (Isaiah 10:23). Return to your throne and stay there.' She thereupon left His presence and returned to her place.

"The letter י (*yod*) entered. She said to Him, 'Master of the world, may it please You to create the world by me, for I am the beginning of the holy Name.[99] It is fitting for You to create the world by me!'

"He replied, 'It is enough for you to be engraved in Me, to be inscribed in Me. My desire culminates in you. You should not be uprooted from My name.'

"The letter ט (*tet*) entered. She said to Him, 'Master of the world, may it please You to create the world by me, for by me You are called טוב וישר (*tov ve-yashar*), *good and upright* (Psalms 25:8).'

"He replied, 'I will not create the world by you, for your goodness is concealed and hidden within you,[100] as is written: *How abundant is Your goodness that You have hidden away for those in awe of You* (Psalms 31:20). Since it is hidden within you, it plays no part in this world that I am about to create, but rather in the world to come.[101] Furthermore, because your goodness is hidden within you, the gates of My Temple will sink, as is written: *Her gates* טבעו (*tave'u*), *have sunk, into the earth* (Lamentations 2:9). Further, facing you is ח (*ḥet*),[102] and when you join together you spell חטא (*ḥet*), sin.'[103] So these two letters are not inscribed in the holy tribes.[104] She immediately left His presence.

"The letter ז (*zayin*) entered. She said to Him, 'Master of the world, may it please You to create the world by me, for by me Your children observe the Sabbath, as is written: זכור (*Zakhor*), *Remember, the Sabbath day, to hallow it* (Exodus 20:8).'

15

99. **beginning**... The first letter of יהוה (*YHVH*).

100. **hidden within you** The point at the upper right of the ט (*tet*) is turned inward. See *Zohar* 1:30b.

101. **rather in the world to come** See BT *Ḥagigah* 12a (cited above, note 10); *Bereshit Rabbah* 3:6; 41:3; *Shemot Rabbah* 35:1; *Tanḥuma, Shemini* 9; *Bahir* 97–98 (147); *Zohar* 1:31b–32a, 45b–46a, 47a; 2:127a, 148b–149a, 220a–b; 3:88a, 173b.

102. **facing you is ח (*ḥet*)** The letter preceding ט (*tet*) in the alphabet.

103. חטא (*ḥet*), sin Which ends with a quiescent א (*alef*). See *Zohar* 1:204a.

104. **these two letters are not inscribed**... The letters ח (*ḥet*) and ט (*tet*) do not appear in the names of the twelve tribes, which were engraved on the jewels of the breast-plate worn by the high priest. See BT *Yoma* 73b; JT *Yoma* 7:7, 44c; *Zohar* 2:152a, 230a; 3:188b.

"He replied, 'I will not create the world by you, for you imply war—a sharp sword and a spear for battle, like a ן (*nun*).'[105] She immediately left His presence.

"The letter ו (*vav*) entered. She said to Him, 'Master of the world, may it please You to create the world by me, for I am a letter of Your name.'[106]

"He replied, 'ו (*Vav*), it is enough for you and ה (*he*) to be letters of My name, included in the mystery of My name, engraved and carved in My name. I will not create the world by either of you.'

"The letters ד (*dalet*) and ג (*gimel*) entered and made the same request. He replied to them as well, 'It is enough for you to be with each other, since the poor will never cease from the world[107] and need to be treated kindly. ד (*Dalet*) is poor; ג (*gimel*) גומל (*gomel*), renders, goodness to her.[108] Do not separate from one another! It is enough for one of you to sustain the other.'

"The letter ב (*bet*) entered. She said to Him, 'Master of the world, may it please You to create the world by me, for by me You are blessed above and below.'[109]

16

"The blessed Holy One replied, 'Indeed, by you I will create the world. You will be the beginning of Creation.'

"The letter א (*alef*) stood and did not enter. The blessed Holy One said to her, 'א, א (*Alef, alef*), why do you not enter My presence like all the other letters?'

"She replied, 'Master of the world! Because I saw all the letters leaving Your presence fruitlessly. What could I do there? Furthermore, look, [3b] You have given this enormous gift to the letter ב (*bet*), and it is not fitting for the exalted King to take back a gift He has given to His servant and give it to another!'

"The blessed Holy One said, 'א, א (*Alef, alef*)! Although I will create the world with the letter ב (*bet*), you will be the first of all the letters. Only through you do I become one.[110] With you all counting begins and every deed in the world. No union is actualized except by א (*alef*).'

"The blessed Holy One fashioned high, large letters and low, small letters.[111] So, ב, ב (*Bet, bet*): בראשית ברא (*Be-reshit bara*); א, א (*Alef, alef*): אלהים את

---

105. **like a ן (*nun*)**   Like the straight line of a ן (final *nun*). The word זין (*zayin*) means "weapon."

106. **letter of Your name**   The third letter of the name יהוה (*YHVH*).

107. **poor will never cease...**   See Deuteronomy 15:11.

108. **ד (*Dalet*) is poor...**   The letter ד (*dalet*) signifies דל (*dal*), "poor." See BT *Shabbat* 104a: "גימ״ל דל״ת — גמול דלים (*Gimel dalet: gemol dallim*), Render kindness to the poor."

109. **by me You are blessed...**   ב (*Bet*) stands for ברכה (*berakhah*), "blessing." See JT *Ḥagigah* 2:1, 77c; *Bereshit Rabbah* 1:10; *Midrash ha-Gadol*, Genesis 1:1, 10.

110. **Only through you do I become one**   The א (*alef*) stands for the number one and also for *Keter*, the first *sefirah*. The word אחד (*eḥad*), "one," begins with א (*alef*).

111. **high, large letters and low, small letters**   The initial letters of the first four words of the Torah are ב, ב (*bet, bet*), then

(*Elohim et*). Letters above and letters below. They were all as one, from the upper world and the lower world.

בראשית (*Be-reshit*), *In the beginning.*

Rabbi Yudai said, "What is בראשית (*Be-reshit*)? With Wisdom.[112] This is the Wisdom on which the world stands—through which one enters hidden, high mysteries. Here were engraved six vast, supernal dimensions, from which everything emerges, from which issued six springs and streams, flowing into the immense ocean.[113] This is ברא שית (*bara shit*), created six,[114] created from here. Who created them? The unmentioned, the hidden unknown."[115]

Rabbi Ḥiyya and Rabbi Yose were walking on the way. As they reached the site of a certain field, Rabbi Ḥiyya said to Rabbi Yose, "What you have said—ברא שית (*bara shit*)—is certainly true, for there are six supernal days in the Torah, not more; the others are concealed.[116] But in the Secrets of Creation we have discovered this:

"'The holy hidden one[117] engraved an engraving in the innards of a recess, punctuated by a thrust point.[118] He engraved that engraving, hiding it away, like one who locks up everything under a single key, which locks everything

17

א, א (*alef, alef*). Although the first word, בראשית (*be-reshit*), does open with a large ב (*bet*), the emphasis here is not on the size of the letters but rather their origin. The first of each pair derives from *Binah*, the higher world; the second of each from *Shekhinah*, the lower world.

See *Zohar* 1:159b; 2:132a, 174a, 180b; 3:2a, 220a; *ZḤ* 66c (*ShS*), 74c (*ShS*).

112. בראשית (*Be-reshit*)? **With Wisdom** See *Targum Yerushalmi* (frag.), Genesis 1:1: "With wisdom God created." Wisdom (*Ḥokhmah*) is the second *sefirah*, the primordial point of emanation.

The identification of ראשית (*reshit*), *beginning*, with Wisdom appears widely. See Wolfson, *Philo*, 1:242–45, 266–69; *Bereshit Rabbah* 1:1; Azriel of Gerona, *Peirush ha-Aggadot*, 81; Naḥmanides on Genesis 1:1; *Zohar* 1:2a, 15a, 16b, 20a, 145a; Moses de León, *Sheqel ha-Qodesh*, 21–22 (25–26); Scholem, *Major Trends*, 391, n. 80.

113. **six vast, supernal dimensions...** Within *Ḥokhmah*, the six *sefirot* from *Ḥesed* to *Yesod* are etched, subsequently emerging

and flowing to the ocean of *Shekhinah*. See *Sefer Yetsirah* 1:13.

114. ברא שית (*bara shit*)... The word בראשית (*Be-reshit*) is divided in two and read as ברא שית (*bara shit*), "created six." See *Midrash ha-Gadol*, Genesis 1:1, 11–12; *Seder Rabbah di-Vreshit*, 1 (*Battei Midrashot*, 1:19), where it is said that the world was created by six letters (the divine names יה [*YH*] and יהוה [*YHVH*]); BT *Sukkah* 49a; *Zohar* 1:15b, 39b.

115. **The unmentioned, the hidden unknown** The hidden source of emanation, *Ein Sof* or *Keter*; the unnamed subject of the verb ברא (*bara*), "created."

116. **six supernal days...the others...** The mystical Torah, *Tif'eret*, includes the six *sefirot* from *Ḥesed* to *Yesod*, the six primordial days of Creation, whereas the higher *sefirot* are concealed.

117. **holy hidden one** Apparently *Keter*. See *Zohar* 1:10a; 3:66b.

118. **recess...thrust point** *Binah* is the recess, or womb, penetrated by the primordial point of *Ḥokhmah*.

within a single palace.[119] Although everything is hidden away within that palace, the essence of everything lies in that key, which closes and opens. Within that palace lie hidden treasures, one greater than the other. Within that palace stand gates built cryptically, fifty of them. Carved into four sides, they were forty-nine. One gate has no side. No one knows whether it is above or below; it is shut.[120] In those gates is one lock and one precise place for inserting the key,[121] marked only by the impress of the key, known only to the key. Concerning this mystery it is written: בראשית ברא אלהים (Be-reshit bara Elohim), *In the beginning God created.* בראשית (Be-reshit) is the key enclosing all, closing and opening. Six gates are contained in that key that closes and opens.[122] When it closes those gates, enclosing them within itself, then indeed: בראשית (Be-reshit)—a revealed word combined with a concealed word. ברא (Bara), *Created,* is always concealed, closing, not opening.'"[123]

Rabbi Yose said, "Certainly so! I heard the Holy Lamp[124] say so, that ברא (bara) is a concealed word, closing, not opening. As long as the world[125] was locked within the word ברא (bara), it was not, did not exist. Enveloping

18

119. **a single key...a single palace** The key of *Ḥokhmah* opens and closes the palace of *Binah*.

120. **Carved into four sides...forty-nine...** Forty-nine gates of *Binah* are revealed in four lower *sefirot,* corresponding to the four directions: *Ḥesed* (south), *Gevurah* (north), *Tif'eret* (east), and *Shekhinah* (west). The fiftieth gate remains hidden; it "has no side" and "is shut."

See BT *Rosh ha-Shanah* 21b: "Rav and Shemu'el both said, 'Fifty gates of בינה (binah), understanding, were created in the world, all of which were given to Moses except for one, as is said: *You made him little less than God* (Psalms 8:6).'"

Instead of "forty-nine" (preferred by *OY* and *OL*), several witnesses (C12, Ms3, M, Cr) read "forty." *KP* suggests that the original reading was מי (Mi), "Who," indicating *Binah* and Her fifty (the *gimatriyya* of מי) gates, and that this word was misread as מ' (mem), "forty."

121. **one lock...** The opening within *Binah*. The "precise place" is the subtle link between the primordial point of *Ḥokhmah* and the womb of the Divine Mother, *Binah*. Elsewhere in the *Zohar* this site is identified

as *a path unknown to any vulture* (Job 28:7). See 1:29a–b; 2:122b–123a; 3:61b.

122. **Six gates...** The six *sefirot* hidden within *Ḥokhmah*. See *Zohar* 2:177a (*SdTs*).

123. **revealed word...concealed word...** The word בראשית (Be-reshit) contains two words: ברא (bara), "created," referring to the hidden mystery of creation, and שית (shit), "six," referring to the revelation of the six *sefirot.*

Yehuda Liebes argues that the insistence on the concealed nature of ברא (bara) alludes to a different pronunciation and meaning: ברא (bera), "son," the Divine Son. See *Zohar* 2:178b (*SdTs*); and Liebes, *Studies in the Zohar,* 146–52.

124. **Holy Lamp** בוצינא קדישא (Botsina Qaddisha), the Zoharic title of Rabbi Shim'on son of Yoḥai. See *Zohar* 1:4a, 156a, 197b; 3:171a; *ZḤ 85d* (MhN, Rut).

See 2 Samuel 21:17; *Bereshit Rabbah* 85:4; BT *Ketubbot* 17a, where Rabbi Abbahu is called: בוצינא דנהורא (Botsina di-Nhora), "Lamp of Light"; and *Berakhot* 28b, where Rabban Yoḥanan son of Zakkai is called נר ישראל (Ner Yisra'el), "Lamp of Israel."

125. **world** The lower *sefirot,* which constitute the pattern of all the worlds.

everything was תהו (*tohu*), *chaos*,[126] and as long as תהו (*tohu*) reigned, the world was not, did not exist. When did that key open gates? When was it fit to be fruitful, to generate offspring? When Abraham arrived,[127] as is written: *These are the generations of heaven and earth* בהבראם (*be-hibbare'am*), *when they were created* (Genesis 2:4), and we have learned: באברהם (*be-Avraham*), through Abraham.[128] Whereas everything was concealed in the word ברא (*bara*), now the letters were transposed and rendered fruitful. A pillar emerged, generating offspring: אבר (*ever*), organ—Holy Foundation on which the world stands.[129]

"When אבר (*ever*) was inscribed in the word ברא (*bara*), the supernal concealed one inscribed another inscription for its glorious name. This is מי ברא אלה (*Mi vara elleh*), *Who created these* (Isaiah 40:26).[130] The holy blessed name מה (*Mah*), *What*, was also inscribed.[131] Out of ברא (*bara*) it generated אבר (*ever*), inscribing אלה (*elleh*) at one end and אבר (*ever*) at the other.[132] Holy concealed one! אלה (*Elleh*) exists, אבר (*ever*) exists. As one was completed, so was the other. In אבר (*ever*) it engraved ה (*he*); in אלה (*elleh*), י (*yod*). Letters were aroused to complete one side and the other. It produced מ״ם (two *mems*), moving one to this side, one to that. The holy name was completed— becoming אלהים (*Elohim*)—and the name אברהם (*Avraham*) as well. [4a] As one was completed, so was the other.[133] Then life was generated and the complete

19

126. תהו (*tohu*), *chaos* Ḥokhmah, the primordial divine substance representing pure potential, corresponding to the Greek philosophical concept of *hyle,* primordial matter.

127. **When Abraham arrived** Abraham symbolizes the *sefirah* of Ḥesed, first of the lower *sefirot* emanating from *Binah*.

128. **באברהם (*be-Avraham*)** . . . According to Rabbi Yehoshu'a son of Korḥah (*Bereshit Rabbah* 12:9), בהבראם (*be-hibbare'am*), *when they were created,* is an anagram of באברהם (*be-Avraham*), "through Abraham," indicating that the world was created for his sake.

See *Zohar* 1:86b, 91b, 93a, 105b, 128b, 154b, 230b; 3:117a.

129. **Whereas everything was concealed . . . אבר (*ever*)** . . . The letters of the word ברא (*bara*) were rearranged into אבר (*ever*), which not only forms the beginning of אברהם (*Avraham*) but also signifies the male "organ," *Yesod* ("Foundation"), the divine phallus and cosmic pillar.

130. **מי ברא אלה (*Mi vara elleh*)** . . . *Binah,*

known as מי (*Mi*), *Who* (see above, pages 5–9), emanated *elleh* (*these*), the lower *sefirot.* The transition from מי (*mi*) to אלה (*elleh*) corresponds to the transposition of ברא (*bara*) into אבר (*ever*).

131. **מה (*Mah*), *What* . . .** *Shekhinah* is known as מה (*mah*), *What* (see above, pages 6–9). When מה (*mah*) was added to אבר (*ever*), the name אברהם (*Avraham*) was formed.

132. **אלה (*elleh*) at one end and אבר (*ever*) at the other** The verse *These are the generations of heaven and earth, when they were created* contains אלה (*elleh*), *these*, at one end and אבר (*ever*) (included in the word בהבראם [*be-hibbare'am*], *when they were created*) at the other.

133. **As one was completed . . .** The letters ה (*he*) and מ (*mem*) were added to אבר (*ever*) to complete the name אברהם (*Avraham*); the letters י (*yod*) and מ (*mem*) were added to אלה (*elleh*) to complete the name אלהים (*Elohim*).

Name emerged, unlike before, as is written: *These are the generations of heaven and earth* בהבראם *(be-hibbare'am), when they were created.* All remained suspended until the name of Abraham was created.[134] Once that name was completed, the holy name was completed, as the verse concludes: *on the day that* יהוה אלהים *(YHVH Elohim) made earth and heaven* (Genesis 2:4)."[135]

Rabbi Ḥiyya prostrated himself on the ground, kissing the dust and weeping. He cried out, "Dust, dust, how stubborn you are, how impudent! All delights of the eye decay in you. All pillars of light in the world you consume and pulverize. How insolent you are! The Holy Lamp[136] who has illumined the world, majestic ruler, prince whose merit sustains the world, decays in you. O Rabbi Shim'on, radiance of the lamp, radiance of the worlds, you decompose in the dust, yet you subsist and guide the world!"[137]

For a moment he was shocked, and then exclaimed, "Dust, dust, do not boast! The pillars of the world will not be surrendered to you. Rabbi Shim'on has not decayed in you!"[138]

Still weeping, Rabbi Ḥiyya rose and walked on together with Rabbi Yose. From that day on, he fasted forty days to envision Rabbi Shim'on.[139] He was

20

134. **until the name of Abraham...** See the remark by Rabbi Yehoshu'a son of Korḥah (*Bereshit Rabbah* 12:9) referred to above: בהבראם *(be-hibbare'am)* is an anagram of באברהם *(be-Avraham)*.

135. *on the day...* יהוה אלהים *(YHVH Elohim)...* In rabbinic literature these two names represent, respectively, the divine qualities of compassion and justice.

See *Sifrei*, Deuteronomy 26; *Bereshit Rabbah* 12:15; 33:3; and 13:3, where *YHVH Elohim* is called "a complete name." Cf. *Zohar* 1:20a, 48b; 2:161a, 229a; 3:138b (*IR*); *ZḤ* 70d (*ShS*).

136. **Holy Lamp** Rabbi Shim'on, who had recently died; see above, note 124. On the following passage see Wineman, *Mystic Tales from the Zohar*, 19–32.

137. **yet you subsist...** The soul of Rabbi Shim'on endures in the Garden of Eden, and his spiritual power still guides the world.

138. **has not decayed...** The bodies of the righteous do not decay. See BT *Bava Metsi'a* 84b, concerning Rabbi El'azar son of Rabbi Shim'on.

139. **he fasted forty days to envision Rabbi Shim'on** See *Qohelet Rabbah* on 9:10:

"Resh Lakish (according to another version: Rabbi Yehoshu'a son of Levi) was longing to see Rabbi Ḥiyya Rabbah [in a dream]. He was told, 'You are not worthy.' 'Why?' he asked. 'Didn't I study Torah as he did?' They replied, 'You did not teach Torah as he did; and not only that, he exiled himself [wandering for the sake of Torah].' He said to them, 'Didn't I exile myself?' They replied, 'You exiled yourself to learn; he exiled himself to teach.' He sat for 300 fasts, and then he [Rabbi Ḥiyya] appeared to him in a dream, saying, 'If someone is a nobody but speaks of himself as though he were somebody—better for him if he had never been created.' Rabbi Assi fasted for thirty days to envision Rabbi Ḥiyya Rabbah but did not see him. He was told, 'You are not worthy.' He said to them, 'Show him to me, and let happen what happens!' He saw his steps [the steps of Rabbi Ḥiyya's throne in heaven], and his eyes grew dim." See JT *Kil'ayim* 9:4, 32b; Lerner, in *Sinai* 59 (1966): 20–21.

In the *Zohar* Rabbi Ḥiyya is no longer the saint whose appearance is sought by fasting, but rather the devotee who seeks. Rabbi

told, "You are not entitled to see him." He wept and fasted another forty days. In a vision he was shown Rabbi Shim'on and his son Rabbi El'azar, studying the word that Rabbi Yose had spoken,[140] with thousands listening. Meanwhile he noticed many huge celestial wings,[141] which Rabbi Shim'on and his son Rabbi El'azar mounted, and they soared to the Academy of Heaven. All those wings waited for them. He saw them returning, their splendor renewed, and they shone more brilliantly than the dazzle of the sun.

Rabbi Shim'on opened, saying, "Let Rabbi Ḥiyya enter and see how the blessed Holy One intends to rejuvenate the faces of the righteous in the time to come.[142] Happy is one who enters here without shame. Happy is one who stands in that world[143] as a sturdy pillar."

Rabbi Ḥiyya saw himself entering. Rabbi El'azar rose together with the other pillars sitting there. Embarrassed, he drew back, then entered and sat at the feet of Rabbi Shim'on. A voice issued: "Lower your eyes, do not raise your head, do not gaze!" Lowering his eyes, he saw a light shining in the distance. The voice returned: "O high, hidden, concealed ones, open-eyed, roaming the

21

Shim'on, who has replaced him as the spiritual hero, welcomes him to heaven.

On Mount Sinai Moses fasted for forty days (Exodus 34:28). According to Rabbi Tanḥum son of Ḥanilai (*Midrash Mishlei* 1:1), Solomon did the same "so that God would give him a spirit of wisdom and understanding." See BT *Bava Metsi'a* 85a, where Rabbi Yosef is said to have fasted forty fasts, then forty more, then forty more, in order to ensure that Torah not depart from him. On the following page (85b) we read of Rabbi Ḥiyya's glorious state in heaven, a passage that influences the *Zohar*'s description here of Rabbi Shim'on and Rabbi El'azar: "Rabbi Ḥaviva said, 'Rabbi Ḥaviva son of Surmaki told me: "I saw one of the rabbis whom Elijah used to frequent. In the morning his eyes were lovely, but in the evening they looked as if they had been burnt by fire. I asked him, 'What is this?' He told me that he had asked Elijah, 'Show me the [departed] rabbis as they ascend to the Heavenly Academy.' He [Elijah] replied: 'You can gaze at all of them except for the carriage of Rabbi Ḥiyya, at which you cannot gaze.' 'What is their sign? [How can I distinguish between them?]' 'All are accompanied by angels as they as-

cend and descend, except for Rabbi Ḥiyya's carriage, which ascends and descends on its own.' 'Unable to restrain myself, I gazed at it. Two sparks of fire shot forth and struck that man [i.e., me], blinding him. The next day I went and prostrated myself upon his [Rabbi Ḥiyya's] grave, crying, "Your mishnah is my mishnah," and I was healed.""'"

On the special relationship between Rabbi Ḥiyya and Rabbi Shim'on, see *Zohar* 2:14a (*MhN*). On weeping as a technique for attaining a vision, see Idel, *Kabbalah: New Perspectives,* 75–88.

140. **the word that Rabbi Yose had spoken**   Rabbi Yose had transmitted a teaching of Rabbi Shim'on's concerning בראשית ברא (*Be-reshit bara*). See above, pages 18–20.

141. **wings**   Of angels, or "winged beings."

142. **rejuvenate the faces...**   See *Qohelet Rabbah* on 1:7: "Rabbi Yirmeyah son of Rabbi El'azar said, 'In the time to come, the blessed Holy One will rejuvenate the light of the faces of the righteous, as is said: *But may those that love him be as the sun going forth in its might* (Judges 5:31).'"

143. **in that world**   On earth.

entire world, gaze and see![144] O low, sleeping ones, close-eyed, awake![145] Who among you turns darkness into light, bitter into sweet before arriving here?[146] Who among you awaits each day the light that shines when the King visits the doe[147] and is glorified—declared King of all kings of the world? Whoever does not await this each day in that world has no portion here."[148]

Meanwhile he noticed many of the Companions surrounding him—all those erect pillars—and he saw them being raised to the Academy of Heaven, some ascending, some descending.[149] Above them all, he saw the Master of Wings[150] approaching. When he arrived, he solemnly swore that he had heard from behind the curtain[151] that the King remembers the doe who lies in the dust and visits Her every day. At that moment He kicks the 390 firmaments,[152] which all

144. **O high, hidden, concealed ones...** Referring to the angels or perhaps the souls of the righteous. See *ZH* 76d (*MhN, Rut*); and Zechariah 4:10: *the eyes of YHVH roaming the whole earth.*

145. **O low, sleeping ones...** Human beings.

146. **darkness into light...** By acting righteously on earth.

147. **visits the doe** Joins *Shekhinah* and redeems Her from exile. The *Zohar* identifies *Shekhinah* with the *doe of love* (Proverbs 5:19) and the *doe of dawn* (Psalms 22:1). See *Zohar* 2:7b; 3:21b, 25b; JT *Berakhot* 1:1, 2c.

148. **Whoever does not await...** See BT *Shabbat* 31a: "Rava said, 'When a human is led in for judgment, he is asked, "Were you honest in your business dealings, did you set aside time for Torah, did you generate new life, did you await salvation, did you engage in the dialectics of wisdom, did you understand one thing from another?"'"

149. **saw them being raised to the Academy...** See the passage from BT *Bava Metsi'a* 85b, cited above, note 139. Again, what is said in rabbinic literature about Rabbi Ḥiyya is transferred here to Rabbi Shim'on.

150. **Master of Wings** מארי דגדפי (*Marei de-gadpei*). Apparently Metatron, the chief angel. Cf. Proverbs 1:17; Ecclesiastes 10:20 (in both of which the corresponding Hebrew expression means simply "a winged creature," "a bird"); BT *Shabbat* 49a (where the title is applied to Elisha, who wore *tefillin* despite a Roman prohibition). Elsewhere in the *Zohar*, the expression means simply "angel." See 1:44a, 92a, 152a; 2:13a, 122b; 3:80b. At times (e.g., above; 2:171a), גדפין (*gadpin*), "wings," itself means "angels"; so "the Master of wings" would be the chief angel.

Metatron is often associated with the Heavenly Academy. See BT *Avodah Zarah* 3b; *Bereshit Rabbati* 5:24; *Sefer Ḥanokh* (*Beit ha-Midrash*, 2:115–16); *Seder Gan Eden* (*Beit ha-Midrash*, 3:134–35); *Zohar* 2:169b; *ZH* 36b (*ST*).

In *Targum Qohelet* 10:20 and *Ma'yan Ḥokhmah* (*Beit ha-Midrash*, 1:60), Elijah is identified as "Master of Wings." See BT *Bava Metsi'a* 85b, a passage which influences the *Zohar* here (cited above, note 139): "He [Rabbi Ḥaviva] had asked Elijah, 'Show me the [departed] rabbis as they ascend to the Heavenly Academy.'"

151. **behind the curtain** The curtain concealing God from the world. See BT *Ḥagigah* 15a; *Ma'yan Ḥokhmah* (*Beit ha-Midrash*, 1:60).

152. **He kicks the 390 firmaments** See *Derekh Erets Rabbah*, 2, 56a: "He is one and dwells in 390 firmaments." The *gimatriyya* of שמים (*shamayim*), "heaven," is 390.

On kicking the firmament, see BT *Berakhot* 59a; *Zohar* 1:231a; 2:195b–196a; *ZH* 53b.

tremble and quake [4b] before Him. He sheds tears over this,[153] and those tears of bubbling fire fall into the vast ocean. From those tears the Prince of the Ocean[154] emerges—by them he is sustained. And he hallows the name of the Holy King, agreeing to swallow up all the waters of Creation and absorb them when all the nations gather against the holy people,[155] so that the waters will dry up and they will pass through on dry land.[156]

Meanwhile he[157] heard a voice proclaiming, "Make way, make way—for King Messiah is coming to the Academy of Rabbi Shim'on!" For all the righteous present there are heads of academies, and those academies are designated there; and all members of each academy ascend from the Academy here[158] to the Academy of Heaven. The Messiah visits all those academies, setting his seal on the Torah issuing from the mouths of the rabbis.[159] At that moment the Messiah arrived, adorned by the heads of the academies with celestial crowns. At that moment all the Companions rose and Rabbi Shim'on rose, his light radiating to the vault of heaven.

He said to him,[160] "Happy are you, Rabbi, for your Torah ascends in 370 lights,[161] each and every light refracting into 613 senses,[162] ascending and bathing in rivers of pure balsam.[163] The blessed Holy One sets His seal on the

23

153. **sheds tears over this**   Over the exile of *Shekhinah*. See BT *Berakhot* 59a: "When the blessed Holy One remembers His children, who are plunged in suffering among the nations of the world, He sheds two tears into the Great Sea, and His voice resounds from one end of the world to the other."

See *Zohar* 2:9a, 19a–b (*MhN*), 195b; 3:172a–b; *Seder Gan Eden* (*Beit ha-Midrash*, 3:133).

154. **Prince of the Ocean**   Apparently Leviathan, mentioned below, page 24.

155. **to swallow up all the waters...**   See *Tanḥuma, Ḥuqqat* 1, and BT *Bava Batra* 74b (in the name of Rav), where God commands the Prince of the Ocean to swallow the chaotic waters of creation. When he refuses, God kicks and slays him. Here, the prince obeys the divine command.

On the parallel between the waters and the nations, see *Avot de-Rabbi Natan* A, 35, where both gatherings (of the water and of the nations) are peaceful. Cf. *Zohar* 1:119a; Wineman, *Mystic Tales from the Zohar*, 30–31.

156. **pass through on dry land**   Recalling the crossing of the Red Sea. See Micah 7:15:

As in the days when You went forth from the land of Egypt, I will show him wonders. Cf. Exodus 14:21–22; Isaiah 11:15–16; *Vayiqra Rabbah* 27:4.

157. **he**   Rabbi Ḥiyya.

158. **the Academy here**   In the Garden of Eden.

159. **setting his seal...**   Endorsing their teachings. See *Zohar* 3:173a; *ZḤ* 80b (*MhN, Rut*); BT *Ḥagigah* 15b. The image of sealing Torah originates in Isaiah 8:16: *Bind up the testimony, seal Torah among my disciples.*

160. **He said to him**   The Messiah said to Rabbi Shim'on.

161. **370 lights**   Apparently the number 300 signifies the three highest *sefirot*, while the number 70 represents the seven lower *sefirot* emanating from them. See *OY*; *Zohar* 2:14a–b (*MhN*); 3:128b (*IR*). *KP* reads: 390, corresponding to the 390 firmaments.

162. **613 senses**   Corresponding to the 613 *mitsvot* of the Torah. See *Zohar* 3:128a (*IR*).

163. **pure balsam**   Thirteen rivers of balsam await the righteous in the world that is coming. See BT *Ta'anit* 25a; *Bereshit Rabbah*

Torah of your academy, and of the academy of Hezekiah, king of Judah,[164] and of the academy of Ahiyah of Shiloh.[165] I have not come to set my seal on what issues from your academy. Rather, the Master of Wings has entered here, for I know he enters no academy but yours."[166]

Then Rabbi Shim'on told him[167] the oath that the Master of Wings had sworn. The Messiah began trembling and cried aloud. The heavens trembled, the vast ocean trembled, Leviathan trembled, and the world verged on over-turning. At that moment, he noticed Rabbi Ḥiyya sitting at the feet of Rabbi Shim'on. He said, "Who placed a human here, clothed in the garb of that world?"[168]

Rabbi Shim'on answered, "This is Rabbi Ḥiyya, radiance of the lamp of Torah!"

The Messiah said, "Let him be gathered in,[169] together with his sons,[170] so that they become members of your academy."

Rabbi Shim'on said, "Let him be granted time."[171]

24

62:2. In the *Zohar* (2:127a; 3:181a), the rivers of balsam are the fragrant flow of emanation from *Binah* to *Shekhinah*.

164. **Hezekiah . . .**   King of Judah toward the end of the eighth century B.C.E. According to rabbinic tradition, Hezekiah was extremely devoted to the study and teaching of Torah. See *Shir ha-Shirim Rabbah* on 4:8; BT *Sanhedrin* 94b. According to Rabbi Ḥizkiyah (*Bereshit Rabbah* 35:2), there was no need of the covenantal sign of the rainbow in the generations of Hezekiah and of Rabbi Shim'on because of the righteousness of those two figures.

165. **Ahiyah of Shiloh**   Ahiyah was the prophet who revealed to King Jeroboam that Solomon's kingdom would be divided (1 Kings 11:29–39). According to rabbinic tradition, he was a master of the secrets of Torah (BT *Sanhedrin* 102a; *Midrash Tehillim* 5:8) and the teacher of Elijah (JT *Eruvin* 5:1, 22b).

Rabbi Shim'on associates himself with Ahiyah in *Bereshit Rabbah* 35:2; *Zohar* 3:287b (*IZ*); *ZḤ* 19a (*MhN*). Hasidic legend portrays Ahiyah as the mentor of Israel Ba'al Shem Tov, founder of Hasidism.

166. **I have not come . . .**   Your teachings do not need my confirmation, as your

teachings have been confirmed by God. Rather, I have come to hear the words of Metatron.

167. **told him**   Told the Messiah.

168. **clothed in the garb of that world**   In a physical body. See the reaction of the angels when Moses ascends to receive the Torah (BT *Shabbat* 88b): "Rabbi Yehoshu'a son of Levi said, 'When Moses ascended on high, the ministering angels said before the blessed Holy One, "Master of the Universe! What is one born of woman doing here among us?"'"

169. **"Let him be gathered in"**   Let his life on earth come to an end. Cf. the biblical idiom "to be gathered to one's people" (Genesis 25:8; 35:29; 49:29).

170. **together with his sons**   The *amora'im* Rabbi Ḥizkiyah and Rabbi Yehudah. In BT *Bava Metsi'a* 85b (which, as already noted, influences the *Zohar* here), Elijah compares Rabbi Ḥiyya and his sons with the patriarchs. See *Qohelet Rabbah* on 9:10 (which also influences this *Zohar* passage).

171. **"Let him be granted time"**   Let Rabbi Ḥiyya remain alive on earth a while longer. See *ZḤ* 8oc (*MhN, Rut*); and *Zohar* 1:217b–218b, where Rabbi Shim'on intercedes with God to spare the life of Rabbi

Time was granted to him. He emerged trembling, his eyes streaming with tears. Quivering, he cried, "Happy is the share of the righteous in that world! Happy is the share of the son of Yoḥai who has attained this! Of him is written: *So that I may endow those who love Me with substance and fill their treasuries* (Proverbs 8:21)."[172]

בראשית (*Be-reshit*), *In the beginning.* Rabbi Shim'on opened, "*I have put My words in your mouth* (Isaiah 51:16). How vital it is for a human being to engage in Torah day and night! For the blessed Holy One listens to the voice of those who occupy themselves with Torah, and every word innovated in Torah by one engaged in Torah fashions one heaven.

"We have learned: The moment a new word of Torah originates from the mouth of a human being, that word ascends and presents herself before the blessed Holy One,[173] who lifts that word, kisses her, and adorns her with seventy crowns—engraved and inscribed.[174] But an innovated word of wisdom[175] ascends and settles on the head of צדיק (*Tsaddiq*), Righteous One— Vitality of the Worlds.[176] From there, it flies and soars through 70,000 worlds,[177] ascending to the Ancient of Days.[178] All the words of the Ancient

25

Yitsḥak when it was decreed that he was to die.

The theme of a holy person remaining on earth appears in a contemporary thirteenth-century Spanish hagiography, *Vida de Santa Oria,* composed by Gonzola de Berceo. There St. Orea ascends to heaven and sees her reward as a throne but is told that for now she must return to earth and continue her spiritual practice. See Wineman, *Mystic Tales from the Zohar,* 28–29.

172. *So that I may endow those who love Me with substance . . .* According to rabbinic tradition, this verse describes the reward of the righteous in the afterlife. See M *Avot* 5:19; *Uqtsin* 3:12; *Pesiqta de-Rav Kahana, nispaḥim, Vezot Haberakhah,* 451; BT *Sanhedrin* 100a; *Zohar* 1:158a, 206a, 242b; 2:166b.

173. **the blessed Holy One** *Tif'eret.*

174. **seventy crowns . . .** The number seventy appears in the context of revelation in BT *Shabbat* 88b: "Rabbi Yoḥanan said, '. . . Every utterance emerging from the mouth of Power branched into seventy languages.'" See *Bemidbar Rabbah* 13:16, where

Torah is compared to wine: "Just as יין (*yayin*), wine, is numerically equivalent to seventy, so Torah assumes seventy faces."

See *Sefer Ḥanokh (Beit ha-Midrash,* 2:116); Ibn Ezra, introduction to Commentary on the Torah; *Zohar* 1:26a (*TZ*), 47b, 54a.

175. **innovated word of wisdom** A new mystical insight, which rises higher than other new interpretations. Cf. *OY:* "One is able to innovate in Torah matters that Moses himself was not permitted to reveal."

176. צדיק (*Tsaddiq*), **Righteous One— Vitality of the Worlds** *Yesod,* who channels the flow of emanation to *Shekhinah* and the worlds below.

On various senses of the title "Vitality of the Worlds," see Daniel 12:7; *Mekhilta, Pisḥa* 16; *Bereshit Rabbah* 1:5; Schäfer, *Synopse zur Hekhalot-Literatur,* § 275; *Zohar* 1:132a, 135b, 167b.

177. **70,000 worlds** Corresponding to the seven lower *sefirot.*

178. **Ancient of Days** עתיק יומין (*Attiq yomin*). See Daniel 7:9: *The Ancient of Days sits, the hair on His head like clean fleece, His*

of Days are words of wisdom, conveying supernal, concealed mysteries.[179] When that secret word of wisdom, innovated here, ascends, it joins those words of the Ancient of Days. Along with them, it ascends and descends, entering eighteen hidden worlds, which *no eye has seen, O God, but You* (Isaiah 64:3).[180] Emerging from there, they roam until they arrive, full and complete, presenting themselves before the Ancient of Days. At that moment, the Ancient of Days inhales the aroma of that word and it pleases Him more than anything. Lifting that word, He adorns her with 370,000 crowns.[181] The word flies, ascending and descending, and is transformed into a heaven. So each and every word of wisdom is transformed into a heaven, existing enduringly in the presence of the Ancient of Days. He calls them *new heavens*, newly created heavens, hidden mysteries of supernal wisdom. As for all other innovated words of Torah,[182] they stand before [5a] the blessed Holy One, then ascend and are transformed into *earths of the living* (Psalms 116:9). Then they descend, crowning themselves upon one earth,[183] which is renewed and transformed into a *new earth* through that renewed word of Torah. Concerning this is written: *As the new heavens and the new earth that I am making endure before Me....* (Isaiah 66:22). The verse does not read *I have made,*[184] but rather *I am making,* for He makes them continually out of those innovations and mysteries

26

throne—flames of fire. In the *Zohar* this name designates the primordial *sefirah* of *Keter.*

179. **words of the Ancient of Days...** In BT *Pesahim* 119a, secrets of Torah are referred to as "things hidden by the Ancient of Days." See the rabbinic blessing in BT *Berakhot* 17a: "May your steps run to hear words of the Ancient of Days."

See BT *Bava Batra* 91b; *Zohar* 1:9a; 2:168a; 3:105b, 138b (*IR*), 232b; and 3:20a: "Rabbi Yose said to Rabbi Ḥiyya, 'Let us engage in words of Torah, in words of the Ancient of Days.'"

180. **eighteen hidden worlds...** Recalling the phrase above, חי עלמין (*ḥei almin*), "vitality of the worlds," describing *Yesod*; the word חי (*ḥei*) has a numerical value of eighteen. See BT *Avodah Zarah* 3b: "Rabbi Abba said to Rabbi Naḥman son of Yitshak, '...What does [God] do at night?...He rides his light cherub and sails through 18,000 worlds.'"

See BT *Berakhot* 34b: "Rabbi Ḥiyya son of Abba said in the name of Rabbi Yoḥanan,

'All the prophets prophesied only concerning the days of the Messiah, but as for the world that is coming, *No eye has seen, O God, but You,* [*what You will do for one who awaits You*]...All the prophets prophesied only concerning masters of return [those who succeed in turning back to God], but as for the completely righteous, *No eye has seen, O God, but You.'"*

181. **370,000...** An allusion to the three higher *sefirot* (3 × 100,000) and seven lower *sefirot* (7 × 10,000). See *Zohar* 1:4b; 2:14a–b (*MhN*); 3:128b (*IR*).

182. **all other innovated words of Torah** Nonmystical insights.

183. **earths of the living...one earth** *Shekhinah* is the singular "earth of the living," who is adorned and renewed by human insights of Torah, which have been transformed into planetoids, miniature *earths of the living* orbiting Her.

184. **The verse does not read *I have made*** In the past tense, referring to the original creation of heaven and earth.

of Torah. Of this is written: *I have put My words in your mouth and covered you with the shadow of My hand, to plant heavens and establish earth* (Isaiah 51:16). The verse does not read *the heavens,* but rather *heavens.*"[185]

Rabbi El'azar asked, "What is the meaning of: *I have covered you with the shadow of My hand?*"

He replied, "When Torah was transmitted to Moses, myriads of celestial angels came to scorch him with flames from their mouths, but the blessed Holy One sheltered him.[186] Now when this word ascends, is aroused, and stands before the blessed Holy One, He shelters that word and covers that person so that he will not be discovered by them—arousing their jealousy—before that word is transformed into new heavens and a new earth, as is written: *I have covered you with the shadow of My hand, to plant heavens and establish earth.* From this we learn that every word concealed from the eyes attains supernal value,[187] as is written: *I have covered you with the shadow of My hand.* Why was it covered and hidden from view? For the sake of supernal value, as is written: *to plant heavens and establish earth,* as already explained.

"*To say to Zion: 'You are* עמי *(ammi), My people!'* (ibid.). *To say to* those gates, those distinguished words,[188] these above those: '*You are* עמי *(ammi).*'"

27

---

185. **The verse does not read *the heavens*...** The reference is not to the existing heavens, but to new heavens. See BT *Sanhedrin* 99b: "Rav said, '[Concerning one who studies Torah for her own sake,] it is as though he built heavenly and earthly palaces, as is written: *I have put My words in your mouth and covered you with the shadow of My hand, to plant heavens and establish earth.*'" Rabbi Shim'on amplifies this teaching and radicalizes it; note how the phrase "it is as though" has disappeared.

186. **angels came to scorch him...** Jealous that a mere mortal dared to enter the celestial realm. See *Pesiqta Rabbati* 20: "When Moses ascended on high....a band of angels of destruction...sought to scorch him with the breath of their mouths. What did the blessed Holy One do? He spread over him some of His splendor."

See *Ma'yan Ḥokhmah* (*Beit ha-Midrash*, 1:58–60); and BT *Shabbat* 88b: "Rabbi Yehoshu'a son of Levi said, 'When Moses ascended on high, the ministering angels said before the blessed Holy One, "Master of the Universe! What is one born of woman doing

here among us?" He answered, "He has come to receive Torah." They said, "That precious treasure hidden by You for 974 generations before the world was created, You desire to give to flesh and blood! *What is a human that You are mindful of him, a human being that You take note of him?*" (Psalms 8:5). "Answer them," said the blessed Holy One to Moses. "Master of the Universe," he replied, "I fear they could scorch me with the breath of their mouths." He said, "Grasp My throne of Glory, and answer them...."'" Rabbi Naḥman observed, 'This teaches that the Almighty spread some of the luster of His *Shekhinah* and His cloud over him.'" See *Zohar* 2:58a, 156b.

187. **every word concealed...** See BT *Ta'anit* 8b: "Blessing is not found in anything weighed, measured, or counted, but only in that which is hidden from the eye." Cf. *Zohar* 1:64b, 202a.

188. **Zion...gates...distinguished words** In BT *Berakhot* 8a, the phrase *gates of* ציון (*Tsiyyon*), *Zion* (Psalms 87:2) is interpreted in the name of Rav Ḥisda as "gates מצויינים (*metsuyyanim*), distinguished, by *halakhah.*" Based on this passage, Rabbi Shim'on iden-

Do not read 'You are עמי (*ammi*), *My people*,' but rather 'You are עמי (*immi*), *with Me*, becoming My partner! Just as I made heaven and earth by speaking, as is said: *By the word of YHVH, the heavens were made* (Psalms 33:6), so do you.' Happy are those engaged in Torah!

"Now if you say that the word of any ignorant person has the same effect, come and see: One who is unaccustomed to the mysteries of Torah and innovates words he does not fully understand—when that word ascends, *a man of perversity, tongue of falsehood* (Proverbs 16:28; 6:17)[189] bursts forth from the chasm of the immense abyss,[190] leaping 500 parasangs[191] to obtain that word. Grabbing her, he takes that word back to his chasm and transmogrifies her into a distorted heaven called 'chaos.' The *man of perversity* flies through that heaven—6,000 parasangs in one glide.[192] As soon as the distorted heaven is established, *a woman of whoredom* (Hosea 1:2)[193] emerges, clinging to it, joining with it. From there she sets out, killing thousands, myriads. For as long as she endures in that heaven, she is empowered to swoop through the entire world in a single moment.[194] Concerning this is written: *Woe unto them who haul iniquity with cords of falsehood, and sin as with a cart rope* (Isaiah 5:18).[195] *Iniquity* is the male. Who is *sin*? The female. He[196] hauls the one called *iniquity* with those *cords of falsehood*, and then *sin as with a cart rope*, that female called *sin*, who is empowered there to fly and kill human beings. So, *Many are those she has struck dead* (Proverbs 7:26). Who has struck them dead? This *sin* who slays human beings. Who causes this? A disciple unqualified to teach who teaches.[197] May the Compassionate One save us!"

28

tifies original interpretations of Torah as Zion.

189. *man of perversity*... Samael, the male demon who schemes and accuses falsely.

190. **chasm of the immense abyss** The abode of demons.

191. **parasangs** The Greek parasang equals about 3.5 miles.

192. **in one glide** The distorted heaven empowers Samael, providing him a fast celestial highway.

193. *woman of whoredom* Lilith, the female demon, wife of Samael. Together they comprise *Sitra Aḥra*, "the Other Side." See *Zohar* 1:148a (*ST*); 2:245a; Scholem, *Kabbalah*, 356–61.

194. **in a single moment** See BT *Berakhot* 4b: "A *tanna* taught: 'Michael [reaches his destination] in one [glide], Gabriel in two, Elijah in four, and the Angel of Death in eight—in time of plague, however, in one.'"

195. *Woe unto them*... See BT *Sukkah* 52a: "Rabbi Assi said, 'The evil impulse at first resembles the thread of a spider but ultimately it resembles cart ropes, as is said: *Woe unto them who haul iniquity with cords of vanity, and sin as with a cart rope.*'" Cf. *Zohar* 1:57a.

196. **He** The sinner or the distorted heaven.

197. **A disciple unqualified**... See BT *Sotah* 22a: "Rav said, 'What is the meaning of the verse *Many are those she has struck dead, numerous are her slain? Many are those she has struck dead*—this refers to a disciple unqualified to teach [to decide questions of law] who teaches. *Numerous are her slain*—this refers to a disciple qualified to teach who does not.'"

Rabbi Shim'on said to the Companions, "I beg of you not to utter a word of Torah that you do not know and have not heard properly from a lofty tree,[198] lest you enable *sin* to slay multitudes without cause."[199]

They all opened, saying, "May the Compassionate One save us! May the Compassionate One save us!"

"Come and see: With Torah the blessed Holy One created the world. This has been established, as is written: *I was with Him as a nursling, I was a daily delight* (Proverbs 8:30).[200] He gazed upon her once, twice, three and four times, then spoke, creating through her.[201] To teach human beings not to err in her,[202] as is written: *Then He saw and declared her, arranged her and probed her. He told humanity* (Job 28:27).[203] The blessed Holy One created what He created corresponding to those four times: *He saw and declared her, arranged her and probed her.*[204] Before generating His work, He introduced four words: בראשית ברא אלהים את (*Be-reshit bara Elohim et*), *In the beginning God created.* First, these four; then, השמים (*ha-shamayim*), *the heavens.* These correspond to the four times that the blessed Holy One contemplated Torah before actualizing His work of art."

29

198. **from a lofty tree** From a recognized authority. See the similar expression: "from high tamarisks" (BT *Beitsah* 27a). One of the five things that the imprisoned Rabbi Akiva taught Rabbi Shim'on (BT *Pesahim* 112a) was: "If you want to be strangled, then be hanged on a large tree," which according to Rashi (ad loc.) means: If you must depend on an authority, see that it is a great one.

See *Kallah Rabbati*, 2; *Zohar* 2:87a; 3:76a–b; and BT *Berakhot* 27b: "Rabbi Eli'ezer says, '...One who says something that he has not heard from his teacher causes *Shekhinah* to depart from Israel.'"

The conservative attitude here contrasts with the preceding encouragement to innovate. See *OY* and *KP*.

199. **slay multitudes without cause** Righteous and sinful die together in the plagues and disease brought by Lilith.

200. **With Torah... This has been established...** According to M *Avot* 3:14, Torah is the "precious instrument by which the world was created." See *Bereshit Rabbah* 1:1: "Rabbi Osha'ya opened, '*I was with Him as* אמון (*amon*), *a nursling*... אמון (*amon*)—אומן (*umman*), *an artisan.* Torah says, "I was the artistic tool of the blessed Holy One."'... The blessed Holy One gazed into Torah and created the world.'"

See *Zohar* 1:47a, 134a–b; 2:161a–b; 3:35b; Wolfson, *Philo*, 1:243–45.

201. **then spoke...** Only after perusing Torah did God proclaim her words, thereby creating the world.

202. **not to err...** But rather to imitate God and study Torah thoroughly. Cf. BT *Eruvin* 54b: "Rabbi Eli'ezer said, 'One must teach his student four times.'"

203. ***Then He saw... declared... arranged... probed...*** See *Bereshit Rabbah* 24:5. The four verbs correspond to the four times that God gazed into Torah, perhaps also to the four methods of interpretation: literal, allegorical, midrashic, and mystical. After creating the world, God *told humanity* to imitate Him by studying Torah intensively.

204. **corresponding to those four times...** Apparently a reference to the four worlds, containing respectively the *sefirot*, the Chariot, the angels, and the physical world.

Rabbi El'azar was going to see Rabbi Yose son of Rabbi Shim'on son of Lekonya, his father-in-law.[205] [5b] Rabbi Abba accompanied him, and a man was goading the donkeys behind them.

Rabbi Abba said, "Let us open openings of Torah, for the time is ripe to adorn ourselves on our way."

Rabbi El'azar opened, saying, "*My Sabbaths you are to observe* (Leviticus 19:30). Come and see: In six days the blessed Holy One created the world. Every single day revealed its work, transmitting its power through that day.[206] When did it reveal its work and transmit its power? On the fourth day,[207] for those first three days were all concealed, not revealed. When the fourth day arrived, it generated the work and power of them all, since fire, water, and air—although they are three ethereal elements[208]—were all suspended, their work unrevealed until earth revealed them. Then the skill of each one of them was made known.

"Now you might say this happened on the third day, concerning which is written: *Let the earth sprout vegetation*, and *The earth brought forth vegetation* (Genesis 1:11–12). But although written of the third day, it was really the fourth,

30

205. **Rabbi Yose son of Rabbi Shim'on son of Lekonya, his father-in-law** See the similar setting in *Pesiqta de-Rav Kahana* 11:20: "Rabbi El'azar son of Rabbi Shim'on was going to Rabbi Shim'on son of Rabbi Yose son of Lekonya, his father-in-law...." According to this rabbinic tradition, El'azar's father-in-law was named Shim'on son of Yose.

See JT *Ma'aserot* 3:8, 50d; *Shir ha-Shirim Rabbah* on 4:11; *Devarim Rabbah* 7:11; *Seder ha-Dorot*, s.v. Shim'on ben Yose ben Lekonya. (In BT *Bava Metsi'a* 85a the name of Rabbi El'azar's brother-in-law is given as Rabbi Shim'on son of Issi [Yose] son of Lekonya, which would make Yose his father-in-law, as here in the *Zohar*, but nowhere in rabbinic literature is he named Yose son of Shim'on.)

The author(s) of the *Zohar* consistently switches father and son, transforming Shim'on son of Yose into Yose son of Shim'on. See 1:61b, 143b; 3:84b, 188a, 193a; *ZḤ* 10d, 14a (*MhN*), 22c (*MhN*). El'azar's own father, of course, is Rabbi Shim'on son of Yoḥai. Note who accompanies Rabbi El'azar: Rabbi

Abba ("father"). Soon another father and son appear.

206. **In six days...** The six days of Creation correspond to six primordial days, the *sefirot* from *Ḥesed* through *Yesod*, through which God fashioned the world. Each sefirotic day displayed its creative power on the corresponding day of the week.

207. **On the fourth day** Corresponding to *Shekhinah*. Although usually pictured as seventh of the lower *sefirot*, She can also be characterized as the fourth primordial day (the middle of the cosmic week), completing the triad of *Ḥesed, Gevurah,* and *Tif'eret*. *Shekhinah* actualizes the potential of the other *sefirot*.

208. **three ethereal elements** According to Empedocles and later Greek and medieval thought, the four elements—water, fire, air, and earth—are the ultimate root of all things. By their combination and separation, everything in nature comes into being and passes away.

See *Sefer Yetsirah* 3:3; *Bemidbar Rabbah* 14:12; Maimonides, *Mishneh Torah, Hilkhot Yesodei ha-Torah* 4:1. In the *Zohar*, the four

included in the third to be one without division.[209] From the fourth day on, its work was revealed, yielding an artisan for each and every skill,[210] for the fourth day constitutes the fourth leg of the celestial throne.[211] All the work of all of them, both earlier and later days, was dependent on the Sabbath day,[212] as is written: *God included*[213] *in the seventh day His work that He had made* (Genesis 2:2). This is *Sabbath,* fourth leg of the throne.

"Now you might ask, 'If so, why *My Sabbaths you are to observe,* two?' The answer is: the Sabbath of Sabbath eve and the Sabbath of the day itself, which are indivisible."[214]

That rambling donkey-driver[215] goading behind them said, "And what is *My sanctuary you are to hold in awe* (Leviticus 19:30)?"[216]

He replied, "This is the holiness of the Sabbath."

He said, "What is the holiness of the Sabbath?"

He replied, "This is the holiness drawn down from above."

---

elements symbolize the quartet of *sefirot*: *Ḥesed, Gevurah, Tif'eret,* and *Shekhinah.*

209. included in the third... The third primordial day is *Tif'eret,* the male *sefirah.* The activity of the female, *Shekhinah,* symbolized by earth, took place on the fourth day but is included in His day to ensure and demonstrate their union.

210. From the fourth day on... an artisan... Beginning on the fourth day, the lower triad of *sefirot* emerged: *Netsaḥ, Hod,* and *Yesod.* These three artisans completed the work of the preceding skilled trio: *Ḥesed, Gevurah,* and *Tif'eret.* See *OY.*

211. fourth leg... The four *sefirot* (*Ḥesed, Gevurah, Tif'eret,* and *Shekhinah*), the four elements, also constitute the four legs of the divine throne upon which sits *Binah.* See *Zohar* 1:20a.

212. earlier and later days... Sabbath *Shekhinah* completes the triad of *Ḥesed, Gevurah,* and *Tif'eret,* as well as the next triad: *Netsaḥ, Hod,* and *Yesod.* She is the Sabbath, culmination of the primordial week of Creation.

213. *included* ויכל (*Vaykhal*), "And He completed," from the root כלה (*klh*). Rabbi El'azar understands this word in light of the related root כלל (*kll*), "include, comprise, gather."

214. Sabbath of Sabbath eve... There are two aspects of the Sabbath: the feminine Sabbath eve, symbolized by *Shekhinah,* and the masculine Sabbath day, symbolized by *Tif'eret* or *Yesod.* Cf. Moses de León, *Sefer ha-Mishqal,* 110.

215. rambling donkey-driver טייעא (*Tayya'a*), "Arab," Arabian caravanner, derived from the name of the Arabian tribe *Ṭayyi'.* The prophet Elijah returns to earth to appear as a *tayya'a* in BT *Berakhot* 6b, and as an ערבי (*aravi*), "Arab" in *Rut Zuta* 1:20; 4:11. See *Rosh ha-Shanah* 26b; *Yevamot* 120b; *Bava Batra* 73b; *Sanhedrin* 110a; *Ḥullin* 7a.

In the *Zohar, tayya'a* indicates one of several wandering donkey-drivers who annoy, perplex, and enlighten the Companions on the road. See 2:45b, 94b–114a, 145b, 155b–157a; 3:21a–23a, 186b; *ZḤ* 83a–d (*MhN, Rut*); *TZ* 23, 69a. Cf. *Tosefta, Ḥagigah* 2:1 (BT *Ḥagigah* 14b; JT *Ḥagigah* 2:1, 77a); BT *Mo'ed Qatan* 25a–b; *Bereshit Rabbah* 32:10; *Shir ha-Shirim Rabbah* on 4:3; Steinschneider, *Polemische und apologetische Literatur,* 248–54; Pushinski, in *Yavneh* 2 (1940): 140–47; Scholem, *Major Trends,* 165, 388, n. 46; idem, *Kabbalah,* 227.

216. *My sanctuary...* The continuation of the verse with which Rabbi El'azar opened: *My Sabbaths you are to observe...* (Leviticus 19:30).

31

He said, "If so, you have turned the Sabbath into something not holy except for the holiness that rests upon it from above!"

Rabbi Abba said, "So it is: *Call the Sabbath a delight, the holy of YHVH honored* (Isaiah 58:13). *Sabbath* and *holy of YHVH* are each mentioned separately."

He said, "If so, who is *holy of YHVH?*"

He replied, "Holiness that descends from above, resting upon it."

He said, "If holiness drawn down from above is called *honored*, then it appears that the Sabbath is not *honored*. Yet it is written: *And honor it* (ibid.)!"

Rabbi El'azar said to Rabbi Abba, "Let this man be! Within him lies a new word we do not know."

They said to him, "Speak!"

He opened, saying, "את שבתותי (*Et Shabbetotai*), *My Sabbaths.* את (*Et*)[217] amplifies the meaning to include[218] the range of Sabbath, which is 2000 cubits in every direction.[219] So the meaning is expanded: את שבתותי (*Et Shabbetotai*), *My Sabbaths*—one is the higher Sabbath; the other, the lower Sabbath;[220] both included as one, concealed as one.

"Another Sabbath[221] was left unmentioned and felt ashamed. She said before Him, 'Master of the universe, since the day You created me, I have been called Sabbath—and there can be no day without night.'[222] He replied, 'My daughter, you are Sabbath—I call you Sabbath—but I am about to crown you with a higher crown.' He issued a proclamation: *My sanctuary you are to hold in awe.* This is the Sabbath of Sabbath eve, who is awe and in whom awe dwells.[223]

32

217. את (*Et*) Grammatically, the accusative particle את (*et*) has no ascertainable independent sense, but Naḥum of Gimzo and his disciple Rabbi Akiva taught that when *et* appears in a biblical verse, it amplifies the original meaning.

See BT *Pesaḥim* 22b; *Ḥagigah* 12a–b; *Zohar* 1:79b, 247a; 2:90a, 135b.

218. **amplifies the meaning to include** לאסגאה (*Le-asga'ah*), "To increase," a Zoharic rendering of the rabbinic Hebrew לרבות (*le-rabbot*), "to increase"—that is, to include, amplify, or widen the scope of meaning.

219. **2000 cubits...** The traditional limitation on how far one may walk beyond the city limits on the Sabbath. See *Mekhilta, Vayassa* 6; cf. *Zohar* 2:207a. Here it refers to the range of holiness beyond the realm of the *sefirot;* according to *KP,* the feet of the divine chariot.

220. **the higher Sabbath...the lower Sabbath** The higher Sabbath is *Binah,* the seventh *sefirah* counting up from *Yesod.* The lower Sabbath is *Yesod,* the seventh *sefirah* counting down from *Binah.*

221. **Another Sabbath** Sabbath eve, symbolizing *Shekhinah.*

222. **there can be no day...** The sefirotic day of *Yesod* needs the night of *Shekhinah.* See *Bereshit Rabbah* 11:8, where according to Rabbi Shim'on son of Yoḥai, the Sabbath complains to God that she has no partner among the days of the week, and she is told: "The Assembly of Israel is your partner." See BT *Ḥullin* 60b.

223. **who is awe...** The "Sabbath of Sabbath eve" (Friday night) is *Shekhinah,* who conveys the attribute of Judgment, inspiring awe and fear. The *sefirah* of *Hokhmah,* the father of *Shekhinah,* is also called

Who is that? The one included by the blessed Holy One when He said *I am YHVH*.[224]

"I heard my father say so precisely: את (*Et*) includes the range of Sabbath. *My Sabbaths* are a circle with a square inscribed within.[225] They are two, corresponding to which are two hallowings we should recite. One is ויכלו (*Vaykhullu*), *And they [heaven and earth] were completed*…(Genesis 2:1–3);[226] the other, קדוש (*qiddush*), hallowing.[227] *Vaykhullu* contains thirty-five words, and in the *qiddush* that we recite there are thirty-five words,[228] altogether amounting to seventy names of the blessed Holy One,[229] with which Assembly of Israel is adorned.[230] Since this circle and square are *My Sabbaths*, they are both included in שמור (*Shamor*), *Observe* (Deuteronomy 5:12), as is written: תשמורו (*Tishmoru*), *You are to observe* (Leviticus 19:30),[231] whereas the higher

---

"awe" and is reflected in His daughter, who is lower *Ḥokhmah*.

224. *I am YHVH* The full verse reads: *My Sabbaths you are to observe, My sanctuary you are to hold in awe, I am YHVH* (Leviticus 19:30). Through *Shekhinah*, God reveals the full spectrum of divine personality and is thus called *I*. In this phrase, *I* is joined with *YHVH* (*Tif'eret*). *Shekhinah* manifests in both sacred time (*Sabbath*) and sacred space (*sanctuary*).

225. **circle with a square inscribed within** The phrase derives from BT *Eruvin* 76b; cf. *Bahir* 83 (114–16). Here the reference is to the higher *sefirot* (beginning with *Binah* and culminating in *Yesod*) and *Shekhinah*.

See *KP*; Scholem. Cf. *Zohar* 2:127a, where the circle of the letter ס (*samekh*) symbolizes *Binah*, while the square of the letter ם (final *mem*) symbolizes *Shekhinah*.

226. ויכלו (*Vaykhullu*)… The opening lines of the *qiddush* ("hallowing, sanctification"), the prayer recited over wine Friday evening to hallow the Sabbath.

227. קדוש (*qiddush*)… The rest of the prayer, which includes the blessing over wine and the blessing of hallowing the Sabbath.

228. **in the *qiddush* that we recite…
thirty-five words** This total requires the omission of the following ten words from the *qiddush*: כי הוא יום (*ki hu yom*), "for it is the day," and כי בנו בחרת ואותנו קדשת מכל

העמים (*ki vanu vaharta ve-otanu qiddashta mi-kol ha-ammim*), "for You have chosen us and hallowed us from among all nations."

See Scholem, 493 (unnumbered); Ta-Shma, *Ha-Nigleh she-ba-Nistar*, 63, 138–39, n. 159. The *Zohar*'s phrase "that we recite" indicates a particular custom, which differs from the standard *qiddush*.

229. **seventy names**… See *Bemidbar Rabbah* 14:12; Naḥmanides, *Kitvei Ramban*, 1:135; cf. *Zohar* 2:207b. For various lists of these names, see *Alfa Beita de-Rabbi Aqiva* (*Battei Midrashot*, 2:350–51); *Shir ha-Shirim Zuta* 1:1; *Midrash ha-Gadol*, Genesis 46:8; and *Ba'al ha-Turim*, Numbers 11:16.

230. **Assembly of Israel**… כנסת ישראל (*Keneset Yisra'el*). In rabbinic Hebrew this phrase denotes the people of Israel. The midrash on the Song of Songs describes the love affair between the maiden (the earthly community of Israel) and her lover (the Holy One, blessed be He). See *Shir ha-Shirim Rabbah* on 2:1. In the *Zohar*, *Keneset Yisra'el* can refer to the earthly community but also (often primarily) to *Shekhinah*, the divine feminine counterpart of the people, the aspect of God most intimately connected with them. The lovers in the Song of Songs are pictured as the divine couple: *Tif'eret* and *Shekhinah*.

231. **they are both included**… Both aspects of the Sabbath, the masculine *Yesod* and the feminine *Shekhinah*, are included in

33

Sabbath is not included here in שמור (*Shamor*), *Observe*, but rather in זכור (*Zakhor*), *Remember* (Exodus 20:8), for the supreme King is completed by זכור (*zakhor*).[232] So He is called 'the King who possesses peace,' and His peace is זכור (*zakhor*).[233] That is why there is no strife above, because of the two peaces below: one, Jacob; the other, Joseph.[234] So it is written twice: *Peace, peace to the far and the near* (Isaiah 57:19). *To the far* refers to Jacob, [6*a*] *and the near* refers to Joseph. *To the far*, as is said: *From afar, YHVH appeared to me* (Jeremiah 31:2),[235] *His sister stood far off* (Exodus 2:4).[236] *And the near*, as is said: *New [gods] who came from nearby* (Deuteronomy 32:17).[237] *From afar* is the highest point, standing in its palace.[238] So it is written: תשמורו (*Tishmoru*), *You are to observe*, included in שמור (*Shamor*), *Observe*.[239] *My sanctuary you are to hold in*

34

the feminine, which is signified by the opening word of the fourth of the Ten Commandments: שמור (*Shamor*), *Observe, the Sabbath day to keep it holy*. This word signifies the feminine because the other version of the Ten Commandments (Exodus 20:8) reads: זכור (*Zakhor*), *Remember, the Sabbath day,* and זכור (*zakhor*) suggests זכר (*zakhar*), "male." In the verse in Leviticus 19, the plural verb תשמורו (*tishmoru*), *you are to observe,* indicates the union of male and female.

See BT *Berakhot* 20b; *Bahir* 124 (182); Ezra of Gerona, *Peirush Shir ha-Shirim,* 496–97; Naḥmanides on Exodus 20:8; *Zohar* 1:47b, 48b, 164b; Moses de León, *Sefer ha-Rimmon,* 118.

232. **completed by** זכור (***zakhor***) *Binah,* the supreme King and higher Sabbath, finds its completion in the masculine *sefirah* of Yesod, signified by זכור (*zakhor*), which implies זכר (*zakhar*), "male." Although often depicted as the Divine Mother, *Binah* is also described as "World of the Male," encompassing the entire configuration of *sefirot* from *Ḥesed* through *Yesod.* Together they constitute a masculine entity ready to join *Shekhinah.*

See *Zohar* 1:96a, 147a, 149a, 160b, 246a, 248b; 2:127b; *ZḤ* 72b (*ShS*). Cf. 1:17b, 46b, 163a; 2:4a.

233. **'the King who possesses peace'...** In midrashic literature this phrase is applied to God. See *Pesiqta de-Rav Kahana* 1:2; *Shir ha-Shirim Rabbah* on 1:2. Here it designates

Binah, who contains *Yesod,* who is called "peace" either because He mediates between the right and left poles of the *sefirot,* or because He unites *Tif'eret* with *Shekhinah.* See BT *Shabbat* 152a, where Rabbi Shim'on son of Ḥalafta refers to the phallus as "peacemaker of the home."

234. **two peaces below**... Jacob symbolizes *Tif'eret;* Joseph symbolizes *Yesod,* the divine phallus, since he withstood the test of sexual temptation in Egypt (Genesis 39). See *TZ* 21, 43b, 45b. Both of these mediate between right and left, and unite with *Shekhinah,* insuring peace in the sefirotic realm.

235. *From afar, YHVH appeared*... *Tif'eret,* who is called *YHVH,* appeared *from afar.* See Rashi, ad loc.; *Zohar* 1:120a.

236. *His sister stood far off* Miriam, the subject of the sentence, symbolizes *Shekhinah,* who faces *Tif'eret.* See BT *Sotah* 11a.

237. *from nearby* Idiomatic for "recently." Joseph, *Yesod,* represents a more recent emanation than Jacob, *Tif'eret.* This citation is striking, since the verse in Deuteronomy refers to false gods.

238. *From afar* **is the highest point**... *Ḥokhmah,* the primordial point of emanation, is situated in the palace of *Binah. Tif'eret* issues from them, *from afar.*

239. **So it is written**...שמור (***Shamor***), *Observe* Referring back to the two Sabbaths, *Yesod* and *Shekhinah,* who are indicated together by the plural verb תשמורו (*Tishmoru*), *You are to observe.*

awe is the point standing in the center,[240] which one should fear more than anything, for its punishment is death, as is written: מחלליה (*Meḥaleleha*), *Those who profane it, shall surely be put to death* (Exodus 31:14). Who are מחלליה (*meḥaleleha*), *those who profane it*? Whoever enters the חלל (*ḥalal*), hollow, of the circle and the square—the site where that point rests—and damages it[241] *shall surely be put to death*. So it is written: *You are to hold in awe*. That point is called *I*,[242] and on it rests that high concealed one, unrevealed.[243] This is *YHVH*, and all is one."[244]

Rabbi El'azar and Rabbi Abba dismounted[245] and kissed him. They said, "All this wisdom in your hand, and you are goading our donkeys behind us? Who are you?"

He replied, "Do not ask who I am! Rather, let us go together, engaging in Torah. Let each one speak words of wisdom to illumine the way."

They said to him, "Who appointed you to go here, goading donkeys?"

He replied, "יוד (*Yod*) waged war with two letters, כף (*kaf*) and סמך (*samekh*), to be bound together with me.[246] כף (*Kaf*) did not want to depart and be bound, since it cannot survive for a moment anywhere else.[247] סמך (*Samekh*) did not want to depart, so it could support those who fall, for without סמך (*samekh*) they cannot survive.[248] Alone, יוד (*yod*) came to me, kissing and

35

240. **point standing in the center** The central point of *Shekhinah* inside the square inscribed within the circle.

See *Zohar* 2:204a–b; 3:250a; Moses de León, *Sefer ha-Mishqal*, 110; Joseph Gikatilla, cited in Elijah de Vidas, *Reshit Ḥokhmah, Sha'ar ha-Qedushah*, 2. On the Sabbath as sacred center, see Ginsburg, *The Sabbath in the Classical Kabbalah*, 85–92.

241. **Whoever enters…damages it** Profaning the Sabbath damages the core of *Shekhinah*. See Moses de León, *Sefer ha-Rimmon*, 332–35; idem, *Sefer ha-Mishqal*, 111.

242. **called *I*** *Shekhinah*, who fully expresses the personality of God, is called *I*.

243. **that high concealed one…** *Tif'eret*, more concealed than *Shekhinah*.

244. **all is one** The conclusion of the verse, *I am YHVH*, indicates that *Tif'eret* and *Shekhinah* are united.

245. **dismounted** Out of respect for the sanctity of Torah. See *Tosefta, Ḥagigah* 2:1, where Yoḥanan son of Zakkai dismounts from his donkey to hear an exposition of

ma'aseh merkavah, "the account of the chariot," from El'azar son of Arakh, who had been driving the donkey from behind.

See BT *Ḥagigah* 14b; JT *Ḥagigah* 2:1, 77a; *Zohar* 1:160a.

246. **to be bound together…** These three letters spell the word כיס (*kis*), "pocket." If all three had joined together, then the wandering donkey-driver would have been wealthy, but such was not the case.

247. **כף (*Kaf*) did not want…** כף (*Kaf*) wanted to remain at the head of the word כסא (*kisse*), the divine "throne." See above, pages 14-15 (transmitted in the name of Rav Hamnuna Sava), where the throne begins to tremble when כף (*kaf*) descends from it.

248. **סמך (*Samekh*) did not want…** The letter סמך (*samekh*) stands for the word סומך (*somekh*), "supporting." See above, page 14, where God tells her: "You are needed where you are; do not move! If you leave, what would happen to the fallen, who depend on you?"

embracing me. She wept with me, saying, 'My son, what can I do for you? But look, I will ascend and fill myself with goodness—with hidden, celestial, splendid letters! Then I will come to you, serving as your support. I will endow you with two letters, higher than those that departed, namely, יש (yesh), substance—celestial יוד (yod) and שין (shin)—as your treasuries filled with everything. So, my son, go and goad donkeys.' That is why I go like this."[249]

Rabbi El'azar and Rabbi Abba rejoiced and wept. They said, "Go ride! We will goad the donkeys behind you."

He said to them, "Didn't I tell you it is the command of the King, until the one driving donkeys arrives?"[250]

They said to him, "But you haven't told us your name. The site you inhabit—what is it?"

He replied, "The site I inhabit is fine and lofty for me: a certain tower soaring in the air, grand and splendid.[251] Those dwelling in this tower are the blessed Holy One and a certain poor person.[252] This is where I reside, but I have gone into exile, goading donkeys."

36

249. יש (yesh), substance... Composed of the two letters יוד (yod) and שין (shin). יש (Yesh) designates the flow of emanation from Ḥokhmah ("Wisdom") and Binah ("Understanding"), which is the ultimate substance, more valuable than wealth.

The gimatriyya of יש (yesh) is 310, and according to Rabbi Yehoshu'a son of Levi (M Uqtsin 3:12), "In the world to come, the blessed Holy One will endow every righteous person with 310 worlds, as is written: So that I may endow those who love Me with יש (yesh), substance, and fill their treasuries (Proverbs 8:21)." See Gikatilla, Sha'arei Orah, 93a–b.

250. until the one driving... Until the Messiah arrives riding on a donkey. See Zechariah 9:9: Behold, your king is coming to you. He is righteous and triumphant, humble [or: poor] and riding on a donkey, on a colt, the foal of an ass.

251. tower soaring in the air... The expression originates in the Talmud (BT Ḥagigah 15b; Sanhedrin 106b), where the phrase counter of the towers (Isaiah 33:18) is interpreted as: "one who counted 300 fixed laws concerning a tower soaring in the air." The laws are apparently laws of defilement (see M Oholot 4:1). Rashi (on both Talmudic

passages) offers several interpretations, including one from his teacher that the tower refers to the letter ל (lamed), highest letter of the alphabet. Todros Abulafia, in Otsar ha-Kavod, discusses this interpretation of the Ḥagigah passage (ad loc.); cf. Shoshan Sodot, 108. In several Qumran texts the ל (lamed) is written above the normal line of letters. See Birnbaum, The Hebrew Scripts, 1:127, 143.

In the Zohar, the tower is Binah, towering over the lower sefirot. See 2:91a, 102a; ZḤ 58a, 70a (ShS), and 66a–b (ShS), where the connection between ל (lamed) and the tower is cited from the Book of Rav Hamnuna Sava. Cf. Moses de León, Sheqel ha-Qodesh, 89–90 (112–14); Zohar 1:9a, 37b, 96b; 3:164a–b.

252. the blessed Holy One and a certain poor person Tif'eret and Shekhinah, who is poor in the sense that She has no emanation of Her own but receives emanation from the other sefirot. These two sefirot are joined in the tower of Binah, the ל (lamed). According to Todros Abulafia, Otsar ha-Kavod, Ḥagigah 15b, the ל (lamed) is composed of the two letters ד (dalet) and ו (vav). In Kabbalah ד (dalet) symbolizes Shekhinah, who is דלה (dallah), "poor," while ו (vav),

Rabbi Abba and Rabbi El'azar gazed at him. He had flavored his words for them as sweet as manna and honey.

They said to him, "If you tell us the name of your father, we will kiss the dust of your feet."

He said, "Why? It is not my habit to boast of Torah.[253] But my father's dwelling was in the great ocean. He was a fish,[254] circumnavigating the vast ocean from one end to the other. So grand and splendid, ancient of days, he would swallow all the other fish in the ocean, then spew them out alive, thriving, filled with all goodness of the world. So strong, he could swim the ocean in one moment. He shot me out like an arrow from the hand of a mighty warrior,[255] secreting me in that site I described. Then he returned to his site, disappearing into the ocean."

Rabbi El'azar contemplated his words. He said, "You are the son of the Holy Lamp![256] You are the son of Rav Hamnuna Sava,[257] son of the radiance of Torah, and you are goading donkeys behind us?"

37

whose numerical value is six, symbolizes *Tif'eret,* who joins with the five *sefirot* around Him (*Ḥesed, Gevurah, Netsaḥ, Hod,* and *Yesod*) to form the sixfold sefirotic torso. The three letters joined together spell לוד (*Lod*), the city of Lydda (cf. *KP*), and the donkey-driver is apparently hinting that on the material plane he resides there. On the messianic implication of "poor," see Zechariah 9:9, cited above, note 250.

253. **It is not my habit to boast...** See *Sefer Ḥasidim,* ed. Wistinetzki, par. 1945 (ed. Margaliot, par. 522): "A person whose father is called 'Rabbi,' e.g., 'Rabbi Ya'akov,' and his son [i.e., he himself] is called 'Reu'ven,' should not sign his name 'Reu'ven son of Rabbi Ya'akov,' but rather simply 'Reu'ven.'"

254. **fish** נונא (*Nuna*), swimming in the ocean of Torah. Sefirotically, the fish is *Yesod,* swimming the ocean of divinity.

255. **like an arrow...** See Psalms 127:4: *Like arrows in the hand of a warrior, so are the children of one's youth.* Cf. BT *Ḥagigah* 15a: "Shemu'el said, 'Any emission of semen that does not shoot forth like an arrow does not fructify.'"

256. **Holy Lamp** בוצינא קדישא (*Botsina Qaddisha*), the title usually reserved by the

Zohar for Rabbi Shim'on son of Yoḥai. See above, note 124.

257. **Rav Hamnuna Sava** Rav Hamnuna the Elder, a Babylonian teacher who lived in the third century, though the *Zohar* assumes that he died in the lifetime of Rabbi Shim'on, before the story related here. The donkey-driver had hinted at the name Hamnuna by saying that his father was a נונא (*nuna*), "fish."

See *Zohar* 3:187a; *Tosafot, Qiddushin* 25a, s.v. *hamnuna qarnuna; Bereshit Rabbah* 97:3. The fish carries messianic overtones in both Judaism and Christianity; see Stroumsa, "The Early Christian Fish Symbol Reconsidered."

In the Talmud Rav Hamnuna occasionally transmits teachings of Rabbi Shim'on (e.g., BT *Ḥullin* 21a; *Temurah* 15a), and several prayers are attributed to him (BT *Berakhot* 11b, 17a, 58a). Cf. BT *Gittin* 39b. In the *Zohar* roles are reversed and Rabbi Shim'on cites Rav Hamnuna (e.g., 1:8a–b). Throughout the *Zohar* Hamnuna is greatly revered, and several original ritual acts are attributed to him.

See 1:240a, 250a; 2:88a, 124a, 136b; 3:87b, 103b, 145b (*IR*), 188a; Scholem, *Das Buch Bahir,* 68; idem, *Major Trends,* 368, n. 134;

They both wept together, kissed him, and went on.

They said to him, "If it pleases our master, let him reveal his name to us."

He opened, saying, "*Benayahu son of Yehoyada* (2 Samuel 23:20).[258] This verse has been established[259]—which is fine—but this verse alludes to supernal mysteries of Torah. *Benayahu son of Yehoyada* appears on behalf of a mystery of wisdom—a concealed word, and the name prevails. *Son of a living man* (ibid.)—צדיק (*Tsaddiq*), Righteous One—Vitality of the Worlds.[260] *Master of deeds* (ibid.)[261]—Master of all action, of all celestial powers, for all emerge from Him. He is יהוה צבאות (*YHVH Tseva'ot*), Lord of Hosts, insignia of all His hosts.[262] Distinguished and supreme, He is called *Master of deeds.*

"*From Qavtse'el* (ibid.)—this grand and dignified tree, supreme above all,[263] from which site did it emerge? From which rung did it come? The verse goes on to say: *From Qavtse'el*[264]—a high, concealed rung that [6b] *no eye has seen . . .* (Isaiah 64:3),[265] a rung containing all, gathered in from upper light, and from which all emerges. It is the holy, hidden palace, in which all rungs are

38

Liebes, in *Eshel Be'er Sheva* 4 (1996): 198–201; Goldreich, in *Massu'ot*, 486–91.

258. *Benayahu son of Yehoyada* The verse continues: *son of a living man, abounding in deeds, from Qavtse'el. He smote the two Ariel of Moab. He went down and slew the lion within the pit on a snowy day.* The donkey-driver begins to answer the question of his identity with a verse about Benayahu, a loyal follower of King David, one of the heroes mentioned in 2 Samuel 23.

259. **This verse has been established** See BT *Berakhot* 18a–b: "Rabbi Ḥiyya said . . . , '*Son of a living man.* Are all other people then sons of dead men? Rather, *son of a living man,* for even in his death he was called *living.* . . .'"

Cf. Gikatilla, *Sha'arei Tsedeq,* 7a; *Zohar* 1:132a, 136a.

260. **the name prevails . . .** צדיק (*Tsaddiq*), **Righteous One . . .** The name בניהו (*Benayahu*) indicates *Yesod,* who is בן (*ben*), "son of," יהו (*yod, he, vav*), three letters symbolizing *Ḥokhmah, Binah,* and *Tif'eret.* See *Zohar* 1:136a, 164a.

Yesod, "Vitality of the Worlds," animates all of existence. On various senses of this title see above, note 176. On the notion that "the

name prevails," see BT *Berakhot* 7b; *Zohar* 1:58b; 2:179b.

261. *Master of deeds* The donkey-driver interprets the biblical word רב (*rav*), *abounding,* according to its alternate meaning: "master."

262. **insignia of all His hosts** See BT *Ḥagigah* 16a, in the name of Rabbi Yoḥanan: "He is the insignia among His myriad." Cf. *Zohar* 2:232a.

263. **this grand and dignified tree . . .** *Yesod,* often identified with the Tree of Life.

264. *Qavtse'el* The root קבץ (*qvts*) means "to gather," and *Qavtse'el* refers to *Binah,* who gathers in the upper light of *Ḥokhmah.*

265. *no eye has seen* The verse continues: *O God, but You, what You will do for one who awaits You.* See BT *Berakhot* 34b: "Rabbi Ḥiyya son of Abba said in the name of Rabbi Yoḥanan, 'All the prophets prophesied only concerning the days of the Messiah, but as for the world that is coming, *No eye has seen, O God, but You,* [*what You will do for one who awaits You*] . . . All the prophets prophesied only concerning masters of return [those who succeed in turning back

gathered and concealed.[266] In the trunk of this tree all worlds exist; from it, all holy powers are nourished and deployed.

"*He smote the two Ariel of Moab* (2 Samuel, ibid.). Two sanctuaries existed because of Him, were nourished by Him: First Temple and Second Temple.[267] As soon as He departed, the flow flowing from above ceased. *He,* as it were, *smote* them, destroying and obliterating them, and the Holy Throne fell,[268] as is written: *And I was in the midst of the exile* (Ezekiel 1:1)—that rung called *I*[269] was *in the midst of the exile.* Why? *By the River Kevar* (ibid.), River of Already,[270] on account of the river gushing and flowing, whose waters and springs ceased, so that it did not flow as before, as is written: *A river dries up and is parched* (Job 14:11).[271] *Dries up*—in the First Temple; *is parched*—in the Second. So *He smote the two Ariel of Moab.* מואב (Mo'av), *Moab*—for they originated מאב (me-av), from Father, in heaven and were destroyed and obliterated because of Him.[272] All the lights illumining Israel darkened.

"Further, *He went down and slew the lion* (2 Samuel, ibid.).[273] In former times, when this river gushed its waters below, [the people of] Israel were fulfilled, offering offerings and sacrifices to atone for their souls. Then from above would descend the image of a lion, whom they could see on the altar,

39

to God], but as for the completely righteous, *No eye has seen, O God, but You.*'"

In the *Zohar* this verse often refers to *Binah,* who is identified with "the world that is coming." See 1:4b; 2:97b, 163a; above, note 19.

266. **holy, hidden palace...** *Binah,* the Divine Mother, contains within Herself—and then gives birth to—all the lower *sefirot.*

267. *two Ariel...* **Two sanctuaries...** The meaning of the word *Ariel* in the verse in Samuel is unclear. In Ezekiel 43:15–16 it apparently means "hearth" of an altar; in Isaiah 29:1 the name is applied to Jerusalem. In rabbinic sources *Ariel of Moab* refers to the Temple, since King David was descended from Ruth the Moabite. See M *Middot* 4:7; and BT *Berakhot* 18a–b: "Rabbi Ḥiyya said..., '*He smote the two Ariel of Moab,* for he did not leave his like in either the First Temple or the Second.'"

268. **Holy Throne fell** *Shekhinah* fell into exile.

269. **that rung called *I*** *Shekhinah,* who reveals the full spectrum of divine personality.

270. *River Kevar...* **River of Already** The prophet Ezekiel experienced his vision by the River Kevar, a stream near Nippur in Babylon. In Hebrew, though, the word כבר (kevar) means "already," "long ago." The point here is that the river of *Yesod* was of the past and had ceased to flow, causing the destruction of the Temple and the exile of *Shekhinah.*

See *Re'uyyot Yeḥezqel,* ed. Gruenwald, in *Temirin* 1 (1972): 111–14; Matt, *Essential Kabbalah,* 126, 205; *Zohar* 1:85a, 149a–b.

271. *A river dries up and is parched* See *Zohar* 1:26a (*TZ*), 67a; 2:166b; 3:150b.

272. **originated...were destroyed...** The two Temples came into being through the flow of divine emanation, and when that flow ceased they were destroyed.

273. *He went down and slew the lion* The verse continues: *within the pit on a snowy day.*

crouching over its prey,[274] consuming sacrifices like a fierce warrior, while all dogs[275] hid themselves away, not venturing out.

"When sins prevailed, He descended to the rungs below,[276] and He killed that lion, no longer willing to provide its prey. He, as it were, killed it. *He slew the lion,* really! *Within the pit* (ibid.)—in plain sight of the evil Other Side.[277] Seeing this, that Other Side was emboldened to send a dog to eat the offerings. What is the name of that lion? אוריאל (Uri'el), for his face is the face of אריה (aryeh), a lion.[278] What is the name of that dog? בלאדן (Bal'adan) is its name, for it is excluded from the category of אדם (adam), human, but is rather a dog—its face a dog.[279] *On a snowy day*—a day when sins prevailed, and

274. **image of a lion...** See BT *Yoma* 21b: "Five things were reported about the fire of the pile of wood on the Temple altar: it crouched like a lion, it was as clear as sunlight, its flame was of substance, it devoured wet wood like dry wood, and it caused no smoke to rise." Cf. *Zohar* 3:32b, 211a, 241a; Todros Abulafia, *Sha'ar ha-Razim,* 90.

275. **dogs** The demonic powers.

276. **He descended...** Sin severed the connection between *Yesod* and *Shekhinah,* and the flow of emanation became available to "the rungs below," the demonic forces. The holy lion no longer received its prey and was thus killed, as it were, by *Yesod.*

277. **evil Other Side** סטרא אחרא בישא (Sitra aḥra bisha), the demonic realm, which represents the shadow of the divine.

278. **אוריאל (Uri'el)...** Literally, "God is my light," though here connected by the *Zohar* with the similar-sounding אריה (aryeh), "lion" and with אריאל (Ariel), symbol of the Temple. Uriel is one of the four angels of the Presence (along with Michael, Gabriel, and Raphael), who surround the divine throne. In Kabbalah these angels of the Presence are identified with the four holy creatures seen by Ezekiel. Uriel appears sometimes as the figure of the eagle, sometimes as the lion.

See 1 Enoch 9:1; 2 Esdras 4:1; *Pesiqta Rabbati* 46; *Bemidbar Rabbah* 2:10; *Midrash Konen* (*Beit ha-Midrash,* 2:39); cf. *Zohar* 3:32b, 211a.

279. **name of that dog? בלאדן (Bal'adan)...** The name derives from Merodach Baladan, king of Babylon (722–710 B.C.E.), with whom King Hezekiah of Judea had contact. See 2 Kings 20:12–13; Isaiah 39:1–2, where he is named Merodach Baladan son of Baladan. On this the Talmud (BT *Sanhedrin* 96a) comments: "Why was he called [Merodach-]Baladan the son of Baladan? It has been told: Baladan was a king whose face turned into that of a dog, so his son sat upon his throne instead. In his documents he wrote his own name and the name of his father, King Baladan." Baladan's dog-face is probably a rabbinic explanation of the dogs seen on Assyrian-Babylonian monuments (Ginzberg, *Legends,* 6:368, n. 82).

Here בלאדן (Bal'adan) is a demonic figure whose name is taken to mean: בל אדם (bal adam), "not human." *KP* refers to non-Jewish magical traditions concerning בילאד (Bil'ad), prince of the demons. See *OY; Shoshan Sodot,* 104; Scholem, in *Madda'ei ha-Yahadut* 1 (1926): 112–27. In the continuation of the passage cited above (note 274), BT *Yoma* 21b observes that in the First Temple the fire on the altar appeared crouching like a lion, while in the Second Temple it crouched like a dog. See *Zohar* 3:32b, 211a.

Here the donkey-driver blends several of these traditions to describe a demonic figure with the face of a dog who is empowered to devour the sacrifices.

judgment was decreed above by the celestial court.[280] Of this is written: *She is not afraid of snow for her household* (Proverbs 31:21)—Judgment on high.[281] Why? Because *her whole household is clothed in crimson*[282] (ibid.) and can endure the fierce fire.

"Until here, mystery of the verse. What is written next? *He slew an Egyptian, a man of good appearance* (2 Samuel, ibid., 21). Here the mystery of the verse discloses that whenever Israel sinned He[283] departed, withholding from them all the goodness, all the light illumining them. *He slew an Egyptian man*—the light of that light illumining Israel. Who is it? Moses,[284] as is written: *They said, 'An Egyptian man rescued us'* (Exodus 2:19).[285] There he was born, there he was raised, there he rose to the highest light.[286] *A man of* מראה (*mar'eh*), *good appearance,* as is said: ומראה (*u-mar'eh*), *in appearance, not in riddles* (Numbers 12:8).[287] *Man,* as is said: *Man of Elohim* (Deuteronomy 33:1)—husband, as it were, of that מראה (*mar'eh*), *appearance, of the Presence of YHVH,*[288] for he was worthy of conducting this rung on earth in any way he wished—something no other human attained.

41

280. *On a snowy day...sins...judgment...* Water symbolizes *Ḥesed,* but snow symbolizes *Gevurah* and *Din* ("Judgment"), the congealing and hardening of water. See *Zohar* 1:16a; and *Aggadat Olam Qatan* (*Beit ha-Midrash,* 5:58): "Snow is human sin." According to rabbinic literature, the yearlong punishment of the wicked in Hell is equally divided between fire and snow. See JT *Sanhedrin* 10:3, 29b; *Pesiqta de-Rav Kahana* 10:4; *Zohar* 1:62b, 68b, 107b, 238b.

In *Zohar* 2:97b, 104a, 109a, the donkey-driver who confounds the rabbis refers cryptically to a snowy day on which he and Rabbi Shim'on son of Yoḥai "sowed beans in fifty-two colors," alluding to the fifty-two-letter name of God and to the word בן (*ben*), "son," whose *gimatriyya* is fifty-two. See Liebes, in *Eshel Be'er Sheva* 4 (1996): 200.

281. *She is not afraid...* The *She* of Proverbs 31 is understood as *Shekhinah,* who does not fear the power of *Din* ("Judgment").

282. *clothed in crimson...* *Shekhinah* has an affinity with *Gevurah* and *Din,* symbolized by the color red, and She executes the decrees of Judgment, so She does not

fear Judgment's fire or snow. See *Zohar* 1:238b.

283. **He** *Yesod.*

284. **the light of that light...Moses** Moses attained the *sefirah* of *Tif'eret* and transmitted some of its light.

285. *'An Egyptian man...'* A description of Moses given by Jethro's daughters to their father after Moses rescued them from aggressive shepherds.

286. **There...there...there...** In Egypt. See *Zohar* 2:34a.

287. ומראה (*u-mar'eh*), *in appearance...* In plain sight. God appears to Moses directly, unlike the experience of other prophets.

288. *Man of Elohim*—husband, as it were, of that מראה (*mar'eh*)... *Shekhinah* is the מראה (*mar'eh*), *appearance of the Presence of YHVH,* the site of divine manifestation. She is also known as *Elohim.* Moses is on such intimate terms with *Shekhinah* that he is called Her husband, as indicated by his title: *Man of Elohim* (Deuteronomy 33:1; Psalms 90:1).

See *Midrash Tehillim* 90:5; *Pesiqta de-Rav Kahana,* nispaḥim, Vezot Haberakhah, 443–44, 448 (variants); *Tanḥuma,* Vezot Habe-

"*The Egyptian had a spear in his hand* (2 Samuel, ibid.). This is the staff of God, handed down to him,[289] as is said: *with the staff of God in my hand* (Exodus 17:9). This is the staff created on the eve of Sabbath at twilight,[290] engraved with the holy name,[291] a holy graving. With this he sinned at the rock, as is said: *He struck the rock with his staff twice* (Numbers 20:11). The blessed Holy One said to him, 'Moses, I did not give you My staff for this. By your life! From now on, it will no longer be in your hand.' Immediately *He went down to him with a club* (2 Samuel, ibid.)[292]—with severe judgment. *And wrenched the spear out of the Egyptian's hand,* for from that moment it was withheld from him and was never again in his hand. *And killed him with his own spear.* Because of the sin of striking with that staff,[293] he died and did not enter the Holy Land, and this light was withheld from Israel.

"*From the thirty, he was most honored* (2 Samuel, ibid., 23).[294] These are the thirty celestial years,[295] on which He drew, conveying Them below. Drawing on

42

rakhah 2 (*Ets Yosef,* ad loc.); *Devarim Rabbah* (Lieberman), on 33:1; *Zohar* 1:21b–22a, 148a, 152a–b, 236b, 239a; 2:22b, 235b, 238b, 244b (*Heikh*).

According to rabbinic tradition, after encountering God on Mount Sinai, Moses abstained from sexual contact with his wife and maintained union with *Shekhinah.*

See *Sifrei,* Numbers 99; BT *Shabbat* 87a; *Tanḥuma, Tsav* 13; Maimonides, *Mishneh Torah, Hilkhot Yesodei ha-Torah* 7:6; *Zohar* 1:22a, 152b, 234b; 2:222a; 3:148a, 180a.

289. **staff of God, handed down to him** The staff with which Moses performed miracles before Pharaoh, split the Red Sea, and struck the rock to produce water. According to *Pirqei de-Rabbi Eli'ezer* 40, the rod had previously been in the possession of Adam, Enoch, Noah, Shem, Abraham, Isaac, Jacob, Joseph, and Jethro. See *Targum Yerushalmi,* Exodus 2:21; Ginzberg, *Legends,* 6:106, n. 600.

290. **staff created on the eve of Sabbath...** One of the ten things created in the last moments of the week of Creation, just before the first Sabbath began. See M *Avot* 5:6.

291. **engraved with the holy name** The Ineffable Name, YHVH. See *Targum Yerushalmi,* Exodus 2:21; *Devarim Rabbah* 3:8;

Midrash Tehillim 114:9; *Sefer ha-Yashar, Shemot,* 307; *Zohar* 2:28a, 48a.

292. **He went down to him with a club** The verse continues: *and wrenched the spear out of the Egyptian's hand and killed him with his own spear.* As the donkey-driver interprets the verse, the subject, Benayahu, is really *Yesod,* who confronts Moses the Egyptian. See *Zohar* 2:114b (*RM*).

293. **And killed him with his own spear ...that staff** Benayahu killed Moses the Egyptian *with* Moses' own staff, i.e., because of Moses' own misuse of the staff. The notion that Moses was an Egyptian who was killed by an Israelite foreshadows Freud's thesis. See Amado Lévy-Valensi, *Le Moïse de Freud;* Goldreich, in *Massu'ot,* 486–87.

294. **From the thirty, he was most honored** The verse continues: *but the three he did not attain. David set him over his guard.* The actual biblical verse does not include the word *most* (הכי [*ha-khi*]). Apparently the *Zohar*'s author or a later scribe replaced this phrase with a different one, several verses earlier, describing another of King David's warriors, Avishai: *Of the three, he was most honored* (2 Samuel 23:19). See *Zohar* 1:105b.

295. **thirty celestial years** The three sefirot *Ḥesed, Gevurah,* and *Tif'eret* each reflect

Them, He drew near. *But the three he did not attain.* They approached Him, giving to Him wholeheartedly, but He did not approach Them.[296] Still, although He was not counted as one of Them, *David set him over his body-guard,* for He never faded from the tablet of His heart.[297] [7a] They are never separated. David set Him close—not conversely—for with the praises, songs, and love that the moon offers to the sun,[298] She draws Him toward Her, so that He dwell with Her. This is: *David set him over his bodyguard.*"

Rabbi El'azar and Rabbi Abba fell before him. Meanwhile they did not see him. They rose, looking in every direction, but could not see him. They sat down and wept, and could not speak to one another. After a while Rabbi Abba said, "This is precisely what we learned: On whatever path the righteous walk, with words of Torah between them, virtuous ones of that world come to them.[299] This was indeed Rav Hamnuna Sava,[300] coming to us from that world to reveal these words to us. Before we could recognize him, he vanished!"

the full decade of the *sefirot;* so together They form a total of thirty, which flow into and through *Yesod.* See Gikatilla, *Sha'arei Orah,* 48a.

296. **They approached Him...** The highest triad of *sefirot, Keter, Hokhmah,* and *Binah,* emanate to *Yesod,* but He has no direct contact with Them.

297. *David set him...bodyguard...* King David, who symbolizes *Shekhinah,* yearns to unite with *Yesod. Bodyguard* renders the Hebrew משמעתו (*mishma'ato*), "his obedient band," from the root שמע (*shm'*), "to hear."

Liebes (oral communication) suggests that the use of the word in this passage is influenced by the Arabic Sufi term *sama,* "hearing," the ecstatic song and dance of the Dervishes. Note the following reference to "songs and love." One Sufi defense of *sama* invokes the Koranic tradition (34:10) that David sang praises to God (*Encyclopedia of Religion,* 13:30–31). See Schimmel, *Mystical Dimensions of Islam,* 178–86.

298. **moon...sun** *Shekhinah* and Her partner, *Yesod.*

299. **On whatever path...with words of Torah...** See M *Avot* 3:2: "Rabbi Hananya son of Teradyon said, '...If two are sitting engaged in words of Torah, *Shekhinah* dwells between them.'" Here the seekers are walking, not sitting, and they are visited not by *Shekhinah,* but by a righteous soul who has reincarnated and comes to puzzle and enlighten them.

On the importance of engaging in Torah while on a journey, see Deuteronomy 6:7; BT *Eruvin* 54a; *Ta'anit* 10b; *Zohar* 1:58b, 69b–70a, 76a, 87a, 115b.

300. **Rav Hamnuna Sava** Earlier, the donkey-driver had hinted at the name Hamnuna when he said that his father was a נונא (*nuna*), "fish" (above, page 37). The rabbis concluded that he was the son of the late Hamnuna, but now they realize that he was really Hamnuna himself, reincarnated as a lowly donkey-driver. Father and son are one and the same. Hamnuna's reincarnation is referred to (by his son) in *Zohar* 3:186a–88a; cf. *Zohar* 2:94b–95a; *ZH* 97b–c (*Tiq*).

According to BT *Berakhot* 18a–b, the phrase *son of a living man* (2 Samuel 23:20) describing Benayahu refers to the fact that Benayahu (or the righteous in general) are called *living* even in death. In the *Zohar,* Rav Hamnuna, the donkey-driver, embodies Benayahu anew.

They rose and tried to goad the donkeys, but they would not move. They tried to goad them, but they would not move. Frightened, they left the donkeys behind. Still today that spot is called Donkeys' Site.

Rabbi El'azar opened, saying, "*How immense is Your goodness that You have hidden away for those in awe of You!...* (Psalms 31:20). How great is the precious, supernal goodness the blessed Holy One intends to lavish upon humanity—for the supremely righteous, dreading sin, engaging in Torah—when they enter that world! The verse does not read *Your goodness,* but rather *Your immense goodness.* Who is that? *The memory of Your immense goodness they express* (Psalms 145:7)[301]—joy of life flowing from the world that is coming[302] to Vitality of the Worlds,[303] who is *the memory of Your immense goodness— immense goodness for the house of Israel...* (Isaiah 63:7).[304]

"Further, *How immense is Your goodness.* Here is engraved a mystery of wisdom, all mysteries intimated here. מה (*Mah*), *How,* as has been explained.[305] *Immense*—the *immense* and mighty tree,[306] for there is another, smaller tree,[307] but this one is *immense,* penetrating the vault of heaven. *Your*

44

---

301. *memory...* זכר (*Zekher*), connected by Rabbi El'azar with זכר (*zakhar*), "male," denoting *Yesod,* the divine male who transmits the flow of emanation from the upper *sefirot* to *Shekhinah.* The cited verse is fitting because *Yesod* is also known as "good."

302. **world that is coming** עלמא דאתי (*Alma de-atei*), the Aramaic equivalent of the rabbinic Hebrew העולם הבא (*ha-olam ha-ba*), "the world that is coming." This concept is often understood as referring to the hereafter and is usually translated as "the world to come." From another point of view, however, "the world that is coming" already exists, occupying another dimension. See *Tanḥuma, Vayiqra* 8: "The wise call it *ha-olam ha-ba* not because it does not exist now, but for us today in this world it is still to come." Cf. Maimonides, *Mishneh Torah, Hilkhot Teshuvah* 8:8; and Guttmann, *Philosophies of Judaism,* 37: "'The world to come' does not succeed 'this world' in time, but exists from eternity as a reality outside and above time, to which the soul ascends."

In Kabbalah "the world that is coming" often refers to *Binah,* the continuous source of emanation. See *Zohar* 3:290b (*IZ*): "the world that is coming, constantly coming, never ceasing."

Cf. *Bahir* 106 (160); Asher ben David, *Peirush Shelosh Esreh Middot,* in *Kabbalah* 2 (1997): 293; Moses de León, *Sheqel ha-Qodesh,* 26 (30); idem, *Sod Eser Sefirot,* 375; *Zohar* 1:83a, 92a.

303. **Vitality of the Worlds** *Yesod,* who channels the flow of emanation to *Shekhinah* and the worlds below. On this title, see above, note 176.

304. *house of Israel* *Shekhinah,* also known as Assembly of Israel. See above, note 230.

305. מה (*Mah*), *How,* as has been explained Earlier (above, page 6) Rabbi El'azar had explained that מה (*mah*), "what" or "how," is a name for *Shekhinah.*

306. *immense* and mighty tree *Tifer'et,* trunk of the cosmic tree. See Daniel 4:8.

307. **another, smaller tree** *Shekhinah.* See *Zohar* 2:99b; 3:170a; Tishby, *Wisdom of the Zohar,* 2:696.

goodness—the light created on the first day.[308] *That you have hidden away for those in awe of You,* for He concealed it for the righteous in that world.[309]

"*That You made* (Psalms 31:20)[310]—the upper Garden of Eden,[311] as is written: *The place You have made to dwell in, O YHVH* (Exodus 15:17). This is *that You made for those who take refuge in You. In the presence of human beings*—the lower Garden of Eden, where all the righteous abide in spirit clothed in a splendid garment resembling the image of this world.[312] This is נגד (*neged*), *in the presence of, human beings*—in the image of *human beings* of this world.[313] There they stand, then fly through the air, ascending to the Academy of Heaven in that upper Garden of Eden.[314] They soar and bathe in the dew of rivers of pure balsam,[315] then descend and dwell below. Sometimes

308. **light created on the first day** *Ḥesed*, the first of the lower seven *sefirot*, the seven primordial days. In the Torah, the word "good" appears for the first time in the verse describing this light: *God saw that the light was good* (Genesis 1:4).

309. **He concealed it...** See BT *Ḥagigah* 12a: "Rabbi El'azar said, 'With the light created by the blessed Holy One on the first day, one could gaze and see from one end of the universe to the other. When the blessed Holy One foresaw the corrupt deeds of the generation of the Flood and the generation of the Dispersion [the generation of the Tower of Babel], He immediately hid it from them, as is written: *The light of the wicked is withheld* (Job 38:15). For whom did He hide it? For the righteous in the time to come.'"

See *Bereshit Rabbah* 3:6; 41:3; *Shemot Rabbah* 35:1; *Tanḥuma, Shemini* 9; *Bahir* 97–98 (147); *Zohar* 1:31b–32a, 45b–46a, 47a; 2:127a, 148b–149a, 220a–b; 3:88a, 173b.

310. *That You made* The verse continues: *for those who take refuge in You, in the presence of human beings.* Rabbi El'azar now concludes the verse that he began.

311. **upper Garden of Eden** *Shekhinah*, the divine presence and dwelling, the culmination of the emanation that was *made*. *Shekhinah* actualizes the various divine qualities.

312. **all the righteous abide...** Righteous souls who have departed this world

abide in the Garden of Eden clothed in an ethereal body resembling their previous human form. The soul is clothed in this garment before descending to earth, retains it while in the physical body until shortly before death, and then regains it upon ascending.

See *Zohar* 1:38b (*Heikh*), 81a (*ST*), 90b–91a, 131a, 219a, 220a, 227b; 2:96b, 150a, 161b; 3:43a–b, 104a–b; Scholem, in *Tarbiz* 24 (1955): 293–95; idem, *Kabbalah*, 158–59; idem, *On the Mystical Shape of the Godhead*, 251–73; Tishby, *Wisdom of the Zohar*, 2:770–73. Cf. Rashi on BT *Ḥagigah* 12b, s.v. *ve-ruḥot unshamot.*

313. נגד (*neged*), *in the presence of...* *in the image of...* The Hebrew word means both "in the presence of" and "corresponding to."

314. **Academy of Heaven...** Where the souls of the righteous study Torah with God.

315. **dew of rivers of pure balsam** Thirteen rivers of pure balsam await the righteous in the world that is coming. See BT *Ta'anit* 25a; *Bereshit Rabbah* 62:2.

In the *Zohar* the rivers of balsam are the fragrant flow of emanation from *Binah,* who is known as "the world that is coming, constantly coming, never ceasing" (*Zohar* 3:290b [*IZ*]; see 2:127a; 3:181a).

The reference to dew recalls the rabbinic notion that God will resurrect the dead with dew. See BT *Shabbat* 88b; JT *Berakhot* 5:2, 9b.

45

they appear *in the presence of human beings,* enacting miracles for them like celestial angels[316]—as we just saw the radiance of the High Lamp,[317] though we were not privileged to contemplate and discover further mysteries of wisdom."

Rabbi Abba opened, saying, "*Manoah said to his wife, 'We will surely die, for we have seen God!'* (Judges 13:22). Even though Manoah did not know its nature,[318] he said, 'Since it is written: *No human shall see Me and live* (Exodus 33:20), and we certainly have seen, so *we will surely die.'* As for us, we have seen and attained this light moving with us,[319] yet we are still alive, for the blessed Holy One sent him to us to reveal mysteries of wisdom. Happy is our share!"

They went on. They reached a certain mountain, as the sun was inclining. The branches of the tree on the mountain began lashing one another, emitting a song. As they were walking, they heard a resounding voice proclaim: "Holy sons of God,[320] dispersed among the living of this world! Luminous lamps, initiates of the Academy! Assemble at your places to delight with your Lord in Torah!"

They were frightened, stood in place, then sat down. Meanwhile a voice called out as before, proclaiming: "Mighty boulders, towering hammers,[321] behold the Master of Colors,[322] embroidered in figures, standing on a dais.[323] Enter and assemble!" That moment, they heard the branches of the trees resounding intensely, proclaiming: *The voice of YHVH breaks cedars* (Psalms 29:5).[324] Rabbi El'azar and Rabbi Abba fell on their faces, immense fear falling upon them. They rose hastily, went on, and heard nothing. Leaving the mountain, they walked on.

46

316. **Sometimes they appear...** See Naḥmanides on Genesis 49:33.

317. **High Lamp** Rav Hamnuna Sava.

318. **its nature** The divine nature of the angel, as indicated in Judges 13:16: *Manoah did not know that he was an angel of YHVH.* See BT *Berakhot* 61a; Gikatilla, *Sha'arei Orah,* 36b.

319. **this light...** Rav Hamnuna Sava.

320. **Holy sons of God...** Souls of the righteous, such as Rav Hamnuna, who circulate among humanity, spreading wisdom.

321. **towering hammers** See BT *Berakhot* 28b, where Yoḥanan son of Zakkai is addressed by his students as "Mighty Hammer." Cf. *Zohar* 3:206a, and 187a: "Rabbi Yehudah wept and said, 'Rabbi Shim'on, happy is your share! Happy is the genera-

tion! On account of you, even schoolchildren are towering, mighty hammers!'"

322. **Master of Colors** Apparently Metatron (see *KP*). According to *TZ*, intro, 7a; 70, 119b, Metatron has *the appearance of the rainbow* (Ezekiel 1:28). He is often associated with the Heavenly Academy.

See BT *Avodah Zarah* 3b; *Bereshit Rabbati* 5:24; *Sefer Ḥanokh* (*Beit ha-Midrash,* 2:115–16); *Seder Gan Eden* (*Beit ha-Midrash,* 3:134–35); *Zohar* 2:169b; *ZH* 36b (*ST*).

323. **a dais** אצטוונא (Itstevana). See Targum to 2 Kings 11:14; Radak, ad loc.

324. **branches of the trees...** In *Pereq Shirah* (2:80), an early mystical text according to which every created thing sings a biblical verse to God, the trees of the field sing differently: *Then all the trees of the forest*

Upon reaching the house of Rabbi Yose son of Rabbi Shim'on son of Lekonya,[325] they saw Rabbi Shim'on son of Yoḥai and rejoiced. [7b] Rabbi Shim'on rejoiced, saying to them, "Indeed you have traversed a path of heavenly miracles and signs. For I was just now sleeping, and I saw you and Benayahu son of Yehoyada, who was sending you two crowns[326] by the hand of a certain old man to crown you. This was certainly a path of the blessed Holy One! Further, I see your faces transfigured."

Rabbi Yose said, "Well have you said, 'A sage is preferable to a prophet.'"[327]

Rabbi El'azar approached, placed his head between the knees of his father,[328] and told him what happened. Rabbi Shim'on was frightened and wept. He said, "*YHVH, I heard what You made heard; I am awed* (Habakkuk 3:2). This verse was spoken by Habakkuk when he saw his death and was restored to life by Elisha.[329] Why was he named חבקוק (*Ḥavaqquq*), Habakkuk? Because it is written: *At this time next year, you will be* חובקת (*ḥoveqet*), *embracing, a son* (2 Kings 4:16). He[330] was the son of the Shunammite! Furthermore there were two embracings[331]—one by his mother, one by Elisha—as is written: *He placed his mouth on his mouth* (ibid., 34).

47

will sing before YHVH *because He is coming to judge the earth* (Psalms 96:12–13; 1 Chronicles 16:33).

Elsewhere too the trees exult in song at the revelation of secrets of Torah. See JT *Ḥagigah* 2:1, 77a; BT *Ḥagigah* 14b; *Zohar* 1:77a; *Seder Gan Eden* (*Beit ha-Midrash*, 3:138).

325. **Rabbi Yose son of Rabbi Shim'on son of Lekonya** See the beginning of this story, above, page 30. As noted there, the *Zohar* changes Shim'on son of Yose into Yose son of Shim'on, transposing father and son. Similarly, the apparent son of Rav Hamnuna turned out to be Hamnuna himself.

326. **two crowns** Two new words of Torah, each of which becomes a crown. The donkey-driver presented the rabbis with new interpretations of two biblical passages, one concerning the Sabbath, the other concerning Benayahu son of Yehoyada. See BT *Shabbat* 88a; *Zohar* 1:4b; 3:291a (*IZ*).

327. **A sage is preferable to a prophet** See BT *Bava Batra* 12a, in the name of Amemar; *Zohar* 1:183b; 2:6b; 3:35a. Rabbi Shim'on's visionary power is unrivaled.

328. **placed his head…** Placing one's head between one's own knees was a meditative posture in early rabbinic mysticism. See 1 Kings 18:42; *Zohar* 3:166b. Here Rabbi El'azar places his head between his father's knees before relating what has happened to them on the road.

329. **spoken by Habakkuk when he saw his death…** The son of the Shunammite, who was born miraculously, died suddenly, and was restored to life by the prophet Elisha (2 Kings 4), is identified by the *Zohar* with the prophet Habakkuk. See 2:44b–45a; 3:195a; and El'azar of Worms, *Rimzei Haftarot* for *Shavu'ot* (Scholem).

Habakkuk's desire to know secrets and his special intimacy with God are noted in *Midrash Tehillim* 7:17; 77:1; cf. BT *Ta'anit* 23a. He appears as a paradigmatic mystic in *Bahir* 46–47 (68–69). This particular verse, which opens Habakkuk's theophany, appears again in *Zohar* 2:45a; 3:128a, 138b (*IR*). See Liebes, *Studies in the Zohar*, 34–35.

330. **He** Habakkuk.

331. **two embracings** חבוקין (*Ḥibbuqin*), which explains the doubling in the name חבקוק (*Ḥavaqquq*).

"I have discovered in *The Book of King Solomon:*[332] He inscribed on him[333] in words the engraved name of seventy-two names.[334] For the letters of the alphabet that his father had originally inscribed on him[335] flew away from him when he died. Now that Elisha embraced him, he inscribed on him all those letters of the seventy-two names. The letters of these seventy-two engraved names are 216 letters,[336] all of which Elisha inscribed with his breath to restore him to life through the letters of the seventy-two names. He called him חבקוק (Ḥavaqquq), a name fulfilling all sides: fulfilling embracings, as explained, and fulfilling the mystery of the 216 letters of the holy name.[337] He was revived with words,[338] restoring his spirit, and with letters,[339] reviving his entire body

48

332. *The Book of King Solomon* One of the many volumes housed in the real or imaginary library of the author(s) of the *Zohar*. See 1:13b, 33b, 225b; Matt, *Zohar*, 25; and the comment on this passage by Shim'on Lavi, *KP*: "All such books mentioned in the *Zohar*...have been lost in the wanderings of exile....Nothing is left of them except what is mentioned in the *Zohar*."

333. **He inscribed on him** Elisha inscribed on Habakkuk, the son of the Shunammite woman.

334. **engraved name of seventy-two names** The divine name derived from the description of the splitting of the Red Sea: Exodus 14:19–21. Each of these three verses contains seventy-two letters. The name is composed of seventy-two triads (or "words"), according to the following pattern: the first letter of the first verse, the last letter of the second verse, the first letter of the third verse (forming the first triad); the second letter of the first verse, the penultimate letter of the second verse, the second letter of the third verse (the second triad); etc.

Revival by means of a divine name recalls the legend of the Golem, according to which dust could be animated by the recitation of magical names, and in fact Abraham Abulafia notes that the seventy-two-letter name animates the Golem. See Idel, *Golem*, 98–101; Liebes, in *Kiryat Sefer* 63 (1991): 1318–21. According to a magical text (British Museum MS 752:17, 107a), Elisha used the forty-two-letter name of God to revive the son of the

Shunammite (see Scholem). *Sefer Ḥasidim* (ed. Wistinetzki, par. 219) states that Elisha was punished with illness for using the forty-two-letter name of God to curse a group of children who had insulted him by calling him "Baldhead" (2 Kings 2:23–24). As a result of his curse, forty-two of the children were killed by two she-bears.

On the seventy-two-letter name, see *Leqaḥ Tov*, Exodus 14:21; *Bereshit Rabbah* 44:19; *Vayiqra Rabbah* 23:2; *Shir ha-Shirim Rabbah* on 2:2; Hai Gaon, *Otsar ha-Ge'onim, Ḥagigah*, 23; Rashi on BT *Sukkah* 45a, s.v. *ani*; Ibn Ezra on Exodus 14:19; *Bahir* 79 (110); *Zohar* 1:17a; 2:51b, 132b, 270a; 3:150b–151a; Trachtenberg, *Jewish Magic and Superstition*, 95–97; Kasher, *Torah Shelemah*, 14:67, 284–86.

335. **letters...that his father...** Habakkuk, the son of the Shunammite, was born through the power of the letters of the alphabet, but not the particular combination of seventy-two triads of letters that Elisha employed.

336. **216 letters** The total number of letters in the seventy-two triads derived from the three verses (Exodus 14:19–21).

337. חבקוק **(Ḥavaqquq)...216 letters...** The name חבקוק has a numerical value of 216.

338. **with words** The seventy-two triads, whose greater spiritual potency is required for the restoration of the spirit.

339. **with letters** The 216 individual letters, whose potency suffices to restore the body.

enduringly. So he was called Habakkuk; it was he who said, '*YHVH, I heard what You made heard; I am awed.* I heard what happened to me, my tasting of that world,[340] and I am frightened.' He began begging for compassion for his soul, exclaiming, '*YHVH, Your action* that You did for me, *in the midst of years* חייהו (*hayyehu*), *may its life be*' (Habakkuk, ibid.). חייהו (*Hayyehu*), like חייו (*hayyav*): its life.[341] Whoever is bound to those primordial years,[342] life is bound to him. *Convey it in the midst of years* (ibid.)—*Convey it* to that level that has no life at all."[343]

Rabbi Shim'on wept and said, "From what I have heard, I, too, am afraid of the blessed Holy One."

Raising his hands above his head, he exclaimed: "What a privilege that you saw Rav Hamnuna Sava, radiance of Torah, face-to-face! I was not so privileged."

He fell on his face and saw him[344] uprooting mountains,[345] kindling lights in the palace of King Messiah.[346] He said to him,[347] "Rabbi, in that world you will be neighbors, empowered masters in the presence of the blessed Holy One."

From that day on, he called Rabbi El'azar, his son, and Rabbi Abba פניאל (*Peni'el*), *Face of God*, as is said: *For I have seen God face-to-face* (Genesis 32:31).[348]

49

בראשית (*Be-reshit*), *In the beginning.*

Rabbi Ḥiyya opened, "*The beginning of wisdom is awe of YHVH; all who actualize it gain good insight. His praise endures forever* (Psalms 111:10). *The beginning of wisdom*—this verse should read *The end of wisdom is awe of YHVH,* because *awe of YHVH* is really

---

340. **my tasting of that world** My brief experience of death.

341. *Your action... in the midst of years* ... The verse concludes: חייהו (*hayyehu*), *revive it.* Rabbi Shim'on reads this last word not as a verb but as a noun: *its life.*

342. **those primordial years** See Malachi 3:4. Here the phrase refers to the *sefirot* from *Ḥesed* through *Yesod,* flowing into *Shekhinah.* See *Zohar* 1:238b; 2:105b; 3:134b, 138b (*IR*). They are also the six primordial days of the week culminating in the Sabbath of *Shekhinah.*

343. **that level that has no life at all** *Shekhinah,* who has nothing of Her own and is dependent on the flow from above.

344. **him** Rav Hamnuna Sava.

345. **uprooting mountains** In BT *Berakhot* 64a, Rabbah son of Naḥmani is called "Uprooter of Mountains," based on his sharp mind.

346. **palace of King Messiah** Also known in the Zohar as "the bird's nest" (2:7b–8b). Cf. 3:164b; *Seder Gan Eden* (*Beit ha-Midrash,* 3:132).

347. **He said to him** Rav Hamnuna said to Rabbi Shim'on.

348. *For I have seen God face-to-face* The verse continues: *and my life has been saved.* After surviving his wrestling match with the angel, Jacob names the site *Peni'el.* Perhaps here the name is understood in the plural: *Penei El, Faces of God,* referring to both rabbis.

the end of Wisdom.[349] However, it enables one to enter the level of supernal Wisdom, as is written: *Open for me gates of righteousness. This is the gate to YHVH* (Psalms 118:19–20).[350] Truly! For unless one enters this gate, one will never enter.

"This can be compared to an exalted king—high, concealed, and hidden away—who built gates for himself, one above the other. At the end of all the gates, he fashioned one gate with many locks, openings, palaces—one above the other. He said, 'Whoever wishes to enter my presence, this gate will be first. Whoever enters, will enter through this gate.'

"Similarly, the first gate to supernal Wisdom is *awe of YHVH*.[351] This is ראשית (*reshit*), *beginning;* ב (*bet*)—two joined together as one.[352] These are two points: one hidden and concealed, one existing overtly.[353] Since they are inseparable, they are called ראשית (*reshit*), *beginning*—one, not two. Whoever attains one attains the other.[354] All is one, for He and His name are one,[355] as is written: *They will know that You, YHVH, alone are Your name* (Psalms 83:19).

"Why is it called *awe of YHVH*? Because it is the Tree of Good and Evil.[356] If a person is deserving, it is good; if not, evil. [8a] So awe abides at this site, gateway to all goodness of the world.

50

349. *awe of YHVH* **is really the end of Wisdom** Shekhinah is called *awe of YHVH* because She is characterized by the power of Judgment and inspires awe. See above, page 32. She is also lower Wisdom, culmination of the process of emanation that begins at upper Wisdom.

350. *gates of righteousness. This is the gate...* Shekhinah is called Righteousness. Through Her one enters the realm of *sefirot* and can eventually ascend to Wisdom. See *Zohar* 1:11b, 36b–37a, 141b; Gikatilla, *Sha'arei Orah*, 4b.

351. **Similarly...** The king in the parable symbolizes supernal Wisdom, who has fashioned the various gates (*sefirot*). The last gate, first to be encountered, is Shekhinah, but even before reaching Her, one must pass through several levels of camps of angels, chariots, and palaces. See BT *Shabbat* 31a–b.

352. **This is** ראשית (*reshit*), *beginning;* ב (*bet*)—**two...** The opening word of the

Torah, בראשית (*Be-reshit*), *In the beginning,* alludes to both Wisdom (Ḥokhmah) and Shekhinah. The letter ב (*bet*), the second letter of the alphabet, signifies "two," and both of these *sefirot* are called ראשית (*reshit*), *beginning:* Wisdom is the beginning of emanation, while Shekhinah is the first gate on the spiritual path.

353. **two points...** Ḥokhmah and Shekhinah. See above, pages 34–35.

354. **Whoever attains one...** Upon entering Shekhinah, lower Wisdom, one encounters higher Wisdom, reflected in Her.

355. **He and His name are one** Shekhinah reveals the *sefirot*, the various divine qualities, and is therefore called the name of God. See *Zohar* 1:18a; 2:134a, 161b.

356. **Tree of Good and Evil** The Tree of the Knowledge of Good and Evil, whose fruit was eaten by Adam and Eve. In Kabbalah this Tree symbolizes Shekhinah, who transmits either reward or punishment, depending on human behavior.

"*Good insight*—two gates as one."[357]

Rabbi Yose said, "*Good insight* is the Tree of Life[358]—*good insight* with no evil at all.[359] Since no evil abides there, it is *good insight* without evil. *All who actualize it—David's loyal acts of love* (Isaiah 55:3), supporters of Torah.[360] Those supporting Torah, as it were, actualize.[361] All those studying Torah attain no actualization while they study, while those supporting them do. Through this power, *His praise endures forever,* and the throne stands fittingly firm.[362]

Rabbi Shim'on was sitting engaged in Torah on the night when the Bride is joined with Her Husband.[363] For we have learned: All those Companions initiated into the bridal palace[364] need—on that night when the Bride is destined the next day to be under the canopy with Her Husband[365]—to be with Her all night, delighting with Her in Her adornments in which She is arrayed,[366] engaging in Torah, from Torah to Prophets, from Prophets to

51

357. **two gates as one**   *Yesod* and *Shekhinah,* the union of male and female. *Yesod* is often called "good," and *Shekhinah* is lower Wisdom or, in this verse, *insight* (שכל [*sekhel*]).

358. **Tree of Life**   The other tree mentioned in the Garden story, identified by the rabbis with Torah, based on the description of wisdom in Proverbs 3:18: *She is a tree of life to those who grasp her.* See BT *Berakhot* 32b, 61b. In Kabbalah this tree symbolizes *Tif'eret,* who is known as Written Torah. Here Rabbi Yose contrasts *Tif'eret,* the Tree of Life, with *Shekhinah,* Tree of Good and Evil.

359. ***good insight* with no evil at all**   Rabbi Yose interprets שכל טוב (*sekhel tov*), *good insight,* as שכלו טוב (*she-kullo tov*), "entirely good."

360. ***David's loyal acts of love*...**   *Netsaḥ* and *Hod,* representing the legs (or genitals) of the sefirotic body. They transmit love to *Shekhinah,* known as David, while above they support and strengthen *Tif'eret,* Written Torah. See *Zohar* 1:219a; 2:169a; Moses de León, *Sheqel ha-Qodesh,* 48 (59).

361. **Those supporting Torah...actualize**   Those who support the study of Torah on earth actualize (עבדין [*avedin*], "make, do")

their divine archetypes, the supports of *Tif'eret,* Written Torah: *Netsaḥ* and *Hod.* On actualizing the divine, see BT *Sanhedrin,* 99b; *Vayiqra Rabbah* 35:7; Idel, *Kabbalah,* 187–91.

362. ***His praise...the throne...***   *Shekhinah,* known as both Praise and the throne of *Tif'eret,* is sustained by those who support Torah. Thereby divine union is stimulated.

363. **on the night when the Bride...**   On the eve of *Shavu'ot* (Festival of "Weeks"), the celebration of the revelation of Torah, *Shekhinah* prepares to join Her groom, *Tif'eret.* See *Zohar* 3:97b–98b; Moses de León, *Sod Ḥag ha-Shavu'ot,* 87a–b.

364. **Companions initiated...**   The חברייא (*ḥavrayya*) who accompany *Shekhinah.*

365. **next day...**   The marriage between the masculine and feminine takes place on the day of *Shavu'ot,* when the Torah was actually given at Mt. Sinai. *Tif'eret* is symbolized by the Written Torah, while *Shekhinah* is alluded to by the Oral Torah, and together they convey revelation.

366. **all night...**   On other nights, the Companions rise at midnight and study Torah until dawn, chanting to *Shekhinah.* On this night of *Shavu'ot,* they adorn Her all night long. This all-night study ritual

Writings,[367] midrashic renderings of verses and mysteries of wisdom: these are Her adornments and finery.[368]

She enters, escorted by Her maidens,[369] standing above their heads. Adorned by them, She rejoices with them the whole night. The next day She enters the canopy only with them, and they are called "members of the canopy."[370] As soon as She enters the canopy, the blessed Holy One inquires about them,[371] blesses them, and crowns them with bridal crowns. Happy is their share!

Rabbi Shim'on and all the Companions were singing the song of Torah,[372] innovating words of Torah, each one of them. Rabbi Shim'on and all the other Companions rejoiced.

Rabbi Shim'on said, "My children, happy is your share! For tomorrow the Bride will enter the canopy only with you. For all those arranging Her adornments tonight, rejoicing with Her, will be recorded and inscribed in the Book

became known as *tiqqun leil Shavu'ot*, "the *tiqqun* of the eve of *Shavu'ot*." See Wilhelm, "Sidrei Tiqqunim," 125–30.

The root תקן (*tqn*) appears throughout the *Zohar*, ranging widely in meaning: "mend, restore, correct, perfect, prepare, arrange, array, adorn, establish, institute."

Philo (*On the Contemplative Life*, 10:75–90) describes a similar night vigil of study and song practiced by the Therapeutae. Cf. the account of revelation through the Holy Spirit at Pentecost in Acts 2, and Revelation 21:2: "I saw the holy city, new Jerusalem, coming down from God out of heaven, prepared as a bride adorned for her husband." See Liebes, *Studies in the Zohar*, 74–82.

367. **from Torah to Prophets...** The three divisions of the Bible. See *Vayiqra Rabbah* 16:4: "Ben Azzai was sitting and expounding, and fire was blazing around him. They [his disciples] came and told Rabbi Akiva.... He went to him and said, 'Perhaps you are engaged in the chambers of the Chariot [the secrets of Ezekiel's vision of the Chariot].' He replied, 'No, I am stringing words of Torah to the Prophets, and words of the Prophets to the Writings, and the words of Torah are as joyous as on the day they were given from Sinai.'"

368. **Her adornments and finery** See *Shir ha-Shirim Rabbah* on 4:11, in the name

of Rabbi Shim'on son of Lakish: "Just as a bride is adorned with twenty-four ornaments [see Isaiah 3:18–24] and lacking one of them, she is considered worthless, so a disciple must be fluent in twenty-four books [of the Bible]—lacking in one of them, he is worthless."

See *Tanḥuma, Ki Tissa* 18; *Zohar* 1:4b–5a; *ZH* 63d–64a (*ShS*); *OY*, where Cordovero lists the biblical and rabbinic passages read on the eve of *Shavu'ot*; and Vital's list in *Sha'ar ha-Kavvanot*, 2:202a–203b. It became customary to read this passage from the *Zohar* ("Rabbi Shim'on was sitting... sealed in a man's flesh") as part of the *tiqqun*.

369. **She enters...** *Shekhinah* enters the Companions' house of study with Her attending angels.

370. **members of the canopy** A rabbinic phrase meaning "members of the wedding party." The Companions participate in the divine union.

371. **inquires about them** See *Zohar* 3:98a: "Happy is the share of the Companions when the King asks the Consort who adorned Her in jewelry, polished Her crown, and arrayed Her adornments."

372. **singing the song of Torah** Torah is referred to as song in BT *Eruvin* 18b; *Ḥagigah* 12b. Cf. BT *Megillah* 32a; Targum to Lamentations 2:19; *Zohar* 3:23b; *KP*.

52

of Memory.[373] The blessed Holy One blesses them with seventy blessings[374] and crowns of the supernal world."

Rabbi Shim'on opened, saying, "*Heaven declares the glory of God...* (Psalms 19:2).[375] We have already established this verse;[376] but at this time, when the Bride is aroused to enter the canopy the next day, She is arrayed and illumined with Her adornments, together with the Companions rejoicing with Her that whole night, while She rejoices with them. The following day, countless troops, soldiers, and camps[377] assemble with Her, and She waits together with all of them for each and every one who adorned Her this night.[378] As soon as they join together, and She sees Her Husband, what is written? *Heaven declares the glory of God. Heaven*—the Groom entering the canopy.[379] מספרים (*Mesapperim*), *Declares*—sparkles with the radiance of ספיר (*sappir*), sapphire, sparkling and radiating from one end of the universe to the other. *The glory of God*—glory of the Bride, who is called *God*, as is written: *God rages every day* (Psalms 7:12).[380] Every day of the year, She is called *God*, but now that She has entered the canopy, She is called *Glory* as well as *God*, glory upon glory, radiance upon radiance, dominion upon dominion. Then, at the moment when *Heaven* enters the canopy, coming to illumine Her,[381] all those Companions who adorned Her are designated there by name, as is written: *The sky proclaims the work of His hands* (Psalms 19:2). *The work of His hands*—masters of the covenant with the Bride, Her partners.[382] Those masters of the covenant are called *the work of His

53

373. **Book of Memory** The celestial book in which all human actions are recorded. Later in this passage, it is identified with *Yesod*. See Ezra 4:15; Targum to Esther 6:1; *Zohar* 1:62b; 2:70a, 200a, 217a, 246a.

374. **seventy blessings** Corresponding to the seven *sefirot* from *Ḥesed* to *Shekhinah*.

375. *Heaven declares the glory of God* The verse continues in parallelism: *the sky proclaims the work of His hands*.

376. **We have already established this verse** The verse is cited frequently in rabbinic literature. See BT *Ketubbot* 5a; *Zohar* 2:136b.

377. **troops, soldiers, and camps** Countless angels.

378. **She waits...for each...** For each Companion who adorned Her with a gem of Torah.

379. **Groom...** *Tif'eret*, who is called *Heaven*. See *Bahir* 68 (100), citing 1 Kings

8:32; *Zohar* 2:85a–b. Several verses later in this psalm, the sun is identified as a groom: *He* [*the sun*] *is like a groom coming forth from his chamber* [or: *canopy*] (Psalms 19:6).

380. *God rages every day* אל (*El*), "God," is a name of *Shekhinah*, who manifests the power of judgment and is angered daily by the evil of humanity. See *Zohar* 1:91a; 3:119b, 176b.

381. **illumine Her** The verse is taken to mean: *Heaven* (*Tif'eret*) illumines *the glory of God* (*Shekhinah*).

382. **masters of the covenant...Her partners** Literally, "masters of the oath of covenant with the Bride." The expression מארי קיימא דברית (*marei qeyama divrit*), "masters of the oath of covenant," reflects the Hebrew בעל ברית (*ba'al berit*), "master of the covenant," or "partner." The covenant is that of circumcision, and the masters of this covenant are those who have mastered the sexual

hands, as is said: *The work of our hands, establish it* (Psalms 90:17). This is the covenant sealed in a man's flesh.[383]

"Rav Hamnuna Sava[384] said as follows: '*Do not let your mouth induce your flesh to sin* (Ecclesiastes 5:5). One should not let his mouth reach evil fantasies,[385] causing that holy flesh in which the holy covenant is sealed to sin.[386] If he does, he is dragged into Hell. The one appointed over Hell is named Dumah,[387] who is escorted by many myriads of angels of destruction. He stands at the door of Hell, but he is not permitted to approach any of those who guarded the holy covenant in this world.[388]

'King David—when that incident befell him[389]—was frightened. That moment, Dumah rose in the presence of the blessed Holy One and said to Him, "Master of the universe, [8b] it is written in the Torah: *A man who commits adultery with a man's wife...* (Leviticus 20:10),[390] and: *To your neighbor's*

54

urge, leading holy sexual lives. Since they embody the quality of *Yesod,* the divine phallus, their virtue is proclaimed by *Yesod,* symbolized by *the sky.* These Companions are invited to participate in the union with *Shekhinah.*

See *Tanḥuma, Lekh Lekha* 17, where Abraham's circumcision is compared to marrying the king's daughter.

383. **The work...establish it...** The mark of circumcision, made by hand, is called *the work of our hands.* The interpretation of the verse is: May God *establish* (help us control and purify) *the work of our hands* (our sexual conduct). A similar phrase, *the work of your hands* (Ecclesiastes 5:5, cited later in this passage) is linked to sexuality in BT *Shabbat* 32b: "Rabbi says, '...What is the work of one's hands? You must conclude: one's sons and daughters.'"

384. **Rav Hamnuna Sava...** Rabbi Shim'on now cites Rav Hamnuna at length to support his interpretation of *the work of His hands.* In the Talmud their roles are reversed: it is Rav Hamnuna who cites Rabbi Shim'on.

385. **reach evil fantasies** One should not speak of things that can incite lust.

386. **that holy flesh...** Sexual misconduct defaces the sign of covenant sealed in the flesh. See *Zohar* 2:87a–b. Cf. *Sefer Yetsi-*

rah 1:3, where covenant is linked to both tongue and phallus.

387. **Dumah** Literally, "silence," a name for the netherworld in the Bible, e.g., Psalms 94:17: *Unless YHVH had been my help, my soul would soon have dwelt in dumah* (cited later in this passage). Cf. Psalms 115:17.

In rabbinic literature Dumah is the angel in charge of souls of the dead (BT *Berakhot* 18b, *Shabbat* 152b, *Sanhedrin* 94a). In the *Zohar* he retains this role but also oversees Hell. See 1:94a, 102a, 124a (*MhN*), 237b.

388. **any of those who guarded...** See *Bereshit Rabbah* 48:8: "Rabbi Levi said, 'In the time to come, Abraham [who initiated circumcision] will be sitting at the door to Hell, and he will not let any circumcised Israelite descend there.'" Cf. BT *Eruvin* 19a; *Zohar* 1:93a, 94a, 95b.

389. **that incident...** With Bathsheba, the wife of Uriah the Hittite (2 Samuel 11–12). Seeing her bathing, David was attracted to her and slept with her. He then arranged for her husband, Uriah, to die in battle, after which he married her.

390. ***A man who commits adultery with a man's wife*** The verse continues: *—who commits adultery with his neighbor's wife—is surely to be put to death, the adulterer and the adulteress.*

wife . . . (Leviticus 18:20).[391] David, who ruined the covenant by lewdness, what shall be done to him?"

'The blessed Holy One said to him, "David is innocent, and the holy covenant stands arrayed, for it is revealed before Me that Bathsheba was destined for him since the day the world was created."[392]

'He replied, "Even if it is revealed before You, before him it was not!"

'He said, "Further, what happened happened with permission, for of all those entering battle, no one would enter until he legally divorced his wife."[393]

'He replied, "If so, he should have waited three months,[394] and he didn't."

'He said, "Concerning which case was that rule established? Where we fear she might be pregnant. But it is revealed before Me that Uriah never approached her, for look, My name is sealed within him as evidence: it is spelled both אוריה (*Uriyyah*) and אוריהו (*Uriyyahu*).[395] My name is sealed in him, proving he never cohabited with her."

'He replied, "Master of the universe, as I already said, even if before You it is revealed that Uriah did not lie with her, was it revealed to him?[396] He

55

391. *To your neighbor's wife* The verse continues: *you are not to give your emission of seed, defiling yourself through her.*

392. **Bathsheba was destined** . . . See BT *Sanhedrin* 107a: "Rava expounded, '. . . Ever since the six days of Creation, Bathsheba, daughter of Eliam, was designated for David, but she came to him with suffering.' The school of Rabbi Yishma'el taught likewise: 'She was designated for David, but he ate her unripe [prematurely, while she was still married to Uriah].'" See *Zohar* 1:73b; 2:107a; 3:78b.

393. **of all those entering battle** . . . See BT *Shabbat* 56a: "Rav said, 'Rabbi [Yehudah the Prince], who is descended from David, seeks to defend him, and expounds [the verse] in David's favor: *You have taken his wife to be your wife* (2 Samuel 12:9) implies that you have marriage rights to her [since the verb *to take* denotes marriage, as in Deuteronomy 24:1], for Rabbi Shemu'el son of Nahmani said in the name of Rabbi Yonatan: "Everyone who went to war in the dynasty of David would first write a writ of divorce for his wife."'"

394. **waited three months** To determine whether Bathsheba was pregnant or not.

Otherwise, if a baby were born seven months after the new marriage, it would be unclear whether the newborn's father was David or Uriah. See M *Yevamot* 4:10; BT *Yevamot* 42a.

395. **spelled both אוריה (*Uriyyah*) and אוריהו (*Uriyyahu*)** The first spelling ends with the divine name יה (*yah*), the second with יהו (*yahu*), three of the four letters of יהוה (*YHVH*). The sacredness of Uriah's name indicates his chaste character (see *Vayiqra Rabbah* 23:10). Note how the prophet Nathan describes the relationship between Uriah and Bathsheba (2 Samuel 12:3): *she was like a daughter to him*. In the Bible, the spelling אוריהו (*Uriyyahu*) is never applied to Uriah the Hittite; it is the name of an entirely different figure, a prophet contemporary with Jeremiah who was executed by King Jehoiakim (Jeremiah 26:20–23). Rabbinic sources identify this prophet Uriahu with Uriah the priest, mentioned in Isaiah 8:2 (*Sifrei*, Deuteronomy 7; BT *Makkot* 24b), but Rav Hamnuna is apparently the first to blend the identity of Uriahu the prophet with David's victim, Uriah the Hittite.

396. **to him** To David.

should have waited three months for her. Furthermore, if he knew[397] that he[398] never lay with her, why did David send for him and order him to have intercourse with his wife, as is written: *Go down to your house and bathe your feet* (2 Samuel 11:8)?"[399]

'He said, "He certainly did not know.[400] But he waited longer than three months—actually four, for so have we learned: On the twenty-fifth of Nisan[401] David issued a proclamation throughout Israel,[402] and by the seventh of Sivan, they had assembled under Joab; then they set out and destroyed the land of the children of Ammon. They lingered there for Sivan, Tammuz, Av, and Elul, and on the twenty-fourth of Elul happened what happened with Bathsheba. On Yom Kippur the blessed Holy One forgave him that sin. Some say: he issued the proclamation on the seventh of Adar,[403] they assembled on the fifteenth of Iyyar, on the fifteenth of Elul happened what happened with Bathsheba, and on Yom Kippur he was assured: *YHVH has removed your sin; you will not die* (2 Samuel 12:13). What does *you will not die* mean? *You will not die* at the hand of Dumah."

'Dumah replied, "Master of the universe, I still have one thing against him: he opened his mouth and said[404] *As YHVH lives, the man who did this deserves to die* (ibid., 5).[405] He condemned himself. I claim him!"

'He said, "You are not entitled! He confessed to Me, saying, *I have sinned against YHVH* (ibid., 13), even though he did not sin! But as for his sin against Uriah,[406] I sentenced him to punishment, which he received."[407]

397. **if he knew** If David knew.

398. **that he** That Uriah.

399. *Go down to your house and bathe your feet* Understood as a euphemism for intercourse. See 2 Samuel 11:11; Ruth 3:7; *Tosafot, Eruvin* 63b, s.v. *kol zeman*.

Similarly, God's command to Moses, *Remove your sandals from your feet* (Exodus 3:5), is interpreted to mean: "Refrain from intercourse with your wife." See *Zohar* 2:222a; 3:148a, 180a; *ZH* 59b. Cf. 1:112b.

400. **He certainly did not know** David certainly did not know.

401. **Nisan** The first month of spring, followed by Iyyar, Sivan, Tammuz, Av, Elul, and Tishrei. Yom Kippur is the tenth of Tishrei. According to this chronology, Uriah died in battle at the beginning of the month of Sivan, and David had intercourse with Bathsheba nearly four months later, at the end of Elul. The Bible mentions simply that David sent Israel out to war *at the time when*

kings go out [to battle] (2 Samuel 11:1), in springtime.

402. **issued a proclamation...** Calling the people to assemble for war.

403. **Adar** The month preceding Nisan. According to this chronology, David waited four full months, from the middle of Iyyar to the middle of Elul.

404. **he opened his mouth...** Recalling the saying attributed to Rabbi Yose (BT *Berakhot* 19a): "One should not open his mouth to Satan," i.e., speak in such a way as to give him an opening.

405. *the man who did this...* David's incriminating response to the parable told him by Nathan the prophet. Nathan replies, *You are the man!* (2 Samuel 12:7).

406. **his sin against Uriah** Arranging for Uriah's death in battle.

407. **punishment...** As Nathan prophesies, David's dynasty is wracked by war, his wives are violated, and the child born

'Immediately Dumah returned in despair to his site. Concerning this, David said *Unless YHVH had been my help, my soul would soon have dwelt with Dumah* (Psalms 94:17). *Unless YHVH had been my help,* my guardian, *my soul would soon have dwelt*.... What does *would soon have* mean? By a thread as fine as a filament of hair, separating me from the Other Side.[408] By that measure *my soul* did not *dwell with Dumah.*

'So a person should be on guard not to speak as David did,[409] since one will not be able to plead with Dumah *that it was an error* (Ecclesiastes 5:5),[410] as happened with David, when the blessed Holy One defeated him legally.[411] *Why should God be angry at your voice?*—at the voice in which one speaks.[412] *And destroy the work of your hands*—holy flesh, holy covenant that he damages,[413] and he is dragged into Hell by Dumah.'

"So[414] *The sky proclaims the work of His hands* (Psalms 19:2)—the Companions who join this Bride, masters of Her covenant, Her partners.[415]

of David's union with Bathsheba dies (ibid., 9–23).

408. **separating me from the Other Side** In Kabbalah David symbolizes *Shekhinah,* whose realm borders the demonic realm of *Sitra Aḥra* ("the Other Side"). According to *Qohelet Rabbah* on 7:22, the separation between Heaven and Hell is slight: "*This opposite that* (Ecclesiastes 7:14)—Hell and the Garden of Eden. What is the distance between them? A handbreadth. Rabbi Yoḥanan said, 'A wall.' The Rabbis say, 'They are parallel, so that they will gaze at one another.'"

409. **not to speak as David did** Apparently the words with which David condemned himself, cited above: *As YHVH lives, the man who did this deserves to die.* Or perhaps a reference to Psalms 26:2: *Probe me, YHVH, and test me.* With his confident words, David tempted Satan, providing him an opening. (The entire phrase is missing in C12, Ms3, Cr, and *OY*.)

410. *that it was an error* From the conclusion of the verse with which Rav Hamnuna opened (above, page 54): *Do not let your mouth induce your flesh to sin, and do not plead before the messenger that it was an error. Why should God be angry at your voice and destroy the work of your hands?*

411. **defeated him legally** Defeated Dumah with valid arguments.

412. **voice in which one speaks** The suggestive words that a person might utter, inducing him to sin.

413. **holy flesh...that he damages** Apparently "he" refers to the person who damages the covenant through immoral speech and behavior. Galante and *OY* interpret the subject as Dumah, who damages the sign of covenant and thereby condemns the sinner to Hell. See above, pages 53–54: "*The work of His hands*—masters of the covenant with the Bride, Her partners. Those masters of the covenant are called *the work of His hands,* as is said: *The work of our hands, establish it* (Psalms 90:17). This is the covenant sealed in a man's flesh.... He [Dumah, standing at the door of Hell] is not permitted to approach any of those who guarded the holy covenant in this world."

414. **So** Rabbi Shim'on resumes his interpretation of Psalm 19 after transmitting this long teaching from Rav Hamnuna, which was cited to demonstrate that the phrase *the work of His hands* refers to the covenant in the flesh. See Liebes, *Studies in the Zohar,* 57–60.

415. **masters of Her covenant, Her partners** This renders two senses of one term, מארי קיימא דילה (*marei qeyama dilah*), "masters of Her covenant." The expression reflects the Hebrew בעל ברית (*ba'al berit*),

Proclaims—inscribing every single one. Who is *the sky*? The sky embracing sun, moon, stars, and constellations[416]—the Book of Memory.[417] He *proclaims* and inscribes them, recording them as initiates of the palace, constantly fulfilling their desires.

"*Day to day pours forth speech* (Psalms 19:3)[418]—a holy day of those supernal days of the King.[419] They praise the Companions and repeat the word[420] each one told his companion. *Day to day expresses* that *speech* and praises it.

"*Night to night* (ibid.)—every rung ruling the night extols to one another each Companion's *knowledge*,[421] ecstatically becoming their companions and lovers.[422]

"*There is no speech, there are no words* (ibid., 4)[423]—any other, mundane words, not heard in the presence of the holy King, nor does He wish to hear them. But as for these words, *their line extends throughout the earth* (ibid., 5)— these words extend [9a] a cord,[424] measuring above and below. From some of them skies are made; from others, earth, through that praise.[425] Do not suppose that those words stay in one place; they roam the world: *Their words extend to the end of the world* (ibid.). Once transformed into skies, who dwells in them? The verse goes on to say: *In them He set a tent for the sun* (ibid.)— that sacred sun abides in them, is crowned by them.[426] Dwelling in those skies, crowned in them, *he is like a groom coming forth from his chamber*

58

"master of the covenant," i.e., "partner." See above, page 53.

416. **sky embracing...** See BT Ḥagigah 12b: "Resh Lakish said, 'There are seven heavens....In the one called רקיע (raqi'a), "sky," sun, moon, stars, and constellations are set.'" Here the sky symbolizes *Yesod*, through which the divine male and female, symbolized by sun and moon, unite. Cf. *Zohar* 1:17a–b, 34a; 2:2a, 246a.

417. **Book of Memory** *Yesod*. See above, pages 52–53.

418. *Day to day pours forth speech* The verse continues in parallelism: *night to night declares knowledge.*

419. **those supernal days of the King** The *sefirot* from *Ḥesed* through *Yesod*, which surround *Tif'eret*.

420. **word** The interpretation offered as an adornment to *Shekhinah* during the all-night study session.

421. **every rung ruling the night...** *She-khinah* and the forces under Her command

exchange the past day's innovations of To-rah. See *Zohar* 2:137a.

422. **ecstatically becoming...** *Shekhinah* and those under Her become companions of the Companions.

423. *There is no speech, there are no words* The verse continues in parallelism: *their sound is not heard.*

424. **cord** משיחא (Meshiḥa), identified by the *Zohar* with "the line of measure," which maps out the paths and stages of emanation. See *ZH* 56d–58d; *Zohar* 1:15a.

425. **skies are made...earth...** See above, page 26, where it is said that new kabbalistic interpretations of Torah are transformed into *new heavens*, while other new interpretations are transformed into *earths of the living*. Here Rabbi Shim'on adds that the praise offered by the *sefirot* to these interpretations serves as the catalyst.

426. **that sacred sun...** The divine male, *Yesod*, abides in mystical innovations. See *Zohar* 1:33b; 2:136b–137b, 205b, 224b;

(ibid., 6),[427] running joyously through those skies. Emerging from them, He enters and runs through a certain other tower at another site.[428] *His going forth is at one end of the heaven* (ibid., 7)[429]—indeed He emerges from the upper world, *the end of heaven* above.[430] *And his circuit* (ibid.)—who is *his circuit*? *The end of heaven* below, who is *the circuit of the year* (Exodus 34:22), encircling all endings, linking heaven with this sky.[431] *Nothing is hidden from his heat* (Psalms 19:7)—from the heat of this *circuit* and the *circuit* of the sun,[432] encircling all sides. *Nothing is hidden*—not one of the supernal rungs[433] is concealed from Him, for they all come encircling Him; not one of them hides from Him, *from his heat*, when He arouses himself, desiring them totally. All this praise and exaltation stems from Torah,[434] as is written: *The Torah of YHVH is pure* (ibid., 8). Six times *YHVH* is written here,[435] and there are six verses from *Heaven declares* (ibid., 2) to *The Torah of YHVH is pure* (ibid., 8). Concerning this mystery it is written: בראשית (*Be-reshit*), *In the beginning*—look, six letters![436] ברא אלהים את השמים ואת הארץ (*Bara Elohim et ha-shamayim ve-et ha-arets*), *God created the heavens and the earth*—look, six more words, corresponding to the six times *YHVH* appears! Six verses for six letters here; six names for six words here.

While they were sitting,[437] Rabbi El'azar, his son, and Rabbi Abba entered. He said to them, "The face of *Shekhinah* has indeed arrived![438] That is why

---

3:12a, 225b; Moses de León, *Sod Eser Sefirot*, 381; idem, *Shushan Edut*, 338; idem, *Sheqel ha-Qodesh*, 50 (61).

427. **he is like a groom coming forth from his chamber** The verse continues in parallelism: *rejoicing like a hero to run his course*.

428. **a certain other tower at another site** *Shekhinah*, who is referred to as *a tower of strength* (Proverbs 18:10; *Zohar* 1:37b, 96b; 3:164a–b), as distinguished from the "tower soaring in the air" (above, page 36), symbolizing *Binah*.

Here the divine bridegroom runs through the tower, uniting with *Shekhinah*. See Galante; Liebes, *Studies in the Zohar*, 59–60. For other interpretations, see *OY*; the fragment in *OH* 12b; and Scholem.

429. **His going forth is at one end of the heaven** The verse continues in parallelism: *and his circuit reaches the other; nothing is hidden from his heat.*

430. **the end of heaven above** *Binah*. She and *Shekhinah* comprise the two ends of

heaven, above and below *Tif'eret*, known as Heaven. See *Zohar* 1:1b; 2:137a.

431. **the end of heaven** below ... **the circuit of the year** ... *Shekhinah*, who includes all the *sefirot* and unites with *Tif'eret* and *Yesod*.

432. **this circuit and the circuit of the sun** The divine female and male.

433. **supernal rungs** The *sefirot*.

434. **All this praise and exaltation...** New readings of Torah here on earth garner sefirotic praise, which, in turn, stimulates the divine union.

435. **Six times YHVH ...** This divine name appears six times in the following three verses (Psalms 19:8–10). See *Zohar* 2:137b.

436. **six letters** The opening word of the Torah, בראשית (*Be-reshit*), *In the beginning*, contains six letters.

437. **While they were sitting** Adorning *Shekhinah* with new insights of Torah on the night of *Shavu'ot* (Festival of "Weeks").

438. **face of Shekhinah has indeed arrived** See *Mekhilta, Amaleq* (*Yitro*) 1: "Whoever

I called you 'פניאל (*Peni'el*), Face of God,' for you have seen the face of *Shekhinah* face-to-face.[439] Now that you know, and he[440] has revealed to you the verse *Benayahu son of Yehoyada*, it is certainly a word of the Holy Ancient One,[441] and the following verse as well. The concealed one of all spoke it,[442] and this verse appears similarly elsewhere."[443]

He opened, saying, "*He slew the Egyptian, a man of measure,*[444] *five cubits high* (1 Chronicles 11:23). All one mystery. What does *the Egyptian* mean?[445] That well-known one, *very great in the land of Egypt* (Exodus 11:3),[446] grand and splendid, as revealed by that old man. This verse was discussed in the Academy on High.[447] *A man of measure.* All is one. *A man of good appearance* (2 Samuel 23:21). Why *measure*?[448] All is one, for it is the Sabbath and her range, as is

---

receives the face of [i.e., welcomes] the wise, it is as if he receives the face of *Shekhinah.*" Cf. JT *Eruvin* 5:1, 22b: "Rabbi Shemu'el said in the name of Rabbi Ze'eira, '...Whoever receives the face of his teacher, it is as if he receives the face of *Shekhinah.*'...Rabbi Yishma'el taught...'One who receives the face of his friend, it is as if he receives the face of *Shekhinah.*'" Cf. Genesis 33:10; *Tanḥuma, Ki Tissa* 27; *Shir ha-Shirim Rabbah* on 2:5.

The *Zohar* transforms the rabbinic simile into an actual description of the Ḥavrayya, the Companions, who "are called the face of *Shekhinah* because *Shekhinah* is hidden within them. She is concealed, they are revealed" (*Zohar* 2:163b). See 1:94b; 2:5a, 50a; 3:6b, 148a, 298a; *ZH* 11c (*MhN*).

439. פניאל (*Peni'el*), Face of God... Earlier, Rabbi Shim'on gave this name because in meeting Rav Hamnuna they had encountered the Divine Presence. See above, page 49: "From that day on, he called Rabbi El'azar, his son, and Rabbi Abba פניאל (*Peni'el*), Face of God, as is said: *For I have seen God face-to-face [and my life has been saved]* (Genesis 32:31)."

440. he Rav Hamnuna Sava. See above, pages 38–44.

441. word of the Holy Ancient One *Keter,* the first *sefirah.* New revelations of kabbalistic wisdom are called "words of the Ancient of Days" (above, pages 25–26). In BT *Pesaḥim* 119a, the secrets of Torah are referred to as "things hidden by the Ancient

of Days." Cf. the rabbinic blessing in BT *Berakhot* 17a: "May your steps run to hear words of the Ancient of Days."

See BT *Bava Batra* 91b; *Zohar* 2:168a; 3:105b, 138b (*IR*), 232b; and 3:20a: "Rabbi Yose said to Rabbi Ḥiyya, 'Let us engage in words of Torah, in words of the Ancient of Days.'"

442. The concealed one of all... *Keter,* the highest *sefirah,* also known as the Holy Ancient One.

443. this verse appears similarly elsewhere The verse that follows (1 Chronicles 11:23) is a variant of 2 Samuel 23:21, which Rav Hamnuna interpreted above, pages 41–42. Here Rabbi Shim'on expounds on the slight differences between the two verses.

444. *a man of measure* Meaning *a man of stature.*

445. the Egyptian... In Samuel the verse reads *an Egyptian.* The definite article in Chronicles is intentional and significant.

446. *very great in the land of Egypt* The full verse reads: *The man Moses was very great in the land of Egypt, in the eyes of Pharaoh's servants and in the eyes of the people.* Thus, the definite article in the phrase *the Egyptian* refers to Moses.

447. Academy on High The Heavenly Academy, where the souls of the righteous study Torah with God.

448. *A man of good appearance...Why measure?* What is the significance of this difference between the two verses?

60

written: *You are to measure outside the city* (Numbers 35:5),[449] and similarly: *You are not to commit corruption in justice—in measure* (Leviticus 19:35).[450] So he is *a man of measure*—really *a man of measure*, his length extending from one end of the universe to the other, as with Adam.[451] Now if you say, 'Look at what is written: *five cubits high!*' those *five cubits* extended from one end of the universe to the other.[452]

"*In the Egyptian's hand was a spear*—as he said.[453] *Like a weaver's beam* (1 Chronicles, ibid.)—the staff of God in his hand,[454] engraved with the graven, explicit name,[455] with the radiance[456] of permutations of letters engraved by Bezalel, called *weaver*, together with his academy,[457] as is written: *the engraver, the designer, the embroiderer...* (Exodus 35:35).[458] That staff was radiating the engraved name in every direction with radiance of the wise who engraved the

---

449. **the Sabbath and her range...** *You are to measure outside the city*   The verse continues: *two thousand cubits on the east side, two thousand on the south side, two thousand on the west side, and two thousand on the north side, with the town in the center. That shall be the pasture for their towns.* The measure of two thousand cubits for the pasture lands of the Levitical cities served as the basis for the "range of Sabbath," the maximum distance one may walk beyond the city on the Sabbath. See *Mekhilta, Vayassa* 6; cf. *Zohar* 1:5b; 2:207a.

Earlier (above, page 41), Rav Hamnuna had interpreted *a man of good appearance* as meaning "husband of *Shekhinah*"; Rabbi Shim'on now applies the same interpretation to the variant in Chronicles: *a man of measure*. *Shekhinah* is the Sabbath, whose holiness extends beyond the realm of the *sefirot*.

450. *in justice—in measure*   The full concluding phrase reads: *in measure, weight, or capacity*. *Tif'eret* is called *justice*, and *Shekhinah* is *measure*.

451. **from one end of the universe to the other, as with Adam**   Moses symbolizes *Tif'eret*, who spans the *sefirot* from *Binah*, at one end of the divine realm, to *Shekhinah* at the other.

See *Bereshit Rabbah* 8:1; *Vayiqra Rabbah* 14:1; and BT *Ḥagigah* 12a: "Rabbi Yehudah said in the name of Rav, 'Adam extended from one end of the universe to the other.'"

452. **those *five cubits* extended...**   The five cubits symbolize the realm of five *sefirot* surrounding *Tif'eret*: *Ḥesed, Gevurah, Netsaḥ, Hod,* and *Yesod*. Alternatively, this group of six can be pictured as five, since *Yesod* and *Tif'eret* are often counted together as one.

453. **as he said**   As Rav Hamnuna explained. See above, page 42.

454. **staff of God...**   The staff with which Moses performed miracles before Pharaoh, split the Red Sea, and struck the rock to produce water.

455. **explicit name**   The Ineffable Name, YHVH. See *Devarim Rabbah* 3:8; *Midrash Tehillim* 114:9; *Zohar* 2:48a.

456. **radiance** נהירו (*Nehiru*). Apparently Rabbi Shim'on interprets the Hebrew word מנור (*menor*), "beam," as מנורה (*menorah*), "lamp," or as מנור (*mi-nur*), "from fire."

457. **permutations of letters...Bezalel...**   See BT *Berakhot* 55a: "Rabbi Yehudah said in the name of Rav, 'Bezalel knew how to permute the letters by which heaven and earth were created.'" By weaving together various combinations of letters, Bezalel was able to fashion the vessels of the Tabernacle in the desert. Similarly, permutations of the name YHVH flashed from the staff of Moses.

458. **the engraver, the designer, the embroiderer**   The verse continues: *in blue, purple, crimson yarns and in fine linen, and the weaver....*

61

explicit name in forty-two colors.[459] From here on, the verse accords with what he said.[460] Happy is his share!

"Sit, dear ones, sit! Let us renew the adornment of the Bride tonight.[461] For everyone joining Her on this night will be protected, above and below, that entire year and will live through the year in peace. Of them is written: *The angel of YHVH encamps around those in awe of Him and delivers them. Taste and see that YHVH is good* (Psalms 34:8–9)."

Rabbi Shim'on opened, saying, "*In the beginning God created* (Genesis 1:1). This verse calls for contemplation, for anyone claiming that there is another god[462] is extirpated from worlds, as is said: *Thus shall you say to them: The gods who did not make heaven and earth shall perish from earth and from under these heavens* (Jeremiah 10:11), for there is no god other than the blessed Holy One alone. Now this [9b] verse is in Aramaic,[463] except for the word ending the verse.[464] If you suppose that this is because holy angels do not attend to Aramaic nor recognize it,[465] then this word[466] should have been spoken in the holy tongue,

62

459. **radiance of the wise...in forty-two colors** The name YHVH was permuted on the staff in forty-two ways. See *Zohar* 2:260a. On the forty-two-letter name of God, see above, page 2: "the engraved, explicit name is sown in forty-two letters of the act of Creation." Cf. *Zohar* 2:175b: "the forty-two holy letters of the holy name, by which heaven and earth were created."

The forty-two-letter name is mentioned in the name of Rav, though not recorded, in BT *Qiddushin* 71a. According to one later view, it consists of the first forty-two letters of the Torah, from the ב (*bet*) of בראשית (*Be-reshit*) through the ב (*bet*) of בהו (*bohu*), *void* (Genesis 1:2).

See *Tosafot, Ḥagigah* 11b, s.v. *ein doreshin; KP* 1:46c–d; Trachtenberg, *Jewish Magic and Superstition*, 94–95; cf. Maimonides, *Guide of the Perplexed* 1:62. Cordovero (*OY*) on the passage in 1:1a describes how the name YHVH can be permuted into a forty-two-letter name. In his commentary here, Cordovero describes permutations of the forty-two-letter name itself. In *Zohar* 2:97b, 104a, 109a, the donkey-driver who confounds the rabbis refers cryptically to a snowy day on which he and Rabbi Shim'on son of Yoḥai

"sowed beans in fifty-two colors," alluding to the fifty-two-letter name of God.

460. **with what he said** With what Rav Hamnuna said. See above, pages 42–43.

461. **tonight** The night of *Shavu'ot*, when *Shekhinah*, the Bride, is adorned by the Companions' new words of Torah.

462. **there is another god** As could be heretically inferred from the apparently plural form of the word אלהים (*Elohim*), *gods*, in the opening verse of the Torah.

463. **in Aramaic** Hebrew, תרגום (*targum*), "translation," often referring to an Aramaic translation of the Bible. By referring to Aramaic as *targum*, the *Zohar* betrays the fact that its author(s) lived at a time when Aramaic was no longer spoken. See *Zohar* 1:88b–89a (*ST*); 2:129b, 132b–133a; Tishby, *Wisdom of the Zohar*, 1:75.

464. **the word ending the verse** Namely, the Hebrew word אלה (*elleh*), *these*.

465. **do not attend to Aramaic...** See BT *Shabbat* 12b: "Rabbi Yoḥanan said, 'If one petitions for his needs in Aramaic, the ministering angels do not attend to him, for they do not know Aramaic.'" Cf. *Zohar* 1:74b (*ST*), 88b–89a (*ST*).

466. **this word** This verse.

so that holy angels will listen and be obliged to acknowledge it. But indeed, precisely because of this it is written in Aramaic, for since holy angels do not attend to it, they will not become jealous of a human and harm him.[467] For those holy angels are included in this verse, since they are called אלהים (*Elohim*), *gods*.[468] They are included in the category of *gods*, though *they did not make heaven and earth.*

"וארקא (*Ve-arqa*), *And earth*—the verse should read וארעא (*ve-ar'a*),[469] but ארקא (*arqa*) is one of those seven earths below,[470] site of descendants of Cain. After he was banished from the face of the earth,[471] he descended there, generating offspring.[472] He blundered there, knowing nothing. It is a dual earth, dualized by darkness and light.[473] Two officials rule there, one ruling darkness, the other light, inciting one another. When Cain descended there, they joined together—were completed as one—entirely befitting the offspring of Cain. So they have two heads[474] like two snakes, but the one of light rules—prevailing, defeating the other. So those of darkness merged in those of light, and they became one. Those two officials are Afrira and Kastimon,[475] who resemble six-winged holy angels. One resembles an ox, the other an eagle, but when they join they are transformed into the image of a human being.[476] In darkness they

63

467. **become jealous...** See *Tosafot, Berakhot* 3a, s.v. *ve-onin*.

468. **they are called אלהים (*Elohim*), *gods***
See Maimonides, *Guide of the Perplexed* 1:2: "Every Hebrew knew that the term *Elohim* is equivocal, designating the deity, the angels, and the rulers governing the cities." Cf. *Zohar* 1:111b; 3:113a; *ZH* 4a (*MhN*).

469. **the verse should read וארעא (*ve-ar'a*)**
The common Aramaic word for "earth."

470. **those seven earths below** Corresponding to the seven heavens. See *Vayiqra Rabbah* 29:11; *Sefer Yetsirah* 4:12; *Zohar* 1:39b–40a, 54b, 157a; 3:9b–10a; *ZH* 8c–9b (*SO*); 87b (*MhN, Rut*).

471. **banished from the face of the earth**
See Cain's statement in Genesis 4:14: *Behold, You have banished me today from the face of the earth.*

472. **generating offspring** On the demonic descendants of Cain, see El'azar of Worms, *Ḥokhmat ha-Nefesh*, 26c; *Zohar* 1:36b, 54a, 178a–b; 3:76b, 122a.

473. **dual earth, dualized by darkness and light** Both manifesting in confusion. See *KP*. Cf. *Zohar* 3:285b.

474. **two heads** On the two-headed descendants of Cain, see *Beit ha-Midrash*, 4:151–52; Judah ben Barzillai, *Peirush Sefer Yetsirah*, 173; *Tosafot, Menaḥot* 37a, s.v. *o qum gelei*; *Zohar* 1:157a; 2:80a; *ZH* 9b; Ginzberg, *Legends*, 5:143 n. 34; Ta-Shma, *Ha-Nigleh she-ba-Nistar*, 125, n. 84.

475. **Afrira and Kastimon** Ruling darkness and light, respectively. Afrira's name derives from עפר (*afar*), "dust," and, as noted below, his earth is not fruitful (see *Zohar* 2:266b). For the second name, *KP* reads: Kastiron, who also appears in *Sefer Razi'el*, 41a. Cf. קוסטור (*qustor*), "quaestor," a Roman prosecutor (e.g., JT *Eruvin* 6:2, 23b).

In *Zohar* 1:151a the word קסטוטירא (*qastutira*) apparently means "luster" and seems to derive from the Greek *kassiteros*, "tin." See *Targum Yerushalmi* and *Targum Yerushalmi* (frag.), Numbers 31:22; *Zohar* 1:125a; 2:24b; *Bei'ur ha-Millim ha-Zarot*, 188.

476. **ox...eagle...human being** In his vision, Ezekiel sees four creatures, each of whom has four faces: the face of a human being in front, the face of a lion on the right, the face of an ox on the left, and the

turn into the image of a two-headed serpent, moving like a serpent, then swooping into the abyss,[477] bathing in the vast ocean. Reaching the chains of Uzza and Azael,[478] they agitate and arouse them. These then leap into the dark mountains, thinking the blessed Holy One is about to call them to judgment.[479] Those two officials swim the vast ocean and fly through the night to Na'amah, mother of demons, after whom the primordial deities strayed.[480] They intend to approach her, but she leaps 60,000 parasangs, transmogrifying herself into countless figures confronting human beings, so that they stray after her. These two officials fly and roam throughout the world, then return to their abode, arousing those descendants of Cain to generate offspring by the spirit of evil impulses.[481]

"The heavens ruling there do not resemble these,[482] nor does the earth bear seed and harvest through their power as does this,[483] and they only cycle once in many years of seasons.[484] These *gods who did not make heaven and earth shall perish from the* higher *earth* of the world,[485] so that they will not rule over it nor roam through it, causing humans to defile themselves through a nocturnal mishap.[486] So, *they shall perish from the earth and from under the heavens*

64

face of an eagle at the back (Ezekiel 1:10). Here the demonic officials Afrira and Kastimon resemble the creatures who appear on the left and the back before combining into a human image.

477. **abyss** Home of all demons.

478. **Uzza and Azael** These two angels opposed the creation of Adam and Eve, fell from heaven, and were attracted by *the daughters of men* (Genesis 6:2). They were punished by being bound in chains of iron in the mountains of darkness, from where they still manage to wreak havoc, teaching sorcery to humans.

See 1 Enoch 6–8; Jubilees 5; BT *Yoma* 67b; *Aggadat Bereshit*, intro, 39; *Midrash Avkir*, 7 (cited in *Yalqut Shim'oni*, Genesis, 44); *Pirqei de-Rabbi Eli'ezer* 22; *Zohar* 1:23a (*TZ*), 37a, 37a (*Tos*), 58a, 126a; 3:208a–b, 212a–b; *ZH* 81a–b (*MhN, Rut*).

479. **call them to judgment** For their deeds of lust.

480. **Na'amah, mother of demons...** Na'amah, whose name means "lovely," was the sister of Tuval-Cain and the great-great-great-great-granddaughter of Cain (Genesis 4:22). According to rabbinic tradition, the

fallen angels were attracted by her beauty. See ibid. 6:1–4; *Tanhuma* (Buber), *Huqqat*, add. 1; *Midrash Aggadah* and *Midrash ha-Gadol*, Genesis 4:22.

In the *Zohar*, Na'amah is the mother of Ashmedai, king of the demons, and she generates demons by seducing men in their sleep. See Nahmanides, ad loc.; *Zohar* 1:19b, 55a; 3:76b–77a; *ZH* 19d (*MhN*).

481. **by the spirit of evil impulses** Through lustful desire, in the style of Na'amah.

482. **these** The heavens above our earth.

483. **seed and harvest...** Which depend on the influence of heaven. Only on our earth ("this") do the various species of grain grow. See *Zohar* 1:157a; *ZH* 9b, 87b (*MhN, Rut*).

484. **they only cycle...** The heavenly spheres of that lower earth revolve slowly. Alternatively, the reference is to vegetation, which fails to sprout annually.

485. **world** Hebrew, תבל (*tevel*), referring to our earth, the most desirable of all. See *Vayiqra Rabbah* 29:11.

486. **nocturnal mishap** A nocturnal emission, an involuntary emission of semen.

fashioned by the name אלה (*elleh*), *these*, as explained.[487] That is why this verse is written in Aramaic: so that the celestial angels will not think it is being said about them and denounce us. So the mystery of אלה (*elleh*) accords with what has been said; it constitutes a sacred word, not to be exchanged for Aramaic."

Rabbi El'azar said to him,[488] "This verse that is written: *Who would not be in awe of You, O King of the nations? For it befits You* (Jeremiah 10:7)[489]—what kind of praise is that?"[490]

He replied, "El'azar, my son, this verse has been discussed in various places,[491] but it is certainly not so, for it is written: *since among all the wise of the nations and among all their kingdoms* [*there is none like You*] (ibid.), providing a pretext for sinners who think that the blessed Holy One does not know their thoughts and fantasies.[492] So their stupidity must be exposed.

"Once a Gentile philosopher came to me and said, 'You claim that your God rules all the heights of heaven, that all the hosts and camps[493] cannot grasp or know His site.[494] Well, this verse does not exalt Him very well: *since among all the wise of the nations and among all their kingdoms there is none like You.* What kind of comparison is this—to human beings who do not [10a] endure? Furthermore, you say: "*Never again did there arise in Israel a prophet like Moses* (Deuteronomy 34:10)—In Israel none arose, but among the nations of the world one did!"[495] Similarly I can say: Among all the wise of nations there is none like Him, but among the wise of Israel there is! If so, a God who has an equal among the wise of Israel is not a God who reigns supreme. Look closely at the verse, and you will find I have been fittingly precise.'

65

See Deuteronomy 23:11. According to the *Zohar,* such semen impregnates Na'amah, producing a new generation of demons.

See *Tanḥuma* (Buber), *Bereshit* 26; *Bereshit Rabbah* 20:11; BT *Eruvin* 18b; *Zohar* 1:34b, 54b–55a, 2:231b, 3:76b.

487. **as explained**   See above, pages 8–10, 19–20.

488. **to him**   To his father, Rabbi Shim'on.

489. *Who would not be in awe of You...*   This verse appears shortly before the verse that Rabbi Shim'on has just interpreted.

490. **what kind of praise is that?**   God is not merely *King of the nations;* He rules the entire cosmos.

491. **discussed in various places**   See *Shemot Rabbah* 29:9; *Midrash Tehillim* 93:1; Maimonides, *Mishneh Torah, Hilkhot Avodat Kokhavim* 1:1; *Zohar* 2:38a, 95b–96a.

492. **pretext for sinners...**   Apparently, since the verse compares God with *the wise of the nations* (although contrasting the two), sinners could conclude that just as those wise ones cannot conceive the thoughts of other humans, neither can God.

See *KP; OY; MmD.* For other interpretations, see Galante; Scholem.

493. **camps**   Camps of angels.

494. **cannot grasp or know His site**   See BT *Ḥagigah* 13b: "It is written [that the angels exclaimed]: *Blessed be the Presence of YHVH in His place* (Ezekiel 3:12)—because no one knows His place."

See *Pirqei de-Rabbi Eli'ezer* 4; *Bahir* 90 (131); *Zohar* 1:103a; 3:159a.

495. **but among the nations...one did**   See *Sifrei,* Deuteronomy 357: "*Never again did there arise in Israel a prophet like Moses*—In Israel none arose, but among the na-

"I replied, 'You have certainly spoken well. Who revives the dead? The blessed Holy One alone. Along came Elijah and Elisha, and they revived the dead! Who makes the rain fall? The blessed Holy One alone. Along came Elijah and withheld it—and then brought it down through his prayer.[496] Who created heaven and earth? The blessed Holy One alone. Abraham came, and they were firmly established because of him.[497] Who controls the sun? The blessed Holy One. Joshua came and calmed it down, commanding it to stand in place, and it stood still, as is written: *The sun stood still, and the moon halted* (Joshua 10:13). The blessed Holy One issues decrees. Similarly Moses issued decrees, which were fulfilled. Further, the blessed Holy One issues decrees, and the righteous of Israel abolish them, as is written: *The righteous one rules the awe of God* (2 Samuel 23:3).[498] Further, He commanded them to walk in His ways, literally, imitating Him consummately.'[499]

"That philosopher went and converted in the village of Shiḥlayim.[500] They called him Yose the Small.[501] He studied Torah intensively and is considered one of the righteous sages of that place.

"Now we should contemplate the verse. Isn't it already written: *All the nations are as nothing before Him* (Isaiah 40:17)? What amplification appears here? But, *Who would not be in awe of You, O King of the nations?* Is He then *King of the nations* and not King of Israel? The blessed Holy One always desires to be glorified through Israel—and is named for Israel alone, as is written: *God of Israel, God of the Hebrews* (Exodus 5:1, 3), and similarly: *Thus says YHVH, King of Israel* (Isaiah 44:6). *King of Israel*, indeed! The nations of the world said, 'We have another patron in heaven, since your King rules only over you, not over us.' So the verse comes and says: *Who would not be in awe of You,*

66

tions of the world one did! Who is this? Balaam son of Beor."

See *Bemidbar Rabbah* 14:20; *Zohar* 2:21b (*MhN*); 3:193b.

496. **Who revives the dead?...Who makes the rain fall?...** See 1 Kings 17:1, 7, 17–24; 18:41–45; 2 Kings 4:8–37; *Bereshit Rabbah* 77:1.

497. **Abraham came...** See *Bereshit Rabbah* 12:9; above, page 19.

498. **righteous of Israel abolish them...** See BT *Mo'ed Qatan* 16b: "*The righteous one rules the awe of God....*Rabbi Abbahu said, '...I rule over humanity. Who rules over Me? The righteous one. For I issue a decree and he abolishes it.'"

See *Zohar* 1:45b; 2:15a (*MhN*), 262a; 3:15a.

499. **to walk in His ways...** See Deuteronomy 8:6; 11:22; 13:5; 28:9; 30:16. In rabbinic literature (*Sifrei*, Deuteronomy 49; BT *Sotah* 14a) this biblical idiom is understood as *imitatio dei*. Here Rabbi Shim'on implies that such imitation includes the exercise of Godlike powers.

500. **Shiḥlayim** Mentioned in BT *Gittin* 57a, as one of three cities with a population twice the size of the total number of Israelites who left Egypt. See *Eikhah Rabbah* 2:4. Its name is said to derive from its major business: *shiḥlayim*, "watercress."

501. **Yose the Small** יוסי קטינאה (*Yose Qattina'ah*). See the reference in M *Sotah* 9:15 to יוסי קטנותא (*Yose Qatnuta*), so called because he was the last, or tail end, of the

O King of the nations? Supreme King, ruling them, punishing them, implementing His will upon them. *For it befits You*—to be in awe of You, above and below. *Since among all the wise of the nations*—the mighty rulers appointed over them.[502] *And among all their kingdoms*[503]—in that kingdom on high, for there are four kingdoms reigning above,[504] reigning by His will over all other nations; nevertheless, none of them does even the slightest thing unless He commands them, as is written: *He does as He wishes with the host of heaven and with the inhabitants of earth* (Daniel 4:32). *The wise of the nations*—princes appointed on high, whose wisdom issues from His mouth. *And among all their kingdoms*—the reigning kingdom, as explained.

"This is the simple meaning of the verse, but: *Among all the wise of the nations and among all their kingdoms*—In the books of the ancients I have found as follows: Although those camps[505] and hosts have been empowered over affairs of the world, and He has commanded each and every one to enact his action, מאין כמוך (*mi ayin kamokha*), *who is Ayin like You?* (Jeremiah 10:7).[506] Who else is the holy concealed one? It is not His will that any of them act *like You*. For You are distinguished in esteem, distinguished from all of them in action and speech. This is מאין כמוך יהוה (*Mi ayin kamokha YHVH*), *Who is Ayin like You, YHVH?* (ibid., 6).[507] Who is the holy concealed one that would act or be *like You*, above or below, that would resemble You at all? The act of the holy King is heaven and earth, but they are *chaos, and what they desire is worthless* (Isaiah 44:9).[508] Of the blessed Holy One is written: *In the beginning God*

67

ḥasidim. A story with a similar ending appears in *Pesiqta Rabbati* 14.

502. **mighty rulers appointed...** According to rabbinic tradition, the seventy nations of the world are governed by seventy angels or heavenly princes appointed by God.

See Daniel 10:20; Septuagint, Deuteronomy 32:8–9; Jubilees 15:31–32; *Targum Yerushalmi*, Genesis 11:8, Deuteronomy 32:8–9; *Tanḥuma, Re'eh* 8; *Leqaḥ Tov*, Genesis 9:19; *Pirqei de-Rabbi Eli'ezer* 24; *Zohar* 1:46b, 61a, 108b; 2:33a, 151b; 3:298b; Ginzberg, *Legends*, 5:204–5, n. 91.

503. *And among all their kingdoms* The verse continues: *there is none like You.*

504. **four kingdoms...** The book of Daniel (chapters 2 and 7) suggests a framework of four world-kingdoms: Babylonians, Medes, Persians, and Greeks, to be succeeded by the everlasting kingdom of God.

505. **camps** Camps of angels.

506. מאין כמוך (*mi ayin kamokha*), *who is Ayin like You* The final two words of the verse are read not as מאין כמוך (*me-ein kamokha*), *there is none like You*, but rather as מי אין כמוך (*mi ayin kamokha*), *who is Ayin like You? Ayin*, "nothingness," is a name for *Keter*, the highest *sefirah*. This ultimate stage of divinity is inconceivable, the divine nothingness, also called "the holy concealed one." See *OY*.

507. **This is** מאין כמוך יהוה (*Mi ayin kamokha YHVH*)... This verse immediately precedes the verse being discussed (Jeremiah 10:7). Here, too, Rabbi Shim'on reads מאין (*me-ein*), *there is none*, as מי אין (*mi ayin*), *who is Ayin?*

508. *chaos, and what they desire...* The subject of the biblical verse is *the makers of idols.*

created... (Genesis 1:1); of *their kingdoms*, it is written: *The earth was chaos and void* (Genesis 1:2)."[509]

Rabbi Shim'on said to the Companions, "Members of this wedding party, let each one of you adorn the Bride with one adornment."[510]

He said to Rabbi El'azar, his son, "El'azar, give one present to the Bride, for tomorrow when He enters the canopy[511] He will gaze upon those songs of praise bestowed upon Her by initiates of the palace, to stand in His presence."

Rabbi El'azar opened, saying, "*Who is this that ascends from the wilderness*...? (Song of Songs 3:6). *Who is this?*—sum of two sanctities, two worlds in one bond, one nexus.[512] *Ascends*, literally, to become the holy of holies,[513] for the holy of holies is *Who* and is joined with *This*, so that She[514] *ascends*, becoming the holy of holies. *From the wilderness*—for in the desert She inherited the role of Bride, entering the canopy.[515]

"Further, *From the* מדבר (*midbar*), *wilderness*, She *ascends*, as is said: ומדברך (*u-midbarekh*), *and your speech, is lovely* (ibid. 4:3). By that מדבר (*midbar*), *speech* [10b]—by the whispering of lips—She *ascends*.[516] We have learned: What is the meaning of the verse *These mighty gods—these are the gods who smote the Egyptians with every kind of plague* במדבר (*ba-midbar*), *in the wilderness* (1 Samuel 4:8)?[517] Was it in the wilderness that the blessed Holy One

68

---

509. **of *their kingdoms*... *chaos*...** See *Bereshit Rabbah* 2:4, where Genesis 1:2 is similarly applied to the four kingdoms.

510. **Members of this wedding party...** On the eve of *Shavu'ot* (Festival of "Weeks"), the Companions are invited to adorn *Shekhinah* with new interpretations of Torah, preparing Her for Her union with *Tif'eret*. See above, pages 51–52.

511. **when He enters...** When *Tif-'eret* enters the canopy to be united with *Shekhinah*.

512. ***Who is this?—sum of two*...** *Who* is a name of *Binah*, the Divine Mother, whose nature can be questioned and explored, though She remains a mystery. See above, page 5. *This* is a name of *Shekhinah*, who is more revealed. See *Zohar* 1:176b; 2:37b (*MhN*); 3:145b.

513. ***Ascends*, literally...** עולה (*Olah*) is also the name for the offering on the altar that is totally consumed by fire—that "as-

cends" to God. In M *Zevahim* 5:4, the *olah* offering is classified as one of the קדשי קדשים (*qodshei qodashim*), "holies of holies," i.e., the most sacred offerings. Here Rabbi El'azar indicates that *Shekhinah* ascends to *Binah*, the "holy of holies," and is united with Her. See *Zohar* 2:239a; 3:26a–b.

514. **She** *This*, that is, *Shekhinah*.

515. **in the desert She inherited...** *Shekhinah* is also called *Keneset Yisra'el*, "Assembly of Israel," since She is the divine counterpart of the people, that aspect of God most intimately connected with them. At Mount Sinai on *Shavu'ot*, when the Torah was given to Israel, *Keneset Yisra'el* was wedded to *Tif'eret*, the blessed Holy One.

516. **by the whispering of lips...** Through fervent, meditative prayer or study, *Shekhinah* ascends to *Binah*.

517. ***These mighty gods*...** This verse records the frightened reaction of the Philistines when the ark of the covenant was

did everything to them? It was in inhabited land! Rather, במדבר (*ba-midbar*) means בדבורא (*be-dibbura*), *by speech,* as is said: ומדברך (*u-midbarekh*), *and your speech, is lovely.*[518] Similarly, ממדבר הרים (*mi-midbar harim*), *from wilderness mountains* (Psalms 75:7): *from speech he raised.*[519] So, too: *She ascends from* המדבר (*ha-midbar*), indeed *from ha-midbar!* By that word of the mouth, She ascends, nestling between the Mother's wings.[520] Afterward through speech She descends, hovering over the heads of the holy people.[521]

"How does She ascend by speech? First, upon rising in the morning, one should bless his Lord, the moment he opens his eyes.[522] How can he bless?[523] This is what the ancient *ḥasidim* used to do:[524] In front of them was a receptacle of water, and when they awoke at night they would wash their hands, rise, and study Torah—and offer a blessing over the crowing of the rooster.[525] For the moment that the rooster crows is precisely midnight, when

brought into the Israelite camp in the midst of battle.

518. **Rather,** במדבר **(*ba-midbar*) means** בדבורא **(*be-dibbura*), *by speech*...** See *Shemot Rabbah* 2:4; Radak on 1 Samuel 4:8.

519. ממדבר הרים **(*mi-midbar harim*), *from wilderness mountains*...** In *Bemidbar Rabbah* 22:8 the word הרים (*harim*) is interpreted by Rabbi Abba as הרים (*herim*), "he raised." See *Tanḥuma, Mattot* 6; *Tanḥuma* (Buber), *Mattot* 9; *Midrash Tehillim* 75:3.

Here Rabbi El'azar combines this interpretation with the midrashic rendering of מדבר (*midbar*).

520. **By that word of the mouth...** Through the power of prayer and study, *Shekhinah* ascends to the realm of *Binah*.

521. **Afterward through speech...** Holy speech also draws down emanation.

522. **bless...the moment he opens his eyes** See BT *Berakhot* 60b: "Upon opening his eyes, one should say: 'Blessed is He who opens the eyes of the blind.'"

523. **How can he bless?** Seeing that he has not yet washed his hands.

524. **ancient *ḥasidim*...** This group is referred to in rabbinic literature, but here Rabbi El'azar may be alluding to the German *ḥasidim* of the twelfth and thirteenth centuries. See Scholem, who cites *Sefer Ḥasidim*, ed. Wistinetzki, par. 798 (ed. Marga-

liot, par. 992), where a rabbi instructs young men to sleep with "a vessel filled with [cold] water by their beds" and to immerse themselves in the water in order to overcome the evil impulse. Cf. par. 1066 (Margaliot, par. 371), where advice is given that "at night one place next to him water in a cup" to purify oneself from nocturnal emission. See *Orḥot Ḥayyim*, par. 10: "Be careful to have a cup of water next to your bed, and when you rise in the morning do not put on your garment without first washing your hands."

525. **blessing over the crowing of the rooster** See BT *Berakhot* 60b: "When one hears the rooster crowing he should say: 'Blessed is He who has given the rooster understanding to distinguish between day and night.'" Here the rooster marks the moment of midnight, the beginning of the union of *Tif'eret* and *Shekhinah*. See Rashi on BT *Eruvin* 53b, s.v. *maggidei ba-alatah*, according to whom the rooster's crows mark the various divisions of the night. See *Pereq Shirah*, 2:57 (s.v. *tarnegol*): "When the blessed Holy One comes to the righteous in the Garden of Eden, all the trees of the Garden sprinkle spices before Him. Then he [the rooster] praises."

See Naḥmanides on Job 38:36; *Zohar* 1:77b, 218b; 2:196a; 3:22b–23b, 171b; *ZḤ* 88a (*MhN, Rut*).

the blessed Holy One appears with the righteous in the Garden of Eden.[526] It is forbidden to bless with impure, filthy hands,[527] and similarly at all times.[528] For when a person is sleeping, his spirit flies away from him, and as his spirit flies off, an impure spirit is ready to settle on his hands, defiling them.[529] So it is forbidden to offer a blessing with them without first washing. Now if you ask, 'If so, then during the daytime (when one has not been sleeping, and his spirit has not flown away and no impure spirit rests upon him), why is one who enters the bathroom forbidden to bless or read Torah—even a single word—until after washing his hands? If you say the reason is that his hands are dirty—not so: how have they become dirty?' The answer is: Woe to the inhabitants of the world who fail to consider, who are unaware of the glory of their Lord, who do not realize the foundation of the world's existence. There is one spirit in every bathroom of the world,[530] dwelling there, reveling in that dirt and filth, and it settles immediately on the fingers of one's hands."[531]

70

Rabbi Shim'on opened, saying, "Whoever rejoices on the festivals without giving the blessed Holy One His share—that stingy one, evil-eyed Satan, Arch-

526. **midnight…** See Psalms 119:62; and BT *Berakhot* 3b: "Rabbi Shim'on the Ḥasid said, 'There was a harp suspended above [King] David's bed. As soon as midnight arrived, a north wind came and blew upon it, and it played by itself. He immediately arose and engaged in Torah until the break of dawn.'"

In the *Zohar,* this legendary custom is expanded into a ritual: all kabbalists are expected to rise at midnight and adorn *Shekhinah* with words of Torah and song in preparation for Her union with *Tif'eret.* See Scholem, *On the Kabbalah,* 146–50. This parallels the midnight vigil, common among Christian monks from early medieval times. In *Zohar* 3:119a Rabbi Yehudah alludes to the Christian practice: "I have seen something similar among the nations of the world." At midnight God delights in the souls of the righteous in the Garden of Eden, and those who study Torah here below partake of the celestial joy.

See *Sifra, Beḥuqqotai* 3:3, 111b; *Aggadat Bereshit* 23:5; BT *Sanhedrin* 102a; 2 Enoch 8:3; *Seder Gan Eden* (*Beit ha-Midrash,* 3:138); *Zohar* 1:72a, 77a, 82b, 92a–b, 136b, 178a, 231b;

2:46a, 130a–b, 136a, 173b, 195b–196a; 3:21b–22b, 52b, 193a; *ZH* 13c (*MhN*). Cf. Matthew 25:6.

527. **forbidden to bless with impure, filthy hands** See BT *Berakhot* 53b: "R. Zuhamai said, 'Just as a filthy [person or animal] is unfit for the Temple service, so filthy hands render one unfit for reciting a blessing [after eating].'" Cf. *Zohar* 1:184b; 3:186a; *Orḥot Ḥayyim,* par. 12.

528. **at all times** When a person rises from sleep, even during the day.

529. **his spirit flies away…an impure spirit…** During sleep one's spirit soars upward and an impure spirit arrives. See BT *Shabbat* 109a; *Ḥullin* 107b; *Zohar* 1:53b, 169b, 184b; 3:67a; *Orḥot Ḥayyim,* par. 10.

Cf. *Bereshit Rabbah* 14:9: "It was said in the name of Rabbi Me'ir: 'This soul fills the body, and when a person sleeps she ascends, drawing down life from above.'"

530. **one spirit in every bathroom…** See "the demons of the bathroom" mentioned in BT *Qiddushin* 72a; cf. *Berakhot* 62b.

531. **on the fingers of one's hands** The passage is apparently incomplete. See *KP; Scholem.*

enemy, appears and accuses him, removes him from the world.[532] How much compounded suffering he brings upon him!

"The share of the blessed Holy One consists in gladdening the poor as best as one can.[533] For on these days the blessed Holy One comes to see those broken vessels of His.[534] Entering their company and seeing they have nothing to celebrate, He weeps over them—and then ascends to destroy the world!

"Many members of the Academy[535] come before Him and plead: 'Master of the universe! You are called Compassionate and Gracious.[536] May your compassion be aroused for your children!'

"He answers them, 'Don't the inhabitants of the world realize that I based the world solely on love? As is written: *I said, "The world shall be built on love"* (Psalms 89:3). By this the world endures.'[537]

"The angels on high declare before Him, 'Master of the universe! Look at so-and-so who is eating and drinking his fill. He could be generous with the poor, but he gives them nothing!'

"The Accuser comes, claims permission, and sets out in pursuit of that human being.[538]

"Who in the world was greater than Abraham, who acted kindly to all creatures?[539] What is written concerning the day that he prepared a feast? *The*

71

532. **removes him from the world** Satan and the Angel of Death are two manifestations of *Sitra Aḥra,* "the Other Side," the demonic. See BT *Bava Batra* 16a: "Resh Lakish said, 'Satan, the evil impulse, and the Angel of Death are one and the same.'" Cf. *Zohar* 1:35b, 52a, 202a; 2:262b–263a; Moses de León, *Sefer ha-Rimmon,* 394–95.

See the description of Satan's itinerary in *Bava Batra,* loc cit.: "He descends and seduces, ascends and arouses wrath, obtains authorization, and seizes the soul." Cf. Rashi on BT *Shabbat* 89a, s.v. *ba ha-satan; Zohar* 1:46b, 125a, 148a (*ST*), 152b; 2:33b, 268b.

533. **gladdening the poor . . .** See *ZḤ* 87b (*MhN, Rut*): "The blessed Holy One enjoys the food that one gives to a poor person because that food satisfies the poor person and makes him happy." Cf. *Orḥot Ḥayyim,* par. 65; *Zohar* 2:88b; 3:103b–104a; Maimonides, *Mishneh Torah, Hilkhot Yom Tov* 6:18.

534. **those broken vessels of His** See Psalms 34:19: *YHVH is close to the broken-hearted.* According to midrashic sources, Rabbi Alexandri, referring to such suppli-

cants, says, "All of God's vessels are broken" (*Vayiqra Rabbah* 7:2; cf. *Pesiqta de-Rav Kahana* 24:5).

In the *Zohar* God's broken vessels are the poor, who are compared to *Shekhinah* because, like Her, they have nothing at all of their own (3:113b). As She is provided for by the other *sefirot,* so other humans must provide for the poor, and "anyone who mistreats a poor person mistreats *Shekhinah*" (2:86b). See 2:218a; *ZḤ* 77c (*MhN, Rut*).

535. **Many members of the Academy** The souls of the righteous reside in heaven, imbibing the deepest secrets of Torah.

536. **Compassionate and Gracious** See Exodus 34:6: *YHVH, YHVH, a God compassionate and gracious, slow to anger, abounding in love and faithfulness.*

537. **By this the world endures** Without deeds of love, the world will collapse.

538. **The Accuser . . .** Satan, who claims permission to punish the selfish person.

539. **Abraham . . . acted kindly . . .** On Abraham's hospitality, see *Avot de-Rabbi Natan* A, 7; *Bereshit Rabbah* 54:6; BT *Sotah*

child grew and was weaned, and Abraham held a great feast on the day that Isaac was weaned (Genesis 21:8). He made a feast, inviting all the dignitaries of his generation.[540]

"We have learned:[541] Whenever there is a joyous meal, the Accuser comes to observe. If the host has first provided for the poor or invited them into his home, then the Accuser departs from the house without entering. If not, he enters and witnesses the chaos of revelry,[542] without any poor, without prior generosity toward the poor. Then he ascends, accusing the host.

"As Abraham welcomed the dignitaries, the Accuser descended and stood at the door, disguised as a poor man. No one paid him any attention. Abraham was waiting on those kings and princes. Sarah was suckling all their babies because they did not believe that she had given birth;[543] they said, 'It is a foundling from off the streets!' So when they brought along their babies, Sarah took them and suckled them in front of everyone, as is written: *Who would have said* [11a] *to Abraham: Sarah will suckle children?* (ibid. 21:7). *Children,* literally![544]

"Meanwhile the Accuser was still at the door. She[545] said, '*God has made a laughingstock of me*' (ibid. 21:6).

"At once, the Accuser rose to face the blessed Holy One. He exclaimed, 'Master of the universe! You called Abraham *My beloved* (Isaiah 41:8)? He held a feast and gave me nothing,[546] and nothing to the poor. To You, he

72

10a–b. According to the *Zohar* (1:83a; 3:104a, 267a), Abraham's devotion to God and love of his fellow creatures elevated him to the rung of *Hesed* ("Love").

540. **inviting all the dignitaries...** See *Bereshit Rabbah* 53:10: "Rabbi Yehudah said, '*A great feast* means a feast of the great. Og [king of Bashan, who was a giant (Deut. 3:11)] and all the great ones were there.'"

541. **We have learned...** The following teaching has no known source in rabbinic literature.

542. **chaos of revelry** On this expression, see *Vayiqra Rabbah* 20:10; Moses de León, *Sheqel ha-Qodesh,* 64 (79).

543. **they did not believe...** That Sarah, aged ninety, had really given birth to Isaac.

544. *Children,* **literally!** In the plural. See *Pirqei de-Rabbi Eli'ezer* 52; *Bereshit Rabbah* 53:9; *Pesiqta de-Rav Kahana* 22:1; and BT *Bava Metsi'a* 87a: "*She* [Sarah] *said, Who would have said to Abraham: Sarah will*

suckle children? How many children did Sarah suckle? Rabbi Levi said, 'On the day that Abraham weaned his son Isaac, he held a great feast. All the nations of the world mocked him, saying, "Have you seen that old man and woman, who brought a foundling from off the streets, and now claim him as their son! Furthermore they hold a great feast to establish their claim!" What did Abraham our father do? He invited all the dignitaries of his generation, and Sarah our mother invited their wives. Each one brought her baby with her, but not her wetnurse, and a miracle happened to Sarah our mother: her breasts opened like two fountains, and she suckled them all.'"

545. **She** That is, Sarah.

546. **gave me nothing** Elsewhere the *Zohar* indicates that the demonic powers should be assuaged by giving them their share, as a bone is thrown to a dog. See *Pirqei de-Rabbi Eli'ezer* 46: "They gave him

didn't offer even a single dove![547] Furthermore, Sarah said that You made fun of her!'

"The blessed Holy One replied, 'Who in the world is like Abraham?'[548]

"But he held his ground[549] until he ruined all that joy, and the blessed Holy One commanded that Isaac be offered as a sacrifice,[550] and it was decreed that Sarah die in anguish over her son's ordeal.[551] All that suffering came about because he[552] gave nothing to the poor."

Rabbi Shim'on opened, saying, "What is the meaning of the verse: *Hezekiah turned his face to the wall and prayed to YHVH* (Isaiah 38:2)?[553] Come and see how potent is the power of Torah, how supreme above all! For whoever engages in Torah has no fear of those above and those below, nor of any grave sickness in the world, since he grasps the Tree of Life and learns from it every day.[554] For Torah teaches a person to follow the true path, advises him how to

[Satan] a bribe on Yom Kippur [i.e., the scapegoat] so that he would not nullify Israel's sacrifice."

According to Leviticus 16, a goat bearing the sins of Israel is designated for Azazel, a wilderness demon. Similarly, in the Babylonian Akitu ritual a goat, substituted for a human being, is offered to Ereshkigal, goddess of the Abyss.

See Naḥmanides on Leviticus 16:8; *Zohar* 1:64a, 65a, 113b–114b, 138b, 174b, 190a, 210b; 2:154b, 237b; 266b; 3:63a (*Piq*), 102a, 202b–203a, 258b; *ZḤ* 87b–c (*MhN, Rut*); Moses de León, *She'elot u-Tshuvot*, 49; Tishby, *Wisdom of the Zohar*, 3:890–95.

547. **even a single dove** See BT *Sanhedrin* 89b: "Rabbi Yoḥanan said in the name of Rabbi Yose son of Zimra, '... Satan said in the presence of the blessed Holy One, "Master of the universe! You bestowed upon this old man the fruit of the womb at the age of one hundred! From his entire feast could he not offer a single dove or pigeon to You?"'"

See *Bereshit Rabbah* 55:4. Leviticus 5:7 specifies doves or pigeons as the offering that a poor person may bring if he cannot afford a sheep.

548. **Who in the world is like Abraham?** See *Sefer ha-Yashar, Vayera,* 117; Job 1:8.

549. **he held his ground** Satan, the Accuser, would not leave God's presence or relent.

550. **that Isaac be offered as a sacrifice** According to BT *Sanhedrin* 89b (the continuation of the passage cited above), God commanded Abraham to offer up Isaac in order to prove to Satan that Abraham was a loyal servant. Here in the *Zohar,* the tone is different: the binding of Isaac is a punishment for Abraham's selfishness and neglect of the poor, a substitute offering to God.

See *Bereshit Rabbah* 55:4–5, where Rabbi Yehoshu'a in the name of Rabbi Levi cites Micah 6:7: *Shall I offer my firstborn for my transgression, the fruit of my body for my own sin?* See *Zohar* 1:119b.

551. **that Sarah die in anguish...** When she heard the details of the binding of Isaac. See *Vayiqra Rabbah* 20:2; *Pesiqta de-Rav Kahana* 26:3; *Tanḥuma, Vayera* 23; *Pirqei de-Rabbi Eli'ezer* 32.

552. **he** Abraham.

553. *Hezekiah turned his face to the wall and prayed...* When King Hezekiah of Judah fell dangerously ill, Isaiah prophesied to him that he would die (Isaiah 38:1). See *Zohar* 1:132a, 228a–b; 2:44a, 133a; 3:260a–b.

554. **learns from it every day** In *Zohar* 3:260a the reading is: "eats from it every day."

return to his Lord, nullifying that decree.[555] Even if it has been ordained that the decree not be nullified, it is annulled immediately and removed from him, looming over him no longer in this world. So one should engage in Torah day and night, never departing from her, as is written: *Meditate on it day and night* (Joshua 1:8). If one departs from Torah or separates from her, it is like separating oneself from the Tree of Life.[556]

"Come and see this advice: When one climbs into bed at night, he should accept upon himself wholeheartedly the Kingdom on high[557] and in advance deliver to Him the pledge of his soul.[558] At once he is protected from any grave illness[559] or maleficent spirit, which are powerless against him.

"In the morning, upon rising from bed, one should bless his Lord, enter His house, bow down in great awe before His sanctuary,[560] and then offer his prayer. He should seek advice from those holy Patriarchs,[561] as is written: *As for me, through Your abundant love, I will enter Your house; I will bow down at Your holy sanctuary in awe of You* (Psalms 5:8). So they have established:[562] A person should not enter the synagogue without first consulting Abraham, Isaac, and Jacob, for they innovated prayer to the blessed Holy One,[563] as is written: *As for me, through Your abundant love, I will enter Your house*—Abraham; *I will bow down at Your*

74

555. **that decree** Whatever has been decreed against him, as the decree against King Hezekiah was nullified when he turned back to God in sincere prayer (Isaiah 38:4–8).

556. **Tree of Life** Torah is identified with the Tree of Life, based on the description of wisdom in Proverbs 3:18: *She is a tree of life to those who grasp her.* See BT *Berakhot* 32b, 61b.

557. **accept...the Kingdom on high** Before going to sleep, one should recite the *Shema* (*Hear O Israel! YHVH is our God, YHVH is one* [Deuteronomy 6:4]), thereby accepting upon oneself "the yoke of the Kingdom of Heaven."

See BT *Berakhot* 4b: "Rabbi Yehoshu'a son of Levi said, 'Even if one has recited the *Shema* in the synagogue, it is a *mitsvah* to recite it upon his bed.'" Cf. *Zohar* 1:183a; 3:211a; and on the phrase "the yoke of the Kingdom of Heaven," see M *Berakhot* 2:2.

558. **in advance deliver to Him the pledge...** During sleep the soul ascends to heaven. On account of one's daily sins, the soul should not be restored in the morning, but by consciously delivering the soul as

a pledge to God before sleep, one ensures that God will return the pledge. See *Zohar* 1:36b; 3:119a, 260a; *ZH* 18b–c (*MhN*), 89a (*MhN, Rut*).

The nightly delivery of the pledge is announced by reciting Psalms 31:6: *Into Your hand I entrust* [or: *deposit*] *my spirit; You redeem me, YHVH, faithful God.* See BT *Berakhot* 5a, where this verse is recommended by Abbaye.

559. **any grave illness** As with Hezekiah, sincere prayer wards off illness.

560. **His house...His sanctuary** The synagogue and the ark.

561. **He should seek advice from those holy Patriarchs** One should meditate on the sefirotic triad symbolized by Abraham, Isaac, and Jacob: Ḥesed, Gevurah, and Tif'eret.

562. **So they have established** In the *Zohar*, this formula often refers to Talmudic traditions, but here it refers to the Spanish custom of reciting this verse from Psalms upon entering the synagogue. See *Abudarham*, 349; Scholem; *Zohar* 3:8b.

563. **they innovated prayer...** See BT *Berakhot* 26b: "Rabbi Yose son of Rabbi

holy sanctuary—Isaac; *in awe of You*—Jacob.[564] One should embrace them first, then enter the synagogue and offer one's prayer. So it is written: *He said to me, 'You are My servant, Israel, in whom I will be glorified'* (Isaiah 49:3)."[565]

Rabbi Pinḥas[566] used to frequent Rabbi Reḥumai[567] by the shore of Lake Ginnosar.[568] He[569] was distinguished, advanced in years, and his eyes had transcended seeing.[570]

Ḥanina said, 'The patriarchs instituted the prayers'.... Abraham instituted the morning prayer, ... Isaac, the afternoon prayer, ... Jacob, the evening prayer." See *Bereshit Rabbah* 68:9.

564. **Abraham... Isaac... Jacob** The verse is applied to all three patriarchs. Abraham is often identified with *Ḥesed* ("Love"). The correlation of the next part of the verse with Isaac is not clear. Jacob and awe are linked in Genesis 28:17, where the third patriarch declares: *How awesome is this place!* (cf. Genesis 32:8). The *Zohar* links the divine name נורא (*Nora*), *Awesome* (Deuteronomy 10:17; Nehemiah 9:32), with Jacob and *Tif'eret* (see *Zohar* 1:19a; 2:78b–79a, 261a).

There are various alternate readings in the manuscripts and commentaries. See Vital and Galante; *KP;* Scholem; Meir ibn Gabbai, *Tola'at Ya'aqov, sod ha-tefillin,* 9a; cf. *Zohar* 3:8b.

565. ***Israel, in whom I will be glorified*** Through contemplative prayer, the Jew (*Israel*) unites the triad of *sefirot,* imitating *Tif'eret* ("Glory"), who synthesizes *Ḥesed* and *Gevurah*.

566. **Rabbi Pinḥas** Son of Ya'ir, a second-century rabbi who lived in Palestine, renowned for his saintliness and ability to work miracles. See BT *Ḥullin* 7a; JT *Demai* 1:3, 22a. In the *Zohar,* he is accorded special status. In recognition of his *ḥasidut* ("saintliness, piety, love of God"), Rabbi Shim'on affirms that Pinḥas has attained the *sefirah* of *Ḥesed* (3:62a; cf. 201a, 240b). Generally he is in a class by himself among the Companions. See 3:59b–60b, 62a–b, 200b–202a, 203a, 225b, 288a, 296b (*IZ*); *ZḤ* 12b, 19a (*MhN*).

Such special treatment is to be expected given that, according to BT *Shabbat* 33b (a passage on which the following story is based), Rabbi Pinḥas was the son-in-law of Rabbi Shim'on. However, the *Zohar* elevates Pinḥas further by transforming him into Rabbi Shim'on's father-in-law. This new role could be the result of a simple mistake: confusing חתן (*ḥatan*), "son-in-law," and חותן (*ḥoten*), "father-in-law." However, the switch may also be deliberate, another instance of interchanging father and son (see above, notes 300 and 325). The fantastic or contrived contexts in which the son-in-law appears as the father-in-law support this possibility. In the following lines, Rabbi Reḥumai alludes cryptically to the relationship; Rabbi El'azar meets Pinḥas on the road and quotes an appropriate verse (3:36a); Rabbi Shim'on quotes another verse to his son, El'azar, and interprets it as referring to El'azar's mother, Pinḥas's daughter (3:240b, on the Torah portion *Pinḥas*); the prophet Elijah appears and tells Rabbi Shim'on: "Today for your sake, your father-in-law, Rabbi Pinḥas son of Ya'ir, has been crowned with fifty crowns!" (3:144b [*IR*]). In 3:200b–202a, the relationship is given narrative substance: Rabbi Pinḥas is on his way to see his sick daughter, the wife of Rabbi Shim'on (cf. 3:64a). Yet this setting is provided only to highlight the fabricated relationship and set the tone for a fantastic tale. Pinḥas's daughter never appears in the story.

567. **Rabbi Reḥumai** One of the main characters in *Sefer ha-Bahir.*

568. **Lake Ginnosar** The Sea of Galilee, Lake Kinneret.

569. **He** Rabbi Reḥumai.

570. **transcended...** אסתלקו (*Istallaqu*), "had ascended, departed, withdrawn." His eyes had ceased seeing in the normal way.

He said to Rabbi Pinḥas, "Truly I have heard that our Companion Yoḥai has a pearl, a precious stone.[571] I gazed at the light of that pearl, issuing like the radiance of the sun from its sheath, illuminating the entire world.[572] That light extends from heaven to earth, illumining the entire world until the Ancient of Days[573] comes and sits fittingly upon the throne.[574] That light is contained totally in your house,[575] and from the light contained in your house emanates a fine, threadlike ray, radiating, illumining the entire world.[576] Happy is your share! Go, my son, go out after that pearl illuminating the world, for the time is ripe."

He left him[577] and was about to board a boat along with two other men, when he saw two birds come flying over the lake.[578] He shouted to them, "Birds, birds, flying over the lake! Have you seen the site of the son of Yoḥai?"

He paused a while, and then said, "Birds, birds, go and bring me a reply!" They flew off.

They embarked, setting off across the lake.[579] Before he had disembarked, those birds returned, and in the mouth of one of them was a note on which was written: "The son of Yoḥai has emerged from the cave along with his son Rabbi El'azar."[580]

He went to him and found him transfigured, his body full of moldy sores.[581] He wept [11b] together with him and said, "Alas, that I see you so!"

571. **a pearl, a precious stone** The son of Yoḥai: Rabbi Shim'on. Together with his son, Rabbi El'azar, Rabbi Shim'on hid from the Roman authorities in a cave for thirteen years.

See *Bereshit Rabbah* 79:6; *Qohelet Rabbah* on 10:9; BT *Shabbat* 33b; JT *Shevi'it* 9:1, 38d; *Pesiqta de-Rav Kahana* 11:16; *Midrash Tehillim* 17:13; *ZH* 59c–60a; *Zohar* 1:216b.

On the tradition that the *Zohar* was composed in this cave, see Tishby, *Wisdom of the Zohar,* 1:13; Huss, "Hofa'ato shel Sefer ha-Zohar," 528.

572. **issuing...** Alluding to Rabbi Shim'on's emergence from the cave.

573. **Ancient of Days** עתיק יומין (*Attiq yomin*). See Daniel 7:9: *The Ancient of Days sits, the hair on His head like clean fleece, His throne—flames of fire.* In the *Zohar,* this name designates *Keter,* the first, primordial *sefirah.*

574. **throne** The *sefirot* below *Keter.* Until then, the light of Rabbi Shim'on unifies the *sefirot.*

575. **contained totally in your house** According to the *Zohar,* Rabbi Shim'on is married to the daughter of Rabbi Pinḥas and thus contained in his house. See above, note 566; below, page 81.

576. **a fine, threadlike ray, radiating...** Rabbi El'azar, son of Rabbi Shim'on, is now "radiating" (נפיק לבר [*nafeiq le-var*], "coming out" of the cave).

577. **He left him** Rabbi Pinḥas left Rabbi Reḥumai.

578. **two birds...** See *ZH* 59c–60a, where a dove transmits a message from the Companions to Rabbi Shim'on in the cave and brings back his response to them. Cf. *Zohar* 2:6b; 3:201a–b; *Bereshit Rabbah* 79:6.

579. **They embarked...** Rabbi Pinḥas and his two companions.

580. **emerged from the cave...** The cave in which Rabbi Shim'on and his son hid themselves for thirteen years. See above, note 571.

581. **full of moldy sores** From living in the cave. See *Bereshit Rabbah* 79:6. Accord-

76

He replied, "Happy is my share that you see me so, for had you not seen me so, I would not be so."[582]

Rabbi Shim'on opened with the commandments of Torah, saying, "The commandments of Torah given by the blessed Holy One to Israel are all written in Torah in general terms.[583]

"*In the beginning God created* (Genesis 1:1). This is the first commandment of all, called *awe of YHVH,* which is called *beginning,* as is written: *The beginning of wisdom is awe of YHVH* (Psalms 111:10), *Awe of YHVH is the beginning of knowledge* (Proverbs 1:7). For this entity is named *beginning;* it is the gate through which one enters faith.[584] The entire world is based upon this commandment.[585]

"Awe branches in three directions, two of which are not fittingly rooted, one of which is essence[586] of awe. There is the person who fears the blessed Holy One so that his children may live and not die, or who fears physical or material punishment. Because of this he fears Him constantly, but his awe is not focused on the blessed Holy One.[587]

"Then there is the person who fears the blessed Holy One because he is afraid of the punishment of the other world and the punishment of Hell. Neither of these is the essential root of awe.

"The essence of awe is that a person be in awe of his Lord because He is immense and sovereign—essence and root of all worlds—before whom every-

77

ing to BT *Shabbat* 33b, "A miracle occurred: A carob tree and a spring of water were created for them [Rabbi Shim'on and Rabbi El'azar]. They took off their clothes and sat up to their necks in the sand. All day long they studied; when it was time to pray they put on their clothes, prayed, and then took them off again, so as not to wear them out."

582. **I would not be so** I would not have attained the high level that I attained in the cave. See BT *Shabbat* 33b. According to *ZH* 59c, Elijah taught Rabbi Shim'on and Rabbi El'azar in the cave twice daily.

583. **in general terms** The commandments are alluded to in the opening verses of Genesis and spelled out later in the Torah. On the following list of fourteen commandments, see Gottlieb, *Meḥqarim,* 215, n. 1; Wolfson, introduction to *Sefer ha-Rimmon,* by Moses de León, 32–33.

584. **gate...** *Shekhinah* is the gate through which one enters the divine realm of faith. She is also called *awe,* since She is associated with the *sefirah* of *Din,* Judgment. See *Zohar* 1:7b; Moses de León, *Sefer ha-Rimmon,* 24–32.

585. **The entire world is based...** The letter ב (*bet*) of בראשית (*Be-reshit*), *In the beginning,* means not only "in," but also "with." Rabbi Shim'on reads the verse: *With beginning* (awe), *God created the heavens and the earth.*

586. **essence** עקרא (*Iqqara*), "Root, essence." On the distinction between different types of awe, see Baḥya ibn Paquda, *Ḥovot ha-Levavot* 10:6; Tishby, *Wisdom of the Zohar,* 3:975–989.

587. **his awe is not focused...** See Moses de León, *Sefer ha-Rimmon,* 31; *TZ* 33, 77a; *Zohar* 2:33b.

thing is considered as nothing, as is said: *All the inhabitants of the earth are considered as nothing* (Daniel 4:32). One should direct his desire to the site called Awe."[588]

Rabbi Shim'on wept and exclaimed, "Woe is me if I speak! Woe is me if I do not speak! If I speak, the wicked will know how to serve their Lord. If I do not speak, the Companions will be deprived of this word."[589]

"At the site where holy awe dwells, below is evil awe, beating, striking, accusing.[590] It is a lash to whip the wicked. Whoever fears the punishment of flogging and accusation, as mentioned—that awe called *awe of YHVH leading to life* (Proverbs 19:23)[591] does not hover over him. Who then hovers over him? Evil awe. So that lash deploys above him—evil awe, not *awe of YHVH*.[592]

"So the site called *awe of YHVH* is called *beginning*, and therefore this commandment is included here.[593] This is the root and foundation of all the other commandments in Torah. Whoever adheres to awe adheres to all; one who does not, does not keep the commandments of Torah, for this is the gate to all.

"So it is written: בראשית (*Be-reshit*), *Because of beginning*, which is awe, *God created heaven and earth*.[594] Whoever violates this violates the commandments

78

588. **site called Awe** *Shekhinah,* the focus of genuine devotion.

589. **Woe is me if I speak!...** See BT *Bava Batra* 89b, where Rabbi Yoḥanan son of Zakkai says, concerning the details of illegal practices, "Woe is me if I say it! Woe is me if I do not say it! If I say it, the deceivers will learn. If I do not say it, the deceivers will say, 'Scholars are not expert in our practices.'"

See M *Kelim* 17:16; *Tosefta, Kelim (Bava Metsi'a)* 7:9; *Zohar* 2:100b, 257b (*Heikh*); and *Zohar* 3:74b: "Rabbi Shim'on clapped his hands and wept. He exclaimed, 'Woe is me if I speak and reveal the secret! Woe is me if I do not speak, for the Companions will be deprived of the word.'" See 3:127b (*IR*): "Rabbi Shim'on sat down. He wept and exclaimed, 'Woe is me if I reveal! Woe is me if I do not reveal!'"

Given the rabbinic and kabbalistic emphasis on repentance, it seems startling that Rabbi Shim'on would not want the wicked to learn how to serve God, but apparently he feels that in certain cases they are irredeemable and must be punished; cf. Isaiah 6:9–10.

OY and Galante suggest that Rabbi Shim'on doesn't want the wicked to discover this secret because if they then persist in sinning willfully, they would be even more evil. According to *KP,* Rabbi Shim'on fears that revealing the secret to the wicked would lead them to serve the demonic, "their lord."

See also *Nefesh David;* Zeitlin, "*Haqdamat Sefer ha-Zohar*"; *Sullam;* Tishby, *Wisdom of the Zohar,* 3:1065; *YN; MmD.*

590. **below is evil awe...** Below *Shekhinah,* holy awe, lies the demonic realm, *Sitra Aḥra* ("the Other Side"), who accuses human sinners and is then empowered to punish them. See *TZ* 30, 73a; 33, 76b–77a.

591. **that awe called** *awe of YHVH...* *Shekhinah,* who dwells only with those whose awe is genuine.

592. **Who then hovers over him?...** By fearing punishment, one attracts the demonic lash.

593. **this commandment is included here** The commandment of awe is indicated in the opening word of the Torah.

594. בראשית (*Be-reshit*), *Because of beginning,* which is awe...* The letter ב (*bet*)

of Torah, and his punishment is the evil lash. This is: *The earth was chaos and void, with darkness over the face of the abyss, and the wind of God* (Genesis 1:2). These are four types of punishment by which the wicked are punished.[595] *Chaos* is strangulation, as is written: *a line of chaos* (Isaiah 34:11),[596] *a measuring rope* (Zechariah 2:5).[597] *Void* is stoning, stones sunk in the immense abyss[598] for punishing the wicked. *Darkness* is burning, as is written: *When you heard the voice from the midst of the darkness* (Deuteronomy 5:20),[599] *and the mountain was ablaze with fire to the heart of heaven, darkness* (ibid. 4:11).[600] This is the fierce fire licking the heads of the wicked to consume them.[601] *And the wind* is death by sword, *a stormy wind* (Ezekiel 1:4), a sharp sword flashing in it, as is said: *the flaming, ever-turning sword* (Genesis 3:24), called *wind*.[602]

"Such is the punishment awaiting one who violates the commandments of Torah. It is written after awe, *beginning,* sum of all.[603] Then follow the other commandments of Torah.

"The second commandment: one to which the commandment of awe is linked, never departing. This is love, loving one's Lord consummately.[604] What is consummate love? Abounding love,[605] as is written: *Walk in My presence and*

79

---

of בראשית (*Be-reshit*), usually translated "in," can also mean "because of."

595. **four types of punishment . . .** According to M *Sanhedrin* 7:1, there are four types of capital punishment: stoning, burning, beheading, and strangulation.

596. **line of chaos** The verse reads: *He will stretch over it a line of chaos and plummet-stones of void.* See BT *Ḥagigah* 12a: "Chaos is a green line encompassing the whole world, from which darkness issued." Cf. Moses de León, *Or Zaru'a,* 268.

597. **measuring rope** The full verse reads: *I raised my eyes and looked, and behold: a man with a measuring rope in his hand.* Together, the two prophetic verses indicate that *chaos* is a line, which is a rope—implying strangulation.

598. **Void is stoning, stones sunk . . .** See BT *Ḥagigah* 12a: "*Void*—the slimy stones sunk in the abyss, from which water issues, as is said: *He will stretch over it a line of chaos and plummet-stones of void.*" The immense abyss is the home of demonic powers.

599. **When you heard the voice from the midst of the darkness** The verse con-

tinues: *while the mountain was ablaze with fire.*

600. **the mountain was ablaze . . . heaven . . .** The verse concludes: *darkness, cloud, and fog.*

601. **fierce fire . . .** See BT *Ḥagigah* 13b: "Where does the river of fire pour forth? Rabbi Zutra son of Toviah said in the name of Rav, 'Upon the heads of the wicked in Hell.'" Cf. *Zohar* 1:16a; and Maimonides, *Guide of the Perplexed* 2:30: "The elemental fire was designated by this term [*darkness*] because it is not luminous, but only transparent."

602. **called wind** The sword of punishment swishes through the air.

603. **It is written after awe, *beginning* . . .** The verse alluding to the various types of punishment (Genesis 1:2) follows the verse *In the beginning . . .,* which alludes to awe, the all-inclusive commandment.

604. **loving one's Lord consummately** See Moses de León, *Sefer ha-Rimmon,* 44–45.

605. **Abounding love** Hebrew, אהבה רבה (*ahavah rabbah*), "great love," a designation of *Ḥesed,* while *Shekhinah* is אהבה

be wholehearted (Genesis 17:1)—consummate in love.[606] This is what is written: *God said, 'Let there be light'* (ibid. 1:3)—consummate love, called 'abounding love.'[607] Here is the commandment to love one's Lord fittingly."

Rabbi El'azar said, "Father, I have heard something about consummation of love."

He replied, "Speak, my son, in the presence of Rabbi Pinḥas, for he stands on this rung."[608]

Rabbi El'azar said, "Abounding love is consummate love, consummate in two aspects. Unless embracing both, it is not [12a] consummate fittingly. So we have learned: Love—love of the blessed Holy One—branches in two directions.[609] There is the person who loves Him because he has wealth, longevity, children surrounding him; he dominates his enemies, his paths are paved. Because of this he loves Him. If things were overturned—the blessed Holy One turning the wheel of strict judgment against him—then he would hate Him, not love Him at all. So this love is not rooted.[610]

"The love called consummate abides both aspects, whether judgment or favor.[611] The ripening of the way is to love one's Lord as we have learned: 'even if He plucks your soul.'[612] Such love is consummate, embracing both

זוטא (ahavah zuta), "small love." See *Zohar* 2:254b; *ZH* 52b.

606. *be wholehearted*—consummate in love   By fulfilling this command, Abraham attained the rung of Ḥesed ("Love").

607. *Let there be light...*   The primordial light of Creation is Ḥesed (*Zohar* 1:16b), so the commandment of love is alluded to in the phrase *Let there be light*, following the allusion to the commandment of awe in the first verse (see above, page 77).

608. **Pinḥas...stands on this rung**   Rabbi Pinḥas has attained the *sefirah* of Ḥesed ("Love"). See *Zohar* 3:62a, where Rabbi Shim'on describes him as "crown of Ḥesed, supernal head." Cf. 3:201a, 240b, where he is called חסידא (hasida), "devotee, saint, pious one, lover of God."

Mishnah *Sotah* 9:15 attributes to Rabbi Pinḥas the following teaching: "Zeal leads to cleanliness, cleanliness leads to purity, purity leads to restraint, restraint leads to holiness, holiness leads to humility, humility leads to fear of sin, fear of sin leads to *hasidut* ("love, devotion"), *hasidut* leads to Holy Spirit, Holy

Spirit leads to resurrection of the dead, and resurrection of the dead comes through Elijah, remembered for good."

The order of stages varies; see JT *Shabbat* 1:3, 3c; *Sheqalim* 3:3, 47c; *Shir ha-Shirim Rabbah* 1:9 (on 1:1); and BT *Avodah Zarah* 20b, where Rabbi Pinḥas concludes that "*hasidut* is greater than any of these."

609. **love of the blessed Holy One—branches in two directions**   On the various types of love of God, see Baḥya ibn Paquda, *Ḥovot ha-Levavot* 10:2.

610. **this love is not rooted**   The line can also be rendered: "this love is not love, for it is based on something." See M *Avot* 5:16: "Any love dependent on something—if that thing ceases, love ceases. Love not dependent on anything never ceases." Cf. Moses de León, *Sefer ha-Rimmon*, 44.

611. **whether judgment or favor**   Consummate love of God endures whatever comes.

612. **'even if He plucks your soul'**   See BT *Berakhot* 61b: "Rabbi Akiva said, '[*You shall love YHVH your God*] *with all your soul*

aspects. So the light of the act of Creation radiated and was then hidden away.[613] When it was hidden, severe Judgment flashed,[614] and two aspects merged, consummating love fittingly."[615]

Rabbi Shim'on, his father, took hold of him and kissed him.

Rabbi Pinḥas came and kissed him, then blessed him, saying, "The blessed Holy One certainly sent me here. This is the fine ray of light I was told is contained in my house, about to illumine the entire world."[616]

Rabbi El'azar said, "Awe should certainly not be forgotten in any of the commandments and should cleave especially to this commandment. How does it cleave? In one aspect, love is gracious—as explained—bestowing wealth, goodness, long life, children, and sustenance. So one should arouse awe, fearing the sway of sin. Therefore it is written: *Happy is one who always fears* (Proverbs 28:14), for awe is embraced by love.

"Similarly on the other side—of severe Judgment[617]—one should arouse awe. When one sees severe Judgment befalling him, he should then arouse awe and

(Deuteronomy 6:5)—even if He plucks your soul.'...When Rabbi Akiva was brought out to be executed [by the Romans], it was the time for reciting the *Shema*. While they were combing his flesh with iron combs, he accepted upon himself the Kingdom of Heaven [by reciting the *Shema*]. His disciples asked him, 'Our teacher, even this far?' He replied, 'All my days I have been troubled by this verse: *with all your soul,* [which I interpret] "even if He plucks your soul." I said, "When will I have the opportunity to fulfill this?" Now that I have the opportunity, shall I not fulfill it?' He prolonged the word אחד (eḥad), *one* [in the verse: *Hear O Israel! YHVH is our God, YHVH is one* (Deuteronomy 6:4)] until his soul departed with *one*. A voice echoed from heaven: 'Happy are you, Akiva, whose soul has departed with *one*!'"

See M *Berakhot* 9:5; *Sifrei*, Deuteronomy 32; *Zohar* 3:68a; *TZ, Haqdamah,* 10b; Moses de León, *Sefer ha-Rimmon,* 43–44.

613. **light...radiated and was then hidden away** The primordial light of the first day of Creation was hidden away. See BT *Ḥagigah* 12a: "Rabbi El'azar said, 'With the light created by the blessed Holy One on the first day, one could gaze and see from one end of the universe to the other. When the

blessed Holy One foresaw the corrupt deeds of the generation of the Flood and the generation of the Dispersion [the generation of the Tower of Babel], He immediately hid it from them, as is written: *The light of the wicked is withheld* (Job 38:15). For whom did He hide it? For the righteous in the time to come.'"

See *Bereshit Rabbah* 3:6; 41:3; *Shemot Rabbah* 35:1; *Tanḥuma, Shemini* 9; *Bahir* 97–98 (147); *Zohar* 1:31b–32a, 45b–46a, 47a; 2:127a, 148b–149a, 220a–b; 3:88a, 173b.

614. **severe Judgment flashed** The primordial light symbolizes *Ḥesed,* while its concealment symbolizes the next stage of emanation, *Gevurah,* or *Din* ("Judgment").

615. **two aspects merged...** The *sefirah* of *Tif'eret,* also known as רחמים (Raḥamim), Compassion, represents the blending of *Ḥesed* and *Din.* Complete love must include both extremes: grace and judgment.

616. **This is the fine ray of light I was told...** Rabbi Reḥumai had told Rabbi Pinḥas about this ray of light, which he now realizes is his grandson, Rabbi El'azar, who emerged from the cave with Rabbi Shim'on (see above, pages 75–76).

617. **on the other side—of severe Judgment** The other aspect of love, mediated

fear his Lord fittingly, not hardening his heart. So it is written: *But one who hardens his heart falls into evil* (ibid.)—into that other side called *evil*.[618]

"So awe is linked to both aspects,[619] embraced by them. This is fittingly consummate love."

"The third commandment:[620] to realize that God exists[621]—vast and controlling the world—and to unify Him fittingly each day in those six supernal directions,[622] unifying them through the six words of שמע ישראל (*Shema Yisra'el*), *Hear, O Israel!* (Deuteronomy 6:4),[623] directing one's desire above along with them.[624]

"So one should prolong אחד (*eḥad*), *one,* to the length of six words, as is written: *Let the waters under heaven be gathered to one place* (Genesis 1:9)—let the rungs beneath heaven be gathered together to unite with it, to be fittingly

by Judgment. "The other side" (סטרא אחרא [*sitra aḥra*]) alludes to the demonic realm, mentioned several lines later. The *Zohar* plays with various senses of this phrase.

618. **that other side . . .** The other side is the realm of evil. To avoid falling into its clutches, one should arouse awe when harsh Judgment arrives.

619. **both aspects** Both aspects of love: grace (good fortune) and judgment (suffering). Awe is essential in either case to consummate love.

620. **third commandment** Rabbi Shim-'on continues, linking the third commandment with the third day of Creation, on which God said: *Let the waters under heaven be gathered to one place* (Genesis 1:9).

621. **to realize that God exists** See Maimonides, *Mishneh Torah, Hilkhot Yesodei ha-Torah* 1:1: "The ultimate foundation and pillar of wisdom is to realize that there is a first existent who brings every existent into existence. Every existent in heaven and earth and what is between has come into existence solely out of His genuine existence."

While for Maimonides, the primal commandment is to realize that God exists, for the *Zohar*, awe and love of God take precedence.

622. **six supernal directions** See BT *Berakhot* 13b, in the name of Rabbi Ḥiyya son

of Abba: "Once you have enthroned Him above and below and in the four directions of heaven, you need do nothing more." These six directions (above, below, north, south, east, and west) symbolize the six *sefirot* from *Ḥesed* through *Yesod,* which join in preparation for the union with *Shekhinah.*

See *Sefer Yetsirah* 1:13; *Zohar* 1:158a; 2:216b; *Shulḥan Arukh, Oraḥ Ḥayyim* 61:6.

623. **through the six words . . .** The first line of the *Shema* contains six words in Hebrew: שמע ישראל יהוה אלהינו יהוה אחד (*Shema Yisra'el YHVH Eloheinu YHVH eḥad*), *Hear O Israel! YHVH is our God, YHVH is one.* By reciting these words with כונה (*kavvanah*), "intention," one unifies the corresponding six *sefirot.*

See Tishby, *Wisdom of the Zohar,* 3:971–74. Cf. BT *Berakhot* 13b: "Our Rabbis taught: '*Hear O Israel! YHVH is our God, YHVH is one.* Until here *kavvanah* is required.'"

624. **directing one's desire above along with them** While reciting the first six words, one should focus on the six corresponding *sefirot,* but one should then aim toward the three highest *sefirot* (*Keter, Ḥokhmah,* and *Binah*) and ultimately to that which is beyond all words: *Ein Sof.* Here lies the source and goal of the lower *sefirot,* and so one's desire ascends "along with them." See *Zohar* 2:216b.

complete in six directions.[625] Yet, with that unity one should bind awe,[626] prolonging the ד (dalet) of אחד (eḥad), one, since the ד (dalet) of אחד (eḥad) is large, as is written: *Let the dry land appear* (ibid.)—let ד (dalet), who is *dry land, appear* and be bound in that union.[627] After She is bound there above, one should bind Her below with Her forces, in six other directions below: ברוך שם כבוד מלכותו לעולם ועד (*Barukh shem kevod malkhuto le-olam va-ed*), Blessed be the name of His glorious kingdom forever and ever, comprising six other words of unification.[628] Then, what was *dry land* is transformed into *earth*, generating fruit, verdure, planting trees.[629] This corresponds to what is written: *God called the dry land Earth* (ibid., 10)—through that unification below, ארעא (*ar'a*), *Earth*, fittingly consummates רעוא (*ra'ava*), desire.[630] So, *it was good, it was good* (ibid. 1:10, 12), twice:[631] one for the unification above, one for the unification below. Once It[632] was unified in both aspects, from then on: *Let the*

---

625. **one should prolong אחד (eḥad), one . . . to be fittingly complete . . .** The word אחד (eḥad), one, completes the first line of the *Shema*. See BT *Berakhot* 13b: "It has been taught: Symmachus says, 'Whoever prolongs the word אחד (eḥad), one, has his days and years prolonged.' . . . Rabbi Yirmeyah was sitting in the presence of Rabbi Ḥiyya son of Abba. [Rabbi Ḥiyya] saw that he was prolonging [the word eḥad] greatly. He said to him, 'Once you have declared Him king over what is above and below and in the four directions of heaven, you need do nothing more.'"

Here Rabbi Shim'on teaches that by prolonging eḥad to the length of all six words of the first line of the *Shema*, one fulfills the mystical meaning of Genesis 1:9: *Let the waters* (the sefirot) *under heaven* (around Tif'eret) *be gathered to one place* (Yesod), thus forming a union of six directions. Cf. *Zohar* 1:18a–b.

626. **awe** *Shekhinah*. See above, page 77.

627. **prolonging the ד (dalet) of אחד (eḥad), one . . .** The ד (dalet) is the final letter of אחד (eḥad). According to Rabbi Aḥa son of Ya'akov (BT *Berakhot* 13b), one should prolong this letter specifically, and in the Torah scroll it is written large. See *Zohar* 2:160b; 3:236b.

In the *Zohar*, ד (dalet) symbolizes *Shekhinah*, who is called both דלה (dallah), "poor," and *dry land* before She receives the flow of emanation from the higher sefirot.

628. **with Her forces, in six other directions . . .** *Shekhinah* should be united with Her retinue of angels, who parallel the six sefirot above. The six Hebrew words of the second line of the *Shema*, ברוך שם כבוד מלכותו לעולם ועד (*Barukh shem kevod malkhuto le-olam va-ed*), "Blessed be the name of His glorious kingdom forever and ever," allude to these angels, the six other directions below, accompanying *Shekhinah*, who is known as *Malkhut* ("Kingdom").

See BT *Pesaḥim* 56a; *Zohar* 1:18b; 2:139b; 3:264a.

629. **dry land is transformed into earth . . .** *Shekhinah* becomes fertile, engendering new life.

630. **ארעא (ar'a), Earth fittingly consummates רעוא (ra'ava), desire** Literally, "*Earth* is fittingly consummate favor [or: will, desire]." See *Bereshit Rabbah* 5:8: "*God called the dry land Earth.* Why ארץ (erets), *Earth*? Because she wanted to fulfill רצונו (retsono), His will." The Aramaic רעוא (ra'ava) and Hebrew רצון (ratson) both mean "will, favor, desire."

631. **it was good, it was good, twice** The phrase *God saw that it was good* appears twice in the account of the third day of Creation.

632. **It** *Shekhinah*.

83

earth sprout vegetation (ibid., 11)[633]—arrayed to generate fruit and verdure fittingly.

"The fourth commandment:[634] to realize that יהוה (YHVH) is האלהים (*ha-Elohim*), God,[635] as is said: *Know today and take to heart that* יהוה (YHVH) *is* האלהים (*ha-Elohim*), *God* (Deuteronomy 4:39). To include the name אלהים (*Elohim*) in the name יהוה (YHVH), realizing they are one, indivisible. This is the mystery written: *Let there be* מארת (*me'orot*), *lights, in the expanse of heaven to shine upon earth* (Genesis 1:14–15), that the two names be one, with absolutely no division—that מארת (*me'orot*), *lights,* spelled deficiently, merge in the name of *heaven:*[636] one together and indivisible, black light with white light,[637] indivisible, and all is one. [12b] This is the white cloud of day and the cloud of fire in the night,[638] as they have said: 'Quality of day and quality of night'[639]— to be arrayed by each other to shine, as is said: *to shine upon earth.*

84

633. **Let the earth sprout vegetation** The verse continues: *—seed-bearing plants, fruit trees of every kind on earth bearing fruit with the seed in it.*

634. **fourth commandment** Linked with the fourth day of Creation, on which God said *Let there be lights in the expanse of heaven* (Genesis 1:14).

635. יהוה **(YHVH) is** האלהים **(*ha-Elohim*), God** Rabbi Shim'on is alluding to the first line of the *Shema,* discussed above, which contains both these names and concludes with the word *one.* In rabbinic literature the two names represent the divine qualities of compassion and justice, respectively. See *Sifrei,* Deuteronomy 26; *Bereshit Rabbah* 12:15; 33:3; and 13:3, where יהוה אלהים (*YHVH Elohim*) is called "a complete name."

In Kabbalah the two names often designate *Tif'eret* and *Shekhinah,* who are essentially one and should not be separated. See *Zohar* 1:4a, 20a, 48b, 91a; 2:161a, 229a; 3:138b (*IR*); *ZH* 70d (*ShS*).

636. מארת **(*me'orot*)...deficiently...** In Genesis 1:14, the word מארת (*me'orot*) is written without *vavs,* the vowel letters. This deficient spelling is interpreted as alluding to *Shekhinah,* the moon, who is incomplete without Her partner, *Tif'eret,* sun or heaven.

See Proverbs 3:33; JT *Ta'anit* 4:4, 68b; *Pesiqta de-Rav Kahana* 5:1; *Soferim* 17:4; Rashi and *Minḥat Shai* on Genesis 1:14; *Zohar* 1:1a, 19b, 33b.

On the diminution of the moon, see BT *Ḥullin* 60b: "Rabbi Shim'on son of Pazzi pointed out a contradiction. 'It is written: *God made the two great lights* (Genesis 1:16), and it is written: *the greater light...and the lesser light* (ibid.). The moon said before the blessed Holy One, "Master of the Universe! Can two kings possibly wear one crown?" He answered, "Go, diminish yourself!"...'"

637. **black light with white light** *Shekhinah* and *Tif'eret,* also known, respectively, as "the speculum that does not shine" and "the speculum that shines." See *Zohar* 1:51a, 77b, 83b. On "speculum," see below, p. 209, n. 824.

638. **white cloud of day...** See Exodus 13:21: *YHVH walks before them in a pillar of cloud by day, to guide them along the way, and in a pillar of fire by night, to give them light.* The white cloud symbolizes *Tif'eret,* often associated with the day; the cloud of fire, *Shekhinah,* associated with the night.

639. **Quality of day...of night** In BT *Berakhot* 11b, Rava and Abbaye indicate that light is mentioned in the evening prayers, and darkness in the morning prayers, "in

"This is the sin of the primordial serpent: he joined below and it separated above.[640] So he caused what he caused to the world. For one should separate below and join above. The black light should be united above in a single bond, then united with Her forces of unification[641] and separated from the evil side.

"Nevertheless one should realize that אלהים יהוה (*Elohim YHVH*) is entirely one, indivisible. יהוה (*YHVH*) *is* האלהים (*ha-Elohim*). Once one realizes all is one and does not impose division, even that Other Side will disappear from the world, not be drawn below.[642]

"This is the mystery written: *Let them be* מאורות (*me'orot*), *lights* (ibid., 15). The shell rises in the wake of the kernel.[643] The kernel is אור (*or*), light; the other side, מות (*mavet*), death. אור (*Or*) in letters joined together, מות (*mavet*) in separation.[644] When this אור (*or*) disappears from there, the letters of separation join together.[645] From these letters Eve began, bringing evil upon the world, as is written: ותרא האשה (*Va-tere ha-ishshah*), *The woman saw* (ibid. 3:6),[646] reversing the letters. מ"ו (*Mem, vav*) were left; they went and took the letter ת (*tav*) along with them, inflicting death upon the world, as is written: ותרא (*Va-tere*), *She saw*."[647]

85

order to mention the quality of day during the night and the quality of night during the day."

See *Zohar* 1:120b, 259a (*Hash*); 2:162a; 3:260b, 264a.

640. **he joined below...** The serpent united the demonic powers below, thereby ruining the divine harmony above. Alternatively, he united *Shekhinah* with the demonic powers. On the nature of the sin in the Garden of Eden, see *Zohar* 1:35b–36b, 51a–53b, 221a–b; Scholem, *Major Trends*, 231–32, 236, 404–5, n. 105; Tishby, *Wisdom of the Zohar*, 1:373–76.

641. **Her forces of unification** The angels beneath *Shekhinah* with whom She is joined through the unification of the second line of the *Shema*. See above, page 83.

642. **that Other Side...** *Sitra Aḥra*, "The Other Side," the demonic realm.

643. **The shell rises in the wake of the kernel** The demonic follows the lead of the holy.

644. אור (*Or*) **in letters joined together,** מות (*mavet*) **in separation** The word מאורות (*me'orot*), *lights*, contains the letters of the word אור (*or*), "light," in proper sequence,

while the letters of the word מות (*mavet*), "death," are interrupted. Whereas in Genesis 1:14 מארת (*me'orot*) is written without either ו (*vav*), in this next verse it is spelled מאורות, with one ו (*vav*), and Rabbi Shim'on reads it as if it contained two *vavs*.

645. **letters of separation...** The letters of the word מות (*mavet*), "death," which until now had been separated. The command *Let them be* מאורות (*me'orot*), *lights*, was intended to ensure that the letters of death remain apart.

646. ותרא האשה (***Va-tere ha-ishshah***), *The woman saw* The verse continues: *that the tree was good for eating and a delight to the eyes, and that the tree was desirable to contemplate. She took of its fruit and ate, and also gave to her husband beside her, and he ate.*

647. **reversing the letters...** The verse describing Eve's sin opens with the word ותרא (*va-tere*), *she saw*. This word contains the letters of the word אור (*or*), but now out of order and interrupted by the ת (*tav*), whereas in the word מאורות (*me'orot*) they appeared in correct sequence. Through her sin, Eve reversed the letters. Furthermore she removed the letters of the word ותרא

Rabbi El'azar said, "Father, I have learned that מ (mem) was left alone.[648] ו (Vav), who is always life, was transformed,[649] then went and took ת (tav), as is written: ותקח...ותתן (Va-tiqqaḥ...va-titten), She took...and she gave (ibid.).[650] This word[651] was completed, the letters joined."

He said to him, "Blessed are you, my son! We have established this word."

"The fifth commandment. It is written: *Let the waters swarm with a swarm of living souls* (Genesis 1:20).[652] This verse contains three commandments: to study Torah, to be fruitful and multiply, and to circumcise on the eighth day, removing the foreskin.[653]

"To study and contemplate Torah, expanding her every day,[654] not letting her be forgotten, as is written: *Let the waters swarm*—Torah.[655] One should engage in her every day—enhancing one's soul and spirit. For when a person studies Torah he is adorned with another holy soul,[656] as is written: *with a swarm of*

86

(va-tere) from the word מאורות (me'orot), which was left with only two letters: מ"ו (mem, vav). These two letters joined together with the letter ת (tav) of ותרא (va-tere), which interrupts the disordered letters of the word אור (or). The combination of מ"ו (mem, vav) and ת (tav) formed the word מות (mavet), "death." See Genesis 2:17.

648. מ (*mem*) was left alone Rabbi El'azar insists on reading the word מאורת (me'orot) exactly as it is spelled in Genesis 1:15, with one ו (vav). Without the letters of the word ותרא (va-tere), She saw, only the מ (mem) is left.

649. ו (*Vav*), who is always life, was transformed The letter ו (vav), whose numerical value is six, symbolizes Tif'eret, the Tree of Life, together with the five sefirot surrounding Him (Ḥesed to Yesod). See Zohar 1:33b, 241b; 2:137a; 3:176b. Sin changes this letter from a symbol of life to a component of death, as Rabbi El'azar goes on to explain. The word "transformed" (אתהפכת [ithappakhat]) may allude to the grammatical term ו' המהפכת (vav ha-mehappekhet), "the conversive [or: transformative] vav," which transforms the imperfect tense to the perfect, as in the two examples that follow.

650. went and took ת (*tav*)...*She took ...and she gave* The verse reads: She took

of its fruit and ate, and she gave also to her husband beside her, and he ate. Rabbi El'azar indicates that the first two letters of the verbs ותקח (va-tiqqaḥ), she took, and ותתן (va-titten), she gave, are ו (vav) and ת (tav). Once these two letters joined, they needed only the letter מ (mem) to produce מות (mavet), "death." See Zohar 3:237a.

651. This word The word מות (mavet), "death."

652. fifth commandment...*Let the waters swarm*... The verse continues: *and let birds fly above the earth.* The fifth commandment is linked with the fifth day of Creation, on which God gave the command recorded here.

653. on the eighth day... A male infant is circumcised normally on the eighth day.

654. expanding her... Expanding one's understanding of Torah and thereby expanding Torah herself.

655. *Let the waters swarm—Torah* Torah is often compared to water. See BT *Bava Qamma* 82a: "Those who interpret metaphorically said, 'Water means solely Torah, as is said: *Ho, all who thirst, come for water* (Isaiah 55:1).'" Cf. *Ta'anit* 7a; *Bereshit Rabbah* 54:1; Zohar 2:60a.

656. another holy soul If one engages in Torah and purifies oneself, then this higher

נפש חיה (*nefesh ḥayyah*)—a נפש (*nefesh*), *soul,* of that holy חיה (*ḥayyah*), *living being.*[657] For when a person does not study Torah, he has no holy soul;[658] supernal holiness does not rest upon him. When he is engaged with Torah, through his murmuring[659] he attains that *living soul,* becoming like the holy angels, as is written: *Bless YHVH, O His angels* (Psalms 103:20)—those engaged in Torah, called *His angels* on earth.[660] This is what is written: *and let birds fly above the earth* (Genesis, ibid.),[661] referring to this world.[662] Regarding that world, we have learned that the blessed Holy One intends to provide them with wings like eagles to roam throughout the world, as is written: *They who await YHVH shall renew their strength; they shall mount up with wings as eagles* (Isaiah 40:31).[663] This is what is written: [*Let the waters swarm with a swarm of living souls*] *and let birds fly above the earth*—Torah, called water,[664] let it *swarm* and generate the movement of a *living soul,* drawing her down from the site of the *living being,* as explained. Concerning this David declared, *Create in me a pure heart, O God,* to study Torah, and then, *renew in me a steadfast spirit* (Psalms 51:12).[665]

87

"The sixth commandment: to be fruitful and multiply. For whoever engages in this causes that river to flow constantly, its waters never ceasing, and the sea is

soul (נשמתא [*nishmeta*], "soul") is added to the two lower levels: נפשא (*nafsha*), "soul," and רוחא (*ruḥa*), "spirit."

See *Zohar* 1:62a; 3:70b; *TZ* 45, 82b. On the various levels of soul, see Tishby, *Wisdom of the Zohar,* 2:677–722.

657. **that holy** חיה (*ḥayyah*)**, living being** *Shekhinah,* who gives birth to the highest level of soul. See Ezra of Gerona, *Peirush Shir ha-Shirim,* 508–9; *Zohar* 1:46b–47a, 242a; 2:48b, 177b–178a (*SdTs*); 3:46b.

Shekhinah, the *ḥayyah,* controls and sustains the holy *ḥayyot* ("living creatures, animals") who support the Chariot, the divine throne.

658. **no holy soul** The highest level.

659. **his murmuring** רחישו דרחיש (*Reḥishu de-raḥeish*). The root means "to move," here, to move the lips, whisper. *Targum Onqelos* employs the same root to translate *swarm* in Genesis 1:20; see *Zohar* 2:177b (*SdTs*).

660. **those engaged in Torah, called *His angels...*** The sages are compared to, or

described as, angels in BT *Nedarim* 20b; *Qiddushin* 72a.

661. **and let birds fly...** This verse is applied to the angels in *Bereshit Rabbah* 1:3. See *Devarim Rabbah* 8:2.

662. **referring to this world** To their reward in this world.

663. **to provide them wings...** See BT *Sanhedrin* 92a–b: "It was taught in the school of Elijah: The righteous whom the blessed Holy One will resurrect will...endure forever....The blessed Holy One will provide them wings like eagles, and they will fly above the water, as is written, *They who await YHVH shall renew their strength; they shall mount up with wings as eagles; they shall run and not grow weary; and they shall walk and not grow faint.*" See *Zohar* 3:163a.

664. **Torah, called water** See above, note 655.

665. **renew in me a steadfast spirit** Through the study of Torah, one attains a new soul.

filled from every direction.⁶⁶⁶ New souls are innovated, emerging from that tree,⁶⁶⁷ while above, numerous powers⁶⁶⁸ increase along with them, as is written: *Let the waters swarm with a swarm of living souls [and let birds fly above the earth]* (Genesis, ibid.). This is the holy sealed covenant, a river streaming forth,⁶⁶⁹ its waters swelling, swarming with swarms of souls for that living being.⁶⁷⁰ With those souls entering that living being, emerge many birds,⁶⁷¹ flying, soaring throughout the world. As a soul emerges into this world, the bird flying forth with this soul from that tree emerges with her.

"How many emerge with each and every soul? Two, one on the right and one on the left. If one is virtuous they protect him, as is written: *For He will order His angels [to guard you in all your ways]* (Psalms 91:11). If not, they accuse him."⁶⁷²

Rabbi Pinḥas said, [13a] "There are three who serve as the guardians of a human being, as is written: *If he has an angel over him, an advocate, one among a thousand, to vouch for his uprightness* (Job 33:23). *If he has an angel over him*—here is one. *An advocate*—two. *To vouch for his uprightness*—here is three."

Rabbi Shim'on said, "Five, since it is written further: *Then he is gracious to him and he says, ["Deliver him from descending to the Pit, I have found a ransom"]* (ibid., 24). *Then he is gracious to him*—one. *And he says*—two."

He replied, "Not so! Rather, *Then He is gracious to him*—the blessed Holy One alone, for no one but He has the authority."⁶⁷³

He said to him, "You have spoken well!

88

666. **causes that river...** By fulfilling the commandment *Be fruitful and multiply* (Genesis 1:28), one stimulates *Yesod*, the divine river and phallus, and ensures that it will flow into *Shekhinah*, the sea, transmitting to Her the emanation from the higher *sefirot*. See *Zohar* 1:186b; *TZ* 43, 82b.

667. **New souls...** The flow of emanation from *Yesod* to *Shekhinah* consummates the union of the divine male and female, engendering new souls, which emerge from the tree (*Tif'eret* or *Yesod*).

668. **powers** Angels, soon described also as birds.

669. **holy sealed covenant, a river** streaming forth *Yesod*, the divine phallus, is referred to as "the sign of covenant," site of circumcision. The flow of *Yesod* is symbolized by *the waters* of Genesis 1:20. The

phrase "a river streaming forth" derives from Daniel 7:10: *A river of fire streams forth before Him.*

670. **that living being** *Shekhinah.*

671. **many birds** Angels. See *Zohar* 1:34a, 46b. The verse is interpreted: *Let the waters (Yesod) swarm with a swarm of souls* (for the) *living being (Shekhinah), and let birds (angels) fly above the earth.*

672. **on the right...on the left...** Corresponding to *Ḥesed* ("Love") and *Din* ("Judgment"). Though the angels stem from opposite sides, they act in concert, according to each person's conduct.

See BT *Shabbat* 119b; *Ta'anit* 11a; *Zohar* 1:144b, 165b; 2:106b, 239a; *ZH* 47a; *ZH* 84d (*MhN, Rut*).

673. **has the authority** To grant a pardon. See *Zohar* 2:252a.

"Whoever avoids engendering new life diminishes, as it were, the image comprising all images,[674] causing the waters of that river to flow no more, damaging the holy covenant on all sides.[675] Concerning him it is written: *They will go out and stare at the corpses of the people who rebelled against Me* (Isaiah 66:24), indeed![676] This is for the body.[677] As for his soul, it does not pass through the curtain at all; it is banished from that world.[678]

"The seventh commandment: to circumcise on the eighth day, removing the filth of the foreskin.[679] For the living being is the eighth of all rungs,[680] and the soul that has flown from Her should appear before Her on the eighth day, since She is the eighth rung.[681] Then it is clearly seen that she is נפש חיה (*nefesh ḥayyah*), *a soul of* that holy *living being* (Genesis 1:20), not from

674. **Whoever avoids ... diminishes ...** Whoever fails to fulfill the commandment *Be fruitful and multiply* disrupts the union of the divine couple and thereby diminishes *Shekhinah*, who ideally comprises all the higher *sefirot* and reflects those images.

See *Zohar* 1:186b; *ZH* 59a (*MhN*), 89b (*MhN, Rut*); and BT *Yevamot* 63b: "Rabbi Eli'ezer said, 'Whoever does not engage in procreation is as though he sheds blood....' Rabbi Ya'akov said, 'As though he diminishes the [divine] image.'" Because human beings are created in the image of God, by failing to bring new life into the world, one diminishes the manifestation of that divine image.

675. **that river ... the holy covenant ...** The flow of emanation culminating in *Yesod*, the divine phallus, symbolized by the covenant of circumcision.

676. *against Me,* **indeed!** Failure to fulfill this vital commandment renders the body a mere corpse and damages the *sefirot*.

677. **This is for the body** The conclusion of the verse in Isaiah describes the punishment: *their worms shall not die, nor their fire be quenched; they shall be a horror to all flesh.* Cf. *ZH* 59a (*MhN*), 89b (*MhN, Rut*).

678. **does not pass through the curtain ...** The soul of such a person is not allowed to enter the divine realm and must

transmigrate into a different body, where it is given another opportunity to fulfill this vital commandment.

See BT *Bava Batra* 116a: "Rabbi Yoḥanan said in the name of Rabbi Shim'on son of Yoḥai, 'Whoever does not leave a son to succeed him incurs the full wrath of the blessed Holy One.'"

Cf. *Zohar* 1:48a, 90a, 115a, 186b, 228b; *ZH* 89b (*MhN, Rut*); Scholem, in *Tarbiz* 16 (1945): 146–47.

679. **filth of the foreskin** Symbolizing the demonic. See below; and Moses de León, *Sheqel ha-Qodesh*, 55 (68).

680. **the living being is the eighth ...** *Shekhinah* is the eighth *sefirah*, counting from *Binah*, who is the first *sefirah* about whom one can inquire (see above, page 5). Elsewhere the *Zohar* identifies *Yesod* as the eighth *sefirah*, counting from *Ḥokhmah*, called "Beginning." See 3:11a and, in the context of circumcision, 43b (*Piq*); Moses de León, *Sefer ha-Rimmon*, 228.

681. **soul that has flown from Her ... eighth day ...** The soul that has emerged from *Shekhinah* into the world should appear before Her.

See *Zohar* 1:12b, 33a; cf. *Pesiqta de-Rav Kahana* 9:10; Moses de León, *Sefer ha-Rimmon*, 228.

the Other Side.[682] This is *Let the waters swarm* (ibid.).[683] In *The Book of Enoch*:[684] Let the water of the holy seed be inscribed with the mark of נפש חיה (*nefesh ḥayyah*), *a soul of the living being*.[685] This is the mark of the letter י (*yod*),[686] inscribed in the holy flesh in preference to all other marks of the world.

"*Let birds fly above the earth* (ibid.). This is Elijah, who sweeps through the entire world in four glides to be present at that holy circumcision. One must prepare a chair for him and declare: 'This is the chair of Elijah.' If not, he does not abide there.[687]

682. **Other Side** The demonic realm.

683. *Let the waters swarm* *with a swarm of* נפש חיה (*nefesh ḥayyah*), *living souls* [or: *a soul of the living being*].

684. *The Book of Enoch* Concerning Enoch, Genesis 5:24 states: *He was no more, for God took him.* In postbiblical literature this verse is taken to mean that God transported Enoch through the heavens, a journey recorded extensively in the Enoch literature. The *Zohar's Book of Enoch,* though influenced by this literature, is not identical with any of its particular volumes. It comprises one of the many books housed in the real or imaginary Zoharic library.

See 1:37b, 72b; 2:55a, 100a, 105b, 180b, 192b, 217a; 3:10b, 236b, 240a, 248b, 253b, 307a; *ZH* 2c (*SO*). See Matt, *Zohar,* 25; Ginzberg, *Legends,* 5:158, 163, nn. 60, 61; Margaliot, *Mal'akhei Elyon,* 80–83; and *KP,* 22d: "All such books mentioned in the *Zohar*... have been lost in the wanderings of exile... Nothing is left of them except what is mentioned in the *Zohar.*"

685. **Let the water of the holy seed...** Let the phallus of the holy people, which symbolizes the flowing river of *Yesod,* be inscribed with the mark of circumcision and thereby distinguished as *a soul of Shekhinah, the living being.* The biblical command ישרצו (*yishretsu*), *Let* [*the waters*] *swarm,* is interpreted freely as יתרשמון (*yitrashshemun*), "Let [the water] be inscribed."

686. **mark of the letter י (*yod*)** The mark of circumcision is pictured as the smallest of the Hebrew letters. In *Tanḥuma,*

Tsav 14, *Shemini* 8, this mark is identified with the י (*yod*) of the divine name שדי (*Shaddai*). A German Hasidic tradition identifies the mark with the *yod* of יהוה (*YHVH*). In the *Zohar,* it signifies the divine name as well as *Yesod* (and occasionally *Shekhinah*).

See *Zohar* 1:2b, 56a, 95a–b; 2:36a, 216b; 3:142a (*IR*), 215b, 220a, 256a (*RM*); Wolfson, in *JQR* 78 (1987): 77–112; idem, *Circle in the Square,* 29–48.

687. **Elijah...in four glides...** According to 2 Kings 11:12, the prophet Elijah did not die a normal death but was carried off to heaven in a chariot of fire. See *Midrash Tehillim* 8:7: "*The bird of heaven* (Psalms 8:9)—this is Elijah, who flies through the world as a bird." Cf. *Targum Qohelet* 10:20; *Zohar* 1:46b. See BT *Berakhot* 4b: "A *tanna* taught: 'Michael [reaches his destination] in one [glide], Gabriel in two, Elijah in four, and the Angel of Death in eight—in time of plague, however, in one.'"

According to *Pirqei de-Rabbi Eli'ezer* 29, when the Israelites neglected the commandment of circumcision, "Elijah, may his memory be a blessing, was passionately zealous and adjured the heavens not to send down dew or rain upon the earth. [Queen] Jezebel heard and sought to kill him. Elijah immediately prayed before the blessed Holy One. The blessed Holy One said to him, 'Are you better than your ancestors? Jacob fled [from Esau] and escaped.... Moses fled [from Pharaoh] and escaped.... David fled [from Saul] and escaped....' Elijah immediately fled from the land of Israel and

90

"*God created the great sea monsters* (ibid., 21)—two: foreskin and uncovering, cutting the foreskin and afterward uncovering. They are male and female.[688]

"*And every soul of the living being that moves* (ibid.)[689]—inscription of the sign of the holy covenant,[690] indicating that she is a *soul of the* holy *living being*, as we have said.

"*Which the waters brought forth in swarms* (ibid.)—the upper waters were drawn toward this inscribed sign.[691] Consequently Israel is inscribed with the holy, pure mark below. Just as they are inscribed to distinguish between the holy side and the other side, of impurity,[692] so Israel is inscribed to distinguish

---

escaped [to Horeb].... The blessed Holy One appeared to him and said, '*What are you doing here, Elijah?*' (1 Kings 19:9). He answered, '*I have been very zealous* [*for YHVH, the God of Hosts, for the Children of Israel have abandoned Your covenant*]' (ibid., 10). The blessed Holy One said, 'You are always zealous! You were zealous in Shittim on account of sexual immorality [Numbers 25; Elijah is identified with Phinehas]..., and here, too, you are zealous. By your life! Israel will not enact the covenant of circumcision until you see it with your own eyes.' Because of this the sages ordained that a seat of honor be arranged for the Angel of the Covenant [Elijah; see Malachi 3:1]."

Traditionally, at a circumcision the chair of Elijah is placed at the right of the *sandaq* ("godfather") and left unoccupied. The *mohel* ("circumciser") declares in the opening prayer: "This is the chair of Elijah, may his memory be a blessing."

See *Halakhot Gedolot* (according to *Shibbolei ha-Leqet* 376:6); *Sefer Ḥasidim*, ed. Wistinetzki, par. 585; *Zohar* 1:93a, 209b; 2:190a; *Shulḥan Arukh, Yoreh De'ah* 265:11; Ginzberg, *Legends*, 6:338, n. 103.

688. **foreskin and uncovering...male and female** In the ritual of circumcision, first the foreskin is cut and removed, disclosing the mucous membrane, which is then torn down the center and pulled back, revealing the corona. The act of tearing and pulling back the membrane is called פריעה (*peri'ah*), "uncovering" the corona. See M *Shabbat* 19:6: "If one circumcises but does

not uncover the circumcision, it is as if he has not circumcised." See Moses de León, *Sheqel ha-Qodesh*, 55 (67).

Here the two acts designate the two monsters, the demonic couple Samael and Lilith. See *Zohar* 1:34b; 2:34a–b. Through the double ritual of circumcision, one overcomes them. Elsewhere the two acts symbolize the sefirotic couple of *Yesod* and *Shekhinah*. Through the double procedure, one unites, and communes with, both of these *sefirot*. See 1:32a (*Tos*), 96b; 3:91b; Moses de León, *Sefer ha-Mishqal*, 133.

Although the wording here implies that the foreskin symbolizes the male, and the uncovering symbolizes the female, the reverse is maintained in *Zohar* 2:40a, 125b; 3:91b, 95b; *Sefer ha-Mishqal*, loc. cit.

689. *every soul...* The verse continues: *which the waters brought forth in swarms*.

690. **inscription...** The words ואת כל (*ve-et kol*), *and every*, are interpreted as referring to *Yesod*, who is referred to both as את (*at*), "sign, letter"—the sign of covenant and the letter י (*yod*)—and כל (*kol*), "everything," since He includes the entire flow of the upper *sefirot*. There is also a play on the words רומשת (*romeset*), *moves*, and רשימו (*reshimu*), "inscription."

691. **upper waters were drawn...** The flow of emanation from the higher *sefirot* descended to the את (*at*), "sign," or "letter," of *Yesod*.

692. **Just as they are inscribed...** As the *sefirot* themselves are inscribed. See *Zohar* 3:44a (*Piq*): "When the holy people

91

between holiness and other nations, deriving from the other, impure side, as explained. As He marks them, so He marks off their animals and birds from the animals and birds of other nations.[693] Happy is their share!

"The eighth commandment: to love the convert[694] coming to circumcise himself, to enter beneath the wings of *Shekhinah*.[695] Under Her wings She brings those separating themselves from the impure Other Side[696] and approaching Her, as is written: *Let the earth bring forth* חיה נפש (*nefesh ḥayyah*), *souls of the living being*,[697] *according to their kind* (ibid., 24).

"Now if you say that the *soul of the living being* contained in Israel is designated for everyone, the verse continues: *according to their kind*. How many rooms and parlors, one within the other, are located in this *earth*,[698] *the living being*, beneath Her wings! Her right wing includes two parlors, branching from it for two other nations closely related to Israel,[699] to bring them into these

92

gather to remove that foreskin from the covenant, the blessed Holy One gathers His entire household and openly reveals Himself in order to remove that foreskin above from the covenant of the holy oath [*Yesod*]. For behold, every action that Israel enacts below arouses an action above."

693. **so He marks off their animals...** Through the signs distinguishing permitted and forbidden animals, birds, and fish. See Leviticus 11; Deuteronomy 14; *Zohar* 1:20b; and the continuation of the verse interpreted here (Genesis 1:21): *and every living creature that moves, according to its kind, which the waters brought forth in swarms, and every winged bird, according to its kind.*

694. **convert** גיורא (*Giyyora*), "Stranger, convert"; cf. Deuteronomy 10:19: *Love the* גר (*ger*), *stranger, for you were strangers in the land of Egypt.*

695. **to enter beneath the wings of Shekhinah** See Ruth 2:11–12, where Boaz says to Ruth: *I have been told of all that you did for your mother-in-law after the death of your husband, how you left your father and mother and the land of your birth and came to a people you had not known before. May YHVH reward your deed, and may you have a full recompense from YHVH, the God of Israel, under whose wings you have sought refuge.* Based on this verse, the metaphor of coming

under the divine wings is used in rabbinic literature to describe conversion. See BT *Shabbat* 31a; *Mekhilta de-Rashbi*, Exodus 18:6; and *Vayiqra Rabbah* 2:9: "Thus have the sages taught in the Mishnah: If a convert comes to convert, one should extend a hand to him to bring him beneath the wings of *Shekhinah*."

See *Zohar* 2:70a; 3:168a; Moses de León, *Sefer ha-Rimmon*, 16, 212–13; Wijnhoven, "The *Zohar* and the Proselyte," 123–25.

696. **Other Side** *Sitra Aḥra*, "The Other Side," the demonic realm.

697. **souls of the living being** Souls deriving from *Shekhinah*.

698. **this earth** *Shekhinah*.

699. **closely related to Israel** Apparently referring to the descendants of Ishmael (son of Abraham and Hagar), and Edom, descended from Esau (son of Isaac and Rebecca). See Vital. Cordovero interprets "closely related" as referring to those who *may be admitted to the Assembly of YHVH in the third generation* (Deuteronomy 23:9), namely, Edom and Egypt.

In medieval Jewish literature Edom symbolizes Christianity, while both Ishmael and Egypt represent Islam (see Scholem; *Zohar* 2:87a). Cryptically, Rabbi Shim'on teaches that Christians and Muslims are closely related to Israel, and *Shekhinah* prepares a

parlors. Beneath Her left wing are two other parlors, branching off for two other nations, namely, Ammon and Moab.[700] All of them are called *souls of the living being.*

"Countless other concealed rooms and palaces abide in each wing, from which spirits emerge, to be distributed to all converting converts. They are called *souls of the living being,* but *according to their kind.* They all enter beneath the wings of *Shekhinah,* no further.[701] But as for Israel, their soul emerges from the trunk of that tree,[702] whence souls fly into *earth,* into Her womb, deep within. The secret is: *You shall be an earth of delight* (Malachi 3:12).[703] So Israel is *a precious son,* for whom Her *innards yearn,*[704] and they are called *borne from the womb* (Isaiah 46:3), not from the wings, outside. Furthermore, [13b] converts have no share in the celestial tree, certainly not its trunk;[705] rather, their share is in the wings, no higher. A convert is beneath the wings of *Shekhinah,* no higher. They are converts of Righteousness,[706] for there they dwell, uniting, not within, as explained.

"So, *Let the earth bring forth souls of the living being, according to their kind. Which kind? Cattle, crawling things, and living creatures of the earth, according*

93

---

special place for them, inviting them to convert. The *Zohar*'s reluctance to explicitly name the two sister religions is understandable, given the strict prohibition against conversion to Judaism in thirteenth-century Spain.

The manuscripts C12 and Ms3, as well as *OY, OL,* and *KP,* support the reading קריבין ביחוסא לישראל (*qerivin be-yiḥusa le-yisra'el*), "closely related to Israel," while M and Cr read קריבין ביחודא לישראל (*qerivin be-yiḥuda le-yisra'el*), "[who] approach Israel in unity," i.e., in monotheism, also implying Christianity and Islam.

See *Zohorei Ya'bets;* Naḥmanides on Genesis 2:3 (end); *Zohar* 2:237a; *ZH* 38b; Moses de León, *Sefer ha-Mishqal,* 62–63.

700. **Ammon and Moab** According to Deuteronomy 23:4–5, *No Ammonite or Moabite shall be admitted into the Assembly of YHVH; none of their descendants, even in the tenth generation, shall ever be admitted... because they did not meet you with food and water on your journey after you left Egypt, and because they hired Balaam... to curse you.* According to later Jewish law, however, any foreigner may convert.

701. **no further** Such souls ascend no higher. See Judah Halevi, *Kuzari* 1:27; *Zohar* 1:96a; 2:87a; 3:14a–b.

702. **from the trunk of that tree** *Tif'eret.* C12 and C13 read here: נופא (*nofa*), "boughs, crown," instead of גופא (*gufa*), "trunk." See *Bahir* 67 (98); Scholem, *Das Buch Bahir,* 71, n. 3.

703. *an earth of delight* *Shekhinah,* who unites with *Tif'eret* in joy and gives birth to the soul. See *Zohar* 2:275b.

704. *precious son...* See Jeremiah 31:20: *Truly Ephraim is a precious son to Me, a child that is dandled! Whenever I speak against him, My thoughts still dwell on him. That is why My innards yearn for him. I will surely love him, says YHVH.*

705. **the celestial tree...its trunk** The body of the *sefirot...Tif'eret.*

706. **converts of Righteousness** In rabbinic literature the term גר צדק (*ger tsedeq*), "convert of righteousness, righteous convert," denotes a full convert; here it indicates that the convert has an intimate connection with *Shekhinah,* who is called צדק (*tsedeq*), "righteousness." See *Zohar* 1:96a; 2:87a; 3:14a–b, 168a.

to their kind (Genesis 1:24).[707] All of them draw a *soul* from that *living being,* but each *according to its kind,* fittingly.

"The ninth commandment: to be generous to the poor and provide them with food, for it is written: *Let us make a human being in our image, according to our likeness* (Genesis 1:26). *Let us make a human being*—jointly, including male and female;[708] *in our image*—the wealthy; *according to our likeness*—mystery of the poor.[709] For the wealthy derive from the side of the male, the poor from the side of the female. Just as they constitute a single partnership[710]—one caring for the other, providing for the other, and rendering goodness—so should human beings below be rich and poor in a single bond, one providing for the other and rendering goodness.

"*They shall have dominion over the fish of the sea, [the birds of the sky, the animals, the whole earth, and all crawling things that crawl on earth]* (ibid.). This secret we have seen in *The Book of King Solomon:*[711] If one cares for the poor wholeheartedly, his image never mutates from that of Adam;[712] and since the image of Adam is impressed on him, he controls all creatures of the world,[713] as is written: *Fear and dread of you shall be upon all the beasts of the*

94

707. *Cattle, crawling things, and living creatures...* The continuation of the verse—which, according to Rabbi Shim'on, specifies various kinds of souls. See *Zohar* 1:47a.

708. **jointly...** The original human being was androgynous, engendered by the masculine and feminine aspects of the *sefirot, Tif'eret* and *Shekhinah,* who together constitute the *image* and *likeness* of God.

See *Bereshit Rabbah* 8:1: "Rabbi Yirmeyah son of El'azar said, 'When the blessed Holy One created Adam, He created him androgynous, as is said: *Male and female He created them* (Genesis 1:27).' Rabbi Shemu'el son of Naḥmani said, 'When the blessed Holy One created Adam, He created him with two faces. Then He sawed him and gave him two backs, one on this side and one on that.'"

See BT *Berakhot* 61a; *Eruvin* 18a; Plato, *Symposium* 189d–191d; *Zohar* 1:47a; 2:55a; 3:5a, 44b; Matt, *Zohar,* 217.

709. *in our image*—**the wealthy...** *Our image* indicates *Tif'eret,* who transmits the rich flow of emanation to *Shekhinah, our*

likeness, who "has nothing at all of Her own" (*Zohar* 1:181a). See 3:35b.

710. **Just as they...** As *Tif'eret* and *Shekhinah.*

711. **The Book of King Solomon** One of the many volumes housed in the real or imaginary library of the author(s) of the *Zohar.* See above, note 684.

712. **his image...that of Adam** By fulfilling the *mitsvah* of caring for the poor, one imitates God and regains the pristine divine image in which Adam was created. See BT *Bava Batra* 58a; *Zohar* 1:71a.

713. **since the image of Adam...** See *Pirqei de-Rabbi Eli'ezer* 11: "[Adam] stood on his feet and was adorned with the divine image. The creatures saw him and were frightened, thinking that he was their Creator, and they all approached to bow down to him."

See *Shir ha-Shirim Rabbah* on 3:7: "It was taught: Before a person sins, he inspires awe and fear, and creatures are afraid of him. Once he sins, he is filled with awe and fear, and he is afraid of others." Cf. *Sifrei,* Deu-

earth [*and upon all the birds of the sky, everything with which the earth teems and all the fish of the sea—into your hand they are given*] (ibid. 9:2). All of them fear and tremble from that image impressed on him because of all the commandments this[714] is the finest for attaining the image of one's Lord.

"How do we know? From Nebuchadnezzar. Even though he dreamed that dream,[715] as long as he was generous to the poor, his dream did not befall him.[716] As soon as he cast a stingy, evil eye, no longer acting generously to them,[717] what is written? *The word was still in the king's mouth,* [*when a voice fell from heaven, "To you it is decreed, O King Nebuchadnezzar: The kingdom has departed from you. You are being driven away from human beings, and your habitation shall be with the beasts of the field. You shall be fed grass like cattle"*] (Daniel 4:28–29). Immediately his image mutated and he was banished from humankind.

"So, נעשה (Na'aseh), *Let us make, a human being* [*in our image*]. Here is written עשיה (asiyyah), *making*, and there is written: *The name of the man with whom* עשיתי (asiti), *I worked, today is Boaz* (Ruth 2:19).[718]

95

teronomy 50; and BT *Shabbat* 151b: "Rami son of Abba said, 'A wild beast has no power over a person until he appears to it as an animal.'"

See *Zohar* 1:38a, 71a, 191a, 221b; 2:55a, 125b; 3:107b; *ZH* 38c; Moses de León, *Sefer ha-Rimmon*, 337–38; Ginzberg, *Legends*, 5:119–20, n. 113.

714. **this**   The commandment to care for the poor.

715. **dreamed that dream**   According to Daniel 4, King Nebuchadnezzar of Babylon dreamed of a huge tree reaching to the sky, providing food for all creatures. A heavenly messenger then decrees that the tree be cut down and that Nebuchadnezzar share the grass of the earth with the beasts. The messenger adds: *Let his heart be changed from that of a human, and let him be given the heart of a beast* (4:13).

716. **as long as he was generous...**   Daniel interpreted the dream to the king: *You will be driven away from human beings and have your habitation with the beasts of the field* (ibid., 22). He then advised him: *Redeem your sins by charity and your iniquities by generosity to the poor; then your serenity*

may be extended (24). According to rabbinic tradition, the king followed Daniel's advice for one year.

See *Aggadat Shir ha-Shirim*, 25; *Tanḥuma, Mishpatim* 4; *Shemot Rabbah* 30:24; BT *Bava Batra* 4a; Ginzberg, *Legends*, 6:423–24, n. 104.

717. **As soon as he cast a stingy, evil eye...**   One year later King Nebuchadnezzar bragged *as he was walking on the roof of the royal palace...: "Is this not great Babylon, which I have built by my vast power to be a royal residence for the glory of my majesty!"* (Daniel 4:26–27). He decided against spending any more of his resources on the poor, and this selfish refusal ensured the fulfillment of his tragic dream.

718. *with whom* עשיתי (*asiti*), *I worked...*   See *Vayiqra Rabbah* 34:8. The appearance of the verb עשה (*asah*), "to make, work," in both biblical verses implies a parallel: just as in the story of Ruth the verb indicates an act of generosity toward the poor, so, too, in the story of Creation. By accepting Boaz's generosity, Ruth "made" him a complete *man*. Generosity is inherent in the makeup of humanity, the clearest sign of our original divine nature.

"The tenth commandment: to put on תפילין (*tefillin*),[719] perfecting oneself in the image on high, for it is written: *God created the human being in His image* (Genesis 1:27)."[720]

He opened, saying, "*Your head upon you is like Carmel* (Song of Songs 7:6).[721] We have established this verse and it has been discussed,[722] but *Your head upon*

---

719. תפילין (*tefillin*) Phylacteries, two black leather boxes containing passages from the Torah (Exodus 13:1–10, 11–16; Deuteronomy 6:4–9; 11:13–21) written on parchment. The *tefillin* (singular, *tefillah*) are bound by black leather straps on the left arm and on the head and are worn during weekday morning services. Each of the biblical passages indicates that the Israelites should place a sign upon their hand and a frontlet (or reminder) between their eyes. In the *tefillah* of the hand, all four passages are written on one piece of parchment in the order of their occurrence in the Torah. The *tefillah* of the head, however, is divided into four compartments, and each of the four passages, written on a separate piece of parchment, is inserted in one compartment. The exact order of the biblical passages in the *tefillah* of the head was a matter of dispute in the time of the Second Temple, and in the twelfth century this dispute was renewed. According to Rashi, they are inserted in the order of their occurrence in the Torah, while according to his grandson, Rabbeinu Tam, the passage from Deuteronomy 11:13–21 precedes that of Deuteronomy 6:4–9. See BT *Menahot* 34b; Maimonides, *Mishneh Torah, Hilkhot Tefillin* 3:5.

The commandment of *tefillin* was widely disregarded in France and Spain in the twelfth and thirteenth centuries. The *Zohar*, seeking to reinforce the commitment to this *mitsvah*, emphasizes its mystical significance. See *Tosafot, Shabbat* 49a, s.v. *ke-elisha ba'al kenafayim*; Baer, *History* 1:250; Tishby, *Wisdom of the Zohar*, 3:1161–65.

720. **perfecting oneself in the image on high...** By wearing *tefillin*, one imitates God. See BT *Berakhot* 6a: "Rabbi Avin son of Rabbi Adda said in the name of Rabbi

Yitshak, 'How do we know that the blessed Holy One puts on *tefillin*? For it is said: *YHVH has sworn by His right hand and by the arm of His strength* (Isaiah 62:8). *By His right hand*—this is Torah, as is said: *At His right hand was a fiery law unto them* (Deuteronomy 33:2). *And by the arm of His strength*—this is *tefillin,* as is said: *YHVH will give strength unto His people* (Psalms 29:11). How do we know that *tefillin* are a strength to Israel? For it is written: *All the peoples of the earth shall see that the name of YHVH is proclaimed upon you, and they shall be in awe of you* (Deuteronomy 28:10), and it has been taught: Rabbi Eli'ezer the Great says, "This refers to the *tefillin* of the head."' Rabbi Nahman son of Yitshak asked Rabbi Hiyya son of Avin, 'These *tefillin* of the Master of the Universe—what is written in them?' He replied, '*Who is like Your people Israel, a unique nation on earth?* (1 Chronicles 17:21).'"

See Isaac the Blind, *Peirush Sefer Yetsirah,* 4; Ezra of Gerona, *Peirush Shir ha-Shirim,* 525; Azriel of Gerona, *Peirush ha-Aggadot,* 4; Todros Abulafia, *Otsar ha-Kavod,* ad loc.; *Zohar* 1:141a; 3:81a, 140a (*IR*), 262a–263a, 264a, 269a–b; Moses de León, *Sefer ha-Rimmon,* 235–39; Tishby, *Wisdom of the Zohar,* 3:1161–65.

721. **He opened, saying, "*Your head upon you is like Carmel*** Rabbi Shim'on continues his mystical explanation of the commandments. The verse concludes: *the locks of your head are like purple; a king is held captive in the tresses.*

722. **We have established...** See *Vayiqra Rabbah* 31:5; *Shir ha-Shirim Rabbah* on 7:6; *Tanhuma, Tetsavveh* 6; *Zohar* 1:113a–b (*MhN*).

you is like Carmel—the head on high, *tefillin* of the head,[723] name of the holy
King on high, יהוה (*YHVH*), inscribed in letters. Each and every letter—one
portion; the holy name engraved fittingly, in the order of the letters.[724]

"We have learned: [*All the peoples of the earth shall see*] *that the name of
YHVH is proclaimed upon you, and they shall be in awe of you* (Deuteronomy
28:10)—the *tefillin* of the head, the holy name in the order of its letters.[725]

"The first portion is: *Hallow to Me every firstborn* (Exodus 13:1–10)[726]—
י (*yod*), holiness, firstborn of all the holy above.[727] *Breacher of every womb*
(ibid.)—by that narrow path descending from the י (*yod*), opening the womb
to generate fruit and verdure fittingly.[728] That is holiness above.

"The second portion is: *So when YHVH brings you* [*to the land…*] (ibid., 11–
16)—ה (*he*), the palace, whose womb was opened by י (*yod*) through fifty
openings, parlors, and concealed rooms of *Binah*.[729] That opening made by י
(*yod*) in the palace is intended to trumpet the sound issuing from the shofar,[730]

723. **head on high…** The divine head, which also wears *tefillin*. See Rashi on Song of Songs 7:6, who interprets *Your head upon you is like Carmel* as referring to the *tefillin* on the head of Israel.

724. **Each and every letter…** Each letter of the name יהוה (*YHVH*) corresponds to one of the four portions in the *tefillin* (Exodus 13:1–10, 11–16; Deuteronomy 6:4–9; 11:13–21), as Rabbi Shim'on goes on to explain. He follows the view of Rashi, according to whom the order of these passages in the *tefillah* of the head follows their order in the Torah. See above, note 719; *Orḥot Ḥayyim*, par. 15.

725. **We have learned…** See BT *Bera-khot* 6a: "Rabbi Avin son of Rabbi Adda said in the name of Rabbi Yitsḥak, '…It is written: *All the peoples of the earth shall see that the name of YHVH is proclaimed upon you, and they shall be in awe of you* (Deuteronomy 28:10), and it has been taught: Rabbi Eli'ezer the Great says, "This refers to the *tefillin* of the head."'"

726. *Hallow to Me every firstborn* The verse continues: —*breacher of every womb among the Children of Israel, of human or beast—it is Mine.*

727. י (*yod*)… The first portion of the *tefillin* symbolizes *Ḥokhmah*, the first *sefirah* (excluding *Keter*, so concealed that it cannot

be counted). *Ḥokhmah* is the primordial point of holiness, indicated by the letter י (*yod*), first letter of the name יהוה (*YHVH*). See *Zohar* 2:43a–b.

728. **that narrow path…** The thin stroke that tapers off at the bottom of the י (*yod*) symbolizes the subtle connection between the primordial point of *Ḥokhmah* and the womb of the Divine Mother, *Binah*. Elsewhere in the *Zohar* (1:29a–b; 2:122b–123a; 3:61b), this path is identified as *a path unknown to any vulture* (Job 28:7).

729. ה (*he*)… The second portion symbolizes *Binah*, whose identifying letter is the feminine marker ה (*he*), second letter of the name יהוה (*YHVH*). According to BT *Rosh ha-Shanah* 21b, Rav and Shemu'el taught: "Fifty gates of בינה (*binah*), understanding, were created in the world, all of which were given to Moses except for one, as is said: *You made him little less than God* (Psalms 8:6)." The fifty gates of *Binah* figure prominently in Kabbalah; here the number constitutes the product of the numerical equivalent of the י (*yod*) of *Ḥokhmah* (10) times the numerical equivalent of the ה (*he*) of *Binah* (5).

730. **the shofar** *Binah*, who expresses the raw power of revelation. See *Zohar* 1:114a–b; 2:81b.

for this shofar was stopped up on every side, and י (*yod*) came and opened it, bringing forth its sound. As soon as He opened it, He blew it, bringing forth a sound to bring forth slaves to freedom.[731] Through the sounding of this shofar Israel went forth from Egypt, as destined once again at the end of days.[732] Every deliverance issues from this shofar. So the Exodus from Egypt is included in this portion,[733] for it emerged from this shofar through the power of י (*yod*), who opened Her womb, bringing forth its sound for the deliverance of the slaves. This is ה (*he*), second letter of the holy name.

"The third portion is the mystery of unification: *Hear, O Israel!* [*YHVH is our God, YHVH is one...*] (Deuteronomy 6:4–9). This is ו (*vav*)—including all, unifying all; in Him they unite, and He carries all.[734]

"The fourth portion is: *If you listen* (Deuteronomy 11:13–21),[735] totality of two sides, [14a] with whom Assembly of Israel, Power below, is united.[736] This is the final ה (*he*),[737] receiving them, comprised by them.

98

731. **to bring forth slaves...** *Binah* is also symbolized by the Jubilee, celebrated every fifty years, when slaves were released and land reverted to its original owner (Leviticus 25:8–55). The Jubilee was proclaimed by the blast of the shofar.

732. **at the end of days** See Isaiah 27:13: *On that day a great shofar shall be sounded.* Cf. the daily *amidah*: "Sound the great shofar for our redemption."

733. **the Exodus from Egypt is included...** See Exodus 13:14–15: *When, in the time to come, your son asks you, "What is this?"* [i.e., "Why are you setting apart to God the firstborn?"], *you shall say to him, "By strength of hand YHVH brought us out of Egypt, out of the house of bondage...."* See *Zohar* 1:21b; 2:83a–b, 85b.

734. **mystery of unification...This is** ו **(vav)...** The first line of the *Shema* contains six words in Hebrew: שמע ישראל יהוה אלהינו יהוה אחד (*Shema Yisra'el YHVH Eloheinu YHVH eḥad*), *Hear O Israel! YHVH is our God, YHVH is one.* By reciting these words with כונה (*kavvanah*), "intention," one unifies *Tif'eret* and the five *sefirot* surrounding Him (*Ḥesed* to *Yesod*). *Tif'eret* then channels the entire flow of emanation to *Shekhinah*, consummating the union. See above, page 82; Tishby, *Wisdom of the Zohar*, 3:971–74.

The letter ו (*vav*), whose numerical value is six, symbolizes *Tif'eret* and constitutes the third letter of the name יהוה (*YHVH*). *Tif'eret* is also symbolized by Jacob, who is called Israel. See *Zohar* 2:43a, 160b; BT *Pesaḥim* 56a.

735. **If you listen** closely to *My commandments that I command you this day, to love YHVH your God and to serve Him with all your heart and with all your being....*

736. **totality of two sides...Assembly of Israel, Power below...** The two sides are *Ḥesed* and *Gevurah*, divine love and power, which both flow into *Shekhinah*, Assembly of Israel (the divine counterpart of the people Israel, that aspect of God most intimately connected with them). *Shekhinah* is also called "*Gevurah* below" because She manifests, in a more mild way, the rigor of *Gevurah*. The fourth portion of the *tefillin* contains both grace and rigor, *Ḥesed* and *Gevurah*: if Israel obeys God's commands, they will be blessed with rain and abundance (Deuteronomy 11:13–15), but they are threatened with drought and famine if they worship false gods (ibid., 16–17).

737. **final** ה **(he)** As *Binah*, the Divine Mother, is symbolized by the initial ה (*he*) of the name יהוה (*YHVH*), so *Shekhinah*, daughter of *Binah*, is symbolized by the final ה (*he*).

"*Tefillin* are the actual letters of the holy name. So, *Your head upon you is like Carmel*—*tefillin* of the head. ודלת (*Ve-dallat*), *The locks, of your head are like purple* (Song of Songs, ibid.)—*tefillah* of the hand, who is poor compared to those above.[738] Nevertheless, She is complete, as above. *A king is held captive in the tresses* (ibid.)—He is bound and held within those compartments,[739] uniting with that holy name fittingly.

"So one adorned in them is *in the image of God* (Genesis 1:27).[740] Just as the holy name is united with God, so is the holy name united with him, fittingly. *Male and female He created them* (ibid.)—*tefillin* of the head and *tefillah* of the hand.[741] All is one.

"The eleventh commandment: to tithe the tithe of the earth.[742] Here are two commandments: one to tithe the tithe of the earth, the other the first fruits of the tree,[743] for it is written: *See, I have given you every seed-bearing plant that is upon the face of all the earth* [*and every tree that has seed-bearing fruit; they shall be yours for food*] (ibid., 29). Here is written: *See, I have given*, and there is

99

738. ודלת (*Ve-dallat*)…poor… Rabbi Shim'on interprets דלה (*dallah*), *lock*, according to its homonym, דלה (*dallah*), "poor." *Shekhinah*, symbolized by the *tefillah* of the hand, is poor in relation to the upper *sefirot*, who provide Her with the flow of emanation. See *Zohar* 1:168b; 2:43a.

739. **He is bound…within those compartments** *Tif'eret* is bound by the *tefillin*, held within the four compartments of the *tefillah* of the head. By wearing *tefillin*, one "captures" God. Rabbi Shim'on is playing with the two meanings of רהטים (*rehatim*): "tresses" and "troughs."

See *Vayiqra Rabbah* 31:4; *Shir ha-Shirim Rabbah* on 7:6; *Tanḥuma, Tetsavveh* 6; *Zohar* 1:161a–b; 162a (*ST*), 3:140a (*IR*), 269b; *TZ* 6, 21b; *TZ* (2) 6, 144b. Cf. the phrase רהיטי מוחא (*rehitei moḥa*), "channels (or cavities) of the brain," in the last two citations (from *TZ*) and *Zohar* 3:136a (*IR*), 293a–b (*IZ*).

740. *in the image of God* From the verse with which Rabbi Shim'on began his discussion of this commandment: *God created the human being in His image; in the image of God He created him, male and female He created them.*

741. *Male and female…tefillin* **of the head…of the hand** Symbolizing *Tif'eret* with the *sefirot* surrounding Him, and *Shekhinah*. By wearing both *tefillin*, one imitates and unites the divine couple.

742. **to tithe…** The Torah commands that all produce be tithed. The first tithe is given to the Levite. The second tithe is eaten by the owner himself at the site of the sanctuary or exchanged for its value, which is then taken to the site of the sanctuary together with an additional fifth and spent there. In the third and sixth years of each seven-year cycle, instead of eating this second tithe, it is given to the poor. See Leviticus 27:30–31; Numbers 18:21–24; Deuteronomy 14:22–29.

The eleventh and twelfth commandments differ from the others listed by Rabbi Shim'on in that they did not apply in medieval times nor were they required outside the land of Israel. Neither is interpreted here mystically.

743. **first fruits…** The first ripe fruits are to be brought to the Temple (Exodus 23:19; Deuteronomy 26:1–11).

written: *See, I have given the Levites every tithe in Israel* (Numbers 18:21),[744] and similarly: *Every tithe of the earth, from the seed of the earth or from the fruit of the tree, belongs to YHVH* (Leviticus 27:30).

"The twelfth commandment: to bring the first fruits of the tree, for it is written: *Every tree that has seed-bearing fruit* (Genesis 1:29). 'Everything designated for Me, which I have forbidden you to eat, I permitted to them and gave them—all tithes and first fruit of the trees.' *I have given you* (ibid.)—*you*, not to the generations after you.[745]

"The thirteenth commandment: to redeem one's son,[746] binding him to life. For there are two appointees, one of life and one of death, standing above a person.[747] When he redeems his son, he redeems him from the hand of that one of death, who now has no power over him. The secret is: *God saw all that He had made*—in general; [*and behold, it was very good*] (Genesis 1:31): *and behold, it was good*—Angel of Life; *very*—Angel of Death.[748] So through that redemption, this one of life is sustained, that one of death weakened. Through this redemption, he acquires life for him,[749] as explained, and that evil side leaves him, cannot seize him.

100

744. *See, I have given the Levites every tithe in Israel* The verse continues: *as an inheritance in return for the services that they perform, the services of the Tent of Meeting.* Both verses contain the phrase *See, I have given.* By applying the hermeneutical principle of analogy, Rabbi Shim'on concludes that they refer to the same topic: tithes.

745. **Everything designated for Me...** The tithes and first fruits belong to God, and according to the Torah, Israel is forbidden to eat them, but in the Garden of Eden, before the Torah was revealed, God gave them to Adam and Eve.

746. **redeem one's son** During the night of the Exodus, when the Egyptian firstborn were slain, the Israelite firstborn were spared. In return for their deliverance, they were originally to be consecrated to God, forming a priesthood. Instead, the tribe of Levi was selected to serve God. Among the other tribes, each father is commanded to redeem the firstborn son on the mother's side by paying five shekels or its equivalent to the priest when the infant is thirty days old.

See Exodus 13:1–16; Numbers 3:11–13; *Teshuvot ha-Ge'onim, Sha'arei Teshuvah*, 47; Ta-Shma, *Minhag Ashkenaz ha-Qadmon*, 336–42.

747. **two appointees...** Two angels accompany each human being. See BT *Shabbat* 119b; *Ta'anit* 11a; *Zohar* 1:12b, 52a, 144b, 165b; 2:106b, 239a.

748. *good*—**Angel of Life;** *very*—**Angel of Death** See *Bereshit Rabbah* 9:10 (according to Oxford MS 147; cf. Paris MS 149 and *Yalqut Shim'oni* [in the variants in Theodor-Albeck's edition]): "Rabbi Shemu'el son of Rav Yitsḥak said, '*Behold, it was good*—this is the Angel of Life; *very*—this is the Angel of Death.'"

According to Rabbi Shemu'el, the Angel of Death is *very good* because he kills those who fail to accumulate good deeds. According to *Zohar* 2:149b, he is *very good* because the awareness of mortality stimulates a person to return to God. See 1:47a, 144b; 2:68b, 103a, 149b, 163a, 249a.

749. **acquires...** קני (*Qanei*), "Buys, purchases, acquires." With the ransom of

"The fourteenth commandment: to observe the Sabbath day, day of rest from all acts of Creation.[750] Here two commandments coalesce: one, observing the Sabbath day; the other, endowing that day with its holiness.

"To observe the Sabbath day, as I have mentioned, whose meaning I have aroused, for it is a day of rest for the worlds,[751] on which all acts were consummated and enacted before the day was hallowed. Once the day was hallowed, the creation of spirits remained—for them no body had been created.[752] Now, didn't the blessed Holy One know to delay hallowing the day until bodies had been created for these spirits? The answer is: the Tree of Knowledge of Good and Evil[753] aroused that other, evil side,[754] who verged on seizing power in the world, and countless spirits of varied species spread out to empower themselves in bodies. As soon as the blessed Holy One saw this, He aroused a gust of wind from the Tree of Life,[755] which struck another tree,[756] arousing the other, good side, and the day was hallowed. For the creation of bodies and the arousal of spirits derive from the side of goodness on this night,[757] not from the other side. If on this night the other side had preceded the side of goodness, the world could not have withstood them for even a moment.[758] But the blessed Holy One provided a remedy in advance, for the

101

the five shekels (see above, note 746), the father purchases life for his son.

750. **to observe the Sabbath day...** For this commandment, unlike the preceding ones, Rabbi Shim'on cites no verse from the opening section of Genesis, apparently because the connection is obvious: *On the seventh day God completed the work that He had done, and He ceased on the seventh day from all the work that He had done. God blessed the seventh day and hallowed it, for on it He ceased from all His work that God created to make* (Genesis 2:2–3).

751. **for the worlds** לעלמין (*Le-almin*), "For the worlds" or "forever, eternally." The worlds above and below share the tranquility of the Sabbath.

752. **for them no body had been created** See *Tanḥuma* (Buber), *Bereshit* 17: "It is not written here: [*He ceased from all His work*] *that* [*God*] *created and made*, but rather [*that God created*] *to make* (Genesis 2:3), for the Sabbath came first, with the work not yet completed. Rabbi Benaya said, 'This refers to the demons, for He created their

souls, and as He was creating their bodies, the Sabbath day was hallowed. He left them, and they remained soul without body.'"

See *Bereshit Rabbah* 7:5; 11:9; *Zohar* 1:20b, 47b–48a, 178a; 2:155b; 3:142b (*IR*); and M *Avot* 5:6: "Ten things were created on Sabbath eve at twilight:...Some say, 'Also the demons.'"

753. **Tree of Knowledge of Good and Evil** Adam and Eve ate the forbidden fruit of this tree. In Kabbalah it symbolizes *Shekhinah*, who transmits either reward or punishment, depending on human behavior (see above, page 50). By eating its fruit, Adam and Eve stimulated the power of evil.

754. **that other, evil side** The demonic realm, known as *Sitra Aḥra*, "the Other Side."

755. **Tree of Life** The other tree mentioned in the Garden story. In Kabbalah it symbolizes *Tif'eret*, husband of *Shekhinah*.

756. **another tree** *Shekhinah*, the Tree of Knowledge of Good and Evil. See *Zohar* 2:95b.

757. **on this night** On Sabbath eve.

758. **could not have withstood them...** The embodied maleficent spirits.

hallowing of the day skipped ahead,[759] forestalling the other side, and the world stood firm.

"Whereas the other side had schemed to be constructed in the world, empowered, on this night the side of goodness was constructed and empowered. Holy bodies and spirits were constructed on this night from the side of goodness—so the conjugal interval of the wise, who know this, is from Sabbath [14b] to Sabbath.[760] Once the other side saw that the side of holiness had done what she[761] had intended to do, she began roaming with her countless forces and her flanks, observing all those having intercourse in the nude by the light of a lamp. All children issuing from there are epileptic, possessed by spirits of that other side, naked spirits of the wicked called demons,[762] or possessed by Lilith who slays them.

759. **remedy...the hallowing of the day skipped ahead** The Sabbath began ahead of time, before sunset. See *Shir ha-Shirim Rabbah* on 4:5: "Rava said in the name of Rabbi Shim'on, 'A human being does not prepare a compress until he sees the wound. Not so the One by whose word the world came into being: He first prepares the compress and then strikes.'"

See BT *Megillah* 13b: "Resh Lakish said, 'The blessed Holy One does not strike Israel unless He has created healing for them beforehand.'"

760. **conjugal interval of the wise...** The Mishnah (*Ketubbot* 5:6) discusses how often husbands of various professions are required to fulfill the commandment of עונה (*onah*), "conjugal rights," i.e., to satisfy their wives sexually. According to Rabbi Eli'ezer, "The *onah* mentioned in the Torah [applies as follows]: Those who are unoccupied, every day; laborers, twice a week; donkey-drivers, once a week; camel-drivers, once every thirty days; sailors, once every six months."

The Talmud (BT *Ketubbot* 62b) adds: "When is the *onah* of the disciples of the wise? [I.e., What is the proper interval between two successive times of fulfilling this *mitsvah*?] Rav Yehudah said in the name of Shemu'el, 'From one Sabbath eve to the next.'"

In the *Zohar*, the union of the devotee of Torah with his wife on the eve of Sabbath

symbolizes and stimulates the union of the divine couple, *Tif'eret* and *Shekhinah*. The sacred human act engenders a holy body and draws down a holy soul. See *Zohar* 1:50a, 112a (*MhN*); 2:63b, 89a–b; 3:49b, 78a.

761. **she** Lilith, the demonic feminine, married to Samael. See *Zohar* 1:148a (*ST*); 2:96a–b, 245a; Scholem, *Kabbalah*, 356–61.

762. **intercourse in the nude...epileptic...possessed...** See BT *Pesaḥim* 112b: "It has been taught: 'One who stands naked in front of a lamp will become an epileptic. One who engages in sexual intercourse by the light of a lamp will have epileptic children.'" The *Zohar* combines both motifs.

The rabbinic Hebrew word for epileptic, נכפה (*nikhpeh*), means "forced, overtaken," hence, overtaken and possessed by demons, epileptic. Similarly, the Greek word for epilepsy derives from *lambanein*, "to seize."

According to *Pirqei de-Rabbi Eli'ezer* 34 (see the version in *Yalqut Shim'oni*, Isaiah, 429), the souls of the generation of the Flood will not arise at the resurrection of the dead; rather, they turn into bodiless spirits harming human beings. According to the *Zohar*, souls of the wicked in general turn into bodiless demons who roam in search of vulnerable bodies.

See 1:28b–29a (*TZ*), 48a, 100a, 129b; 2:99b, 118a (*RM*); 3:25a, 70a, 143a–b (*IR*); *ZH* 11a (*MhN*); *Sefer Ḥasidim*, ed. Margaliot, par. 770.

As soon as the day is hallowed and holiness rules the world, that other side diminishes itself, hiding away throughout the night and day of Sabbath. Except for Asimon[763] and his entire band who pass secretly over lamps, observing naked intercourse, then hide themselves away in the chasm of the immense abyss until Sabbath departs.[764] As soon as Sabbath departs, countless forces and companies fly, roaming through the world. So the song against maleficent spirits[765] was instituted to prevent their ruling the holy people. Where do they fly on that night? After they issue in a rush—intending to rule in the world over the holy people—and they see them in prayer and song, first enacting *havdalah* during prayer and then again over the cup,[766] they fly away, roaming till they reach the desert.[767]

"Concerning the departure of Sabbath, they have said, may their memory be a blessing: Three bring evil upon themselves. One, whoever curses himself.[768] The second, whoever throws out bread or crumbs amounting to the size of an olive.[769] The third, whoever lights a lamp at the departure of Sabbath before

103

763. **Asimon** Hebrew, אסימון (*asimon*), derived from the Greek *asemon*, "without mark, uncoined, shapeless, formless, unperceived." In rabbinic literature (e.g., M *Bava Metsi'a* 4:1) the term refers to uncoined metal and unmarked coin. Here Asimon designates an amorphous, unperceived demon. In *Zohar* 2:249b Asimon appears in holy form as one of the four multicolored, eight-winged angels (*ofanim*).

764. **chasm of the immense abyss...** The demonic abode. According to *Midrash Tehillim* 92:5, on the first Sabbath, "demons ceased from the world."

765. **song against maleficent spirits** Psalms 91:1–9, traditionally recited to ward off demons and maleficent spirits. Since Gaonic times, this psalm has been recited at the conclusion of the Sabbath, following the *amidah* prayer of the evening service.

See BT *Shevu'ot* 15b; JT *Shabbat* 6:2, 8b; *Midrash Tehillim* 91:1, and Buber's nn. 12–13; Scholem, in *Tarbiz* 50 (1982): 248, 251; *Zohar* 1:48a.

766. **enacting *havdalah*...** The *havdalah* ("separation") is the ritual marking the end of Sabbath (and in an abbreviated form, the end of festivals). The *havdalah* at the conclu-

sion of the Sabbath is first recited in the fourth blessing of the *amidah* prayer of the evening service and then over a cup of wine. This second, longer ritual consists of blessings over wine, spices, and the light of a candle (or here, a lamp).

See Ginsburg, *The Sabbath in the Classical Kabbalah*, 256–84; idem, in *Mehqerei Yerushalayim be-Mahashevet Yisra'el* 8 (1989): 189–90, n. 19.

767. **desert** Abode of the demons. See *Zohar* 1:126a, 169b, 178b; 2:157a, 184a, 236b–237a; 3:63b.

768. **whoever curses himself** According to M *Shevu'ot* 4:13, "One who curses himself or his neighbor by any of them [any of the divine names] violates a negative commandment." Further, BT *Shevu'ot* 36a adds the verse *But take care, take exceeding care for yourself* (Deuteronomy 4:9), implying that such a curse is dangerous.

See *Zohar* 2:266a; 3:155b, 246a (*RM*).

769. **whoever throws out bread...** See BT *Berakhot* 52b: "Rabbi Yohanan said, 'One may willfully [literally: with the hand] destroy crumbs smaller than an olive.'"

Cf. *Tosafot*, ad loc., s.v. *peirurin*; *Pesahim* 111b; *Hullin* 105b.

Israel has reached the hallowing of the portion,[770] because by this fire he
prematurely kindles the fire of Hell. For there is a place reserved in Hell for
those who violate Sabbaths; and those punished in Hell curse the one who
lights a lamp prematurely,[771] exclaiming: *YHVH is going to hurl you with a
mighty hurl, winding you round and round. He will wrap you up as a turban, a
ball—off to a vast land* (Isaiah 22:17–18).[772] For it is not right to kindle fire as
Sabbath departs until Israel enacts *havdalah* during prayer and then over the
cup, because until then it is still Sabbath and the holiness of Sabbath reigns
over us. At the moment they enact *havdalah* over the cup, all those forces and
companies empowered over the days of the week return, each and every one to
its station and task. For when Sabbath enters and the day is hallowed, holiness
is aroused and rules the world, while the profane is divested of its rule. Until
Sabbath has departed they do not return. Even as Sabbath departs, they do not
return to their places till the moment Israel says: 'Blessed are You, *YHVH,* who
separates the holy from the profane.'[773] Then holiness withdraws, and the
companies empowered over the weekdays are aroused and return to their
posts, each to its assigned watch. Even so, they do not assume control until
they shine through the mystery of the lamp. They are all called 'lights of the

104

770. **hallowing of the portion** קדושא
דסדרא (*Qiddusha de-sidra*), a version of the
qedushah in Hebrew and Aramaic usually
included in the prayer ובא לציון גואל (*U-va
le-tsiyyon go'el*), *A redeemer will come to
Zion* (Isaiah 59:20), and originally recited
after studying passages from the Prophets
following daily prayer. This *qedushah* appears in the liturgy near the end of the
morning service, on Sabbath afternoon,
and at the close of Sabbath, following the
evening prayer. See BT *Sotah* 49a, and Rashi, ad loc.

Rabbi Shim'on here goes beyond the
Talmud (BT *Shabbat* 150b), according to
which one is allowed to engage in work after
reciting *havdalah* in the evening prayer before
reciting it again over the cup of wine.

See *Zohorei Ya'bets;* Ta-Shma, *Minhag
Ashkenaz ha-Qadmon,* 217–20.

771. **prematurely kindles the fire of
Hell...a place reserved...** According to
Tanhuma, Ki Tissa 33, one of the dwellers
in Hell reports: "Whoever does not observe
the Sabbath properly [*Bereshit Rabbah* 11:5:

"willingly"] in your world comes here and
observes it against his will.... All week long
we are punished and on the Sabbath we
rest, and [we continue resting] as Sabbath
departs until the portions [i.e., *qiddusha de-
sidra,* "the hallowing of the portion" (see
previous note)] have been completed. Once
they are completed, an angel named Dumah, appointed over souls, comes and takes
the souls of those people [i.e., our souls]
and slings them...."

By lighting a lamp before the completion
of *qiddusha de-sidra,* one cuts short the
Sabbath rest of the sinners in Hell and
returns them to their suffering prematurely.

See *Zohar* 1:197b; 2:31b, 88b, 150b–151a,
203b, 207a; 3:94b; *ZH* 17a–b (*MhN*).

772. *YHVH is going to hurl you...off to
a vast land* The person who lights a lamp
too soon will himself be cast into Hell. See
BT *Menahot* 99b–100a; *Aggadat Bereshit* 61:1.

773. **Blessed are You...** The main blessing of *havdalah,* recited over the cup of wine.
See BT *Pesahim* 103b.

fire,' for they all spring from the mysterious stream of elemental fire[774] and rule over the lower world.

"All this applies when one lights a lamp before Israel has completed the hallowing of the portion. However, if one waits until they have completed it, those sinners in Hell acknowledge the justice of the blessed Holy One and confirm for that person all the blessings declared by the congregation: *May God give you of the dew of heaven* [*and the fat of the earth, abundance of grain and new wine*] (Genesis 27:28). *Blessed be you in the city, blessed be you in the field* (Deuteronomy 28:3)."[775] [15a]

---

774. **lights of the fire … elemental fire** The blessing over the flame in *havdalah* concludes: "… who creates the lights of the fire." The forces that dominate the week are beneath *Shekhinah*, symbolized by fire, while She herself derives from the *sefirah* of *Gevurah*, elemental fire. See *Zohar* 1:20b–21a; 2:207b–208b.

775. *May God give you …* These verses are recited at the conclusion of the evening service as Sabbath departs.

פרשת בראשית

Parashat Be-Reshit

"IN THE BEGINNING" (GENESIS 1:1–6:8)

בראשית (Be-reshit), *In the beginning* (Genesis 1:1).

t the head of potency of the King,[1] He engraved engravings[2] in luster on high.[3] A spark of impenetrable darkness[4] flashed within the concealed of the con-

1. **potency of the King** הורמנותא דמלכא (Hurmanuta de-malka), "Authority [or: decree] of the king." The phrase הרמנא דמלכא (harmana de-malka), "authority [or: decree] of the king," appears in BT *Berakhot* 58a, *Gittin* 57b, *Bava Metsi'a* 83b–84a, *Ḥullin* 57b.

See *Zohar* 1:76b, 97a, 108a, 109b (all *ST*), 147a (*Tos*); 2:123a; *ZḤ* 67c (*ShS*), 121d. Here the King is *Ein Sof*, arousing Itself to manifest through the process of emanation.

2. **engraved engravings** These engravings eventually manifest as the *sefirot*. See *Zohar* 1:3b, 38a; 2:126b; 3:128a (*IR*).

3. **luster on high** The brilliance of the first *sefirah*, *Keter*, represented in the *Zohar* as coeternal with *Ein Sof*.

4. **spark of impenetrable darkness** בוצינא דקרדינותא (Botsina de-qardinuta), "A lamp of impenetrability." Though בוצינא (botsina) usually means "lamp," here "spark" is likely. See the wealth of material collected and analyzed by Liebes, *Peraqim*, 145–51, 161–64. *OY* and *OL* record the variant בוציצא (botsitsa), "spark." Cf. *Zohar* 3:139a (*IR*), 295a (*IZ*); and the phrase בוציצא דקרדינותא (botsitsa de-qardinuta), which appears several times in *ZḤ* 56d–58d (*QhM*). קרדינותא (Qardinuta) recalls a phrase in BT *Pesaḥim* 7a: חיטי קורדניתא (ḥittei qurdanaita), "wheat from Kurdistan," which, according to Rashi,

is very hard. *OY*, *OL*, and *DE* record the variants קדרינותא (qadrinuta) or קדרוניתא (qadrunita), "darkness." See *ZḤ* 2a, where קרדנותא דסיהרא (qardenuta de-sihara) means "eclipse of the moon," corresponding to the Hebrew קדרות הירח (qadrut ha-yareaḥ), "darkening of the moon." Shim'on Lavi (*KP*) retains the reading בוצינא דקרדינותא (botsina de-qardinuta) but renders it שביב הקדרות (sheviv ha-qadrut), "the spark of darkness." Cf. Tishby, *Mishnat ha-Zohar*, 1:163: שביב של קדרות (shaviv shel qadrut), "a spark of darkness"; Tishby, *Wisdom of the Zohar*, tr. Goldstein, 1:309: "a spark of blackness." See *Tanḥuma, Shemot* 15.

The spark is so potently brilliant that it overwhelms comprehension. Many mystics convey similar paradoxical images: "a ray of divine darkness" (Dionysius, *Mystical Theology* 1:1); "the luminous darkness" (Gregory of Nyssa, *Life of Moses* 2:163); "the black light" (Iranian Sufism; see Corbin, *The Man of Light in Iranian Sufism*, 99–120). Prior to the *Zohar*, Azriel of Gerona and the author of *Ma'yan ha-Ḥokhmah* mention "the light darkened from shining." See Verman, *The Books of Contemplation*, 59–60, 158–59; Scholem, *Origins of the Kabbalah*, 336. Cf. Maimonides, *Guide of the Perplexed* 1:59: "We are dazzled by His beauty, and He is hidden

cealed,[5] from the head of Infinity[6]—a cluster of vapor forming in formlessness, thrust in a ring,[7] not white, not black, not red, not green, no color at all.[8] As a cord surveyed,[9] it yielded radiant colors. Deep within the spark gushed a flow, splaying colors below, concealed within the concealed of the mystery of *Ein Sof*.[10] It split and did not split its aura,[11] was not known at all, until under the

from us because of the intensity with which He becomes manifest, just as the sun is hidden to eyes too weak to apprehend it."

Here the blinding spark is the first impulse of emanation flashing from *Ein Sof* through *Keter* and proceeding to delineate the various *sefirot*. (On the connection between *qardinuta* and measurement, see Liebes, *Peraqim*, 146–49, 162–63.) The goal of meditation is to attain this spark and participate in the primal flow of being. See *ZH* 57d–58a (*QhM*); cf. *Zohar* 1:18b, 86b, 172a; 2:133b, 177a, 233a, 254b, 260a; 3:48b–49a, 135b, 139a (*IR*), 292b, 295a–b (*IZ*).

Other renderings of the phrase include: מנורה חשוכה (*menorah ḥashukhah*), "a dark lamp" (Galante); ניצוץ חזק (*nitsots ḥazaq*), "powerful spark" (*DE*); נר של חשך (*ner shel ḥoshekh*), "a lamp of darkness" (Elijah of Vilna, *Yahel Or*); "a dark flame" (Scholem, *Zohar*, 27); "a very powerful light" (Scholem, *Kabbalah*, 228); "a lamp of scintillation [or: darkness, measurement]" (Sperling and Simon, *The Zohar*); "a blinding spark" (Matt, *Zohar*, 49); *une flamme obscure* (Mopsik, *Le Zohar*); "the hardened spark" (Wolfson, "Woman—The Feminine as Other in Theosophic Kabbalah," 178–82). On the phallic connotations of the phrase, see Wolfson's discussion there and in his *Circle in the Square*, 60–62, and index, s.v. "hardened spark"; Liebes, "*Zohar ve-Eros,*" 73–80.

5. **concealed of the concealed** The luster on high, the first and most hidden *sefirah*, *Keter*.

6. **Infinity** Hebrew, אין סוף (*Ein Sof*), "there is no end," the ultimate divine reality. On the evolution of this term, see Scholem, *Kabbalah*, 88–89.

7. **cluster of vapor forming in formlessness...** קוטרא בגולמא (*Qutra be-gulma*). *Qutra* means both "knot" and "smoke" in

the *Zohar*. See 1:172a, and 30a, 33b, 94b, 106a, 161b; 2:80a, 124a; 3:45b, 51a–b, 107a, 289b, 295b (*IZ*).

Some commentators (Galante, *OY, Sullam*) suggest translating *qutra* as "form." Cf. קטורין (*qeturin*) in *Vayiqra Rabbah* 23:12; *Arukh*, s.v. *qtr*. The phrase would then mean: "a form in formlessness," which resonates with "a spark of darkness." The ring is *Keter*, the "Crown."

8. **not white, not black...** These four colors are associated with four *sefirot*: *Ḥesed, Shekhinah, Gevurah*, and *Tif'eret*, none of which appears until a later stage of emanation. See *ZH* 57a (*QhM*); Liebes, *Studies in Jewish Myth*, 84.

9. **As a cord surveyed** The spark that is a vapor is also a cord (משיחא [*meshiḥa*]), referred to elsewhere in the *Zohar* as קו המדה (*qav ha-middah*), "the line of measure," based on Jeremiah 31:38.

See Azriel of Gerona, *Peirush ha-Aggadot*, 89–90; Jacob ben Sheshet, *Meshiv Devarim Nekhoḥim*, 113; *Zohar* 1:18b; 2:233a–b, 258a; *ZH* 56d–58d (*QhM*); *TZ* 18, 37b.

The cord, or measuring line, maps out the paths and stages of emanation, the spectrum of divine colors, each with its own wavelength.

10. **concealed within the concealed...** The flow of emanation has just begun; everything is still hidden within the mystery of *Ein Sof*.

11. **It split and did not split...** בקע ולא בקע (*Beqa ve-la beqa*). The flow somehow broke through, but the nature of the breakthrough is impossible to describe, so the act is stated and immediately denied. See Scholem's remarks on expressions of this kind in *Major Trends*, 166–67.

The aura (אוירא [*avira*], "air, space, ether, aura") is *Keter*. See *Zohar* 1:16b; 3:135b (*IR*); Altmann, *Studies*, 174; Scholem, "*Iqvotav shel*

108

impact of splitting, a single, concealed, supernal point shone. Beyond that point, nothing is known, so it is called ראשית (*Reshit*), *Beginning*,[12] first command of all.[13]

The enlightened[14] *will shine like the* זהר (*zohar*), *radiance*,[15] *of the sky, and those who lead many to righteousness, like the stars forever and ever* (Daniel 12:3).

זהר (*Zohar*), *Radiance!* Concealed of concealed struck its aura, which touched and did not touch

this point.[16] Then this *beginning* expanded, building itself a palace worthy of

Gevirol be-Qabbalah," 167–68; idem, *Origins of the Kabbalah*, 331–47 (especially 342); Pines, in *Tarbiz* 50 (1981): 339–47; Liebes, in *Meḥqerei Yerushalyim be-Maḥashevet Yisra'el* 6:3–4 (1987): 80–86; Verman, *The Books of Contemplation*, 153–56.

See *Sefer Yetsirah* 2:6: "Out of chaos He formed substance, making what is not into what is. He hewed enormous pillars out of ether that cannot be grasped."

See Solomon ibn Gabirol, *Keter Malkhut* 9:101: "He called to אין (*ayin*), nothingness, ונבקע (*ve-nivqa*), and it was split, to יש (*yesh*), something, and it was thrust." On the parallel between the *Zohar*'s description and the Orphic myth of the hatching of the cosmic egg, see Liebes, *Studies in Jewish Myth*, 79–84.

12. **a single, concealed, supernal point…** *Beginning*   The flow of emanation manifests as a point of light. This is the second *sefirah: Hokhmah* ("Wisdom"), which is called *Beginning* because it is the first ray of divine light to appear outside of *Keter*, the first aspect of God that can be known.

The identification of ראשית (*reshit*), *beginning*, with Wisdom appears widely. See *Targum Yerushalmi* (frag.), Genesis 1:1; Wolfson, *Philo*, 1:242–45, 266–69; *Bereshit Rabbah* 1:1; Azriel of Gerona, *Peirush ha-Aggadot*, 81; Naḥmanides on Genesis 1:1; *Zohar* 1:2a, 3b, 16b, 20a, 145a; Moses de León, *Sheqel ha-Qodesh*, 21–22 (25–26); Scholem, *Major Trends*, 391, n. 80.

13. **first command of all**   According to M *Avot* 5:1, "The world was created through ten commands." Only nine explicit commands appear in Genesis 1, but the decade is completed by counting the phrase *In the beginning*.

See BT *Rosh ha-Shanah* 32a, *Megillah* 21b; Ezra of Gerona, *Peirush Shir ha-Shirim*, 506; *Zohar* 1:16b, 30a; *TZ* 32, 76a. In Kabbalah the ten commands symbolize the ten *sefirot*, the first of which establishes the basis for the other nine.

14. **The enlightened** המשכילים (*Ha-maskilim*).   Both philosophers and kabbalists described themselves by this term, which originally may have designated the community of those who shared Daniel's vision. See Scholem, *Origins of the Kabbalah*, 224. On the following pages of the *Zohar* (15b–16a), the term is applied to the letters and vowels, as well as to the *sefirot*. The *Zohar* on Exodus opens with the same verse and applies it to the kabbalists: "*The enlightened* are those who contemplate the secret of wisdom" (2:2a).

See *Bahir* 95 (139); *Zohar* 2:23a; *ZH* 58c (*QhM*), 93d–94b (*Tiq*); Wolfson, *Through a Speculum That Shines*, 383–84; Liebes, "*Zohar ve-Eros*," 73–75.

15. זהר (*zohar*), *radiance*   The word designates the hidden power of emanation and provides the title of the book. See below, and *Zohar* 1:100a (*ST*); 3:124b, 153b (*RM*); Liebes, "*Zohar ve-Eros*," 73–86.

16. זהר (*Zohar*), *Radiance!…this point*   The spark of emanation flashes again, and *Keter*, the aura, subtly transmits the impulse to *Hokhmah*, the point of Wisdom. See *Zohar* 1:16b, 65a; 2:268b.

glorious praise. There it sowed seed to give birth, availing worlds.[17] The secret is: *Her stock is seed of holiness* (Isaiah 6:13).[18]

זהר (*Zohar*), *Radiance!* Sowing seed for its glory, like the seed of fine purple silk wrapping itself within, weaving itself a palace,[19] constituting its praise, availing all.

With this *beginning*, the unknown concealed one[20] created the palace. This palace is called אלהים (*Elohim*), *God.*[21] The secret is: בראשית ברא אלהים (*Bereshit bara Elohim*), *With beginning, ____ created God* (Genesis 1:1).[22]

17. **palace worthy of glorious praise.... sowed seed...** The purpose of emanation is to display the glory of the hidden God, which is achieved through a rhythm of revelation and concealment: only by concealing itself can the overwhelming light be revealed. The point expands into a circle, a palace—the third *sefirah: Binah* ("Understanding"). She is the divine womb, where the seed of *Ḥokhmah,* the divine father, is sown. *Binah* gives birth to the seven lower *sefirot,* which engender the rest of creation. See *Zohar* 2:68b (*Tos*). The idea that the sperm originates in the brain is based on the theory of the second-century Greek physician Galen, common in medieval literature.

18. *Her stock is seed of holiness* The prophet Isaiah refers to one-tenth of the people of Israel, who will be saved. The *Zohar* cites the verse as an allusion either to *Binah* or *Shekhinah,* the mystical Assembly of Israel, the tenth *sefirah,* whose origin is the seed of *Ḥokhmah* (known as "Holiness") sown in *Binah.* See Azriel of Gerona, *Peirush ha-Aggadot,* 20; *Zohar* 2:121a.

19. **fine purple silk wrapping itself within...** As the silkworm spins a cocoon out of its own substance, so *Ḥokhmah,* the point of *beginning,* expands into the palace of *Binah.* (The silk industry was extensive in Andalusia, south of Castile, where the *Zohar* emerged.)

See *Bereshit Rabbah* 21:5: "like the locust whose garment is of itself." Cf. Shneur Zalman of Lyady, *Sha'ar ha-Yiḥud ve-ha-Emunah,* chap. 7; and the spider simile in the Upanishads (Hume, ed., *The Thirteen Principal Upanishads,* 95, 367).

20. **the unknown concealed one** The hidden source of emanation, *Ein Sof* or *Keter.*

21. אלהים (*Elohim*), *God* Here the name signifies *Binah,* the Divine Mother who gives birth to the seven lower *sefirot.* See *Zohar* 1:3b, 15b.

22. **The secret is...** The *Zohar* offers its mystical reading of the opening words of Genesis. It translates the first word, בראשית (*Be-reshit*), as *With beginning* rather than *In the beginning,* relying on an alternative meaning of the preposition ב (*be*). See *Targum Yerushalmi* (frag.) and Naḥmanides, ad loc.; *Bereshit Rabbah* 1:1; Azriel of Gerona, *Peirush ha-Aggadot,* 81.

The subject of the verse, אלהים (*Elohim*), *God,* follows the verb ברא (*bara*), *created.* In its typical hyperliteral fashion, the author(s) of the *Zohar* insists on reading the words in the exact order in which they appear, thereby transforming *God* into the object! This means that the subject is now unnamed, but that is perfectly appropriate because the true subject of emanation is unnamable. The opening words of the Bible no longer mean: *In the beginning God created,* but rather: *With beginning* [by means of the point of *Ḥokhmah*], the ineffable source *created Elohim* [the palace of *Binah*].

The rabbis of the Talmud were aware of the danger of misinterpreting *Elohim* as the object of the sentence, which could promote Gnostic dualism (see BT *Megillah* 9a; Rashi and Tosafot, ad loc.). Various early kabbalists also adopt such a reading. See *Kiryat Sefer* 6 (1929–30): 415; Verman, *The Books of Contemplation,* 139–41; Isaac ibn Latif, *Sha'ar ha-Shamayim* 2:10; *Ma'arekhet ha-Elohut,* 82b–

110

זהר (*Zohar*), *Radiance!* From here all commands were created through the mysterious expansion of this point of concealed radiance. If *created* is written here, no wonder it is written: *God created the human being in His image* (Genesis 1:27).[23]

זהר (*Zohar*), *Radiance!* Mystery! בראשית (*Be-reshit*), *In the beginning,* first of all. אהיה (*Ehyeh*), *I will be* (Exodus 3:14), a sacred name engraved in its sides;[24] אלהים (*Elohim*), *God,* engraved in the crown.[25] אשר (*Asher*), *Who* (ibid.)—a hidden, treasured palace, beginning of the mystery of ראשית (*reshit*).[26] אשר (*Asher*)—ראש (*rosh*), head, emerging from ראשית (*reshit*).[27] When [15b] afterward point and palace were arrayed as one, then בראשית (*Be-reshit*) comprised supernal ראשית (*reshit*) in wisdom.[28] Afterward the color of the palace transformed and it was called בית (*bayit*), house, while the supernal point was called ראש (*rosh*), merging in one another in the mystery of בראשית (*Be-reshit*), when all was as one in one entirety, before the house was inhabited.[29]

83a; Scholem, *Major Trends,* 402, n. 55; Liebes, *Studies in the Zohar,* 152–54. For Gnostic parallels, see Robinson, ed., *The Nag Hammadi Library,* index, s.v. Autogenes, Self-begotten One.

23. **If *created*...no wonder...** The verb ברא (*bara*), *created,* thought to be reserved for creation *ex nihilo,* refers in the opening verse of Genesis to an act of emanation, the emanation of *Binah* (*Elohim*) from the primordial point of *Ḥokhmah* (*Reshit*). See below, page 113: "*Bara*—concealed mystery, from which all expands." If so, no wonder the same verb is employed to describe the creation of Adam and Eve, a further stage of divine unfolding.

For alternative interpretations, see Scholem; *KP; OY;* Galante; *MM;* Tishby, *Wisdom of the Zohar,* 1:310. Liebes ("*Zohar ve-Eros,*" 75) suggests: If, by means of זהר (*zohar*), *radiance,* God created heaven and earth, no wonder that it is written: *God created the human being in His image,* a verse that perplexed those medieval interpreters who denied anthropomorphism. The verse is not comparing the human and divine forms, but rather the creative power called *zohar,* common to both God and humans. In creating the human being, God emanated and imparted this creative potential.

24. **אהיה (*Ehyeh*), *I will be*...** A name of *Keter.* At the burning bush, God reveals His name to Moses: אהיה אשר אהיה (*Ehyeh asher ehyeh*), *I will be who I will be* [or: *I am who I am*]. Here the first two of the three Hebrew words are applied to *Keter* and *Binah* respectively. See *Zohar* 3:11a, 65a–b.

25. **אלהים (*Elohim*), *God*...** As noted above, this name applies to *Binah,* but it also alludes to *Shekhinah,* known as עטרה (*atarah*), "crown."

26. **אשר (*Asher*), *Who*...** Referring to *Binah,* the palace, the first *sefirah* to emanate from *Ḥokhmah,* known as ראשית (*reshit*), *beginning.* On *Asher* as a name of *Binah,* see *Zohar* 1:158a, 246a.

27. **אשר (*Asher*)—ראש (*rosh*), head...** אשר (*Asher*), signifying *Binah,* is an anagram of ראש (*rosh*), the initial letters of ראשית (*reshit*), signifying *Ḥokhmah. Binah* emerges from *Ḥokhmah.*

28. **then בראשית (*Be-reshit*)...in wisdom** The opening word of the Torah indicates both the primordial point of *Ḥokhmah* (*reshit*) and the palace of *Binah* (*be*).

29. **the color...transformed...** *Binah* develops further and is no longer called by the single letter ב (*bet*) (i.e., the preposition *be,* "in" or "with"), but by the word בית (*bayit*), "house," though it is still joined with

Once it was sown, arraying habitation, it was called אלהים (Elohim)—hidden, concealed.[30]

זהר (Zohar), *Radiance!* Concealed and treasured, while offspring lay within, yet to be born, and the house expanded, arrayed by that seed of holiness.[31] Until it conceived, expanding into habitation, it was not called אלהים (Elohim), rather all combined: בראשית (Be-reshit). Once arrayed in the name אלהים (Elohim), it generated offspring from that seed sown within.

What is that seed? Those engraved letters, mystery of Torah, emerging from that point.[32] Within that palace the point sowed the seed of three points—חולם (ḥolem), שורק (shuruq), חירק (ḥireq)[33]—merging together, becoming a single mystery: a voice emerging in unison.[34] As it emerged, its consort emerged with it, comprising all letters, as is written: את השמים (et ha-shamayim), *the heavens*—voice and consort.[35] This voice, *heaven*, is the final אהיה (ehyeh), *I will be.*[36]

112

the point of Ḥokhmah, called ראש (rosh), "head," and together they comprise בראשית (Be-reshit). At this stage, the house of Binah is still uninhabited by the primordial seed or by any of the lower *sefirot.* See ZḤ 5a (MhN).

30. **Once it was sown...אלהים (Elohim)...** Once the seed of emanation from Ḥokhmah flows into Her, Binah attains the independent name *Elohim.* "Hidden, concealed" may refer to the lower *sefirot* gestating within Binah or to the fact that Binah is assigned the letters of the name יהוה (YHVH) with the vowels of the name אלהים (Elohim). See *Zohar* 3:65a; OY; Tishby, *Wisdom of the Zohar,* 1:311.

31. **while offspring...** The lower *sefirot* exist potentially within the primordial seed of Ḥokhmah, which has not yet impregnated Binah, though the primordial point has already expanded into a circle, the house of Binah, and begun to enter Her.

32. **Those engraved letters...** The emanation is depicted as a stream of the letters of the alphabet flowing from Ḥokhmah, who is known as primordial Torah.

33. **the seed of three points—חולם (ḥolem), שורק (shuruq), חירק (ḥireq)** These three vowels appear, respectively, as points placed above, within, and beneath the letter. Here they apparently represent the three lines of emanation: right, left, and center.

See Isaac ha-Kohen, *Ta'amei ha-Nequddot,* ed. Scholem, *Madda'ei ha-Yahadut* 2 (1927): 265–68; *Zohar* 1:17a; Judah Ḥayyat, *Ma'arekhet ha-Elohut,* 136a. According to Moses de León, *Sefer ha-Rimmon,* 328–30 (see Wolfson's note, 329:2), the three points symbolize Ḥokhmah, Tif'eret, and Shekhinah.

34. **a voice...** The *sefirah* of Tif'eret, known as Written Torah.

35. **its consort emerged with it...** The partner of Tif'eret is Shekhinah, who is called את (Et), comprising the entire alphabet of divine speech, the letters from א (alef) to ת (tav). See the Christian parallel in Revelation 1:8: "I am *alpha* and *omega.*"

Grammatically, the accusative particle *et* has no ascertainable independent sense, but Naḥum of Gimzo and his disciple Rabbi Akiva taught that when *et* appears in a biblical verse, it amplifies the original meaning. See BT *Pesaḥim* 22b; *Ḥagigah* 12a–b; *Zohar* 1:247a; 2:90a, 135b.

את (Et), the range of the alphabet, is an appropriate name for Shekhinah, who is known as both the mystical realm of speech and Oral Torah. In the opening verse of Genesis, the phrase את השמים (et ha-shamayim) refers to Shekhinah and Her partner, Tif'eret, the voice, also known as *shamayim, heaven.*

36. **the final אהיה (ehyeh), *I will be*** In the name revealed by God to Moses, אהיה

זהר (*Zohar*), *Radiance!* Comprising all colors in this way, till here. יהוה אלהינו יהוה (*YHVH Eloheinu YHVH*), *YHVH, our God, YHVH* (Deuteronomy 6:4)—three rungs, corresponding to the supernal mystery.[37] בראשית ברא אלהים (*Be-reshit bara Elohim*), *In the beginning God created. Be-reshit*—primordial mystery.[38] *Bara*—concealed mystery, from which all expands.[39] *Elohim*—mystery sustaining all below.[40] את השמים (*Et ha-shamayim*), *the heavens*—so as not to separate them, male and female as one.[41] את (*Et*)—conveying all those letters, entirety of them all: beginning and end. Afterward ה (*he*) was added, so all those letters would be combined with *he*, and it was called אתה (*Attah*), *You.*[42] So, ואתה (*Ve-Attah*), *And You, enliven them all* (Nehemiah 9:6). *Et*—mystery of אדני (*Adonai*), *Lord*, and so it is called.[43] *Ha-shamayim—YHVH*, supernal mystery.[44] ואת (*Ve-et*)—array of male and female.[45] ואת (*Ve-et*)—mystery of ויהוה (*va-YHVH*), *and YHVH*, and all is one.[46] הארץ (*Ha-arets*), *The*

אשר אהיה (*Ehyeh asher ehyeh*), *I will be who I will be* [or: *I am who I am*] (Exodus 3:14), the first *ehyeh* refers to *Keter*, *asher* refers to *Binah*, and the second *ehyeh* refers to *Tif'eret*. See above, page 111.

37. **יהוה אלהינו יהוה (*YHVH Eloheinu YHVH*), *YHVH, our God, YHVH*...** This triad of divine names from the opening line of the *Shema* corresponds to the triad interpreted above, אהיה אשר אהיה (*Ehyeh asher ehyeh*), *I am who I am*. Both triads symbolize *Keter* (or *Hokhmah*), *Binah*, and *Tif'eret*. The triad immediately following, בראשית ברא אלהים (*Be-reshit bara Elohim*), *In the beginning God created* (along with the continuation of the verse), conveys a similar meaning. On the possibility of trinitarian influence on the *Zohar's* interpretation of triads such as these, see Tishby, *Wisdom of the Zohar*, 3:973; Liebes, *Studies in the Zohar*, 140–45.

38. **primordial mystery** The primordial point of *Hokhmah*.

39. **concealed mystery...** The hidden source of emanation, *Keter* or *Ein Sof*.

40. **mystery sustaining all below** *Binah*, who gives birth to the lower seven *sefirot*.

41. **male and female...** *Tif'eret* and *Shekhinah*, whose union is vital to the cosmos.

42. **ה (*he*) was added...** The final ה (*he*) in the name יהוה (*YHVH*) symbolizes *Shekhinah*. When this letter is added to Her

name את (*Et*), She attains an expanded name: אתה (*Attah*), *You*.

See *Zohar* 1:37a, 154b, 158b; 2:138b, 261a (*Heikh*).

43. **mystery of אדני (*Adonai*), *Lord*, and so it is called** *Shekhinah* is also called אדני (*Adonai*), which is pronounced as it is written, unlike the more concealed name יהוה (*YHVH*), which is also pronounced *Adonai*, differently than it is written.

44. **supernal mystery** *Tif'eret*.

45. **ואת (*Ve-et*)—array of male and female** The word ואת (*ve-et*) immediately precedes הארץ (*ha-arets*), *the earth*, in the opening verse of Genesis. While את (*et*) signifies *Shekhinah*, the prefix ו (*ve*), *and*, signifies *Tif'eret*, since the numerical value of the letter ו (*vav*) is six, and *Tif'eret* together with the five *sefirot* associated with Him (*Hesed, Gevurah, Netsah, Hod, and Yesod*) constitute a sixfold entity. See *Zohar* 1:29b.

46. **mystery of ויהוה (*va-YHVH*), *and YHVH*...** See *Bereshit Rabbah* 51:2: "Rabbi El'azar said, 'Wherever it is said: *and YHVH*, this implies: He and His Court.'" In Kabbalah this court symbolizes *Shekhinah*, who derives from the *sefirah* of *Din* ("Judgment") and pronounces the divine decree, so the phrase *and YHVH* encompasses "He [*Tif'eret*, known as *YHVH*] and His Court [*Shekhinah*]." Whereas the ו (*vav*) of the word ואת (*ve-et*) refers to *Tif'eret*, the ו (*vav*) of ויהוה

earth—Elohim, as above, generating fruit and verdure.[47] This name is embraced at three sites, branching from there variously.[48]

Until here, mystery of secret of secrets, which He engraved, fashioned, vivified in hidden ways, through the mystery of a single verse.[49] From here on,[50] בראשית—ברא שית (*Be-reshit—bara shit*), He created six, *from one end of heaven to the other* (Deuteronomy 4:32), six directions extending from the supernal mystery[51] through the expansion that He created from the primordial point. ברא (*Bara*), *Created*—expansion of a single point on high. Here is engraved the mystery of the name of forty-two letters.[52]

The enlightened will shine like the זהר (*zohar*), *radiance, of the sky* (Daniel 12:3)[53]—like musical intonations,[54] whose melody is followed by the letters and

(*va-YHVH*) refers to *Shekhinah,* but "all is one."

See JT *Berakhot* 9:5, 14b; Rashi on Exodus 12:29; *Zohar* 1:64b, 107b; 2:37b, 44b; 3:149a. The hermeneutical significance of *and* was championed by Rabbi Akiva. See BT *Yevamot* 68b; *Sanhedrin* 51b.

47. **fruit and verdure** Souls. See *Bahir* 14 (22); Ezra of Gerona, *Peirush Shir ha-Shirim,* 489, 504; *Zohar* 1:19a, 33a, 59b–60a, 82b, 85b, 115a–b; 2:223b; Moses de León, *Sefer ha-Mishqal,* 51; idem, *Sheqel ha-Qodesh,* 56 (69). Cf. Ibn Ezra on Psalms 1:3.

48. הארץ (*Ha-arets*), *The earth—Elohim, as above...at three sites...* *Shekhinah* is called *Earth,* and She shares the name *Elohim* with *Binah* ("as above"). As *Binah* reigns over the lower *sefirot, Shekhinah* reigns over the lower worlds. The name *Elohim* is also applied to *Gevurah* (thus to three *sefirot* in all) and—outside of the *sefirot*—to angels, false gods, and human judges.

49. **which He engraved, fashioned, vivified...** The opening verse of the Torah discloses the most secret divine activities: the initial engraving within the luster of *Keter,* fashioning the primordial point of *Hokhmah* into the palace of *Binah,* and the gestation of the lower *sefirot.*

50. **From here on** Now the opening word of the Torah is interpreted as referring directly to the lower *sefirot.*

51. ברא שית – בראשית (*Be-reshit—bara shit*)... The word בראשית (*Be-reshit*) is divided in two and read as ברא שית (*bara*

shit), "created six." See *Midrash ha-Gadol,* Genesis 1:1, 11–12; *Seder Rabbah di-Vreshit,* 1 (*Battei Midrashot,* 1:19), where it is said that the world was created by six letters (the divine names יה [*YH*] and יהוה [*YHVH*]); BT *Sukkah* 49a; *Zohar* 1:3b, 39b.

The six directions are north, south, east, west, up, and down (see *Sefer Yetsirah* 1:13), which symbolize the six *sefirot* from *Hesed* through *Yesod,* emanating from the hidden source. At the center stands *Tif'eret, Heaven,* so all six extend *from one end of heaven to the other.*

52. **the mystery of the name of forty-two letters** The forty-two-letter name is mentioned in the name of Rav, though not recorded, in BT *Qiddushin* 71a. According to one later view, it consists of the first forty-two letters of the Torah, from the ב (*bet*) of בראשית (*Be-reshit*) through the ב (*bet*) of בהו (*bohu*), *void* (Genesis 1:2).

See *Tosafot, Hagigah* 11b, s.v. *ein doreshin; KP* 1:46c–d; Trachtenberg, *Jewish Magic and Superstition,* 94–95. Cf. Maimonides, *Guide of the Perplexed* 1:62; *Zohar* 1:1a, 30a; 2:130b, and 175b: "...the forty-two holy letters of the holy name, by which heaven and earth were created."

53. *The enlightened will shine like the* זהר (*zohar*), *radiance, of the sky* The verse continues: *and those who lead many to righteousness, like the stars forever and ever.*

54. **musical intonations** The cantillation signs in the biblical text impart meaning to the words of each verse, thereby illuminat-

vowels, undulating after them like troops behind their king. The letters are body; the vowels, spirit.[55] All of them range in motion after the intonations and halt with them. When the melody of the intonation moves, letters and -vowels follow; when it stops, they do not move but stand in place.

The enlightened will shine—letters and vowels. *Like the* זהר (*zohar*), *radiance*—melody of the notes. *Of the sky*—extension of the melody, like those extending, prolonging the melody.[56] *And those who lead many to righteousness*—pausal notes, halting their movement, as a result of which the word is heard.[57] *Will shine*—letters and vowels shining as one on their journey into a mystery of concealment, a journey on concealed paths. From this all expands.[58]

We have learned: Every *Solomon* mentioned in the Song of Songs connotes the King to whom peace belongs, while *king*, anonymous, connotes the female, lower connoting upper.[59] The mystery is that lower inherits upper, both as

ing the letters and vowels, which are soon identified as *the enlightened*. The word משכילים (*maskilim*), *enlightened*, is perhaps associated here with the biblical word משכיל (*maskil*), an obscure musical term appearing in the title of various psalms. See *TZ* 21, 48b–49a; Wolfson, "Biblical Accentuation in a Mystical Key."

55. **The letters are body; the vowels, spirit** See *Bahir* 83 (115): "[The vowels] in the letters resemble the breath of life in the human body."

See Judah Halevi, *Kuzari* 4:3; Ibn Ezra on Exodus 20:1; Ezra of Gerona, *Peirush Shir ha-Shirim*, 487; Todros Abulafia, *Sha'ar ha-Razim*, 73–76; Gikatilla, *Ginnat Egoz*, 413–16; Moses de León, *Sefer ha-Rimmon*, 328; Scholem, *Das Buch Bahir*, 87–89, n. 5; Liebes, *Peraqim*, 174–76; *ZH* 73c (*ShS*), 84b, 104a–b (*TZ*), 107d (*TZ*); *TZ* 5, 20b.

56. **those extending, prolonging...** The cantillation signs that extend the melody are compared to *the sky*, stretched out above the earth.

57. **pausal notes, halting their movement...** Cantillation signs that bring the melody to a halt. By indicating the appropriate pauses, they *lead many* letters and words to the correct syntax and phrasing. See BT *Megillah* 3a; *Bereshit Rabbah* 36:8.

58. **all expands** The flow of letters and vowels, guided by musical intonation, sym-

bolizes the expansion of the primordial point of emanation. The divine manifests through speech.

59. **We have learned...** This paragraph appears here in several manuscripts (L2, P1, P4, V5) and witnesses (*OY*, Cr), while in other manuscripts and in M it appears in 1:29a with slight variations.

See *Shir ha-Shirim Rabbah* 1:11 (on 1:1): "Rabbi Yudan and Rabbi Levi said in the name of Rabbi Yoḥanan, 'Wherever in this scroll [the Song of Songs] the expression *King Solomon* appears, the text speaks of King Solomon, while *the king*, anonymous, connotes the blessed Holy One.' The Rabbis say, 'Wherever *King Solomon* appears, the text speaks of the King to whom peace belongs [deriving שלמה (*Shelomoh*), *Solomon*, from שלום (*shalom*), peace], while *the king*, anonymous, connotes the Assembly of Israel.'"

In rabbinic Hebrew the phrase כנסת ישראל (*Keneset Yisra'el*), "Assembly of Israel," denotes the people of Israel, and the Song of Songs is read as a love poem between them and God. In the *Zohar*, *Keneset Yisra'el* refers to *Shekhinah*, described here as נוקבא (*nuqba*), "female." She is the divine counterpart of the people, that aspect of God most intimately connected with them. The lovers depicted in the Song of Songs symbolize *Shekhinah* and Her partner, *Tif'eret*. *Shekhinah* is described there as *King*, reflecting Her name *Malkhut*

one.[60] This is ב (*bet*), as is written: *By wisdom* בית (*bayit*), *a house is built* (Proverbs 24:3).[61] Similarly, *King Solomon made himself a pavilion from the trees of Lebanon* (Song of Songs 3:9).[62] *Pavilion* is the adorning of the lower world by the upper world.[63] For before the blessed Holy One created the world, He and His name were enclosed within Him, one.[64] Nothing existed until there arose within the will of thought[65] actualizing all by impress of the signet,[66] creating

("Kingdom"). See *Zohar* 1:47a, 84a. Here, apparently, King Solomon denotes *Binah*, "to whom peace belongs," namely, *Yesod*, who conveys the flow of *Binah* and thereby links the two lovers. See BT *Shabbat* 152a, where Rabbi Shim'on son of Ḥalafta refers to the phallus as "peacemaker of the home." Cf. *Zohar* 1:5b; 2:127b. The lower (plain, earthly) meaning of the text connotes the upper, divine sense. See below, page 170.

60. **lower inherits upper...** Through Her union with *Tif'eret, Shekhinah* absorbs the flow of emanation from Her mother above, *Binah*. See *Zohar* 2:215a: "... for Daughter inherits Mother," and above, page 9: "Mother lends Daughter Her garments."

61. **This is ב (*bet*)...** The opening letter of the Torah, the ב (*bet*) of בראשית (*Bereshit*), *In the beginning*, stands for בית (*bayit*), *house*. The letter *bet*, the second letter of the alphabet, is equivalent to two, and here indicates two sefirotic structures: *Binah*, fashioned from the primordial point of *Ḥokhmah*, divine wisdom; and *Shekhinah*, comprising the *sefirot* from *Ḥesed* through *Yesod*.

62. *a pavilion...* אפריון (*Appiryon*), a biblical hapax legomenon, often translated "palanquin" but apparently referring to a stationary structure. In the Midrash, it is interpreted as referring to the Tabernacle and to the Temple in Jerusalem (*Pesiqta de-Rav Kahana* 1:2; *Shir ha-Shirim Rabbah* and *Targum*, ad loc.).

In the *Zohar*, the *appiryon* is *Shekhinah*, the divine palace (1:29a; 2:127a). This *pavilion* is constructed of the *sefirot* from *Ḥesed* through *Yesod*, known as *the trees of Lebanon*, namely, of *Ḥokhmah*. See *Zohar* 1:31a, 35a–b; 2:127b.

63. **adorning of the lower world by the upper world** *Shekhinah* is adorned by the light radiating from *Binah*.

64. **before the blessed Holy One created...** See *Pirqei de-Rabbi Eli'ezer* 3: "Rabbi Eli'ezer son of Hyrcanus [said], '...Before the world was created, there existed only the blessed Holy One and His great name. The thought of creating the world arose in His mind. He traced the world, but it did not endure. They told a parable. To what can this be compared? To a king who wishes to build his palace. If he does not trace in the earth its foundations, exits, and entrances, he cannot begin to build. Similarly, the blessed Holy One traced the world in front of Himself, but it did not endure until He created *teshuvah* ("returning, turning back" to God).'" Cf. Maimonides, *Guide of the Perplexed* 1:61; *ZH* 2d (*MhN*).

In Kabbalah the *sefirot* are considered God's names since they reveal the divine identity. In particular, *Shekhinah*, the culminating expression of the *sefirot*, is called "the name" of God. Before the process of emanation, all of the *sefirot* existed potentially within *Ein Sof*.

65. **the will of thought** *Keter*, the impulse within the divine mind. See Azriel of Gerona, *Peirush ha-Aggadot*, 92, 94, 107; *Zohar* 1:45b; 2:259b, 268b; *ZH* 1b, 6c (*ST*).

66. **the signet** סמיטרא (*Samitra*), apparently based on סימנטיר (*simanteir*), derived from the Greek *semanterion*, "seal, signet, stamp." *Bei'ur ha-Millim ha-Zarot*, 182, defines *samitra* as "turban," based on the *Arukh*; see *KP, OY*.

The process of emanation begins with a gesture of royal authority. See above, note 1.

116

the world. He traced and built, but it did not endure[67] until He enwrapped Himself in a wrapping of radiance, supernal right, creating *the heavens*.[68] With this first radiance of all He created *the heavens*. The mystery is this verse: *With beginning Elohim created the heavens and the earth* (Genesis 1:1).[69]

The enlightened will shine like the זהר (*zohar*), *radiance, of the sky*—these are pillars and sockets of that *pavilion*.[70] המשכילים (*Ha-maskilim*), *The enlightened*—supernal pillars and sockets, contemplating in wisdom everything needed by that *pavilion* and its supports. This mystery accords with what is said: *Happy is* משכיל (*maskil*), *one who considers, the poor* (Psalms 41:2).[71]

Will shine—for unless they shine and radiate, they cannot contemplate that *pavilion*, looking out for all it needs.

Like the זהר (*zohar*), *radiance, of the sky*—standing [16a] above *the enlightened*, of whom is written: *An image above the heads of the living being: a sky, like awesome ice* (Ezekiel 1:22).[72]

---

67. **but it did not endure**   See *Bereshit Rabbah* 9:2: "*He fashioned everything at its appropriate time* (Ecclesiastes 3:11).... Rabbi Abbahu said, 'From here [we learn] that the blessed Holy One kept creating worlds and destroying them until He created these [i.e., heaven and earth]. Then He declared, "These please Me, those do not."'"

See *Bereshit Rabbah* 1:7; *Pirqei de-Rabbi Eli'ezer* 3, cited above. The theme of previous worlds that did not endure appears in the *Idrot* (*Zohar* 3:128a [*IR*], 292b [*IZ*]) and inspired Isaac Luria's theory of "the breaking of the vessels."

68. **wrapping of radiance...**   See *Tanhuma* (Buber), *Vayaqhel* 7: "Rabbi Shim'on son of Rabbi Yehotsadak asked Rabbi Shemu'el son of Nahman, 'Since you are a master of Aggadah, tell me how the blessed Holy One created the world.' He replied, 'When the blessed Holy One wished to create the world, He enwrapped Himself in light and created the world, as is said: *He wraps in light as in a garment* (Psalms 104:2), and afterward: *He spreads out the heavens like a curtain*.'"

See *Bereshit Rabbah* 3:4 (and Theodor, ad loc.); *Pirqei de-Rabbi Eli'ezer* 3. The image of God wrapping Himself in a garment of light appears in Greek, Iranian, Gnostic, and kab-

balistic sources. See Matt, *Zohar*, 212; Ezra of Gerona, *Peirush Shir ha-Shirim*, 493–94; Ezra's letter, ed. Scholem, in *Sefer Bialik*, 157–58; Azriel of Gerona, *Peirush ha-Aggadot*, 110–11; *Zohar* 1:2a, 29a, 90a (*ST*), 245a; 2:39b, 164b; Moses de León, *Mishkan ha-Edut*, 5a.

Here the garment of light is the *sefirah* of Hokhmah, located on the upper right side of the sefirotic tree. Divinity clothes itself in this radiant wrapping, thereby mediating the intense primordial energy and generating *Tif'eret*, known as *heaven*.

69. **With beginning...**   See above, note 22.

70. **pillars and sockets of that** *pavilion*   The pillars and sockets allude to the *sefirot* (as well as to the kabbalists) who sustain *Shekhinah* (the *pavilion*). See above, note 14.

71. ***Happy is*** משכיל (*maskil*)...*the poor*   This verse alludes to the *sefirot* as well as to the kabbalists, both of whom sustain *Shekhinah*. She is called *poor*, having nothing at all of Her own. See BT *Bava Batra* 8b.

72. **standing above** *the enlightened*, **of whom is written...**   The *sky* is *Tif'eret*, who stands above *the enlightened*, specifically *Netsah* and *Hod*, also called *the heads*. The *living being* (חיה [*hayyah*]) is *Shekhinah*, who controls and sustains the holy *hayyot* ("living

זהר (*Zohar*), *Radiance*—illumining Torah.[73] זהר (*Zohar*)—illumining the *heads* of that *living being*. Those *heads* are *the enlightened*, who constantly radiate and shine, contemplating that *sky*, the radiance flashing from there, radiance of Torah, sparkling constantly, never ceasing.

The earth was תהו ובהו (*tohu va-vohu*), *chaos and void*... (Genesis 1:2).[74]

Was, precisely: previously.[75] Snow in water. Through the potency of snow in water emerged slime.[76] Blazing fire struck it, refuse came to be, and תהו (*tohu*), *chaos*, was produced—abode of slime, nest of refuse.[77] ובהו (*Va-vohu*), *And void*—sifting sifted from refuse, settling upon it.[78]

creatures, animals"), who support the Chariot, the divine throne.

See Ezra of Gerona, *Peirush Shir ha-Shirim*, 508–9; *Zohar* 1:12b, 242a; 2:48b, 177b–178a (*SdTs*); 3:46b.

73. **illumining Torah** The radiance illumines *Tif'eret*, called Written Torah, and through Him, the lower *sefirot*.

74. *The earth was* תהו ובהו (*tohu va-vohu*), *chaos and void* The verse continues: *with darkness over the face of the abyss, and the wind of God hovering over the face of the waters*.

75. *Was*, precisely: previously See *Bereshit Rabbah* 1:15: "Rabbi Ḥanin said, '... The earth was—it already had been [i.e., it preceded the creation of heaven].'" In the *Bahir* 2 (2), the midrashic interpretation of *was* is applied specifically to *tohu*: the earth was originally in a state of תהו (*tohu*) and then changed to בהו (*bohu*), which is interpreted as בו הוא (*bo hu*), "in it is something," i.e., something with substance, as opposed to chaos.

The early kabbalists, drawing on Jewish Neoplatonism, understood *tohu* and *bohu* as referring to primordial matter and form, respectively. *Tohu*, primordial matter, was seen as the root of evil (a Platonic notion developed in Gnosticism and Neoplatonism), while *bohu*, form, was the origin of good.

See *Bahir* 9 (11), 109 (163); Abraham bar Ḥiyya, *Hegyon ha-Nefesh*, 2a; Isaac the Blind, *Peirush Sefer Yetsirah*, 2:6; Azriel of Gerona, *Peirush Sefer Yetsirah*, 1:11; 2:6; idem, *Peirush*

ha-Aggadot, 89, 102–5; Jacob ben Sheshet, *Meshiv Devarim Nekhoḥim*, 118–21; Naḥmanides on Genesis 1:2.

Here the *Zohar* indicates that *Shekhinah*, known as *earth*, was originally in a chaotic state before *tohu* (matter) and *bohu* (form) emerged from Her. This process, described in the following lines, produces the demonic realm.

See *Zohar* 1:11b, 30a, 39b, 262b–263a (*Hash*); Tishby, *Wisdom of the Zohar*, 2:460–64. In several passages (e.g., 1:39b; *ZH* 6d [*MhN*]), *tohu*, *bohu*, *darkness*, and *wind* symbolize the four elements: fire, water, earth, and air.

76. **Snow in water...** Water symbolizes *Ḥesed*, while snow symbolizes *Gevurah* and *Din* ("Judgment"), the congealing and hardening of water. The two were mingled in *Shekhinah*, yielding a slime. See *Zohar* 1:6b; and *Pirqei de-Rabbi Eli'ezer* 3: "From where was the earth created? From the snow beneath the Throne of Glory. He took it and threw it upon the waters, and the waters congealed and dust was made."

77. **Blazing fire...** The fire of *Gevurah* struck *Shekhinah*, and the slime turned into refuse and then *tohu*, primordial matter, the domain of evil. On the dregs of primordial matter, see Jacob ben Sheshet, *Meshiv Devarim Nekhoḥim*, 120.

78. **sifting sifted from refuse...** *Bohu*, form, was sifted out of the refuse and then joined to matter.

118

חשך (Ḥoshekh), *Darkness* (ibid.)[79]—mystery of blazing fire.[80] That *darkness* covers *tohu,* over the refuse, and thereby it is empowered.[81]

ורוח אלהים (Ve-ruaḥ Elohim), *And a wind of God* (ibid.)—רוח קודשא (Ruaḥ Qudsha), Holy Spirit, emerging from the living God,[82] *hovering over the face of the waters* (ibid.). Once this *wind* blew, one fine film clarified from that refuse, like filthy froth flying off, clarified, refined again and again, till that filth is left lacking any filth at all.[83] So was *tohu* clarified and refined, from it emerging *a great, mighty wind, splitting mountains and shattering rocks* (1 Kings 19:11), the one seen by Elijah.[84] *Bohu* was clarified and refined, from it emerging *an earthquake,* as is written: *After the wind—an earthquake* (ibid.). *Darkness* clarified, embracing fire within its mystery, as is written: *After the earthquake—fire* (ibid., 12). *Wind* clarified, and embraced in its mystery was *the sound of sheer silence* (ibid.).

Tohu—a colorless, formless realm, not embraced by the mystery of form. Now within form—as one contemplates it, no form at all.[85] Everything has a garment in which to be clothed, except for this: though appearing upon it, it does not exist at all, never did.[86]

119

79. חשך (**Ḥoshekh**), *Darkness* The verse continues: *over the face of the abyss and the wind of God hovering over the face of the waters.*

80. **mystery of blazing fire** The fire of *Gevurah,* called *Darkness.* This designation apparently derives from Maimonides (*Guide of the Perplexed* 2:30), who identifies the *darkness* of Genesis 1:2 with "elemental fire": "The elemental fire was designated by this term [*darkness*] because it is not luminous, but only transparent." The other three elements (earth, air [*ruaḥ*], and water) are mentioned explicitly in Genesis 1:2.

See Azriel of Gerona, *Peirush ha-Aggadot,* 111; Jacob ben Sheshet, *Meshiv Devarim Nekhoḥim,* 124.

81. **it is empowered** *Tohu,* matter, is empowered by *Gevurah.*

82. **Holy Spirit...** *Tif'eret,* emanating from *Binah,* "the living God." רוח (Ruaḥ) means both "wind" and "spirit." The *ruaḥ* of Genesis 1:2 is identified with Holy Spirit in *Midrash Konen* (*Beit ha-Midrash,* 2:24).

83. **one fine film...** The *wind,* or Holy Spirit, of *Tif'eret* refines the refuse, yielding *bohu,* form. The process is described as the smelting of dross off molten metal.

84. *a great, mighty wind...* **seen by Elijah** The passage reads (1 Kings 19:11–12): [*God*] *said* [*to Elijah*]: *"Go out and stand on the mountain before YHVH." Behold, YHVH was passing by. A great, mighty wind, splitting mountains and shattering rocks before YHVH; YHVH was not in the wind. After the wind—an earthquake; YHVH was not in the earthquake. After the earthquake—fire; YHVH was not in the fire. After the fire—the sound of sheer silence.* The four elements referred to in Genesis 1:2 (*tohu, bohu, darkness,* and *wind*) are each clarified, and from them emerge the four refined manifestations experienced by Elijah: *a great, mighty wind, an earthquake, fire,* and *the sound of sheer silence.*

On the demonic aspect of Elijah's vision, see *Zohar* 2:203a; *ZḤ* 38a; cf. 3:30a. Similarly, the four phenomena of Ezekiel's vision (1:4: *a stormy wind, a huge cloud, flashing fire,* and *a radiance*) are described as four demonic shells enclosing a kernel. See Tishby, *Wisdom of the Zohar,* 2:463–64.

85. *Tohu—...* **no form at all** Primordial matter is formless, despite transient appearances. See *Zohar* 1:40a.

86. **Everything has a garment...** All things comprise matter and form, the latter

Bohu—this has shape and form: stones sunk within the shell of *tohu*,[87] emerging from the shell in which they are sunk, conveying benefit to the world. Through the form of a garment they convey benefit from above to below, ascending from below to above.[88] So they are hollow and moist,[89] suspended in the air[90]—sometimes suspended in the air, sometimes concealed on a cloudy day, generating water from the abyss to nourish *tohu*,[91] for then frivolity and folly prevail as *tohu* spreads through the world.

Darkness is black fire, potent in color; red fire, potent in appearance; green fire, potent in shape; white fire, embracing all.[92] *Darkness,* most powerful fire, empowers *tohu*. *Darkness* is fire but not dark fire until it empowers *tohu*.[93] This is the mystery of: *His eyes were too dim to see, and he called Esau...* (Genesis 27:1). *Darkness*—face of evil, for he greeted evil with a friendly face.[94] Then it is called *darkness,* for it settles upon it,[95] empowering it. This is the mystery of: *Darkness over the face of the abyss* (Genesis 1:2).

רוח (*Ruaḥ*), *Wind,* is a voice hovering over *bohu,* empowering and conducting it with whatever is needed. This is the mystery of: *The voice of YHVH is upon the waters* (Psalms 29:3), and similarly: *The wind of God hovering over the face of the waters* (Genesis 1:2)—stones sunk in the abyss, from which water issues. So it is called *face, face of the abyss* (ibid.). The wind conducts and empowers that *face, face of the waters,* each one receiving what it needs.[96]

120

pictured as a garment, but primordial matter is formless and naked.

87. **stones sunk within the shell of *tohu*** See BT *Ḥagigah* 12a: "*Bohu*—these are the slimy stones sunk in the abyss, from which water issues." The potential forms of *bohu* are sunk in the abyss, or shell, of *tohu* before they are clarified and emerge. On the shell of *tohu,* see *Zohar* 3:227a (*RM*); *ZḤ* 32c, 55b.

88. **conveying benefit...** Once the forms of *bohu* emerge from *tohu,* they clothe matter and enable the things of the world to exist. They transmit the stream of emanation from the *sefirot* above to the world below.

89. **hollow and moist** Channeling the flow of emanation.

90. **suspended in the air** Linking the *sefirot* with the physical world.

91. **on a cloudy day...** When human sin evokes harsh judgment, the flow of emanation is blocked and the forms descend to the abyss, nourishing the demonic powers of

tohu. See *Zohar* 3:32a; and BT *Ta'anit* 8b: "Rabbah son of Shila said, 'A day of rain is as harsh as a day of judgment.'" The *Zohar* understands תהום (*tehom*), *abyss,* as equivalent to תהו (*tohu*), *chaos*.

92. ***Darkness* is black fire...** *Gevurah* includes several aspects, pictured as various colors of fire. See *Pesiqta de-Rav Kahana* 1:3. Cf. *Tanḥuma, Shemot* 15.

93. ***Darkness...dark fire...empowers tohu*** *Gevurah* manifests as dark fire when it strengthens the demonic.

94. ***His eyes...*** The verse describes the aged Isaac preparing to bless his firstborn son, Esau. Isaac symbolizes *Gevurah,* while Esau symbolizes the demonic. Because Isaac greeted Esau with a friendly face, his eyes grew dim. See *Bereshit Rabbah* 65:6; *Zohar* 2:46b. As *Gevurah* empowers evil, it grows dark or *dim*.

95. **upon it** Upon evil.

96. ***face of the abyss...face of the waters...each one receiving...*** *Darkness* empow-

Tohu—upon it rests the name שדי (Shaddai).[97] Bohu—upon it rests the name צבאות (Tseva'ot), Hosts.[98] Darkness—upon it rests the name אלהים (Elohim).[99] Wind—upon it rests the name יהוה (YHVH).[100] A [great,] mighty wind, splitting mountains and shattering rocks... YHVH was not in the wind (1 Kings 19:11). This name was not in it, for Shaddai controls it through the mystery of tohu. After the wind, an earthquake; YHVH was not in the earthquake—for the name Tseva'ot controls it through the mystery of bohu. So bohu is called earthquake, for it does not exist without quaking. After the earthquake, fire; YHVH was not in the fire—for the name Elohim controls it, from the side of darkness. After the fire, the sound of sheer silence—here is found the name YHVH.[101]

Here are four sections, constituting well-known sections of the limbs of the body, numbering four,[102] numbering twelve.[103] Here is the engraved name of twelve letters, transmitted to Elijah in the cave.[104] [16b]

ers tohu, the face of the abyss, while wind empowers bohu, which is equated with the face of the waters. See BT Ḥagigah 12a: "Bohu—these are the slimy stones sunk in the abyss, from which water issues." Wind is a name for Tif'eret, also known as voice and YHVH.

97. שדי (Shaddai) An obscure divine name, which may mean "of the mountain." The traditional rendering "Almighty" is unjustified. Here Shaddai designates the sefirah of Yesod, limiting the destructive power of tohu. See BT Ḥagigah 12a, where Resh Lakish interprets Shaddai as a reference to God's command to limit the universe at creation: "I am the one ש (she), who, said to the world: 'די (dai), Enough!'"

98. צבאות (Tseva'ot), Hosts This divine name, associated with the sefirot of Netsaḥ and Hod, refers here to the hosts of forms emerging from bohu.

99. אלהים (Elohim) This name designates Gevurah, known as Darkness.

100. יהוה (YHVH) This name designates Tif'eret, known as Ruaḥ, Wind (or: Spirit).

101. This name was not in it... here is found the name YHVH The name YHVH is not associated with the mighty wind, earthquake, or fire, each of which has its own distinct divine name, corresponding to its primordial element: tohu, bohu, and darkness,

respectively. YHVH is reserved for the sound of sheer silence, corresponding to ruaḥ. Tif'eret, known as YHVH and Ruaḥ, is also called Qol (voice or sound). See ZḤ 38a; Zohar 3:227a (RM).

102. four sections... sections of the limbs... The four parts of Elijah's vision correspond to four parts of the body of the sefirot: the trunk (Tif'eret), the left arm (Gevurah), the thighs (Netsaḥ and Hod, taken together), and the phallus (Yesod).

103. numbering twelve Each of the four limbs apparently comprises three parts. See the passage from Bahir cited below.

104. name of twelve letters... Perhaps referring to the fact that the four-letter name YHVH appears three times in the phrases: YHVH was not in the wind... YHVH was not in the earthquake... YHVH was not in the fire (1 Kings 19:11–12). Taken together, the letters of these three occurrences total twelve. The name of twelve letters is mentioned but not identified in BT Qiddushin 71a. It was later associated with the three occurrences of YHVH in the priestly blessing (Numbers 6:24–26). See Bahir 80 (111): "... numbering three, numbering twelve."

Cf. Zohar 1:19b; 2:58a; 3:78a–b, 172b; Trachtenberg, Jewish Magic and Superstition, 92, 290, n. 32. Zohar 2:201b refers to "the holy name of twelve letters... ruling the air. This

God said, "Let there be light!"
And there was light (Genesis 1:3).

Here begins the discovery of hidden treasures: how the world was created in detail. For until here was general, and afterward general returns, constituting general-particular-general.[105] Till here, all was suspended in space,[106] from the mystery of *Ein Sof*. Once the force spread through the supernal palace, mystery of *Elohim*, saying is ascribed: ויאמר אלהים (*Va-yomer Elohim*), *God said.*[107] Above, saying is not specified. Although בראשית (*Be-reshit*), *In the beginning*, is a saying,[108] *said* is not ascribed. This *said* is susceptible to questioning and knowing.[109] ויאמר (*Va-yomer*), *Said*—a power raised, ארמותא

is the name with which Elijah flew, ascending to heaven." See 2 Kings 2:11.

105. **general-particular-general** כלל ופרט וכלל (*Kelal ufrat ukhlal*), "Generality, particularity, and generality." According to one of Rabbi Yishma'el's thirteen hermeneutical rules (*Sifra*, intro, 1a–b), if a biblical law is stated in general terms, followed by particular instances and then followed by another generality, one may derive only things similar to those specified. For example, Deuteronomy 14:26 states: *You may spend the money on anything that your appetite desires* (generality), *cattle, sheep, wine, or intoxicant* (particularity), *or anything that your appetite seeks* (generality). According to the principle of *kelal ufrat ukhlal*, one may purchase things other than those specified, but only if they are food or drink similar to those specified.

Here the *Zohar* indicates that the opening verse of Genesis describes the emergence of *Hokhmah* and *Binah* out of *Keter*. These three *sefirot* contain the entirety of emanation (generality). Then, beginning with *Let there be light!*, the emanation of the seven lower *sefirot* is spelled out in detail (particularity). Finally, generality returns in Genesis 2:4: *This is the story of heaven and earth when they were created, on the day when YHVH Elohim made earth and heaven.* Applying the hermeneutical principle of *kelal ufrat ukhlal*, one should understand the emanation of the initial *sefirot* in light of the detailed account of the further emanation.

106. **space** אוירא (*Avira*), "Air, space, ether, aura." The *avira* is *Keter*, the original

sefirah. See *Sefer Yetsirah* 2:6: "Out of chaos He formed substance, making what is not into what is. He hewed enormous pillars out of אויר (*avir*), ether, that cannot be grasped."

See *Zohar* 1:15a; 3:135b (*IR*); Altmann, *Studies*, 174; Scholem, "*Iqvotav shel Gevirol be-Qabbalah*," 167–68; idem, *Origins of the Kabbalah*, 331–47 (especially 342); Pines, in *Tarbiz* 50 (1981): 339–47; Liebes, in *Meḥqerei Yerushalyim be-Maḥashevet Yisra'el* 6:3–4 (1987): 80–86; Verman, *The Books of Contemplation*, 153–56.

107. **Once the force spread . . .** Once the primordial seed of *Hokhmah* impregnated the divine womb of *Binah*, known as *Elohim*, the subsequent process of emanation can be described in terms of speech. Until that stage, the appropriate metaphor is not speech but thought.

108. **Although בראשית (*Be-reshit*) . . .** According to M *Avot* 5:1, "The world was created through ten utterances [or: sayings, commands]." Only nine explicit commands appear in Genesis 1, but the decade is completed by counting the phrase *In the beginning*.

See BT *Rosh ha-Shanah* 32a, *Megillah* 21b; Ezra of Gerona, *Peirush Shir ha-Shirim*, 506; *Zohar* 1:15a, 30a; *TZ* 32, 76a. In Kabbalah the ten commands symbolize the ten *sefirot*, the first of which establishes the basis for the other nine.

109. **This *said* is susceptible to questioning . . .** Only beginning with the rung of *Binah* does speech manifest, so She is characterized by the verb *said*. She is also known as the primordial question, Who. A spiritual

122

(*armuta*), rising, silently from the mystery of *Ein Sof*, in the origin of thought.[110] *God said*—now that palace, impregnated by the seed of holiness, gave birth, giving birth silently, while outside the newborn was heard.[111] The one giving birth gave birth silently, was not heard at all. As the emergent one emerged, a voice was generated, heard outside: יהי אור (*Yehi or*), *Let there be light!* All that emerged, emerged through this mystery. יהי (*Yehi*), *Let there be*, alluding to the mystery of Father and Mother, namely, י״ה (*yod he*),[112] afterward turning back to the primordial point, to begin expanding into something else: *light.*[113]

And there was light—light that already was.[114] This light is concealed mystery, an expansion expanding, bursting from the mysterious secret of the hidden supernal aura.[115] First it burst, generating from its mystery a single con-

---

seeker may inquire about Her, but such questions do not yield ordinary answers. The identity of the divine is discovered only in a realm beyond words. The mystical name "Who" becomes a focus of meditation, as question turns into quest. See Shim-'on Lavi, *KP*, 1:91a: "Concerning everything that cannot be grasped, its question constitutes its answer."

See *Zohar* 1:1b, 29b–30a, 45b, 85b–86a, 237b; 2:126b–127a, 138a, 139b, 226a, 231b.

110. **a power raised...** *Binah* represents the subtle beginnings of speech, the inner voice emerging silently through thought, *Hokhmah*. ויאמר (*Va-yomer*), *Said*, is interpeted here as ארמותא (*armuta*), "rising." On the subtle nature of the verb אמר (*amr*), "to say," see *Zohar* 1:234b; 2:17a (*MhN*), 25b; 3:132b–133a (*IR*).

111. **while outside the newborn was heard** *Tif'eret*, the son born to *Binah*, is known as Voice and was now heard.

See *Zohar* 1:50b, 74a, 141b; Moses de León, *Sheqel ha-Qodesh*, 89 (113). Cf. BT *Berakhot* 15b: "The womb, which takes in silently, gives forth loudly."

112. **Father and Mother...** *Hokhmah* and *Binah*, symbolized by the first two letters of יהוה (*YHVH*), which are also the first two letters of יהי (*yehi*), *let there be*. See *Zohar* 2:22a.

113. **afterward turning back...** The final letter of יהי (*yehi*), *let there be*, is once again י (*yod*), symbolizing the primordial

point of *Hokhmah*, from which emerges the first of the lower seven *sefirot*: *Hesed*, known as *light*.

114. **light that already was** The primordial light emerging from the depths of the first *sefirah*. See *Bereshit Rabbah* 3:2: "It is not written here והיה אור (*Ve-hayah or*) [which could mean either *And there will be light* or *And there was light*], but rather ויהי אור (*Vayhi or*) [which can mean only] *And there was light*—it already was." Theodor (ad loc.) regards this as a scribal gloss. In any case, the point in the Midrash is that the creation of light was instantaneous and effortless, whereas here the *Zohar* emphasizes that the light preexisted—it already *was*.

See *Bahir* 17 (25), elaborating on *Bereshit Rabbah*: "Rabbi Berekhiah said, 'Why is it written: *God said, "Let there be light!"* ויהי אור (*Vayhi or*), *And there was light*, and not: והיה (*Ve-hayah*) [which could mean either *And there will be* or *And there was*]? This can be compared to a king who had a beautiful object and set it aside until he had prepared a place for it; then he placed it there. As is written: *"Let there be light!" And there was light*. For it already *was*.'"

See Ezra of Gerona, *Peirush Shir ha-Shirim*, 494; Azriel of Gerona, *Peirush ha-Aggadot*, 109; *Zohar* 1:45b; 3:245b (*RM*); *ZH* 1a, 37d; Recanati on Genesis 1:3, 3c.

115. **the hidden supernal aura** *Keter*. See above, note 106.

cealed point,[116] for *Ein Sof* burst out of its aura, revealing this point: י (*yod*). Once this *yod* expanded, what remained was found to be: אור (*or*), *light,* from that mystery of concealed אויר (*avir*), aura.[117] After the primordial point, *yod,* emerged from it into being, it manifested upon it, touching yet not touching.[118] Expanding, it emerged; this is אור (*or*), *light* remaining from אויר (*avir*), aura, namely, the light that already was. This endured, emerged, ascended, was treasured away, and a single point remained, so that by a hidden path it constantly touches that point, touching yet not touching, illumining it through the primordial point that emerged from it.[119] So all is linked, one to another, illumining this and that.[120] As it ascends, all ascend, merging in it.[121] Attaining the realm of *Ein Sof,* it is hidden away, and all becomes one.

That point of light is *light.*[122] It expanded, and seven letters of the alphabet shone within, not congealing, still fluid.[123] Then *darkness* emerged, and seven other letters of the alphabet emerged within, not congealing, remaining fluid.[124] An *expanse* emerged, dissipating the discord of two sides, and eight other letters emerged within, making twenty-two.[125] Seven letters jumped from this side and seven from that, and all were engraved in that *expanse,* remaining fluid. The *expanse* congealed, and the letters congealed, folding into shape, forming forms.[126] Torah was engraved there, to shine forth.[127]

124

116. **single concealed point** The primordial point of *Ḥokhmah,* which broke through the aura of *Keter.* See above, page 109.

117. **what remained...** Once the י (*yod*) left אויר (*avir*), "aura," what remained was אור (*or*), "light." See *Zohar* 3:245b (*RM*).

118. **it manifested upon it...** The light remaining from the aura of *Keter* shone subtly upon the primordial point of *Ḥokhmah.* See *Zohar* 1:15a, 65a.

119. **emerged, ascended... a single point remained...** After emerging, the light returns to its source within *Keter.* A single point, the *sefirah* of *Ḥesed,* now stands revealed, and the light beyond maintains contact with the point of *Ḥesed* through the primordial point of *Ḥokhmah.*

120. **illumining this and that** The light hidden away within *Keter* illumines both points: *Ḥokhmah* and *Ḥesed.*

121. **all ascend, merging in it** As the light ascends, all the *sefirot* follow and merge into it.

122. **That point of light is** *light* The point is *Ḥesed,* revealed when most of the

light withdrew to its hidden source in *Keter.*

123. **seven letters...** Emanation continues to unfold, manifesting as divine speech.

124. *darkness* **emerged, and seven other letters...** The *sefirah* of *Gevurah,* symbolized by *darkness,* emanates, generating the next set of letters.

125. **An** *expanse* **emerged... twenty-two** *Tif'eret,* the *expanse* (רקיע [*raqi'a*], "firmament, expanse, sky" [Genesis 1:6]), is also known as רחמים (*Raḥamim*), Compassion, and this central *sefirah* balances the contending forces of *Ḥesed* and *Gevurah,* Love and Judgment. Its accompanying eight letters bring the total to twenty-two, the number of letters in the Hebrew alphabet.

126. **The** *expanse* **congealed...** See *Bereshit Rabbah* 4:2: "Rav said, 'The works of Creation [i.e., the heavens] were fluid, and on the second day they congealed. *Let there be an expanse [in the midst of the waters]!* (Genesis 1:6), Let the expanse be firm!'"

See *Zohar* 2:167b; *ZH* 68d (*ShS*); Moses de León, *Sheqel ha-Qodesh,* 88 (111).

127. **Torah was engraved there...** The

Let there be light! Namely, גדול אל (*El gadol*), great God,[128] the mystery emerging from the primordial aura. ויהי (*Vayhi*), *And there was*—mystery of *darkness,* called אלהים (*Elohim*).[129] *Light*—left merging in right. Then from the mystery of אל (*El*) came to be אלהים (*Elohim*), right merging in left, left in right.[130]

God saw that the light was good (Genesis 1:4)—the central pillar.[131] *Good,* illumining[132] above and below and all other directions, through the mystery of *YHVH,* the name embracing all sides.[133]

God separated the light from the darkness (ibid.), dissipating discord, so that all would be perfect.

God called the light Day (ibid., 5). What does *called* mean? He called forth and summoned this perfect light, standing in the center, to emit a radiance— foundation of the world, upon which worlds are established. From that perfect light, the central pillar, extended יסודא (*Yesoda*), Foundation, Vitality of the Worlds, *Day,* from the right side.[134]

And the darkness He called Night (ibid.). He called forth, summoned and gen-erated from the side of *darkness* a female, the moon ruling by night, called *Night,* mystery of אדני (*Adonai*), אדון (*Adon*), *Lord, of all the earth* (Joshua 3:11).[135]

125

twenty-two letters of Creation, now fully formed, spell out the text of Torah within *Tif'eret,* who is known as Written Torah.

128. גדול אל (*El gadol*), great God *Ḥe-sed,* who is known both as אל (*El*), God, and גדולה (*Gedullah*), Greatness.

129. ויהי (*Vayhi*), *And there was*—mystery of *darkness...* See BT *Megillah* 10b: "Rab-bi Levi, or some say Rabbi Yonatan, said, 'This matter is a tradition handed down to us from the Men of the Great Assembly: Wherever it is said ויהי (*vayhi*), *and there was* [or: *and it came to pass*], this denotes distress.'" The word ויהי (*vayhi*), *it came to pass,* is split into וי היה (*vai hayah*), "there was woe," or וי הי (*vai, hi*), "woe, wailing."

See *Bereshit Rabbah* 41(42):3 (on Genesis 14:1); *Vayiqra Rabbah* 11:7; BT *Megillah* 11a; *Zohar* 1:119b; 2:140b, 167a; 3:231a; *ZH* 77a (*MhN, Rut*).

Here the distress is the *darkness* and judg-ment of the left side, also known as *Elohim.*

130. *Light*—left merging in right... The repetition of the word *light* indicates the resolution of the conflict between light and darkness, right and left. The mingling

of the two forces is also indicated by the fact that אל (*El*) is included in אלהים (*Elohim*).

131. the central pillar *Tif'eret,* who me-diates between the polar opposites, *Ḥesed* and *Gevurah.* See *Zohar* 2:167a.

132. illumining אנהיר (*Anhir*). Recanati on Genesis 1:4, 4c reads: אדליק (*adliq*), "kindling," based on an Aramaic rendering of בהיטיבו (*be-heitivo*), *as he tends* [or: *trims*] (Exodus 30:7): באדלקותיה (*be-adlequteih*), *as he kindles.*

See Ezra of Gerona, *Peirush Shir ha-Shirim,* 485; Azriel of Gerona, *Peirush ha-Aggadot,* 89.

133. all other directions... All of the lower *sefirot* surrounding *Tif'eret,* who is symbolized by the name *YHVH.*

134. to emit a radiance... *Tif'eret* is summoned to emanate *Yesod,* "foundation" of the world, also known as *Day,* with the help of *Ḥesed,* the *sefirah* of the right side. *Yesod* channels the vivifying flow of emana-tion to *Shekhinah* and the worlds below.

135. generated from the side of *dark-ness...* From the *sefirah* of *Gevurah,* known

The right entered that perfect pillar in the center, embracing the mystery of the left,[136] and ascended to the primordial point [17a], grasping there the power of three points: חולם (ḥolem), שורק (shuruq), חירק (ḥireq), seed of holiness,[137] for without this mystery no seed is sown. All was united in the central pillar, generating the foundation of the world, who is therefore called כל (Kol), All, for He embraces all in a radiance of desire.[138]

The left blazed potently, inhaling, inhaling fragrance on all those rungs. Out of that blazing flame, it generated the female, the moon.[139] That blaze was dark, deriving from *darkness*. These two sides generated these two rungs, one male and one female.[140]

Foundation was linked to the central pillar by the increase of light within it, for as the central pillar was consummated, pacifying all sides, its radiance was increased from above, from all sides in all-encompassing joy. Out of that increased joy emerged the foundation of the worlds, called Increase.[141] From here emerge all forces[142] below and holy spirits and souls through the mystery of יהוה צבאות (*YHVH Tseva'ot*), Lord of Hosts, אל אלהי הרוחות (*El Elohei ha-ruḥot*), *God, God of spirits* (Numbers 16:22).[143]

Night, Lord of all the earth, derives from the left side, from *darkness*. Since *darkness* yearns to merge in the right, and its strength weakened, *night* spread out

126

---

as *darkness,* emanates *Shekhinah,* symbolized by the moon and called *Night.* One of Her other many names is אדני (*Adonai*), *Lord.* See *Zohar* 1:228b.

136. **embracing the mystery of the left** *Tif'eret,* the central pillar, balances right and left.

137. **three points: חולם (*ḥolem*), שורק (*shuruq*), חירק (*ḥireq*)...** These three vowels appear, respectively, as points above, within, and beneath the letter. Here they apparently represent three lines of emanation (right, left, and center) extending from the primordial point (or seed) of *Ḥokhmah.*

See Isaac ha-Kohen, *Ta'amei ha-Nequddot,* ed. Scholem, *Madda'ei ha-Yahadut* 2 (1927): 265–68; *Zohar* 1:15b; Judah Ḥayyat, in *Ma-'arekhet ha-Elohut,* 136a. According to Moses de León, the three points symbolize *Ḥokhmah, Tif'eret,* and *Shekhinah.* See his *Sefer ha-Rimmon,* 328–30, and Wolfson's note, 329:2.

138. **generating the foundation of the world...** *Ḥesed* transmits the seed of holiness, *Ḥokhmah,* through the central pillar,

thereby generating *Yesod,* who embodies all of the *sefirot* as He streams joyously toward union with *Shekhinah.* On *Yesod* as כל (*Kol*), All, see *Zohar* 1:130b, 195b; 2:157a.

139. **The left blazed...** *Gevurah,* drawing power from the various *sefirot,* generates *Shekhinah.*

140. **These two sides...** The right and left sides generate *Yesod* and *Shekhinah,* respectively.

141. **Increase** מוסף (*Musaf*), "Additional," the additional service for Sabbaths, festivals, and fast days. The word is a cognate of the name יוסף (*Yosef*), Joseph—the biblical hero who symbolizes *Yesod,* the divine phallus, since he withstood the test of sexual temptation in Egypt (Genesis 39). See Moses de León, *Sheqel ha-Qodesh,* 10 (12–13).

142. **forces** Angels.

143. אל יהוה צבאות (*YHVH Tseva'ot*)... אלהי הרוחות (*El Elohei ha-ruḥot*)... Both of these names are associated with *Yesod,* who by uniting with *Shekhinah* generates human souls.

from it.[144] As this *night* began to spread, before being completed,[145] that *darkness* entered and merged in the right, right embracing it, and *night* was left wanting.[146] As *darkness* yearns to merge into *light*, so *night* yearns to merge into *day*. *Darkness* lacked its light, so it generated a level lacking, not radiant. *Darkness* does not shine unless it merges into *light*. *Night,* emerging from it, does not shine unless it merges into *day*. *Night*'s lack is filled solely through Increase. What is increased here, decreases there. Increase comprised mystery of the primordial point and mystery of the central pillar along with all sides.[147] So two letters were added to it, while from *night* these two letters were subtracted. Hence, קרא (qara), *He called*. It is written: ויקרא (Va-yiqra), *And He called*. Then ו"י (vav, yod) were subtracted, and it is written: קרא (Qara), *He called, Night.*[148] Here lies mystery of the name of seventy-two engraved letters[149] of the supernal crown.

God said, "Let there be an expanse in the midst of the waters..." (Genesis 1:6).[150]

Here is mystery in detail,[151] separating upper waters from lower through mystery of the left.[152] Here conflict was created through the left side. For until here was mystery of the

144. **Since *darkness* yearns...**   As *Gevurah* approaches *Ḥesed*, its harshness weakens, and *Shekhinah,* known as Lenient Judgment, emerges.

145. **before being completed**   Instead of אסתיים (istayyam), "it was completed," *OY* reads here: אתבסים (itbesim), "it was sweetened," i.e., sweetened by the light of *Ḥesed*.

146. ***night* was left wanting**   *Shekhinah* lacks the full power of *Gevurah,* now softened by *Ḥesed*. Emanating from *darkness,* She also lacks light.

147. **Increase comprised mystery of the primordial point...**   *Yesod* includes the emanation of *Ḥokhmah* and *Tif'eret.*

148. **two letters were added...subtracted...**   The word ויקרא (va-yiqra), *and He called*, describing the emergence of *day* (*Yesod*), contains two more letters than קרא (qara), *He called*, describing the emergence of *night* (*Shekhinah*). These two extra letters, ו, י (vav, yod), symbolize *Tif'eret* and *Ḥokhmah,* which constitute the increase of *Yesod.*

149. **the name of seventy-two engraved letters**   The divine name derived from the description of the splitting of the Red Sea: Exodus 14:19–21. Each of these three verses

begins with the letters י, ו (vav, yod) and contains seventy-two letters. The name is actually composed of seventy-two triads of letters, according to the following pattern: the first letter of the first verse, the last letter of the second verse, the first letter of the third verse (forming the first triad); the second letter of the first verse, the penultimate letter of the second verse, the second letter of the third verse (the second triad); etc.

See *Leqaḥ Tov,* Exodus 14:21; *Bereshit Rabbah* 44:19; *Vayiqra Rabbah* 23:2; *Shir ha-Shirim Rabbah* on 2:2; Rashi on BT *Sukkah* 45a, s.v. *ani;* Hai Gaon, *Otsar ha-Ge'onim, Ḥagigah* 23; *Bahir* 79 (110); *Zohar* 1:7b; 2:51b, 132b, 270a; 3:150b–151a; Trachtenberg, *Jewish Magic and Superstition,* 95–97; Kasher, *Torah Shelemah,* 14:67, 284–86. The *Zohar* associates the seventy-two-letter name with *Ḥesed, Gevurah,* and *Tif'eret,* whose emanation is alluded to in the verses discussed here. See *Zohar* 2:132b; 3:150b–151a.

150. ***"Let there be an expanse in the midst of the waters...*   *that it may separate water from water."*

151. **in detail**   See above, page 122: "*God said, 'Let there be light!' And there was light*

right,[153] and here is mystery of the left, so conflict raged between this and the right. Right is consummate of all, so all is written by the right,[154] for upon it depends all consummation. When the left aroused, conflict aroused, and through that conflict blazed the fire of wrath.[155] Out of that conflict aroused by the left, emerged Hell. Hell aroused on the left and clung.[156]

The wisdom of Moses: he contemplated this, gazing into the act of Creation. In the act of Creation a conflict arose between left and right, and in that conflict aroused by the left, Hell emerged, clinging there. The central pillar, who is the third day,[157] entered between them, mediating the conflict, reconciling the two sides. Hell descended, left merged in right, and peace prevailed over all.[158]

Similarly the conflict between Korah and Aaron was left against right.[159] Moses, contemplating the act of Creation, said, "It is fitting that I mediate the conflict between left and right."[160] He endeavored to reconcile them, but the left was unwilling, and Korah stiffened his resistance.[161] He[162] said, "Hell must

128

(Genesis 1:3). Here begins the discovery of hidden treasures: how the world was created in detail. For until here was general...." The opening verse of Genesis describes the emergence of *Ḥokhmah* and *Binah* out of *Keter*. These three *sefirot* contain the entirety of emanation. Then, beginning with *Let there be light!*, the emanation of the seven lower *sefirot* is spelled out in detail. Now the *Zohar* proceeds with the second day of creation, on which conflict arose. See *Bereshit Rabbah* 4:6.

152. **separating upper waters from lower...** Separating *Binah* from *Shekhinah* through the mystery of *Gevurah*, the *sefirah* of the left side, manifesting on the second day. See *Zohar* 1:46a, 2:149b.

153. **mystery of the right** *Ḥesed*, the *sefirah* of the right side, manifesting in the light of the first day.

154. **all is written by the right** The act of writing is usually performed with the right hand.

155. **blazed the fire of wrath** The harsh power of the left side was aroused.

156. **emerged Hell...** See BT *Pesaḥim* 54a, "Rabbi Bana'ah son of Rabbi Ulla said, 'Why was the expression *that it was good* not said concerning the second day of Creation? Because on that day the fire of Hell was created.'"

Here the *Zohar* indicates that Hell was generated by the fiery wrath of the left side and remained attached there. Cf. *Bereshit Rabbah* 4:6; *Pirqei de-Rabbi Eli'ezer* 4; *Midrash Konen* (*Beit ha-Midrash*, 2:25); Ezra of Gerona, *Peirush Shir ha-Shirim*, 506; *Zohar* 1:33a, 46a; 2:149b; Moses de León, *Sheqel ha-Qodesh*, 41 (49).

157. **The central pillar...** *Tif'eret*, symbolized by the third day of Creation, who mediates between the polar opposites, *Ḥesed* and *Gevurah*.

158. **Hell descended...** The extreme manifestation of harsh Judgment separated from the left side and descended, while the left side itself was harmonized.

159. **Korah and Aaron...** Aaron the high priest symbolizes *Ḥesed*, the right side, while the rebel Korah, who was a Levite, symbolizes the left side, *Gevurah*. See Numbers 16; *Zohar* 3:176a.

160. **It is fitting that I mediate...** Moses, who symbolizes the harmonizing *sefirah* of *Tif'eret*, can mediate the conflict.

161. **but the left was unwilling...** According to *Zohar* 3:176a, Korah "sought to reverse right and left."

162. **He** Moses.

certainly join in the heat of the conflict of the left.[163] Since he[164] does not want to join above, merging in the right, he will certainly descend below by the intensity of his rage." Korah did not want this conflict to be harmonized by Moses because it was not for the sake of heaven;[165] he cared nothing about the supernal glory and denied the act of Creation.[166] As soon as Moses saw that he had denied the act of Creation and been thrust outside,[167] *Moses became very angry* (Numbers 16:15). *Moses became angry* because they had denied him the opportunity to harmonize that conflict. *Very*—because they had denied the act of Creation. Korah denied everything, [17b] above and below, as is written: *who strove against Moses and Aaron as part of Korah's band when they strove against YHVH* (ibid. 26:9), below and above.[168] So he joined what befitted him.[169]

A conflict arrayed as above, ascending, not descending, established rightly, is the conflict of Shammai and Hillel.[170] The blessed Holy One mediated between them, harmonizing them.[171] This was a conflict for the sake of heaven, so

163. **Hell must certainly join...** As in the second day of Creation.

164. **he** Korah.

165. **not for the sake of heaven** See M *Avot* 5:17: "Every conflict that is for the sake of heaven is destined to endure, while every conflict not for the sake of heaven is not destined to endure. Which conflict is for the sake of heaven? The conflict between Hillel and Shammai. Which conflict is not for the sake of heaven? The conflict of Korah and his entire band." See *Zohar* 1:33a.

166. **denied the act of Creation** By refusing to harmonize with the right side, he denied the process of Creation.

167. **been thrust outside** Korah was now beyond the pale.

168. **below and above** Korah rebelled against Moses and Aaron, the human leaders of Israel, as well as against the divine creative process.

169. **what befitted him** Hell, or Sheol, to which Korah descended. See Numbers 16:33, cited below: *They and all that belonged to them went down alive into Sheol.*

170. **the conflict of Shammai and Hillel** See M *Avot* 5:17: "Every conflict that is for the sake of heaven is destined to endure, while every conflict not for the sake of heav-

en is not destined to endure. Which conflict is for the sake of heaven? The conflict between Hillel and Shammai. Which conflict is not for the sake of heaven? The conflict of Korah and his entire band."

Numerous disputes between the disciples of Hillel and Shammai are recorded in rabbinic literature. One of these (*Bereshit Rabbah* 1:15; *Pirqei de-Rabbi Eli'ezer* 18) concerns the order of Creation, the school of Shammai insisting that the heavens were created before the earth, the school of Hillel the reverse. Another dispute between them continued for years, according to BT *Eruvin* 13b: "Rabbi Abba said in the name of Shemu'el: 'For three years the school of Shammai and the school of Hillel disputed, the former contending: "The *halakhah* accords with our view," the latter contending: "The *halakhah* accords with our view." A heavenly voice came forth, saying: "Both these and those are the words of the living God, but the *halakhah* accords with the school of Hillel."'" According to Isaac Luria (*MM*), in messianic times Shammai's views will prevail.

171. **harmonizing them** אסכים לון (*Askim lon*). See *Pirqei de-Rabbi Eli'ezer* 18: "The school of Shammai said, 'The heavens

Heaven mediated the conflict, and upon this conflict the world was established.[172] This resembled the act of Creation, whereas Korah totally denied the act of Creation, disputing heaven, seeking to deny the words of Torah.[173] He certainly adhered to Hell, so there he clung.[174] This secret appears in *The Book of Adam*.[175] When *darkness*[176] aroused, it aroused intensely, thereby creating Hell, clinging to it in that conflict. As the seething fury subsided, conflict of a different type arose: a conflict of love.[177] There were two conflicts: one, beginning; one, ending. This is the way of the righteous: beginning harshly, ending gently.[178] Korah was the beginning of the conflict: seething in wrath, he was compelled to cling to Hell. Shammai was the end of the conflict,

---

were created first, and the earth afterward....' The school of Hillel said, 'The earth was created first....' Contention arose between them over this matter, until *Shekhinah* rested between them and they agreed (הסכימו [*hiskimu*]) with one another that both were created simultaneously." See *Zohar* 1:29b.

172. **for the sake of heaven, so Heaven...** As noted above, M *Avot* 5:17 cites the dispute between Hillel and Shammai as the prototypical "conflict for the sake of heaven," destined להתקיים (*le-hitqayyem*), "to endure." Appropriately, the *sefirah* of *Tif'eret,* known as Heaven, mediates this conflict, and thus "the world אתקיים (*itqayyam*), was established." See the reference to the heavenly voice, above, note 170. Cf. *Zohar* 1:33a, 252b; Moses de León, *Sefer ha-Rimmon,* 113–14.

173. **deny the words of Torah** According to which, Aaron was designated to be the priest; or according to which, the process of Creation involved the harmonizing of left and right.

174. **so there he clung** Descending to Sheol: *They and all that belonged to them went down alive into Sheol* (Numbers 16:33).

175. *The Book of Adam* One of the many volumes housed in the real or imaginary library of the author(s) of the *Zohar*. According to BT *Bava Metsi'a* 85b–86a, Rabbi Yehudah the Prince once saw *The Book of Adam,* which contained the genealogy of the entire human race. See Genesis 5:1; Be-

reshit Rabbah 24:1; BT *Sanhedrin* 38b. This book is not to be confused with the Apocryphal *Book of Adam,* known in various versions, though the Apocryphal book may have influenced the *Zohar*'s depiction of the *Book of Adam*. According to various medieval traditions, the angel Raziel transmitted a magical book to Adam. Later, probably in the seventeenth century, *Sefer Razi'el* was compiled in its present form, comprising ancient magical, mystical, and cosmological teachings.

See *Zohar* 1:37b, 55a–b, 58b, 72b, 90b; 2:70a–b, 131a, 143b, 180a, 181a, 197a; 3:10a, 68b; *ZH* 37b; Ginzberg, *Legends,* 5:117–18, n. 110; Liebes, *Peraqim,* 85–87; Matt, *Zohar,* 25; Wineman, *Mystic Tales from the Zohar,* 35–54. Note the comment by Shim'on Lavi, *KP,* on *Zohar* 1:7a: "All such books mentioned in the *Zohar*...have been lost in the wanderings of exile...Nothing is left of them except what is mentioned in the *Zohar*."

176. *darkness* The *sefirah* of *Gevurah,* on the left.

177. **a conflict of love** The tension between left and right, when resolved, yields the harmony of *Tif'eret,* also known as רחמים (*Raḥamim*), Compassion, who eventually unites with *Shekhinah*.

178. **the way of the righteous...** See BT *Qiddushin* 30b: "Rabbi Ḥiyya son of Abba said, 'Even father and son, master and disciple, who are engaged in Torah at the same gate become each other's enemies. Yet, they do not stir from there until they come to

130

when wrath subsides and one must arouse the conflict of love and be reconciled by heaven.

This is the mystery of: *Let there be an expanse in the midst of the waters, that it may separate*—the first conflict, outburst of seething fury. He[179] sought to mediate, but before the fury cooled, Hell aroused. Then *God fashioned the expanse and separated* (Genesis 1:7)[180]—arousing a conflict of passionate love, endurance of the world.[181] In accord with this mystery was the conflict of Shammai and Hillel, for Oral Torah approached Written Torah in love, together consummating existence.[182]

Separation is certainly on the left. Here separation is written: *that it may separate*, and *He separated*; and there is written: *Is it too little for you that the God of Israel has separated you from the community of Israel...?* (Numbers 16:9).[183] Similarly: *At that time YHVH separated the tribe of Levi* (Deuteronomy 10:8).[184] Separation, indeed, is solely on the second, on the left.[185] Now you might say, "Indeed, separation is on the second, so why is it associated with Levi, who is third? It should be with Simeon, who is second."[186] But although Levi is third, in Jacob's mind he was second,[187] and separation is always on the second. Everything follows the straight path perfectly.

131

love one another.'" See *Zohar* 1:174; 2:56a; 3:42a (*RM*).

179. **He**   God.

180. ***God fashioned the expanse...***   The *expanse* of *Tif'eret*.

181. **a conflict of... love, endurance of the world**   See *Bereshit Rabbah* 4:6: "... a conflict that promoted the ordering of the world and civilization."

182. **Oral Torah... Written Torah...**   *Shekhinah* and *Tif'eret*.

183. ***has separated you from the community of Israel***   The verse continues: *to bring you near to Him, to perform the duties of the Dwelling of YHVH, to stand before the community and serve them?* These are Moses' words to the rebellious Korah, who was privileged to be a Levite.

184. ***At that time YHVH separated the tribe of Levi***   The verse continues: *to carry the ark of the covenant of YHVH, to stand before YHVH to serve Him, and to bless in His name.*

185. **on the second, on the left**   Separation occurred on the second day of Creation, symbolizing the *sefirah* of the left side, *Gevurah*, which is also symbolized by the tribe of Levi.

186. **Levi, who is third... Simeon, who is second**   The birth order of the eldest sons of Jacob was: Reuben, Simeon, and Levi.

187. **in Jacob's mind he was second**   When Jacob had sexual relations with Leah, he thought she was Rachel (Genesis 29:23, 25), so the child who was conceived (Reuben) was in his mind Rachel's. Simeon was therefore considered Leah's firstborn, and Levi was the second. Furthermore, Reuben's primogeniture was disavowed by Jacob following the incident of the mandrakes (ibid. 30:14–17) or after Reuben slept with his father's concubine, Bilhah (ibid. 35:22).

See ibid. 49:4; 1 Chronicles 5:1; *Bereshit Rabbah* 98:4; *Zohar* 1:155a (*ST*), 176b, 222b, 236a.

הבדלה (*Havdalah*), Separation, as Sabbath departs, separates those who rule the weekdays from Sabbath.[188] As soon as Sabbath departs, a specter,[189] an evil officer, ascends from Hell, intent on seizing power the moment Israel recites: *Let the work of our hands prosper* (Psalms 90:17).[190] Emerging from the rung known as Sheol,[191] he desires to mingle in the seed of Israel and dominate them. But Israel takes action with myrtle and wine,[192] reciting *havdalah*, so he departs from them. As soon as they recite the blessing of separation over the cup, that specter sinks into his place in Sheol, site of Korah and his gang, as is written: *They and all that belonged to them went down alive into Sheol* (Numbers 16:33). They did not descend there until Israel separated from them, as is written: *Separate yourselves from the midst of this community...!* (ibid., 21).[193]

So separation is always on the second, which is the left,[194] at the outbreak of intense fury aroused by the left in the conflict, before it subsides into calm. On

188. הבדלה (*Havdalah*)... *Havdalah* ("separation") is the ritual marking the end of Sabbath (and, in an abbreviated form, the end of festivals). The *havdalah* at the conclusion of the Sabbath is first recited in the fourth blessing of the *amidah* prayer of the evening service and then over a cup of wine. This second, longer ritual consists of blessings over wine, spices, and the light of a candle. For the kabbalist, the end of Sabbath is fraught with danger, for now the harsh powers of judgment, banished for the duration of the Sabbath, are aroused and stand poised to dominate the weekdays. The wicked, who enjoyed a day's respite from their torment in Hell, resume their suffering.

See *Tanhuma, Ki Tissa* 33; *Zohar* 1:14b, 21a; 2:207a; Ginsburg, *The Sabbath in the Classical Kabbalah*, 256–84.

189. **specter** טסירא (*Tesira*), a neologism appearing several times in the *Zohar* (1:20b, 178a ["*tesirin* without a body"]; 2:29a). See *Tanhuma* (Buber), *Bereshit* 17: "It is not written here: [*He ceased from all His work*] *that* [*God*] *created and made*, but rather [*that God created*] *to make* (Genesis 2:3), for the Sabbath came first and their work was not completed. Rabbi Benaya said, 'This refers to the demons, for He created their souls, and as He was creating their bodies, the Sabbath day was hallowed. He left them, and they remained soul without body.'"

See *Bereshit Rabbah* 7:5; 11:9; *Zohar* 1:14a, 47b–48a, 178a; 2:155b; 3:142b (*IR*); and M *Avot* 5:6: "Ten things were created on Friday eve at twilight:.... Some say, 'Also the demons.'"

An alternative rendering here is "warden"; cf. טסורא (*tesora*) in JT *Ketubbot* 11:3, 34b, a corruption of סנטירא (*santeira*), "guardsman." See *Zohar* 1:14b.

190. *Let the work of our hands prosper* This verse, recited as Sabbath departs, is intended to ward off demonic forces, but it also signals their return. See *Zohar* 1:197b.

191. **Sheol** The biblical term for the abode of the dead, later identified with גיהנם (*geihinnom*), "Hell."

192. **myrtle and wine** Used in the ritual of *havdalah*. See *Zohar* 2:20a (*MhN*), 208b–209a; 3:35a–b; J. Lauterbach, in *Hebrew Union College Annual* 15 (1940): 367–86; Ginsburg, *The Sabbath in the Classical Kabbalah*, 259–67; Ta-Shma, *Ha-Nigleh she-ba-Nistar*, 125, n. 84; Hallamish, *Ha-Qabbalah*, 323.

193. *Separate yourselves from the midst of this community* The verse continues: *that I may annihilate them in an instant!* The command is actually spoken to Moses and Aaron, not the entire people.

194. **on the second, which is the left** On the second day of Creation, symbolizing the *sefirah* of *Gevurah*.

it, Hell was created,[195] and then all those angels who denounce their Master above and are burned, consumed by fire;[196] and all those others who vanish, unenduring, devoured by fire.[197] Similarly Korah below,[198] entirely the same.

Let there be an expanse—Let an expanse expand, one from the other.[199]

אל (*El*), God, cluster on the right, אל גדול (*El gadol*), Great God.[200] From the midst of the waters an expanse expanded to complete this name, אל (*El*), to merge in that expansion, one in the other, and from אל (*El*) expanded אלהים (*Elohim*), God.[201] The letters הי"ם (*he, yod, mem*) expanded and were transposed into lower waters, ימ"ה (*yod, mem, he*). That expansion

195. **Hell was created**   As noted above, page 128.

196. **all those angels who denounce...** Apparently referring to the angels who opposed the creation of the human being. See BT *Sanhedrin* 38b: "Rav Yehudah said in the name of Rav: 'When the blessed Holy One sought to create the human being, He [first] created a company of ministering angels and asked them, "Is it your desire that we make the human being in our image?" They responded, "Master of the Universe, what are his deeds?" He replied, "Such and such are his deeds." They exclaimed, "Master of the Universe, *What is a human that You are mindful of him, a human being that You take note of him? (Psalms 8:5)." He stretched out His little finger among them and burned them. The same thing happened with a second company. The third company said to Him, "Master of the Universe, the former ones who spoke in Your presence—what did they accomplish? The entire world is Yours! Whatever You wish to do in Your world, do it." When He reached the members of the generation of the Flood and the generation of the Dispersion [the Tower of Babel], whose deeds were corrupt, they [the angels] said to Him, "Master of the Universe, didn't the first ones speak well?" He responded, "*Till* [*your*] *old age, I am He; till* [*you turn*] *grey, I will carry you.* [*I have made and I will bear* (*your sins*); *I will carry and deliver*] (Isaiah 46:4).'"

197. **all those others...**   According to Rabbi Yoḥanan (*Bereshit Rabbah* 1:3), all the angels were created on the second day. In

the *Zohar,* those angels created on the second day are angels of Judgment, deriving from the side of *Gevurah.* Consisting solely of strict Judgment, they cannot survive.

On the notion of angels vanishing, see BT Ḥagigah 14a: "Shemu'el said to Rabbi Ḥiyya son of Rav, 'O son of a lion! Come, I will tell you one of those fine words said by your father: Every single day ministering angels are created from the fiery stream, chant a song, then cease to be, as is said: *New every morning, immense is Your faithfulness!* (Lamentations 3:23)."

See *Zohar* 1:18b; 2:213b–214a, 247a; Ezra of Gerona, *Peirush Shir ha-Shirim,* 507, 510; Moses de León, *Sefer ha-Mishqal,* 65; idem, *Sefer ha-Rimmon,* 205; Tishby, *Wisdom of the Zohar,* 2:624–25.

198. **Similarly Korah below**   He was descended from Levi, considered the second son (see above, page 131), and he embodied the left side.

199. **Let an expanse expand...**   Let the *sefirot* emanate from *Binah.* See Ezra of Gerona, *Peirush Shir ha-Shirim,* 506.

200. **אל (*El*), God, cluster...**   *Ḥesed* is known as both אל (*El*) and גדולה (*Gedullah*), Greatness, and therefore אל גדול (*El gadol*). See *Zohar* 1:16b; 2:253a.

"Cluster" renders קטפא (*qitpa*). See BT *Ketubbot* 112a, *Avodah Zarah* 72b: קטופי (*qeto-phei*), "clusters, fruit ready to be plucked"; *Bei'ur ha-Millim ha-Zarot,* 190.

201. **From the midst of the waters...** From *Binah,* the upper waters, the letters הי"ם (*he, yod, mem*) emanated and thus אל

expanding on the second day is the upper waters: הי״ם (*he, yod, mem*), *this vast* הים (*ha-yam*), *sea* (Psalms 104:25). הי״ם (*He, yod, mem*) is the upper waters; the transposition of these letters, ימ״ה (*yod, mem, he*), is the lower waters.[202] Once arrayed, all became one entity, this name extending to various realms.[203] The upper waters are male; the lower waters, female.[204] At first water intermingled with water,[205] until they were separated, to distinguish upper from lower: these are אלהים (*Elohim*), *God,* and these are אדני (*Adonai*), *Lord,* upper ה (*he*) and lower ה (*he*).[206] What is written? *Elohim fashioned the expanse* (Genesis 1:7)— this expansion took this name: *Elohim,* upper waters,[207] while the lower waters [18a] are *Adonai.* Nevertheless, once male waters were completed by female waters, the name *Elohim* extended over all.[208]

Even though He separated the upper waters from the lower, the conflict did not cease until the third day[209] arrived, harmonizing the conflict, and every-

(*El*), *Ḥesed,* expanded into אלהים (*Elohim*), the next *sefirah: Gevurah.*

134

202. **transposed into lower waters...** The letters הי״ם (*he, yod, mem*) emanate from *Binah,* who is known as upper waters and as הים (*ha-yam*), "the sea." As this alphabetic flow proceeds, it is gradually transposed into ימ״ה (*yod, mem, he*), which spell ימה (*yammah*), "sea," indicating the lower waters of *Shekhinah.* (The homonym ימה [*yammah*], "west," also refers to *Shekhinah.*)

203. **this name extending...** The name אלהים (*Elohim*) refers not only to *Binah* and *Gevurah,* but now also to *Shekhinah,* angels, and even "other gods."

204. **upper waters are male...** See *Bereshit Rabbah* 13:13: "Rabbi Shim'on son of El'azar said, 'Every single handbreadth [of water] descending from above is met by two handbreadths emitted by the earth. What is the reason? *Deep calls to deep...* (Psalms 42:8).' Rabbi Levi said, 'The upper waters are male; the lower, female. The former cry to the latter, "Receive us! You are creatures of the blessed Holy One and we are His messengers." They immediately receive them, as is written: *Let the earth open* (Isaiah 45:8)—like a female opening to a male.'"

See *Tosefta, Ta'anit* 1:4; 1 Enoch 54:8; *Seder Rabbah di-Vreshit,* 10 (*Battei Midrashot,* 1:25); *Pirqei de-Rabbi Eli'ezer* 23; *Zohar* 1:29b, 46a, 60b, 244a–b, 245b; 3:223b.

Although often depicted as the Divine Mother, *Binah* is also described as "World of the Male," encompassing the entire configuration of *sefirot* from *Ḥesed* through *Yesod.* Together they constitute a masculine entity ready to join *Shekhinah.*

See *Zohar* 1:96a, 147a, 149a, 160b, 246a, 248b; 2:127b; *ZḤ* 72b (*ShS*). Cf. 1:17b, 46b, 163a; 2:4a.

205. **water intermingled with water** Aramaic and Hebrew, הוו מים במים (*havo mayim be-mayim*). See *Tanḥuma, Vayaqhel* 6: "When the blessed Holy One created His world, היה העולם כלו מים במים (*hayah ha-olam kullo mayim be-mayim*), it was entirely water intermingled with water."

See JT *Ḥagigah* 2:1, 77a; *Pesiqta Rabbati* 1; *Shemot Rabbah* 50:1; *Zohar* 1:56b, 68a.

206. **these are אלהים (*Elohim*), *God,* and these are אדני (*Adonai*), *Lord...*** *Binah* is *Elohim* and the first ה (*he*) of יהוה (*YHVH*); *Shekhinah* is *Adonai* and the second ה (*he*).

See *Bahir* 20 (29); *Zohar* 1:62a; 2:177a (*SdTs*); 3:74b, 89b; *ZḤ* 82c (*MhN, Rut*).

207. **this expansion took this name...** The emanation proceeded from *Binah,* first to *Ḥesed* and then to *Gevurah,* which took the name *Elohim,* previously associated with *Binah,* the upper waters.

208. **the name *Elohim* extended over all** Once *Shekhinah* completed the array of *sefirot,* the name *Elohim* was extended to Her as well.

209. **the third day** *Tif'eret.*

thing settled fittingly in place. Because of this conflict, although it sustains the world, *that it was good* is not written of the second day, for the act was incomplete.[210] Upper waters and lower waters mingled, and nothing generated in the world until they were separated and distinguished, thereby generating offspring. Even so, although the separation took place on the second day, and the conflict arose then, the third day harmonized everything, for it is the name engraved with the engravings הו״ה (*he, vav, he*), harmonizing upper and lower waters: upper ה (*he*), lower ה (*he*), ו (*vav*) between them, pacifying the two sides.[211] This is the sign: the waters of the Jordan, upper waters, *rose in one heap* (Joshua 3:16), the lower waters flowed down into the sea, and Israel passed between.[212]

Five *expanses* are written here.[213] Vitality of the Worlds moves through them, conducts by them,[214] all comprising one another.[215] Were it not for this conflict, harmonized by the middle, they would not merge or be at peace with

210. ***that it was good* is not written of the second day...** In the biblical account of Creation, the statement *God saw that it was good* (or a variant) is included in the description of each of the six days except for the second. See *Bereshit Rabbah* 4:6: "Why is *that it was good* not written concerning the second day? Rabbi Yoḥanan said..., 'Because on that day Hell was created....' Rabbi Ḥanina said, 'Because on that day conflict was created: *that it may separate water from water.*'.... Rabbi Shemu'el son of Naḥman said, 'Because the work of the water was not completed. Therefore *that it was good* is written twice on the third day: once for the work of the water [see Genesis 1:9–10] and once for the work of the [third] day [ibid., 11].'"

In the *Zohar,* the second day marks the emergence of *Gevurah,* characterized by strict justice, which conflicts with *Ḥesed,* divine love. On the third day, these polar opposites were balanced and synthesized.

See BT *Pesaḥim* 54a; *Pirqei de-Rabbi Eli'ezer* 4; *Midrash Konen* (*Beit ha-Midrash,* 2:25); Ezra of Gerona, *Peirush Shir ha-Shirim,* 506; *Zohar* 1:17a–b, 33a; 46a; 2:149b; Moses de León, *Sheqel ha-Qodesh,* 41 (49).

211. **the name engraved with the engravings...** In the name יהוה (*YHVH*), the letter ו (*vav*)—whose numerical value is six—symbolizes *Tif'eret* together with the five se-

firot surrounding Him (*Ḥesed* to *Yesod*). *Tif'eret* harmonizes *Binah* and *Shekhinah,* the upper and lower waters, symbolized by the first and second ה (*he*), respectively.

212. **This is the sign...** See Joshua 3:16, describing Israel's crossing the Jordan: *The waters coming down from above* [upstream] *rose in one heap a great way off, at Adam, the town next to Zarethan; and those flowing down* [downstream] *toward the Sea of the Aravah, the Dead Sea, ran out completely. So the people crossed near Jericho.* Here *the waters from above* symbolize *Binah,* those flowing *down toward the Sea* symbolize *Shekhinah,* and *the people* (of Israel) symbolize *Tif'eret.*

213. **Five *expanses*...** The word רקיע (*raqi'a*), *expanse,* appears five times in the description of the second day (Genesis 1:6–8), alluding to the five *sefirot* from *Ḥesed* through *Hod.* See Moses de León, *Sheqel ha-Qodesh,* 11 (14).

214. **Vitality of the Worlds...** *Yesod,* the river of emanation, flows through these five *sefirot* and, drawing on them, conducts the lower worlds by means of *Shekhinah.*

On various senses of the title "Vitality of the Worlds," see Daniel 12:7; *Mekhilta, Pisḥa* 16; *Bereshit Rabbah* 1:5; Schäfer, *Synopse zur Hekhalot-Literatur,* §275; *Zohar* 1:4b, 132a, 135b, 167b.

215. **all comprising...** Each *sefirah* reflects the entire array of *sefirot.*

one another. There are five hundred years to which the Tree of Life clings, generating verdure and offspring for the world. All the waters of Creation, drawn and flowing from the beginning, branch beneath it, through it.[216] King David captures it all and then distributes,[217] as is written: *He distributed among all the people, the entire multitude of Israel…a cake made in a pan and a raisin cake* (2 Samuel 6:19).[218] Similarly, *You give to them, they gather* (Psalms 104:28), and *She rises while it is still night, and gives food to her household* (Proverbs 31:15).

When conflict was aroused by the potency of the left, Colonel Ember[219] glowed and flared. Out came two specters, male and female, immediately congealing with no moisture at all.[220] From them split off various maleficent species; from here infusion of impure spirit into all those fierce specters, mystery of foreskin.[221] They were empowered by virulent species—viper and serpent—turning into one. The viper bears at seventy years, but in union all reverts to the seven years of the serpent.[222] Here lies the mystery of Hell, called by seven names.[223] The evil impulse is called by seven names.[224] From here,

136

216. There are five hundred years… See *Bereshit Rabbah* 15:6: "Rabbi Yehudah son of Rabbi Il'ai said, 'The Tree of Life extends over a journey of five hundred years, and all the waters of Creation branch off beneath it.'"

The five hundred years symbolize the five *sefirot* from Ḥesed through Hod, which channel the emanation from Ḥokhmah (known as ראשית [*Reshit*], "Beginning" or "Creation") and nourish *Yesod,* the Tree of Life.

See *Zohar* 1:35a, 78b (*ST*); Moses de León, *Sheqel ha-Qodesh,* 56 (69).

217. King David… David, the ideal king, symbolizes *Shekhinah,* who is often called *Malkhut* ("Kingdom"). *Shekhinah* receives the flow of emanation from *Yesod* and distributes it to the lower worlds.

218. *He distributed among all the people…* After defeating the Philistines.

219. Colonel Ember הורפילא דטיפסא (*Hurpila de-tifsa*). *Hurpila* derives from the Aramaic רופילא (*rufila*) and Latin *rufulus,* a military tribune appointed by the general. See BT *Bava Metsi'a* 49b, 107b; *Shevu'ot* 6b; *Avodah Zarah* 33b, 61b. *Tifsa* means "ember" in *Zohar* 1:242a; 3:111a. See *DE; Bei'ur ha-Millim ha-Zarot,* 176, 178–79.

Here the demonic Colonel Ember is empowered and enflamed by the harsh conflict.

220. congealing… The male and female demonic forces unite. Congealing typifies the second day, according to *Bereshit Rabbah* 4:2: "Rav said, 'The works of Creation [i.e., the heavens] were fluid, and on the second day they congealed. *Let there be an expanse* [*in the midst of the waters*]! (Genesis 1:6), Let the expanse be firm!'" See above, page 124.

221. mystery of foreskin The foreskin, removed in the ritual of circumcision, symbolizes the demonic. See *Zohar* 1:13a; Moses de León, *Sheqel ha-Qodesh,* 55 (68).

222. viper and serpent… See BT *Bekhorot* 8a: "A viper bears at seventy years;… a serpent at seven years." Cf. *Bereshit Rabbah* 20:4; *Zohar* 2:220a. The gestation period of snakes is actually several months.

223. Hell, called by seven names See BT *Eruvin* 19a: "Rabbi Yehoshu'a son of Levi said, 'Hell has seven names: Sheol, Ruin, Pit of Destruction, Tumultuous Pit, Miry Clay, Shadow of Death, and Netherworld.'" Cf. *Zohar* 2:150b.

224. The evil impulse…seven names See BT *Sukkah* 52a: "Rabbi Avira, or some say Rabbi Yehoshu'a son of Levi, expounded, 'The evil impulse has seven names. The blessed Holy One called it Evil…; Moses called it Uncircumcised…; David called it

through countless rungs, impurity spreads through the world, all from the mystery of the left. Good and evil diverge—cultivation of the world.[225] Here is the engraved name of eighteen letters,[226] presiding over rain of favor and blessing, cultivating the world.

<table>
<tr><td>

God said, "Let the waters under heaven be gathered to one place!" (Genesis 1:9).[227]

</td><td>

יקוו (Yiqqavu), Let [the waters] be gathered—in קו (qav), a line, following a straight path.[228]

</td></tr>
</table>

For out of the mystery of the primordial point,[229] all emerges secretly, till reaching, clustering in the supernal palace.[230] From there it radiates in a straight line to the other rungs, until reaching that *one place,* which gathers all in the totality of male and female. Who is that? Vitality of the Worlds.[231] *The waters*—flowing from above, from upper ה (he).[232] *Under heaven*—small ו (vav); so, ו"ו (vav): one is *heaven;* the other, *under heaven.*[233] Then, *Let the dry land appear!* (ibid.)—lower ה (he).[234]

137

Impure...; Solomon called it Enemy...; Isaiah called it Stumbling Block...; Ezekiel called it Stone...; Joel called it Hidden One.'" See *Zohar* 2:262b–263a.

225. **cultivation of the world** The world is maintained through a rhythm of light and darkness, good and evil. Human choice and action determine which power will manifest on earth: the divine or the demonic. The demonic forces, too, serve a sacred function by punishing human evil.

226. **engraved name of eighteen letters** Apparently referring to the six different permutations of the three letters יה"ו (yod, he, vav), which compose the name יהוה (YHVH): יה"ו, יו"ה, הי"ו, הו"י, וי"ה, וה"י.

227. *Let the waters under heaven be gathered to one place* The verse continues: *and let the dry land appear! And it was so.*

228. קו (*qav*), **a line...** The flow of emanation, proceeding in a line, referred to elsewhere in the *Zohar* as קו המדה (qav ha-middah), "the line of measure."

See Jeremiah 31:38; Azriel of Gerona, *Peirush ha-Aggadot,* 89–90; Jacob ben Sheshet, *Meshiv Devarim Nekhohim,* 113; *Zohar* 1:15a; 2:233a–b, 258a; *ZH* 56d–58d (*QhM*); *TZ* 18, 37b.

See *Bereshit Rabbah* 5:1: "יקוו המים (Yiqqavu ha-mayim). Rabbi Berekhiah said in the name

of Rabbi Abba son of Yama, 'Let a measure be made for the waters, as is said: וקו (Veqav), *And a line, will be stretched out over Jerusalem* (Zechariah 1:16).'"

229. **the primordial point** Ḥokhmah, the point of light issuing from *Keter.*

230. **the supernal palace** *Binah,* the divine womb.

231. **Vitality of the Worlds** *Yesod,* who channels the entire flow of emanation to *Shekhinah,* thereby uniting male and female. See above, note 214.

232. **upper ה (he)** *Binah,* symbolized by the first ה (he) in the name יהוה (YHVH), and perhaps alluded to by the ה (he) of המים (ha-mayim), *the waters.*

233. **small ו (vav)...** *Yesod,* which emerges from, yet remains joined to, *Tif'eret.* Whereas *Tif'eret* is known as *heaven* and is symbolized by the large ו (vav), *Yesod* is *under heaven* and symbolized by the small ו (vav). Together they spell out the name of the letter, וו (vav), as well as the double ו (vav) in the word יקוו (yiqqavu), *let [the waters] be gathered.*

See *Zohar* 1:119a; 2:9b; 3:11a, 53b, 74b. On the question of the small ו (vav), see *Minḥat Shai* on Psalms 24:4.

234. **lower ה (he)** *Shekhinah,* symbolized by the second ה (he) of the name יהוה

This is revealed, the rest all concealed—so mystery of blessings revealed and concealed[235]—none but this lower one being revealed. From this one, *let it appear!*—through contemplation the concealed one is perceived.[236] *To one place*—for here is the nexus of unity of the upper world.[237]

YHVH is one and His name is one (Zechariah 14:9). Two unifications: one of the upper world, to be unified in its rungs,[238] and one of the lower world to be unified in its rungs.[239] Nexus of unity of the upper world extends till here.[240] Vitality of the Worlds is consummated there, the upper world bound in unity. So it is called *one place*. All levels and limbs[241] gather there, all unified within, completely indivisible. On no level but this are they unified; within, they are all secretly concealed in a single desire.[242] Here, on this rung, the revealed world joins the concealed.[243]

Similarly the revealed world is unified below, and this revealed world is the world of *let it appear!* (Genesis 1:9). *I saw YHVH* (Isaiah 6:1).[244] *They saw the God of Israel* (Exodus 24:10). *The presence of YHVH appeared* (Numbers 14:10). *The presence of YHVH appeared* (ibid. 17:7). *Like the appearance of the bow in the cloud on a rainy day, so was the appearance of the surrounding radiance—the*

138

(*YHVH*), and perhaps alluded to by the ה (*he*) of היבשה (*ha-yabbashah*), *the dry land*. Without the *waters* of emanation, *Shekhinah* is *dry land*. Of all the *sefirot,* She is the one revealed, the one who reveals the others.

235. **mystery of blessings revealed and concealed**   The Hebrew formula of blessing begins by addressing God directly in the second person (revealed): "Blessed are You, *YHVH*," but then it switches to the third person (concealed): "...who has hallowed us by His commandments...."

See *Bahir* 125 (184); Scholem, *Das Buch Bahir,* 134–35; Naḥmanides on Exodus 15:26; Todros Abulafia, *Otsar ha-Kavod, Berakhot* 12a; *Zohar* 1:158a–b; 3:271b, 289a (*IZ*) (*NZ,* n. 6); *TZ* 39, 79b; *Kolbo* 1.

236. **From this one, *let it appear!*...**   By contemplating the revealed *sefirah* of *She-khinah,* one is able to perceive concealed realms.

237. **the nexus of unity...**   In *Yesod* all the higher *sefirot* are united in preparation for joining *Shekhinah*.

238. **one of the upper world...**   The six *sefirot* from *Ḥesed* through *Yesod,* centering on *Tif'eret,* who is symbolized by the name *YHVH*.

239. **one of the lower world...**   *Shekhinah* and the powers accompanying Her. She is called *His name* because through Her revealed nature *YHVH* becomes known and recognized. See *Zohar* 2:133b–134b.

240. **till here**   To *Yesod*.

241. **limbs**   שייפין (*Shaifin*), from a root meaning "to smooth, rub, slip." In the *Zohar,* the word signifies "limbs," perhaps based on the Talmudic expression (BT *Sotah* 7b) על איבריה לשפא (*al eivreih le-shafa*), "each limb entered its socket"—"slipping" into place—or "...the chest."

See *Arukh,* s.v. *shaf;* Rashi, ad loc., and on Job 33:21, citing BT *Ḥullin* 42b; *Zohar* 3:170a.

242. **in a single desire**   As *Yesod* verges on union with *Shekhinah*. See *Zohar* 2:128b, 133b.

243. **the revealed world joins the concealed**   *Shekhinah* joins the more hidden *sefirot*.

244. *I saw **YHVH***   The verse actually reads *I saw* אדני (*Adonai*). See *Zohar* 1:60a; 2:81b. The key root in each of the following verses is ראה (*r'h*), "to see," or, in its passive conjugation, "to appear." All these theophanies are linked by the *Zohar* with the command of Genesis: תראה (*Tera'eh*), *Let it*

appearance of the image of the presence of YHVH (Ezekiel 1:28). This is the mystery of: *Let the dry land appear!* (Genesis 1:9).

I have set My bow in the cloud (ibid. 9:13)—since the day the world was created.[245] On a cloudy day, [18b] when the קשת (*keshet*), rainbow, appears, *the appearance of the image of the presence of YHVH,* the left is aroused to be empowered.[246] Rachel emerges, ותקש (*va-teqash*), *and she had hard, labor* (ibid. 35:16).[247] Michael on one side, Gabriel on another, Raphael on a third—these are the colors appearing in that *image:* white, red, and green.[248] *So was the appearance of the surrounding radiance*—a radiance concealed in revolving the

appear!, which is taken to mean: "Let the divine appear through *Shekhinah!*" *Shekhinah* is often referred to as אדני (*Adonai*), "Lord," and כבוד (*kavod*), *presence.*

245. *I have set My bow in the cloud . . .* God's declaration to Noah after the Flood, assuring him of the divine covenant with humanity. According to M *Avot* 5:6, the rainbow was one of the ten things created at the end of the week of Creation, "at twilight on Sabbath eve."

See Ibn Ezra and Radak on Genesis 9:13; Naḥmanides on 9:12; Judah ben Barzillai, *Peirush Sefer Yetsirah,* 139; *Zohar* 1:71b; Kasher, *Torah Shelemah,* Genesis 9:13, n. 81.

In the *Zohar,* the bow often symbolizes *Yesod,* the divine phallus and site of the covenant (the sign of circumcision). *Yesod* comprises the various colors of the *sefirot,* set in *the cloud* of *Shekhinah* since the beginning of time. *Bow* is a euphemism for phallus in rabbinic literature (e.g., *Bereshit Rabbah* 87:7; BT *Sanhedrin* 92a) and also refers to the Divine Presence. See BT *Ḥagigah* 16a: "'Whoever shows no concern for the glory of his Maker, it were better for him if he had not come into the world' (M *Ḥagigah* 2:1). What does this mean? Rabbi Abba said: 'It refers to one who gazes at the rainbow,' . . . for it is written: *Like the appearance of the bow in the cloud on a rainy day, so was the appearance of the surrounding radiance— the appearance of the image of the presence of YHVH* (Ezekiel 1:28)."

See BT *Berakhot* 59a; Isaac ben Jacob ha-Kohen, *Commentary on the Merkavah,* ed. Scholem, *Tarbiz* 2 (1931): 200; Naḥmanides

on Genesis 9:12; *Zohar* 1:71b; 2:51b, 66b, 99a; 3:84a, 215a; *TZ* 30, 74b; Scholem, "Colours and Their Symbolism," 69–71; Wolfson, *Through a Speculum That Shines,* 336–40.

246. **On a cloudy day . . .** On a day when judgment prevails. See Naḥmanides on Genesis 9:12; he identifies the rainbow (קשת [*qeshet*]) as the quality of Judgment (*Din*) or *Gevurah*—which is harsh (קשה [*qasheh*]). Cf. Baḥya ben Asher on Genesis 9:13. According to BT *Ketubbot* 77b, the rainbow appears when no righteous human is present. See *Zohar* 1:225a; 3:15a, 36a, 215a.

247. *and she had hard labor* The full verse reads: *They set out from Bethel; but when they were still some distance short of Efrat, Rachel went into childbirth, and she had hard labor.* Rachel dies giving birth to Benjamin. The word ותקש (*va-teqash*), *and she had hard* [*labor*], indicates harsh judgment, and it also contains the letters of the word קשת (*qeshet*), "rainbow" (cf. *TZ* 69, 99b). *Shekhinah,* symbolized by Rachel, transmits divine judgment; She shares the symbol of the rainbow with *Yesod,* displaying the colors of the *sefirot.*

248. **Michael . . . Gabriel . . . Raphael . . .** These angels (together with Uriel) are the angels of the Presence, surrounding the divine throne. In Kabbalah these angels of the Presence are identified with the four holy creatures seen by Ezekiel (1:5–14). Here the *Zohar* indicates that they accompany *Shekhinah,* displaying the spectrum of colors: white (associated with the right side), red (the left), and green (the middle). See *Zohar* 1:98b–99a (*ST*).

139

vision of the eye.[249] *The appearance of the image of the presence of YHVH—* colors, for the lower unity is unified in accord with the unity above.[250] יהוה אלהינו יהוה (*YHVH Eloheinu YHVH*), *YHVH, our God, YHVH* (Deuteronomy 6:4)—colors concealed, unrevealed, banding together *to one place,* one unity above.[251] The colors of the rainbow below, uniting white, red, and green, match the concealed colors,[252] composing another unity, mystery of *His name is one* (Zechariah 14:9), "Blessed be the name of His glorious kingdom forever and ever," the unity below.[253] The unity above is: *Hear, O Israel!* יהוה אלהינו יהוה (*YHVH Eloheinu YHVH*), *YHVH is our God, YHVH is one* (Deuteronomy 6:4). One parallels the other: six words here, six words there.[254]

יקוו (*Yiqqavu*), *Let [the waters] be gathered*—surveying by קו (*qav*), line, and measure.[255] Measure, plumb of dark brilliance,[256] as is written: *Who measured*

249. **revolving the vision of the eye** An allusion to a technique for seeing the concealed colors of the *sefirot.* By closing one's eye and pressing a finger on the eyeball until it is moved to one side, one gains a vision of colors (white, red, and green), symbolizing *Ḥesed, Gevurah,* and *Tif'eret.* See *Zohar* 2:23b: "The secret is: close your eye and roll your eyeball. Those colors that shine and sparkle will be revealed."

See 1:42a, 43a, 97a–b (*ST*); 2:43b, 247a; Moses de León, *Sheqel ha-Qodesh,* 96–97 (123–24); *KP* on *Zohar* 1:18b; Scholem, "Colours and Their Symbolism," 66–67; Liebes, *Peraqim,* 291–93; Wolfson, *Through a Speculum That Shines,* 380–83.

250. **the lower unity … the unity above** The unity of *Shekhinah* (*presence*) with Her powers, and the unity of *Tif'eret* with the *sefirot* surrounding Him.

251. יהוה אלהינו יהוה (*YHVH Eloheinu YHVH*)… The opening line of the *Shema* (*Hear O Israel! YHVH is our God, YHVH is one*) contains these three divine names, symbolizing the colors of the triad of *sefirot: Ḥesed, Gevurah,* and *Tif'eret,* which band together in *Yesod.* See *Zohar* 2:43b.

252. **The colors of the rainbow…** On the rainbow's colors, see *Sefer Ḥasidim,* ed. Wistinetzki, par. 1445 (ed. Margaliot, par. 484); Moses of Burgos, *Commentary on the Merkavah,* ed. Scholem, *Tarbiz* 5 (1934): 183; Baḥya ben Asher on Genesis 9:13; *Zohar* 1:71b, 98b (*ST*), 136b; 3:215a.

253. **another unity, mystery of *His name is one*…** The unity of *Shekhinah,* who "names" or reveals the divine. She is often called *Malkhut* ("Kingdom").

254. **six words here, six words there** The first line of the *Shema* contains six words in Hebrew: שמע ישראל יהוה אלהינו יהוה אחד (*Shema Yisra'el YHVH Eloheinu YHVH eḥad*), *Hear O Israel! YHVH is our God, YHVH is one.* These six words symbolize the unity above: *Tif'eret* and the five *sefirot* surrounding Him (*Ḥesed* to *Yesod*). The second line of the *Shema* (a nonbiblical response) also contains six words: ברוך שם כבוד מלכותו לעולם ועד (*Barukh shem kevod malkhuto le-olam va-ed*), "Blessed be the name of His glorious kingdom forever and ever." These six words symbolize *Shekhinah* (known as *Malkhut* ["Kingdom"]) and Her accompanying powers. The two realms correspond and eventually unite.

See *Zohar* 1:12a; 2:133b–134a; 3:264a.

255. **surveying by קו (*qav*)…** As the waters of emanation flow, the various *sefirot* take shape, assuming size and dimension. See above, page 137: "יקוו (*Yiqqavu*), *Let [the waters] be gathered*—in קו (*qav*), a line, following a straight path," and note 228.

256. **plumb of dark brilliance** בוצינא דקרדינותא (*Botsina de-qardinuta*), "Lamp of impenetrability." See above, page 107: "a spark of impenetrable darkness," and note 4; *ZḤ* 56d–58d (*QhM*). Liebes (*Peraqim,* 146–49, 162–63) notes the connection between *qardinuta* and measurement and, citing an

the waters with the hollow of His hand? (Isaiah 40:12).[257] This is יקוו המים
(*Yiqqavu ha-mayim*), *Let the waters be aligned.* Here is the measure of the
Creator of the worlds: יוד, הא, ואו, הא (*yod, he, vav, he*).[258] *Holy, holy, holy!
YHVH of Hosts!* (Isaiah 6:3). *Holy, holy, holy—Let the waters be aligned.*[259] *YHVH
of Hosts—to one place,* in the mystery of this name.[260] *The whole earth is full of
His presence* (ibid.)—*Let the dry land appear,* engraved mystery, name of unity:
כוזו במוכסז כוזו (*Kuzu be-mukhsaz kuzu*).[261]

*Let the earth sprout vegetation—
seed-bearing plants* (Genesis 1:11).[262]

Now *Earth* generates Her powers with
those waters gathered *to one place*,[263]
flowing into Her in hidden secrecy,
emerging within Her as supernal se-
crecies, sacred forces, arrayed in an array of faith by all those scions of faith by

early *Zohar* dictionary, suggests the translation: "a plumb of darkened light."

257. *Who measured the waters with the
hollow of His hand* The verse continues:
*gauged the skies with a span, meted the dust
of the earth with a measure, and weighed the
mountains with a scale and the hills with a
balance?*

258. **the measure of the Creator of the
worlds...** The *sefirot* constitute the limbs
of the divine body and represent the full
articulation of the divine name. The *Zohar*
sees the divine anatomy alluded to in both
Genesis 1:9 and Isaiah 6:3.

שעורא (*Shi'ura*), "Measure," recalls שעור
קומה (*shi'ur qomah*), "the measure of the
stature," a term describing the vision of the
divine form in early Jewish mysticism. יוצר
עלמין (*Yotser almin*), "Creator of the worlds,"
recalls the early mystical term יוצר בראשית
(*Yotser Bereshit*), "Creator of the Beginning."

See Schäfer, *Synopse zur Hekhalot-Literatur*, index, s.v. *shi'ur, yotser*; 3 Enoch 11:1;
Seder Rabbah di-Vreshit, 17 (*Battei Midrashot*,
1:28); *Sefer ha-Temunah*, 71b; *Zohar* 2:175b–
176a; Scholem, *Major Trends*, 65.

259. *Holy, holy, holy!... Let the waters...*
The beginning of the verse in Isaiah refers to
the emanation flowing from *Binah* through
the triad of *Ḥesed, Gevurah,* and *Tif'eret.*

260. *YHVH of Hosts—to one place...*
Yesod is called צבאות יהוה (*YHVH Tseva'ot*),
YHVH of Hosts (see above, page 126), and as

noted above, page 137, *one place*—the place
where the entire flow of emanation gathers
before streaming into *Shekhinah.*

261. *The whole earth is full of His
presence* *Shekhinah* is known as the Divine
Presence (כבוד [*kavod*]), as well as *earth* and
dry land. Her more mysterious name is כוזו
במוכסז כוזו (*Kuzu be-mukhsaz kuzu*), an
encoded version of יהוה אלהינו יהוה (*YHVH
Eloheinu YHVH*), formed by replacing each
letter of this triple divine name with the
following letter in the alphabet. Whereas
יהוה אלהינו יהוה (*YHVH Eloheinu YHVH*)
denotes the triad of *sefirot* culminating in
Tif'eret, כוזו במוכסז כוזו (*Kuzu be-mukhsaz
kuzu*) denotes *Shekhinah.* See *Zohar* 1:23a
(*TZ*). As noted in *Zohar* 2:134a, "the letters
of the female are transposed."

The formula כוזו במוכסז כוזו (*Kuzu be-
mukhsaz kuzu*) is written on the back of the
parchment in the *mezuzah,* opposite the
words on the front: יהוה אלהינו יהוה (*YHVH
Eloheinu YHVH*). See Asher ben Yeḥiel, on
Alfasi, *Hilkhot Mezuzah* (end); *Tur, Yoreh
De'ah* 288; Ta-Shma, *Ha-Nigleh she-ba-Nistar*, 31, 121, n. 58.

262. *Let the earth sprout vegetation—
seed-bearing plants* The verse continues:
*fruit trees of every kind on earth bearing fruit
with the seed in it.*

263. **Now *Earth* generates...** *Shekhinah*
receives the flow of emanation from *Yesod*
(*one place*) and transmits it in the form of

worshiping their Lord.[264] This is the mystery of: *Who makes the grass grow for the* בהמה (*behemah*), *beast, and plants for the work of humanity, to bring forth food from the earth* (Psalms 104:14). *Who makes the grass grow for the behemah*—the behemoth crouching on a thousand mountains, which grow that *grass* for her every day.[265] *Grass* is the angels ruling momentarily, created on the second day,[266] existing as food for this *behemah,* for there is fire consuming fire.[267] *And plants for the work of humanity. Plants* are the אופנים (*ofanim*), whirling angels; חיות (*hayyot*), living creatures; and כרובים (*keruvim*), cherubs[268]—all arrayed, standing ready to be arrayed the moment that human beings come to worship their Lord in offering and prayer,[269] which is *the work of humanity.*[270] These *plants* are designated, destined for *the work of humanity,* to be fittingly arrayed and enhanced. Once they are enhanced by that *work of humanity,* nutriment and food emerge for the world, as is written: *to bring*

angels who accompany Her. See above, page 138.

142

264. **arrayed in an array...** The angels are arrayed and adorned through the human act of prayer, as performed by the kabbalists—the "scions of faith," Aramaic בני מהימנותא (*benei meheimanuta*).

265. **behemoth crouching on a thousand mountains...** See *Vayiqra Rabba* 22:10: "Rabbi Yoḥanan said, 'It is one beast [interpreting the apparent plural, בהמות (*behemot*), *beast,* in Psalms 50:10], crouching on a thousand mountains—and a thousand mountains grow all kinds of herbs for her and she eats.'"

See *Pirqei de-Rabbi Eli'ezer* 11; BT *Bava Batra* 74b; *Zohar* 1:223a; 3:189a, 217a, 240b; Moses de León, *Sefer ha-Rimmon,* 201. Here the *beast* symbolizes *Shekhinah.*

266. **created on the second day** The angels created on the second day of Creation are angels of Judgment, deriving from the side of *Gevurah.* Consisting solely of strict Judgment, they cannot survive. See above, page 133.

267. **fire consuming fire** See BT *Yoma* 21b, where *Shekhinah* is called "fire consuming fire" because of God's burning the angels who opposed human creation (as related in *Sanhedrin* 38b). Here the fire of *Shekhinah* consumes the angels created on the second day, who consist of "flashing

fire" (*Zohar* 3:217a) and derive from the fire of *Gevurah.*

See Psalms 104:4; BT *Ḥagigah* 14a; *Zohar* 1:50b, 69a; Moses de León, *Sefer ha-Mishqal,* 65.

268. אופנים (*ofanim*), **whirling angels...** Various families of angels. The term אופנים (*ofanim*), "wheels," derives from Ezekiel's vision of the throne-chariot (Ezekiel 1:15–21), where it refers to "wheels" rimmed with eyes, moving in perfect unison with the חיות (*hayyot*), "living creatures, animals" (1:5–26) and together transporting the throne, turning it into a chariot.

The כרובים (*keruvim*), "cherubs," modeled on human-animal-bird figures of the Fertile Crescent, are the only pictorial representation permitted in biblical religion. They guard the path to the Tree of Life (Genesis 3:24). Two golden *keruvim* with outstretched wings covered the ark in the Tabernacle in the wilderness (Exodus 25:18–22), and from between them issued the divine voice speaking to Moses (Numbers 7:8–9). Ezekiel identifies them with the *hayyot* (Ezekiel 10:20). In the *Zohar,* all three types of angels emanate from *Shekhinah* and are here symbolized by *plants.*

269. **to be arrayed...** Through human prayer, the angels are arrayed and adorned.

270. *the work...* עבודה (*Avodah*) means both "work" and "worship."

forth food from the earth.[271] This is *seed-bearing plants,* for grass is not *seed-bearing* but rather destined for food for the holy fire,[272] whereas *plants* maintain the world. All this: *to bring forth food from the earth.* All the tending that humans provide these *plants* in that *earth* by worshiping their Lord is intended entirely to generate food and nutriment from that *earth* for this world, ensuring that humanity will be blessed from above.[273]

Fruit trees bearing fruit (Genesis 1:11)—rung upon rung, male and female.[274] As the *fruit tree* generates the potency of *bearing fruit,* similarly She generates. Who are these? Cherubs and columns. What are columns? Those ascending in the smoke of sacrifice, arrayed therein, called *columns of smoke* (Song of Songs 3:6).[275] They all abide in full array through *the work of humanity,*[276] whereas *grass* does not, for it is destined to be consumed, as is written: *Behold behemoth, whom I fashioned along with you, eating grass like an ox* (Job 40:15).

Fruit trees bearing fruit—image of male and female.[277] *The image of their face was a human face* (Ezekiel 1:10).[278] These differ from those cherubs; these are large faces, in concealed color, while כרובים (*keruvim*), cherubs, are small faces, כרביין (*ke-ravyan*), like children.[279] All images are comprised in the *human*

143

271. *from the earth* From *Shekhinah.*

272. **the holy fire** *Shekhinah,* the "fire consuming fire." See *OY.*

273. **All the tending...** Human worship ensures the continued flow of divine sustenance and blessing.

274. **male and female** *Shekhinah* is the *fruit tree,* conveying the fructifying power of *Yesod,* known as *bearing fruit.* See *Zohar* 1:33a, 238a.

275. **Those ascending in the smoke...** Angels accompanying the offering in the Temple. See *Zohar* 3:307a.

276. **through *the work of humanity*** The act of human worship adorns the angelic *columns of smoke.*

277. **male and female** *Yesod* and *Shekhinah.*

278. ***The image of their face was a human face*** The opening of Ezekiel's description of the faces of the ḥayyot, which include also the faces of lion, ox, and eagle. Here the *human face* alludes to the divine couple. See Liebes, *Studies in Jewish Myth,* 76–77.

279. **differ from those cherubs... large faces... small faces...** See BT *Sukkah* 5b: "Rabbi Aḥa son of Ya'akov said, 'We have learned that the face of the cherubim was no less than a handbreadth....' What is a כרוב (*keruv*), cherub? Rabbi Abbahu said, 'כרבייא (*Ke-ravya*), Like a child, for in Babylon they call a child רביא (*ravya*).' Abbaye said to him, 'If so, how do you explain the verse: *The face of one was the face of a cherub, and the face of the second the face of a human* (Ezekiel 10:14), seeing that [the faces of] a cherub and a human are the same?'—'A large face and a small face [i.e., *The face of a human* is large, while *the face of a cherub* is small].'"

See *Zohar* 1:228b; 3:60b, 217b. Cf. 3:201a, where Rabbi Shim'on and his son Rabbi El'azar are called "the large face and the small face."

According to BT *Yoma* 54a, the cherubs in the Temple were depicted in sexual embrace: "Rabbi Katina said, 'When Israel ascended [to Jerusalem] for the Festival, the curtain would be rolled open for them and the cherubs revealed, their bodies intertwined. They [the people] would be addressed: "Look! You are beloved by God [as intensely] as man loves woman."'"

face,[280] for it is a large face, traced with tracings, engraved with engravings of the explicit name[281] in the four directions of the world: East, West, North, and South.

Michael is inscribed on the South.[282] All faces gaze at the *human face: face of a lion, face of an ox, face of an eagle* (ibid.) *A human* is male and female, and is otherwise not called *human*.[283] From it are traced figures of *the chariots of God, myriads upon myriads*, as is written: *The chariots of God, myriads upon myriads, thousands of* שנאן (*shin'an*) (Psalms 68:18). שנאן (*Shin'an*)—totality of all those figures: שור (*shor*), *ox;* נשר (*nesher*), *eagle;* אריה (*aryeh*), *lion;* ן (final *nun*)—the *human*, [19a] an extension merging as one through the mystery of male and female.[284] All those thousands and myriads[285] emerge from this mystery: שנאן (*shin'an*). From these images, each one spreads out fittingly. These are the ones interlaced, interwoven, included in one another: *ox, eagle, lion, human*,[286] conducted by the mystery of four engraved names, ascending to be guided and to gaze.

Ox ascends to the *human face*. A name ascends, crowned and engraved in the mystery of two colors: אל (*El*).[287] Then it turns back—is inscribed and engraved on the throne—designated to be conducted by the mystery of this name.[288]

Eagle ascends to the *human face*, to be guided and to gaze. Another name ascends, crowned and engraved in the mystery of two faces, radiant colors,

144

---

280. **All images are comprised...** Identical language appears in the *Zohar*'s section on physiognomy. See 2:73a (*RR*); cf. 74a.

281. **the explicit name** The Ineffable Name, *YHVH*. See *Devarim Rabbah* 3:8; *Midrash Tehillim* 114:9; *Zohar* 2:48a.

282. **Michael... the South** Michael, one of the *ḥayyot,* is associated with the South, the side of *Ḥesed.* See *Bereshit Rabbah* 1:3; *Zohar* 2:254a; 3:118b.

283. *A human* **is male and female...** The human face seen by Ezekiel was complete, combining male and female characteristics, reflecting the union of *Yesod* and *Shekhinah.* See BT *Yevamot* 63b: "Rabbi El'azar said, 'Any אדם (*adam*), man, without a woman is not an *adam,* as is said: *Male and female He created them... and He named them adam* (Genesis 5:2).'"

284. שנאן (*Shin'an*)... This word from Psalms 68:18, of uncertain origin and meaning, is interpreted here as an acronym alluding to the four faces of the *ḥayyot:* שור

(*shor*), *ox;* נשר (*nesher*), *eagle;* אריה (*aryeh*), *lion;* and finally אדם (*adam*), *human,* symbolized by the last letter, ן (final *nun*), whose extended length implies the fullness of male and female.

See *Bahir* 56 (83); *Zohar* 1:147a–b (*Tos*), 149b (*ST*); 2:118a (*RM*); 3:66b, 155a, 156b, 285b.

285. **All those thousands and myriads** Of angels.

286. **included in one another** The *ḥayyot* have four faces each. See Ezekiel 1:5–11.

287. *Ox* **ascends... A name ascends...** The *ox* symbolizes *Gevurah,* the left side (see Ezekiel 1:10), yet its name is אל (*El*), symbolizing *Ḥesed,* the right. As the *ox* ascends to gaze, the two opposite forces harmonize in a pattern of two colors: white (symbolizing the right side) and red (symbolizing the left).

288. **Then it turns back...** After gazing at the *human face,* the ox returns and is engraved on the throne, *Shekhinah.* Thereafter it is guided by the name אל (*El*), "God."

ascending in the ascent of the crown above: גדול (Gadol), Great.[289] Then it turns back—is inscribed and engraved on the throne—designated to be conducted by the mystery of this name.

Lion ascends to the *human face,* to be guided and to gaze. Another name ascends, crowned and engraved in the mystery of two faces, bold colors, aligned in power: גבור (Gibbor), Mighty.[290] Then it turns back, is inscribed and engraved on the throne, designated to be conducted by the mystery of this name.

Human gazes at them all, while all ascend and gaze at him. Then they are all traced in their engravings, in this tracing, in the mystery of one name called נורא (Nora), Awesome.[291] So it is written of them: *The image of their face was a human face.* They are all comprised in this image, an image comprising them.[292] Because of this mystery, the blessed Holy One is called *the great, mighty, and awesome God* (Deuteronomy 10:17),[293] for these names are engraved above in the mystery of the supernal chariot, comprised of four letters: יהוה (YHVH), the name comprising all.[294]

These images are engraved, carved in the throne, a throne engraved, embroidered in them:[295] one on the right, one on the left, one in front, one behind, inscribed in the four directions of the world. The throne, ascending, is inscribed with these four images.[296] These four supernal names[297] carry this

145

289. *Eagle* ascends... Another name ascends... The *eagle* symbolizes the middle (see *Zohar* 2:80b), and its name is גדול (Gadol), Great, symbolizing Ḥesed, the right. The colors are white (symbolizing the right side) and green (symbolizing the middle).

290. *Lion* ascends... Another name ascends... The *lion* symbolizes the right side (see Ezekiel 1:10); its name is גבור (Gibbor), Mighty, symbolizing Gevurah, the left. The two colors are white and red. For "aligned in power" (ולאתישרא בתוקפא [ul-ityashshara be-tuqpa]), the parallel in *Zohar* 3:274a (as well as Recanati) reads: ולאתקשרא בתוקפיה [ul-itqashshara be-tuqpeih], "to be bound in its power."

291. נורא (Nora), Awesome Associated with Tif'eret, who is symbolized by the humanlike figure seated on the throne of Shekhinah. See Ezekiel 1:26; *Zohar* 2:78b–79a, 261a.

292. *The image of their face...* The ḥayyot all combine into the *human face.*

293. *the great, mighty, and awesome God* Designating Tif'eret (the blessed Holy One, awesome), who harmonizes the qualities of right (*great*) and left (*mighty*).

294. *the supernal chariot...* The sefirot, specifically Ḥesed, Gevurah, Tif'eret, and Shekhinah, which constitute a throne for Binah. See Tishby, *Wisdom of the Zohar*, 2:588–89. The name יהוה (YHVH) represents both Tif'eret and the entirety of the sefirot: י (yod) symbolizing the primordial point of Ḥokhmah; the feminine marker ה (he) symbolizing Binah, the Divine Mother; ו (vav), whose numerical value is six, symbolizing the six sefirot from Ḥesed through Yesod; and the final ה (he) symbolizing Shekhinah.

295. **These images...** The images of the ḥayyot are engraved in the throne of Shekhinah.

296. **The throne, ascending...** To unite with Tif'eret.

297. **These four supernal names** אל, גדול, גבור, נורא (El, Gadol, Gibbor, Nora), God, Great, Mighty, Awesome.

throne—a throne comprised of them—as it grasps and gathers souls, delights, and yearnings.[298] Having grasped and gathered those delights and yearnings, it descends full, like a tree full of branches in every direction, filled with fruit.[299] Once it descends, these four images emerge, traced in their tracings, engraved, radiant, sparkling, flashing, scattering seed upon the world. Then they are called *seed-bearing plants,* for they scatter seed upon the world. The *human* image emerges, embracing all images.[300] Then this verse applies: *fruit trees of every kind, bearing fruit with the seed in it upon earth* (Genesis 1:11). It emits seed only purposefully, *upon earth.*[301] *With the seed in it.* Precisely! From here we learn that one is not permitted to emit seed in vain.[302]

The *vegetation* here[303] is not *seed-bearing,* so it is undone and does not endure like those others, having no image to be traced or engraved in any image or figure at all, rather seen and unseen. All those untraced in figure and image do not endure, existing momentarily, consumed by the fire-consuming fire, then returning as before, and so on every day.[304]

146

The human being below has an image and figure,[305] yet does not endure in the manner above. The figure and image above[306] are drawn as they are, with no other garment to be drawn, so they endure constantly. The human figure below is drawn in a garment,[307] in no other manner, so they endure for a set

298. **as it grasps and gathers souls...** As *Shekhinah* unites with Her partner (*Tif'e-ret* or *Yesod*), She gathers in the ecstatic flow of new souls.

299. **it descends...** *Shekhinah* descends, now filled with the fruit of new souls.

On souls as fruit, see *Bahir* 14 (22); Ezra of Gerona, *Peirush Shir ha-Shirim,* 489, 504; *Zohar* 1:15b, 33a, 59b–60a, 82b, 85b, 115a–b; 2:223b; Moses de León, *Sefer ha-Mishqal,* 51; idem, *Sheqel ha-Qodesh,* 56 (69). Cf. Ibn Ezra on Psalms 1:3.

300. **embracing all images** See *Zohar* 1:44a; 2:73a (*RR*), 74a; 3:241b; Liebes, *Pera-qim,* 50–51.

301. **It emits seed...** *Yesod* channels its flow to *Shekhinah,* known as *earth,* in order to engender new life.

302. **Precisely!...** The wording of Genesis (*in it*) implies that *Yesod* retains its flow, channeling it only *on earth,* i.e., to *Shekhi-nah.* Similarly, human seed should remain within the male except when fulfilling the *mitsvah* of procreation. According to the *Zo-har,* masturbation is a heinous sin.

See *Kallah Rabbati* 2; BT *Niddah* 13a; *Zohar* 1:56b–57a, 188a, 219b; Moses de León, *Shushan Edut,* 353; Tishby, *Wisdom of the Zohar,* 3:1365–66.

303. **The *vegetation* here** The angels created on the second day, who rule momentarily and are then consumed by *Shekhi-nah.* Above, page 142, they are referred to as *grass.*

304. **and so on every day** See BT *Ḥagi-gah* 14a: "Shemu'el said to Rabbi Ḥiyya son of Rav, 'O son of a lion! Come, I will tell you one of those fine words said by your father: Every single day ministering angels are created from the fiery stream, chant a song, then cease to be, as is said: *New every morning, immense is Your faithfulness!* (Lamentations 3:23).'"

See *Bereshit Rabbah* 78:1; above, pages 133, 142.

305. **an image and figure** A soul.

306. **The figure and image above** Of the angels who endure.

307. **in a garment** In a body.

time. Every single night, the spirit strips itself of that garment and ascends,[308] and the consuming fire consumes it. Later they are restored as before, figured in clothes. So they do not endure as those figures and images above, and of this is written: *New every morning* (Lamentations 3:23)—human beings who are *new* every single day.[309] [19b] What is the reason? *Immense is Your faithfulness!* (ibid.)—immense, not small.[310] *Immense is Your faithfulness!—immense,* indeed! For it can grasp all creatures of the world, absorbing them in itself, higher and lower. A place immense and vast, absorbing all, filled no further. This is the mystery: *All the rivers flow into the sea, yet the sea is not full; to the place the rivers flow, they flow back again* (Ecclesiastes 1:7).[311] They flow toward the sea, who grasps them, consumes them, and is filled no fuller. Then it pours them out as before, so they flow on.

Your faithfulness is immense, absorbing all, consuming them, filled no fuller, restoring them as before; they are *new* in the world every single day. Of this day is written: *it was good, it was good* (Genesis 1:10, 12), twice,[312] for this day united two sides, mediating the conflict.[313] It said to this side: *It was good,* and to the other side: *It was good,* reconciling them. So it includes *He said, he said,* twice.[314] Mystery of the four-letter name,[315] engraved and carved, ascending to twelve letters in four images on four sides,[316] inscribed on the holy throne.

147

308. **the spirit strips itself...** The spirit divests itself of the body and ascends to *Shekhinah.* See El'azar of Worms, *Ḥokhmat ha-Nefesh,* 4b.

309. *New every morning...* In BT *Ḥagigah* 14a, this verse is applied to the angels. See above, note 304; *Zohar* 2:213b–214a, 247a; *ZḤ* 18b (*MhN*). Here the reference is to the daily miracle of human rebirth.

310. *faithfulness...* One of the many names of *Shekhinah.* See *Zohar* 2:214a; 3:35b.

311. *All the rivers...* Each night souls stream into the sea of *Shekhinah,* each morning they reemerge. See *Zohar* 1:235a.

312. **Of this day is written...** The phrase *God saw that it was good* appears twice in the account of the third day of Creation.

313. **this day united two sides...** The third day symbolizes *Tif'eret,* third of the lower *sefirot,* who mediates the extremes of *Ḥesed* and *Gevurah.* See above, page 128.

314. **So it includes...** God gives two commands (*He said*) on the third day (Gen-

esis 1:9, 11), each of which is followed by the phrase *God saw that it was good.*

315. **the four-letter name** יהוה (*YHVH*), the divine name associated with *Tif'eret.*

316. **ascending to twelve...** Formed into twelve letters. A name of twelve letters is mentioned but not identified in BT *Qiddushin* 71a. It was later associated with the three occurrences of *YHVH* in the priestly blessing (Numbers 6:24–26). See *Bahir* 80 (111): "...numbering three, numbering twelve."

Cf. *Zohar* 1:16a; 2:58a; 3:78a–b, 172b; Trachtenberg, *Jewish Magic and Superstition,* 92, 290, n. 32. *Zohar* 2:201b refers to "the holy name of twelve letters that...rules the air. This is the name with which Elijah flew, ascending to heaven [see 2 Kings 2:11]."

KP interprets the twelve-letter name as the full spelling of אדני (*Adonai*): אלף, דלת, נון, יוד (*alef, dalet, nun, yod*). *Adonai* ("My Lord") is the traditional, circumlocutional pronunciation of יהוה (*YHVH*) and a name of *Shekhinah,* the throne. Scholem provides a conceivable

Let there be מארת *(me'orot), lights, in the expanse of heaven* (Genesis 1:14)—spelled deficiently: מארת *(me'erat), curse,* for diphtheria was created for children.[317] After the radiance of primordial light was treasured away,[318] a shell was created for the kernel.[319] That shell expanded, generating another shell.[320] Emerging, she ascended and descended, arriving at the small faces.[321] She desired to cling to them, be portrayed in them, and never depart.[322] The blessed Holy One separated her from there, bringing her down below when He created Adam, so that this would be perfected in this world.[323] As soon as she saw Eve cleaving to the side of Adam, beauty above, as soon as she saw the

diagram of יהוה *(YHVH)* written four times in a square using twelve letters.

317. **spelled deficiently: מארת (me'erat), curse...** In Genesis 1:14, the word מארת *(me'orot)* is written without *vavs*, the vowel letters. This deficient spelling is interpreted to mean that something was missing on the fourth day of Creation: the light of *Shekhinah*—symbolized by the moon—diminished; and this lack represents the potential for evil or "curse": מארה *(me'erah)*.

See JT *Ta'anit* 4:4, 68b: "On the fourth day [of the week, Wednesday] they would fast for infants, so that diphtheria not enter their mouths. *God said, 'Let there be מארת (me'orot), lights'*—spelled מארת *(me'erat), curse.*"

Cf. Proverbs 3:33; BT *Ta'anit* 27b, *Ḥullin* 60b; *Pesiqta de-Rav Kahana* 5:1; *Soferim* 17:4; Rashi and *Minḥat Shai* on Genesis 1:14; *Zohar* 1:1a, 12a, 33b; 2:167b, 205a.

Diphtheria here alludes to Lilith, the female demon who strikes children with this dread disease. See BT *Berakhot* 8a; *Zohar* 2:264b. In *Zohar* 2:267b Lilith and diphtheria appear as two distinct but kindred spirits.

318. **After the radiance of primordial light...** The primordial light of the first day of Creation was hidden away. See BT *Ḥagigah* 12a: "Rabbi El'azar said, 'With the light created by the blessed Holy One on the first day, one could gaze and see from one end of the universe to the other. When the blessed Holy One foresaw the corrupt deeds of the generation of the Flood and the generation of the Dispersion [the generation of the Tower of Babel], He immediately hid it from them, as is written: *The light of the wicked is withheld* (Job 38:15). For whom

did He hide it? For the righteous in the time to come.'"

See *Bereshit Rabbah* 3:6; 41:3; *Shemot Rabbah* 35:1; *Tanḥuma, Shemini* 9; *Bahir* 97–98 (147); *Zohar* 1:12a, 31b–32a, 45b–46a, 47a; 2:127a, 148b–149a, 220a–b; 3:88a, 173b.

319. **a shell was created...** Surrounding, concealing, and protecting the kernel of light. This shell is the demonic realm of *Sitra Aḥra*—or, according to *KP, Shekhinah*.

320. **another shell** Lilith, the female demon, wife of Samael. See *Zohar* 1:34b; 3:19a; *ZḤ* 16c *(MhN)*; Scholem, *Kabbalah*, 356–61.

321. **the small faces** The cherubim, guarding the heavenly gates. See above, page 142; *Zohar* 1:228b; 3:60b, 217b; and BT *Sukkah* 5b: "Rabbi Aḥa son of Ya'akov said, 'We have learned that the face of the cherubim was not less than a handbreadth'.... What is a כרוב *(keruv)*, cherub? Rabbi Abbahu said, 'כרביא *(Ke-ravya)*, Like a child, for in Babylon they call a child רביא *(ravya)*.' Abbaye said to him, 'If so, how do you explain the verse: *The face of one was the face of a cherub, and the face of the second the face of a human* (Ezekiel 10:14), seeing that [the faces of] a cherub and a human are the same?'—'A large face and a small face [i.e., *The face of a human* is large, while *the face of a cherub* is small].'"

322. **She desired...** The demonic seeks to assume higher form. See above, pages 144–45, where the four faces of the *ḥayyot* are engraved on the divine throne.

323. **so that this would be perfected in this world** Through overcoming evil, Lilith herself is perfected (see *OY, Sullam, YN*). Alternatively, Adam is perfected (Scholem,

148

complete image, she flew away,[324] desiring as before to cleave to the small faces. Those guardians of the gates on high did not allow her. The blessed Holy One rebuked her and cast her to the bottom of the sea, where she dwelled until Adam and his wife sinned. Then the blessed Holy One plucked her from there, and she rules over all those children—small faces of humanity—who deserve to be punished for the sins of their fathers.[325] She flies off, roaming through the world. Approaching the earthly Garden of Eden, she sees cherubs guarding the gates of the Garden, and she dwells there by that *flaming sword* (Genesis 3:24),[326] for she emerged from the side of that *flame*.[327] As the flame revolves she flees and roams the world, finding children who deserve to be punished; she toys with them and kills them.[328] This happens in the waning of the moon, whose light diminishes;[329] this is מארת (*me'orot*), *lights,* deficient.[330]

Until Cain was born, she could not cling to him.[331] Later she drew close to him and gave birth to spirits and flying demons.[332] For 130 years Adam

---

MmD), or the world is perfected by Adam (*KP*; Tishby, *Wisdom of the Zohar,* 2:540). See Moses de León, *Sefer ha-Mishqal,* 157.

324. **As soon as she saw Eve...** According to *Alfa Beita de-Ven Sira,* 232–34, Lilith was Adam's first wife, created from the earth. Insisting on her equality, she refused to lie beneath Adam; uttering the name *YHVH,* she flew away. Here Lilith flees once she sees Eve. Adam's beauty reflects that of the *sefirot,* Primordial Adam. Together, he and Eve constitute an image of the divine couple, *Tif'eret* and *Shekhinah.*

325. **children...who deserve...** See *Qohelet Rabbah* on 4:1: "*I further observed all the oppression that goes on under the sun....* Rabbi Yehudah says, 'These are the children who are hidden away [taken away early] in life through the sins of their fathers in this world....'" Adam and Eve's sin empowers Lilith to kill.

326. **cherubs...** These cherubs are lower than the ones mentioned above. According to Genesis 3:24, cherubs along with *the flaming, ever-turning sword* guard the Garden of Eden and its path to the Tree of Life. See *Zohar* 3:167a.

327. **she emerged from the side of that flame** Lilith emerged from the left side, Judgment, symbolized by fire. See *Bereshit Rabbah* 21:9: "*Ever-turning*—changing: some-times male, sometimes female; sometimes spirits, sometimes angels."

328. **As the flame revolves...** As the *flaming sword* revolves, Judgment and Love manifest alternately. When Judgment prevails, Lilith strikes. Or, according to *MM,* when Judgment prevails, Lilith abides by the flame; when Love prevails, she flees. See *Zohar* 1:221b.

329. **in the waning of the moon...** When *Shekhinah,* symbolized by the moon, is weakened, the power of the demonic grows dominant. See *Zohar* 1:70b, 146a.

330. מארת (*me'orot*), *lights,* deficient See above, page 148.

331. **Until Cain was born...** Until then, Lilith could not cling to Adam, who was united with Eve. Once Cain killed Abel, Adam saw no reason to have any more children, so he separated from Eve, whereupon maleficent spirits copulated with him.

See *Tanḥuma* (Buber), *Bereshit* 26; *Bereshit Rabbah* 20:11; BT *Eruvin* 18b; *Zohar* 1:34b, 54b–55a; 2:231b; 3:76b.

According to various sources, Cain himself was engendered by the union of Eve and the serpent. See *Targum Yerushalmi,* Genesis 4:1 (variants); *Pirqei de-Rabbi Eli'ezer* 21; *Zohar* 1:36b–37a, 54a; Stroumsa, *Another Seed,* 38–53.

332. **Later she drew close to him...** to Adam.

copulated with female spirits[333] until the arrival of Na'amah,[334] whose beauty seduced *the sons of Elohim,* Uzza and Azael.[335] By them she gave birth; from her, maleficent spirits and demons spread through the world. In the night she roams; they[336] roam the world and titillate humans, causing them to spill seed accidentally. Wherever they find people sleeping alone in a house, they hover above them, grab hold of them, cling to them, seize desire from them, and bear offspring.[337] Further, they attack him with disease unawares. All this in the waning of the moon.[338]

מארת (*me'orot*), *lights.* When the moon was restored, letters were rearranged: אמרת (*imrat*), *The word of YHVH is refined; He is a shield to all who seek refuge in*

---

333. For 130 years... Referring to Genesis 5:3: *Adam lived 130 years and engendered a son in his likeness, after his own image.* See *Bereshit Rabbah* 20:11: "Rabbi Simon said, 'Throughout all 130 years that Adam separated himself from Eve, male spirits heated themselves from her and she gave birth, while female spirits heated themselves from Adam and gave birth.'"

See BT *Eruvin* 18b: "Rabbi Yirmeyah son of El'azar said, 'During all those [130] years that Adam was under the ban [for having eaten from the Tree of Knowledge], he engendered spirits, demons, and לילין (*lilin*), female demons, as is said: *Adam lived 130 years and engendered a son in his likeness, after his own image* (Genesis 5:3), from which it follows that until that time he did not engender after his own image'.... That statement refers to semen that he emitted accidentally."

See *Tanḥuma* (Buber), *Bereshit* 26; *Zohar* 1:34b, 54a–55a; 2:231b; 3:76b; Trachtenberg, *Jewish Magic and Superstition,* 51–54.

334. Na'amah Na'amah, whose name means "lovely," was the sister of Tuval-Cain and the great-great-great-great-granddaughter of Cain (Genesis 4:22). According to rabbinic tradition, the fallen angels were attracted by her beauty. See ibid. 6:1–4; *Tanḥuma* (Buber), *Ḥuqqat,* add. 1; *Midrash Aggadah* and *Midrash ha-Gadol,* Genesis 4:22.

According to the *Zohar,* she is the mother of Ashmedai, king of the demons, and she generates demons by seducing men in their

sleep. See Naḥmanides, ad loc.; *Zohar* 1:9b, 55a; 3:76b–77a; *ZH* 19d (*MhN*).

335. Uzza and Azael These two angels opposed the creation of Adam and Eve, fell from heaven, and were attracted by *the daughters of men* (Genesis 6:2), here specifically Na'amah. They were punished by being bound in chains of iron in the mountains of darkness, from where they still manage to wreak havoc, teaching sorcery to humans.

See 1 Enoch 6–8; BT *Yoma* 67b; *Aggadat Bereshit,* intro, 39; *Midrash Avkir,* 7 (cited in *Yalqut Shim'oni,* Genesis, 44); *Pirqei de-Rabbi Eli'ezer* 22; *Zohar* 1:9b, 23a, 37a, 37a (*Tos*), 58a, 126a; 3:208a–b, 212a–b; *ZH* 81a–b (*MhN, Rut*).

336. they Na'amah and her demonic offspring.

337. sleeping alone in a house... seize desire from them... The spirits and demons are succubi, who were created without bodies and are eager to be impregnated by the seminal emission of males sleeping alone.

See *Tanḥuma* (Buber), *Bereshit* 17; *Zohar* 1:55a; 2:264a; Trachtenberg, *Jewish Magic and Superstition,* 51–54; Scholem, *On the Kabbalah,* 154–57; Tishby, *Wisdom of the Zohar,* 3:1366–67. See BT *Shabbat* 151b: "Rabbi Ḥanina said, 'One may not sleep alone in a house [or: in an isolated house], and whoever sleeps alone in a house is seized by Lilith.'" Cf. *Zohar* 3:45a; *Orḥot Ḥayyim,* par. 60.

338. the waning of the moon As the light of *Shekhinah* diminishes.

Him (Psalms 18:31).[339] *He is a shield* against all those maleficent spirits and quaestors[340] who roam the world in her waning, for all those holding fast to faith in the blessed Holy One.

When King Solomon descended to the depth of the nut,[341] as is written: *I descended to the nut garden* (Song of Songs 6:11), he took the shell of a nut, contemplated all those shells, and realized that all the joy and delight of those spirits—shells of the nut—consists solely in clinging to human beings and leading them astray, as is written: *The delights of the sons of men: demon after demon* (Ecclesiastes 2:8).[342] Further, *the delights of the sons of men*, in which they indulge asleep at night, generate *demon after demon*.[343]

The blessed Holy One had to create everything in the world, arraying the world. All consists of a kernel within, with several shells covering the kernel.[344] The entire world is like this, above and below, from the head of the mystery of the primordial point[345] to the end of all rungs: all [20a] is this within that, that within this, so that one is the shell of another, which itself is the shell of another.[346]

151

339. **letters were rearranged...** When the light returned, *Shekhinah* regained Her fullness, manifesting as the divine *word*.

340. **quaestors** קסטירין (*Qastirin*). The rabbinic term קוסטור (*qustor*) derives from Latin *quaestor*, a Roman official or prosecutor. See JT *Eruvin* 6:2, 23b; *Zohar* 1:53b; 2:58b, 208b; 3:13a. *Bei'ur ha-Millim ha-Zarot*, 188 relates the Zoharic term to the rabbinic קוסטינר (*qustinar*), which derives from the Latin *quaestionarius*, "torturer, executioner." Cf. קלסטור (*qalastor*), from the Greek *kolaster*, "torturer, executioner."

341. **descended to the depth of the nut** Solomon explored the nature of reality by examining the structure of the nut, which is composed of a kernel symbolizing divinity surrounded by layers of shells (קליפין [*qelippin*]), symbolizing demonic forces. In the writings of El'azar of Worms, the nut symbolizes the *merkavah* (the divine chariot-throne).

See Scholem, *Major Trends*, 239; Altmann, *Studies*, 172–79; Pope, *Song of Songs*, 574–79. Cf. Moses de León, *Sefer ha-Mishqal*, 156–60; *Zohar* 1:44b; 2:15b (*MhN*), 140b, and 233b: "Just as a nut has a shell surrounding and covering the kernel, the kernel resting within, so, too, with everything holy: holiness with-

in, the other side without." The nut also appears as a cosmic symbol in the Orphic mysteries. See Eisler, *Weltenmantel und Himmelszelt*, 2:521–25.

342. ***The delights of the sons of men...*** Interpreting the verse to mean: The delights of demons are the sons of men.

343. **Further...** Interpreting the verse hyperliterally: *The delights of the sons of men* (i.e., their seminal emissions) impregnate the succubi, thereby generating *demon after demon*.

344. **had to create everything...** Both the shells and the kernel play a role in existence. The ultimate kernel is *Ein Sof*, surrounded, as it were, by the shells of the *sefirot*, which clothe and filter the intense light emanating out. See *Zohar* 2:131a.

345. **the head of the mystery...** Ḥokhmah, the first ray of emanation.

346. **all is this within that...** Each layer of existence is simultaneously the kernel of the shell surrounding it and the shell of the kernel within it. See Maimonides, *Mishneh Torah, Hilkhot Yesodei ha-Torah* 3:2, who describes the many spheres within the eight celestial spheres as arranged "like the skins of an onion."

The primordial point is inner radiance—there is no way to gauge its translucency, tenuity, or purity until an expanse expanded from it.[347] The expansion of that point became a palace, in which the point was clothed—a radiance unknowable, so intense its lucency.[348] This palace, a garment for that concealed point, is a radiance beyond measure, yet not as gossamer or translucent as the primordial point, hidden and treasured. That palace expanded an expanse: primordial light.[349] That expansion of primordial light is a garment for the palace, which is a gossamer, translucent radiance, deeper within. From here on, this expands into this, this is clothed in this, so that this is a garment for this, and this for this. This, the kernel; this, the shell. Although a garment, it becomes the kernel of another layer.

Everything is fashioned the same way below, so that a human in this world manifests this image: kernel and shell, spirit and body.[350] All for the arrayal of the world, and so the world is.

When the moon shared a single cleaving with the sun, she was radiant.[351] As soon as she was separated from the sun and appointed over her forces, she diminished herself, diminished her light. Shells upon shells were created for concealing the kernel, all for arraying the kernel.[352] So, *Let there be* מארת (*me'orot*), *lights*, is spelled deficiently.[353] All this for arraying the world, as is written: *to shine upon earth* (Genesis 1:15).[354]

347. **until an expanse...** Until the circle of *Binah* expanded from the point of *Hokhmah*. See above, pages 109–12.

348. **radiance unknowable...** Apparently the radiance of the point of *Hokhmah*, though some commentators specify the palace of *Binah*, also unknowable.

349. **primordial light** *Hesed*, symbolized by the light of the first day of Creation.

350. **kernel and shell, spirit and body** The human being, fashioned *in the image of God* (Genesis 1:27), manifests the structure of kernel and shell. See Moses de León, *Sefer ha-Mishqal*, 159.

351. **When the moon shared...** When *Shekhinah* and *Tif'eret* were united, She was radiant. Originally the moon and the sun were equally radiant. See BT *Hullin* 60b: "Rabbi Shim'on son of Pazzi pointed out a contradiction. 'It is written: *God made the two great lights* (Genesis 1:16), and it is written [in the same verse]: *the greater light...*

and the lesser light. The moon said before the blessed Holy One, "Master of the Universe! Can two kings possibly wear one crown?" He answered, "Go, diminish yourself!"....'"

352. **Shells upon shells...** The shells conceal the kernel of light, yet also filter it. Even the outermost shells, the demonic forces, serve this function by testing and punishing humanity.

353. מארת **(*me'orot*), *lights*, is spelled deficiently** As noted above (page 148), in Genesis 1:14, the word מארת (*me'orot*) is written without *vavs*, the vowel letters. This deficient spelling alludes to the diminished light of *Shekhinah*, the moon, now surrounded by shells, which culminate in evil or "curse": מארה (*me'erah*).

354. *to shine upon earth* The arrayal of the kernel within a series of shells actually benefits the world; now the light is filtered, shining with a bearable intensity.

152

God made the two great lights (Genesis 1:16). *Made*—enhancement and arrayal of all, fittingly. *The two great lights*—at first in a single bond, mystery of the name complete as one: יהוה אלהים (*YHVH Elohim*),[355] though not revealed, rather in a manner concealed.[356] *Great*—for they were enhanced in name, both alike, to be called by the mystery of all: מצפץ מצפץ (*MTsPTs, MTsPTs*), supernal names of the thirteen qualities of compassion.[357] *Great*—these were enhanced, ascending, for they are supernal, from the mystery on high, ascending for the benefit of the world, so that through them worlds endure.[358]

Similarly, *the two lights,* both ascending as one, in one enhancement. The moon was uneasy with the sun, ashamed in its presence.[359] The moon said, "*Where do you pasture your sheep? Where do you let them rest at noon?* (Song of

355. **The two great lights...** Originally, *Tif'eret* and *Shekhinah,* symbolized by the sun and moon, were united. Their union is indicated by the full name: יהוה אלהים (*YHVH Elohim*). In rabbinic literature these two names represent, respectively, the divine qualities of compassion and justice. See *Sifrei,* Deuteronomy 26; *Bereshit Rabbah* 12:15; 33:3; and 13:3, where *YHVH Elohim* is called "a complete name."

In Kabbalah the two names often designate *Tif'eret* and *Shekhinah,* who were originally one and whose reunion represents the goal of religious life. See *Zohar* 1:4a, 20a, 48b; 2:161a, 229a; 3:138b (*IR*); *ZH* 70d (*ShS*).

356. **in a manner concealed** Concealed within divine thought prior to emanation (*KP*), or concealed by not appearing in this verse in its full form but only as אלהים (*Elohim*), *God.* An encoded form of the other half of the name follows.

357. מצפץ מצפץ (*MTsPTs, MTsPTs*)... An encoded form of the name יהוה יהוה (*YHVH YHVH*), according to the system of letter substitution known as א״ת ב״ש (*at bash*), in which the last letter of the alphabet is substituted for the first, the penultimate for the second, etc. See *Zohar* 2:132a–b. The double name יהוה יהוה (*YHVH YHVH*) appears at the beginning of the thirteen qualities of compassion, derived from Exodus 34:6–7. See BT *Rosh ha-Shanah* 17b; *Zohar* 1:1a. According to Kabbalah these qualities originate in *Keter,* the highest *sefirah,* the

realm of total compassion untainted by judgment.

358. **these were enhanced...** *Tif'eret* and *Shekhinah* return to their source in *Keter,* the mystery on high, and draw down a flow of emanation to the worlds.

359. **The moon was uneasy...** See BT *Ḥullin* 60b: "Rabbi Shim'on son of Pazzi pointed out a contradiction. 'It is written: *God made the two great lights* (Genesis 1:16), and it is written [in the same verse]: *the greater light... and the lesser light.* The moon said before the blessed Holy One, "Master of the Universe! Can two kings possibly wear one crown?" He answered, "Go, diminish yourself!" She said before Him, "Master of the Universe! Because I have suggested something proper I should make myself smaller?" He replied, "Go and rule by day and night." She said, "But what is the value of this? What good is a lamp at noon?"... Seeing that her mind was uneasy [that she could not be consoled], the blessed Holy One said, "Bring an atonement for Me for making the moon smaller."' As was said by Rabbi Shim'on son of Lakish: 'Why is the goat offered on the new moon distinguished by the phrase *to* [or: *for*] *YHVH* (Numbers 28:15)? The blessed Holy One said, "Let this goat be an atonement for My having made the moon smaller."'"

See BT *Rosh ha-Shanah* 23b; *Zohar* 1:146a; *ZH* 70d–71a (*ShS*); Moses de León, *Sefer ha-Rimmon,* 189; idem, *Mishkan ha-Edut,* 35b.

153

Songs 1:7).[360] How can a little lamp shine at noon?[361] *Lest I be like one enwrapped* (ibid.)—how can I abide in shame?" So she diminished herself, becoming head of those below,[362] as is written: *Go forth in the footsteps of the flock, and graze your goats* (ibid., 8). The blessed Holy One said to her, "Go, diminish yourself!" From that point on, she has light only from the sun.[363] Whereas at first they dwelled as one, evenly, later she diminished herself on all her rungs, though heading them, for a woman is enhanced only together with her husband.

The greater light (Genesis, ibid.)—יהוה (*YHVH*); *and the smaller light*—אלהים (*Elohim*), end of all rungs, end of thought.[364] At first she was inscribed above among the letters of the holy name, its fourth letter.[365] Afterward she diminished herself, to be called by the name *Elohim*. Nevertheless she ascended in all directions above in the letter ה (*he*), through the joining of letters of the holy name.[366] Then rungs expanded on this side and that. Rungs expanding from the higher side are called *ruling the day;* rungs expanding from the lower side are called *ruling the night* (ibid.).[367] *And the stars* (ibid.)—other forces and camps, innumerable,[368] all suspended in that *expanse of heaven*, Vitality of the Worlds,[369] as is written: *God placed them in the expanse of heaven* (ibid., 17).

154

360. *Where do you pasture... Where do you let them rest...* OY suggests the rendering: *Where will she pasture... Where will she let them rest...*, referring to the moon herself (the pronominal prefix ת [*tav*] denotes either *you* or *she*). See *MM;* and *ZḤ* 71a (*ShS*), where the verse is addressed by the moon to the blessed Holy One.

361. **How can a little lamp shine at noon?** The moon is ashamed to reveal its own meager light in the face of the sun's light. See the moon's complaint cited above, note 359: "What good is a lamp at noon?" Cf. *ZḤ* 71a (*ShS*).

362. **head of those below** Of the angelic forces beneath her and of the lower worlds.

363. **she has light only from the sun** Reflecting its light. Similarly, *Shekhinah* reflects the light of *Tif'eret*, lacking light of Her own. The expression derives from a medieval astronomic description of the moon.

See Radak on Genesis 1:16; Moses de León, *Shushan Edut*, 338; idem, *Sod Eser Sefirot*

Belimah, 381; *Zohar* 1:31a, 132b, 181a, 238a; 2:43a, 142a, 218b.

364. *The greater light... and the smaller light...* Tif'eret, whose name is *YHVH*, and *Shekhinah*, known as *Elohim*. As the final *sefirah*, She is the culmination of divine thought.

365. **inscribed above among the letters...** *Shekhinah* is symbolized by the final letter in the name יהוה (*YHVH*).

366. **Nevertheless she ascended...** *Shekhinah*, symbolized by the letter ה (*he*), regained union with the higher *sefirot*, symbolized by the first three letters of the name יהוה (*YHVH*).

367. **Rungs expanding...** Both *Tif'eret*, who rules the day, and *Shekhinah*, ruling the night, generate angelic forces.

368. **other forces and camps...** Of angels.

369. **that *expanse of heaven*...** *Yesod*, who encompasses the angels. He is also known as "Vitality of the Worlds," since He channels the flow of emanation, animating all of existence. See above, note 214.

On this day the kingdom of David was established, fourth leg and support of the throne.[370] The letters were arrayed and aligned.[371] Yet even so, until the sixth day, when the image of Adam was fully arrayed, it did not stabilize.[372] Then the upper throne and the lower throne were established,[373] all the worlds settled in place, and all the letters were arrayed [20b] in their wheels[374] by the expanding scribal matrix of the nexus.[375]

The fourth day is a day rejected by builders, as is said: *the stone that the builders rejected* (Psalms 118:22), and similarly: *My mother's sons were incensed at me* (Song of Songs 1:6).[376] For this light diminished herself and her radiance, and shells were arrayed at their sites.[377] All those radiant lights are suspended

370. **On this day the kingdom of David...** *Shekhinah*, who is known as *Malkhut* ("Kingdom"), is symbolized by the ideal kingdom of David and by the fourth day of Creation, on which the sun and moon were fashioned. She together with the sefirotic triad of *Ḥesed, Gevurah,* and *Tif'eret* (symbolized by Abraham, Isaac, and Jacob) constitute the four legs of the divine throne upon which sits *Binah*. See *Zohar* 1:5b, 82a, 89b (*ST*), 154b.

See *Bereshit Rabbah* 47:6: "Resh Lakish said, 'The patriarchs themselves constitute the [divine] Chariot.'" Cf. Azriel of Gerona, *Peirush ha-Aggadot,* 57; *Zohar* 1:60b, 99a, 150a, 173b, 248b; 2:144a; 3:38a, 99a.

On the relation between David and the patriarchs, see Acts 2:29; *Mekhilta, Pisḥa* 1; BT *Berakhot* 16b; *Pesaḥim* 117b; *Sanhedrin* 107a; *Midrash Tehillim* 18:8, 25; Moses de León, *Sheqel ha-Qodesh,* 45 (54); Jacob ben Sheshet, *Ha-Emunah ve-ha-Bittaḥon,* 396; Baḥya ben Asher on Genesis 32:10; Ginzberg, *Legends,* 6:265, n. 94. Cf. *Zohar* 1:82a and note 164 there.

371. **The letters were arrayed...** The letters of the name יהוה (*YHVH*) were arranged, no longer encoded, with the final ה (*he*) symbolizing *Shekhinah*.

372. **until the sixth day...** The creation of the human being on the sixth day symbolizes the full emanation of the *sefirot,* envisioned as the limbs of Primordial Adam. Only at this point did *Shekhinah* stabilize.

373. **the upper throne and the lower throne...** Here the upper throne symbol-

izes *Tif'eret* and the *sefirot* around Him, enthroning *Binah,* while the lower throne symbolizes *Shekhinah,* enthroning *Tif'eret*.

374. **arrayed in their wheels** The letters of the alphabet, by which the world was created, were arrayed in correct order. See *Sefer Yetsirah* 2:4: "Twenty-two elemental letters. God set them in a wheel with 231 gates, turning forward and backward." Cf. Liebes, *Peraqim,* 293.

375. **scribal matrix of the nexus** טופסירא דקוטרא (*Tufsira de-qutra*). In the *Zohar, tufsira* (or *tufsera*) means either "mold, form, configuration" (based on טופסא [*tufsa*], derived from the Greek *tupos*), or "royal dignitary" (based on טפסרא [*tafsera*], derived from biblical טפסר [*tifsar*], "marshal, scribe").

See Jeremiah 51:27; Nahum 3:17; *Zohar* 1:30b, 96b, 157a, 241b, 242b, 243b; 2:235b (*Tos*); 3:120a, 270b; *Bei'ur ha-Millim ha-Zarot,* 178–80, 185; *KP*; Scholem. Here the letters are linked in a creative pattern.

376. **a day rejected...** When *Shekhinah,* symbolized by the fourth day of Creation, diminished Her light, She excluded Herself from the brilliance of *the builders,* the triad of *sefirot* (*Ḥesed, Gevurah,* and *Tif'eret*) symbolized by the first three days of Creation who together construct the pattern of the *sefirot*. See *Bahir* 131 (190); *Zohar* 1:89b (*ST*). *Shekhinah* refers to them as *My mother's sons,* the offspring of *Binah,* the Divine Mother.

377. **shells were arrayed...** Concealing the light. See above, pages 151–52.

155

in this *expanse of heaven,* so that in them the throne of David will be arrayed.[378] These lights depict a figure below, arraying a figure of all those included in the category *human,* an intrinsic figure.[379] Every intrinsic figure is so called, so every figure comprised in this expansion is called *human,* as is written: *You are human* (Ezekiel 34:31). *You are human;* the other nations are not.[380] Every spirit is called *human;* the body of the spirit of the holy side[381] is a garment of the *human,* and so it is written: *You clothed me in skin and flesh, wove me of bones and sinews* (Job 10:11).[382] Flesh is the garment of the *human,* as is written everywhere: *flesh of a human* (Exodus 30:32)—*human,* within; *flesh,* garment of the *human,* its body.

Specters[383] below, melted in the smelting of this spirit,[384] were figured into figures clothed in another garment, such as figures of pure animals: *ox, sheep, goat, deer, gazelle, roebuck, wild goat, ibex, antelope,* and *mountain sheep* (Deuteronomy 14:4–5), who desire to be interwoven in the garment of the *human,* flesh of the *human.*[385] The inner spirit of those figures attains the name applied

156

378. All those radiant lights... The lights of the *sefirot* (from Ḥesed through Hod) converge in *Yesod* in order to adorn *Shekhinah,* the throne of David.

379. all those included in the category human... Those creatures (ox, lion, eagle) comprised in the *human* face of the *ḥayyot.* See above, page 145: "*The image of their face was a human face* (Ezekiel 1:10). They are all comprised in this image, an image comprising them."

380. *You are human*... See BT *Yevamot* 60b–61a: "Rabbi Shim'on son of Yoḥai said, 'The graves of Gentiles do not impart impurity by a tent [i.e., one who stands on or bends over such a grave, thereby constituting a tent with his body, is not rendered impure], as is said: *You, My sheep, sheep of My pasture, are human* [*and I am Your God*] (Ezekiel 34:31). You are called *human;* Gentiles are not called *human.*'"

Rabbi Shim'on assumes a connection between *human* and "impurity by a tent," based on the wording of Numbers 19:14: *When a human dies in a tent, whoever enters the tent and whoever is in the tent shall be impure seven days.*

See *Zohar* 1:131a, 220a; 2:25b, 86a.

381. the spirit of the holy side Emanating from the world of the *sefirot.*

382. body...is a garment... The body clothes the soul. See *Zohar* 2:75b–76a; *ZH* 78c (*MhN, Rut*). The identical teaching appears in Moses de León's *Sefer ha-Mishqal,* 44: "They have said in *Secrets of the Torah....*" Cf. ibid., 159.

383. Specters טסירין (*Tesirin*), a neologism appearing several times in the *Zohar* (1:17b, 178a ["*tesirin* without a body"]; 2:29a). See *Tanḥuma* (Buber), *Bereshit* 17: "It is not written here: [*He ceased from all His work*] *that* [*God*] *created and made,* but rather [*that God created*] *to make* (Genesis 2:3), for the Sabbath came first and their work was not completed. Rabbi Benaya said, 'This refers to the demons, for He created their souls, and as He was creating their bodies, the Sabbath day was hallowed. He left them, and they remained soul without body.'"

Cf. *Bereshit Rabbah* 7:5; 11:9; *Zohar* 1:14a, 47b–48a, 178a; 2:155b; 3:142b (*IR*); and M *Avot* 5:6: "Ten things were created on Friday eve at twilight.... Some say, 'Also the demons.'"

384. melted in the smelting of this spirit As the spirit (called *human*) is refined, lower spirits ("specters") are produced, which are then clothed in the form of ten pure animals, permitted to be eaten.

385. who desire to be interwoven... To be included in the category of *human.*

to its body, the garment of that name. Flesh of an ox: ox is the interior of that body; its flesh, a garment; and so with them all.

Similarly on the other side, side of impurity: the spirit spreading through the other nations emerges from the side of impurity.[386] It is not *human,* and so does not attain this name. The name of that spirit is Impure, not attaining the name *human,* having no share in it. Its body is a garment of that Impure, flesh of Impure—impure within; flesh, its garment. So as long as that spirit abides in that body, it is called Impure.[387] Once the spirit emerges from that garment, it is not called Impure; that garment does not attain the name.[388]

Specters[389] below, melted in the smelting of this spirit,[390] are figured into figures clothed in another garment, such as figures of animals of impurity, of which the Torah opens: *These shall be impure for you* (Leviticus 11:29), such as the pig and the birds and animals of that side.[391] The spirit attains that name; the body is its garment and is called "flesh of pig"—pig within; flesh, its garment.

So the two sides diverge. These are comprised in the mystery of *human;* those, in the mystery of Impure. Each kind follows its own, returning to its own kind.[392]

The radiant lights above shine in that *expanse of heaven,*[393] so that figures are drawn below fittingly, as is written: *God placed them in the expanse of heaven to shine upon earth and to rule the day and the night* (Genesis 1:17–18). The reign of two lights is a fitting reign: *greater light* ruling by day; *smaller light,* by night.[394] From here derives this secret: The rule of the male by day

157

386. **the other side...** The demonic realm, source of other nations' souls. The claim that the souls of the nations derive from the demonic is supposedly based on the rabbinic source cited above (note 380), but is amplified far beyond its original context. For parallel medieval Christian views of the demonic nature of the Jews, see Trachtenberg, *The Devil and the Jews.* Cf. *Zohar* 1:47a, 131a; *ZḤ* 10c (*MhN*).

387. **it is called Impure** The body shares the impurity of the spirit.

388. **Once the spirit emerges...** Once that person dies, the garment ("it"), that is, the body, is no longer called Impure, which explains why "the graves of Gentiles do not impart impurity" (BT *Yevamot* 61a, cited above, note 380).

See *Zohar* 1:131a, 220a; *ZḤ* 78d (*MhN, Rut*); Moses de León, *Mishkan ha-Edut,* 48a.

389. **Specters** טסירין (*Tesirin*). See above, note 383.

390. **this spirit** The spirit of impurity.

391. **that side** The side of impurity.

392. **Each kind follows its own...** See BT *Bava Qamma* 92b: "It was taught in the Mishnah: 'Anything attached to something subject to impurity is itself subject to impurity. Anything attached to something that remains pure will itself remain pure.' It was taught in a *baraita* [a tannaitic tradition]: Rabbi Eli'ezer said, 'Not for nothing did the starling follow the raven, but because it is of its kind.'"

See *Bereshit Rabbah* 65:3; *Zohar* 1:137b, 167b.

393. **The radiant lights above shine...** The *sefirot* emanate through *Yesod.*

394. *greater light...smaller light...* *Tif'eret,* symbolized by the sun, and *Shekhinah,* by the moon.

consists in filling His house with all that is needed, bringing in food and nutriment.[395] As night enters and the female grasps all, the house is ruled solely by Her—for then the reign belongs to Her, not to the male—as is written: *She rises while it is still night, and gives food to her household and a portion to her maidens* (Proverbs 31:15)—*She*, not *He. Ruling the day* (Genesis 1:16) belongs to the male; *ruling the night* (ibid.), to the female.

And the stars (Genesis 1:16). Once the female commands Her household and retires with Her husband,[396] the house is ruled solely by the maidens who remain in the house to array it consummately.[397] Afterward the house returns to the rule of the male by day, all fittingly.

God made the two great lights (Genesis 1:16)—this one, a *light;* that one, a *light.*[398] So those lights ascending are called "luminaries of light,"[399] while those descending are called "luminaries of fire"—rungs below, controlling all the weekdays.[400] Therefore when Sabbath departs, a blessing is recited over a lamp, for they have been granted authority to rule.[401]

158

The fingers of a human being are the secret of rungs and mysteries on high,[402] including front and back.[403] The backs are outside, alluding to the fingernails, so one is [21a] permitted to gaze at the fingernails as Sabbath

395. **The rule of the male...** The *sefirot* function as a traditional household: the male, *Tif'eret,* gathers the flow of emanation from left and right, while the female, *Shekhinah,* channels this flow, thereby nourishing the world.

396. **commands Her household...** Once *Shekhinah* arranges the powers under Her and retires with *Tif'eret.*

397. **the maidens who remain...** Angels serving *Shekhinah.*

398. ***God made the two great lights...*** The verse is taken to mean: *Binah,* known as אלהים (*Elohim*), *God,* gave birth to *Tif'eret* and *Shekhinah, the two great lights.* See above, page 153.

399. **"luminaries of light"** A phrase appearing in the morning liturgy: "May You be blessed, *YHVH* our God, for the exquisite work of Your hands, for the luminaries of light You fashioned; they glorify You." See Ezekiel 32:8. Here the phrase refers to the emanation flowing between *Ḥesed* and *Shekhinah.*

400. **"luminaries of fire"...** The ritual of *havdalah,* marking the end of Sabbath, consists of blessings over wine, spices, and the light of a candle (here, a lamp). The blessing over the flame concludes: "...who creates the lights of the fire." Here "luminaries of fire" are the forces dominating the weekdays and sustained by *Shekhinah,* who is symbolized by fire. See *Zohar* 1:14b; 2:207b–208b.

401. **for they have been granted...** The weekday forces have been empowered by *Shekhinah,* the divine lamp. The ceremony of *havdalah* symbolizes and actualizes this transition of authority.

402. **fingers of a human being...** The ten fingers of the human hand symbolize the ten *sefirot.*

See *Sefer Yetsirah* 1:3; *Midrash Tadshe* 10 (*Beit ha-Midrash,* 3:174); *Bahir* (87) 124; Naḥmanides on Exodus 30:19; *Zohar* 2:67a, 208a; 3:143a (*IR*), 186a, 195b.

403. **front and back** The fronts of the fingers (adjoining the palm) symbolize the

departs, for they shine from that lamp, from that fire, to rule.[404] These may be viewed, but the inside of the fingers may not be viewed by the light of that lamp, for they shine from above and are called "inner faces."[405] This is the mystery of: *You will see My back, but My face will not be seen* (Exodus 33:23). *You will see My back*—the outer face, alluded to by the fingernails. *But My face will not be seen*—the inside of the fingers. This rules on Sabbath; that, during the week.[406] On the Sabbath day, the blessed Holy One rules alone through those inner faces on His throne of glory,[407] all embraced by Him; dominion belongs to Him. So He conveys rest to all the worlds, and the holy people, called "a people unique on earth,"[408] inherit the heritage of this day: luminaries of light from the side of the right,[409] primordial light prevailing on the first day.[410] On the Sabbath day those luminaries of light shine alone, ruling, and from them shine all those below. When Sabbath departs, luminaries of light are treasured away, no longer revealed, and luminaries of fire rule, each in its position. When do they rule? From the departure of Sabbath until the entrance of Sabbath.[411] So as Sabbath departs, they must be illumined by that lamp.[412]

159

sefirot, while the backs of the fingers symbolize the forces beneath *Shekhinah* who rule the weekdays.

404. **permitted to gaze at the fingernails...** As one recites the blessing over the flame, one bends the fingers in toward the palm and gazes at the light reflected off the fingernails, which symbolize the weekday forces illumined and empowered by the fire of *Shekhinah.*

See *Pirqei de-Rabbi Eli'ezer* 20, and David Luria, ad loc., n. 20; *Teshuvot ha-Ge'onim, Sha'arei Teshuvah,* 104; *Zohar* 2:208a–b; S. Finesinger, in *Hebrew Union College Annual* 12–13 (1937–38): 347–65; D. Noy, in *Maḥanayim* 85–86 (1963): 166–73; Ginsburg, *The Sabbath in the Classical Kabbalah,* 272–74; Hallamish, *Ha-Qabbalah,* 322–23.

405. **the inside of the fingers may not be viewed...** The fronts of the fingers, symbolizing the *sefirot,* should be concealed.

406. **This rules on Sabbath...** On Sabbath the *sefirot* rule through *Shekhinah,* while the rest of the week is dominated by the forces beneath *Shekhinah.*

407. **the blessed Holy One...His throne of glory** *Tif'eret* and *Shekhinah.*

408. **"a people unique on earth"** See 2 Samuel 7:23: *Who is like Your people, like Israel, a nation unique on earth...?*

409. **the side of the right** The side of *Ḥesed.*

410. **primordial light...** See BT *Ḥagigah* 12a: "Rabbi El'azar said, 'With the light created by the blessed Holy One on the first day, one could gaze and see from one end of the universe to the other. When the blessed Holy One foresaw the corrupt deeds of the generation of the Flood and the generation of the Dispersion [the generation of the Tower of Babel], He immediately hid it from them, as is written: *The light of the wicked is withheld* (Job 38:15). For whom did He hide it? For the righteous in the time to come.'"

See *Bereshit Rabbah* 3:6; 41:3; *Shemot Rabbah* 35:1; *Tanḥuma, Shemini* 9; *Bahir* 97–98 (147); *Zohar* 1:12b, 31b–32a, 45b–46a, 47a; 2:127a, 148b–149a, 220a–b; 3:88a, 173b. According to *Zohar* 1:1a, this primordial light was concealed in the covenant, a name for *Yesod,* also known as the Sabbath day.

411. **From the departure of Sabbath...** All week long.

412. **by that lamp** *Shekhinah.*

The creatures darting to and fro (Ezekiel 1:14).[413] No eye catches them since they are *darting to and fro*. They are revealed *creatures,* within whom stands that *wheel.*[414] Who is that? Metatron,[415] more grand and splendid than the other forces, 500 parasangs higher.[416] The hidden creatures[417] crouch beneath two supernal letters concealed: י״ה (*yod, he*), letters ruling over ו״ה (*vav, he*), these a chariot of those,[418] while Concealed of all Concealed,[419] totally unknown, rules over all, rides all. The revealed creatures are below, beneath these hidden supernal ones, illumined by them, moving because of them. The supernal creatures are all comprised *in the expanse of heaven,*[420] and of them is written: *Let there be lights.... Let them serve as lights in the expanse of heaven* (Genesis 1:14–15). They are all suspended in that *expanse of heaven.*

The expanse above the creatures[421] is the one of which is written: *An image above the heads of the creature: an expanse like awesome ice, spread out above their heads* (Ezekiel 1:22). This is primordial ה (*he*), beyond which no one can contemplate or know.[422] What is the reason? Because it is enclosed in

160

413. ***The creatures darting to and fro*** The verse continues: *with the appearance of sparks.* This is from Ezekiel's vision of the חיות (*ḥayyot*), "living creatures, animals," who carry the divine throne. The long passage that follows soon refers to *the expanse of heaven* (Genesis 1:15) encompassing the *ḥayyot* and concludes with the same verse.

414. ***wheel*** אופן (*Ofan*), one of the אופנים (*ofanim*) described by Ezekiel (1:15–21). There the wheels are rimmed with eyes and move in perfect unison with the *ḥayyot,* transporting the throne together with them. Here the *ofan* is identified with Metatron.

415. **Metatron** The chief angel, variously described as Prince of the World, Prince of the Presence, celestial scribe, and even יהוה קטן (*YHVH Qatan*), "Lesser *YHVH*" (3 Enoch 12:5, based on Exodus 23:21). In Heikhalot literature Metatron is also identified with Enoch, who ascended to heaven (based on Genesis 5:24). See BT *Sanhedrin* 38b; Scholem, *Kabbalah,* 377–81; Margaliot, *Mal'akhei Elyon,* 73–108.

416. **500 parasangs higher** The Greek parasang equals about 3.5 miles. See BT *Ḥagigah* 13b, on Ezekiel 1:15: "*As I beheld the creatures, behold, one wheel on the ground alongside the creatures.* Rabbi Eleazar said, 'This is a certain angel who stands on earth

and whose head extends close to the living creatures.' In a *matnita* [tannaitic tradition] it is taught: His name is Sandalfon, who is taller than his companion [Munich MS: companions] by a journeying distance of five hundred years. He stands behind the Chariot, binding crowns for his Lord." Here in the *Zohar,* Metatron replaces Sandalfon. Cf. 3 Enoch 9:1–2: "Rabbi Yishma'el said, 'Metatron, Prince of the Presence, said to me: "....I was enlarged and increased in size till I matched the world in length and breadth.""'"

417. **The hidden creatures** *Ḥesed, Gevurah, Tif'eret,* and *Shekhinah.*

418. **beneath two supernal letters...** The quartet of *sefirot* lies beneath the divine parents, *Ḥokhmah* and *Binah,* symbolized by the first two letters of יהוה (*YHVH*), who rule over the lower *sefirot,* symbolized by the last two letters. The highest *sefirah, Keter,* is alluded to by the tip of the initial letter, י (*yod*).

419. **Concealed of all Concealed** *Ein Sof.*

420. ***the expanse of heaven*** *Yesod.* See above, page 154.

421. **above the creatures** Above the hidden creatures, the quartet of *sefirot.*

422. **primordial ה (*he*)...** *Binah,* the Divine Mother, symbolized by the second

thought.[423] The thought of the blessed Holy One is the concealed, enveloped, supernal א (*alef*);[424] no human thought in the entire world can either grasp or know it. If what is suspended in supernal thought[425] cannot be grasped by anyone, all the more so thought itself! Within thought—who can conceive an idea? Understanding fails to even pose a question, much less to know. *Ein Sof* contains no trace at all;[426] no question applies to It, nor conceiving contemplating any thought. From within concealing of the concealed, from the initial descent of *Ein Sof*,[427] radiates a tenuous radiance, unknown, concealed in tracing like the point of a needle, mystery of concealment of thought.[428] Unknown, until a radiance extends from it to a realm containing tracings of all letters, issuing from there.[429]

First of all, א (*alef*), first and last of all the rungs, a tracing traced by all the rungs,[430] yet called "One," to demonstrate that although containing many images, it is only one. This is certainly a letter on which above and below depend. The beginning of the א (*alef*) is a single secrecy of the mystery of supernal thought.[431] The expansion of the celestial expanse is entirely concealed in that beginning, for when א (*alef*) issues from that expanse, it issues in the form of mystery of the beginning of thought. The middle of the א (*alef*) comprises six rungs, mystery of all those hidden, supernal *creatures* suspended in thought.[432]

161

letter of יהוה (*YHVH*). See *Zohar* 2:22a. She is also known as מי (*Mi*), "Who." See above, pages 5–9. A spiritual seeker inquires about Her, but such questions do not lead to ordinary verbal answers.

423. **it is enclosed in thought** *Binah* is concealed within the realm of divine thought, which is impenetrable.

424. **The thought of the blessed Holy One...א (*alef*)** Divine thought is identified with the open-ended א (*alef*) in *Bahir* 48 (70).

425. **what is suspended...** The lower *sefirot*.

426. **no trace at all** Similar language appears in *Zohar* 3:289b (*IZ*).

427. **the initial descent of *Ein Sof*** *Keter*, out of which all emanation proceeds.

428. **a tenuous radiance...** *Hokhmah*, the primordial point of light. See above, page 109; Moses de León, *Sheqel ha-Qodesh*, 21–22 (25–26).

429. **a realm containing tracings of all**

letters... *Binah*, who generates the letters of the alphabet.

430. **first and last of all the rungs...** The graphic shape of the letter א (*alef*) encompasses the entire range of *sefirot*: on the top right is a י (*yod*), symbolizing the primordial point of *Hokhmah* (along with *Keter* and *Binah*); the central shaft of the א (*alef*) is a ו (*vav*), whose numerical value of six symbolizes *Tif'eret* and the five *sefirot* surrounding Him (*Hesed* to *Yesod*); and finally the י (*yod*) on the bottom left of the א (*alef*) symbolizes *Shekhinah*, (lower *Hokhmah*), also pictured as a point.

See *Zohar* 3:73a, 193b; *ZH* 5c (*ST*); Moses de León, *Sheqel ha-Qodesh*, 87–89 (111–12).

431. **a single secrecy...** The primordial point represented by the י (*yod*) on the top right of the א (*alef*).

432. **six rungs...** The six *sefirot* from *Hesed* through *Yesod* suspended in the divine mind (*Keter*, *Hokhmah*, and *Binah*).

One is the radiance that shone and was treasured away,⁴³³ the radiance of the letter ט (*tet*) of Creation,⁴³⁴ *the heat of the day*—mystery of Abraham sitting *at the opening of the tent* (Genesis 18:1), the opening from below to above, while *the heat of the day* shines on that opening, shining from there.⁴³⁵

Second, a radiance that darkens away as evening turns,⁴³⁶ mystery of the prayer of Isaac to mend this rung, as is written: *Isaac went out to meditate in the field* לפנות ערב (*lifnot erev*), *as evening turned* (Genesis 24:63)—toward that *turning of the evening*.⁴³⁷ Contemplation of the *evening* and all the darkness focused on him. In this *turning of the evening* Jacob was endangered by the Prince of Esau.⁴³⁸

Third, a radiance combining both of [21b] these,⁴³⁹ a radiance radiant with healing, mystery written of Jacob: *The sun rose upon him as he passed Penu'el* (Genesis 32:32)⁴⁴⁰—indeed, once he had merged in that פנות ערב (*penot erev*),

433. **the radiance that shone...** Ḥesed, first of the six rungs, identified with the primordial light of the first day of Creation. See BT Ḥagigah 12a, cited above, note 410.

434. **the letter ט (*tet*) of Creation** The first appearance of the letter ט (*tet*) in the Creation story is in Genesis 1:4: *God saw that the light was* טוב (*tov*), *good.* The primordial light of Ḥesed was hidden away in Yesod, the ninth *sefirah* (matching the numerical value of *tet*), who is also called *tov.* Thus *tet* indicates the light of Ḥesed concealed within Yesod.

See BT *Bava Qamma* 55a; *Zohar* 1:3a, 30b; 2:152a, 230a; *ZḤ* 63b (*ShS*).

435. **the heat of the day... at the opening of the tent...** From the description of Abraham's theophany: *YHVH appeared to him by the oaks of Mamre; he was sitting at the opening of the tent in the heat of the day.* In the *Zohar*, Abraham symbolizes Ḥesed, who shines on Shekhinah, *the opening of the tent,* the opening of the divine realm. *The heat of the day* alludes to Ḥesed, Abraham's day within the cosmic week, and Yesod, through whose passion Ḥesed joins Shekhinah.

See *Zohar* 1:97b–98b (*ST*), 98a–b, 103b; 2:36a; 3:14a.

436. **a radiance that darkens away...** Gevurah, second of the six rungs, on the left side, which tends toward judgment and severity.

437. **the prayer of Isaac to mend this rung...** See BT *Berakhot* 26b: "Rabbi Yose son of Rabbi Ḥanina said, 'The patriarchs instituted the prayers'.... Abraham instituted the morning prayer..., Isaac instituted the afternoon prayer, as is said: *Isaac went out to meditate in the field as evening turned.* ...Jacob instituted the evening prayer." See *Bereshit Rabbah* 68:9.

The three patriarchs each symbolize one of the sefirotic triad: Ḥesed, Gevurah, and Tif'eret. Isaac embodies Gevurah, also known as *the turning of the evening.* His prayer focused on restoring this darkened radiance and sweetening its harsh judgment.

438. **the Prince of Esau** The story of Jacob wrestling with *a man* (Genesis 32:25) is interpreted by Rabbi Ḥama son of Rabbi Ḥanina (*Bereshit Rabbah* 77:3) as a wrestling match with "the Prince of Esau," Esau's guardian angel. *Tanḥuma, Vayishlaḥ* 8 identifies this figure as Samael. Both Esau and Samael are empowered by Gevurah on the left side.

439. **a radiance combining both of these** The third rung is Tif'eret, who balances the sefirot of Ḥesed and Gevurah. He is symbolized by both Jacob and the sun.

440. *The sun rose upon him as he passed Penu'el, limping on his thigh,* following his wrestling ordeal. On the healing power of the sun, see Malachi 3:20; BT *Bava Batra* 16b.

turning of the evening.[441] From here on, *he was limping on his thigh* (ibid.)—נצח ישראל (*Netsaḥ Yisra'el*), *Eternity of Israel* (1 Samuel 15:29).[442] It is written: *his thigh;* not: *his thighs.* This is the fourth rung, from which no human prophesied until Samuel arrived, and of which is written: *Moreover,* נצח ישראל (*Netsaḥ Yisra'el*), *the Eternal One of Israel, does not lie or change His mind* (1 Samuel 15:29).[443] Then this rung was mended, for it had been weak ever since Jacob was endangered by the Prince of Esau. *He touched the socket of his thigh* (Genesis 32:26).[444] When he reached Jacob, he seized power from that *turning of the evening* in severe Judgment.[445] Jacob had merged with it, so he could not prevail against him.[446] *When he saw that he could not prevail against him, he touched the socket of his thigh*—he seized the power of judgment from there, for the thigh is outside the torso.[447] Jacob was the torso,[448] comprising mystery of two rungs, mystery called אדם (*adam*), *human.*[449] Once he seized power outside the torso, immediately *the socket of Jacob's thigh was wrenched* (ibid.), and no human prophesied from there until Samuel arrived. So concerning נצח ישראל (*Netsaḥ Yisra'el*), *the Eternal One of Israel,* it is written: *For He is not human*

163

441. **once he had merged . . .** Jacob wrestled with the power of the left, the *turning of the evening,* and integrated it with the right. Thereby he attained the rung of *Tif'eret,* the sun. The *Zohar* relates פנות ערב (*penot erev*), *turning of the evening,* to פנואל (*Penu'el*).

442. נצח ישראל (*Netsaḥ Yisra'el*), *Eternity of Israel . . .* The verse reads: *Moreover, the Eternal One of Israel does not lie or change His mind, for He is not human that He should change His mind. Netsaḥ* is symbolized as one thigh of Primordial Adam, paired with *Hod,* the other thigh. Together these two *sefirot* constitute the source of prophecy.

443. **the fourth rung, from which no human prophesied . . .** When Jacob was wounded in his thigh, *Netsaḥ* (one of the two rungs of prophecy) was weakened and therefore such prophecy was suspended until the time of Samuel, who restored the *sefirah* of *Netsaḥ* and referred to it in the verse cited here. See 1 Samuel 3:1: *In those days the word of YHVH was rare; vision was not widespread.*

See *Zohar* 1:170b–171a; 2:111b; Moses de León, *Sheqel ha-Qodesh,* 10–12 (13–14); idem, *Sefer ha-Rimmon,* 82–83.

444. *He touched the socket of his thigh*

The full verse reads: *When he saw that he could not prevail against him* [Jacob], *he touched the socket of his thigh, so the socket of Jacob's thigh was wrenched as he wrestled with him.*

445. **from that *turning of the evening* . . .** The Prince of Esau was empowered by *Din* ("Judgment"), the *sefirah* of the left side.

446. **had merged with it . . .** Jacob had balanced left and right.

447. **from there, for the thigh . . .** The Prince of Esau could not overpower Jacob, who symbolizes *Tif'eret,* the harmony of left and right, but he succeeded in wounding Jacob's thigh, symbolizing *Netsaḥ,* which is outside the torso of the body, and from there he derived power. See *Zohar* 1:146a, 166a; 2:227a.

448. **the torso** *Tif'eret,* torso of the sefirotic body.

449. **mystery of two rungs, mystery called** אדם (*adam*), *human Ḥesed* and *Gevurah,* the *sefirot* of the right and the left, are balanced in *Tif'eret,* the torso of the body of Primordial Adam. *Tif'eret* is symbolized by Jacob, of whom it is said (BT *Bava Metsi'a* 84b): "Jacob's beauty was a reflection of Adam's."

(1 Samuel, ibid.).[450] Joshua prophesied from the הוד (*Hod*), *Splendor* of Moses, as is written: *Confer* מהודך (*me-hodekha*), *of your splendor, upon him* (Numbers 27:20).[451] This is the fifth rung, נצח (*Netsaḥ*), *Eternity*, left thigh of Jacob.[452] So David came and combined it with the right, as is written: *Delights in Your right hand* נצח (*netsaḥ*), *for eternity* (Psalms 16:11)—not *Your right hand*, but *in Your right hand*.[453]

Why was Jacob's thigh weakened? Because the side of impurity[454] approached, seizing power from it, and it was delayed until Samuel. So he[455] pointed out that this is the thigh of Israel, as is written: *Moreover*, נצח ישראל (*Netsaḥ Yisra'el*), *the Eternal One of Israel* (1 Samuel, ibid.). So, too, all his words were stern, at the beginning and at the end.[456] Further, the blessed Holy One later merged him in הוד (*Hod*), *Splendor*. When? After he had anointed kings.[457]

450. *He is not human* The full verse reads: *Moreover, the Eternal One of Israel does not lie or change His mind, for He is not human that He should change His mind.* The *sefirah* of *Netsaḥ*, being outside the torso of the body, lacks the balance of *Tif'eret* ("the mystery called *human*") and is therefore vulnerable to the Prince of Esau. See above, page 163; Moses de León, *Sheqel ha-Qodesh*, 11 (14).

By wounding Jacob's thigh, this demonic power damages the source of prophecy in the sefirotic thigh, *Netsaḥ*, and thereby prophecy is delayed until the arrival of Samuel. See *Zohar* 3:136b (*IR*).

451. *Confer* מהודך (*me-hodekha*), *of your splendor, upon him* The verse continues: *so that the entire community of the Children of Israel hearken*. In the biblical passage, God instructs Moses to impart his charisma to Joshua. Here in the *Zohar*, הודך (*hodekha*), *your splendor*, indicates the *sefirah* of *Hod*, companion of *Netsaḥ*, who together inspire prophecy. Joshua, living before Samuel, did not have access to *Netsaḥ*.

452. **the fifth rung,** נצח **(Netsaḥ),** *Eternity,* **left thigh...** M7 deletes the word נצח (*Netsaḥ*), *Eternity*, which simplifies the line, since in Kabbalah *Hod* is usually described as the fifth lower *sefirah* and the left thigh, while *Netsaḥ* is the fourth, the right thigh. The commentators wrestle with this inconsistency and attempt various solutions; see *OY, KP, MM, Sullam*. Apparently, here the

Zohar adopts the view that *Netsaḥ* is on the left, and *Hod* on the right.

See Moses de León, *Sheqel ha-Qodesh*, 10–11, 47–48 (13–14, 57, 59); idem, *Sefer ha-Rimmon*, 82–83, and Wolfson's note on 82:17.

453. **David came and combined it with the right... in Your right hand...** David combined left with right, so that *Netsaḥ* was included *in Your right hand*, on the right side.

See *Zohar* 2:168b–169a; *ZḤ* 44a; Moses de León, *Sheqel ha-Qodesh*, 11 (13): "But I have seen in the Midrash...."

454. **the side of impurity** The demonic power embodied by the Prince of Esau.

455. **So he** Samuel.

456. **all his words were stern...** Samuel devoted himself to restoring the *sefirah* of *Netsaḥ*, which had been attacked by the Prince of Esau on the left side, so his prophecy was characterized by the severe quality of the left side. Samuel's career began with the condemnation of the house of the high priest Eli, delivered by *a man of God* (1 Samuel 2:27–36), who is identified in rabbinic sources as Elkanah, Samuel's father.

See *Midrash Tanna'im*, 208; *Seder Olam Rabbah* 20:6; *Battei Midrashot*, 2:121; Rashi on BT *Eruvin* 18b, s.v. *Elqanah*; Ginzberg, *Legends*, 6:222, n. 28.

Samuel's final prophecy was a condemnation of King Saul. See 1 Samuel 15:10–34; 28:15–19.

457. **anointed kings** Saul and David.

Thus he is equivalent to Moses and Aaron: just as Moses and Aaron occupy two sides above,[458] so does he below, like those two sides. Who are they? *Netsaḥ and Hod*.[459] So Samuel is equivalent to Moses and Aaron. All those rungs are linked to one another, as is written: *Moses and Aaron among His priests, Samuel among those invoking His name* (Psalms 99:6),[460] for six aspects are interlaced, interlinked. Just as these—Moses, Aaron, and Samuel—are linked, so are Jacob, Moses, and Joseph.[461] Jacob, master of the house.[462] When Jacob died, Moses took over the house, enjoining it in his lifetime.[463] Joseph was righteous through Jacob and Moses, both of whom performed in the house[464] only

458. **two sides above** *Ḥesed* and *Gevurah,* on the left and the right, symbolized by Aaron the priest and Moses the Levite.

459. **Netsaḥ and Hod** The source of prophecy, situated beneath *Ḥesed* and *Gevurah,* and actualized by the prophet Samuel.

460. **Samuel is equivalent...** See BT *Berakhot* 31b, where Hannah's prayer, *Give your handmaid the seed of men* [i.e., offspring], is interpreted by Rabbi Yoḥanan as referring to: "Seed equivalent to two men. Who are they? Moses and Aaron, as is said: *Moses and Aaron among His priests, Samuel among those invoking His name*."

Cf. *Zohar* 2:148a; 3:19b; *ZḤ* 43c.

461. **six aspects...** All six *sefirot* from *Ḥesed* through *Yesod* are encompassed by the six named figures. Moses, Aaron, and Samuel symbolize *Ḥesed, Gevurah, Netsaḥ,* and *Hod* (see above), while Jacob as well as Moses symbolize *Tif'eret,* and Joseph symbolizes *Yesod*.

462. **master of the house** Jacob, symbolizing *Tif'eret,* is the husband of *Shekhinah,* known as "house." In the *Zohar,* the phrase "master of the house" is applied to both Jacob and Moses (1:138b, 152b, 236b, 239a; 2:22b, 235b, 238b, 244b [*Heikh*]) as well as to the mystic who masters the secrets of Torah (2:99b). See Numbers 12:7: *Throughout My house he* [Moses] *is trusted.*

On Jacob and Moses in the *Zohar,* see Liebes, in *Eshel Be'er Sheva* 4 (1996): 193–98.

463. **Moses took over...** During his lifetime Moses united with *Shekhinah,* thereby becoming "master of the house" while still in the body, whereas Jacob atttained

this state only at death. See *Zohar* 1:152b, 236b; 3:187b.

According to rabbinic tradition, after encountering God on Mount Sinai, Moses abstained from sexual contact with his wife and maintained union with *Shekhinah*.

See *Sifrei,* Numbers 99; BT *Shabbat* 87a; *Tanḥuma, Tsav* 13; Maimonides, *Mishneh Torah, Hilkhot Yesodei ha-Torah* 7:6; *Zohar* 1:152b, 234b; 2:222a; 3:148a, 180a.

On the theme of Moses the husband commanding God, see *Midrash Tehillim* 90:5, in the name of Rabbi Shim'on son of Lakish: "Why was he [Moses] called איש האלהים (*ish ha-elohim*), *man* [or: *husband*] *of God* (Psalms 90:1)? Just as a husband can, if he wishes, either nullify his wife's vow or confirm it, as is said: אישה (*Ishah*), *Her husband may confirm it, her husband may nullify it* (Numbers 30:14), so, as it were, Moses said to the blessed Holy One, *Arise, O YHVH!... Return, O YHVH!* (ibid. 10:35–36)."

See *Pesiqta de-Rav Kahana, nispaḥim, Vezot Haberakhah,* 443–44, 448 (variants); *Tanḥuma, Vezot Haberakhah* 2 (*Ets Yosef,* ad loc.); *Devarim Rabbah* (Lieberman), on 33:1; *Zohar* 1:6b, 21b–22a, 148a, 152a–b, 236b; 239a; 2:22b, 235b, 238b, 244b (*Heikh*).

464. **performed in the house** שמשו בביתא (*Shimmeshu be-veita*), "Served in the house," based on the rabbinic euphemism for sexual intercourse: "performed [the function of] the house," "house" itself being a euphemism for "vulva." See M *Miqva'ot* 8:4; *Niddah* 1:7; 10:8.

Here "the house" is *Shekhinah,* with whom both Jacob and Moses unite. See *Zohar* 1:133a.

165

through Joseph because he was righteous.[465] Jacob took over the house through Joseph, as is written: *These are the generations of Jacob: Joseph* (Genesis 37:2).[466] Moses did not perform with Her until he carried Joseph—when *Shekhinah* emerged from exile,[467] he could join with Her only through Joseph, as is written: *Moses took the bones of Joseph with him* (Exodus 13:19).[468] Since it is written: *Moses took the bones of Joseph,* why *with him*? Because the body does not join the female before joining with the covenant.[469] So Moses carried Joseph with him, and being with him, he performed with the female fittingly. Thus Jacob, Moses, and Joseph go together.[470] When Jacob died, his body was brought into the Holy Land.[471] When Joseph died, his body was not buried in the Holy Land, rather his bones.[472] Moses, neither one.[473] Why? Because Jacob was first husband of the Consort.[474] When Jacob died, She joined Moses, and

465. **he was righteous** Since Joseph resisted the sexual advances of Potiphar's wife, he is called "righteous" in rabbinic literature. See BT *Yoma* 35b; *Bereshit Rabbah* 93:7; *Pesiqta de-Rav Kahana, nispaḥim,* 460. Cf. *Tanḥuma, Bereshit* 5; *Pirqei de-Rabbi Eli'ezer* 38, which cite Amos 2:6.

In Kabbalah Joseph symbolizes the divine phallus, *Yesod* ("Foundation"), also known as Righteous One, based on Proverbs 10:25: וצדיק יסוד עולם (*Ve-tsaddiq yesod olam*). The verse literally means *The righteous one is an everlasting foundation* but is understood as *The righteous one is the foundation of the world.* See BT *Ḥagigah* 12b; *Bahir* 71 (102); Azriel of Gerona, *Peirush ha-Aggadot,* 34.

The point here is that both Jacob and Moses could unite with *Shekhinah* only through the *sefirah* of *Yesod,* symbolized by Joseph. See *Zohar* 1:180a.

466. *These are the generations of Jacob: Joseph* The *Zohar* conveniently breaks off the citation here with the mention of the two males, so that the verse now implies that they must be together. By means of *Yesod* (Joseph), Jacob united with *Shekhinah* and generated new life. See *Bereshit Rabbah* 84:6.

467. **emerged from exile** From the exile of Egyptian slavery, which She shared with the Children of Israel.

468. *Moses took the bones of Joseph...* Joseph, at his death, had made his brothers promise to eventually take his bones out of

Egypt (Genesis 50:25), a promise fulfilled by Moses at the Exodus. Joseph's bones were reinterred in Canaan at the end of the conquest (Joshua 24:32).

469. **the body...with the covenant** As a male body unites with a female through the phallus, which is marked with the sign of the covenant of circumcision, so Moses, symbolizing *Tif'eret,* the torso of the body of the *sefirot,* unites with the divine female, *Shekhinah,* only by means of the divine phallus, *Yesod,* known as Covenant. See Moses de León, *Sheqel ha-Qodesh,* 10 (12–13).

470. **Jacob, Moses, and Joseph...** Jacob and Moses both symbolize *Tif'eret,* while Joseph symbolizes *Yesod.*

471. **When Jacob died...** See Genesis 50:13. Jacob symbolizes *Tif'eret,* the torso of the sefirotic body, so when he died his body entered the Holy Land, symbolizing *Shekhinah.*

472. **When Joseph died...** Joseph symbolizes *Yesod,* the phallus protruding from the torso of the body, so his body did not enter the land; rather, it was his bones (whose symbolism is clarified below). See *Zohar* 2:141b.

473. **Moses, neither one** Moses died just outside the land of Israel on Mt. Nebo and was buried in the valley below. See Deuteronomy 34:1–6.

474. **first husband of the Consort** Jacob was the first to wed *Shekhinah,* who is called

166

as long as Moses existed in this world, he enjoined Her fittingly; he was Her second husband. Jacob was brought into the land with his entire body because he is the body.[475] Joseph, his bones and not his body because bones are soldiers and companies above, all emerging from that צדיק (*Tsaddiq*), Righteous One, that *Tsaddiq* called צבאות (*Tseva'ot*), Hosts.[476] Why? Because all supernal hosts and companies emerge from Him. So his bones, which are hosts, entered the land. Moses was outside and did not enter there, neither his body nor his bones. Rather, after Moses died, *Shekhinah* entered the land and returned to Her first husband from there, namely, Jacob. From here we learn that a female married to two, returns to the first in that world.[477] Moses was outside since Her first husband was in the land. Moses enjoined Her in his lifetime, something Jacob did not attain. Jacob performed with Her in that world; Moses, in this world.

Now if you say this shows Moses' inferiority, not so![478] Rather, when Israel went forth from Egypt, it was from the aspect of Jubilee.[479] All those 600,000 were from the upper world,[480] [22a] and in that image they wandered through the desert. Not one of them entered the land, just their children, their off-

---

מטרוניתא (*Matronita*), an aramaized form of the Latin *matrona*, "matron, married woman, noble lady."

475. **he is the body** Jacob symbolizes *Tif'eret*, torso of the divine body.

476. **bones are soldiers...** The bones symbolize camps of angels emerging from *Yesod*, who is known both as צדיק (*Tsaddiq*), "Righteous One" (see above, note 465) and צבאות (*Tseva'ot*), "Hosts," referring to these hosts of angels. See *Zohar* 3:296a (*IZ*).

477. **a female married to two...** If a woman marries two men, in the future world when all are resurrected, she will be reunited with her first husband.

See Matthew 22:28; Mark 12:23; *Zohar* 2:102a–b; Moses de León, *She'elot u-Tshuvot*, 59; *NZ*, here, n. 9, and *millu'im*, 15; Mordechai Shpielman, *Tif'eret Tsevi*, 1:248a–249a.

478. **this shows Moses' inferiority...** The fact that he did not enter the land and maintain his union with *Shekhinah* apparently indicates failure.

479. **the aspect of Jubilee** *Binah*, the Divine Mother, is symbolized by the Jubilee, proclaimed every fifty years, when slaves

were released and land reverted to its original owner (Leviticus 25:8–55). In general She is characterized by the number fifty, based on BT *Rosh ha-Shanah* 21b, where Rav and Shemu'el teach: "Fifty gates of בינה (*binah*), understanding, were created in the world, all of which were given to Moses except for one, as is said: *You made him little less than God* (Psalms 8:6)." *Binah* is the source of redemption and liberation, specifically the Exodus from Egypt.

See *Zohar* 1:47b; 2:46a, 83b, 85b; 3:262a.

480. **All those 600,000...** According to the Torah, the total number of male Israelites above the age of twenty who left Egypt was approximately 600,000. See Exodus 12:37; Numbers 11:21. The precise total of the first census taken in the Sinai Desert was 603,550. See Exodus 38:26; Numbers 1:46; cf. Numbers 26:51; *Leqah Tov*, Numbers 1:46.

The 600,000 Israelites redeemed from Egypt derive from *Binah*, the upper world, and symbolize the six *sefirot* from *Hesed* through *Yesod* generated by *Binah*. See *Zohar* 1:2a–b.

spring, fittingly, for they constitute the mending of the moon.[481] All the cultivation of earth was the mending of the moon.[482] Moses performed with the moon while still in the body, enjoining her as he wished. Departing from this world, he ascended in sublime ascent through his holy spirit,[483] returning by spirit to upper Jubilee, where he joined those 600,000 who were his.[484] Not so with Jacob, who returned by spirit to Sabbatical;[485] not so in his lifetime, since he had another house.[486] The Holy Land was restored below through the power above.[487] So it was not fitting for them all to be as one: those of the upper world were apart, all in spirit; those of the lower world were apart, all in body.[488] It was not fitting for both of these to be within the moon, rather

481. **Not one of them entered...** The generation redeemed from Egypt was condemned to die in the desert because of their faithlessness, except for Caleb and Joshua. See Numbers 14:26–35. The offspring who do enter the Holy Land thereby restore *Shekhinah*, who is symbolized by both the land and the moon.

482. **All the cultivation of earth...** *Shekhinah* was restored and arrayed by the labor of those who entered the land and cultivated it, whereas the generation of the Exodus who died in the desert derived from *Binah* and were sustained effortlessly by the manna, known as *bread from heaven* (Exodus 16:4); they were not meant to enter the land. What appears to be a tragic punishment is actually a cosmic necessity.

483. **through his holy spirit** Through his soul, or through *Shekhinah*, known as Holy Spirit.

484. **those 600,000...** When the generation of the Exodus, who derived from *Binah* (Jubilee), died in the desert, their souls returned to Her. There they united with Moses, whose soul also derives from *Binah*. They symbolize the six *sefirot* from *Ḥesed* to *Yesod*, while Moses symbolizes the core of those six, *Tif'eret*, also designated by the letter ו (*vav*), whose numerical value is six. Moses did not need to enter the land (symbolizing *Shekhinah*). Having already united with Her during his lifetime, he was now destined to return directly to *Binah*, the Divine Mother.

485. **Sabbatical** שמטה (*Shemittah*), "Release." Every seventh year is a year of *shemittah*, during which the land must lie fallow and at the end of which all debts are remitted. See Leviticus 25:1–24; Deuteronomy 15:1–3. In Kabbalah *shemittah* symbolizes *Shekhinah*, the seventh of the lower *sefirot*. See *Zohar* 1:153b.

486. **another house** As the *Zohar* indicates below, Jacob was married to earthly partners, namely Leah, Rachel, and their two handmaids, Bilhah and Zilpah, so he could not unite with *Shekhinah*. Moses, on the other hand, is said to have abstained from sexual contact with his wife after encountering the divine on Mount Sinai. See BT *Shabbat* 87a; and below. Maintaining intimacy with *Shekhinah* throughout his life, he became master of the house while still in the body; at death his spirit joined with *Binah*. See *Zohar* 2:23a.

487. **The Holy Land was restored below through the power above** *Shekhinah* was restored by the generation entering and working the land who derived power from their parents, whose souls had returned to *Binah*.

488. **not fitting for them all to be...** It was inappropriate for both generations to enter the land. Rather, the generation that wandered in the desert rose in spirit to *Binah*, the upper world, whereas the next generation physically entered the land, symbolizing *Shekhinah*. Similarly, with Moses and Jacob: one rose to *Binah*, remaining outside

168

these within the moon and those outside, so that those would be illumined by these.[489]

All those who entered the land resembled the originals[490] but did not experience an ascent as high. For there will never be, nor has there ever been, a generation like those originals, shown the splendid luster of their Lord face-to-face.[491]

Jacob performed with his wives in the body, later cleaving spirit to spirit.[492] Moses separated himself from his wife, performing while in the body with that Holy Spirit.[493] Later his spirit cleaved to a high, hidden spirit above.[494] So all levels cleaved as one. The spirit of Moses derives from Jubilee; his body, from Sabbatical. The spirit of Jacob, cleaving to Sabbatical; his body belonged to his wives in this world.

All those upper lights appear in their image below on earth; all are suspended in *the expanse of heaven* (Genesis 1:15).[495] Mystery of two names merging into one,[496] their perfection three, turning back into one, corresponding to one

169

the land, whereas the other was buried in the land and joined *Shekhinah*.

489. **these within the moon and those outside...** The younger generation entered the land, symbolizing *Shekhinah,* also identified with the moon. The generation of the Exodus were "outside": having risen in spirit to *Binah,* they could illumine their descendants below.

490. **the originals** The generation of the Exodus.

491. **For there will never be...** Despite the failures and faithlessness of the generation of the Exodus, they are later described in glowing terms. See *Mekhilta de-Rashbi,* Exodus 19:11: "There never arose, nor will there ever arise, a generation as worthy to receive the Torah as these." Cf. Jeremiah 2:2; and *Mekhilta, Shirta* 3: "Rabbi Eli'ezer said, '...A handmaiden at the [Red] Sea saw what Isaiah, Ezekiel, and all the other prophets never saw.'"

See *Zohar* 2:60a, 64b, 82a, 93b–94a; 3:22b, 287a; and Isaac ibn Latif, *Iggeret ha-Teshuvah,* 25: "The generation of the desert comprehended the intellectual forms while still in the body... Their world was the world to come." The phrase "face-to-face" derives from the description of the revelation at

Mount Sinai (Deuteronomy 5:4): *Face-to-face YHVH spoke to you on the mountain out of the fire.*

492. **spirit to spirit** His soul united with *Shekhinah,* Holy Spirit.

493. **Moses separated himself from his wife...** See above, note 463.

494. **a high, hidden spirit above** *Binah.*

495. **All those upper lights...** Various *sefirot* are reflected and embodied by the biblical heroes mentioned above: Jacob (*Tif-'eret*), Joseph (*Yesod*), Moses (*Gevurah, Tif'eret*), Aaron (*Ḥesed*), Samuel (*Netsaḥ, Hod*). These *sefirot* gather in *Yesod,* known as *the expanse of heaven,* from which they illumine *Shekhinah.* See above, pages 154, 156–57, 159.

496. **Mystery of two names...** Apparently יהוה אלהים (*YHVH Elohim*). In rabbinic literature these two names represent, respectively, the divine qualities of compassion and justice. See *Sifrei,* Deuteronomy 26; *Bereshit Rabbah* 12:15; 33:3; and 13:3, where *YHVH Elohim* is called "a complete name."

In Kabbalah the two names often designate *Tif'eret* and *Shekhinah,* who were originally one and whose reunion represents the goal of religious life. See *Zohar* 1:4a, 20a, 48b; 2:161a, 229a; 3:138b (*IR*); *ZḤ* 70d (*ShS*). *OY* suggests two other possiblities: יהוה (*YHVH*) and אדני

another.[497] This is the name inscribed and engraved, embraced by the mystery of faith.[498]

[29a] בראשית (Be-reshit), In the beginning.[499]

We have learned: Every Solomon mentioned in the Song of Songs connotes the King to whom peace belongs, while king, anonymous, connotes the female, lower reflecting upper.[500] Mystery of the matter: lower inherits upper, both as one.[501] This is בית (bayit), house, as is written: By wisdom a house is built (Proverbs 24:3),[502] and similarly: King Solomon made himself a pavilion from the trees of

(Adonai) merged into one name, יאהדונהי (YAHDVNHY); or יהוה (YHVH) and אהיה (Ehyeh) merged into יאההויהה (YAHHVYHH).

497. **their perfection three...** Apparently אהיה יהוה אדני (Ehyeh, YHVH, Adonai), names of Keter, Tif'eret, and Shekhinah, respectively, all three of which are aligned in the middle column of the sefirot. The gimatriyya of יהוה אלהים (YHVH Elohim), 112, is equivalent to that of אהיה יהוה אדני (Ehyeh, YHVH, Adonai). See KP; Scholem; cf. OY.

498. **the mystery of faith** The mystery of the union of the sefirot, symbolized by the unification of the divine names. See Zohar 2:9a; 3:65b.

499. **[29a] בראשית (Be-reshit), In the beginning** The section comprising 1:22a–29a belongs to Tiqqunei ha-Zohar, a later stratum of Zoharic literature, so it is not included in this translation. See Scholem, Kabbalah, 218–19.

500. **We have learned...** See Shir ha-Shirim Rabbah 1:11 (on 1:1): "Rabbi Yudan and Rabbi Levi said in the name of Rabbi Yoḥanan, 'Wherever in this scroll [the Song of Songs] the expression King Solomon appears, the text speaks of King Solomon, whereas the king, anonymous, connotes the blessed Holy One.' The Rabbis say, 'Wherever King Solomon appears, the text speaks of the King to whom peace belongs [deriving שלמה (Shelomoh), Solomon, from שלום (shalom), "peace"], whereas the king, anonymous, connotes the Assembly of Israel.'"

In rabbinic Hebrew, the phrase כנסת ישראל (Keneset Yisra'el), "Assembly of Isra-

el," denotes the people of Israel, and the Song of Songs is read as a love poem between them and God. In the Zohar, Keneset Yisra'el refers to Shekhinah, described here as נוקבא (nuqba), "female." She is the divine counterpart of the people, that aspect of God most intimately connected with them. The lovers depicted in the Song of Songs symbolize Shekhinah and Her partner, Tif'eret. Shekhinah is described there as King, reflecting Her name Malkhut ("Kingdom"). See Zohar 1:47a, 84a. Here, apparently, King Solomon denotes Binah, "to whom peace belongs," namely, Yesod, who conveys the flow of Binah and thereby links the two lovers. See BT Shabbat 152a, where Rabbi Shim'on son of Ḥalafta refers to the phallus as "peacemaker of the home." Cf. Zohar 1:5b; 2:127b. The lower (plain, earthly) meaning of the text connotes the upper, divine sense. See above, page 115.

501. **lower inherits upper...** Through Her union with Tif'eret, Shekhinah absorbs the flow of emanation from Her mother above, Binah. See Zohar 2:215a: "...for Daughter inherits Mother." Cf. above, page 9: "Mother lends Daughter Her garments."

502. **This is בית (bayit), house...** The opening letter of the Torah, the ב (bet) of בראשית (Be-reshit), In the beginning, stands for בית (bayit), house. The letter bet, second letter of the alphabet, is equivalent to two, and here indicates two sefirotic structures: Binah, fashioned from the primordial point of Ḥokhmah ("Wisdom"), and Shekhinah, comprising the sefirot from Ḥesed through Yesod.

170

Lebanon (Song of Songs 3:9).[503] *Pavilion* is the adorning of the lower world by the upper world.[504] For before the blessed Holy One created the world, He and His name were enclosed within Him, one.[505] Nothing existed—He alone— until there arose within the will of thought[506] actualizing all by impress of the signet,[507] creating the world. He traced and built, but it did not endure[508] until He enwrapped Himself in a wrapping of contemplative radiance[509] and created

503. **pavilion...** אפריון (*Appiryon*), a biblical hapax legomenon of uncertain meaning, often translated "palanquin," but apparently referring to a stationary structure. In the Midrash it is interpreted as referring to the Tabernacle and to the Temple in Jerusalem. See *Pesiqta de-Rav Kahana* 1:2; *Shir ha-Shirim Rabbah* and *Targum,* ad loc.

In the *Zohar* the *appiryon* is *Shekhinah,* the divine palace (2:127a). This *pavilion* is constructed out of the *sefirot* from *Ḥesed* through *Yesod,* known as *the trees of Lebanon,* namely, of *Ḥokhmah.* See *Zohar* 1:31a, 35a–b; 2:127b.

504. **the adorning of the lower world by the upper world** *Shekhinah* is adorned by the light radiating from *Binah.*

505. **before the blessed Holy One created...** See *Pirqei de-Rabbi Eli'ezer* 3: "Rabbi Eli'ezer son of Hyrcanus opened, '...Before the world was created, there existed only the blessed Holy One and His great name. The thought of creating the world arose in His mind. He traced the world, but it did not endure. They told a parable. To what can this be compared? To a king who wishes to build his palace. If he does not trace in the earth its foundations, exits, and entrances, he cannot begin to build. Similarly the blessed Holy One traced the world in front of Himself, but it did not endure until He created *teshuvah* ("returning, turning back" to God).'" Cf. Maimonides, *Guide of the Perplexed* 1:61; *ZḤ* 2d (*MhN*).

In Kabbalah the *sefirot* are considered God's names since they reveal the divine identity. In particular, the final *sefirah, Shekhinah,* is called "the name" of God. Before the process of emanation, all of the *sefirot* existed potentially within *Ein Sof.*

506. **the will of thought** *Keter,* the impulse within the divine mind. See Azriel of

Gerona, *Peirush ha-Aggadot,* 92, 94, 107; *Zohar* 1:45b; 2:259b, 268b; *ZḤ* 1b, 6c (*ST*).

507. **the signet** סמיטרא (*Samitra*), apparently based on סימנטיר (*simanteir*), derived from the Greek *semanterion,* "seal, signet, stamp." *Bei'ur ha-Millim ha-Zarot,* 182, defines *samitra* as "turban," based on the *Arukh;* see *KP, OY.*

The process of emanation begins with a gesture of royal authority. Cf. above, page 107: "At the head of potency ["authority, decree"] of the King, He engraved engravings in luster on high."

508. **but it did not endure** See *Bereshit Rabbah* 9:2: "*He fashioned everything at its appropriate time* (Ecclesiastes 3:11)....Rabbi Abbahu said, 'From here [we learn] that the blessed Holy One kept creating worlds and destroying them until He created these [i.e., heaven and earth]. Then He declared, "These please Me, those do not."'"

See *Bereshit Rabbah* 1:7; *Pirqei de-Rabbi Eli'ezer* 3, cited above (note 505). The theme of previous worlds that did not endure appears in the *Idrot* (*Zohar* 3:128a [*IR*], 292b [*IZ*]) and inspired Isaac Luria's theory of "the breaking of the vessels."

509. **wrapping of contemplative radiance** See *Tanḥuma* (Buber), *Vayaqhel* 7: "Rabbi Shim'on son of Rabbi Yehotsadak asked Rabbi Shemu'el son of Naḥman, 'Since you are a master of Aggadah, tell me how the blessed Holy One created the world.' He replied, 'When the blessed Holy One wished to create the world, He enwrapped Himself in light and created the world, as is said: *He wraps in light as in a garment* (Psalms 104:2), and afterward: *He spreads out the heavens like a curtain.*'"

See *Bereshit Rabbah* 3:4 (and Theodor, ad loc.); *Pirqei de-Rabbi Eli'ezer* 3. The image of

171

the world, generating trees, supernal, grand cedars,[510] from the light, that supernal luster. He set His chariots on twenty-two engraved letters, carved in ten utterances, settling.[511] So it is written: *from the trees of Lebanon,* and similarly: *the cedars of Lebanon that He planted* (Psalms 104:16), for from these He fashioned that *pavilion.*

King Solomon made himself. Himself—for Himself; *himself*—for His arrayal; *himself*—displaying supernal splendor; *himself*—proclaiming that He is one and His name one,[512] as is said: *YHVH will be one and His name one* (Zechariah 14:9), and that He and His name are one, as is written: *They will know that You alone are Your name: YHVH* (Psalms 83:19).

By the impact of His truncheons,[513] ramparts[514] are revealed. Trickling to this side above, trickling to the right, deviating to the left, descending below, and so in four directions.[515] Dominion extends above, below, and in four directions,[516] becoming one supernal stream, flowing down, forming a vast sea,[517] as is said: *All the streams flow into the sea, yet the sea is not full* (Ecclesiastes 1:7), for it gathers all, drawing it within, as is said: *I am the rose of Sharon* (Song of Songs 2:1), *Sharon* being none other than the site drawing all waters of the world.[518] So this brings forth and that draws in, one illumining the other by

172

God wrapping Himself in a garment of light appears in Greek, Iranian, Gnostic, and kabbalistic sources. See Matt, *Zohar,* 212; Ezra of Gerona, *Peirush Shir ha-Shirim,* 493–94; Ezra's letter, ed. Scholem, in *Sefer Bialik,* 157–58; Azriel of Gerona, *Peirush ha-Aggadot,* 110–11; *Zohar* 1:2a, 15b, 90a (*ST*), 245a; 2:39b, 164b; Moses de León, *Mishkan ha-Edut,* 5a. Here the wrapping of radiance filters the intense primordial energy.

510. **generating trees, supernal, grand cedars** The *sefirot* from *Ḥesed* through *Yesod,* generated by the union of *Ḥokhmah* and *Binah.* See *Bereshit Rabbah* 15:1; *Zohar* 1:35b.

511. **twenty-two engraved letters, carved in ten utterances...** The twenty-two letters of the Hebrew alphabet spell out the ten utterances by which the world was created (according to M *Avot* 5:1). The ten utterances parallel both the ten *sefirot* and the Ten Commandments, which contain all twenty-two letters (in the version of the Decalogue in Deuteronomy 5:6–18). According to *Sefer Yetsirah* 1:1–2, God created the world by means of "thirty-two wondrous

paths of wisdom," namely, the twenty-two letters and the ten *sefirot.*

See Naḥmanides, *Peirush Sefer Yetsirah,* 401; *Zohar* 1:109a (*ST*); 3:290a (*IZ*).

512. **himself—for His arrayal...** The divine King is arrayed in the *pavilion, Shekhinah,* who reveals the royal glory and is known as "the name" of God.

513. **His truncheons** קלפוי (*Qulpoi*), "His clubs." The flow of emanation is stimulated by a divine blow.

514. **ramparts** קסטורין (*Qastorin*), derived from the Latin *castra,* "fortifications," referring here to the sefirotic structures beginning to emerge.

515. **Trickling...** Emanation begins to trickle down the sefirotic tree. See *Zohar* 1:245a.

516. **above, below...** The six directions correspond to the six *sefirot* from *Ḥesed* through *Yesod.* See *Sefer Yetsirah* 1:13.

517. **a vast sea** *Shekhinah,* who gathers the stream of emanation.

518. **Sharon...the site drawing all waters of the world** The Sharon is the coastal plain from Jaffa to Mount Carmel.

well-known paths.[519] Thus, *By wisdom a house is built* (Proverbs 24:3), and so ב
(*bet*), בראשית (*Be-reshit*), *In the beginning*: the upper house is built *by wisdom,*
and the lower one, as well,[520] though the upper house is grand, cultivation of
the world, while *king,* anonymous, is the lower house.

The king will rejoice in אלהים (*Elohim*), *God* (Psalms 63:12). When supernal
גבורה (*Gevurah*), Power, is aroused to embrace Him beneath His head, drawing Him close in joy, so that all will be one, then *the king will rejoice,*[521] the joy
of a stream issuing through a single secret, hidden channel,[522] flowing into
him. ב (*Bet*), two who are one, and so the world is consummated in existence.
The king will rejoice in Elohim—the lower world rejoicing in the upper, deep
world, a joy streaming forth.[523] Where does He rejoice? *In Elohim.* In Him, He
rejoices; by Him, He transmits life to all.[524] He is called "life of the king."[525]
This is the essence [29b] of the house.[526] This house built the house of the
world, built the world.[527] The secret is: בראשית (*Be-reshit*), *In the beginning*—
ב ראשית (*bet reshit*), two, beginning, *beginning of wisdom.*[528]

Then it gathers all into itself[529] and is transformed into a vast sea to imbibe
all, a sea whose waters congeal, imbibing all waters of the world, gathering

173

519. **So this brings forth and that draws
in...** *Binah* generates the stream of emanation, which pours into *Shekhinah* through
sefirotic channels.

520. *By wisdom a house is built...*
ב (*bet*)... The opening letter of the Torah,
ב (*bet*), indicates בית (*bayit*), "house," and
the number two. The two houses are: *Binah,*
built out of the primordial point of *Hokhmah,* and *Shekhinah,* constructed by the *sefirot* emerging from *Binah.*

521. **When supernal** גבורה (*Gevurah*),
Power, is aroused... *Shekhinah* is embraced by *Gevurah,* as indicated by the verse:
The king (Shekhinah) *will rejoice in Elohim*
(which denotes both *Binah* and *Gevurah*).
The phrase "beneath His head" derives from
Song of Songs 2:6: *His left hand beneath my
head, his right embracing me,* a verse applied
in the *Zohar* to sefirotic embrace.

522. **a single secret, hidden channel** Yesod, who conveys the flow of emanation to
Shekhinah.

523. **the lower world rejoicing in the
upper...** *Shekhinah* rejoicing in *Binah.*

524. **In Him, He rejoices...** In *Binah,*
Shekhinah rejoices.

525. **"life of the king"** *Binah* is called by

this epithet because it is the source of life
for *Shekhinah,* "the king."

See *Zohar* 2:115b; 3:58a; cf. *Sifrei,* Numbers
153; Nahmanides on Genesis 2:7 and Numbers 30:3.

526. **the essence of the house** *Binah* animates the entire divine realm as well as the
world below.

On this phrase, see Psalms 113:9; *Bereshit
Rabbah* 71:2; *Pesiqta de-Rav Kahana* 20:2;
Tanhuma (Buber), *Vayetse* 15; *Bemidbar
Rabbah* 14:8; *Zohar* 1:50a, 149b, 154a, 157b.

527. **This house built the house of the
world, built the world** *Binah,* the primordial house, generated *Shekhinah,* "the house
of the world," and through Her, the world.
See *Zohar* 1:33a.

528. ב ראשית (*bet reshit*)... The letter ב
(*bet*) indicates the number two and בית
(*bayit*), "house." The two houses, *Binah* and
Shekhinah, originate in the primordial point
of *Hokhmah* ("Wisdom"), known as ראשית
(*reshit*), *Beginning,* while *Shekhinah* is known
as *beginning of wisdom* (Psalms 111:10), the
starting point of the search for *Hokhmah.*
See *Zohar* 1:7b, 31b.

529. **Then it gathers...** *Shekhinah* gathers the flow of emanation.

them into itself, so waters continually flow and are absorbed within. This emerges from above. The sign of this secret: *From the womb of* מי (*mi*), *whom, emerged the ice* (Job 38:29),[530] its waters congealing to draw others in. This ice, this frozen sea—its waters flow only when the power of the South reaches it, drawing it close.[531] Then the waters that were congealed on the side of the North[532] are released and flow, for on the side of the North the waters congeal, and from the side of the South they are released and flow, watering all those beasts of the field, as is said: *watering all beasts of the field* (Psalms 104:11).[533] These are called *cleft mountains* (Song of Songs 2:17), mountains of separation,[534] all of whom are watered when the side of the South begins to draw near it.[535] Then waters flow, and through this supernal energy, all streams in joy.

When thought arises in joyous desire,[536] from the Concealed of all Concealed,[537] a concealed river is drawn forth from it.[538] They approach one another on a single path unknown above or below;[539] here lies the beginning of all. ב (*Bet*), anonymous *king*, was consummated by this beginning.[540] With this

174

530. *From the womb of* מי (*mi*), *whom, emerged the ice* Shekhinah emerged from the womb of *Binah*, known as מי (*Mi*), "Who" (or "Whom"). A spiritual seeker may inquire about Her, but such questions do not yield ordinary answers. The identity of the divine is discovered only in a realm beyond words. The mystical name "Who" becomes a focus of meditation, as question turns into quest. See Shim'on Lavi, *KP*, 1:91a: "Concerning everything that cannot be grasped, its question constitutes its answer."

See *Zohar* 1:1b, 45b, 85b–86a, 237b; 2:126b–127a, 138a, 139b, 226a, 231b.

531. **its waters flow only...** The frozen sea of *Shekhinah* thaws only through the warmth of *Ḥesed*, the *sefirah* of flowing love, associated with the warm South. See *Zohar* 1:152a, 161b; 2:30a; Moses de León, *Shushan Edut*, 341.

532. **on the side of the North** Due to the influence of *Gevurah*, or *Din* (severe "Judgment"), associated with the North.

533. **all those beasts of the field...** The forces, including the *ḥayyot* ("living creatures, animals, beasts") beneath *Shekhinah*, who is known as "field" or Holy Apple Orchard.

See *Zohar* 1:107a, 122a, 128b, 142b, 224b; 2:61b; 3:84a. Cf. BT *Ta'anit* 29b; *Bereshit Rabbah* 65:22; Azriel of Gerona, *Peirush ha-Aggadot*, 35–37.

534. *cleft mountains...* הרי בתר (*Harei vater*). The word בתר (*vater*) in Song of Songs is interpreted variously and is probably derived from the root meaning "to cut, divide," thus denoting "jagged, craggy" mountains. In the *Zohar*, *cleft mountains* refers to the forces outside *Shekhinah* that are not included in the unified realm of the *sefirot*. See *Zohar* 1:62a, 158a; 2:234a–b.

535. **near it** Near *Shekhinah*, the frozen sea.

536. **When thought arises...** When *Ḥokhmah* emerges from *Keter*, known as Desire.

537. **Concealed of all Concealed** *Ein Sof* or *Keter*, the most hidden recesses of divinity. See *Zohar* 2:234b.

538. **concealed river...** *Binah* emanates from *Ḥokhmah*.

539. **They approach one another...** *Ḥokhmah* and *Binah* meet on a secret path described below.

540. ב (*Bet*), anonymous *king*... The opening letter of the Torah, the ב (*bet*) of

energy,[541] אלהים (*Elohim*), *God, created heaven* (Genesis 1:1)—the hidden one, hidden river whose waters flow forth, created, generated a voice from within, called "voice of the shofar."[542] This is: אלהים (*Elohim*), *God, created heaven.* *Heaven* rules over *earth* by the life of the supernal king, as indicated by: *The son of Jesse lives on earth* (1 Samuel 20:31), for life depends on *the son of Jesse.*[543] Through that life He[544] rules over all, and earth is thereby nourished, as is written: ואת הארץ (*ve-et ha-arets*), *and earth* (Genesis, ibid.)—the ו (*vav*) added to regulate the nourishment of earth;[545] את (*et*) above, the lower power comprising twenty-two letters generated by *God* for *heaven,* as is written: *the crown with which his mother crowned him on his wedding day* (Song of Songs 3:11).[546] This is: את השמים (*et ha-shamayim*), *heaven,* merging one with the other, joining them together,[547] to endure as one through that life of the king, the anonymous king,[548] so that *heaven* thereby is nourished. ואת הארץ (*Ve-et ha-arets*),

בראשית (*Be-reshit*), *In the beginning,* stands for בית (*bayit*), *house,* and here indicates *Shekhinah,* who is also known as the anonymous *king.* See above, note 500. *Shekhinah* is emanated (or "consummated") through the union of *Ḥokhmah* and *Binah.* So the opening word of the Torah spans the range of *sefirot,* from *Shekhinah* (ב [*bet*]) to *Ḥokhmah,* known as ראשית (*reshit*), *beginning.* Alternatively, *king* here refers to *Binah.*

541. **With this energy**   With the energy of *Ḥokhmah.* See above, page 110.

542. **the hidden one…**   *Binah,* known as אלהים (*Elohim*), generated *Tif'eret* (*heaven*), who emerges from Her as a blast from the shofar.

543. ***Heaven* rules over *earth* by the life…**   *Tif'eret* rules over *Shekhinah* by the vivifying energy that flows from *Binah* to *Yesod,* who is known as *the son of Jesse* and "Vitality of the Worlds." See above, note 214; *Zohar* 1:29a; 2:175b.

544. **He**   *Tif'eret.*

545. **the ו (*vav*) added…**   The ו (*vav*), meaning *and,* has a numerical value of six, alluding to *Tif'eret* and the five *sefirot* surrounding Him (*Ḥesed* to *Yesod*). The appearance of the letter here in the phrase ואת הארץ (*ve-et ha-arets*), *and earth,* indicates that *Tif'eret* conducts nourishment to *Shekhinah,* known as both את (*et*) and *earth.* See above, pages 112–14.

546. **את (*et*) above, the lower power…**

Grammatically, the accusative particle *et* has no ascertainable independent sense, but Naḥum of Gimzo and his disciple Rabbi Akiva taught that when *et* appears in a biblical verse, it amplifies the original meaning. See BT *Pesaḥim* 22b; *Ḥagigah* 12a; *Zohar* 1:247a; 2:90a, 135b.

את (*Et*) comprises the entire alphabet, the letters from א (*alef*) to ת (*tav*), and is therefore an appropriate name for *Shekhinah,* last of the *sefirot,* who is known as both the mystical realm of speech and Oral Torah. See the Christian parallel in Revelation 1:8: "I am *alpha* and *omega.*"

Here the *Zohar* indicates that the letters were generated by *Binah,* the Divine Mother, for the wedding of *Tif'eret* and *Shekhinah,* who is also known as *Atarah* ("Crown"). The word "above" (in "את [*et*] above") may refer to the preceding occurrence of את (*et*) in the phrase את השמים (*et ha-shamayim*), *heaven.*

547. **את השמים (*et ha-shamayim*), *heaven*…**   The words imply the union of *Shekhinah,* known as את (*et*), and *Tif'eret,* *heaven.*

548. **life of the king, the anonymous king**   The flow of emanation from *Binah* is called "life of the king" because it animates *Shekhinah,* the anonymous king.

See above, pages 170 and 173 (and note 500); *Zohar* 3:58a; Naḥmanides on Genesis 2:7; Numbers 30:3. Alternatively, *king* here refers to *Binah.*

And earth—union of male and female,[549] graved in traced letters, and the life of the king drawn from the world above to *heaven*, sustaining *earth* and all her habitants.[550]

The mystery of supreme אלהים (*Elohim*)[551] fashioned *heaven* and *earth* to endure, generating them as one by supreme energy, beginning of all.[552] Similarly the supreme mystery descended, and the final one fashioned *heaven* and *earth* below.[553] The mystery of all: ב (*bet*). Both of them are worlds,[554] which created worlds, this one an upper world, this one a lower world, one corresponding to the other; this one *heaven* and *earth*, this one *heaven* and *earth*.[555] So, ב (*bet*): there are two worlds, one generating two worlds, the other generating two worlds, all through the energy of supernal ראשית (*reshit*), *beginning*.[556] Above descended below,[557] who was filled by way of a certain rung resting upon Her,[558] corresponding to that secret, hidden path, concealed above,[559] though one is a narrow path and one is a way. The one below is a way, as is said: *The way of the righteous is like gleaming light* (Proverbs 4:18),[560] while the one above is a path, as is written: *a path unknown to any vulture* (Job 28:7). The mystery of all is: *who makes a way through the sea and a path through raging waters* (Isaiah 43:16). Similarly it is written: *Your way is through the sea, Your path through mighty waters* (Psalms 77:20).[561]

176

549. ואת הארץ (*Ve-et ha-arets*), *And earth*... Here, too, the wording implies the union of *Tif'eret*, known as ו (*vav*), and *Shekhinah*, known as both את (*et*) and *earth*. See above notes 545–46.

550. **the world above... heaven... earth...** *Binah, Tif'eret*, and *Shekhinah*.

551. **The mystery of supreme אלהים (*Elohim*)** *Binah*.

552. **beginning of all** An allusion to *Hokhmah, Binah's* origin and partner.

553. **the supernal mystery descended...** The process of emanation continued until *Shekhinah*, last of the *sefirot*, who generated the physical *heaven* and *earth*.

554. **Both of them are worlds** See *Bereshit Rabbah* 1:10: "Rabbi Yehudah son of Pazzi expounded on the act of Creation together with Bar Kappara. 'Why was the world created with ב (*bet*)? To inform you that there are two worlds: this world and the world that is coming.'" Here the *Zohar* alludes to two sefirotic realms: *Binah* and *Shekhinah*.

555. **which created worlds...** *Binah* and *Shekhinah* each yield a world comprising *heaven* and *earth*. *Binah* emanates *Tif'eret* and *Shekhinah*, while *Shekhinah* generates *heaven* and *earth* below.

See *Zohar* 1:240b; Moses de León, *Sefer ha-Rimmon*, 192.

556. **supernal ראשית (*reshit*), *beginning*** *Hokhmah*, the primordial point of emanation. See above, page 109.

557. **Above descended below** *Tif'eret* joined *Shekhinah*.

558. **certain rung...** *Yesod*, who channels the flow of emanation to *Shekhinah*.

559. **that secret, hidden path...** The subtle link between the primordial point of *Hokhmah* and the womb of the Divine Mother, *Binah*.

See *Zohar* 1:3b; 2:122b–123a; 3:61b.

560. ***The way of the righteous...*** The verse associates *way* with *righteous*, a name of *Yesod*.

561. ***who makes a way...*** Both verses connect *way* (symbolizing *Yesod*) with the

When the world above was filled and impregnated, like a female impregnated by a male, it generated two children as one, male and female, who are *heaven* and *earth,* as above.[562] *Earth* is nourished by the waters of *heaven,*[563] released into her, though the upper are male and the lower female,[564] the lower nourished by the male. The lower waters call to the upper, like a female opening to the male, pouring out water toward the water of the male to form seed.[565] The female is nourished by the male, as is written: ואת הארץ (*ve-et ha-arets*), *and earth,* with the additional ו (*vav*), as mentioned.[566]

It is written: *Lift your eyes on high and see: Who created these?* (Isaiah 40:26). Letters were engraved [30a] in actualizing all, in actualizing above and below.[567] Subsequently letters were traced and inscribed in Scripture. ב (*Bet*): ברא (*bara*), *created;* א (*alef*): את (*et*).[568] ב (*Bet*): ברא (*bara*), *created,* indeed, as explained.[569]

---

sea (*Shekhinah*), and *path* (the subtle link) with powerful *waters* (*Binah*).

562. **When the world above...** After *Binah* was impregnated by Her partner, *Ḥokhmah,* She gave birth to *Tif'eret* and *Shekhinah,* known as *heaven* and *earth,* who resembled their parents. See *Zohar* 2:85b–86a.

563. ***Earth* is nourished by the waters of *heaven*** *Shekhinah* is fed the flow of emanation from *Tif'eret.*

564. **the upper are male and the lower female** See *Bereshit Rabbah* 13:13: "Rabbi Shim'on son of El'azar said, 'Every single handbreadth [of water] descending from above is met by two handbreadths emitted by the earth. What is the reason? *Deep calls to deep...*(Psalms 42:8).' Rabbi Levi said, 'The upper waters are male; the lower, female. The former cry to the latter, "Receive us! You are creatures of the blessed Holy One and we are His messengers." They immediately receive them, as is written: *Let the earth open* (Isaiah 45:8)—like a female opening to a male.'"

See *Tosefta, Ta'anit* 1:4; 1 *Enoch* 54:8; *Seder Rabbah di-Vreshit,* 10 (*Battei Midrashot,* 1:25); *Pirqei de-Rabbi Eli'ezer* 23; *Zohar* 1:17b, 46a, 60b, 244a–b, 245b; 3:223b. Here the upper and lower waters symbolize *Tif'eret* and *Shekhinah.*

565. **pouring out water...** *Shekhinah* stimulates the flow from *Tif'eret.* According

to the second-century Greek physician Galen, sperm is generated by both male and female. See Leviticus 12:2: *When a woman yields seed.* Cf. Ibn Ezra, Naḥmanides, Baḥya ben Asher, and Sforno, ad loc.; BT *Berakhot* 60a; *Niddah* 31a.

566. **with the additional ו (*vav*)...** Indicating *Tif'eret,* who nourishes *Shekhinah,* known as both את (*et*) and *earth.* See above, note 545.

567. **Letters were engraved...** The process of emanation above and physical creation below unfolded through the medium of language, conveyed by the letters of the alphabet. According to *Sefer Yetsirah* 1:1–2, God created the world by means of "thirty-two wondrous paths of wisdom," namely, the twenty-two letters of the Hebrew alphabet and the ten *sefirot.*

568. **ב (*Bet*): ברא (*bara*), *created;* א (*alef*): את (*et*)** The first two letters of the Hebrew alphabet appear as the initial letters of the first four words of the Torah. The first two words, בראשית ברא (*Be-reshit bara*), *In the beginning created,* begin with the letter ב (*bet*); the next two words, אלהים את (*Elohim et*), *God,* begin with א (*alef*). Some manuscripts and witnesses include all four words, but apparently the focus is on these two.

569. **ב (*Bet*): ברא (*bara*), *created,* indeed...** The letter ב (*bet*) symbolizes *Binah* (above, pages 173–76), who emanated

177

ב (*Bet*): ברא (*bara*), *created,* indeed, by supreme energy.[570] ב (*Bet*), female; א (*alef*), male.[571] As ב (*bet*) *created,* so א (*alef*) generated letters, totality of twenty-two letters.[572] ה (*He*) generated שמים (*shamayim*), *heaven:* השמים (*ha-shamayim*), *the heaven,* enlivening it, embedding it.[573] ו (*Vav*) generated הארץ (*ha-arets*), *earth,* to nourish her, array her, provide her the gratification she deserves.[574] ואת הארץ (*Ve-et ha-arets*), *And earth,* for ו (*vav*) takes את (*et*), totality of twenty-two letters, and *earth* is nourished, absorbing them within, as is said: *All the rivers flow into the sea* (Ecclesiastes 1:7).[575] This is the mystery of: ואת הארץ (*ve-et ha-arets*), *and earth,* union of male and female.[576] All is gathered to the female, who absorbs them. *Earth* received ואת (*ve-et*), absorbing them as nourishment.

The impact of a word[577] is discovered in its cudgels.[578] The fortress of vapor is discovered on earth.[579]

When flashing fire flows, aroused on the left, it seizes Her and smoke ascends, as is said: *Mount Sinai was all in smoke, for YHVH had descended upon it in fire* (Exodus 19:18)—this is fire, this is smoke.[580] And it is written: *the mountain smoking* (Exodus 20:15). For as fire descends, they cling to each other:

178

the lower *sefirot.* The rest of this paragraph appears with slight variation in *Zohar* 2:234b.

570. **by supreme energy** By the power of *Ḥokhmah.*

571. **ב (*Bet*), female; א (*alef*), male** The two letters symbolize *Binah* and *Ḥokhmah.* See *Zohar* 1:200a; 2:228a; *ZḤ* 74c (*ShS*).

572. **so א (*alef*) generated letters...** From *Hokhmah* emanation streamed in the form of letters to *Binah* and below.

573. **ה (*He*) generated...heaven...** The fifth word of the Torah, השמים (*ha-shamayim*), *the heaven,* consists of the letter ה (*he*), the second letter of יהוה (*YHVH*), alluding to *Binah,* and שמים (*shamayim*), *heaven,* signifying *Tif'eret,* who emanated from *Binah.*

See *Zohar* 1:12b, 33b, 241b; 2:137a; 3:176; and the parallel in 2:234b.

574. **ו (*Vav*) generated הארץ (*ha-arets*), *earth*...** The letter ו (*vav*), the third letter of יהוה (*YHVH*), has a numerical value of six and symbolizes *Tif'eret* together with the five *sefirot* surrounding Him. *Tif'eret* emanated *Shekhinah,* symbolized by *earth.*

575. **for ו (*vav*) takes את (*et*)...** The word ואת (*ve-et*), *and,* consists of ו (*vav*), *and,* symbolizing *Tif'eret* (see above, note 574), and את (*et*), representing all twenty-two letters of the alphabet, from א (*alef*) to ת (*tav*), the entire flow of emanation (see above, note 546). *Tif'eret* conveys this flow to *Shekhinah,* who is symbolized by both *earth* and *sea.* She is the sea into which stream all the rivers, the lower *sefirot.*

576. **male and female** *Tif'eret* and *Shekhinah.*

577. **a word** מלה (*Millah*), "Word" or "thing."

578. **its cudgels** קולפוי (*Qulpoi*), "Its clubs." See above, note 513.

579. **The fortress of vapor...** קוסטרא דקוטרא (*Qustera de-qutra*). *Qustera* derives from the Latin *castrum* (pl. *castra*), "fortress, castle." See above, note 514. The phrase here alludes to *Shekhinah;* see immediately below.

580. **When flashing fire flows...** When the *sefirah* of *Gevurah,* symbolized by fire, is aroused, it stimulates *Shekhinah,* symbolized by smoke. See *Zohar* 1:70a–b.

smoke and fire. So all endures on the side of the left.[581] This is the mystery of: *My own hand founded earth, My right hand spread out heaven* (Isaiah 48:13), by the power of the right above.[582] In this manner *heaven* was fashioned, for He is male, and the male emerges from the side of the right, while the female emerges from the side of the left,[583] as is written: *My own hand founded earth.*

Lift your eyes on high and see: Who created these? (Isaiah 40:26). Words extend till here; beyond, one does not inquire.[584] For Wisdom was consummated by Nothingness[585] and is insusceptible to questioning, for it is concealed deep; no one fathoms it. Once a deep river emanates,[586] it becomes susceptible to question, though concealed from everything below,[587] and in accord with questioning is called מי (*Mi*), Who.[588] מי (*Mi*), *Who, created these.*[589] This is the secret of which we have spoken: *From the womb of* מי (*mi*), *whom, emerged the ice* (Job 38:29)—*the womb of mi*, indeed:[590] the one susceptible to question— though one does not ask, "What is above?" "What is below?"[591]—seeking rather

581. **So all endures on the side of the left** By stimulating *Shekhinah* to join *Tif'eret*, the fire of *Gevurah* ensures the continued flow of emanation and the generation of the lower worlds.

582. *My own hand founded earth...* Since both *hand* and *right hand* are mentioned in the verse, it is assumed that *hand* denotes the left hand (symbolizing *Gevurah*), who *founded earth* (symbolizing *Shekhinah*). *Tif'eret*, on the other hand, emanated from *Hesed*, the divine *right hand*.

583. **the male emerges from the side of the right...** The male is associated with *Hesed*, the female with *Gevurah*.

584. **Words extend till here...** Concerning *Binah*, known as *Who*, one can speak, or at least pose a question. Beyond this realm, the divine mind is impenetrable.

585. **For Wisdom was consummated by Nothingness** The *sefirah* of *Hokhmah* ("Wisdom") emerged from *Keter*, who is known as אין (*Ayin*), "Nothingness," because this ultimate stage of divinity is inconceivable, the divine no-thingness. Wisdom shares in the incomprehensibility of *Ayin*.

586. **Once a deep river emanates** Once *Binah* emanates from the primordial point of *Hokhmah*.

587. **concealed from everything below** Even from the *sefirot* emerging from Her. According to the Gnostic *Gospel of Truth*

(22:27–29), the aeons (divine emanations) below *Nous* ("Intellect") are unaware of hidden divinity: "It was quite amazing that they were in the Father without knowing Him." The phrase here can also be rendered: "concealed more than anything below."

588. **it is called מי (*Mi*), Who** Or, "they [namely, the lower *sefirot*] call it Who." *Binah* is known as מי (*Mi*), Who, because when a spiritual seeker inquires about Her, the questions do not yield ordinary answers. The identity of the divine is discovered only in a realm beyond words. The mystical name Who becomes a focus of meditation, as question turns into quest. See Shim'on Lavi, *KP*, 1:91a: "Concerning everything that cannot be grasped, its question constitutes its answer."

See *Zohar* 1:1b, 45b, 85b–86a, 237b; 2:126b– 127a, 138a, 139b, 226a, 231b.

589. מי (*Mi*), *Who, created these* The question is transformed into a declaration: *Binah* emanated the lower seven *sefirot*, known as *these*. See above, pages 5–9.

590. *From the womb of* מי (*mi*), *whom, emerged the ice...* *Shekhinah*, the sea whose waters congeal and thaw, emerged from the womb of *Binah*. See above, page 174.

591. **"What is above?" "What is below?"** See M *Hagigah* 2:1: "Whoever contemplates four things, it would be better for him if he

the site of their issuance,[592] knowing yet not knowing it,[593] for we cannot. Susceptible to questioning, not knowing.

בראשית: ב' ראשית (*Be-reshit: bet reshit*), *bet, beginning*.[594] Is ראשית (*reshit*), *beginning*, an utterance, or should we say that בראשית (*Be-reshit*), *In the beginning*, is an utterance?[595] As long as its energy has not emerged and expanded, all concealed within, it is בראשית (*Be-reshit*), *In the beginning*, an utterance.[596] Once potencies emerge and expand, it is called ראשית (*reshit*), *beginning*, an utterance of its own.

מי (*Mi*), *Who*, a question, the one who created אלה (*elleh*), *these*.[597] Afterward, once it expanded and consummated itself, it became ים (*yam*), ocean,[598] creating below, fashioning everything exactly as above, one corresponding to the other, reflecting one another, both of them ב (*bet*).[599]

It is written: *While the king was reclining* (Song of Songs 1:12).[600] *Reclining*—settling with the lower kingdom in the mystery of that intimacy of delight in

180

had not come into the world: what is above, what is below, what before, and what after."

These Mishnaic restrictions on cosmological speculation recall the Gnostic striving after "the knowledge of who we were, what we have become, where we were, where we have been thrown, where we hasten, from what we are redeemed, what birth is, and what is rebirth" (Clement of Alexandria, *Excerpts from Theodotus* 78:2). Here the restriction is applied to probing the origin and essence of *Binah*.

592. **the site of their issuance**   Where the lower *sefirot* emerge from *Binah*.

593. **yet not knowing it**   Not knowing the essence of *Binah* Herself.

594. בראשית: ב' ראשית (***Be-reshit: bet reshit***), ***bet, beginning***   The opening word of the Torah, בראשית (*Be-reshit*), *In the beginning*, is divided into the letter ב (*bet*), and ראשית (*reshit*), *beginning*. In KP this paragraph appears several paragraphs below, following the phrase "constituting peace for the world."

595. **Is** ראשית (***reshit***), ***beginning*, an utterance...**   According to M *Avot* 5:1, "The world was created through ten utterances [or: sayings, commands]." Only nine explicit commands appear in Genesis 1, but the decade is completed by counting the phrase *In*

the beginning. See BT *Rosh ha-Shanah* 32a, *Megillah* 21b; cf. *Zohar* 1:15a, 16b; *TZ* 32, 76a.

Here the *Zohar* asks whether the tenth command is represented by the entire word בראשית (*Be-reshit*), *In the beginning*, or just by ראשית (*reshit*), *beginning*.

596. **As long as its energy...**   As long as the primordial point of Ḥokhmah has not expanded, it is called בראשית (*Be-reshit*), *In the beginning*, which signifies that Ḥokhmah, known as ראשית (*reshit*), *beginning*, includes what will emerge as *Binah*, symbolized by the initial ב (*bet*). See above, page 111.

597. אלה (***elleh***), ***these***   The lower seven *sefirot*, who emerge from *Binah*.

598. ים (***yam***), **ocean**   *Shekhinah*, who collects all the rivers, the *sefirot*. The letters of מי (*mi*) and ים (*yam*) are identical; *Shekhinah* consummates *Binah*. See *Zohar* 1:86a.

599. **fashioning everything exactly as above...**   *Shekhinah* creates the world below, which corresponds to the world of the *sefirot*, emanated by *Binah*. Both creative forces are indicated by the letter ב (*bet*), whose numerical value is two. See above, pages 173–76.

600. ***While the king was reclining***   The verse continues: *my spikenard spread its fragrance*.

Eden above,[601] by that hidden, concealed, unknown path by which He is filled, issuing in well-known streams.[602] *My spikenard spread its fragrance*—the lower king who created a world below resembling the one above.[603] A redolent, supreme fragrance ascends to preside and perform, enduring, prevailing, sparkling with transcendent light.[604]

The world was created in two modes, by the right and by the left, by six transcendent days.[605] Six days were fashioned to radiate, as is said: *Six days YHVH made, heaven and earth* (Exodus 31:17).[606] These dug pathways and drilled sixty holes into the immense abyss—hollows conducting the water of streams into the abyss.[607] So we have learned: "The hollows were formed from the six days of Creation,"[608] constituting peace for the world.

The earth was תהו ובהו (*tohu va-vohu*), *chaos and void* (Genesis 1:2)—dregs of an inkwell in seepage.[609] For at first it existed but did not endure: *was*

601. **settling with the lower kingdom...** *Binah,* the supreme *king,* joins *Shekhinah,* who is often called *Malkhut* ("Kingdom"). Their union reflects that between *Hokhmah*—known as *Eden*—and *Binah.* See *Zohar* 2:227b.

602. **by that hidden, concealed, unknown path...** The subtle link between *Hokhmah* and *Binah.* See *Zohar* 1:3b, 29a; 2:122b–123a; 3:61b. Once filled by this path, *Binah* emanates the lower *sefirot,* the "well-known streams."

603. **lower king...** *Shekhinah.*

604. **A redolent, supreme fragrance ascends...** The arousal of *Shekhinah* stimulates the forces above.

605. **by the right and by the left...** By *sefirot* on the right side, characterized by *Hesed,* and on the left, characterized by *Gevurah.* The *sefirot* from *Hesed* to *Yesod* are symbolized by the six days of Creation.

606. **Six days were fashioned to radiate...** The six cosmic days, the *sefirot* from *Hesed* to *Yesod,* emanated from *Binah,* culminating in *Shekhinah* and the creation below. The plain meaning of the verse, *For in six days YHVH made heaven and earth,* is abandoned in favor of a hyperliteral reading, which emphasizes the lack of the preposition ב (*be*), *in,* before *six days,* thereby turning the *six days* into the object of YHVH's

creative power: the *six days* were themselves fashioned, or emanated. The phrase *heaven and earth* refers to *Tif'eret* and *Shekhinah,* whose union marks the consummation of the cosmic week. See *Bahir* 55 (82).

607. **These dug pathways...** These six *sefirot* channeled the flow of emanation to *Shekhinah,* "the immense abyss," through sixty openings. The *Zohar* is playing on the homonyms שיתין (*shittin*), "sixty," and שיתין (*shitin*), "hollows, pits."

608. **So we have learned...** See BT *Sukkah* 49a: "Rabbah son of Bar Hana said in the name of Rabbi Yohanan, 'The hollows [under the Temple altar into which the wine and water of libation flowed] were formed during the six days of Creation.'" The *Zohar* indicates that the openings into *Shekhinah* were formed not just *during* the six days of Creation but *by* "the six days of Creation," by the six *sefirot.*

According to Rabbi Yose (*Tosefta, Sukkah* 3:15), the hollows penetrated to the abyss. Cf. *Zohar* 1:56a; *ZH* 62d–63a (*ShS*).

609. **dregs of an inkwell in seepage** סוספיתא דקמרי גו קולטוי (*Suspita de-qamrei go qultoi*), one of the *Zohar's* typical mystifying phrases constructed out of rare or invented words.

סוספיתא (*Suspita*) is a neologism apparently based on Aramaic כוספא (*kuspa*), "pomace,

already,⁶¹⁰ later enduring. In forty-two letters the world was engraved and endured, all of them crowning the holy name.⁶¹¹ As they permutate, letters ascend [30b] and descend, crowning themselves in the four directions of the world, so the world may endure, while these endure through the doings of the world.⁶¹² Scribal patterns of impress appear here by the seal of the signet.⁶¹³ They entered and emerged, letter by letter, and the world was created. They entered the seal, permutated, and the world endured by the cudgels of the

husk, residue." See *Zohar* 1:71b, 118b, 228a; 2:24b, 203a, 224b, 236b; *Bei'ur ha-Millim ha-Zarot,* 182; *KP; Scholem, Major Trends,* 389, n. 54; Liebes, *Peraqim,* 336–38.

קמרי (*Qamrei*) is a variation on קלמרין (*qalmarin*), "inkwell," and the Greek *qala-marion;* see *Arukh,* s.v. *qamrin.* As for קולטוי (*qultoi*), rendered here "seepage," the root קלט (*qlt*) means "to absorb, receive."

The dregs are the forces of evil left over after the refining process of emanation, the residue of ink remaining after the divine writer has sketched the *sefirot.* Here the *Zohar* indicates that *Shekhinah,* known as *earth,* was still in a chaotic state, since the dregs had not been completely separated from the sefirotic realm of holiness.

See *Bereshit Rabbah* 10:2: "*Remove the dross from the silver... [and a vessel emerges for the refiner]* (Proverbs 25:4). Rabbi Eli'ezer said, 'This can be compared to a bath full of water, in which were two beautiful sculptured disks. As long as it was full of water, the artistry of the disks could not be seen, but as soon as it was unplugged and the water emptied, the artistry could be seen. Similarly, as long as תהו ובהו (*tohu va-vohu*), *chaos and void,* was in the world, the artistry of heaven and earth could not be seen, but as soon as *tohu va-vohu* was eradicated from the world, the artistry of heaven could be seen: *A vessel emerges for the refiner.*" See Azriel of Gerona, *Peirush ha-Aggadot,* 104–5.

610. *was* **already** See *Bereshit Rabbah* 1:15: "Rabbi Ḥanin said, '... *The earth was* —it already had been [i.e., it preceded the creation of heaven].'"

Here the point is that before She attained enduring existence, *Shekhinah* (the *earth*) was

in chaos. Cf. above, page 118 (and note 75), *Zohar* 1:39b, 262b–263a (*Hash*); Tishby, *Wisdom of the Zohar,* 2:460–64.

611. **In forty-two letters...** The forty-two-letter name is mentioned in the name of Rav, though not recorded, in BT *Qiddu-shin* 71a. According to one later view, it consists of the first forty-two letters of the To-rah, from the ב (*bet*) of בראשית (*Be-reshit*) through the ב (*bet*) of בהו (*bohu*), *void* (Genesis 1:2).

See *Tosafot, Ḥagigah* 11b, s.v. *ein doreshin; KP* 1:46c–d; Trachtenberg, *Jewish Magic and Superstition,* 94–95; cf. Maimonides, *Guide of the Perplexed* 1:62; *Zohar* 1:1a, 15b; 2:130b, 132b, 175b, 234a–b.

The forty-two letters crown the name יהוה (*YHVH*) or *Shekhinah,* known as "the name" of God. See *MM; Sullam; Zohar* 2:132b.

612. **while these endure through the doings...** The permutations of letters animate the world, while they themselves are sustained by righteous action below.

613. **Scribal patterns of impress...** טופסרא דקילטא (*Tufsera de-qilta*). In the *Zohar, tufsera* (or *tufsira*) means either "mold, form, configuration" (based on טופסא [*tufsa*], derived from the Greek *tupos*), or "royal dignitary" (based on טפסרא [*tafsera*], derived from biblical טפסר [*tifsar*], "marshal, scribe"). See above, page 155: "All the letters were arrayed in their wheels by the expanding טופסירא דקוטרא (*tufsira de-qutra*), scribal matrix of the nexus."

See Jeremiah 51:27; Nahum 3:17; *Zohar* 1:96b, 157a, 241b, 242b, 243b; 3:120a, 270b; *Bei'ur ha-Millim ha-Zarot,* 178–80, 185.

As mentioned previously (note 609), the root קלט (*qlt*) means "to absorb, receive." Cf.

182

mighty serpent.[614] They struck and penetrated chasms of dust 1500 cubits.[615] Then the immense abyss ascended in darkness, and darkness covered all, until light emanated, split the darkness, and radiated, as is written: *Revealing depths out of darkness, bringing pitch-blackness to light* (Job 12:22).[616] Water was measured by the handful,[617] 1500 by fingers dripping thrice into the balance,[618] half for sustenance, half entering below, these rising, these falling. Once they rise by the handful, the balance stands even, inclining neither right nor left, as is written: *Who measured the waters with the hollow of His hand...?* (Isaiah 40:12).[619] All was within Earth, concealed and unrevealed.[620] Energy, power, and water congealed within Her, neither flowing nor expanding until a light from above shone upon Her. The light struck sponginess,[621] and Her energy

---

Zohar 2:235b (*Tos*): טיפסרא דקולטא (*tifsera de-qulta*). Here letters of creation are being stamped by the divine seal.

614. **by the cudgels of the mighty serpent** See *Pirqei de-Rabbi Eli'ezer* 9, where it is said of Leviathan: "Between his fins stands the axis of Earth." Cf. *Seder Rabbah di-Vreshit*, 17 (*Battei Midrashot*, 1:28): "The entire world stands on one fin of Leviathan." See *Midrash Konen* (*Beit ha-Midrash*, 2:26); *Zohar* 2:34b, 108b; 3:279a (*RM*).

615. **1500 cubits** The letters penetrate 1500 cubits beneath the surface of the earth. The number appears in rabbinic discussions of the abyss. According to JT *Sanhedrin* 10:2 (29a), "When [King] David began digging the foundations of the Temple, he dug 1500 cubits without finding the abyss." When he finally penetrated the abyss, "it rose and threatened to drown the world." David's adviser, Ahitophel, managed to subdue the abyss by reciting a divine name, upon which David sang the fifteen Psalms of Ascent (Psalms 120–134), one psalm for each 100 cubits.

See the tradition reported in the name of Rabbi Yoḥanan (BT *Sukkah* 53a–b): "When David dug the hollows [beneath the site of the Temple], the abyss arose and threatened to drown the world.... [David] inscribed the [divine] Name on a shard and cast it into the abyss, and it subsided 16,000 cubits. When he saw that it had subsided so far, he said, 'The higher it is raised, the more the earth

will be watered.' So he sang the fifteen Ascents and raised it 15,000 cubits, leaving it 1000 cubits [below the surface]." Cf. *Zohar* 3:198b.

616. **split the darkness, and radiated...** See the *Zohar*'s description of the beginning of emanation (1:15a): "It split and did not split its aura."

617. **the handful** תיקלא (*Tiqla*), a Zoharic neologism derived from the root תקל (*tql*), "weigh." The word has a wide range of meaning: "hollow of the hand, fist, water clock (1:92b), potter's wheel, scale." See *Bei-'ur ha-Millim ha-Zarot*, 178; Baer, *History*, 1:437, n. 24; Liebes, *Peraqim*, 331; and Isaiah 40:12, cited several lines below.

618. **1500 by fingers dripping thrice...** Three handfuls of water, each including five fingers, drip into the balance, thereby conveying a total of fifteen (hundred) units. See Rashi on BT *Menaḥot* 29b, s.v. *aḥat be-he va-aḥat be-yod*.

619. *Who measured the waters with the hollow of His hand* The verse continues in parallelism: *gauged the skies with a span, meted the dust of the earth with a measure, and weighed the mountains with a scale and the hills with a balance?*

620. **All was within Earth...** Concealed within *Shekhinah*.

621. **sponginess** קולטוי (*Qultoi*), "Its absorption," the congealed substance within *Shekhinah*. See above, page 181: "dregs of an inkwell in seepage," and note 609 there.

was released, as is written: *God said, "Let there be light!" And there was light* (Genesis 1:3)—primordial, transcendent light, already existent.[622] From here issued all powers and forces, so Earth turned firm and fragrant,[623] generating Her potencies. As the light shone, its radiance blazed from one end of the universe to the other. When it gazed upon the wicked of the world, it hid itself away, emerging only by its paths, concealed, unrevealed.[624]

God saw that the light כי טוב *(ki tov), was good* (Genesis 1:4). We have learned: Every dream enjoying the status of כי טוב *(ki tov), that it was good,* fosters peace above and below.[625] One sees letters corresponding to his ways, every single

622. primordial, transcendent light, already existent   The light of *Ḥesed,* which manifested on the first day of Creation but existed primordially. See *Bereshit Rabbah* 3:2: "It is not written here אור והיה (*Ve-hayah or*) [which could mean either *And there will be light* or *And there was light*], but rather ויהי אור (*Vayhi or*) [which can mean only] *And there was light*—it already was." Theodor (ad loc.) regards this as a scribal gloss. In any case, the point in the Midrash is that the creation of light was instantaneous and effortless, whereas here the *Zohar* emphasizes that the light preexisted—it already *was.*

See *Bahir* 17 (25), elaborating on *Bereshit Rabbah*: "Rabbi Berekhiah said, 'Why is it written *God said, "Let there be light!"* ויהי אור (*Vayhi or*), *And there was light,* and not והיה (*Ve-hayah*) [which could mean either *And there will be* or *And there was*]? This can be compared to a king who had a beautiful object and set it aside until he had prepared a place for it; then he placed it there. As is written: *"Let there be light!" And there was light.* For it already *was.*'"

See Ezra of Gerona, *Peirush Shir ha-Shirim,* 494; Azriel of Gerona, *Peirush ha-Aggadot,* 109; *Zohar* 1:16b, 45b; 3:245b (*RM*); *ZḤ* 1a, 37d; Recanati on Genesis 1:3, 3c.

623. turned firm and fragrant   אתבסמת (*Itbassamat*), "Was sweetened" or "was firmly established." The root *bsm* conveys both senses.

See *Bereshit Rabbah* 66:2; *Midrash She-mu'el* 26:4; *Zohar* 1:31a, 34a, 37a, 56a, 137a; 2:143a, 168a, 227a; 3:18a; N. Bronsnick, in *Sinai* 63 (1968): 81–85; Scholem, *Major Trends,* 165, 388, n. 44; idem, *Kabbalah,* 228.

624. its radiance blazed...   See BT *Ḥagigah* 12a: "Rabbi El'azar said, 'With the light created by the blessed Holy One on the first day, one could gaze and see from one end of the universe to the other. When the blessed Holy One foresaw the corrupt deeds of the generation of the Flood and the generation of the Dispersion [the generation of the Tower of Babel], He immediately hid it from them, as is written: *The light of the wicked is withheld* (Job 38:15). For whom did He hide it? For the righteous in the time to come.'"

See *Bereshit Rabbah* 3:6; 41:3; *Shemot Rabbah* 35:1; *Tanḥuma, Shemini* 9; *Bahir* 97–98 (147); *Zohar* 1:31b–32a, 45b–46a, 47a; 2:127a, 148b–149a, 220a–b; 3:88a, 173b.

625. Every dream...   See BT *Bava Qamma* 55a: "Rabbi Yehoshu'a said, 'One who sees [the letter] ט (*tet*) in a dream should regard it as a good omen. Why so?...Because Scripture inaugurated it with goodness, for from בראשית (*Be-reshit*), *In the beginning,* up to *God saw the light,* no ט (*tet*) occurs.'" Since the first ט (*tet*) in Scripture begins the word טוב (*tov*), *good,* it is a good omen to see ט (*tet*) in a dream.

See *Zohar* 2:152a, 230a; *ZḤ* 63b (*ShS*); Liebes, *Peraqim,* 366.

one.[626] If he sees ט (*tet*)—טב (*tav*), *good* for him, *good* for his dream,[627] for the Torah inaugurated it with כי טוב (*ki tov*), *that it was good,*[628] radiating from one end of the universe to the other. ט (*Tet*)—טב (*tav*), *good,* consummate radiance. ט (*Tet*), ninth of all,[629] a letter radiating from Primordial One above, contained within,[630] coming to be in the secrecy of the point, mystery of י (*yod*), singular point.[631] From its energy emerged ו (*vav*), whereby heaven came into being.[632] When it culminated in a single point and was hidden within a letter, ב (*bet*) glowed.[633] From it emerged above and below—above, concealed; below, revealed—in the mystery of two,[634] existing by the energy above. This is טוב (*tov*), *good.* These three letters, טו"ב (*tet, vav, bet*), later merged into the Righteous One of the world, who embraces all, above and below, as is said: *Say of the righteous one* כי טוב (*ki tov*), *that he is good* (Isaiah 3:10),[635] for a supernal radiance is contained within him,[636] as is written: *YHVH is* טוב (*tov*), *good, to all* (Psalms 145:9)—*to all,* unspecified, illuminating one day illumining all, supreme above all.[637] Until here, obscurity of words.[638]

185

בראשית (*Be-reshit*), *In the beginning, God created* (Genesis 1:1)—mystery of: ראשית (*Reshit*), *At the beginning of, your baking, offer a loaf as a gift* (Numbers

626. **One sees letters...** One's daily conduct determines the contents of the dream.

627. **good for his dream** A dream is vulnerable to various interpretations, which affect its outcome. See *Zohar* 1:183a–b.

628. **for the Torah inaugurated it...** See above, note 625.

629. **ninth of all** The letter ט (*tet*) is the ninth letter of the Hebrew alphabet and symbolizes the ninth *sefirah, Yesod.* In this *sefirah* the primordial light of *Ḥesed* was hidden away. See *Zohar* 1:3a, 21a; 2:230a. On the primordial light, see above, note 624.

630. **Primordial One above...** *Ḥokhmah,* known as Beginning, since it is the first *sefirah* that can be even faintly known. For a different rendering and interpretation of the phrase "contained within," see *KP, OY.*

631. **the secrecy of the point...** The primordial point of *Ḥokhmah,* symbolized by the letter י (*yod*). See above, page 109.

632. **From its energy emerged ו (*vav*)...** From the point represented by the letter י (*yod*) extended the line of the letter ו (*vav*), whose numerical value is six, symbolizing *Tif'eret* (known as Heaven) and the five *sefirot* surrounding Him.

633. **When it culminated...** When the point of *Ḥokhmah* was implanted within the womb of *Binah,* symbolized by the letter ב (*bet*), She glowed.

634. **From it emerged above and below...** From *Ḥokhmah* emerged the Divine Mother, *Binah,* and Her daughter, *Shekhinah,* both alluded to by the letter ב (*bet*), whose numerical value is two. See above, pages 173–76.

635. **These three letters...** As noted above, these letters stand for different stages of emanation: ט (*tet*) for *Yesod,* ו (*vav*) for *Tif'eret,* and ב (*bet*) for *Binah.* The entire flow of emanation gathers in *Yesod,* also known as Righteous One, who then unites with *Shekhinah.* See BT *Yoma* 38b.

636. **supernal radiance...** The primordial light of *Ḥesed* is concealed within *Yesod.*

637. ***to all,* unspecified...** *Yesod,* who contains and conveys the totality of emanation, is called All. He is the sixth cosmic day of Creation, animating the universe.

638. **obscurity of words** The mysteries of the process of emanation hidden within Scripture.

15:20).[639] ב (*Bet*) is ביתא (*beita*), house, of the world[640]—watered by that river entering it, the mystery written: *A river issues from Eden to water the garden* (Genesis 2:10).[641] This river gathers all from the high depth,[642] its waters never ceasing to saturate the garden. That high depth, initial ב (*bet*)—letters are sealed inside it by a single narrow path hidden within.[643] Out of that depth emerged two forces,[644] as is written: את השמים (*et ha-shamayim*), *the heavens* (Genesis 1:1). Not שמים (*shamayim*), *heavens,* but השמים (*ha-shamayim*), *the heavens,* from that depth, a mystery utterly concealed.[645] *And the earth* (ibid.)—the concealed one generated this *earth,* but included with *heaven,* emerging together, cleaving side by side.[646] When the *beginning* of all was

639. *At the beginning of, your baking, offer a loaf...* The loaf (חלה [*ḥallah*]) was offered as the first fruits of baking. See *Bereshit Rabbah* 1:4: "Rav Huna said in the name of Rav Mattanah, 'The world was created for the sake of three things: for the sake of *ḥallah,* tithes, and first fruits. For it is said: בראשית (*Be-reshit*), *In the beginning* [taken to mean: *For the sake of beginning*], and *beginning* is *ḥallah,* as is written: *At the beginning of your baking* [*offer* חלה (*ḥallah*), *a loaf, as a gift*]....'"

Here ראשית (*reshit*), *beginning,* symbolizes the second *sefirah, Ḥokhmah* ("Wisdom"), which is the first aspect of God that can be known, since the initial *sefirah, Keter,* is transcendently unknowable.

The identification of *beginning* with Wisdom appears widely. See *Targum Yerushalmi* (frag.), Genesis 1:1; Wolfson, *Philo,* 1:242–45, 266–69; *Bereshit Rabbah* 1:1; Azriel of Gerona, *Peirush ha-Aggadot,* 81; Naḥmanides on Genesis 1:1; *Zohar* 1:2a, 3b, 15a, 16b, 20a, 145a; Moses de León, *Sheqel ha-Qodesh,* 21–22 (25–26).

640. ב (*Bet*) is ביתא (*beita*), house, of the world The opening letter of the Torah, the ב (*bet*) of בראשית (*Be-reshit*), *In the beginning,* symbolizes *Shekhinah,* the Divine Presence encompassing the world. See *Zohar* 1:29b, 33a, 172a.

641. that river entering it... The flow of emanation channeled by *Yesod* to *Shekhinah, the garden.* This proof text from Genesis appears approximately fifty times in the *Zohar.*

642. the high depth *Binah,* source of emanation for the lower *sefirot.* See *Sefer Yetsirah* 1:5: "...depth of above, depth of below...."

643. That high depth, initial ב (*bet*)... The ב (*bet*) of בראשית (*Be-reshit*), *In the beginning,* alludes also to *Binah,* who unites with *Ḥokhmah,* known as ראשית (*Reshit*), *Beginning,* and receives from Him the stream of emanation in the form of letters. The narrow path is the subtle link between *Ḥokhmah* and *Binah.* See *Zohar* 1:3b, 29a–b; 2:122b–123a; 3:61b.

644. two forces *Tif'eret* and *Shekhinah,* known as *heaven* and *earth.*

645. Not שמים (*shamayim*), *heavens,* but השמים (*ha-shamayim*), *the heavens...* The definite article ה (*ha*) in השמים (*ha-shamayim*) symbolizes *Binah,* who is often identified with the first ה (*he*) in the divine name יהוה (*YHVH*).

646. *And the earth...* *Shekhinah,* known as *earth,* also emanated from *Binah,* not as a separate entity but joined together with *Tif'eret* (*heaven*), side by side, or back-to-back. See the description of the original androgynous nature of the human being in *Bereshit Rabbah* 8:1: "Rabbi Yirmeyah son of El'azar said, 'When the blessed Holy One created Adam, He created him androgynous, as is said: *Male and female He created them* (Genesis 1:27).' Rabbi Shemu'el son of Naḥman said, 'When the blessed Holy One created Adam, He created him with two faces. Then He sawed him and gave him

186

illumined, *heaven* carried Her and set Her in Her site,[647] as is written: ואת הארץ (*ve-et ha-arets*), *and the earth*—ו (*vav*) and totality of letters.[648] When She turned to dwell in Her place, separating [31a] from His side, She was confounded and bewildered,[649] yearning to cleave to *heaven* as one, as before, for She saw *heaven* beaming and Herself darkened.[650] But then a transcendent light shone upon Her, illumining Her, and She returned to Her place, gazing at *heaven* face-to-face.[651] So *earth* was mended, rendered firm and fragrant.[652]

Light radiated on the right side, darkness on the left.[653] He then separated them, so they would merge, as is written: *God separated the light from the darkness* (Genesis 1:4). Now if you say an actual separation—no; rather, *Day* came from the side of light, which is right, and *Night* from the side of darkness,

two backs, one on this side and one on that.'"

See BT *Berakhot* 61a; *Eruvin* 18a; Plato, *Symposium* 189d–191d; *Zohar* 1:2b, 13b, 47a; 2:55a; 3:5a, 44b; Matt, *Zohar*, 217.

647. **When the *beginning* of all…** When *Ḥokhmah* received further emanation from *Keter,* the flow extended to *Tif'eret* (*heaven*), empowering Him to install *Shekhinah* in Her position as the culmination of the *sefirot.*

648. **ו (*vav*) and totality of letters** The word ואת (*ve-et*) is divided into ו (*vav*) and את (*et*). *Vav,* the third letter of יהוה (*YHVH*), is numerically equivalent to six and symbolizes *Tif'eret* together with the five *sefirot* surrounding Him (*Ḥesed* to *Yesod*). את (*Et*) represents the totality of emanation from א (*alef*) to ת (*tav*), which is transmitted by *Tif'eret* to *Shekhinah* (*earth*), enabling Her to attain independent existence. See above, pages 112, 175, 178.

649. **confounded and bewildered** תוהה ובוהה (*Tohah u-vohah*), playing on תהו ובהו (*tohu va-vohu*), [*The earth was*] *chaos and void* (Genesis 1:2). The pun derives from *Bereshit Rabbah* 2:2, where *earth* is said to be "confounded and bewildered" by the inferior position of earthly creatures relative to heavenly creatures. See *Zohar* 1:24b (*TZ*).

On the Gnostic connotation of this phrase, see Van Winden, in *Studies in Gnosticism,* 458–66.

650. **for She saw *heaven* beaming and Herself darkened** On the diminution of

Shekhinah, see BT *Ḥullin* 60b: "Rabbi Shim'on son of Pazzi pointed out a contradiction. 'It is written: *God made the two great lights* (Genesis 1:16), and it is written [in the same verse]: *the greater light…and the lesser light.* The moon said before the blessed Holy One, "Master of the Universe! Can two kings possibly wear one crown?" He answered, "Go, diminish yourself!" She said before Him, "Master of the Universe! Because I have suggested something proper I should make myself smaller?" He replied, "Go and rule by day and night." She said, "But what is the value of this? What good is a lamp at noon?"'"

See BT *Rosh ha-Shanah* 23b; *Zohar* 1:19b–20a; *ZḤ* 70d–71a (*ShS*); Moses de León, *Mishkan ha-Edut,* 35b.

651. **gazing at *heaven* face-to-face** *Shekhinah* achieves reunion with *Tif'eret,* but now face-to-face, rather than back-to-back. See the description of the original nature of the human being from *Bereshit Rabbah* 8:1, cited above (note 646): "Rabbi Shemu'el son of Naḥman said, 'When the blessed Holy One created Adam, He created him with two faces. Then He sawed him and gave him two backs, one on this side and one on that.'"

See *Zohar* 3:296a (*IZ*); BT *Bava Batra* 99a.

652. **rendered firm and fragrant** See above, note 623.

653. **Light radiated…** As *Tif'eret* and *Shekhinah* emerge from *Binah, Tif'eret* derives from *Ḥesed* on the right side (identified with

which is left,[654] and when they emerged as one, He separated them, dividing them along their sides, so they could gaze face-to-face, cleaving to one another, all becoming one. He is called *Day*—He named him *Day*[655]—and She is called *Night*, as is written: *and the darkness He called Night* (Genesis 1:5),[656] for *darkness* seizes Her; She has no light of Her own.[657] Though deriving from the side of fire, which is *darkness*, still She is dark until illumined from the side of *Day*.[658] *Day* illumines *Night*, but *Night* does not shine until the time of which is written: *Night will shine as day; darkness and light will be the same* (Psalms 139:12).[659]

Rabbi El'azar jumped in first,[660] expounding: "*The voice of YHVH is over the waters: the God of glory thunders, YHVH over mighty waters* (Psalms 29:3). *The voice of YHVH*—the supernal *voice* appointed over *the waters* flowing from rung to rung until they gather at one site, in one throng.[661] That supernal *voice* conducts the *waters* in their courses, each in its own way, like a gardener appointed over water to conduct it to each site fittingly. So *the voice of YHVH* is appointed *over the waters*.

"*The God of glory thunders*, as is said: *Who can contemplate the thunder of His might?* (Job 26:14). This is the side extending from *Might*,[662] emerging therefrom.

188

light), while *Shekhinah* derives from *Gevurah* on the left side (identified with darkness). See above, page 125.

654. *Day... Night...* Tif'eret, Shekhinah.

655. **He is called *Day*...** Tif'eret is called *Day*.

656. **and the darkness He called Night** The verse reads: *God called the light Day, and the darkness He called Night*.

657. **darkness seizes Her...** Gevurah seizes *Shekhinah*, who reflects the light of the other *sefirot* but has none of Her own. The expression "She has no light of Her own" derives from a medieval astronomic description of the moon.

See Radak on Genesis 1:16; Moses de León, *Shushan Edut*, 338; idem, *Sod Eser Sefirot Belimah*, 381; Zohar 1:20a, 132b, 181a, 238a; 2:43a, 142a, 218b.

658. **Though deriving from the side of fire, which is *darkness*...** Though *Shekhinah* derives from *Gevurah*, symbolized by both fire and *darkness*, She receives no light from this fire but rather remains dark until illumined by *Tif'eret*.

On the combination of fire and *darkness*, see Maimonides, *Guide of the Perplexed* 2:30, where the *darkness* of Genesis 1:2 is identified with "elemental fire": "The elemental fire was designated by this term [*darkness*] because it is not luminous, but only transparent."

659. **until the time of which is written...** Until Messianic time, when *Shekhinah* will shine on Her own.

660. **Rabbi El'azar jumped in first** The beginning of this passage appears to be missing. See KP. This is the first occurrence of the name of one of the Ḥavrayya ("Companions") in "Parashat Be-Reshit" of the *Zohar*.

661. **the supernal *voice*...** The transcendent voice of *Binah* regulates the flow of emanation through the lower *sefirot* until they collect in *Yesod*.

662. **the side extending from *Might*** *Shekhinah*, the Divine Presence is also known as כבוד (*kavod*), *glory*. She emanates via *Gevurah* ("might, power"), located on the left side of the sefirotic tree.

"Alternatively, *The God of glory thunders*—the right, from which left emerges.[663]

"*YHVH over mighty waters*—transcendent Wisdom, who stands *over mighty waters*—over that concealed depth emerging therefrom, as is said: *Your path through mighty waters* (Psalms 77:20)."[664]

Rabbi Shim'on resolved the conflict,[665] opening with a verse: "It is written, *Next to the enclosure are the rings to be, as housings for the poles* (Exodus 25:27).[666] Who is that *enclosure*? A closed site, opened only by a single narrow path, intimated secretly.[667] Thereby it is filled, and traces gates to kindle lamps.[668] Because it is a site hidden and concealed, it is called *enclosure*; this is the world that is coming.[669]

"*Are the rings to be*—supernal rings linked to one another, water from air, air from fire, fire from water, all linked to each other, emerging from one another, like rings.[670] They all gaze at that *enclosure*, into which merges the supernal river to water them,[671] and they merge in it.

663. **the right...** *Ḥesed*, also known as אל (*El*), *God* (*Zohar* 3:30b), and located on the right side. From here *Gevurah* emerges on the left as thunder.

664. **that concealed depth...** *Binah*, who emerges from *Ḥokhmah* and remains linked to Him by a narrow path.

665. **resolved the conflict** The conflict between *Ḥesed* and *Gevurah*, right and left sides of the sefirotic tree symbolizing light and darkness, or the conflict between the waters of Creation. See above, pages 124–36.

666. *Next to the enclosure are the rings to be, as housings for the poles* *to carry the table.* In the desert Tabernacle, each week twelve loaves of bread were placed on a portable table, which was fitted with rings and poles and topped with a rim (*enclosure*).

667. **A closed site...** *Binah*, joined intimately to *Ḥokhmah*. See *Zohar* 1:3b, 29a–b, 30b; 2:122b–123a; 3:61b.

668. **traces gates...** *Binah*, filled by the flow from *Ḥokhmah*, begins to emanate the lights of the lower *sefirot* ("gates").

669. **the world that is coming** עלמא דאתי (*Alma de-atei*), the Aramaic equivalent of the rabbinic Hebrew העולם הבא (*ha-olam ha-ba*), "the world that is coming." This concept is often understood as referring to the hereafter and is usually translated as "the world to come." From another point

of view, however, "the world that is coming" already exists, occupying another dimension. See *Tanḥuma, Vayiqra* 8: "The wise call it *ha-olam ha-ba* not because it does not exist now, but for us today in this world it is still to come." Cf. Maimonides, *Mishneh Torah, Hilkhot Teshuvah* 8:8; and Guttmann, *Philosophies of Judaism*, 37: "'The world to come' does not succeed 'this world' in time, but exists from eternity as a reality outside and above time, to which the soul ascends."

In Kabbalah "the world that is coming" often refers to *Binah*, the continuous source of emanation. See *Zohar* 3:290b (*IZ*): "the world that is coming, constantly coming, never ceasing."

Cf. *Bahir* 106 (160); Asher ben David, *Peirush Shelosh Esreh Middot*, in *Kabbalah* 2 (1997): 293; Moses de León, *Sheqel ha-Qodesh*, 26 (30); idem, *Sod Eser Sefirot*, 375; *Zohar* 1:83a, 92a.

670. **supernal rings...** The triad of *sefirot* emerging from *Binah*: *Ḥesed, Gevurah*, and *Tif'eret*, symbolized respectively by water, fire, and air. See *Sefer Yetsirah* 1:9–12; *Zohar* 1:110a, 118b. The *sefirot* are links in the cosmic chain of being. See Matt, intro to *Mar'ot ha-Ẓove'ot*, by David ben Judah he-Ḥasid, 34, n. 238.

671. **the supernal river...** The flow of emanation from *Ḥokhmah* to *Binah*.

"*Housings for the poles*—these supernal rings are *housings* designated *for the poles,* the chariots below,[672] for one derives from the side of fire, one from the side of water, one from the side of air, and so with them all, constituting a chariot for the ark.[673] So whoever approaches should approach these *poles,* not what lies within.[674] As we say to the Nazarite, 'Go around, around! Do not come near the vineyard!'[675] Except for those worthy of serving within, privileged to enter and draw near. Of this is written: *An outsider who comes near shall be put to death* (Numbers 1:51)."

Rabbi Yose asked him, "These six days of Creation (בראשית [*Be-reshit*], *In the beginning*) that we study, who are they?"

190

He replied, "The same as is written: *The cedars of Lebanon that He planted* (Psalms 104:16). As these *cedars* emerge from *Lebanon,* so those six days emerge from בראשית (*Be-reshit*), *In the beginning* (Genesis 1:1).[676] Scripture designates these six supernal days explicitly, as is written: *Yours, YHVH, are* גדולה (*gedullah*), *greatness;* גבורה (*gevurah*), *power;* [תפארת (*tif'eret*), *beauty;* נצח (*netsah*), *victory;* הוד (*hod*), *splendor—yes, all...*] (1 Chronicles 29:11).[677] [31b] So בראשית (*Be-reshit*), *In the beginning*—ב ראשית (*Bet, reshit*), 'two, *beginning,*' for though second by count, it is called *beginning.* For the supernal, concealed Crown is first, but since it is not included in the count, the second is *beginning.* So: ב ראשית (*Bet, reshit*), 'two, *beginning.*'[678]

672. **the chariots below** As the *poles* in the Tabernacle carried the table (and the ark), so the chariots beneath *Shekhinah* carry Her. Each of these lower forces derives from one of the *housings: Ḥesed, Gevurah,* or *Tif'eret.*

673. **the ark** *Shekhinah.* According to Exodus 25:12–15, *the ark of the covenant* in the Tabernacle was also fitted with rings and poles.

674. **not what lies within** *Shekhinah* and the entire sefirotic realm.

675. **As we say to the Nazarite...** See BT *Shabbat* 13a; cf. *Zohar* 2:125b; 3:127b. A Nazarite vows not to eat grapes or drink wine (Numbers 6:1–3). As a precaution, he is forbidden even to approach a vineyard. Here, the unproven spiritual seeker is directed toward the chariot but not its occupant, *Shekhinah,* who is known as "vineyard."

676. **As these *cedars* emerge from Lebanon...** The six *sefirot* from Ḥesed through

Yesod are symbolized by *cedars* rooted in *Lebanon* (Ḥokhmah). See *Bereshit Rabbah* 15:1; above, pages 170–72. Alternatively, they are the six cosmic days of Creation, emerging from Ḥokhmah, known as בראשית (*Be-reshit*), *In the beginning.*

677. ***Yours, YHVH, are*** גדולה (***gedullah***), ***greatness*...** הוד (***hod***), ***splendor—yes, all...*** The verse continues: *that is in heaven and on earth....* This verse appears often in kabbalistic literature as a designation of the lower *sefirot:* Ḥesed (also called *Gedullah*), Gevurah, Tif'eret, Netsaḥ, Hod, Yesod (known as *all*), and Shekhinah (symbolized by *earth*), who is joined with Tif'eret (symbolized by *heaven*).

678. ב ראשית (***Bet, reshit***), 'two, *beginning*'... Ḥokhmah, the second *sefirah,* is the first that can be known at all, since Keter, the first *sefirah,* shares the unknowable infinity of *Ein Sof* and is therefore "not included in the count." See *Zohar* 3:269a.

"ברא (Bara), *Created* (Genesis, ibid.)—as is written: *A river issues from Eden to water the garden* (ibid. 2:10), to water and maintain it, attending to all its needs.[679]

"אלהים (Elohim), *God* (ibid. 1:1)—אלהים חיים (Elohim ḥayyim), *Living God*.[680] So the meaning of בראשית ברא אלהים (Be-reshit bara Elohim), *In the beginning God created,* is certainly: By means of that river, generating, saturating all.[681]

"את השמים (Et ha-shamayim), *heaven* (ibid.)—the expansion of the river, expanding and gushing after being generated by *beginning*.[682] Once this generated all, and all settled in its site as one, the last link became a *beginning*.[683] Through this *beginning* it channeled the river, pouring water to flow below.[684]

"So, בראשית (Be-reshit), *By means of beginning,* indeed, *God created*—by it He created the lower world, by it He radiated lights, by it He energized everything."[685]

Rabbi Yehudah said, "Concerning this is written: *Should the axe boast over him who hews with it?* (Isaiah 10:15). To whom does praise belong—not to the craftsman? Similarly, with this ראשית (reshit), *beginning,* the transcendent *God created heaven.* To whom does praise belong? To *God.*"

Rabbi Yose said, "It is written: *To whom* אלהים (Elohim), *God, are close* (Deuteronomy 4:7). *Are close?* The verse should read: *is close.* However, transcendent *Elohim, Elohim* of *the fear of Isaac,* final *Elohim;* therefore, *are close.*[686] Many powers emerge from one, all being one."

191

679. *A river issues from Eden...* The act of Creation described in the opening verse of Genesis is the flow of emanation from *Ḥokhmah* (known as *Eden*) through *Binah* and the *sefirot* below Her to *Shekhinah,* the garden. The *Zohar* may be associating the Hebrew word יוצא (yotse), *issues,* "goes out," with the Aramaic word ברא (bara), "outside."

680. אלהים חיים (Elohim ḥayyim), *Living God* The phrase appears in Deuteronomy 5:23; Jeremiah 10:10. Here it is a name of *Binah,* source of life and emanation. See *Zohar* 1:74a; 2:140a.

681. **By means of that river...** The opening word of the Torah, בראשית (Be-reshit), is understood as meaning not *In the beginning,* but *With beginning,* "by means of the primordial river emanating from *Ḥokhmah,* known as *beginning.*" This interpretation relies on the fact that the Hebrew preposition ב (be) means "with" as well as "in."

See *Targum Yerushalmi* (frag.) and Naḥmanides, ad loc.; *Bereshit Rabbah* 1:1; Azriel of Gerona, *Peirush ha-Aggadot,* 81; above, page 110.

682. **the expansion of the river...** The river, generated by *Ḥokhmah,* emerges from *Binah* and emanates *Tif'eret,* known as *heaven.*

683. **the last link...** *Shekhinah,* last of the *sefirot,* is the *beginning* of the creation of the world below.

684. **it channeled the river...** *Binah* channeled the flow of emanation.

685. **by it He created the lower world...** By means of *Shekhinah,* the lower *beginning, Binah* (known as אלהים [Elohim], *God*) created the world below.

686. **However, transcendent *Elohim*...** The name אלהים (Elohim), *God,* applies to several *sefirot: Binah* (transcendent *Elohim*), *Gevurah* (associated with Isaac and known as *the fear of Isaac;* see Genesis 31:42), and

God said, "Let there be light!" (Genesis 1:3). This is the light that the blessed Holy One created at first.[687] It is the light of the eye.[688] This is the light that the blessed Holy One showed Adam, who gazed with it from one end of the universe to the other.[689] It is the light that the blessed Holy One showed David, who praised it, declaring: *How abundant is Your goodness that You have hidden away for those in awe of You!* (Psalms 31:20). This is the light that the blessed Holy One showed Moses; by it he saw from Gilead to Dan.[690]

When the blessed Holy One saw that three wicked generations would arise—the generation of Enosh, the generation of the Flood, and the generation of Dispersion—He hid it away to prevent them from using it.[691] The blessed

Shekhinah (final *Elohim*). So, the plural is justified. See BT *Sanhedrin* 38b; *Devarim Rabbah* 2:13.

687. **the light... created at first** The primordial light of the first day of Creation, identified with the *sefirah* of *Ḥesed*, the first to emerge from *Binah*. See *Zohar* 1:20a; 2:137a, 166b.

688. **the light of the eye** Vision derives from the primordial light and was originally boundless. According to rabbinic tradition, the primordial light was overwhelming. See *Bereshit Rabbah* 3:6: "The light created during the six days of Creation cannot shine during the day because it dims [i.e., overwhelms] the globe of the sun."

See Isaiah 30:26; and *Bahir* 97 (147): "No creature could look at the primordial light." Cf. *ZH* 15b (*MhN*); Philo, *On the Creation of the World*, 29–31. An alternate view appears in *Shemot Rabbah* 35:1: "Its light was pleasant for the world and did not cause harm like the sun."

Elsewhere the *Zohar* refers to a technique for seeing the concealed colors of the *sefirot*. By closing one's eye and pressing a finger on the eyeball until it is moved to one side, one gains a vision of colors (white, red, and green), symbolizing *Ḥesed, Gevurah,* and *Tif'eret*. See *Zohar* 2:23b: "The secret is: close your eye and roll your eyeball. Those colors that shine and sparkle will be revealed."

Cf. 1:18b, 42a, 43a, 97a–b (*ST*); 2:43b, 247a; Moses de León, *Sheqel ha-Qodesh*, 96–97 (123–24); *KP* on *Zohar* 1:18b; Scholem, "Colours and Their Symbolism," 66–67;

Liebes, *Peraqim*, 291–93; Wolfson, *Through a Speculum That Shines*, 380–83.

689. **who gazed with it from one end of the universe to the other** See BT *Ḥagigah* 12a: "Rabbi El'azar said, 'With the light created by the blessed Holy One on the first day, one [or "Adam"] could gaze and see from one end of the universe to the other. When the blessed Holy One foresaw the corrupt deeds of the generation of the Flood and the generation of the Dispersion [the generation of the Tower of Babel], He immediately hid it from them, as is written: *The light of the wicked is withheld* (Job 38:15). For whom did He hide it? For the righteous in the time to come.'"

See *Bereshit Rabbah* 3:6; 41:3; *Shemot Rabbah* 35:1; *Tanḥuma, Shemini* 9; *Bahir* 97–98 (147); *Zohar* 1:30b, 45b–46a, 47a; 2:127a, 148b–149a, 220a–b; 3:88a, 173b.

690. **from Gilead to Dan** When he was about to die, Moses ascended Mt. Nebo in Moab and was shown the entire land of Israel from a distance. See Deuteronomy 34:1–5, where *Gilead as far as Dan* refers to just one part of the entire landscape.

See *Sifrei*, Deuteronomy 338, where Rabbi Yehoshu'a says that Moses was able to view the entire land because God "placed power in Moses' eyes and he saw from one end of the world to the other." According to the *Zohar*, this power derives from the primordial light.

691. **three wicked generations...** Concerning the generation of Enosh, Genesis 4:26 states: *Then for the first time the name*

192

Holy One gave it to Moses, who used it for the three remaining months of his gestation, as is said: *She hid him for three months* (Exodus 2:2).[692] When three months later he was brought before Pharaoh,[693] the blessed Holy One took it away from him, until he stood upon Mount Sinai to receive the Torah, when He restored that light to him. He wielded it[694] all his days, and the Children of Israel could not approach him until he placed a veil over his face, as is said: *They were afraid to come near him* (Exodus 34:30).[695] He enwrapped Himself in it as in a *tallit*, as is written: *He wraps in light as in a garment* (Psalms 104:2).[696]

YHVH was invoked. In the Midrash this is taken to mean that Enosh's generation was the first to worship idols and address them by the name YHVH.

See *Mekhilta, Baḥodesh* 6; *Bereshit Rabbah* 23:7; *Targum Yerushalmi* and Rashi, ad loc.; Maimonides, *Mishneh Torah, Hilkhot Avodah Zarah* 1:1; Ginzberg, *Legends*, 5:151, n. 54.

The generation of the Flood was notoriously corrupt (Genesis 6:5–13). "The generation of Dispersion" refers to the generation of the Tower of Babel who attempted to assault heaven and were punished by being dispersed and by their having their common language divided into many tongues (ibid. 11:1–9; cf. 10:25). All three generations are mentioned in *Shemot Rabbah* 35:1 and *Pesiqta Rabbati* 23.

692. **the three remaining months...** According to one midrashic tradition, Moses was born three months premature in order to deceive the Egyptians, who were planning to kill him; the wording in Exodus 2:2, *She hid him for three months,* refers to the last three months of the normal period of pregnancy, which were the first three months of Moses' life. The Midrash also connects the preceding phrase, *She saw that he was good,* with Genesis 1:3: *God saw that the light was good,* implying that Moses radiated supernal light.

See *Mekhilta de-Rashbi,* Exodus 6:2; *Targum Yerushalmi* and *Midrash ha-Gadol,* Exodus 2:2; Rashi on Exodus 2:3; as well as BT *Sotah* 12a; *Shemot Rabbah* 1:20; *Zohar* 2:11b; Ginzberg, *Legends,* 5:397, nn. 42, 44.

The *Zohar* may also have in mind the teaching of Rabbi Simlai (BT *Niddah* 30b)

that a fetus in the womb has "a lamp kindled above its head, and it gazes from one end of the world to the other."

693. **he was brought before Pharaoh** By Pharaoh's daughter, who found him in the Nile. See Exodus 2:3–10.

694. **He wielded it** אשתמש ביה (*Ishtammash beih*), "He used it." The verb has theurgic connotations.

See M *Avot* 1:13; *Zohar* 1:55b; Scholem, *Jewish Gnosticism,* 54, n. 36; idem, *Major Trends,* 358, n. 17.

695. *They were afraid to come near him* The full verse reads: *Aaron and all the Children of Israel saw Moses, and behold, the skin of his face was radiant! They were afraid to come near him.*

696. **He enwrapped Himself in it as in a** *tallit...* *Tallit* originally meant a "gown, cloak" worn by distinguished scholars and the wealthy. Later it came to mean "prayer shawl." The image applied here to Moses derives from an esoteric rabbinic description of God. See *Midrash Tehillim* 104:4: "Rabbi Shim'on son of Rabbi Yehotsadak asked Rabbi Shemu'el son of Naḥman, 'How did the blessed Holy One create the light?' He replied, 'He enwrapped Himself in a white *tallit,* and the world shone from His light.' He said this to him in a whisper. [Rabbi Shim'on] said, 'Is this not stated explicitly in Scripture: *He wraps in light as in a garment* (Psalms 104:2)?' He replied, 'As I received it in a whisper, so I told it to you in a whisper.'"

Cf. *Bereshit Rabbah* 3:4 (and Theodor, ad loc.); *Pirqei de-Rabbi Eli'ezer* 3. The image of God wrapping Himself in a garment of light

193

"Let there be light!" And there was light (Genesis, ibid.). Every subject of the phrase *and there was* exists in this world and in the world that is coming.[697]

Rabbi Yitsḥak said, "The light created by the blessed Holy One in the act of Creation flared from one end of the universe to the other, and was hidden away. Why was it hidden away? So the wicked of the world would not enjoy it, nor the worlds enjoy it because of them.[698] It is preserved for the righteous—for the righteous, precisely, [32a] as is written: *Light is sown for the righteous, joy for the upright in heart* (Psalms 97:11).[699] Then the worlds will be fragrant and all will be one. But until the day when the world that is coming arrives, it is preserved, treasured away.

"That light radiated from the midst of darkness hewn by truncheons of the Concealed of All,[700] until a single secret path[701] was carved by the hidden light,

appears in Greek, Iranian, Gnostic, and kabbalistic sources.

See Matt, *Zohar*, 212; Ezra of Gerona, *Peirush Shir ha-Shirim*, 493–94; Ezra's letter, ed. Scholem, in *Sefer Bialik*, 157–58; Azriel of Gerona, *Peirush ha-Aggadot*, 110–11; *Zohar* 1:2a, 29a, 90a (*ST*), 245a; 2:39b, 164b; Moses de León, *Mishkan ha-Edut*, 5a.

697. **Every subject of the phrase...** This exegetical principle derives from older rabbinic models. See *Tanḥuma* (Buber), *Naso* 24: "Rabbi Shim'on son of Yoḥai said, 'Wherever the phrase *and there was* appears, it refers to something that was and ceased for many days and returned to its original state.'" Cf. *Bereshit Rabbah* 41:3: "Rabbi Shim'on said in the name of Rabbi Yoḥanan, 'Wherever the phrase *and there was* appears, it serves for sorrow and for joy. If sorrow, there is none like it; if joy, there is none like it.' Rabbi Shemu'el son of Naḥman came and made a distinction: 'Wherever it says, *and there was,* there is sorrow; wherever it says, *and there will be,* there is joy.' It was objected: 'But it is written: *God said, "Let there be light!" And there was light.*' He responded, 'There is no longer any joy, for the world was not worthy to use that light.'" Cf. BT *Megillah* 10b.

The *Zohar* alludes here to the primordial light, which appeared briefly in this world and was hidden away for the righteous in the hereafter. *Bahir* 106 (160) identifies the hidden light with the world that is coming,

which it takes to mean "the world that already came." The phrase *And there was light* is similarly taken to mean "There already was light," i.e., the primordial light.

See *Bahir* 17 (25); *Zohar* 1:16b, 30b, 45b; *Bereshit Rabbah* 3:2, along with the variant readings and Theodor, ad loc.

698. **nor the worlds enjoy it because of them** The wicked deprive the world of the primordial light.

699. **for the righteous, precisely...** The word "righteous" alludes to the *sefirah* of Yesod ("Foundation"), based on Proverbs 10:25: וצדיק יסוד עולם (*Ve-tsaddiq yesod olam*). The verse literally means *The righteous one is an everlasting foundation* but is understood as *The righteous one is the foundation of the world*. See BT *Ḥagigah* 12b; *Bahir* 71 (102); Azriel of Gerona, *Peirush ha-Aggadot*, 34.

The primordial light is hidden in *Yesod*, the procreative power of God. See *Zohar* 1:3a, 21a, 45b; 2:35a, 148b–149a; 166b–167a, 230a.

The Midrash links the verse *Light is sown for the righteous* with the hidden light. See *Tanḥuma, Shemini* 9; *Shemot Rabbah* 35:1; *Midrash Tehillim* 27:1.

700. **by truncheons...** בקלפוי (*Bequlpoi*), "By His clubs." The darkness is carved by divine blows. See above, note 513.

701. **a single secret path...** The path of emanation or, specifically, *Yesod,* who conveys the emanation to *Shekhinah*.

194

leading to darkness below, where light dwells. Who is darkness below? The one called *Night,* of whom is written: *And the darkness He called Night* (Genesis 1:5).[702] So we have learned: *Revealing depths out of darkness* (Job 12:22)."[703]

Rabbi Yose said, "If you say they are revealed from sealed *darkness,*[704] we can see they are concealed—all those supernal crowns—[705] and we call them *depths.* Why, then, *revealing?*[706] Because all those supernal concealments are revealed only from the *darkness* abiding in the mystery of *Night.*[707]

"Come and see: All those concealed depths emerging from thought, conveyed by the voice, are not revealed until the word reveals them.[708] Who is the word? Speech. This speech is called Sabbath,[709] and because Sabbath is called Speech, mundane speech is forbidden on Sabbath, for this speech must prevail, no other.[710] This speech deriving from the side of *darkness*[711] reveals depths."

Rabbi Yitsḥak said, "If so, what is the meaning of the verse: *God separated the light from the darkness* (Genesis 1:4)?"

He replied, "*Light* generated day, *darkness* generated night.[712] Afterward He joined them together and they became one, as is written: *There was evening, there was morning: day one* (ibid. 1:5), for night and day are called *one.*[713] As to what is written: *God separated the light from the darkness,* this pertains to the time of exile, when division prevails."[714]

195

702. **The one called** *Night*...   *Shekhinah,* who is called "darkness below" because She has no light of Her own but simply reflects the light of the other *sefirot.*

703. *Revealing depths*...   See above, page 183: "Then the immense abyss ascended in darkness, and darkness covered all, until light emanated, split the darkness, and radiated, as is written: *Revealing depths out of darkness, bringing pitch-blackness to light.*"

704. **from sealed** *darkness*   From the source of emanation.

705. **all those supernal crowns**   The *sefirot.*

706. **Why, then,** *revealing?*   Such an explicit description is incompatible with the hidden nature of the emanation.

707. **from the** *darkness* **abiding**...   From *Shekhinah,* the "darkness below."

708. **All those concealed depths**...   The *sefirot* emerge from within the recesses of the divine mind and are conveyed by the "voice," the central *sefirah* of *Tif'eret,* until fully articulated in the divine word, *Shekhinah.*

709. **This speech is called Sabbath**   *Shekhinah,* the divine word, is the last of the seven lower *sefirot* and is symbolized by the Sabbath, the seventh day of the week.

710. **mundane speech is forbidden on Sabbath**...   See BT *Shabbat* 113b: "Your speech on the Sabbath should not resemble your speech on weekdays." Mundane speech mars the holiness of Sabbath and arouses demonic powers.

See *Zohar* 2:47b, 63b–64a; 3:105a–b.

711. **from the side of** *darkness*   From the left side.

712. *Light* **generated day**...   The *sefirah* of *Ḥesed,* symbolized by light, emanated *Tif'eret,* whereas *Gevurah,* symbolized by darkness, emanated *Shekhinah.* See above, pages 125–26.

713. **for night and day are called** *one*   *Shekhinah* and *Tif'eret* are intended to unite. See *Zohar* 1:31a, 46a.

714. **the time of exile**...   When the divine couple is separated.

Rabbi Yitsḥak said, "Until now the male was in *light;* now the female is in *darkness,* reflecting its light.[715] Later they join together, becoming one. How are they differentiated, distinguishing light from dark? Rungs differentiate, yet both are as one, for there is no light without darkness, no darkness without light.[716] Though one, they diverge in color;[717] even so, they are one, as is written: *day one.*"

Rabbi Shim'on said, "Through a covenant the world was created and established, as is written: *Were it not for My covenant with day and night, I would not have established the laws of heaven and earth* (Jeremiah 33:25).[718] Who is *Covenant?* צדיק (*Tsaddiq*), Righteous One.[719] So the world endures by *Covenant, day and night* together,[720] as is written: *Were it not for My covenant with day and night, I would not have established the laws of heaven and earth—the allowance of heaven and earth,* flowing forth from Eden."[721]

He opened, saying, "*From the voice of* מחצצים (*meḥatsatsim*), *dividers, between the water drawers—there they will chant the righteous acts of YHVH, His righteous deliverance of Israel. Then the people of YHVH descended to the gates* (Judges 5:11). *From the voice of* מחצצים (*meḥatsatsim*), *dividers*—the voice of Jacob. מחצצים (*Meḥatsatsim*), *Dividers,* as is said: *Man of the space between* (1 Samuel 17:4).[722]

196

---

715. **Until now...** First, *Tif'eret* emerged from *Ḥesed.* Then *Shekhinah* emerged from *Gevurah* and had no light of Her own, only what She reflected.

716. **Rungs differentiate...** The *sefirot* are differentiated, yet still unified. On the interdependence of light and darkness, see *Zohar* 2:187a; 3:47b.

717. **they diverge in color** As different frequencies of the wavelengths of light yield different colors.

718. *Were it not for My covenant...* See BT *Shabbat* 137b, where this verse is applied to the covenant of circumcision: "Were it not for the blood of the covenant, heaven and earth would not endure, as is said: *Were it not for My covenant with day and night, I would not have established the laws of heaven and earth.*"

See *Zohar* 1:56a, 59b, 66b, 89a, 93b.

719. **Who is** *Covenant?* צדיק (*Tsaddiq*), **Righteous One** *Covenant* alludes to *Yesod,* the divine phallus, site of the covenant of

circumcision. On his title *Tsaddiq,* see above, note 699.

720. *day and night* **together** Symbolizing *Tif'eret* and *Shekhinah,* who unite by means of *Yesod,* the *Covenant.*

721. *the allowance of heaven and earth,* **flowing forth from Eden** The word חקות (*ḥuqqot*), *laws,* is understood to mean "prescribed portion, allowance," i.e., the emanation intended for *Tif'eret* (*heaven*) and *Shekhinah* (*earth*), which emerges from *Ḥokhmah* (*Eden*).

722. *From the voice of* מחצצים (*meḥatsatsim*)...**the voice of Jacob...** In Deborah's song (Judges 5), the rare word מחצצים (*meḥatsatsim*) may mean "archers," "singers," "musicians," or "thunder peals." Here Rabbi Shim'on understands it hyperliterally as *dividers,* alluding to *Tif'eret,* symbolized by Jacob, who mediates between right and left, *Ḥesed* and *Gevurah.*

The phrase "the voice of Jacob" originates in Genesis 27:22. The verse in Samuel refers

Between the water drawers, for He dwells between those drawing water from above and receives on two sides, blending them within Himself.[723]

"There they will chant the righteous acts of YHVH—there is the site of faith cleaving.[724] *There the righteous acts of YHVH will chant*—there *the righteous acts of YHVH* suck, imbibe.[725]

"His righteous deliverance—Righteous One of the world, Holy Covenant, drawing, conveying all, delivering, dispersing supernal water into the vast ocean.[726]

"Of Israel—for *Israel* inherited this covenant, the blessed Holy One conveying it to them eternally.[727] When Israel abandoned it by not פרעין (*pare'in*), uncovering—cutting and not uncovering[728]—what is written? *Then the people of YHVH descended to the gates*—gates of righteousness. They sat by the gates but did not enter.[729] Of that time [32b] is written: *The Children of Israel forsook YHVH* (Judges 2:12),[730] until Deborah appeared, inspiring them to offer themselves for this, as is written: בפרוע פרעות (*Biphro'a pera'ot*), *When uncoverings are uncovered, in Israel; when the people willingly offer themselves* (ibid. 5:2).[731] So it is written: *Deliverance ceased, ceased in Israel* (ibid., 7). *Deliverance—His*

197

---

to Goliath, who stood *between* the Israelites and Philistines.

723. **He dwells between those drawing water...** *Tif'eret* stands between *Ḥesed* and *Gevurah,* who draw the emanation from above.

724. **the site of faith cleaving...** *Tif'eret,* symbolized by the name יהוה (*YHVH*), is the focus of human belief and also the partner of *Shekhinah,* known as Faith (מהימנותא [*Meheimanuta*]).

725. **there *the righteous acts*...** From *Tif'eret* the next two *sefirot, Netsaḥ* and *Hod,* draw their sustenance. Now the verse is being read: *There* (at *Tif'eret*) *the righteous acts of YHVH* (*Netsaḥ* and *Hod*) *will chant.*

726. **Righteous One...** *Yesod* (see above, notes 699, 719), who channels the rivers of emanation to the ocean of *Shekhinah.*

727. **for *Israel* inherited this covenant...** The covenant between God and Israel is embodied in the rite of circumcision.

728. **cutting and not uncovering** In the ritual of circumcision, first the foreskin is cut and removed, disclosing the mucous membrane, which is then torn down the center and pulled back, revealing the corona. The act of tearing and pulling back the mem-

brane is called פריעה (*peri'ah*), "uncovering" the corona. See M *Shabbat* 19:6: "If one circumcises but does not uncover the circumcision, it is as if he has not circumcised."

See *Zohar* 1:13a, 32a (*Tos*), 93b, 96b, 98b (*ST*); 2:3b, 40a, 125b; 3:91b; Moses de León, *Sefer ha-Mishqal,* 133; idem, *Sheqel ha-Qodesh,* 55 (67).

729. ***gates of righteousness*...** *Shekhinah,* who is known as *righteousness.* Those who fail to complete the act of circumcision remain outside the divine realm. The phrase *gates of righteousness* derives from Psalms 118:19.

730. **The Children of Israel forsook *YHVH*** The verse actually reads: *They forsook YHVH.* See *Zohar* 1:93b; 3:42b.

731. **until Deborah appeared...** Deborah renewed Israel's commitment to complete the rite of circumcision by uncovering the corona. Literally, the opening words of the verse (בפרוע פרעות [*Biphro'a pera'ot*]) apparently mean *When locks go untrimmed,* an expression of dedication (see Numbers 6:5). Here, though, Rabbi Shim'on intends another meaning of the root: "uncover," alluding to the act of פריעה (*peri'ah*), "uncovering." See *Zohar* 1:93b.

deliverance (ibid., 11), of which we spoke. *Deliverance ceased*—the holy covenant, for they failed to uncover.[732] *Until I, Deborah, arose; I arose, mother in Israel* (ibid., 7). What is the meaning of *mother*? 'I channeled supernal water from above, sustaining worlds.'[733] *In Israel*—unspecified, above and below, showing that the world is erected only on this covenant.[734] Mystery of all: *The righteous one is the foundation of the world* (Proverbs 10:25).[735]

"Three emerge from one; one stands in three, enters between two; two suckle one, one suckles many sides,[736] so all is one, as is written: *There was evening, there was morning: day one* (Genesis 1:5), a *day* embracing *evening* and *morning* as *one*, namely, the mystery of *covenant with day and night*, in which all is one."[737]

God said, "Let there be an expanse in the midst of the waters, and let it separate water from water" (Genesis 1:6). Rabbi Yehudah said, "There are seven expanses above, all abiding in supernal holiness,[738] and through them the holy name is consummated.[739] This *expanse* lies in the middle of the

198

732. **His deliverance...** *Deliverance* alludes to *Yesod*, who delivers the flow of emanation to *Shekhinah*. By failing to uncover the corona, one interrupts their union.

733. **What is the meaning of *mother*? ...** By inspiring Israel, Deborah stimulated *Binah*, the Divine Mother, to channel life and sustenance.

734. ***In Israel*—unspecified...** *Israel* refers to both the earthly people and the central *sefirah* named *Tif'eret Yisra'el* ("Beauty of Israel"), both of whom are included in the covenant of circumcision and dependent upon it.

735. ***The righteous one is the foundation of the world*** The verse applies below and above. The righteous human who fulfills the commandments maintains the world, just as *Yesod* constitutes the cosmic pillar. *Yesod* ("Foundation") is known as Righteous One, based on this verse: וצדיק יסוד עולם (*Ve-tsaddiq yesod olam*), which literally means *The righteous one is an everlasting foundation* but is understood as *The righteous one is the foundation of the world.*

See BT *Ḥagigah* 12b; *Bahir* 71 (102); Azriel of Gerona, *Peirush ha-Aggadot*, 34.

736. **Three emerge from one...** A multivalent riddle, one of whose meanings may be: *Keter, Ḥokhmah,* and *Binah* emerge from *Ein Sof; Tif'eret* stands in the next triad, which includes *Ḥesed* and *Gevurah.* The flow continues to *Netsaḥ* and *Hod,* who suckle *Yesod,* who disperses the flow through *Shekhinah* to many sides.

For other interpretations see *OY; KP;* Scholem; and *MM,* who after listing many meanings, writes: "Perhaps Rabbi Shim'on son of Yoḥai intended all of these interpretations." Similar numerical riddles appear in *Zohar* 1:72b, 77a, 151b (*Tos*); 2:12b, 95a; 3:162a.

737. **a *day* embracing *evening* and *morning*...** *Yesod* binds *Shekhinah* and *Tif'eret.*

738. **seven expanses above...** See BT *Ḥagigah* 12b: "Resh Lakish said, 'There are seven heavens [רקיעים (*reqi'im*), expanses or firmaments].'" Here the expanses are the *sefirot* from *Ḥesed* to *Shekhinah.* See *Zohar* 1:85b; 2:56b.

739. **the holy name is consummated** In Kabbalah the name יהוה (*YHVH*) represents the entirety of the *sefirot:* י (*yod*) symbolizes the primordial point of *Ḥokhmah;* the feminine marker ה (*he*) symbolizes *Binah,* the Divine Mother; ו (*vav*), whose numerical value is six, symbolizes the six *sefirot* from *Ḥesed* through *Yesod;* and the final ה (*he*) symbolizes *Shekhinah. Ḥokhmah* and *Binah*

waters,[740] above other creatures,[741] separating upper waters from lower waters. The lower waters call to the upper and imbibe them through this *expanse separating them*,[742] for all those waters merge in it, and then it sheds them upon these creatures, drawing from there.

"It is written: *A locked garden is my sister, bride; a locked fountain, a sealed spring* (Song of Songs 4:12). *A locked garden,* for within all is enclosed, all is embraced.[743] *A locked fountain,* for that river gushes, flows, and enters it, and it absorbs without releasing, the water congealing within.[744] Why is this? Because the north wind blows on those waters and they congeal, unable to flow out, eventually turning into ice.[745] Were it not for the wind from the side of the South whose power smashes this ice,[746] the waters would never flow. The appearance of that supernal *expanse* is like this ice congealing, gathering all those waters within.[747] Similarly, that supernal one above gathers all those waters and separates upper from lower.

by themselves spell out the name יה (*Yah*), while the final seven *sefirot*, "the seven expanses," complete the name יהוה (*YHVH*).

740. **This *expanse* lies in the middle...** *Yesod,* the *expanse,* separates the upper *sefirot* from *Shekhinah,* through whom the flow extends to the worlds below.

See *Targum Onqelos,* Genesis 1:6; *Zohar* 1:20a, 21a; Moses de León, *Sefer ha-Rimmon,* 198.

741. **other creatures** The *ḥayyot* ("living creatures, animals") who transport the divine throne (*Shekhinah*). See Ezekiel 1:22: *There was a shape above the heads of the creature, of an expanse that looked like awesome ice, stretched above their heads.* Here the *ḥayyot* are called "other creatures" in contradistinction to the "creatures" within the world of the *sefirot: Ḥesed, Gevurah, Tif'eret,* and *Shekhinah.* See above, page 160.

742. **The lower waters call to the upper...** The lower powers seek the streaming energy of the *sefirot.* See *Bereshit Rabbah* 13:13: "Rabbi Shim'on son of El'azar said, 'Every single handbreadth [of water] descending from above is met by two handbreadths emitted by the earth. What is the reason? *Deep calls to deep...* (Psalms 42:8).' Rabbi Levi said, 'The upper waters are male; the lower, female. The former cry to the latter, "Receive us! You are creatures of the blessed Holy One and we are His messen-

gers." They immediately receive them, as is written: *Let the earth open* (Isaiah 45:8)— like a female opening to a male.'"

See *Tosefta, Ta'anit* 1:4; 1 Enoch 54:8; *Seder Rabbah di-Vreshit,* 10 (*Battei Midrashot,* 1:25); *Pirqei de-Rabbi Eli'ezer* 23; *Zohar* 1:29b, 46a, 60b, 244a–b, 245b; 3:223b.

743. **for within all is enclosed...** *Shekhinah* contains the entire flow of emanation.

744. **that river gushes, flows...** The river of emanation empties into *Shekhinah,* which absorbs the waters but does not release them.

745. **Because the north wind blows...** The harsh power of *Gevurah* freezes the waters that have gathered in *Shekhinah,* preventing them from streaming on to the worlds below.

See *Bereshit Rabbah* 4:2: "Rav said, 'The works of Creation [i.e., the heavens] were fluid, and on the second day they congealed. *Let there be an expanse [in the midst of the waters]!* (Genesis 1:6), Let the expanse be firm!'" Cf. *Zohar* 1:29b; 2:167b.

746. **wind from the side of the South...** The warmth of *Ḥesed,* which thaws the frozen sea of *Shekhinah.*

747. **The appearance of that supernal *expanse*...** *Yesod.* See Ezekiel 1:22: *There was a shape above the heads of the creature, of an expanse that looked like awesome ice, stretched above their heads.*

"As to what we said: *Let there be an expanse in the midst of the waters,* meaning 'in the middle,' it is not so! Rather, it is written: *Let there be*—the one emerging from it lies in the middle of the waters, while it lies above, resting on the heads of the creatures."[748]

Rabbi Yitsḥak said, "There is a membrane in the midst of the innards of the human body, partitioning below and above, drawing from above, issuing below.[749] Similarly the *expanse* is in the middle, resting upon those creatures below, separating upper from lower waters.

"Come and see: Those waters conceived and bore darkness.[750] Concerning this mystery it is written: *The curtain will serve you as a partition between the Holy and the Holy of Holies* (Exodus 26:33)."[751]

Rabbi Abba opened, "*Setting the rafters of His lofts in the waters, making the clouds His chariot, walking on the wings of the wind* (Psalms 104:3). *In the waters*—the uppermost waters, by which He established the house, as is said: *By wisdom a house is built, by understanding established* (Proverbs 24:3).[752]

"*Making* עבים (avim), *the clouds, His chariot.* Rabbi Yeisa Sava divides עבים (avim) into עב ים (av yam), cloud, sea—a cloud that is darkness on the left abiding above this sea.[753]

"*Walking on the wings of the wind*—spirit of the supernal sanctuary,[754] mystery of *two cherubim of gold* (Exodus 25:18).[755] It is written: *He rode upon*

200

748. **it is not so!...** The *expanse, Yesod,* does not divide between the upper and lower waters; rather, it contains the upper waters—whereas *Shekhinah,* who emerges from *Yesod,* separates the two realms.

749. **There is a membrane...** The diaphragm, permeable only from above to below. The phrase "partitioning below and above" can also be rendered "impermeable below to above." According to medieval physiology, the diaphragm transmits moisture from the lungs to the lower parts of the body. Similarly, within the sefirotic body, *Yesod,* the *expanse,* separates the waters and channels emanation from above to below.

750. **Those waters conceived...** See *Shemot Rabbah* 15:22: "Water conceived and bore darkness." Here apparently the lower waters give birth to darkness. Cf. *Zohar* 1:103b, where the waters of *Ḥesed* give birth to the darkness of *Gevurah.*

751. ***The curtain will serve you as a partition...*** The curtain in the Tabernacle parallels the diaphragm in the human body and the *expanse* in the cosmos. Here *the curtain* symbolizes *Yesod,* who separates *Shekhinah* and *Binah,* symbolized respectively by *the Holy* and *the Holy of Holies.* See *Zohar* 2:178b (*SdTs*).

752. **the uppermost waters...the house...** The emanation emerging from *Hokhmah* (*wisdom*) and *Binah* (*understanding*) culminates in *Shekhinah,* the *house.*

753. **a cloud that is darkness...** *Gevurah,* on the left side of the sefirotic tree, hovering above the sea of *Shekhinah.*

754. **spirit of the supernal sanctuary** *Tif'eret,* known as רוח (*ruaḥ*), "spirit, wind," who emanates from *Binah,* the sanctuary above.

755. ***two cherubim...*** *Tif'eret* and *Shekhinah,* the divine couple. According to BT *Yoma* 54a, the cherubs in the Temple were depicted in sexual embrace: "Rabbi Katina

a cherub and flew, gliding on the wings of the wind (Psalms 18:11). *He rode upon a cherub*—one; afterward He manifested *on the wings of the wind.* Until this aroused, He did not manifest on that."[756]

Rabbi Yose said, "It is written: *He meted the waters by measure* (Job 28:25)— literally, *in measure,*[757] arraying them as they arrived in Her for the harmony of the world, as they arrived from the side of *Gevurah.*"[758]

Rabbi Abba said, "When the ancients arrived at this site, they would say: 'The lips of the wise move but they say nothing lest they be punished.'"[759]

Rabbi El'azar said, "First letter of all[760] flitted on the surface of pure vapor,[761] was crowned below and above, ascended [33a] and descended. Waters carved in carvings settle in their sites, merging in one another.[762] So all the letters combine with each other, crown one another until a structure is soundly constructed.[763] Once all were constructed and crowned, upper waters mingled with lower, generating the house of the world.[764] So ב (*bet*) appears at the be-

said, 'When Israel ascended [to Jerusalem] for the Festival, the curtain would be rolled open for them and the cherubs revealed, their bodies intertwined. They [the people] would be addressed: "Look! You are beloved by God as intensely as the love between man and woman."'"

756. **Until this aroused...** Until *Shekhinah*, the *cherub*, was aroused, *Tif'eret* did not fully reveal Himself.

757. **literally, *in measure*...** In *Shekhinah*, last of the *sefirot*, through which the Infinite becomes finite.

758. **from the side of *Gevurah*** *Shekhinah* is influenced by this *sefirah*, located on the left.

759. **When the ancients arrived at this site...** At the stage of mystical ascent described in BT *Ḥagigah* 14b: "Rabbi Akiva said to them [his companions on the mystical journey: Ben Azzai, Ben Zoma, and Elisha son of Avuyah], 'When you arrive at the stones of pure marble, do not say, "Water, water!" For it is said, *One who speaks falsehood shall not remain in My sight* (Psalms 101:7).'"

"This site" may also allude to the verse: *God said, "Let there be an expanse in the midst of the waters, and let it separate water from water"* (Genesis 1:6). This verse served as a focus of speculation and contemplation. See

the various estimates of the size of the separation in *Ḥagigah* 15a, including that of Ben Zoma: "I was gazing between the upper and lower waters, and there is merely three fingers' breadth between them."

760. **First letter of all** The letter א (*alef*), which symbolizes the first *sefirah*, *Keter*. See *Bahir* 48 (70). Its shape (a line separating two points) symbolizes the *expanse* separating the upper and lower waters.

761. **pure vapor** קיטרא דכיא (*Qitra dakhya*), referring to *Keter*, the first *sefirah*, also known as אוירא דכיא (*avira dakhya*), "pure ether, air."

See above, page 108: "a cluster of vapor forming in formlessness." Cf. 3:135b (*IR*), 292b (*IZ*); Scholem, *Origins of the Kabbalah*, 331–47; and *Sefer Yetsirah* 2:6: "Out of chaos He formed substance, making what is not into what is. He hewed enormous pillars out of ether that cannot be grasped."

762. **Waters carved...** Emanation assumes the form of the *sefirot*.

763. **So all the letters...** The letters of the alphabet permutate and spell out words, thereby constituting spiritual entities. See *Sefer Yetsirah* 4:12: "Two stones [letters] build two houses...."

764. **the house of the world** *Shekhinah*, the Divine Presence who includes all of creation. See above, page 173.

ginning.[765] Waters ascend and descend until this *expanse* comes to be, separating them. Division occurred on the second, on which Hell was created,[766] a blazing fire—as is said: *He is a consuming fire* (Deuteronomy 4:24)—destined to rain upon the heads of the wicked."

Rabbi Yehudah said, "From here we learn that every division of opinion for the sake of heaven is destined to endure,[767] for here is a division for the sake of heaven, and through it heaven endured, as is written: *God called the expanse Heaven* (Genesis 1:8).[768]

"In a waterskin of lofts they appear by the pint and endure.[769] For we have learned that it is written: *The curtain shall serve you as a partition between the Holy and the Holy of Holies* (Exodus 26:33), precisely, for this is an *expanse* dividing in the middle.[770]

765. **So ב (*bet*) appears at the beginning** The initial letter of the Torah, the ב (*bet*) of בראשית (*Be-reshit*), *In the beginning,* symbolizes the בית (*bayit*), "house," of the world.

766. **Division occurred on the second...** The upper waters were separated from the lower waters on the second day of Creation, corresponding to the second of the seven lower *sefirot,* *Gevurah,* who administers strict justice and conflicts with divine love, *Ḥesed.* Hell and conflict emerged on the second day, according to *Bereshit Rabbah* 4:6: "Why is *that it was good* not written concerning the second day? Rabbi Yoḥanan said..., 'Because on that day Hell was created....' Rabbi Ḥanina said, 'Because on that day conflict was created: *that it may separate water from water.'...* Rabbi Shemu'el son of Naḥman said, 'Because the work of the water was not completed. Therefore *that it was good* is written twice on the third day: once for the work of the water [see Genesis 1:9–10] and once for the work of the [third] day [ibid., 11].'"

See BT *Pesaḥim* 54a; *Pirqei de-Rabbi Eli-'ezer* 4; *Midrash Konen* (Beit ha-Midrash, 2:25); Ezra of Gerona, *Peirush Shir ha-Shirim,* 506; *Zohar* 1:17a–b, 18a, 46a; 2:149b; Moses de León, *Sheqel ha-Qodesh,* 41 (49).

767. **every division of opinion for the sake of heaven...** See M *Avot* 5:17: "Every conflict that is for the sake of heaven is destined to endure, while every conflict not for the sake of heaven is not destined to endure.

Which conflict is for the sake of heaven? The conflict between Hillel and Shammai. Which is not for the sake of heaven? The conflict of Korah and his entire band."

768. **through it heaven endured...** *Tif'eret,* known as *Heaven,* endured as a result of the conflict between the *sefirot* on the right and left, *Ḥesed* and *Gevurah. Yesod,* the *expanse,* is an extension of *Tif'eret* and shares His name. See above, pages 127–31.

769. **In a waterskin of lofts...** One of the *Zohar*'s neologistic gnomes, apparently alluding to the waters measured in heaven. See Liebes, *Peraqim,* 349. קטפירא (*Qatpira*)—perhaps an expansion of קטרא (*qitra*), "knot, bond, connection"—carries several meanings in the *Zohar,* including "waterskin," which here refers to the waters above. See Psalms 119:83; and Job 38:37: *Who can tilt the waterskins of the sky?*

The "lofts" are the heavens, as in Psalms 104:3, cited above (page 200): *Setting the rafters of His lofts in the waters.*

"By the pint" renders בקסטייהו (*be-qistaihu*), "in their pints." The singular, קסטא (*qista*), derives from the Greek *xestes,* a measure about the size of a pint. See Job 28:25, also cited above: *He meted the waters by measure.* Cf. *Bereshit Rabbah* 4:5: "Ben Pazzi said, 'The upper waters exceed the lower waters by about thirty *xestes.'*"

770. **The curtain shall serve you...** As *the curtain* divides *between the Holy and the Holy of Holies,* so *Yesod, the expanse,* sepa-

202

"Come and see what is written next: *Let the waters under heaven be gathered to one place* (Genesis 1:9)[771]—*under heaven*, literally![772] *To one place*—to a place called *One*, namely, the lower sea, completing *One*, without whom He is not called *One*.[773] *Let them be gathered* means that there all those waters converge, as is said: *All the rivers flow into the sea* (Ecclesiastes 1:7)."[774]

Rabbi Yeisa said, "*To one place*—the place of which is written: *My covenant of peace will not be shaken* (Isaiah 54:10), for He carries all and casts it into the sea.[775] By Him Earth is arrayed, as is written: *Let the dry land appear* (Genesis, ibid.)—Earth, as is said: *God called the dry land Earth* (ibid., 10).[776]

"Why is it called *dry land*?"[777]

Rabbi Yitsḥak said, "This corresponds to what is written: לחם עוני (*leḥem oni*), *bread of affliction* (Deuteronomy 16:3), spelled: לחם עני (*leḥem ani*), *impoverished bread*.[778] Since it is *impoverished bread*, it is called *dry land*, though it absorbs all the waters of the world. She remains *dry* until this *place* fills Her; then water streams through those springs.[779]

"*And the gathering of waters He called Seas* (Genesis, ibid.)—house of convergence above, where all waters converge, whence they flow and gush."[780]

Rabbi Ḥiyya said, "*The gathering of waters* is the Righteous One,[781] for when the text reaches *the gathering of waters*, it is written: *God saw that it was good*

203

---

rates the upper and lower waters. See above, page 200; cf. *Zohar* 2:178b (*SdTs*).

771. **what is written next...** In the account of the third day of Creation.

772. *under heaven*, **literally!** In the *Zohar*, the term ממש (*mammash*), "really, literally," often implies one of the *sefirot*, the realm of ultimate reality. Here the allusion is to *Tif'eret*, known as *heaven*, beneath whom streams of emanation gather.

773. **to a place called *One*...** To *Shekhinah*, the lower sea, who joins Her partner, *Tif'eret*, thereby completing the unity of the *sefirot*.

774. *All the rivers flow into the sea* The streams of emanation flow into the sea of *Shekhinah*.

775. **the place of which is written: *My covenant*...** Rabbi Yeisa offers a different interpretation: *One place* implies *Yesod*, the divine phallus—symbolized by the covenant of circumcision, who pours into the sea of *Shekhinah*. See above, pages 137–41.

776. **Earth...** *Shekhinah*.

777. **Why is it called *dry land*?** How can *Shekhinah*, who is called Sea, also be *dry land*?

778. **לחם עוני (*leḥem oni*), *bread of affliction*...** Referring to *matstsah*, unleavened bread eaten on Passover.

779. **Since it is *impoverished bread*...** *Shekhinah* on Her own lacks the waters of emanation, so She is impoverished and dry until filled by the flow of *Yesod*.

See BT *Pesaḥim* 36a–b, 115b–116a; *Zohar* 1:157a; 2:40a–b; Moses de León, *Sefer ha-Rimmon*, 112, 133.

780. **house of convergence above...** *Shekhinah*.

781. **the Righteous One** *Yesod* ("Foundation"), who channels the waters from above. He is known as Righteous One, based on Proverbs 10:25: וצדיק יסוד עולם (*Ve-tsaddiq yesod olam*), which literally means *The righteous one is an everlasting foundation* but is understood as *The righteous one is the foundation of the world*.

See BT *Ḥagigah* 12b; *Bahir* 71 (102); Azriel of Gerona, *Peirush ha-Aggadot*, 34.

(ibid.), and it is similarly written: *Say of the righteous one that he is good* (Isaiah 3:10).[782] So, too, the primordial light is called *good*,[783] and on all of them is written: *that it was good,* except for the second day, of which *good* is not written.[784]

Rabbi Yose said, "This מקוה (*miqveh*), *gathering,* is Israel, as is written: מקוה ישראל (*Miqveh Yisra'el*), *Hope of Israel—YHVH* (Jeremiah 17:13)."[785]

Rabbi Ḥiyya said, "It is the Righteous One, corresponding to what is written: *He called Seas* (Genesis, ibid.), for He conveys all springs, streams, and rivers;[786] He is the source of all, conveying all. So, *Seas,* and therefore: *God saw that it was good* (ibid.), and similarly: *Say of the righteous one that he is good* (Isaiah, ibid.). Since He is distinguished, the first day is separated from the third, and between them *that it was good* is not declared.[787] For on the third day Earth generated verdure from the power of this Righteous One, as is written: *God said, 'Let the earth sprout vegetation, seed-bearing plant, fruit tree'* (Genesis 1:11).[788] What is *fruit tree*? The Tree of Knowledge of Good and Evil, who generates fruit.[789] *Bearing fruit*—the Righteous One.[790] *Of its kind*—for every human being endowed with a holy spirit, fruit of that tree, is signed with an insignia *of its kind.*[791] What is that? Covenant of holiness, covenant of

782. *Say of the righteous one that he is good* This verse links *righteous one* with the phrase כי טוב (*ki tov*), *that he is good;* so by analogy the same phrase in Genesis, כי טוב (*ki tov*), *that it was good,* also implies the *righteous one,* namely, *Yesod.* See BT *Yoma* 38b.

783. **the primordial light is called** *good* See Genesis 1:4: *God saw that the light was good.*

784. **on all of them is written...** In the biblical account of Creation, the statement *God saw that it was good* (or a variant) is included in the description of each of the six days except for the second. See above, note 766.

785. **This** מקוה (*miqveh*), *gathering,* **is Israel...** Rabbi Yose contends that the word מקוה (*miqveh*) alludes to the central *sefirah, Tif'eret Yisra'el,* who is the third of the lower *sefirot* and associated with the third day of Creation.

786. *He called Seas...* *And the gathering of waters He called Seas.* This name fits *Yesod* since He includes the entire flow.

787. **Since He is distinguished...** Since *Yesod* is so full, the text highlights its crea-

tion on the third day by separating it from the first day with the account of the second day, in which the phrase כי טוב (*ki tov*), *that it was good,* does not appear. The third day is further distinguished by a double mention of *ki tov.*

788. **For on the third day...** *Shekhinah,* known as Earth, sprouted with life. The verse reads literally: *Let the earth sprout vegetation, seed-bearing plant, fruit tree bearing fruit of its kind with its seed in it on earth.*

789. **the Tree of Knowledge of Good and Evil...** Adam and Eve ate from this tree. In Kabbalah it symbolizes *Shekhinah,* who transmits either reward or punishment, depending on human behavior.

790. *Bearing fruit*—**the Righteous One** *Yesod,* the divine phallus. See *Zohar* 1:18b, 238a.

791. *Of its kind...* Souls are generated by *Yesod.* When a male infant is circumcised, he is linked with the source of his soul, the divine phallus.

On souls as fruit, see *Bahir* 14 (22); Ezra of Gerona, *Peirush Shir ha-Shirim,* 489, 504; *Zohar* 1:15b, 19a, 59b–60a, 82b, 85b, 115a–b;

peace.[792] Scions of faith are found, each *of its kind,* on the tree, not parting from it.[793] The Righteous One *bears fruit,* and the tree conceives, generating fruit *of its kind,* of the kind of that one *bearing fruit,* resembling Him.[794] Happy is the share of the one who resembles his mother and father! Therefore the holy insignia on the eighth day, so that he resemble his mother, and when the insignia is uncovered and revealed, he resembles his father.[795] So *fruit tree* is mother; *bearing fruit,* his father; *of its kind,* resembling him, marked by him.

"*With its seed in it on earth* (ibid.). זרעו (Zar'o), *Its seed, in it.* The verse should read: זרע (zera), *seed, in it.*[796] Why זרעו (zar'o), *its seed, in it*? So that the word may be read זרע ו׳ (zera vav), *the seed of* ו (vav), *in it on earth.* So it is indeed, for He pours that seed on Earth.[797]

"Happy is the share of Israel, for they are holy, resembling holy ones. Certainly of this is written: *Your people, all of them righteous* (Isaiah 60:21)— *all of them righteous,* indeed, for they emerged from these and resemble them. Happy are they in this world and in the world that is coming!"[798]

205

2:223b; Moses de León, *Sefer ha-Mishqal,* 51; idem, *Sheqel ha-Qodesh,* 56 (69). Cf. Ibn Ezra on Psalms 1:3.

792. **Covenant of holiness...** *Yesod,* symbolized by the covenant of circumcision.

793. **Scions of faith...** בני מהימנותא (*Benei meheimanuta*). The faithful ripen on the tree of *Shekhinah,* each fruit still linked with its source, *Yesod.*

794. **the tree conceives...** *Shekhinah* gives birth to humans who resemble *Yesod.*

795. **the one who resembles his mother and father...** When a male infant is circumcised on the eighth day, he resembles the divine couple: *Shekhinah* (the eighth *sefirah* counting from *Binah*) and *Yesod* (the divine phallus). The ritual of circumcision involves two stages. First, in מילה (*milah*), "cutting," the foreskin is cut and removed, disclosing the mucous membrane, which is then torn down the center and pulled back, revealing the corona. The act of tearing and pulling back the membrane is called פריעה (*peri'ah*), "uncovering" the corona. See M *Shabbat* 19:6: "If one circumcises but does not uncover the circumcision, it is as if he has not circumcised." The removal of the foreskin links the infant with *Shekhinah,*

while the act of *peri'ah* binds him with *Yesod.*

See *Zohar* 1:13a, 32a (*Tos*), 93b, 96b, 98b (*ST*); 2:3b, 40a, 125b; 3:91b; Moses de León, *Sefer ha-Mishqal,* 133; idem, *Sheqel ha-Qodesh,* 55 (67).

796. **The verse should read...** The pronominal suffix ו (vav), indicating *its,* in the word זרעו (zar'o), *its seed,* appears superfluous.

797. **So that the word may be read...** The letter ו (vav) has a numerical value of six and indicates *Tif'eret* together with the five *sefirot* surrounding Him (*Ḥesed* to *Yesod*). This entire flow of emanation pours into *Shekhinah,* the Earth. See above, page 146.

798. *all of them righteous,* indeed... They resemble the divine couple, *Yesod* and *Shekhinah,* known individually as צדיק (*Tsaddiq*), "Righteous One," and צדק (*Tsedeq*), "Righteousness," and together as צדיקים (*Tsaddiqim*), *Righteous.*

The verse from Isaiah, appearing frequently in the *Zohar,* reads in full: *Your people, all of them righteous, will inherit the land forever—sprout of My planting, work of My hands, that I may be glorified.* In M *Sanhedrin* 10:1, it is cited to demonstrate that "all of Israel have a share in the world that is coming."

[33b] Rabbi Ḥiyya said, "It is written: *He makes Earth by His power* (Jeremiah 10:12). Why *makes Earth*? The verse should read: *made Earth*. But indeed, *makes,* continuously! The blessed Holy One illumines and arrays this Earth.[799] *By His power*—the Righteous One.[800]

"*He establishes the world by His wisdom* (ibid.). *The world* is the earth below.[801] *By His wisdom*—Righteousness, as is written: *He will judge the world with righteousness* (Psalms 9:9).[802]

"*He makes Earth*—the blessed Holy One, who arrays Earth and its pathways. How? *By His power,* as we have explained."

Rabbi Yehudah said, "In *The Engraved Letters of Rabbi El'azar*[803] are clusters of letters, twenty-two clustered as one, two letters, one ascending, one descending—the descending, ascending; the ascending, descending—the sign being: אכ״ב ב״ך א״ל (*Akh bakh el*), *Surely God is in you* (Isaiah 45:14)."[804]

---

799. **The blessed Holy One illumines...** *Tif'eret* shines upon *Shekhinah.*

800. **the Righteous One** *Yesod.*

801. **the earth below** The physical universe.

802. **Righteousness...** *Shekhinah,* partner of *Yesod,* the Righteous One. She is also known as Lower Wisdom, daughter of *Ḥokhmah* ("Wisdom").

803. ***The Engraved Letters of Rabbi El'azar*** A manual of letter permutations attributed to the son of Rabbi Shim'on son of Yoḥai. This book, one of many housed in the real or imaginary library of the author(s) of the *Zohar,* is cited again in *Zohar* 3:175b, 285a, 286b; cf. 1:224a; 2:139b; 3:180b.

See Matt, *Zohar,* 25; and the comment by Shim'on Lavi, *KP,* on *Zohar* 1:7a: "All such books mentioned in the *Zohar*...have been lost in the wanderings of exile...Nothing is left of them except what is mentioned in the *Zohar.*"

804. **clusters of letters, twenty-two clustered as one...** A veiled description of the permutation of the twenty-two letters of the Hebrew alphabet, one of the primary methods of kabbalistic contemplation. According to *Sefer Yetsirah* (2:2, 4–5), the world was created by a divine act of permutation: "Twenty-two elemental letters. He engraved them, carved them, weighed them, permuted them, and transposed them—forming with them everything formed and everything destined to be formed....Twenty-two elemental letters. He set them in a wheel with 231 gates, turning forward and backward....How did He permute them? א (*Alef*) with them all, all of them with א (*alef*); ב (*bet*) with them all, all of them with ב (*bet*); and so with all the letters, turning round and round, within 231 gates."

The "231 gates" represent the number of two-letter combinations that can be formed from the twenty-two letters, provided that the same letter is not repeated. The permutations are often arranged in a table consisting of twenty-one rows, each containing eleven two-letter combinations (21 × 11 = 231). The biblical phrase cited here by the *Zohar* apparently indicates such a table: the word אך (*akh*) is numerically equivalent to twenty-one, the number of rows; the next word, בך (*bakh*), equals twenty-two, the number of letters in the alphabet; the final word, אל (*el*), is the opening combination of the middle row, according to a particular scheme of permutation (see the chart printed in *KP*). In this permutation the opening letters of the two-letter combinations "ascend" from א (*alef*) to ת (*tav*), while the second letters "descend" in reverse order.

See *OY; MM; Zohar* 2:9a–b, 132b; Isaac of Acre, *Peirush Sefer Yetsirah,* 385; Kaplan, *Sefer Yetsirah,* 108–24.

206

Rabbi Yose said, "The lip of the balance stands in the middle.[805] The sign: *In measuring or* משקל (*mishqal*), *weighing* (Leviticus 19:35).[806] *Mishqal, Weighing*—tongue standing in the middle, mystery of שקל הקדש (*sheqel ha-qodesh*), *the weight of holiness* (Exodus 30:13), from which scales are suspended and balanced.[807] Who are the scales? As is said: *Scales of justice* (Leviticus, ibid.), all suspended in the balance, *sheqel of holiness*."[808]

Rabbi Yehudah said, "*Sheqel of holiness*—spirit of holiness."[809]

Rabbi Yitsḥak said, "It is written: *By the word of YHVH the heavens were made, by the breath of His mouth all their host* (Psalms 33:6). *By the word of YHVH the heavens were made*—the heavens below, fashioned *by the word of* the heavens above through a breath generating a voice reaching that river flowing forth, whose waters never cease.[810] *By the breath of His mouth all their host*—all those below endure *by the breath*, namely, *the word*.

"*Watering mountains from His lofts; from the fruit of Your work, Earth is sated* (ibid. 104:13). This is well known. *Watering mountains from His lofts*. Who are *His lofts*? As we have explained, for it is written: *Setting the rafters of His lofts in the waters* (ibid., 3).[811] *From the fruit of Your work, Earth is sated*—mystery of that river flowing forth below, as is written: *bearing fruit with its seed in it*... (Genesis 1:11), as explained."[812]

Let there be מארת (*me'orot*), *lights, in the expanse of heaven*.... (Genesis 1:14). *Let there be* מארת (*me'erat*), *curse*, spelled deficiently.[813]

805. **The lip**... סיפתא (*Sifta*), apparently a playful reference to the tongue in the middle of the balance. The verse cited in the preceding line may refer to the middle row of a particular scheme of permutation (see previous note).

806. **In measuring**... The full verse reads: *You are not to commit corruption in justice—in measure, weight, or capacity.*

807. **mystery of** שקל הקדש (*sheqel ha-qodesh*), *the weight of holiness*... Referring to a cosmic scale or to *Shekhinah*. See Moses de León, *Sefer ha-Rimmon*, 169.

808. *Scales of justice*... Referring to scales in the celestial palaces or to *Netsaḥ* and *Hod*. See *Zohar* 2:95b, 175b, 252a; *TZ, Haqdamah*, 17b; 5, 19b.

809. **spirit of holiness** Holy Spirit, often identified with *Shekhinah*. See *Zohar* 1:67a; 2:97b, 238b; 3:61a.

810. **fashioned** *by the word of* **the heavens above**... The heavens below were generated by the power of *Tif'eret*, "the heavens above," channeled through the river of *Yesod*. On breath, voice, and word, see *Sefer Yetsirah* 1:9.

811. **As we have explained**... See above, page 200. Cf. *Zohar* 2:98b, where *His lofts* refers to *Netsaḥ* and *Hod*.

812. **mystery of that river flowing forth**... *Yesod*, who is indicated by the phrase *bearing fruit*. See above, page 204. He flows into *Shekhinah*, the Earth, who is referred to in the conclusion of the verse from Genesis: *bearing fruit with its seed in it of its kind on earth*.

813. מארת (*me'erat*), *curse*, spelled deficiently In Genesis 1:14, the word מארת (*me'orot*) is written without *vavs*, the vowel letters. This deficient spelling is interpreted

Rabbi Ḥizkiyah said, "מארת (*Me'erat*), *Curse*, for there abides the rigor of the seepage of judgment."[814]

Rabbi Yose said, "*Let there be* מארת (*me'erat*), *curse*, below, for diphtheria in the world's children depends upon her,[815] and she depends upon this מארת (*me'orot*), smallest of all the lights, sometimes darkened, receiving no light.[816]

"*In the expanse of heaven*—the expanse that is the sum of them all, for it receives all lights and illumines the light that does not shine because that מארה (*me'erah*), curse, clung to it.[817] All those other species below depend upon it because of the diminution of the light."[818]

Rabbi Yitsḥak said, "Even this expanse that does not shine is called *expanse of heaven*, and similarly Kingdom of Heaven, Land of Israel.[819] This expanse derives from Heaven. So, *Let there be* מארת (*me'erat*), *curse*, missing the ו (*vav*).[820] Why? Because without ו (*vav*) death appears in the world.[821] *Let there be* מארת (*me'erat*), *curse*—everything depends upon this, including Lilith in the

208

to mean that something was missing on the fourth day of Creation: the light of *Shekhinah*, symbolized by the moon, diminished, and this lack represents the potential for evil or "curse": מארה (*me'erah*).

See JT *Ta'anit* 4:4, 68b: "On the fourth day [of the week, Wednesday] they would fast for infants, so that diphtheria not enter their mouths. *God said, 'Let there be* מארת (*me'orot*), *lights'*—spelled מארת (*me'erat*), curse."

See Proverbs 3:33; BT *Ta'anit* 27b, *Ḥullin* 60b; *Pesiqta de-Rav Kahana* 5:1; *Soferim* 17:4; Rashi and *Minḥat Shai* on Genesis 1:14; *Zohar* 1:1a, 12a, 19b; 2:167b, 205a.

814. **the rigor of the seepage of judgment** *Shekhinah* is influenced by the left side of the *sefirot*, dominated by *Gevurah*, the *sefirah* of *Din* ("Judgment"). On קילטא (*qilta*), "absorbing, seepage," see above, page 181: "dregs of an inkwell in seepage," and note 609.

815. **diphtheria...** This dread disease originates in Lilith, the demoness below the divine realm, who strikes children.

See *Zohar* 1:19b; 2:264b, 267b; and above, note 813.

816. **she depends upon...** Lilith depends on *Shekhinah*, last of the *sefirot*, who inclines toward Judgment.

817. **the expanse that is the sum...** *Yesod, the expanse of heaven*, includes the light

of all the *sefirot* above Him and illumines *Shekhinah*, the light that does not shine.

818. **All those other species...** External powers are nourished by the dimmed light of *Shekhinah*, symbolized by the moon. See BT *Ḥullin* 60b: "Rabbi Shim'on son of Pazzi pointed out a contradiction. 'It is written: *God made the two great lights* (Genesis 1:16), and it is written [in the same verse]: *the greater light... and the lesser light*. The moon said before the blessed Holy One, "Master of the Universe! Can two kings possibly wear one crown?" He answered, "Go, diminish yourself!"'"

819. **this expanse that does not shine...** *Shekhinah* does not shine with light of Her own and is dependent on *Tif'eret*. Her link to this source of light is indicated by Her names *expanse of heaven*, Kingdom of Heaven, and Land of Israel—since *Tif'eret* is known as both Heaven and Israel.

820. **missing the ו (*vav*)** See above, note 813.

821. **without ו (*vav*)...** The letter ו (*vav*), whose numerical value is six, symbolizes *Tif'eret*, the Tree of Life, together with the five *sefirot* surrounding Him (*Ḥesed* to *Yesod*). Without the vivifying vav, the life force no longer flows through *Shekhinah* to the world.

See *Zohar* 1:12b, 241b; 2:137a; 3:176b.

world.[822] It is written: *Small and great alike are there* (Job 3:19), and similarly: *There YHVH shall be majestic for us* (Isaiah 33:21), and so: *There Lilith shall repose and find herself a resting place* (ibid. 34:14)."[823]

Rabbi El'azar said, "*Let there be* מארת (*me'orot*)—a speculum that does not shine on its own[824] but like a lantern absorbing light and glowing.

"It is written: *Behold the ark of the covenant, Lord of all the earth* (Joshua 3:11). *Behold the ark*—מארת (*me'orot*);[825] *the ark*—the chest containing Written Torah.[826] *The covenant*—the sun illumining Her, to illumine the world.[827] *The ark of the covenant*—precisely, *Lord of all the earth*. *The covenant* is *Lord of all the earth,* so this *ark* is *Lord* because of the sun illumining it, illumining the whole world.[828] [34a] From Him this *ark* takes its name, being called in the mystery of אל״ף, דל״ת, נו״ן, יו״ד (*alef, dalet, nun, yod*).[829] As we say: 'Righteous One and Righteousness,'[830] and similarly: אדון (*Adon*), *Lord;* אדני (*Adonai*), one dependent on the other.

822. **Lilith in the world** The demoness Lilith is the wife of Samael, and together they oversee *Sitra Aḥra,* "the Other Side." See *Zohar* 1:148a (*ST*); 2:245a; Scholem, *Kabbalah,* 356–61.

823. *Small and great alike are there... There ... There Lilith...* The biblical word *there* signifies *Shekhinah,* the Divine Presence. The deficient spelling of מארת (*me'orot*) indicates the potential for evil, symbolized by Lilith, who dwells in the vicinity of *Shekhinah.*

824. **speculum...** אספקלריא (*Ispaqlarya*), "Glass, mirror, lens, speculum." See BT *Yevamot* 49b: "All the prophets gazed through a dim glass [literally: an *ispaqlarya* that does not shine], whereas Moses our Rabbi gazed through a clear glass [literally: an *ispaqlarya* that shines]." Cf. 1 Corinthians 13:12: "For now we see through a glass darkly, but then face-to-face."

Shekhinah is the "speculum [or: mirror] that does not shine on its own" but rather reflects the other *sefirot.* See *Zohar* 1:183a; 2:23b. The deficient spelling of מארת (*me'orot*) indicates the lack of independent light.

825. מארת (*me'orot*) *Shekhinah.* See above, note 813.

826. **Written Torah** *Tif'eret.*

827. **the sun...** *Yesod, the covenant,* illumines *Shekhinah.*

On *Yesod* as sun, see *Zohar* 1:9a; 2:3b, 136b–137b; 3:12a, 225b; Moses de León, *Sod Eser Sefirot,* 381; idem, *Shushan Edut,* 338; idem, *Sheqel ha-Qodesh,* 50 (61).

828. *The ark of the covenant*—*precisely...* *Shekhinah* is *the ark* housing *the covenant, Yesod,* and She thereby inherits His name: אדון (*Adon*), *Lord.*

See *Zohar* 1:2a, 59b, 228b; Moses de León, *Sheqel ha-Qodesh,* 75 (95).

829. **the mystery of** אל״ף, דל״ת, נו״ן, יו״ד (*alef, dalet, nun, yod*) *Shekhinah* is called אדני (*Adonai*), "My Lord," because of Her link with *Yesod,* called אדון (*Adon*), *Lord.* See *Zohar* 2:235b.

830. **Righteous One and Righteousness** *Yesod* and *Shekhinah.* See *Zohar* 1:32a (*Tos*), 49a; 3:287a.

Yesod ("Foundation") is known as Righteous One, based on Proverbs 10:25: וצדיק יסוד עולם (*Ve-tsaddiq yesod olam*), which literally means *The righteous one is an everlasting foundation* but is understood as *The righteous one is the foundation of the world.* See BT *Ḥagigah* 12b; *Bahir* 71 (102); Azriel of Gerona, *Peirush ha-Aggadot,* 34.

Shekhinah, partner of Righteous One, is called Righteousness.

"Come and see: Stars and constellations endure through a covenant, which is indeed *the expanse of heaven* (Genesis, ibid., 15), in which stars and constellations are traced and engraved, in which they are suspended to shine."[831]

Rabbi Yeisa Sava used to say: "*Let there be* מארת (*me'orot*), suspended *in the expanse of heaven*—the moon.[832] Once it is written: *Let them be for* מאורת (*me'orot*), *lights* (ibid.)—behold, the sun....[833] *For seasons* (ibid., 14),[834] because times, festivals, months, and Sabbaths depend upon them. All through the supernal, primordial act, linked with His holy name.[835] He is all.

"There are seven planets corresponding to seven heavens, all of them conducting the world, and above them the upper world.[836] There are two worlds: the upper world and the lower world, lower resembling upper, for it is written: *From world to world* (Psalms 106:48), upper king and lower king.[837] It is written: 'YHVH is king, YHVH was king, YHVH will be king for eternity.'[838] YHVH is king—above; YHVH was king—in the middle; YHVH will be king—below."

Rabbi Aḥa said, "YHVH is king—the upper world, the world that is coming.[839]

210

831. **Stars and constellations...** See BT *Ḥagigah* 12b: "Resh Lakish said, 'There are seven heavens....The one called רקיע (*raqi'a*), expanse, is that in which the sun, moon, stars, and constellations are set.'"

Here *the expanse* symbolizes *Yesod*, known as Covenant. See *Zohar* 1:8b, 17a–b; 2:2a, 246a.

832. *Let there be* מארת (*me'orot*), suspended... The deficient spelling of מארת (*me'orot*) indicates a lack, as in the diminution of the moon. See above, notes 813 and 818.

833. **Once it is written...** In the following verse, the word is spelled out more completely (מאורת [*me'orot*], with a *vav*), thus indicating the fuller light of the sun, symbolizing *Tif'eret* and *Yesod*. See *Minḥat Shai*, ad loc. The ellipsis points at the end of this sentence indicate a lacuna in the text, as attested by several of the manuscripts (C9, V7, O2).

834. *For seasons...* The full verse reads: *God said, "Let there be lights in the expanse of heaven to separate the day from the night, that they may be for signs and for seasons, for days and years."*

835. **linked with His holy name** Creation was enacted through the power of the divine name.

836. **seven planets...** The seven planets correspond to the seven lower *sefirot*, known as רקיעין (*reqi'in*), "heavens, expanses."

837. **two worlds...** Though the statement could refer to the physical world and the spiritual world (see *Zohar* 1:38a), the continuation of the passage concerns the two worlds within the *sefirot*: *Binah* and *Shekhinah*, known as upper and lower kings (above, pages 170–73).

See *Zohar* 1:153b, 158b, 248b; 2:22a, 53b; 3:145b, 285b, 297b.

838. **It is written...** This is not a biblical verse but rather a liturgical formula. See *Bahir* 80 (111), 88 (127).

839. **the world that is coming** עלמא דאתי (*Alma de-atei*), the Aramaic equivalent of the rabbinic Hebrew העולם הבא (*ha-olam ha-ba*), "the world that is coming." This concept is often understood as referring to the hereafter and is usually translated as "the world to come." From another point of view, however, "the world that is coming" already exists, occupying another dimension. See *Tanḥuma, Vayiqra* 8: "The wise call it *ha-olam ha-ba* not because it does not exist now, but for us today in this world it is still to come." Cf. Maimonides, *Mishneh Torah, Hilkhot Teshuvah* 8:8; and Guttmann,

YHVH was king—*Tif'eret Yisra'el*.[840] YHVH will be king—*the ark of the covenant*.[841] Another time David reversed them, from below to above, saying: *YHVH is king forever and ever* (Psalm 10:16). *YHVH is king*, below; *forever*—in the middle; ועד (*va-ed*), *and ever*—above, site of ויעודא (*vi'uda*), convening, and enduring in the consummation of all.[842] *King*, above; *king*, below."[843]

Rabbi Abba said, "All these lights join *in the expanse of heaven to shine upon earth* (Genesis 1:15), to illumine Earth. Who is the expanse illumining Earth? You must admit, this is the river flowing forth from Eden, as is written: *A river issues from Eden to water the garden* (Genesis 2:10).[844]

"Come and see: Once the moon prevails, illumined by that river flowing forth, all those heavens below and their hosts are augmented with light.[845] The stars empowered over the world prevail, raising plants and trees.[846] Earth grows in its entirety—even the waters and fish of the sea abound. Countless wardens of judgment roam the world, overjoyed and empowered.[847] When joy prevails in the king's palace, even the gatekeepers, even crag dwellers[848] all revel and roam the world, and children of the world must beware."

Philosophies of Judaism, 37: "'The world to come' does not succeed 'this world' in time, but exists from eternity as a reality outside and above time, to which the soul ascends."

In Kabbalah "the world that is coming" often refers to *Binah*, the continuous source of emanation. See *Zohar* 3:290b (*IZ*): "the world that is coming, constantly coming, never ceasing."

Cf. *Bahir* 106 (160); Asher ben David, *Peirush Shelosh Esreh Middot*, in *Kabbalah* 2 (1997): 293; Moses de León, *Sheqel ha-Qodesh*, 26 (30); idem, *Sod Eser Sefirot*, 375; *Zohar* 1:83a, 92a.

840. *Tif'eret Yisra'el*   "Beauty of Israel," the central *sefirah*.

841. *the ark of the covenant*   *Shekhinah*, the last *sefirah*, who houses *Yesod*, *the covenant*.

842. site of ויעודא (*vi'uda*), convening . . .   *Binah*, source and perfection of all.

843. *King*, above; *king*, below   *Binah* and *Shekhinah*.

844. the river flowing forth from Eden . . .   *Yesod*, who conveys the flow of emanation to *Shekhinah*, known as Earth.

845. the moon . . .   Symbolizing *Shekhinah*.

846. **raising plants and trees**   See *Bereshit Rabbah* 10:6: "Rabbi Simon said, 'You cannot find a single blade of grass [Oxford MS 147 adds: 'below'] that does not have a constellation in the sky, striking it and telling it: "Grow!"'"

Cf. *Zohar* 1:251a (*Hash*); 2:171b; 3:86a; Moses de León, *Sefer ha-Rimmon*, 181, 294; idem, *Sefer ha-Mishqal*, 135; Maimonides, *Guide of the Perplexed* 2:10.

847. **wardens of judgment . . .**   Harsh powers. The Zoharic term גרדיני (*gardinei*), "wardens, guardians," derives from the Castilian *guardián*. See Corominas, *Diccionario*, 3:246–48.

848. **crag dwellers**   מדבי טרטשי (*Mi-devei tarteshei*). *Tarteshei* may derive from טרש (*teresh*), "crag, stony ground," here the hiding place of the demons. Alternatively, it could be a corruption of תיאטראות (*ti'atra'ot*), "theaters, spectacles" (see Jastrow, *Dictionary*, 552a, 1663a), in which case the phrase would mean: "crowds from the stadium," "those of the theaters."

The point of the saying is that the overflow from *Shekhinah* ("the king's palace") also energizes demonic powers, who run rampant, threatening innocent children. At any mo-

Rabbi Aḥa said, "*God placed them in the expanse of heaven* (Genesis 1:17).[849] When all of them are present there, joy prevails between one another.[850] Then the moon diminishes herself in the presence of the sun,[851] and whatever he conveys is designed to illumine her, as is written: *to shine upon earth* (ibid.)."[852]

Rabbi Yitsḥak said, "It is written: *The light of the moon shall be like the light of the sun, and the light of the sun shall be sevenfold, like the light of the seven days* (Isaiah 30:26). Who are *the seven days*? The seven days of Creation."[853]

Rabbi Yehudah said, "These are the seven days of מלואים (*millu'im*), investiture—*millu'im*, filling, indeed, for at that time the world is rendered firm and fragrant, restored to fullness.[854] The moon is not tainted by the evil serpent, of whom is written: *A whisperer separates an intimate* (Proverbs 16:28).[855] When is this? When *He will swallow up death forever* (Isaiah 25:8). Then this verse will be fulfilled: *On that day YHVH will be one and His name one* (Zechariah 14:9)."

212

Let the waters swarm with a swarm of living souls (Genesis 1:20).

Rabbi El'azar said, "These are the lower waters, teeming with species as above, those higher, these lower."[856]

ment, Lilith, Mother of the Demons, may strike with diphtheria.

849. *God placed them in the expanse of heaven to shine upon earth.*

850. **When all of them are present...** When the *sefirot* gather in *Yesod*.

851. **Then the moon diminishes herself...** See BT Ḥullin 60b: "Rabbi Shim'on son of Pazzi pointed out a contradiction. 'It is written: *God made the two great lights* (Genesis 1:16), and it is written [in the same verse]: *the greater light... and the lesser light.* The moon said before the blessed Holy One, "Master of the Universe! Can two kings possibly wear one crown?" He answered, "Go, diminish yourself!"'" Cf. *Zohar* 3:191a.

852. **whatever he conveys...** Whatever *Tif'eret* receives from above is intended for *Shekhinah*.

853. **seven days of Creation** The seven *sefirot* from *Ḥesed* to *Shekhinah*, each of which manifests on one day of the primal week of Creation. See *Vayiqra Rabbah* 11:1.

854. **seven days of מלואים (*millu'im*), investiture...** The weeklong ceremony of installing the priests described in Leviticus 8.

The literal meaning of the word מלואים (*millu'im*), "filling," alludes to the restoration of the full brightness of the moon (and of *Shekhinah*). See *Vayiqra Rabbah* 11:4.

On the phrase "rendered firm and fragrant," see above, note 623.

855. **not tainted by the evil serpent...** See *Bereshit Rabbah* 20:2: "*A whisperer separates an intimate....A whisperer*—[this is the serpent] for he whispered rebelliously against his Creator, saying: *You surely will not die* (Genesis 3:4). *Separates an* אלוף (*aluf*), *intimate*—for he separated the אלוף (*Aluf*), Chief, of the world [he caused *Shekhinah* to depart] and was immediately cursed." Cf. *Bereshit Rabbah* 19:7.

The serpent's advice led to the eating of the Tree of Knowledge and the separation of *Tif'eret* and *Shekhinah*, symbolized by the diminution of the moon.

856. **These are the lower waters...** The waters emerging from the *sefirot* are a continuation of the upper waters within the world of the *sefirot*. Both generate souls. See *Zohar* 1:46b.

Rabbi Ḥiyya said, "The higher generated *a living soul.* What is that? The soul of Adam, as is said: האדם (*Ha-adam*), *The human, became a living soul* (Genesis 2:7).[857]

"*And let birds fly upon the earth* (ibid. 1:20)—messengers from above appearing to humans in human appearance, as implied by the wording *fly upon the earth.*[858] For there are others who appear only in genuine spirit, according to human awareness.[859] [34b] So of these is not written: *after its kind,* as with those others, of whom is written: *every winged bird after its kind* (ibid., 21), for these never change their kind, like these others, of whom is not written: *after its kind.*[860]

"Now if you say, 'Some of them differ from one another'—certainly so, some of them do differ, and so it is written: *From there it divides* (ibid. 2:10).[861]

"*God created the great sea serpents* (ibid. 1:21)[862]—Leviathan and his mate.[863]

"*And every* נפש החיה (*nefesh ha-ḥayyah*), *soul of the living being, who glides—* the soul of that *living being* gliding in all four directions of the world. Who is She? Night.[864]

213

857. **The soul of Adam...** See *Tanḥuma* (Buber), *Tazri'a* 2: "Rabbi El'azar son of Pedat says, '... [Of the six things created on the sixth day,] the soul of Adam was created first, as is said: *Let earth bring forth a living soul* (Genesis 1:24). *A living soul* means the soul of Adam, as is said: *The human became a living soul.*"

See *Bereshit Rabbah* 7:5; *Zohar* 3:39b.

858. **messengers...** Angels, symbolized by birds, who manifest in human form, that is, *upon the earth.* See *Bereshit Rabbah* 1:3; *Devarim Rabbah* 8:2; *Zohar* 1:13a, 46b; 3:39b.

859. **only in genuine spirit...** Without assuming bodily form.

860. **So of these is not written:** *after its kind...* Of those angels who *fly upon earth,* i.e., who appear in human form on earth, the biblical text does not say: *after its kind,* since by appearing on earth, they change their *kind.* The phrase *after its kind* is reserved for angels of genuine spirit, who never appear in physical form and so never change their *kind.*

861. *From there it divides* The full verse reads: *A river issues from Eden to water the garden, and from there it divides and becomes four stream-heads.* Once the flow of

emanation reaches *Shekhinah, the garden,* it branches off into various kinds of angels.

See *Zohar* 3:40a; Tishby, *Wisdom of the Zohar,* 2:556–57.

862. *God created the great sea serpents* The verse continues: *and every soul of the living being who glides, with which the waters swarmed after their kind, and every winged bird after its kind.*

863. **Leviathan and his mate** See BT *Bava Batra* 74b: "*God created the great sea serpents.*... Rabbi Yoḥanan said, 'This is Leviathan the elusive serpent and Leviathan the twisting serpent [see Isaiah 27:1]....' Rav Yehudah said in the name of Rav, 'Everything that the blessed Holy One created in His world, He created male and female. Even Leviathan the elusive serpent and Leviathan the twisting serpent He created male and female, and if they mated with another, they would destroy the entire world. What did the blessed Holy One do? He castrated the male and killed the female, salting her for the righteous in the world to come, as is written: *He will slay the dragon of the sea* (ibid.).'"

See Ezra of Gerona, *Peirush Shir ha-Shirim,* 510; *Zohar* 1:46b.

864. **that** *living being* **gliding... Night** *Shekhinah,* the Divine Presence who spreads

"With which the waters swarmed, after their kind—for waters nourish them.[865] When South arrives, waters are released, flowing in all directions.[866] Ships of the sea sail away, plying, as is said: *There ships travel, Leviathan whom You formed to play with* (Psalms 104:26).[867]

"And every winged bird after its kind—as is said: *For a bird of heaven will carry the sound, a winged creature will report the word* (Ecclesiastes 10:20)."[868]

Rabbi Yose said, "All of them are six-winged, never changing, so it is written: *after its kind.* What does this mean? After a supernal kind.[869] These sweep through the world in six,[870] observing the actions of human beings, conveying them above.[871] So, *even in your thoughts do not curse the king, even in your bedroom do not curse the rich, for a bird of heaven will carry the sound* (ibid.)."[872]

Rabbi Ḥizkiyah said, "הרומשת (*Ha-romeset*), *Who glides*—the verse should read: השורצת (*ha-shoretset*), *who swarms.*[873] But as we say: 'Night רמש (*remash*), dusked.'[874] So, *when all creatures of the forest* תרמוש (*tirmos*), *creep* (Psalms 104:20),[875] for when She reigns they all reign, opening with song in three

214

over the entire world. The word רומשת (*romeset*), *glides*, is here identified with רמש (*remesh*), "evening."

On *Shekhinah* as *ḥayyah*, see Ezra of Gerona, *Peirush Shir ha-Shirim*, 508–9; *Zohar* 1:12b, 242a; 2:48b, 177b–178a (*SdTs*); 3:46b.

865. **for waters nourish them** Emanation flowing from the *sefirot* nourishes the souls emerging from *Shekhinah*.

866. **When South arrives...** The waters within *Shekhinah* tend to congeal due to the influence of *Gevurah*, or *Din* (severe "Judgment"), associated with the North. These waters are released through the warmth of *Ḥesed*, the *sefirah* of flowing love, associated with the South.

See *Zohar* 1:29b, 152a, 161b; 2:30a; Moses de León, *Shushan Edut*, 341.

867. **Ships of the sea...** Powers extending from *Shekhinah*. See *Zohar* 1:40b.

868. *For a bird of heaven will carry the sound...* The verse is understood as alluding to angels in *Devarim Rabbah* 6:10; *Zohar* 1:92a; 3:138a; Moses de León, *Sefer ha-Rimmon*, 203. Cf. above, page 213.

869. **All of them are six-winged...** All the angels have six wings (see Isaiah 6:2),

corresponding to the six *sefirot* from *Ḥesed* to *Yesod*, who together constitute the supernal paradigm, known as *Ze'eir Anpin*, the Impatient One.

870. **in six** In six glides, playing on BT *Berakhot* 4b: "A *tanna* taught: 'Michael [reaches his destination] in one [glide], Gabriel in two, Elijah in four, and the Angel of Death in eight—in time of plague, however, in one.'"

871. **conveying them above** Where they are recorded and weighed.

872. *for a bird of heaven will carry the sound* a winged creature will report the word (cited above).

873. **the verse should read:** השורצת (*ha-shoretset*), *who swarms...* Matching the wording in the preceding verse (Genesis 1:20): *Let the waters swarm with a swarm of living souls.*

874. **But as we say: 'Night** רמש (*remash*), **dusked'** Rabbi Ḥizkiyah refers to the idiom of the *Zohar*. See 2:36b, 171a, 173a, 188a; 3:21a, 149b, 166b; cf. above, note 864.

875. *when all creatures...* The full verse reads: *You make darkness and it is night, when all creatures of the forest creep.* Here in the *Zohar*, the *creatures of the forest* are

watches, segments of the night, chanting without subsiding.[876] Of them is written: *O you, who call upon YHVH, be not silent!* (Isaiah 62:6)."[877]

Rabbi Shim'on rose and said, "I was gazing:[878] When the blessed Holy One was about to create Adam, above and below trembled.[879] The sixth day was ascending its rungs[880] as the supernal will arose[881] and the origin of all lights dawned,[882] opening the gate of the East, whence light issues.[883] South displayed the power of the light inherited from the head[884] and was empowered by the

the angels singing at night while *Shekhinah* reigns.

876. **opening with song in three watches . . .** The night is divided into three watches, during each of which a different choir of angels sings.

See BT *Berakhot* 3b; *Zohar* 1:230b; 2:195b–196a; *ZH* 17d (*MhN*), 88a (*MhN, Rut*).

877. **O you, who call upon YHVH, be not silent!** The verse begins: *Upon your walls, O Jerusalem, I have set watchmen, who shall never be silent day or night.*

878. **I was gazing** Upon the secrets of Creation. See the testimony of Shim'on son of Zoma (*Tosefta, Ḥagigah* 2:6): "I was gazing upon the act of Creation, and not even a handbreadth separates the upper waters from the lower waters."

See *Bereshit Rabbah* 2:4; BT *Ḥagigah* 15a; JT *Ḥagigah* 2:1, 77a–b.

879. **above and below trembled** On heavenly opposition to human creation, see BT *Sanhedrin* 38b: "Rav Yehudah said in the name of Rav: 'When the blessed Holy One sought to create the human being, He [first] created a company of ministering angels and asked them, "Is it your desire that we make the human being in our image?" They responded, "Master of the Universe, what are his deeds?" He replied, "Such and such are his deeds." They exclaimed, "Master of the Universe, *What is a human that You are mindful of him, a human being that You take note of him?*" (Psalms 8:5)." He stretched out His little finger among them and burned them. The same thing happened with a second company. The third company said to Him, "Master of the Universe, the former ones

who spoke in Your presence—what did they accomplish? The entire world is Yours! Whatever You wish to do in Your world, do it." When He reached the members of the generation of the Flood and the generation of the Dispersion [the Tower of Babel], whose deeds were corrupt, they [the angels] said to Him, "Master of the Universe, didn't the first ones speak well?" He responded, "*Till your old age, I am He; till you turn grey, I will carry you* [*I have made and I will bear; I will carry and deliver*] (Isaiah 46:4).""

See *Alfa Beita de-Rabbi Aqiva*, Version 2 (*Battei Midrashot*, 2:412): "At first, Adam was created extending from earth to heaven. When the ministering angels saw him, they trembled and recoiled from him. Immediately they presented themselves before the blessed Holy One and said, 'Master of the world! There are two powers in the world: one in heaven and one on earth.' What did the blessed Holy One do at that moment? He placed His hand on him and reduced him to one thousand cubits."

880. **The sixth day . . .** The *sefirah* of Yesod, sixth of the lower seven *sefirot*, the cosmic week of Creation.

881. **the supernal will . . .** *Keter*, the first *sefirah*.

882. **the origin of all lights . . .** *Ḥokhmah*, first *sefirah* to emerge from *Keter*.

883. **the gate of the East . . .** The four directions (east, south, north, west) symbolize *Tif'eret, Ḥesed, Gevurah,* and *Shekhinah,* respectively. See *Pirqei de-Rabbi Eli'ezer* 3.

884. **from the head** From the highest *sefirot*.

215

East. East empowered North; North aroused and expanded, calling potently to the West to draw near, to join him.[885] Then West rose to the North, bonding with him. Afterward South approached, embracing West, now encompassed by South and North, mystery of the hedges of the garden.[886] Then East draws near West,[887] and West abides in joy, inviting them all: *Let us make a human being in our image, according to our likeness* (Genesis 1:26), resembling this in four directions, above and below.[888] East cleaved to West, generating him, and so we have learned: 'Adam emerged from the site of the Temple.'[889]

"Further, *Let us make* אדם (*adam*), *a human being*—the blessed Holy One imparted to these lower beings, who emerged from the aspect above,[890] the secret of the name amounting to אדם (*adam*), from the sealed supernal mystery.[891] אדם, mystery of letters, for אדם embraces above and below: א (*alef*), beyond, beyond;[892] ם (final *mem*), who is למרבה (*le-marbeh*), *for the abundance of, dominion* (Isaiah 9:6);[893] lower ד (*dalet*), concealed in the

216

885. **North aroused and expanded...** *Gevurah*, stimulated by *Tif'eret*, seeks to join *Shekhinah*, the West.

886. **Afterward South approached...** Once *Gevurah* joins *Shekhinah*, so does *Ḥesed*. Thus South and North (*Ḥesed* and *Gevurah*) surround Her, hedging the garden of *Shekhinah*.

887. **East draws near West** *Tif'eret* approaches *Shekhinah*.

888. *Let us make a human being...* *Shekhinah* invites the other *sefirot* to join in creating the human being, who will reflect all dimensions of the divine realm. See *Zohar* 1:38a. Rabbi Shim'on thus explains the plural construction *Let us make*, which perplexed many biblical readers. See *Bereshit Rabbah* 8:3, where various answers are offered to the question: "Whom did He consult?"

889. **Adam emerged from the site of the Temple** See *Pirqei de-Rabbi Eli'ezer* 12: "He created him from a pure, holy site. From where did He take him? From the site of the Temple."

See 2 Enoch 30:13; *Bereshit Rabbah* 14:8 (and Theodor, ad loc.); JT *Nazir* 7:2, 56b; *Tanḥuma, Pequdei* 3; *Pirqei de-Rabbi Eli'ezer* 11; *Targum Yerushalmi*, Genesis 2:7; *Zohar* 1:130b, 205b; 2:23b, 24b; 3:83a.

Here the Temple symbolizes *Shekhinah*, the Divine Presence dwelling there.

890. **these lower beings...** The angels who emerged from the divine realm.

891. **the secret of the name amounting to אדם (*adam*)...** The divine name יהוה (*YHVH*) spelled out according to its letters—יוד (*yod*), הא (*he*), ואו (*vav*), הא (*he*)—whose *gimatriyya* is forty-five, equal to אדם (*adam*).

892. **א (*alef*), beyond, beyond** א (*Alef*) symbolizes *Keter*, the highest *sefirah*.

893. **ם (final *mem*), who is למרבה (*le-marbeh*), *for the abundance of, dominion*** This is the only time in the entire Bible that a final ם (*mem*) appears out of place, before the end of the word—a peculiarity that stimulated the rabbinic mind. See BT *Sanhedrin* 94a; *Soferim* 7:3; *Midrash Ḥaserot Vi-Yterot* 185 (*Battei Midrashot*, 2:302); *Minḥat Shai*, ad loc.

Here the ם (*mem*), shaped like a house, signifies *Binah*, who houses the lower *sefirot*. See *ZḤ* 5c (*SO*); cf. *Zohar* 2:127a–b; 3:156b, 285b.

On the esoteric nature of the ם (final *mem*), see BT *Shabbat* 104a: "The Rabbis told Rabbi Yehoshu'a son of Levi: 'Children have now come to the house of study and said things unparalleled even in the days of Joshua son of Nun:...Open מ (*mem*) and closed ם (*mem*): open saying and sealed saying.'"

West.[894] This is the entirety of above and below, arrayed above, arrayed below. When these letters descended, all was as one in consummation: male and female.[895] The female cleaved to his side until He cast sleep upon him and he slumbered, lying on the site of the Temple below.[896] The blessed Holy One sawed him, adorned her as one adorns a bride, and brought her to him, as is written: *He took one of his sides and closed up the flesh in its place* (Genesis 2:21).[897] *He took one*—precisely! In the books of the ancients I have discovered: This is the original Lilith, who accompanied him, was impregnated by him, and taken away from him.[898] She was no *fitting helper* for him[899]—What is *a helper?* סמך (*Semakh*), A support.[900] Till finally it is written: *It is not good for Adam to be alone. I will make him a fitting helper* (ibid., 18).[901]

894. **lower** ד (***dalet***), **concealed in the West** Symbolizing *Shekhinah,* who is דלה (*dallah*), "poor," before She receives the rich flow of emanation from the higher *sefirot.* See BT *Bava Batra* 25a: "Rabbi Abbahu said, '*Shekhinah* is in the West.'"

895. **When these letters descended…** Through the creative power of the letters אדם (*adam*), an androgynous being emerged, reflecting the male and female aspects of the *sefirot.*

896. **until He cast sleep upon him…** See Genesis 2:21: *YHVH Elohim cast a deep sleep upon the human and he slept.* On the Temple, see above, note 889.

897. **The blessed Holy One sawed him…** God split the original androgynous human into two: Adam and Eve. See *Bereshit Rabbah* 8:1: "Rabbi Yirmeyah son of El'azar said, 'When the blessed Holy One created Adam, He created him androgynous, as is said: *Male and female He created them* (Genesis 1:27).' Rabbi Shemu'el son of Naḥman said, 'When the blessed Holy One created Adam, He created him with two faces. Then He sawed him and gave him two backs, one on this side and one on that.'" The word צלע (*tsela*) in Genesis 2:21, often translated as "rib," also means "side."

See Exodus 26:20; BT *Berakhot* 61a; *Eruvin* 18a; Plato, *Symposium* 189d–191d; *Zohar* 1:2b, 47a, 48b; 2:55a; 3:5a, 44b; Matt, *Zohar,* 217.

On the adorning of Eve, see *Bereshit Rabbah* 18:1: "*YHVH Elohim fashioned the rib* (Genesis 2:22).… It was taught in the name of Rabbi Shim'on son of Yoḥai: 'He adorned her like a bride and brought her to him.'"

Cf. BT *Berakhot* 61a: "Rabbi Shim'on son of Menasia expounded, 'Why is it written: *YHVH Elohim fashioned the rib* (Genesis 2:22)? This teaches that the blessed Holy One braided Eve's hair and brought her to Adam.'"

898. **In the books of the ancients…** Alluding to the tenth-century text *Alfa Beita de-Ven Sira,* 232–34, according to which Lilith was Adam's original wife. Insisting on her equality, Lilith refused to lie beneath Adam and flew away.

See *Zohar* 1:19b; 3:19a; *ZḤ* 16c (*MhN*); Scholem, *Kabbalah,* 356–61.

אתעברת (*It'abbarat*) is rendered here "was impregnated … and taken away," since the Aramaic word conveys both meanings. According to *Tanḥuma* (Buber), *Bereshit* 26, after Cain killed Abel, Adam saw no reason to have any more children, so he separated from Eve, whereupon maleficent spirits copulated with him.

See *Bereshit Rabbah* 20:11; BT *Eruvin* 18b; *Zohar* 1:54b, 2:231b, 3:76b.

899. ***fitting helper…*** See Genesis 2:20: *But for Adam no fitting helper was found.*

900. **What is *a helper?*** סמך (***Semakh***), **A support** *Targum Onqelos* renders עזר (*ezer*) *a helper* (Genesis 2:18, 20) by the Aramaic סמך (*semakh*), "support, help."

901. **Till finally…** Until Eve was created to replace Lilith.

217

"Come and see: Adam was last of all, fittingly, so as to arrive in a consummate world."[902]

Rabbi Shim'on said further, "It is written: *No bush of the field was yet on earth, no plant of the field had yet sprouted, for YHVH Elohim had not rained upon earth…*(ibid. 2:5).[903] *No bush of the field*—[35a] magnificent trees planted later, still tiny.[904]

"Come and see: Adam and Eve were created side by side.[905] Why not face-to-face? Because, as is written, *YHVH Elohim had not rained upon earth*, and the coupling was not yet fittingly arrayed.[906] When the one below was arrayed, and they turned face-to-face, then so it was above.[907] How do we know?[908] From the *Dwelling*, as is written: *The Dwelling was erected* (Exodus 40:17), from which we learn that another *Dwelling* was erected along with it, and until erected below, it was not erected above.[909] Similarly here, once arrayed below, it was arrayed above. Since until now it had not been arrayed above, they were not created face-to-face, as proven by Scripture: *for YHVH Elohim had not rained upon earth*. Consequently, *there was no human*, for he was not arrayed.[910]

"This secret is implied by the fact that up to this point in the portion the letter ס (*samekh*) does not appear. Although the Companions have commented, still ס (*samekh*) is *a helper*, namely, *a helper* above, for above turned face-to-

218

902. **Adam was last of all…** See BT *Sanhedrin* 38a: "Our Rabbis taught: 'Adam was created on the eve of Sabbath. Why? …So he could immediately go to the banquet. A parable: A king of flesh and blood built palaces and decorated them, prepared a banquet, and only then brought in the guests.'"

903. *for YHVH Elohim had not rained upon earth… and there was no human to till the soil.*

904. **magnificent trees planted later, still tiny** The nascent *sefirot*, seedlings in the divine mind, planted later in the field of *Shekhinah*.

905. **created side by side** As an androgynous being with two faces in opposite directions. See above, note 897.

906. *YHVH Elohim had not rained upon earth…* The upper *sefirot* had not flowed into *Shekhinah*, symbolized by *earth*, so the union was incomplete.

907. **When the one below…** When the androgynous human was split in two (Adam and Eve), and they turned face-to-face, then the union above was actualized.

908. **How do we know?** How do we know that actions on earth affect the divine realm?

909. **From the *Dwelling*…** The Tabernacle in the desert. The passive construction, *The Dwelling was erected* (instead of the active, *Moses erected the Dwelling*), alludes to the erection of a heavenly Dwelling, *Shekhinah*.

See *Bemidbar Rabbah* 12:12: "Rabbi Simon said, 'When the blessed Holy One told Israel to erect the Dwelling, he hinted to the angels that they, too, construct a Dwelling. When it was erected below, it was erected above.'"

See *Tanḥuma, Naso* 18; *Zohar* 2:143a, 159a; 3:3b.

910. *there was no human…* The verse concludes: *for YHVH Elohim had not rained upon earth, and there was no human to till the soil.* Since Adam and Eve could not face each other, the human being was incomplete.

face, male and female supported by each other, indeed, *supported eternally, fashioned in truth and integrity* (Psalms 111:8).[911] *Supported*—male and female, supported as one. The world of which we have spoken depends upon the world below, for as long as the world below was not arrayed, neither was the world of which we have spoken.[912]

"*YHVH Elohim had not rained upon earth,* for one supports the other. This lower world, once arrayed—once turned and arrayed face-to-face—became a support above, for previously the work was in disarray. Each depends on the other.

"What is written next? *A flow welled up from earth* (Genesis 2:6). This is the arrayal below, afterward *watering the whole face of the ground* (ibid.). This is the desire of female for male.[913]

"Alternatively, why *had* He *not rained*? Because no arrayal *welled up from earth*. So from earth below action is aroused above.[914] Come and see: Vapor ascends from earth at first, a cloud is aroused, and then all conjoins. Similarly, smoke of sacrifice is aroused below, consummates above, and all conjoins in consummation.[915] Similarly above, arousal begins from below, then all is consummated.[916] If Assembly of Israel did not initiate arousal, the one above would not be aroused toward Her.[917] By desire below, all is consummated."

219

911. **up to this point in the portion... the Companions have commented...** The ס (*samekh*) under discussion appears in Genesis 2:21: *He took one of his sides,* ויסגר (*va-yisgor*), *and He closed up, the flesh in its place.* See *Bereshit Rabbah* 17:6: "Rabbi Ḥanina son of Rav Adda said, 'From the beginning of the book until here, no ס (*samekh*) appears. Once she was created, סטן (*Satan*), Satan, was created with her. Now, if someone cites for you: "הסובב (*Ha-sovev*), *Circling* (Genesis 2:11, 13, an earlier occurrence of the letter ס [*samekh*]),'' answer him: "The text refers there to rivers [and not the creation of the human being].''''

In contrast to this demonic interpretation, Rabbi Shim'on claims that the ס (*samekh*) signifies help. The root סמך (*smkh*) means "to support," and *Targum Onqelos* renders עזר (*ezer*) *a helper* (Genesis 2:18) by the Aramaic סמך (*semakh*). With Eve's help, the human couple united face-to-face, thereby stimulating a similar union above between the divine couple *Tif'eret* and *Shekhinah*.

912. **The world of which we have spoken...** The divine realm depends upon the human realm.

913. *A flow welled up*...**the desire of female...** *Shekhinah* is stimulated by humans below and in turn stimulates *Tif'eret*.

914. **from earth below action is aroused above** A general principle of Kabbalah. See *Zohar* 1:77b, 82b, 86b, 88a, 164a, 244a; 2:31b, 265a; 3:92a, 110b.

915. **Similarly, smoke of sacrifice...** The ritual of sacrifice unites the *sefirot*.

916. **Similarly above...** In the divine realm *Shekhinah* arouses the passion of *Tif'eret*.

917. **Assembly of Israel...** כנסת ישראל (*Keneset Yisra'el*). In rabbinic Hebrew this phrase denotes the people of Israel. The midrash on the Song of Songs describes the love affair between the maiden (the earthly community of Israel) and her lover (the Holy One, blessed be He). In the *Zohar*, *Keneset Yisra'el* can refer to the earthly community but also (often primarily) to *Shekhinah*,

Rabbi Abba said, "It is written: *the tree of life in the middle of the garden, and the tree of knowledge of good and evil* (Genesis 2:9). *The tree of life*—we have learned that it extends over a journey of five hundred years, and all the waters of Creation branch off below.[918] *The tree of life* is precisely in the middle of the garden, conveying all waters of Creation, branching below, for that flowing, gushing river spreads into the garden, whence waters branch in many directions. Receiving them all is the ocean, from which they emerge in numerous streams below, as is said: *watering all beasts of the field* (Psalms 104:11).[919] Just as they emerge from that world above, watering those towering mountains of pure balsam,[920] subsequently upon reaching *the tree of life*, they branch below by paths in every direction.

"*And the tree of knowledge of good and evil.* Why is it called so? It is not in the middle.[921] But what does *knowledge of good and evil* mean? Since it suckles on two sides and knows them as one suckling sweet and bitter, since it suckles on two sides, knowing them and dwelling among them, it is called so.[922] All those plants dwell above it,[923] while within it dwell other plants, supernal plants called *cedars of Lebanon*. Who are those *cedars of Lebanon*? The six days of Creation of which we have spoken, *the cedars of Lebanon that He planted* (Psalms 104:16), certainly saplings, later firmly implanted.[924]

220

the divine feminine counterpart of the people, the aspect of God most intimately connected with them. The lovers in the Song of Songs are pictured as the divine couple: *Tif-'eret* and *Shekhinah*.

918. **The tree of life... five hundred years...** See *Bereshit Rabbah* 15:6: "Rabbi Yehudah son of Rabbi Il'ai said, 'The Tree of Life extends over a journey of five hundred years, and all the waters of Creation branch off beneath it.'"

For Rabbi Abba, the five hundred years symbolize the five *sefirot* from Ḥesed through Hod, which channel the emanation to *Yesod*, *the tree of life*. See *Zohar* 1:18a, 78b (*ST*); Moses de León, *Sheqel ha-Qodesh*, 56 (69).

919. **precisely in the middle of the garden...** *Yesod*, *the tree of life*, is planted in the middle of the garden, *Shekhinah*. Similarly, *Yesod* is the river of emanation flowing into the ocean of *Shekhinah*, from whom water streams to the powers beneath Her.

920. **Just as they emerge...** The waters emanate from *Binah*, the Divine Mother, and flow through the *sefirot* from Ḥesed to Yesod,

the mountains of pure balsam. In rabbinic tradition thirteen rivers of balsam await the righteous in the world that is coming.

See BT *Ta'anit* 25a; *Bereshit Rabbah* 62:2; cf. *Zohar* 1:4b; 2:87b, 127a; 3:91a, 181a.

921. **It is not in the middle** According to Genesis 3:3, the Tree of Knowledge of Good and Evil was planted in the middle of the Garden of Eden. However, as we have seen, the Tree of Life was planted precisely in the middle of the garden. Furthermore, the Tree of Knowledge of Good and Evil symbolizes *Shekhinah*, who is not precisely in the middle but rather tends toward the left side of the *sefirot*. If She is not in the middle, how can She know the two extremes?

922. **Since it suckles...** *Shekhinah* is called *the tree of knowledge of good and evil* because She imbibes from both sides of the *sefirot*, the sweet right side and the bitter left side.

923. **All those plants...** Apparently offshoots of the right and left sides.

924. *cedars of Lebanon*...**The six days of Creation...** The six *sefirot* from Ḥesed

"From here on, ס (*samekh*). What is it? ויסגור (*Va-yisgor*), *He closed up, the flesh at that place* (Genesis 2:21). She was attached to his side, one to the side of the other. Indeed the blessed Holy One uprooted them, transplanting [35b] them elsewhere, where they turned face-to-face for endurance.[925] Similarly, the worlds were adjoined; the blessed Holy One uprooted them, transplanting them elsewhere, where they endured."[926]

Rabbi Abba said, "How do we know that Adam and Eve were saplings? For it is written: *sprout of My planting, work of My hands, that I may be glorified* (Isaiah 60:21)[927]—*work of My hands*, precisely, for no other creature engaged in them.[928] Similarly it is written: *On the day of your planting, you become debased* (ibid. 17:11), for the very day they were planted in the world, they united and decayed.[929] We have learned: 'They resembled antennae of grasshoppers,' for their light was tenuous and they did not shine. Once planted firmly, their light increased and they were called *cedars of Lebanon*.[930] Adam and Eve, as well, did

to *Yesod,* which began as saplings in the higher sefirotic realm and were later transplanted into *Shekhinah.* See *Bereshit Rabbah* 15:1: "*YHVH Elohim planted a garden in Eden* (Genesis 2:8)....As is written: *The trees of YHVH drink their fill, the cedars of Lebanon that He planted.* Rabbi Ḥanina said, 'They resembled antennae of grasshoppers, and the blessed Holy One uprooted them, transplanting them in the Garden of Eden.'"

See Ezra of Gerona, *Peirush Shir ha-Shirim,* 504; *Zohar* 1:31a, 37a; 2:127b; 3:4b, 217b; and below.

925. **From here on, ס (*samekh*)...** See above, notes 897 and 911. Eve and Adam were attached side to side, or back-to-back, until God split them, enabling them to unite face-to-face.

926. **Similarly, the worlds were adjoined...** The *sefirot* were originally united in their source. Alternatively, *Tif'eret* and *Shekhinah* were united as an androgyne, back-to-back. Once the *sefirot* emerged individually, *Tif'eret* and *Shekhinah* reunited face-to-face. See above, note 924.

927. ***sprout of My planting, work of My hands, that I may be glorified*** The verse opens: *Your people, all of them righteous, will inherit the land forever.*

928. **no other creature engaged...** Adam and Eve had no human parents.

929. ***On the day of your planting, you become debased...*** The word תשגשגי (*tesagsegi*), *you make it grow,* is interpreted as if deriving from the root סיג (*sig*), "dross." Cf. *Vayiqra Rabbah* 18:3; *Bemidbar Rabbah* 7:4.

See *Bereshit Rabbah* 22:2: "Rabbi El'azar son of Azariah said, 'Three wonders were performed on that day: On that very day they were created; on that very day they engaged in sexual union; on that very day they generated offspring.'" According to BT *Sanhedrin* 38b, "In the seventh hour [of the first day] Eve was joined with him...In the tenth hour he decayed [i.e., sinned]."

See Moses de León, *Mishkan ha-Edut,* 63b: "Because Adam did not want to wait until Sabbath eve [to unite with Eve]...evil and death came upon his descendants." According to BT *Ketubbot* 62b (in the name of Shemu'el), Sabbath eve is the appropriate time for scholars to engage in sexual union. In the *Zohar,* the union of the devotee of Torah with his wife on the eve of Sabbath symbolizes and stimulates the union of the divine couple, *Tif'eret* and *Shekhinah.* The human couple thereby engenders a holy body and draws down a holy soul.

See *Zohar* 1:50a, 112a (*MhN*); 2:63b, 89a–b; 3:49b, 78a.

930. **We have learned...** See above, note 924.

221

not grow until planted, gave forth no fragrance; indeed they were uprooted, transplanted, fittingly arrayed."[931]

YHVH Elohim commanded [*the human, saying...*] (Genesis 2:16).[932] We have learned: "*Command* means idolatry; *saying*—this is woman..."[933] That is fine. *From every tree of the garden you are free to eat*—everything was permitted to him if eaten in oneness.[934] For we see that Abraham ate, Isaac, and Jacob—they all ate and endured.[935] But this tree is a tree of death; whoever takes it alone dies, for he has taken deadly poison.[936] So, *on the day you eat from it, you will surely die* (ibid., 17), for he separates saplings.[937]

931. **uprooted, transplanted, fittingly arrayed**   Split apart and then reunited face-to-face.

932. ***YHVH Elohim commanded*** [***the human, saying...***]   The passage continues: "*From every tree of the garden you are free to eat; but as for the tree of knowledge of good and evil, do not eat from it, for on the day you eat from it, you will surely die*" (Genesis 2:16–17).

933. **"*Command* means idolatry; *saying*—this is woman..."**   A Zoharic revision of a midrashic interpretation found in *Bereshit Rabbah* 16:6: "*YHVH Elohim commanded the human, saying, 'From every tree of the garden you are free to eat.'* Rabbi Levi said, 'He issued him six commands. *He commanded,* concerning idolatry...; *YHVH,* concerning blasphemy...; *Elohim,* these are the judges...; *the human,* this is murder...; *saying,* concerning גלוי עריות (*gillui arayot*), exposing nudity (fornication)— *Saying: If a man divorces his wife* (Jeremiah 3:1); *From every tree of the garden you are free to eat,* commanding him concerning theft.'"

In this midrash the word *saying* connotes "adultery" (based on the verse *Saying: If a man divorces his wife* [literally: *woman*]), while for the *Zohar, saying* alludes to the divine woman, *Shekhinah.*

See BT *Sanhedrin* 56a–b; *Zohar* 2:83b, 239b; 3:27a.

934. **everything was permitted...**   Adam could partake of anything in the

garden as long as he preserved its unity with all.

935. **Abraham ate, Isaac...**   All of the patriarchs partook of *Shekhinah,* the Tree of Knowledge, without separating Her from the other *sefirot.* See the expression "feasted their eyes on *Shekhinah*" (*Pesiqta de-Rav Kahana* 26:9).

936. **a tree of death...**   See Genesis 2:17. According to *Seder Eliyyahu Rabbah* 5, the Tree of Knowledge of Good and Evil is called the Tree of Death because when Adam and Eve ate its fruit, death ensued. Here *Shekhinah* is given this name because anyone who partakes of Her alone separates Her from the other *sefirot,* thereby cutting off the vivifying flow of emanation, which is replaced by a deadly potion.

On the nature of Adam and Eve's sin, see *Zohar* 1:12b, 51a–53b, 221a–b; Scholem, *Major Trends,* 231–32, 236, 404–5, n. 105; Tishby, *Wisdom of the Zohar,* 1:373–76. On the relation between *Shekhinah* and the demonic, see Scholem, *On the Mystical Shape of the Godhead,* 189–92; Tishby, *Wisdom of the Zohar,* 1:376–79.

937. **separates saplings**   פריש נטיעין (*Pareish neti'in*). See BT *Ḥagigah* 14b, the famous account of the four rabbis who engaged in mystical search: "Four entered פרדס (*pardes*), an orchard [whence: paradise]: Ben Azzai, Ben Zoma, Aḥer, and Rabbi Akiva....Ben Azzai glimpsed and died.... Ben Zoma glimpsed and went mad.... Aḥer קיצץ בנטיעות (*qitstsets ba-neti'ot*), sev-

222

Rabbi Yehudah asked Rabbi Shim'on, "We have learned: 'Adam stretched his foreskin.'[938] What does this mean?"

He replied, "That he separated the holy covenant from its site.[939] He certainly stretched the foreskin, for he abandoned the holy covenant, cleaved to the foreskin, was seduced by the word of the serpent."[940]

But from the fruit of the tree in the middle of the garden (ibid. 3:3)[941]—this is woman.[942]

Do not eat from it (ibid.), for it is written: *Her feet descend to death . . .* (Proverbs 5:5).[943] On this one there is fruit, on the other there is not.[944]

For on the day you eat from it, you will surely die (ibid. 2:17), for it is a tree of death, as we have said: *Her feet descend to death.*

Now the serpent was slier than any creature of the field (ibid. 3:1).

Rabbi Yose said, "The tree of which we have spoken was watered, flourished, and rejoiced, as is said: *A river issues from Eden to water the garden* (Genesis 2:10). *The garden*—this is woman, the *river* entering Her, watering Her, and all

ered the saplings. Rabbi Akiva emerged in peace."

See *Tosefta, Ḥagigah* 2:2; JT *Ḥagigah* 2:1, 77c; *Shir ha-Shirim Rabbah* on 1:4; *Devarim Rabbah* 7:4.

Aḥer, "the other," is the nickname of Elisha son of Avuyah, the most famous heretic in rabbinic literature. The metaphor of "severing the saplings" may allude to his conversion to Gnostic dualism. In Kabbalah "severing the saplings" refers to splitting the unity of the *sefirot,* specifically separating *Shekhinah* from the others.

938. **'Adam stretched his foreskin'** See BT *Sanhedrin* 38b: "Rabbi Yitsḥak said, 'He [Adam] stretched his foreskin.'" The phrase refers to epispasm, an attempt to disguise circumcision by cutting and pulling forward the loose skin of the penis to form a partial foreskin. According to rabbinic tradition, Adam was one of those rare individuals born circumcised. See *Avot de-Rabbi Natan* A, 2; *Tanḥuma, Noaḥ* 5.

939. **he separated the holy covenant . . .** Adam separated *Yesod*—the divine phallus, symbolized by the covenant of circumcision—from *Shekhinah.*

940. **the foreskin . . .** Symbolizing the demonic. See *Zohar* 1:13a, 18a; Moses de

León, *Sheqel ha-Qodesh,* 55 (68).

941. **But from the fruit of the tree in the middle of the garden** The verse continues: *God said: "Do not eat from it and do not touch it, lest you die."* Cf. Genesis 2:17.

942. **this is woman** See *Pirqei de-Rabbi Eli'ezer* 21: "*But from the fruit of the tree in the middle of the garden.* It has been taught: Rabbi Ze'eira said, '*But from the fruit of the tree*—this *tree* means man, who is compared to a tree, as is said: *Man is a tree of the field* (Deuteronomy 20:19). *In the middle of the garden*—the middle of the garden is a euphemism for what lies in the middle of the body. *In the middle of the garden*—in the middle of the woman, for *garden* means woman, who is compared to a garden, as is said: *A locked garden is my sister, bride* (Song of Songs 4:12).'"

Here *woman* alludes to the divine woman, *Shekhinah.* See above, note 933.

943. **Her feet descend to death** The verse alludes to the fatal aspect of *Shekhinah* and the demonic realm that lies below Her. See *Zohar* 1:221b; 2:48b.

944. **On this one there is fruit . . .** *Shekhinah,* symbolized by the Tree of Knowledge, yields fruit, unlike the demonic realm, which is barren. See *Zohar* 2:103a.

was one, while from there below is division, as is written: *From there it divides* (ibid.)."⁹⁴⁵

Now the serpent. Rabbi Yitsḥak said, "This is the evil impulse."

Rabbi Yehudah said, "An actual *serpent.*"

They came before Rabbi Shim'on, who said to them, "Indeed, all is one. It was Samael appearing on a *serpent,* and the form of *the serpent* is Satan; all is one.⁹⁴⁶

"We have learned: 'At that moment Samael descended from heaven, riding on this *serpent,* and when all creatures saw his form they fled from him.⁹⁴⁷ They got to the woman with words, inflicting death upon the world. Indeed through wisdom Samael brought curses on the world, destroying the primordial tree created in the world by the blessed Holy One.⁹⁴⁸

"This matter loomed over Samael until another holy tree arrived—namely, Jacob—who wrested blessings from him, so that he would not be blessed above, nor Esau below.⁹⁴⁹ For Jacob was patterned on Adam; the beauty of Jacob was the beauty of Adam.⁹⁵⁰ Just as Samael withheld blessings from the primordial tree, so Jacob, a tree patterned on Adam, withheld blessings from Samael above and below. Jacob took what was his entirely. So, *a man wrestled with him* (Genesis 32:25).⁹⁵¹

945. *A river issues from Eden...* The flow of emanation proceeds from the highest *sefirot* to *Shekhinah, the garden.* Below Her, the unity of the divine yields multiplicity.

946. **all is one...** Both interpretations are valid, since the demonic power, which activates the evil impulse, appeared on an actual *serpent.* See BT *Bava Batra* 16a: "Resh Lakish said, 'Satan, the evil impulse, and the Angel of Death are one and the same.'"

Cf. *Zohar* 1:35b, 52a, 202a; 2:262b–263a; Moses de León, *Sefer ha-Rimmon,* 394–95.

947. **At that moment Samael descended...** See *Pirqei de-Rabbi Eli'ezer* 13: "Samael...took his band and descended and saw all the creatures created by the blessed Holy One. He determined that the most cunningly evil was the serpent, as is said: *Now the serpent was slier than any creature of the field that YHVH Elohim had made.* He [the serpent] looked like a camel, and he [Samael] mounted and rode him."

See *Zohar* 1:64a, 137b, 146a, 153a.

948. **through wisdom...** Through shrewdness. See *Targum Onqelos,* Genesis 3:1. The primordial tree symbolizes Adam and Eve, who are modeled on the sefirotic tree.

949. **until another holy tree arrived...** Jacob, who symbolizes *Tif'eret,* the Tree of Life, took blessings away from his brother, Esau, thereby depriving Samael, Esau's heavenly guardian, of blessing above.

See *Zohar* 1:145b; Moses de León, *She'elot u-Tshuvot,* 45–46.

950. **For Jacob was patterned on Adam...** See BT *Bava Metsi'a* 84a: "The beauty of our father Jacob resembled the beauty of Adam." The *Zohar* transforms the Talmudic comparison into an affirmation of identity. Jacob manifested Adam's beauty and by his bold act rectified the demonic flaw of Adam's sin.

See *Bava Batra* 58a; *Zohar* 1:142b, 145b–146a, 222a.

951. **Jacob took what was his...** The blessings that Jacob took from Esau be-

"*The serpent was slier*—evil impulse, Angel of Death.[952] Being the Angel of Death, he inflicted death upon the whole world. This is the mystery written: *End of all flesh has come before Me* (ibid. 6:13)—*End of all flesh* who takes the soul of all flesh and is so named."[953]

*He said to the woman, "*אַף *(Af), Really…"* (ibid. 3:1).[954]

Rabbi Yose said, "He opened with אַף (*af*), *really,* and cast אַף (*af*), wrath, into the world.[955] He said to her, [36a] 'With this tree the blessed Holy One created the world. Eat from it and you will really *be like* אלהים (*Elohim*), *God, knowing good and evil!* (ibid., 5).' For so it is: *Elohim* is its name, *the tree of knowledge of good and evil.*[956] So, *You will be like Elohim, knowing good and evil.*"

Rabbi Yehudah said, "That is not what he said. For if he had said: 'With this tree the blessed Holy One created the world,' it would have been correct.[957] What he said was, rather: 'The blessed Holy One ate from this tree and then created the world, and every artisan hates his fellow. Eat from it and you will be creating worlds! So, *God knows that on the day you eat from it [your eyes will be opened and you will become like God…]* (ibid., 5). Because He knew this, He commanded you concerning it.'"[958]

Rabbi Yitsḥak said, "He spoke lies entirely. The very first thing he said was a lie, as is written: *Even though God said, 'Do not eat from any of the trees in the*

225

longed to Jacob, having originally been taken away from Adam (Jacob's paradigm) by Samael (Esau's heavenly guardian). Before Jacob's reunion with Esau, *Jacob was left alone, and a man wrestled with him until the rising of dawn.* This *man* is identified by Rabbi Ḥama son of Rabbi Ḥanina (*Bereshit Rabbah* 77:3) as "the Prince of Esau," and in *Tanḥuma, Va-yishlaḥ* 8, he is explictly named Samael.

952. **evil impulse, Angel of Death** See BT *Bava Batra* 16a: "Resh Lakish said, 'Satan, the evil impulse, and the Angel of Death are one and the same.'" See above, note 946.

953. *End of all flesh…* Angel of Death. See *Zohar* 1:54a.

954. *He said to the woman, "*אַף *(Af), Really…"* The verse reads: *He said to the woman, "Did God really say: 'Do not eat from any of the trees in the garden'?"*

955. **He opened with** אַף (*af*)… See *Bereshit Rabbah* 19:2: "Rabbi Ḥanina son of

Sansan said, 'Four opened with אַף (*af*) [which has a range of meanings] and perished in אַף (*af*), "wrath": the serpent, the chief baker [Genesis 40:16], Korah's band [Numbers 16:14], and Haman [Esther 5:12].'"

956. **Elohim is its name…** The tree of knowledge, symbolizing *Shekhinah,* is called *Elohim.*

957. **it would have been correct** *Shekhinah* channels the vivifying flow of emanation beyond the sefirotic realm, and so the world is brought into being.

958. **The blessed Holy One ate from this tree…** See *Bereshit Rabbah* 19:4: "Rabbi Yehoshu'a of Sikhnin said in the name of Rabbi Levi: 'He [the serpent] began defaming his Creator, saying: "From this tree He ate and created the world. Then He said to you, 'Do not eat from it,' so that you not create other worlds. Every person hates his fellow craftsman."'"

garden' (ibid., 1).⁹⁵⁹ It was not so, for it is written: *From every tree of the garden you are free to eat* (ibid. 2:16)⁹⁶⁰—He permitted him all of them."⁹⁶¹

Rabbi Yose said, "We have learned: 'The blessed Holy One commanded him concerning idolatry, as is written: *commanded* (ibid.); *YHVH,* concerning blasphemy; *Elohim,* concerning judges; *the human,* concerning murder; *saying,* concerning the woman, concerning exposing nudity.'⁹⁶² Now, how many people existed in the world, necessitating this?⁹⁶³ But certainly all touched upon this tree, by which they are embraced.⁹⁶⁴ Whoever takes it by itself, takes it together with hordes below embraced by it, takes idolatry, murder, and exposing nudity.⁹⁶⁵ Idolatry toward those empowered princes.⁹⁶⁶ Murder engendered by this tree, which is *Gevurah*; Samael is appointed over this.⁹⁶⁷ Exposing nudity— She is Woman, so named, and it is forbidden to invite a woman by herself, only with her husband, that one not be suspected of exposing nudity.⁹⁶⁸ So in

959. ***Even though God said...*** Usually translated: *"Did God really say: 'Do not eat from any of the trees in the garden'?"* See above, page 225.

960. ***From every tree of the garden you are free to eat*** The passage reads: *YHVH Elohim commanded the human, saying: "From every tree of the garden you are free to eat; but as for the tree of knowledge of good and evil, do not eat from it, for on the day you eat from it, you will surely die"* (Genesis 2:16–17).

961. **He permitted him all of them** If eaten in oneness. See above, page 222.

962. **We have learned...** See above, page 222; and *Bereshit Rabbah* 16:6: *"YHVH Elohim commanded the human, saying, 'From every tree of the garden you are free to eat.'* Rabbi Levi said, 'He issued him six commands. *He commanded,* concerning idolatry...; *YHVH,* concerning blasphemy...; *Elohim,* these are the judges...; *the human,* this is murder...; *saying,* concerning גלוי עריות (*gillui arayot*), exposing nudity (fornication)—*Saying: If a man divorces his wife* (Jeremiah 3:1); *From every tree of the garden you are free to eat,* commanding him concerning theft.'"

See BT *Sanhedrin* 56a–b; *Zohar* 2:239b; 3:27a.

963. **Now, how many people...** Since Adam and Eve were the only inhabitants

of the earth, what need was there for these laws?

964. **all touched upon this tree...** All the various commands implied by the verse concerned *the tree of knowledge,* namely *Shekhinah.*

965. **Whoever takes it by itself...** Whoever separates *Shekhinah* from the other *sefirot* becomes prey to powers of judgment beneath Her. The phrase "exposing nudity" is the literal rendering of the Hebrew term גלוי עריות (*gillui arayot*), fornication.

966. **Idolatry toward those empowered princes** In separating *Shekhinah* from the other *sefirot,* one becomes fixated on Her and the powers beneath Her, thus committing idolatry.

967. **Murder engendered by this tree...** Murder has its roots in *Shekhinah,* who is known as the Tree of Death and derives from *Gevurah,* the *sefirah* of harshness on the left side. See Genesis 2:17; above, page 222.

According to *Seder Eliyyahu Rabbah* 5, the Tree of Knowledge of Good and Evil is called the Tree of Death, because when Adam and Eve ate its fruit, death ensued.

968. **She is Woman...** *Shekhinah,* the divine feminine. See BT *Qiddushin* 70b: "So said Shemu'el: 'One should greet a woman only via her husband.'" By invoking *Shekhi-*

them all he was commanded concerning this tree. When he ate from it, he violated them all, for it embraces all."

Rabbi Yehudah said, "Indeed this is so, for it is forbidden to be alone with a woman, only together with her husband.[969] What did that wicked one do? He said, 'Look, I touched this tree and did not die. You, too, come and touch it with your hand; you won't die.' This he added for her on his own.[970]

"Immediately, *The woman saw that the tree was good* (ibid. 3:6).[971] What did she see?"

Rabbi Yitsḥak said, "That tree gave forth an aroma, as is said: *like the fragrance of a field blessed by YHVH* (ibid. 27:27).[972] Because of that aroma ascending, she desired eating of it."

Rabbi Yose said, "It was vision."

Rabbi Yehudah said to him, "But it is written: *The eyes of both of them were opened* (ibid. 3:7)!"[973]

He replied, "The vision she beheld was the measure of the tree, as is written: ותרא האשה (*Va-tere ha-ishshah*), *She saw the Woman,* precisely![974]

"*The woman saw that it was good* (ibid., 6). She saw and did not see. She saw *that it was good,* but she was unsettled. What is written next? *She took of its fruit*

227

---

nah alone, without Her husband, *Tif'eret,* one commits sexual sin in the sefirotic world.

969. **it is forbidden to be alone with a woman...** See M *Qiddushin* 4:12; BT *Qiddushin* 81a; *Sanhedrin* 21a–b; Moses de León, *Sefer ha-Rimmon,* 232–33. Cf. *Zohar* 1:67a.

970. **Look, I touched this tree...** Based on the account in *Pirqei de-Rabbi Eli'ezer* 13 and *Avot de-Rabbi Natan* A, 1. Although the last sentence here describes the serpent's action, it derives from the tradition in *Avot de-Rabbi Natan* that when Adam informed Eve of the divine command not to eat from the tree, he added the restriction against touching it.

971. *The woman saw that the tree was good* The verse continues: *for eating and a delight to the eyes, and that the tree was desirable to contemplate. She took of its fruit and ate, and also gave to her husband beside her, and he ate.*

972. **as is said:** *like the fragrance of a field blessed by YHVH* The field of *Shekhinah,* also known as the Holy Apple Orchard. See BT *Ta'anit* 29b; *Bereshit Rabbah* 65:22;

Tanḥuma, Toledot 11; Azriel of Gerona, *Peirush ha-Aggadot,* 35–37; *Zohar* 1:85a–b, 122a, 128b, 142b, 143b, 224b, 249b; 2:60b, 61b; 3:74a, 84a, 133b (*IR*), 135b (*IR*), 286b–287a, 288a (*IZ*); Moses de León, *Shushan Edut,* 365.

973. *The eyes of both of them were opened and they knew that they were naked.* Rabbi Yehudah's point is that only after eating from the tree could they see. How could Eve see before eating?

974. **the measure of the tree...** *She saw the Woman,* **precisely!** Eve beheld a vision of *Shekhinah.* שיעורא (*Shi'ura*), "Measure," recalls שיעור קומה (*shi'ur qomah*), "the measure of the stature," a term describing the mystical vision of the divine form, also known as גוף השכינה (*guf ha-shekhinah*), "the body of *Shekhinah.*"

Here the biblical phrase, ותרא האשה (*Va-tere ha-ishshah*), *The woman saw,* is read hyperliterally, according to the exact word order: ותרא האשה (*Va-tere ha-ishshah*), *She saw the woman,* transforming *the woman* from the subject of the sentence (Eve) into its object (*Shekhinah*).

(ibid.), not *She took of it.* She cleaved to the site of death, inflicting death upon the whole world, separating life from death, which are not to be separated.[975] For voice is never separate from speech, and whoever separates voice from speech turns dumb, speechless.[976] Deprived of speech, he turns to dust."[977]

Rabbi Shim'on said, "It is written: *I was dumb with silence, stilled, bereft of goodness, my pain aroused* (Psalms 39:3). This verse was spoken by Assembly of Israel, who is in exile.[978] Why? Because voice conducts speech.[979] When She is in exile, voice separates from Her, no word is heard, and so: *I was dumb with silence.* Why? Because *I was stilled, bereft of goodness*—for voice no longer accompanies Her, and Israel declares: *To You, praise is silent* (ibid. 65:2). Who is *silent*? *Praise, praise of David* (Psalms 145:1), who turns *silent* in exile, voiceless."[980]

Rabbi Yitsḥak said, "What does *to you* mean? Because of You, She is *silent*, for You abandoned Her."[981]

She took of its fruit and ate.[982] We have learned: She squeezed grapes and offered them to him,[983] and they inflicted death upon the whole world, for death abides in this tree, a tree ruling by night.[984] [36b] When She rules, all

228

---

975. *She took of its fruit,* not *She took of it...* In separating the fruit from its source, Eve caused separation above. Deprived of the flow of emanation, *Shekhinah* generates death.

See *ZḤ* 18c (*MhN*); cf. Genesis 2:17.

976. **For voice is never separate from speech...** The flow of emanation is described in terms of divine speech. *Tif'eret,* the primal voice, should never be separate from *Shekhinah,* articulated speech.

See *Zohar* 1:145a–b, 246b; 2:3a, 25b.

977. **he turns to dust** As in the divine decree to Adam: *For dust you are, and to dust you shall return* (Genesis 3:19). The wording here recalls the Talmudic legend of the Golem animated by permutating letters of the alphabet (BT *Sanhedrin* 65b): "Rava created a man and sent him to Rabbi Zeira. He [Rabbi Zeira] conversed with him, but he did not respond. He said to him, 'You are from the Companions. Return to your dust!'"

978. **Assembly of Israel...** כנסת ישראל (*Keneset Yisra'el*). In rabbinic Hebrew this phrase denotes the people of Israel. The midrash on the Song of Songs describes the love affair between the maiden (the earthly

community of Israel) and her lover (the Holy One, blessed be He). In the *Zohar, Keneset Yisra'el* can refer to the earthly community but also (often primarily) to *Shekhinah,* the divine feminine counterpart of the people, the aspect of God most intimately connected with them. Here Assembly of Israel, suffering in exile, yearns for Her partner, *Tif'eret.* See Moses de León, *Shushan Edut,* 336.

979. **voice conducts speech** *Tif'eret* conducts *Shekhinah.*

980. *To You, praise is silent...* Literally, the verse may mean: *To You, silence is praise.* Here Rabbi Shim'on interprets it to mean that *Shekhinah,* known as *praise of David,* turns *silent* in exile without the resounding voice of *Tif'eret.*

981. **Because of You...** *Tif'eret* is responsible for the silencing of *Shekhinah.*

982. *She took of its fruit and ate* The verse continues: *and also gave to her husband beside her, and he ate.*

983. **She squeezed grapes...** See *Bereshit Rabbah* 19:5: "Rabbi Aivu said, 'She squeezed grapes and offered them to him.'" Cf. *Zohar* 1:192a; 2:267b.

984. **for death abides in this tree...** *Shekhinah,* symbolized by night and the Tree

creatures of the world taste a taste of death,[985] but those scions of faith first
pledge their souls to Him, and since pledged, the souls return to their sites. So,
Your faithfulness every night (Psalms 92:3).[986]

The eyes of both of them were opened (Genesis 3:7).[987]

Rabbi Ḥiyya said, "Opened to perceive the evil of the world, unknown to
them till now.[988] Once they knew and were open to knowing evil, then *they
knew that they were naked* (ibid.), for they had lost the supernal radiance
enveloping them, which disappeared, leaving them *naked.*[989]

"They sewed together fig leaves (ibid.). They knew to be covered by the shade
of that tree from which they had eaten, called 'leaves of the tree.'"[990]

And made themselves loincloths (ibid.). Rabbi Yose said, "Once they knew of
this world and clung to it, they saw that this world is conducted by those leaves
of the tree. So they built themselves a stronghold, fortifying themselves with
them in this world, discovering every kind of magic. They sought to gird
themselves with the weapons of those leaves of the tree for protection."[991]

Rabbi Yehudah said, "Then three were brought to justice and convicted, and
the lower world was cursed[992] and could not firmly endure due to the slime of
the serpent until Israel stood at Mount Sinai.[993] Afterward the blessed Holy

229

of Knowledge, is also known as the Tree
of Death. See Genesis 2:17; above, pages
222–26.

985. **a taste of death** See BT *Berakhot*
57b: "Sleep is one-sixtieth of death."

986. **scions of faith . . .** בני מהימנותא
(*Benei meheimanuta*). They entrust their souls
to *Shekhinah,* confident that She will restore
each soul to its body the next morning,
even if the person be undeserving.

See *Zohar* 1:11a, 92a, 183a; 3:119a, 120b; *ZḤ*
18b–c (*MhN*), 89a (*MhN, Rut*); and BT *Berakhot* 5a: "Abaye said, 'Even a disciple of
the wise should recite one verse of compassion [before going to bed], such as: *Into
Your hand I entrust my spirit; You redeem
me, YHVH, God of truth* (Psalms 31:6).'"

987. *The eyes of both of them were
opened* The verse continues: *and they knew
that they were naked. They sewed together fig
leaves and made themselves loincloths.*

988. **Opened to perceive the evil of the
world . . .** See Maimonides, *Guide of the
Perplexed* 1:2; *Zohar* 3:261b.

989. **they had lost the supernal radiance . . .** Their original aura.

See *Zohar* 1:52a–b, 224a; cf. *Bereshit Rabbah* 12:6 (and Theodor, ad loc.); 19:6; *Targum
Yerushalmi,* Genesis 3:7; *Pirqei de-Rabbi Eli-
'ezer* 14; *Bahir* 141 (200).

990. **that tree from which they had
eaten . . .** According to Rabbi Neḥemiah
(BT *Berakhot* 40a), Adam and Eve sinned
by eating from the fruit of a fig tree. The
leaves of this Tree of Knowledge convey the
knowledge of magic.

See *Zohar* 1:53b, 56a, 63b. Cf. BT *Bava
Metsi'a* 114b.

991. **They sought to gird themselves . . .**
Adam and Eve sought the protection of magical knowledge.

992. **Then three were brought . . .** See
Bereshit Rabbah 5:9: "It was taught in the
name of Rabbi Natan: 'Three were brought
to justice and four were convicted: Adam,
Eve, and the serpent were brought to justice,
and the earth was cursed along with them:
Cursed is the ground (Genesis 3:17).'"

993. **the slime of the serpent . . .** זוהמא
דנחש (*Zohama de-naḥash*), "The filth of the
serpent." See BT *Shabbat* 145b–146a: "Rav
Yosef taught: '. . . When the serpent copu-

One clothed them in garments soothing to the skin, as is written: כתנות עור (*kotnot or*), *garments of skin* (ibid., 21).[994] At first they wore כתנות אור (*kotnot or*), *garments of light,* and he was waited upon by the highest beings, for the angels on high came to bask in that light, as is written: *You made him little less than God, adorned him with glory and majesty!* (Psalms 8:6).[995] Now that they sinned, כתנות עור (*kotnot or*), *garments of skin,* soothing the skin, not the soul.[996]

"Afterward they bore their first son, son of slime. Two copulated with her; she conceived and bore two.[997] Each emerged according to his kind; by their spirit they separated, one to this side, one to the other, each resembling its side. From the side of Cain emerge all the haunts of maleficent species, spirits, demons, and sorcerers.[998] From the side of Abel, a side of greater compassion, yet incomplete—good wine adulterated with bad, immature until Seth appeared, from whom descended all righteous generations, by whom the world was sown.[999] From Cain descended all those insolent, wicked sinners of the world."

230

lated with Eve, he injected her with זוהמא (*zohama*), filth [or: slime, lewdness]. Israel, who stood at Mount Sinai—their *zohama* ceased. Star-worshipers, who did not stand at Mount Sinai—their *zohama* did not cease.'"

See *Targum Yerushalmi,* Genesis 4:1 (variants); *Pirqei de-Rabbi Eli'ezer* 21; *Zohar* 1:37a, 52a, 54a, 122b.

994. **garments soothing to the skin...** The verse reads: *YHVH Elohim made garments of skin for Adam and his wife, and clothed them.* See BT *Sotah* 14a: "*Garments of skin.* Rav and Shemu'el. One said: 'Deriving from skin.' The other said: 'Soothing to the skin.'"

995. **and he was waited upon...** Adam's brilliance attracted the angels. See *Bereshit Rabbah* 8:10: "Rabbi Hosha'ya said, 'When the blessed Holy One created Adam, the ministering angels mistook him and sought to recite in his presence: *Holy!*'" Cf. *Zohar* 1:55b.

996. כתנות אור (*kotnot or*), *garments of light...*כתנות עור (*kotnot or*), *garments of skin...* The verse in Genesis reads: כתנות עור (*kotnot or*), *garments of skin,* but a variant reading is: כתנות אור (*kotnot or*), *garments of light,* suggesting the original aura. See above, note 989. See *Bereshit Rabbah* 20:12: "In the Torah [scroll] of Rabbi Me'ir, it was found

written: 'כתנות אור (*kotnot or*), *garments of light.*' These are the clothes of Adam....'"

As a result of eating the fruit of the Tree of Knowledge, thereby splitting the divine, Adam and Eve lost their luster and were clothed in skin.

See *Zohar* 1:224a; 2:229b; 3:261b; cf. Origen, *Contra Celsum* 4:40; *Apocryphon of John* 23:31–32; *Hypostasis of the Archons* 90:16; Irenaeus, *Adversus haereses* 1:5:5; Scholem, *Major Trends,* 404, n. 87.

997. **son of slime...** Cain, born from the union of the serpent and Eve. See *Pirqei de-Rabbi Eli'ezer* 21: "The serpent-rider [Samael] copulated with her and she conceived Cain. Afterward Adam copulated with her and she conceived Abel."

See *Targum Yerushalmi,* Genesis 4:1 (variants); *Zohar* 1:37a, 52a, 54a; Stroumsa, *Another Seed,* 38–53.

998. **From the side of Cain...** On the demonic descendants of Cain, see El'azar of Worms, *Ḥokhmat ha-Nefesh,* 26c; *Zohar* 1:9b, 54a, 178a–b; 3:76b, 122a.

999. **until Seth appeared...** Even Abel was not fully refined, since he was still tainted by the demonic. Seth, the third child of Adam and Eve, generated the righteous.

See BT *Eruvin* 18b; *Pirqei de-Rabbi Eli'ezer* 22; *Zohar* 1:54a, 55a; 3:77a, 143b (*IR*); *ZḤ* 8c

Rabbi El'azar said, "When Cain sinned he was terrified, for he saw several armed camps confronting him, coming to kill him. When he returned to God,[1000] what did he say? *Behold, You have banished me today from the face of the soil, and from Your face I will be hidden* (Genesis 4:14). What is the meaning of: *from Your face* אסתר (essater), *I will be hidden*? His structure סתיר (setir), destroyed."

Rabbi Abba said, "As is written: *He will hide His face from them* (Micah 3:4).[1001] So, *From Your face I will be hidden*—it will not watch over me, *and whoever finds me will kill me* (Genesis, ibid.).

"*YHVH put* אות (ot), *a mark, on Cain* (ibid., 15). What is אות (ot), *a mark*? He placed upon him one אות (ot), letter, of the twenty-two letters of Torah to protect him."[1002]

Rabbi Yehudah said, "Why is it written: *When they were in the field* (ibid., 8)? This is a woman. Because of this he killed him, for from this side he inherited killing, the side of Samael, who inflicted death upon the whole world. Cain was jealous of Abel because of his female."[1003]

Rabbi Ḥiyya said, "But we have seen it written: *Cain was very angry and his face fell* (ibid., 5) because his offering was not accepted."

He replied, "So it is! All this confronted him."[1004]

Rabbi Yehudah said, "Why is it written: *Surely if you do well, there is dignity. But if you do not do well, sin crouches at the opening* (ibid., 7)? Because the verse

231

(SO). Cf. *Bemidbar Rabbah* 14:12: "*He named him* שת (Shet), *Seth* (Genesis 5:3), because on him the world הושתת (hushtat), was founded."

See *Aggadat Bereshit*, intro, 37; Ginzberg, *Legends*, 5:148, n. 50; Liebes, *Peraqim*, 372–73; Stroumsa, *Another Seed*, 74.

1000. **returned to God**   Repenting sincerely.

1001. *He will hide His face from them*   The full verse reads: *Then they will cry out to YHVH, but He will not answer them; He will hide His face from them at that time, in accordance with the wrongs they have committed.*

1002. **He placed upon him one** אות **(ot), letter...**   See *Pirqei de-Rabbi Eli'ezer* 21: "Cain said in the presence of the blessed Holy One, 'Now some righteous person will arise and recite Your name and kill me!' What did the blessed Holy One do? He took one of the twenty-two letters and placed it

on Cain's arm, so that he would not be killed.'"

See *Yalqut Re'uveni*, Genesis 4:15; *TZ* 69 (118b–119a).

1003. *When they were in the field*? **This is a woman...**   See *Pirqei de-Rabbi Eli'ezer* 21: "Rabbi Tsadok said, 'Envy and hatred toward his brother Abel entered Cain's heart because his [Abel's] offering had been accepted. Further, Abel's wife and twin sister was the most beautiful of women. He said, "I will kill my brother Abel and take his woman," as is said: *When they were in the field...*, and *in the field* means "woman," who is compared to a field, as is said: *Man is a tree of the field* (Deuteronomy 20:19).'"

See *Bereshit Rabbah* 22:7; 63:12; BT *Bava Batra* 16b; *Zohar* 1:35b, 54b; 3:202a–b.

1004. **All this confronted him**   He was angry both because of the offering and because of a woman.

declares this: *If you do well, there is dignity*. What is *dignity*? As is written: *surpassing in dignity* (ibid. 49:3), for the firstborn is entirely praiseworthy, depending on his deeds.[1005] So, *if you do well, there is dignity. But if you do not do well, sin crouches at the opening*. What is *the opening*? The opening [37a] above, from whom judgments issue for evil deeds of the world. *Opening*, as is said: *Open for me the gates of justice* (Psalms 118:19).[1006] At that *opening, sin crouches*, namely, the Angel of Death, poised to punish you.

"Come and see: On Rosh Hashanah Adam was born.[1007] On Rosh Hashanah, indeed, mystery above and below: Rosh Hashanah above, Rosh Hashanah below.[1008] On Rosh Hashanah barren women are attended.[1009] How do we know this happens on Rosh Hashanah? As is written: ויהוה (*Va-YHVH*), *And YHVH, attended to Sarah* (Genesis 21:1)—ויהוה (*Va-YHVH*), *And YHVH*, precisely: this is Rosh Hashanah.[1010] Since Adam emerged from Rosh Hashanah, he emerged through judgment, and the world endures through judgment.[1011]

232

1005. *surpassing in dignity...* From the blessing given by Jacob to Reuben, his first-born: *Reuben, you are my firstborn, my strength and first fruit of my vigor! Surpassing in dignity, surpassing in power!* Cain, the firstborn of Adam and Eve, can also attain such *dignity* if he behaves well.

See Naḥmanides on Genesis 4:7; *Zohar* 1:54b; *ZḤ* 19c–d (*MhN*); Kasher, *Torah Shelemah*, Genesis 4:7, n. 68.

1006. **The opening above...** *Shekhinah*, known as Justice, through whom divine punishment is delivered.

1007. **On Rosh Hashanah Adam was born** See *Pesiqta de-Rav Kahana* 23:1: "Rabbi Eli'ezer taught, 'The world was created on the twenty-fifth of Elul.'... Consequently Adam was created on Rosh Hashanah."

See *Vayiqra Rabbah* 29:1; *Pirqei de-Rabbi Eli'ezer* 8, and David Luria, ad loc., n. 1; BT *Rosh ha-Shanah* 10b; Asher ben Yeḥiel, on *Rosh ha-Shanah* 8a; *Ḥiddushei ha-Ran* on *Rosh ha-Shanah* 16a; *Tosefot Yom Tov, Rosh ha-Shanah* 1:2.

1008. **Rosh Hashanah above... below** Rosh Hashanah is both the beginning of the year and the Day of Judgment. It symbolizes *Shekhinah*, who administers justice and constitutes the beginning of the *sefirot* from a human perspective.

1009. **barren women are attended** See *Bereshit Rabbah* 73:1; *Tanḥuma, Vayera* 17; and BT *Rosh ha-Shanah* 11a: "Rabbi Yehoshu'a says, '...On Rosh Hashanah Sarah, Rachel, and Hannah were attended.'" All barren until then, they miraculously conceived on Rosh Hashanah.

1010. **How do we know...** See *Bereshit Rabbah* 51:2: "Rabbi El'azar said, 'Wherever it is said: *And YHVH*, this implies: He and His Court.'" In Kabbalah this court symbolizes *Shekhinah*, who derives from the *sefirah* of *Din* ("Judgment") and pronounces the divine decree, so the phrase *And YHVH* encompasses "He [*Tif'eret*, known as YHVH] and His Court [*Shekhinah*]."

See JT *Berakhot* 9:5, 14b; Rashi on Exodus 12:29; *Zohar* 1:15b, 64b, 107b; 2:37b, 44b; 3:149a. The hermeneutical significance of *and* was championed by Rabbi Akiva. See BT *Yevamot* 68b; *Sanhedrin* 51b.

On Rosh Hashanah, the Day of Judgment, YHVH is accompanied by His Court, *Shekhinah*, also known as Rosh Hashanah. Thus the opening word of the verse in Genesis, ויהוה (*Va-YHVH*), *And YHVH*, alludes to Rosh Hashanah. Further, the verse opens the Torah portion read on the first day of Rosh Hashanah.

1011. **Since Adam emerged...** Adam's origin, *Shekhinah*, is characterized by judgment, essential to the world.

So, *at the opening,* indeed, *sin crouches* to punish you. *His desire is toward you* (ibid. 4:7), till you are destroyed. ואתה (*Ve-attah*), *And you, will rule over him* (ibid.)—a mystery, as is written: ואתה (*Ve-Attah*), *And You, enliven them all* (Nehemiah 9:6).[1012] From here they have concluded that the blessed Holy One reigns only when the wicked of the world are destroyed.[1013] So, once the Angel of Death destroys them, He rules over him, preventing him from putrefying the world, as is written: ואתה (*Ve-attah*), *And you, will rule over him*—ואתה (*Ve-Attah*), *And You,* precisely!"[1014]

Rabbi Yitsḥak said, "In a grapple of strife a potentate appears."[1015]

Rabbi Yehudah said, *"And you will rule over him,* by returning to God."

Rabbi Yose said, "The generations of Cain resembled beings above and below: walking upon the earth, they pulverized the ground."[1016]

Rabbi Yitsḥak said, "When Uzza and Azael fell from their holy site above, they saw the daughters of human beings, sinned, and engendered sons.[1017]

1012. ואתה (*Ve-Attah*), *And You, enliven them all* Shekhinah is often called את (*Et*) and is also symbolized by the final ה (*he*) in the name יהוה (*YHVH*). Together these letters spell an expanded name of *Shekhinah:* אתה (*Attah*), *You.* See *Zohar* 1:15b, 154b, 158b; 2:138b, 261a (*Heikh*).

As for the accusative particle *et,* grammatically it has no ascertainable independent sense, but Naḥum of Gimzo and his disciple Rabbi Akiva taught that when *et* appears in a biblical verse, it amplifies the original meaning. See BT *Pesaḥim* 22b; *Ḥagigah* 12a; *Zohar* 1:247a; 2:90a, 135b.

את (*Et*) comprises the entire alphabet, the letters from א (*alef*) to ת (*tav*), and is therefore an appropriate name for *Shekhinah,* who is known in the *Zohar* as both the mystical realm of speech and Oral Torah. See the Christian parallel in Revelation 1:8: "I am *alpha* and *omega.*"

1013. **the blessed Holy One reigns only when...** See *Vayiqra Rabbah* 24:1: "Rabbi Shim'on son of Yoḥai said, 'When is the name of the blessed Holy One exalted in His world? When He executes the quality of judgment upon the wicked. This is demonstrated by many verses....'" Cf. *Zohar* 3:297b.

1014. ואתה (*Ve-Attah*), *And You,* precisely! *Shekhinah,* who is known by this name. See above, note 1012.

1015. **In a grapple of strife...** One of the *Zohar*'s neologistic gnomes. On the simple level, it means apparently that an officer comes to break up a quarrel. The implication may be that in the struggle with the sinful urge, a divine power appears to help, or in the struggle with the Angel of Death, *Shekhinah* appears, restraining him.

The Aramaic neologism קפסירא (*qafsira*) means "ruler, potentate" in *Zohar* 1:177a; 3:152a. Cf. 1:243a; 3:36b.

1016. **pulverized...** מטרטשי (*Metarteshei*), "Crumbled," based on מטרשי (*metareshei*), "make brittle," and טרש (*teresh*), "stony ground." See *Zohar* 1:239b; 2:30a; cf. above, note 848: מדבי טרטשי (*mi-devei tarteshei*), "crag dwellers."

1017. **Uzza and Azael...** These two angels opposed the creation of Adam and Eve, fell from heaven, and were attracted by *the daughters of men* (Genesis 6:2). They were punished by being bound in chains of iron in the mountains of darkness, from where they still manage to wreak havoc, teaching sorcery to humans.

See 1 Enoch 6–8; Jubilees 5; BT *Yoma* 67b; *Aggadat Bereshit,* intro, 39; *Midrash Avkir,* 7 (cited in *Yalqut Shim'oni,* Genesis, 44); *Pirqei de-Rabbi Eli'ezer* 22; *Zohar* 1:9b, 23a, 37a (*Tos*), 58a, 126a; 3:208a, 212a–b; *ZḤ* 81a–b (*MhN, Rut*).

These were נפילים (*nefilim*), *fallen beings,* as is written: *The* נפילים (*nefilim*), *fallen beings, were on earth* (Genesis 6:4)."[1018]

Rabbi Ḥiyya said, "The sons of Cain were *the sons of* אלהים (*Elohim*), *God* (ibid., 2). For when Samael copulated with Eve, injecting her with slime, she conceived and bore Cain.[1019] His features differed from other humans,[1020] and all those issuing from his aspect are called *sons of Elohim.*"

Rabbi Yehudah said, "Even the sons of those *nefilim* are so called.

"*They were the mighty men* (ibid., 4).[1021] There were sixty on earth, corresponding to the number above. Here is written: *They were the mighty men* מעולם (*me-olam*), *of old,* and there is written: *sixty mighty men encircling her* (Song of Songs 3:7)."[1022]

Rabbi Yose said, "*They were the mighty men* מעולם (*me-olam*), *from the world,* literally, *from the world,* precisely![1023]

"*The men of name* (Genesis, ibid.). What does *name* mean? This is *the world* of which we have spoken, *men of the name,* precisely![1024] Here is written: *men of the name,* and there is written: *when he blasphemes the name* (Leviticus 24:16), and similarly: *The son of the Israelite woman blasphemed the name* (ibid., 11)."[1025]

Rabbi Ḥiyya said, "They were מעולם (*me-olam*), *from the world,* literally! *From the world* below, the blessed Holy One took them, as is said: *Remember*

234

1018. **These were** נפילים (***nefilim***), *fallen beings...* Uzza and Azael, referred to also as *the sons of* אלהים (*Elohim*), *God* (Genesis 6:2). See *Zohar* 1:58a; 3:144a (*IR*).

1019. **For when Samael copulated with Eve...** See *Pirqei de-Rabbi Eli'ezer* 21: "The serpent-rider [Samael] copulated with her and she conceived Cain. Afterward Adam copulated with her and she conceived Abel."

Cf. BT *Shabbat* 145b–146a: "Rav Yosef taught: '...When the serpent copulated with Eve, he injected her with זוהמא (*zohama*), filth [or: slime, lewdness].'"

See *Targum Yerushalmi,* Genesis 4:1 (variants); *Zohar* 1:36b, 52a, 54a, 122b; Stroumsa, *Another Seed,* 38–53.

1020. **His features differed...** See *Pirqei de-Rabbi Eli'ezer* 22: "When Adam had lived a hundred and thirty years, he engendered in his likeness, according to his image, [*and named him Seth*] (Genesis 5:3). From here you learn that Cain was not from his seed, nor *in his likeness,* nor *according to his im-*

age. Finally Seth was born, who was *in his likeness* and *according to his image.*" See above, page 63.

1021. **They were the mighty men** The verse continues: *of old, men of name.*

1022. **sixty mighty men encircling her** The female figure in the Song of Songs is identified with *Shekhinah,* who is surrounded by sixty angelic powers. See *Zohar* 2:5a, 51a; 3:60a.

1023. מעולם (***me-olam***), *from the world,* literally, *from the world,* precisely! The word עולם (*olam*) means both "eternity" and "world." Rabbi Yose picks the second meaning, which is also one of the names of *Shekhinah,* the culmination of the upper world. From Her *the mighty men* derived. See *Zohar* 2:179a (*SdTs*); 3:144a (*IR*).

1024. **What does *name* mean?...** *Shekhinah,* known as *the world,* is also the divine name, the full expression of divine being.

1025. **when he blasphemes the name...** Here, too, *the name* is *Shekhinah.* See *Zohar* 3:176b; Moses de León, *Sefer ha-Rimmon,* 360.

Your compassion, YHVH, and Your love, for they are מעולם *(me-olam), from the world*—really *from the world* the blessed Holy One took them to become a holy chariot above.[1026] Similarly here, *They were the mighty men from the world*—really *from the world.*"

Rabbi Yitsḥak said, "מעולם *(Me-olam), From the world*—this is *the bed of Solomon* (Song of Songs 3:7), as is written: *sixty mighty men encircling her* (ibid.)."[1027]

Rabbi Aḥa said, "They are all called *sons of Elohim,* for *the world* was not yet firm and fragrant.[1028]

"Come and see: All those saplings were concealed, tenuously traced in a certain site. Afterward the blessed Holy One uprooted them, transplanting them elsewhere, and they endured."[1029]

Rabbi Yeisa asked, "Concerning what is written: *This is the book of the generations of Adam...* (Genesis 5:1)—"

"This is a supernal mystery," said Rabbi Abba. "We have learned: 'Three books are opened on Rosh Hashanah: one, of the completely righteous....'[1030]

235

1026. **the blessed Holy One took them...** God removed *the sons of Elohim* from the world because of their destructiveness. See above, note 1017. A different removal took place with the patriarchs (Abraham, Isaac, and Jacob), who were transformed into a divine chariot, having attained respectively the rungs of *Ḥesed* (*love*), *Gevurah,* and *Tif'eret,* also known as *Raḥamim* (*compassion*).

See *Bereshit Rabbah* 47:6: "Resh Lakish said, 'The patriarchs themselves constitute the [divine] Chariot.'"

Cf. Azriel of Gerona, *Peirush ha-Aggadot,* 57; *Zohar* 1:60b, 99a, 150a, 154b, 173b, 248b; 2:144a; 3:38a, 99a.

1027. **this is** *the bed of Solomon...* Symbolizing *Shekhinah,* surrounded by angels and married to *Tif'eret,* known as Solomon.

1028. **for** *the world* **was not yet firm and fragrant** *Shekhinah, the world,* was not yet filled with the flow of emanation, and tended toward severe judgment, symbolized by the name אלהים (*Elohim*), *God.*

"Firm and fragrant" renders both senses of אתבסמת (*itbassamat*), "was sweetened" or "was firmly established."

See *Bereshit Rabbah* 66:2; *Midrash Shemu'el* 26:4; *Zohar* 1:30b, 31a, 34a, 56a, 137a; 2:143a, 168a, 227a; 3:18a; N. Bronsnick, in *Sinai* 63 (1968): 81–85; Scholem, *Major Trends,* 165, 388, n. 44; idem, *Kabbalah,* 228.

1029. **All those saplings were concealed...** The six *sefirot* from *Ḥesed* to *Yesod* began as saplings in the higher sefirotic realm and were later transplanted into *Shekhinah.* See *Bereshit Rabbah* 15:1: "*YHVH Elohim planted a garden in Eden* (Genesis 2:8)....As is written: *The trees of YHVH drink their fill, the cedars of Lebanon that He planted.* Rabbi Ḥanina said, 'They resembled antennae of grasshoppers, and the blessed Holy One uprooted them, transplanting them in the Garden of Eden.'"

See Ezra of Gerona, *Peirush Shir ha-Shirim,* 504; *Zohar* 1:31a, 35b; 2:127b; 3:4b, 217b.

1030. **Three books are opened...** See BT *Rosh ha-Shanah* 16b: "Rabbi Keruspedai said in the name of Rabbi Yoḥanan, 'Three books are opened on Rosh Hashanah: one of the completely wicked, one of the completely righteous, and one of those in between. The completely righteous are immediately inscribed and sealed for life. The

[37b] A supernal book whence all emerges, whence emerges writing.[1031] A middle book comprising above and below, embracing all sides, mystery of Written Torah, Primordial Adam.[1032] A book called *Generations of Adam.* Which is that? The one of the completely righteous, as is written: *This is the book,* really! Righteous One engendering generations.[1033]

"*On the day God created Adam in the likeness of God* (ibid.),[1034] for really then was all arrayed above and below, stabilized in a single paradigm.[1035]

"*Male and female He created them* (ibid., 2)—unidentifiable, one merging in the other."[1036]

236

completely wicked are immediately inscribed and sealed for death. Those in between remain pending from Rosh Hashanah until Yom Kippur. If they prove worthy, they are inscribed for life; if not, for death.'"

For Rabbi Abba, the "three books" (ספרים [*sefarim*]) are three *sefirot.* See the play on *sefer* and *sefirot* at the opening of *Sefer Yetsirah.*

1031. **A supernal book...** *Binah,* Divine Mother and source of the linguistic stream of emanation. See *Zohar* 2:200a.

1032. **A middle book...** *Tif'eret,* torso of the sefirotic body of Primordial Adam, including the right and left sides (*Ḥesed* and *Gevurah*). In Him the stream of divine language takes shape as the Written Torah.

1033. **The one of the completely righteous...** The third ספר (*sefer*), "book," is the *sefirah* of *Yesod* ("Foundation"), the procreative force. He is known as Righteous One, based on Proverbs 10:25: וצדיק יסוד עולם (*Ve-tsaddiq yesod olam*), which literally means *The righteous one is an everlasting foundation* but is understood as *The righteous one is the foundation of the world.*

See BT *Ḥagigah* 12b; *Bahir* 71 (102); Azriel of Gerona, *Peirush ha-Aggadot,* 34.

Yesod is also called זה (*Zeh*), "This" (masculine), partner of *Shekhinah,* the Divine Presence, known as זאת (*Zot*), "This" (feminine).

On *the book of the generations,* see BT *Avodah Zarah* 5a: "Did not Resh Lakish say: 'What is the meaning of the verse *This is the book of the generations of Adam...*? Did

Adam possess a book? Rather, this teaches that the blessed Holy One showed Adam every generation with its expounders, every generation with its sages, every generation with its leaders. When he reached the generation of Rabbi Akiva [martyred by the Romans], he rejoiced over his Torah and grieved over his death, saying: *How precious to me are Your companions, O God!* [*How mighty their chiefs!*] (Psalms 139:17).'"

See *Bereshit Rabbah* 24:2; BT *Sanhedrin* 38b; *Zohar* 1:55a–b, 90b, 227b; 2:70a; *ZH* 16d (*MhN*).

1034. **On the day God created Adam in the likeness of God** The verse concludes: *He made him.*

1035. **all was arrayed above and below...** The human being embodies the sefirotic paradigm.

1036. **unidentifiable, one merging in the other** Adam and Eve were not yet differentiated as male and female, having been created as one androgynous entity. See *Bereshit Rabbah* 8:1: "Rabbi Yirmeyah son of El'azar said, 'When the blessed Holy One created Adam, He created him androgynous, as is said: *Male and female He created them* (Genesis 1:27).' Rabbi Shemu'el son of Naḥman said, 'When the blessed Holy One created Adam, He created him with two faces. Then He sawed him and gave him two backs, one on this side and one on that.'"

See BT *Berakhot* 61a; *Eruvin* 18a; Plato, *Symposium* 189d–191d; *Zohar* 1:47b; 2:55a; 3:5a, 44b; Matt, *Zohar,* 217.

Our Mishnah.[1037] It is written: *The name of YHVH is a tower of strength, into which the righteous one runs and is safe* (Proverbs 18:10). This is *the book of the generations of Adam,* who runs into that *tower.*[1038] This *tower*—what is its nature? This is the Tower of David.[1039] This is: מגדל עוז שם יהוה בו ירוץ צדיק ונשגב (*Migdal oz shem YHVH, bo yaruts tsaddiq ve-nisgav*), *The name of YHVH is a tower of strength, into which the righteous one runs and is safe.* All is one. Here is a cipher for scions of faith:[1040]

מיץ	עוי	מבש
יצד	ווה	גרג
היי	זדו	דצב
ונק	שוה	לקה

This is really *the book of the generations of Adam* for scions of faith.

Rabbi Abba said, "An actual book was brought down to Adam, from which he discovered supernal wisdom.[1041] This book reached *the sons of Elohim,* who

237

1037. **Our Mishnah** The *Zohar* often cites teachings from a secret, mystical Mishnah known only to its own circle.

See 1:55b, 74a, 91b, 93a, 95b, 96a, 224a, 252a (*Hash*); 3:57b, 61b, 78a, 284b, 285a. This is to be distinguished from the *Matnitin* of the *Zohar,* on which see Scholem, *Kabbalah,* 216.

1038. **This is *the book of the generations of Adam*...** *The righteous one* is *Yesod,* the generative power of the *sefirot,* who unites with *Shekhinah,* the divine name—symbolized by the *tower.* See *Zohar* 1:9a, 96b; 3:164a–b.

1039. **the Tower of David** *Shekhinah,* known as *Malkhut* ("Kingdom") and symbolized by the ideal king, David.

1040. **Here is a cipher for scions of faith** A lexical labyrinth, a kabbalistic permutation of letters consisting of twelve triads, encoding the verse from Proverbs. Begin at the top right and read down the first column of letters: מגדל. Proceed to the middle column of triads and read down the first column of letters and continue likewise with the final column of triads on the left: עוז שם יהו. The final ה (*he*) of יהוה appears at the end of the last triad of the first column of triads on the right. Now return to the starting point and read the second letter of each

triad from right to left: בו ירוץ צדיק ון. To complete the verse, return to the starting point and read the final letter of each triad from top to bottom: שגב. Skip the final letter of the last triad of the first column of triads (ה [*he*], since this already completed the name יהוה), and continue with the second and third columns of triads, reading the final letters from top to bottom, which encapsulate the verse: יהוה צדיק.

1041. **An actual book was brought down to Adam...** According to various medieval traditions, the angel Raziel transmitted a magical book to Adam, though after his departure from the Garden of Eden. Here the book preserves the primordial wisdom of paradise for Adam and his generations. (Later, probably in the seventeenth century, *Sefer Razi'el* was compiled in its present form, comprising ancient magical, mystical, and cosmological teachings.)

According to BT *Bava Metsi'a* 85b–86a, Rabbi Yehudah the Prince once saw *The Book of Adam,* which contained the genealogy of the entire human race. See *Sanhedrin* 38b; *Bereshit Rabbah* 24:2. This is not to be confused with the Apocryphal *Book of Adam,* known in various versions, though the Apocryphal book may have influenced the

contemplate and know it.[1042] This book was brought down by the master of mysteries, preceded by three envoys.[1043] When Adam departed the Garden of Eden he grasped that book, but as he was leaving it flew away from him to the gate. He prayed and cried before his Lord, and it was restored to him as before, so wisdom would not be forgotten by humanity and they would strive to know their Lord.

"Similarly we have learned: חנוך (*Ḥanokh*), Enoch, had a book—a book from the site of *the book of the generations of Adam,* mystery of wisdom—for he was taken from Earth, as is written: *He was no more, for God took him* (Genesis 5:24).[1044] He is the Lad, as is written: חנוך (*Ḥanokh*), *Train, the lad* (Proverbs 22:6).[1045] All hidden treasures above were entrusted to him, and he transmits, carrying out the mission. A thousand keys were handed to him; he conveys one hundred blessings every day, wreathing wreaths for his Lord.[1046] The blessed

238

Zohar's *Book of Adam*. The book is referred to frequently, sometimes in the context of physiognomy and chiromancy.

See 1:17b, 55a–b, 58b, 72b, 90b; 2:70a–b, 70a–b (*RR*), 77a, 131a, 143b, 180a, 181a, 197a; 3:10a, 68b; *ZḤ* 37b; Ginzberg, *Legends,* 5:117–18, n. 110; Liebes, *Peraqim,* 85–87; Wineman, *Mystic Tales from the Zohar,* 35–54. Cf. *Otsar ha-Ge'onim, Ḥagigah* 11b; Naḥmanides on Genesis 5:2.

1042. *the sons of Elohim,* **who contemplate and know it**   On *sons of Elohim,* see above, pages 234–35. Several manuscripts and the printed editions read here: "*the sons of Elohim,* wise of the generation, and whoever are privileged to contemplate it discover higher wisdom."

1043. **the master of mysteries...**   The angel Raziel, whose name means "mystery of God." See *Zohar* 1:55b.

1044. **חנוך** (*Ḥanokh*)**, Enoch, had a book...**   In postbiblical literature the phrase *for God took him* was taken to mean that God transported Enoch through the heavens, a journey recorded in his book, *The Book of Enoch*. The *Zohar*'s *Book of Enoch,* though influenced by the Enoch literature, is not identical with any of its particular volumes.

See *Zohar* 1:13a, 55b, 72b; 2:55a, 100a, 105b, 180b, 192b, 217a; 3:10b, 236b, 240a, 248b, 253b, 307a; *ZḤ* 2c (*SO*). Cf. *Aggadat Bereshit,*

intro, 38; *Midrash Aggadah,* Genesis 5:24; Ginzberg, *Legends,* 5:156–64, nn. 58–61; Margaliot, *Mal'akhei Elyon,* 80–83.

1045. **He is the Lad...**   Through his heavenly journey, Enoch was transformed into the chief angel, Metatron, also known as the Lad (heavenly servant). Rabbi Abba proves the identification of Enoch with the Lad by citing the phrase from Proverbs: חנוך לנער (*ḥanokh la-na'ar*), *train the lad,* which is understood to mean that Ḥanokh (Enoch) was transformed into *the lad*.

See 3 Enoch 4:1–10; BT *Yevamot* 16b, and *Tosafot,* s.v. *pasuq zeh; Targum Yerushalmi,* Genesis 5:24; *Zohar* 1:223b; 2:179a (*SdTs*), Ginzberg, *Legends,* 5:162–63, n. 61; Scholem, *Kabbalah,* 378–79; Margaliot, *Mal'akhei Elyon,* 89–90.

1046. **he conveys one hundred blessings...**   See *Shemot Rabbah* 21:4: "Rabbi Pinḥas said in the name of Rabbi Me'ir and Rabbi Yirmeyah said in the name of Rabbi Abba, 'When Israel prays, you do not find them all praying as one, but rather each assembly prays on its own, one after the other. When they have all finished, the angel appointed over prayers gathers all the prayers offered in all the synagogues and weaves them into wreaths, which he places on the head of the blessed Holy One.'"

In BT *Ḥagigah* 13b, it is reported that the angel Sandalfon "stands behind the Chariot,

Holy One took him from the world to serve Him, as is written: *for God took him.* By him a book was transmitted, a book was conveyed called *The Book of Enoch.*[1047] When the blessed Holy One grasped him, He showed him all the treasures above, the Tree of Life in the middle of the garden, including its leaves and branches.[1048] All this we see in his book. Happy are the devout of the world, to whom supernal wisdom is revealed, never to be forgotten, as is said: *The secret of YHVH is for those in awe of Him; to them He reveals His covenant* (Psalms 25:14)."[1049]

YHVH said, "My spirit shall not abide in humanity forever, since they, too, are flesh" (Genesis 6:3).[1050] Rabbi Aḥa said, "At that time the flowing, gushing river was gushing a supernal spirit from the Tree of Life, pouring into the tree where death abides,[1051] so spirits were drawn into human beings recurrently, until maleficent species ascended, presenting themselves at the opening. Then, as human souls were flying off, the supernal spirit departed from that tree, as is written: *My spirit shall not abide in humanity* לעולם (*le-olam*), *forever,* given לעולם (*la-olam*), to the world."[1052]

    Since they, too, are flesh. Members of the academy of Rabbi El'azar said, "בשגם (*Be-shaggam*), *Since too*—this is משה (*Mosheh*), Moses, who illumines the moon, by whose energy humanity endures for many days in the world.[1053]

239

binding crowns for his Lord." See *Pesqita Rabbati* 20; *Midrash Tehillim* 88:2; Ezra of Gerona, *Peirush Shir ha-Shirim,* 495; *Zohar* 1:37b, 167b; 2:58a, 146b, 202b, 209a, 245b–246a (*Heikh*); Green, *Keter,* 37–38.

Here Metatron weaves wreaths out of the one hundred blessings recited each day by Israel. See BT *Menaḥot* 43b: "Rabbi Me'ir used to say: 'One should offer one hundred blessings each day.'"

1047. *The Book of Enoch*   See above, note 1044.

1048. **the Tree of Life in the middle of the garden...**   As described in Genesis 2:9. The leaves of the Tree of Knowledge convey the knowledge of magic.

See *Zohar* 1:36b, 56a, 63b. Cf. BT *Bava Metsi'a* 114b.

1049. **Happy are the devout of the world...**   Alluding to those who discover wisdom, including the Companions.

1050. *My spirit shall not abide in humanity forever, since they, too, are flesh   Let his days be a hundred and twenty years.*

1051. **the flowing, gushing river...**   In antediluvian history *Yesod* conveyed the supernal spirit from *Tif'eret,* the Tree of Life, to *Shekhinah,* from whom human souls emerge. She is characterized by judgment and associated with death. See Genesis 2:17; above, pages 222–23, 228–29.

According to *Seder Eliyyahu Rabbah* 5, the Tree of Knowledge of Good and Evil is called the Tree of Death, because when Adam and Eve ate its fruit, death ensued.

1052. **maleficent species ascended...the supernal spirit departed...**   Human wickedness activated demonic powers who blocked the opening, *Shekhinah.* See *Zohar* 1:36b–37a, 58a. Consequently the supernal spirit departed from Her as souls were beginning to emanate, thereby diluting each soul and reducing human longevity, as the verse concludes: *Let his days be a hundred and twenty years.*

1053. בשגם (*Be-shaggam*), *Since too*—this is משה (*Mosheh*), Moses...   The word בשגם (*be-shaggam*) in the verse in Genesis is nu-

"*Let his days be a hundred and twenty years* (ibid.), alluding to Moses, through whom Torah was given and who thereby poured life lavishly for humanity from that Tree of Life.[1054] So it would have been, had Israel not sinned, as is written: חרות (*ḥarut*), *engraved, on the tablets* (Exodus 32:16)—חרות (*ḥerut*), *freedom*, from the Angel of Death, for the Tree of Life extended to those below.[1055] So, בשגם (*be-shaggam*), *since [he,] too, is flesh,* the event transpires: the spirit of life is lavishly poured.[1056] בשגם (*Be-shaggam*), *Since too*— embraced below and above. So we have learned: 'Moses did not die, but was rather gathered [38a] from the world and illumines the moon.'[1057] For even when the sun is gathered from the world, it does not die but illumines the moon. So too, Moses."

Alternatively, *since it, too, is flesh*—when the spirit extends long within human beings, it turns into *flesh*, being drawn after the body.[1058]

Rabbi Yitsḥak said, "All the generations perfected by Seth were entirely righteous and devout.[1059] Subsequently spreading and multiplying, they learned

240

merically equivalent to the word משה (*Mosheh*), Moses, and alludes to Moses' life span, specified in the continuation of the verse: 120 years. The wordplay appears in BT *Ḥullin* 139b, in the name of Rabbi Mattanah. Here Moses, symbolizing the sun and *Tif'eret*, illumines the moon (*Shekhinah*), thereby ensuring longevity on earth.

1054. **alluding to Moses...** Who lived for 120 years (see Deuteronomy 34:7).

Torah is identified with the Tree of Life, based on the description of wisdom in Proverbs 3:18: *She is a tree of life to those who grasp her.* See BT *Berakhot* 32b, 61b. Here the tree symbolizes *Tif'eret*, who is both Written Torah and source of the spirit.

1055. **had Israel not sinned...** If Israel had not sinned at Sinai with the Golden Calf (Exodus 32), they would have become immortal. See *Tanḥuma, Ki Tissa* 16; and *Shir ha-Shirim Rabbah* on 8:6: "חרות (*Ḥarut*), *Engraved, on the tablets* [describing the divine writing on the tablets of stone, spelling out the Ten Commandments]. Do not read חרות (*ḥarut*), *engraved*, but rather חירות (*ḥeirut*), *freedom*. Rabbi Yehudah, Rabbi Neḥemiah, and the Rabbis: Rabbi Yehudah says, 'Freedom from the Angel of

Death.' Rabbi Neḥemiah says, 'Freedom from foreign rulers.' The Rabbis say, 'Freedom from suffering.'"

1056. **So, בשגם (*be-shaggam*), *since [he,] too, is flesh*...** As noted above, Moses' name is equivalent to בשגם (*be-shaggam*). When he appears in bodily form on earth and transmits Torah, spirit pours into the world.

1057. **Moses did not die...** See *Sifrei*, Deuteronomy 357: "Some say: Moses did not die, but rather stands ministering above."

See BT *Sotah* 13b; *Zohar* 1:21b–22a; 3:284a; Ginzberg, *Legends*, 6:161–62, n. 951.

1058. **when the spirit extends long...** When humans live long, the spirit is gradually transformed into matter and inured to material pursuits.

1059. **All the generations perfected by Seth...** Seth, the third child of Adam and Eve, generated the righteous. See *Bemidbar Rabbah* 14:12: "He named him שת (*Shet*), *Seth* (Genesis 5:3), because on him the world הושתת (*hushtat*), was founded."

See BT *Eruvin* 18b; *Pirqei de-Rabbi Eli'ezer* 22; *Zohar* 1:36b, 54a, 55a; 3:77a, 143b (*IR*); *ZḤ* 8c (*SO*); Liebes, *Peraqim*, 372–73.

the art of annihilation: spears and swords.[1060] Finally Noah appeared and rearranged the world for them, preparing and cultivating the soil. For at first they neither sowed nor reaped, which afterward they found essential, as is written: *So long as the earth endures, [sowing and harvest...shall not cease]* (Genesis 8:22)."[1061]

Rabbi El'azar said, "God will one day mend the world and ripen the spirit within human beings so they prolong their days forever, as is written: *For as the days of a tree shall the days of My people be* (Isaiah 65:22), and similarly: *He will swallow up death forever...* (ibid. 25:8)."

[45b][1062] *God said, "Let there be light!" And there was light* (Genesis 1:3). as indicated by the expression: *And there was.*"[1063]

Rabbi Yitsḥak said, "From here we learn that the blessed Holy One uprooted these saplings and transplanted them,

Rabbi Yehudah said, "A light that already was. We have learned that it is written: ויהי (*Vayhi*), *And there was, light.* Not והיה (*ve-hayah*), but rather

241

1060. **the art of annihilation: spears and swords** According to Genesis 4:22, Tuval-Cain, a descendant of Cain, *forged every blade of copper and iron.* According to *Bereshit Rabbah* 23:3, "Rabbi Yehoshu'a said in the name of Rabbi Levi, 'This one [Tuval-Cain] refined the sin of Cain. Cain killed without any instrument, whereas this one *forged every blade....*'" See Rashi, ad loc.

1061. **Finally Noah appeared...** See Genesis 5:29: *He* [Lamech] *named him* נח (*Noaḥ*), *Noah, saying:* "May this one ינחמנו (*yenaḥamenu*), *provide us relief, from our labor and from the painful toil of our hands caused by the soil that YHVH cursed.*" Commenting on this verse, *Tanḥuma, Bereshit* 11 relates: "Before Noah was born, people did not reap what they sowed. If they sowed wheat, they reaped thorns and thistles. Once Noah was born, the world became arable once again. They reaped what they sowed, sowing wheat and reaping wheat, sowing barley and reaping barley. Furthermore, until Noah was born, they worked by hand.... Once Noah was born, he invented plows, scythes, spades, and all kinds of tools." See *Zohar* 1:58b, 97b.

1062. **[45b]** The folios 1:38a–45b comprise one of two Zoharic sections entitled *Heikhalot*, descriptions of the heavenly "Palaces." This section, not connected exegetically with Torah portion *Be-Reshit,* does not appear here in manuscripts representing an earlier recension of the *Zohar.* Therefore the *Heikhalot* have not been translated here and are scheduled to appear in a subsequent volume.

1063. **the blessed Holy One uprooted these saplings...** The image derives from *Bereshit Rabbah* 15:1: "*YHVH Elohim planted a garden in Eden* (Genesis 2:8)....As is written: *The trees of YHVH drink their fill, the cedars of Lebanon that He planted.* Rabbi Ḥanina said, 'They resembled antennae of grasshoppers, and the blessed Holy One uprooted them, transplanting them in the Garden of Eden.'"

Here the saplings symbolize the six *sefirot* from *Ḥesed* to *Yesod,* which sprouted in the higher sefirotic realm and were later transplanted into *Shekhinah.* See Ezra of Gerona, *Peirush Shir ha-Shirim,* 504; *Zohar* 1:31a, 35b, 37a; 2:127b; 3:4b, 217b.

Rabbi Yitsḥak reads the phrase *and there was* as alluding to the initial stage of the emanation of the *light.*

vayhi.[1064] When the blessed Holy One contemplated the generations of the wicked, who would prove unworthy of that light, He treasured it away, as is written: *The light of the wicked is withheld* (Job 38:15). For whom did He hide it? For the righteous—the righteous, precisely, as is written: *Light is sown for the righteous, joy for the upright in heart* (Psalms 97:11).[1065]

"God said, 'Let there be light!' As is written: *Who aroused from the East...?* (Isaiah 41:2).[1066]

"*God saw that the light was good* (Genesis 1:4). What did He see?"

Rabbi Ḥiyya said, "As we have said, He saw the acts of the wicked and treasured it away."

Rabbi Abba said, "*God saw the light,* its radiance flashing from one end of the universe to the other.[1067]

1064. **A light that already was...** The primordial light emerging from the depths of the highest *sefirot*. See *Bereshit Rabbah* 3:2: "It is not written here אור והיה (*Ve-hayah or*) [which could mean either *And there will be light* or *And there was light*], but rather ויהי אור (*Vayhi or*) [which can mean only] *And there was light*—it already was." Theodor (ad loc.) regards this as a scribal gloss. In any case, the point in *Bereshit Rabbah* is that the creation of light was instantaneous and effortless, whereas here Rabbi Yehudah emphasizes that the light preexisted—it already *was*.

See *Bahir* 17 (25), elaborating on *Bereshit Rabbah*: "Rabbi Berekhiah said, 'Why is it written: *God said, "Let there be light!"* ויהי אור (*Vayhi or*), *And there was light,* and not והיה (*Ve-hayah*) [which could mean either *And there will be* or *And there was*]? This can be compared to a king who had a beautiful object and set it aside until he had prepared a place for it; then he placed it there. As is written: *"Let there be light!" And there was light.* For it already was.'"

See Ezra of Gerona, *Peirush Shir ha-Shirim,* 494; Azriel of Gerona, *Peirush ha-Aggadot,* 109; *Zohar* 1:16b, 45b; 3:245b (*RM*); *ZH* 1a, 37d; Recanati on Genesis 1:3, 3c.

1065. **When the blessed Holy One contemplated...** See BT *Ḥagigah* 12a: "Rabbi El'azar said, 'With the light created by the blessed Holy One on the first day, one could gaze and see from one end of the universe to the other. When the blessed Holy One

foresaw the corrupt deeds of the generation of the Flood and the generation of the Dispersion [the generation of the Tower of Babel], He immediately hid it from them, as is written: *The light of the wicked is withheld* (Job 38:15). For whom did He hide it? For the righteous in the time to come.'"

See *Bereshit Rabbah* 3:6; 41:3; *Shemot Rabbah* 35:1; *Tanḥuma, Shemini* 9; *Bahir* 97–98 (147); *Zohar* 1:31b–32a, 45b–46a, 47a; 2:127a, 148b–149a, 220a–b; 3:88a, 173b.

In the *Zohar,* the word *righteous* indicates the *sefirah* of *Yesod* ("Foundation"), based on Proverbs 10:25: וצדיק יסוד עולם (*Ve-tsaddiq yesod olam*). The verse literally means *The righteous one is an everlasting foundation* but is understood as *The righteous one is the foundation of the world.*

See BT *Ḥagigah* 12b; *Bahir* 71 (102); Azriel of Gerona, *Peirush ha-Aggadot,* 34.

The primordial light is hidden in *Yesod,* the procreative power of God (*Zohar* 1:3a, 21a; 2:35a, 148b–149a, 166b–167a, 230a). Righteous humans are linked with this *sefirah* and thereby experience the light.

1066. **God said... Who aroused from the East...?** Alluding to the process of emanation from *Binah,* the Divine Mother, who is called *Elohim, God,* as well as *Who,* since She can be questioned and sought.

See *Zohar* 1:1b, 30a, 85b–86a; 2:127a, 138a, 139b, 226a, 231b.

1067. **its radiance flashing...** See BT *Ḥagigah* 12a (cited above): "Rabbi El'azar

242

"*That it was good* [46a]—to hide it, so that the wicked of the world would not enjoy it."

Rabbi Shim'on said, "*God saw that the light was good*—without a trace of wrath. Here is written *that it was good*, and there is written: *that it was good in the eyes of YHVH to bless Israel* (Numbers 24:1).[1068] The end of the verse proves it: *God separated the light from the darkness* (Genesis, ibid.), so no wrath could be found, although the blessed Holy One joined them as one.[1069]

"Come and see: Supreme radiance, so this light would glow, and from that radiance, delight to all—the right, by which gravings of engravings are wreathed.[1070] This has been said, as is written: *How abundant is Your goodness that You have hidden away for those in awe of You* (Psalms 31:20). This is the primordial light treasured away by the blessed Holy One for the righteous, as we have said.[1071]

"*There was evening* (Genesis, ibid., 5), from the side of darkness; *there was morning*, from the side of light. Since they join as one, it is written: *day of oneness*."[1072]

Rabbi Yehudah said, "Why is it written of every single day: *There was evening, there was morning*? To reveal that there is no day without night, no night without day; they must not be parted."[1073]

Rabbi Yose said, "That day, on which primordial light radiated, extended through all those days, for on all of them is written: *day*."[1074]

Rabbi El'azar said, "This is implied by the fact that on all of them is written *morning*, and *morning* is solely from the side of primordial light."[1075]

Rabbi Shim'on said, "The first day accompanies all of them, and all inhabit it, showing there is no separation between them. All is one.

said, 'With the light created by the blessed Holy One on the first day, one could gaze and see from one end of the universe to the other....'"

1068. **without a trace of wrath...** The primordial light of Ḥesed was untainted by the harshness of the left side. The verse from Numbers indicates that *good* connotes blessing, the opposite of wrath.

1069. **although the blessed Holy One joined them as one** The polar opposites Ḥesed and Gevurah merged.

1070. **the right, by which gravings...** Ḥesed, on the right, conveying emanation to entities below.

1071. *How abundant is Your goodness...* The primordial light of Ḥesed was hidden away. See above, page 242.

1072. *day of oneness* The verse reads literally: *There was evening, there was morning: one day*. Here the last two words are taken to mean "day of oneness," referring to the union of the opposites: dark and light, left and right.

1073. **there is no day without night...** The opposites are interdependent. See Zohar 1:93a–b.

1074. **That day...extended...** The primordial light of Ḥesed, the first day, radiated through all the lower *sefirot*, symbolized by the other six days of the week of Creation. See *Zohar* 1:141b–142a.

1075. *morning* **is solely from the side of primordial light** Morning derives from the light of Ḥesed.

243

"*God said, 'Let there be light!'*—an extension of this light below. These are angels created on the first day, abiding enduringly on the right side.[1076]

"*God saw* את האור (*et ha-or*), *the light.* את (*Et*), including the speculum that does not shine together with the speculum that shines, of which is written: *that it was good.*"[1077]

Rabbi El'azar said, "את (*Et*)—amplifying, including all those angels issuing from the side of this light, all radiant as at first, enduringly."

Let there be an expanse in the midst of the waters (Genesis 1:6).[1078]

Rabbi Yehudah said, "By this, upper waters were separated from lower waters. *An expanse*—an expansion of the waters, as has been explained. *That it may separate water from water,* upper waters from lower waters.[1079]

"*God fashioned the expanse* (Genesis 1:7), fashioning it lavishly. The verse does not read: *There was an expanse,* but rather: *God fashioned,* expanding it immensely."

Rabbi Yitshak said, "On the second day Hell was created for the wicked of the world. On the second, conflict was created. On the second, work was not completed, so *that it was good* is not written of it, until the third day arrived,

244

1076. **These are angels...** In the world of the *Zohar* most of the angels were created on the fifth day, but angels of Judgment emerged on the second day from *Gevurah*, while angels of Love emerged on the first day from *Ḥesed*.

See *Bereshit Rabbah* 1:3; Jubilees 2; *Zohar* 1:17b, 18b, 34a, 46b; Tishby, *Wisdom of the Zohar*, 2:623–24.

1077. את (*Et*), **including the speculum that does not shine...** Grammatically, the accusative particle את (*et*) has no ascertainable independent sense, but Naḥum of Gimzo and his disciple Rabbi Akiva taught that when *et* appears in a biblical verse it amplies the original meaning. See BT *Pesaḥim* 22b; *Ḥagigah* 12a.

את (*Et*) comprises the entire alphabet, the letters from א (*alef*) to ת (*tav*). In the *Zohar*, it becomes a name for *Shekhinah*, who is known as both the mystical realm of speech and Oral Torah.

See *Zohar* 1:29b, 247a; 2:90a, 135b; and the Christian parallel in Revelation 1:8: "I am *alpha* and *omega*."

Shekhinah is also known as the "speculum (אספקלריא [*ispaqlarya*]) [or: glass, mirror, lens] that does not shine." She does not shine on Her own but rather reflects the other *sefirot,* who are centered in *Tif'eret,* the speculum that shines. See *Zohar* 1:33b, 48b, 183a; 2:23b.

See BT *Yevamot* 49b: "All the prophets gazed through an opaque glass [literally: an *ispaqlarya* that does not shine], whereas Moses our Rabbi gazed through a translucent glass [literally: an *ispaqlarya* that shines]." Cf. 1 Corinthians 13:12: "For now we see through a glass darkly, but then face-to-face."

1078. *Let there be an expanse in the midst of the waters* The verse continues: *that it may separate water from water.*

1079. **upper waters were separated from lower waters...** On the second day of Creation, *Gevurah* emerged, separating the upper flow of emanation (channeled through *Binah* to *Ḥesed*) from the *sefirot* below. Alternatively, the *expanse* of *Yesod* separated the upper flow of emanation (channeled through *Binah* to *Yesod*) from *Shekhinah* and Her lower waters. The comment that follows (on *God fashioned...*) apparently relates to *Yesod.* See *Zohar* 1:17a–b, 32b; 2:149b.

when work was completed, so *that it was good* is written twice, once for the completion of the second day's work and once for itself. On the third day, the second day was mended, the conflict mediated.[1080] Then compassion ripened for the wicked in Hell. On the third day sparks of Hell subside, so by it the second day is embraced, consummated."[1081]

Rabbi Ḥiyya was sitting in the presence of Rabbi Shim'on. He said to him, "This light on the first day, and darkness on the second, when waters were separated and conflict arose—why was it not consummated on the first day, since right embraces left?"[1082]

He replied, "This was precisely the conflict, so the third had to intervene, harmonizing, extending peace between them."[1083]

God said, "Let the earth sprout vegetation" (ibid., 11)[1084]—upper waters joined with lower, yielding fruit. Upper waters swell and generate; lower call to upper, as female to male, for upper waters are male, and lower, female.[1085]

245

1080. **On the second day...On the third day...**   In the biblical account of Creation, the statement *God saw that it was good* (or a variant) is included in the description of each of the six days except for the second. See *Bereshit Rabbah* 4:6: "Why is *that it was good* not written concerning the second day? Rabbi Yoḥanan said..., 'Because on that day Hell was created....' Rabbi Ḥanina said, 'Because on that day conflict was created: *that it may separate water from water.*' ....Rabbi Shemu'el son of Naḥman said, 'Because the work of the water was not completed. Therefore *that it was good* is written twice on the third day: once for the work of the water [see Genesis 1:9–10] and once for the work of the [third] day [ibid., 11].'"

In the *Zohar*, the second day marks the emergence of *Gevurah*, characterized by strict justice, which conflicts with *Ḥesed*, divine love. On the third day, these polar opposites were balanced and synthesized.

See BT *Pesaḥim* 54a; *Pirqei de-Rabbi Eli'ezer* 4; *Midrash Konen* (*Beit ha-Midrash*, 2:25); Ezra of Gerona, *Peirush Shir ha-Shirim*, 506; *Zohar* 1:17a–b, 18a, 33a; 2:149b; Moses de León, *Sheqel ha-Qodesh*, 41 (49).

1081. **compassion ripened...**   On the third day emerged *Tif'eret*, also known as *Raḥamim* (Compassion), who mitigates the harsh judgment of Hell, stemming from *Gevurah*.

1082. **why was it not consummated on the first day...**   Since *Ḥesed*, the first cosmic day, includes within itself the following *sefirot*, why was the work not completed then?

1083. **This was precisely the conflict...**   *Ḥesed* and *Gevurah* manifested two extremes, which were harmonized only by the appearance of the third day.

1084. *Let the earth sprout vegetation*   The verse continues: —*seed-bearing plants, fruit trees of every kind on earth bearing fruit with the seed in it.*

1085. **upper waters joined with lower...**   See *Bereshit Rabbah* 13:13: "Rabbi Shim'on son of El'azar said, 'Every single handbreadth [of water] descending from above is met by two handbreadths emitted by the earth. What is the reason? *Deep calls to deep...* (Psalms 42:8).' Rabbi Levi said, 'The upper waters are male; the lower, female. The former cry to the latter, "Receive us! You are creatures of the blessed Holy

Rabbi Shim'on said, "All this transpires both above and below."[1086]

Rabbi Yose said, "If so, אלהים (Elohim), God, mentioned here—who is Elohim?"[1087]

He replied, "Elohim unspecified is אלהים חיים (Elohim Ḥayyim), Living God, above.[1088] If you say 'below,' not so;[1089] rather, below is generation, [46b] as is said: *These are the generations of heaven and earth בהבראם* (be-hibbare'am), *when they were created* (Genesis 2:4), and we have explained: בה' בראם (be-he bera'am), with he He created them,[1090] while the one above is Patriarchs Supreme.[1091] She is activity, so earth activated *generations,* for She conceives, like female from male."[1092]

Rabbi El'azar said, "All forces were in earth, though she did not issue her forces, namely *generations,* until the sixth day, as is written: *Let the earth bring forth living beings* (ibid. 1:24).[1093] If you say, 'But it is written: *The earth*

One and we are His messengers." They immediately receive them, as is written: *Let the earth open* (Isaiah 45:8)—like a female opening to a male.'"

See *Tosefta, Ta'anit* 1:4; 1 *Enoch* 54:8; *Seder Rabbah di-Vreshit,* 10 (*Battei Midrashot,* 1:25); *Pirqei de-Rabbi Eli'ezer* 23; *Zohar* 1:17b, 29b, 46a, 60b, 244a–b, 245b; 3:223b.

According to the second-century Greek physician Galen, sperm is generated by both male and female. See Leviticus 12:2: *When a woman yields seed.* Cf. Ibn Ezra, Naḥmanides, Baḥya ben Asher and Sforno, ad loc.; BT *Berakhot* 60a; *Niddah* 31a.

1086. **both above and below** In both the sefirotic realm and the physical universe. Above, *Binah* and the six *sefirot* beneath Her (*Ḥesed* to *Yesod*) constitute the upper waters, which join the lower waters flowing from *Shekhinah.* On the masculine aspect of *Binah,* see below.

1087. **who is Elohim?** To whom does the word *Elohim,* the subject of this verse, refer? *Elohim* is the name of several *sefirot: Binah, Gevurah,* and *Shekhinah.*

1088. **Elohim unspecified…** The most general, inclusive *Elohim* is the Divine Mother, *Binah,* also known as *Elohim Ḥayyim.*

1089. **If you say 'below,' not so** *Elohim* does not refer here to the lower *sefirah, Shekhinah.*

1090. **rather, below is generation…** *Shekhinah* generates the worlds beneath Her

including the physical universe. See BT *Menaḥot* 29b: "As Rabbi Yehudah son of Il'ai expounded…: '*These are the generations of heaven and earth בהבראם* (be-hibbare'am), *when they were created.* Do not read בהבראם (be-hibbare'am), *when they were created,* but rather בה' בראם (be-he bera'am), "With ה (he) He created them."'"

Here *he* symbolizes *Shekhinah,* often identified with the final letter of יהוה (YHVH). See *Bereshit Rabbah* 12:10; JT *Ḥagigah* 2:1, 77c; *Alfa Beita de-Rabbi Aqiva,* Version 1 (*Battei Midrashot,* 2:363); *Zohar* 1:91b.

1091. **Patriarchs Supreme** From *Binah* emerge *Ḥesed, Gevurah,* and *Tif'eret,* identified with the three patriarchs, so *Binah* assumes their title. Although often depicted as the Divine Mother, *Binah* is also described as "World of the Male," encompassing the entire configuration of *sefirot* from *Ḥesed* through *Yesod.* Together they constitute a masculine entity ready to join *Shekhinah.*

See *Zohar* 1:96a, 147a, 149a, 160b, 246a, 248b; 2:127b; *ZH* 72b (*ShS*). Cf. 1:17b, 46b, 163a; 2:4a.

1092. **She is activity…** *Shekhinah,* symbolized by *earth,* conceives by the patriarchal power above Her and generates life, thus actualizing the emanation of *Binah.*

1093. **All forces were in earth…** The living beings latent in earth were brought forth on the sixth day of Creation.

246

brought forth vegetation (ibid., 12),' this means she arrayed her forces so they would be fittingly deployed, all hidden away within her until necessary.[1094] For at first is written: *desolate and void* (ibid., 2), as translated.[1095] Afterward she was arrayed and inhabited, receiving seed, grass, vegetation, and trees fittingly, generating them afterward.[1096] Similarly with *the lights*, not functioning until necessary.[1097]

"*Let there be* מארת (*me'orot*), *lights, in the expanse of heaven* (ibid., 14)—spelled deficiently: מארת (*me'erat*), *curse*,[1098] to include the evil serpent who injected slime, causing separation, for the sun does not perform with the moon.[1099] מארת (*Me'erot*), *Curses*, causing earth to be cursed, as is written: *Cursed is the ground* (ibid. 3:17). So it is spelled: מארת (*me'erat*).

1094. **But it is written:** *The earth brought forth vegetation...* Already on the third day. See BT Ḥullin 60b: "Rabbi Assi pointed out a contradiction: It is written: *The earth brought forth vegetation*, on the third day, but it is written: *No bush of the field was yet on earth* [*and no plant of the field had yet sprouted, for YHVH Elohim had not rained upon earth and there was no human to till the soil*] (ibid. 2:5), on the eve of Sabbath. This teaches that plants began to grow but stopped as they verged on breaking through the soil, until Adam came and prayed for them; then rain fell and they sprouted. This teaches you that the blessed Holy One yearns for the prayers of the righteous." See Zohar 1:97a.

1095. *desolate and void...* צדיא וריקניא (*Tsadeya ve-reiqanya*), from *Targum Onqelos*, ad loc., rendering the Hebrew תהו ובהו (*tohu va-vohu*), *chaos and void*. The full verse reads: *The earth was chaos and void, with darkness over the face of the abyss, and the wind of God hovering over the face of the waters.*

1096. **Afterward she was arrayed...generating them afterward** On the third day, earth was arrayed with seed and vegetation, though these emerged only on the sixth day.

1097. **Similarly with *the lights*...** Though fashioned on the fourth day, they began to function only as Creation culminated on the sixth day.

1098. **spelled deficiently:** מארת (*me'erat*), *curse* In Genesis 1:14, the word מארת (*me'orot*) is written without *vavs*, the vowel letters. This deficient spelling is interpreted to mean that something was missing on the fourth day of Creation: the light of the moon, diminished, and this lack represents the potential for evil or "curse": מארה (*me'erah*).

See JT *Ta'anit* 4:4, 68b: "On the fourth day [of the week, Wednesday] they would fast for infants, so that diphtheria not enter their mouths. *God said, 'Let there be* מארת (*me'orot*), *lights*'—spelled מארת (*me'erat*), *curse*."

See Proverbs 3:33; BT *Ta'anit* 27b, *Ḥullin* 60b; *Pesiqta de-Rav Kahana* 5:1; *Soferim* 17:4; Rashi and *Minḥat Shai* on Genesis 1:14; *Zohar* 1:1a, 12a, 19b, 33b; 2:167b, 205a.

1099. **to include the evil serpent who injected slime...** The unusual spelling of the word alludes to the cursed serpent. See BT *Shabbat* 145b–146a: "Rav Yosef taught: '...When the serpent copulated with Eve, he injected her with זוהמא (*zohama*), filth [or: slime, lewdness].'"

See *Targum Yerushalmi*, Genesis 4:1 (variants); *Pirqei de-Rabbi Eli'ezer* 21; *Zohar* 1:36b–37a, 52a, 54a, 122b; Stroumsa, *Another Seed*, 38–53.

The serpent's act ruined the union of *Tif'eret* and *Shekhinah*, the sun and the moon.

"*Let there be* מארת (*me'orot*), *lights*—the moon.[1100] *In the expanse of heaven*—the sun.[1101] Both in a single entity, coupling, illumining worlds above and below, as indicated by the expression על הארץ (*al ha-arets*), *above the earth*, rather than בארץ (*ba'arets*), *on the earth*, implying above and below. Calculation of all is by the moon."[1102]

Rabbi Shim'on said, "Numerologies and calculations of equinoxes, solstices, and intercalations derive entirely from the mystery of the moon, no higher."[1103]

Rabbi El'azar said to him, "No? But the Companions perform numerous calculations and measurements."[1104]

He replied, "Not so! Calculation abides in the moon, whence one enters to discover above."[1105]

He said to him, "But it is written: *that they may be for signs and for seasons.*"[1106]

He replied, "Spelled deficiently: לאתת (*le-otot*), *for signs.*"[1107]

248

1100. **the moon** The singular imperative יהי (*yehi*), *let there be*, as well as the deficient spelling of מארת (*me'orot*), *lights*, imply only one light, namely, the moon, symbolizing *Shekhinah*.

1101. **the sun** Symbolizing *Yesod*, who unites with *Shekhinah*. See *Zohar* 1:19b–20a.

1102. **Calculation of all is by the moon** The Jewish calendar is lunar and derives from *Shekhinah*, symbolized by the moon. See BT *Sukkah* 29a: "Our Rabbis taught:... 'Israel counts by the moon.'" Cf. *Zohar* 1:239a.

1103. **Numerologies...** These various numerical operations derive from the tenth *sefirah, Shekhinah*, mother of the bounded world, not from the higher *sefirot*, where unity prevails and the numerical multiplicity is irrelevant. "Numerologies" (גימטריאות [*gi-matriyya'ot*]) refers to the numerical values of the letters of the alphabet. "Intercalation" refers to the insertion of an additional day in a lunar month (to harmonize the month with the lunar cycle) or an additional month in a lunar year (to harmonize the lunar and solar years).

See M *Avot* 3:18: "Rabbi Eli'ezer son of Ḥisma said, '[Laws concerning] bird offerings and commencements of the menstrual cycle are essential laws. Determining equi-

noxes and solstices, and mathematical calculations (גימטריאות [*gimatriyya'ot*]) are wisdom's dessert.'" Cf. *Zohar* 3:220b.

1104. **But the Companions perform numerous calculations and measurements** The kabbalists engage in numerology concerning the higher *sefirot* as well. Furthermore, they measure the divine body, as recorded in *Shi'ur Qomah* (Measure of the Stature) and the *Idrot* of the *Zohar*.

1105. **Not so!...** All calculations derive from *Shekhinah*, whence one can enter more deeply into the divine. The various divine measurements are perceived through the lens of *Shekhinah*, and "the measure of the stature" concerns גוף השכינה (*guf ha-shekhinah*), "the body of *Shekhinah*." See above, page 227.

1106. *that they may be for signs and for seasons* The full verse reads: *God said, "Let there be lights in the expanse of heaven to separate the day from the night, that they may be for signs and for seasons, for days and years."* The plural, *signs*, indicates not only the moon (*Shekhinah*) but also the sun (*Tif'eret*).

1107. **Spelled deficiently:** לאתת (*le-otot*), *for signs* The word לאתת (*le-otot*), *for signs*, is spelled without a ו (*vav*), and this deficiency implies just one *sign*.

He said to him, "But it is written: *that they may be.*"[1108]

He replied, "All those essences that will inhabit Her, like a treasure ship filled with all,[1109] but calculation of all is by the moon.

"Come and see: There is a single point, origin of counting, for what lies within that point is unknown, uncountable.[1110] There is a point above, concealed, totally unrevealed and unknown, origin of constructing everything concealed and profound.[1111] Similarly there is a point below, revealed, origin of every calculation and reckoning.[1112] So here is the site of all equinoxes and solstices, numerologies, intercalations, festivals, holidays, and Sabbaths. Israel, cleaving to the blessed Holy One, calculate by the moon, cleaving to Her and raising Her, as is written: *You, cleaving to YHVH your God* (Deuteronomy 4:4)."[1113]

Let the waters swarm with a swarm of living creatures (Genesis, ibid., 20).[1114]

Rabbi El'azar said, "They have established that those waters teemed and generated as above. This has already been said.[1115]

"*And let birds fly above the earth* (ibid.). The verse should read: יעוף (ya'uf), *let fly.* Why יעופף (ye'ofef)?"[1116]

Rabbi Shim'on said, "It is a mystery. ועוף (Ve-of), *And a bird*—Michael, as is written: *One of the serafim* ויעף (va-ya'af), *flew, to me* (Isaiah 6:6). יעופף

249

1108. **But it is written: *that they may be*** The plural is explicit.

1109. **All those essences...like a treasure ship...** All the *sefirot* who will pour into *Shekhinah.* "Treasure ship" renders אסקופא (isquppa), which may mean both "yard of a ship" and "threshold." Cf. Greek *skaphe* and אסקפא (isqapha), "skiff, light boat." The image here apparently derives from *Midrash Mishlei* 31:14, where Joseph is compared to "a ship filled with all the best of the world."

In *ZH* 3a (*MhN*), isquppa refers to the "threshold" beneath which household valuables were buried. See BT *Berakhot* 18b; Rashi on BT *Mo'ed Qatan* 11a, s.v. *tsinnor;* idem on Joshua 24:26.

See *Zohar* 1:67a; 2:83b; 3:69a; *ZH* 88c (*MhN, Rut*); *Bei'ur ha-Millim ha-Zarot,* 173; Scholem, *Major Trends,* 165, 388, n. 47.

1110. **There is a single point, origin of counting...** Apparently *Ḥesed,* first of the seven lower *sefirot,* beyond whom lie un-

fathomable divine qualities. See *Zohar* 1:16b. Other commentators understand this phrase as referring to *Shekhinah* (*OY*) or *Ḥokhmah* (*KP*).

1111. **There is a point above, concealed...** The primordial point of *Ḥokhmah,* from which the sefirotic world is constructed.

1112. **Similarly there is a point below, revealed...** *Shekhinah.*

1113. **Israel, cleaving...** By following the moon, Israel cleaves to *Shekhinah,* stimulating Her union with YHVH.

1114. *Let the waters swarm with a swarm of living creatures* and let birds fly above the earth, across the face of the expanse of heaven.

1115. **They have established that those waters teemed...** The waters of *Shekhinah* generated life below. See above, page 212.

1116. **Why יעופף (ye'ofef)?** With a double פ (fe).

(*Ye'ofef*), *Let fly*—Gabriel, as is written: *The man Gabriel whom I had previously seen in the vision* מועף ביעף (*mu'af bi'af*), *was flown in flight* (Daniel 9:21).[1117]

"על הארץ (*Al ha-arets*), *Upon the earth*[1118]—Elijah, appearing continually on earth, not from the aspect of father and mother,[1119] arriving in four glides,[1120] as is written: *The spirit of YHVH will carry you off I know not where* (1 Kings 18:12).[1121] *The spirit of YHVH*—one; *will carry you off*—two; *where*—three; *I know not*—four.

"*Across the face of* (Genesis, ibid.)—Angel of Death, who darkens the face of the world and of whom is written: *darkness over the face of the abyss* (ibid., 2).[1122]

"*The expanse of heaven* (ibid.), as we have said: 'He ascends and accuses…'"[1123]

1117. **Michael…Gabriel…** Two of the four angels of the Presence (along with Raphael and Uriel), who surround the divine throne. The phrase ועוף יעופף (*ve-of ye'ofef*), *and let birds fly*, alludes to these two archangels. Michael is identified as *one of the birdlike serafim* in BT *Berakhot* 4b, while the double פ (*fe*) of יעופף (*ye'ofef*) suggests the doublet describing Gabriel in the book of Daniel: מועף ביעף (*mu'af bi'af*), *was flown in flight*. Furthermore, the *gimatriyya* of גבריאל (*Gavri'el*), Gabriel, is equal to יעופף (*ye'ofef*), *let fly*.

See *Zohar* 2:239a; 3:26b; Baḥya ben Asher on Genesis 1:20; cf. *Devarim Rabbah* 8:2.

1118. על הארץ (*Al ha-arets*), *Upon the earth* In the verse this phrase means *above the earth*, but the word על (*al*) also means "on, upon," as in the interpretation that follows.

1119. **Elijah, appearing continually…** According to the Bible (2 Kings 2:11–12), the prophet Elijah did not die a normal death but was carried off to heaven in a chariot of fire. He became associated with the Messianic age (Malachi 3:23–24) and in rabbinic tradition is described as "still existing" (BT *Bava Batra* 121b) and revealing divine secrets to righteous humans (*Bava Metsi'a* 59b).

See *Midrash Tehillim* 8:7: "*The bird of heaven* (Psalms 8:9)—this is Elijah, who flies through the world as a bird." He is identified as "Master of Wings" in *Targum Qohelet* 10:20 and *Ma'yan Ḥokhmah* (*Beit ha-Mid-*

rash, 1:60). See BT *Berakhot* 4b; *Pirqei de-Rabbi Eli'ezer* 29, and David Luria, ad loc., nn. 66–67.

In Kabbalah Elijah appears in various guises, e.g., a guest at each rite of circumcision, or a wanderer encountered on the road by the Companions. Mystical experiences are known as revelations of Elijah. See Scholem, *On the Kabbalah*, 19–21; *Zohar* 1:13a; 3:221a, 231a; *ZH* 59d.

In the passage here, Elijah is described as an angel, "not from the aspect of father and mother." This accords with the view of Moses de León, according to whom the angel Elijah assumed bodily form in descending to earth. See his *She'elot u-Tshuvot*, 63, 68–71. Cf. *Zohar* 1:151b, 209a, 245b (*NZ*, n. 2); 2:197a; 3:88b; *ZH* 84c–d (*MhN, Rut*). Moses de León's view is criticized by Moses Cordovero (*Pardes Rimmonim* 24:14).

1120. **in four glides** See BT *Berakhot* 4b: "A *tanna* taught: 'Michael [reaches his destination] in one [glide], Gabriel in two, Elijah in four, and the Angel of Death in eight—in time of plague, however, in one.'" See *Zohar* 1:13a, 93a.

1121. *The spirit of YHVH will carry you off…* Spoken to Elijah by Obadiah, steward of King Ahab.

1122. **Angel of Death, who darkens the face of the world…** See *Tanḥuma, Shemot* 17.

1123. **He ascends and accuses…** See the description of Satan's itinerary in BT *Bava*

250

Rabbi Abba said, "But the Angel of Death was created on the second day![1124] Rather, *upon the earth*—Raphael, empowered to heal the earth,[1125] thanks to whom earth is restored to health along with all her forces and the human being endures thereon.

"*Across the face of the expanse of heaven*—Uriel. All is contained within the text.[1126] So afterward is written: *God created the great sea serpents* (ibid., 21)."[1127]

Rabbi El'azar said, "These are Leviathan and his mate.[1128] Alternatively, these are seventy princes appointed over the seventy nations, all created to rule over earth.[1129]

"*And every* נפש חיה (*nefesh ḥayyah*), *soul of the living being, that moves* (ibid.)[1130]—Israel, who are [47a] the actual *soul* of that *living being*[1131] and are called *a nation unique on earth* (2 Samuel 7:23).[1132]

Batra 16a: "He descends and seduces, ascends and arouses wrath, obtains authorization, and seizes the soul." On the same page, Satan is identified with the Angel of Death: "Resh Lakish said, 'Satan, the evil impulse, and the Angel of Death are one and the same.'"

See Rashi on BT *Shabbat* 89a, s.v. *ba hasatan; Zohar* 1:10b, 125a, 148a (*ST*), 152b; 2:33b, 268b.

1124. **the Angel of Death was created on the second day** Along with all the angels of Judgment, not on the fifth day, which is the context of the verse under discussion.

See *Bereshit Rabbah* 1:3; *Zohar* 1:17b, 46a; Tishby, *Wisdom of the Zohar*, 2:623–24.

1125. **Raphael...** Whose name derives from a root meaning "to heal."

1126. **All is contained within the text** The verse alludes to all these angels.

1127. **So afterward is written...** The *sea serpents* allude to other angelic forces.

1128. **Leviathan and his mate** See BT *Bava Batra* 74b: "*God created the great sea serpents*.... Rabbi Yoḥanan said, 'This is Leviathan the elusive serpent and Leviathan the twisting serpent [see Isaiah 27:1]....' Rav Yehudah said in the name of Rav, 'Everything that the blessed Holy One created in His world, He created male and female. Even Leviathan the elusive serpent and Leviathan the twisting serpent He created male and female, and if they mated

with another, they would destroy the entire world. What did the blessed Holy One do? He castrated the male and killed the female, salting her for the righteous in the world to come, as is written: *He will slay the dragon of the sea* (ibid.).'"

See Ezra of Gerona, *Peirush Shir ha-Shirim*, 510; above, 34b.

1129. **seventy princes...** According to rabbinic tradition, the seventy nations of the world are governed by seventy angels or heavenly princes appointed by God.

See Daniel 10:20; Septuagint, Deuteronomy 32:8–9; Jubilees 15:31–32; *Targum Yerushalmi*, Genesis 11:8, Deuteronomy 32:8–9; *Tanḥuma*, *Re'eh* 8; *Leqaḥ Tov*, Genesis 9:19; *Pirqei de-Rabbi Eli'ezer* 24; *Zohar* 1:61a, 108b; 2:33a, 151b; 3:298b; Ginzberg, *Legends*, 5:204–5, n. 91.

1130. *And every soul of the living being that moves* The verse continues: *which the waters brought forth in swarms, according to its kind, and every winged bird, according to its kind.*

1131. **the actual *soul* of that *living being*** The souls of Israel derive from *Shekhinah*, who is known as *ḥayyah*, *living being*. On *Shekhinah* as *ḥayyah*, see Ezra of Gerona, *Peirush Shir ha-Shirim*, 508–9; *Zohar* 1:12b, 242a; 2:48b, 177b–178a (*SdTs*); 3:46b.

1132. *a nation unique on earth* The verse begins: *Who is like Your people, like Israel, a nation unique on earth...?* The

251

"*Which the waters brought forth in swarms, according to its kind* (ibid.), for they engage in Torah.[1133]

"*And every winged bird*—the righteous among them, who are therefore נפש חיה (*nefesh ḥayyah*), *living souls*.[1134] Alternatively, *and every winged bird*, as has been explained: messengers of the world."[1135]

Rabbi Abba said, "נפש חיה (*Nefesh ḥayyah*), *Soul of the living being*, namely, Israel, for they are scions of the blessed Holy One and their holy souls derive from Him.[1136] The soul of other nations—whence does it come?"

Rabbi El'azar said, "From those impure aspects of the left, defiling them and anyone approaching them.[1137]

"*God said, 'Let the earth bring forth* נפש חיה (*nefesh ḥayyah*), *living beings, according to their kind'* (ibid., 24)—all the other creatures, each according to its kind."[1138]

Rabbi El'azar added, "This supports what we have said: נפש חיה (*Nefesh ḥayyah*), *Souls of the living being*—Israel, who are *souls of the* supernal, holy *living being*.[1139]

"*Cattle, crawling things, and living creatures of the earth* (ibid.)[1140]—other nations, who are not *souls of the living being*, but rather foreskin, as we have said."[1141]

252

---

phrase can also be translated *a single nation* [or: *a nation of oneness*] *on earth*, perhaps connected here to the singular *soul*.

1133. **for they engage in Torah** Often compared to water. See BT *Bava Qamma* 82a: "Those who interpret metaphorically said, 'Water means solely Torah, as is said: *Ho, all who thirst, come for water* (Isaiah 55:1).'"

See *Ta'anit* 7a; *Bereshit Rabbah* 54:1; *Zohar* 2:12b, 60a.

1134. **who are therefore** נפש חיה (*nefesh ḥayyah*), *living souls* The righteous, who resemble the winged angels, attain the status of *living souls*, or they are linked by their souls to *Shekhinah*, the חיה (*ḥayyah*), *living being*.

1135. **as has been explained: messengers of the world** Angels. See above, notes 858 and 1117.

1136. **Israel, for they are scions...** The souls of Israel derive from the union of the blessed Holy One and *Shekhinah*.

1137. **From those impure aspects of the left...** From demonic powers stemming from the left side of the *sefirot*. For parallel medieval Christian views of the Jewish soul, see Trachtenberg, *The Devil and the Jews*. Cf. *Zohar* 1:20b, 131a; *ZH* 10c (*MhN*).

1138. **all the other creatures...** All the other creatures on earth created on the sixth day, or all the other angelic powers, who derive from *Shekhinah*.

1139. **This supports what we have said...** See above, page 251.

1140. *Cattle, crawling things, and living creatures of the earth according to their kind.* See *Zohar* 1:13b, where Rabbi Shim-'on applies this verse to various kinds of souls.

1141. **other nations...** Who derive from the demonic aspect, known as (uncircumcised) "foreskin." See *Zohar* 1:13a, 18a, 35b; Moses de León, *Sheqel ha-Qodesh*, 55 (68).

Let us make a human being in our image, according to our likeness (ibid., 26), embracing six aspects comprising all, as above,[1142] with smooth members[1143] arrayed fittingly in the mystery of wisdom, an entirely supernal array. *Let us make a human being*—mystery of male and female, entirely in supernal, holy wisdom.[1144] *In our image, according to our likeness*—to be consummated by one another, so that he will be unique in the world, ruling over all.[1145]

God saw all that He had made, and behold it was very good (ibid., 31). Here was restored the omission of *it was good* on the second day, omitted because death was created then. Here is stated: *and behold, it was* טוב מאד (*tov me'od*), *very good.*[1146]

1142. **embracing six aspects...** Reflecting the structure of the cosmos. See *Sefer Yetsirah* 4:3, where six directions are specified: above, below, east, west, north, and south. Cf. *Pirqei de-Rabbi Eli'ezer* 11.

The six aspects also represent the core of the *sefirot*, composed of *Tif'eret* together with the five *sefirot* from *Ḥesed* through *Yesod*. The limbs of the human body are modeled on those of the divine body.

1143. **smooth members** Rendering two senses of one term, שייפי (*shaifei*). Deriving from a root meaning "to smooth, rub, slip," the word signifies "limbs" in the *Zohar*, perhaps based on the Talmudic expression (BT *Sotah* 7b): על איבריה לשפא (*al eivreih le-shafa*), "each limb entered its socket"—"slipping" into place—or "...the chest."

See *Arukh*, s.v. *shaf;* Rashi, ad loc., and on Job 33:21, citing BT *Ḥullin* 42b; *Zohar* 3:170a.

1144. **mystery of male and female...** The original human being was androgynous, reflecting the masculine and feminine aspects of the *sefirot*, *Tif'eret* and *Shekhinah*, who together constitute the *image* and *likeness* of God. See *Bereshit Rabbah* 8:1: "Rabbi Yirmeyah son of El'azar said, 'When the blessed Holy One created Adam, He created him androgynous, as is said: *Male and female He created them* (Genesis 1:27).' Rabbi Shemu'el son of Naḥman said, 'When the blessed Holy One created Adam, He created him with two faces. Then He sawed him and gave him two backs—one on this side and one on that.'"

See BT *Berakhot* 61a; *Eruvin* 18a; Plato, *Symposium* 189d–191d; *Zohar* 1:2b, 13b, 48b; 2:55a; 3:5a, 44b; Matt, *Zohar*, 217.

1145. **ruling over all** See *Tanḥuma* (Buber), intro, 77b: "What is the meaning of: *In our image, according to our likeness*? Similar to us, that he will rule below as I do above."

1146. **Here was restored the omission...** In the biblical account of Creation, the statement *God saw that it was good* (or a variant) is included in the description of each of the six days except for the second. See *Bereshit Rabbah* 4:6: "Why is *that it was good* not written concerning the second day? Rabbi Yoḥanan said..., 'Because on that day Hell was created....' Rabbi Ḥanina said, 'Because on that day conflict was created: *that it may separate water from water.*'...Rabbi Shemu'el son of Naḥman said, 'Because the work of the water was not completed. Therefore *that it was good* is written twice on the third day: once for the work of the water [see Genesis 1:9–10] and once for the work of the [third] day [ibid., 11].'"

See BT *Pesaḥim* 54a; *Pirqei de-Rabbi Eli'ezer* 4; *Midrash Konen* (*Beit ha-Midrash*, 2:25); Ezra of Gerona, *Peirush Shir ha-Shirim*, 506; *Zohar* 1:18a, 46a; 2:149b; Moses de León, *Sheqel ha-Qodesh*, 41 (49).

According to *Zohar* 1:46b, the Angel of Death was created on the second day along with all the angels of Judgment. See *Bereshit Rabbah* 1:3; *Zohar* 1:17b; Tishby, *Wisdom of the Zohar*, 2:623–24.

Here the *Zohar* suggests that the omission of *that it was good* was restored not on the

253

This parallels what the Companions say: *And behold,* טוב מות (*tov mavet*), *death is good.*[1147]

God saw all that He had made. Had He not seen it before? The blessed Holy One had certainly seen everything, but the mention of את כל (*et kol*), *all,* amplifies the meaning to include all following generations, and all that would newly emerge in the world in every generation, before it actually existed.[1148]

That He had made—all the works of Creation, for there was created the elemental essence of all that would later emerge anew. So the blessed Holy One saw it before it existed, deploying all in the act of Creation.[1149]

יום הששי (*Yom ha-shishi*), *The sixth day* (ibid.). What is different about all the other days, lacking the letter ה (*he*)?[1150] Here, when the world was consummated, female united with male in single union, ה (*he*), with ששי (*shishi*), *sixth,* so that all would be one.[1151]

254

third day but on the sixth, by the phrase *very good.*

1147. *And behold,* טוב מות (*tov mavet*), *death is good* See *Bereshit Rabbah* 9:5: "In the Torah of Rabbi Me'ir it was found written: '*And behold it was* טוב מאד (*tov me'od*), *very good: And behold* טוב מות (*tov mavet*), *death is good.*'"

See *Bereshit Rabbah* 9:10: "Rabbi Shemu-'el son of Rav Yitsḥak said, '*Behold, it was very good*—this is the Angel of Life; *And behold, it was very good*—this is the Angel of Death.'"

According to Rabbi Shemu'el, the Angel of Death is *very good* because he kills those who fail to accumulate good deeds. According to *Zohar* 2:149b, he is *very good* because the awareness of mortality stimulates a person to return to God. See 1:14a, 144b; 2:68b, 103a, 163a, 249a.

1148. the mention of את כל (*et kol*), *all,* amplifies the meaning... Grammatically, the accusative particle את (*et*) has no ascertainable independent sense, but Naḥum of Gimzo and his disciple Rabbi Akiva taught that when *et* appears in a biblical verse, it amplifies the original meaning. See BT *Pesaḥim* 22b; *Ḥagigah* 12a; *Zohar* 1:247a; 2:90a, 135b.

Here the word *et* expands the meaning of

all to include all future generations and events. See *Zohar* 2:198b–199a.

1149. *That He had made*—all the works of Creation... God not only foresaw everything; through the power of the divine gaze, He included everything potentially in the primal act of Creation.

1150. **What is different about all the other days...** The definite article ה (*ha*), *the,* appears only in the phrase יום הששי (*yom ha-shishi*), *the sixth day,* not in any of the corresponding phrases describing the other five days of Creation. See BT *Shabbat* 88a: "Resh Lakish said, 'Why is it written: *There was evening and there was morning:* יום הששי (*yom ha-shishi*), *the sixth day*? Why the extra letter ה (*ha*), *the*? This teaches that the blessed Holy One stipulated a condition with the works of Creation, saying to them: "If Israel accepts the Torah [given at Mount Sinai on the sixth day of the month Sivan], you will endure. If not, I will return you to *chaos and void* (Genesis 1:2).""" See *Zohar* 2:63b.

1151. **female united with male...** With the completion of Creation, *Shekhinah* united with *Yesod. Shekhinah* is symbolized by the feminine marker ה (*he*), which is also the final letter of the name יהוה (*YHVH*), while *Yesod* is the sixth of the lower seven *sefirot.*

They were completed (ibid. 2:1)—all consummated as one, totally perfect and complete.[1152]

The heavens and the earth were completed (ibid.).

Rabbi El'azar opened, "*How abundant is Your goodness that You have hidden away for those in awe of You . . .* (Psalms 31:20).[1153] Come and see: The blessed Holy One fashioned the human being in the world and prepared him to become perfect through his service, to mend his ways, so as attain the supernal light treasured away by the blessed Holy One for the righteous, as is written: *No eye has seen, O God, but You, what You will do for one who awaits You* (Isaiah 64:3).[1154] How does one attain that light? Through Torah, for whoever is engaged with Torah attains each day a share in the world that is coming.[1155]

1152. **They were completed . . .** The full verse reads: *The heavens and the earth were completed, with all their array.* See *Targum Onqelos*, Genesis 2:1; Gikatilla, *Sha'arei Orah*, 8a.

1153. **How abundant is Your goodness that You have hidden away for those in awe of You** The verse continues: *that You made for those who take refuge in You, in the presence of human beings.*

1154. **the supernal light treasured away . . .** See BT Ḥagigah 12a: "Rabbi El'azar said, 'With the light created by the blessed Holy One on the first day, one could gaze and see from one end of the universe to the other. When the blessed Holy One foresaw the corrupt deeds of the generation of the Flood and the generation of the Dispersion [the generation of the Tower of Babel], He immediately hid it from them, as is written: *The light of the wicked is withheld* (Job 38:15). For whom did He hide it? For the righteous in the time to come.'"

See *Bereshit Rabbah* 3:6; 41:3; *Shemot Rabbah* 35:1; *Tanḥuma, Shemini* 9; *Bahir* 97–98 (147); *Zohar* 1:7a, 31b–32a, 45b–46a; 2:127a, 148b–149a, 220a–b; 3:88a, 173b.

See BT *Berakhot* 34b: "Rabbi Ḥiyya son of Abba said in the name of Rabbi Yoḥanan, 'All the prophets prophesied only concerning the days of the Messiah, but as for the world that

is coming, *No eye has seen, O God, but You,* [*what You will do for one who awaits You*]. . . . All the prophets prophesied only concerning masters of return [those who succeed in turning back to God], but as for the completely righteous, *No eye has seen, O God, but You.*'"

1155. **whoever is engaged with Torah . . .** On the link between Torah and the primordial light, see *Bahir* 97–99 (147–49); *Zohar* 2:149a, 167a.

See BT *Niddah* 73a: "It was taught in the school of Elijah: 'Whoever studies laws each day is guaranteed admission into the world that is coming.'" Rabbi El'azar introduces a significant variation: by studying Torah, one attains here and now a share in the world that is coming.

"The world that is coming" (Aramaic, עלמא דאתי [*alma de-atei*]; Hebrew, העולם הבא [*ha-olam ha-ba*]) is often understood as referring to the hereafter and is usually translated as "the world to come." From another point of view, however, "the world that is coming" already exists, occupying another dimension. See *Tanḥuma, Vayiqra* 8: "The wise call it *ha-olam ha-ba* not because it does not exist now, but for us today in this world it is still to come." Cf. Maimonides, *Mishneh Torah, Hilkhot Teshuvah* 8:8; and Guttmann, *Philosophies of Judaism*, 37: "'The world to

255

He is deemed a builder of worlds,[1156] for by Torah the world was built and consummated, as is written: *YHVH founded the earth by wisdom* (Proverbs 3:19), and similarly: *I was with Him as a nursling, I was a daily delight* (Proverbs 8:30).[1157] Whoever engages in her consummates and sustains the world.

"Come and see: By breath the blessed Holy One made the world,[1158] and by breath it is sustained[1159]—the breath of those studying Torah, especially the breath of schoolchildren.[1160]

"*How abundant is Your goodness*—the *goodness* hidden away *for those in awe of You*, those fearing sin.

"*That You made for those who take refuge in You* (Psalms, ibid.). What is the meaning of: *You made*? The act of Creation."

Rabbi Abba said, "This is the Garden of Eden, for the blessed Holy One fashioned it exquisitely on earth, resembling the one above, so that the righteous would be invigorated therein,[1161] [47b] as is written: *that You made for those who take refuge in You, in the presence of human beings* (ibid.)—for that

256

come' does not succeed 'this world' in time, but exists from eternity as a reality outside and above time, to which the soul ascends."

In Kabbalah "the world that is coming" often refers to *Binah,* the continuous source of emanation, who gives birth to the lower *sefirot.* See *Zohar* 3:290b (*IZ*): "the world that is coming, constantly coming, never ceasing."

Cf. *Bahir* 106 (160); Asher ben David, *Peirush Shelosh Esreh Middot,* in *Kabbalah* 2 (1997): 293; Moses de León, *Sheqel ha-Qodesh,* 26 (30); idem, *Sod Eser Sefirot,* 375; *Zohar* 1:83a, 92a.

1156. **He is deemed a builder of worlds** By engaging in Torah, one creates entire worlds. See BT *Shabbat* 114a: "What does 'builders' mean? Rabbi Yoḥanan said, 'These are the disciples of the wise, who are engaged all their days in building the world.'" See *Zohar* 1:4b–5a.

1157. **by Torah the world was built...** According to M *Avot* 3:14, Torah is the "precious instrument by which the world was created." See *Bereshit Rabbah* 1:1: "Rabbi Osha'ya opened, '*I was with Him as* אמון (*amon*), *a nursling*... אמון (*amon*)—אומן (*umman*), *an artisan.* Torah says, "I was the artistic tool of the blessed Holy One."'...

The blessed Holy One gazed into Torah and created the world.'"

See *Zohar* 1:5a, 134a–b; 2:161a–b; 3:35b; Wolfson, *Philo,* 1:242–45, 266–69.

1158. **By breath the blessed Holy One made the world** See Psalms 33:6: *By the word of YHVH the heavens were made, by the breath of His mouth all their host.*

See *Sefer Yetsirah* 1:9; and Shabbetai Donnolo, *Sefer Ḥakhmoni,* on *Sefer Yetsirah* 1:10 (in Matt, *Essential Kabbalah,* 92, 194): "God, great, mighty, and awesome, powerfully breathed out a breath, and cosmic space expanded to the boundary determined by divine wisdom, until God said, 'Enough!'"

1159. **by breath it is sustained** See *Tanḥuma, Bereshit* 5; *Midrash Temurah,* 2 (*Beit ha-Midrash,* 1:109); *Zohar* 1:148a.

1160. **the breath of schoolchildren** See BT *Shabbat* 119b: "Resh Lakish said in the name of Rabbi Yehudah the Prince, 'The world endures only for the sake of the breath of schoolchildren.'"

1161. **resembling the one above, so that the righteous would be invigorated therein** The earthly Garden of Eden is modeled on the one above and invigorates the souls of the righteous. See *Zohar* 1:106b (*MhN*).

one is *in the presence of human beings,* while the other is *in the presence of* holy celestial beings."[1162]

Rabbi Shim'on said, "Even the other one is *in the presence of human beings,* so that the righteous who fulfill the will of their Lord will be gathered there."[1163]

They were completed (Genesis 2:1)[1164]—for acts above and below *were completed. The heavens and the earth*—above and below.[1165]

Rabbi Shim'on said, "Act and artistry of Written Torah, act and artistry of Oral Torah.[1166]

"*With all their array* (ibid.)—the details of Torah, faces of Torah. 'Torah assumes seventy faces.'[1167]

"*They were completed*—sustained and consummated by one another.[1168]

"*Heaven and earth*—particular and general.[1169]

"*With all their array*—secrets of Torah, purities of Torah, impurities of Torah.[1170]

1162. **that one is *in the presence of human beings*...** The earthly Garden of Eden is in the human realm, whereas the heavenly Garden of Eden is in the angelic realm.

1163. **Even the other one...** Even the heavenly Garden of Eden is accessible to souls of the righteous.

1164. ***They were completed*** The full verse reads: *The heavens and the earth were completed, with all their array.*

1165. **for acts above and below *were completed*...** The emanation of the *sefirot* and the creation of the world were both completed.

1166. **Act and artistry of Written Torah... Oral Torah** The emergence of *Tif'eret* and *Shekhinah,* each of whom conveys more explicitly the unwritten, unspoken Primordial Torah of Ḥokhmah, divine Wisdom.

1167. **Torah assumes seventy faces** See *Bemidbar Rabbah* 13:16, where Torah is compared to wine: "Just as יין (yayin), wine, is numerically equivalent to seventy, so Torah assumes seventy faces."

See *Sefer Ḥanokh* (*Beit ha-Midrash,* 2:116); Ibn Ezra, introduction to Commentary on the Torah; *Zohar* 1:4b, 26a (*TZ*), 54a. Cf. the description of the revelation at Mount Sinai in BT *Shabbat* 88b: "Rabbi Yoḥanan said, '...Every utterance emerging from the mouth of Power branched into seventy languages.'"

1168. **sustained and consummated by one another** At the climax of Creation, *Tif'eret* and *Shekhinah* (*heaven* and *earth*) unite. See *Targum Onqelos,* Genesis 2:1; Gikatilla, *Sha'arei Orah,* 8a.

1169. **particular and general** פרט וכלל (*Perat ukhlal*), a halakhic term referring to legal details and their general formulations, included in Rabbi Yishma'el's thirteen hermeneutical rules (*Sifra,* intro, 1a–b). Cf. *Zohar* 1:16b.

Here the term is applied to *heaven* and *earth,* symbolizing the divine couple, *Tif'eret* and *Shekhinah.* The former includes various individual *sefirot,* which culminate and coalesce in *Shekhinah.* Alternatively, the Written Torah (*Ti'feret*) conveys generalities, which unfold into the endless particularities of Oral Torah (*Shekhinah*).

1170. **purities of Torah, impurities of Torah** The various detailed laws of ritual purity and impurity. See *Pesiqta de-Rav Kahana* 4:4: "[Israel] knows how to expound Torah according to forty-nine aspects [literally, "faces"] of purity and forty-nine aspects of impurity."

See *Shir ha-Shirim Rabbah* on 2:4; BT *Eruvin* 13b.

"*On the seventh day God completed* (ibid., 2).[1171] This is Oral Torah, for She is *the seventh day*. Through Her the world was consummated, for She sustains all.[1172]

"*The work that He had done*—not *all His work,* for Written Torah generated all through the potency of Writing, issuing from Wisdom.[1173]

"Three times here: *on the seventh day. On the seventh day God completed. He rested on the seventh day. God blessed the seventh day* (ibid., 2–3). Look, three![1174] *On the seventh day God completed*—Oral Torah, for with this *seventh day* the world was consummated, as we have said. *He rested on the seventh day*—Foundation of the world.[1175] In *The Book of Rav Yeiva Sava:*[1176] This is Jubilee,[1177] so here is written: *from all the work* (ibid., 2),[1178] for all issues

258

1171. **On the seventh day God completed** The verse continues: *the work that He had done, and He ceased on the seventh day from all the work that He had done.*

1172. **This is Oral Torah . . . the seventh day . . .** *Shekhinah,* seventh of the lower *sefirot,* seventh day of the cosmic week of Creation.

1173. **not *all His work* . . .** As phrased later in the same verse. *Shekhinah,* Oral Torah, derives from *Tif'eret,* Written Torah, who derives from the Divine Mother, *Binah,* known as Writing, who Herself emerges from the Primordial Torah of *Hokhmah* ("Wisdom").

See *Zohar* 2:85a, 200a. Cf. *Bereshit Rabbah* 17:5: "Rabbi Avin [said] . . . , 'Torah is an unripe fruit of supernal Wisdom.'"

1174. **Three times here . . .** A different interpretation of the tripled phrase appears in Moses de León, *Sefer ha-Mishqal,* 111.

1175. **Foundation of the world** יסודא דעלמא (*Yesoda de-alma*), referring to the ninth *sefirah, Yesod* ("Foundation"), also known as Righteous, based on Proverbs 10:25: וצדיק יסוד עולם (*Ve-tsaddiq yesod olam*). The verse literally means *The righteous one is an everlasting foundation* but is understood as *The righteous one is the foundation of the world.*

See BT *Hagigah* 12b; *Bahir* 71 (102); Azriel of Gerona, *Peirush ha-Aggadot,* 34.

Yesod is the seventh *sefirah* counting from the Divine Mother, *Binah.*

1176. **The Book of Rav Yeiva Sava** One of the many volumes housed in the real or imaginary library of the author(s) of the *Zohar.* It is cited frequently: 1:79b, 117b; 2:6a, 60b, 206b; 3:7b, 155b, 289b, 290a, 295a (*IZ*).

See Matt, *Zohar,* 25; and the comment by Shim'on Lavi, *KP,* 22d: "All such books mentioned in the *Zohar* . . . have been lost in the wanderings of exile . . . Nothing is left of them except what is mentioned in the *Zohar.*"

1177. **This is Jubilee** *Binah,* the Divine Mother, giving birth to all. She is symbolized by the Jubilee, proclaimed every fifty years, when slaves were released and land reverted to the original owner (Leviticus 25:8–55). Here fifty (seven squared plus one) is linked to the phrase *on the seventh day. Binah* is often characterized by the number fifty, based on BT *Rosh ha-Shanah* 21b, where Rav and Shemu'el teach: "Fifty gates of בינה (*binah*), understanding, were created in the world, all of which were given to Moses except for one, as is said: *You made him little less than God* (Psalms 8:6)." *Binah* is the source of redemption and liberation, specifically the Exodus from Egypt.

See *Zohar* 1:21b; 2:46a, 83b, 85b; 3:262a. Cf. Solomon ibn Adret, *She'elot u-Tshuvot* 1:9.

1178. **from all the work** The verse reads: *He ceased on the seventh day from all the work that He had done.*

therefrom. But as for us: This is Foundation, as we have said, for the rest thereon is best of all.[1179] *God blessed the seventh day*—the High Priest, who blesses all and receives first share.[1180] Blessing inheres in Him, begins blessing from Him,[1181] and He is called *seventh*.

"Rabbi Yeisa Sava said, 'These two refer respectively to Foundation and Central Pillar,[1182] but these three correspond to the entry of Sabbath at night, the day, and the world that is coming, namely Great Sabbath.'[1183]

"*He hallowed* אותו (*oto*), *it* (ibid., 3).[1184] Whom did He hallow? That site where את (*at*), sign, of the covenant abides, as is said: *He will show me* אותו (*oto*), *His sign, and His habitation* (2 Samuel 15:25).[1185] At this site abides all

1179. **the rest thereon is best of all** *Yesod* represents the culmination of the process of emanation, when all is released into *Shekhinah*.

1180. **the High Priest...** *Ḥesed*, the first *sefirah* to emerge from *Binah*, conveys emanation to those below Him. Counting upward from *Shekhinah*, He is the seventh.

According to M *Yoma* 1:2, the high priest chooses his sacrificial portion first. See the formulation attributed to Rava in BT *Nedarim* 62a: "A priest receives first," which is included here in most printed versions but not in the manuscripts.

See *Zohar* 1:147a; 2:225a; *ZḤ* 43a.

1181. **inheres in... begins...** שריין (*Shareyan*) conveys both these meanings.

1182. **These two refer respectively to...** Apparently the two phrases, *He rested on the seventh day* and *God blessed the seventh day*, refer respectively to *Yesod* (as just indicated by Rabbi Shim'on) and *Tif'eret* (the seventh *sefirah* from *Keter*), who constitutes the Central Pillar of the sefirotic structure and conveys the blessings of emanation. For other interpretations, see *OY; KP.*

1183. **but these three correspond to...** Rabbi Yeisa Sava offers an alternative interpretation, based on the triplicate phrase *the seventh day*. See Moses de León, *Sefer ha-Mishqal*, 111. (Some commentators suggest that "these three" refers to the three occurrences of the word אלהים [*Elohim*], *God*, in Genesis 2:2–3; see *OY*.) The three phases of the Sabbath (Sabbath Eve, Sabbath Day, and

Great Sabbath) symbolize respectively *Shekhinah* (the Sabbath Bride arriving with sunset on Friday evening), *Tif'eret* or *Yesod* (the masculine Day), and *Binah*, the Divine Mother, known as שבת הגדול (*Shabbat ha-Gadol*). This name, traditionally designating the last Sabbath before Passover, means literally "Sabbath of *the great*," referring to the phrase *the great day of YHVH* (Malachi 3:23), the climax of the prophetic portion read on that Sabbath. On the various sefirotic aspects of the Sabbath, see Tishby, *Wisdom of the Zohar*, 3:1223–26.

1184. **He hallowed** אותו **(*oto*), *it*** The full verse reads: אלהים (*Elohim*), *God, blessed the seventh day and hallowed it, for on it He rested from all His work that God created to make.*

1185. **That site where** את **(*at*), sign, of the covenant abides...** *Yesod*, the phallus in the sefirotic body, is the site of circumcision, sign of the covenant. The phrase *He* (namely, *Elohim*) *hallowed it* implies that *Binah*, known as *Elohim*, emanated holiness to *Yesod*. The word אותו (*oto*), *it*, is identified with Hebrew אות (*ot*) and Aramaic את (*at*), "sign." So the verse now reads: *He hallowed His sign*, meaning: *Binah* hallowed *Yesod*. Similarly, in the verse in Samuel, the word אותו (*oto*), *it*, is understood to mean *His sign*, namely *Yesod*, while *His habitation* refers to *Shekhinah*.

A similar midrashic reading appears in *Shemot Rabbah* 1:20. See *Zohar* 1:94a, 112b; 3:184a.

holiness from above, issuing from there to Assembly of Israel[1186] to provide Her delectable pastry.[1187] This accords with what is written: *Out of Asher his bread is rich, he will yield delicacies of a king* (Genesis 49:20). *Out of Asher*— consummate covenant.[1188] *His bread is rich*—what had been *bread of affliction* (Deuteronomy 16:3) was transformed into pastry.[1189] *He will yield delicacies of a king.* Who is *king*? Assembly of Israel.[1190] He provides Her all the delights of the world.[1191] All holiness issuing from above issues from this site. So *He hallowed* אותו (oto), *His sign.*

"*For on it He rested* (ibid. 2:3).[1192] *On it*, repose of all, repose above and below. *On it* earth *rested* in repose.[1193]

"*That God created* (ibid.)—from the totality of *Remember* emerged *Observe*, arraying the works of the world.[1194]

"*To make* (ibid.)—Artisan of the world, fashioning the works of all."[1195]

1186. **Assembly of Israel** כנסת ישראל (*Keneset Yisra'el*). In rabbinic Hebrew this phrase denotes the people of Israel. The midrash on the Song of Songs describes the love affair between the maiden (the earthly community of Israel) and her lover (the Holy One, blessed be He). In the *Zohar*, *Keneset Yisra'el* can refer to the earthly community but also (often primarily) to *Shekhinah*, the divine feminine counterpart of the people, the aspect of God most intimately connected with them. The lovers in the Song of Songs are pictured as the divine couple: *Tif'eret* and *Shekhinah*.

1187. **pastry** לחם פנג (*Leḥem pannag*), "Bread of *pannag*," a biblical hapax legomenon (Ezekiel 27:17) apparently meaning "meal, ground seeds of grain."

1188. *Out of Asher*—consummate covenant **** *Asher* derives from אושר (*osher*), "happiness," and symbolizes *Yesod*, site of the sign of covenant of circumcision, who delights *Shekhinah*. She is named similarly Asherah.

See *Zohar* 1:49a, 245b; Patai, *The Hebrew Goddess*, 39, 296–97, n. 15.

1189. *bread of affliction* was transformed into pastry **** *Bread of affliction* refers to *matstsah*, the unleavened bread eaten on Passover. *Shekhinah*, symbolized by *matstsah*, had been in a state of affliction or impover-

ishment until She was filled by the riches of *Yesod*.

See BT *Pesaḥim* 36a–b, 115b; *Zohar* 1:33a, 157a, 235b, 245b–246a; 2:40a–b; Moses de León, *Sefer ha-Rimmon*, 112, 133.

1190. **Who is *king*? Assembly of Israel** *Shekhinah* reigns over the lower worlds and is known as *Malkhut* ("Kingdom"). See *Zohar* 1:122a.

1191. **He provides Her...** *Yesod* provides *Shekhinah*, known as *king*, with delights.

1192. *For on it He rested* **** The verse continues: *from all His work that God created to make.*

1193. *On it*, repose of all... **** At the stage of *Yesod*, all the *sefirot* culminated, emptying into *Shekhinah*, symbolized by earth.

1194. **from the totality of *Remember* emerged *Observe*...** **** The command to observe the Sabbath appears differently in the two versions of the Ten Commandments in Exodus and Deuteronomy. Exodus 20:8 reads: זכור (*Zakhor*), *Remember, the Sabbath Day*, while Deuteronomy 5:12 reads: שמור (*Shamor*), *Observe, the Sabbath Day*. To the kabbalists, זכור (*zakhor*) suggests זכר (*zakhar*), "male," and is identified with *Yesod*, while שמור (*shamor*) is identified with the female, *Shekhinah*.

See BT *Berakhot* 20b; *Bahir* 124 (182); Ezra of Gerona, *Peirush Shir ha-Shirim*, 496–97;

Rabbi Shim'on further elucidated the word, saying: "It is written: *Guarding the covenant and the love* (Deuteronomy 7:9). *Guarding*—Guardian of Israel;[1196] *the covenant,* as we have explained;[1197] *and the love*—Abraham.[1198] Assembly of Israel is *guarding the covenant and the love.* This one guards the gate of all; on it depend all works of the world.[1199] Indeed, *that God created to make*—perfecting and arraying all, every single one, every single day,[1200] generating spirits and souls, even demonic spirits. Now if you say that these[1201] do not enhance the world—yes they do, by whipping the wicked of the world, for they confront and chastise them. Whoever wends to the left is seized by them on the left side.[1202] So they came into being to mend the world.

"Come and see what is written of Solomon: *I will chastise him with a human rod, with blows of the children of Adam* (2 Samuel 7:14). What are *blows of the children of Adam?* These are demons.[1203]

Naḥmanides on Exodus 20:8; *Zohar* 1:5b; 48b, 164b; Moses de León, *Sefer ha-Rimmon,* 118.

Here Rabbi Shim'on indicates that *Shekhinah* emerged from *Yesod.* The phrase אשר ברא אלהים (*asher bara Elohim*), *that God created,* is read: *Asher, That* (namely, *Yesod,* known as *Asher* [see above, note 1188]) *created Elohim* (namely, *Shekhinah*).

1195. **Artisan of the world...** *Shekhinah,* who actualizes the potential of the *sefirot* and fashions the world.

1196. *Guarding*—**Guardian of Israel** The first word of the biblical phrase denotes *Shekhinah,* who protects the people of Israel. See *Zohar* 3:239b. The phrase "Guardian of Israel" originates in Psalms 121:4.

1197. *the covenant,* **as we have explained** Symbolizing *Yesod,* the phallus in the sefirotic body, which is the site of circumcision, sign of the covenant. See above, page 259.

1198. *and the love*—**Abraham** Referring to *Ḥesed* ("Love"), first of the seven lower *sefirot,* symbolized by Abraham, who manifested love on earth.

1199. **Assembly of Israel is** *guarding...* *Shekhinah* (known as Assembly of Israel; see above, note 1186) constitutes the gateway to the realm of the *sefirot.* By entering Her, one encounters the various aspects of the divine—in particular, the *sefirot* from *Ḥesed* through *Yesod.* She actualizes the other *sefirot* and brings about Creation.

1200. **every single one, every single day** Each of the cosmic days, the *sefirot* from *Ḥesed* through *Yesod,* manifests in *Shekhinah* and subsequently in Creation. See *Zohar* 2:127b.

1201. **these** The demonic spirits.

1202. **Whoever wends to the left...** Whoever sins, succumbing to the demonic, is attacked and punished by demonic spirits.

1203. **What are** *blows of the children of Adam?* **These are demons** See *Tanḥuma* (Buber), *Bereshit* 26: "Rabbi Simon said, 'For 130 years Adam separated from his wife, Eve, for once Cain was killed, Adam said, "Why should I engender children if they become cursed?" What did he do?... Female spirits approached him and heated themselves from him. As the blessed Holy One said to David, "... *When he* [Solomon] *does wrong, I will chastise him with a human rod, with blows of the children of Adam*" (2 Samuel 7:14)..., namely, the demons.'"

See *Bereshit Rabbah* 20:11: "Rabbi Simon said, 'Throughout all 130 years that Adam separated himself from Eve, male spirits heated themselves from her and she gave birth, while female spirits heated themselves from Adam and gave birth, as is written: *When he does wrong, I will chastise him with a human rod, with blows of the children of* אדם (*adam*), namely, children of Adam.'"

See BT *Eruvin* 18b; *Zohar* 1:19b, 34b, 54a–

261

"Come and see: As they were being created, the day was hallowed, and they were left spirit without body.[1204] These are creatures never [48a] completed, from the left side, dross of gold.[1205] Since they are incomplete and defective, the holy name does not abide in them nor do they cleave to it. Their terror is provoked by the holy name, before which they tremble and panic, for the holy name does not abide in a defective site.[1206]

"Come and see: A person flawed by not leaving a son in this world does not cleave to the holy name when he departs, nor is he admitted within the curtain because he is defective, incomplete.[1207] An uprooted, barren tree must be transplanted, for the holy name is consummate from every angle and no defect can cleave to it.[1208]

"Come and see: These creatures are defective from above and below, so they cleave neither above nor below.[1209] These *God created to make* (Genesis 2:3), for they were completed neither above nor below.[1210] Now if you say, 'Look, they are spirits! Why not above?'[1211] Since they were not completed below, on earth,

262

55a; 2:231b, 3:76b; Trachtenberg, *Jewish Magic and Superstition*, 51–54.

1204. **As they were being created...** At twilight on the eve of the first Sabbath, as the six days of Creation drew to a close. See *Tanḥuma* (Buber), *Bereshit* 17: "It is not written here: [*He ceased from all His work*] *that* [*God*] *created and made*, but rather [*that God created*] *to make* (Genesis 2:3), for the Sabbath came first and their work was not completed. Rabbi Benaya said, 'This refers to the demons, for He created their souls, and as He was creating their bodies, the Sabbath day was hallowed. He left them, and they remained soul without body.'"

See *Bereshit Rabbah* 7:5; 11:9; *Zohar* 1:14a, 178a; 2:155b; 3:142b (*IR*); and M *Avot* 5:6: "Ten things were created on Friday eve at twilight:.... Some say, 'Also the demons.'"

1205. **from the left side, dross of gold** The demonic derives from the dregs of *Gevurah* or *Din* (strict Judgment), located on the left side of the sefirotic tree and symbolized by gold.

See *Zohar* 1:52a, 73a, 193a; 2:236b.

1206. **Their terror is provoked by the holy name...** If adjured by the divine name, demons flee in terror. See BT *Gittin* 68a.

1207. **A person flawed...** One who fails to fulfill the first command of the Torah, *Be fruitful and multiply* (Genesis 1:28), is flawed. Consequently, at death his soul is excluded from the divine realm.

See BT *Bava Batra* 116a: "Rabbi Yoḥanan said in the name of Rabbi Shim'on son of Yoḥai, 'Whoever does not leave a son to succeed him incurs the full wrath of the blessed Holy One.'"

See *Zohar* 1:13a, 90a, 115a, 186b, 228b; *ZḤ* 89b (*MhN, Rut*); Scholem, in *Tarbiz* 16 (1945): 146–47.

1208. **An uprooted, barren tree must be transplanted...** The soul of such a person must transmigrate into another body, where it is given another opportunity to fulfill this vital commandment. See *ZḤ* 89b (*MhN, Rut*).

1209. **These creatures...** The demons.

1210. **These *God created to make*...** According to Rabbi Shim'on, the unusual wording implies that the creation of the demons was incomplete. See *Tanḥuma* (Buber), *Bereshit* 17, cited above, note 1204.

1211. **Why not above?** In the spiritual realm.

they were not completed above.[1212] All deriving from the left side, they are invisible to human beings, whom they menacingly confront.

"Three features they share with the ministering angels and three with human beings, as has been established.[1213] Having been created, those spirits were plunged behind the millstones of the chasm of the immense abyss for the duration of Sabbath eve and Sabbath day.[1214] Once the holiness of the day departed and they were not completed, they erupted into the world, roaming in every direction.[1215] The world must defend itself against them, for then the entire left side is aroused, fire of Hell flashes, and all denizens of the left roam the world, craving to clothe themselves in a body, but they cannot. We must protect ourselves against them, so a song against maleficent spirits has been prescribed for whenever their dread prevails in the world.[1216]

"Come and see: When the day is hallowed at the entrance of Sabbath, a canopy of peace hovers, spreading over the world. Who is Canopy of Peace? Sabbath, when all spirits, whirlwinds, demons, and the entire dimension of impurity are hidden away within the eye of the millstone of the chasm of the immense abyss.[1217] For as soon as holiness arouses over the world, the spirit of impurity cannot arouse; one flees the other. Then the world enjoys supernal shelter, and we need not pray for protection, for example: 'who guards His people Israel forever.' This has been prescribed for weekdays,

263

1212. **Since they were not completed below, on earth…** Even a spiritual entity is incomplete unless actualized in the physical realm.

1213. **Three features…** See BT Ḥagigah 16a: "Our Rabbis taught: 'Six things have been said concerning the demons, three of which correspond to the ministering angels and three to human beings. Three correspond to the ministering angels: they have wings, they fly from one end of the world to the other, and they know what will happen in the future…. Three correspond to human beings: they eat and drink, they are fruitful and multiply, and they die.'"

1214. **plunged behind the millstones of the chasm of the immense abyss…** The chasm of the immense abyss is the abode of the demons, where they are confined throughout each Sabbath. According to *Midrash Tehillim* 92:5, on the first Sabbath, "demons ceased from the world." See *Zohar* 1:14b.

The phrase "behind the millstones" derives from Exodus 11:5: *the slave girl who is behind the millstones.* See *Zohar* 1:118a, 177a, 223b; 2:28a, 37b, 80a, 191b.

1215. **and they were not completed…** They were still not furnished with bodies.

1216. **a song against maleficent spirits has been prescribed…** Psalms 91:1–9, traditionally recited to ward off demons and maleficent spirits. Since Gaonic times this psalm has been recited at the conclusion of the Sabbath, following the *amidah* prayer of the evening service.

See BT *Shevu'ot* 15b; JT *Shabbat* 6:2, 8b; *Midrash Tehillim* 91:1, and Buber's nn. 12–13; Scholem, in *Tarbiz* 50 (1982): 248, 251; *Zohar* 1:14b.

1217. **Who is Canopy of Peace? Sabbath…** *Shekhinah*, identified with Sabbath eve, when peace reigns and the demonic dimension disappears.

See *Zohar* 2:135a–b; Moses de León, *Sefer ha-Mishqal*, 111–12.

when the world does need protection,[1218] but on Sabbath a canopy of peace spreads over the world, which is sheltered on every side. Even the wicked in Hell are protected;[1219] all bask in peace, those above and those below. So in hallowing the day, we bless: 'who spreads a canopy of peace over us, over His entire people Israel, and over Jerusalem.'[1220] Why 'over Jerusalem'? Because this is the abode of that canopy, and we should invite that canopy to spread over us, abide with us, and protect us, like a mother hovering over her children, who are thereby free of fear from any direction. So, 'who spreads a canopy of peace.'

"Come and see: When Israel blesses and invites this canopy of peace—holy guest—by reciting 'who spreads a canopy of peace,' supernal sanctity descends, spreading Her wings over Israel, covering them like a mother over her children. All maleficent species are rounded up from the world, and Israel dwells beneath the holiness of their Lord. Then this canopy of peace issues new souls to Her children.[1221] Why? Because then is the time of coupling, and She receives souls, abiding in Her, emerging from Her. As She hovers, spreading Her wings over Her children, She pours new souls upon every single one."

Rabbi Shim'on said further, "So we have learned: 'Sabbath is patterned on the world that is coming.'[1222] Certainly so! Sabbatical and Jubilee are paradigms of

264

1218. 'who guards His people Israel forever'... The conclusion of the second blessing following the *Shema* in the weekday evening liturgy.

1219. Even the wicked in Hell are protected According to *Tanḥuma, Ki Tissa* 33, one of the dwellers in Hell reports: "Whoever does not observe the Sabbath properly in your world comes here and observes it against his will.... All week long we are punished and on the Sabbath we rest."

See *Bereshit Rabbah* 11:5; BT *Sanhedrin* 65b; *Zohar* 1:14b, 197b; 2:31b, 88b, 150b–151a, 203b, 207a; 3:94b; *ZḤ* 17a–b.

1220. 'who spreads a canopy of peace over us...' According to an Ashkenazic custom promoted by the *Zohar*, on Sabbath eve the wording of the second blessing following the *Shema* changes.

See *Zohar* 2:205a; *ZḤ* 79b–c (*MhN, Rut*); Moses de León, *Sefer ha-Mishqal*, 112–13; *Teshuvot ha-Ge'onim, Sha'arei Teshuvah*, 80;

Tishby, *Wisdom of the Zohar*, 3:1266, n. 139; Ta-Shma, *Minhag Ashkenaz ha-Qadmon*, 142–56.

1221. this canopy of peace issues new souls... See BT *Beitsah* 16a: "Rabbi Shim'on son of Lakish said, 'On Sabbath eve, the blessed Holy One imparts an extra soul to a human being. When Sabbath departs, it is taken from him.'" Medieval Jewish philosophers disregarded this teaching or reinterpreted it rationalistically, while the *Zohar* revels in the literalness of the image and embellishes it.

See Tishby, *Wisdom of the Zohar*, 3:1230–33; *Zohar* 2:135b, 204a; 3:173a; and 2:136b: "Every Sabbath eve, a human being sits in the world of souls."

1222. 'Sabbath is patterned on the world that is coming' See BT *Berakhot* 57b: "Three [things] reflect the world to come: Sabbath, sunshine, and sexual union."

one another,[1223] as are Sabbath and the world that is coming.[1224] That supplement to the soul comes to this canopy of peace from the mystery of זכור (*Zakhor*), *Remember* (Exodus 20:8), as received [48b] from the world that is coming.[1225] She bestows this supplement upon the holy people, who rejoice in it, and all fear, trouble, and sorrow sink into oblivion, as is said: *On the day that YHVH gives you rest from your sorrow and anxiety, and from the hard bondage imposed on you* (Isaiah 14:3).

"On Sabbath eve one should taste everything, to show that this canopy of peace encompasses all, provided one doesn't mar one course for the day— some say two, for the two other meals of the day, and this is fine.[1226]

1223. **Sabbatical and Jubilee...** Symbolizing *Shekhinah* and *Binah,* divine daughter and mother, who reflect one another.

According to the Bible, every seventh year is a Sabbatical (שמטה [*shemittah*], "release"), during which the land must lie fallow and at the end of which all debts are remitted (Leviticus 25:1–24; Deuteronomy 15:1–3). In Kabbalah the Sabbatical symbolizes *Shekhinah,* seventh of the lower *sefirot.* See *Zohar* 1:153b.

In the biblical cycle, after seven Sabbaticals comes the Jubilee, proclaimed every fifty years, when slaves are released and land reverts to its original owner (Leviticus 25:8–55). In Kabbalah the Jubilee symbolizes *Binah* —the Divine Mother—who is characterized by the number fifty, based on BT *Rosh ha-Shanah* 21b, where Rav and Shemu'el teach: "Fifty gates of בינה (*binah*), understanding, were created in the world, all of which were given to Moses except for one, as is said: *You made him little less than God* (Psalms 8:6)." *Binah* is the source of redemption and liberation, specifically the Exodus from Egypt. See *Zohar* 1:21b, 47b; 2:46a, 83b, 85b; 3:262a.

1224. **as are Sabbath and the world that is coming** Symbolizing, respectively, *Shekhinah* and *Binah.* The rabbinic concept of העולם הבא (*ha-olam ha-ba*), "the world that is coming" (Aramaic, עלמא דאתי [*alma de-atei*]), is often understood as referring to the hereafter and is usually translated as "the world to come." From another point of view, however, "the world that is coming" already exists, occupying another dimen-

sion. See *Tanḥuma, Vayiqra* 8: "The wise call it *ha-olam ha-ba* not because it does not exist now, but for us today in this world it is still to come." Cf. Maimonides, *Mishneh Torah, Hilkhot Teshuvah* 8:8; and Guttmann, *Philosophies of Judaism,* 37: "'The world to come' does not succeed 'this world' in time, but exists from eternity as a reality outside and above time, to which the soul ascends."

In Kabbalah "the world that is coming" often refers to *Binah,* the continuous source of emanation. See *Zohar* 3:290b (*IZ*): "the world that is coming, constantly coming, never ceasing."

Cf. *Bahir* 106 (160); Asher ben David, *Peirush Shelosh Esreh Middot,* in *Kabbalah* 2 (1997): 293; Moses de León, *Sheqel ha-Qodesh,* 26 (30); idem, *Sod Eser Sefirot,* 375; *Zohar* 1:83a, 92a.

1225. **from the mystery of** זכור **(*Zakhor*), *Remember*...**   From *Yesod,* who receives the additional soul from *Binah,* "the world that is coming." *Yesod,* the masculine potency, is called זכור (*Zakhor*), *Remember,* because of the association with זכר (*zakhar*), 'male.'

1226. **one should taste everything...** By tasting many foods on Sabbath eve, one demonstrates that the divine Sabbath, *Shekhinah,* includes all. Yet one course (or two) should remain untouched until the Sabbath day. See *TZ* 24 (69b).

On the significance of the three Sabbath meals, see BT *Shabbat* 118b; *Zohar* 2:88a–b; Tishby, *Wisdom of the Zohar,* 3:1234–36.

"Kindling the lamp of Sabbath has been entrusted to the women of the holy people.[1227] The Companions have said that she extinguished the lamp of the world and darkened it. . . .[1228] This is fine, but here is the mystery of the matter: This canopy of peace is the Consort of the world, and souls constituting the supernal lamp abide within Her.[1229] So the consort should kindle, for linked to her site, she performs the act.[1230] A woman should kindle the Sabbath lamp in joy to attain supernal honor and merit, to be worthy of holy sons who will become lamps of the world in Torah and reverence, spreading peace through the world.[1231] She also provides her husband long life; so she should be careful.[1232]

"Come and see: Sabbath, night and day, זכור (zakhor), *remember,* and שמור (shamor), *observe,* as one. So it is written: *Remember the Sabbath day, to hallow it* (Exodus 20:8), and: *Observe the Sabbath day* (Deuteronomy 5:12). זכור (*Zakhor*), *Remember,* for דכורא (dekhora), male; and שמור (shamor), *observe,* for female—all is one.[1233]

266

1227. **Kindling the lamp of Sabbath...** See M *Shabbat* 2:6; *Zohar* 2:166a.

1228. **she extinguished the lamp of the world...** See *Tanḥuma* (Buber), *Metsora* 17: "Why were [the commandments of kindling the Sabbath lights, separating a portion of dough before baking, and menstrual purity] given to the woman? The blessed Holy One said, 'She [i.e., Eve] extinguished the lamp of the world [i.e., the soul of Adam]..., so she [the woman of the house] should keep the commandment of the lamp.'"

See JT *Shabbat* 2:4, 5b; *Tanḥuma* (Buber), *Noaḥ* 1 (and n. 15); *Bereshit Rabbah* 17:8 (and Theodor, ad loc.).

1229. **the Consort...** מטרוניתא (*Matronita*), an aramaized form of the Latin *matrona* ("matron, married woman, noble lady"). *Matronita* is one of the many names of *Shekhinah,* the feminine partner of *Tif'eret.* She transmits souls deriving from the lamp of the higher sefirotic realms.

1230. **So the consort should kindle...** By kindling the Sabbath lights, the woman of the house, who corresponds to *Shekhinah,* stimulates the transmission of souls.

1231. **to be worthy of holy sons...** Rabbi Shim'on blends two Talmudic traditions (BT *Shabbat* 23b, *Berakhot* 64a): "Rav Huna said, 'One who regularly lights the lamp will have sons who are disciples of the wise.'" "Rabbi El'azar said in the name of Rabbi Ḥanina, 'Disciples of the wise spread peace through the world.'"

1232. **she should be careful**   In fulfilling this commandment.

1233. **night and day,** זכור **(zakhor),** *remember,* **and** שמור **(shamor),** *observe...* Sabbath eve (when light is kindled by the woman of the house) and Sabbath day symbolize, respectively, the feminine and masculine *sefirot: Shekhinah* and *Yesod,* who unite on the Sabbath. Each of the two aspects of Sabbath is alluded to by one version of the opening word of the fourth of the Ten Commandments. The version in Exodus 20:8 reads זכור (*Zakhor*), *Remember, the Sabbath day,* which suggests the Hebrew זכר (*zakhar*) and Aramaic דכורא (*dekhora*), "male." The version in Deuteronomy 5:12 reads שמור (*Shamor*), *Observe, the Sabbath day,* and this alternate formulation suggests the other, feminine aspect of Sabbath. According to *Mekhilta, Baḥodesh* 7, both versions of the fourth Commandment were spoken by God simultaneously.

See BT *Berakhot* 20b; *Bahir* 124 (182); Ezra of Gerona, *Peirush Shir ha-Shirim,* 496–97; Naḥmanides on Exodus 20:8; *Zohar*

"Happy are Israel, portion of the blessed Holy One, His share and heritage. Of them is written: *Happy the people who have it so; happy the people whose God is YHVH* (Psalms 144:15)."

YHVH Elohim fashioned הצלע *(ha-tsela), the side,*[1234] *that He had taken from the human into a woman, and He brought her to the human* (Genesis 2:22).

Rabbi Shim'on said, "It is written: *Elohim understands her way, He knows her site* (Job 28:23). This verse bears numerous nuances,[1235] but *Elohim* הבין *(hevin), understands, her way* corresponds to what is said: ויבן יהוה אלהים *(Va-yiven YHVH Elohim), YHVH Elohim fashioned, the side*—namely, Oral Torah, who contains a way, as is said: *who makes a way through the sea* (Isaiah 43:16).[1236] So, *Elohim understands her way.*

"*He knows her site.* Who is *her site*? Written Torah, containing knowledge.[1237]

"*YHVH Elohim*—a complete name, arraying Her with all, so it is called both Wisdom and Understanding, for it bore the complete name entirely—*YHVH Elohim*—consummating two names.[1238]

267

1:5b, 47b, 164b; Moses de León, *Sefer ha-Rimmon,* 118.

1234. הצלע *(ha-tsela), the side* The word צלע *(tsela)* is often translated "rib," but it also means "side," which is the meaning adopted here by Rabbi Shim'on.

See Exodus 26:20; *Bereshit Rabbah* 8:1 (cited in note 1236, below); *Zohar* 1:34b.

1235. **This verse bears numerous nuances** A similar expression appears in *Zohar* 1:54a, 81b, 197b.

1236. **namely, Oral Torah...** *Shekhinah* is known as both the mystical realm of speech and Oral Torah. She represents one *side* of the primordial androgynous figure of Primordial Adam, the other side being *Tif'eret.* The image derives from *Bereshit Rabbah* 8:1: "Rabbi Yirmeyah son of El'azar said, 'When the blessed Holy One created Adam, He created him androgynous, as is said: *Male and female He created them* (Genesis 1:27).' Rabbi Shemu'el son of Naḥman said, 'When the blessed Holy One created Adam, He created him with two faces. Then He sawed him and gave him two backs, one on this side and one on that.'"

See BT *Berakhot* 61a; *Eruvin* 18a; Plato,

Symposium 189d–191d; *Zohar* 1:13b, 34b, 47a; 2:55a; 3:5a, 44b; Matt, *Zohar,* 217.

The *way through the sea* symbolizes *Yesod,* coursing into the sea of *Shekhinah* (*Zohar* 1:29b). *Elohim* symbolizes *Binah* ("Understanding"), mother of both *Yesod* and *Shekhinah,* intimate with both of them.

1237. **Written Torah...** *Tif'eret,* who together with *Shekhinah* (Oral Torah) emerges from *Ḥokhmah* (Primordial Torah). The hidden *sefirah* of *Da'at* ("Knowledge") is enclosed within *Tif'eret.*

1238. **YHVH Elohim—a complete name...** In rabbinic literature these two names represent, respectively, the divine qualities of compassion and justice. See *Sifrei,* Deuteronomy 26; *Bereshit Rabbah* 12:15; 33:3; and 13:3, where *YHVH Elohim* is called "a complete name."

Here the complete name *YHVH Elohim* indicates the divine parents, *Ḥokhmah* and *Binah* ("Wisdom" and "Understanding"), who transmit their qualities to their daughter, *Shekhinah.*

See *Zohar* 1:49a; 3:296a (*IZ*). Cf. *Zohar* 1:4a, 20a; 2:161a, 229a; 3:138b (*IR*); *ZḤ* 70d (*ShS*).

"הצלע (Ha-tsela), *The side*—the speculum that does not shine, as is said: ובצלעי (Uv-tsal'i), *At my stumbling, they rejoiced...* (Psalms 35:15).[1239]

"*That He had taken from* האדם (ha-adam), *the human*—for She issued from Written Torah.[1240]

"*Into a woman*—to be joined to the flame of the left side, for Torah was given from the side of Power.[1241] לאשה (Le-ishshah), *Into a woman*—to be אש ה' (esh he), fire of *he,* bound together as one.[1242]

"*And He brought her to* האדם (ha-adam), *the human*—for She should not be alone but rather embraced by, joined with Written Torah.[1243] Once She joins with Him, He will nourish and adorn Her, providing Her what She needs. From here we learn that when one offers his daughter in marriage, until she enters her husband's domain her parents prepare and provide all she needs, but once she joins her husband, he nourishes her and provides what she needs.[1244]

"Come and see: At first is written, *YHVH Elohim fashioned the side,* for Father and Mother array Her. Afterward *He brought her to the human,* so that all is bound as one, joined to one another, and He provides Her what She needs.[1245]

268

1239. **speculum...** אספקלריא (*Ispaqlar-ya*), "Glass, mirror, lens, speculum." See BT *Yevamot* 49b: "All the prophets gazed through a dim glass [literally: an *ispaqlarya* that does not shine], whereas Moses our Rabbi gazed through a clear glass [literally: an *ispaqlarya* that shines]." Cf. 1 Corinthians 13:12: "For now we see through a glass darkly, but then face-to-face."

Shekhinah is the "speculum [or: mirror] that does not shine on its own" but rather reflects the other *sefirot.* See *Zohar* 1:33b, 183a; 2:23b. Her incomplete state is implied here by another meaning of the root צלע (*tsl'*), "to stumble."

1240. **for She issued from Written Torah** *Shekhinah* (Oral Torah) emanates from *Tif'eret,* symbolized by Written Torah and Primordial Adam.

1241. **the flame of the left side...** *Shekhinah* is associated with *Gevurah* ("Power"), on the left side of the sefirotic tree. For the connection between revelation and the divine name *Gevurah,* see BT *Shabbat* 88b: "Rabbi Yoḥanan said, '...Every utterance [at Sinai] emerging from the mouth of Power branched into seventy languages.'"

See *Tanḥuma, Yitro* 11; BT *Makkot* 24a; *Zohar* 2:81a, 84a.

1242. **to be אש ה' (esh he), fire of *he*...** The word אשה (*ishshah*), *woman,* is divided into two elements linked together: the fire of *Gevurah,* and *Shekhinah,* who is symbolized by the second ה (*he*) of the name יהוה (*YHVH*).

1243. **She should not be alone...** *Shekhinah* (Oral Torah) should be joined with Her partner, *Tif'eret,* who is known as Primordial Adam and Written Torah.

1244. **when one offers his daughter in marriage...** See the husband's declaration to his wife in M *Ketubbot* 4:11: "The female children born from our marriage will dwell in my house and be maintained out of my estate until they are married."

1245. **for Father and Mother array Her...** The complete name *YHVH Elohim* indicates the divine parents, *Ḥokhmah* and *Binah,* who sustain and adorn their daughter, *Shekhinah.* Once She is wed to *Tif'eret,* He sustains Her.

See *Bereshit Rabbah* 18:1: "*YHVH Elohim fashioned the rib* [or: *side*].... It was taught in the name of Rabbi Shim'on son of Yoḥai: 'He adorned her like a bride and brought her to him.'"

Cf. BT *Berakhot* 61a: "Rabbi Shim'on son of Menasia expounded, 'Why is it written:

"Alternatively, *Elohim understands her way*. When the daughter resides in her mother's house, she watches out every day for everything her daughter needs, as is written: *Elohim understands her way*.[1246] Once she joins her husband, he provides her all she needs and arranges her affairs, as is written: *He knows her site*.

[49a] "Alternatively, this verse was spoken concerning supernal wisdom and linked to supernal secrets. The primordial point is totally unknown to anyone, but *Elohim understands her way*—this is the world that is coming.[1247] *He*— hidden of all hidden, concealed of all concealed, called *He*, unknown by any name.[1248]

"It is written: ויײצר יהוה אלהים (*Va-yitser YHVH Elohim*), *YHVH Elohim formed, the human* (Genesis 2:7). Here he was perfected consummately, on the right and on the left. We have already established that he encompassed the good impulse and the evil impulse.[1249] Why? The good impulse, for himself; the evil impulse, to arouse toward his female.[1250] Arousal always arises from the left side toward the female, linking itself with her, so she is called אשה (*ishshah*), woman.[1251]

269

YHVH Elohim fashioned the rib? This teaches that the blessed Holy One braided Eve's hair and brought her to Adam.'"

1246. **she watches out every day...** The name *Elohim* indicates the Divine Mother, *Binah*, who provides for Her daughter, *She-khinah*, until She is wed to *Tif'eret*. The same pattern is followed on earth.

1247. **The primordial point is totally unknown...** The point of *Ḥokhmah* ("Wisdom") is incomprehensible even to the *sefirot* emerging from it, except for *Binah* ("Understanding"), known as "the world that is coming." According to the Gnostic *Gospel of Truth* (22:27–29), the aeons (divine emanations) below *Nous* ("Intellect") are unaware of the hidden divinity: "It was quite amazing that they were in the Father without knowing Him."

On the rabbinic concept of העולם הבא (*ha-olam ha-ba*), "the world that is coming," see above, note 1224.

1248. *He*—**hidden of all hidden...** *Keter*, the highest *sefirah*, cannot be identified precisely, only by the vague term *He*. See *Zohar* 3:129b (*IR*), 290a (*IZ*).

1249. **he encompassed the good impulse and the evil impulse** See BT *Berakhot* 61a: "Rav Naḥman son of Rav Ḥisda expounded, 'Why is it written: ויײצר (*Va-yitser*), [*YHVH Elohim*] *formed...*, spelled with two *yods*? Because the blessed Holy One created two impulses, one good and the other evil.'"

See *Bereshit Rabbah* 14:4; *Targum Yerushalmi*, ad loc.

The good impulse derives from *Ḥesed* ("Love") on the right side of the sefirotic tree, while the evil impulse derives from *Gevurah* ("Power"), also known as *Din* ("Judgment") on the left.

1250. **to arouse toward his female** See *Bereshit Rabbah* 9:7: "Naḥman said in the name of Rabbi Shemu'el: '*Behold, it was very good*—this is the good impulse; *And behold, it was very good* (Genesis 1:31)—this is the evil impulse. Is the evil impulse *very good*? How astonishing! Yet were it not for the evil impulse, no man would ever build a house, marry a woman, or engender children.'"

1251. **so she is called אשה (*ishshah*), woman** See above, page 268.

"Come and see the good impulse and the evil impulse, for the female is embraced by them, linked with them, though not until the evil impulse arouses toward her and they join one another. Once they do, the good impulse, who is joy, arouses, drawing her close to him. Above, genuine North, who is joy without the filth of evil impulse, holds Her first, as is written: *His left hand beneath my head*, and afterward, *his right embracing me* (Song of Songs 2:6).[1252] She is positioned between right and left, to be nourished, so: *YHVH Elohim formed*—a complete name, corresponding to these two sides.[1253]

"*The human* (Genesis, ibid.). We have already established that this implies male and female as one, not separated to be face-to-face.[1254]

"What is written? *Dust of the earth* (ibid.),[1255] now poised to be arrayed.[1256]

"Come and see: When a woman is joined with her husband, she is called by his name: איש אשה (*ish ishshah*), man, woman; צדיק צדק (*tsaddiq tsedeq*), righteous, righteousness.[1257] He is עופר (*ofer*), fawn, and she is עפר (*afar*), dust. Then he is צבי (*tsevi*), hart, and she is צביה (*tseviyyah*), doe; צבי (*tsevi*), *fairest, of all lands* (Ezekiel 20:6).[1258]

"It is written: *Do not plant* אשרה (*asherah*)[1259] *or any tree-like object beside the altar that you make for YHVH your God* (Deuteronomy 16:21). *Beside the altar*—Is it permitted above the altar or anywhere else? Rather, we have established: אשר (*Asher*) is her husband, and she is named after him: אשרה

270

1252. **Above, genuine North...** In the realm of the *sefirot, Gevurah,* symbolized by the direction north and the left hand, arouses toward *Shekhinah.* Then *Ḥesed,* the right hand, embraces Her.

1253. **YHVH Elohim formed—a complete name...** In rabbinic literature these two names represent, respectively, the divine qualities of compassion and judgment. Here they correspond to *Ḥesed* ("Love") and *Gevurah,* also known as *Din* ("Judgment"). Cf. above, note 1238.

1254. **this implies male and female as one...** The original human was an androgynous being. Similarly, the sefirotic couple *Tif'eret* and *Shekhinah* were originally joined. See above, note 1236.

1255. **Dust of the earth** The verse reads: *YHVH Elohim formed the human from the dust of the earth.*

1256. **now poised to be arrayed** *Dust* alludes to *Shekhinah,* as Rabbi Shim'on goes on to explain. Originally part of the androg-

ynous being, She was now about to manifest as a separate entity.

1257. צדיק צדק (*tsaddiq tsedeq*), **righteous, righteousness** Symbolizing *Yesod* and *Shekhinah,* respectively (see *Zohar* 1:132b). *Yesod* ("Foundation") is called Righteous, based on Proverbs 10:25: וצדיק יסוד עולם (*Ve-tsaddiq yesod olam*). The verse literally means *The righteous one is an everlasting foundation* but is understood as *The righteous one is the foundation of the world.*

See BT *Ḥagigah* 12b; *Bahir* 71 (102); Azriel of Gerona, *Peirush ha-Aggadot,* 34.

1258. צבי (*tsevi*), **fairest, of all lands** Alluding to *Shekhinah,* often identified with the land of Israel.

1259. אשרה (*asherah*) This term denotes a standing wooden object apparently symbolizing the Canaanite goddess Asherah. The following, remarkable passage (until "So, *dust of the earth*") is missing in many manuscripts.

(Asherah). So it is written: *For Baal and Asherah* (2 Kings 23:4).[1260] So, *Do not plant* אשרה *(Asherah)... beside the altar that you make for* YHVH *your God—* over against *the altar of* YHVH, for *the altar of* YHVH is based on this, so *do not plant* another *Asherah* over against Her.[1261]

"Come and see: All those sun-worshipers are always called worshipers of Baal, and those who worship the moon are called worshipers of Asherah, so *for Baal and Asherah,* Asherah being named after her husband, Asher. If so, why was this name displaced?[1262] Because Asherah derives from the verse באשרי *(Be-oshri), Happy am I! For daughters will deem me happy* (Genesis 30:13), while the other nations did not deem Her happy, substituting another in Her place.[1263] Further it is written: *All who honored her despise her* (Lamentations 1:8). So this name was displaced in order that those worshiped by other nations not be empowered.[1264] We call Her *altar* made of *earth,* as is written: *altar of earth...* (Exodus 20:22). So, *dust of the earth.*[1265]

"*He blew into his nostrils the breath of life* (Genesis 2:7). The word is inclusive, but *He blew into his nostrils the breath of life*—into that *dust,* like a female impregnated by a male, for they join and this *dust* is filled with all.[1266] With whom? Spirits and souls.

"*And* האדם *(ha-adam), the human, became a living soul* (ibid.)—now *the human* was arrayed enduringly, to adorn and nourish the *living soul.*[1267]

271

1260. אשר *(Asher)* is her husband... *For Baal and Asherah*   Baal was the most prominent Canaanite god, often paired in the Bible with Asherah. Here Rabbi Shim'on plays on the literal meaning of the word בעל *(ba'al),* "husband." Elsewhere in the *Zohar* (1:47b, 245b), the name Asher is associated with the male sefirotic potency, *Yesod;* so *Shekhinah,* wife of *Yesod,* is named after Him: Asherah. This startling name of *Shekhinah* and Her intimacy with the masculine divinity mirror the ancient Israelite worship of YHVH and *Asherah.* An inscription from the eighth century B.C.E. found in Khirbet el-Qom (Northern Israel) reads: "To YHVH, my Protector and to His *Asherah.*" Another in Kuntillet Arjud (Sinai) reads: "YHVH of Yemen and His *Asherah.*"

See Patai, *The Hebrew Goddess,* 39, 296–97, n. 15; *Anchor Bible Dictionary,* s.v. "Kom, Khirbet el-," "Kuntillet Arjud."

1261. over against *the altar of* YHVH... The verse is understood to mean: Do not substitute the false goddess Asherah ("an-other *Asherah*") for *Shekhinah,* the original Asherah, who is the genuine *altar of* YHVH.

1262. why was this name displaced? Why was the name Asherah, which originally designated *Shekhinah,* removed from Her and applied only to the Canaanite goddess?

1263. the other nations did not deem Her happy... The other nations did not recognize *Shekhinah* and in Her place worshiped the Canaanite goddess.

1264. So this name was displaced... The name Asherah was removed from *Shekhinah* so that the false goddess would not be empowered by the invocation of that name.

1265. We call Her *altar* made of *earth...* *dust of the earth*   *Shekhinah* is symbolized by earth.

1266. The word is inclusive... Nostrils is plural, but the object here is specifically *Shekhinah,* known as *dust,* into whom *Tif'eret* blows *the breath of life.*

1267. now *the human* was arrayed enduringly... Now *Tif'eret,* Primordial Adam,

"*YHVH Elohim fashioned* (ibid., 22).[1268] Here, too, with the complete name, for Father and Mother adorned Her before She approached Her husband.[1269]

"*The side,* as is said: *I am black but beautiful* (Song of Songs 1:5), the speculum that does not shine,[1270] but Father and Mother adorned Her so that Her husband be pleased with Her.

"*And He brought her to the man* (ibid.). From here we learn that the father and mother of the bride should bring her into the domain of the groom, as is said: *I have given my daughter to this man* (Deuteronomy 22:16). From now on, her husband comes to her, for the house is hers, as is written: *He came in to her* (Genesis 29:23), *He came in to Rachel also* (ibid., 30).[1271] First, *He brought her to the man,* for up to this point the father and mother should act. Afterward, he should come to her, for the entire house is hers and he must obtain her permission.[1272]

"We have aroused our awareness of this, as is written: *He approached the place and stayed there for the night* (ibid. 28:11), first obtaining permission.[1273] From here we learn that one who joins [49b] his wife should entreat her and sweeten her with words, or otherwise not spend the night with her, so that their desire be as one, with no coercion.

272

was prepared to emanate to *Shekhinah,* known as *living soul.*

1268. **YHVH Elohim fashioned**   The verse continues: *the side that He had taken from the human into a woman, and He brought her to the human.*

1269. **Here, too, with the complete name...**   As in Genesis 2:7 (see above, page 270). In rabbinic literature these two names represent, respectively, the divine qualities of compassion and justice. Here the complete name *YHVH Elohim* indicates the divine parents, *Ḥokhmah* and *Binah,* who sustain and adorn their daughter *Shekhinah.* Once She is wedded to *Tif'eret,* He sustains Her.

See above, note 1238; and *Bereshit Rabbah* 18:1 and BT *Berakhot* 61a, cited above, note 1245.

1270. **speculum...**   אספקלריא (*Ispaqlarya*), "Glass, mirror, lens, speculum." See BT *Yevamot* 49b: "All the prophets gazed through a dim glass [literally: an *ispaqlarya* that does not shine], whereas Moses our Rabbi gazed through a clear glass [literally: an *ispaqlarya* that shines]." Cf. 1 Corinthians 13:12: "For now we see through a glass darkly, but then face-to-face."

Shekhinah is the "speculum [or: mirror] that does not shine on its own" but rather reflects the other *sefirot.* See *Zohar* 1:33b, 183a; 2:23b. Her incomplete state is indicated by the root צלע (*tsl'*), which in addition to "side" or "rib," also means "to stumble." See above, page 268: "הצלע (*Ha-tsela*), *The side*—the speculum that does not shine, as is said: ובצלעי (*Uv-tsal'i*), *At my stumbling, they rejoiced...* (Psalms 35:15)." Once adorned, She turns *beautiful.*

1271. **He came in to her... He came in to Rachel also**   Jacob united with Leah and later with Rachel.

1272. **he must obtain her permission**   The husband must not force himself on the wife.

1273. **He approached...**   ויפגע (*Va-yifga*), *He encountered* (or: *reached*), understood here according to another sense of the root, *entreated.* Jacob's journey to *the place* symbolizes the union of *Tif'eret* with *Shekhinah.* Proper union requires a gentle approach.

See *Mekhilta, Beshallaḥ* 2; *Bereshit Rabbah* 68:9; BT *Berakhot* 26b; *Zohar* 1:148b, 165a.

In rabbinic literature, מקום (*maqom*), "place," is a name of God, emphasizing di-

"*He stayed there for the night, for the sun had set* (ibid.), showing that one is forbidden to engage in intercourse in the daytime.[1274]

"*He took one of the stones of the place and put it under his head* (ibid.). Here we learn that if a king has golden beds and precious spreads in which to spend the night, and his consort prepares him a bed arranged with stones, he should leave his own and sleep in the one that she prepares, as is written: *He lay down in that place* (ibid.).[1275]

"Come and see what is written here: *The man said, 'This one at last...'* (ibid. 2:23).[1276] Behold the fragrance of words, to draw love with her, draw her toward his desire, arouse passion together. See how sweet, how full of love: *Bone of my bones, flesh of flesh*, showing her they are one, inseparable.[1277]

"Now he begins praising her: *This one shall be called Woman* (ibid.). This one is unparalleled, glory of the house! All women compared with her are like an ape compared with humans.[1278] Certainly *this one shall be called Woman*, perfection of all, *this one* and no other, as is written: *Many daughters have done virtuously, but you surpass them all* (Proverbs 31:29).[1279]

"*Therefore a man leaves his father and mother and cleaves to his wife* [*and they become one flesh*] (Genesis 2:24)—all to draw her in love, to cleave to her.[1280] Once he had aroused her with all these words, what is written? *Now the serpent was slier than any creature of the field* ... (ibid. 3:1). The evil impulse aroused to seize her, binding her with bodily desire, arousing in her other things in which evil impulse delights, until eventually what is written? *The woman saw that the tree was good for eating and a delight to the eye,*[1281] *and she took of its fruit and*

273

vine immanence and omnipresence. Here it designates *Shekhinah*. See *Bereshit Rabbah* 68:9; Urbach, *Sages*, 1:66–79.

1274. **one is forbidden to engage in intercourse in the daytime** See BT *Niddah* 17a: "Rav Ḥisda said, 'One is forbidden to engage in intercourse in the daytime.'"

1275. **if a king has golden beds...** See *Zohar* 1:148b; 3:242a.

1276. *This one at last* In the verse, the man continues: *is bone of my bones, flesh of flesh! This one shall be called Woman, for from Man was she taken.*

1277. **Behold the fragrance of words...** According to Rabbi Shim'on, Adam spoke these words romantically to Eve.

1278. **like an ape compared with humans** See BT *Bava Batra* 58a: "Rabbi Bana'ah said, '...Compared with Sarah, all others are like

an ape compared with a human. Compared with Eve, Sarah was like an ape compared with a human. Compared with Adam, Eve was like an ape compared with a human. Compared with *Shekhinah*, Adam was like an ape compared with a human.'"

1279. *this one...* Referring to Eve, and alluding to *Shekhinah* (the Divine Presence), who is known as זאת (*zot*), "this." The hymn to the virtuous woman in Proverbs 31:10–31 is interpreted in the *Zohar* as applying to *Shekhinah*.

1280. **all to draw her in love...** This verse, too, is understood as part of Adam's approach to Eve.

1281. *and a delight to the eye* Rabbi Shim'on omits the phrase: *and that the tree was desirable to contemplate.*

ate (ibid., 6)—receiving it willingly[1282]—*and also gave to her husband beside her,* for now she aroused desirously toward him, offering passionate love. This shows human beings how the act corresponds above."[1283]

Rabbi El'azar said, "If so, how can we demonstrate the evil impulse above, seizing the female?"[1284]

He replied, "We have already aroused our awareness of the mystery of left and right, corresponding to the good impulse and the evil impulse—good impulse on the right, evil impulse on the left—these above and those below.[1285] The left above grasps the body to join with Her as one, as is said: *His left hand beneath my head...* (Song of Songs 2:6).[1286] So until here words are interpretable above and below. From here on, words with a residue of tar, interpretable by tiny children.[1287] By this the Companions have already been aroused."

Rabbi Shim'on was traveling to Tiberias, accompanied by Rabbi Yose, Rabbi Yehudah, and Rabbi Ḥiyya. On the way they saw Rabbi Pinḥas approaching. Upon joining as one, they dismounted and sat beneath the trees of the hillside.

Rabbi Pinḥas said, "Now that we are sitting, I am eager to hear some of those sublime words you convey every day!"[1288]

Rabbi Shim'on opened, saying, "*He went on his journeys from the Negev as far as Bet-El* (Genesis 13:3).[1289] *He went on his journeys.* The verse should read: *his journey.* Why *his journeys?* Because there are two journeys: one, his; one, of

274

1282. **receiving it willingly** Seduced by the evil impulse, Eve indulged in physical desire.

1283. **how the act corresponds above** In the realm of the *sefirot,* male and female interact similarly.

1284. **how can we demonstrate the evil impulse above...** How can an evil component appear in the realm of the *sefirot?*

1285. **the mystery of left and right...** The good and evil impulses derive, respectively, from the *sefirot* of *Ḥesed* on the right and *Gevurah* on the left.

See BT *Berakhot* 61a; *Zohar* 1:144b, 155b, 165b, 174b; 3:263b.

1286. *His left hand beneath my head* The verse continues: *his right embracing me.* In the divine romance, the left hand (*Gevurah*) arouses the body of *Shekhinah,* then the right hand (*Ḥesed*) completes the embrace, uniting Her with *Tif'eret.* See above, page 270.

1287. **So until here...** Perhaps meaning: until this point in Genesis (3:6), the verses apply both on the earthly plane and the sefirotic plane. From here on, they apply primarily on the corporeal level (as indicated by "a residue of tar") and their interpretation requires no profound insight.

See *KP; Bei'ur ha-Millim ha-Zarot,* 176–77; Scholem; Tishby, *Wisdom of the Zohar,* 3:1390.

1288. **I am eager to hear some of those sublime words...** The expression derives from the Talmud and appears often in the *Zohar.* See BT *Berakhot* 8a; *Ta'anit* 20b; *Ḥagigah* 14a; *Zohar* 1:87a, 96b, 197b; 2:31a; 3:148a, 209b, 231a.

1289. *He went on his journeys...* Describing the journeyings of Abraham on his way back to Canaan from Egypt. See *Bereshit Rabbah* 40:3 (on Genesis 13:3); *Zohar* 1:83b.

Shekhinah. For every human being should manifest as male and female to fortify faith; then *Shekhinah* never separates from him.[1290]

"You might say: 'If one sets out on the road and is no longer male and female, *Shekhinah* separates from him.'[1291] Come and see: Whoever sets out on the road should offer his prayer to the blessed Holy One to draw upon himself *Shekhinah* of his Lord before he leaves, while still male and female.[1292] Once he has offered his prayer and *Shekhinah* rests upon him, he can leave, for *Shekhinah* has coupled with him so that he will be male and female: male and female in town, male and female in the countryside,[1293] as is written: *Righteousness goes before him, and he sets out on his way* (Psalms 85:14).[1294]

"Come and see: As [50a] long as one lingers on the way, he must guard his conduct, so that supernal coupling will not separate from him, leaving him defective, lacking male and female.[1295] In town he must, when his female is

1290. **every human being should manifest as male and female...** When a human couple unites, they stimulate the union of *Shekhinah* and Her partner, *Tif'eret*, thereby strengthening the entirety of the *sefirot*, the realm of faith. A married man is constantly accompanied by *Shekhinah* (*Zohar* 1:228b).

See BT *Sotah* 17a: "Rabbi Akiva expounded: איש ואשה (*Ish ve-ishshah*), Man and woman: If they are worthy, *Shekhinah* abides between them; if not, fire consumes them.'" As indicated by Rashi (ad loc.), the two Hebrew words איש ואשה (*ish ve-ishshah*), "man and woman," share the letters א (*alef*) and ש (*shin*), which spell אש (*esh*), "fire"; in addition each contains one of the two letters of the divine name יה (*Yah*). Without divinity between them, only fire remains.

1291. **no longer male and female...** If he travels without his wife, *Shekhinah* would apparently desert him.

1292. **should offer his prayer... before he leaves...** Before setting out on a journey, one should pray, including (or specifically) *tefillat ha-derekh* ("the prayer for the way"). See BT *Berakhot* 29b: "Elijah said to Rav Yehudah the brother of Rabbi Sala the Ḥasid, 'Do not let your anger boil and you will not sin; do not get drunk and you will not sin; and when you set out on the way, consult your Creator and then set out.' What is meant by 'consult your Creator and then set

out'? Rabbi Ya'akov said in the name of Rav Ḥisda, 'This is *tefillat ha-derekh*.'"

By praying before leaving home and while still with his wife, the husband ensures that *Shekhinah* will abide with him throughout his journey.

See BT *Berakhot* 14a (cited in the note after next), 30a; *Zohar* 1:58b, 121a (*MhN*), 178a, 230a–b, 240b; 2:130b; *Shulḥan Arukh, Oraḥ Ḥayyim* 110:7; David ben Samuel ha-Levi, *Turei Zahav*, ad loc.; Issachar Ber Eilenburg, *Be'er Sheva*, 45; Mordechai Shpielman, *Tif-'eret Tsevi*, 1:351–53.

1293. **in town... in the countryside** In town with his wife, in the countryside with *Shekhinah*.

1294. *Righteousness...* See BT *Berakhot* 14a: "Rav Idi son of Avin said in the name of Rabbi Yitsḥak son of Ishyan, 'Whoever prays and then sets out on the way, the blessed Holy One fulfills his desires, as is said: *Righteousness goes before him, and he sets out on his way.*'"

In this Talmudic passage, *righteousness* (or: *justice*) implies justification by prayer, which guarantees a successful journey. Here in the *Zohar, Righteousness* is a name of *Shekhinah*, who symbolizes divine justice. By praying, one secures Her accompanying presence. See *Zohar* 1:49a, 58b.

1295. **supernal coupling...** *Shekhinah*, his partner on the road.

with him; how much more so here, for supernal coupling is linked with him! Further, this coupling protects him on the way, not parting from him until he returns home.

"Upon entering his house he should delight the lady of his house, for she engendered that supernal coupling.[1296] As soon as he reaches her he should delight her anew, for two nuances. First, because the joy of this coupling is joy of *mitsvah*, and joy of *mitsvah* is joy of *Shekhinah*.[1297] Further, he increases peace below,[1298] as is written: *You will know that your tent is at peace, attend to your abode and not sin* (Job 5:24). Is it a sin if one does not attend to his wife? Certainly so, for he diminishes the splendor of supernal coupling coupled with him, engendered by the lady of his house.[1299] Second, if his wife conceives, supernal coupling pours into it a holy soul,[1300] for this covenant is called Covenant of the blessed Holy One.[1301] So one should focus on this joy as on the joy of Sabbath, coupling of the wise.[1302] So, *You will know that your tent is*

276

1296. **he should delight the lady of his house...** Upon returning home, he should unite with his wife, thanks to whom *Shekhinah* accompanied him. See the question posed by King David to Uriah in 2 Samuel 11:10: *You just returned from a journey; why didn't you go down to your house?*

See BT *Yevamot* 62b: "Rabbi Yehoshu'a son of Levi said, 'A man must attend to his wife when he is about to set out on the road, as is said: *You will know that your tent is at peace...* [*you will attend to your abode and not sin*].'"

1297. **the joy of this coupling is joy of *mitsvah*...** Uniting with one's wife upon returning from a journey is a religious obligation and stimulates the union of *Shekhinah* with Her partner, *Tif'eret*. See BT *Shabbat* 30b: "*Shekhinah* abides neither through gloom nor laziness nor frivolity nor levity nor talk nor idle chatter [or: vain pursuits], but only through the joy of *mitsvah*."

1298. **he increases peace below** He guarantees peace and harmony in his house. See BT *Shabbat* 152a, where Rabbi Shim'on son of Ḥalafta refers to the phallus as "peacemaker of the home."

1299. **he diminishes the splendor...** If on returning home, the husband fails to unite with his wife, he dishonors *Shekhinah*,

who united with him because of his wife, and he hinders Her union with *Tif'eret*.

1300. **supernal coupling pours into it...** *Shekhinah* emanates to the fetus a holy soul generated from Her union with *Tif'eret* (through *Yesod*).

1301. **this covenant is called Covenant of the blessed Holy One** The human phallus, inscribed with the covenant of circumcision, symbolizes the *sefirah* of *Yesod*, the divine phallus. Human sexual union stimulates the divine union of *Yesod* and *Shekhinah*, which generates the soul.

1302. **the joy of Sabbath, coupling of the wise** The Mishnah (*Ketubbot* 5:6) discusses how often husbands of various professions are required to fulfill the commandment of עונה (onah), "conjugal rights," i.e., to satisfy their wives sexually. According to Rabbi Eli'ezer, "The *onah* mentioned in the Torah [applies as follows]: Those who are unoccupied, every day; laborers, twice a week; donkey-drivers, once a week; camel-drivers, once every thirty days; sailors, once every six months."

The Talmud (BT *Ketubbot* 62b) adds: "When is the *onah* of the disciples of the wise? [i.e., What is the proper interval between two successive times of fulfilling this *mitsvah*?] Rav Yehudah said in the name of

at peace, for *Shekhinah* accompanies you and dwells in your house; therefore, *you will attend to your abode and not sin.* What is the meaning of *not sin*? Not fail to perform the joy of *mitsvah* in the presence of *Shekhinah*.[1303]

"Similarly, when disciples of the wise part from their wives all days of the week to engage in Torah, supernal coupling couples with them, not parting from them, so that they be male and female.[1304] Once Sabbath enters, disciples of the wise should delight their wives anew for the sake of the splendor of supernal coupling, focusing their hearts on the will of their Lord, as has been explained.

"Similarly, when a man's wife undergoes days of impurity and he waits for her fittingly,[1305] supernal coupling couples with him all those days, so he is male and female. Once his wife is purified, he should delight her anew—joy of *mitsvah,* supernal joy!

"All the reasons we have offered rise to a single rung.[1306] The gist of the word: All scions of faith should focus their heart and will on this.[1307]

"Now you might say, 'If so, it is more admirable for a person to set out on the road than to stay at home because of supernal coupling who couples with him.' Come and see: When a man is at home, the essence of the home is his wife, for on account of her, *Shekhinah* does not leave the house. So we have learned: *Isaac brought her into the tent of his mother Sarah* (Genesis 24:67), for the lamp was kindled. Why? Because *Shekhinah* entered the home.[1308]

277

Shemu'el, 'From one Sabbath eve to the next.'"

See *Zohar* 1:112a (*MhN*); 2:63b, 89a–b; 3:49b, 78a.

1303. **What is the meaning of *not sin*? Not fail...** The Hebrew verb חטא (*ḥt'*) means both "to sin" and "to fail, miss."

1304. **when disciples of the wise part from their wives...** See above, note 1302. All week long *Shekhinah* joins the solitary male devotees of Torah.

1305. **undergoes days of impurity...** During and immediately following menstruation, when the husband must avoid contact with her.

1306. **All the reasons we have offered rise to a single rung** The reasons for delighting one's wife upon returning from a journey apply as well to sexual union on Sabbath eve and following the wife's purification. All pertain to *Shekhinah.*

1307. **All scions of faith...** Those who

believe in the reality of the *sefirotic* realm are called בני מהימנותא (*benei meheimanuta*), "children of faith."

1308. **the lamp was kindled...** See *Bereshit Rabbah* 60:16: "*Isaac brought her [Rebekah] into the tent of his mother Sarah* ...As long as Sarah existed...the lamp would burn in her tent from one Sabbath eve until the next. As soon as she died, it went out. As soon as Rebekah arrived, it returned."

Rabbi Shim'on alludes to this midrash to demonstrate that the presence of the light of *Shekhinah* in the home depends upon the presence of the essence of the home (the wife): first Sarah, and upon her death, Rebekah. See *Zohar* 1:133a.

On the phrase "essence of the home," see Psalms 113:9; *Bereshit Rabbah* 71:2; *Pesiqta de-Rav Kahana* 20:2; *Tanḥuma* (Buber), *Vayetse* 15; *Bemidbar Rabbah* 14:8; *Zohar* 1:29a–b, 149b, 154a, 157b.

"Mystery of the matter: Supernal Mother appears with the male only when the house is arrayed, when male and female join. She then pours blessings upon them.[1309] Similarly, Lower Mother appears with the male only when the house is arrayed, when the male approaches his female and they join as one. She then pours blessings upon them.[1310] So a man at home is adorned with two females, as above.[1311] This corresponds to the mystery written: *until the desire of hills of eternity* (ibid. 49:26). *The desire of hills of eternity* extends to this *until:* supernal female, to array, adorn, and bless Him; lower female, to unite with Him, be nourished by Him.[1312]

"Similarly below, when a male is married, *the desire of hills of eternity* verges toward him, and he is adorned with two females, one above and one below: the upper to pour blessings upon him, the lower to be nourished by him, unite with him.[1313] A man at home is the focus of *the desire of hills of eternity,* with whom he is adorned. Not so when he sets out on the road: Supernal Mother unites with him, while the lower is left behind.[1314] Upon returning home he should adorn himself with two females, as we have said."

Rabbi Pinḥas said, "Even in a skein of scales and fins,[1315] no one [50b] dares challenge you."

Rabbi Shim'on said, "Similarly Torah stands between two houses, as is written: *for the two houses of Israel* (Isaiah 8:14), one concealed on high, the

278

1309. **Supernal Mother appears...** *Binah,* the Divine Mother, manifests only when *Tif-'eret* and *Shekhinah* join.

1310. **Lower Mother appears...** *Shekhinah* manifests only when husband and wife establish a home and join together.

1311. **adorned with two females, as above** Adorned with both his wife and *Shekhinah,* as in the sefirotic realm *Tif'eret* is adorned both with His partner, *Shekhinah,* and the Divine Mother, *Binah*. See *Zohar* 1:66b, 153b.

1312. ***The desire of hills of eternity* extends to this *until*...** *Binah* and *Shekhinah* are the *hills of eternity,* towering, respectively, over the lower *sefirot* and the lower worlds. See BT *Rosh ha-Shanah* 11a; *Targum Yerushalmi,* Genesis 49:26; *Pirqei de-Rabbi Eli'ezer* 48, and David Luria, ad loc., n. 20; *Zohar* 2:112b.

Both of these female divine entities desire the male divine potency (*Tif'eret* or *Yesod*), who is known as עד (*ad*), *until*. See *Zohar* 1:150b, 247b; 2:22a.

1313. **he is adorned with two females...** The human husband is adorned by both *Shekhinah* and his wife.

1314. **Supernal Mother unites...** On the road, *Shekhinah* joins him, while his wife remains at home.

1315. **in a skein of scales and fins...** בקילפי סנפירי קטרא (*Be-qilpei senappirei qitra*). According to Leviticus 11:9 (see *Targum Onqelos,* ad loc.), fins and scales are the distinguishing features of kosher seafood. Perhaps Rabbi Pinḥas's point is that in all realms, ranging from mystical truth to the fine points of dietary law, Rabbi Shim'on's wisdom is unchallenged. More likely, the phrase is metaphorical: Rabbi Shim'on has mastered not only the holy but also the demonic realm. See *Pirqei de-Rabbi Eli'ezer* 9, where it is said of the monstrous Leviathan: "Between his fins stands the axis of Earth."

Cf. *Seder Rabbah di-Vreshit,* 17 (*Battei Midrashot,* 1:28): "The entire world stands

other more revealed.[1316] The concealed one on high is the *mighty voice,* as is written: *a mighty voice unceasing* (Deuteronomy 5:19). This voice is inward, inaudible, and unrevealed, as the larynx wells, whispering ה (*he*), flowing incessantly, tenuous, internal, eternally unheard.[1317]

"From here emerges Torah, *voice of Jacob,* audible issuing from inaudible.[1318] Afterward speech merges in it, resounding from its potency.[1319] The voice of Jacob, Torah, is embraced by two females: this inner, inaudible one, and this outer one, audible.[1320]

"Two are inaudible, two audible. Of the two inaudible, this is supernal, concealed Wisdom abiding in Thought, unrevealed, unheard. Afterward it emerges, revealing itself slightly in a whisper unheard, called *mighty voice,* tenuous whispering.[1321]

"Two who are audible issue from here: voice of Jacob and speech merging in it. The *mighty voice* in a whisper unheard is בית (*bayit*), a house, for supernal Wisdom—every female is called 'house'—while final speech is a house for the voice of Jacob, mystery of Torah.[1322] Therefore Torah begins with בית (*bet*): ב׳ ראשית (*Bet reshit*), *Two-house beginning* (Genesis 1:1)."[1323]

He opened, saying, "בראשית (*Be-reshit*), *In the beginning, created* אלהים (*Elohim*), *God* (Genesis 1:1), corresponding to what is written: *YHVH Elohim fash-*

on one fin of Leviathan." See *Midrash Konen* (*Beit ha-Midrash,* 2:26); *Zohar* 2:34b, 108b; 3:279a (*RM*).

1316. **Torah stands between two houses...** Torah symbolizes *Tif'eret Yisra'el,* the core of the *sefirot,* God's self-revelation. *Tif'eret* is situated between *Binah* and *Shekhinah,* the two feminine houses.

1317. **the *mighty voice*...** *Binah* is *mighty,* powerful in Her silence. Through Her, the divine voice begins to emerge as the whispered letter ה (*he*), the second letter of the name יהוה (*YHVH*). This ה (*he*) expands from the primordial point of Wisdom, the initial letter י (*yod*).

See *Zohar* 2:226b; 3:261a; Moses de León, *Sheqel ha-Qodesh,* 89 (113).

1318. **Torah, *voice of Jacob*...** See Genesis 27:22. *Tif'eret,* identified with the third patriarch, Jacob, harmonizes the qualities of *Ḥesed* and *Gevurah,* symbolized by Abraham and Isaac. With the emergence of *Tif'eret,* silent revelation becomes audible.

See *Zohar* 1:16b, 74a, 97b–98a, 141b; 2:226b. Cf. BT *Berakhot* 15b: "The womb, which takes in silently, gives forth loudly."

1319. **speech merges in it...** *Shekhinah,* symbolized by speech, resounds from the power of the voice.

1320. **two females...** *Binah* and *Shekhinah.*

1321. **Two are inaudible...** *Ḥokhmah* and *Binah.*

1322. **every female is called 'house'...** As indicated in BT *Shabbat* 118b; *Yoma* 2a; *Sotah* 44a; cf. 2 Samuel 11:10. In the sefirotic realm, *Binah* houses *Ḥokhmah,* while *Shekhinah* houses *Tif'eret.*

1323. **Therefore Torah begins with בית (*bet*)...** The initial letter of the Torah, the ב (*bet*) of בראשית (*Be-reshit*), *In the beginning,* is numerically equivalent to two and suggests the word בית (*bayit*), "house." Thus the Torah opens with an allusion to two houses: *Binah* and *Shekhinah.* The word ראשית (*reshit*), *beginning,* signifies the pri-

ioned the side (ibid. 2:22).[1324] את השמים (*Et ha-shamayim*), *Heaven,* correspond-ing to: *He brought her to the human* (ibid.). ואת הארץ (*Ve-et ha-arets*), *and earth,* as is written: *Bone of my bones* (ibid., 23)."[1325]

Rabbi Shim'on opened, saying, "*YHVH declares to my Lord, 'Sit at My right hand until I make your enemies your footstool'* (Psalms 110:1). *YHVH declares to my Lord*—the upper rung says to the lower rung:[1326] *Sit at My right hand,* so that West will be linked with South, left with right, to smash the power of other nations.[1327] *YHVH declares to my Lord. YHVH declares*—this is Jacob;[1328] *to my Lord*—the ark of the covenant, Lord of all the earth (Joshua 3:11).[1329]

mordial point of Ḥokhmah as well as Torah, symbol of *Tif'eret.* See *Bereshit Rabbah* 1:1; cf. *Zohar* 1:29b.

1324. בראשית (*Be-reshit*), *In the beginning,* created אלהים (*Elohim*), *God...* Rabbi Shim'on understands the phrase to mean that Ḥokhmah and Binah (implied by the word בראשית [*Be-reshit*]; see previous note) emanated *Shekhinah,* who is called *Elohim.* The verse thus corresponds to the account of the creation of Eve, where Ḥokhmah and Binah (YHVH Elohim) fashion *Shekhinah* (*the side*). See *Zohar* 1:15a, 48b–49a.

1325. את השמים (*Et ha-shamayim*), *Heaven,* corresponding to...* Grammatically, the accusative particle את (*et*) has no ascertainable independent sense, but Naḥum of Gimzo and his disciple Rabbi Akiva taught that when *et* appears in a biblical verse, it amplifies the original meaning. See BT *Pesaḥim* 22b; *Ḥagigah* 12a; *Zohar* 1:247a; 2:90a, 135b.

את (*Et*) comprises the entire alphabet, the letters from א (*alef*) to ת (*tav*), and serves as an appropriate name for *Shekhinah,* who is known as both the mystical realm of speech and Oral Torah. See the Christian parallel in Revelation 1:8: "I am *alpha* and *omega.*"

According to Rabbi Shim'on, the phrase את השמים (*et ha-shamayim*) refers to *Shekhinah* and Her partner, *Tif'eret,* who is also called *shamayim, heaven.* This corresponds to the phrase *He brought her to the human,* which is interpreted as meaning that *Ḥokhmah* and *Binah* (YHVH Elohim) brought *Shekhinah* to *Tif'eret* (האדם [*ha-adam*], *the man*

[or: *human*], i.e., primordial Adam). See above, page 268.

The conclusion of the first verse of the Torah, ואת הארץ (*ve-et ha-arets*), *and earth,* also refers to the union of *Tif'eret* and *Shekhinah.* The letter ו (*vav*), whose numerical value is six, denotes *Tif'eret,* along with the five *sefirot* surrounding Him (*Ḥesed* to *Yesod*). את (*Et*) here symbolizes either *Shekhinah* or the flow of emanation conveyed by *Tif'eret* to *Shekhinah,* who is called *earth.* The phrase ואת הארץ (*ve-et ha-arets*), *and earth,* thus corresponds to *bone of my bones,* which similarly expresses the intimacy of the divine couple.

1326. the upper rung says to the lower rung *Tif'eret* (YHVH) says to *Shekhinah* (אדני [*Adoni*], *my Lord,* identified here with the divine name אדני [*Adonai*], "my Lord").

1327. so that West will be linked with South...* *Shekhinah* is symbolized by West, based on BT *Bava Batra* 25a: "Rabbi Abbahu said, '*Shekhinah* is in the West.'" *Ḥesed,* the warm love of God, is symbolized by South and located on the right side of the sefirotic tree. Here *Shekhinah,* who is influenced by the left side, is invited by *Tif'eret* to join the right.

1328. Jacob Symbolizing *Tif'eret,* who harmonizes the qualities of *Ḥesed* and *Gevurah,* symbolized by Abraham and Isaac.

1329. *the ark of the covenant...* *Shekhinah* is the ark housing the *sefirah* of *Yesod,* the covenant. See *Zohar* 1:2a, 33b, 59b, 228b; Moses de León, *Sheqel ha-Qodesh,* 75 (95).

280

"Alternatively, *YHVH declares*—this is Jubilee; *to my Lord*—Sabbatical,[1330] of whom is written: *I love my lord* (Exodus 21:5).[1331] *Sit at My right hand,* for right abides in Jubilee, and Sabbatical yearns to be linked with right.[1332]

"Come and see: Since the day She came to be, Sabbatical was never linked enduringly to right and left.[1333] When She yearned to be linked, He extended His left arm toward Her and created this world.[1334] Since it derived from the left side, it remains unstable till the seventh millennium, when it will be named One.[1335] Then She will be linked to the right, abide enduringly between right and left.[1336] *New heavens* and *new earth* will come to be;[1337] then She will never depart.

"If so, how can we establish the meaning of *Sit at My right hand?*[1338] This implies until a certain time, as is written: *until I make your enemies your*

1330. **Jubilee…Sabbatical**   Symbolizing *Binah* and *Shekhinah,* Divine Mother and Daughter.

According to the Bible, every seventh year is a Sabbatical (שמטה [*shemittah*], "release"), during which the land must lie fallow and at the end of which all debts are remitted (Leviticus 25:1–24; Deuteronomy 15:1–3). In Kabbalah the Sabbatical symbolizes *Shekhinah,* seventh of the lower *sefirot.* See *Zohar* 1:153b.

In the biblical cycle, after seven Sabbaticals comes the Jubilee, proclaimed every fifty years, when slaves are released and land reverts to its original owner (Leviticus 25:8–55). In Kabbalah the Jubilee symbolizes *Binah*—the Divine Mother—who is characterized by the number fifty, based on BT *Rosh ha-Shanah* 21b, where Rav and Shemu-'el teach: "Fifty gates of בינה (*binah*), understanding, were created in the world, all of which were given to Moses except for one, as is said: *You made him little less than God* (Psalms 8:6)." *Binah* is the source of redemption and liberation, specifically the Exodus from Egypt. See *Zohar* 1:21b, 47b; 2:46a, 83b, 85b; 3:262a.

1331. *I love my lord*   According to the Torah, at the start of the Sabbatical Hebrew slaves were to be set free, though they could refuse by declaring these words.

1332. **right abides in Jubilee…**   *Ḥesed,* on the right, is the first *sefirah* to emerge from *Binah. Shekhinah,* influenced by the left,

yearns to complete Herself by linking with the right.

1333. **Since the day She came to be…**   *Shekhinah* was unable to join *Tif'eret* and be embraced by both *Ḥesed* and *Gevurah,* His right and left arms, without an arousal from the world below, which had not yet been created.

1334. **He extended His left arm…**   The world was created through the power of *Gevurah,* the left arm of God.

1335. **it remains unstable till the seventh millennium…**   At the end of the seventh millennium, the world will be perfected and renewed, with right balancing left. Then *Shekhinah* will attain complete union with *Tif'eret,* and oneness will prevail. See BT *Sanhedrin* 97a: "Rabbi Katina said, 'The word will exist for six thousand years and for one thousand lie desolate.'"

1336. **Then She will be linked…**   Then *Shekhinah* will be perfectly balanced between right and left, *Ḥesed* and *Gevurah,* and united with *Tif'eret.*

1337. *New heavens* and *new earth*…   See Isaiah 66:22: *As the new heavens and the new earth, which I am making, rise before Me.…Heavens* and *earth* symbolize, respectively, *Tif'eret* and *Shekhinah.*

1338. **If so, how can we establish the meaning…**   If *Shekhinah* will remain imbalanced until the next eon, how does this verse apply in the present eon?

footstool, not permanently. But then You will never depart from there, as is written: *For you shall burst forth right and left* (Isaiah 54:3), all becoming one.[1339]

"Come and see: את השמים (*Et ha-shamayim*), *Heaven* (Genesis 1:1) is upper *Shekhinah*; ואת הארץ (*ve-et ha-arets*), *and earth* (ibid.) is lower *Shekhinah*, in a merging of male and female as one.[1340] This has been explained, as discussed arousingly by the Companions."

They rose and were about to leave, when Rabbi Shim'on said, "A word lingers here with us."

He opened, saying, "Two verses are written: *YHVH your God is a devouring fire* (Deuteronomy 4:24), and *You, cleaving to YHVH your God, are alive every one of you today* (ibid., 4). We have established these verses in various places, and the Companions have been aroused by them.[1341]

"Come and see: *For YHVH your God is a devouring fire.* The word has been discussed among the Companions: There is a fire devouring fire, devouring and consuming it, for there is fire fiercer than fire, as they have established.[1342] But come and see: Whoever desires to penetrate the wisdom of

282

1339. **But then...** When the world is perfected and renewed.

1340. את השמים (*Et ha-shamayim*), *Heaven...* ואת הארץ (*ve-et ha-arets*), *and earth...* On the word את (*et*), see above, note 1325. Here, apparently, את (*et*) refers not to a specific *sefirah*, but to the flow of emanation from א (*alef*) to ת (*tav*). את השמים (*Et ha-shamayim*), *Heaven*, refers to *Binah* (upper *Shekhinah*), from whom emanation flows to *Tif'eret* (*heaven*). The following words, ואת הארץ (*ve-et ha-arets*), *and earth*, refer to *Shekhinah* (lower *Shekhinah*), known as *earth*, who, by uniting with *Tif'eret*, receives the flow. The letter ו (*vav*) in the word ואת (*ve-et*), whose numerical value is six, may symbolize *Tif'eret* together with the five *sefirot* surrounding Him (*Hesed* through *Yesod*).

1341. **We have established these verses...** The apparent contradiction between the two verses is discussed in BT *Ketubbot* 111b: "Rabbi El'azar said, . . . '*You, cleaving to YHVH your God, are alive every one of you today.* Now is it possible to cleave to *Shekhinah*, of whom is written: *YHVH your God is a*

devouring fire? Rather the meaning is: Whoever marries his daughter to a disciple of the wise, conducts business on their behalf, or benefits them from his assets is regarded by Scripture as if he cleaves to *Shekhinah*.'"

In BT *Sotah* 14a, Rabbi Hama son of Hanina explains that one can approach and withstand the consuming fire of *Shekhinah* by imitating the divine, e.g., by clothing the naked, visiting the sick, comforting mourners, and burying the dead. See the discussion by Heschel, *Torah min ha-Shamayim*, 1:153–55.

A mystical response to this dilemma is offered by Gikatilla, *Sha'arei Orah*, 166: "As to what the rabbis have said: 'Now is it possible for one to cleave to *Shekhinah*?'—it certainly is!"

1342. **There is a fire devouring fire...** See BT *Yoma* 21b, where the fire of *Shekhinah* is identified as "a fire devouring fire," i.e., consuming the fiery angels.

Cf. *Zohar* 3:27b; Moses de León, *Sefer ha-Mishqal*, 63–65.

holy unification should contemplate the flame ascending from a glowing ember or a burning candle.[1343] For flame ascends only [51a] when grasped by coarse substance.

"Come and see! In a flame ascending are two lights: one, a white light, radiant; the other, a light tinged with black or blue.[1344] The white light is above, ascending unswervingly, while beneath it is the blue or black light, a throne for the white, which rests upon it, each embracing the other, becoming one. This black light colored blue, below, is a throne of glory for the white— here lies the mystery of the thread of blue.[1345] This blue-black throne is grasped by another substance below, so it can flame, arousing it to embrace the white light.[1346] Sometimes this blue-black turns red,[1347] while the white light above never wavers, constantly white. This blue one, though, changes color: sometimes blue or black, sometimes red. This is grasped in two directions: above, by that white light; below, by what lies beneath, by which it is fueled, primed to glow. This constantly consumes and devours what is placed beneath it, for the blue light consumes anything cleaving below, anything it rests upon, since by nature it consumes and devours. On it depends destruction and death of all.[1348]

"So it consumes anything cleaving below, while that white light hovering over it never devours or consumes, nor does its light waver. Therefore Moses said, '*For YHVH your God is a devouring fire*'—really *devouring*, devouring and

283

1343. **candle** ברצינא (*Botsina*), "Lamp," employed by *Targum Onqelos* (e.g., Exodus 27:20; 30:7–8) to render the Hebrew word נר (*ner*), "lamp" and later "candle."

Wax candles are discussed in a thirteenth-century treatise commissioned by Alfonso X of Castile (1252–1284); see *Libro del saber de astrologia* (University of Madrid MS 156), fol. 194r. See *Bereshit Rabbah* 85:4; *Tosafot, Shabbat* 20b, s.v. *ad kan; Zohar* 1:83b.

1344. **a white light … a light tinged with black or blue** Symbolizing, respectively, *Tif'eret* and *Shekhinah*. The last *sefirah* has no light of Her own but reflects the light of the other *sefirot*.

See *Zohar* 1:12a, 77b, 83b. On *Shekhinah* and the color blue, see the next note; *Zohar* 2:139a, 152a–b.

1345. **the mystery of the thread of blue** The blue thread woven into the tassels of one's garment, according to Numbers 15:38. See *Sifrei*, Numbers 115: "Rabbi Me'ir says,

'… Whoever fulfills the *mitsvah* of *tsitsit* (the "tassel") is considered to have greeted the face of *Shekhinah*, as it were; for blue resembles the sea, and the sea resembles the sky, and the sky resembles the Throne of Glory.'"

1346. **another substance below…** The flame of the candle (or lamp) feeds on the wick and wax (or oil). Similarly, *Shekhinah* feeds on the realms beneath Her and is thereby enabled to flame and unite with *Tif'eret*.

1347. **Sometimes this blue-black turns red** When *Shekhinah* is influenced by *Gevurah*, the attribute of strict judgment, She is tinged with its color: red.

1348. **destruction and death of all** *Shekhinah* is identified with the Tree of Knowledge of Good and Evil, which—according to *Seder Eliyyahu Rabbah* 5—is called the Tree of Death, because when Adam and Eve ate its fruit, death ensued. See Genesis 2:17; *Zohar* 1:35b.

consuming anything found below. That is why he said *your God*, not *our God*, for Moses inhabited that white light above, which does not consume or devour.[1349]

"Come and see: The only arousal kindling this blue light, to be grasped by the white light, is Israel cleaving below.[1350]

"Come and see: Although by nature this blue-black light consumes anything cleaving below, Israel cleaves below and abides enduringly, as is written: *You, cleaving to YHVH your God, are alive. To YHVH your God*, not *our God; to YHVH your God*, to that blue-black light devouring, consuming whatever cleaves below—yet you cleave and endure, as is written: *alive every one of you today.*

"Above the white light hovers a concealed light, encompassing it.[1351] Here abides supernal mystery. You will discover all in the ascending flame, wisdoms of the highest."[1352]

284

Rabbi Pinḥas approached and kissed him, saying, "Blessed be the Compassionate One, that we happened to meet here."

They escorted Rabbi Pinḥas for three miles.[1353] When Rabbi Shim'on and the Companions returned, he said, "What we have discussed is a mystery of wisdom concerning holy unification, for the final ה (*he*) of the holy name is blue-black light, grasped by יה"ו (*yod, he, vav*), radiant white light.[1354]

1349. *your God*, not *our God*... Moses specified *your God*, indicating the *sefirah* pertaining to Israel, namely, *Shekhinah*, who devours and consumes. Moses, himself, attained the rung of *Tif'eret*, the white light, who does not consume.

See *Zohar* 2:79b; Moses de León, *Sefer ha-Mishqal*, 67.

1350. **Israel cleaving below** Their devotion fuels the passion of the divine couple.

1351. **Above the white light hovers a concealed light...** The encompassing light of *Binah*, the Divine Mother.

1352. **You will discover all in the ascending flame...** See the remark of the nineteenth-century physicist Michael Faraday at the beginning of his *Chemical History of a Candle*: "There is not a law under which any part of this universe is governed which does not come into play and is touched upon in these phenomena. There is no better, there is no more open door by which you can

enter into the study of natural philosophy, than by considering the physical phenomena of a candle."

1353. **for three miles** According to Rav Sheshet (BT *Sotah* 46b), one should escort his teacher a distance of a parasang. A distinguished teacher, however, is to be escorted for three parasangs. (The Greek parasang equals about 3.5 miles.)

See *Pesiqta de-Rav Kahana* 18:5; *Bereshit Rabbah* 32:10; *Zohar* 1:87a, 96b, 150b; 2:14a, 164a, 187a; 3:8b.

1354. **the final ה (*he*) of the holy name...** The name יהוה (*YHVH*) represents the entirety of the *sefirot*: י (*yod*) symbolizing the primordial point of *Ḥokhmah*; the feminine marker ה (*he*) symbolizing *Binah*, the Divine Mother; ו (*vav*), whose numerical value is six, symbolizing *Tif'eret* and the five *sefirot* surrounding Him (from *Ḥesed* to *Yesod*); and the final ה (*he*) symbolizing *Shekhinah*. Here Rabbi Shim'on focuses on the final ה (*he*),

"Come and see: Sometimes this blue light is ד (dalet), sometimes ה (he). When Israel does not cleave below, kindling it to be grasped by the white light, it is ד (dalet). When they arouse it to join the white light, it is called ה (he).[1355] How do we know? For it is written: *If there is* נערה (na'arah), *a girl, a virgin* (Deuteronomy 22:23), spelled נער (na'ara), without a ה (he). Why? Because She has not joined a male, and wherever male and female are not found, ה (he) is not found but rather ascends, leaving ד (dalet).[1356] Whenever She is joined to the radiant white light, She is called ה (he), for all is as one: She cleaves to the white light, and Israel cleaves to Her, enduring beneath Her to kindle Her. Then all is one.

"This is the mystery of sacrifice. For the smoke ascending arouses this blue light to kindle, and when it kindles, it joins [51b] the white light, and the candle burns in oneness.[1357] Since this blue light by nature consumes and devours anything cleaving below, when favor prevails and the candle burns indivisibly, then this verse applies: *Fire descended from heaven and consumed the offering...* (1 Kings 18:38).[1358] Then it is known that the candle burns in a single union, a single bond: blue light cleaving to white light, and it is one. Below, it consumes fat and flesh of the offerings, though only when it ascends, joined to the white light. Then peace pervades all worlds, all linked inseparably.

"Once the blue light has finished consuming below, priests, Levites, and Israel cleave to it below, whether in joy of song, in heart's desire, or in prayer,[1359] while above them glows the candle, lights merging as one, worlds glimmering, above and below in bliss. Then, ואתם (Ve-attem), *And you, cleaving to YHVH your God, are alive every one of you today.* ואתם (Ve-attem), *And you—*

---

symbolizing the blue-black light of *Shekhinah,* and the first three letters, combining in the white light of *Tif'eret.*

1355. **Sometimes this blue light is ד (dalet), sometimes ה (he)...** When *Shekhinah* is not aroused by the devotion of Israel below, She cannot join the white light of *Tif'eret* and is symbolized by the letter ד (dalet), signifying that She is דלה (dallah), "poor," lacking the rich flow of emanation from above. When the human arousal from below stimulates Her union with *Tif'eret,* the ד (dalet) is enhanced by the straight line of the letter ו (vav), whose numerical value of six symbolizes *Tif'eret* and the five *sefirot* surrounding Him. Thereby the ד (dalet) is transformed into ה (he).

See *Zohar* 1:60a; 2:104a, 123b, 188b (*SdTs*).

1356. **spelled נער (na'ara), without a ה (he)...** The lack of the final letter indicates the incomplete status of *Shekhinah.*

See BT *Ketubbot* 40b; *Zohar* 2:38b; Moses de León, *Sefer ha-Rimmon,* 115.

1357. **the candle...** שרגא (Sheraga), "Lamp." See above, note 1343.

1358. *Fire descended from heaven...* The verse reads: *The fire of YHVH descended and consumed the offering,* which is adopted by Cr. The ritual offering stimulates the union of the divine couple, symbolized by the blue and white lights. Their passionate embrace ignites the fire that consumes the sacrifice.

1359. **priests, Levites, and Israel cleave to it...** The ritual devotion of the priests is accompanied by the singing of the Le-

285

the verse should read: אתם (*attem*), *you*. But ו (*vav*), *and*, surpasses the fat and flesh of the offerings: while they, cleaving to it, are devoured and consumed, you cleave to that blue-black devouring light and endure, as is written: *alive every one of you today*.[1360]

"'In a dream all colors bode well, except blue,'[1361] for it devours and consumes continuously. It is a tree of death spreading over the lower world, and since all abides beneath, it consumes and devours.[1362]

"Now you might say, 'It also prevails in heaven above, yet countless powers above endure.'[1363] Come and see: All those above are encompassed by the blue light,[1364] but those below, not so, for they constitute coarse substance upon which it alights, so it devours and consumes them. Nothing in the world escapes destruction, for the blue light consumes whatever it bestrides."

The universe diffracts into forty-five hues of colored light.[1365] Seven disperse into seven abysses, each one striking its own abyss, stones gyrating.[1366] The light penetrates those stones, piercing them, and water issues from them, each one sinking within an abyss, covering both sides.[1367] Water flows through those

286

vites and the prayers of Israel. See *Zohar* 2:238b.

1360. **But ו (*vav*), *and*, surpasses...** The apparently superfluous conjunction here connotes *but*. As opposed to the sacrifice, which is consumed by the fire of *Shekhinah*, *you* (Israel) endure.

1361. **In a dream all colors bode well, except blue** See BT *Berakhot* 57b: "In a dream all kinds of color bode well, except blue." Cf. *Zohar* 2:135a, 152a.

1362. **It is a tree of death...** *Shekhinah* is identified with the Tree of Knowledge of Good and Evil, which according to *Seder Eliyyahu Rabbah* 5 is called the Tree of Death, because when Adam and Eve ate its fruit, death ensued. See Genesis 2:17; above, page 283. *Shekhinah* governs this world, and everything is eventually consumed by Her.

1363. **countless powers above endure** The heavenly hosts and angels are not consumed by *Shekhinah*. According to another tradition, certain angels are consumed daily by *Shekhinah*. See BT *Ḥagigah* 14a: "Shemu'el said to Rabbi Ḥiyya son of Rav, 'O son of a lion! Come, I will tell you one of those fine words said by your father: Every single day ministering angels are created from the fiery

stream, chant a song, then cease to be, as is said: *New every morning, immense is Your faithfulness!* (Lamentations 3:23).'"

See *Zohar* 1:17b, 18b; 2:213b–214a, 247a; Ezra of Gerona, *Peirush Shir ha-Shirim*, 507, 510; Moses de León, *Sefer ha-Mishqal*, 65; idem, *Sefer ha-Rimmon*, 205; Tishby, *Wisdom of the Zohar*, 2:624–25.

1364. **encompassed by the blue light** The heavenly powers are included within *Shekhinah*, thereby escaping destruction.

1365. **The universe diffracts...** In the following cryptic passage (which reappears in *Zohar* 2:228b–229a), I have chosen not to impose any sefirotic interpretation, but rather to let the reader encounter the imagery in its raw, pristine form. The number forty-five may allude to the *gimatriyya* of the divine name יהוה (*YHVH*), spelled out according to its letters: יוד (*yod*), הא (*he*), ואו (*vav*), הא (*he*), which is equal to the *gimatriyya* of אדם (*adam*). See *Zohar* 1:34b.

1366. **seven abysses...** The seven abysses are mentioned in *Seder Rabbah di-Vreshit*, 9 (*Battei Midrashot*, 1:24–25).

1367. **water issues from them...** On the connection between abyss, stones, and water, see BT *Ḥagigah* 12a: "תהו ובהו (*Tohu*

holes, light penetrates, striking all four sides of the abyss. Each light whirls around its partner, converging as one, splitting the water. All seven seize seven abysses, delving their darkness, which mingles with them.[1368] Waters rise and fall, swirling amidst those lights. Light, darkness, and water blend as one, yielding darkened, invisible lights. Each strikes its partner, splaying into seventy-five abyssal channels, water streaming through. Every channel roars, abysses quake. As the roar sounds, each abyss calls to its partner: "Split your waters and I will enter you," as is written: *Abyss calls to abyss in the roar of Your channels* (Psalms 42:8).[1369]

Beneath these lie 365 sinews, some white, some black, some red, intertwining, turning into one color.[1370] These sinews interweave into seventeen webs, each one called a sinew web.[1371] Interwoven, they sink to the depths of the abysses. Beneath these abide two webs like iron and two others like copper. Upon them stand two thrones, one on the right and one on the left. All those webs join as one, and water pours down from the channels through the webs. Those two thrones—one is the throne of black expanse; the other, the throne of multicolored expanse. When they rise, they rise through the throne of black expanse; when they fall, they fall through the throne of multicolored expanse.[1372] These two thrones appear on the right and the left—of black expanse on the right, of multicolored expanse on the left. [52a] When they rise through the throne of black expanse, the throne of the expanse on the left sinks and through it they fall. Spinning around one another, the thrones catch

287

va-vohu), *Chaos and void* (Genesis 1:2) . . . *Void*—the slimy stones sunk in the abyss, from which water issues, as is said: *He will stretch over it a line of chaos and plummet-stones of void* (Isaiah 34:11)."

1368. **All seven . . .** All seven lights.

1369. **each abyss calls to its partner . . .** See BT *Ta'anit* 25b: "Rabbi Eli'ezer said, 'When water libations are poured [on the Temple altar] on *Sukkot* [Festival of "Booths"], one abyss calls to its partner, "Let your waters gush, I hear the voice of two friends [the two vessels used for libation]," as is said: *Abyss calls to abyss in the roar of Your channels.*'"

See *Bereshit Rabbah* 13:13: "Rabbi Shim'on son of El'azar said, 'Every single handbreadth [of water] descending from above is met by two handbreadths emitted by the earth. What is the reason? *Abyss calls to abyss. . . .*' Rabbi Levi said, 'The upper waters are male;

the lower, female. The former cry to the latter, "Receive us! You are creatures of the blessed Holy One and we are His messengers." They immediately receive them, as is written: *Let the earth open* (Isaiah 45:8)—like a female opening to a male.'"

See *Tosefta, Ta'anit* 1:4; 1 *Enoch* 54:8; *Seder Rabbah di-Vreshit* 10 (*Battei Midrashot* 1:25); *Pirqei de-Rabbi Eli'ezer* 23; *Zohar* 1:17b, 29b, 46a, 60b, 244a–b, 245b; 3:223b.

1370. **365 sinews . . .** Corresponding to the number of sinews in the human body, according to rabbinic tradition. See *Targum Yerushalmi*, Genesis 1:27; *Zohar* 1:170b. Cf. BT *Makkot* 23b. The human body is a microcosm.

1371. **seventeen webs . . .** The *gimatriyya* of the word גיד (*gid*), "sinew," is seventeen.

1372. **When they rise . . .** When the waters rise.

all those webs, drawing them into the depths of the lowest abyss. One throne ascends above all the abysses, the other lies below, while in between all channels are inserted, all abysses swirl.

There are seventy-five channels: seven, highest of all; all the others connected to them. All are implanted in the wheels of the throne on this side and in the wheels of the throne on that. Through them waters rise and fall. Falling, they delve the abysses, splitting them. Rising, they penetrate the holes in the stones, filling seven seas. Till here, seven colors of light in supernal mystery.

Seven other lights disperse into seven seas, one sea encompassing them.[1373] That one sea is supernal, all seas merging within. These seven lights enter that sea, striking it on seven sides, each side splitting into seven torrents, as is written: *He will smite it into seven torrents . . .* (Isaiah 11:15). Each torrent splits into seven rivers, each river into seven channels, each channel into seven conduits, and all the waters of the sea entirely flow through.[1374]

Seven lights ascend and descend on seven sides. Seven supernal lights enter the sea—six radiating from one supreme.[1375] As the sea receives, so it disperses its waters to all those seas, all those rivers.

One monster below, on the left side, swims through all those rivers.[1376] He approaches the side, all his scales iron-hard, stretches to suck, and defiles the site. All lights darken before him. His mouth and tongue flame with fire, his tongue sharp as a steely sword, till he penetrates the sanctuary within the sea.[1377] Then the sanctuary is desecrated, lights extinguished, supernal lights ascend from the sea.[1378] The waters of the sea split on the left side, and the sea congeals, its waters flowing no more.[1379]

So the mystery of the word is as written: *Now the serpent was slier than any creature of the field that YHVH Elohim had made* (Genesis 3:1)—mystery of the evil serpent descending from above, skimming the surface of bitter waters, seducing below till they fall into his nets.[1380] This serpent is death of the world,[1381]

288

1373. **Seven other lights . . .** Apparently the seven *sefirot* from *Binah* through *Yesod*, which flow into the sea of *Shekhinah*.

1374. **all the waters of the sea . . .** The emanation gathered in the sea of *Shekhinah* flows through a multitude of channels to the worlds below.

1375. **six radiating from one supreme** The six *sefirot* from *Ḥesed* through *Yesod* radiate from the Divine Mother, *Binah*.

1376. **One monster below . . .** The chief demonic power, who approaches *Shekhinah* from his domain below on the left side. See *Zohar* 2:27b, 34a–35b.

1377. **the sanctuary within the sea** The sacred space of *Shekhinah*.

1378. **supernal lights ascend from the sea** The lower *sefirot* abandon *Shekhinah*.

1379. **The waters of the sea split on the left side . . .** Abandoned by the other *sefirot*, *Shekhinah* provides sustenance to the demonic serpent and then congeals. See *Zohar* 1:32b.

1380. **till they fall into his nets** Until human beings fall into his trap.

1381. **This serpent is death of the world** The demonic power and the Angel of Death are both manifestations of *Sitra Aḥra*, "the Other Side." See BT *Bava Batra* 16a:

penetrating a person's blind gut.[1382] He is on the left, while another, of life, is on the right, both accompanying each human, as they have established.[1383]

Than any creature of the field. For no other creature of the field is as cunning in perpetrating evil, for he is dross of gold.[1384] Woe to one drawn toward him, for he inflicts death upon him and upon all those following him! This they have established.[1385]

Adam was drawn down toward him, descending to know everything below.[1386] As he descended, his will and ways were drawn toward them,[1387] until they reached that serpent, discovering worldly desire, straying at that site.[1388] Then he rose,[1389] drawn toward Adam and his wife, clung to them, inflicted death upon them and upon all subsequent generations. Until Israel arrived at Mount Sinai, his slime never ceased infecting the world, as has been explained.[1390]

Once they sinned, clinging to the tree where death abides,[1391] what is written? *They heard the voice of YHVH Elohim moving about in the garden*

289

"Resh Lakish said, 'Satan, the evil impulse, and the Angel of Death are one and the same.'"

See *Zohar* 1:35b, 202a; 2:262b–263a; Moses de León, *Sefer ha-Rimmon*, 394–95.

1382. **blind gut** מעוי דסתים (*Me'oi distim*), "His hidden intestine," the cecum, beginning of the large intestine; corresponding to the Latin *intestinum caecum*, "blind gut," so called because it is prolonged behind the opening of the ilium into a cul-de-sac.

See *Avot de-Rabbi Natan* A, 16: "…the evil impulse in his intestines." Cf. *Zohar* 1:190b.

1383. **while another, of life, is on the right…** The demonic serpent (corresponding to the evil impulse) is balanced by the holy serpent (corresponding to the good impulse). See *TZ* 21 (43a).

According to rabbinic tradition, two angels—one good and one bad—accompany each person. See BT *Shabbat* 119b; cf. *Ta'anit* 11a; *Zohar* 1:12b, 14a, 144b, 165b; 2:106b, 239a.

1384. **dross of gold** The demonic derives from the dregs of *Gevurah* or *Din* (strict Judgment), located on the left side of the sefirotic tree and symbolized by gold.

See *Zohar* 1:48a, 73a, 193a; 2:236b.

1385. **he inflicts death upon him…** The serpent inflicts death upon anyone drawn toward him. See *Zohar* 1:35b.

1386. **descending to know everything below** Adam explored the demonic realm.

1387. **drawn toward them** Toward the demonic powers.

1388. **until they reached…** Until Adam and Eve reached.

1389. **Then he rose** The serpent rose, aroused by Adam.

1390. **Until Israel arrived at Mount Sinai…** See BT *Shabbat* 145b–146a: "Rav Yosef taught: '…When the serpent copulated with Eve, he injected her with זוהמא (*zohama*), filth [or: slime, lewdness]. Israel, who stood at Mount Sinai—their *zohama* ceased. Star-worshipers, who did not stand at Mount Sinai—their *zohama* did not cease.'"

See *Targum Yerushalmi*, Genesis 4:1 (variants); *Pirqei de-Rabbi Eli'ezer* 21; *Zohar* 1:36b–37a, 52a, 54a, 122b; Stroumsa, *Another Seed*, 38–53.

1391. **Once they sinned, clinging to the tree where death abides** Adam and Eve sinned by eating from the Tree of Knowledge of Good and Evil. According to *Seder Eliyyahu Rabbah* 5, this tree is called the Tree of Death, because as a result of their sin, death ensued. In Kabbalah the tree is identified with *Shekhinah,* and the sin consists in separating Her from the other *sefirot,*

(ibid. 3:8). The verse does not read: מהלך (*mehallekh*), *moving,* but rather: מתהלך (*mithallekh*), *moving about.*[1392]

Come and see: Until Adam sinned, he ascended and abode in supernal, radiant wisdom, never parting from the Tree of Life.[1393] Once he indulged in desire to descend and know below, he was drawn toward them until he parted from the Tree of Life, knowing evil, abandoning good.[1394] So it is written: *You are not a God who delights in wickedness; evil cannot abide with You* (Psalms 5:5). [52b] Whoever is drawn toward evil cannot abide with the Tree of Life. Until they sinned, they used to hear a voice from above, perceive supernal wisdom, endure supernal radiance fearlessly. Once they sinned, even a voice below they could neither understand nor withstand.[1395]

Similarly, when Israel stood at Mount Sinai, before sinning, the slime of this serpent was eliminated from them, for the evil impulse was repulsed by them, universally abolished.[1396] So they grafted to the Tree of Life, ascending, not descending; knowing, seeing supernal specula;[1397] eyes glistening, delighting in discovery, in listening. Then the blessed Holy One girded them with belts of

290

thereby cutting off the vivifying flow of emanation.

See Genesis 2:17; *Zohar* 1:12b, 35b–36a, 51a–b, 53b, 221a–b; Scholem, *Major Trends,* 231–32, 236, 404–5, n. 105; Tishby, *Wisdom of the Zohar,* 1:373–76.

1392. **but rather:** מתהלך (***mithallekh***), *moving about* This form of the verb includes the additional letter ת (*tav*), often a feminine marker, which in the *Zohar* implies the divine feminine, *Shekhinah,* identified with the Tree of Death. With the added letter, the word now begins: מת (*met*), "dead."

See *Bereshit Rabbah* 19:7: "Rabbi Abba son of Kahana said, 'The verse does not read: מהלך (*mehallekh*), *moving,* but rather: מתהלך (*mithallekh*), *moving about, leaping up.* The essence of *Shekhinah* was in the lower realms. As soon as Adam sinned, it withdrew to the first heaven.'"

See Naḥmanides on Genesis 3:8; Gikatilla, *Sha'arei Orah,* 15–17; *Zohar* 1:76a; *ZḤ* 18d (*MhN*).

1393. **the Tree of Life** Symbolizing *Tif'eret,* trunk of the sefirotic tree.

1394. **he was drawn toward them...** Toward the demonic powers. Splitting the

Tree of Knowledge of Good and Evil, Adam abandoned good and clung to evil.

1395. **Until they sinned...** See *Shir ha-Shirim Rabbah* on 3:8: "It was taught: Until a person sins, he inspires awe and fear; creatures are terrified of him. Once he has sinned, he himself is filled with awe and fear; he is terrified of others. The proof of this was offered by Rabbi [Yehudah the Prince], who said, 'Until Adam sinned, he could listen to the divine voice while standing upright, fearlessly. Once he sinned, when he heard the divine voice he was frightened and hid himself, as is said: *I heard Your voice...* [*and I was afraid*] (Genesis 3:10); *The man* [*and his wife*] *hid* (ibid., 8).'" Cf. *Pesiqta de-Rav Kahana* 5:3; *Zohar* 1:36b

Here the "voice from above" alludes to *Tif'eret,* who is known as Voice, while the "voice below" apparently refers to *Shekhinah,* subject of the verb מתהלך (*mithallekh*), *moving about.* See above, note 1392.

1396. **the slime of this serpent was eliminated from them...** See above, note 1390.

1397. **specula** אספקלריאן (*Ispaqlaryan*), "Specula [or: glasses, mirrors, lenses]." Here the word implies *sefirot.*

letters of the holy name, so the serpent could not dominate or defile them as before. Once they sinned, all those supernal lights and rungs were removed from them, along with the belts bristling with crowns of the supreme name. Attracting the evil serpent as before, they inflicted death upon the whole world.[1398]

What is written next? *The Children of Israel saw the face of Moses, and behold, the skin of his face was radiant! They were afraid to come near him* (Exodus 34:30).[1399] Come and see what is written previously: *Israel saw the great hand* (ibid. 14:31).[1400] All were seeing supernal radiancies, being enlightened by the resplendent speculum, as is written: *All the people were seeing the voices* (ibid. 20:15).[1401] By the sea they were gazing fearlessly, as is written: *This is my God and I will adorn Him* (ibid. 15:2).[1402] After they sinned, what is written? *They were afraid to come near him.*[1403]

Come and see what is written of them: *The Children of Israel were stripped of their ornaments from Mount Horeb on* (ibid. 33:6), for they were divested of the weapons girded on them at Mount Sinai, preventing the evil serpent from

291

1398. **the blessed Holy One girded them with belts of letters...** See *Tanḥuma* (Buber), *Shelaḥ*, add. 1: "Rabbi Shim'on son of Yoḥai said, 'He adorned them with weapons engraved with the Ineffable Name [*YHVH*], and as long as they possessed these, no evil could touch them, neither the Angel of Death nor anything else. As soon as they sinned [with the Golden Calf], Moses said to them: *Now take off your ornaments, and I will decide what to do to you* (Exodus 33:5). At that moment, *When the people heard this evil word, they mourned,* [*and no one put on his ornaments*] (ibid., 4). What is written? *The Children of Israel were stripped of their ornaments....*'"

See *Targum Onqelos* and *Targum Yerushalmi*, Exodus 33:4, 6; *Targum Shir ha-Shirim* 2:17; *Eikhah Rabbah, Petiḥta* 24; *Shir ha-Shirim Rabbah* on 1:4; *Pirqei de-Rabbi Eli'ezer* 47; BT *Shabbat* 88a; *Avodah Zarah* 5a; Naḥmanides on Exodus 33:6; *Zohar* 1:63b, 126b; Green, *Keter*, 70–71.

1399. *The Children of Israel saw the face of Moses* The verse actually reads: *Aaron and all the Children of Israel saw Moses...,* which is adopted in later printed editions of the *Zohar*.

1400. *Israel saw the great hand* The verse continues: *that YHVH had wielded against Egypt* (at the Red Sea).

1401. **the resplendent speculum...** אספקלריא דנהרא (*Ispaqlarya de-nahara*), "Glass [or: mirror, speculum] that shines," symbolizing *Tif'eret*, who is also known as Voice. See BT *Yevamot* 49b: "All the prophets gazed through a dim glass [literally: an *ispaqlarya* that does not shine], whereas Moses our Rabbi gazed through a clear glass [literally: an *ispaqlarya* that shines]." Cf. 1 Corinthians 13:12: "For now we see through a glass darkly, but then face-to-face."

1402. **By the sea they were gazing fearlessly...** See *Mekhilta, Shirta* 3: "*This is my God and I will adorn Him.* Rabbi Eli'ezer says, '...A maidservant by the [Red] Sea saw that which Ezekiel and all the other prophets did not see.'"

1403. **After they sinned, what is written?...** See *Pesiqta de-Rav Kahana* 5:3: "Rabbi Abba son of Kahana said, '[At Mount Sinai] seven realms of fire were devouring one another, yet Israel gazed fearlessly. Once they sinned, they could not even look at the face of the intermediary, as is written: *Aaron and all the Children of Israel saw Moses* [*and*

dominating them. Once they were deprived of these, what is written? *Moses took the Tent and pitched it outside the camp, far from the camp* (ibid. 33:7).

Rabbi El'azar said, "What is this verse doing next to that?[1404] Since Moses knew that those supernal weapons had been removed, he thought, 'Certainly from now on, the evil serpent will come dwell among them. If the sanctuary remains standing here among them, it will be defiled.[1405] Immediately, *Moses took the Tent and pitched it outside the camp, far from the camp,* for he saw that, unlike before, the evil serpent was poised to prevail."

He called it Tent of Meeting (ibid.). Was it not so previously? At first, it was simply *Tent;* now, *Tent of Meeting.* Why מועד (mo'ed), *meeting*? Rabbi El'azar explained it positively; Rabbi Abba, negatively.

Rabbi El'azar explained positively, "Just as מועד (mo'ed), festival, is a day of joy for the moon, when her holiness waxes and she is free of defect,[1406] so now he called Her by this name, showing She had been removed far from them and not been tainted.[1407] So it is written: *He called it Tent of Mo'ed, Festival.*"

Rabbi Abba explained negatively, "At first, it was simply *Tent,* as is said: *a tent not to be moved, whose pegs will never be pulled up* (Isaiah 33:20). Now, *Tent of Mo'ed, Slated Time.*[1408] At first, extending long life eternally, so death would not prevail.[1409] From now on, *Tent of Mo'ed,* as is said: *the house mo'ed, slated, for all living* (Job 30:23).[1410] Now time is allotted, life rationed to the world. At

behold, the skin of his face was radiant! They were afraid to come near him].'"

See Deuteronomy 5:5; *Shir ha-Shirim Rabbah* on 3:8.

1404. **What is this verse doing next to that?** What is the connection between Israel being *stripped of their ornaments* and Moses pitching the tent *outside the camp*? See *Shemot Rabbah* 45:3; BT *Shabbat* 88a; *Zohar* 2:236a; 3:114a.

1405. **it will be defiled** *Shekhinah,* symbolized by the sanctuary in the tent, will be defiled by the serpent.

1406. **Just as מועד (mo'ed), festival, is a day of joy for the moon...** One of the meanings of the word מועד (mo'ed) is "festival," and many festivals begin on the full moon.

1407. **he called Her by this name...** Moses called *Shekhinah* Tent of מועד (Mo'ed), indicating that She was full and free of any defect.

1408. **Mo'ed, Slated Time** The word מועד

(mo'ed) can also mean "appointed time."

1409. **At first, extending long life eternally...** At Sinai, the serpent's slime was eliminated from Israel, so they could have lived forever, nourished by the vivifying flow from *Shekhinah.* Unfortunately, they committed the sin of the Golden Calf and forfeited the gift of immortality.

See *Tanḥuma, Ki Tissa* 16; and *Shir ha-Shirim Rabbah* on 8:6: "חרות (Ḥarut), *Engraved, on the tablets* (Exodus 32:16) [describing the divine writing on the tablets of stone, spelling out the Ten Commandments]. Do not read: חרות (ḥarut), *engraved,* but rather: חירות (ḥeirut), *freedom.* Rabbi Yehudah, Rabbi Neḥemiah, and the Rabbis: Rabbi Yehudah says, 'Freedom from the Angel of Death.' Rabbi Neḥemiah says, 'Freedom from foreign rulers.' The Rabbis say, 'Freedom from suffering.'" Cf. *Zohar* 1:37b.

1410. **the house mo'ed, slated, for all living** The verse begins: *I know You will bring me to death...*

first, untainted; now tainted. At first, joining and coupling of the moon with the sun unceasingly.[1411] Now, *Tent of Mo'ed, Slated Time,* coupling from time to time. So unlike before, *He called it Tent of Mo'ed.*"

One night Rabbi Shim'on was sitting, plying Torah. Sitting in front of him were Rabbi Yehudah, Rabbi Yitsḥak, and Rabbi Yose.

Rabbi Yehudah said, "Look at what is written: *The Children of Israel were stripped of their ornaments from Mount Horeb on* (Exodus 33:6)! We assert that from that moment on they inflicted death upon themselves; that evil serpent they had just thrown off now dominated them.[1412] This may be true of the Israelites, but what of Joshua, who did not sin?[1413] Was he, too, divested of that supernal weapon he received with them at Mount Sinai or not? [53a] If you say not, then why did he die like all other human beings? If you say he was, why, seeing that he had not sinned, for he was with Moses when Israel was sinning? And if you say he did not receive the same crown received by Israel at Mount Sinai, why not?"

He opened, saying,[1414] "*For YHVH is righteous, loving righteousness; the upright shall behold His face* (Psalms 11:7). The Companions have discussed this verse,[1415] but: *For YHVH is righteous*—He is righteous and His name is Righ-

293

1411. **joining and coupling of the moon with the sun...** The union of *Shekhinah* and Her partner, *Tif'eret.*

1412. **from that moment on they inflicted death upon themselves...** See *Tanḥuma* (Buber), *Shelaḥ,* add. 1: "Rabbi Shim'on son of Yoḥai said, 'He adorned them with weapons engraved with the Ineffable Name [YHVH], and as long as they possessed these, no evil could touch them, neither the Angel of Death nor anything else. As soon as they sinned [with the Golden Calf], Moses said to them: *Now take off your ornaments, and I will decide what to do to you* (Exodus 33:5). At that moment, *When the people heard this evil word, they mourned,* [*and no one put on his ornaments*] (ibid., 4). What is written? *The Children of Israel were stripped of their ornaments....*'"

See above, note 1398.

1413. **what of Joshua, who did not sin?** Joshua was outside of the camp during the sin of the Golden Calf, waiting for Moses to

descend from Mount Sinai. See Exodus 24:13; 32:17.

1414. **He opened...** The subject could be Rabbi Yehudah, answering his own questions, though the parallel passage in *Zohar* 2:194a reads: "Rabbi Shim'on opened," which accords with the style of the *Zohar* and with the interpretation of *MmD* and Soncino. See 3:15a.

1415. **The Companions have discussed this verse** See *Bereshit Rabbah* 32:2: "*For YHVH is righteous, loving righteousness; the upright shall behold His face.* Rabbi Tanḥuma said in the name of Rabbi Yehudah, and Rabbi Menaḥem said in the name of Rabbi El'azar, 'No one loves his fellow artisan. A sage, however, loves his fellow artisan; for example, Rabbi Ḥiyya loves his colleagues, and Rabbi Hosha'ya his. The blessed Holy One loves His fellow artisan: *For YHVH is righteous, loving righteousness....*'"

See *Midrash Tehillim* 11:6; *Zohar* 1:241b; 3:15a.

teous, so: *loving righteousness.*[1416] *Upright*—He is *upright,* as is said: *Righteous and upright is He* (Deuteronomy 32:4). So all inhabitants of the world *shall behold His face,* mending their ways to follow the straight path fittingly.[1417]

"Come and see: When the blessed Holy One judges the world, He does so according to the majority of human beings.[1418]

"Come and see: When Adam sinned by eating from the tree, he transmogrified that tree into a universal source of death; he caused a defect, separating the Woman from Her Husband.[1419] The fault of this defect stood out in the moon, until Israel stood at Mount Sinai, when that defect disappeared from the moon, enabling Her to constantly shine.[1420] Once Israel sinned with the calf, She relapsed into defectiveness; the evil serpent prevailed and seized Her, dragging Her to him.[1421] When Moses discovered that Israel had sinned and been divested of their supernal, sacred weapons, he knew for sure that the serpent had seized the moon to drag Her to him, that She had been tainted. So he

294

1416. He is righteous... *loving righteousness* The *sefirah* of *Yesod* ("Foundation") is called Righteous, based on Proverbs 10:25: וצדיק יסוד עולם (*Ve-tsaddiq yesod olam*). The verse literally means *The righteous one is an everlasting foundation* but is understood as *The righteous one is the foundation of the world.* See BT *Ḥagigah* 12b; *Bahir* 71 (102); Azriel of Gerona, *Peirush ha-Aggadot,* 34.

The phrase *loving* צדקות (*tsedaqot*), *righteousness,* may allude to *Shekhinah,* known as צדק (*Tsedeq*), "Righteousness," or (reflecting the plural form *tsedaqot*) to both *Shekhinah* and *Binah.*

1417. Upright—He is upright... The word *upright* refers primarily to God, not to human beings. Humans who succeed in imitating God *shall behold His face.* See *Shir ha-Shirim Zuta* 1:13.

1418. according to the majority of human beings See BT *Qiddushin* 40b: "Rabbi El'azar son of Rabbi Shim'on said, '...The world is judged by its majority, and similarly an individual is judged by his majority [of deeds, good or bad].'" So although Joshua did not sin in the incident of the Golden Calf, he was still punished along with the majority.

1419. he transmogrified that tree... Adam sinned by separating *Shekhinah* from

the other *sefirot*—in particular, from Her partner, *Tif'eret.* Divorced from the vivifying flow of emanation, *Shekhinah* was transformed from the Tree of Knowledge of Good and Evil into the Tree of Death. See Genesis 2:17. According to *Seder Eliyyahu Rabbah* 5, the Tree of Knowledge is called the Tree of Death, because as a result of Adam and Eve's sin, death ensued.

See *Zohar* 1:12b, 35b–36a, 51a–b, 52a, 53b, 221a–b; Scholem, *Major Trends,* 231–32, 236, 404–5, n. 105; Tishby, *Wisdom of the Zohar,* 1:373–76.

1420. The fault of this defect stood out in the moon... The moon symbolizes *Shekhinah,* who waxes and wanes according to the conduct of Israel.

See BT *Shabbat* 145b–146a: "Rav Yosef taught: '...When the serpent copulated with Eve, he injected her with זוהמא (*zohama*), filth [or: slime, lewdness]. Israel, who stood at Mount Sinai—their *zohama* ceased. Star-worshipers, who did not stand at Mount Sinai—their *zohama* did not cease.'"

See *Targum Yerushalmi,* Genesis 4:1 (variants); *Pirqei de-Rabbi Eli'ezer* 21; *Zohar* 1:36b–37a, 52a–b, 54a, 122b; Stroumsa, *Another Seed,* 38–53.

1421. the evil serpent prevailed and seized Her... The demonic, empowered

brought Her outside.[1422] Even though Joshua maintained his armored crown, since She was susceptible to turning defective and defect abode in Her and She slipped back into the defectiveness caused by Adam's sin, no human being can perdure except for Moses, who controlled Her and whose death ensued from another aspect.[1423] So She was not empowered to sustain Joshua forever, nor anyone else. Therefore he called Her *Tent of* מועד (*Mo'ed*), *Slated Time* (Exodus 33:7), a tent housing allotted time for the entire world.[1424]

"So the mystery of the word: There is right above, there is right below. There is left above, there is left below.[1425] Right above in supernal sanctity; right below on the other side. Left above in supernal sanctity, arousing love, linking the moon with a sacred site to shine.[1426] Left below, blocking love from above, preventing Her from reflecting the sun and drawing near. This is the side of the evil serpent, for when this lower left arouses, it pulls the moon, separating Her from above, so Her light darkens and She cleaves to the serpent. Then She draws death for all, distancing Herself from the Tree of Life,[1427] inflicting death upon the whole world. Consequently the sanctuary is defiled for a fixed time till the moon is restored and resumes shining; therefore, *Tent of* מועד (*Mo'ed*),

295

and emboldened by human sin, seized *Shekhinah*.

1422. **So he brought Her outside** Moses brought the Tent of Meeting, symbolizing *Shekhinah,* outside of the camp, so that it would not be tainted any further by Israel's impurity and the demonic power. See Exodus 33:7 (discussed above, page 292): *Moses took the Tent and pitched it outside the camp, far from the camp.*

1423. **Moses, who controlled Her and whose death ensued...** Moses attained the rung of *Tif'eret* and became the master, or husband, of *Shekhinah,* as indicated by his title איש האלהים (*Ish ha-Elohim*), *Man of Elohim* (Deuteronomy 33:1; Psalms 90:1).

See *Midrash Tehillim* 90:5; *Pesiqta de-Rav Kahana, nispaḥim, Vezot Haberakhah,* 443–44, 448 (variants); *Tanḥuma, Vezot Haberakhah* 2 (*Ets Yosef,* ad loc.); *Devarim Rabbah* (Lieberman), on 33:1; *Zohar* 1:6b, 21b, 148a, 236b; 239a; 2:22b.

Having mastered *Shekhinah,* Moses was invulnerable to Her. His death ensued from striking the rock to bring forth water (Numbers 20:11–12) and derived from a higher *sefirah:* the Divine Mother, *Binah* (*Zohar* 1:21b–22a).

According to rabbinic tradition, Moses, Aaron, and Miriam died by a kiss of God. See BT *Bava Batra* 17a; *Shir ha-Shirim Rabbah* on 1:2; *Tanḥuma, Va'etḥannan* 6.

1424. **Therefore he called Her *Tent of* מועד (*Mo'ed*), *Slated Time*...** See Exodus 33:7: *Moses took the Tent and pitched it outside the camp, far from the camp. He called it Tent of* מועד (*Mo'ed*), *Meeting* [understood here as *Slated Time*]. *Shekhinah* rations the lifetime of every human being. See above, page 292.

1425. **There is right above...below... There is left above...below** In the sefirotic realm, *Ḥesed* and *Gevurah* represent the right and left sides, respectively. In the demonic realm below, powers are also arrayed right and left.

1426. **arousing love, linking the moon with a sacred site...** *Gevurah* arouses *Shekhinah,* symbolized by the moon, and links Her with Her partner, *Tif'eret,* symbolized by the sun.

1427. **the Tree of Life** Symbolizing *Tif'eret.*

Slated Time.[1428] So Joshua died only through the incitement of the serpent, who approached and tainted the Dwelling as at first.[1429] This is the mystery written: *Joshua son of Nun, a lad*—although he was *a lad* below, absorbing light, *he would not depart from the Tent* (Exodus 33:11): as one was defective, so was the other.[1430] Even though he possessed the sacred weapon, since he was tainted he was certainly not singularly saved from that very stain.

"Come and see: Similarly, once Adam sinned, the blessed Holy One deprived him of those weapons of sacred sparkling letters with which he was arrayed. Then they were frightened, knowing they had been stripped of them, as is written: *They knew that they were naked* (Genesis 3:7).[1431] At first they were adorned with those precious studded crowns—absolute freedom.[1432] Once they sinned, they were stripped of them; then they knew that death was calling them, that they were stripped of absolute freedom, that they had inflicted death upon themselves and upon the whole world. [53b]

"*They sewed together fig leaves* (ibid.). We have already established that they discovered every kind of sorcery and magic, grasping the one below, as has

296

1428. **the sanctuary is defiled...** *Shekhinah,* symbolized by the sanctuary in Jerusalem and the Dwelling in the desert, is defiled by the demonic serpent. See above, page 292.

1429. **Joshua died only through the incitement of the serpent...** See BT *Shabbat* 55b: "Four died through the incitement of the serpent, namely: Benjamin the son of Jacob, Amram the father of Moses, Jesse the father of David, and Chileab the son of David." According to this view, these four individuals did not sin on their own but died only because of the sin of Adam and Eve, who were enticed by the serpent. Here the *Zohar* specifies Joshua, who did not participate in the sin of the Golden Calf. See *Zohar* 1:57b, where Levi is substituted for Chileab.

1430. **although he was *a lad* below...** Joshua's description, נער (na'ar), lad, suggests the chief angel, Metatron—known as the Lad who serves beneath *Shekhinah,* receiving Her light. Joshua displayed the qualities of Metatron, yet he also reflected the defective nature of *Shekhinah,* symbolized by *the Tent.*

See BT *Yevamot* 16b, and *Tosafot,* s.v. *pasuq zeh;* above, note 1045; *Zohar* 1:223b; 2:179a (*SdTs*), Scholem, *Kabbalah,* 378–79; Margaliot, *Mal'akhei Elyon,* 89–90.

1431. **the blessed Holy One deprived him of those weapons...** Adam and Eve were stripped of their original potent splendor, here identified with the weapons bestowed upon Israel at Sinai.

See *Zohar* 1:36b, 52a–b, 224a. Cf. *Bereshit Rabbah* 19:6; *Targum Yerushalmi,* Genesis 3:7; *Pirqei de-Rabbi Eli'ezer* 14; *Bahir* 141 (200).

1432. **absolute freedom** Another motif from midrashic tradition concerning Israel at Sinai, here applied to Adam and Eve. See *Tanḥuma, Ki Tissa* 16; and *Shir ha-Shirim Rabbah* on 8:6: "חרות (Ḥarut), *Engraved, on the tablets* (Exodus 32:16) [describing the divine writing on the tablets of stone, spelling out the Ten Commandments]. Do not read: חרות (ḥarut), *engraved,* but rather: חירות (ḥeirut), freedom. Rabbi Yehudah, Rabbi Neḥemiah, and the Rabbis: Rabbi Yehudah says, 'Freedom from the Angel of Death.' Rabbi Neḥemiah says, 'Freedom from foreign rulers.' The Rabbis say, 'Freedom from suffering.'" Cf. *Zohar* 1:37b, 52b.

been said.[1433] At that moment the erect stature of Adam diminished by one hundred cubits.[1434] Separation ensued, Adam was arraigned, earth was cursed, as we have established."

He drove out את האדם (*et ha-adam*), *Adam* (ibid., 24).[1435]

Rabbi El'azar said, "We do not know who divorced whom: if the blessed Holy One divorced Adam, or not.[1436] But the word is transposed: *He drove out* את (*Et*)—precisely![1437] Who drove out *Et*? *Adam. Adam* actually drove

---

1433. *fig leaves...they discovered every kind of sorcery...* According to Rabbi Neḥemiah (BT *Berakhot* 40a), Adam and Eve sinned by eating from the fruit of a fig tree. The leaves of this Tree of Knowledge convey the knowledge of magic. See *Zohar* 1:56a, 63b, and 36b: "Once they knew of this world and clung to it, they saw that this world is conducted by those leaves of the tree. So they built themselves a stronghold, fortifying themselves with them in this world, discovering every kind of magic. They sought to gird themselves with the weapons of those leaves of the tree for protection." Cf. BT *Bava Metsi'a* 114b.

"The one below" apparently refers to the demonic realm, though perhaps to *Shekhinah,* identified with the Tree of Knowledge and split off from the other *sefirot* by Adam's sinful act. See *Zohar* 1:35b–36a, 52a, and below.

1434. **the erect stature of Adam diminished...** See BT *Ḥagigah* 12a: "Rabbi El'azar said, 'Adam extended from earth to heaven.... As soon as he sinned, the blessed Holy One placed His hands upon him and diminished him....' Rabbi Yehudah said in the name of Rav, 'Adam extended from one end of the world to the other.... As soon as he sinned, the blessed Holy One placed His hand upon him and diminished him.'"

See *Bereshit Rabbah* 12:6: "Rabbi Aivu said, 'His stature was reduced to one hundred cubits.... Rabbi Shim'on said, '[His stature was originally] two hundred cubits.'" Cf. *Sifra, Beḥuqqotai* 3:3, 111b; BT *Bava Batra*

75a; *Sanhedrin* 100a; *Araqim* 6 (*Otsar Midrashim* 1:70–71); *Zohar* 1:142b; and Rashbam, *Bava Batra* 75a, who suggests, matching the view here, that his original stature was two hundred cubits and was reduced by half.

For Iranian and Gnostic parallels, see Altmann, "The Gnostic Background of the Rabbinic Adam Legends"; Urbach, *The Sages,* 227–32.

1435. *He drove out* את האדם (*et ha-adam*), *Adam* Literally, *He drove out the human.* The preceding verse reads similarly: *YHVH Elohim expelled him from the Garden of Eden.* The apparent redundancy stimulates the following mystical midrash.

1436. **We do not know who divorced whom...** Several midrashim interpret the biblical word ויגרש (*vaygaresh*), *He drove out,* in the sense of גירושין (*geirushin*), "divorce." See *Bereshit Rabbah* 21:8; *Midrash Avkir,* in *Yalqut Shim'oni,* Genesis, 34; and *Seder Eliyyahu Rabbah* 1: "*He drove out Adam.* This teaches that the blessed Holy One divorced him like a wife." Cf. *Ziqquqin de-Nura,* ad loc.; and *Midrash ha-Gadol* on this verse: "This teaches that he was divorced like a wife divorced from her husband because of some indecency."

Adam's harmonious and intimate relationship with God is ruined by sin. Rabbi El'azar adopts this midrashic view but reassigns the roles.

1437. את (*Et*)—**precisely!** Grammatically, the accusative particle את (*et*) has no ascertainable independent sense, but Naḥum of Gimzo and his disciple Rabbi Akiva taught that when *et* appears in a biblical

out *Et!*[1438] Consequently it is written: *YHVH Elohim expelled him from the Garden of Eden* (ibid., 23). Why did He expel him? Because Adam drove out *Et,* as we have explained.[1439]

"*He placed* [... *the cherubim*] (ibid., 24).[1440] He installed them in this site; he was the cause, closing pathways, inflicting punishment on the world, extending curses from that day on.[1441]

298

verse, it amplifies the original meaning. See BT *Pesaḥim* 22b; *Ḥagigah* 12a.

Here, as often in the *Zohar,* את (et) becomes a name of *Shekhinah,* who comprises the totality of divine speech, the entire alphabet from א (alef) to ת (tav). See *Zohar* 1:29b, 247a; 2:90a, 135b; and the Christian parallel in Revelation 1:8: "I am *alpha* and *omega.*"

1438. *Adam* **actually drove out** *Et!* By dividing the biblical sentence, *He drove out* את (et) *Adam,* into two units, Rabbi El'azar transforms its meaning. The first unit consists of: *He drove out* את (et). The second unit identifies the subject of the sentence, which is shockingly not God, but *Adam.* His sin consists in divorcing *Shekhinah.*

In the *Zohar,* the exact nature of Adam's sin is a tightly guarded secret; the biblical account of the Garden story is seen as hiding the true meaning. See *ZH* 19a (*MhN*), where Rabbi Shim'on recounts a conversation he had with Adam while selecting his future site in Paradise: "Adam... was sitting next to me, speaking with me, and he asked that his sin not be revealed to the whole world beyond what the Torah had recounted. It is concealed in that tree in the Garden of Eden." The Tree of Knowledge of Good and Evil symbolizes *Shekhinah.* Adam's sin was that he worshiped and partook of *Shekhinah* alone, splitting Her off from the other *sefirot* and divorcing Her from Her husband, *Tif'eret,* the Tree of Life. See *Zohar* 1:12b, 35b–36a, 221a–b; Scholem, *Major Trends,* 231–32, 236, 404–5, n. 105; Tishby, *Wisdom of the Zohar,* 1:373–76.

On the psychological plane, the sin corresponds to the splitting off of consciousness from the unconscious. See Jung, *Collected Works,* 8:157; Neumann, *Origins and History*

of *Consciousness,* 102–27; Jaynes, *Origin of Consciousness,* 299; cf. Scholem, *Major Trends,* 216, 236–37.

By his midrashic transposition, Rabbi El'azar teaches that Adam divorced *Shekhinah,* divorcing Her from *Tif'eret* and consequently also from himself. See above, page 294: "When Adam sinned by eating from the tree,... he caused a defect, separating the Woman from Her Husband." Cf. Isaiah 50:1: *Because of your transgressions your mother was divorced.* See *Bereshit Rabbah* 19:7: "Rabbi Abba son of Kahana said, 'The essence of *Shekhinah* was in the lower realms. As soon as Adam sinned, it withdrew to the first heaven.'" Cf. Naḥmanides on Genesis 3:8; Gikatilla, *Sha'arei Orah,* 15–17.

Adam's sin has driven *Shekhinah* from the Garden and dissolved Her union with *Tif'eret,* so She finds Herself abandoned in a no-man's-land. Meanwhile, as a result of his sin, Adam is banished from the Garden. Wandering outside, he finds *Shekhinah,* and together they go into exile. See *Zohar* 3:114a–115b, and 1:237a: "Come and see the secret of the word: Adam was caught in his own sin, inflicting death upon himself and the whole world, causing that tree with which he sinned to be divorced, driven away with him, driven away with his children forever, as is written: *He drove out* את (et) *Adam.*"

1439. **Consequently it is written**... The apparent redundancy is eliminated. Adam was expelled because he divorced *Shekhinah.*

1440. **He placed**... The verse continues: *east of the Garden of Eden the cherubim and a blazing, ever-turning sword to guard the way to the Tree of Life.*

1441. **He installed them**... As in the beginning of the verse, the subject is not God

"And a blazing, ever-turning sword (ibid.)—all those projectiles of judgment deployed against the world in the hollow of a sling,[1442] turning countless shades to chastise the world,[1443] sometimes male, sometimes female,[1444] flashing fire, winds—unbearable, unfathomable. All this *to guard the way to the Tree of Life* (ibid.), so they would commit no further wrong, as before.

"*A blazing sword*—flashing fiery torment[1445] upon the heads of sinners, turning various shades according to human conduct. So, *blazing*, as is said: *The day that is coming shall set them ablaze...* (Malachi 3:19), as has been explained.

"*Sword—the sword of YHVH*, as is said: *the sword of YHVH filled with blood...* (Isaiah 34:6)."[1446]

Rabbi Yehudah said, "*A blazing sword.* Even all those quaestors below, constantly transforming, are empowered over the world to harass and accuse sinners violating their Lord's commands.[1447]

"Come and see: When Adam sinned, he drew upon himself countless maleficent species and wardens of judgment,[1448] before all of whom he trembled, overwhelmed. Solomon knew supernal wisdom, was crowned with royalty by the blessed Holy One, feared by the entire world. Yet once he sinned, he drew upon himself countless maleficent species and wardens of judgment, before all of whom he trembled, so they were able to torment him, snatching his possessions.[1449]

299

---

but Adam, who by his divisive act installed *the cherubim*. Here *the cherubim* represent harsh powers.

See Rashi and Baḥya ben Asher on Genesis 3:24; Theodor's note on *Bereshit Rabbah* 21:9.

1442. **projectiles...the hollow of a sling** קוזפי (*Quzpei*), a Zoharic neologism perhaps deriving from the Arabic root *qdph*, "to throw." Cf. the neologism קוספיתא (*quspita*), "hollow of a sling"; Liebes, *Peraqim*, 347; *Bei'ur ha-Millim ha-Zarot*, 189; and the similar forms קזטיפי (*qaztiphei*) (*Zohar* 1:167a), קיזפא (*qizpa*) (2:175b), and קסטיפא דשמשא (*qastipha de-shimsha*), "ray of the sun" (3:283b).

1443. **turning countless shades...** See BT *Yoma* 75a, where demons are said to "turn many colors."

1444. **sometimes male, sometimes female** See *Bereshit Rabbah* 21:9: "*Ever-turning*—changing: sometimes male, sometimes female; sometimes spirits, sometimes angels." See *Zohar* 1:44a, 165a (*ST*), 237a; 3:19b.

1445. **torment** קוסטירי (*Qustirei*). Cf. the rabbinic term קוסטור (*qustor*) from Latin *quaestor*, a Roman official or prosecutor. See JT *Eruvin* 6:2, 23b; *Zohar* 1:19b; 2:19b, 58b, 208b; 3:13a. *Bei'ur ha-Millim ha-Zarot*, 188 relates the Zoharic term to the rabbinic קוסטינר (*qustinar*), deriving from Latin *quaestionarius*, "torturer, executioner."

1446. **the sword of YHVH...** Symbolizing *Shekhinah*, who executes the divine judgment of *Gevurah*. See *Zohar* 2:28b.

1447. **quaestors...** קסטרין (*Qisterin*). See above, note 1445.

1448. **wardens of judgment** Harsh powers. The Zoharic term גרדיני (*gardinei*), "wardens, guardians" derives from the Castilian *guardián*. See Corominas, *Diccionario*, 3:246–48.

1449. **Yet once he sinned...** According to midrashic tradition, when Solomon sinned by marrying many foreign wives and worshiping false gods (1 Kings 11:1–13), he was replaced on the throne by the demon Ash-

"So as a person tends, according to his pursued path, he draws upon himself an appointed power encountering him.[1450] Thus Adam attracted another, impure power defiling him and all humanity.

"Come and see: When Adam sinned he drew upon himself an impure power, defiling him and all humanity. This is the evil serpent, impure, defiling the world. For we have learned: When he plucks out souls from human beings, the body is left impure, defiling the house and anyone coming near, as is written: *Whoever touches a corpse*... (Numbers 19:11).[1451] Once he seizes the soul and defiles the body, permission is granted to all those impure aspects to hover over it, for that body has been defiled by the aspect of the evil serpent settling upon it. So wherever that serpent prevails, he defiles.

"Come and see: When night spreads her wings and all inhabitants of the world lie asleep in bed, they taste a taste of death.[1452] Due to this taste, the impure spirit roams the world, defiling the world with its whirlwind,[1453] alighting on the hands of a human being, now contaminated.[1454] Upon awakening, his soul restored, he defiles whatever his hands draw near because the impure spirit settles upon them. So when dressing, one should not take his clothes from anyone who has not washed his hands, for he thereby draws upon himself that impure spirit and is contaminated. This impure spirit is empowered to settle anywhere it detects a trace of its side. So one should not let his hands be washed by anyone who has not washed his hands, for he draws upon him that impure spirit, received by the one whose hands are being washed, empowered to settle upon him.[1455] [54a]

300

medai and forced to wander as a commoner for years.

See *Midrash Tehillim* 78:12; *Bemidbar Rabbah* 11:3; *Beit ha-Midrash*, 6:106–7; BT *Gittin* 68a–b; Ginzberg, *Legends*, 6:299–300, n. 86.

1450. **So as a person tends...** See BT *Shabbat* 104a: "Resh Lakish said, '...If one comes to defile himself, he is provided an opening; if one comes to purify himself, he is assisted.'"

Cf. *Makkot* 10b: "Rabbah son of Bar Ḥana said in the name of Rabbi Huna (some say, Rabbi Huna said in the name of Rabbi El'azar), 'From the Torah, the Prophets, and the Writings it can be demonstrated that one is led on the path one wishes to take.'"

See *Zohar* 1:54a, 125b, 169b, 198b; 2:50a; 3:47a.

1451. ***Whoever touches a corpse...*** The verse continues: *of any human being shall be impure for seven days.* See *Zohar* 3:88a–b.

1452. **they taste a taste of death** See BT *Berakhot* 57b: "Sleep is one-sixtieth of death." Cf. *Zohar* 1:36b.

1453. **whirlwind** קפטירא (Qaftira), a Zoharic neologism. See *Zohar* 2:178a (*SdTs*); Liebes, *Peraqim*, 351.

1454. **the hands of a human being, now contaminated** During sleep one's spirit soars upward and an impure spirit arrives.

See BT *Shabbat* 109a; *Ḥullin* 107b; *Zohar* 1:10b, 169b, 184b; 3:67a; *Orḥot Ḥayyim*, par. 10. Cf. *Bereshit Rabbah* 14:9: "It was said in the name of Rabbi Me'ir: 'This soul fills the body, and when a person sleeps she ascends and draws down life from above.'"

1455. **one should not take his clothes from anyone...** See BT *Berakhot* 51a: "Rabbi Yishma'el son of Elisha said, 'Three things were told to me by Suriel, Prince of

"So one should guard every side against the side of this evil serpent, lest it dominate him. In the world to come the blessed Holy One intends to exterminate him from the world, as is written: *I will eliminate the spirit of impurity from earth* (Zechariah 13:2). Then *He will swallow up death forever . . .* (Isaiah 25:8)."

The man knew Eve his wife . . . (Genesis 4:1).[1456]

Rabbi Abba opened, "*Who knows if the spirit of the sons of men ascends on high and the spirit of a beast descends into earth?* (Ecclesiastes 3:21). This verse bears numerous nuances,[1457] as does every word of Torah, each and every one including countless colors, all fitting. So they are, the entire Torah assuming seventy aspects, seventy faces.[1458] So it is with every single word of Torah, and whatever emerges from each and every word diverges into numerous nuances in countless directions.

"Come and see: When one follows the path of truth, he tends toward the right, drawing upon himself a supernal holy spirit from above.[1459] This spirit ascends in holy desire to unite above, cleaving to supernal holiness irremovably. But when one follows the path of evil and strays, he draws upon himself an impure spirit of the left side, defiling him, so he becomes defiled,[1460] as is said: *Do not defile yourselves with them, and thus become defiled* (Leviticus 11:43). If one turns toward defiling himself, he is defiled.[1461]

301

the [Divine] Countenance: Do not take your shirt from the hand of the attendant when dressing in the morning, do not let your hands be washed by anyone who has not washed his hands, and do not return a cup of asparagus to anyone other than the one who has handed it to you. For a band of demons (some say: a cluster of angels of destruction) lies in wait, saying: "When will a human do one of these things, so we can capture him!"'"

Cf. *Orḥot Ḥayyim*, par. 10; *Zohar* 1:198b.

1456. *The man knew Eve his wife* The verse continues: *and she conceived and bore* קין (Qayin), *Cain, saying* "קניתי (Qaniti), *I have created, a male along with YHVH.*"

1457. **This verse bears numerous nuances** A similar expression appears in *Zohar* 1:48b, 81b, 197b.

1458. **seventy aspects, seventy faces** See *Bemidbar Rabbah* 13:16, where Torah is compared to wine: "Just as יין (yayin), wine,

is numerically equivalent to seventy, so Torah assumes seventy faces."

See *Sefer Ḥanokh* (*Beit ha-Midrash*, 2:116); Ibn Ezra, introduction to Commentary on the Torah; *Zohar* 1:4b, 26a (*TZ*), 47b.

See the description of the revelation at Mount Sinai in BT *Shabbat* 88b: "Rabbi Yoḥanan said, '. . . Every utterance emerging from the mouth of Power branched into seventy languages.'"

1459. **toward the right . . .** The right side is characterized by Ḥesed ("Love").

1460. **the left side . . .** The left side is characterized by harshness and generates the demonic realm.

1461. **If one turns toward defiling himself . . .** See BT *Shabbat* 104a: "Resh Lakish said, '. . . If one comes to defile himself, he is provided an opening; if one comes to purify himself, he is assisted.'"

Cf. *Yoma* 39a: "Our Rabbis taught: '*Do not defile yourselves with them, and thus become*

"Come and see: When one follows the path of truth, drawing upon himself a supernal, holy spirit, cleaving to it, he draws supernal holiness upon the son he engenders, who issues from him into the world, who is thereby endowed with the holiness of his Lord, as is written: *Hallow yourselves and you will be holy*... (ibid., 44).[1462] But when he follows the left side, drawing upon himself an impure spirit, cleaving to it, he draws an impure spirit upon the son who issues from him into the world, who is thereby defiled by the impurity of that side.

"So it is written: *Who knows if the spirit of the sons of men ascends on high?* When he cleaves to the right, she ascends, but when he cleaves to the left, that side of the left, spirit of impurity, descends and possesses him unyieldingly, so whatever son he engenders derives from that impure spirit.[1463]

"Adam cleaved to that impure spirit,[1464] while his wife cleaved to it first, receiving, absorbing its slime, from which a son was engendered—son of impure spirit. So there were two sons: one from that impure spirit and one

302

defiled. If one defiles himself slightly, he is defiled greatly; below, he is defiled from above; in this world, he is defiled in the world to come.'"

See *Zohar* 1:53b, 125b, 169b, 198b; 2:50a; 3:47a; and *Makkot* 10b: "Rabbah son of Bar Ḥana said in the name of Rabbi Huna (some say, Rabbi Huna said in the name of Rabbi El'azar), 'From the Torah, the Prophets, and the Writings it can be demonstrated that one is led on the path one wishes to take.'"

1462. *Hallow yourselves and you will be holy* The verse continues: *for I am holy.* See BT *Yoma* 39a: "Our Rabbis taught: 'Hallow yourselves and you will be holy. If one sanctifies himself slightly, he is sanctified greatly; below, he is sanctified from above; in this world, he is sanctified in the world to come.'"

Here Rabbi Abba applies the verse specifically to the act of sexual union, which should be fulfilled in purity to ensure a holy soul for the fetus. Cf. BT *Shevu'ot* 18b; *Bemidbar Rabbah* 9:7.

1463. **when he cleaves to the left...** If he engages in sexual union impurely, acting like *a beast* (Ecclesiastes, ibid.), then his son's soul will be tainted.

1464. **Adam cleaved to that impure spirit**

See *Tanḥuma* (Buber), *Bereshit* 26: "Rabbi Simon said, 'For 130 years Adam separated from his wife Eve, for once Cain was killed, Adam said, "Why should I engender children if they become cursed?" What did he do?...Female spirits approached him and heated themselves from him. As the blessed Holy One said to David, "...*When he* [Solomon] *does wrong, I will chastise him with a human rod, with blows of the children of* אדם *(adam)*" (2 Samuel 7:14)..., namely, the demons.'"

See *Bereshit Rabbah* 20:11: "Rabbi Simon said, 'Throughout all 130 years that Adam separated himself from Eve, male spirits heated themselves from her and she gave birth, while female spirits heated themselves from Adam and gave birth, as is written: *When he does wrong, I will chastise him with a human rod, with blows of the children of* אדם *(adam)*, namely, children of Adam.'"

See BT *Eruvin* 18b: "Rabbi Yirmeyah son of El'azar said, 'During all those [130] years that Adam was under the ban [for having eaten from the Tree of Knowledge], he engendered spirits, demons, and female demons.'"

Cf. *Zohar* 1:19b, 34b, 55a; 2:231b; 3:76b; Trachtenberg, *Jewish Magic and Superstition,* 51–54.

when Adam returned to God;[1465] this from the impure side, this from the pure."[1466]

Rabbi El'azar said, "When the serpent injected that slime into Eve, she absorbed it, so when she copulated with Adam she bore two sons: one from that impure side and one from the side of Adam,[1467] Cain resembling both the higher image and the lower.[1468] So their paths diverged from one another. Cain was certainly son of the impure spirit, and deriving from the side of the Angel of Death, he killed his brother.[1469] Being from his side, from him emerged all evil haunts, goblins, spirits, and demons."[1470]

Rabbi Yose said, "קין (Qayin), Cain—קינא (qina), nest, of evil lairs materializing from the side of impurity.[1471] Afterward they brought an offering, each from his own side, as is written: *It came to pass at the end of days that Cain brought an offering to YHVH from the fruit of the soil [and as for Abel, he, too, brought— from the firstlings of his flock, from their fat portions]* (Genesis 4:3–4)."[1472]

Rabbi Shim'on said, "ויהי מקץ ימים (Vayhi mi-qets yamim), *It came to pass at the end of days.*[1473] What is מקץ ימים (mi-qets yamim), *at the end of days*? This is

303

1465. **returned to God** Repenting sincerely.

1466. **while his wife cleaved to it first...**
See *Pirqei de-Rabbi Eli'ezer* 21: "The serpent-rider [Samael] copulated with her and she conceived Cain. Afterward Adam copulated with her and she conceived Abel."

Cf. BT *Shabbat* 145b–146a: "Rav Yosef taught: '...When the serpent copulated with Eve, he injected her with זוהמא (zohama), filth [or: slime, lewdness].'"

See *Targum Yerushalmi*, Genesis 4:1 (variants); *Zohar* 1:36b–37a, 52a; *KP* on this passage; Stroumsa, *Another Seed*, 38–53.

1467. **so when she copulated with Adam...** According to Rabbi El'azar, both sons were engendered by Adam, though Cain inherited the slime of the serpent. See *ZH* 83b (*MhN, Rut*).

1468. **Cain resembling both the higher image and the lower** Through the fallen angel Samael, Cain inherited traits of the upper world; through Adam, he inherited traits of the lower world. Alternatively, the lower image derived from the slime of the serpent; the higher, from Adam, created in the divine image. See *Zohar* 2:231a; *ZH* 63c (*ShS*).

1469. **the side of the Angel of Death...**
The Angel of Death is a demonic manifestation. See BT *Bava Batra* 16a: "Resh Lakish said, 'Satan, the evil impulse, and the Angel of Death are one and the same.'"

Cf. *Zohar* 1:35b, 52a, 202a; 2:262b–263a; Moses de León, *Sefer ha-Rimmon*, 394–95.

1470. **from him emerged all evil haunts...**
On the demonic descendants of Cain, see El'azar of Worms, *Ḥokhmat ha-Nefesh*, 26c; *Zohar* 1:9b, 36b, 178a–b; 3:76b, 122a.

1471. קין (*Qayin*), Cain—קינא (*qina*), nest... The same play on words appears in *Zohar* 2:178a (*SdTs*).

1472. **each from his own side...** See *Bereshit Rabbah* 22:5: "Cain brought [*an offering to YHVH*] *from the fruit of the soil*— from the inferior crops." In this midrash the phrase *from the fruit* is taken to mean: "not from the first fruit."

Cf. *Tanḥuma, Bereshit* 9; *Pirqei de-Rabbi Eli'ezer* 21.

1473. ויהי מקץ ימים (*Vayhi mi-qets yamim*),
It came to pass at the end of days The phrase מקץ ימים (mi-qets yamim) is usually taken to mean *in the course of time,* but here Rabbi Shim'on focuses on the literal meaning.

end of all flesh (ibid. 6:13). Who is that? Angel of Death.[1474] Cain brought an offering precisely from that *end of days,* for it says: מקץ ימים (*mi-qets yamim*), *from the end of days,* and not מקץ ימין (*mi-qets yamin*), *from the end of the right.*[1475] So of Daniel it is written: *As for you, go till the end and take your rest; you will rise for your reward* לקץ הימין (*le-qets ha-yamin*) (Daniel 12:13). He asked, 'לקץ הימים (*Le-qets ha-yamim*), *At the end of days,* or לקץ הימין (*le-qets ha-yamin*), *at the end of the right?*' He responded, 'לקץ הימין (*Le-qets ha-yamin*), *At the end of the right.*'[1476] [54b] Whereas Cain brought (*mi-qets ha-yamim*), *from the end of days.*

"*Cain brought from the fruit of the soil,* as is said: *from the fruit of the tree* (Genesis 3:3)."[1477]

Rabbi El'azar said, "*From the fruit of the soil,* as is said: *Woe to the wicked! Disaster! What his hands have done shall be done to him. For they shall eat the fruit of their deeds* (Isaiah 3:10–11). *For they shall eat the fruit of their deeds*— Angel of Death.[1478] *They shall eat*—for he is drawn to them, clings to them, to kill and defile them. So Cain offered from his side.

"*As for Abel, he brought* גם הוא (*gam hu*), *Him, too*—amplifying the meaning to include the supernal side deriving from the side of holiness.[1479] So *YHVH*

304

1474. **end of all flesh...Angel of Death** A manifestation of the demonic. See BT *Bava Batra* 16a: "Resh Lakish said, 'Satan, the evil impulse, and the Angel of Death are one and the same.'"

See *Zohar* 1:35b, 52a, 202a; 2:262b–263a; Moses de León, *Sefer ha-Rimmon,* 394–95. On the phrase *end of all flesh,* see *Zohar* 1:58a, 62b.

1475. **not מקץ ימין (*mi-qets yamin*), *from the end of the right*** Whereas *the end of days* symbolizes the demonic power of death, *the end of the right* symbolizes *Shekhinah,* the culmination of the flow of emanation, characterized by the divine grace of the right side. See *Zohar* 1:75a (*ST*), 152b; 2:134a–b.

1476. **He asked...** Daniel asked God which *end* He intended, the demonic or the divine. See *Eikhah Rabbah* 2:6; *Pesiqta de-Rav Kahana* 17:5; *Zohar* 1:63a, 210b; 2:34a, 181b.

1477. *from the fruit of the tree* The verse continues: *in the middle of the garden, God said: "Do not eat from it and do not touch it, lest you die."* See Genesis 2:17: *As*

for the tree of knowledge of good and evil, do not eat from it, for on the day you eat from it, you will surely die.

In Kabbalah the Tree of Knowledge of Good and Evil symbolizes *Shekhinah.* Adam's sin was that he worshiped and partook of *Shekhinah* alone, splitting Her off from the other *sefirot* and divorcing Her from Her husband, *Tif'eret,* the Tree of Life. See above, note 1438. Here Rabbi Shim'on compares Cain's sin to that of Adam: Cain, too, separated *Shekhinah,* symbolized by the soil, from the other *sefirot.*

1478. *For they shall eat the fruit of their deeds...* This phrase, addressed by Isaiah to the righteous, is here applied to the wicked Cain and paired with the phrase *the fruit of the soil.* See Genesis 4:10: *Your brother's blood cries out to Me from the soil.* Cain's murderous act arouses the Angel of Death to avenge his brother.

1479. **amplifying the meaning to include...** לאסגאה (*Le-asga'ah*), "To increase," a Zoharic rendering of the rabbinic

gazed upon Abel and his offering with favor, but upon Cain and his offering He gazed not, not accepting them, so *Cain was very angry and his face fell* (Genesis 4:4–5), for *his face*, the facet of his side, was not accepted,[1480] whereas Abel was. Consequently it is written: *And when they were out in the field* (ibid., 8)[1481]—this is a woman, as has been said.[1482]

"*If you do right, is there not* שאת (*se'et*), *uplift?* (ibid., 7), as has been explained,[1483] but according to Rabbi Abba, שאת (*se'et*), *uplift* means: You will ascend, not descend."

Rabbi Yose said, "This word has now been said and is fitting, but I have heard as follows: שאת (*Se'et*)—He will remove from you, forgive you this clinging of impure spirit.[1484] If not, *sin crouches at the opening* (ibid.). What is the meaning of *at the opening?* Supernal judgment, opening of all, as is said: *Open for me the gates of justice* (Psalms 118:19).[1485] *Sin crouches*—that side to which you clung, extending toward you, lies in wait for you to punish you, as translated."[1486]

305

Hebrew לרבות (*le-rabbot*), "to increase"—that is, to include, amplify, or widen the scope of meaning. In rabbinic hermeneutics the word גם (*gam*), "also, too," amplifies the literal meaning of a biblical word or phrase. See *Bereshit Rabbah* 1:14; JT *Berakhot* 9:5, 14b.

Here the phrase גם הוא (*gam hu*), referring to Abel and usually translated *he, too*, is apparently understood as the object of the sentence: *Him, too*, referring to the divine male. Whereas Cain's demonic offering split *Shekhinah* from Her partner (*Tif'eret*), Abel united Her with Him. See *Zohar* 2:34a, 181b.

1480. **the facet of his side . . .** The demonic side.

1481. *And when they were out in the field* The verse continues: *Cain set upon his brother Abel and killed him.*

1482. **this is a woman, as has been said** See *Pirqei de-Rabbi Eli'ezer* 21: "Rabbi Tsadok said, 'Envy and hatred toward his brother Abel entered Cain's heart because his [Abel's] offering had been accepted. Further, Abel's wife and twin sister was the most beautiful of women. He said, "I will kill my brother Abel and take his woman," as is said: *When they were in the field . . .*, and *in the field* means "woman," who is

compared to a field, as is said: *Man is a tree of the field* (Deuteronomy 20:19).'"

See *Bereshit Rabbah* 22:7; 63:12; BT *Bava Batra* 16b; *Zohar* 1:35b, 36b; 3:202a–b.

In Kabbalah, *field* symbolizes *Shekhinah*, whom Abel, unlike Cain, successfully united with *Tif'eret*. See *Zohar* 1:142b; 2:61b. Cf. BT *Ta'anit* 29b; *Bereshit Rabbah* 65:22; Azriel of Gerona, *Peirush ha-Aggadot*, 35–37.

1483. **as has been explained** The root נשא (*ns'*) has a range of meaning, including: "lift, remove, forgive." The reference here may be to the interpretation offered by *Targum Onqelos* and adopted by Rashi: "You will be forgiven." Cf. the views of Naḥmanides and Ibn Ezra, ad loc.; *Zohar* 1:36b; ZH 19c–d (MhN); Kasher, *Torah Shelemah*, Genesis 4:7, n. 68.

1484. **He will remove from you, forgive you . . .** God will remove and forgive. Here שאת (*se'et*) is interpreted according to two of its root meanings: "remove" and "forgive."

1485. **Supernal judgment . . . the gates of justice** *Shekhinah* is called Justice (or: Righteousness); through Her gate one enters the realm of the *sefirot*. See *Zohar* 1:7b, 11b, 36b–37a; Gikatilla, *Sha'arei Orah*, 4b.

1486. **as translated** See *Targum Onqelos*, ad loc.

Rabbi Yitsḥak said, "Come and see: As Cain was killing Abel, he did not know how his soul would expire, as the Companions have established.[1487] At that moment the blessed Holy One cursed him, and he wandered the world, everywhere rejected, till finally he slapped himself on the head and returned to the presence of his Lord.[1488] Then Earth admitted him to a stratum below."[1489]

Rabbi Yose said, "Earth permitted him to walk on her surface, as is written: *YHVH put a mark on Cain* (Genesis, ibid., 15)."[1490]

Rabbi Yitsḥak said, "Not so! Rather, a certain stratum below her, as is written: *For You have banished me today from the face of the earth* (ibid., 14). He was banished *from the face of the earth*, but not below. Where did Earth admit him? To *Arqa*, concerning all of whose denizens is written: *They shall perish from the earth and from under these heavens* (Jeremiah 10:11).[1491] There he resided, as is written: *He settled in the land of Nod, east of Eden* (Genesis, ibid., 16)."[1492]

Rabbi Yitsḥak said further, "From that time on, Adam separated from his wife and bore spirits and demons who roam the world.[1493] This should not seem strange to you, for when a man abides in his dream, female spirits

306

1487. **as the Companions have established** See BT *Sanhedrin* 37b: "Rabbi Yehudah son of Rabbi Ḥiyya said, '... Cain inflicted many blows and wounds upon his brother Abel because he did not know whence the soul departs, until he reached his neck.'"

Cf. *Tanḥuma, Bereshit* 9; and *Zohar* 2:231a–b: "We have found in ancient books that when Cain killed Abel he bit him with bites like a snake till he plucked out his soul and killed him." See Ginzberg, *Legends,* 5:139–40, n. 20.

1488. **returned to the presence of his Lord** Repenting sincerely.

1489. **Earth admitted him to a stratum below** To one of the levels beneath the surface of the earth. See *Vayiqra Rabbah* 29:11; *Sefer Yetsirah* 4:12; *Zohar* 1:9b, 39b–40a, 157a; 3:9b–10a; *ZḤ* 8c–9b (*SO*); 87b (*MhN, Rut*).

1490. **YHVH put a mark on Cain** The verse continues: *so that whoever came upon him would not strike him.*

1491. **Arqa ... They shall perish from the earth ...** *Arqa* is one of the levels below Earth, alluded to in the Aramaic verse from Jeremiah: *Thus shall you say to them: "The gods who did not make heaven* וארקא *(ve-*

arqa), and earth, shall perish from the earth and from under these heavens."

See *Vayiqra Rabbah* 29:10; *Avot de-Rabbi Natan* A, 37; *Seder Rabbah di-Vreshit* 9 (*Battei Midrashot,* 1:24); *Zohar* 1:9a–b, 39b.

1492. **the land of Nod ...** This region, whose name derives from the root "to wander," is here identified with *Arqa*.

1493. **Adam separated from his wife ...** See *Tanḥuma* (Buber), *Bereshit* 26: "Rabbi Simon said, 'For 130 years Adam separated from his wife Eve, for once Cain was killed, Adam said, "Why should I engender children if they become cursed?" What did he do? ... Female spirits approached him and heated themselves from him. As the blessed Holy One said to David, "... When he [Solomon] does wrong, I will chastise him with a human rod, with blows of the children of אדם *(adam)*" (2 Samuel 7:14) ..., namely, the demons.'"

See *Bereshit Rabbah* 20:11: "Rabbi Simon said, 'Throughout all 130 years that Adam separated himself from Eve, male spirits heated themselves from her and she gave birth, while female spirits heated themselves from Adam and gave birth, as is written: *When he does wrong, I will chastise him with a*

approach and titillate him, are inflamed by him, and subsequently give birth to those called *blows of the children of Adam* (2 Samuel 7:14).[1494] These transform solely into the image of human beings[1495] and have no hair on their heads.[1496] So of Solomon is written: *I will chastise him with a human rod, with blows of the children of Adam.* Similarly male spirits approach women of the world, who are impregnated by them and bear spirits, all called *blows of the children of Adam.*

"After 130 years Adam wrapped himself [55a] in jealousy and united with his wife,[1497] engendering a son he called שת (*Shet*), Seth—mystery of consummation of letters engraved in clusters."[1498]

Rabbi Yehudah said, "Mystery of vanished spirit, enveloped bodily in the world, as is written: *For God* שת (*shat*), *has granted, me another seed in place of Abel* (Genesis, ibid., 25)."[1499]

He said further, "It is written: *He engendered in his likeness, according to his image* (ibid. 5:3), implying that the other sons were not in his likeness or image, which accords with what Rabbi Shim'on said in the name of Rabbi

307

human rod, with blows of the children of אדם (*adam*), namely, children of Adam.'"

See BT *Eruvin* 18b; *Zohar* 1:19b, 34b, 54a, 55a; 2:231b, 3:76b; Trachtenberg, *Jewish Magic and Superstition,* 51–54.

1494. **female spirits approach and titillate him...** These female demons desire to be impregnated by human semen. See *Zohar* 1:9b, 19b, 47b, 169b; and the citation of the verse from Samuel in *Tanḥuma* (Buber), *Bereshit* 26 and *Bereshit Rabbah* 20:11 (in the previous note).

1495. **solely into the image of human beings** Other demons assume the form of various creatures.

1496. **have no hair on their heads** According to *Tanḥuma* (Buber), *Bo* 16, "Demons have no hair." See *Rut Rabbah* 6:1; Trachtenberg, *Jewish Magic and Superstition* 275–76, n. 18; Ginzberg, *Legends,* 6:192, n. 58. Cf. *Zohar* 3:48b: "Holiness depends on the hair," based on the description of the Nazirite in Numbers 6:5: *He shall be holy, letting the locks of the hair on his head grow untrimmed.*

1497. **After 130 years...** See Genesis 5:3: *When Adam had lived 130 years, he engendered in his likeness, according to his image, and named him Seth.* Cf. above, note 1493. Adam was jealous of Eve's illicit partner, the serpent.

On the phrase "wrapped himself in jealousy," see Isaiah 59:17; *Zohar* 2:231b.

1498. שת (*Shet*), Seth—mystery of consummation of letters... This name is composed of the final two letters of the alphabet, all of which were engraved in the process of creation. See *Sefer Yetsirah* 2:2, 4–5: "Twenty-two elemental letters. He engraved them, carved them, weighed them, permuted them, and transposed them— forming with them everything formed and everything destined to be formed.... Twenty-two elemental letters. He set them in a wheel with 231 gates, turning forward and backward.... How did He permute them? א (*Alef*) with them all, all of them with א (*alef*); ב (*bet*) with them all, all of them with ב (*bet*); and so with all the letters, turning round and round, within 231 gates."

The "231 gates" represent the number of two-letter combinations that can be formed from the twenty-two letters, provided that the same letter is not repeated. Cf. *Zohar* 1:33b; *ZḤ* 8c–9a (SO); 83b (MhN, Rut).

1499. **Mystery of vanished spirit, enveloped bodily...** According to Rabbi Yehudah, the soul of Abel disappeared and was then reincarnated in his newborn brother, Seth. On reincarnation in Kabbalah, see Scholem, *Kabbalah,* 344–50.

Yeisa Sava: 'The other sons derived from the clinging of the slime of the serpent to its rider, so they were not in the image of Adam.'[1500]

"If you object, 'But you stated that Abel derived from the other side!'[1501] So it is, but neither one was in the image below."[1502]

Rabbi Yose said, "Look at what is written: *Adam knew Eve his wife, and she conceived and bore Cain* (ibid. 4:1). Certainly so! It is not written: *and he engendered Cain.* Even of Abel, it is not written: *He engendered,* but rather: *She continued bearing—his brother, Abel* (ibid., 2). This is the mystery of the word. But of this one, what is written? *He engendered in his likeness, according to his image.*"[1503]

Rabbi Shim'on said, "For 110 years Adam separated from Eve,[1504] and throughout that time he engendered spirits and demons in the world through the potency of the slime he had absorbed.[1505] Once that slime was eliminated, he returned jealously to his wife and engendered a son, as is written: *He engendered in his likeness, according to his image.*

"Come and see: When a human follows the left side, defiling his ways,[1506] he draws upon himself all sorts of impure spirits, clinging to him relentlessly, clinging to him alone, clinging only to those who cling to them. Happy are the

308

1500. **the other sons derived...** See BT *Eruvin* 18b: "Rabbi Yirmeyah son of El'azar said, 'During all those [130] years that Adam was under the ban [for having eaten from the Tree of Knowledge], he engendered spirits, demons, and female demons, as is said: *Adam lived 130 years and engendered a son in his likeness, after his own image* (Genesis 5:3), from which it follows that until that time he did not engender after his own image'.... That statement refers to semen that he emitted accidentally."

According to BT *Shabbat* 145b–146a: "Rav Yosef taught: '... When the serpent copulated with Eve, he injected her with זוהמא (*zohama*), filth [or: slime, lewdness].'"

See *Pirqei de-Rabbi Eli'ezer* 21: "The serpent-rider [Samael] copulated with her and she conceived Cain. Afterward Adam copulated with her and she conceived Abel." Here Rabbi Yehudah and Rabbi Shim'on contend that even Abel was tainted by the serpent's slime.

See *Targum Yerushalmi*, Genesis 4:1 (variants); *Pirqei de-Rabbi Eli'ezer* 22; *Zohar* 1:19b, 34b, 36b–37a, 52a, 54a; 2:231b; 3:76b; *ZH* 8c (SO); Stroumsa, *Another Seed*, 38–53.

1501. **Abel derived from the other side** From the side of holiness. See above, page 303.

1502. **in the image below** In the image of Adam.

1503. **It is not written: *and he engendered...*** Adam's name is linked with neither Cain nor Abel, only with Seth, who was born *in his likeness, according to his image.* See *Zohar* 2:167b–168a.

1504. **For 110 years...** Both the midrashic tradition and the preceding passage in the *Zohar* (above, pages 302–7) specify 130 years, based on Genesis 5:3: *Adam lived 130 years and engendered in his likeness, according to his image.* However, nearly all of the witnesses on this passage (manuscripts and printed editions) read "110 years." *KP* suggests that Abel was killed at age twenty, following which Adam separated from Eve for 110 years.

1505. **the slime he had absorbed** When Adam united with Eve, he was contaminated by the slime previously injected into her by the serpent.

1506. **When a human follows the left side...** When he is seduced by evil.

righteous who follow the straight path! They are truly righteous, their children eternally righteous."

Rabbi Ḥiyya said, "Why is it written: *The sister of Tuval-Cain was* נעמה (*Na'amah*), *Na'amah* (ibid., 22)? What is the point of Scripture specifying her name?[1507] Because human beings stray after her, even spirits and demons."[1508]

Rabbi Yitsḥak said, "Those *sons of Elohim* (ibid. 6:4), Uzza and Azael, strayed after her."[1509]

Rabbi Shim'on said, "She was the mother of demons, having issued from the side of Cain,[1510] and was appointed together with Lilith over children's diphtheria."[1511]

Rabbi Abba objected, "But Master has said she was appointed to titillate humans."[1512]

He replied, "Certainly so! She approaches and titillates them, sometimes bearing them spirits in the world. Still now she persists, toying with humans."

Rabbi Abba said, "But they die like human beings! How can she have survived till now?"[1513]

309

1507. **What is the point of Scripture specifying her name?** Nothing further is said of her, so why is she mentioned?

1508. **Because human beings stray after her...** Na'amah, whose name means "lovely," was the great-great-great-great-granddaughter of Cain. According to rabbinic tradition, the fallen angels were attracted by her beauty.

See Genesis 6:1–4; *Tanḥuma* (Buber), *Ḥuqqat*, add. 1; *Midrash Aggadah* and *Midrash ha-Gadol*, Genesis 4:22; and the next note. According to the *Zohar* (1:9b, 19b; 3:76b–77a), Na'amah generates demons by seducing men in their sleep.

1509. **Those *sons of Elohim*, Uzza and Azael...** These two angels opposed the creation of Adam and Eve, fell from heaven, and were attracted by *the daughters of men* (Genesis 6:2). They were punished by being bound in chains of iron in the mountains of darkness, from where they still manage to wreak havoc, teaching sorcery to humans.

See 1 Enoch 6–8; Jubilees 5; BT *Yoma* 67b; *Aggadat Bereshit*, intro, 39; *Midrash Avkir*, 7 (cited in *Yalqut Shim'oni*, Genesis, 44); *Pirqei de-Rabbi Eli'ezer* 22; *Zohar* 1:23a (*TZ*), 37a,

37a (*Tos*), 58a, 126a; 3:208a–b, 212a–b; *ZḤ* 81a–b (*MhN, Rut*).

1510. **She was the mother of demons...** In the *Zohar*, Na'amah is the mother of Ashmedai, king of the demons.

See Naḥmanides, ad loc.; *Zohar* 1:9b, 19b; 3:76b–77a; *ZḤ* 19d (*MhN*).

1511. **appointed together with Lilith over children's diphtheria** This dread disease originates in Lilith, the demoness who attacks children.

See *Zohar* 1:19b, 33b; 2:264b, 267b; cf. JT *Ta'anit* 4:4, 68b: BT *Berakhot* 8a.

1512. **she was appointed to titillate humans** See above, page 150: "From her [Na'amah], maleficent spirits and demons spread through the world. In the night she roams; they [Na'amah and her offspring] roam the world and titillate humans, causing them to spill seed accidentally. Wherever they find people sleeping alone in a house, they hover above them, grab hold of them, cling to them, seize desire from them, and bear offspring."

1513. **But they die like human beings...** See BT *Ḥagigah* 16a: "Our Rabbis taught: 'Six things have been said concerning the

He replied, "So it is, but Lilith, Na'amah, and Agrat daughter of Maḥalat—
who issued from their side[1514]—all endure until the blessed Holy One exterminates the impure spirit from the world, as is written: *I will eliminate the spirit
of impurity from earth* (Zechariah 13:2)."

Rabbi Shim'on said, "Woe to human beings who do not know, consider, or
see![1515] They are all obtuse, unaware how full the world is of strange, invisible
creatures, of hidden things. If the eye were empowered to see, humans would
be amazed how they themselves can endure.[1516]

"Come and see: This Na'amah was mother of demons. From her side issue
all those inflamed by human beings, absorbing their spirit of lust, titillating
them, turning them into casualties of ejaculation.[1517] Since such a casualty derives from the side of impure spirit, he must bathe to purify himself, as established by the Companions."[1518]

310

*This is the book of the
generations of Adam...* (Genesis 5:1).

Rabbi Yitsḥak said, "The blessed Holy One showed Adam images of every
generation that would arise in the
world, all the wise of the world, and
kings of the world destined to dominate Israel.[1519] When he caught sight of

demons, three of which correspond to the
ministering angels and three to human beings. Three correspond to the ministering
angels: they have wings, they fly from one
end of the world to the other, and they
know what will happen in the future....
Three correspond to human beings: they
eat and drink, they are fruitful and multiply,
and they die.'"

1514. **Agrat daughter of Maḥalat...** Maḥalat was the daughter of Ishmael and wife
of Esau (Genesis 28:9). According to rabbinic
tradition, her daughter Agrat rules over myriads of demonic powers. See BT *Pesaḥim*
112b: "One should not go out alone at night,
neither on the eve of Wednesday nor of
Sabbath, for Agrat daughter of Maḥalat along
with 180,000 thousand angels of destruction
emerge, each independently empowered."

Cf. *Bemidbar Rabbah* 12:3; *Zohar* 3:113b–
114a; Baḥya ben Asher, on Genesis 4:22.

1515. **Woe to human beings who do not
know, consider, or see!** See BT *Ḥagigah* 12b:
"Rabbi Yose said, 'Woe to creatures, for they
see but do not know what they see, they
stand but do not know on what they stand.'"

1516. **If the eye were empowered to
see...** See BT *Berakhot* 6a: "Abba Binya-
min says, 'If the eye were empowered to see,
no creature could endure the demons.'" Cf.
Zohar 2:142a; 3:104b.

1517. **all those inflamed by human beings...** The demons issuing from Na'a-
mah seduce human beings, inciting them to
spill semen (see above, note 1512). The
phrase בעלי קריין (ba'alei qerayin), "casualties
of ejaculation," means literally "masters
[owners] of mishaps," those to whom mishaps happen, those who succumb to nocturnal emission.

1518. **he must bathe to purify himself...**
See the law concerning nocturnal emission
in Deuteronomy 23:11: *If any man among
you becomes impure due to nocturnal mishap,
he must go outside the camp; he must not
enter the midst of the camp. Toward evening
he shall bathe in water, and when the sun sets
he may come inside the camp.*

1519. **The blessed Holy One showed
Adam...** See BT *Avodah Zarah* 5a: "Did
not Resh Lakish say: 'What is the meaning
of the verse *This is the book of the genera-*

David, king of Israel, who died at birth, he said, 'I will lend him some of my own years.' So these were deducted from Adam and reserved by the blessed Holy One for David, who sang praise for this: '*For You have gladdened me* [55b] *by Your deed, YHVH; I sing for joy at Your handiwork* (Psalms 92:5).[1520] Who brought me joy in this world? *Your deed*—Adam, deed of the blessed Holy One, not of flesh-and-blood, *handiwork* of the blessed Holy One, not of human beings.[1521] So those seventy years were deducted from Adam, from the thousand that were his to endure.[1522]

"The blessed Holy One showed him the wise of every single generation until he reached the generation of Rabbi Akiva. Seeing his Torah, he rejoiced; seeing his death, he grieved. He opened, saying, '*How precious to me are Your companions, O God! How mighty their chiefs!* (ibid. 139:17).'[1523]

"*This is the book*—an actual book, as we have established. When Adam was in the Garden of Eden, the blessed Holy One brought down a book for him by the hand of Raziel, the holy angel appointed over supernal, sacred mysteries.[1524] In it were engraved supernal engravings, sacred wisdom. Seventy-two species

311

tions of Adam . . . ? Did Adam possess a book? Rather, this teaches that the blessed Holy One showed Adam every generation with its expounders, every generation with its sages, every generation with its leaders. When he reached the generation of Rabbi Akiva [martyred by the Romans], he rejoiced over his [vast knowledge of] Torah and grieved over his death, saying: *How precious to me are Your companions, O God!* [*How mighty their chiefs!*] (Psalms 139:17).'"

See *Bereshit Rabbah* 24:2; BT *Sanhedrin* 38b; *Zohar* 1:37a–b, 90b, 227b; 2:70a; *ZH* 16d (*MhN*).

1520. **David, king of Israel, who died at birth . . .** According to a midrashic tradition, King David was destined to die at childbirth, but Adam offered him 70 of his own 1000 allotted years, so David lived for 70 years and Adam for 930.

See Genesis 5:5; Jubilees 4:30; *Pirqei de-Rabbi Eli'ezer* 19, and David Luria, ad loc., n. 31; *Midrash Tehillim* 92:10; *Bemidbar Rabbah* 14:12; *Bereshit Rabbati* 5:5; *Yalqut Shim'oni*, Genesis, 41; *Zohar* 1:91b, 140a, 168a, 233b, 248b; 2:103b, 235a; *ZH* 67d (*ShS*), 81a (*MhN*, *Rut*); Moses de León, *Sheqel ha-Qodesh*, 68 (85); idem, *Sod Eser Sefirot Belimah*, 383.

1521. **Adam, deed of the blessed Holy One . . .** Adam, unlike all his descendants, was fashioned solely by God without the participation of human parents.

1522. **the thousand that were his to endure** According to *Bemidbar Rabbah* 14:12, this was Adam's intended life span, "as is said: *On the day you eat from it, you will surely die* (Genesis 2:17), and a day of the blessed Holy One is a thousand years, as is said: *For a thousand years in Your eyes are like a day just gone by* (Psalms 90:4)."

1523. **Seeing his Torah, he rejoiced; seeing his death, he grieved . . .** See above, note 1519. According to BT *Menaḥot* 29b, Moses also saw Akiva's Torah and his death.

1524. *This is the book*—**an actual book . . .** According to various medieval traditions, the angel Raziel (whose name derives from רז [*raz*], "secret") transmitted a magical book to Adam, though after his departure from the Garden of Eden.

According to BT *Bava Metsi'a* 85b–86a, Rabbi Yehudah the Prince once saw *The Book of Adam*, which contained the genealogy of the entire human race. Cf. *Bereshit Rabbah* 24:1; BT *Sanhedrin* 38b. *The Book of Adam* figures prominently in the *Zohar*,

of wisdom expanded, were expounded into 670 engravings of supernal secrets.[1525] In the middle of the book, an engraving of wisdom revealing 1500 keys not transmitted to sacred celestial beings, all concealed in the book until it reached Adam.[1526] As soon as it did, supernal angels thronged to discover and listen; then they declared: *Be exalted above the heavens, O God! Let Your glory manifest over all the earth!* (ibid. 57:12).

"Just then the holy angel Hadraniel[1527] encountered him and exclaimed: 'Adam, Adam, treasure away the precious glory of your Lord, for permission has not been granted to supernal beings to know it, only to you!' So he kept it hidden until he left the Garden of Eden, daily wielding treasures of his Lord,[1528] discovering supernal mysteries of which supernal ministers are unaware.

"As soon as he sinned, violating his Lord's command, that book flew away from him. Adam slapped himself on the head and wept. He entered the waters of Gihon up to his nape, till the water moldered his skin and his luster faded.[1529]

312

sometimes in the context of physiognomy and chiromancy.

See 1:17b, 37b, 58b, 72b, 90b; 2:70a–b, 70a–b (*RR*), 77a, 131a, 143b, 180a, 181a, 197a; 3:10a, 68b; *ZH* 37b; Ginzberg, *Legends*, 5:117–18, n. 110; Liebes, *Peraqim*, 85–87; Wineman, *Mystic Tales from the Zohar*, 35–54. Cf. *Otsar ha-Ge'onim, Ḥagigah* 11b; Naḥmanides on Genesis 5:2.

1525. **Seventy-two species of wisdom...** Corresponding to the seventy-two names of God, a complex divine name derived from the description of the splitting of the Red Sea: Exodus 14:19–21. Each of these three verses contains seventy-two letters. The name is composed of seventy-two triads (or "words"), according to the following pattern: the first letter of the first verse, the last letter of the second verse, the first letter of the third verse (forming the first triad); the second letter of the first verse, the penultimate letter of the second verse, the second letter of the third verse (the second triad); etc.

See *Leqaḥ Tov*, Exodus 14:21; *Bereshit Rabbah* 44:19; *Vayiqra Rabbah* 23:2; *Shir ha-Shirim Rabbah* on 2:2; Rashi on BT *Sukkah* 45a, s.v. אני (*ani*); Hai Gaon, *Otsar ha-Ge'onim, Ḥagigah* 23; *Bahir* 79 (110); *Zohar* 1:7b, 17a; 2:51b, 132b, 270a; 3:150b–151a; Trachten-

berg, *Jewish Magic and Superstition*, 95–97; Kasher, *Torah Shelemah*, 14:67, 284–86.

The 670 engravings may symbolize the seven lower *sefirot*: 600 corresponding to the first six of them, 70 corresponding to the seventh, *Shekhinah*.

1526. **1500 keys...** See *Zohar* 1:37b, where Enoch, also possessing a heavenly book, is said to have one thousand keys. Cf. 1:56b, 92a, 223b.

1527. **Hadraniel** According to *Pesiqta Rabbati* 20, Hadraniel blocked Moses' ascent up Mount Sinai until he was rebuked by God, whereupon he became Moses' guide. See *Zohar* 2:58a, 247a.

1528. **wielding...** משתמש (*Mishtammash*), "Using." The verb has theurgic connotations. See M *Avot* 1:13; *Zohar* 1:31b; Scholem, *Jewish Gnosticism*, 54, n. 36; idem, *Major Trends*, 358, n. 17.

1529. **He entered the waters of Gihon...** On Adam's repentance, see *Bereshit Rabbah* 22:13; BT *Avodah Zarah* 8a; and *Pirqei de-Rabbi Eli'ezer* 20: "On the first day of the week, Adam entered the waters of the upper Gihon until the waters reached his neck, and he fasted seven weeks until his body became like a sieve." Gihon is the name of one of the four rivers of the Garden of Eden (Genesis

"At that moment the blessed Holy One signaled to Raphael, who returned the book to him.[1530] Adam engaged in it and left it to his son Seth, and so to all those generations until it reached Abraham, who thereby discovered how to contemplate the glory of his Lord, as has been said. Similarly a book was given to Enoch, and he contemplated supernal glory."[1531]

Male and female
He created them (Genesis 5:2).

Rabbi Shim'on said, "Supernal secrets are revealed in these two verses.[1532] *Male and female He created them*—revealing supernal glory, mystery of faith, for out of this mystery Adam was created.[1533]

"Come and see: With the secret by which heaven and earth were created, Adam was created. Of them is written: *These are the generations of heaven and earth* (ibid. 2:4). Of Adam is written: *This is the book of the generations of Adam* (ibid. 5:1). Of them is written: *when they were created* (ibid. 2:4). Of Adam is written: *on the day they were created* (ibid. 5:2).[1534]

313

2:13) as well as the spring providing water for Jerusalem. See David Luria on *Pirqei de-Rabbi Eli'ezer* 20, n. 30; *Zohar* 2:35a.

The phrase "moldered his skin" derives from the story of Rabbi Shim'on son of Yoḥai and his son, Rabbi El'azar, who hid from the Roman authorities in a cave for thirteen years "until their bodies were afflicted with moldy sores" (*Bereshit Rabbah* 79:6). See *Zohar* 1:11a. On Adam's luster, see *Bereshit Rabbah* 12:6 (and Theodor, ad loc.).

1530. **Raphael...**   The angel of healing.

1531. **Similarly a book was given to Enoch...**   Concerning Enoch, Genesis 5:24 states: *He was no more, for God took him.* In postbiblical literature this verse is taken to mean that God transported Enoch through the heavens, a journey recorded in the Enoch literature. The *Zohar*'s *Book of Enoch,* though influenced by this literature, is not identical with any of its particular volumes.

See *Zohar* 1:13a, 37b, 72b; 2:55a, 100a, 105b, 180b, 192b, 217a; 3:10b, 236b, 240a, 248b, 253b, 307a; *ZH* 2c (*SO*). Cf. *Aggadat Bereshit,* intro, 38; *Midrash Aggadah,* Genesis 5:24; Ginzberg, *Legends,* 5:156–64, nn. 58–61; Margaliot, *Mal'akhei Elyon,* 80–83.

1532. **Supernal secrets are revealed...**   These two verses (Genesis 5:1–2) are cited elsewhere as biblical indications of the secret arts of physiognomy and chiromancy. See above, note 1524; Scholem, *Kabbalah,* 317–19.

Such techniques were employed by the Merkavah mystics to ascertain whether a potential initiate was fit to receive esoteric teachings. *The book of the generations of Adam* was taken to mean "the book of human character and fate." *Male and female He created them* implied that chiromantic prediction varied according to sex, the right hand being the determining factor for the male, the left hand for the female.

1533. **revealing supernal glory, mystery of faith...**   The human being mirrors the structure of divinity, the ten *sefirot,* in which masculine and feminine are balanced. The union of the divine couple engenders all human souls and constitutes רזא דמהימנותא (*raza dimheimanuta*), "the mystery of faith," the belief system of Kabbalah.

See *Bahir* 55 (82); *Zohar* 1:101b, 160a; 3:117a, 141b (*IR*).

1534. **heaven and earth...Adam...**   Rabbi Shim'on proves the correspondence between Adam's creation and the creation

"*Male and female He created them.* From here we learn: Any image not embracing male and female is not fittingly supernal. So we have established in the mystery of our Mishnah.[1535]

"Come and see: Anywhere male and female are not found as one, the blessed Holy One does not place His abode. Blessings are found solely where male and female are found,[1536] as is written: *He blessed them and named them Adam* (ibid.). It is not written: *He blessed him and named him Adam.* One is not even called אדם (*adam*), human, unless male and female are as one."[1537]

Rabbi Yehudah said, "Ever since the day the Temple was destroyed, blessings are found nowhere in the world;[1538] they are lost every day, as is written: *The righteous one loses* (Isaiah 57:1). What does *loses* mean? He loses the blessings found within Him, as is written: *blessings upon the head of the righteous* (Proverbs 10:6). It is written as well: *Faith has lost* (Jeremiah 7:28).[1539]

314

of heaven and earth by verbal analogy (*gezerah shavah,* "equal category"), a common rabbinic technique of interpretation. The human being is a microcosm.

See *Tanḥuma, Pequdei* 3; *Avot de-Rabbi Natan* A, 31; *Qohelet Rabbah* on 1:4; *Zohar* 1:90b, 134b, 186b.

1535. **mystery of our Mishnah** This formulation appears nowhere in the Mishnah. Rabbi Shim'on is apparently alluding to a secret, mystical Mishnah known only to his circle. See *Zohar* 1:37b, 91b, 93a, 95b, 96a, 224a, 252a (*Hash*); 3:57b, 61b, 78a, 284b, 285a. (This is to be distinguished from the *Matnitin* of the *Zohar,* on which see Scholem, *Kabbalah,* 216).

See BT *Bava Batra* 74b: "Rabbi Yehudah said in the name of Rav, 'Everything that the blessed Holy One created in His world He created male and female.'" See *Zohar* 1:157b; 2:144b.

1536. **Blessings are found solely...** See BT *Yevamot* 62b: "Rabbi Tanḥum said in the name of Rabbi Ḥanilai, 'Any man without a wife is without joy, without blessing, without goodness.'"

See *Zohar* 1:165a, 182a; 3:74b; 296a (*IZ*).

1537. **One is not even called אדם (*adam*), human...** See BT *Yevamot* 63b: "Rabbi El'azar said, 'Any אדם (*adam*), man, without a wife is not an *adam,* as is said: *Male and*

*female He created them...and He named them adam.'" See *Bereshit Rabbah* 17:2.*

Rabbi Shim'on is also alluding to the original androgynous nature of Adam, reflecting the divine union of male and female, *Tif'eret* and *Shekhinah.* See *Bereshit Rabbah* 8:1: "Rabbi Yirmeyah son of El'azar said, 'When the blessed Holy One created Adam, He created him androgynous, as is said: *Male and female He created them* (Genesis 1:27).' Rabbi Shemu'el son of Naḥman said, 'When the blessed Holy One created Adam, He created him with two faces. Then He sawed him and gave him two backs, one on this side and one on that.'"

See BT *Berakhot* 61a; *Eruvin* 18a; Plato, *Symposium* 189d–191d; *Zohar* 1:2b, 13b, 47a; 2:55a, 144b; 3:5a, 44b; Matt, *Zohar,* 217.

1538. **Ever since the day the Temple was destroyed...** See M *Sotah* 9:12: "Rabban Shim'on son of Gamli'el says in the name of Rabbi Yehoshu'a, 'Ever since the day that the Temple was destroyed, there is no day without a curse, dew has not descended as a blessing, and flavor has departed from fruit.'"

In Kabbalah the destruction of the Temple symbolizes the separation of the divine couple. See *Zohar* 1:70b, 134a; 3:74b.

1539. *The righteous one loses...* Usually translated: *The righteous one perishes.* Rabbi

Similarly, *He blessed them* (Genesis, ibid.), and *God blessed them* (ibid. 1:28).[1540]

"Back to שת (*Shet*), Seth, all generations trace, all truly righteous of the world."[1541]

Rabbi Yose said, "These are the final letters found in Torah.[1542] For Adam violated all the letters of Torah, [56a] and when he returned to the presence of his Lord[1543] he grasped these two, whereupon the letters were restored, though not fully arrayed until Israel stood at Mount Sinai. Then they were restored consummately as on the day heaven and earth were created, and the world turned fragrant and firm, erected enduringly."[1544]

Rabbi Abba said, "On the day Adam violated the command of his Lord, heaven and earth sought to uproot themselves. Why? Because they were based solely on the covenant, as is written: *Were it not for My covenant with day and night, I would not have established the laws of heaven and earth* (Jeremiah 33:25),[1545] and Adam violated the covenant, as is said: *Like Adam, they violated*

Yehudah understands the verse to mean that *Yesod* ("Foundation"), known as *Righteous One*, loses the flow of emanation intended for *Shekhinah*, known as *Faith*. See *Zohar* 1:182a; 3:16b. *Yesod*'s title, *Righteous One*, is based on Proverbs 10:25: וצדיק יסוד עולם (*Ve-tsaddiq yesod olam*). The verse literally means *The righteous one is an everlasting foundation* but is understood as *The righteous one is the foundation of the world*.

See BT *Ḥagigah* 12b; *Bahir* 71 (102); Azriel of Gerona, *Peirush ha-Aggadot*, 34.

1540. **Similarly, *He blessed them*...** Both passages specify that the human being was created *male and female*, a condition essential to receiving blessing.

1541. **Back to שת (*Shet*), Seth, all generations trace...** See *Bemidbar Rabbah* 14:12: "He named him שת (*Shet*), Seth (Genesis 5:3), because on him the world הושתת (*hushtat*), was founded."

On the righteous descending from Seth, see *Pirqei de-Rabbi Eli'ezer* 22; *Zohar* 1:36b, 38a, 54a, 55a; 3:77a.

1542. **These are the final letters...** The letters ש (*shin*) and ת (*tav*), which spell שת (*Shet*), Seth, are the final letters of the Hebrew alphabet.

1543. **when he returned to the presence of his Lord** Repenting sincerely.

1544. **Adam violated all the letters of Torah...** By his sin, Adam ruined the creative flow of emanation, pictured as a linguistic stream. So the letters of the alphabet were reversed. By turning back to God, he began to restore the letters to their proper order; the first two to be restored were ש (*shin*) and ת (*tav*), which Adam employed to name his son שת (*Shet*), Seth. The process of alphabetic restoration was completed at Mount Sinai, when language manifested perfectly through the revelation of Torah, a renewal of the act of Creation.

See *Zohar* 1:67b; 2:51b; *ZḤ* 66c–d (*ShS*), 83b (*MhN, Rut*). On the letters appearing in reverse order at Creation, see *Zohar* 1:2b, 205b; *ZḤ* 88c–d (*MhN, Rut*).

The phrase "turned fragrant and firm" renders both senses of אתבסם (*itbassam*), "was sweetened" or "was firmly established."

See *Bereshit Rabbah* 66:2; *Midrash Shemu'el* 26:4; *Zohar* 1:30b, 31a, 34a, 37a, 137a; 2:143a, 168a, 227a; 3:18a; N. Bronsnick, in *Sinai* 63 (1968): 81–85; Scholem, *Major Trends*, 165, 388, n. 44; idem, *Kabbalah*, 228.

1545. **heaven and earth sought to uproot themselves...** See *Shemot Rabbah* 47:4: "[God said to Israel,] 'Had you not accepted My Torah, I would have returned the world to *chaos and void* (Genesis 1:2), as is said:

315

the covenant (Hosea 6:7).[1546] If it had not been revealed to the blessed Holy One that Israel was destined to stand firm at Mount Sinai, affirming this covenant, this world would not have endured."

Rabbi Ḥizkiyah said, "Whoever confesses his sin is forgiven and pardoned by the blessed Holy One. Come and see: When the blessed Holy One created the world, He fashioned this covenant, upon which the world was established. How do we know? As it is written: בראשית (Be-reshit), In the beginning (Genesis 1:1): ברא שית (bara shit), created foundation. This is the covenant upon which the world stood firm, a conduit through which blessings flow and gush to the world.[1547] Adam violated this covenant, wrenching it from its site.[1548]

"This covenant is intimated by the letter י (yod), a tiny letter, root and foundation of the world.[1549] When he engendered a son he confessed his sin,

316

Were it not for My covenant with day and night, [I would not have established the laws of heaven and earth]. Why? Because with Torah I created heaven and earth.... If you annul the covenant [of Torah], you cause Me to return the upper and lower realms to chaos and void.'"

See BT Shabbat 33a, 88a, and 137b, where the verse from Jeremiah is applied to the covenant of circumcision: "Were it not for the blood of the covenant, heaven and earth would not endure, as is said: Were it not for My covenant with day and night, I would not have established the laws of heaven and earth."

Cf. Zohar 1:32a, 59b, 66b, 89a, 93b.

1546. Adam violated the covenant... Adam's sin is related specifically to the covenant of circumcision. See BT Sanhedrin 38b: "Rabbi Yitsḥak said, 'He [Adam] stretched his foreskin. Here is written: Like Adam, they violated the covenant, and there is written: He has broken My covenant [by not fulfilling the command of circumcision] (Genesis 17:14).'" The phrase "stretched his foreskin" refers to epispasm, an attempt to disguise circumcision by cutting and pulling forward the loose skin of the penis to form a partial foreskin.

In the Zohar, Adam's sin is understood as ruining the union of Shekhinah and Yesod, the divine phallus, site of the covenant. See Zohar 1:35b, 53b.

1547. בראשית (Be-reshit), In the beginning: ברא שית (bara shit), created foundation The opening word of the Torah, בראשית (Be-reshit), is divided in two. See BT Sukkah 49a: "It was taught in the school of Rabbi Yishma'el: 'Be-reshit ... Do not read בראשית (Be-reshit) but rather ברא שית (bara shit),'" referring to the שיתין (shitin), "hollows, pits," beneath the main Temple altar, into which the wine and water of libation flowed.

Here Rabbi Ḥizkiyah alludes to the covenant of Yesod ("Foundation"), upon which the world is based and through which it receives the flow of emanation. Elsewhere the phrase ברא שית (bara shit) means "created six," which also applies to Yesod, sixth of the seven lower sefirot.

See Seder Rabbah di-Vreshit, 1 (Battei Midrashot, 1:19); Midrash ha-Gadol, Genesis 1:1, 11–12; Zohar 1:3b, 15b, 30a, 39b.

1548. wrenching it from its site Disrupting the union of Yesod and Shekhinah.

1549. This covenant is intimated by the letter י (yod)... The mark of circumcision is pictured as the smallest of the Hebrew letters. In Tanḥuma, Tsav 14, Shemini 8, this mark is identified with the י (yod) of the divine name שדי (Shaddai). A German Hasidic tradition identifies the mark with the yod of יהוה (YHVH). Here the י (yod) signifies Yesod ("Foundation").

See Zohar 1:2b, 13a, 95a–b; 2:36a, 216b; 3:142a (IR), 215b, 220a, 256a (RM); Wolfson,

naming him שת (*Shet*), Seth, not enunciating י (*yod*) and thereby forming שית (*shit*), foundation, for this he had violated.[1550] So from here the blessed Holy One sowed the world; to here all generations of the righteous trace.[1551]

"Come and see: When Israel stood at Mount Sinai, between these two letters entered the mystery of covenant.[1552] Who is that? ב (*Bet*), entering between the two surviving letters and transmitted to Israel.[1553] When ב (*bet*)—mystery of covenant—entered between these two letters, שבת (*shabbat*), Sabbath, entered into being, as is said: *The Children of Israel shall observe the Sabbath, celebrating the Sabbath throughout their generations as an eternal covenant* (Exodus 31:16).[1554] As at the beginning of the world all generations stood poised to descend from the two letters, ש״ת (*shin, tav*), so these two remained suspended until the world was perfected and the holy covenant entered between them, consummating, becoming שבת (*shabbat*), Sabbath."[1555]

Rabbi Yose said, "These two letters were consummated by the letter ב (*bet*). When the letters were reversed, from the day Seth was born letters were restored in every single generation until Israel reached Mount Sinai and they were perfectly arrayed."[1556]

Rabbi Yehudah said, "They were restored below, and in every single generation the world was embraced by letters, but they did not settle in their sites. When Torah was transmitted to Israel, all was arrayed."

in *JQR* 78 (1987): 77–112; idem, *Circle in the Square*, 29–48.

1550. **When he engendered a son...** When Adam engendered his third son, he named him שת (*shet*), Seth, and not שית (*shit*), "foundation," which contains the letter י (*yod*). The missing letter implied that he had impaired *Yesod* ("Foundation"). See *TZ* 69 (110a, 119a).

1551. **So from here the blessed Holy One sowed the world...** Since Adam repented. אשתיל (*Ashtil*), "Sowed, planted" is a play on the midrashic wording (*Bemidbar Rabbah* 14:12): "*He named him* שת (*Shet*), *Seth* (Genesis 5:3), because on him the world הושתת (*hushtat*), was founded."

See *Aggadat Bereshit*, intro, 37; *Pirqei de-Rabbi Eli'ezer* 22; *Zohar* 1:36b, 38a, 54a, 55a–b; 3:77a; Ginzberg, *Legends*, 5:148, n. 50; Liebes, *Peraqim*, 372–73; Stroumsa, *Another Seed*, 74.

1552. **between these two letters...** Between the letters ש (*shin*) and ת (*tav*).

1553. ב (***Bet***), **entering between the two surviving letters...** The letter ב (*bet*) symbolizes ברית (*berit*), "covenant." ש (*Shin*) and ת (*tav*), the final letters of the alphabet, were the first to be restored to their proper order after Adam violated all the letters of Torah (see above, page 315).

1554. שבת (***shabbat***), **Sabbath...** Composed of all three letters and identified as the *covenant* of *Yesod*.

1555. **As at the beginning of the world...** Following the tragedy of Cain and Abel, שת (*Shet*), Seth, represented a new beginning of humanity. Similarly at Mount Sinai, the letters ש (*shin*) and ת (*tav*) symbolized a new beginning, which unfolded when they were joined by the letter ב (*bet*).

1556. **When the letters were reversed...** See above, note 1544.

Rabbi El'azar said, "In the days of Enosh humans became skilled in the wisdom of sorcery and magic, in the art of blocking heavenly powers.[1557] Ever since Adam left the Garden of Eden, taking with him the wisdom of the leaves of the tree,[1558] no human had engaged in it, for Adam, his wife, and his descendants until Enosh abandoned it. When Enosh appeared he saw them,[1559] saw their wisdom transforming upper beings. They engaged, achieving effects, performing sorcery and magic, till that wisdom spread through the generation of the Flood, all of whom enacted their acts wickedly. Defying Noah with those forms of wisdom, they asserted that universal justice could not prevail against them, for they were actualizing wisdom to repel all those masters of judgment.[1560] So from the time of Enosh they all began to engage in these forms of wisdom, as is written: *Then the name of YHVH was invoked profanely* (Genesis 4:26)."[1561]

Rabbi Yitsḥak said, "All the righteous who appeared later among that generation—such as Jered, Methuselah, and Enoch[1562]—tried to thwart them but failed, so the wicked proliferated, rebelling against their Lord, exclaiming: *What is Shaddai that we should serve Him?* (Job 21:15).[1563] Did they really speak such stupidity? Rather, since they knew all those modes of wisdom and all the officials of the world appointed over them, they relied upon them,[1564] till finally the blessed Holy One turned the world back into what it had been. For [56b] originally it was water intermingled with water,[1565] and afterward He

318

1557. **In the days of Enosh...** According to rabbinic tradition, the generation of Enosh was the first to commit idolatry by worshiping the heavenly bodies.

See *Mekhilta, Baḥodesh* 6; *Bereshit Rabbah* 23:7; *Targum Yerushalmi*, Genesis 4:26; Rashi on Genesis, ibid.; Maimonides, *Mishneh Torah, Hilkhot Avodah Zarah* 1:1; Ginzberg, *Legends*, 5:151, n. 54.

Here the sin is sorcery and specifically interfering with heavenly powers.

1558. **the wisdom of the leaves of the tree** The leaves of the Tree of Knowledge convey the knowledge of magic. See *Zohar* 1:36b, 53b, 63b. Cf. BT *Bava Metsi'a* 114b.

1559. **saw them** Saw the leaves of the tree.

1560. **Defying Noah...** According to a rabbinic tradition, Noah attempted to warn his contemporaries and induce them to repent, but he was unsuccessful. See *Bereshit Rabbah* 30:7; *Tanḥuma, Noaḥ* 5; BT *Sanhedrin* 108a–b. Armed with magical knowledge,

the sinners of Noah's generation were confident that they could repel the powers of judgment.

1561. *Then the name of YHVH was invoked profanely* The verse means literally: *Then* הוחל (huḥal), *it was begun, to invoke the name YHVH.* Here, following midrashic tradition, the word הוחל (huḥal) is derived from the root meaning "profane" and applied to the practice of sorcery. See above, note 1557.

1562. **Jered, Methuselah, and Enoch** See Genesis 5:15–27; *Sefer ha-Yashar, Noaḥ*, 56.

1563. *What is Shaddai that we should serve Him?* See *Bereshit Rabbah* 38:6.

1564. **since they knew all those modes of wisdom...** They thought that with their magical knowledge they could block any form of heavenly punishment.

1565. **it was water intermingled with water** הוה מים במים (Havah mayim be-mayim). See *Tanḥuma, Vayaqhel* 6: "When the blessed Holy One created His world, היה העולם כלו

returned the world to its original state, though not completely devastated, since He gazed upon it compassionately, as is written: *YHVH sat enthroned at the Flood* (Psalms 29:10), not *Elohim*.[1566]

"In the days of Enosh even children of those days all gazed upon supernal modes of wisdom, contemplating them."

Rabbi Yeisa said, "If so, they were stupid, since they did not know that the blessed Holy One intended to inundate them with waters of the Flood, in which they would perish!"

Rabbi Yitsḥak replied, "They certainly did know, yet their minds embraced stupidity, for they knew the angel empowered over fire and the one empowered over water, and they knew how to block them, preventing them from executing judgment upon them. But they did not know that the blessed Holy One rules over earth, that from Him issues judgment upon the world.[1567] Rather, they saw that the world was entrusted to those officials, who controlled all mundane matters, so they failed to contemplate the blessed Holy One or consider His exploits until the earth was destroyed and Holy Spirit proclaimed daily: *Let sinners be consumed from the earth, and the wicked be no more* (Psalms 104:35). The blessed Holy One delayed patiently as long as those righteous ones endured in the world.[1568] As soon as they departed from the world, He brought judgment upon them and they perished, as is said: *They were obliterated from the earth* (Genesis 7:23)."

319

מים במים (hayah ha-olam kullo mayim be-mayim), it was entirely water intermingled with water."

Cf. JT *Ḥagigah* 2:1, 77a; *Pesiqta Rabbati* 1; *Shemot Rabbah* 50:1; *Zohar* 1:17b. Only on the second day of Creation were the waters separated (see Genesis 1:6–7).

1566. *YHVH sat enthroned at the Flood, not Elohim* In rabbinic literature these two names represent, respectively, the divine qualities of compassion and justice.

See *Sifrei*, Deuteronomy 26; *Bereshit Rabbah* 12:15; 33:3; *Zohar* 1:64b; 2:187a, 227b.

1567. **they knew the angel empowered over fire...** See *Eikhah Rabbah* 2:5, describing the scene in Jerusalem on the eve of the Babylonian attack: "Before the vicious enemy came, Jeremiah kept calling to them, 'Turn back to God so that you will not go into exile.' They retorted, 'If the enemy comes, what can they do to us?' One said,

'[By invoking the aid of the appropriate heavenly prince] I will surround the city with a wall of water.' Another said, 'I will surround it with a wall of fire.' Another said, 'I will surround it with a wall of iron.' The blessed Holy One replied, 'You are exploiting what is Mine!' He immediately changed the names of the angels, empowering the angel in charge of water over fire, and the one in charge of fire over iron, so when they invoked their names below, they did not respond."

Here Rabbi Yitsḥak adapts the midrashic account to the eve of the Flood. See Moses de León, *Sefer ha-Rimmon*, 281–82; Maimonides, *Mishneh Torah, Hilkhot Avodah Zarah* 1:1–2.

1568. **as long as those righteous ones...** Such as Jered, Methuselah, and Enoch (see above, page 318).

Enoch walked with God;
then he was no more,
for God took him (Genesis 5:24).

Rabbi Yose opened, "*While the king was on his couch, my spikenard spread its fragrance* (Song of Songs 1:12). This verse has been discussed,[1569] but come and see! Such are the ways of the blessed Holy One: When a person cleaves to Him, so He plants His abode upon him, yet knowing that one day he will decay, He culls his fragrance ahead of time, plucking him from the world,[1570] as is written: *While the king was on his couch, my spikenard spread its fragrance. While the king*—the blessed Holy One. במסבו (*Bimsibbo*), *On his couch*—a person cleaving to Him, walking in His ways.[1571] *My spikenard spread its fragrance*—good deeds, on account of which he is plucked from the world prematurely.

"Concerning this King Solomon said, *There is futility befalling earth: there are righteous people* [*treated according to the conduct of the wicked, and there are wicked people treated according to the conduct of the righteous*] (Ecclesiastes 8:14). *There are righteous people treated according to the conduct of the wicked,* as we have established: because of their good deeds, the blessed Holy One removes them from the world prematurely, executing judgment upon them. *And there are wicked people treated according to the conduct of the righteous,* for the blessed Holy One prolongs their days and postpones His anger, as has all been explained: these, so that they not decay; those, so they turn back to Him, or so virtuous children issue from them.[1572]

"Come and see: Enoch was pure, but the blessed Holy One saw that he would eventually decay, so He gathered him in beforehand, as is written: *to gather lilies* (Song of Songs 6:2)—because of their fragrance the blessed Holy One gathers them before they decay.[1573] *Then he was no more, for God took him.*

1569. **This verse has been discussed** See BT *Shabbat* 88b, where the verse is applied to the Children of Israel at Sinai. Cf. *Shir ha-Shirim Rabbah* on 1:12.

1570. **one day he will decay...** Since God knows that the person will degenerate morally, He plucks him prematurely from the world. See *Qohelet Rabbah* on 7:23, and below.

1571. במסבו (*Bimsibbo*), *On his couch*—a **person cleaving to Him...** The human devotee has transformed himself into a dwelling place for God.

1572. **those, so they turn back to Him...** The days of the wicked are prolonged to enable them to turn back to God or to engender worthy children.

See BT *Bava Qamma* 38b; *Vayiqra Rabbah* 32:4; *Zohar* 1:118a (*MhN*), 140a, 227a.

1573. **Enoch was pure...** See *Bereshit Rabbah* 25:1: "*Enoch walked with God; then he was no more, for God took him....* Rabbi Aivu said, 'Enoch was a hypocrite, sometimes righteous, sometimes wicked. The blessed Holy One said, "While he is righteous I will remove him."'"

See Theodor, ad loc.; *Wisdom of Solomon* 4:10–11; *Shir ha-Shirim Rabbah* on 6:2; *Zohar* 2:10b, 96a; *ZH* 20a–b (*MhN*), 36b (*ST*); cf. M *Sanhedrin* 8:5; *Sifrei*, Deuteronomy 218.

Then he was no more—not living as long as other humans. Why? Because the blessed Holy One *took him* before his time."

Rabbi El'azar said, "He *took him* from the earth, raised him to the highest heavens, and transmitted to him all supernal treasures, along with forty-five secret engraved keys, wielded by highest angels. All these were handed to him, as we have established."[1574]

YHVH saw that human evil on earth was immense, and every thought devised by their mind [was nothing but evil all day] (Genesis 6:5).

Rabbi Yehudah opened, "*You are not a God who delights in wickedness; evil cannot abide with You* (Psalms 5:5). This verse has been discussed and established,[1575] but come and see! Whoever clings to the evil impulse and is drawn after it, defiles himself and is defiled, as has been said.[1576] *That human evil on earth was immense*—they committed all sorts of evil, but their guilt was incomplete until they spilled blood upon the earth fruitlessly.[1577] Who wasted their ways upon earth?[1578] As is written: *nothing but evil all day.* Here is written: *nothing but evil,* [57a] and there is written: *Evil cannot abide*

1574. **He *took him* from the earth, raised him to the highest heavens...** God transported Enoch through the heavens, a journey recorded in *The Book of Enoch*.

See *Aggadat Bereshit*, intro, 38; *Midrash Aggadah*, Genesis 5:24; *Zohar* 1:37b, 55b; Ginzberg, *Legends*, 5:156–64, nn. 58–61; Margaliot, *Mal'akhei Elyon*, 80–83.

The number forty-five may allude to the numerical value of the divine name יהוה (*YHVH*) spelled out according to its letters: יוד (*yod*), הא (*he*), ואו (*vav*), הא (*he*), which equals the value of the word אדם (*adam*). See *Zohar* 1:34b.

In Heikhalot literature Enoch is identified with the chief angel, Metatron, sometimes described as יהוה קטן (*YHVH Qatan*), "Lesser YHVH." See BT *Yevamot* 16b, and *Tosafot*, s.v. *pasuq zeh; Sanhedrin* 38b; *Targum Yerushalmi*, Genesis 5:24; *Zohar* 1:21a, 37b, 223b; 2:179a (*SdTs*), Scholem, *Kabbalah*, 378–79; Margaliot, *Mal'akhei Elyon*, 89–90.

1575. **This verse has been discussed...** See BT *Sotah* 42a; *Niddah* 13b.

1576. **defiles himself and is defiled...** See BT *Shabbat* 104a: "Resh Lakish said,

'...If one comes to defile himself, he is provided an opening; if one comes to purify himself, he is assisted.'"

See *Yoma* 39a: "Our Rabbis taught: '*Do not defile yourselves with them, and thus become defiled* (Leviticus 11:43). If one defiles himself slightly, he is defiled greatly; below, he is defiled from above; in this world, he is defiled in the world to come.'"

Cf. *Zohar* 1:53b–54a, 169b, 198b; 2:50a; 3:47a.

1577. **spilled blood upon the earth fruitlessly** An allusion to masturbation. See BT *Niddah* 13a: "Rabbi Yitshak and Rabbi Ammi said, '[Whoever emits semen fruitlessly] is as though he sheds blood.'"

See *Zohar* 1:188a, 219b; Moses de León, *Shushan Edut*, 353; Tishby, *Wisdom of the Zohar*, 3:1365–66.

1578. **Who wasted their ways upon earth?** See Genesis 6:12: *God saw the earth, and behold, it was corrupt, for all flesh had corrupted their way upon earth.* The expression *corrupted their way* is interpreted as referring to masturbation in *Kallah Rabbati* 2, which cites Genesis 38:9: שחת ארצה [*Shiḥet*

with You, and similarly: *Er, firstborn of Judah, was evil in the eyes of YHVH* (Genesis 38:7)."[1579]

Rabbi Yose said, "Isn't *evil* the same as *wicked*?

He replied, "No. One is called *wicked* even if he merely raises his hand against his fellow without harming him at all,[1580] but one is only called *evil* if he wastes his way, defiling himself, defiling the earth, empowering the impure spirit called *evil,* as is written: *nothing but evil all day.*[1581] He never enters the palace nor gazes upon the face of *Shekhinah,* for on account of this *Shekhinah* withdraws from the world.[1582]

"How do we know? From Jacob, for when *Shekhinah* departed from him, he thought there was a blemish in his sons,[1583] on account of whom the impure spirit was empowered in the world, the light of the moon diminished, the moon tainted.[1584]

artsah], *He* [Onan] *wasted* [his seed] *on the ground.*

322

See *Pirqei de-Rabbi Eli'ezer* 22; *Bereshit Rabbah* 26:4; Rashi on BT *Shabbat* 41a, s.v. *ke-illu mevi mabbul la-olam; Zohar* 1:62a, 69a.

1579. *Er, firstborn of Judah, was evil...* Genesis does not specify the nature of Er's sin, but rabbinic tradition maintains that it was the same as that of his younger brother, Onan, who let his seed *waste on the ground* (Genesis 38:9).

See BT *Yevamot* 34b; *Bereshit Rabbah* 85:4 (and Theodor, ad loc.); *Targum Yerushalmi,* Genesis 38:7.

1580. **One is called *wicked*...** רשע (Rasha) means both "wicked" and "guilty." See BT *Sanhedrin* 58b: "Resh Lakish said, 'One who raises his hand against his fellow, even if he does not strike him, is called *rasha,* wicked, as is written: *He* [Moses] *said to the* rasha, *guilty one: Why will you strike your fellow?* (Exodus 2:13). It is not written *Why did you strike?* but rather *Why will you strike?* Even though he had not yet struck him, he was called *rasha.*'"

1581. **one is only called *evil* if he wastes his way...** The act of masturbation nourishes the demonic.

See *Zohar* 1:19a, 188a, 219b; 3:90a, 158a; Tishby, *Wisdom of the Zohar,* 3:1365–66. Above (pages 309–10) it is said that Na'amah,

mother of demons, titillates men in their sleep, causing nocturnal emissions.

1582. **He never enters the palace...** See BT *Niddah* 13b: "Rabbi Ammi said, 'Whoever excites himself lustfully is not allowed to enter the domain of the blessed Holy One.'" Cf. *Zohar* 1:69a; Moses de León, *Mishkan ha-Edut,* 23b.

Sexual purity is a prerequisite for encountering *Shekhinah,* who in general flees from sin. See BT *Ḥagigah* 16a: "Rabbi Yitsḥak said, 'Whoever sins secretly, it is as if he thrusts away the feet of *Shekhinah.*'"

1583. **he thought there was a blemish in his sons** See BT *Pesaḥim* 56a: "Rabbi Shim'on son of Lakish said, '... [Upon his death bed] Jacob wished to reveal to his sons the end of days, but *Shekhinah* departed from him. He said, "Perhaps, Heaven forbid, there is someone unfit in my bed [i.e., among my children], like Abraham, from whom issued Ishmael, or like my father Isaac, from whom issued Esau." His sons answered him, "*Hear, O Israel!* [i.e., Jacob]. *YHVH is our God, YHVH is one* (Deuteronomy 6:4): just as there is only *one* in your heart, so there is only *one* in ours." At that moment our father Jacob opened and exclaimed, "Blessed be the name of His glorious kingdom forever and ever."'"

1584. **impure spirit was empowered... light of the moon diminished...** Human

"If you ask, 'Why?' Because this defiles the sanctuary, so She withdrew from Jacob.[1585] All the more so, one defiling his way and defiling himself empowers the impure spirit; so in becoming defiled he is called *evil*.

"Come and see: When a person defiles himself, he is not visited favorably by the blessed Holy One, but rather visited continually, malevolently by that one called *evil*,[1586] as is written: *Passing the night in contentment, he will not be visited by evil* (Proverbs 19:23)—when he walks on the straight path, *he will not be visited by evil*.[1587] Concerning this is written: *nothing but evil all day*, and similarly: *Evil cannot abide with You*. Such a one is called *evil*, not *wicked*. So, too, is written: *Though I walk through the valley of the shadow of death, I fear no evil, for You are with me* (Psalms 23:4)."

וינחם יהוה (Va-yinnaḥem YHVH), *YHVH was sorry, that He had made humankind on earth, and His heart was saddened* (Genesis 6:6).

Rabbi Yose opened, "*Woe unto them who haul iniquity with cords of* שוא (shav), *falsehood, and sin as with a cart rope* (Isaiah 5:18). *Woe unto them who haul iniquity*—people who sin in the presence of their Lord every day, and in whose eyes those sins appear like *cords of* שוא (shav), *nothingness*, the sin they commit like nothing at all, unnoticed by the blessed Holy One, till eventually they make that sin as thick and strong *as a cart rope*, so strong as to be indestructible.[1588]

"Come and see: When the blessed Holy One executes judgment upon the wicked, even though they have sinned in His presence, provoking Him daily, He does not want to exterminate them from the world. Observing their works, He feels *sorry* for them, work of His hands, and prolongs them in the world. Since they are the work of His hands, He takes compassion upon them, feels *sorry* for them, pities them. On the verge of executing judgment upon them, He is *saddened*, as it were, as is said: *No entertainment was brought before him*

323

misconduct diminishes the light of *Shekhinah*, symbolized by the moon, and empowers the demonic.

See BT *Ḥullin* 60b; *Zohar* 1:19b–20a, 146a.

1585. **this defiles the sanctuary...** Sin, especially sexual sin, defiles *Shekhinah*, symbolized by the sanctuary.

1586. **by that one called *evil*** By the demonic, which manifests as the evil impulse. See BT *Bava Batra* 16a: "Resh Lakish said, 'Satan, the evil impulse, and the Angel of Death are one and the same.'"

Cf. *Zohar* 1:35b, 52a, 198a–b, 202a; 2:262b–263a; Moses de León, *Sefer ha-Rimmon*, 394–95.

1587. *Passing the night in contentment...* Not being seduced by lust. See BT *Sukkah* 52b: "Rabbi Yoḥanan said, 'Man has a small organ. If he starves it, it is satisfied; if he satisfies it, it is hungry.'"

1588. **till eventually they make that sin as thick and strong *as a cart rope*...** See BT *Sukkah* 52a: "Rabbi Assi said, 'The evil impulse at first resembles the thread of a

(Daniel 6:19),[1589] for since they are the work of His hands, He feels sad for them."[1590]

"But it is written: *Splendor and majesty are before Him, power and joy in His place* (1 Chronicles 16:27)."[1591]

Rabbi Yose said, "Come and see! It is written: *His heart was saddened—His heart*, no other place; *His heart*, as is said: *who will act according to what is in My heart and in My soul* (1 Samuel 2:35)."[1592]

Rabbi Yitsḥak said, "וינחם יהוה (*Va-yinnaḥem YHVH*), *YHVH renounced*, as is said: וינחם יהוה (*Va-yinnaḥem YHVH*), *YHVH renounced, the evil He had intended to bring upon His people* (Exodus 32:14)."[1593]

Rabbi Yeisa explained it positively; Rabbi Ḥizkiyah, negatively.

Rabbi Yeisa explained it positively, as has been said, that the blessed Holy One feels *sorry* for those works of His hands, feels compassion for them. He is *saddened* because they sin in His presence.

Rabbi Ḥizkiyah explained it negatively, for when the blessed Holy One wants to exterminate the wicked from the world, He is consoled over them, as it were, like one reconciled to a loss. Once He has been consoled, judgment is

324

spider but ultimately it resembles cart ropes, as is said: *Woe unto them who haul iniquity with cords of nothingness, and sin as with a cart rope.*' Cf. *Zohar* 1:5a.

1589. *No entertainment was brought before him* Describing the scene in the palace of King Darius, after he sent Daniel to the lions' den. Here the verse is applied to God.

1590. **since they are the work of His hands...** See BT *Megillah* 10b: "Rabbi Yoḥanan said, '[At the Red Sea] the ministering angels wanted to sing, but the blessed Holy One said, "The work of My hands is drowning in the sea, and you are singing?"'" Rabbi Yose understands the verse in Genesis to mean: *YHVH was sorry* [about punishing them] *because He had made humankind on earth, and His heart was saddened.*

1591. **But it is written...** See BT *Ḥagigah* 5b: "*If you will not listen, My soul will weep in secret because of the arrogance* (Jeremiah 13:17).... But is there weeping in the presence of [i.e., on the part of] the blessed Holy One? Look, Rabbi Papa has said: 'There is no sadness in the presence of the blessed Holy One, as is said: *Splendor and majesty are before Him, power and joy in His*

place.' There is no contradiction: this refers to the inner chambers; that refers to the outer chambers." The last sentence is usually taken to mean: "This [the weeping] refers to the inner chambers; that [the joy] refers to the outer chambers."

1592. *His heart*, **no other place...** The divine sadness is confined to *Shekhinah*, the last *sefirah*, known as *heart* and *soul*, while in the higher realms joy prevails. This view accords with Ḥanan'el ben Ḥushi'el's interpretation of the passage cited from *Ḥagigah* in the previous note: "This [the joy] refers to the inner chambers; that [the weeping] refers to the outer chambers."

See *Zohar* 1:163a (and *KP*, ad loc.); 2:17b–18a; 3:15b; Margaliot, *Sha'arei Zohar*, *Ḥagigah* 5b.

1593. *YHVH renounced, the evil...* In this verse, the word וינחם (*va-yinnaḥem*) can be rendered variously: "changed His mind, retracted, renounced, relented, repented, regretted, was sorry." Rabbi Yitsḥak apparently understands the word in the sense of "renounced," and similarly in Genesis 6:6: *YHVH renounced having made humankind on earth.*

certainly executed, independent of returning to God.[1594] When does it depend on returning? Until He is consoled over them. Once He is, it does not depend on returning at all, and judgment is executed. Then judgment is added to judgment, intensifying that site of judgment, and He exterminates the wicked from the world.[1595] All in the text, as is written: וינחם יהוה (*Va-yinnaḥem YHVH*), *YHVH was comforted*—He was consoled. Afterward, ויתעצב אל לבו (*Va-yit'atstsev el libbo*), *His heart was embittered*—He empowered Judgment to execute judgment.[1596]

Rabbi Ḥiyya said, "*YHVH was comforted when He had made Adam on earth.* The blessed Holy One was comforted and overjoyed *when He had made Adam on earth,* for he resembled the supernal, and upon seeing his supernal image, all the supernal angels praised the blessed Holy One, saying: [57b] *You made him little less than God, adorned him with glory and majesty!* (Psalms 8:6). Afterward when Adam sinned, He *was saddened,* for he provided a rationale to the supernal angels who had exclaimed before Him: *What is a human that You are mindful of him, a human being that You take note of him?* (Psalms 8:5)."[1597]

Rabbi Yehudah said, "*His heart was saddened* because He had to execute judgment upon them, as is said: *going forth before the warriors,* [*exclaiming:*] *'Praise YHVH, for His love endures forever'* (2 Chronicles 20:21), and Rabbi Yitsḥak has said, 'Why is it not written here: *for it is good?* Because He was about to destroy the work of His hands in the presence of Israel.' Correspondingly when Israel was crossing the sea, the celestial angels came that night to

325

1594. **returning to God** Repenting sincerely.

1595. **that site of judgment...** *Shekhinah,* who receives the power of judgment from *Gevurah* and executes it upon humans. See *Zohar* 1:70b.

1596. ויתעצב אל לבו (*Va-yit'atstsev el libbo*), *His heart was embittered...* *Shekhinah,* known as both *heart* and Judgment, was empowered by the harshness of *Gevurah.*

1597. *What is a human that You are mindful of him...* See BT *Sanhedrin* 38b: "Rav Yehudah said in the name of Rav: 'When the blessed Holy One sought to create the human being, He [first] created a company of ministering angels and asked them, "Is it your desire that we make the human being in our image?" They responded, "Master of the Universe, what are his deeds?" He replied, "Such and such are his deeds." They exclaimed, "Master of the Uni-

verse, *What is a human that You are mindful of him, a human being that You take note of him?*" He stretched out His little finger among them and burned them. The same thing happened with a second company. The third company said to Him, "Master of the Universe, the former ones who spoke in Your presence—what did they accomplish? The entire world is Yours! Whatever You wish to do in Your world, do it." When He reached the members of the generation of the Flood and the generation of the Dispersion [the Tower of Babel], whose deeds were corrupt, they [the angels] said to Him, "Master of the Universe, didn't the first ones speak well?" He responded, "*Till your old age, I am He; till you turn grey, I will carry you* [*I have made and I will bear; I will carry and deliver*] (Isaiah 46:4).'" Cf. *Bereshit Rabbah* 8:6; 31:12.

sing before Him, but the blessed Holy One said to them, 'The work of My hands is drowning in the sea, and you are singing?' So, *one did not approach the other all night long* (Exodus 14:20).[1598] Similarly whenever the wicked are being eliminated, sadness hovers over them."

Rabbi Abba said, "When Adam sinned in the presence of the blessed Holy One, violating His commands, sadness appeared before Him. The blessed Holy One said to him, 'Woe to you, Adam! You have weakened supernal power!'[1599] That moment one light darkened.[1600] He immediately drove him out of the Garden of Eden, saying, 'I brought you into the Garden of Eden to bring an offering, but you impaired the altar, so no offering can be brought.[1601] From now on, *to till the ground* (Genesis 3:23).'[1602] He decreed death upon him. Yet taking pity upon him, as he was about to die the blessed Holy One treasured him away close to the Garden. What did Adam do? He dug a cave and hid himself inside together with his wife. How did he know? He saw a ray of light

326

1598. **as is said: *going forth before the warriors*...**   When King Jehoshaphat of Judah was attacking Moab and Ammon, he stationed singers ahead of the troops. See BT *Megillah* 10b: "Does the blessed Holy One rejoice in the downfall of the wicked? Look at what is written: *going forth before the warriors, exclaiming: 'Praise YHVH, for His love endures forever,'* and Rabbi Yoḥanan has said, 'Why isn't the phrase *for He is good* [which usually follows *Praise YHVH* and is here interpreted as *for it is good*] omitted from this praise? Because the blessed Holy One does not rejoice in the downfall of the wicked.' And Rabbi Yoḥanan said further, 'What is the meaning of the verse: *One did not approach the other all night long*? [In its literal sense, this verse refers to the Israelites and the Egyptians.] The ministering angels [referred to as *one* and *the other* in Isaiah 6:3] wanted to sing, but the blessed Holy One said, "The work of My hands is drowning in the sea, and you are singing?"'"

This midrash is sometimes cited to explain the reduced version of the *Hallel* prayer on the latter days of Passover, commemorating the crossing of the Red Sea.

1599. **You have weakened supernal power!**   Human sin impairs the divine. See *Eikhah Rabbah* 1:33: "Rabbi Azariah said in the name of Rabbi Yehudah son of Rabbi Simon, 'When Israel enact the will of the Omnipresent, they strengthen heavenly power, as is said: *In God we generate strength* (Psalms 60:14). When Israel do not enact the will of the Omnipresent, they weaken, as it were, the great power of the One above, as is written: *You weakened the Rock that engendered you* (Deuteronomy 32:18).'"

See *Sifrei*, Deuteronomy 319; *Vayiqra Rabbah* 23:12; *Pesiqta de-Rav Kahana* 25:1; *Zohar* 2:32b, 64a, 65b.

In the *Zohar*, Adam's sin is understood as ruining the union of the divine couple, *Shekhinah* and *Tif'eret*. See *Zohar* 1:35b, 53b.

1600. **one light...**   The light of *Shekhinah*, now separated from Her partner, *Tif'eret*.

1601. **I brought you into the Garden of Eden to bring an offering...**   See *Bereshit Rabbah* 16:5: "[*YHVH Elohim took the human and placed him in the Garden of Eden*] *to work it and tend it* (Genesis 2:15)—these are the offerings." *Zohar* 1:141b, 199b; 2:165b; 3:263a.

Here, "to bring an offering" means to bring the *sefirot* together by uniting *Shekhinah* and *Tif'eret*. *Shekhinah* is symbolized by both the altar and the Garden.

1602. ***to till the ground***   Having failed to serve *Shekhinah*, symbolized by earth, Adam is banished from the Garden and condemned to till the earth.

glinting on that spot, gleaming from the Garden of Eden, and desired a desire for his grave. Right there is a site bordering the gate of the Garden of Eden.[1603]

"Come and see: No one departs from the world without first seeing Adam, who asks him why he is leaving the world and how he is exiting. He replies, 'Woe to you! On account of you, I am leaving the world.'[1604] He responds, 'My son, I violated one command and was punished for it. Look at all your sins! Look how many of your Lord's commands you have violated!'"[1605]

Rabbi Ḥiyya said, "To this day Adam endures, gazing at the patriarchs twice a day, confessing his sins, showing them the site where he dwelled in supernal splendor.[1606] He goes to see all the righteous and devout who issued from him, who inherited that supernal splendor in the Garden of Eden. All the patriarchs offer praise, saying: *How precious is Your love, O God! The children of Adam shelter in the shadow of Your wings* (Psalms 36:8)."

Rabbi Yeisa said, "At the moment he departs from the world, every inhabitant of the world sees Adam to bear witness that due to his own sins he is departing, not because of Adam[1607]—except for those three who departed due to the incitement of the primordial serpent, namely, Amram, Levi, and Benjamin; some say: also Jesse.[1608] They never sinned; no trace of sin could be found upon them to warrant their death, but that incitement of the serpent was brought to bear upon them, as we have said.

327

1603. **the blessed Holy One treasured him away close to the Garden...** Guided by a ray of light emanating from the Garden, Adam dug a cave close by, a cave later known as the Cave of Machpelah (Genesis 23), where all the patriarchs and matriarchs (except for Rachel) were buried. According to rabbinic tradition, Adam and Eve were buried there as well.

See *Bereshit Rabbah* 58:8; BT *Eruvin* 53a; *Pirqei de-Rabbi Eli'ezer* 20, 36; *Midrash ha-Gadol*, Genesis 23:9; *Zohar* 1:81a (*ST*), 127a–128b, 248b; 3:164a; *ZH* 21a (*MhN*), 79d (*MhN*).

1604. **On account of you, I am leaving the world** Because of Adam's sin, death was decreed upon humanity.

1605. **No one departs from the world without first seeing Adam...** See *Bemidbar Rabbah* 19:18: "Death is decreed upon all the righteous who spring from him [Adam]. They do not depart this life without first gazing upon the face of *Shekhinah* and reproving Adam, saying: 'You inflicted death

upon us!' Adam responds: 'As for me, I possess only one sin, while in your case, every single one of you possesses more than four.'"

See *Tanḥuma, Ḥuqqat* 16; *Tanḥuma* (Buber), *Ḥuqqat* 39; *Zohar* 1:65b, 81a (*ST*), 127a.

1606. **Adam endures, gazing at the patriarchs...** Adam points out to them his former site in the Garden.

1607. **due to his own sins...** As opposed to the doctrine of original sin. See *Tanḥuma* (Buber), *Bereshit* 29; and BT *Shabbat* 55a: "Rabbi Ammi said, 'There is no death without sin; there is no suffering without iniquity. There is no death without sin, for it is written: *The soul who sins is the one who will die. The son will not share the guilt of the father, nor the father the guilt of the son....* (Ezekiel 18:20).'"

1608. **except for those three...** See BT *Shabbat* 55b: "Four died through the incitement of the serpent, namely: Benjamin the son of Jacob, Amram the father of Moses, Jesse the father of David, and Chileab the son of David." According to this view, these

"Come and see: All generations in the days of Noah exposed their sins to the world brazenly, in sight of all.[1609] One day Rabbi Shim'on was walking through the gates of Tiberias when he saw some men drawing the bow taut with the shaft of a centaur.[1610] He exclaimed, 'What! Such brazen sin, provoking their Lord?' He cast his eyes upon them; they were hurled into the sea and drowned.[1611]

"Come and see: Every sin committed openly repels *Shekhinah* from earth, so She removes Her abode from the world.[1612] These walked haughtily, with head erect, perpetrating their sins brazenly, thrusting *Shekhinah* from the world,[1613] till finally the blessed Holy One thrust them away. Concerning this is written: *Remove the wicked from the presence of the king.... Remove the dross from silver* (Proverbs 25:5, 4)."[1614]

YHVH said, "My spirit shall not abide in humanity לעלם *(le-olam), forever, since they, too, are flesh..."* (Genesis 6:3).[1615]

328

Rabbi El'azar said, "Come and see: When the blessed Holy One created the world, He fashioned this world to perform [58a] as above.[1616] When the inhabitants of the world are virtuous, walking the straight path, the blessed Holy One

four individuals did not sin on their own but died only because of the sin of Adam and Eve, who were enticed by the serpent.

Here the *Zohar* substitutes Levi for Chileab; see Ta-Shma, *Ha-Nigleh she-ba-Nistar* (1st ed.), 115. Cf. above, page 296, where only Joshua (who did not participate in the sin of the Golden Calf) is specified.

1609. **brazenly, in sight of all** See *Pirqei de-Rabbi Eli'ezer* 22; *Zohar* 1:60b.

1610. **drawing the bow taut with the shaft of a centaur** A cryptic reference to masturbation. On the phallic association of the bow, see *Bereshit Rabbah* 87:7; BT *Sanhedrin* 92a. Cf. BT *Ḥagigah* 15a: "Shemu'el said, 'Any emission of semen that does not shoot forth like an arrow does not fructify.'"

קולפא (*Qulpa*) means "pole, lance, shaft, club, strap" (see *Zohar* 1:29a, 32a). קנטיר (*Qantir*), is "centaur," the mythical creature who is half-human, half-horse. See *Bereshit Rabbah* 23:6; *Ma'arikh*, s.v. qtr.

1611. **He cast his eyes upon them...** On the destructive power of Rabbi Shim'on's gaze, see BT *Shabbat* 33b–34a; JT *Shevi'it* 9:1, 38d; *Bereshit Rabbah* 79:6; *Pesiqta de-Rav Kahana* 11:16; *Qohelet Rabbah* on 10:9;

Midrash Tehillim 17:13; *Eikhah Zuta* 1:43. In all of these sources (except the last), the context is the purification of Tiberias. The sea mentioned here is the Sea of Galilee.

1612. **Every sin committed openly repels** *Shekhinah*... See BT *Ḥagigah* 16a: "Rabbi Yitsḥak said, 'Whoever sins secretly, it is as if he thrusts away the feet of *Shekhinah*.'" Cf. *Zohar* 1:57a, 61a, 68b–69a.

1613. **haughtily, with head erect...** ברישא זקיף (*Be-reisha zeqif*), "With head erect." See BT *Berakhot* 43b: "Whoever walks with a haughty [literally, "erect"] stature even for four cubits, it is as if he thrusts away the feet of *Shekhinah*."

1614. *Remove the wicked from the presence of the king...* The first of the cited verses continues: *and his throne will be established in justice.* The second verse reads: *Remove the dross from silver, and a vessel emerges for the smith.*

1615. *My spirit shall not abide in humanity forever, since they, too, are flesh* The verse continues: *Let his days be a hundred and twenty years.*

1616. **to perform as above** The world below is modeled on the divine realm and arouses the spirit of life above until that life reaches the site where Jacob abides.[1617] From there life flows until the spirit is drawn to this world in which King David abides.[1618] From there blessings flow to all those below. Since that supernal spirit is drawn and conducted below, they are able to endure in the world. So, לעלם (le-olam), *forever,* without a ו (vav)—עולם (olam), world, of King David, spelled without a ו (vav).[1619] For when that spirit flows into this world, from there blessings and life issue to all, to be sustained. Now that humans sinned, all was withdrawn to prevent the spirit of life from reaching this world, benefiting, sustaining those below.[1620]

"*Since he, too, is flesh*—so spirit would not be poured into this world. Why? Amplifying the meaning to include the serpent, lowest of rungs, who would thereby be empowered—so that holy spirit not mingle with impure spirit.[1621]

"*Since he, too, is flesh*—primordial serpent, who would be blessed. So, *he is flesh,* as is said: *End of all flesh has come before Me* (ibid. 6:13), concerning which Rabbi Shim'on has said: 'This is the Angel of Death.'[1622]

329

sustained by the stream of emanation.

See *Zohar* 1:38a, 129a, 145b, 156b, 158b, 205b; 2:15b (*MhN*), 20a (*MhN*), 48b, 82b, 251a (*Heikh*); 3:40b, 65b; Tishby, *Wisdom of the Zohar,* 1:273.

1617. **the spirit of life above...** The flow of emanation, which emerges from the highest realms of the *sefirot* and proceeds to *Tif'eret,* symbolized by Jacob.

1618. **this world in which King David abides** *Shekhinah,* also known as *Malkhut* ("Kingdom"), symbolized by the ideal king, David.

1619. **לעלם (le-olam), *forever,* without a ו (vav)...** In the verse in Genesis (*My spirit shall not abide in humanity* לעלם [*le-olam*], *forever*), the word לעלם (*le-olam*) is written without the letter ו (*vav*), a spelling that alludes to *Shekhinah* without Her partner, *Tif'eret.* He together with the five *sefirot* surrounding Him (*Hesed* to *Yesod*) is symbolized by this letter whose numerical value is six.

See *Minhat Shai* on Genesis 6:3; Exodus 3:15; 31:17; BT *Pesahim* 50a.

1620. **Now that humans sinned...** In the generation of the Flood.

1621. **Amplifying the meaning to include...** לאסגאה (*Le-asga'ah*), "To increase," a Zoharic rendering of the rabbinic

Hebrew לרבות (*le-rabbot*), "to increase"— that is, to include, amplify, or widen the scope of meaning. In rabbinic hermeneutics the word גם (*gam*), "also, too," amplifies the literal meaning of a biblical word or phrase. See *Bereshit Rabbah* 1:14; JT *Berakhot* 9:5, 14b.

Here the word *too* amplifies the meaning to include the serpent, who lurks beneath *Shekhinah,* craving the rich nourishment of emanation.

1622. **he is flesh, as is said: *End of all flesh...*** The demonic primordial serpent is known as *End of all flesh* (see *Zohar* 1:35b, 54a, 62b) and identified with the Angel of Death. See BT *Bava Batra* 16a: "Resh Lakish said, 'Satan, the evil impulse, and the Angel of Death are one and the same.'" Cf. *Zohar* 1:52a, 202a; 2:262b–263a; Moses de León, *Sefer ha-Rimmon,* 394–95.

Rabbi El'azar apparently reads the verse: *My spirit shall not abide in* אדם (*adam*) [namely, *Ti'feret,* known as Primordial Adam, so that the flow of emanation will not continue] לעלם (*le-olam*), *to the world* [of *Shekhinah*], *since he, too* [the serpent, lurking beneath *Shekhinah*], *is flesh* [and would be nourished]. Alternatively, *My spirit shall not abide in humanity* לעלם (*le-olam*) [because *Shekhinah* is lacking ו (*vav*) due to Adam's sin], *since he, too* [the serpent, lurking be-

"*Let his days be a hundred and twenty years* (ibid., 3)—duration of banded diadem."[1623]

The נפילים *(nefilim), fallen beings, were on earth in those days* (Genesis 6:4).

Rabbi Yose teaches: "These are Uzza and Azael, as has been stated, cast down by the blessed Holy One from supernal sanctity."[1624]

But how could they survive in this world?

Rabbi Ḥiyya said, "They were among those of whom is written: *Let birds fly upon the earth* (ibid. 1:20), and as explained, these appear to humans in human appearance.[1625] If you ask: 'How can they transform?'—it has been stated: 'They turn countless shades,'[1626] and as they descend they materialize in the atmosphere, appearing as human beings. These are Uzza and Azael, who rebelled above, were cast down by the blessed Holy One, and materialized on earth, abiding on it, unable to strip themselves of it.[1627] Subsequently they strayed after earthly women, and to this day they endure, teaching sorcery to human beings. They engendered children, whom they called Mighty Giants,[1628] while the *nefilim* themselves are called *sons of Elohim*, as has been explained."[1629]

YHVH said, "I will exterminate humankind, whom I have created, from the face of the earth" (ibid. 6:7).

Rabbi Yose opened, "*For My thoughts are not your thoughts* [*nor are your ways My ways, says YHVH*] (Isaiah 55:8). Come and see: When a person seeks vengeance on another, he keeps silent, saying nothing, for if he lets him know, he will be on

---

neath *Shekhinah*], *is flesh* [and would be nourished].

1623. **duration of banded diadem** One of the *Zohar*'s neologistic phrases, apparently alluding to the splendid bond of body and soul. On קוזפירא (*quzpira*), "diadem," see *Zohar* 2:175a; 3:154a.

1624. **These are Uzza and Azael...** These two angels opposed the creation of Adam and Eve, fell from heaven, and were attracted by *the daughters of men* (Genesis 6:2). They were punished by being bound in chains of iron in the mountains of darkness, from where they still manage to wreak havoc, teaching sorcery to humans.

See 1 Enoch 6–8; Jubilees 5; BT *Yoma* 67b; *Aggadat Bereshit*, intro, 39; *Midrash Avkir*, 7 (cited in *Yalqut Shim'oni*, Genesis, 44); *Pirqei de-Rabbi Eli'ezer* 22; *Zohar* 1:9b, 23a, 37a, 37a

(*Tos*), 126a; 3:208a–b, 212a–b; *ZḤ* 81a–b (*MhN, Rut*).

1625. *Let birds fly upon the earth...* Certain angels, symbolized by birds, manifest in human form *upon the earth*.

See *Bereshit Rabbah* 1:3; *Devarim Rabbah* 8:2; *Zohar* 1:13a, 34a–b, 46b, 101a, 144a; 3:39b.

1626. **'They turn countless shades'** See BT *Yoma* 75a, where demons are said to "turn many colors." Cf. *Bereshit Rabbah* 21:9, commenting on *a blazing, ever-turning sword* (Genesis 3:24): "*Ever-turning*—changing: sometimes male, sometimes female; sometimes spirits, sometimes angels."

See *Zohar* 1:44a, 53b, 165a (*ST*), 237a; 3:19b.

1627. **abiding on it, unable to strip themselves of it** They had materialized so fully that they could not escape the physical realm. See *ZḤ* 81a (*MhN, Rut*).

330

guard, invulnerable. Not so the blessed Holy One. He does not execute judgment upon the world until He proclaims to them once, twice, thrice,[1630] for *there is no one who can stay His hand or say to Him, 'What are You doing?'* (Daniel 4:32), nor can one guard against Him nor withstand Him.

"Come and see: *YHVH said, 'I will exterminate humankind, whom I have created, from the face of the earth.'* He announced it to them through Noah, warning them several times, but they would not listen.[1631] After they failed to listen He brought judgment upon them, eliminating them from the face of the earth.

"Come and see: What is written of Noah? *He named him* נח (Noaḥ), *Noah, saying: This one* ינחמנו (yenaḥamenu), *will provide us relief, from our labor* (Genesis 5:29).[1632] How did he know? When [58b] he was born, he saw that he was circumcised, inscribed with the sign of *Shekhinah;* he saw *Shekhinah* cleaving to him.[1633] So *he named him* for what he would later do. At first they did not know how to sow, reap, or plow. Once Noah appeared, he innovated techniques for them along with all the implements required to cultivate the soil to yield fruit.[1634]

331

1628. **Mighty Giants** See *Zohar* 3:160b.

1629. **the *nefilim* themselves are called *sons of Elohim*...** See Genesis 6:2–4; *Zohar* 1:19b, 37a, 55a; 3:144a (*IR*).

1630. **When a person seeks vengeance...** See *Tanḥuma, Va'era* 14: "The way the world operates, if a person wants to do something evil to his enemy, he does it suddenly to catch him unawares. But the blessed Holy One warned Pharaoh before every single plague [so that he might turn back to God]."

Cf. BT *Yoma* 86b, citing Job 33:29.

1631. **He announced it to them through Noah, warning them...** Noah attempted to warn his contemporaries and induce them to repent, but he was unsuccessful. See *Bereshit Rabbah* 30:7; *Tanḥuma, Noaḥ* 5; BT *Sanhedrin* 108a–b.

1632. **He named him** נח **(Noah), Noah, saying...** The full verse reads: *He named him* נח (Noaḥ), *Noah, saying: This one* ינחמנו (yenaḥamenu), *will provide us relief, from our labor and from the painful toil of our hands caused by the soil that YHVH cursed.* Here Noah is named by his father Lamech.

1633. **How did he know?...** How did Lamech, Noah's father, know that his son would *provide relief*? See *Tanḥuma, Bereshit* 11: "How did he know to say, *This one will provide us relief from our labor...*? Was he a prophet? Rabbi Shim'on son of Yehotsadak said, 'They had been taught that when the blessed Holy One said to Adam, *Cursed is the ground because of you; by painful toil will you eat of it all the days of your life* (Genesis 3:17), Adam asked, "Master of the world, for how long?" He replied, "Until a human is born circumcised." When Noah was born circumcised, Lamech immediately knew and said, "Indeed, *this one will provide us relief...!*"'"

See *Avot de-Rabbi Natan* A, 2; *Tanḥuma, Noaḥ* 5; *Zohar* 1:59b. According to the *Zohar*, the mark of circumcision signifies union with *Shekhinah;* see *Zohar* 1:2b, 13a.

1634. **At first they did not know how to sow...** See *Tanḥuma, Bereshit* 11: "Before Noah was born, people did not reap what they sowed. If they sowed wheat, they reaped thorns and thistles. Once Noah was born, the world became arable once again.

"*From our labor and from the painful toil of our hands caused by the soil [that YHVH cursed]*. For he liberated the earth from her curse and was therefore called איש האדמה (*ish ha-adamah*), *man of the soil* (ibid. 9:20)."

Rabbi Yehudah said, "איש האדמה (*Ish ha-adamah*), *Husband of the soil,* as is said: איש נעמי (*ish no'omi*), *husband of Naomi* (Ruth 1:3), for he was called Righteous, and by bringing an offering he liberated her from her curse,[1635] as is written: *Never again will I curse the soil because of humankind* (Genesis 8:21). He was therefore called *husband of the soil* and named for the future."

Rabbi Yehudah opened, "*Come, gaze upon the works of Elohim, how He has brought* שמות (*shammot*), *desolation, on earth* (Psalms 46:9).[1636] If it had been *the works of* יו״ד ה״א וא״ו ה״א (*yod he vav he*), YHVH, He would have *brought existence to earth,* but being *the works of* this name, He brought desolation on earth."[1637]

Rabbi Ḥiyya said, "Now this I would not say, for whether it be one name or the other, all is praise, but I say as the Companions have aroused: He brought names—actual שמות (*shemot*), *names, He brought to earth.* Why? So the world would wield them, be sustained by them."[1638]

332

They reaped what they sowed, sowing wheat and reaping wheat, sowing barley and reaping barley. Furthermore, until Noah was born, they worked by hand... Once Noah was born, he invented plows, scythes, spades, and all kinds of tools." Cf. *Zohar* 1:38a, 97b.

1635. **as is said: איש נעמי (*ish no'omi*), *husband of Naomi*...** This verse demonstrates that איש (*ish*) can mean "husband." Noah was not simply *man of the soil,* but *husband of Shekhinah,* who is symbolized by earth. He fulfilled the role of *Yesod,* known as Righteous, uniting with the divine feminine. Similarly, Moses is called איש האלהים (*ish ha-Elohim*), *husband of Elohim.* See above, pp. 41–42, n. 288. Cf. 1:59b, 62b.

The mystical purpose of an offering is to redeem *Shekhinah* by uniting Her with Her partner.

1636. **the works of Elohim...** The Masoretic text reads: *the works of YHVH.* See Psalms 66:5: *Come, see the works of Elohim.* The entire discussion here is based on the assumption that Psalms 46:9 reads *Elohim* rather than *YHVH;* cf. *ZḤ* 12a (*MhN*). Such a reading is attested in biblical manuscripts as well as the Septuagint (codex Alexan-

drinus), and the Zoharic rabbis are aware of both variants. Note the comment by Rabbi Ḥiyya in the following lines: "Whether it be one name or the other, all is praise."

See *Bereshit Rabbah* 84:8; 88:3 (and Theodor, ad loc.); *Tanḥuma, Vayelekh* 1; Radak on Psalms 46:9; *Zohar* 1:60a, 157b (*ST*); 2:5a; *ZḤ* 73a (*ShS*); Moses de León, *Sefer ha-Rimmon,* 288; *OY, KP, MM,* and *Zohorei Ya'bets* on this passage; *Minḥat Shai* on Numbers 23:9; Psalms 46:9; 66:5; Menaḥem Azariah of Fano, *Yonat Elem,* 99; Margaliot, *Sha'arei Zohar, Berakhot* 7b.

1637. **works of יו״ד ה״א וא״ו ה״א (*yod he vav he*), YHVH... works of this name...** In rabbinic literature the names *YHVH* and *Elohim* represent, respectively, the divine qualities of compassion and justice. See *Sifrei,* Deuteronomy 26; *Bereshit Rabbah* 12:15; 33:3; *Zohar* 1:64b; 2:187a, 227b.

Strict justice demands punishment, namely, *desolation.*

1638. **He brought names...** God imparted divine names to the world so that human beings could wield them theurgically, drawing down the rich flow of emanation. See BT *Berakhot* 7b: "How do we know that a name determines destiny? Rabbi El'a-

Rabbi Yitsḥak said, "Even what Rabbi Yehudah said is fine! For if the world were conducted by the name of compassion, it would endure, but since it was founded on justice and abides by justice, *He has brought desolation on earth.* This is fine, for otherwise the world could not endure human sin.[1639]

"Come and see: When נח (Noaḥ), Noah, was born, he was named for נחמה (neḥamah), comfort, so that the name would determine his destiny.[1640] Not so, the blessed Holy One: נח (Noaḥ), is the reverse of חן (ḥen), favor, as is said: ונח (Ve-Noaḥ), *But Noah, found* חן (ḥen), *favor* [*in the eyes of YHVH*] (Genesis 6:8)."[1641]

Rabbi Yose said, "חן (Ḥen), *Favor,* is נח (Noaḥ), *Noah.* Names of the righteous are auspicious; names of the wicked, ominous. Of Noah is written: ונח (Ve-Noaḥ), *But Noah, found* חן (ḥen), *favor, in the eyes of YHVH,* while the letters of ער (Er), Er, firstborn of Judah, were reversed for evil: ער (Er), Er—רע (ra), evil; *ra, evil, in the eyes of YHVH* (ibid. 38:7).[1642]

"Come and see: When Noah was born he saw the deeds of human beings, sinning in the presence of the blessed Holy One, so he hid himself away, engaging in devotion to his Lord, so as not to follow in their paths. If you ask, 'In what did he engage?'—that *Book of Adam* and *The Book of Enoch,* engaging in them to worship his Lord.[1643]

333

zar said, 'For Scripture states: *Come, gaze upon the works of YHVH, how He has brought* שמות (shammot), *desolation, on earth.* Do not read שַׁמּוֹת (shammot), *desolation,* but rather שֵׁמוֹת (shemot), *names.'"*

1639. **For if the world were conducted by the name of compassion...** As noted above, the two divine names, *YHVH* and *Elohim,* symbolize, respectively, compassion and justice. See *Bereshit Rabbah* 12:15, explaining the appearance of both names in Genesis 2:4, *On the day YHVH Elohim created heaven and earth:* "The blessed Holy One said, 'If I create the world by the quality of compassion, its sins will abound; by the quality of justice, the world will not endure. Rather, I will create it by both the quality of justice and the quality of compassion. Oh that it may endure!' So, *YHVH Elohim.*"

Here Rabbi Yitsḥak's point is that the name *Elohim* in Psalms 46:9 denotes justice (or: judgment) and the consequent punishment of *desolation,* whose purging power ensures the continued existence of the world.

1640. **so that the name would determine his destiny** So that Noah would succeed in providing comfort and relief to the world. See BT *Berakhot* 7b (cited above, note 1638); *Zohar* 1:6a; 2:179b.

1641. **Not so, the blessed Holy One...** God favored a different etymology of Noah's name.

1642. **Of Noah is written...while the letters of ער (Er), Er...** See *Kallah Rabbati* 2: "It was taught: [ער (Er), Er] spelled backward is רע (ra), evil. Similarly, נח (Noaḥ), Noah, spelled backward is חן (ḥen), favor." Genesis does not specify the nature of Er's sin, but rabbinic tradition maintains that it was the same as that of his younger brother, Onan, who spilled his semen on the ground (38:9).

See *Bereshit Rabbah* 85:4 (and Theodor, ad loc.); BT *Yevamot* 34b; *Kallah Rabbati,* ibid.; *Targum Yerushalmi,* Genesis 38:7; *Zohar* 1:56b–57a.

1643. **That *Book of Adam* and *The Book of Enoch*...** See *Sefer Noaḥ* (*Beit ha-Midrash,* 3:158–60). Both of these books are referred to frequently in the *Zohar.* According

"Come and see: So it was, for how did he know to bring an offering to his Lord? He discovered the wisdom of how the world is sustained and realized it is sustained by offering. Without offering, those above and those below would not endure."[1644]

Rabbi Shim'on was walking on the way together with his son Rabbi El'azar, Rabbi Yose, and Rabbi Ḥiyya. While they were walking, Rabbi El'azar said to his father, "The way before us is smooth. We want to hear words of Torah!"[1645]

Rabbi Shim'on opened, saying, "*Even when a fool walks on the way,* לבו (*libbo*), *his mind, is lacking, and he reveals to everyone that he is a fool* (Ecclesiastes 10:3). When a person wants to smooth his way before the blessed Holy One, before setting out on the way he should consult Him and pray for his way before Him, as we have learned, for it is written: *Righteousness goes before him, and he sets out on his way* (Psalms 85:14). Then *Shekhinah* does not part from him.[1646]

334

to BT *Bava Metsi'a* 85b–86a, Rabbi Yehudah the Prince once saw *The Book of Adam,* which contained the genealogy of the entire human race. See Genesis 5:1; *Bereshit Rabbah* 24:1; BT *Sanhedrin* 38b. According to various medieval traditions, the angel Raziel transmitted a magical book to Adam. Later, probably in the seventeenth century, *Sefer Razi'el* was compiled in its present form, comprising ancient magical, mystical, and cosmological teachings.

See *Zohar* 1:17b, 37b, 55a–b, 72b, 90b; 2:70a–b, 131a, 143b, 180a, 181a, 197a; 3:10a, 68b; *ZḤ* 37b; Ginzberg, *Legends,* 5:117–18, n. 110; Liebes, *Peraqim,* 85–87; Wineman, *Mystic Tales from the Zohar,* 35–54.

Concerning Enoch, Genesis 5:24 states: *He was no more, for God took him.* In postbiblical literature this verse is taken to mean that God transported Enoch through the heavens, a journey recorded in the Enoch literature. The *Zohar's Book of Enoch,* though influenced by this literature, is not identical with any of its particular volumes. It comprises one of the many books housed in the real or imaginary Zoharic library.

See *Aggadat Bereshit,* intro, 38; *Midrash Aggadah,* Genesis 5:24; *Zohar* 1:13a, 37b, 55b, 72b; 2:55a, 100a, 105b, 180b, 192b, 217a; 3:10b,

236b, 240a, 248b, 253b, 307a; *ZḤ* 2c (*SO*); Ginzberg, *Legends,* 5:156–64, nn. 58–61; Margaliot, *Mal'akhei Elyon,* 80–83.

1644. **how did he know to bring an offering...** When the waters of the Flood receded, Noah emerged from the ark and offered sacrifices (Genesis 8:20). According to the *Zohar,* the purpose of such offerings is to unite the *sefirot* and ensure the flow of blessing and sustenance to the world. Noah discovered this mystical truth by studying the books of Adam and Enoch.

See BT *Ta'anit* 27b: "Rabbi Ya'akov son of Aḥa said in the name of Rabbi Assi: 'Were it not for the *ma'amadot* [representatives accompanying the Temple sacrifices], heaven and earth would not endure.'" Cf. Tishby, *Wisdom of the Zohar,* 3:878–90.

1645. **The way before us is smooth. We want to hear words of Torah!** Since the road is clear, let us focus on Torah. On the importance of engaging in Torah while on a journey, see Deuteronomy 6:7; BT *Eruvin* 54a; *Ta'anit* 10b; *Zohar* 1:7a, 69b–70a, 87a, 115b.

1646. **before setting out on the way...** Before setting out on a journey, one should pray, including (or specifically) *tefillat ha-derekh* ("the prayer for the way"). See BT *Be-*

"Concerning one who does not trust His Lord, what is written? [59a] *Even when a fool walks on the way,* לבו (libbo), *his heart, is lacking.*[1647] Who is *his heart?* The blessed Holy One, who will not accompany him on the way.[1648] So that person lacks his escort since, not trusting His Lord, he failed to seek His companionship and support before setting out. Even while walking on the way he does not engage in words of Torah, so *his heart is lacking,* for his Lord does not walk along with him, is absent from his way.

"*And he says to everyone:* סכל הוא (Sakhal hu), *It is foolish.* Even when he hears a word of faith in his Lord, he says *it is foolish* to engage in it. Like the time someone was asked about the sign of covenant engraved in a man's flesh, and he replied, 'That's irrelevant to belief!'[1649] Rabbi Yeisa Sava heard, stared at him, and he turned into a heap of bones.[1650]

"As for us, look, we are being accompanied on the way by the blessed Holy One, so we should speak words of Torah!"

He opened, saying, "*Teach me Your way, O YHVH, that I may walk in Your truth; unify my heart to be in awe of Your name* (Psalms 86:11). This verse presents a difficulty, for we have learned: 'All is in the hand of the blessed Holy One except being virtuous or wicked.'[1651] So how could David ask this of the blessed Holy One?[1652] Rather, this is what David declared: *Teach me Your way,*

335

rakhot 29b: "Elijah said to Rav Yehudah the brother of Rabbi Sala the Ḥasid, 'Do not let your anger boil and you will not sin; do not get drunk and you will not sin; and when you set out on the way, consult your Creator and then set out.' What is meant by 'consult your Creator and then set out'? Rabbi Ya'akov said in the name of Rav Ḥisda, 'This is *tefillat ha-derekh.*'"

See *Berakhot* 14a: "Rav Idi son of Avin said in the name of Rabbi Yitsḥak son of Ishyan, 'Whoever prays and then sets out on the way, the blessed Holy One fulfills his desires, as is said: *Righteousness goes before him, and he sets out on his way.*'" In this Talmudic passage, *righteousness* (or: *justice*) implies justification by prayer, which guarantees a successful journey. Here, for Rabbi Shim'on, *Righteousness* is a name of *Shekhinah,* who symbolizes divine justice. By praying, one secures Her accompanying presence. See above, note 1292.

1647. לבו (**libbo**), *his heart*... לב (Lev) means both "heart" and "mind."

1648. **Who is *his heart*? The blessed Holy One...** God is identified as "heart" in *Eikhah Rabbah, Petiḥta* 16; *Shir ha-Shirim Rabbah* on 5:2; and *Shemot Rabbah* 33:3.

1649. **the sign of covenant engraved in a man's flesh...** The mark of circumcision. Some radical critics of tradition contended that belief in God did not require fulfilling the commandments; the *Zohar* insists on integrating belief and observance.

1650. **he turned into a heap of bones** On the destructive power of the rabbinic gaze, see BT *Berakhot* 58a; *Shabbat* 33b–34a; *Bava Batra* 75a; cf. above, page 328; *Zohar* 3:221a.

1651. **'All is in the hand of the blessed Holy One except being virtuous or wicked'** See BT *Berakhot* 33b: "Rabbi Ḥanina said, 'All is in the hands of heaven except the awe of heaven, as is said: *Now, Israel, what does YHVH your God ask of you but to be in awe?* (Deuteronomy 10:12).'" Cf. *Niddah* 16b.

1652. **So how could David...** How could David (traditionally, the author of

O YHVH—that straight, smooth way, opening my eyes so I can know it. Then, *I will walk in Your truth*—I will walk the true way, not deviating right or left. *Unify my heart.* Who is *my heart*? As is said: *Rock of my heart and my portion* (ibid. 73:26).[1653] All this I request *to be in awe of Your name*—cleaving to awe,[1654] guarding my way fittingly. *To be in awe of Your name*—my allotted site, where awe strikes awe.[1655]

"Come and see: Faith abides fittingly with every human being in awe of the blessed Holy One,[1656] for such a human consummates the service of his Lord. Faith does not abide with anyone devoid of the awe of his Lord; he is unworthy of sharing the world that is coming."[1657]

He opened further, saying, "*The path of the righteous is like gleaming light, shining ever brighter until full day* (Proverbs 4:18). Happy are the righteous in this world and in the world that is coming, for the blessed Holy One desires to glorify them! Come and see what is written: *The path of the righteous is like gleaming light*. What does this mean: *like gleaming light*? Like that radiant light created by the blessed Holy One in the act of Creation, treasured away for the righteous in the world that is coming.[1658] *Shining ever brighter*, for it constantly

336

Psalms) ask God to make him virtuous, since this is dependent on free will?

1653. **Who is *my heart*?...** As noted above, God is identified as "heart" in *Eikhah Rabbah, Petiḥta* 16; *Shir ha-Shirim Rabbah* on 5:2; and *Shemot Rabbah* 33:3, all of which cite Psalms 73:26. Here the reference is specifically to *Shekhinah*, associated with David; see below.

1654. **cleaving to *awe*** Cleaving to *Shekhinah*, known as awe.

1655. **my allotted site...** David, the ideal king, symbolizes *Shekhinah*, the divine name, who is also known as *Malkhut* ("Kingdom").

1656. **Faith abides fittingly...** *Shekhinah*, known as Faith, accompanies one who lives in awe of God.

1657. **the world that is coming** עלמא דאתי (*Alma de-atei*), the Aramaic equivalent of the rabbinic Hebrew העולם הבא (*ha-olam ha-ba*), "the world that is coming." This concept is often understood as referring to the hereafter and is usually translated as "the world to come." From another point of view, however, "the world that is coming" already exists, occupying another dimen-

sion. See *Tanḥuma, Vayiqra* 8: "The wise call it *ha-olam ha-ba* not because it does not exist now, but for us today in this world it is still to come." Cf. Maimonides, *Mishneh Torah, Hilkhot Teshuvah* 8:8; and Guttmann, *Philosophies of Judaism*, 37: "'The world to come' does not succeed 'this world' in time, but exists from eternity as a reality outside and above time, to which the soul ascends."

In Kabbalah "the world that is coming" often refers to *Binah*, the continuous source of emanation, who gives birth to the lower *sefirot*. See *Zohar* 3:290b (*IZ*): "the world that is coming, constantly coming, never ceasing."

Cf. *Bahir* 106 (160); Asher ben David, *Peirush Shelosh Esreh Middot*, in *Kabbalah* 2 (1997): 293; Moses de León, *Sheqel ha-Qodesh*, 26 (30); idem, *Sod Eser Sefirot*, 375; *Zohar* 1:83a, 92a.

1658. **treasured away for the righteous...** See BT *Ḥagigah* 12a: "Rabbi El'azar said, 'With the light created by the blessed Holy One on the first day, one could gaze and see from one end of the universe to the other. When the blessed Holy One foresaw the corrupt deeds of the generation of the Flood and the generation of the Dispersion [the

intensifies, never fading. But of the wicked, what is written? *The way of the wicked is like deep darkness; they do not know what will make them stumble* (ibid., 19). *They do not know*—Don't they know? Rather, the wicked walk this world on a crooked path, not caring to contemplate that the blessed Holy One intends to judge them in that world and cast them into the chastisements of Hell, where they scream: 'Woe to us that we did not stretch our ears and listen in that world!'[1659] Every day, this 'Woe'!

"Come and see: The blessed Holy One intends to enlighten the righteous in the world that is coming, providing them their due reward, penetrated, perceived by no eye, as is said: *No eye has seen, O God, but You, what You will do for one who awaits You* (Isaiah 64:3).[1660] Whereas it is written: *They will go out and stare at the corpses of the people who rebelled against Me* (ibid. 66:24). Similarly, *You will trample the wicked, for they will be ashes under the soles of your feet* (Malachi 3:21). Happy are the righteous in this world and in the world that is coming! Of them is written: *The righteous will inherit the land forever* (Isaiah 60:21), and similarly: *Surely the righteous will praise Your name; the upright will dwell in Your presence* (Psalms 140:14).[1661] *Blessed be YHVH forever! Amen and Amen* (ibid. 89:53)." [59b]

337

generation of the Tower of Babel], He immediately hid it from them, as is written: *The light of the wicked is withheld* (Job 38:15). For whom did He hide it? For the righteous in the time to come.'"

See *Bereshit Rabbah* 3:6; 41:3; *Shemot Rabbah* 35:1; *Tanḥuma, Shemini* 9; *Bahir* 97–98 (147); *Zohar* 1:7a, 31b–32a, 45b–46a, 47a; 2:127a, 148b–149a, 220a–b; 3:88a, 173b.

1659. **listen in that world** While on earth.

1660. *No eye has seen, O God, but You...* See BT *Berakhot* 34b: "Rabbi Ḥiyya son of Abba said in the name of Rabbi Yoḥanan, 'All the prophets prophesied only concerning the days of the Messiah, but as for the world that is coming, *No eye has seen, O God, but*

You, [what You will do for one who awaits You]... All the prophets prophesied only concerning masters of return [those who succeed in turning back to God], but as for the completely righteous, *No eye has seen, O God, but You.'*"

In the *Zohar*, this verse often refers to *Binah*, who is identified with "the world that is coming." See 1:4b, 6b; 2:97b, 163a.

1661. *The righteous will inherit the land forever...* This verse, appearing frequently in the *Zohar*, reads in full: *Your people, all of them righteous, will inherit the land forever—sprout of My planting, work of My hands, that I may be glorified.* In M *Sanhedrin* 10:1, it is cited to demonstrate that "all of Israel have a share in the world that is coming."

Parashat Noaḥ

"NOAH" (GENESIS 6:9–11:32)

These are the offspring of Noah (Genesis 6:9).

R abbi Ḥiyya opened, "*Your people, all of them righteous, will inherit the land forever...* (Isaiah 60:21). Happy are Israel who engage in Torah and know her ways, for on account of her they will attain the world that is coming![1]

"Come and see: All of Israel have a share in the world that is coming.[2] Why? Because they uphold the covenant upon which the world is erected, as is said: *Were it not for My covenant day and night, I would not have established the laws of heaven and earth* (Jeremiah 33:25).[3] So Israel, who embraced the covenant

1. **world that is coming** עלמא דאתי (*Alma de-atei*), the Aramaic equivalent of the rabbinic Hebrew העולם הבא (*ha-olam ha-ba*), "the world that is coming." This concept is often understood as referring to the hereafter and is usually translated as "the world to come." From another point of view, however, "the world that is coming" already exists, occupying another dimension. See *Tanḥuma, Vayiqra* 8: "The wise call it *ha-olam ha-ba* not because it does not exist now, but for us today in this world it is still to come." Cf. Maimonides, *Mishneh Torah, Hilkhot Teshuvah* 8:8; and Guttmann, *Philosophies of Judaism,* 37: "'The world to come' does not succeed 'this world' in time, but exists from eternity as a reality outside and above time, to which the soul ascends."

In Kabbalah "the world that is coming" often refers to *Binah,* the continuous source of emanation, who gives birth to the lower *sefirot.* See *Zohar* 3:290b (*IZ*): "the world that is coming, constantly coming, never ceasing."

Cf. *Bahir* 106 (160); Asher ben David, *Peirush Shelosh Esreh Middot,* in *Kabbalah* 2 (1997): 293; Moses de León, *Sheqel ha-Qodesh,* 26 (30); idem, *Sod Eser Sefirot,* 375; *Zohar* 1:83a, 92a.

Here "the world that is coming" is identified with *the land* mentioned in Isaiah.

2. **All of Israel have a share...** See M *Sanhedrin* 10:1: "All of Israel have a share in the world that is coming, as is said: *Your people, all of them righteous, will inherit the land forever—sprout of My planting, work of My hands, that I may be glorified.*"

3. **Because they uphold the covenant...** The covenant of circumcision, which is upheld by living in sexual purity. See BT *Shabbat* 137b: "Were it not for the blood of the covenant, heaven and earth would not endure, as is said: *Were it not for My covenant day and night, I would not have established the laws of heaven and earth.*"

Cf. *Zohar* 1:32a, 56a, 66b, 89a, 93b. See BT *Sanhedrin* 110b: "An infant—from when may

and uphold it, have a share in the world that is coming. Moreover, they are therefore called *righteous*. From here we learn that anyone upholding this covenant, upon which the world is erected, is called *righteous*. How do we know? From Joseph. Because he upheld the covenant of the world, he attained the title Righteous. So, *Your people, all of them righteous, will inherit the land forever.*"[4]

Rabbi El'azar said, "We have learned that *these are* always invalidates the preceding.[5] Come and see: What is written above? *A river issues from Eden to water the garden* (Genesis 2:10). That *river* gushes and flows, entering *the garden*, drenching it with supernal saturation, satisfying it, generating fruit and seed.[6] Then, satisfaction for all: satisfaction for *the garden*, who satisfies Him, as is said: *for* בו (vo), *on it, He rested,*[7] and: *He rested on the seventh day* (ibid., 2–3).[8] This is the mystery of the word: this generated *offspring*, no other.[9]

he enter the world that is coming? ... Rabbi Naḥman son of Yitsḥak said, 'From the moment he is circumcised.'"

Rabbi Ḥiyya's concern with sexual purity reflects the promiscuity prevalent in the Jewish community in thirteenth-century Castile. On this issue, see Moses de León, *Sheqel ha-Qodesh,* 51–54 (63–67); Baer, in *Zion* 2 (1937): 31–33, 36–44; idem, *History,* 1:250–63; Tishby, *Wisdom of the Zohar,* 3:1371–72; Assis, "Sexual Behavior in Mediaeval Hispano-Jewish Society."

4. **From Joseph ...** Joseph upheld the covenant by resisting the sexual advances of Potiphar's wife, and he is therefore called "righteous" in rabbinic literature. See Genesis 39; BT *Yoma* 35b; *Bereshit Rabbah* 93:7; *Pesiqta de-Rav Kahana, nispaḥim,* 460. Cf. *Tanḥuma, Bereshit* 5 and *Pirqei de-Rabbi Eli-'ezer* 38, which cite Amos 2:6.

According to Kabbalah, because of his sexual purity Joseph attained the level of *Yesod* ("Foundation"), the divine phallus and site of the covenant. *Yesod* is known as Righteous, based on Proverbs 10:25: וצדיק יסוד עולם (Ve-tsaddiq yesod olam). The verse, which literally means *The righteous one is an everlasting foundation,* is understood as *The righteous one is the foundation of the world.* See BT *Ḥagigah* 12b; *Bahir* 71 (102); Azriel of Gerona, *Peirush ha-Aggadot,* 34. The righteous who follow the example of Joseph participate in *Yesod* and attain the world that is coming.

5. *these are* always invalidates ... See *Bereshit Rabbah* 30:3: "Rabbi Abbahu said, 'Wherever *these are* is written, it invalidates the preceding, whereas *and these are* adds to the preceding. Here [namely, *These are the offspring of Noah*], the wording *these are* invalidates the preceding. What is invalidated? The generation of the Flood.'"

Cf. *Bereshit Rabbah* 12:3 (based on Genesis 2:4); *Zohar* 2:223a.

6. **That** *river* **gushes and flows ...** The stream of emanation flows from *Hokhmah* (known as *Eden*) through *Binah* and the *sefirot* below Her, and via *Yesod* enters *Shekhinah, the garden,* who yields souls.

On souls as fruit, see *Bahir* 14 (22); Ezra of Gerona, *Peirush Shir ha-Shirim,* 489, 504; *Zohar* 1:15b, 19a, 33a, 60a, 82b, 85b, 115a–b; 2:223b; Moses de León, *Sefer ha-Mishqal,* 51; idem, *Sheqel ha-Qodesh,* 56 (69). Cf. Ibn Ezra on Psalms 1:3.

7. *for* בו (vo), *on it, He rested* On *Yesod, Shekhinah* rested. See *Zohar* 1:47b.

8. *He rested on the seventh day* *Yesod* rested on *Shekhinah,* seventh of the lower *sefirot.* Rabbi El'azar is playing with the various meanings of נייחא (neyaḥa): "satisfaction, pleasure, rest" and alluding to נח (Noaḥ), Noah, who symbolizes *Yesod.*

9. **this generated** *offspring,* **no other** *Yesod* alone engenders new life, as implied by the wording: *These are the offspring of Noah.*

340

"Come and see: Noah below embodied the covenant, modeled on above,[10] so he was called איש האדמה (*ish ha-adamah*), *husband of earth* (ibid. 9:20).[11] We have learned a secret: Noah needed the ark—to unite with it, to sustain the seed of all, as is written: *to keep seed alive* (ibid. 7:3). Who is the ark? *Ark of the covenant* (Joshua 3:11).[12] Noah and the ark followed this paradigm.[13] Of Noah, *covenant* is written: *I will erect My covenant with you* (Genesis 6:18).[14] Until the covenant was erected with him, he did not enter the ark, as is written: *I will erect My covenant with you, and you will enter the ark.* Then the ark was *ark of the covenant,* ark of Noah, corresponding consummately above. Since this covenant above generates offspring, similarly Noah generates offspring. So, *these are the offspring of Noah.*

"*Noah was a righteous man* (ibid. 6:9). Certainly so, corresponding above, and so it is written: *The righteous one is the foundation of the world* (Proverbs 10:25). Upon this, earth is established, for it is the pillar on which the world stands. Who is He? Righteous One, and Noah is called *righteous* below.[15] Mystery of all: *Noah walked with* אלהים (*Elohim*), *God* (Genesis, ibid.), existing on earth as above.[16]

"*A righteous man,* foundation of the world, *covenant of peace* (Ezekiel 34:25), peace of the world, *husband of earth,* indeed![17] So, *Noah found favor in the eyes of YHVH* (Genesis, ibid., 8).

341

10. **Noah below embodied the covenant...** Noah lived in sexual purity, unlike the rest of the generation of the Flood (see above, pages 321–23), so he attained the level of *Yesod,* the divine phallus and site of the covenant. According to rabbinic tradition (see below, note 18), Noah was born circumcised, already embodying the covenant.

11. איש האדמה (*ish ha-adamah*), *husband of earth* The phrase is normally rendered *man of the soil,* but Rabbi El'azar understands it as *husband of earth.* Having embodied *Yesod,* Noah unites with *Shekhinah,* symbolized by *earth.* See 1:58b, 62b.

Similarly, Moses is called איש האלהים (*ish ha-Elohim*), *husband of Elohim.* See Deuteronomy 33:1; Psalms 90:1; *Midrash Tehillim* 90:5; *Pesiqta de-Rav Kahana, nispaḥim, Vezot Haberakhah,* 443–44, 448 (variants); *Tanḥuma, Vezot Haberakhah* 2 (*Ets Yosef,* ad loc.); *Devarim Rabbah* (Lieberman), on 33:1; *Zohar* 1:6b, 21b–22a, 148a, 152a–b, 236b; 239a; 2:22b, 235b, 238b, 244b (*Heikh*).

12. *Ark of the covenant* *Shekhinah,* who houses *the covenant* of *Yesod.* See *Zohar* 1:2a, 33b, 228b; Moses de León, *Sheqel ha-Qodesh,* 75 (95).

13. **Noah and the ark followed this paradigm** Noah, embodying *Yesod,* enters the ark, symbolizing *Shekhinah,* thereby ensuring the continuity of life.

14. *I will erect...* והקימותי (*Va-haqimoti*), *I will establish.* Rabbi El'azar focuses on the literal meaning: "raise up, erect."

See *Zohar* 1:66b; Moses de León, *Sod Eser Sefirot Belimah,* 381–82; Liebes, *Peraqim,* 378–79; idem, in *Da'at* 1 (1978), 107.

15. **Righteous One...** As explained above in note 4, *Yesod* ("Foundation") is known as Righteous One, based on this verse in Proverbs.

16. *Noah walked with* אלהים (*Elohim*), *God...* He accompanied *Shekhinah,* known as *Elohim.*

17. *covenant of peace* (Ezekiel 34:25), **peace of the world...** *Yesod,* the divine

"*Perfect in his generations* (ibid., 9). What does this mean: *in his generations?* Those issuing from him: perfecting them all, he was more perfect than all of them.

"*Perfect,* for he was born circumcised, as is written: *Walk before Me and be perfect* (ibid. 17:1).[18]

"*In his generations,* not the generations of the world, for from him issued offspring to the world.[19]

"Come and see: Since the day the world was created, Noah was destined to be united with the ark, to enter her. Until they joined as one, the world was unfit. Afterward what is written? *From these the whole earth dispersed* (ibid. 9:19). What does *dispersed* mean? As is said: *from there it divides* (ibid. 2:10).[20] From there division appeared, offspring scattered in every direction. All is as one, according to a single paradigm. So, *these are the offspring of Noah. These,* indeed! For Foundation of the World is the one who generates [60a] offspring enduring on earth."[21]

Rabbi Abba came and kissed him, saying, "A lion in his potency pierces, pulverizes rock![22] So, indeed! Come and see: So, too, from the measurement of the ark."[23]

Rabbi El'azar opened, saying, "*Come, gaze upon the works of Elohim, how He has brought desolation on earth* (Psalms 46:9).[24] *Come, gaze.* What does חזו

342

phallus and site of the covenant, brings peace by uniting *Tif'eret* with *Shekhinah.* See BT *Shabbat* 152a, where Rabbi Shim'on son of Ḥalafta refers to the phallus as "peacemaker of the home."

18. *Perfect,* **for he was born circumcised...** According to rabbinic tradition, Noah was one of those rare individuals born circumcised. See *Avot de-Rabbi Natan* A, 2; *Tanḥuma, Noah* 5; *Zohar* 1:58a–b. The verse in Genesis 17 is addressed by God to Abraham immediately preceding the command of circumcision; see *Bereshit Rabbah* 46:1, 4.

19. *In his generations,* **not the generations of the world...** The wording implies that all future generations are considered Noah's generations, but Rabbi El'azar is apparently also alluding to the tradition that Noah was only relatively righteous: "*In his generations,* not in other generations" (*Tanḥuma, Noah* 5, according to the view of Rabbi Yehudah).

20. *from there it divides* The full verse reads: *A river issues from Eden to water the*

garden, *and from there it divides and becomes four stream-heads.* In Kabbalah this verse is interpreted as a description of the flow of emanation from *Hokhmah* (*Eden*) to *Shekhinah* (*the garden*), below whom *it divides,* generating the lower worlds. Noah's entrance into the ark symbolizes the union of *Yesod* and *Shekhinah,* which ensures proliferation. See *Zohar* 1:60b–61a.

21. **Foundation of the World...** *Yesod,* embodied by Noah.

22. **A lion in his potency pierces, pulverizes rock!** The mighty Rabbi El'azar penetrates even the hardest passage.

23. **So, too, from the measurement of the ark** Perhaps, as follows: The ark was 300 cubits long, 50 cubits wide and 30 cubits high, totaling 380, which is the *gimatriyya* (numerical value) of two divine names symbolizing *Yesod* and *Shekhinah:* שדי (*Shaddai*) and אדני (*Adonai*), with the addition of one indicating their unification.

24. *works of Elohim...* The Masoretic text reads: *the works of YHVH.* Cf. Psalms

(ḥazu), *gaze*, mean? As is said, *A harsh* חזות (ḥazut), *vision, has been conveyed to me* (Isaiah 21:2). Through the acts of the blessed Holy One, supernal prophecy is revealed to human beings.[25]

"*How He has brought* שַׁמּוֹת (shammot), *desolation*—שֵׁמוֹת (shemot), *names*, indeed, for the name determines destiny entirely.[26]

"It is written: *He named him Noah, saying: This* (Genesis 5:29).[27] Why *saying*? Why *this*? *Saying* implies Woman;[28] *this*, Righteous One,[29] as the blessed Holy One named him: נח (*Noaḥ*), Noah, נייחא (*neyaḥa*), satisfaction, of the earth.[30] What does *saying* mean? This site named him Noah.[31] Who is that? Holy Land,[32] who said: *This one* ינחמנו (yenaḥamenu), *will provide us relief*. The blessed Holy One fashioned him below corresponding above.

66:5: *Come, see the works of Elohim.* The reading *Elohim* in Psalms 46:9 is attested in many manuscripts and the Septuagint (codex Alexandrinus), and the Zoharic rabbis are aware of both variants. Note the comment by Rabbi Ḥiyya, above, page 332: "Whether it be one name or the other, all is praise."

See *Bereshit Rabbah* 84:8; 88:3 (and Theodor, ad loc.); *Tanḥuma, Vayelekh* 1; Radak on Psalms 46:9; *Zohar* 1:157b (*ST*); 2:5a; *ZH* 12a (*MhN*), 73a (*ShS*); Moses de León, *Sefer ha-Rimmon*, 288; *OY, KP, MM*, and *Zohorei Ya'bets* on 1:58b; *Minḥat Shai* on Numbers 23:9; Psalms 46:9, 66:5; Menaḥem Azariah of Fano, *Yonat Elem*, 99; Margaliot, *Sha'arei Zohar, Berakhot* 7b.

25. *A harsh* חזות (ḥazut), *vision...* Rabbi El'azar explains the word חזו (ḥazu), *gaze*, by relating it to the word חזות (ḥazut), prophetic *vision*.

26. **name determines destiny entirely** See BT *Berakhot* 7b: "How do we know that a name determines destiny? Rabbi El'azar said, 'For Scripture states: *Come, gaze upon the works of YHVH, how He has brought* שמות (shammot), *desolation, on earth.* Do not read שַׁמּוֹת (shammot), *desolation*, but rather: שֵׁמוֹת (shemot), *names*.'" Cf. *Zohar* 1:6a, 58b; 2:179b.

Here the point is that the name given to a child determines and predicts his future character.

27. *saying: This* The full verse reads: *He named him Noah, saying: This one* ינחמנו (yenaḥamenu), *will provide us relief, from our*

labor and from the painful toil of our hands caused by the ground that YHVH cursed.

28. *Saying* implies Woman Literally, "*Saying:* this is woman." A Zoharic revision of a midrashic interpretation found in *Bereshit Rabbah* 16:6: "*YHVH Elohim commanded the human, saying, 'From every tree of the garden you are free to eat.'* Rabbi Levi said, 'He issued him six commands..., [one of which was implied by] *saying*, concerning גלוי עריות (gillui arayot), exposing nudity (fornication) [as shown by analogy from this proof text]: *Saying: If a man divorces his wife* (Jeremiah 3:1).'"

See BT *Sanhedrin* 56a–b; *Zohar* 1:35b; 2:83b, 239b; 3:27a. Here Rabbi El'azar alters the interpretation of the word *saying* from "concerning adultery" (based on the verse *Saying: If a man divorces his wife* [literally: *woman*]) to "this is Woman," alluding to the divine woman, *Shekhinah*.

29. *this*, Righteous One The biblical word זה (zeh), *this*, refers to *Yesod*, known as Righteous One, while the feminine form, זאת (zot), *this*, refers to his partner, *Shekhinah*, the Divine Presence.

30. נח (*Noaḥ*), Noah, נייחא (*neyaḥa*), satisfaction, of the earth Noah's name implies that by embodying *Yesod* he satisfied *Shekhinah*, symbolized by earth.

31. This site... *Shekhinah*, implied by the word *saying*. Rabbi El'azar reads the verse: *He named him Noah.* [Who named him Noah?] *Saying* [i.e., *Shekhinah*].

32. Holy Land *Shekhinah*.

343

"Here is written: *This,* and there is written: *This is YHVH for whom we have waited* (Isaiah 25:9).[33] Happy are the righteous, inscribed with the inscription of the royal signet, inscribed with His name.[34] He has brought names to earth fittingly.

"It is written: *He called* את שמו (*et shemo*), *his name, Noah.* Yet it is written: *He called* שמו (*shemo*), *his name, Jacob* (Genesis 25:26). Why is את (*et*) not written?[35] There, another rung; here, another rung, as is written: *I saw* את (*et*) *YHVH* (Isaiah 6:1)—not *I saw YHVH,* but את (*et*) *YHVH.* Similarly here: *He called his name Jacob*—his rung, the blessed Holy One Himself, named him Jacob. But here: את (*et*), encompassing *Shekhinah.*[36]

These are the offspring of Noah.

Rabbi Yehudah opened, "*A good man lends graciously and conducts his affairs with justice* (Psalms 112:5). *A good man*— the blessed Holy One, who is called *good,* as is written: *YHVH is good to all* (ibid. 145:9).[37] *Lends graciously*—to the site possessing nothing of its own, nourished by Him.[38] *Conducts his affairs with justice*—for that *affair* is nour-

344

---

33. **Here is written: *This,* and there is written: *This is YHVH . . .*** The second verse specifies the divine male, *YHVH,* thereby demonstrating that *this* conveys that meaning.

34. **inscribed with the inscription of the royal signet, inscribed with His name** In *Tanḥuma, Tsav* 14, *Shemini* 8, the mark of circumcision is identified with the י (*yod*) of the divine name שדי (*Shaddai*). A German Hasidic tradition identifies the mark with the *yod* of יהוה (*YHVH*). In the *Zohar,* it signifies the divine name as well as *Yesod* (and occasionally *Shekhinah*).

See *Zohar* 1:2b, 13a, 56a, 95a–b; 2:36a, 216b; 3:142a (*IR*), 215b, 220a, 256a (*RM*); Wolfson, in *JQR* 78 (1987): 77–112; idem, *Circle in the Square,* 29–48.

35. **Why is את (*et*) not written?** Grammatically, the accusative particle את (*et*) has no ascertainable independent sense; but Naḥum of Gimzo and his disciple Rabbi Akiva taught that when *et* appears in a biblical verse, it amplifies the original meaning. See BT *Pesaḥim* 22b; *Ḥagigah* 12a; *Zohar* 1:247a; 2:90a, 135b.

36. **There, another rung; here, another rung . . .** In the *Zohar,* the word את (*et*) symbolizes *Shekhinah,* who comprises the entire alphabet of divine speech, from א (*alef*) to ת (*tav*). She is also known as Oral Torah. See the Christian parallel in Revelation 1:8: "I am *alpha* and *omega.*"

Here Rabbi El'azar's point is that *Shekhinah* named Noah; he reads the verse: את (*Et*) [*Shekhinah*] *called his name Noah.* Jacob, on the other hand, was named by his *sefirah, Tif'eret,* known as the blessed Holy One, so in that verse the word את (*et*) does not appear. See *Bereshit Rabbah* 63:8; *Tanḥuma, Shemot* 4; *Midrash Aggadah,* Genesis 25:26; Rashi, ad loc.; *Zohar* 1:138a, 186a–b.

The verse from Isaiah is cited to show that את (*et*) symbolizes *Shekhinah,* who is paired with יהוה (*YHVH*), symbolizing *Tif'eret,* though actually in that verse the divine name is written: אדני (*Adonai*). See *Zohar* 1:18a, 247a; 2:81b.

37. **the blessed Holy One . . .** *Tif'eret,* known as *YHVH.*

38. **site possessing nothing of its own . . .** *Shekhinah,* who receives emanation from Her partner.

ished only *with justice*, as is said: *Righteousness and justice are the foundation of Your throne* (ibid. 89:15).[39]

"Alternatively, *a good man*—this is Righteous One, as is written: *Say of the righteous one that he is good* (Isaiah 3:10)."[40]

Rabbi Yose said, "This is Noah, as is written: *a righteous man* (Genesis 6:9)."

Rabbi Yitsḥak said, "This is Sabbath who opened with *good*, as is written: *It is good to praise YHVH* (Psalms 92:1)."[41]

Rabbi Ḥiyya said, "All is one! All have spoken one word.[42] This generates offspring in the world.[43] Who are the offspring of the world? Souls of the righteous, fruit of the handiwork of the blessed Holy One."[44]

Rabbi Shim'on said, "When the blessed Holy One adorns Himself in His crowns, He crowns Himself above and below.[45] Above, from the site deepest of all;[46] below, with what? With souls of the righteous. Then vitality is lavished above and below, embracing the site of the sanctuary on all sides.[47] The cistern is filled, the ocean consummated, providing for all.[48]

"It is written: *Drink water from your cistern, flowing water from your well* (Proverbs 5:15). Why first *your cistern*, then *your well*? A *cistern* is empty, un-flowing, while a *well* bubbles with water.[49] Yet all is one site. The site embracing the poor is called *cistern*, possessing nothing of its own, only what is de-

345

39. that *affair* is nourished only *with justice*... Shekhinah is known as דבר (*davar*), "affair" or "word," since She is the realm of divine speech. She is nourished by *Tif'eret*, known as *justice*. Shekhinah is also known as *righteousness*, and together with *Tif'eret* constitutes the foundation of the divinity.

40. Righteous One   *Yesod* ("Foundation"), who is called Righteous One based on Proverbs 10:25; see above, note 4.

See BT *Ḥagigah* 12b; *Bahir* 71 (102); Azriel of Gerona, *Peirush ha-Aggadot*, 34.

41. Sabbath who opened with *good*   According to *Midrash Tehillim* 92:3, the Sabbath Day herself recited this psalm together with Adam. Cf. the Sabbath morning liturgy: "The Sabbath Day exclaims in praise: *A psalm, a song for the Sabbath Day. It is good to praise YHVH.*"

42. All is one! All have spoken one word   All these different interpretations harmonize. *Tif'eret* and *Yesod* represent two aspects

of the divine masculine potency, while Noah embodies *Yesod*, who is also symbolized by the Sabbath day.

43. This generates offspring...   *Yesod* generates life.

44. Souls of the righteous...   Souls are engendered by the union of *Tif'eret* (or *Yesod*) and *Shekhinah*. On souls as fruit, see above, note 6.

45. adorns Himself in His crowns...   Divinity is adorned both by the *sefirot* and by righteous human souls. See *Zohar* 3:291a (*IZ*).

46. site deepest of all   The highest sefirotic realm is also the deepest.

47. site of the sanctuary...   *Shekhinah*.

48. cistern...ocean...   Other names of *Shekhinah*, who receives the divine flow and channels it to the lower worlds.

49. Why first *your cistern*, then *your well*?...   The words בור (*bor*), *cistern*, and באר (*be'er*), *well*, are nearly identical. See BT *Avodah Zarah* 19a.

posited there.[50] Who is that? ד (*Dalet*). Subsequently it becomes a well, filled from all directions. Who is that? ה (*He*), filled from above, [60b] bubbling from below. Filled from above, as we have explained; bubbling from below, from souls of the righteous.[51]

"Alternatively, *Drink water from your cistern*—this is King David, of whom is written: *Who will get me a drink of water from the cistern of Bethlehem?* (2 Samuel 23:15).[52] *Flowing water*—this is Abraham.[53] *From the midst of*—this is Jacob, in the middle.[54] *Your well*—this is Isaac, called *well of living water* (Genesis 26:19).[55] Look, in this verse appears the supernal holy chariot, composed of the patriarchs joined by King David![56]

"Desire of the female toward the male arouses only when a spirit enters her and she gushes water toward upper, masculine waters.[57] Similarly Assembly of Israel arouses desire toward the blessed Holy One only by the spirit of the

---

346

50. **site embracing the poor is called *cistern*...** *Shekhinah* is symbolized by poverty and by the empty cistern, since She possesses nothing of Her own and is dependent on the higher *sefirot*. See *Zohar* 1:235a.

51. **Who is that? ד (*Dalet*)... ה (*He*)...** When *Shekhinah* is empty, She is symbolized by the letter ד (*dalet*), signifying that She is דלה (*dallah*), "poor," lacking the flow of emanation from above. Once the human arousal from below stimulates Her union with *Tif'eret*, the ד (*dalet*) is enhanced by the straight line of the letter ו (*vav*), the third letter of יהוה (*YHVH*) whose numerical value of six symbolizes *Tif'eret* and the five *sefirot* surrounding Him. Thereby *Shekhinah* is enriched, and ד (*dalet*) is transformed into ה (*he*), the final letter of יהוה (*YHVH*). See *Zohar* 2:51a, 104a, 123b, 188b (*SdTs*).

52. **King David...** David, the ideal king, symbolizes *Shekhinah*, who is also known as *Malkhut* ("Kingdom").

53. **Abraham** Symbolizing the free-flowing love of *Hesed*.

54. **Jacob, in the middle** Jacob symbolizes *Tif'eret*, the central pillar and core of the *sefirot*, who mediates between *Hesed* and *Gevurah*.

55. **Isaac...** Whose servants discovered *a well of living water*. See *Zohar* 1:135b.

56. **supernal holy chariot, composed of the patriarchs...** The three patriarchs

symbolize the sefirotic triad *Hesed*, *Gevurah*, and *Tif'eret*, which is completed by *Shekhinah*, symbolized by King David.

See *Bereshit Rabbah* 47:6: "Resh Lakish said, 'The patriarchs themselves constitute the [divine] Chariot.'" Cf. Azriel of Gerona, *Peirush ha-Aggadot*, 57; Jacob ben Sheshet, *Ha-Emunah ve-ha-Bittahon*, 396; *Zohar* 1:5b, 20a, 89b (*ST*), 99a, 150a, 154b, 173b, 248b; 2:144a; 3:38a, 99a; Bahya ben Asher on Genesis 32:10.

57. **Desire of the female toward the male arouses...** On the spirit entering the female, cf. *Zohar* 2:102a. See *Bereshit Rabbah* 13:13: "Rabbi Shim'on son of El'azar said, 'Every single handbreadth [of water] descending from above is met by two handbreadths emitted by the earth. What is the reason? *Deep calls to deep*... (Psalms 42:8).' Rabbi Levi said, 'The upper waters are male; the lower, female. The former cry to the latter, "Receive us! You are creatures of the blessed Holy One and we are His messengers." They immediately receive them, as is written: *Let the earth open* (Isaiah 45:8)—like a female opening to a male.'"

See *Tosefta, Ta'anit* 1:4; 1 Enoch 54:8; *Seder Rabbah di-Vreshit*, 10 (*Battei Midrashot*, 1:25); *Pirqei de-Rabbi Eli'ezer* 23; *Zohar* 1:17b, 29b, 35a, 46a, 85b, 244a–b, 245b; 3:223b.

According to the second-century Greek physician Galen, sperm is generated by both

righteous entering Her.[58] Then waters flow from within Her toward waters of the male, all becoming one desire, one cluster, one nexus. Rapture, total rapture! An amble ambled by the blessed Holy One with souls of the righteous.[59]

"Come and see: All those offspring of the Garden of Eden issue from Righteous One only when He enters this ark in a single bond.[60] All are treasured away in Her, afterward issuing. Similarly here, Noah, *righteous man* (ibid. 6:9), did not generate offspring, becoming fruitful in the world, until he entered the ark, in which all was gathered and treasured, afterward issuing, becoming fruitful in the world, enduring on earth.[61] Had they not issued from the ark, they would not have endured in the world. All corresponding above: issuing from the ark above, issuing from the ark below, corresponding to one other. From here the world was firmly established, not previously, and so it is written: *The earth was corrupt before God* (ibid. 6:11)."

Rabbi Yehudah said, "Since it is written: *The earth was corrupt*, why *before God*? Because they perpetrated their sins brazenly, in the eyes of all, it is written: *before God*."[62]

347

male and female. See Leviticus 12:2; Ibn Ezra, Naḥmanides, Baḥya ben Asher, and Sforno, ad loc.; BT *Berakhot* 60a; *Niddah* 31a.

58. **Assembly of Israel...** כנסת ישראל (*Keneset Yisra'el*). In rabbinic Hebrew this phrase denotes the people of Israel. The midrash on the Song of Songs describes the love affair between the maiden (the earthly community of Israel) and her lover (the Holy One, blessed be He). In the *Zohar*, *Keneset Yisra'el* can refer to the earthly community but also (often primarily) to *Shekhinah*, the divine feminine counterpart of the people, the aspect of God most intimately connected with them. The lovers in the Song of Songs are pictured as the divine couple, *Tif'eret* and *Shekhinah*.

Here Rabbi Shim'on teaches that *Shekhinah*'s passion for *Tif'eret* is stimulated by righteous souls of Israel "assembled" within Her. See *Zohar* 1:235a, 244a–b, 245b. This ascent of "female waters" is emphasized by Isaac Luria.

59. **amble ambled by the blessed Holy One...** See *Sifra, Beḥuqqotai* 3:3, 111b: "*I will walk among you* (Leviticus 26:12).... In the time to come the blessed Holy One will stroll with the righteous in the Garden of Eden."

See Genesis 3:8; *Aggadat Bereshit* 23:5; BT *Sanhedrin* 102a; 2 Enoch 8:3; *Pereq Shirah*, 2:57 (s.v. *tarnegol*); *Seder Gan Eden* (*Beit ha-Midrash*, 3:138).

According to the *Zohar*, at midnight God delights in the souls of the righteous in the Garden of Eden, and those who study Torah here below partake of the celestial joy.

See *Zohar* 1:10b, 72a, 77a–b, 82b, 92a–b, 132b, 136b, 178b, 231b; 2:46a, 130a–b, 136a, 173b, 195b–196a; 3:21b–22b, 52b, 193a; *ZḤ* 13c (*MhN*). Cf. BT *Berakhot* 3b; Scholem, *On the Kabbalah*, 146–50.

60. **All those offspring of the Garden of Eden...** Souls emerge only from the union of *Yesod*, known as Righteous One, with *Shekhinah* (known as both "Garden of Eden" and "ark").

61. **Similarly here, Noah, *righteous man*...** Noah, embodying *Yesod*, had to enter the ark, symbolizing *Shekhinah*, in order to generate offspring.

62. **Because they perpetrated their sins brazenly...** See *Pirqei de-Rabbi Eli'ezer* 22; *Zohar* 1:57b.

Rabbi Yose said, "I say the opposite. *The earth was corrupt before God.* At first, *before God,* for they did not act openly: they acted *before God,* not before human beings. Eventually they acted brazenly, as is written: *and the earth was filled with violence* (ibid.), for nowhere on earth was it unexposed. So the verse conveys two modes."[63]

These are the offspring of Noah.

Rabbi Abba said, "From the day Adam violated the command of his Lord, all children of the world born thereafter are called 'children of Adam'[64]—not admiringly, but as if to say: 'the children of that one who violated his Lord's command.' Once Noah appeared, children of the world are named after him: *offspring of Noah,* for he actualized their existence in the world,[65] not *offspring of Adam,* who removed them from the world, inflicting death upon them all."[66]

Rabbi Yose said, "If so, look at what is written later: *YHVH came down to see the city and tower that the children of Adam had built* (ibid. 11:5)—*the children of Adam,* not *the children of Noah!*"[67]

He replied, "Because of Adam, who sinned in the presence of his Lord. Better for him had he never been created, so that this verse would not have been written. But come and see what is written: *A wise son delights a father* (Proverbs 10:1).[68] When a son is good, all the inhabitants of the world speak well of his father, but when he is bad, all speak ill of his father. Since Adam sinned, violating the command of his Lord, when rebels arose against their Lord, what is written? *That the children of Adam had built*—children of Adam who rebelled against his Lord, violating the command.[69] So *these are the offspring*—

348

---

63. **verse conveys two modes** The first half of the verse (*The earth was corrupt before God*) conveys hidden sin, known only to God, while the second half (*and the earth was filled with violence*) denotes brazen sin. Both interpretations of *before God* presented here by Rabbi Yehudah and Rabbi Yose derive from Ibn Ezra, ad loc., who prefers a different interpretation. See BT *Keritot* 25b; *Leqaḥ Tov,* ad loc.

64. **'children of Adam'** בני האדם (*Benei ha-adam*), "The children of the human," i.e., human beings. Rabbi Abba understands the phrase as "children of Adam."

65. **he actualized their existence in the world** By entering the ark, he saved humanity.

66. **inflicting death upon them all** By eating the forbidden fruit, he brought death into the world. See Genesis 2:17; *Zohar* 1:36a.

67. *the children of Adam,* not *the children of Noah* Even though the account of the Tower of Babel appears after Noah, it still includes the phrase: *the children of Adam.* Why?

68. *A wise son delights a father* The verse continues in parallelism: *but a foolish son is his mother's grief.*

69. **when rebels arose against their Lord...** By building the Tower of Babel. See *Bereshit Rabbah* 38:9, which compares the sinful ingratitude of Adam and the generation of the Tower of Babel: "*That* בני האדם (*benei ha-adam*), *the children of the*

these, not the earlier ones. *These,* who emerged from the ark and generated offspring for the world, not *the offspring of Adam,* who emerged from the Garden of Eden without generating them from there.[70]

"Come and see: If Adam had generated offspring from the Garden of Eden, they would never have been destroyed[71] and the light of the moon would never have darkened.[72] They all would have lived forever, and even the supernal angels could not have withstood their radiant luster and wisdom. But since [61a] sin compelled him to leave the Garden of Eden and he generated offspring outside, they did not endure in the world and were imperfect."

Rabbi Ḥizkiyah said, "How could they have generated offspring there? For if the evil impulse had not been drawn toward him, enticing him to sin, he would have existed alone in the world, generating no offspring.[73] Similarly if Israel had not sinned, drawing to themselves the evil impulse, they would never have generated offspring and no other generations would have come into the world."[74]

He replied, "If Adam had not sinned, he would not have generated offspring like this. For now he generates only from the side of the evil impulse, and since all human offspring derive from that side, they do not endure and are incapa-

349

human, had built. Rabbi Berekhiah said, 'Would we have thought it was built by the children of donkeys or camels? Rather, it means *the children of Adam.* "Just as Adam, after all the good that I bestowed upon him, said *The woman whom You gave to be beside me [she gave me of the tree, and I ate]* (Genesis 3:12), so although the generation of the Dispersion [the generation of the Tower of Babel] followed the generation of the Flood by only two years [as is said:] *two years after the Flood* (ibid. 11:10), yet [they rebelled, displaying gross ingratitude]."'" See *Zohar* 1:74b (*ST*), 75a.

70. **these, not the earlier ones...** See above, p. 340 and n. 5. Here Noah's offspring are contrasted with Adam's, who were generated only after he was banished from the Garden.

71. **If Adam had generated offspring from the Garden...** If he had engendered children while still in the Garden, they would have lived forever. Actually, according to various rabbinic sources, Adam did engender children in the Garden.

See *Bereshit Rabbah* 22:2; BT *Sanhedrin*

38b; *Avot de-Rabbi Natan* A, 1; Rashi on Genesis 4:1.

72. **light of the moon would never have darkened** The light of *Shekhinah,* symbolized by the moon, would not have diminished. See *Zohar* 1:1a, 12a, 19b, 33b.

73. **How could they have generated offspring there?...** Procreation is linked with the evil impulse, so if Adam had not sinned, he would have remained childless. See *Bereshit Rabbah* 9:7: "Naḥman said in the name of Rabbi Shemu'el: '*Behold, it was very good*—this is the good impulse; *And behold, it was very good* (Genesis 1:31)—this is the evil impulse. Is the evil impulse *very good?* How astonishing! Yet were it not for the evil impulse, no man would ever build a house, marry a woman, or engender children.'"

See *Yoma* 69b; *Zohar* 1:49a; 3:189a.

74. **Similarly if Israel had not sinned...** At Sinai with the Golden Calf. See BT *Avodah Zarah* 5a: "Resh Lakish said, 'Let us be grateful to our ancestors, for if they had not sinned [with the Golden Calf], we would never have come into the world!'"

ble of the other side.[75] But if Adam had not sinned and not been banished from the Garden of Eden, he would have generated offspring from the side of Holy Spirit, holy as supernal angels, enduring forever, corresponding above. Since he sinned and engendered children outside the Garden, and was unworthy of generating them from the Garden, they did not endure even long enough to take root in the world, until Noah appeared and entered the ark. From the ark issued all generations of the world, dispersing from there to all four directions of the world."[76]

God saw the earth, and behold, it was corrupt (Genesis 6:12). Why was it corrupt? *For all flesh had corrupted their way* (ibid.), as has been explained.[77]

Rabbi Ḥiyya opened with a verse, saying, "*God saw their deeds, how they turned from their evil ways* (Jonah 3:10). Come and see: When human beings are virtuous, observing the commandments of Torah, earth is invigorated, pervaded with joy. Why? Because *Shekhinah* hovers over earth, so all delight, above and below. But when human beings corrupt their ways, failing to observe the commandments of Torah, sinning in the presence of their Lord, then, as it were, they thrust *Shekhinah* out of the world, and earth is left ruined.[78] For *Shekhinah* no longer hovers over her, so she is ruined. Why? Because another spirit hovers over her, ruining the world.[79]

"You might think this applies even to the land of Israel, yet we have learned that no other spirit or official hovers over the land of Israel, only the blessed Holy One.[80] Come and see! So it is in the land of Israel: no official or emissary

350

75. **incapable of the other side** They cannot endure on the other, holy side. Alternatively, they are incapable of enduring on "the other side," the side of evil, which is barren.

76. **From the ark issued…** See Genesis 9:18–19.

77. *For all flesh had corrupted their way…* The verse concludes: *upon earth.* Immorality, especially sexual sin, contaminates the earth. The phrase *corrupted their way upon earth* is elsewhere interpreted as referring to masturbation (spilling seed on earth) or crossbreeding.

See BT *Sanhedrin* 108a; *Bereshit Rabbah* 28:8; *Kallah Rabbati* 2; *Pirqei de-Rabbi Eli-'ezer* 22; Rashi on BT *Shabbat* 41a, s.v. *ke-illu mevi mabbul la-olam*; *Zohar* 1:56b–57a, 61b–62a, 69a. Cf. *Sanhedrin* 57a; *Bereshit Rabbah* 26:4.

78. **they thrust *Shekhinah* out of the world…** See BT *Ḥagigah* 16a: "Rabbi Yitsḥak said, 'Whoever sins secretly, it is as if he thrusts away the feet of *Shekhinah*.'" Cf. *Zohar* 1:57a–b, 69a, 84b.

79. **another spirit hovers over her…** A demonic spirit fills the vacuum left by *Shekhinah*.

80. **no other spirit or official hovers over the land of Israel…** See BT *Ta'anit* 10a: "The land of Israel is watered by the blessed Holy One Himself, whereas the rest of the world is watered by an emissary."

Cf. *Tanḥuma, Re'eh* 8; BT *Ketubbot* 110b; *Zohar* 1:84b, 108b; 2:33a, 151b. According to *Bereshit Rabbah* 33:6, "Rabbi Levi said, '…The land of Israel was not inundated by the Flood.'"

According to rabbinic tradition, the seventy nations of the world are governed by

hovers over her, only the blessed Holy One. But for a moment it does hover to destroy human beings.[81] How do we know? From David, for it is written: *David saw the angel of YHVH [standing between earth and heaven], with a drawn sword in his hand extended over Jerusalem* (1 Chronicles 21:16), so the land was ruined."

Rabbi El'azar said, "Even that time, it was the blessed Holy One. Here is written: *angel,* and there is written: *the angel who redeems me* (Genesis 48:16), and similarly: *The angel of YHVH moved* (Exodus 14:19).[82] Whether for good or for ill, the blessed Holy One reigns over her. For good, so that other officials and all inhabitants of earth will be ashamed of their deeds.[83] For ill, so that they will not rejoice in ruling over her.[84]

"Now you might say, 'No? Look at what is written: *For she has seen heathens invade her sanctuary* (Lamentations 1:10) and destroy the House.[85] If those officials were not in charge, the Temple would not have been destroyed!' Come and see! It is written: *For You have done it* (ibid. 1:21), and similarly: *YHVH has done what He devised* (ibid. 2:17).

"Come and see! It is written: *God saw the earth, and behold, it was corrupt. Corrupt,* indeed, as has been explained.[86] Correspondingly, *God saw their deeds, how they turned from their evil ways.* For then, earth called above, adorning her face like a woman for a man.[87] So, *God saw the earth, and behold, it was corrupt,* like a woman rendered impure, hiding her face from her husband. When the sins of humanity abounded brazenly, the face of earth transmogrified into that of a woman totally shameless, as is said: *Earth was defiled under*

351

seventy angels or heavenly princes appointed by God. See Daniel 10:20; Septuagint, Deuteronomy 32:8–9; Jubilees 15:31–32; *Targum Yerushalmi,* Genesis 11:8, Deuteronomy 32:8–9; *Tanḥuma, Re'eh* 8; *Leqaḥ Tov,* Genesis 9:19; *Pirqei de-Rabbi Eli'ezer* 24; *Zohar* 1:46b, 84b, 108b; 2:33a, 151b; 3:298b; Ginzberg, *Legends,* 5:204–5, n. 91.

81. **But for a moment it does hover...** A destructive power hovers even over the land of Israel.

82. **Here is written: *angel*...** In all these passages *angel* refers to *Shekhinah.* See *Zohar* 1:113a, 120b, 166a, 230a; 3:187a. Cf. *Mekhilta, Shirta* 3.

83. **For good, so that other officials...** In good times, when Israel acts virtuously, God rules over the land of Israel directly, lavishing blessing, so that all others will

witness His intimacy with Israel and be ashamed of their own failings.

84. **For ill, so that they will not rejoice...** When Israel sins, God Himself administers the punishment, so as not to give her enemies the satisfaction of dominating her. See *Eikhah Rabbah* 1:41; BT *Sanhedrin* 96b.

85. **the House** The Temple.

86. ***Corrupt,* indeed, as has been explained** See above, note 77. The word נשחתה (nishḥatah), *corrupt,* can also mean "destroyed," alluding to the destruction of the Temple described above.

87. **earth called above...** Earth symbolizes *Shekhinah,* who, stimulated by human repentance, adorns Herself for Her partner, *Tif'eret.* See *Zohar* 1:72b; 2:232b.

her inhabitants (Isaiah 24:5). So, *it was corrupt*, indeed! Why? *For all flesh had corrupted* [61b] *their way upon earth.*"[88]

Rabbi El'azar went to visit Rabbi Yose son of Rabbi Shim'on son of Lekonya, his father-in-law.[89] As soon as he saw him, he set up a canopied carpet with wooden poles,[90] and they sat.

His father-in-law asked him, "Did you happen to hear from your father anything about this verse: *YHVH has done what He devised; He has executed His utterance that He ordained in days of old* (Lamentations 2:17)?"

He replied, "The Companions have already established it: *He has executed His utterance*—He rent His purple raiment.[91] *That he ordained in days of old,* for He ordained that purple from those supernal, primordial days;[92] and on the

---

88. **So, *it was corrupt*, indeed!...** Immorality defiles both the earth and *Shekhinah*.

89. **Rabbi Yose son of Rabbi Shim'on son of Lekonya, his father-in-law** See the similar setting in *Pesiqta de-Rav Kahana* 11:20: "Rabbi El'azar son of Rabbi Shim'on was going to Rabbi Shim'on son of Rabbi Yose son of Lekonya, his father-in-law..." According to this rabbinic tradition, El'azar's father-in-law was named Shim'on son of Yose.

See JT *Ma'aserot* 3:8, 50d; *Shir ha-Shirim Rabbah* on 4:11; *Devarim Rabbah* 7:11; *Seder ha-Dorot*, s.v. Shim'on ben Yose ben Lekonya. (In BT *Bava Metsi'a* 85a, the name of Rabbi El'azar's brother-in-law is given as Rabbi Shim'on son of Issi [Yose] son of Lekonya, which would make Yose his father-in-law, as here in the *Zohar*; but nowhere in rabbinic literature is he named Yose son of Shim'on.)

The author(s) of the *Zohar* consistently switches father and son, transforming Shim'on son of Yose into Yose son of Shim'on. See 1:5a–b, 143b; 3:84b, 188a, 193a; *ZH* 10d, 14a (*MhN*), 22c (*MhN*). El'azar's own father, of course, is Rabbi Shim'on son of Yoḥai.

90. **canopied carpet with wooden poles** טופסיסא דקומרא במטון דקולפא (*Tufsisa de-qumra be-matun de-qulpa*). One of the Zo-

har's neologistic phrases, describing the gracious welcome given Rabbi El'azar by his father-in-law. *Tufsisa* derives from the Greek *tapes*, "carpet, rug." See *Bereshit Rabbah* 33:1; *Bei'ur ha-Millim ha-Zarot*, 178.

Qumra derives from the Greek *qamara*, "arched cover." See *Bereshit Rabbah* 31:11 (describing Noah's ark); M *Eruvin* 8:9–10; *Arukh*, s.v. qmr.

The word *qulpa* means "pole, lance." See *Zohar* 1:29a, 32a, 57b.

91. **Companions have already established...** This interpretation appears in *Vayiqra Rabbah* 6:5 (and parallels) in the name of Rabbi Ya'akov of Kefar Ḥanin, who interprets אמרתו (*emrato*), *His utterance*, as *imrato*, "His hemmed garment," the royal purple torn by God in mourning over the destruction of the Temple. According to rabbinic tradition, the Temple curtain was slashed by the Roman general Titus.

See *Sifrei*, Deuteronomy 328; *Bereshit Rabbah* 10:7; *Vayiqra Rabbah* 20:5; BT *Gittin* 56b. Cf. *Midrash Tehillim* 9:13; *Ester Rabbah* 7:10; *Yalqut Shim'oni*, Numbers, 785; *Zohar* 1:39a, 41a (*Heikh*), 224b; 2:8b; 3:140b (*IR*).

92. **He ordained that purple...** The royal purple symbolizes *Shekhinah*, known as *Malkhut* ("Kingdom"). She culminates the emanation of the "primordial days," the six *sefirot* from Ḥesed to Yesod.

352

day the Temple was destroyed, He rent it because this purple robe is His glory and adornment—so He rent it."[93]

He said to him, "*YHVH has done what He devised.* Does a king devise evil against his children before they sin?"

He replied, "This can be compared to a king who possessed a precious vessel.[94] Every day he feared it might be broken, so he gazed upon it constantly, eyeing its perfection. One day the king's son provoked him. The king took that precious vessel and smashed it, as is written: *YHVH has done what He apprehended.*[95]

"Come and see: From the day the Temple was built, the blessed Holy One would gaze upon it, so precious was it to Him. He feared Israel might sin and the Temple be destroyed. Whenever He entered, He would don that purple robe.[96] Afterward, when sins prevailed, provoking the King, the Temple was destroyed and He rent that purple raiment, as is written: *YHVH has done what He apprehended, He has executed His utterance.*

"This applies to the time when the Temple was destroyed; but at other times, nothing delights the blessed Holy One as much as the elimination of the wicked of the world and those who have provoked Him, as is written: *When the wicked perish, jubilation!* (Proverbs 11:10). So in every generation that He punishes the wicked of the world, joyous song resounds in the presence of the blessed Holy One.

"Now you might say, 'But we have learned that joy vanishes from the presence of the blessed Holy One when He punishes the wicked!'[97] Come and see: When judgment is executed upon the wicked, joyous song does resound in His presence over their elimination from the world—but only when the extension He patiently granted them has expired and they have still

353

93. **on the day the Temple was destroyed, He rent it...** *Shekhinah,* corresponding to the Temple, was torn from Her partner, *Tif'eret,* and thrown into exile along with Israel.

94. **This can be compared to a king...** See the similar parable in *Bahir* 23 (33).

95. *He apprehended* זמם (Zamam), which means both "devise" and "consider." Rabbi El'azar adopts the latter meaning, in the sense of "being apprehensive."

96. **Whenever He entered, He would don...** Whenever the blessed Holy One manifested in the Temple, for example, during the three pilgrimage festivals, He would be robed in *Shekhinah,* uniting with Her.

97. **But we have learned that joy vanishes...** See BT *Megillah* 10b: "Rabbi Yoḥanan has said, '...The blessed Holy One does not rejoice in the downfall of the wicked.' And Rabbi Yoḥanan said further, 'What is the meaning of the verse *One did not approach the other all night long* (Exodus 14:20)? [In its literal sense, this verse refers to the Israelites and the Egyptians encamped at the Red Sea.] The ministering angels [referred to as *one* and *the other* in Isaiah 6:3] wanted to sing, but the blessed Holy One said, "The work of My hands is drowning in the sea, and you are singing?"'" Cf. *Zohar* 1:57a–b.

not turned back to Him from sinning.[98] If, however, they are punished prematurely—with incomplete guilt, as is said: *for the guilt of the Amorites is not yet complete* (Genesis 15:16)—then joy vanishes from His presence due to their perishing.[99]

"You might ask, 'If their time has not yet come, why does He punish them?' But the blessed Holy One punishes them prematurely only because they interfere with Israel, harassing them. So He punishes them prematurely, eliminating them from the world. This is why He was distressed when He drowned the Egyptians in the sea and when he destroyed the enemies of Israel in the days of Jehoshaphat,[100] and so with all of them, for they were eliminated prematurely on account of Israel.

"But when the extension He has granted them expires without their having returned to God, then joyous song resounds in His presence over their elimination from the world. Except for the time when the Temple was destroyed, for even though their time was up—for they had provoked Him[101]—joy vanished from His presence, and ever since that time, there has been no joy above or below."[102]

For in another seven days I will make it rain upon the earth forty days and forty nights... (Genesis 7:4).

Rabbi Yehudah said, "What is the nature of these forty days and forty nights? Forty, to lash sinners, as is written: *Forty he is to be struck, no more* (Deuteronomy 25:3),[103] corresponding to the four directions of the world, ten in each, because the human

---

98. **extension He patiently granted them...** The days of the wicked are prolonged to enable them to turn back to God or to engender worthy children.

See BT *Bava Qamma* 38b; *Vayiqra Rabbah* 32:4; *Zohar* 1:56b, 62b, 65b, 118a (*MhN*), 227a; 2:12b.

99. **punished prematurely—with incomplete guilt...** See BT *Sotah* 9a: "Rav Hamnuna said: 'The blessed Holy One does not punish a person until his peck is full.'"

Cf. *Zohar* 1:113b, 121b. The verse from Genesis explains why Abraham's descendants can inherit the Promised Land only in the distant future.

100. **Egyptians in the sea...enemies of Israel...** On the drowning of the Egyptians, see above, note 97, citing BT *Megillah* 10b. Earlier in the same Talmudic passage,

reference is made to the sad fate of the soldiers of Moab and Ammon who died in battle against King Jehoshaphat of Judah. See *Zohar* 1:57b.

101. **even though their time was up...** Even though Israel had sinned and deserved punishment.

102. **there has been no joy...** See M *Sotah* 9:12: "Rabban Shim'on son of Gamli'el says in the name of Rabbi Yehoshu'a: 'Ever since the day the Temple was destroyed, there is no day without a curse, dew has not descended as a blessing, and the flavor of fruit has been eliminated.'"

See *Zohar* 1:70b, 177a, 181a–b, 203a; 3:15b, 74b.

103. **Forty, to lash sinners...** This interpretation by Rabbi Yehudah accords with the view attributed to him in the Mishnah

being was created from these four.[104] So, *I will obliterate all existing things* (Genesis, ibid.).[105] Forty were required for lashing, for the world to be obliterated."

Rabbi Yitsḥak was in the presence of Rabbi Shim'on. He asked him, "This verse: *The earth was corrupt* [62a] *before God* (ibid. 6:11)—given that humans sinned, but how did earth?"

He replied, "Since it is written: *for all flesh had corrupted their way* [*upon earth*] (ibid., 12), as has been said.[106] Similarly, *The earth was defiled, and I inflicted her punishment upon her* (Leviticus 18:25). It was human beings who sinned. If you ask 'How did earth?' the answer is: Human beings constitute the essence of earth—they ruin earth and she is ruined. The verse proves it, as is written: *God saw the earth, and behold, it was corrupt, for all flesh had corrupted their way upon earth* (Genesis, ibid.).

"Come and see: All sins of a human being are entirely his ruination, yet are susceptible to return;[107] but the sin of spilling seed, wasting his way, emitting seed upon earth,[108] ruining both himself and earth—of this is written: *Stained is your iniquity before Me* (Jeremiah 2:22). Similarly, *You are not a God who delights in wickedness; evil cannot abide with You* (Psalms 5:5).[109] Similarly, *Er,*

355

(M *Makkot* 3:10) that forty full lashes should be administered by the court, not thirty-nine, as ruled by the majority of rabbis.

See *Tanḥuma, Qoraḥ* 12; Maimonides, *Mishneh Torah, Hilkhot Sanhedrin* 17:1; *Zohar* 2:184a, 249b (*Heikh*). For other associations of the forty days and nights of the Flood, see *Bereshit Rabbah* 32:5.

104. **the human being was created from these four** See *Tanḥuma, Pequdei* 3: "He began assembling the body of Adam from the four directions of the world."

See 2 *Enoch* 30:13; *Targum Yerushalmi*, Genesis 2:7; BT *Sanhedrin* 38b; *Pirqei de-Rabbi Eli'ezer* 11; *Zohar* 1:130b, 205b; 2:23b, 24b; 3:83a.

105. *I will obliterate all existing things* The verse continues: *that I have made, from the face of the earth.* Rabbi Yehudah is playing with two senses of מחה (*mḥh*): "wipe out" and "strike."

106. *for all flesh had corrupted their way...* Human immorality, especially sexual sin, contaminates earth. Rabbi Shim-

'on understands the expression השחית דרכו (*hishḥit darko*), *corrupted their way*, as an allusion to masturbation.

See *Kallah Rabbati* 2, citing Genesis 38:9: שחת ארצה (*shiḥet artsah*), *he* [Onan] *wasted* [his seed] *on the ground* (or: *let it go to ruin*). Cf. *Pirqei de-Rabbi Eli'ezer* 22; *Bereshit Rabbah* 26:4, 31:7; Rashi on BT *Shabbat* 41a, s.v. *ke-illu mevi mabbul la-olam; Zohar* 1:56b–57a, 69a.

In the world of the *Zohar*, masturbation is a heinous sin. See 1:188a, 219b; Moses de León, *Shushan Edut*, 353; Tishby, *Wisdom of the Zohar*, 3:1365–66. Cf. BT *Niddah* 13a: "Rabbi Yitsḥak and Rabbi Ammi said, '[Whoever emits semen fruitlessly] is as though he sheds blood.'"

107. **return** Turning back to God in sincere repentance.

108. **emitting seed upon earth** Instead of על ארעא (*al ar'a*), "upon earth," several manuscripts read על זרעא (*al zar'a*), "upon seed."

109. *evil cannot abide with You* See *Zohar* 1:56b–57a; cf. BT *Niddah* 13b. Later

firstborn of Judah, was evil in the eyes of YHVH...(Genesis 38:7).[110] This has already been explained."

He asked, "Why did the blessed Holy One punish the world with water, and not with fire or some other element?"

He replied, "It is a mystery! For they wasted their ways, so that the upper waters and lower waters failed to unite fittingly.[111] Who has ever ruined like this: male and female waters? So they were punished with water, just like they sinned. The water was boiling, peeling off their skin, just as they wasted their ways with boiling water.[112] A fitting punishment, as is written: *All the springs of the great abyss burst forth* (ibid. 8:2)—lower waters; *and the sluices of heaven opened* (ibid.)—upper waters. Upper and lower waters."

Rabbi Ḥiyya and Rabbi Yehudah were walking on the way and reached some huge mountains, in whose ravines they discovered human bones from victims

356

editions include a qualifying gloss here: "except through great returning [repentance]." See *Zohar* 1:219b; Moses de León, *Shushan Edut*, 353.

110. *Er, firstborn of Judah, was evil*... The verse concludes: *and YHVH put him to death*. As noted in *Kallah Rabbati* 2, "[ער (Er), Er] spelled backward is רע (ra), evil." Genesis does not specify the nature of Er's sin, but rabbinic tradition maintains that it was the same as that of his younger brother, Onan, who *wasted* [his seed] *on the ground* (Genesis 38:9).

See *Targum Yerushalmi*, Genesis 38:7; BT *Yevamot* 34b; *Bereshit Rabbah* 85:4 (and Theodor, ad loc.); *Zohar* 1:56b–57a.

111. **upper waters and lower waters failed to unite fittingly** Human immorality ruins the union of the divine couple, *Tif'eret* and *Shekhinah*, symbolized by the upper and lower waters. See *Pirqei de-Rabbi Eli'ezer* 23: "Rabbi Tsadok said, '...The waters of the Flood came down upon the earth—namely, the male waters—and they rose from the depths—namely, the female waters. Joining one another, they prevailed and destroyed the world.'" Cf. *Bereshit Rabbah* 32:7.

See *Bereshit Rabbah* 13:13: "Rabbi Shim'on son of El'azar said, 'Every single handbreadth [of water] descending from above

is met by two handbreadths emitted by the earth. What is the reason? *Deep calls to deep*...(Psalms 42:8).' Rabbi Levi said, 'The upper waters are male; the lower, female. The former cry to the latter, "Receive us! You are creatures of the blessed Holy One and we are His messengers." They immediately receive them, as is written: *Let the earth open* (Isaiah 45:8)—like a female opening to a male.'"

See *Tosefta, Ta'anit* 1:4; 1 Enoch 54:8; *Seder Rabbah di-Vreshit*, 10 (*Battei Midrashot*, 1:25); *Zohar* 1:17b, 29b, 46a, 60b, 244a–b, 245b; 3:223b.

According to the second-century Greek physician Galen, sperm is generated by both male and female. See Leviticus 12:2; Ibn Ezra, Naḥmanides, Baḥya ben Asher, and Sforno, ad loc.; BT *Berakhot* 60a; *Niddah* 31a.

112. **The water was boiling...just as they wasted their ways**... See BT *Sanhedrin* 108b: "It has been taught: The waters of the Flood were as thick as semen....Rav Ḥisda said: 'With boiling [passion] they sinned, and with boiling [water] they were punished.'"

See *Yalqut Shim'oni*, Job, 906; *Pirqei de-Rabbi Eli'ezer* 22; *Targum Yerushalmi*, Genesis 7:10; *Zohar* 1:66a.

of the Flood. They paced three hundred paces along one bone.[113] Amazed, they exclaimed, "Just as our companions have said: They did not fear the judgment of the blessed Holy One, as is written: *They say to God, 'Leave us alone! We have no desire to know Your ways* (Job 21:14). What did they do? With their feet they dammed up the springs of the abyss, but the waters bubbled up boiling and they could not endure, finally slipping, falling to the ground, and dying."[114]

Noah engendered three sons... (Genesis 6:10).[115]

Rabbi Ḥiyya said to Rabbi Yehudah, "Come and I'll tell you a word I heard regarding this. It can be compared to a man who implants in a female the fruit of her womb simultaneously, two or three children, diverging from one another in character and conduct: this one virtuous, that one wicked.[116] Here, too, three clusters of spirit roaming, embraced by three worlds.[117]

113. **bones from victims of the Flood ... three hundred paces...** According to rabbinic tradition, the generation of the Flood were giants, of whom only Og, King of Bashan, survived. See *Midrash ha-Gadol*, Genesis 7:20: "Each of them was fifteen cubits [approximately twenty-two feet] high, and they said, 'Let's climb to the top of the mountains!' Therefore the waters swelled fifteen cubits above the mountains."

See *Targum Yerushalmi*, Deuteronomy 3:11; *Bereshit Rabbah* 31:12; BT *Niddah* 61a; *Pirqei de-Rabbi Eli'ezer* 22–23, 34.

The immense size of the bone recorded here derives from (and is dwarfed by) the description in BT *Niddah* 24b: "Abba Sha'ul (or, as some say, Rabbi Yoḥanan) stated: 'I used to be a grave digger. Once while chasing a deer, I entered the thighbone of a corpse. I pursued it for three parasangs [about ten miles] but did not catch the deer and the thighbone did not end. When I returned I was told that the bone belonged to Og, King of Bashan.'"

114. **With their feet they dammed up the springs...** See *Pirqei de-Rabbi Eli'ezer* 22: "They said, 'If He brings the waters of the Flood upon us, behold, we are of high stature, and the waters will not reach our necks. If He brings up the waters of the depths against us, behold, the soles of our feet can

dam up the depths.' What did they do? They spread the soles of their feet and dammed up all the depths. What did the blessed Holy One do? He boiled the waters of the depths, which seethed their flesh and peeled off their skin."

115. ***Noah engendered three sons*** The verse continues: —*Shem, Ham, and Japheth.*

116. **this one virtuous, that one wicked** A gloss preserved in M and several other witnesses adds: "this one average." See Philo, *Questions and Answers on Genesis*, 1:88, where Shem symbolizes good; Ham, evil; and Japheth, indifference.

117. **Here, too, three clusters of spirit roaming...** Noah, symbolizing divine potency, generates the soul in her three aspects: נשמה (*neshamah*), "soul, breath," the highest aspect, followed by רוח (*ruaḥ*), "spirit, wind," and נפש (*nefesh*), "vitality, being." These three dimensions of soul correspond to three worlds. In *ZḤ* 6d (*MhN*) the three aspects of the soul correspond to the upper, middle, and lower worlds. In *Maskiyyot Kesef*, 9–11, Moses de León writes that the soul partakes of three worlds: the World of Creation, the World of Formation, and the World of Action. In later Kabbalah these three worlds contain, respectively, the divine throne, the angels, and the physical cosmos. Here the worlds may sym-

"Come and see: The soul emerges, navigating the mountains of separation,[118] and spirit is joined to soul.[119] As it descends, vitality joins spirit,[120] all of them descending, joining one another."

Rabbi Yehudah said, "Vitality and spirit intertwine, while soul abides in one's ways—a hidden abode, her site unknown.[121] If one strives to purify himself, then he is assisted by a holy soul, purified, sanctified, called 'holy.' If he is unvirtuous, not trying to purify himself, then he has two openings—vitality and spirit—but is devoid of the holy soul—supernal boost—suiting his way."[122]

TOSEFTA[123] Incredible clusters![124] Impregnable castles! Quaestors of quaestory![125] Those of open eyes, open ears! A voice—voice of voices—descends from above, pulverizing mountains and boulders:[126]

bolize the sefirotic triad of Ḥesed, Gevurah, and Tif'eret.

See Zohar 2:155a; Moses de León, Sefer ha-Mishqal, 39–40. On the variety of worlds in the Zohar, see Tishby, Wisdom of the Zohar, 2:555–60; on the soul, 2:677–722, especially 687–89.

Noah's middle son, Ham, saw . . . the nakedness of his father (Genesis 9:22), for which he was cursed. In the Midrash ha-Ne'lam (ZH 21c) he symbolizes the evil impulse, while here he symbolizes the lowest level of soul, nefesh ("vitality"), which originates, according to the Zohar, outside the divine realm and on its own is prone to evil.

See 1:81a (ST); 3:25a–b; Moses de León, Sheqel ha-Qodesh 29 (35).

118. **mountains of separation** Angels or the forces surrounding the divine throne who are situated outside the unified realm of the sefirot. See Zohar 1:29b, 158a; 2:234a–b (which all cite Song of Songs 2:17); Tishby, Wisdom of the Zohar, 2:556.

119. **spirit is joined to soul** The soul (neshamah) is clothed in spirit (ruaḥ).

120. **vitality joins spirit** The spirit (ruaḥ) is clothed in vitality (nefesh).

121. **while soul abides in one's ways . . .** The lower two aspects of the soul, vitality (nefesh) and spirit (ruaḥ), appear simultaneously at the beginning of life, but the highest aspect, neshamah, manifests only if one lives virtuously. Until then she remains

hidden within the deepest recesses of divinity.

122. **If one strives to purify himself . . .** See BT Shabbat 104a: "Resh Lakish said, '. . . If one comes to defile himself, he is provided an opening; if one comes to purify himself, he is assisted.'"

Cf. Yoma 39a: "Our Rabbis taught: 'Do not defile yourselves with them and thus become defiled (Leviticus 11:43). If one defiles himself slightly, he is defiled greatly; below, he is defiled from above; in this world, he is defiled in the world to come.' Our Rabbis taught: 'Hallow yourselves and you will be holy (ibid., 44). If one sanctifies himself slightly, he is sanctified greatly; below, he is sanctified from above; in this world, he is sanctified in the world to come.'"

See Makkot 10b: "Rabbah son of Bar Ḥana said in the name of Rabbi Huna (some say, Rabbi Huna said in the name of Rabbi El'azar), 'From the Torah, the Prophets, and the Writings it can be demonstrated that one is led on the path one wishes to take.'"

Cf. Zohar 1:54a, 56b, 169b, 198b; 2:50a; 3:47a. The reference to "two openings" plays on the wording in BT Shabbat 104a, cited above: "If one comes to defile himself, he is provided an opening."

123. **TOSEFTA** "Addenda." The Matnitin and Tosefta of the Zohar, strewn throughout the text, consist mostly of anonymous enigmatic revelations addressed to the Compan-

"Who are those who see without seeing,[127] ears blocked, eyes shut? Neither seeing, nor hearing, nor knowing through contemplation the one encompassed by two within them, cast away by them.[128] They cling to those two, while one, artisan of artisans, does not abide within them.[129] [62b] They are not inscribed in the Books of Memory,[130] are erased from the Book of Life, as is said: *May they be erased from the Book of Life, and not be inscribed among the righteous* (Psalms 69:29).

ions, urging them to open their hearts to the mysteries. The terseness of these passages recalls the style of the Mishnah. See Scholem, *Kabbalah,* 216.

The *Matnitin* and *Tosefta* are not formally part of the *Zohar's* running commentary on the Torah and will consequently be translated separately in a subsequent volume. I have included this passage of *Tosefta* here because it appears here in nearly all of the manuscripts.

124. **Incredible clusters!** קטורי רמאי (*Qeturei rama'ei*), "Exalted bonds," referring to the kabbalists, whose souls link up with divinity. In the preceding passage, the three aspects of soul are referred to as "three clusters of spirit."

The phrase *qeturei rama'ei,* reappearing in *Zohar* 1:107b (*ST*), 251a (*Hash*), could conceivably be rendered "Conspiratorial impostors!" The Hebrew cognate קשר (*qesher*) means "knot, band, conspiracy," while the root *rmy* means "deceive," as in *Zohar* 1:137a (*MhN*), 204b; 2:71a, 72b, 71b–72a (*RR*); *ZH* 32a. (See also note 208, below.) The phrase would then refer to the pseudepigraphic circle of the *Zohar* who present their teachings in the guise of ancient Mishnaic rabbis.

125. **Impregnable castles! Quaestors of quaestory!** קטורי דקוסטרי (*Qastorei dequsterei*). The root *qstr* appears in two senses in the *Zohar:* one deriving from Latin *castrum* (pl. *castra*), "castle, fortress" (as in *Zohar* 1:29a, 30a); the other from Latin *quaestor,* a Roman official (JT *Eruvin* 6:2, 23b; *Zohar* 1:19b, 53b; 2:19b, 58b, 208b; 3:13a). Either sense applies here to the kabbalists, impregnable in their faith, appointed from above.

126. **A voice—voice of voices—descends...** A heavenly voice manifests. See *Zohar* 1:77a, 161b (*Mat*); 2:81a.

127. **who see without seeing** See BT *Ḥagigah* 12b: "Rabbi Yose said, 'Woe to creatures, for they see but do not know what they see, they stand but do not know on what they stand.'"

128. **the one encompassed by two within them...** As indicated above (in the passage immediately preceding this *tosefta*), the deepest aspect of soul (*neshamah*) is clothed in spirit (*ruaḥ*), which is itself clothed in vitality (*nefesh*). So the *neshamah* is "the one encompassed by two [dwelling] within them," yet rejected by them through their conduct.

129. **They cling to those two, while one...** They desire only to stay alive through the power of the lower aspects of the soul, *nefesh* and *ruaḥ,* making no effort to attain the deeper spirituality of *neshamah,* who consequently flees from them.

The *neshamah* is "artisan of artisans," the source of creativity, emanating from *Shekhinah,* who is called "Artisan of the world" (*Zohar* 1:47b) and derives from *Binah,* also called Artisan (2:167b; 3:219b; 1:22a [*TZ*]). See *Bereshit Rabbah* 1:1: "Rabbi Osha'ya opened, '*I was with Him as an artisan, I was a daily delight* (Proverbs 8:30)....Torah says, "I was the instrument of the blessed Holy One."...The blessed Holy One gazed into Torah and created the world.'" Cf. *Zohar* 2:161a–b.

130. **Books of Memory** The celestial books in which all human actions are recorded. Elsewhere in the *Zohar,* the Book of Memory is identified with *Yesod.* See Ezra

"Woe to them when they leave this world! Woe to their lives! Who will plead for them? They are to be handed over to Dumah,[131] burned in blazing fire from which they cannot escape—except on new moons and Sabbaths, as is said: *From new moon to new moon and from Sabbath to Sabbath, all flesh shall come to bow down before Me, says YHVH* (Isaiah 66:23).[132] Afterward[133] a herald in the North proclaims: *Let the wicked return to Sheol!* (Psalms 9:18).[134] How many ravaging bands of truculent stingers[135] gather against them! In four directions fire flames in the Valley of Ben Hinnom;[136] three times a day they are burned.

"Moreover, when Israel responds aloud: 'Amen! May His great name be blessed!' the blessed Holy One is filled with compassion and takes pity upon all.[137] He signals to the angel appointed over the gates of Hell—Samriel is his name.[138] Three keys are in his hand; he opens three gates on the side of the

4:15; Targum to Esther 6:1; *Zohar* 1:8a–b; 2:70a, 200a, 217a, 246a.

131. **Dumah** Literally, "silence," a name for the netherworld in the Bible. See Psalms 94:17: *Unless YHVH had been my help, my soul would have nearly dwelt in dumah.* Cf. Psalms 115:17.

In rabbinic literature Dumah is the angel in charge of souls of the dead (BT *Berakhot* 18b, *Shabbat* 152b, *Sanhedrin* 94a). In the *Zohar*, he retains this role but also oversees Hell. See 1:8a–b, 94a, 102a, 124a (*MhN*), 237b.

132. **except on new moons and Sabbaths...** According to *Tanḥuma, Ki Tissa* 33, one of the dwellers in Hell reports: "Whoever does not observe the Sabbath properly [*Bereshit Rabbah* 11:5: "willingly"] in your world comes here and observes it against his will.... All week long we are punished and on the Sabbath we rest."

See BT *Sanhedrin* 65b; *Zohar* 1:14b, 41a (*Heikh*), 48a, 197b; 2:31b, 88b, 150b–151a, 203b, 207a; 3:94b; *ZḤ* 17a–b.

The notion that the suffering of the wicked in Hell also abates on new moons derives from Ashkenazic sources. See Ta-Shma, *Ha-Nigleh she-ba-Nistar*, 40.

133. **Afterward** At the close of each Sabbath or new moon.

134. **herald in the North...** Associated with the left side and characterized by harsh judgment.

135. **ravaging bands of truculent stingers** חבילי טריקין (*Ḥavilei teriqin*). The first word

derives from either חבל (*ḥevel*), "band, group," or the verb חבל (*ḥvl*), "to injure, destroy." The second word derives from the root טרק (*trq*), "to sting, bite."

See *Zohar* 1:130a, 237b, 243b–244a; 3:52b, 62b, 154b, 181a, 291b (*IZ*).

136. **Valley of Ben Hinnom** גי בן הנם (*Gei Ven Hinnom*). Originally, the valley outside the western wall of Jerusalem where the god Molech was worshiped, perhaps through child sacrifice. See 2 Kings 23:10; Jeremiah 7:31–32. Jeremiah prophesied that it would be known as *the Valley of Slaughter* and serve as a burial site. In postbiblical literature *Geihinnom* became the name of Hell.

137. **when Israel responds aloud: 'Amen! May His great name be blessed!'...** The response of the congregation in the middle of the Kaddish prayer. See BT *Shabbat* 119b: "Rabbi Yehoshu'a son of Levi said, 'Whoever responds with all his strength: "Amen! May His great name be blessed!"—his decreed sentence is torn up.'"

See *Tosafot*, ad loc.; *Zohar* 1:38b (*Heikh*); 3:285b; *ZḤ* 49a–b, 84c (*MhN, Rut*); *Alfa Beita de-Rabbi Aqiva*, Version 1 (*Battei Midrashot*, 2:368); *Yalqut Shim'oni*, Isaiah, 429; *Seder Eliyyahu Zuta* 17 (22–23); Nissim of Kairouan, *Ḥibbur Yafeh me-ha-Yeshu'ah*, 104–5; *Maḥazor Vitri* 144 (112–13); Ta-Shma, *Minhag Ashkenaz ha-Qadmon*, 299–302; Lerner, in *Asufot* 2 (1988): 29–70.

138. **Samriel is his name** Based on the root סמר (*smr*), "to bristle," in Psalm 119:120:

wilderness,[139] and they see the light of this world. Fiery smoke emerges, choking the ways. Then three deputies under his command fan with three spades in their hands, chasing the smoke back to its site, providing them relief for an hour-and-a-half,[140] following which they return to their fire. So it is three times a day and whenever Israel recites: 'Amen! May His great name be blessed...!'[141]

"Happy are the righteous, whose paths in that world radiate in every direction,[142] as is said: *The path of the righteous is like gleaming light, shining ever brighter until full day* (Proverbs 4:18)."

Rabbi Abba said, "In Hell there are abodes upon abodes: second, third, until seven, as the Companions have established.[143] Happy are the righteous who steel themselves against the sins of the wicked, neither following their paths nor becoming defiled through them. Upon reaching that world, whoever has defiled himself descends to Hell, where he is sunk to the lowest abode. There are two abodes adjacent to one another: Sheol and Avadon.[144] One who descends to Sheol is judged there, receives his punishment, and is raised to another, higher abode; and so on—level after level—till they elevate him. But one who descends to Avadon is never raised,[145]

361

My flesh bristles in fear of You. See *Midrash Tehillim,* ad loc.: "*My flesh bristles in fear of You*—in fear of *Geihinnom.*"

139. **three gates on the side of the wilderness**   A somewhat different layout appears in BT *Eruvin* 19a: "Rabbi Yirmeyah son of El'azar said, 'Geihinnom has three gates: one in the wilderness, one in the ocean, and one in Jerusalem.'"

On the demonic nature of the wilderness, see *Zohar* 1:14b, 169b, 178b; 2:157a, 184a.

140. **hour-and-a-half**   See *Zohar* 3:167a, where a person is punished in Hell for an hour-and-a-half.

141. **three times a day and whenever Israel recites: 'Amen!...'**   During the three daily services, which include the Kaddish prayer, and upon completing a session of Torah study, when the prayer is also recited.

142. **in every direction**   Even to Hell, bringing relief to the wicked.

143. **In Hell there are abodes upon abodes...**   On the seven divisions of Hell, see BT *Sotah* 10b; *Midrash Tehillim* 11:6; Zo-

har 1:40a (*Heikh*), 237b; 2:150b, 263a–68b (*Heikh*); 3:178a; Ginzberg, *Legends,* 5:20, n. 56.

144. **Sheol and Avadon**   In the Bible, שאול (*she'ol*) is the underworld, abode of the dead, sometimes paired with אבדון (*avaddon*), "destruction, ruin," which may refer to a distinct area of the underworld reserved for the wicked. See Proverbs 15:11; Job 26:6; and Revelation 9:11, where Avadon is the name of *the angel of the bottomless pit.* Cf. *Zohar* 3:54b, 178a, 285b–86a.

145. **receives his punishment, and is raised... is never raised...**   According to M *Eduyyot* 2:10, the wicked are punished in Geihinnom for twelve months. See BT *Rosh ha-Shanah* 17a: "Transgressors of Israel who sin with their body and transgressors of the Gentiles who sin with their body descend to Geihinnom and are punished there for twelve months. After twelve months their body is consumed, their soul burned, and the wind scatters them under the soles of the feet of the righteous....But as for the heretics, in-

which is why it is called Avadon, for he is totally אביד (*avid*), lost.[146]

"Come and see: Noah warned his contemporaries, but they would not listen,[147] until finally the blessed Holy One inflicted upon them the punishment of Hell. What is that? Fire and snow, water and fire—one freezing, one boiling.[148] All of them were sentenced to the punishment of Hell and eliminated from the world, following which the world fittingly endured.

"Noah entered the ark, bringing with him every species of the creatures of the world. Truly Noah was a *tree bearing fruit* (Genesis 1:11), and all species of the world sprang from the ark, corresponding to the manner above.[149]

"Come and see when this *tree bearing fruit* joins the *fruit tree*:[150] all those supernal species! Living things great and small; countless species, each one unique, as is said: *Living things small and great* (Psalms 104:25).[151] Similarly, Noah in the ark, all of them issuing from the ark, and the world was established, corresponding above.[152] So he is called *Noah, husband of earth* (Genesis 9:20),[153] *Noah, righteous man* (ibid. 6:9), as they have already established."[154]

362

formers, apostates, skeptics, those who rejected Torah and denied the resurrection of the dead, those who abandoned the ways of the community, those who *spread their terror in the land of the living* (Ezekiel 32:23), and those who sinned and made the masses sin..., these descend to *Geihinnom* and are punished there for generation after generation.... *Geihinnom* will be consumed, but they will not be consumed."

146. **totally...lost** Cf. Dante, *Inferno*, 3: "Abandon hope, all you who enter here."

147. **Noah warned his contemporaries...** According to a rabbinic tradition, Noah attempted to warn his contemporaries and induce them to turn back to God, but he was unsuccessful. See *Bereshit Rabbah* 30:7; *Tanhuma, Noah* 5; BT *Sanhedrin* 108a–b.

148. **Fire and snow...** According to rabbinic literature, the year-long punishment of the sinners in Hell is equally divided between fire and snow. See JT *Sanhedrin* 10:3, 29b; *Pesiqta de-Rav Kahana* 10:4; *Zohar* 1:68b, 107b, 238b. Similarly, the generation of the Flood was punished with freezing water raining down from the sky and boiling water surging up from the depths. See *Tanhuma* (Buber), *Bereshit* 33; *Pirqei de-Rabbi Eli'ezer* 22; above, page 356.

149. **Noah was a *tree bearing fruit*...**

Noah symbolizes *Yesod*, the fructiferous phallus, identified with this tree. See *Zohar* 1:1a, 18b, 33a, 238a.

150. **when this *tree bearing fruit* joins the *fruit tree*** When *Yesod* joins with *Shekhinah*, who receives His fruit and is called *fruit tree*.

151. **all those supernal species...** Various heavenly and angelic powers.

152. **Similarly, Noah in the ark...** In entering the ark, Noah both imitated and stimulated the union of *Yesod* and *Shekhinah*.

153. ***Noah, husband of earth*** The phrase איש האדמה (*ish ha-adamah*) is normally rendered as *man of the soil*, but Rabbi Abba understands it as *husband of earth*. Having embodied *Yesod*, Noah unites with *Shekhinah*, symbolized by *earth*. See above, note 11.

154. ***Noah, righteous man...*** Noah symbolizes *Yesod*, who is known as Righteous One, based on Proverbs 10:25: וצדיק יסוד עולם (*Ve-tsaddiq yesod olam*). The verse, which literally means *The righteous one is an everlasting foundation*, is understood as *The righteous one is the foundation of the world*.

See BT *Ḥagigah* 12b; *Bahir* 71 (102); Azriel of Gerona, *Peirush ha-Aggadot*, 34; *Zohar* 1:59b.

Rabbi Ḥiyya said, "For 300 years before the onslaught of the Flood, Noah warned them concerning their deeds, but they would not listen to him,[155] till finally the blessed Holy One completed the span of time He had patiently extended for them, and they were eliminated from the world.[156]

"Come and see: What is written above? *When humans began to multiply on the face of the earth and daughters were born to them* (ibid. 6:1). They walked around naked in sight of all. What is written? *The sons of Elohim saw the human daughters . . .* (ibid., 2).[157] This was the foundation, the root of their persistent sinning, leading finally to their extermination from the world. So they were drawn after the evil impulse, its stem and roots, rejecting holy faith, defiling themselves, as has been explained."[158]

God said to Noah, "End of all flesh has come before Me" (Genesis 6:13). We return to the previous matter.[159] *End of all flesh has come before Me—come before Me,* indeed, as caused by them.[160]

Rabbi Yehudah opened, "*YHVH, let me know my end, what is the measure of my days, that I may know how ephemeral I am* (Psalms 39:5). David said in the presence of the blessed Holy One, 'There are two ends, one on the right and one on the left, these being two paths humans walk to that world.[161]

363

155. **300 years . . .** Rabbinic tradition records 120 years. See *Targum Onqelos* and *Targum Yerushalmi,* Genesis 6:3; *Bereshit Rabbah* 30:7.

156. **completed the span of time He had patiently extended for them . . .** The days of the wicked were prolonged to enable them to turn back to God. See BT *Bava Qamma* 38b; *Vayiqra Rabbah* 32:4; *Zohar* 1:56b, 61b, 65b, 118a (*MhN*), 227a; 2:12b.

157. *The sons of Elohim saw the human daughters . . .* The verse reads: *The sons of Elohim saw how beautiful the human daughters were, and they took themselves wives, whomever they chose.* The myth behind this fragment in Genesis appears in postbiblical sources describing angels who rebelled against God and descended from heaven to earth, where they were attracted by mortal women.

See Isaiah 14:12; 1 Enoch 6–8; Jubilees 5; BT *Yoma* 67b; *Aggadat Bereshit,* intro, 39; *Midrash Avkir,* 7 (cited in *Yalqut Shim'oni,* Genesis, 44); *Pirqei de-Rabbi Eli'ezer* 22; *Zohar*

1:23a (*TZ*), 37a, 37a (*Tos*), 58a, 126a; 3:208a–b, 212a–b; *ZH* 81a–b (*MhN, Rut*); *Targum Yerushalmi,* Genesis 6:2; Ginzberg, *Legends,* 5:153–56, n. 57.

158. **This was the foundation, the root of their persistent sinning . . .** The generation of the Flood, descended from the lustful union of angels with mortal women, persisted in the ancestral sin. Thereby they rejected *Shekhinah,* known as מהימנותא קדישא (*meheimanuta qaddisha*), the realm of "holy faith."

159. **We return to the previous matter** Previously the discussion had focused on Genesis 6:12, then on 6:10, following which there appear a passage from the Zoharic *Tosefta* and a discussion of Noah warning his generation. Now the text returns to Genesis 6:13.

160. *End of all flesh has come before Me . . . caused by them* Human wickedness empowers the Angel of Death, known as *End of all flesh.* See *Zohar* 1:35b, 54a, 58a.

161. **to that world** To the afterlife. See BT *Berakhot* 28b: "When Rabban Yoḥanan

"An end on the right, as is written: לקץ הימין (le-qets ha-yamin), *at the end of the right* (Daniel 12:13).[162] An end on the left, as is written: *He puts an end to darkness, the furthest reaches he explores—earth of pitch-black darkness* (Job 28:3).[163] *He puts an end to darkness. End*—Angel of Death, Serpent, *End of all flesh*.[164] *Puts to darkness*—for he derives from the side of the smelting of gold.[165] *The furthest reaches he explores*—When judgment looms over the world,[166] he *explores*, becoming Accuser of the world,[167] besmirching creatures' faces. [63a]

"An end on the right, as we have said, for it is written: *at the end of the right*. The blessed Holy One said to Daniel, 'As for you, go on till the end; you will rest, and arise' (Daniel, ibid.).[168]

"He asked, 'Where? I don't know what will happen to me in that world.'

"He replied, '*You will rest*.'[169]

"He asked, 'When they rise from the dust, will I rise among them or not?'

"He replied, '*You will arise*.'

"He said, 'I know they will rise in various groups—some genuinely righteous, some the wicked of the world[170]—and I don't know with which of them I will rise.'

364

son of Zakkai fell ill, his disciples came in to visit him. As soon as he saw them, he began to weep. They exclaimed, 'Lamp of Israel! Right-hand Pillar! Mighty Hammer! Why do you weep?' He replied, '... There are two paths before me—one leading to Paradise, the other to Hell—and I do not know on which one I will be led. Should I not weep?'"

162. לקץ הימין (le-qets ha-yamin), *at the end of the right*   The phrase means literally *at the end of days*, the word ימין (yamin) being an aramaized form of the Hebrew ימים (yamim), "days." Rabbi Yehudah, however, understands the word as the Hebrew ימין (yamin), "right."

163. *earth of pitch-black darkness*   The verse actually reads: *rock of pitch-black gloom*. See *Zohar* 1:193a.

164. **Angel of Death, Serpent, *End of all flesh***   The demonic manifests as the Angel of Death. See BT *Bava Batra* 16a: "Resh Lakish said, 'Satan, the evil impulse, and the Angel of Death are one and the same.'" Cf. *Zohar* 1:58a.

165. **he derives from the side of the smelting of gold**   The Angel of Death and the entire demonic realm represent the dark

dross of the *sefirah* of *Gevurah*, who is situated on the left side of the sefirotic tree and symbolized by gold.

166. ***The furthest reaches... When judgment looms...***   Perhaps understanding the biblical word תכלית (takhlit), "end, reaches," according to the intensive form of the root כלה (klh), "to destroy."

167. **Accuser of the world**   See the description of Satan's itinerary in BT *Bava Batra* 16a: "He descends and seduces, ascends and arouses wrath, obtains authorization, and seizes the soul."

See Rashi on BT *Shabbat* 89a, s.v. *ba ha-satan; Zohar* 1:10b, 46b, 125a, 148a (*ST*), 152b; 2:33b, 268b.

168. *As for you, go on till the end; you will rest, and arise*   The verse continues: *for your share at the end of days*. See *Eikhah Rabbah* 2:6; *Pesiqta de-Rav Kahana* 17:5.

169. **He asked, 'Where?... *You will rest***'   Several manuscripts read here: "He asked, 'Rest in this world or in that world?' He replied, 'In that world, as is said: *They will rest on their couches* (Isaiah 57:2).'"

170. **they will rise in various groups...**   See Daniel 12:2; BT *Rosh ha-Shanah* 16b.

"He replied, '*For your share*' (ibid.).

"He said, 'You told me: *As for you, go on till the end*. There is an *end* on the right and an *end* on the left; I don't know to which: to קץ הימין (*qets ha-yamin*), *the end of the right*, or קץ הימים (*qets ha-yamim*), *the end of days*.'[171]

"He replied, 'לקץ הימין (*Le-qets ha-yamin*), *At the end of the right* (ibid.).'

"Similarly here, David said to the blessed Holy One, '*YHVH, let me know my end. What is my allotted share?*' He remained uneasy until he was assured that he would be on the right, as is written: *Sit on My right* (Psalms 110:1).

"Come and see: Similarly, the blessed Holy One said to Noah, '*End of all flesh has come before Me.*' Who is that? The *end* who besmirches creatures' faces: *End of all flesh*.

"*Has come before Me*. From here we learn that the wicked of the world anticipate him, attracting him to themselves to besmirch them.[172] As soon as he is authorized, he seizes the soul, yet not until then.[173] So he *has come before Me* to obtain permission to besmirch faces of the inhabitants of the world. Therefore, *I am about to destroy them along with the earth* (Genesis, ibid.).[174] So, *Make yourself an ark of gopher wood* (ibid., 14) to save yourself, preventing him from overpowering you.

"Come and see: We have learned that when death appears in town or anywhere in the world, one should not show himself on the street because the Destroyer is empowered to destroy everything.[175] So the blessed Holy One said to him, 'You must hide yourself away! Do not show yourself in the presence of the Destroyer, so that he will not overpower you.'

365

171. **I don't know to which...** Daniel asks God which *end* He intends. Whereas *the end of days* symbolizes the demonic power of death, *the end of the right* symbolizes the culmination of emanation, characterized by the grace and bliss of the right side. See *Zohar* 1:54a–b, 152b, 210b; 2:33a–34a, 134a–b, 181b. Cf. BT *Berakhot* 28b (cited above, note 161).

172. **wicked of the world anticipate him...** Those who indulge in immorality stimulate the *End of all flesh*, paving the way for him to approach the divine, ushering him in to seek authorization to strike.

173. **As soon as he is authorized, he seizes the soul...** See above, note 167.

174. **I am about to destroy...** By empowering the Destroyer.

175. **when death appears in town...** See BT *Bava Qamma* 60a–b: "Rabbi Yosef taught: 'What is the meaning of the verse *None of you shall go out the door of his house until morning* (Exodus 12:22)? Once permission has been granted to the Destroyer, he does not distinguish between righteous and wicked.'... Our Rabbis taught: 'A plague in town? Keep your feet indoors.'... Our Rabbis taught: 'A plague in town? One should not walk in the middle of the road, because the Angel of Death walks there—for as soon as permission has been granted him, he strides brazenly.'"

See *Mekhilta, Pisḥa* 11; *Zohar* 1:68a–b, 69a, 101b–102a, 107b, 113a, 182b, 197b, 204b; 2:36a (*MhN*), 196a, 227a; 3:54a–b.

"Now you might say, 'Who deployed the Destroyer here? It was simply water overwhelming.' Come and see: Judgment never manifests in the world, nor is the world obliterated, without that Destroyer surging through the punishments executed upon the world. Similarly here, there was a flood, the Destroyer surging through that flood, called by that name.[176] So the blessed Holy One told Noah to hide himself, not expose himself openly.

"Now you might say, 'The ark was exposed in this world, and the Destroyer was surging.' However, as long as one's face is not visible to the Destroyer, he has no power over him.[177] How do we know? From Egypt, as is written: *None of you shall go out the door of his house until morning* (Exodus 12:22). Why? Because the Destroyer loomed, ready to destroy, and one must not expose himself in his presence. So Noah together with all his companions were hidden away in the ark, and the Destroyer had no power over them."

Rabbi Ḥiyya and Rabbi Yose were walking on the way. They encountered the
mountains of Kurdistan,[178] where they saw traces of crevices in the earth dating from the time of the Flood.[179]

Rabbi Ḥiyya said to Rabbi Yose, "These crevices are vestiges of the Flood, preserved by the blessed Holy One ever since, throughout the generations, so that the sins of the wicked not be obliterated from His sight. For such is the way of the blessed Holy One: He wants the virtuous who do His will to be remembered above and below, their blessed memory unforgotten generation to generation. Similarly He wants the sins of the wicked, who fail to do His will, not to be forgotten, their punishment and evil memory remembered generation to generation, as is written: *Stained is your iniquity before Me* (Jeremiah 2:22)."[180]

Rabbi Yose opened, saying, "*Cry shrilly, O Daughter of Gallim! Listen, Laishah! O poor Anathoth!* (Isaiah 10:30).[181] This verse has been established

366

---

176. **called by that name** Called "Flood."

177. **as long as one's face is not visible...** See *Devarim Rabbah* 4:4; *Zohar* 1:68b, 108b.

178. **mountains of Kurdistan** טורי קרדו (*Turei qardu*), namely, the mountains of Ararat, upon which the ark settled as the waters of the Flood subsided. See Genesis 8:4, and *Targum Onqelos*, ad loc., from whom the *Zohar* borrows this Aramaic expression. Cf. *Zohar* 3:149a; *ZH* 11b (*MhN*), 49a. The neologistic phrase in 1:15a: בוצינא דקרדינותא (*botsina de-qardinuta*), "a spark of impenetrable darkness," may allude to Kurdistan

(see above, p. 107, n. 4).

179. **crevices...from the time of the Flood** See Genesis 7:11: *All the springs of the great abyss burst.*

180. *Stained is your iniquity before Me* See above, page 355.

181. *Cry shrilly, O Daughter of Gallim! Listen, Laishah! O poor Anathoth!* Isaiah calls on the inhabitants of the city of Bat Gallim (literally, *Daughter of Gallim*) to warn the nation (specifically, the residents of Laishah and Anathoth) of the impending Assyrian invasion.

by the Companions, but it was declared for Assembly of Israel.[182] *Cry shrilly, O Daughter of Gallim! Daughter of Abraham; so they have established.*[183]

"*Daughter of Gallim*, as is written: *a sealed* גל (*gal*), *spring* (Song of Songs 4:12). *Gallim—waves*, streams merging, flowing into Her, filling Her, as is written: *Your branches are an orchard of pomegranates* (ibid., 13).[184]

"*Listen, Laishah*, as is written: ליש (*Layish*), *The lion, perishes for lack of prey* (Job 4:11). *Layish* is male; *Laishah*, female. Why is She called *Layish*?[185] Either because of the verse: *Layish, Lion, mighty among beasts* (Proverbs 30:30), or because of: *Layish, The lion, perishes for lack of prey.* But She is all: *Mighty lion*, deriving from upper Might;[186] *The lion perishes for lack of prey*, when those streams disappear, no longer entering Her. Then She is called *Poor Laishah, lioness* (Isaiah, ibid.), perishing for lack of prey, as is written: *The lion perishes for lack of* [63b] *prey, and the cubs of the lioness are scattered.*[187]

---

182. **Assembly of Israel** כנסת ישראל (*Keneset Yisra'el*). In rabbinic Hebrew this phrase denotes the people of Israel. The midrash on the Song of Songs describes the love affair between the maiden (the earthly community of Israel) and her lover (the Holy One, blessed be He). In the *Zohar*, *Keneset Yisra'el* can refer to the earthly community but also (often primarily) to *Shekhinah*, the divine feminine counterpart of the people, the aspect of God most intimately connected with them. The lovers in the Song of Songs are pictured as the divine couple: *Tif- 'eret* and *Shekhinah*.

Here Rabbi Yose cites a verse from Isaiah addressed to the people of Israel and applies it to *Shekhinah*. See *Zohar* 1:249a–b.

183. **O Daughter of Gallim! Daughter of Abraham...** See BT *Sanhedrin* 94b: "Rav Huna said, '...Cry shrilly, O Daughter of Gallim! Daughter of Abraham, Isaac, and Jacob, who enacted *mitsvot* as profusely as גלי הים (*gallei ha-yam*), the waves of the sea.'" Cf. *Eikhah Rabbah, Petiḥta* 1; *Pesiqta de-Rav Kahana* 13:1.

Here Rabbi Yose focuses on Abraham, who according to rabbinic tradition was blessed with a daughter in his old age. In Kabbalah this daughter symbolizes *Shekhi- nah*, who derives from *Ḥesed*, symbolized by

Abraham and by flowing water. See *Tosefta, Qiddushin* 5:17; BT *Bava Batra* 16b; *Bahir* 52 (78); Naḥmanides on Genesis 24:1.

184. *sealed* גל (*gal*), *spring...* streams merging... In the midrashic interpretation of Song of Songs, the beloved described as *a sealed spring* symbolizes the people of Israel (*Shir ha-Shirim Rabbah* on 4:12; *Shemot Rabbah* 20:5). Here the *spring* is *Shekhinah*, Assembly of Israel, filled by the flow of the *sefirot* from *Ḥesed* to *Yesod*, who are known as *Gallim*, "waves" of emanation.

185. *Layish* **is male;** *Laishah*, **female...** The word לישה (*laishah*) means "lioness," while its homonym, *Laishah*, is the name of the city addressed by Isaiah. Usually male and female symbolize the divine couple, *Ye- sod* and *Shekhinah*, though here, as we soon see, both genders characterize *Shekhinah*. See *Zohar* 1:249b–250a and, on the masculine aspect of *Shekhinah*, 1:232a.

186. **deriving from upper Might** *Shekhi- nah*, the lioness, derives from *Gevurah* (Might).

187. **when those streams disappear...** *Poor Laishah...* When She is not nourished by the flow of emanation, *Shekhinah* is impoverished and unable to transmit blessing. See *Zohar* 1:250a.

"*Anathoth*, poorest of the poor, as is said: *of the priests who were in Anathoth* (Jeremiah 1:1),[188] and similarly: *Anathoth, go to your field!* (1 Kings 2:26).[189] What is the point?[190] As long as King David was alive, Abiathar rose in wealth and in all ways. Afterward Solomon said to him, *Anathoth, go to your field!* Why did Solomon call him this? Because he was telling him, 'In your days father was poor; now, *go to your field!*'[191]

"Now still the question may be posed: Why was Abiathar called *Anathoth*? If you say he came from Anathoth, look at what is written: *One son of Ahimelech son of Ahitub escaped—his name was Abiathar* (1 Samuel 22:20),[192] so he must have been from Nob, since Nob was the city of the priests.[193] Even though it is claimed that Nob and Anathoth are one and the same—it being called 'Anathoth' only because the city was reduced to poverty and destroyed by Saul, and the priests eliminated—still Anathoth was a village, not identical with Nob.[194] The real reason he called Abiathar *Anathoth* was as he said: *Because* התענית (*hit'anneita*), *you were afflicted, with all the hardships my father endured* (1 Kings, ibid.).[195] He came from the city of Nob, but because the poverty of David transpired during his lifetime, he was called otherwise."

368

188. *Anathoth,* **poorest of the poor**... Rabbi Yose interprets the name of the priestly village, ענתות (*Anatot*), in the sense of עני (*ani*), "poor," referring to the priests' lack of inheritance (Deuteronomy 18:1–2). The plural form suggests intense poverty. See *Zohar* 1:249b.

189. *Anathoth, go to your field!* The expression means literally: *Go to Anathoth, to your field,* a command given by King Solomon to Abiathar. Abiathar had been a loyal follower of Solomon's father, King David, and was appointed high priest. However, as a result of his support for the succession of Adonijah (another of David's sons), King Solomon banished him to Anathoth. See 1 Samuel 22–23; 1 Kings 1:7; 2:26–27.

190. **What is the point?** Why did Solomon call Abiathar by the name Anathoth?

191. '**In your days father was poor; now,** *go to your field!*' Abiathar initially served David in a period of poverty, as indicated by the name Anathoth. *Shekhinah*, symbolized by David, was then also incomplete. Now in the affluent reign of Solomon, with *Shekhinah* fulfilled, Abiathar is out of place and must return to his humble home.

According to the Midrash, just as the moon does not become full until the fifteenth day of its cycle, so it remained incomplete until the glorious reign of Solomon in the fifteenth generation from Abraham. See *Pesiqta de-Rav Kahana* 5:12; and *Shemot Rabbah* 15:26: "When Solomon appeared, the disk of the moon became full."

See *Zohar* 1:73b, 74a, 150a, 223a, 225b, 249b; 2:85a; 3:61a; *ZH* 83b (*MhN, Rut*); Moses de León, *Shushan Edut,* 342. In Kabbalah the moon symbolizes *Shekhinah*.

192. *One son... his name was Abiathar* The verse concludes: *and he fled to David.*

193. **he must have been from Nob**... When David fled from King Saul, he was assisted by Ahimelech, priest of Nob. Saul then destroyed Nob, killing all its inhabitants—except for Abiathar, Ahimelech's son, who escaped. See 1 Samuel 21–22; *Zohar* 1:224a.

194. **Anathoth was a village, not identical with Nob** The village of Anathoth was located on the outskirts of the city of Nob. See Nehemiah 11:32; *Zohar* 1:249b.

195. *all the hardships my father endured* Abiathar shared the hardships of

Rabbi Ḥiyya said, "The world was impoverished ever since the day Adam violated the commands of the blessed Holy One until Noah arrived and offered an offering, and the world was settled."[196]

Rabbi Yose said, "The world remained unsettled and earth did not escape the slime of the serpent until Israel stood at Mount Sinai, embracing the Tree of Life;[197] then the world was settled. Had Israel not relapsed, sinning before the blessed Holy One, they would have never died, for they had been purged of the slime of the serpent. Then the original tablets were smashed—tablets comprising total freedom, freedom from that serpent: *End of all flesh.*[198] When the Levites rose to deal death,[199] the evil serpent aroused, slithering in front of them, but he could not overpower Israel for they were all girded with armored belts. Once Moses said *Now take off your ornaments* (Exodus 33:5), the serpent was empowered to dominate them.[200]

Solomon's father, David, as he fled from King Saul.

196. **The world was impoverished ... until Noah arrived and offered an offering ...** Adam's sin ruined the union of the *sefirot,* thereby depriving the world of the rich divine flow. When Noah emerged safely from the ark following the Flood, he offered sacrifices (Genesis 8:20–22), which stimulated the union of the *sefirot,* ensuring blessing and harmony for the world.

197. **slime of the serpent ...** זוהמא דנחש (*Zohama de-naḥash*), "The filth of the serpent."

See BT *Shabbat* 145b–146a: "Rav Yosef taught: '...When the serpent copulated with Eve, he injected her with זוהמא (*zohama*), filth [or: slime, lewdness]. Israel, who stood at Mount Sinai—their *zohama* ceased. Star-worshipers, who did not stand at Mount Sinai—their *zohama* did not cease.'" Israel's acceptance of the Torah, symbolized by the Tree of Life, inoculated them against the venomous slime and restored them to a paradisiacal state.

See *Targum Yerushalmi,* Genesis 4:1; *Pirqei de-Rabbi Eli'ezer* 21; *Zohar* 1:36b–37a, 52a, 54a, 122b.

198. **original tablets were smashed ...** When Moses saw the Children of Israel worshiping the Golden Calf, he smashed

the stone tablets inscribed with the Ten Commandments. Later Moses carved a second set, which were again inscribed by God. See Exodus 32:19; 34:1.

According to rabbinic tradition, the first tablets offered immortality. See *Tanḥuma, Ki Tissa* 16; and *Shir ha-Shirim Rabbah* on 8:6: "חרות (*Ḥarut*), *Engraved, on the tablets* [describing the divine writing]. Do not read חרות (*ḥarut*), *engraved,* but rather חירות (*ḥeirut*), freedom. Rabbi Yehudah, Rabbi Neḥemiah, and the Rabbis: Rabbi Yehudah says, 'Freedom from the Angel of Death.' Rabbi Neḥemiah says, 'Freedom from foreign rulers.' The Rabbis say, 'Freedom from suffering.'" See *Zohar* 1:37b, 52a–b.

Here the serpent is identified with the Angel of Death, known as *End of all flesh* (see above, pages 363–65). On the distinction between the original tablets and their copy, see Tishby, *Wisdom of the Zohar,* 3:1103–06.

199. **When the Levites rose to deal death** To kill those who had sinned with the Golden Calf. See Exodus 32:26–28.

200. **they were all girded with armored belts ...** See *Tanḥuma* (Buber), *Shelaḥ,* add. 1: "Rabbi Shim'on son of Yoḥai said, 'He adorned them with weapons engraved with the Ineffable Name [*YHVH*], and as long as they possessed these, no evil could touch them, neither the Angel of Death nor

"Come and see what is written: *The Children of Israel were stripped of their ornaments from Mount Horeb on* (ibid., 6). ויתנצלו (*Va-yitnatstselu*), *They were stripped*—the verse should read וינצלו (*Vaynatstselu*), *They stripped*.[201] But, *they were stripped*, by someone else, for the serpent was empowered to rule. *Their ornaments from Mount Horeb*—that they received *from Mount Horeb* when Torah was given to Israel."[202]

Rabbi Ḥiyya asked, "Since Noah was *a righteous man* (Genesis 6:9), why didn't he abolish death throughout the world?"[203]

Rabbi Yose replied, "Because the slime of the world had not yet disappeared. Furthermore, they did not believe in the blessed Holy One; all of them were grasping the leaves of the tree below and dressing themselves in impure spirit.[204] Further, they later persisted in sinning, clinging to the evil impulse as before, and Torah, Tree of Life, had not yet been brought down to earth by the blessed Holy One."[205]

370

anything else. As soon as they sinned [with the Golden Calf], Moses said to them: *Now take off your ornaments, and I will decide what to do to you* (Exodus 33:5). At that moment, *When the people heard this evil word, they mourned,* [*and no one put on his ornaments*] (ibid., 4). What is written? *The Children of Israel were stripped of their ornaments....* (ibid., 6).'"

Cf. *Targum Onqelos* and *Targum Yerushalmi*, Exodus 33:4, 6; *Targum Shir ha-Shirim* 2:17; *Eikhah Rabbah, Petiḥta* 24; *Shir ha-Shirim Rabbah* on 1:4; *Pirqei de-Rabbi Eli'ezer* 47; BT *Shabbat* 88a; *Avodah Zarah* 5a; Naḥmanides on Exodus 33:6; *Zohar* 1:52b, 126b; 2:227a.

201. **the verse should read וינצלו (*Vaynatstselu*), *They stripped*** Since the Children of Israel stripped off their ornaments, why the construably passive conjugation?

202. **But, *they were stripped*, by someone else...** See BT *Shabbat* 88a: "Rabbi Simai expounded: 'When Israel said *We will do* before *We will listen* (Exodus 24:7) [thereby demonstrating true faith by committing themselves to fulfill God's word before hearing the details], 600,000 ministering angels came to each and every Israelite, setting two crowns upon him, one for *We will do*, and one for *We will listen*. As soon as

Israel sinned, 1,200,000 angels of destruction descended and removed them, as is said: *The Children of Israel were stripped of their ornaments from Mount Horeb.*'"

According to the simple sense of the verse, the phrase *from Mount Horeb* means "from Mount Horeb on," "from when they stood at Mount Sinai," but Rabbi Simai (in the Talmud) and, following him, Rabbi Yose (in the *Zohar*), interpret it differently.

203. **why didn't he abolish death...?** Since, as Rabbi Ḥiyya taught above, Noah repaired the cosmic damage caused by Adam's sin, why could he not also abolish death, which was decreed as a result of that sin? In rabbinic tradition, the righteous are empowered to abolish the divine decree. See BT *Mo'ed Qatan* 16b: "*The righteous one rules the awe of God....* Rabbi Abbahu said, '...I [God] rule over humanity. Who rules over Me? The righteous one. For I issue a decree and he abolishes it.'"

204. **all of them were grasping the leaves of the tree below...** Noah's generation grasped the leaves of the Tree of Knowledge, which convey the knowledge of magic.

See *Zohar* 1:36b, 53b, 56a. Cf. BT *Bava Metsi'a* 114b.

205. **Torah, Tree of Life, had not yet been brought down to earth...** Torah, the source

As they were walking, they saw a Jew approaching.

Rabbi Yose said, "This person is a Jew—he looks so!"[206]

When he reached them, they asked him.

He said, "I am an envoy for a *mitsvah*![207] For we live in the village of Ramin,[208] and the time of the Festival[209] nears, so we need a *lulav* and its fellow species.[210] I'm on my way to pluck them for the *mitsvah*."

They walked on as one.

The Jew said to them, "These four species of the *lulav*, all of which propitiate for water[211]—have you heard why we need them on the Festival?"[212]

They replied, "The Companions have already been aroused by this,[213] but if you possess a new word, say it!"

He said to them, "True, the place we live in is small, but everyone there engages in Torah under the guidance of one inflamed by the rabbis:[214] Rabbi Yitsḥak son of Yose from Maḥoza,[215] who each day tells us new words. He said

---

of life, could have guided and protected them.

Torah is identified with the Tree of Life, based on the description of wisdom in Proverbs 3:18: *She is a tree of life to those who grasp her.* See BT *Berakhot* 32b, 61b.

206. **This person is a Jew—he looks so!** See *Zohar* 1:164a: "While they were walking, they saw a man approaching, accompanied by a child riding on his shoulders. Rabbi Yitsḥak said, "This man is certainly a Jew!""

207. **I am an envoy for a *mitsvah*!** The anonymous Jew is on a spiritual errand, having been sent to fulfill a commandment. See BT *Sukkah* 10b, 26a.

208. **village of Ramin** The name means "high, exalted," though see above, note 124. The village is not mentioned in rabbinic literature, but it reappears in *Zohar* 3:39b.

209. **Festival** The week-long harvest festival of *Sukkot*, celebrated at the end of summer.

210. ***lulav* and its fellow species** Four plants taken and waved during the festival of *Sukkot*: a palm branch (*lulav*), a citron, three sprigs of myrtle, and two willow twigs. See Leviticus 23:40.

211. **all of which propitiate for water** Originally the four species were waved as part of a ritual prayer for rain. Similarly, in

the Temple in Jerusalem on the last six days of *Sukkot,* as the rainy season approached, water was drawn and poured as a libation on the altar. The additional service for *Shemini Atseret* (the day following *Sukkot*) opens with a prayer for rain.

212. **why we need them on the Festival** In his Hebrew writings, Moses de León attacks assimilated Jews who used rationalistic ideology to justify their neglect of *mitsvot*, specifically this *mitsvah*. See his *Sefer ha-Rimmon*, 391–92; Matt, *Zohar*, 5–6.

213. **Companions have already been aroused by this** The symbolic meaning of the four species is discussed in *Zohar* 1:220a–221a; 2:186b; 3:24a, 31b, 104a. See Tishby, *Wisdom of the Zohar*, 3:1249–51.

214. **one inflamed by the rabbis** צורבא מרבנן (*Tsurba me-rabbanan*), a phrase referring to a scholar, perhaps meaning "scorched by the rabbis." See BT *Ta'anit* 4a; and M *Avot* 2:10: "Rabbi Eli'ezer says, '…Warm yourself by the fire of the wise—and beware their glowing coals, so that you'll not be burned. For their bite is the bite of a fox; their sting, the sting of a scorpion; their hiss, the hiss of a serpent; and all their words like coals of fire.'"

215. **Maḥoza** A large trading town on the Tigris River.

that the Festival is the time when all those princes appointed over other nations prevail, blessed from the side of Israel,[216] called by us *raging waters,* as is said: *the raging waters* (Psalms 124:5).[217] In order to overpower them, we approach with the mystery of the holy name—with those four species of the *lulav*[218]—in order to propitiate the blessed Holy One to prevail [64a] against them through the mystery of the holy name, and to arouse holy water upon us, to pour upon the altar.[219]

"He further told us that on Rosh Hashanah the first arousal arises in the world. What is the first arousal? Lower Court of Justice, aroused to judge the world, with the blessed Holy One sitting in judgment over the world.[220] This court remains in session until Yom Kippur, when Her face beams,[221] while the serpent—cosmic informer—is nowhere to be found, being engrossed in that goat they offer to him, deriving from the side of impure spirit, befitting him.[222]

216. **all those princes appointed over other nations...** According to rabbinic tradition, the seventy nations of the world are governed by seventy angels or heavenly princes appointed by God.

See Daniel 10:20; Septuagint, Deuteronomy 32:8–9; Jubilees 15:31–32; *Targum Yerushalmi,* Genesis 11:8, Deuteronomy 32:8–9; *Tanḥuma, Re'eh* 8; *Leqaḥ Tov,* Genesis 9:19; *Pirqei de-Rabbi Eli'ezer* 24; *Zohar* 1:46b, 108b; 3:298b; Ginzberg, *Legends,* 5:204–5, n. 91.

According to rabbinic tradition, the seventy bullocks offered by Israel on *Sukkot* (Numbers 29:12–34) benefit the seventy nations. See BT *Sukkah* 55b; *Eikhah Rabbah* 1:23; *Pesiqta de-Rav Kahana* 28:9; Tishby, *Wisdom of the Zohar,* 3:1251–53.

217. *the raging waters* The full verse reads: *Then over us would have swept the raging waters.* See *Zohar* 2:64b.

218. **In order to overpower them...the holy name...** The four species symbolize the four letters of the name יהוה (*YHVH*), perhaps as follows: myrtle, י; willow, ה; lulav, ו; citron, ה. See *OY; MM; Zohar* 1:220b. Brandishing these species, Israel vanquishes the seventy princes. See *Pesiqta de-Rav Kahana* 27:2.

219. **to arouse holy water upon us, to pour upon the altar** As mentioned above (note 211), in the Temple on the last six days of *Sukkot,* water was drawn and poured as a libation on the altar. Here the water symbolizes the flow of emanation stimulated by Israel's ritual of the four species. This flow pours down upon *Shekhinah,* symbolized by the altar.

220. **Lower Court of Justice...** According to the rabbinic view, "All are judged on Rosh Hashanah" (BT *Rosh ha-Shanah* 16a). Here the court symbolizes *Shekhinah,* who derives from the *sefirah* of *Din* ("Judgment, Justice") and conveys it to the world. See *Zohar* 2:186b, 237b–238a.

221. **when Her face beams** By Yom Kippur, on the tenth of the lunar month, Israel has engaged deeply in turning back to God, and the moon, symbolizing *Shekhinah,* has brightened. See *Zohar* 3:100b.

222. **serpent—cosmic informer—is nowhere...engrossed in that goat...** On Yom Kippur, a scapegoat bearing the sins of Israel is offered to the wilderness demon Azazel (Leviticus 16:10). Similarly, in the Babylonian Akitu ritual a goat, substituted for a human being, is offered to Ereshkigal, goddess of the Abyss. According to *Pirqei de-Rabbi Eli'ezer* 46, the goat is intended to preoccupy Satan: "They gave him [Satan] a bribe on Yom Kippur so that he would not nullify Israel's sacrifice."

See BT *Yoma* 20a: "On Yom Kippur, Satan has no permission to accuse. How do we know? Rami son of Ḥama said, 'השטן

Occupied with that goat, he does not approach the sanctuary.[223] This goat resembles the goat of the new moon, in which he is engrossed,[224] so the face of the sanctuary shines and all of Israel find compassion in the presence of the blessed Holy One, their guilt eliminated.

"One secret he told us, but permission has not been granted to reveal it, except to holy, wise devotees."

Rabbi Yose asked, "What is it?"

He replied, "I haven't examined you yet."[225]

They walked on. After a while he said to them, "When the moon approaches the sun,[226] the blessed Holy One arouses the side of North, who grasps Her lovingly, drawing Her close.[227] South arouses from the other side, and the moon ascends, uniting with East.[228] Then She suckles from two sides, drawing blessing secretly, until the moon is blessed and filled. Here Woman approaches Her Husband.[229] Corresponding to the mysterious image of the smooth members of Adam is the mysterious arrayal of the Female.[230] All is elucidated among us.

373

(Ha-satan), Satan, equals 364 in numerical value, implying that on 364 days he has permission to accuse, while on Yom Kippur he does not.'"

See Naḥmanides on Leviticus 16:8; *Zohar* 1:11a, 113b–114b, 138b, 174b, 190a, 210b; 2:154b, 237b; 266b; 3:63a (*Piq*), 102a, 202b–203a, 258b; *ZH* 87b–c (*MhN, Rut*); Moses de León, *She'elot u-Tshuvot*, 49; Cordovero, *OY*, 4:51b; Tishby, *Wisdom of the Zohar*, 3:890–95.

223. **sanctuary** Symbolizing *Shekhinah*.

224. **goat of the new moon...** According to Numbers 28:15, on each new moon a goat must be brought as a sin-offering. Here, this goat too is intended to preoccupy Satan, leaving Israel and *Shekhinah* (both symbolized by the moon) alone with the blessed Holy One.

See *Zohar* 1:65a, 122b, 138b; 2:33a, 185a, 238a, 269a. Cf. BT *Ḥullin* 60b; *Bereshit Rabbah* 6:3. The sixteenth-century kabbalists of Safed observed the day preceding the new moon as *Yom Kippur Qatan* ("Minor Day of Atonement").

225. **I haven't examined you yet** See *Zohar* 3:186b.

226. **When the moon approaches the sun** At the time of the new moon, *Shekhinah* approaches *Tif'eret* and begins to receive His light.

227. **the blessed Holy One arouses the side of North...** *Gevurah,* symbolized by North, is aroused and embraces *Shekhinah*.

228. **South...East** Symbolizing *Ḥesed* and *Tif'eret*.

229. **Here Woman approaches Her Husband** At the new moon, *Shekhinah* begins to approach Her partner, *Tif'eret*.

230. **smooth members of Adam...arrayal of the Female** The masculine figure of divinity, symbolized by Adam, includes various sefirotic limbs, to which correspond different aspects of *Shekhinah*.

"Smooth members" renders two senses of one term, שייפי (*shaifei*). From a root meaning "to smooth, rub, slip," the word signifies "limbs" in the *Zohar*, perhaps based on the Talmudic expression (BT *Sotah* 7b) על איבריה לשפא (*al eivreih le-shafa*), "each limb entered its socket"—"slipping" into place—or "...the chest."

See *Arukh*, s.v. *shaf*; Rashi, ad loc., and on Job 33:21, citing *Ḥullin* 42b; *Zohar* 3:170a.

"Similarly, below: mysterious arrayal of another, lower Adam beneath the moon.[231] Just as the left arm above[232] grasps Her, arousing toward Her in love, so too, below. This serpent is the left arm, impure spirit; her rider grasps her,[233] approaches the moon and draws Her,[234] sucking from the trough, and She is defiled.[235]

"Then Israel below offer up a goat, to which the serpent is drawn,[236] and the moon is purified, ascending, bound above to be blessed. Her face, darkened below, now shines.

"Similarly here, on Yom Kippur, since that evil serpent is engaged with that goat, the moon breaks away from him, engaging with Israel, and the blessed Holy One blesses them above, forgiving them. Afterward, when Israel arrive at the Festival,[237] they arouse the right side above,[238] so that the moon will bind herself there and her face shine fittingly. Then they distribute a share of blessings to all those deputies below,[239] so that they will occupy themselves with their portion and not approach to suck from the side of Israel's share.[240]

"Similarly below, when the other nations are blessed, they all engage in their inherited share, not meddling with Israel or coveting their share. They therefore convey blessing[241] to all those deputies, so that they will be absorbed with their portion and not interfere with them.

374

231. **Similarly, below...another, lower Adam beneath the moon** The demonic male attempts to seduce *Shekhinah* in Her time of darkness at the new moon. See *Zohar* 2:194b.

232. **left arm above** *Gevurah,* located on the left side of the divine body.

233. **her rider grasps her** The serpent's rider, Samael, grasps the serpent. See *Pirqei de-Rabbi Eli'ezer* 13: "Samael...took his band and descended and saw all the creatures created by the blessed Holy One. He determined that the most cunningly evil was the serpent, as is said: *Now the serpent was slier than any creature of the field that YHVH Elohim had made.* He [the serpent] looked like a camel, and he [Samael] mounted and rode him."

See *Zohar* 1:35b, 137b, 146a, 153a.

234. **draws Her** Draws *Shekhinah.*

235. **sucking from the trough...** ביניקו דקופטא (Biyniqu de-qufta). Qufta means "trough, crib" in *Zohar* 1:236a, perhaps derived from קופסא (qufsa), "box." Cf. *Zohar* 1:33a: קופטרא (quftera), "waterskin"; Liebes, *Peraqim,* 349–50. In *Tosefta, Avodah Zarah*

4:11, קפטא (qafta) apparently means "leeks."

Alternatively, several witnesses read here: קוטפא (qutpa), which could mean either "resin" or "cluster." See BT *Ketubbot* 112a, *Avodah Zarah* 72b: קטופי (qetofei), "clusters, fruit ready to be plucked"; *Zohar* 1:17b; *Bei'ur ha-Millim ha-Zarot,* 190.

In either case, the point is that the demonic draws sustenance from *Shekhinah* and in the process defiles Her.

236. **Then Israel below offer up a goat...** The new-moon offering (see above, note 224) distracts the demonic from *Shekhinah,* enabling Her to join Her divine partner.

237. **Festival** Of *Sukkot,* which begins on the full moon.

238. **right side above** The *sefirah* of Ḥesed, flowing love of God.

239. **all those deputies below** The seventy heavenly princes below *Shekhinah* appointed over the seventy nations of the world.

240. **from the side of Israel's share** Directly from *Shekhinah.*

241. **They...convey blessing** The people of Israel convey blessing.

"When the moon is fittingly filled with blessings above, Israel come and suckle from her all by themselves. Of this is written: *On the eighth day you shall have an assembly* (Numbers 29:35).[242] What is *an assembly*? As translated: 'a gathering.'[243] Everything gathered from those supernal blessings is imbibed by no one except Israel. So it is written: *You shall hold an assembly; you*—no other nation; *you*—no other deputy. Therefore they propitiate for water,[244] to provide them a portion of blessings to keep them occupied, so that later they will not interfere in Israel's joy as they suck supernal blessings. Of that day is written: *My beloved is mine and I am his* (Song of Songs 2:16), for no other interferes with us.

"This may be compared to a king who invited his beloved to a sublime feast he was preparing for him on a designated day.[245] Now the king's beloved knows that the king [64b] delights in him.

"The king said, 'I now want to rejoice with my beloved, but I fear that as we are feasting together, all those appointed quaestors[246] will come in and sit down with us at the table, feasting from the feast of joy with my beloved.'

"What did he do? Anticipating, his beloved brought wickered baskets[247] of greens and meat of oxen, offering them these. Afterward the king sits down with his beloved to that feast more sublime than all delicacies of the world. The king rejoices with his beloved alone, with no others interfering between them.

"Similarly, Israel with the blessed Holy One. So: *On the eighth day you shall have an assembly.*"[248]

Rabbi Yose and Rabbi Ḥiyya said, "The blessed Holy One has paved the way for us. Happy are they who engage in Torah!"

They came up and kissed him.

375

242. **When the moon is fittingly filled...** *an assembly*   The seven-day festival of *Sukkot,* which begins on the full moon, is immediately followed by an additional holy day known as *Shemini Atseret* ("Eighth Day of Assembly"). Now the people Israel rests alone with *Shekhinah.*

243. **As translated...**   From Hebrew into the Aramaic כנישו (*kenishu*). See *Targum Onqelos,* Leviticus 23:36; Numbers 29:35; Deuteronomy 16:8; *Zohar* 3:96b, 259b.

244. **they propitiate for water**   As mentioned above in note 211, during *Sukkot* Israel prays for rain by waving the four species and offering water libations.

245. **This may be compared to a king...**   A similar parable appears in *Pesiqta de-Rav*

Kahana 28:9. See BT *Sukkah* 55b; *Zohar* 3:104b.

246. **quaestors** קסטורי (*Qastorei*), from Latin *quaestor,* a Roman official, referring here to the heavenly princes. See JT *Eruvin* 6:2, 23b; *Zohar* 1:19b, 53b, 62a (*Tos*); 2:19b, 58b, 208b; 3:13a.

247. **wickered baskets** קוסטורין (*Qustorin*), perhaps derived from קלוסטור (*qelustor*), an Aramaic corruption of the Greek *kartallos,* "basket."

248. **Similarly, Israel with the blessed Holy One...**   By offering seventy bullocks on *Sukkot,* Israel assures that the seventy heavenly princes and their earthly nations will be sustained (see above, note 216). Then on the eighth day, Israel feasts alone with God.

Rabbi Yose proclaimed for him, *"All your children will be taught by YHVH . . .* (Isaiah 54:13)."[249]

When they reached the site of a certain field they sat down. That man asked, "Why is it written: *And YHVH rained brimstone and fire on Sodom and Gomorrah* (Genesis 19:24), whereas in the Flood it is everywhere written: *Elohim, Elohim?*[250] Because we have learned: 'Everywhere it is written: *And YHVH*—this means "He and His Court." *Elohim*, unspecified, means Judgment alone.'[251] Now, at Sodom judgment was executed, yet not destroying the world, so He intermingled with Judgment;[252] but in the Flood It[253] destroyed the whole world and all those present in the world.

"Now you might say, 'But look, Noah and his companions were saved!' Come and see: Noah was hidden from sight, invisible! So everything present in the world It destroyed.[254]

"Therefore: *And YHVH*—in the open, not destroying all. *Elohim*—one needs concealment and must seek protection, for It destroys all. So *Elohim* was alone.[255]

376

249. *All your children will be taught by YHVH* The verse continues in parallelism: *and great will be the peace of your children.*

250. **Why is it written: *And YHVH . . . Elohim, Elohim?*** In rabbinic literature the divine names יהוה (*YHVH*) and אלהים (*Elohim*) indicate, respectively, the divine qualities of compassion and judgment. See *Sifrei,* Deuteronomy 26; *Bereshit Rabbah* 12:15; 33:3; and 13:3, where *YHVH Elohim* is called "a complete name." Cf. *Zohar* 1:20a, 48b, 56b, 67a; 2:161a, 229a; 3:138b (*IR*); *ZH* 70d (*ShS*). The following passage reappears in *Zohar* 2:227b.

The name *Elohim* (denoting judgment) appropriately dominates the account of the Flood, though, in fact, the name *YHVH* appears too (Genesis 6:5–8; 7:1, 5, 16). But why does the name *YHVH* (denoting compassion) figure in the destruction of Sodom and Gomorrah?

251. **'Everywhere it is written: *And YHVH . . . Elohim . . .*'** See *Bereshit Rabbah* 51:2: "Rabbi El'azar said, 'Wherever it is said: *And YHVH,* this implies: He and His Court.'" In Kabbalah this court symbolizes *Shekhinah,* who derives from the *sefirah* of *Din* ("Judgment") and pronounces the divine decree, so the phrase *And YHVH* encom-passes "He [*Tif'eret,* known as *YHVH*] and His Court [*Shekhinah*]."

See JT *Berakhot* 9:5, 14b; Rashi on Exodus 12:29; *Zohar* 1:15b, 107b; 2:37b, 44b; 3:149a. The hermeneutical significance of *and* was championed by Rabbi Akiva. See BT *Yevamot* 68b; *Sanhedrin* 51b.

The Jew from Ramin adds to this rabbinic rubric: "*Elohim*, unspecified, means Judgment alone." The name *Elohim* can refer to various *sefirot* (*Binah, Din, Shekhinah*); without further identification it refers to דינא (*dina*), Judgment alone, without the compassion of *YHVH*. See *Zohar* 1:46a; 2:140a.

252. **He intermingled with Judgment** *YHVH,* denoting compassion, mitigated the harsh judgment.

253. **It** Judgment alone. The word can also be rendered "He."

254. **Noah was hidden from sight . . .** The demonic only attacks what is visible. See *Mekhilta, Pisḥa* 11; BT *Bava Qamma* 60a–b; *Zohar* 1:63a, 68a–b, 69a, 107b, 113a, 182b, 197b; 2:196a, 227a.

255. *And YHVH*—in the open . . . *Elohim*—one needs concealment . . . When compassion mingles with judgment, one can venture outside; but if judgment man-

"The secret is: *YHVH sat at the Flood* (Psalms 29:10). What does *sat* mean? If the verse were not written, we could not say it:[256] He sat by, alone, not accompanying Judgment. Here is written: *sat,* and there is written: *Alone he will sit* (Leviticus 13:46)—all alone.[257]

"Since Noah was hidden from view, afterward when judgment had been executed, destroying the world, and His rage subsided, what is written? *Elohim remembered Noah* (Genesis 8:1). For when He destroyed the world, he was not remembered, since he was hidden from sight.

"I have learned a secret: The blessed Holy One—concealed and revealed. 'Revealed'—Lower Court of Justice. 'Concealed'—site from which all blessings flow.[258] So blessings settle upon everything kept concealed,[259] whereas everything revealed is occupied by that site of the Court, it being a site revealed. All within supernal mystery, corresponding above."

Rabbi Yose wept, and said, "Happy is the generation in which Rabbi Shim-'on dwells,[260] for here in the mountains his virtue evoked for us words as high as these!"

Rabbi Yose said, "This person appeared in order to reveal these words to us. The blessed Holy One sent him to us!"

When they reached Rabbi Shim'on and arrayed words before him, he said, "He spoke well indeed!"

Rabbi El'azar was sitting one day in the presence of his father, Rabbi Shim'on. He asked him, "Did that *End of all flesh* enjoy those offerings offered by Israel on the altar?"[261]

377

ifests alone—as in the Flood—one must remain hidden.

256. **If the verse were not written, we could not say it** A rabbinic saying highlighting a radical formulation either in the biblical text or its midrashic interpretation. See *Bereshit Rabbah* 1:5.

257. **He sat by, alone...** *YHVH,* symbolizing Compassion, sat alone, uninvolved in the Flood, while Judgment, symbolized by the name *Elohim,* wrought the catastrophe.

258. **The blessed Holy One—concealed and revealed...** God is revealed through *Shekhinah,* the divine court, yet remains concealed above. The phrase "site from which all blessings flow" refers apparently to *Binah* or *Yesod.* See *Zohar* 1:130b; 3:36a.

259. **blessings settle upon everything kept concealed** See BT *Ta'anit* 8b: "Bless-

ing is not found in anything weighed, measured, or counted, but only in that which is hidden from the eye." Cf. *Zohar* 1:5a, 202a. The success of the *Zohar* itself depends on concealment: the concealment of the medieval author's (or authors') identity behind the pseudepigraphic veil of Rabbi Shim'on.

260. **Happy is the generation in which Rabbi Shim'on dwells** Rabbi Shim'on's potent wisdom enriches his entire generation. See *Bereshit Rabbah* 35:2; *Zohar* 2:156a; 3:79a; Liebes, *Studies in the Zohar,* 28–34.

261. **Did that *End of all flesh* enjoy those offerings...?** As discussed above (pages 372–73), the goats offered on Yom Kippur and the new moon were intended to occupy the demonic and prevent him from accusing Israel in heaven.

He replied, "All were satisfied as one, above and below. Come and see: Priests, Levites, and Israel are called אדם (adam), human,[262] through the union of those sacred aspirations[263] ascending from within them. That sheep or lamb or beast that they offer[264]—before it is offered upon the altar, one must specify over it all one's sins and evil desires, confessing over it. Then it is called entirely 'beast,' within those sins, wrongs, and fantasies. As with the offering of Azazel, of which is written: *He shall confess over it all the iniquities of the Children of Israel* (Leviticus 16:21), so too, here. As it ascends upon the altar, a burden of two on one.[265] So this one ascends to its site, and that one to its site; this in the mystery of human, that in the mystery of beast, as is said: *Human and beast You deliver, O YHVH* (Psalms 36:7).[266]

"Pancakes and all other meal-offerings,[267] to arouse Holy Spirit[268] through the aspiration of priests, the song of Levites, and the prayer of Israel. By that smoke, oil, and flour ascending, all other masters of judgment are saturated and satisfied, [65a] unable to execute the judgment delivered to them. All simultaneously.[269]

"Come and see: All transpires in the mystery of faith, so that one is satisfied by the other,[270] so that the one who must, ascends to *Ein Sof*, Endless."[271]

378

262. **Priests, Levites, and Israel are called אדם (*adam*), human** Rabbi Shim'on's declaration derives from BT *Yevamot* 60b–61a: "Rabbi Shim'on son of Yoḥai says, 'The graves of Gentiles do not impart impurity by a tent [i.e., one who stands on or bends over such a grave, thereby constituting a tent with his body, is not rendered impure], as is said: *You, My sheep, sheep of My pasture, are* אדם (*adam*), *human* [*and I am Your God*] (Ezekiel 34:31). You are called *adam*; Gentiles are not called *adam*.'" Rabbi Shim-'on assumes a connection between *adam* and "impurity by a tent," based on the wording of Numbers 19:14: *When an adam dies in a tent, whoever enters the tent and whoever is in the tent shall be impure seven days.*

Here *adam* alludes to the *sefirot*, configured as a human body. The priests symbolize the right arm (*Ḥesed*); the Levites, the left arm (*Gevurah*); Israel, the trunk of the body (*Tif-'eret*). See *Zohar* 1:20b, 131a, 220a; 2:25b, 86a; 3:219a.

263. **aspirations** רעותין (*Re'utin*), "Desires, wills," referring to the intention of those worshiping and praying.

264. **That sheep or lamb or beast that**

they offer An offering brought by an individual Israelite. See Leviticus 5:5.

265. **burden of two on one** The animal bears a double burden: the aspirations of the worshipers and their confessions.

266. **this one ascends to its site, and that one to its site...** Human aspirations stimulate the union of the *sefirot*, which constitute the divine paradigm of the human being, while confessions and the animal's flesh satisfy the beastly demonic. The verse from Psalms is taken to imply that both the *sefirot* and the demonic are nourished by the divine flow. See *Zohar* 2:238b–239a.

267. **Pancakes and all other meal-offerings** Various meal-offerings, consisting of flour, oil, and frankincense, are specified in Leviticus 2.

268. **Holy Spirit** Often a designation of *Shekhinah*. See *Zohar* 1:67a; 2:238b; 3:61a.

269. **All simultaneously** Both holy and demonic powers are sustained by the offerings.

270. **so that one is satisfied by the other** So that the lower is satisfied by the higher, and vice versa.

271. **so that the one who must, ascends to *Ein Sof*, Endless** So that *Shekhinah* (alter-

Rabbi Shim'on said, "I raise my hands above in prayer![272] When supernal Will, above, above,[273] abides upon the Will unknown, totally ungrasped forever, the head concealed extremely above[274] (and that head generated what it generated, unknown—radiated what it radiated, all in concealment), the desire of supernal Thought is to pursue it, be illumined by it.[275] A single curtain is spread,[276] and from within this curtain, through the pursuit of supernal Thought, it touches and does not touch,[277] until that curtain radiates what it radiates. Then Thought radiates with nameless radiance unknown—unknown even by Thought![278]

"Then this radiance of unknown Thought strikes the radiance of the extended curtain, radiating with that which is unknown, unknowable, unrevealed. So this radiance of unknown Thought strikes the radiance of the curtain, and they radiate as one, forming nine palaces of palaces—neither lights nor spirits nor souls; no one can fathom them.[279] The desire of all nine lights,[280] all existing in Thought—the latter numerically one of them[281]—is to pursue them while existing in Thought,[282] but they remain unapprehended, unknown. These fathom neither Will nor supernal Thought, grasping yet not

379

natively, human intention) ascends through and beyond all the *sefirot* to *Ein Sof*, Divine Infinity. The phrase "to *Ein Sof*" can also be understood adverbially: "endlessly, infinitely."

272. **I raise my hands above in prayer!** Rabbi Shim'on invokes the divine as he prepares to describe the primal origins of emanation. The formula derives from *Targum Onqelos*, Genesis 14:22, and recurs in *Zohar* 2:9a, 70a (*RR*), 268b; 3:195b, 258b, 287a.

273. **supernal Will, above, above** *Ein Sof*, unbounded by the *sefirot*—specifically beyond *Keter*, the first *sefirah*, which itself is known as Will. See *Zohar* 2:268b (*Heikh*).

274. **Will unknown...the head...** *Keter* ("Crown"), head of the *sefirot*.

275. **desire of supernal Thought...** Divine thought, *Ḥokhmah* ("Wisdom"), generated by *Keter*, yearns to return to its source. See Plotinus, *Enneads* 6:7:16. According to *KP*, "supernal Thought" refers to *Keter*, who yearns to rejoin *Ein Sof*.

276. **A single curtain is spread** Between *Keter* and *Ḥokhmah*, Will and Thought. See *Zohar* 2:165b, 259a (*Heikh*); 3:128a (*IR*).

277. **touches and does not touch** The

light of *Keter* shines faintly, subtly through the curtain. See *Zohar* 1:15a.

278. **unknown even by Thought!** Even Thought itself remains unaware of the nature of this radiance. According to the Gnostic *Gospel of Truth* (22:27–29), the aeons (divine emanations) below *Nous* ("Intellect") are unaware of the hidden divinity: "It was quite amazing that they were in the Father without knowing Him." See *Zohar* 1:30a, 49a.

279. **nine palaces of palaces—neither lights...** These entities are the hidden essences of the nine *sefirot* from *Ḥokhmah* downward, so they are not to be identified as "lights," a term designating the *sefirot*, nor as "spirits" or "souls."

280. **all nine lights** Paradoxically, immediately after denying this name to the palaces, Rabbi Shim'on applies it to them. See *Zohar* 3:288a (*IR*).

281. **numerically one of them** *Ḥokhmah*, divine thought, is first of the nine lower *sefirot*, whose essences (the palaces of palaces) are contained within *Ḥokhmah* itself.

282. **pursue them...** The palaces pursue their origin, namely, Will and Thought, but these two cannot be apprehended.

grasping. In these abide all mysteries of faith, and all those lights from the mystery of supernal Thought downward are called *Ein Sof,* Endless.[283] Until here lights extend and do not extend and are unknown. No will here, no thought.[284]

"When Thought illumines—from whom is unknown—it is clothed and enveloped in *Binah,* Understanding, illumining whom it illumines, one entering the other, till all merge as one.[285]

"Through the mystery of the offering, as it ascends, all are bound together, illumining one another. Then all engage in ascent, and Thought is crowned in *Ein Sof.*[286] The radiance from which supernal Thought shines, of which it is totally unaware, is called *Ayin,* Nothingness,[287] whence it comes into being, upon which it stands, illumining whom it illumines. Happy is the share of the righteous in this world and in the world that is coming!

"Come and see this *End of all flesh:*[288] Just as a bond is found above in joy, so too, below, in joyous desire, satisfying all, above and below, with Mother over Israel fittingly.[289]

"Come and see: Every single new moon, as the moon is renewed, this *End of all flesh* is given one portion over and above the offerings,[290] to keep him occupied handling his portion, so that the aspect of Israel is alone to delight with their King. This is the שעיר (*sa'ir*), goat,[291] being the portion of Esau, of whom

380

283. **all those lights…are called *Ein Sof,* Endless** The totality of hidden lights, yearning to return to their source, share in the designation *Ein Sof.* See *ZH* 1b (*SO*), 104c (*Tiq*); Liebes, *Peraqim,* 174–75.

284. **Until here lights extend and do not extend…** Up to this point in the process of emanation, the light cannot be clearly perceived. No will or thought can venture there. Alternatively, these lights are not to be identified with either *Keter* (known as Will) or *Ḥokhmah* (known as Thought).

285. **When Thought illumines…** When *Ḥokhmah* emanates, it fashions the palace of *Binah,* into which it enters.

286. **Through the mystery of the offering…** The sacrificial offering unites the *sefirot,* which then together ascend to the Beyond. Maimonides had relativized the importance of the sacrificial offerings, explaining them away as a concession to the primitive nature of ancient Israel. The *Zohar* counters by emphasizing their vital role in unifying and sustaining the cosmos. See

Maimonides, *Guide of the Perplexed* 3:32; Tishby, *Wisdom of the Zohar,* 3:878–90.

287. ***Ayin,* Nothingness** A name for the primal, unknowable *sefirah,* source of Thought and of all existence, yet not to be identified with any particular "thing," thus best called Nothingness (No-thingness).

288. **this *End of all flesh*** The demonic. See above, pages 377–78.

289. **Just as a bond is found above in joy, so too, below…** The *sefirot* are united through the sacrificial offering, while the powers below revel in their share, not disturbing Israel's intimacy with *Shekhinah.*

290. **over and above the offerings** In addition to his regular share of other offerings, namely, the flesh.

291. **This is the שעיר (*sa'ir*), goat** According to Numbers 28:15, on each new moon a goat must be brought as a sin-offering. Here, this goat is intended to preoccupy Satan, leaving Israel alone with God. See above, note 224.

is written: *Look, my brother Esau is* שעיר איש (*ish sa'ir*), *a hairy man!* (Genesis 27:11).[292] So he handles his portion, and Israel theirs. Hence it is written: *For Yah has chosen Jacob for Himself, Israel as His own treasure* (Psalms 135:4).

"Come and see: This *End of all flesh* desires nothing but flesh constantly, so flesh is arrayed for him constantly[293] and He is called *End of all flesh*. When he rules, he rules over body, not over soul.[294] Soul ascends to her site, while flesh is given to this site. Similarly with an offering: aspiration ascends to one site, flesh to another.[295] A virtuous human being is an actual offering of atonement,[296] while another is not,[297] for he is defective, as is written: *not acceptable* (Leviticus 22:20).[298] So the righteous are an atonement for the world, an offering."

[65b] Rabbi Ḥiyya and Rabbi Yose were walking on the way. One said,[299] "It is written: *Noah did everything YHVH commanded him* (Genesis 7:5). Come and see what is written: *Noah was 600 years old...* (ibid., 6).[300] Why is this calculation reckoned? Because if Noah had not been 600 years old, he would not have entered the ark nor united with her. Once completed by 600 years, he joined her.[301] So from the day that the guilt of the world's inhabitants was complete,

381

---

292. **portion of Esau...** שעיר איש (*ish sa'ir*), *a hairy man* Esau, Jacob's twin and nemesis, symbolizes the demonic. The word שעיר (*sa'ir*) also means "goat, demon, satyr." Further, Esau and his descendants inhabited שעיר (*Se'ir*), Seir (see Genesis 32:4; 36:8–9).

See Genesis 25:25; *Bereshit Rabbah* 65:15; *Zohar* 1:138b, 145b, 153a; 3:64a.

293. **flesh is arrayed for him constantly** The flesh of sacrificial offerings is intended for him.

294. **When he rules, he rules over body...** At death, the demonic power rules over the body, while the soul ascends. See *Zohar* 3:170a, 172b.

295. **aspiration ascends to one site, flesh to another** The intention of the one offering the sacrifice ascends to the *sefirot*, unifying them, while the animal's flesh satisfies the demonic.

296. **A virtuous human being is an actual offering of atonement** See BT *Mo'ed Qatan* 28a: "Rabbi Ammi said, 'Just as the red heifer atones [by the ritual use of its ashes], so does the death of the righteous atone.'" Cf. *Vayiqra Rabbah* 20:12; BT *Shab-*

bat 33b; *Zohar* 2:36b, 38b, 269a; 3:9b, 218a–b; *ZH* 12c–d (*MhN*).

According to one tradition, souls of the righteous are offered by the archangel Michael on a heavenly altar. See *Tosafot, Menaḥot* 110a, s.v. *u-mikha'el; Zohar* 1:80a (*ST*); *ZH* 21a (*MhN*).

297. **while another is not** One unvirtuous is not.

298. *not acceptable* The full verse reads: *Whatever has a defect you are not to offer, for it will not be acceptable on your behalf.*

299. **Rabbi Ḥiyya and Rabbi Yose... One said** In an earlier version of the *Zohar* (preserved in manuscripts V5 and R1, OY, and 1:254b [*Hash*]), the speaker here is neither Rabbi Ḥiyya nor Rabbi Yose, but rather the anonymous Jew encountered earlier by the two rabbis (above, pages 371–77).

300. *Noah was 600 years old* The verse continues: *when the Flood came, waters upon the earth.*

301. **Because if Noah had not been 600 years old...** Noah's ripe age reflects the full sextet of *sefirot* from Ḥesed through Yesod. Through living a long, righteous life,

the blessed Holy One waited patiently for them until Noah was completed by 600 years, his rung fittingly complete, and he became completely righteous.[302] Then he entered the ark, corresponding entirely to the pattern above. *Noah was 600 years old,* as we have said, so the verse does not read *about 600 years old.*"[303]

He opened again,[304] saying, "ואני (*Va-Ani*), *And I, I am about to bring the Flood, waters* (ibid. 6:17).[305] Why *I am about to,* if He already said *Va-Ani, And I*? Because *I* and *I am about to* are one and the same.[306] Come and see: Everywhere *Ani* becomes a body for the soul, receiving what is above,[307] so it is intimated by the sign of the covenant, as is written: *Behold, Ani, I, am My covenant with you* (ibid. 17:4)[308]—*Ani, I,* standing revealed, verging on being known; *Ani, I,* throne to what is above;[309] *Ani, I,* avenging from generation to generation.[310] *Va-Ani, And I,* encompassing male and female as one;[311] afterward designated alone, poised to execute judgment: *I am about to bring the Flood, waters.*[312]

"Since He said *bring the Flood,* don't we know that it's water? However, את (*et*) *the Flood,* amplifying the meaning to include the Angel of Death,[313] for even though there were waters, the Destroyer was coursing through the world, devastating with those waters.

Noah embodied *Yesod,* known as Righteous One, and therefore entered the ark, symbolizing *Shekhinah.* See above, page 341.

302. **from the day that the guilt of the world's inhabitants was complete...** Noah's generation was so wicked that they deserved to be annihilated long before the Flood, but God waited for them to turn back to Him until Noah reached spiritual maturity.

See BT *Bava Qamma* 38b; *Vayiqra Rabbah* 32:4; *Zohar* 1:56b, 61b, 62b, 118a (*MhN*), 227a; 2:12b.

303. **so the verse does not read *about 600 years old*** Noah's precise age corresponds to the six *sefirot* that culminate in *Yesod,* Righteous One.

304. **He opened again** See above, note 299.

305. **And I, I am about to bring the Flood, waters** The verse continues: *upon the earth to destroy all flesh.*

306. **Because *I* and *I am about to* are one and the same** Both refer to *Shekhinah,* through whom the divine manifests, declaring "I am."

307. **Everywhere *Ani* becomes a body for**

the soul... Wherever this word appears in Scripture, it alludes to *Shekhinah,* who receives *Tif'eret* as the body receives the soul.

308. **it is intimated by the sign of the covenant...** *Shekhinah* is linked with the covenant of circumcision, a symbol of *Yesod,* the divine phallus.

309. **throne to what is above** Throne to *Tif'eret.*

310. **avenging from generation to generation** *Shekhinah* executes severe judgment.

311. ***Va-Ani, And I,* encompassing male and female as one** The letter ו (*vav*), whose numerical value is six, symbolizes *Tif'eret* together with the five *sefirot* surrounding Him (*Ḥesed* through *Yesod*).

312. **afterward designated alone...** The wording *I am about to* refers to *Shekhinah* alone. See above, note 306.

313. את (*et*) *the Flood,* **amplifying the meaning to include...** Grammatically, the accusative particle את (*et*) has no ascertainable independent sense; but Naḥum of Gimzo and his disciple Rabbi Akiva taught that when *et* appears in a biblical verse, it amplifies the original meaning. See BT *Pesaḥim* 22b; *Ḥagigah* 12a; *Zohar* 1:247a; 2:90a, 135b.

"אני יהוה (*Ani YHVH*), *I, YHVH* (Leviticus 18:2). We have learned: 'I will faithfully reward the righteous and punish the wicked.'[314] So with *Ani* He promised the righteous their reward, and with *Ani* He threatened the wicked with punishment in the world that is coming.

"*To destroy all flesh* (Genesis 6:17), as we have established, for this is the Destroyer of the world, of whom is written: *He will not allow the Destroyer to enter your homes to strike* (Exodus 12:23).[315] This is: *to destroy all flesh*, from the aspect of *End of all flesh has come before Me* (Genesis, ibid., 13),[316] for as soon as the time extended for them by the blessed Holy One had expired—until Noah completed 600 years[317]—then: *to destroy all flesh*."

He said, "So we have learned in the name of Rabbi Yitsḥak, who told us."[318]

He opened, saying, "*I said, 'I will not see Yah, Yah in the land of the living. I will never see* אדם *(adam), a human, again among the inhabitants of cessation'* (Isaiah 38:11).[319]

"*I said, 'I will not see Yah.'* How obtuse are human beings who neither know nor consider words of Torah nor contemplate matters of that world,[320] so the spirit of wisdom fades from their mind! For when a human departs from this world and renders an account to his Lord of all he did in this world while still existing as spirit and body united,[321] he sees what he sees, finally reaching that world, where he meets Adam, sitting by the gate of the Garden of Eden, gazing upon all those who have observed the commands of their Lord, delighting in them.[322] Around Adam stand many of the righteous, those who have refrained

383

314. **'I will faithfully reward the righteous and punish the wicked'** See *Sifra, Aḥarei Mot* 9:1, 85c; *Sifrei,* Numbers 115; *Vayiqra Rabbah* 23:9.

315. *He will not allow the Destroyer to enter your homes...* During the last of the ten plagues in Egypt: the slaying of the firstborn.

316. **aspect of** *End of all flesh...* The demonic. See above, pages 363–65.

317. **time extended for them...** See above, note 302.

318. **He said...Rabbi Yitsḥak...** See above, note 299. On page 371, the anonymous Jew tells the rabbis: "True, the place we live in is small, but everyone there engages in Torah under the guidance of one inflamed by the rabbis: Rabbi Yitsḥak son of Yose from Maḥoza, who each day tells us new words."

319. *I said, 'I will not see Yah...'* According to Scripture, the verse was sung by King Hezekiah of Judah upon recovering from mortal illness. *Yah* is a divine name, an abbreviated form of *YHVH*. The final word, חדל (*ḥadel*), *cessation,* is usually understood as a metathesis of חלד (*ḥaled*), *world,* but here the anonymous speaker insists on the meaning "cessation."

320. **that world** The spiritual realm.

321. **while still existing as spirit and body united** The phrase applies both to his condition when he acted in this world and to his condition now as he renders his account. See the parable concerning the joint responsibility of body and soul in *Mekhilta de-Rashbi,* Exodus 15:1; *Vayiqra Rabbah* 4:5; BT *Sanhedrin* 91a–b; *Zohar* 1:79a, 130b; 2:199b; 3:126b.

322. **he sees what he sees...meets Adam...** He sees *Shekhinah* and then

from the path of Hell and inclined toward the path of the Garden of Eden.
These are called *inhabitants of* חדל (*ḥadel*), *cessation,* not written: *inhabitants of*
חלד (*ḥaled*), *the world,*[323] but rather: *inhabitants of cessation,* for they desisted
from the path of Hell and overpowered themselves to enter the Garden of Eden.

"Alternatively, *inhabitants of cessation*—masters of return[324] who have refrained from sins of the wicked. Since Adam returned to the presence of his
Lord,[325] he presides over those who have refrained from their sins, who are
children of *ḥadel,* cessation, as is said: *that I may know how ḥadel, ephemeral, I
am* (Psalms 39:5).[326] So he sits at the gate of the Garden of Eden, delighting in
the righteous who come on that path.

"Come and see what is written: *I said, 'I will not see Yah.'* Now, who can see
Yah? But the conclusion of the verse demonstrates the meaning: *Yah in the land
of the living.* Come and see: When souls ascend to the site of the bundle of
life,[327] there they bask in radiance of the resplendent speculum,[328] shining
[66a] from the highest site of all.[329] If the soul did not garb herself in the

384

meets Adam, who is evoked by the verse in
Isaiah. See *Sifra, Vayiqra, dibbura dindavah*
2:12, 4a: "Rabbi Dosa says, 'Scripture states:
No human can see Me and live (Exodus
33:20). In their lifetime they do not see, but
in their death they do!'"

See *Bemidbar Rabbah* 19:18: "Death is
decreed upon all the righteous who spring
from him [Adam]. They do not depart this
life without first gazing upon the face of
Shekhinah and reproving Adam, saying: 'You
inflicted death upon us!' Adam responds: 'As
for me, I possess only one sin, while in your
case, every single one of you possesses more
than four.'"

Cf. *Tanhuma, Ḥuqqat* 16; *Tanhuma* (Buber), *Ḥuqqat* 39; *Pirqei de-Rabbi Eli'ezer* 34;
Zohar 1:57b, 81a (*ST*), 98a (*MhN*), 99a (*ST*),
127a, 218b, 226a; 3:88a.

323. **not written: *inhabitants of* חלד
(*ḥaled*), *the world*** As in Psalms 49:2. The
rare form חדל (*ḥadel*) in Isaiah is usually
understood as a metathesis of חלד (*ḥaled*).

324. **masters of return** Those who succeed in turning back to God.

325. **Adam returned to the presence of
his Lord** On Adam's repentance, see *Bereshit Rabbah* 22:13; BT *Avodah Zarah* 8a; and
Pirqei de-Rabbi Eli'ezer 20: "On the first day

of the week, Adam entered the waters of the
upper Gihon until the waters reached his
neck, and he fasted seven weeks until his
body became like a sieve." Cf. *Zohar* 1:55b.

326. ***that I may know how ḥadel, ephemeral, I am*** The full verse reads: *YHVH, let
me know my end, what is the measure of my
days, that I may know how ephemeral I am*
(Psalms 39:5).

327. **bundle of life** See 1 Samuel 25:29:
*The soul of my lord will be bound in the
bundle of life.* Here the phrase describes *Shekhinah,* destination of the soul. See *Zohar*
1:224b; Moses de León, *Sheqel ha-Qodesh,*
60–61 (75).

328. **resplendent speculum...** אספקלריא
דנהרא (*Ispaqlarya de-nahara*), "Speculum [or:
glass, mirror, lens] that shines," symbolizing
Tif'eret. See BT *Yevamot* 49b: "All the prophets gazed through a dim glass ["an *ispaqlarya*
that does not shine"], while Moses our Rabbi gazed through a clear glass ["an *ispaqlarya*
that shines"]." Cf. 1 Corinthians 13:12: "For
now we see through a glass darkly, but then
face-to-face."

329. **highest site of all** The upper reaches of the *sefirot, Ḥokhmah* and *Binah,* who are
named *Yah.*

radiance of another garment, then she could not draw near to view that light. The mystery of the matter: Just as the soul is given a garment in which to be garbed, to exist in this world,[330] so she is given a garment of supernal radiance in which to exist in that world,[331] to gaze into the speculum that shines from within *the land of the living*.[332]

"Come and see: Moses could not draw near to gaze upon what he gazed until he was garbed in another garment, as is said: *Moses entered the cloud and ascended the mountain* (Exodus 24:18)—into the midst of the cloud.[333] He clothed himself in it, as one clothes himself in a garment, and therefore, *Moses approached the thick darkness where God was* (ibid. 20:18), and *Moses was on the mountain forty days and forty nights* (ibid. 24:18), able to gaze upon what he gazed.

"Similarly, souls of the righteous garb themselves in that world in a garment suiting that world, so they stand gazing at the light radiating into *the land of the living*.

"*I will never see* אדם (*adam*), *a human, again*—this is Adam, as has been explained.[334] Why all this? Because he did not generate children,[335] for anyone who does not generate children in this world is banished, when he leaves, from all that we have mentioned and is not allowed to view that radiant light.[336]

385

330. **garment in which to be garbed, to exist in this world**   The body.

331. **garment of supernal radiance . . . in that world**   To enter and experience higher dimensions, the soul is enveloped in a radiant garment. According to *Zohar* 1:224a–b, this garment is woven out of one's virtuous days. Parallels appear in Islamic and Iranian eschatology—and in Mahayana Buddhism, according to which the Buddha enjoys *sambhogakaya* ("a body of bliss"), generated by merit accrued over aeons.

See *Zohar* 1:7a, 82b, 91a; 2:11a, 150a, 210a–b, 229b, 247a (*Heikh*); 3:70b, 101a, 174b; *Seder Gan Eden* (*Beit ha-Midrash*, 3:133); Scholem, *Major Trends*, 77–78; idem, in *Tarbiz* 24 (1955): 290–306; idem, *Kabbalah*, 158–59; idem, *On the Mystical Shape of the Godhead*, 264–65; Nakamura Hajime, in *Encyclopedia of Religion*, 2:458.

Cf. *Sifrei*, Deuteronomy 36; *Bereshit Rabbah* 19:6; *Shemot Rabbah* 1:35; *Pirqei de-Rabbi Eli'ezer* 14; Matthew 22:1–14.

332. *the land of the living*   Shekhinah, abode of the soul, from where the soul gazes

upon *Tif'eret*, the "speculum that shines." See *Zohar* 1:95b, 115a, 124b, 143b; Moses de León, *Sheqel ha-Qodesh*, 62 (77).

333. **Moses could not draw near . . . until he was garbed in another garment . . .**   See BT *Yoma* 4a: "Moses ascended in the cloud, was enveloped by the cloud, and was sanctified within the cloud—so as to receive Torah for Israel in holiness." Cf. *Pesiqta Rabbati* 20; *Zohar* 2:99a, 197a, 229a.

334. **this is Adam, as has been explained**   As noted above, page 383, Adam greets those who arrive at the Garden of Eden.

335. **he did not generate children**   The subject is King Hezekiah, who sang these lines upon recovering from his illness. See Isaiah 38:9. According to BT *Berakhot* 10a (in the name of Rav Hamnuna), Hezekiah's illness was a punishment for his failure to *be fruitful and multiply* (Genesis 1:28).

336. **anyone who does not generate children in this world . . .**   See BT *Bava Batra* 116a: "Rabbi Yoḥanan said in the name of Rabbi Shim'on son of Yoḥai, 'Whoever does not leave a son to succeed him incurs the

If this was the case with Hezekiah, who possessed ancestral merit[337] and was himself virtuous, righteous, and devout, all the more so with one who lacks ancestral merit and has sinned in the presence of his Lord!

"This garment of which we have spoken is what the Companions call the 'shirt' worn in that world.[338] Happy is the share of the righteous, for whom the blessed Holy One has treasured away such goodness in that world! Of them is written: *No eye has seen, O God, but You, what You will do for one who awaits You* (Isaiah 64:3)."[339]

And I, I am about to bring the Flood, waters upon the earth (Genesis 6:17).[340]

Rabbi Yehudah opened, "*These are the Waters of Quarrel, where the Children of Israel quarreled with YHVH, and through which He was hallowed* (Numbers 20:13). Didn't *the Children of Israel quarrel with YHVH* anywhere else?[341] What's different here, that the verse should state: *These*

386

full wrath of the blessed Holy One.'" Cf. BT *Yevamot* 63b; *Zohar* 1:13a, 48a, 90a, 115a, 228b; *ZH* 89b (*MhN, Rut*).

337. **ancestral merit** Rabbinic Hebrew, זכות אבות (*zekhut avot*), "merit of the fathers," the protecting influence of distinguished ancestry. Hezekiah was descended from King David. See Isaiah 37:35; and BT *Shabbat* 55a: "Since when has ancestral merit ceased?...Rabbi Yoḥanan said, 'Since the days of Hezekiah.'"

338. **'shirt'...** חלוקא (*Ḥaluqa*). See above, note 331. The Hebrew term חלוק (*haluq*) appears in Heikhalot literature describing divine or angelic garments. See *Heikhalot Rabbati*, 3–4 (in *Beit ha-Midrash*, 3:86); Schäfer, *Synopse*, 48–51, §§102, 105; 178, §420.

The printed editions and *DE* (emendations) read חלוקא דרבנן (*haluqa de-rabbanan*), "shirt of the rabbis." See Moses de León, *Sefer ha-Mishqal*, 56. Cf. the later Hebrew phrase איצטלא דרבנן (*itstela de-rabbanan*), "robe of the rabbis." See BT *Mo'ed Qatan* 28b; and *Shabbat* 128a: "It was taught in the name of Rabbi Yishma'el and in the name of Rabbi Akiva: 'All of Israel are worthy of that איצטלא (*itstela*), [royal] robe.'"

339. **for whom the blessed Holy One has treasured away...** See BT *Ḥagigah* 12a: "Rabbi El'azar said, 'With the light created

by the blessed Holy One on the first day, one could gaze and see from one end of the universe to the other. When the blessed Holy One foresaw the corrupt deeds of the generation of the Flood and the generation of the Dispersion [the generation of the Tower of Babel], He immediately hid it from them, as is written: *The light of the wicked is withheld* (Job 38:15). For whom did He hide it? For the righteous in the time to come.'"

See *Bereshit Rabbah* 3:6; 41:3; *Shemot Rabbah* 35:1; *Tanḥuma, Shemini*, 9; *Bahir* 97–98 (147); *Zohar* 1:7a, 31b–32a, 45b–46a, 47a, 59a; 2:127a, 148b–149a, 220a–b; 3:88a, 173b.

See BT *Berakhot* 34b: "Rabbi Ḥiyya son of Abba said in the name of Rabbi Yoḥanan, 'All the prophets prophesied only concerning the days of the Messiah, but as for the world that is coming, *No eye has seen, O God, but You,* [*what You will do for one who awaits You*]... All the prophets prophesied only concerning masters of return [turning back to God], but as for the completely righteous, *No eye has seen, O God, but You.*'"

340. **And I, I am about to bring the Flood, waters upon the earth** The verse continues: *to destroy all flesh.*

341. **Didn't *the Children of Israel quarrel...anywhere else?*** The wandering Isra-

are the Waters of Quarrel, and no others? But these were really *Waters of Quarrel*, potently empowering the masters of judgment.[342] For there are sweet waters and bitter waters, clear waters and turbid waters, waters of peace and waters of strife.[343] So *these are the Waters of Quarrel, where the Children of Israel quarreled with YHVH*, attracting to themselves the one they must not,[344] through whom they became defiled, as is written: ויקדש בם (*va-yiqqadesh bam*), *through which he was tabooed.*"[345]

Rabbi Ḥizkiyah asked, "If so, why ויקדש (*va-yiqqadesh*), *he was tabooed*? The verse should read ויקדשו (*va-yiqqadeshu*), *they were tabooed.*"[346]

He replied, "The word transcends:[347] *va-yiqqadesh*—the one who must not be tainted was, for the moon was tainted, as it were;[348] *va-yiqqadesh*—here implying no praise.[349] *And I, I am about to bring the Flood*, as we have established: to unleash the Destroyer upon them, since through him they had defiled themselves."[350]

Rabbi Yose said, "Woe to the wicked who, having sinned, refuse to return to the blessed Holy One[351] while still in the world! For when a person returns, regretting his sins, the blessed Holy One forgives him, but all those who cling

387

---

elites complained frequently; see Exodus 17:1–7; Numbers 11; 21:4–9.

342. **potently empowering the masters of judgment** Nourishing the powers of harsh judgment. As indicated by the preceding verse (Numbers 20:12), this incident led to the death of Moses and Aaron.

343. **sweet waters and bitter waters…** See *Zohar* 1:80a (*ST*); 3:12b; *ZH* 30c (*MhN*); Numbers 5:17–27 (alluded to below).

344. **the one they must not** The demonic who manifests in bitter, turbid waters of strife.

345. בם ויקדש (*va-yiqqadesh bam*), *through which he was tabooed* The root קדש (*qdsh*) means "to be set apart, consecrated, hallowed" but also "forfeited, tabooed." See Deuteronomy 22:9; *Targum Onqelos*, ad loc. Cf. Genesis 38:21–22; Deuteronomy 23:18; Isaiah 65:5; Haggai 2:12.

The phrase here is normally construed as *through which He was hallowed*, the subject *He* indicating God, who *was hallowed* through the *Waters of Quarrel* or through the subsequent death of Moses and Aaron. Here Rabbi Yehudah identifies the subject as

Israel, who was defiled and tabooed by the waters.

346. **The verse should read ויקדשו (*va-yiqqadeshu*), *they were tabooed*** If the subject is the Children of Israel, the verb should be plural.

347. **The word transcends** The word applies not to Israel but to a higher realm.

348. **the moon was tainted, as it were** *Shekhinah*, symbolized by the moon, was tainted by bitter waters.

349. **here implying no praise** The word does not convey holiness but rather defilement. See Rashi on Deuteronomy 22:9; Ibn Ezra on Numbers 11:18.

350. *And I, I am about to bring the Flood…the Destroyer…* *Shekhinah*, the Divine Presence known as *I*, conveys the attribute of Judgment and here unleashes the waters of the Flood, pervaded by the demonic. The wicked generation of the Flood brought this destruction upon themselves through the defilement of sin. See above, page 382.

351. **to return to the blessed Holy One** Repenting sincerely.

to their sins, refusing to return to the blessed Holy One, will eventually fall into Hell, never to be raised.

"Come and see: Since the entire generation of Noah hardened their hearts, desiring to flaunt their sins, the blessed Holy One executed judgment upon them in a similar manner."[352]

"Rabbi Yitsḥak said, "Even when someone sins in secret, the blessed Holy One exposes him in sight of all.[353] How do we know? From the straying wife.[354] Similarly these wicked ones were obliterated from earth. Obliterated? How? Waters gushed boiling from the abyss, rising and peeling off their skin, then their flesh,[355] leaving nothing but bones, fulfilling the verse: *They were obliterated from the earth* (Genesis 7:23). All those bones disjointed from one another, no longer together,[356] so they were totally eradicated from the world." [66b]

I will establish My covenant with you (Genesis 6:18).[357]

Rabbi El'azar said, "From here we learn that when the righteous appear in the world, the world is established firmly above and below."[358]

Rabbi Shim'on said, "It is a concealed matter, concerning the arousal of a male toward his female when he jealously suspects her.[359] Come and see the mystery of the matter: The moment a righteous man appears in the world,

352. **in a similar manner** Openly and boldly. See above, pages 347–48.

353. **Even when someone sins in secret...** See M *Avot* 4:4: "Rabbi Yoḥanan son of Beroka says, 'Whoever profanes the name of Heaven secretly is punished openly.'"

354. **straying wife** According to the Bible, a wife suspected of infidelity must undergo an ordeal of drinking bitter water. If she is guilty, the water causes her public suffering and disgrace. See Numbers 5:11–31.

355. **Waters gushed boiling from the abyss...** See *Pirqei de-Rabbi Eli'ezer* 22: "[The giants of the generation of the Flood] said, 'If He brings the waters of the Flood upon us, behold, we are of high stature, and the waters will not reach our necks. If He brings up the waters of the depths against us, behold, the soles of our feet can dam up the depths.' What did they do? They spread the soles of their feet and dammed up all the depths. What did the blessed Holy One do? He boiled the waters of the depths, which seethed their flesh and peeled off their skin." Cf. above, pages 356–57.

356. **All those bones disjointed from one another...** See *Bereshit Rabbah* 28:3.

357. *I will establish My covenant with you* The verse continues: *and you will enter the ark—you, your sons, your wife, and your sons' wives with you.*

358. **when the righteous appear in the world...** The verse is addressed to Noah the Righteous but applies to all the righteous. The wording *with you* implies their active participation in stabilizing both this world and the sefirotic world. These virtuous humans embody the *sefirah* of *Yesod,* who is known as Righteous One and symbolized by the *covenant.* Through their virtuous living, they unite the divine couple, *Tif'eret* and *Shekhinah.*

359. **arousal of a male toward his female when he jealously suspects her** See above, note 354. On the visceral link between love and jealousy, see Song of Songs 8:6; *Shir*

388

Shekhinah never leaves him, Her desire drawn toward him. Then supernal desire toward Her in love, like desire of a male for his female when he jealously suspects her.[360] So, *I will erect My covenant with you*—desire arouses because of you.[361] Similarly, *My covenant I will erect with Isaac* (ibid. 17:21).[362]

"*I will erect My covenant with you*—so that you signify My covenant in the world; then *you will enter the ark*. If he had not embodied the covenant, he would not have entered the ark, for only the righteous one unites with the ark. So, *enter the ark,* as has been explained."[363]

Rabbi El'azar said, "As long as people hold fast to the covenant, not abandoning it,[364] no nation or language in the world can harm them. Noah held firmly to this covenant, preserving it,[365] so the blessed Holy One preserved him; but all his contemporaries failed to preserve it, so the blessed Holy One eliminated them from the world. As already explained, they were obliterated from the world in the very same manner as the sin they sinned."[366]

Rabbi Yehudah was in the presence of Rabbi Shim'on, engaging together in this verse: וירפא (Vayrappe), *He healed, the wrecked altar of YHVH* (1 Kings 18:30).[367]

389

ha-Shirim Rabbah, ad loc.; *Zohar* 1:245a; 3:54b.

360. **supernal desire toward Her in love...** The desire of the divine male (*Tif-'eret* or *Yesod*) is aroused toward *Shekhinah,* who was intimate with a righteous man. See *Zohar* 1:49b–50a, 153b.

361. *I will erect...* והקימותי (*Va-haqi-moti*), *I will establish.* Rabbi Shim'on focuses on the literal meaning "raise, erect," suggesting that *Yesod,* the divine phallus bearing the covenant, is stimulated and aroused by righteous humans.

See above, page 341; Moses de León, *Sod Eser Sefirot Belimah,* 381–82; *OY*; Liebes, *Pera-qim,* 378–79; idem, in *Da'at* 1 (1978): 107.

362. *My covenant I will erect with Isaac* Isaac symbolizes the *sefirah* of *Gevurah,* through whose passion *Yesod* is aroused.

363. **If he had not embodied the cove-nant...** If Noah had not embodied *Yesod,* he could not have entered the ark, symbolizing *Shekhinah.* See *Zohar* 1:59b, 65b.

364. **As long as people hold fast to the covenant, not abandoning it** As long as they observe the ritual of circumcision (sign of the covenant) and live in sexual purity.

365. **Noah held firmly to this cove-nant...** Not only did Noah live purely, but according to rabbinic tradition he was one of those rare individuals born circumcised. See *Avot de-Rabbi Natan* A, 2; *Tanhu-ma, Noah* 5; *Zohar* 1:58a–b, 59b.

366. **all his contemporaries failed to pre-serve it...** On the sexual nature of the sins of Noah's generation, see BT *Sanhedrin* 108b: "It has been taught: The waters of the Flood were as thick as semen....Rav Hisda said: 'With boiling [passion] they sinned, and with boiling [water] they were punished.'"

See *Yalqut Shim'oni,* Job, 906; *Pirqei de-Rabbi Eli'ezer* 22; *Targum Yerushalmi,* Gen-esis 7:10; above, page 356.

Rabbi El'azar's condemnation of sexual promiscuity reflects the promiscuity preva-lent in the Jewish community in thirteenth-century Castile. On this issue, see Moses de León, *Sheqel ha-Qodesh,* 51–54 (63–67); Baer, in *Zion* 2 (1937): 31–33, 36–44; idem, *History,* 1:250–63; Tishby, *Wisdom of the Zohar,* 3:1371–72; Assis, "Sexual Behavior in Medi-aeval Hispano-Jewish Society."

367. וירפא (*Vayrappe*), *He healed, the wrecked altar...* The subject is the prophet

"What does *healed* mean? Come and see: All Israel had abandoned the blessed Holy One and abandoned their sealed covenant.[368] When Elijah appeared, he saw that the Israel had abandoned the holy covenant, removing it.[369] Seeing this, he set about repairing the matter. Once he drew the entity to its site,[370] what is written? *He healed the wrecked altar of YHVH*—the sealed covenant coming to repair *the wrecked altar of YHVH;* the sealed covenant, abandoned by the world.[371]

"It is written: *Elijah took twelve stones, corresponding to the number of the tribes of the sons of Jacob* (ibid., 31)—this is the repair of *the altar of YHVH.*[372]

"*To whom the word of YHVH came, saying, 'Israel shall be your name'* (ibid.).[373] Indeed, *Israel shall be your name,* ascending on high, restoring the sealed covenant to its site,[374] corresponding to what is written: *For the Children of Israel have abandoned Your covenant,* and thereby *torn down Your altars* (ibid. 19:10).

"Come and see: As long as Israel preserve the holy covenant, they erect existence above and below.[375] When they abandon this covenant, existence sags above and below, as is written: *Were it not for My covenant day and night, I would not have established the laws of heaven and earth* (Jeremiah 33:25).[376]

390

Elijah on Mount Carmel engaged in a contest with the priests of Ba'al. The word וירפא (vayrappe) means, literally, "he healed," and in this verse, "he repaired."

368. **abandoned their sealed covenant** By neglecting the command of circumcision or indulging in sexual sin. See *Pirqei de-Rabbi Eli'ezer* 29.

369. **abandoned the holy covenant, removing it** Their sinful rejection of the covenant caused the divine covenant, *Yesod,* to abandon *Shekhinah.* The phrase "removing it" may refer to epispasm, the attempt to disguise circumcision by cutting and pulling forward the loose skin of the penis to form a partial foreskin. See BT *Sanhedrin* 38b; JT *Pe'ah* 1:1, 16b; *Zohar* 1:35b.

370. **Once he drew the entity to its site** Once Elijah succeeded in reuniting *Yesod* with *Shekhinah.*

371. **sealed covenant coming to repair** *the wrecked altar of YHVH...* *Yesod* reuniting with *Shekhinah,* who is symbolized by the altar.

372. *twelve stones...* **this is the repair of**

the altar of YHVH The twelve stones of the altar symbolize twelve powers surrounding and adorning *Shekhinah.* See *Zohar* 1:80a (*ST*), 149a–b (*ST*), 241a.

373. *To whom the word of YHVH came, saying, 'Israel shall be your name'* After Jacob wrestled with the angel, he was renamed Israel. See Genesis 32:29; 35:10.

374. **ascending on high...** Ascending to the level of *Tif'eret Yisra'el* ("Beauty of Israel") and reuniting *Yesod* with *Shekhinah.*

375. **erect existence...** עבדי קיומא (*Avedei qiyyuma*). *Qiyyuma* means here both "existence" and "erection." Sexual purity stimulates *Yesod,* unites the divine couple, and ensures a continued flow of sustenance to earth.

376. **When they abandon this covenant...** Sexual sin ruins the divine union, interrupting the vital flow. See BT *Shabbat* 137b: "Were it not for the blood of the covenant, heaven and earth would not endure, as is said: *Were it not for My covenant day and night, I would not have established the laws of heaven and earth.*" Cf. *Zohar* 1:32a, 56a, 59b, 89a, 93b.

So, *He healed the wrecked altar of YHVH*. Now, is that healing? Certainly so! For he sustains the site on which faith depends.[377]

"Come and see, similarly, Phinehas: When he filled with zeal over the act of Zimri, he repaired this covenant in its site, and therefore it is written: *I hereby grant him My covenant of peace* (Numbers 25:12).[378]

"Now, do you think it was for Phinehas? What quarrel did Phinehas have with this covenant?[379] Rather, here an entity was linked with its place.[380] *I hereby grant Him, My covenant*. What will I grant Him? *Peace*, so that each will join its place, so that covenant will join its site.[381] So, *I hereby grant Him, My covenant*. What? *Peace*, its site to join. What had been separated from it by their sins, because of him rejoined.[382] So since he arrayed the entity in its place, from now on: *It shall be for him and for his seed after him a covenant of perpetual priesthood, because he was zealous for his God* (ibid., 13)."[383]

Rabbi Shim'on said, "Nothing in the world so provokes the jealousy of the blessed Holy One as the sin of the covenant,[384] as is said: *A sword avenging with vengeance of the covenant* (Leviticus 26:25). Come and see: The guilt of the generation of the Flood remained incomplete until they sinned by ruining their ways upon earth,[385] even though they robbed one another, as is

391

377. **site on which faith depends** *Shekhinah*, the link between humans and all aspects of the divine.

378. **similarly, Phinehas...** In his zeal, Phinehas killed Zimri together with his forbidden Midianite sexual partner (Numbers 25:1–9). His zeal prefigures that of Elijah, with whom he is often identified.

See Pseudo-Philo 48:1–2; *Targum Yerushalmi*, Exodus 6:18; Numbers 25:12; *Tanḥuma, Pinḥas* 1; *Bemidbar Rabbah* 21:3; *Pirqei de-Rabbi Eli'ezer* 47; *Zohar* 2:190a; 3:214a, 215a (*RM*); Origen on John 6:7; Ginzberg, *Legends*, 6:316–17, n. 3. In Matthew 11:14, John the Baptist is identified with Elijah.

379. **Now, do you think it was for Phinehas?...** Was he in need of a covenant of peace? It was not Phinehas but rather Israel who had rejected the covenant and aroused divine wrath.

380. **an entity was linked with its place** Through his zeal, Phinehas stimulated the union of the divine covenant (*Yesod*) with its abode (*Shekhinah*), yielding harmony and peace.

381. *I hereby grant Him, My covenant.*

What will I grant Him? *Peace*... The object of the verse is not Phinehas, but *Yesod*, the covenant, whose union with *Shekhinah* brings peace.

382. **What had been separated from it by their sins...** Through their sexual contact with the daughters of Moab (Numbers 25:1–9), Israel had separated *Shekhinah* from *Yesod*. Through the zeal of Phinehas, the divine couple reunited.

383. *because he was zealous for his God* The verse continues: *and made atonement for the Children of Israel*.

384. **sin of the covenant** Sexual sin, which betrays the covenant, provoking divine jealousy.

385. **ruining their ways upon earth** The phrase *ruined their way upon earth* (Genesis 6:11) is elsewhere interpreted as referring to masturbation (spilling seed on earth) or crossbreeding. See BT *Sanhedrin* 108a; *Bereshit Rabbah* 28:8; *Kallah Rabbati* 2; *Pirqei de-Rabbi Eli'ezer* 22; Rashi on BT *Shabbat* 41a, s.v. *ke-illu mevi mabbul la-olam; Zohar* 1:56b–57a, 61a–62a, 68a.

written: *The earth was filled with violence* (Genesis 6:11).[386] [67a]

"Come and see how many deputies on high are appointed over the voices of those invoking heavenly judgment against their fellows for what was done to them. So it is written: *For the earth is filled with violence because of them,* and therefore, *Here, I am about to destroy them along with the earth* (ibid., 13)."[387]

YHVH said to Noah, "Come, you and all your household, into the ark!" (ibid. 7:1).

Rabbi Shim'on said, "Throughout, *Elohim,* while here, *YHVH.* What is different here that it should say *YHVH,* supernal name of compassion?[388] It is a mystery, for we have learned: It is not proper for a woman to receive a guest without her husband's permission.[389] Similarly, here: Noah wanted to enter the ark, to unite with Her,[390] but it was unseemly until the husband of the ark gave him permission,[391] as is written: *Come, you and all your household, into the ark!* So here He is called *YHVH,* husband of the ark. Only then did Noah enter, uniting with Her.

"Similarly, we have learned that a guest is not permitted to enter the house without the consent of the woman's husband, master of the house,[392] as is subsequently written: *Noah entered . . .* (ibid., 7).[393]

392

386. **even though they robbed one another . . .** See BT *Sanhedrin* 108a: "Rabbi Yoḥanan said, 'Come and see how great is the power of robbery! For the generation of the Flood violated everything, yet their decree of punishment was sealed only when they stretched out their hands to rob, as is written: *For the earth is filled with violence because of them; here, I am about to destroy them along with the earth* (Genesis 6:13).'"

387. **those invoking heavenly judgment against their fellows . . .** See BT *Bava Qamma* 93a: "Rabbi Ḥanan said, 'One who invokes [heavenly] judgment against his fellow is punished first.'" The proof-text cited there (Genesis 16:5) contains the word *violence,* as does the verse here.

388. **Throughout,** *Elohim,* **while here,** *YHVH . . .* **name of compassion** In rabbinic literature the divine names יהוה (*YHVH*) and אלהים (*Elohim*) indicate, respectively, the divine qualities of compassion and justice. See *Sifrei,* Deuteronomy 26; *Bereshit Rabbah* 12:15; 33:3; and 13:3, where *YHVH Elohim* is called

"a complete name." Cf. *Zohar* 1:20a, 48b, 56b, 64b; 2:161a, 229a; 3:138b (*IR*); *ZH* 70d (*ShS*).

The name *Elohim* dominates the account of the Flood, though the name *YHVH* appears too (Genesis 6:5–8; 7:1, 5, 16). Rabbi Shim'on's point is: The name *Elohim* (denoting judgment) is appropriate to the Flood, so why does the name *YHVH* (denoting compassion) appear here?

389. **It is not proper . . .** See *Zohar* 1:70b–71a; and above, p. 227 and n. 969 there.

390. **to enter the ark, to unite with Her** To unite with *Shekhinah,* symbolized by the ark.

391. **until the husband of the ark gave him permission** Until Her husband, *Tif'eret* (symbolized by the name *YHVH*), permitted Noah to enter.

392. **not permitted to enter . . .** See *Zohar* 1:70b–71a.

393. *Noah entered* The verse continues: *with his sons, his wife, and his sons' wives, into the ark,* after receiving permission.

"Come and see what is written: *For you have I seen as righteous before Me in this generation* (ibid., 1). From here we learn that one should not receive a guest into his home if he seems suspicious, but only if he appears virtuous, beyond all suspicion, as is written: *Come, you and all your household, into the ark!* Why? *For you have I seen as righteous before Me....*[394]

"We also learn that if he grants permission to him alone, and not to all those accompanying him, he should not bring them into the house, as is written: *Come, you and all your household, into the ark*—permitting them all to enter. From this verse we learn the mystery of manners."

Come, you and all your household, into the ark!

Rabbi Yehudah opened, "לדוד מזמור (*Le-David mizmor*), *Of David, a psalm. The earth and her fullness are YHVH's, the world and her inhabitants* (Psalms 24:1). We have learned: לדוד מזמור (*Le-David mizmor*), *Of David, a psalm*—he exclaimed a song, then Holy Spirit dwelled upon him. מזמור לדוד (*Mizmor le-David*), *A psalm of David*—Holy Spirit dwelled upon him, then he exclaimed a song.[395]

393

"*The earth and her fullness are YHVH's.* This verse was uttered for the land of Israel, the Holy Land. *Her fullness* is *Shekhinah,* as is said: *For the Presence of YHVH* מלא (*male*), *filled, the house of YHVH* (1 Kings 8:11), and similarly: *The Presence of YHVH* מלא (*male*), *filled, the Dwelling* (Exodus 40:35).[396] Why מָלֵא (*male*), full, and not מִלֵּא (*mille*), *filled*?[397] But full, indeed! Filled with everything, filled by the sun, a moon complete on every side,[398] male, full, of supernal substance, like a treasure ship filled with all the best of the world.[399]

---

394. *For you have I seen as righteous before Me*   The verse continues: *in this generation.*

395. **We also learn:** לדוד מזמור (*Le-David mizmor*), *Of David, a psalm...A psalm of David...*   These titles, whose precise meaning is unclear, alternate in Psalms. The interpretation formulated here reverses the rabbinic version in BT *Pesaḥim* 117a: "לדוד מזמור (*Le-David mizmor*), *To David, a psalm,* indicates that *Shekhinah* dwelled upon him and then he exclaimed a song. מזמור לדוד (*Mizmor le-David*), *A psalm, to David,* indicates that he exclaimed a song and then *Shekhinah* dwelled upon him." (The preposition ל [*le*] can mean either "of" or "to".) In Rabbi Yehudah's revision, *psalm* becomes a name of *Shekhinah,* who is adorned by human song, so the wording *Le-David mizmor* (*Of David, a psalm*) refers first to David and

then to *Shekhinah* (Holy Spirit), known as *psalm.*

See *Midrash Tehillim* 24:1, 3; Rashi, Psalms 23:1; Jacob bar Sheshet, *Meshiv Devarim Nekhoḥim,* 92; Todros Abulafia, *Sha'ar ha-Razim,* 48; *Zohar* 1:39b; 2:50a, 140a, 170a.

396. *Her fullness* is *Shekhinah,* as is said: *For the Presence...*   *Shekhinah,* the Divine Presence, filled the Tabernacle in the Desert (*the Dwelling*) and the Temple in Jerusalem (*the house of YHVH*).

397. **Why** מָלֵא (*male*), full, and not מִלֵּא (*mille*), *filled*?   Why does Scripture employ the participle and not the intensive verb?

398. **full, indeed!...filled by the sun...**   *Shekhinah,* symbolized by the moon, is filled by the flow of emanation from *Tif'eret,* the sun.

399. **treasure ship...**   אסקופא (*Isquppa*), which may mean both "yard of a ship" and

So, *The earth and her fullness are YHVH's.*[400] *The world and her inhabitants*—the rest of the world.

"Alternatively, *The earth is YHVH's*—the supernal Holy Land, in which the blessed Holy One delights.[401] *And her fullness*—souls of the righteous, all of whom fill Her, by whom She is filled, through the potency of a single pillar upon which the world stands.[402]

"Now if you say, 'It stands upon one,' come and see what is written: *For He founded it upon seas* (Psalms, ibid., 2).[403] *For He.* Who is *He*? The blessed Holy One, as is said: *He made us* (ibid. 100:2), and similarly: *He looks to the ends of earth* (Job 28:24).[404]

"*He founded it upon seas and established it upon rivers* (Psalms 24:2)—seven pillars upon which She stands.[405] They fill Her, She is filled by them. How? When the virtuous abound in the world, this *earth* yields fruit and is filled with all.[406] When the wicked abound in the world, it is written: *Waters vanish from the sea; a river dries up and is parched* (Job 14:11). *Waters vanish from the sea*— the Holy Land we have mentioned, drenched by supernal saturation.[407] *A river*

394

"threshold." Cf. Greek *skaphe* and אסקפא (*isqapha*), "skiff, light boat." The image here apparently derives from *Midrash Mishlei* 31:14, where Joseph is compared to "a ship filled with all the best of the world."

In *ZH* 3a (*MhN*), *isquppa* refers to the "threshold" beneath which household valuables were buried. See BT *Berakhot* 18b; Rashi on BT *Mo'ed Qatan* 11a, s.v. *tsinnor*; idem on Joshua 24:26.

See *Zohar* 1:46b; 2:83b; 3:69a; *ZH* 88c (*MhN, Rut*); *Bei'ur ha-Millim ha-Zarot*, 173; Scholem, *Major Trends*, 165, 388, n. 47.

400. So, *The earth and her fullness are YHVH's* Both the Holy Land and her fullness, *Shekhinah*, derive from *Tif'eret*, known as *YHVH*.

401. supernal Holy Land... *Shekhinah*, in whom *Tif'eret* delights. Rabbi Yehudah is playing with the similar-sounding ארעא (*ar'a*), "land," and אתרעי (*itra'ei*), "delights." See *Zohar* 3:22b.

402. souls of the righteous... potency of a single pillar... Righteous souls are conveyed by the flow of emanation from *Yesod*, the cosmic pillar, to *Shekhinah*. *Yesod* Himself is known as Righteous One, based on Proverbs 10:25: וצדיק יסוד עולם (*Ve-tsaddiq*

yesod olam). The phrase, which literally means *The righteous one is an everlasting foundation,* is understood as *The righteous one is the foundation of the world.* See BT *Ḥagigah* 12b: "Rabbi El'azar son of Shamu'a says, '[The world stands] upon a single pillar named Righteous One, as is said: *The righteous one is the foundation of the world.*'"

Cf. *Bahir* 71 (102); Azriel of Gerona, *Peirush ha-Aggadot*, 34; *Zohar* 3:45b.

403. *For He founded it upon seas* The plural *seas* refers to all of the *sefirot* from *Hesed* through *Yesod*, which flow into *Shekhinah*.

404. Who is *He*? The blessed Holy One... Here apparently referring to *Binah*, from whom the *seas* proceed to *Shekhinah*, known as *earth*. See *Zohar* 1:156b, 158b, 171b; 3:171a, 183b.

405. seven pillars... The *sefirot* from *Hesed* through *Shekhinah* Herself. See *Zohar* 2:23a.

406. When the virtuous abound in the world... The righteous stimulate the union between *Yesod* and *Shekhinah*.

407. Holy Land we have mentioned... *Shekhinah*, watered by the flow of emanation.

dries up and is parched—that single pillar standing above Her, by whom She is illumined.[408] *A river dries up and is parched,* as is said: *The righteous one perishes* (Isaiah 57:1)."[409]

Rabbi Yehudah said further, "When the wicked were annihilated from the world, the blessed Holy One was saddened, seeing no one upon whom it could stand.[410] Now if you say, 'What about Noah?' It was plenty for him to protect himself and to engender generations for the world, as is written: *For you have I seen as righteous before Me in this generation* (Genesis 7:1)—*in this generation,* precisely!"[411]

Rabbi Yose [67b] said, "*In this generation*—a tribute to him, for though living in that wicked generation, he became all this: *a completely righteous man* (ibid. 6:9)—even in the generation of Moses![412] But he could not protect the world, because ten could not be found in the world—as is said: *if I find ten there* (ibid. 18:32), and they could not be found; here, too, ten could not be found: just he and his three sons and their wives, not totaling ten."[413]

Rabbi El'azar asked his father, Rabbi Shim'on, "We have learned that when the world is pervaded by the sins of humanity, and judgment breaks out, woe to the virtuous one found in the world, for he is snared first for the sins of the wicked.[414] How was Noah saved, not seized for their sins?"

395

408. **single pillar standing above Her...** *Yesod.*

409. *The righteous one perishes* The flow channeled through *Yesod* dries up. See *Zohar* 1:55b.

410. **no one upon whom it could stand** No righteous human upon whom the world could stand.

411. **It was plenty for him to protect himself...** *in this generation,* **precisely!** Noah's virtue extended sufficiently to save himself, but he was not righteous enough to redeem his entire generation. See *Devarim Rabbah* 11:3. Rabbi Yehudah's statement matches the one attributed to him in *Bereshit Rabbah* 30:9: "*In his generations* (Genesis 6:9). Rabbi Yehudah and Rabbi Neḥemiah. Rabbi Yehudah said, '*In his generations* he was righteous, but if he had lived in the generations of Moses or Samuel, he would not have been righteous....' Rabbi Neḥemiah said, 'If he was righteous *in his generations* [despite the corrupt environment], all

the more so if he had lived in the generations of Moses or Samuel.'"

412. *In this generation*—**a tribute to him...** Rabbi Yose's view matches the one attributed to Rabbi Neḥemiah. See the preceding note.

413. **ten could not be found in the world...** Ten righteous people would have sufficed to save the generation of Noah, as when Abraham argued with God over the fate of the wicked city of Sodom, convincing Him that even ten innocent Sodomites should suffice to save their city.

The citation *if I find ten there* is a conflation of Genesis 18:30, 32.

414. **he is snared first for the sins of the wicked** See BT *Shabbat* 33b: "Rabbi Gorion (according to others, Rabbi Yosef son of Rabbi Shema'yah) said, 'When there are righteous ones in the generation, the righteous are seized [killed] for the generation. When there are no righteous in the generation, schoolchildren are seized for the generation.'"

He replied, "The blessed Holy One desired to engender from him generations for the world, from out of the ark. Further, judgment could not overpower him because he was hidden away in the ark, concealed from sight.[415]

"Come and see what is written: *Seek righteousness, seek humility; perhaps you
will be hidden on the day of YHVH's wrath* (Zephaniah 2:3). Noah sought righteousness and entered Her,[416] becoming *hidden on the day of YHVH's wrath,* so
judgment could not overpower or denounce him.

"Here is a hint for holy ones of the Most High,[417] to discover the mystery of
supernal letters—reversal of letters, twenty-two—to obliterate the wicked.[418]
Therefore it is written: *They were obliterated from the earth* (Genesis 7:23), and:
בא (*Bo*), *Come... into the ark!* (ibid., 1)."[419]

Rabbi Yitsḥak opened, "*Who sent His glorious arm to be at Moses' right hand,
splitting the waters before them to make Himself an everlasting name* (Isaiah
63:12). Come and see the difference between Moses and other inhabitants of
the world![420] When the blessed Holy One said to Moses, *Now, leave Me alone,
that My wrath may blaze against them and I may consume them, and I will make
of you a great nation* (Exodus 32:10),[421] Moses immediately said, 'Should I

396

---

415. **judgment could not overpower him
because he was hidden away...** See BT
Bava Qamma 60a–b: "Rabbi Yosef taught:
'What is the meaning of the verse *None of
you shall go out the door of his house until
morning* (Exodus 12:22)? Once permission
has been granted to the Destroyer, he does
not distinguish between righteous and wicked.'...Our Rabbis taught: 'A plague in
town? Keep your feet indoors.'...Our Rabbis taught: 'A plague in town? One should
not walk in the middle of the road, because
the Angel of Death walks there—for as soon
as permission has been granted him, he
strides brazenly.'"

See *Mekhilta, Pisḥa* 11; *Zohar* 1:63a, 68a–b,
69a, 107b, 113a, 182b, 197b; 2:196a, 227a.

416. **Noah sought righteousness and entered Her** *Shekhinah* is known as Righteousness, partner of *Yesod* (Righteous One)
and of righteous humans such as Noah.

417. **holy ones of the Most High** In
Daniel 7:18, the phrase refers to Israel; here,
to the kabbalists. See *Zohar* 1:77a, 95b.

418. **mystery of supernal letters—reversal of letters, twenty-two...** According to

Sefer Yetsirah 2:2, God created the world by
permutating the twenty-two letters of the
Hebrew alphabet: "Twenty-two elemental
letters. He engraved them, carved them,
weighed them, permuted them, and transposed them, forming with them everything
formed and everything destined to be
formed." See BT *Berakhot* 55a; BT *Sanhedrin*
65b; *Zohar* 1:33b. Numerous two-letter combinations bring about creation, while the
reversal of letters leads to obliteration. See
Sefer ha-Peli'ah, 51d. The citation from Genesis 7:1 opens with the word בא (*bo*), *come,*
a reversal of the first two letters of the alphabet.

419. **Come... into the ark!** The verse
reads: "*Come, you and all your household,
into the ark!*"

420. **Come and see the difference...**
Moses is contrasted with Noah and others
in *Vayiqra Rabbah* 1:14; *Devarim Rabbah*
11:3; *Zohar* 1:106a; 3:14b–15a; *ZḤ* 23a (*MhN*).

421. **When the blessed Holy One said to
Moses...** When Israel sinned by worship-
ing the Golden Calf. See BT *Berakhot* 32a;
Shemot Rabbah 42:9.

abandon Israel's cause simply for my own advantage? Now all inhabitants of the world will claim that I killed Israel, as Noah did.'

"For when the blessed Holy One told him to save himself in the ark, as is written: *As for Me, I am about to bring the Flood, waters upon the earth.... And I will obliterate all existing things that I have made.... But with you I will establish My covenant, and you will enter the ark* (Genesis 6:17–18; 7:4)—when He told him that he and his sons would be saved, he did not plead for compassion for the world and it perished. Because of this the waters of the Flood are named after him, as is said: *For this is like the waters of Noah to Me: As I swore that the waters of Noah would never again cover* [*the earth*] (Isaiah 54:9).[422]

"Moses said, 'Now the inhabitants of the world will claim that I killed them because He told me, *I will make of you a great nation.* Better, then, that I die and Israel not be destroyed. Immediately, *Moses sweetened the face of YHVH his God* (Exodus 32:11)—pleading for compassion for them, arousing compassion for the world."

Rabbi Yitshak said further, "How did he begin pleading for compassion? *Why, YHVH, should Your wrath blaze against Your people?* (ibid.). How could Moses speak this word: *Why?* They had worshiped strange gods, as is said: *They have made themselves a molten calf, bowed to it, and sacrificed to it* (ibid., 8)—and Moses said *Why?!* But so we have learned: One who appeases another[423] should not magnify the wrong, but rather minimize it before him. Afterward he should maximize it before the other,[424] as is written: *You have sinned a great sin!* (ibid., 30).[425]

"He did not leave the blessed Holy One alone until offering to die, as is written: *Now, if You would only bear their sin! If not, please obliterate me from Your book!* (ibid., 32).[426] Then the blessed Holy One forgave them, as is written: *YHVH renounced the evil* (ibid., 14).[427] But Noah did not act so: he just wanted to save himself, abandoning the entire world.

"Whenever judgment looms over the world, Holy Spirit exclaims, 'Alas, there is no one like Moses to be found! *Where is he who brought them up from the sea?* (Isaiah 63:11).'[428] As is written: *YHVH said to Moses, 'Why are you*

397

---

422. **waters of the Flood are named after him** ... See *Zohar* 3:15a.

423. **One who appeases another** On behalf of someone else who had harmed him.

424. **the other** The one responsible for the wrong.

425. *You have sinned a great sin!* After Moses convinces God not to annihilate Israel, he descends from the mountain and the next day accuses the people in these words.

426. **He did not leave ... until offering to die** ... See BT *Berakhot* 32a: "Shemu'el said, '...He offered to die for them, as is written: *If not, please obliterate me from Your book!*'"

427. *YHVH renounced the evil* The verse continues: *that He had intended to bring upon His people.*

428. *Where is he who brought them up from the sea?* In Isaiah the subject *he* refers to God, but here Rabbi Yitshak understands it as referring to Moses.

crying out to Me?' (Exodus 14:15), which shows that by prayer he raised them from the sea.[429]

"Where is he who placed within them his holy spirit (Isaiah, ibid.)—this is Moses, who ensconced [68a] *Shekhinah* among Israel.[430]

"Who led them through the depths (ibid., 13), when the waters were split, and they walked through the depths on dry land, the water having congealed. All this is ascribed to Moses because he risked his life for Israel."

Rabbi Yehudah said, "Although Noah was virtuous, he was not worthy enough for the blessed Holy One to protect the world for his sake.[431] Come and see: Moses did not depend on his own merit, but rather on the merit of the ancient patriarchs.[432] Noah, however, had no one upon whose merit he could depend."

Rabbi Yitsḥak said, "Even so, once the blessed Holy One said to him, *I will erect My covenant with you* (Genesis 6:18), he should have pleaded for compassion; and the sacrifice he offered afterward[433] he should have offered before, so that the wrath threatening the world would abate."

Rabbi Yehudah said, "The wicked of the world were provoking Him, and he should offer a sacrifice? He must have feared for his life, lest death befall him among the wicked of the world, whose deeds he witnessed every day, their provocation of the blessed Holy One."

Rabbi El'azar said, "Whenever wicked of the world abound, a righteous one found among them is seized first,[434] as is written: *Begin* ממקדשי (*mi-miqdashi*), *at My sanctuary* (Ezekiel 9:6). Do not read ממקדשי (*mi-miqdashi*), *at My sanctuary,* but rather ממקודשי (*mi-mequddashai*), *with My saintly ones.*[435] So here, how was he saved by the blessed Holy One among all those wicked? It was in

429. *Why are you crying out to Me?...* The verse continues: *Tell the Children of Israel to go forward!*

430. **this is Moses...** The subject *he* refers to Moses, who caused *Shekhinah*, Holy Spirit, to dwell among Israel.

431. **not worthy enough...** See *Devarim Rabbah* 11:3; above, page 395.

432. **Moses did not depend on his own merit...** See BT *Berakhot* 10b: "Rabbi Yoḥanan said in the name of Rabbi Yose son of Zimra, '...Whoever depends on the merit of others, is made dependent on his own merit. Moses depended on the merit of others, as is said: *Remember Abraham, Isaac, and Israel, Your servants!* (Exodus 32:13), and he was made dependent on his own merit,

as is said: *He threatened to destroy them, had not Moses His chosen confronted Him in the breach to turn away His wrath from destroying* (Psalms 106:23).

433. **afterward** After the Flood. See Genesis 8:20–22.

434. **a righteous one found among them is seized first** See above, p. 395 and n. 414.

435. **Do not read** ממקדשי (*mi-miqdashi*), *at My sanctuary...* See BT *Avodah Zarah* 4a, in the name of Rabbi Yose. The Talmud goes on to explain: "Since it was in their power to protest [the wickedness being perpetrated] and they did not protest, they are considered incompletely righteous." Cf. *Bava Qamma* 60a; *Zohar* 1:205b.

order for the blessed Holy One to engender generations through him for the world, since he was fittingly righteous.

"Furthermore, he warned them every single day, but they disregarded him.[436] So he himself fulfilled the verse that is written: *Yet if you warn the wicked... you will have saved your life* (ibid. 3:19).[437] From here we learn that whoever warns a sinner—even though his warning is rejected—saves himself, while that sinner is snared in his sin. For how long? This has been established by the Companions."[438]

Rabbi Yose frequented the presence of Rabbi Shim'on. One day he asked him, "Why did the blessed Holy One see fit to annihilate all the beasts of the field and the birds of heaven along with the wicked? If humans sinned, how did animals, birds, and other creatures?"

He replied, "Because it is written: *For all flesh had corrupted their way upon earth* (Genesis 6:12). All of them ruined their ways, abandoning their species, cleaving to another species.[439]

"Come and see: The wicked of the world brought this upon all creatures, seeking to contravene the act of Creation,[440] causing all creatures to ruin their

399

436. **he warned them every single day...** According to a rabbinic tradition, Noah attempted to warn his contemporaries and induce them to turn back to God, but he was unsuccessful. See *Bereshit Rabbah* 30:7; *Tanḥuma, Noaḥ* 5; BT *Sanhedrin* 108a–b; above, page 362.

437. *Yet if you warn the wicked...* The verse continues: *and he does not turn from his wickedness or from his wicked way, he shall die for his iniquity, but you will have saved your life.*

438. **For how long? This has been established...** How long should one keep warning the sinner? Until the sinner strikes the warner. See BT *Arakhin* 16b: "How long reproof? Rav said, 'Until striking.'" Cf. Maimonides, *Mishneh Torah, Hilkhot De'ot* 6:7.

439. **ruined their ways, abandoning their species, cleaving to another species** See *Tanḥuma* (Buber), *Noaḥ* 18: "Why were the animals annihilated, too?...Because even the animals acted corruptly and copulated with species not their own: the horse with the donkey, the lion with the ox, the serpent

with the lizard, as is said: *God saw the earth, and behold, it was corrupt [for all flesh had corrupted their way upon earth]*. It does not say: *all humans*, but rather: *all flesh*, even animals, beasts, and birds. Therefore they were obliterated as well."

See BT *Sanhedrin* 108a: "*For all flesh had corrupted their way upon earth.* Rabbi Yoḥanan said, 'This teaches that they mated beasts with animals, animals with beasts—all of them with humans, and humans with all of them.'"

Rabbi Shim'on understands the biblical expression השחית דרכו (*hishḥit darko*), *corrupted their way*, as an allusion to sexual sin. See *Kallah Rabbati* 2, citing Genesis 38:9: שחת ארצה [*shiḥet artsah*], he [Onan] *wasted* [his seed] *on the ground* (or: *let it go to ruin*). Cf. *Pirqei de-Rabbi Eli'ezer* 22; *Bereshit Rabbah* 26:4, 31:7; Rashi on BT *Shabbat* 41a, s.v. *ke-illu mevi mabbul la-olam; Zohar* 1:56b–57a, 62a, 69a.

440. **seeking to contravene the act of Creation** By intermingling species that had been created distinctly.

ways, as they did themselves.[441] The blessed Holy One said, 'Do you seek to deny the work of My hands? I will fulfill your desire: *I will obliterate all existing things that I have made* (ibid. 7:4). I will return the world to water, as it originally was—water intermingled with water, as has been said.[442] From now on, I will form other, more fitting creatures in the world.'"

Noah entered, with his sons, his wife, and his sons' wives, [into the ark] (Genesis 7:7).

Rabbi Ḥiyya opened, "'*If a man hides in secret places, do I not see him?' says YHVH* (Jeremiah 23:24). How obtuse are human beings, totally unaware of the glory of their Lord, of whom is written: *Do I not fill heaven and earth?* (ibid.). How can humans seek to hide from their sins, saying: *Who sees us? Who knows us?* (Isaiah 29:15). It is written: *Their deeds are in darkness* (ibid.), but where can they hide from His presence?

"This may be compared to a king who built a palace, constructing secret subterranean tunnels.[443] Subsequently the courtiers rebelled against the king. He stormed[444] them with his troops. What did they do? They hid themselves within the recesses of those tunnels. The king said, 'I constructed them, and you want to hide from me?' As is written: '*If a man hides in secret places, do I not see him?' says YHVH*. 'It is I who made those hollow tunnels, who fashioned darkness and light—and you can hide from Me?'[445]

"Come and see: When a person sins in the presence of his Lord and obscures himself, concealing himself, the blessed Holy One executes judgment upon him openly.[446] But when a person purifies himself, the blessed Holy One wants to

441. **to ruin their ways, as they did themselves** See *Tanḥuma* (Buber), *Noaḥ* 5: "Rabbi Aḥa son of Ze'eira said, '...Just as a man copulated with a woman who was not his, so an animal copulated with another species not his own.'"

442. **I will return the world to water, as it originally was...** See *Tanḥuma, Vayaqhel* 6: "When the blessed Holy One created His world, it was entirely water intermingled with water." Cf. JT *Ḥagigah* 2:1, 77a; *Pesiqta Rabbati* 1; *Shemot Rabbah* 50:1; *Zohar* 1:17b, 56b.

443. **tunnels** פציירין (*Petsirin*), apparently based on פצידא (*patsida*), "trench, ditch." See *Targum Yonatan* and Radak on 2 Kings 3:16.

444. **stormed** אסער (*As'ar*). Certain witnesses (*KP* and *DE* [emendations]) preserve an alternative reading: אסחר (*ashar*), "surrounded," besieged.

445. **This may be compared to a king...** See *Bereshit Rabbah* 24:1: "It is written: *Woe to those who go to great depths to hide their plan from YHVH, who perpetrate their deeds in darkness and say, 'Who sees us? Who knows us?'* (Isaiah 29:15). Rabbi Levi said, 'This may be compared to a master builder who constructed a city with chambers, underground conduits, and caves. Subsequently he became a tax-collector, and the inhabitants of the city hid from him in those chambers and caves. He said to them, "It is I who built all these chambers and caves. Why are you hiding?" Similarly, *Woe to those who go to great depths,...who perpetrate their deeds in darkness!*'"

446. **When a person sins...** See M *Avot* 4:4: "Rabbi Yoḥanan son of Beroka says, 'Whoever profanes the name of Heaven secretly is punished openly.'"

400

hide him so that he will be invisible on the day of the wrath of *YHVH*. For one should certainly [68b] not be visible to the Destroyer looming over the world, lest he gaze at him, since he is authorized to destroy all those visible to him.⁴⁴⁷

"This accords with the remark of Rabbi Shim'on: Whoever possesses an evil eye⁴⁴⁸ comes under the spell of the Destroyer's eye and is called Destroyer of the world. One must be on guard against him, not come near him, so as not to be injured by him; it is forbidden to approach him in the open. So what is written of Balaam? *Oracle of the man whose eye is open* (Numbers 24:3),⁴⁴⁹ for he possessed an evil eye and everywhere he gazed he channeled the spirit of the Destroyer.⁴⁵⁰ So he sought to gaze upon Israel in order to destroy wherever his eye gazed. What is written? *Balaam lifted up his eyes* (ibid., 2),⁴⁵¹ raising one eye and lowering one eye,⁴⁵² to gaze upon Israel with an evil eye.

"Come and see what is written: *He saw Israel* שוכן (*shokhen*), *encamped, tribe by tribe* (ibid.)—he saw *Shekhinah* sheltering them, brooding them, adorned by twelve tribes beneath Her,⁴⁵³ and his eye could not overpower them. He said, 'How can I prevail against them? For look, supernal Holy Spirit broods them, sheltering them with Her wings!' As is written: *He crouches, lies down like a lion, like a lioness—who can rouse him?* (ibid., 9).⁴⁵⁴ Who can raise Him from them, so that they will be exposed and the eye will overpower them?

"Therefore the blessed Holy One sought to shield Noah—to hide him from the eye, so that the impure spirit would not overpower him, destroying him, as has already been said."

401

447. **lest he gaze at him...** See *Devarim Rabbah* 4:4; *Zohar* 1:63a, 108b.

448. **Whoever possesses an evil eye** In biblical Hebrew this idiom means "one who is stingy" (Proverbs 23:6; Deuteronomy 15:9). Later, the envious evil eye was thought to exert harmful influence. See *Zohar* 3:63b.

449. *whose eye is open* שתום העין (*Shetum ha-ayin*), a phrase whose meaning is unclear. Elsewhere the *Zohar* interprets שתום (*shetum*) as equivalent to סתום (*setum*), "closed" (see 2:69a, 237a; 3:147b), but here the sense is "open." See BT *Sanhedrin* 105a: "Rabbi Yoḥanan said, 'Balaam was blind in one eye, as is said: *shetum ha-ayin, whose eye is open* [i.e., only one of his eyes was open and capable of vision].'"

450. **he possessed an evil eye...** See M *Avot* 5:19; *Tanḥuma, Balaq* 6; *Zohar* 3:63b, 206b, 211b.

451. *Balaam lifted up his eyes* The verse continues: *and saw Israel encamped tribe by tribe.*

452. **raising one eye and lowering one eye** The verse reads עיניו (*einav*), *his eyes*, but elsewhere the *Zohar* insists on the reading עינו (*eino*), *his eye*. See 3:202b; *Minḥat Shai* on Numbers 24:2.

453. *He saw Israel...encamped, tribe by tribe—he saw Shekhinah...* See BT *Bava Batra* 60a: "Rabbi Yoḥanan said, '...Scripture reads: *Balaam lifted up his eyes and saw Israel encamped tribe by tribe.* What did he see? He saw that the openings of their tents did not face one another, so he exclaimed: "These are worthy of having *Shekhinah* rest upon them!"'"

454. *He crouches, lies down like a lion, like a lioness...* The verse, sung by Balaam, refers to Israel, but Rabbi Ḥiyya applies it to *Shekhinah.*

Noah entered (Genesis 7:7), as has been said, to hide himself from the eye. *Because of the waters of the Flood* (ibid.), for the waters forced him.[455]

Rabbi Yose said, "He saw the Angel of Death coming, so he entered the ark and hid himself there for twelve months. Why twelve months? Because that is the punishment of the wicked."[456]

Rabbi Yehudah said, "For six months they are suspended in water, and for six in fire, but here there was only water, so why twelve months?"[457]

Rabbi Yose replied, "They were inflicted with both punishments of Hell: with water and fire. With water—water from above; with fire—water gushing from below, boiling hot as fire.[458] So they were inflicted with the punishment of Hell—with fire and water—for twelve months, as Rabbi El'azar said, 'The punishment of the wicked in Hell lasts for twelve months,' as has been established. So all those wicked of the world were inflicted with both these punishments, water and fire, until they were exterminated from the world.

"Meanwhile, Noah hid himself in the ark, concealing himself from the eye, so the Destroyer could not come near him; and it floated on the face of the waters, as is said: [*The waters increased*] *and lifted the ark, and it rose above the earth* (ibid. 7:17). For forty days they were lashed, as is written: *The Flood continued forty days upon the earth* (ibid.), and for the rest of the time[459] they were obliterated from the world, as is written: *They were obliterated from the earth* (ibid., 23). Woe to those wicked ones, for they will not rise from the dead to stand at Judgment, as is written: *They were obliterated*, and similarly: *You have obliterated their name forever and ever* (Psalms 9:6), for they will not rise even to stand at Judgment."[460]

402

---

455. *Because of the waters of the Flood, for the waters forced him* See *Bereshit Rabbah* 32:6: "*Noah entered, with his sons, [his wife, and his sons' wives, into the ark because of the waters of the Flood]*. Rabbi Yoḥanan said, 'He was lacking in faith: if the waters had not reached his ankles, he would not have entered the ark.'"

456. *twelve months...the punishment of the wicked* The Flood lasted a full year. See Genesis 7:11; 8:14; and M *Eduyyot* 2:10: "[Rabbi Akiva] said, 'The judgment of the generation of the Flood lasted twelve months....The judgment of the wicked in Hell lasts twelve months.'" Cf. *Bereshit Rabbah* 33:7; *Seder Olam Rabbah* 4; *Zohar* 1:107b.

457. *For six months they are suspended in water, and for six in fire...* According to rabbinic literature, the yearlong punishment of the sinners in Hell is equally divided between fire and snow. See JT *Sanhedrin* 10:3, 29b; *Pesiqta de-Rav Kahana* 10:4; *Zohar* 1:62b, 107b, 238b. Since the Flood consisted only of water, Rabbi Yehudah wonders why it lasted twelve months and not just six.

458. *With water—water from above; with fire...gushing from below* The Flood consisted of freezing water raining down from the sky and boiling water surging up from the depths. See *Tanḥuma* (Buber), *Bereshit* 33; *Pirqei de-Rabbi Eli'ezer* 22; above, pages 356–57.

459. *for the rest of the time* For the rest of the year.

460. *they will not rise from the dead to stand at Judgment...* See M *Sanhedrin*

They lifted the ark, and it rose above the earth (Genesis 7:17).[461]

Rabbi Abba opened, "*Rise, O God, above the heavens! Let Your glory be above all the earth!* (Psalms 57:6).[462] Woe to the wicked who sin and provoke their Lord every day, who through their sins repel *Shekhinah* from earth, making Her disappear from the world.[463]

"Come and see what is written: *They lifted the ark,* for they thrust Her out.[464] *And she rose above the earth,* for She no longer abides on earth but ascends. When She withdraws from the world, there is no one to watch over the world, and Judgment dominates it.[465] Then the wicked of the world are removed, obliterated, and *Shekhinah* restores Her abode to the world."

Rabbi Yeisa asked him, "If so, then what about the land of Israel? The wicked living at that time[466] were obliterated, so why didn't *Shekhinah* return to Her site, as before?"

He replied, "Because the remnant of the righteous of the world did not remain there.[467] But wherever they went She descended, placing [69a] Her abode among them.[468] If She did not part from them in another, foreign land, all the more so if they had remained in the Holy Land.

"As has been said, by all sins of sinners of the world, *Shekhinah* is repelled. One of them is wasting one's way on earth, as we have explained,[469] because

403

10:3: "The generation of the Flood has no share in the world to come, nor will they stand at the [Last] Judgment."

461. **They lifted the ark...** The verse opens: *The waters increased and they lifted the ark.*

462. **Rise, O God...** Usually rendered *Be exalted, O God...,* but here the verse is interpreted in a radically different way.

463. **who through their sins repel Shekhinah from earth...** See BT *Ḥagigah* 16a: "Rabbi Yitsḥak said, 'Whoever sins secretly, it is as if he thrusts away the feet of *Shekhinah*.'" Cf. *Zohar* 1:57a–b, 61a, 69a.

464. **They lifted the ark, for they thrust Her out** For Rabbi Abba, the subject of the verse is no longer *the waters*, but rather, the wicked, who repel *Shekhinah*, symbolized by the ark.

465. **When She withdraws...Judgment dominates it** Without the protection of *Shekhinah*, the world becomes vulnerable to harsh judgment.

466. **at that time** At the time of the destruction of the Temple, the site of *Shekhinah*.

467. **remnant of the righteous of the world did not remain there** All of Israel, including the righteous, were exiled from the land.

468. **wherever they went She descended...** See BT *Megillah* 29a: "Rabbi Shim'on son of Yoḥai says, 'Come and see how beloved are Israel in the sight of the blessed Holy One! Wherever they went in exile, *Shekhinah* accompanied them. When they were exiled to Egypt, *Shekhinah* was with them. ...When they were exiled to Babylon, *Shekhinah* was with them....And even when they are destined to be redeemed, *Shekhinah* will be with them.'" See *Mekhilta, Pisḥa* 14.

469. **wasting one's way on earth...** The biblical expression השחית דרכו (*hishḥit darko*), *corrupted their way,* is interpreted as an allusion to masturbation. See *Kallah Rabbati* 2, citing Genesis 38:9: שחת ארצה

of which one does not see the face of *Shekhinah* nor enter the palace.[470] So of these is written: *They were obliterated from the earth* (Genesis 7:23), obliterated entirely.

"Come and see: When the time comes for the blessed Holy One to revive the dead, He will create suitable bodies for all those located outside in other, foreign lands.[471] For a single bone surviving in a human being underground will become like leaven in dough, upon which the blessed Holy One will build an entire body.[472] But He will provide them with souls only in the land of Israel, as is written: *when I open your graves and raise you from your graves, O My people, and bring you to your land* (Ezekiel 37:12–13),[473] for they will roll underground.[474] What is written next? *I will put My spirit within you and you shall live* (ibid., 14). Look, only in the land of Israel will all inhabitants of the world receive souls, excluding those who defiled themselves and defiled the earth, of whom is written: *They were obliterated from the earth—from the earth*, precisely,[475]

404

[*shiḥet artsah*], he [Onan] *wasted* [his seed] *on the ground.* Cf. *Pirqei de-Rabbi Eli'ezer* 22; *Bereshit Rabbah* 26:4, 31:7; Rashi on BT *Shabbat* 41a, s.v. *ke-illu mevi mabbul la-olam; Zohar* 1:56b–57a, 62a.

In the world of the *Zohar*, masturbation is a heinous sin. See 1:188a, 219b; Moses de León, *Shushan Edut,* 353; Tishby, *Wisdom of the Zohar,* 3:1365–66. Cf. BT *Niddah* 13a: "Rabbi Yitsḥak and Rabbi Ammi said, '[Whoever emits semen fruitlessly] is as though he sheds blood.'"

470. **one does not see the face of *Shekhinah* nor enter the palace** Sexual purity is a prerequisite for encountering *Shekhinah*. See BT *Niddah* 13b: "Rabbi Ammi said, 'Whoever excites himself lustfully is not allowed to enter the domain of the blessed Holy One.'" Cf. *Zohar* 1:57a; Moses de León, *Mishkan ha-Edut,* 23b.

471. **all those located outside in other, foreign lands** All those buried outside the land of Israel.

472. **single bone surviving... like leaven in dough...** According to Rabbi Yehoshu'a son of Ḥananya (*Vayiqra Rabbah* 18:1; *Bereshit Rabbah* 28:3), God will resurrect humans from the vertebra at the base of the spinal column, which does not decompose in the grave. Here Rabbi Abba combines this motif with the tradition in *Pirqei de-*

Rabbi Eli'ezer 34: "Rabbi Shim'on says, 'All bodies crumble into the dust of the earth until nothing remains except a spoonful of decayed matter. This mingles with the dust like leaven mixed with dough. In the time to come... it resurrects the entire body.'" See *Zohar* 1:137a (*MhN*); 2:28b; 3:222a, 270b.

473. ***when I open your graves...*** The citation is actually a conflation of verses 12–14.

474. **roll underground** The resurrected bodies will roll underground until they reach the land of Israel. See BT *Ketubbot* 111a: "Rabbi Yirmeyah son of Abba said in the name of Rabbi Yoḥanan, 'Whoever walks four cubits in the land of Israel is assured membership in the world to come.' Now,... aren't the righteous outside the Land going to be revived? Rabbi Il'a replied, 'By rolling [underground to the land of Israel].' Rabbi Abba Sala the Great objected, 'Rolling will be painful to the righteous!' Abbaye replied, 'Tunnels will be made for them underground.'"

See *Zohar* 1:113b–114b (*MhN*), 131a.

475. ***from the earth*, precisely** Even their one surviving vertebra decomposed in the earth. See *Bereshit Rabbah* 28:3. Alternatively, *the earth* (or: *the land*) refers to the land of Israel, which these wicked will never reach.

although the ancients disputed this and differed.[476] *They were obliterated,* as is said: *May they be obliterated from the Book of Life* (Psalms 69:29)."[477]

Rabbi Shim'on said to him, "They certainly have no share in the world to come, as is written: *They were obliterated from the earth,* and conversely: *They will inherit the earth forever* (Isaiah 60:21).[478] However, they will rise for Judgment, and of them is written: *Many of those who sleep in the dust of earth will awake, some to everlasting life, some to shame and everlasting contempt* (Daniel 12:2)."

He obliterated את כל (*et kol*), *all, existing things over the face of the earth* (Genesis 7:23).

Rabbi Abba said, "Encompassing all those empowered rulers, appointed over earth.[479] This is *existing things over the face of the earth.*[480] For when the blessed Holy One executes judgment upon the world, He first removes those rulers appointed over them, and afterward those abiding beneath their wings, as is written: *YHVH will punish the host of the high heavens on high,* and afterward: *the kings of the earth upon the earth* (Isaiah 24:21).[481] How are they removed from His presence? He removes them with blazing fire, as is written: *For YHVH your God is a consuming fire—a fire con-*

405

476. **although the ancients disputed this and differed** According to M *Sanhedrin* 10:3, "The generation of the Flood has no share in the world to come, nor will they stand at the [Last] Judgment." In *Avot de-Rabbi Natan* A, 32, opinions differ as to whether or not this generation will be judged in the hereafter. See *Tosefta, Sanhedrin* 13:6; BT *Sanhedrin* 108a; *Zohar* 1:68b, 108a; Ginzberg, *Legends,* 5:184, n. 44.

477. ***May they be obliterated from the Book of Life*** They will never be resurrected.

478. ***They will inherit the earth forever*** This verse, appearing frequently in the *Zohar,* reads in full: *Your people, all of them righteous, will inherit the land forever—sprout of My planting, work of My hands, that I may be glorified.* In M *Sanhedrin* 10:1, it is cited to demonstrate that "all of Israel have a share in the world to come." Conversely, according to Rabbi Shim'on, the verse in Genesis indicates that the generation of the Flood has no share in that world.

479. **Encompassing all those empowered rulers...** Rabbi Abba focuses on the word

את (*et*), an accusative particle. Though grammatically it has no ascertainable independent sense, Naḥum of Gimzo and his disciple Rabbi Akiva taught that when *et* appears in a biblical verse, it amplifies the original meaning. See BT *Pesaḥim* 22b; *Ḥagigah* 12a; *Zohar* 1:247a; 2:90a, 135b.

Here the word is understood to imply the heavenly powers appointed over individual nations of the world. See Daniel 10:20; Septuagint, Deuteronomy 32:8–9; Jubilees 15:31–32; *Targum Yerushalmi,* Genesis 11:8, Deuteronomy 32:8–9; *Tanḥuma, Re'eh* 8; *Leqaḥ Tov,* Genesis 9:19; *Pirqei de-Rabbi Eli'ezer* 24; *Zohar* 1:46b, 108b; 3:298b; Ginzberg, *Legends,* 5:204–5, n. 91.

480. **This is *existing things over the face of the earth*** The biblical word יקום (*yequm*), *existing things,* is interpreted to mean the powers who "exist" (קיימים [*qayyamim*]) or "stand" (קמים [*qamim*]) in heaven *over* [i.e., above] *the face of the earth.*

481. **He first removes those rulers appointed over them...** See *Shemot Rabbah* 21:5: "Rabbi El'azar son of Pedat said, '...The blessed Holy One does not cast

suming fire.[482] Those *existing* above them[483]—with fire; those dwelling beneath them[484]—with water. So, *He obliterated all existing things over the face of the earth,*[485] and afterward: *both humans and animals, crawling things and birds of the sky; they were obliterated from the earth* (Genesis, ibid.)—all those below.

"אך (*Akh*), *Only, Noah remained* (ibid.)[486]—limiting,[487] for nothing was left in the world except for Noah and those with him in the ark."

Rabbi Yose said, "He was lame, for a lion bit him, as they have established."[488]

God remembered Noah and all the beasts and all the cattle that were with him in the ark (ibid. 8:1).

Rabbi Ḥiyya opened, "*A prudent person sees evil and hides* (Proverbs 22:3). This verse was spoken for Noah, who entered the ark, hiding himself inside, entering the ark when the waters forced him.[489] As has been said, before entering the ark he saw the Angel of Death walking among them, encircling them.[490] As soon as he saw him, he entered, hiding himself within, as is written: *A prudent person sees evil and hides. Evil*—the Angel of Death. *And hides* from his presence, as is written: *because of the waters of the Flood* (Genesis 7:7)."[491]

down a nation before He first casts down their prince [guardian angel].'" Cf. *Midrash Tehillim* 82:3; *Zohar* 2:6b, 49a.

482. **fire consuming fire** A divine fire consuming the guardian angels, who are themselves composed of fire. In BT *Yoma* 21b, *Shekhinah* is called "a fire consuming fire" because of God's burning the angels who opposed human creation (as related in *Sanhedrin* 38b). See Psalms 104:4; BT *Ḥagigah* 14a; *Zohar* 1:18b, 50b; 2:6b; 3:217a.

483. **Those *existing* above them** The guardian angels.

484. **those dwelling beneath them** The wicked generation of the Flood.

485. **all existing things over the face of the earth** The guardian angels.

486. אך (*Akh*), *Only, Noah remained* The verse continues: *and those with him in the ark.*

487. **limiting** Naḥum of Gimzo and his disciple Rabbi Akiva taught that when the word אך (*akh*), *only*, appears in a biblical verse, it limits or qualifies the original meaning. See JT *Berakhot* 9, 14b. Here Rabbi Ab-

ba does not note any limitation but rather an emphasis.

488. **He was lame, for a lion bit him...** Rabbi Yose insists that the word *akh* implies a limitation. See *Tanḥuma, Noaḥ* 9: "Rabbi Yoḥanan said in the name of Rabbi Eli'ezer son of Rabbi Yose the Galilean, 'Once Noah delayed feeding the lion, so the lion bit him, and he came out [of the ark] limping, as is said: אך (*Akh*), *Only, Noah remained*—*akh,* for he was not intact.'"

489. **entering the ark when the waters forced him** See *Bereshit Rabbah* 32:6: "*Noah entered, with his sons,* [*his wife, and his sons' wives, into the ark because of the waters of the Flood*]. Rabbi Yoḥanan said, 'He was lacking in faith: if the waters had not reached his ankles, he would not have entered the ark.'" See above, page 402.

490. **he saw the Angel of Death walking among them...** Among his contemporaries. The Angel of Death manifested in the waters of the Flood. See above, pages 382, 402.

491. *because of the waters of the Flood* The full verse reads: *Noah entered, with his*

Rabbi Yose said, "*A prudent person sees evil* ונסתר (ve-nistar), *and is hidden*. It is written: ויסתר (va-yissater), *and hides himself*,[492] referring back to what has been said: When death looms over the world, a wise person hides himself, not standing outside, not making himself visible to the Destroyer, who, having been empowered, will destroy anyone found in his presence, anyone passing before him openly.[493] The verse concludes: *But the simple pass and are punished* (Proverbs, ibid.)—they pass before him, are seen by him, *and are punished*.

"Alternatively, [*they*] *pass*—they transgressed this command and were punished.[494]

"Alternatively, *A prudent person sees evil and hides*—this is Noah. *But the simple pass and are punished*—these are his contemporaries.

"When he had hidden himself and stayed there all that time, [69b] finally, *God remembered Noah*."

Rabbi Shim'on said, "*God remembered Noah*. Come and see: When judgment is being executed, זכירה (zekhirah), remembering, is not recorded. Once judgment has been executed and the wicked of the world have been removed, then remembering is recorded. For when judgment looms over the world, unification vanishes and the Destroyer prevails.[495] Once judgment has been executed and wrath subsides, all returns to its site.[496] So here is written: *God remembered Noah*, for זכור (zakhor), remember, inheres in him, as is written: *Noah was a righteous man* (Genesis 6:9).[497]

407

---

sons, his wife, and his sons' wives, into the ark because of the waters of the Flood.

492. **It is written:** ויסתר (**va-yissater**), *and hides himself* The word in this verse is traditionally written as ויסתר (va-yissater), *and hides himself*, although it is read as ונסתר (ve-nistar), which can be rendered *and is hidden*.

493. **referring back to what has been said: When death...** See BT *Bava Qamma* 60a–b: "Rabbi Yosef taught: 'What is the meaning of the verse *None of you shall go out the door of his house until morning* (Exodus 12:22)? Once permission has been granted to the Destroyer, he does not distinguish between righteous and wicked.'... Our Rabbis taught: 'A plague in town? Keep your feet indoors.'... Our Rabbis taught: 'A plague in town? One should not walk in the middle of the road, because the Angel of Death walks there—for as soon as permission has been granted him, he strides brazenly.'"

See *Mekhilta, Pisḥa* 11; *Zohar* 1:63a, 68a–b, 107b, 113a, 182b, 197b; 2:196a, 227a.

494. [*they*] *pass*—they transgressed... The verb עבר (avar) means both "to pass" and "to transgress." By not hiding themselves, Noah's contemporaries transgressed a command.

495. זכירה (*zekhirah*), **remembering, is not recorded...unification vanishes...** During harsh judgment, the unification of the divine masculine and feminine is interrupted, so there is no mention of זכירה (zekhirah), "remembering," alluding to זכר (zakhar), "male." The absence of divine masculine mindfulness creates a vacuum filled by the demonic.

496. **all returns to its site** The divine male and female reunite.

497. זכור (*zakhor*), **remember, inheres in him...** Again, a play on the root זכר (zkhr), which encompasses two meanings:

"It is written: *You rule the raging of the sea. When its waves surge, You still them* (Psalms 89:10). When the sea leaps with its rollers, abysses billowing and plunging,[498] the blessed Holy One transmits a single ray, pulling its waves, assuaging its rage, unknown to anyone.[499]

"Jonah descended into the sea and encountered that destined fish,[500] who swallowed him. Why did his soul not depart and immediately fly away? Because the blessed Holy One *rules the raging of the sea,* and that raging is a single ray swelling the sea, by which it swells. Were it not for the ray reaching it from the right side,[501] it would never swell, for as soon as the ray descends to the sea, grasping it, rollers arouse, roaring to tear prey, until the blessed Holy One turns them back and they return to their place, as is written: *When its waves surge,* תשבחם (*Teshabbeḥem*), *You still them—You still* those waves of the sea. *You still them*—breaking them, restoring them to their place.

"Alternatively, תשבחם (*Teshabbeḥem*), *You praise them,* literally![502] It is their praise, since they ascend in desire to see. From here we learn that whoever yearns to gaze and know, even if incapable, is to be praised. All praise him!"

Rabbi Yehudah said, "When Noah was in the ark, he feared that the blessed Holy One would never remember him. Once judgment had been executed and the wicked of the world removed, what is written? *God remembered Noah.*"

Rabbi El'azar said, "Come and see: When judgment looms over the world, one's name should not be mentioned on high, for if it is, his sins will be mentioned and he will be scrutinized. How do we know? From the Shunammite,[503] for that day was the festival of Rosh Hashanah, when the blessed Holy One judges the world.[504] Then Elisha asked her, *Can we speak on your behalf to the*

408

"remember" and "male." Noah the righteous is appropriately remembered, since he symbolizes the divine male, *Yesod* ("Foundation"), also known as Righteous One, based on Proverbs 10:25: וצדיק יסוד עולם (*Ve-tsaddiq yesod olam*). The verse, which literally means *The righteous one is an everlasting foundation,* is understood as *The righteous one is the foundation of the world.*

See BT *Ḥagigah* 12b; *Bahir* 71 (102); Azriel of Gerona, *Peirush ha-Aggadot,* 34.

498. **When the sea leaps...** See *Zohar* 2:48b, 50b, 56a. The sea often symbolizes *Shekhinah.*

499. **single ray...** A ray of divine grace.

500. **that destined fish** See *Tanḥuma, Vayiqra* 8: "Rabbi Tarfon said, 'Ever since the six days of Creation, that fish was designated to swallow up Jonah, as is said: YHVH

had prepared a huge fish [*to swallow up Jonah*] (Jonah 2:1).'" Cf. *Pirqei de-Rabbi Eli'ezer* 10; *Bereshit Rabbah* 5:5; BT *Bekhorot* 8a; *Zohar* 2:198b.

501. **from the right side** The side of *Ḥesed.* The ray both arouses and calms the sea. See BT *Bava Batra* 73a; *MM.*

502. **Alternatively,** תשבחם **(*Teshabbeḥem*), *You praise them,* literally!** The root שבח (*shvḥ*) can mean "to still," but its more common meaning is "to praise."

503. **Shunammite** The wealthy woman from the town of Shunem who fed and housed the prophet Elisha. She was rewarded with a son, who later died but was resuscitated by Elisha. See 2 Kings 4:8–36; *Zohar* 1:160b; 2:33b, 44b.

504. **that day was the festival of Rosh Hashanah...** The day referred to in 2

king? (2 Kings 4:13)—this is the blessed Holy One, who is then called King, Holy King, King of Judgment.[505] *She replied, 'I dwell among my own people'* (ibid.)—'I do not want to be mentioned or observed except *among my own people.*' Whoever yokes with his own people will not be scrutinized and judged harshly by anyone. So she said: *Among my own people.*

"Come and see: When wrath prevailed in the world, Noah was not recalled.[506] As soon as judgment had been executed, what is written? *God remembered Noah.* Now his name was recalled.

"Alternatively, *God remembered Noah,* corresponding to what is said: *I have remembered My covenant* (Exodus 6:5)."[507]

Rabbi Ḥizkiyah was walking from Cappadocia to Lydda.[508] He met Rabbi Yeisa, who said to him, "I am surprised that you are all alone, for we have learned that one should not set out alone on a journey."[509]

He replied, "A child is walking with me; he's following behind."

Kings 4:8: *One day Elisha was passing through Shunem, where a wealthy woman lived, and she urged him to have a meal.* Similarly, according to a midrashic tradition, the phrase *one day* in Job 1:6 refers to Rosh Hashanah, the Day of Judgment.

See *Targum Yerushalmi, Midrash Iyyov,* Rashi, and Ibn Ezra on Job 1:6; *Battei Midrashot,* 2:158; *Zohar* 3:231a.

505. **who is then called King, Holy King...** Between Rosh Hashanah and Yom Kippur, God is addressed in the liturgy as "Holy King" and "King of Judgment." See BT *Berakhot* 12b.

506. **Noah was not recalled** So he would not be vulnerable to harsh judgment.

507. *God remembered Noah...I have remembered My covenant* Noah symbolizes and embodies *Yesod,* the divine phallus, which is also symbolized by the covenant of circumcision.

508. **from Cappadocia to Lydda** This improbable journey from eastern Asia Minor to a city in Palestine recurs frequently in the *Zohar* and usually includes an encounter with some surprising character. See 1:132a, 138a (*MhN*), 160a, 197b, 223a; 2:31a, 38b, 80b, 86a; 3:35a, 75b, 221b; *ZH* 22a (*MhN*).

The itinerary seems to be intentionally fantastic, though perhaps the author(s) imag-ined that Cappadocia was a Galilean village near Sepphoris, based on the phrase "Cappadocians of Sepphoris" in JT *Shevi'it* 9:5, 39a. According to a dream interpretation in *Bereshit Rabbah* 68:12, Cappadocia is not far at all from Palestine. Cappadocia figures prominently in M *Ketubbot* 13:11 and BT *Ketubbot* 110b, while Cappadocia and Lydda are linked in *Tosefta, Yevamot* 4:5 and BT *Yevamot* 25b.

See Scholem, in *Zion (Me'assef)* 1 (1926): 40–46 (and the appended note by S. Klein, 56); idem, *Major Trends,* 169; idem, *Kabbalah,* 222; Tishby, *Wisdom of the Zohar,* 1:63–64.

509. **one should not set out alone on a journey** See *Tanḥuma, Vayishlaḥ* 8: "Our Rabbis have taught: 'In three situations a person's account book is opened [i.e., his sins will be punished]: One who sets out alone on a journey, one who dwells in a tottering house, and one who vows and does not pay.'" Cf. M *Avot* 3:4: "Rabbi Ḥanina son of Ḥakhinai says, 'One who stays awake at night and one who walks on the way alone and one who makes room in his heart for that which is futile—such a person deserves to die.'" Cf. JT *Shabbat* 2:6, 5b; *Zohar* 1:169b; 2:264b; *Orḥot Ḥayyim,* par. 46.

He said, "I am surprised by that! How can you be accompanied by someone with whom you cannot discuss words of Torah? For whoever walks on the way unaccompanied by words of Torah endangers his life."[510]

He replied, "Certainly so!"

Meanwhile the child arrived. Rabbi Yeisa asked him, "My son, where are you from?"

He answered, "From the town of Lydda. When I heard that this wise man was going there, I offered to serve and accompany him."

He asked, "Do you know any Torah?"

He answered, "I do, because father used to teach me the section of sacrifices, and I inclined my ear when he spoke with my brother, who is older than me."

Rabbi Yeisa said to him, "My son, tell me."

He opened, saying, "*Noah built an altar to YHVH, and took of every pure animal and of every pure bird, and offered ascent-offerings on the altar* (Genesis 8:20).

"*Noah built an altar*—the same altar on which Adam sacrificed.[511] [70a] Why did he bring an ascent-offering, since that is offered only for sinful imagining?[512] How did Noah sin? By imagining, 'Look, the blessed Holy One decreed the destruction of the world! Perhaps because He saved me, all my merit has been expended and none is left.'[513] Immediately, *Noah built an altar to YHVH*—the same one on which Adam sacrificed. If it was the same, why *built*?[514] Because the wicked of the world dislodged it from its site.[515] When Noah appeared, of him is written: *built*.[516]

510. **whoever walks on the way unaccompanied by words of Torah...** See BT *Ta'anit* 10b: "Rabbi Il'ai son of Berekhiah said, 'Two disciples of the wise who are walking on the way and are not engaged in words of Torah deserve to be burned.'"

See Deuteronomy 6:7; BT *Eruvin* 54a; *Zohar* 1:58b, 70a, 76a, 87a, 115b.

511. **altar on which Adam sacrificed** See *Bereshit Rabbah* 34:9: "*Noah built an altar to YHVH...and offered ascent-offerings on the altar.* Rabbi Eli'ezer son of Ya'akov said, 'On the great altar in Jerusalem, where Adam sacrificed.'" According to BT *Avodah Zarah* 8a, "On the day Adam was created, when the sun set, he said, 'Woe is me! Because I have sinned, the world is turning dark and will now revert to chaos and void. This is the death decreed against me from Heaven!' He sat up all night fasting and weeping, and Eve wept facing him. As soon as dawn broke, he said: 'This is the normal

course of the world!' He rose and offered up an ox." See *Targum Yerushalmi*, Genesis 8:20.

512. **that is offered only for sinful imagining** See *Vayiqra Rabbah* 7:3: "Rabbi Shim'on son of Yoḥai taught, 'An ascent-offering is due only for sinful imagining.'" Cf. *Tanḥuma, Lekh Lekha* 10. Having survived the Flood, it would have been more appropriate for Noah to bring a thanksgiving-offering, as Adam did when he survived the darkness.

513. **By imagining...** Noah sinned by lacking faith, by imagining that God would not continue to protect him.

514. **If it was the same, why *built*?** The altar had already been built by Adam.

515. **wicked of the world dislodged it from its site** The altar symbolizes *Shekhinah*, whose union with *Tif'eret* is ruined by human wickedness.

516. **When Noah appeared...*built*** Noah's righteousness restored *Shekhinah*, re-

410

"*And offered up* עולות (*olot*), *ascent-offerings*—spelled עלת (*olat*), *ascent-offering*, one.[517] It is written: *He is* עולה (*olah*), *an ascent-offering, a fire-offering, an aroma pleasing to YHVH* (Leviticus 1:17).[518] Ascent-offering always ascends as male, not female, as is written: *Let him offer it male, unblemished* (ibid., 3). Why is it written: אשה (*ishsheh*), *fire-offering*, since אש (*esh*), fire, must be present there?[519] Because even though ascent-offering is offered as male, offered to his site,[520] female must not part from him.[521] Rather he is offered together with her, uniting one with the other, so female ascends toward male, uniting as one—even though 'אשה (*ishsheh*), *fire-offering*, is intended for אישים (*ishim*), angelic personages.'[522]

"Noah had to offer an ascent-offering, for the blessed Holy One cast him in the sphere of the male, to join and enter the ark, so he offered an ascent-offering.[523]

"*He is an ascent-offering,* אשה (*ishsheh*), *a fire-offering*—אש ה (*esh he*), fire, he, for left unites with female[524]—every female deriving from the left side[525]—

411

uniting Her with Her partner. See above, pages 388–91.

517. spelled עלת (*olat*), *ascent-offering*, one The word עולות (*olot*), *ascent-offerings*, is spelled here without either ו (*vav*): עלת, and so can be read *olat*, *ascent-offering*, in the singular. See *Minḥat Shai*, ad loc. From this spelling, the child concludes that Noah's offering consisted of only one gender.

518. *He is* עולה (*olah*), *an ascent-offering*... The verse would normally be translated: *It is an ascent-offering...*, but here the child emphasizes the masculine sense of the pronoun הוא (*hu*), which means both "it" and "he."

519. Why is it written: אשה (*ishsheh*), *fire-offering*... Why the extra letter ה (*he*), indicating the feminine and suggesting the word אשה (*ishshah*), "woman"? (Actually, the literal meaning of *ishsheh* is probably "gift"; see Milgrom, *Leviticus* 1:161–62.)

520. his site The masculine *sefirah* of *Tif'eret*.

521. female must not part from him The offering must be intended also for the feminine realm, *Shekhinah*.

522. even though 'אשה (*ishsheh*)... is intended for אישים (*ishim*)...' See *Sifra, Vayiqra, dibbura dindavah* 6:9, 7c: "אשה (*Ishsheh*):

for the sake of אישים (*ishshim*), fire-offerings [i.e., not for the sake of charring the flesh]." See M *Zevaḥim* 4:6; BT *Zevaḥim* 46b.

Here the child understands אישים as *ishim*, "angelic personages," who also benefit from the sacrifice. See *Sifrei Zuta*, Numbers 28:2; *Midrash Zuta*, Song of Songs 1:15; *Zohar* 1:81a (*ST*), 164a–b; 2:43a; 3:110a (*RM*), 258b. (On this class of angels, see Maimonides, *Mishneh Torah*, *Hilkhot Yesodei ha-Torah* 2:7.) The child's point is that even though the word *ishsheh* has been interpreted in earlier sources, his new reading is also valid.

523. the blessed Holy One cast him in the sphere of the male... God modeled the righteous Noah on the masculine *sefirah* of *Yesod* (known as Righteous One), so the offering that Noah brought had to be male: an ascent-offering.

524. אש ה (*esh he*), fire, *he*, for left unites with female The word אשה (*ishsheh*), *fire-offering*, is divided into אש ה (*esh he*), "fire, he," indicating the fire of the *sefirah* of *Gevurah*, on the left side, and *Shekhinah*, symbolized by the feminine marker ה (*he*).

525. every female deriving from the left side The left side of the sefirotic tree is associated with the feminine.

cleaving to one another. So female is called אשה (*ishshah*), woman: אשה (*ishshah*) —cluster of love, grasped by the left to raise Her above, to be bound as one.[526] So, *He is an ascent-offering, ishsheh*—nexus of male and female intertwined.

"*YHVH smelled the pleasing aroma* (Genesis, ibid., 21). And it is written: *a fire-offering, a pleasing aroma* (Leviticus, ibid., 17). *A fire offering*—so I have heard: Smoke and fire, joined as one, for there is no smoke without fire, as is written: *Mount Sinai was all in smoke, for YHVH had descended upon it in fire* (Exodus 19:18).

"Come and see: Fire issues from within, and is tenuous, grasped by another substance, without, less tenuous; they are grasped by one another. Then smoke ascends. Why? Because fire is grasped by sensate substance.[527] Your symbol for this is the nose, through which issues smoke out of fire.[528] Of this is written: *They shall place incense in Your nostril* (Deuteronomy 33:10), for fire returns to its site, and through that aroma the nose contracts inward, inward—till all is embraced, returning to its site, all drawn in toward thought, becoming a single desire.[529] Then, ריח ניחח (*reiah nihoah*), *a pleasing aroma*, for wrath נח (*nah*), subsides, yielding נייחא (*neyaha*), tranquility[530]—for smoke is absorbed, condensed in fire, fire grasping smoke, both entering within, within, until wrath subsides. When all intermingles and wrath subsides, then tranquility, a single nexus named 'tranquility'—tranquility of spirit, joy of all as one, radiance of sparkling lamps,[531] radiance of faces. So it is written: *YHVH smelled* [*the pleasing aroma*], like one inhaling, drawing everything in to its site."

Rabbi Yeisa came and kissed him, saying, "All this goodness in your hand, and I was unaware! I will turn around so we can join as one."

They went on.

Rabbi Ḥizkiyah said, "Let us walk on this way together with *Shekhinah,* for it is paved for us."[532]

412

---

526. **to raise Her above...** To raise *Shekhinah* to Her partner, *Tif'eret.*

527. **Fire issues from within...** The fire of *Gevurah* issues from *Binah* and is grasped by *Shekhinah,* less rarified and more sensate, also symbolized by smoke. See *Zohar* 1:30a, 50b–51b.

528. **nose, through which issues smoke out of fire** When the nostrils flare in anger.

529. *They shall place incense in Your nostril...* Divine wrath, symbolized by the fire of *Gevurah,* is assuaged by the offering of incense, and the fire returns to its source in the divine mind. On the divine nose, see

Zohar 2:122b; 3:130a–b (*IR*), 137b–138a (*IR*), 289a (*IZ*), 294a (*IZ*).

530. ריח ניחח (*reiah nihoah*)...נח (*nah*)...נייחא (*neyaha*)... The alliteration extends implicitly to נח (*Noah*), Noah.

531. **sparkling lamps** בוסינין (*Bosinin*), "Lamps." In the *Zohar,* *bosina* or *botsina* may also imply "spark." See above, page 107: בוצינא דקרדינותא (*botsina de-qardinuta*), "lamp of impenetrability," "spark of impenetrable darkness"; and note 4 there.

532. **Let us walk on this way together with *Shekhinah*...** *Shekhinah* accompanies those engaged in Torah. See M *Avot* 3:2: "Rabbi Ḥananya son of Teradyon said,

They grasped the child's hands, and they went on.

They said to him, "Tell us one of those verses your father told you."

He opened, saying, "*O that he would kiss me with the kisses of his mouth* (Song of Songs 1:2).[533] This is supernal desire, for passion issues from the mouth, not from the nose, as does fire. For look, when a mouth merges by kissing, fire issues passionately,[534] in radiant faces, total joy, blissful cleaving. So, *for your caresses are fine, deriving from wine* (ibid.)[535]—from the wine that delights and brightens the face, sparkling the eyes, arousing passion;[536] not from the wine that intoxicates, arousing rage, darkening the face, inflaming the eyes—wine of rage.[537] So, because this good wine brightens the face, delights the eyes, and arouses passionate love, it is offered every day upon the altar [70b] in a quantity satiating and delighting one who drinks it, as is written: *Its wine libation is a quarter of a hin* (Numbers 28:7).[538] So, *for your caresses are fine, deriving from wine*—from that wine arousing love and desire.

"Entirely as below, love arouses above. Two lamps, the light of the upper one extinguished: by the smoke ascending from the one below, the one above is rekindled."[539]

413

Rabbi Ḥizkiyah said, "Certainly so! For the upper world depends upon the lower,[540] and the lower upon the upper. Ever since the day the Temple was destroyed, blessings are not to be found above or below,[541] demonstrating that each depends on the other."

'...If two are sitting engaged in words of Torah, *Shekhinah* dwells between them.'"

On the importance of engaging in Torah while on a journey, see above, page 410 and note 510.

533. *O that he would kiss me...* Having been kissed by Rabbi Yeisa, the child cites an appropriate verse. On the spiritual significance of a kiss, see *Zohar* 2:124b, 146a–147a, 256b (*Heikh*); *ZḤ* 60c (*MhN, ShS*).

534. **fire issues passionately** The fire of love, not the fire of anger.

535. *for your caresses are fine, deriving from wine* The verse would normally be rendered *for your caresses are better than wine*, but here the child understands מיין (*mi-yayin*) not as *than wine*, but rather *from wine*. See Ezra of Gerona, *Peirush Shir ha-Shirim*, 485.

536. **wine that delights and brightens the face...** This wine symbolizes the sweet emanation flowing from *Binah*.

537. **wine that intoxicates... wine of rage** Symbolizing harsh, concentrated judgment.

538. *a quarter of a hin* The quantity of the libation accompanying the daily *olah*, approximately one quart. The word *wine* does not appear in this verse and apparently derives from Leviticus 23:13.

539. **Two lamps, the light of the upper one extinguished...** Similarly, the divine realm—even if temporarily darkened—can be rekindled by human arousal below. See *Sefer ha-Atsamim*, 20; El'azar of Worms, *Ḥokhmat ha-Nefesh*, 15c; *Zohar* 3:35b.

540. **the upper world depends upon the lower** A general principle of Kabbalah. See *Zohar* 1:35a, 77b, 82b, 86b, 88a, 164a, 244a; 2:31b, 265a; 3:92a, 110b.

541. **Ever since the day the Temple was destroyed...** See M *Sotah* 9:12: "Rabban Shim'on son of Gamli'el says in the name of Rabbi Yehoshu'a: 'Ever since the day the Temple was destroyed, there is no day with-

Rabbi Yeisa said, "Blessings are not to be found, curses are! For the sucking of all issues to the world from that side,[542] and blessings do not issue. Why? Because Israel does not dwell in the land and does not perform the vital service: kindling sparkling lamps so that blessings appear.[543] So they disappear above and below, and the worlds remain unfulfilled, unstable."

Rabbi Ḥizkiyah said, "What is the meaning of: לא אוסיף (*Lo osif*), *I will never, again curse the earth because of* האדם (*ha-adam*), *humankind* (Genesis 8:21)?"

Rabbi Yeisa replied, "I have heard as follows from Rabbi Shim'on: As long as fire above אוסיף (*osif*), continues, blazing, smoke—judgment below—rages fiercely, consuming all.[544] For when fire issues, it does not cease until judgment has been completed. When judgment below לא אוסיף (*lo osif*), is no longer, intensified by judgment above,[545] it executes judgment intermittently, consuming incompletely. So it is written: לא אוסיף (*Lo osif*), *I will never,* give תוספת (*tosefet*), an increase, intensifying judgment below."[546]

The child said, "I have heard that it derives from the verse: *Cursed is the earth because of you* (Genesis 3:17).[547] For when the earth was cursed through Adam's sin, she was subjugated to that evil serpent—cosmic destroyer, exterminator of humanity.[548] From the day that Noah offered a sacrifice and the blessed Holy One smelled it,[549] earth was empowered to escape that serpent, escape defilement. So Israel offers a sacrifice to the blessed Holy One to brighten the face of the earth."

Rabbi Ḥizkiyah said, "Correct, but this remained suspended until Israel stood at Mount Sinai."[550]

414

---

out a curse, dew has not descended as a blessing, and the flavor of fruit has been eliminated.'" Cf. *Zohar* 1:61b, 177a, 181a–b, 203a; 3:15b, 74b.

542. **from that side**   From the demonic side.

543. **vital service: kindling sparkling lamps...**   Israel's worship in the Temple stimulates the divine realm.

544. **fire above...smoke—judgment below...**   The fire of *Gevurah* activates the judgment of *Shekhinah*.

545. **judgment below...judgment above**   *Shekhinah* and *Gevurah*.

546. תוספת (*tosefet*), **an increase**   See *Zohar* 3:54a, 115a.

547. **I have heard that it derives from the verse...**   The child offers an alternative to

the interpretation of Rabbi Shim'on. God's promise to Noah—*I will never again curse the earth because of* האדם (*ha-adam*), *humankind*—corresponds to God's decree to Adam: *Cursed is the earth because of you.*

548. **evil serpent—cosmic destroyer, exterminator of humanity**   The serpent is identified with the Angel of Death. See BT *Bava Batra* 16a: "Resh Lakish said, 'Satan, the evil impulse, and the Angel of Death are one and the same.'"

549. **Noah offered a sacrifice...**   See Genesis 8:20–21; above, pages 410–12.

550. **this remained suspended until Israel stood at Mount Sinai**   The venom of the serpent was not remedied until Israel accepted the Torah at Sinai. See BT *Shabbat* 145b–146a: "Rav Yosef taught: '... When the

Rabbi Yeisa said, "The blessed Holy One had diminished the moon and that serpent prevailed,[551] but because of Adam's sin she[552] was cursed, to curse the world. Ever since that day,[553] earth has escaped the curse, while the moon remains defective—except when an offering appears in the world and Israel dwells in their land."[554]

Rabbi Yeisa asked that child, "What is your name?"

He replied, "אבא (*Abba*)."[555]

He said, "You will be אבא (*abba*), father, in everything: in wisdom and in years."[556]

He proclaimed this verse for him: *Your father and mother will be glad; she who bore you will rejoice* (Proverbs 23:25).[557]

Rabbi Ḥizkiyah said, "One day the blessed Holy One will eliminate the impure spirit from the world, as has been said, for it is written: *I will eliminate the spirit of impurity from earth* (Zechariah 13:2). Similarly it is written: *He will*

serpent copulated with Eve, he injected her with זוהמא (*zohama*), filth [or: slime, lewdness]. Israel, who stood at Mount Sinai—their *zohama* ceased. Star-worshipers, who did not stand at Mount Sinai—their *zohama* did not cease.'"

See *Targum Yerushalmi*, Genesis 4:1; *Pirqei de-Rabbi Eli'ezer* 21; *Zohar* 1:36b–37a, 52a, 54a, 63b, 122b.

551. **The blessed Holy One had diminished the moon and that serpent prevailed** See BT *Ḥullin* 60b: "Rabbi Shim'on son of Pazzi pointed out a contradiction. 'It is written: *God made the two great lights* (Genesis 1:16), and it is written [in the same verse]: *the greater light . . . and the lesser light.* The moon said before the blessed Holy One, "Master of the Universe! Can two kings possibly wear one crown?" He answered, "Go, diminish yourself!" She said before Him, "Master of the Universe! Because I have suggested something proper I should make myself smaller?" He replied, "Go and rule by day and night." She said, "But what is the value of this? What good is a lamp at noon?" . . . Seeing that her mind was uneasy [that she could not be consoled], the blessed Holy One said, "Bring an atonement for Me for making the moon smaller." As was said by Rabbi Shim'on son of Lakish: 'Why is

the goat offered on the new moon distinguished by the phrase *to* [or: *for*] *YHVH* (Numbers 28:15)? The blessed Holy One said, "Let this goat be an atonement for My having made the moon smaller."'"

In Kabbalah the moon symbolizes *Shekhinah*. Here Her diminution entails the empowerment of the demonic. See BT *Rosh ha-Shanah* 23b; *Zohar* 1:19b–20a, 146a; *ZḤ* 70d–71a (*ShS*); Moses de León, *Sefer ha-Rimmon*, 189; idem, *Mishkan ha-Edut*, 35b.

552. **she** Apparently, the moon. See 3 *Baruch* 9:7; *Bereshit Rabbah* 12:6. According to some commentators, the earth.

553. **that day** When Noah offered his sacrifice.

554. **except when an offering appears . . .** A sacrificial offering restores the moon to her fullness, reuniting *Shekhinah* with *Tif'eret.*

555. אבא (*Abba*) "Father," an honorary title conferred upon several Talmudic rabbis.

556. אבא (*abba*), **father, in everything: in wisdom and in years** You will be wise and live long. Rabbi Yeisa is playing on the saying of Rabbi Yehudah (*Sifrei*, Deuteronomy 1): "Father in wisdom, tender in years."

557. **He proclaimed this verse for him . . .** See BT *Berakhot* 19a, where Shim'on son of Shetaḥ applies this verse to the miracle-worker Ḥoni.

swallow up death forever. YHVH Elohim will wipe away tears from all faces and remove the disgrace of His people . . . (Isaiah 25:8).

"One day the blessed Holy One will illumine the moon, delivering her from the darkness caused by that evil serpent, as is written: *The light of the moon shall be like the light of the sun, and the light of the sun shall be sevenfold, like the light of the seven days* (Isaiah 30:26). Which light? The light hidden by the blessed Holy One in the act of Creation."[558]

Elohim blessed Noah and his sons . . . (Genesis 9:1).[559]

Rabbi Abba opened, "*The blessing of YHVH— she enriches, and He adds no pain to her* (Proverbs 10:22). *The blessing of YHVH* is *Shekhinah,* appointed over blessings of the world, from whom blessings issue for all.[560]

"Come and see what is written at first: *YHVH said to Noah, 'Come, you and all your household, into the ark!'* (Genesis 7:1). As has been said, the Master of the house gave him permission to enter, while afterward the Woman told him to leave.[561] Initially, he entered with the permission of Her Husband; finally, he emerged with the permission of the Wife. From here we learn that the master [71a] of the house should bring in and the woman send out, as is written: *Elohim said to Noah, 'Go out of the ark!'* (ibid. 8:15–16), for She was empowered to send him out, though not to bring him in.

"Having emerged, he gave Her presents,[562] for She is the house, and the house is in Her hands.[563] Those presents he gave Her were intended to intensify Her Husband's love for Her.[564] From here we learn how a guest should behave.

558. **The light hidden by the blessed Holy One . . .** The primordial light of the first day of Creation was hidden away and reserved for the righteous in the hereafter. See BT *Ḥagigah* 12a: "Rabbi El'azar said, 'With the light created by the blessed Holy One on the first day, one could gaze and see from one end of the universe to the other. When the blessed Holy One foresaw the corrupt deeds of the generation of the Flood and the generation of the Dispersion [the generation of the Tower of Babel], He immediately hid it from them, as is written: *The light of the wicked is withheld* (Job 38:15). For whom did He hide it? For the righteous in the time to come.'"

See *Bereshit Rabbah* 3:6; 41:3; *Shemot Rabbah* 35:1; *Tanḥuma, Shemini,* 9; *Bahir* 97–98 (147); *Zohar* 1:31b–32a, 45b–46a, 47a; 2:127a, 148b–149a, 220a–b; 3:88a, 173b.

559. *Elohim blessed Noah and his sons* The verse continues: *saying to them, "Be fruitful and multiply, and fill the earth."*

560. *Shekhinah,* **appointed over blessings . . .** Receiving the flow of emanation from above, *Shekhinah* transmits it to those below.

561. **Master of the house . . . Woman . . .** YHVH (the masculine *sefirah* of *Tif'eret*) invited Noah into the ark, while *Elohim* (the feminine *sefirah* of *Shekhinah*) told him to leave. See above, page 392.

562. **he gave Her presents** Noah offered sacrifices. See Genesis 8:20.

563. **She is the house . . .** *Shekhinah* is symbolized by the house and the ark. While Noah was inside, She provided for him.

564. **to intensify Her Husband's love for Her** By showing Him how much She was appreciated.

"So once he had given Her presents, She blessed him, as is written: *Elohim blessed Noah.* Therefore, *The blessing of YHVH—she enriches,* indeed, as has been said. *And He adds no pain to her*—mystery of what is written: *By painful toil you will eat of it* (ibid. 3:17).[565] *Painful toil*—pain and anguish, a face lacking radiance, when the moon darkens and blessings are nowhere to be found.[566] *By painful toil*—side of the other spirit,[567] depriving the world of blessings. So, ולא יוסיף (*Ve-lo yosif*), *He adds no, pain to her*—mystery of what is written: לא אוסיף (*Lo osif*), *I will never, again curse the earth* (ibid. 8:21)."[568]

"*Fear and dread of you shall be* [*upon every beast of the earth...*] (ibid. 9:2). From now on, human images, for at first, there were no human images.[569] Come and see: At first, it is written: *In the image of God He made the human being* (ibid. 9:6),[570] and similarly: *He created him in the image of God* (ibid. 5:1).[571] As soon as they sinned, their image mutated from that supernal image and they turned into being frightened by the beasts of the field. At first, all creatures of the world would raise their eyes, see the supernal, sacred image, and be overcome by fear and trembling.[572] Once they sinned, their image transformed in their eyes into another image,[573] and on the contrary, human beings fear and tremble in the presence of other creatures.

"Come and see: All humans who do not sin in the presence of their Lord and do not transgress the words of Torah—their image never wavers from the appearance of the supernal image, so every creature of the world fears and trembles before them. But when humans transgress the words of Torah, their image changes, so they all fear and tremble before other creatures because the supernal image has been exchanged, removed from them. Then beasts of the field dominate them, since they no longer see that worthy image.[574]

417

565. *By painful toil you will eat of it* The curse decreed by God upon Adam: *Cursed is the earth because of you; by painful toil you will eat of it all the days of your life.*

566. **when the moon darkens...** When *Shekhinah,* symbolized by the moon, lacks illumination. See *Zohar* 1:180b; *ZH* 61b (*MhN, ShS*).

567. **side of the other spirit** The demonic realm.

568. לא אוסיף (*Lo osif*), *I will never, again curse the earth* Earth symbolizes *Shekhinah.* See above, pages 414–15.

569. **at first, there were no human images** Before the Flood.

570. *In the image of God He made the human being* See Genesis 1:27.

571. *He created him...* The verse reads: *He made him.*

572. **all creatures of the world...** See *Pirqei de-Rabbi Eli'ezer* 11: "[Adam] stood on his feet and was adorned with the divine image. The creatures saw him and were frightened, thinking that he was their Creator, and they all approached to bow down to him."

See *Zohar* 1:13b, 38a, 191a, 221b; 2:55a, 125b; 3:107b; *ZH* 38c; Moses de León, *Sefer ha-Rimmon,* 337–38; Ginzberg, *Legends,* 5:119–20, n. 113.

573. **their image transformed in their eyes...** The human image transformed in the eyes of other creatures.

574. **All humans who do not sin...** See *Shir ha-Shirim Rabbah* on 3:7: "It was

"So now that the world was renewed, as originally, He bestowed this blessing upon them, granting them dominion over all, as is said: *and all the fish of the sea are given into your hand* (ibid. 9:2)[575]—even the fish of the sea."[576]

Rabbi Ḥiyya said, "*Were given into your hand*, previously,[577] for when the blessed Holy One created the world, He delivered everything into their hands, as is written: *Have dominion over the fish of the sea and the birds of the sky...* (ibid. 1:28)."[578]

Rabbi Ḥizkiyah opened, "*Of David.* משכיל (*Maskil*).[579] *Happy is one whose transgression is lifted,*[580] *whose sin is covered* (Psalms 32:1). This verse has been established,[581] yet it was spoken in the mystery of wisdom. For we have learned: 'With ten varieties of praise, David praised the blessed Holy One,' one of which is משכיל (*maskil*), one of those ten rungs.[582] David attuned himself before this rung settled upon him.[583]

418

taught: Before a person sins, he inspires awe and fear, and creatures are afraid of him. Once he sins, he is filled with awe and fear, and he is afraid of others."

See *Sifrei*, Deuteronomy 50; and BT *Shabbat* 151b: "Rami son of Abba said, 'A wild beast has no power over a person until he appears to it as an animal.'"

575. *and all the fish of the sea are given into your hand* The full verse reads: *Fear and dread of you shall be upon all the beasts of the earth and upon all the birds of the sky, everything with which the earth teems and all the fish of the sea—into your hand they are given.* See above, page 417.

576. *even the fish of the sea* Which, according to one view, were not condemned to die in the Flood and were thus not saved by Noah's merit. See *Bereshit Rabbah* 32:11; BT *Sanhedrin* 108a, *Zevaḥim* 113b; Ginzberg, *Legends,* 5:183, n. 42; Kasher, *Torah Shelemah*, Genesis 7:22, n. 94.

577. *Were given into your hand,* previously The word נתנו (*nittanu*), though usually rendered *are given*, is actually in the past tense: *were given, have been given.*

578. *Have dominion over the fish of the sea and the birds of the sky* The verse continues: *and every living creature that crawls upon the earth.*

579. משכיל (*Maskil*) A literary or musical term whose precise meaning is unclear.

580. *lifted* נשוי (*Nesui*), "Lifted, carried off, taken away, forgiven."

581. **This verse has been established** See *Bereshit Rabbah* 22:6; *Pesiqta Rabbati* 45.

582. **'With ten varieties of praise, David praised the blessed Holy One'...** See BT *Pesaḥim* 117a: "Rabbi Yehoshu'a son of Levi said, 'The Book of Psalms was uttered with ten utterances of praise....'" These ten utterances symbolize the ten *sefirot,* משכיל (*maskil*) symbolizing *Yesod.* Cf. *Zohar* 2:110a–b; 3:101a.

583. **David attuned himself...** King David, the ideal ruler, symbolizes the *sefirah* of *Malkhut* ("Kingdom"), also known as *Shekhinah.* The wording לדוד משכיל (*le-David maskil*), "*Of David. Maskil,*" indicates that David prepared himself to receive *Yesod* (*Maskil*), partner of *Shekhinah.*

See BT *Pesaḥim* 117a: "לדוד מזמור (*Le-David mizmor*), *To David, a psalm,* indicates that *Shekhinah* dwelled upon him and then he exclaimed a song. מזמור לדוד (*Mizmor le-David*), *A psalm, to David,* indicates that he exclaimed a song and then *Shekhinah* dwelled upon him." See above, page 393, where this rabbinic exegesis is reversed.

"Happy is one whose transgression is lifted. For when the blessed Holy One weighs the sins and merits of human beings, the scale on the side of sins ascends, while in the other, merits tip the scale. This is: *whose transgression is lifted.*[584]

"Whose sin is covered, when judgment prevails in the world, so that he will be protected, so the Destroyer will not overpower him.[585] As with Noah, concealed by the blessed Holy One from that sin Adam channeled to him and to the world.[586] For since Adam conveyed this sin to the world, other creatures dominate, humans fear them, and the world lies in disarray. So when Noah emerged from the ark, the blessed Holy One blessed him, as is written: *God blessed Noah and his sons....* (Genesis 9:1–2).[587]

"And as for you, be fruitful and multiply (ibid., 7). In these blessings females are not to be found, just Noah and his sons; the verse does not mention females."[588]

Rabbi Shim'on said, "ואתם (*Ve-attem*), *And as for you*—entirety of males [71b] and females as one.[589] So, *And as for you, be fruitful and multiply,* generating

419

584. **when the blessed Holy One weighs the sins and merits...** See *Midrash Tehillim* 30:4: "Rabbi El'azar said, 'If the scale is evenly balanced—sins on this side, merits on that—what does the blessed Holy One do? He tips it toward love, as is said: *Love is Yours, O YHVH* (Psalms 62:13).' Rabbi Yose son of Rabbi Ḥanina said, 'What does the blessed Holy One do? He snatches one bond of debt from the sins, and instantly the merits tip the scales, as is said: *He lifts iniquity and passes over transgression* (Micah 7:18).'"

See *Pesiqta de-Rav Kahana* 25:2; JT *Pe'ah* 1:1, 16b; BT *Rosh ha-Shanah* 17a.

585. **so that he will be protected...** If one's sin is concealed, then the Destroyer cannot harm him. On concealment and the Destroyer, see BT *Bava Qamma* 60a–b: "Rabbi Yosef taught: 'What is the meaning of the verse *None of you shall go out the door of his house until morning* (Exodus 12:22). Once permission has been granted to the Destroyer, he does not distinguish between righteous and wicked.'...Our Rabbis taught: 'A plague in town? Keep your feet indoors.'...Our Rabbis taught: 'A plague in town? One should not walk in the middle of

the road, because the Angel of Death walks there—for as soon as permission has been granted him, he strides brazenly.'"

See *Mekhilta, Pisḥa* 11; *Zohar* 1:63a, 68a–b, 69a, 107b, 113a, 182b, 197b; 2:196a, 227a.

586. **that sin Adam channeled to him...** Adam's sin of eating the fruit of the Tree of Knowledge affected all future generations.

587. *God blessed Noah and his sons* The passage continues: *saying to them, "Be fruitful and multiply, and fill the earth. Fear and dread of you shall be upon all the beasts of the earth and upon all the birds of the sky, everything with which the earth teems and all the fish of the sea—into your hand they are given."* This divine blessing restored the human dominion over creatures, which had been lost due to Adam's sin. See *Bereshit Rabbah* 34:12.

588. **the verse does not mention females** See Genesis 9:1, cited above: *God blessed Noah and his sons....*

589. ואתם (*Ve-attem*), *And as for you*— **entirety of males and females...** Rabbi Shim'on interprets the ו (*vav*), *and,* preceding the word אתם (*attem*), *you,* as including females. The disagreement between Rabbi Ḥizkiyah and Rabbi Shim'on reflects the

offspring. From here on, *teem on earth* (ibid.).[590] Here the blessed Holy One gave them seven commandments of Torah, for them and all succeeding them, until Israel stood at Mount Sinai and were given all the commandments of Torah as one."[591]

God said to Noah.... This is the sign of the covenant I set between Me and you.... I have set My bow in the cloud (Genesis 9:8, 12–13). *I have set*—previously.[592]

Rabbi Shim'on opened, "*Above the expanse over their heads—appearance of sapphire, semblance of a throne* (Ezekiel 1:26).[593] What is written above? *I heard the sound of their wings like the sound of mighty waters, like the sound of Shaddai, as they moved* (ibid., 24). These are four magnificent, supernal, sacred creatures,[594] above whom that *expanse* is arrayed,[595] all their wings spread, joined to one another, to cover their bodies.[596] As they spread their wings, the sound of all those wings is heard—singing a song, as is written: *like the sound of Shaddai*, never subsiding, as is written: *so that glory may sing to You and not be silent* (Psalms 30:13).[597] What do they exclaim? *YHVH has manifested His salvation; He has revealed His righteousness in the sight of the nations* (ibid. 98:2).[598]

420

---

rabbinic debate over the question of whether women as well as men are commanded to *be fruitful and multiply*. See M *Yevamot* 6:6; BT *Yevamot* 65b.

590. *teem on earth* The verse concludes: *and multiply on it.*

591. **Here the blessed Holy One gave them seven commandments...** See BT *Sanhedrin* 56a: "Our rabbis taught: The sons of Noah were commanded seven commandments: Courts of justice, [not to commit] blaspheming the divine name, idolatry, sexual immorality, bloodshed, robbery, and eating a limb from a living animal." Traditionally, these basic laws of morality apply to all humankind, whereas Israel received 613 commandments. *KP* explains how the seven Noahide commandments emerge from Genesis 9:1–8. See BT *Sanhedrin* 56b; *Bereshit Rabbah* 16:6; *Zohar* 1:36a.

592. *I have set*—previously At the beginning of Creation. According to M *Avot* 5:6, the rainbow was one of the ten things created at the end of the week of Creation, "at twilight on Sabbath eve." See Ibn Ezra

and Radak on Genesis 9:13; Naḥmanides on 9:12; Judah ben Barzillai, *Peirush Sefer Yetsirah*, 139; *Zohar* 1:18a; Kasher, *Torah Shelemah*, Genesis 9:13, n. 81.

593. **Rabbi Shim'on opened...** Rabbi Shim'on begins to draw a parallel between the heavenly sign given to Noah and the heavenly vision of Ezekiel, which constitutes the basis for much of Jewish mysticism.

594. **four magnificent, supernal, sacred creatures** The חיות (*ḥayyot*), "living creatures, animals," who, according to Ezekiel's vision, carry the divine throne.

595. **that *expanse*...** Instead of "expanse," several witnesses read "Creature," alluding to *Shekhinah*.

596. **cover their bodies** See Ezekiel 1:11, 23.

597. ***Shaddai...glory*...** Two names of *Shekhinah*, who sings to Her partner, *Tif'eret*, known as *YHVH*.

598. ***YHVH has manifested His salvation*...** According to Shim'on son of Lakish (BT *Avodah Zarah* 24b), this psalm was chanted by the two cows pulling the cart

"A sound of tumult like the sound of an army camp (Ezekiel, ibid.), like the sound of a holy camp, all supernal hosts gathering above.[599] What do they exclaim? *Holy, holy, holy is YHVH of hosts; the whole earth is full of His glory!* (Isaiah 6:3).[600] Turning south, they sing *holy;* turning north, they sing *holy;* turning east, they sing *holy;* turning west, they sing *blessed.*[601]

"The *expanse* lies above their heads; wherever it moves, it turns faces in that direction, faces encompassed in it.[602] Faces turn to four corners, each revolving within its square, engraved with four faces:[603] face of a lion, face of an eagle, face of an ox, face of a human engraved with them all. Human—face of a lion; human—face of an eagle; human—face of an ox; all coalescing in him. So it is written: *Semblance of their face: a human face* (Ezekiel 1:10).[604]

"In this quadrisected *expanse,* all colors are included, four colors seen within, engraved quadruply,[605] higher and lower secrecies inscribed in four engravings.[606] When the colors of these four scatter, they total twelve: green, red, white, and a color blended of all colors,[607] as is written: *Like the appearance of the bow in the cloud on a rainy day, so was the appearance of the surrounding radiance—the appearance of the semblance of the glory of YHVH* (ibid., 28)— appearance of the colors of all. So, *I have set My bow in the cloud.*[608]

421

---

with the ark of YHVH (1 Samuel 6:10–12). See *Zohar* 1:123a; 2:137b–138a. *Righteousness* symbolizes *Shekhinah.*

599. **holy camp...** A camp of angels.

600. *Holy, holy, holy is YHVH of hosts; the whole earth is full of His glory!* Rabbi Shim'on interweaves the visions of Isaiah and Ezekiel, as does early Jewish mysticism and the *qedushah,* the daily prayer of "sanctification."

601. **blessed** See Ezekiel 3:12: *Blessed be the glory of YHVH from His place!*

602. **wherever it moves, it turns faces...** The faces of the four creatures are engraved in the expanse, so they turn in whichever direction it moves. Alternatively, the subject "it" refers to any one of the creatures. See Ezekiel 1:12.

603. **engraved with four faces** Each creature has four faces. See Ezekiel 1:5–11.

604. **face of a human engraved with them all...all coalescing in him...** The human face comprises all the others. See *Zohar* 1:19a.

605. **engraved quadruply** Apparently

implying that the four colors of the expanse convey the corresponding radiance of the *sefirot:* green—*Tif'eret;* red—*Gevurah;* white—*Ḥesed;* all colors—*Shekhinah.*

606. **higher and lower secrecies...** Of the *sefirot* and of the expanse.

607. **they total twelve...** Each color reflects all the others, but since the fourth is not a specific color, three radiate from each of the four, totaling twelve. As noted above, green, red, and white symbolize, respectively, *Tif'eret, Gevurah,* and *Ḥesed.*

608. **appearance of the colors of all...** *Shekhinah, the glory of YHVH,* includes all the other *sefirot,* reflecting their colors. She is *the cloud,* in which appears the divine rainbow, the full sefirotic spectrum.

On the rainbow's colors, see *Sefer Ḥasidim,* ed. Wistinetzki, par. 1445 (ed. Margaliot, par. 484); Moses of Burgos, *Commentary on the Merkavah,* ed. Scholem, *Tarbiz* 5 (1934): 183; Baḥya ben Asher on Genesis 9:13; *Zohar* 1:18b, 98b (*ST*), 136b; 3:215a; Scholem, "Colours and Their Symbolism," 69–71.

"What is *My bow*? As is said of Joseph: *His bow remained firm* (Genesis 49:24),[609] for Joseph is called Righteous, so *his bow* is covenant of the bow, contained in Righteous One, covenant linking one with the other.[610] Since Noah was righteous, his covenant was a *bow*.[611]

"[*The arms of his hands*] ויפוזו (va-yaphozu), *stayed agile* (ibid.). What is *va-yaphozu*? They sparkled most desirably of all, as is said: *More desirable than gold, even much* פז (paz), *pure gold* (Psalms 19:11). They sparkled in supernal radiance when he kept the covenant,[612] so he was called Joseph the Righteous. Therefore the rainbow is called 'covenant,' embracing one another.

"Luster of supernal glory, vision of all visions, vision resembling hidden vision, hidden colors, revealed colors.[613] It is forbidden to gaze at the rainbow appearing in the world, lest shame be exposed in *Shekhinah*.[614] Furthermore, colors of the rainbow appear as dross[615] clinging to the appearance of supernal glory—not to gaze!

422

609. **Joseph:** *His bow remained firm* This verse is applied to the attempted seduction of Joseph by Potiphar's wife. See *Bereshit Rabbah* 87:7: "Rabbi Samuel said, 'The bow was stretched [i.e., Joseph's phallus became erect] and then returned [to its flaccid state, reading ותשב (va-teshev), *remained*, as *va-tashov*, "returned (from its firmness)"].'" See BT *Sotah* 36b; *Zohar* 1:247a; 3:66b.

610. **Joseph is called Righteous...** Because Joseph resisted the sexual advances of Potiphar's wife, he is called "righteous" in rabbinic literature. See BT *Yoma* 35b; *Bereshit Rabbah* 93:7; *Pesiqta de-Rav Kahana, nispaḥim,* 460. Cf. *Tanḥuma, Bereshit* 5; *Pirqei de-Rabbi Eli'ezer* 38, which cite Amos 2:6.

In Kabbalah Joseph symbolizes the divine phallus, *Yesod* ("Foundation"), also known as Righteous One, based on Proverbs 10:25: וצדיק יסוד עולם (Ve-tsaddiq yesod olam). The verse, which literally means *The righteous one is an everlasting foundation,* is understood as *The righteous one is the foundation of the world.* See BT *Ḥagigah* 12b; *Bahir* 71 (102); Azriel of Gerona, *Peirush ha-Aggadot,* 34; *Zohar* 1:21b.

The phallus of *Yesod* is often symbolized by the *bow* and is also the site of the covenant (the sign of circumcision). Here, though, both *bow* and "covenant" include *Shekhinah,* who is linked to *Yesod,* "contained in Righteous One." See *Zohar* 1:247a; 3:243b (*RM*); Wolf-

son, *Through a Speculum That Shines,* index, s.v. "rainbow."

611. **Since Noah was righteous...** Noah the Righteous symbolizes *Yesod,* Righteous One.

612. **when he kept the covenant** When Joseph withstood the temptation of being seduced.

613. **Luster of supernal glory...hidden colors, revealed colors** The revealed colors of the rainbow symbolize *Shekhinah,* "vision of all visions," who reflects the more hidden colors of the higher *sefirot.*

614. **It is forbidden to gaze at the rainbow...** See BT *Ḥagigah* 16a: "'Whoever shows no concern for the glory of his Maker, it were better for him if he had not come into the world' (M *Ḥagigah* 2:1). What does this mean? Rabbi Abba said: 'It refers to one who gazes at the rainbow,'... for it is written: *Like the appearance of the bow in the cloud on a rainy day, so was the appearance of the surrounding radiance—the appearance of the semblance of the glory of YHVH* (Ezekiel 1:28)." See *Zohar* 2:66b, 99a; 3:84a.

Here, gazing at the rainbow implies gazing at the divine phallus uniting with *Shekhinah.* See Wolfson, *Through a Speculum That Shines,* 336–40.

615. **dross** סוספיתא (Suspita), apparently a deformation of כוספא (kuspa), "pomace,

"Once earth sees this rainbow, the holy covenant is firmly erected.[616] So, *it will be a sign of the covenant between God* [*and the earth*] (Genesis 9:13).[617]

"As to what we have said concerning these colors—three colors and one blended of them—all comprise one mystery, within the cloud ascending to manifest.[618]

"*Above the expanse over their heads—an appearance of sapphire stone* (Ezekiel, ibid., 26). This is the Foundation Stone, centric point of the entire universe, upon which stands the Holy of Holies.[619] This is the supernal sacred throne, appointed over these four.[620] *Semblance of a throne* (ibid.), with four legs—Oral Torah.[621] *Upon the semblance of a throne—semblance of the appearance of a man* (ibid.)—Written Torah.[622] From here we learn that Written Torah is placed [72a] upon Oral Torah,[623] for one is the throne of the other. *Appearance of a man*—image of Jacob, enthroned upon Her."[624]

husk." Dross symbolizes the demonic, the residue of *Gevurah* or *Din* (strict Judgment), which is located on the left side of the sefirotic tree and symbolized by gold. The colors of the rainbow are inferior to divine colors.

See *Zohar* 1:30a, 118b, 228a; 2:24b, 203a, 224b, 236b; *Bei'ur ha-Millim ha-Zarot*, 182; Scholem, *Major Trends*, 389, n. 54; Liebes, *Peraqim*, 336–38.

616. **Once earth sees this rainbow...** See Genesis 9:8–17.

617. *between God* [*and the earth*] The verse reads: *between Me and the earth.* See Genesis 9:16.

618. **all comprise one mystery...** The colors of the rainbow symbolize the divine spectrum manifesting within the cloud of *Shekhinah.*

619. **Foundation Stone...** אבן שתיה (*Even Shetiyyah*), "Rock of Foundation" (upon which the world was founded) or "Rock of Weaving" (from which the world was woven). According to midrashic tradition, the world was created from this rock, located in the Holy of Holies. Here, this stone symbolizes *Shekhinah.*

See M *Yoma* 5:2; *Tosefta, Yoma* 3:6; BT *Yoma* 54b; JT *Yoma* 5:4, 42c; *Vayiqra Rabbah* 20:4; *Pirqei de-Rabbi Eli'ezer* 35; *Zohar* 1:231a; Ginzberg, *Legends*, 5:14–15, n. 39; Tur-Sinai, *Ha-Lashon ve-ha-Sefer*, 3:272; Lieberman, *Tosefta ki-Fshutah*, 4:772–73.

On the phrase "centric point" (נקודה חדא [*nequddah ḥada*], "one point"), see *Zohar* 1:231a; Scholem, *Major Trends*, 391, n. 80.

620. **supernal sacred throne...** *Shekhinah*, carried by the four creatures.

621. **Oral Torah** Symbolizing *Shekhinah.*

622. **Written Torah** Symbolizing Her male partner, *Tif'eret.*

623. **Written Torah is placed upon Oral Torah** See BT *Megillah* 27a: "... One of the Five Books [of Moses may be placed] on the Prophets and Writings, but the Prophets and Writings may not be placed on one of the Five Books." Rabbi Shim'on's formulation here corresponds with the judgment of Joseph ibn Migash, *She'elot u-Tshuvot*, 92.

624. **image of Jacob, enthroned upon Her** According to Genesis 28:12, Jacob dreamed of *a ladder set on earth, its top reaching the heavens, and behold: angels of God were ascending and descending* בו (*bo*), *on it* [or: *on him*]. *Bereshit Rabbah* 68:12 records a dispute between Rabbi Ḥiyya the Elder and Rabbi Yannai concerning this verse: "One said, '*Ascending and descending* the ladder,' while the other said, '*Ascending and descending* Jacob' ... whose image is engraved on high."

See Theodor's note, ad loc.; *Bereshit Rabbah* 82:2 ("engraved on My throne"); *Eikhah Rabbah* 2:1; *Targum Yerushalmi*, Genesis 28:12; BT *Ḥullin* 91b; *Pirqei de-Rabbi Eli'e-*

423

Rabbi Yehudah rose one night to ply Torah at an inn in the town of Meḥasya.[625] There in the house was a certain Jew who arrived with two ragged saddlebags.[626]

Rabbi Yehudah opened, saying, "*This stone that I have set up as a pillar will become the house of God* (Genesis 28:22). This is the Foundation Stone, upon which the world was planted, upon which the Temple was built."[627]

That Jew raised his head[628] and said, "How can that be? The Foundation Stone existed before the world was created; from it the world was sown. Yet you cite: *This stone that I have set up as a pillar,* which implies that Jacob set it up now, as is written: *He took the stone that he had placed under his head* (ibid., 18).[629] Furthermore, Jacob was in Bethel,[630] while this stone was in Jerusalem!"

Without turning his head toward him, Rabbi Yehudah opened, saying, "*Prepare to meet your God, O Israel!* (Amos 4:12). Similarly, *Be silent and listen, O Israel!* (Deuteronomy 27:9). Words of Torah require intention;[631] words of Torah must be arranged with body and will as one."[632]

The Jew arose and dressed himself. He sat beside Rabbi Yehudah and said, "Happy are you righteous, engaging in Torah day and night!"

424

zer 35; Moses de León, Munich MS 47, 338b; Wolfson, *Along the Path*, 1–62.

Based on the midrashic motif of Jacob's image being engraved on the divine throne, Rabbi Shim'on identifies Jacob with the *appearance of a man* seated on the throne, symbolizing *Tif'eret* enthroned upon *Shekhinah*.

625. **Meḥasya** A suburb of Sura on the Euphrates and site of a rabbinic academy. See *Zohar* 1:92b, 101a–b (*MhN*).

626. **ragged saddlebags** קסירי דקטפירא (*Qesirei de-qatpira*), one of the *Zohar*'s neologistic phrases. *Qesirei* apparently derives from קיסר (*qeisar*), "Caesar," whose Latin root was considered related to the stem *caes,* "cut." See *Tosafot, Avodah Zarah* 10b, s.v. *hakhi garsinan kol nesi'eha.*

Qatpira, perhaps an expansion of קטרא (*qitra*), "knot, bond, connection," carries several meanings in the *Zohar,* including "bag, sack, waterskin." See Psalms 119:83; *Zohar* 1:33a, 64a; Liebes, *Peraqim*, 353.

The Jew at the inn is an itinerant merchant transporting his wares.

627. **This is the Foundation Stone, upon which the world was planted...** According

to midrashic tradition, the world was created from this rock, located in the Holy of Holies in the Temple in Jerusalem.

אשתיל (*Ishshetil*), "Was planted," is a play on the rabbinic wording: "from which the world הושתת (*hushtat*), was founded." See the sources cited above, note 619; Moses de León, *Sheqel ha-Qodesh*, 74–75 (95); *Zohar* 1:78a, 82a, 231a; 2:48b, 222a; *ZḤ* 28a (*MhN*); Liebes, *Peraqim*, 372–73.

628. **That Jew raised his head** While still in bed.

629. *He took the stone that he had placed under his head* The verse continues: *and set it up as a pillar.*

630. **Jacob was in Bethel** See Genesis 28:19.

631. **Words of Torah require intention** Directing and preparing one's mind. See BT *Berakhot* 13a, 15b–16a.

632. **with body and will as one** With physical and mental preparation. Rabbi Yehudah is telling the Jew, still lying in bed, that he should prepare himself properly before engaging in Torah.

Rabbi Yehudah replied, "Now that you have prepared yourself, say your word, so that we may join as one, for words of Torah require arraying the body and arraying the mind. Otherwise, I would have lain in bed, expressing words in my mind. But we have learned that even a single person sitting and studying Torah is joined by *Shekhinah*.[633] Now, if *Shekhinah* is here, how can I lie in bed? Furthermore, they require thirsting clarity.[634]

"Moreover, when anyone rises to ply Torah at midnight, as the north wind arouses, the blessed Holy One comes to delight in the righteous in the Garden of Eden, and He together with all the righteous in the Garden listen to him, listening to those words issuing from his mouth.[635] Now, if the blessed Holy One and all the righteous revel in hearing words of Torah at this moment, how can I lie in my bed?"

He said to him,[636] "Now say your word!"

He said, "I asked about what you said concerning the verse *This stone that I have set up as a pillar will become the house of God:* 'This is the Foundation Stone.' How can that be? The Foundation Stone existed before the world was created; from it the whole world was sown. Yet you cite: *that I have set up,*

425

633. **even a single person sitting and studying Torah...** See M *Avot* 3:6: "Rabbi Ḥalafta of Kefar Ḥananya says, 'Ten who are sitting engaged in Torah, *Shekhinah* abides among them.... Even five...; even three...; even two...; even one....'" See *Zohar* 1:58b, 70a, 87a, 115b, 135b.

634. **they require thirsting clarity** Words of Torah require mental clarity, which is difficult while lying in bed. "Thirsting clarity" renders צחותא (*tsaḥuta*), for Rabbi Yehudah is using this Aramaic word meaning "thirst" to play on the Hebrew צחות (*tsaḥut*), "clarity." He has in mind the rabbinic Aramaic saying (BT *Megillah* 28b): "A legal decision requires as much צילותא (*tsiluta*), clarity, as a day of the north wind."

See BT *Eruvin* 65a; *Megillah* 28b; *Targum* on Song of Songs 6:7; *Zohar* 2:89a; 3:23a, 46a, 207b, 221b, 266b; *ZḤ* 13d (*MhN*); Scholem, *Major Trends*, 389, n. 49.

635. **when anyone rises to ply Torah at midnight...** See Psalms 119:62; and BT *Berakhot* 3b: "Rabbi Shim'on the Ḥasid said, 'There was a harp suspended above [King] David's bed. As soon as midnight arrived, a north wind came and blew upon it, and it

played by itself. He immediately arose and engaged in Torah until the break of dawn.'"

In the *Zohar,* this legendary custom is expanded into a ritual: all kabbalists are expected to rise at midnight and adorn *Shekhinah* with words of Torah and song in preparation for Her union with *Tif'eret.* See Scholem, *On the Kabbalah,* 146–50. This parallels the midnight vigil, common among Christian monks from early medieval times. In *Zohar* 3:119a Rabbi Yehudah alludes to the Christian practice: "I have seen something similar among the nations of the world." At midnight God delights in the souls of the righteous in the Garden of Eden, and both He and they listen attentively to anyone studying here below.

See *Sifra, Beḥuqqotai* 3:3, 111b; *Aggadat Bereshit* 23:5; BT *Sanhedrin* 102a; 2 *Enoch* 8:3; *Seder Gan Eden* (*Beit ha-Midrash,* 3:138); *Zohar* 1:10b, 77a–b, 82b, 92a–b, 136b, 178b, 231b; 2:46a, 130a–b, 136a, 173b, 195b–196a; 3:21b–22b, 52b, 193a; *ZḤ* 13c (*MhN*). Cf. Matthew 25:6.

636. **He said to him** Rabbi Yehudah said to the Jew.

which implies that Jacob set it up now, as is written: *He took the stone that he had placed under his head.*[637] Furthermore, Jacob was in Bethel, while this stone was in Jerusalem!"

He replied, "He rolled up the whole land of Israel beneath him, so that stone lay underneath him."[638]

He said to him, "It is written: *that he had placed,* and similarly: *this stone that I have placed.*"[639]

He replied, "If you know something, say it."

He opened, saying,[640] "*As for me, I will behold Your face in righteousness; I will be satisfied, when I awake, with Your likeness* (Psalms 17:15). King David loved and cleaved to this stone, of which he said *The stone that the builders rejected has become the cornerstone* (ibid. 118:22).[641] When he desired to gaze at the sight of the glory of his Lord, he first took this stone in his hand and then entered, for whoever desires to appear before his Lord can enter only through this, as is written: *Through this shall Aaron enter the sanctuary* (Leviticus 16:3).[642] David praises himself, saying: *As for me, I will behold Your face in righteousness.*[643] All David's striving focused on appearing fittingly in this stone, facing above.[644]

426

"Come and see: Abraham innovated morning prayer, revealing the goodness of his Lord to the world, arraying that hour fittingly, as is written: *Abraham*

637. *He took the stone that he had placed under his head* The verse continues: *and set it up as a pillar.*

638. **He rolled up the whole land of Israel beneath him...** See BT *Ḥullin* 91b: "*The land upon which you lie* [*I will give to you and to your seed*] (Genesis 28:13). What is so great about that? [The actual area of land occupied by Jacob's body was minuscule.] Rabbi Yitsḥak said, 'This teaches that the blessed Holy One rolled up the whole land of Israel and placed it beneath our father Jacob, so that it would be easily conquered by his descendants.'"

See *Bereshit Rabbah* 69:4; *Zohar* 1:156a; 3:84a. Here Rabbi Yehudah's point is that by rolling up the entire land of Israel, God brought the Foundation Stone, located in the Temple in Jerusalem, to Bethel.

639. **It is written:** *that he had placed...* Jacob placed the stone when he was at Bethel, so how could it be identical with the Foundation Stone, set in place by God before Creation?

640. **He opened, saying** The Jew opened.

641. **this stone...** *that the builders reject-ed...* Rabbinic tradition applies this verse to David, youngest of Jesse's sons, relegated to tending the flock. See 1 Samuel 16:11; BT *Pesaḥim* 119a; *Midrash Shemu'el* 19:7; *Yalqut ha-Makhiri,* Psalms 118:22, par. 28.

David identifies with *Shekhinah,* the reject-ed stone, whose diminished light excluded Her from the brilliance of *the builders,* the triad of *sefirot* (Ḥesed, Gevurah, and Tif'eret). Eventually he became a triumphant king, while She completed the quartet of *sefirot* (Ḥesed, Gevurah, Tif'eret, and Shekhinah). See *Bahir* 131 (190); *Zohar* 1:20b, 89b (*ST*).

642. **through this...** One who enters the divine realm must begin with *Shekhinah,* the Divine Presence, known as זאת (*zot*), *this.* See *Zohar* 2:51a, 57a; 3:31a.

643. *I will behold Your face in righteousness* I will encounter the divine through *Shekhinah,* known as *righteousness.*

644. **All David's striving focused on appearing fittingly...** David strove to enter

arose early in the morning (Genesis 22:3). Isaac innovated afternoon prayer, revealing to the world that there is judgment and a Judge, capable of saving or condemning the world. Jacob innovated evening prayer, and having arrayed through this prayer what no human had ever fittingly arrayed, he praised himself, saying: [72b] *This stone that I have set up as a pillar,* for until then no one else had set Her as he had.[645] So, *He took the stone that he had placed under his head and set her up as a pillar* (ibid. 28:18). What does *pillar* mean? That She was fallen and he raised Her. *And he poured oil upon her head* (ibid.), for it depended on Jacob to accomplish more than anyone in the world."[646]

Rabbi Yehudah came and kissed him, saying, "All this you know? Then why do you exert yourself in trade, neglecting eternal life?"[647]

He replied, "Times are stressful, and I have two sons attending school every day. I am exerting myself to provide them food and tuition, so that they can exert themselves in Torah."[648]

He opened, saying,[649] "*Solomon sat upon the throne of his father David, and his kingdom was firmly established* (1 Kings 2:12). What is so great about that? It implies, however, that he arrayed the Foundation Stone, setting upon it the Holy of Holies, so then *his kingdom was firmly established.*[650]

427

Shekhinah, identify with Her, and thereby ascend higher.

645. **Abraham innovated morning prayer...** See BT *Berakhot* 26b: "Rabbi Yose son of Rabbi Ḥanina said, 'The patriarchs instituted the prayers.'... Abraham instituted the morning prayer,... Isaac, the afternoon prayer,... Jacob, the evening prayer." See *Bereshit Rabbah* 68:9.

Abraham symbolizes *Ḥesed,* the *sefirah* of light and goodness. Isaac symbolizes *Gevurah* or *Din* ("Judgment"). Jacob symbolizes *Tif'eret,* who unites with *Shekhinah.* Each patriarch adorned *Shekhinah* with the quality of his particular *sefirah,* but Jacob was the first to array *Shekhinah* fittingly, to set up the primordial Foundation Stone as a pillar.

On *the stone* in this verse as *Shekhinah,* see *Zohar* 1:146b, 151a, 231a; 2:229b–230a.

On the expression "There is judgment and a Judge," see *Bereshit Rabbah* 26:6; JT *Sanhedrin* 10:2, 28d; *Zohar* 1:87b.

646. *And he poured oil upon her head...* Jacob stimulated the flow of emanation from the highest *sefirot* to *Shekhinah.*

647. **why do you exert yourself in trade, neglecting eternal life?** Eternal life is guaranteed only by the study of Torah. See BT *Shabbat* 10a, 33b; *Beitsah* 15b; *Ta'anit* 21a.

648. **so that they can exert themselves in Torah** The identical motivation appears in *Zohar* 2:95a.

649. **He opened, saying** The Jew opened.

650. **he arrayed the Foundation Stone...** Solomon arrayed *Shekhinah* with the Holy of Holies (apparently, *Binah* or *Yesod*), so that *Shekhinah,* known as *Malkhut* (*kingdom*), was *firmly established.* Thereby Solomon's own *kingdom was firmly established.*

According to the Midrash, just as the moon does not become full until the fifteenth day of its cycle, so it remained incomplete until the glorious reign of Solomon in the fifteenth generation from Abraham. See *Pesiqta de-Rav Kahana* 5:12; and *Shemot Rabbah* 15:26: "When Solomon appeared, the disk of the moon became full."

See *Zohar* 1:73b, 74a, 150a, 223a, 225b, 249b; 2:85a; 3:61a; *ZḤ* 83b (*MhN, Rut*); Moses

"It is written: *I will see her, to remember the everlasting covenant* (Genesis 9:16).[651] For the desire of the blessed Holy One focuses constantly on Her,[652] and whoever does not appear in Her does not enter the presence of his Lord.[653] So it is written: *I will see her, to remember the everlasting covenant.* What does *I will see her* mean? It is a mystery, as is written: *Make a mark* (Ezekiel 9:4),[654] clearly visible. Some say this is the impress of the sacred insignia in the flesh."[655]

Rabbi Yehudah said, "Certainly it is all![656] However, the rainbow appearing in the world abides in supernal mystery.[657] When Israel emerges from exile, this rainbow is destined to be adorned in its colors, like a bride adorning herself for her husband."[658]

The Jew said to him, "This is what my father told me as he was departing the world: 'Do not expect the footsteps of Messiah until this rainbow appears in the world, adorned in radiant colors, the world resplendent. Then expect Messiah!'[659]

"How do we know? For it is written: *I will see her, to remember the everlasting covenant.*[660] Now when she appears, she appears in dim colors, and *to remember* means: so that the Flood will not return.[661] But at that time she will appear in radiant colors, adorned in her finery. Then, *to remember the everlasting cove-*

428

de León, *Shushan Edut,* 342. In Kabbalah the moon symbolizes *Shekhinah.*

651. *I will see her...*   The verse reads: *When the bow is in the clouds, I will see it* (or: *her*), *to remember the everlasting covenant...* (Genesis 9:16).

652. **on Her**   On *Shekhinah,* symbolized by the rainbow. She displays the full sefirotic spectrum. See above, page 421.

653. **whoever does not appear in Her...**   Whoever does not attain the rung of *Shekhinah* cannot enter further into the divine realm. See Exodus 23:17: *Three times a year all your males shall appear before the presence of the Lord, YHVH.*

654. *Make a mark*   The verse reads: *Pass through the city, through Jerusalem, and make a mark upon the foreheads of the people who moan and groan over all the abominations committed in it.* Only those bearing the mark escape death (ibid. 9:6). Here the Jew's point is that those who appear within *Shekhinah* are designated for life.

655. **Some say this is the impress...**   Alternatively, when God sees the covenantal

sign of circumcision, He remembers the covenant.

656. **Certainly it is all!**   The wording *I will see it* (or: *her*) implies both interpretations, since one who is circumcised attains *Shekhinah.*

657. **rainbow appearing in the world...**   The colors of the rainbow in the sky allude to the colors of the *sefirot.* Specifically, white, red, and green symbolize *Ḥesed, Gevurah,* and *Tif'eret,* respectively. See above, page 421.

658. **this rainbow is destined to be adorned in its colors...**   The rainbow in the sky will display the brilliant colors of the *sefirot.* See *Zohar* 1:1b, 117a.

659. **Do not expect the footsteps of Messiah...**   See *TZ* 18, 36b.

660. *I will see her, to remember the everlasting covenant*   Upon seeing the resplendent rainbow, God will fulfill His promise to redeem Israel.

661. *to remember* means: so that the Flood will not return   The dim colors of the rainbow ensure the preservation of the world but not its redemption.

nant—the blessed Holy One will remember this *covenant* who lies in exile[662] and raise Her from the dust, as is written: *They will seek YHVH their God and David their king* (Hosea 3:5),[663] and similarly: *They will serve YHVH their God and David their king whom I will raise for them* (Jeremiah 30:9)—whom I will raise from the dust, as is said: *I will raise the fallen tabernacle of David* (Amos 9:11).[664] So, *I will see her, to remember the everlasting covenant,* to raise Her from the dust.

"And Father said this: 'Therefore the redemption of Israel and her remembrance are mentioned here in the Torah,[665] as is written: *As I swore that the waters of Noah would never again cover the earth, so I swear not to be angry with you or rebuke you* (Isaiah 54:9)."[666]

The sons of Noah coming out of the ark were [Shem, Ham, and Japheth] (Genesis 9:18).

Rabbi El'azar said, "Since it is written: *The sons of Noah,* why: *coming out of the ark?* Did he have other sons who didn't come out of the ark?"

Rabbi Abba replied, "Yes! For later his sons engendered sons, as is written: *These are the generations of Shem* (ibid. 11:10), and they did not come out of the ark. So it is written: *coming out of the ark: Shem, Ham, and Japheth.*"

Rabbi Shim'on said, "If I had been present in the world[667] when the blessed Holy One issued *The Book of Enoch* to the world and *The Book of Adam,*[668] I would have objected to the presence of human beings, because all the wise did

429

662. **this *covenant* who lies in exile** *Shekhinah,* who participates in Israel's exile. See BT *Megillah* 29a: "Rabbi Shim'on son of Yoḥai says, 'Come and see how beloved are Israel in the sight of the blessed Holy One! Wherever they went in exile, *Shekhinah* accompanied them. When they were exiled to Egypt, *Shekhinah* was with them.... When they were exiled to Babylon, *Shekhinah* was with them.... And even when they are destined to be redeemed, *Shekhinah* will be with them.'" See *Mekhilta, Pisḥa* 14.

663. ***David their king*** David, the ideal king, symbolizes *Shekhinah,* known as *Malkhut* ("Kingdom").

664. **the fallen tabernacle of David** *Shekhinah.* See *Zohar* 2:239b–240a.

665. **here in the Torah** In the verse *I will see her, to remember the everlasting covenant.*

666. ***not to be angry with you or rebuke you*** But rather, to redeem you. See the following verse.

667. **If I had been present in the world** Similar expressions appear in JT *Berakhot* 1:2, 3b (in the name of Rabbi Shim'on son of Yoḥai) and in *ZH* 78b (*MhN, Rut*).

668. ***The Book of Enoch... The Book of Adam*** Two volumes of esoteric knowledge housed in the real or imaginary Zoharic library. Concerning Enoch, Genesis 5:24 states: *He was no more, for God took him.* In postbiblical literature this verse is taken to mean that God transported Enoch through the heavens, a journey recorded in the Enoch literature. The *Zohar's Book of Enoch,* though influenced by this literature, is not identical with any of its particular volumes.

According to BT *Bava Metsi'a* 85b–86a, Rabbi Yehudah the Prince once saw *The Book*

not contemplate them carefully and strayed in strange words, abandoning the supernal domain for the other domain.[669] But now the wise of the world know words and conceal them, invigorating themselves in the service of their Lord.[670]

"I have found this verse[671] in Mystery of Mysteries:[672] When Delight of all Delights[673] arouses—concealed, sealed, Cause of Causes[674]—a tenuous radiance radiates, delight of all delights, lustering right in supernal anointing oil, lustering left in delightfully fine wine, lustering medially in delightful purple.[675] Spirit arouses, spirit rises, rendered to spirit, cleaving to one another.[676] Three enter three,[677] out of three issues one covenant cleaving to covenant.[678] Spirit ascending conceives, conceiving from Him.[679] When She is placed between two sides, spirit cleaves to spirit, [73a] and She conceives three sons.[680] From

430

of Adam, which contained the genealogy of the entire human race. See Genesis 5:1; Bereshit Rabbah 24:1; BT Sanhedrin 38b. The Zohar's Book of Adam is not to be confused with the Apocryphal Book of Adam. According to various medieval traditions, the angel Raziel transmitted a magical book to Adam. Later, probably in the seventeenth century, Sefer Razi'el was compiled in its present form, comprising ancient magical, mystical, and cosmological teachings.

See Zohar 1:13a, 17b, 37b, 55a–b, 90b; 2:55a, 70a–b, 100a, 180a–181a, 197a; 3:10a–b, 68b; ZH 37b; Ginzberg, Legends, 5:117–18, n. 110; 158, 163, nn. 60–61; Liebes, Peraqim, 85–87. Note the comment by Shim'on Lavi, KP, 22d: "All such books mentioned in the Zohar...have been lost in the wanderings of exile....Nothing is left of them except what is mentioned in the Zohar."

669. strayed in strange words... They delved into magic, abandoning the divine realm for the realm of the demonic. See Zohar 1:74b.

670. But now the wise of the world know words and conceal them... The mystics are careful not to reveal their secret knowledge. The reference to concealment may allude to the pseudepigraphic style of the Zohar. See Zohar 1:243a; Scholem, Major Trends, 202, 396–97, nn. 151–52; Matt, Zohar, 22.

671. this verse Namely: The sons of Noah coming out of the ark were Shem, Ham, and Japheth.

672. Mystery of Mysteries Another volume in the Zoharic library. See Zohar 2:70a–78a, 122b; 3:70b; ZH 35b–37c; Glossary, s.v. Raza de-Razin.

673. Delight of all Delights Alluding to Keter, the highest sefirah, known as Ratson ("Will, Desire").

674. Cause of Causes סיבתא דסיבתין (Sibbeta de-sibbatin), reflecting the medieval Hebrew סבת הסבות (sibbat ha-sibbot), based on Latin causa causarum, "cause of causes," the ultimate ground of being. See Zohar 3:288b (IZ); ZH 48b–c; Moses de León, Sheqel ha-Qodesh, 4 (6–7); Scholem, Über einige Grundbegriffe des Judentums, 50.

675. lustering right...left...medially... The flow of emanation spreads on the right, proceeding from Hokhmah to Hesed, and on the left, from Binah to Gevurah. Right and left are balanced in Tif'eret, symbolized by royal purple. On oil and wine, see Zohar 1:88a, 96a; 3:7b, 88b.

676. spirit rises... Shekhinah rises toward Her partner, Tif'eret.

677. Three enter three The triad of Hesed, Gevurah, and Tif'eret enter the following triad: Netsah, Hod, and Yesod.

678. one covenant cleaving to covenant Yesod, the divine phallus, symbolized by the covenant of circumcision, unites with Shekhinah, who shares the symbol of covenant.

679. Spirit ascending... Shekhinah ascends toward Her partner.

680. When She is placed between two sides... Once Shekhinah is embraced by

Noah and the ark issued three, corresponding to the supernal three, namely, those emerging from the ark: *Shem, Ham, and Japheth—Shem* on the right; *Ham* on the left; *Japheth*, purple, blending both.[681]

"*Ham is father of Canaan* (ibid. 9:18)—scoria of gold underneath slag,[682] arousal of impure spirit, primordial serpent. So the verse designates: *Ham is father of Canaan*, who brought curses upon the world, that *Canaan* who was cursed, that *Canaan* who besmirched creatures' faces.[683] So of them all, only this one diverges from them all, as is written: *Ham is father of Canaan*—the one who besmirched the world—whereas of the others is not written: *Shem is father of so-and-so*, or *Japheth is father of so-and-so*. Rather, the verse suddenly skips: *Ham is father of Canaan*, indeed!

"So when Abraham arrived, what is written? *Abram passed through the land* [... *and the Canaanite was then in the land*] (ibid. 12:6), for the patriarchs were still unfulfilled and the seed of Israel had not issued into the world, so that this name leave and the supernal name enter.[684] When Israel proved virtuous, the land was called by this name: land of Israel. When they did not, the land was called by another name: land of Canaan. So it is written: *Cursed be Canaan* (ibid. 9:25), for he brought curses upon the world. What is written of the serpent? *Cursed are you among all animals*... (ibid. 3:14), corresponding to what is written: *slave of slaves* (ibid. 9:25).[685]

431

the right and left arms (*Ḥesed* and *Gevurah*), Her union is consummated and She conceives three spiritual entities or souls.

681. *Shem on the right; Ham on the left; Japheth, purple, blending both*   Noah's three sons embody the souls deriving from the triad of *Ḥesed, Gevurah*, and *Tif'eret*. These souls issue from *Shekhinah* (symbolized by the ark) through the power of *Yesod* (symbolized by Noah).

682. **scoria of gold underneath slag**   Ham, Noah's second son, corresponds to the *sefirah* of *Gevurah* or *Din* (strict Judgment), symbolized by gold and located on the left side of the sefirotic tree. Ham's son, Canaan, symbolizes the demonic, the dross of *Din*. See *Zohar* 1:48a, 52a, 193a; 2:236b.

"Scoria" renders זוהמא (*zohama*), "filth, slime." "Slag" renders the Zoharic neologism קספיטין (*qaspitin*), apparently a deformation of כוספא (*kuspa*), "pomace, husk, residue." See the similar neologism סוספיתא (*suspita*), meaning "dross," in *Zohar* 1:30a, 71b, 118b, 228a; 2:24b, 203a, 224b, 236b; *Bei'ur ha-*

Millim ha-Zarot, 182; Scholem, *Major Trends*, 389, n. 54; Liebes, *Peraqim*, 336–38.

Canaan is dross of dross, "scoria of gold underneath slag."

683. *Ham is father of Canaan, who brought curses upon the world*...   Ham *saw his father's nakedness* (Genesis 9:22) and consequently his son Canaan was cursed by Noah (ibid., 25). Here Canaan is identified with the demonic, specifically the Angel of Death, who "besmirches creatures' faces."

684. **the patriarchs were still unfulfilled**...   Only Abraham had appeared. Until the triad of patriarchs was complete and the people of Israel established, the demonic could not be uprooted from the land.

685. *slave of slaves*   The verse continues: *shall he be to his brothers*. This curse uttered against Canaan parallels the curse pronounced upon the serpent. As the serpent is more cursed than all other animals, who are themselves enslaved to humanity, so Canaan is doomed to be *slave of slaves*.

"Therefore it is written, *Shem, Ham, and Japheth*—these are the three *sons of Noah coming out of the ark,* as we have explained.

"*These three are the sons of Noah* (ibid., 19)—establishing the world, establishing supernal mystery.

"*From these the whole world dispersed* (ibid.)—mystery of three supernal colors. For when that flowing, gushing river waters the garden through the potency of these three supernal ones[686]—from there colors scattering below— each absorbs its companion,[687] showing how the glory of the blessed Holy One extends above and below, how He is one above and below."

Rabbi El'azar said, "These three colors pervade all that derives from the side of holiness, and through reflection they disperse to all those deriving from the side of the other spirit.[688] When you contemplate the mystery of rungs,[689] you will discover how colors scatter in every direction, finally filtering below through the mystery of twenty-seven conduits, sockets of doors covering the abysses.[690]

"All is known to the supernal wise. Happy is the share of the righteous whom the blessed Holy One delights to honor, to whom He reveals supernal secrets of wisdom! Of them is written: *The secret of YHVH is for those in awe of Him* (Psalms 25:14)."

Rabbi El'azar opened, saying, "*YHVH, You are my God; I will exalt You, I will praise Your name. For You have done wonders, plans of long ago, faithful and true* (Isaiah 25:1). How intensely human beings should contemplate the glory of the blessed Holy One, praising His glory! For if one knows how to praise his Lord fittingly,[691] the blessed Holy One fulfills his desire. Further, he multiplies blessings above and below.[692]

432

686. **when that flowing, gushing river waters the garden...** The flow of emanation reaches *Shekhinah,* the garden, through the potency of the sefirotic triad of Ḥesed, Gevurah, and Tif'eret. This triad is characterized by the colors white, red, and green.

687. **each absorbs its companion.** Each aspect reflects and includes the others.

688. **through reflection they disperse...** Indirectly, the sefirotic colors illumine the demonic realm as well.

689. **mystery of rungs** The mystery of emanation extending from the divine to the realms below.

690. **twenty-seven conduits, sockets of doors covering the abysses** The abyss is the domain of the demonic. The number

twenty-seven matches the twenty-seven forces of impurity mentioned in *Zohar* 3:79a. *KP* and *OY* understand the number as referring to the twenty-seven letters of the Hebrew alphabet (including the five final letters), grouped in nine triads. As the world was created through combinations of letters, so certain other combinations obstruct the ever threatening chaos while allowing a measure of divine light to filter through to the demonic realm.

691. **if one knows how to praise his Lord fittingly** According to the various qualities of the *sefirot.* See *Zohar* 3:193b, where Rabbi El'azar interprets this verse sefirotically.

692. **multiplies blessings...** The human worshiper multiplies blessings, drawing

"So one who knows how to praise his Lord and unify His name[693] is beloved above and desirable below.[694] The blessed Holy One prides Himself on him. Of him is written: *He said to me, 'You are My servant, Israel, in whom I will be glorified'* (Isaiah 49:3)."

Noah, a man of the soil, was the first to plant a vineyard (Genesis 9:20).

Rabbi Yehudah and Rabbi Yose. One said, "It was banished from the Garden of Eden, and he planted it here." The other said, "It was in the earth and he uprooted it, then transplanted it. That same day it yielded fruit, blossoming into grapes; he squeezed them, drank of the wine and became drunk."[695]

Rabbi Shim'on said, "There is a mystery here in this verse. When he sought to probe the sin probed by Adam—not to cling but to know, to mend the world—he was incapable.[696] He squeezed grapes to probe that vineyard,[697] but as soon as he arrived, *he became drunk and exposed himself* (ibid., 21),[698] and

433

them down from above, while stimulating divine union from below.

693. **unify His name**   Unify the *sefirot* through contemplation.

694. **beloved above and desirable below** This blessing is linked with knowledge of the divine name in BT *Qiddushin* 71a: "Rav Yehudah said in the name of Rav, 'The forty-two-letter name [of God] is transmitted only to one who is modest, humble, middle-aged, free from anger, sober, and not insistent on retaliating. Whoever knows it, is careful with it, and guards it in purity is beloved above and desirable below, feared by creatures, and endowed with two worlds: this world and the world to come.'" See *Bahir* 80 (111).

695. **One said... the other said...**   Both views derive from *Pirqei de-Rabbi Eli'ezer* 23: "Noah found a vine that had been banished from the Garden of Eden along with its clusters. He took of its fruit and ate and desired them in his heart. He planted a vineyard with it. That same day its fruit flourished... He drank of its wine and was exposed in the tent...."

See 3 Baruch 4:8–17; Origen, *Selecta,* Genesis 9:20–21; *Targum Yerushalmi,* Genesis 9:20;

Tanḥuma (Buber), *Noaḥ* 20; *Zohar* 1:140b; *ZḤ* 22c (*MhN*).

Noah's sin resembles the sin of Adam, who, according to Rabbi Yehudah son of Il'ai and Rabbi Me'ir, ate from a vine. See *Bereshit Rabbah* 15:7; BT *Sanhedrin* 70a; *Apocalypse of Abraham* 23:6.

696. **When he sought to probe the sin probed by Adam...**   Noah attempted to explore the Tree of Knowledge of Good and Evil in order to repair the damage done by Adam. In Kabbalah this tree symbolizes *Shekhinah,* who should be unified with the other *sefirot,* especially with Her partner, *Tif'eret,* symbolized by the Tree of Life. Adam's sin was that he separated Her from Her partner—in effect, banishing Her from the Garden and exposing Her and the world to demonic forces. Noah repeated this sin.

See *Zohar* 1:53b; Recanati on Genesis 9:20–21, 20b. On the relation between *Shekhinah* and the demonic, see Scholem, *On the Mystical Shape of the Godhead,* 189–92; Tishby, *Wisdom of the Zohar,* 1:376–79.

697. **that vineyard**   *Shekhinah.*

698. *he became drunk and exposed himself*   The full verse reads: *He drank of*

was powerless to rise. So, *he exposed himself,* exposing the breach of the world that had been closed.[699] *Inside* אהלה (*oholoh*), *his tent* (ibid.)—spelled with a ה (*he*): inside [73b] *oholah, her tent,* the tent of that vineyard.[700]

"Similarly, the sons of Aaron, for we have learned that they were drunk on wine.[701] Now, who would give them wine to drink at that site? Can you conceive of them being so impudent as to quaff wine like this? Rather, they were actually saturated with that other wine,[702] as is written: *They offered strange fire in the presence of YHVH* (Leviticus 10:1). Here is written: *strange fire,* and there is written: *to protect you from a strange woman* (Proverbs 7:5)—all one and the same.[703]

"Similarly, *He drank of the wine and became drunk, and exposed himself.* So Ham, father of Canaan, aroused, as has been explained, and scope was provided to Canaan to prevail.[704] Whereas he had been righteous, in the mystery of covenant,[705] he castrated him, for we have learned that he removed that covenant from him.[706] Therefore, *He said, 'Cursed be Canaan'* (Genesis 9:25),

434

the wine and became drunk, and exposed himself inside his tent.

699. **breach of the world...** The gap between *Shekhinah* and the other *sefirot,* which had been opened by Adam's sin and then closed when he turned back to God.

700. אהלה (*oholoh*), *his tent*—spelled with a ה (*he*)...*her tent*... In the biblical text the final letter of אהלה (*oholoh*), *his tent,* is a ה (*he*), rather than the normal masculine possessive suffix ו (*vav*). The suffix ה (*he*) usually denotes the feminine possessive, *her.* See *Bereshit Rabbah* 36:4: "Rabbi Yehudah son of Rabbi Simon and Rabbi Ḥanan said in the name of Rabbi Shemu'el son of Rav Yitsḥak, '...It is spelled אהלה (*oholah*), *her tent:* inside the tent of his wife.'" In other words, Noah shamed himself in his wife's tent. See Theodor's note, ad loc.

Here similarly, Rabbi Shim'on reads the word as *oholah, her tent,* but he takes this to mean: "the tent of that vineyard," namely, the tent of *Shekhinah,* site of Noah's sin. See *Zohar* 1:83a.

Instead of "*inside* אהלה (*oholah*), *her tent,* the tent of that vineyard," several manuscripts (V5, R1) read "corresponding to what is written: *Do not come near the door of her house* (Proverbs 5:8)," namely, the house of

the strange woman, symbolizing the demonic. See *Zohar* 2:245a (*Heikh*), 267b (*Heikh*).

701. **Similarly, the sons of Aaron...** Aaron's two eldest sons, Nadab and Abihu, were killed when *they offered strange fire in the presence of YHVH* (Leviticus 10:1–2). According to Rabbi Yishma'el (*Vayiqra Rabbah* 12:1), they died because they "entered while drunk with wine."

702. **that other wine** Of the demonic realm.

703. *strange fire...a strange woman...* The *strange fire* symbolizes the demonic feminine. See Moses de León, *Sheqel ha-Qodesh,* 37 (44).

704. **Ham, father of Canaan, aroused...** Ham, Noah's second son, who saw his father's nakedness, corresponds to the *sefirah* of *Gevurah* or *Din* ("Judgment"), located on the left side of the sefirotic tree. Ham's sin empowered his son Canaan, who symbolizes the demonic refuse of *Din.* See above, page 431.

705. **Whereas he had been righteous...** Noah had been righteous, symbolizing the *sefirah* of *Yesod,* known as Righteous One. *Yesod* is the divine phallus and site of the covenant of circumcision.

706. **he castrated him...** According to Rav (BT *Sanhedrin* 70a), Ham castrated his

for curses aroused, as at first.[707] *Slave of slaves he shall be* (ibid.), as is said: *Cursed are you among all animals and among all beasts of the field* (ibid. 3:14).[708] All will be restored in the time to come, but he will not; all will be liberated, but he will not.[709] This is a mystery intended for those who know the ways and paths of Torah."

He opened, saying, "*For I know my transgressions; my sin confronts me constantly* (Psalms 51:5). How carefully humans should guard themselves from sinning in the presence of the blessed Holy One! For once one has sinned, his sin is inscribed above, inexpungible except through extreme exertion, as is said: *Though you wash yourself with natron and use an abundance of lye, your iniquity is stained before Me* (Jeremiah 2:22).

"Come and see: When a human being sins once in the presence of the blessed Holy One, it leaves a mark. If he repeats, that mark is deepened. If he repeats again, that stain spreads from one side to the other; then, *your iniquity is stained before Me.*

"Come and see: When King David sinned in the presence of the blessed Holy One in the affair of Bathsheba,[710] he thought the sin was marked on him forever. What is written? *YHVH has removed your sin; you shall not die* (2 Samuel 12:13)—He removed that mark from His presence."

Rabbi Abba said to him, "Look, we have learned that Bathsheba was destined for King David since the day the world was created![711] So why did the blessed Holy One give her first to Uriah the Hittite?"

He replied, "Such are the ways of the blessed Holy One. Even though a woman is destined for a certain man, another—anticipating—marries her

435

father, thereby eliminating the covenantal sign of circumcision.

707. **as at first** Following Adam's sin.

708. *Slave of slaves... Cursed are you among all animals...* The curse uttered against Canaan parallels the curse pronounced upon the serpent in the Garden. As the serpent is more cursed than all other animals, who are themselves enslaved to humanity, so Canaan is doomed to be *slave of slaves.* See above, page 431.

709. **All will be restored...** See *Bereshit Rabbah* 20:5: "Rabbi Levi said, 'In the time to come, all will be healed except for the serpent and the Gibeonites [see Joshua 9:23].'" Here Canaan, symbolizing the demonic, shares the eternal curse of the serpent.

710. **When King David sinned... in the affair of Bathsheba** Seeing her bathing, David was attracted to her and slept with her. He then arranged for her husband, Uriah the Hittite, to die in battle, after which he married her. See 2 Samuel 11–12.

711. **Bathsheba was destined for King David...** See BT *Sanhedrin* 107a: "Rava expounded, '...Ever since the six days of Creation, Bathsheba daughter of Eliam was designated for David, but she came to him with suffering.' The school of Rabbi Yishma'el taught likewise: 'She was designated for David, but he ate her unripe [prematurely, while she was still married to Uriah].'" See *Zohar* 1:8b; 2:107a; 3:78b.

before the time of this other one arrives.⁷¹² As soon as his time arrives, the one who had married her is thrust away in favor of this other one coming later, and he departs the world.⁷¹³ It is difficult for the blessed Holy One to remove him from the world before his time arrives, in favor of this other one.⁷¹⁴

"This mystery of Bathsheba who was given first to Uriah the Hittite—go search and you will discover why the Holy Land was given to Canaan before Israel arrived. You will discover it is all one mystery.⁷¹⁵

"Come and see: Even though David confessed his sin and returned,⁷¹⁶ his heart and mind did not depart from those sins he sinned or from that sin regarding Bathsheba, for he feared them constantly, lest one of them prevail and accuse him in time of danger.⁷¹⁷ So he did not obliterate them from his mind.

"Alternatively, *For I know my transgressions*—I know all those rungs from which human sins suspend.⁷¹⁸ *My sin confronts me constantly*—defect of the moon,⁷¹⁹ who did not escape impurity until Solomon appeared and she lustered

<hr>

436

712. **another—anticipating—marries her...** See BT *Mo'ed Qatan* 18b: "Shemu'el said, 'One is allowed to betroth a woman during the intermediate days of a festival, lest another [rival suitor] anticipate him.' ...But could Shemu'el have said, 'Lest another anticipate him'? Surely Rav Yehudah said in the name of Shemu'el, 'Every single day a heavenly echo issues, announcing: "The daughter of so-and-so for so-and-so...."' Rather, 'lest another anticipate him through supplication.'" See *Zohar* 1:91b; 2:101a; 3:78b, 283b.

713. **he departs the world** The first husband dies.

714. **It is difficult for the blessed Holy One...** On God's difficulty in matching couples, see *Bereshit Rabbah* 68:4.

715. **the Holy Land was given to Canaan before Israel arrived...all one mystery** The land was refined through Canaan's prior occupation. Similarly, Bathsheba was prepared for David by her prior marriage to Uriah. See *Zohar* 1:83a.

716. **David confessed his sin and returned** Repenting sincerely. See 2 Samuel 12:13: *David said to Nathan, "I have sinned against YHVH!"*

717. **accuse him in time of danger** See *Bereshit Rabbah* 91:9: "Rabbi Eli'ezer said,

'...Satan accuses only in time of danger.'"

718. **all those rungs from which human sins suspend** The various *sefirot,* each of which is impaired by particular human sins.

719. *My sin confronts me constantly*—**defect of the moon** The Hebrew root חטא (*ḥt'*) includes the meanings "to miss" and "to sin." Here the word implies "something missing," a defect in *Shekhinah,* symbolized by the moon. This *sefirah,* known as *Malkhut* ("Kingdom"), corresponds to King David.

On the defect of the moon, see BT *Ḥullin* 60b: "Rabbi Shim'on son of Pazzi pointed out a contradiction. 'It is written: *God made the two great lights* (Genesis 1:16), and it is written [in the same verse]: *the greater light...and the lesser light.* The moon said before the blessed Holy One, "Master of the Universe! Can two kings possibly wear one crown?" He answered, "Go, diminish yourself!" She said before Him, "Master of the Universe! Because I have suggested something proper I should make myself smaller?" He replied, "Go and rule by day and night." She said, "But what is the value of this? What good is a lamp at noon?"...Seeing that her mind was uneasy [that she could not be consoled], the blessed Holy One said, "Bring an atonement for Me for making the moon smaller.'" As was said by Rabbi Shim'on son

in fullness.[720] Then the world turned firm and fragrant,[721] so Israel dwelled securely, as is written: *Everyone in Israel dwelled under his vine and under his fig tree* (1 Kings 5:5).[722] Nevertheless, *my sin confronts me constantly* and will not be eradicated from the world until King Messiah arrives in the time to come, as is said: *I will eliminate the spirit of impurity from earth* (Zechariah 13:2)."

He was a mighty hunter before YHVH; hence the saying: Like Nimrod, a mighty hunter before YHVH (Genesis 10:9).[723]

Come and see: He was a mighty man, garbed in the garments of Adam, through which he discovered how to hunt creatures.[724]

Rabbi El'azar said, "Nimrod used to entice creatures into worshiping idols. In those garments he prevailed, conquering the inhabitants of the world. He proclaimed himself Ruler of the World, and humanity worshiped him. Why was he called נמרוד (Nimrod), Nimrod? Because he מרד (marad), rebelled, against the supernal King on high, rebelling against those on high, rebelling against those below.[725]

437

of Lakish: 'Why is the goat offered on the new moon distinguished by the phrase *to* [or: *for*] *YHVH* (Numbers 28:15)? The blessed Holy One said, "Let this goat be an atonement for My having made the moon smaller."'"

See BT *Rosh ha-Shanah* 23b; *Zohar* 1:19b–20a, 146a; *ZḤ* 70d–71a (*ShS*); Moses de León, *Sefer ha-Rimmon*, 189; idem, *Mishkan ha-Edut*, 35b.

720. **until Solomon appeared...** During the triumphant reign of Solomon, *Shekhinah* regained Her full splendor.

According to the Midrash, just as the moon does not become full until the fifteenth day of its cycle, so it remained incomplete until the glorious reign of Solomon in the fifteenth generation from Abraham. See *Pesiqta de-Rav Kahana* 5:12; and *Shemot Rabbah* 15:26: "When Solomon appeared, the disk of the moon became full."

See *Zohar* 1:74a, 150a, 223a, 225b, 249b; 2:85a; 3:61a; *ZḤ* 83b (*MhN, Rut*); Moses de León, *Shushan Edut*, 342.

721. **turned firm and fragrant** אתבסם (*Itbassam*), "Was sweetened" or "was firmly established." The root *bsm* conveys both senses.

See *Bereshit Rabbah* 66:2; *Midrash Shemu'el* 26:4; *Zohar* 1:30b, 31a, 34a, 37a, 56a, 137a; 2:143a, 168a, 227a; 3:18a; Bronsnick, in

Sinai 63 (1968): 81–85; Scholem, *Major Trends*, 165, 388, n. 44; idem, *Kabbalah*, 228.

722. ***Everyone in Israel...*** The full verse reads: *Judah and Israel dwelled securely, everyone under his vine and under his fig tree, from Dan to Beer-sheba, all the days of Solomon.*

723. ***Nimrod...*** King of Babylonia and Assyria. See Genesis 10:8–12.

724. **garbed in the garments of Adam...** See *Pirqei de-Rabbi Eli'ezer* 24: "Rabbi Yehudah said, 'The coat made by the blessed Holy One for Adam and his wife [see Genesis 3:21] was with them in the ark. When they emerged from the ark, Ham son of Noah took it out with him and gave it as an inheritance to Nimrod [his grandson]. When he wore it, every animal, beast, and bird came and prostrated itself before him. They [his contemporaries] thought this was due to his own power, so they made him king.'"

See *Bereshit Rabbah* 63:13; 65:16; *Zohar* 1:142b; 2:39a–b; *ZḤ* 65a (*ShS*).

725. **Why was he called נמרוד (*Nimrod*), Nimrod?...** See BT *Pesaḥim* 94a–b. According to rabbinic tradition, Nimrod instigated the building of the Tower of Babel. See *Avodah Zarah* 53b; *Ḥullin* 89a.

"In those [74a] garments he ruled all inhabitants of the world, reigning over them, rebelling against his Lord, proclaiming himself Ruler of the World. He enticed creatures, finally luring humans to abandon the worship of the Lord of the world."

Rabbi Shim'on said, "Concerning these garments, the Companions know a supernal mystery!"[726]

Our Mishnah.[727] *The whole earth was of one language and of identical words* (Genesis 11:1).

Rabbi Shim'on opened, "*The House, in its being built, was built of stone dressed at the quarry, so no hammer, ax, or any iron tool was heard*... (1 Kings 6:7).

"*The House, in its being built.* Didn't Solomon build it along with all those artisans who were there? Why, *in its being built*?[728] But so it was, as is written: *Of hammered work shall the lampstand be made* (Exodus 25:31). If it was *hammered work,* then why *shall it be made*? But indeed, entirely by miracle, made by itself.[729] As soon as they began working, the work taught them how to create what they never knew before. Why? Because the blessing of the blessed Holy One inhabited their hands. So it is written: *in its being built*—it was built by itself,[730] for it taught the artisans how to commence creating, and the actual design of that creation did not vanish from their sight. Contemplating it, they kept working till the entire House was built.

"*Was built* אבן שלמה (*even shelemah*), *of stone dressed, at the quarry*—spelled שלמה (*shelemah*), missing the י (*yod*), *stone of* שלמה (*Shelomoh*), *Solomon,* indeed![731]

438

726. **Concerning these garments, the Companions know a supernal mystery!** See the Zoharic passages cited above, note 724. In 2:39a–b, Rabbi Shim'on maintains that the garments of Adam and Eve were never worn again by anyone else.

727. **Our Mishnah** The *Zohar* often cites teachings from a secret, mystical Mishnah known only to its own circle. See 1:37b, 55b, 91b, 93a, 95b, 96a, 224a, 252a (*Hash*); 3:57b, 61b, 78a, 284b, 285a. This is to be distinguished from the *Matnitin* of the *Zohar,* on which see Scholem, *Kabbalah,* 216.

728. **Didn't Solomon build it...** Didn't Solomon and his artisans build the Temple? Why, then, the wording *in its being built,* which implies that the work was accomplished effortlessly and miraculously?

729. **entirely by miracle, made by itself** Similarly, the lampstand in the Tabernacle took shape miraculously. See *Tanḥuma, Be-ha'alotekha* 3.

730. *in its being built*—**it was built by itself** See *Shir ha-Shirim Rabbah* on 1:1 (5): "Rabbi Berekhiah said, 'It is not written here: *The House that they were building,* but rather: *The House, in its being built.* It was built by itself!'"

731. **spelled** שלמה (*shelemah*), **missing the** י (*yod*)... The defective spelling of the word enables it to be read *Shelomoh, Solomon.* During Solomon's triumphant reign, *Shekhinah* (symbolized by the stone) was complete, and She inspired the construction of the Temple.

See *Zohar* 1:83b, and above, note 720.

"מסע (*Massa*), *Quarry,* Journey[732]—transported, coming and resting upon them, so the work was accomplished.[733] *Massa*—moving their hands to create unconsciously. Here is written: מסע (*massa*), and there is written: *And for* מסע (*massa*), *journeying, the camps* (Numbers 10:2).[734]

"*So no hammer, ax, or any iron tool was heard*—for *shamir*[735] split all soundlessly, so they needed no other tools to work, all miraculously!"

Rabbi Shim'on said, "How beloved are words of Torah! Happy is the share of one engaged in them, knowing how to walk the path of truth! *The House, in its being built.* When it arose in the will of the blessed Holy One to fashion glory for Its glory,[736] from the midst of thought a desire arose to expand—expanding from the site of concealed thought, unknown, expanding and settling in the larynx,[737] a site continuously gushing in the mystery of the spirit of life. When thought expanded and settled in this site, that thought was called אלהים חיים (*Elohim Ḥayyim*), Living God: *He is Living God* (Jeremiah 10:10).

"It sought to expand and reveal Itself further; thence issued fire, air, and water,[738] merging as one. Jacob emerged, Consummate Man,[739] a single voice issuing audibly. Hence, thought, having been concealed in silence, was heard revealing itself.[740]

"Thought expanded further revealing itself, and this voice struck against lips. Then speech issued, consummating all, revealing all.[741] It is perceived that all is concealed thought, having been within, and all is one.[742]

439

732. מסע (*Massa*), *Quarry,* Journey   The Hebrew word bears both meanings.

733. transported, coming and resting upon them...   The presence of *Shekhinah* came upon them.

734. *And for* מסע (*massa*), *journeying, the camps*   Just as *Shekhinah* directed Israel's journey through the desert, so too She guided the building of the Temple. See *Baraita di-Mlekhet ha-Mishkan*, 13.

735. *shamir*   A fabulous worm that could cut through the sharpest stone. According to rabbinic tradition, Solomon employed it in building the Temple. See BT *Gittin* 68a; Ginzberg, *Legends*, 5:53, n. 165.

736. When it arose in the will of the blessed Holy One...   As the infinite divinity verged on manifesting Itself, fashioning *the House*, the sefirotic structure. See *Zohar* 1:246b.

737. larynx   *Binah*, source of the divine voice. See *Zohar* 1:50b.

738. fire, air, and water   *Ḥesed, Gevurah,* and *Tif'eret,* the central triad of *sefirot,* emanating from *Binah.*

739. Jacob emerged, Consummate Man   Jacob, consummation of the patriarchs, symbolizes *Tif'eret,* who balances left and right, expressing the emanation from *Binah.* The phrase גבר שלים (*gevar shelim*), "Consummate Man," derives from *Targum Onqelos,* on Genesis 25:27, where Jacob, in contrast to Esau the hunter, is described as איש תם (*ish tam*), rendered variously: "a simple (or: innocent, plain, mild, quiet, sound, wholesome) man."

740. single voice issuing audibly... concealed in silence...   See *Zohar* 1:16b, 50b, 141b; Moses de León, *Sheqel ha-Qodesh,* 89 (113). Cf. BT *Berakhot* 15b: "The womb, which takes in silently, gives forth loudly."

741. Then speech issued...   *Shekhinah* articulates divine revelation.

742. all is concealed thought...   The entire sefirotic realm evolves from divine thought.

"Once this expansion ripened, generating speech through the potency of that voice, then *The House, in its being built.* The verse does not read *when it was built,* but rather *in its being built,* every single time.[743]

"*Of stone dressed*—as has been said.[744] And it is written: *the crown with which his mother crowned him* (Song of Songs 3:11).[745]

"מסע (*Massa*), *Quarry,* Journey—issuing from within, dwelling, journeying outside; issuing from above, dwelling, journeying below.

"*No hammer, ax, or any iron tool was heard*—other, lower rungs, all dependent upon it, neither heard nor admitted within when She ascends to unite above, to suckle from there.[746]

"This is *in its being built.* Then as She suckles, they all abide in joy, suckling, being filled with blessings. Then all worlds abide in single mystery, in single union, with no division. After each and every one receives his share, they all disperse in their directions, to their appointments.

"Come and see: *The whole earth was of one language and of identical words.* [74b] What is written next? *When they journeyed from* קדם (*qedem*), *the east* (Genesis 11:2)[747]—from קדמאה (*Qadma'ah*), Primordial One, of the world.[748] *They found* בקעה (*biq'ah*), *a valley, in the land of Shinar,* for from there they disperse in all directions, it being the first kingdom to scatter.[749]

"Now if you say, 'Look at what is written: *A river issues from Eden to water the garden, and from there it divides* (Genesis 2:10),' certainly so, for once they journey from there, division ensues.[750] When they gather there to suckle, no

---

743. **every single time** The process unfolds gradually and continuously.

744. **Of stone dressed...** The phrase אבן שלמה (*even shelemah*), *stone dressed,* is read as *even Shelomoh, stone of Solomon,* referring to *Shekhinah.* See above, note 731.

745. **the crown with which his mother crowned him** In Song of Songs this verse applies to King Solomon. Here he symbolizes the male divinity, who is adorned by the Divine Mother (*Binah*) with *Shekhinah,* also known as *Atarah* ("Crown").

746. **other, lower rungs...** The forces and realms below *Shekhinah,* who are nourished by Her. They do not join in Her union with the higher *sefirot.*

747. **When they journeyed from** קדם (*qedem*), *the east* The verse continues: *they found a valley in the land of Shinar and settled there.* The following verses describe the construction of the Tower of Babel.

748. קדמאה (*Qadma'ah*), **Primordial One, of the world** See *Bereshit Rabbah* 38:7: "*When they journeyed from* קדם (*qedem*), *the east.*... Rabbi El'azar son of Rabbi Shim'on said, 'They removed themselves from קדמונו (*Qadmono*), Primordial One, of the world, saying, "We desire neither Him nor His divinity."'"

749. **for from there they disperse...** Rabbi Shim'on interprets בקעה (*biq'ah*), *valley,* according to its root, "to cleave, split." Those who built the Tower of Babel attempted to split the divine unity and were punished by being scattered (Genesis 11:8–9). See Baḥya ben Asher, Genesis 11:4. Similarly, the realms beneath *Shekhinah* are characterized by multiplicity and division.

750. **Now if you say, 'Look at what is written: *A river issues...*** This verse is understood to refer to the flow of emanation to *Shekhinah* (*the garden*) and the division

division; when they journey, division, as is written: *When they journeyed from
qedem, they found a valley,* as has been said.

"*The whole earth was of one language and of identical words.* For then the
world shared a single essential root, a united faith in the blessed Holy One.
What is written? *When they journeyed from qedem*—from *Qadma'ah,* Primordial One, root of the world, faith of all. *They found a valley*—they found a find
by which they forsook supernal faith.

"Come and see: What is written of Nimrod? *The beginning of his kingdom
was Babylon* (ibid. 10:10). From there he journeyed to embrace the other dominion.[751] Similarly here, *They found a valley in the land of Shinar.*[752] From
there they drifted in their hearts, abandoning supernal dominion for the other."

They said, "Come, let us build ourselves a city, and a tower with its top in the heavens, and let us make a name for ourselves" (Genesis 11:4).	Rabbi Ḥiyya opened, "*The wicked are like the banished sea that cannot be still...* (Isaiah 57:20).[753] Now is there such a thing as a *banished sea*? Yes, for when the sea escapes its normal array, surging out of

control, then it is banished, expelled from its site. Like one who is drunk on
wine, agitated, heaving up and down. Why? Because *it cannot be still, and its
waters toss up mire and mud* (ibid.)—casting up all that mud of the sea, all the
muck, onto the shore.[754] Similarly, those wicked who abandon the paved path,
staggering like incoherent drunkards, abandoning the straight path for the
crooked. Why? Because they *cannot be still*—the crookedness of their path
causes them to walk aimlessly, restlessly. Furthermore, all their rage as they
snarl words from their mouths—each word *mire and mud*—all spewing abhor-
rent filth from their mouths until they defile themselves [75a] and are defiled.[755]

"Come and see: *They said, "Come, let us build ourselves a city...."* The expression *Come* denotes mere preparation.[756]

"*Let us build ourselves a city, and a tower with its top in the heavens.* They all
followed bad advice, rebelling against the blessed Holy One. They proceeded
foolishly, stupidly."

beneath Her. Though it appears that the
split begins at the stage of *Shekhinah,* Rabbi
Shim'on explains that it takes effect only
beneath Her, as a result of the journey away
from *the garden.*

751. **other dominion** The demonic
realm.

752. *land of Shinar* Identical with Babylon.

753. *the banished sea...* ים נגרש (*Yam

nigrash*), usually rendered as *the tossing sea*
or *the troubled sea,* but Rabbi Ḥiyya focuses
on the literal meaning.

754. **casting up all that mud of the sea...**
See Radak's explanation of *banished sea,*
ad loc.

755. **defiled** By the demonic powers.

756. **The expression *Come* denotes mere
preparation** See Rashi, ad loc.; *Zohar* 2:18a
(*MhN*).

Rabbi Abba said, "They admitted stupidity into their minds but proceeded with evil wisdom, abandoning supernal dominion for the other,[757] exchanging His glory for alien glory. Everywhere lies a mystery of supernal wisdom.[758]

"*Come, let us build ourselves a city and a tower.* Come and see: When they reached this valley, the alien domain, and the site of its dominion was revealed to them—plunged in the midst of the fish of the sea[759]—they said, 'Here is a place to settle, to harden the heart, and for lower beings to indulge.' Immediately, *Come, let us build ourselves a city*—'let us establish on this site *a city and a tower.*'

"*And let us make a name for ourselves.* 'This site will be our deity, no other;[760] for this site *let us build a city and a tower.* Why ascend any higher, whence we cannot derive pleasure? Here is a perfect place. *Let us make a name for ourselves*—a deity to worship. *Lest we be scattered* (Genesis, ibid.)—to other rungs, in all directions.'

"*YHVH came down to see the city and the tower* (ibid., 5). This is one of the ten times that *Shekhinah* descended to earth.[761] Why *to see?* Didn't He already know?[762] Rather, *to see,* 'to scrutinize in judgment,' as is said: *May YHVH see you and judge!* (Exodus 5:21).

"*The city and the tower.* Here one should contemplate, for the verse does not read *to see the human beings,* but rather *to see the city and the tower.* Why? Because when the blessed Holy One gazes in judgment, at first He gazes at the rung above, then at the rung below; at first at those above, then at those below.[763] Since this matter impinged above, gazing above preceded, as is written: *the city and the tower that* בני האדם (*benei ha-adam*), *the humans,* had

---

757. **proceeded with evil wisdom...**
Consciously seeking the demonic realm.
See above, pages 440–41.

758. **Everywhere...** Even in a sinful act.

759. **plunged in the midst of the fish of the sea** The sea apparently symbolizes *Shekhinah,* who nourishes many powers, including the demonic.

760. **This site will be our deity...** They sought to worship the demonic in place of *Shekhinah,* the divine *name.* Or, they focused on *Shekhinah* alone, thereby splitting Her off from the other *sefirot* and ruining the divine union. The two explanations are related, since the demonic thrives on this cosmic split.

See *Bereshit Rabbah* 38:8: "*And let us make a name for ourselves.* It was taught in the

school of Rabbi Yishma'el: '*Name* means nothing but an idol.'" Cf. *Mekhilta, Mishpatim* 20; Naḥmanides on Genesis 11:2.

761. **one of the ten times that *Shekhinah* descended to earth** These divine manifestations are referred to in various sources, including: *Mekhilta, Baḥodesh* 3; *Bereshit Rabbah* 38:8; *Avot de-Rabbi Natan* A, 34; B, 37; *Pirqei de-Rabbi Eli'ezer* 14.

762. **Didn't He already know?** Since God is omniscient, why should He have to come down *to see?*

763. **at the rung above, then at the rung below...** The sin of the rebels ruined the union of the divine couple, *Yesod* and *Shekhinah,* symbolized by *the city and the tower.* God first inspected the damage above, then gazed below. See *Zohar* 1:74b (*ST*).

built (ibid.). What is the meaning of *benei ha-adam*? 'The children of Adam,' who rebelled against his Lord, inflicting death upon the world.[764] *That the humans had built*—producing an actual building, striving to build above."[765]

Rabbi Shim'on opened, "*Thus says YHVH: The gate of* [75b] *the inner court facing east shall be shut on the six working days, but on the Sabbath it shall be opened, and on the day of the new moon it shall be opened* (Ezekiel 46:1).[766] This verse calls for contemplation, for it is a mystery, as has been explained.

"*It shall be shut on the six working days.* Why *shall it be shut* all those *six working days*? Because these are secular days when this gate should be shut so secular not exploit sacred.[767] *But on the Sabbath it shall be opened, and on the day of the new moon it shall be opened,* for then performance of sacred with sacred; then the moon is illumined to unite with the sun.[768]

"Come and see: This gate is not opened on those six secular days because on those days the lower world is nourished and those six secular days rule the

443

764. 'The children of Adam'... See *Bereshit Rabbah* 38:9, which compares the sinful ingratitude of Adam and the generation of the Tower of Babel: "*That* בני האדם (*benei ha-adam*), *the children of the human, had built*. Rabbi Berekhiah said, 'Would we have thought it was built by the children of donkeys or camels? Rather, it means *the children of Adam,* [by which God implied:] "Just as Adam, after all the good that I bestowed upon him, said *The woman whom You gave to be beside me* [*she gave me of the tree, and I ate*] (Genesis 3:12), so although the generation of the Dispersion [the generation of the Tower of Babel] followed the generation of the Flood by only two years [as is said:] *two years after the Flood* (ibid. 11:10), yet [they rebelled, displaying gross ingratitude].""" See *Zohar* 1:60b, 74b (*ST*).

Adam's sin also ruined the union of the divine couple. See *Zohar* 1:35b–36a, 52a.

765. **striving to build above** Attempting to replace the sefirotic structure with a demonic one.

766. *The gate of the inner court facing east*... The verse is from Ezekiel's vision of the restored Temple in Jerusalem. See *Zohar* 2:248b (*Heikh*); *TZ* 21, 61a; 36, 78a.

767. **Because these are secular days...**

The six weekdays symbolize demonic powers who rule the world on those days. During that time, *Shekhinah,* the gate of the upper world, must remain closed, so that the flow of emanation not flow freely to them.

768. **performance of sacred with sacred...** On these holy days, *Shekhinah* (symbolized by the moon) unites with Her partner, *Tif'eret* (symbolized by the sun). Similarly, according to BT *Ketubbot* 62b (in the name of Shemu'el), scholars should unite with their wives each Sabbath eve. In the *Zohar,* this act symbolizes and stimulates the union of the divine couple, engendering a holy body and drawing down a holy soul.

See Moses de León, *Mishkan ha-Edut,* 63b; *Zohar* 1:14a, 50a, 112a (*MhN*); 2:63b, 89a–b; 3:49b, 78a.

Cf. *Pirqei de-Rabbi Eli'ezer* 51: "Rabbi Yehudah says, 'On Sabbath and new moons, Israel stood there [in the court of the Temple] and saw the doors open by themselves, and they knew that Sabbath had arrived, and they sanctified it. Similarly on the new moons.... Because they stood there and saw the doors open by themselves, they knew that the *Shekhinah* of the blessed Holy One dwelled within.'"

world, except for the land of Israel.[769] They rule because this gate is shut, but *on the Sabbath ... and on the day of the new moon* they are all removed and rule no more, for this gate is open and the world is joyous—nourished from there, not handed over to the other dominion.

"Now if you say those six days rule entirely on their own, come and see: *facing* קדים (qadim), *east*—before they rise to rule, it gazes constantly upon the world,[770] though it is not opened for the world to be nourished from the sacred except on Sabbath and the new moon. All those days cleave to Sabbath, whence they are nourished;[771] for on Sabbath all those gates are opened and tranquility manifests for all, those above and those below.

"Come and see: וירד יהוה (Va-yered YHVH), *YHVH came down, to see,* descending from sacred to secular, with רדיד (redid), a veil, spread,[772] to inspect what they had built, the edifice they had erected to provoke the world to worship them."

444

Rabbi Yitsḥak was sitting in the presence of Rabbi Shim'on and asked him, "How could these people have been so foolish to rebel against the blessed Holy One, unanimously adopting the same plan?"

He replied, "This has already been explained: *When they journeyed from the east*—journeying from above to below, journeying from the land of Israel and descending to Babel.[773] They said, 'Here is a site to embrace. *Let us make a name for ourselves;* then sustenance from below will adhere to this site.[774] For when judgment looms over the world, this site will resist; from here the world will derive pleasure and nourishment, since above is too remote. Further, we will ascend to heaven and wage battle,[775] so that no flood will pour down upon the world as before.'

769. **except for the land of Israel** Ruled and nourished directly by the divine. See BT *Ta'anit* 10a: "The land of Israel is watered by the blessed Holy One Himself, while the rest of the world is watered by an emissary."

Cf. *Tanḥuma, Re'eh* 8; BT *Ketubbot* 110b; *Zohar* 1:61a, 84b, 108b; 2:33a, 151b.

770. *facing* קדים (qadim), *east*—**before they rise to rule...** Rabbi Shim'on connects the word קדים (qadim), *east,* with קודם (qodem), "before." The providential gaze of *Shekhinah* precedes and oversees the dominion of the demonic powers.

771. **All those days cleave to Sabbath...** The weekdays derive their nourishment from Sabbath.

772. **a veil, spread** The veil separates the heavenly and earthly realms.

773. **This has already been explained... journeying from above to below...** See above, pages 440–41; *Pirqei de-Rabbi Eli'ezer* 24. Babel is the site of the demonic.

774. *Let us make a name for ourselves...* Let us replace the divine with the demonic, so that the worship of creatures below will be directed here, empowering the demonic. See above, page 442 and note 760.

775. **we will ascend to heaven and wage battle** See BT *Sanhedrin* 109a.

"*YHVH said, 'Look, they are one people with one language for them all'* (Genesis 11:6). 'Since they are all united as one, they will succeed in their project. Let all rungs disperse, each in its own direction, so that all these below disperse.'[776] What is written? *YHVH scattered them from there* (ibid., 8).[777]

"If you ask, 'Why was their language scattered and scrambled?'—it is because they were all speaking the holy tongue,[778] and that language aided them, for the act of enunciation is essential to attaining one's intention.[779] Thereby they supported the place they sought to erect. So their language was confounded to prevent them from empowering their desire in the holy tongue. As soon as their language mutated, they failed in the project, since the powers above know and recognize only the holy tongue.[780] Once language was scrambled, their power weakened and fractured.

"Come and see: A word spoken by lower creatures in the holy tongue is comprehended by all the powers of heaven, who are thereby invigorated, but any other language they neither comprehend nor recognize. So as soon as their language was scrambled, *they stopped building the city* (ibid.), for their power fractured and despite their desire they could not accomplish anything.

"*Blessed be the name of the blessed Holy One forever and ever, for wisdom and power are His* (Daniel 2:20).[781] Because the blessed Holy One brought secrets of wisdom down to the world, humanity was corrupted by it and sought to attack Him.[782] He gave supernal wisdom to Adam, and through that revealed wisdom [76a] he discovered rungs[783] and clung to the evil impulse until the springs of wisdom vanished. Afterward he returned to the presence of his Lord,[784] and

445

776. **Let all rungs disperse...** Let the heavenly powers disperse, so they will be unable to help the earthly rebels. (According to rabbinic tradition, the seventy nations of the world are governed by seventy angels or heavenly princes appointed by God.)

See Daniel 10:20; Septuagint, Deuteronomy 32:8–9; Jubilees 15:31–32; *Targum Yerushalmi*, Genesis 11:8, Deuteronomy 32:8–9; *Tanḥuma, Re'eh* 8; *Leqaḥ Tov*, Genesis 9:19; *Pirqei de-Rabbi Eli'ezer* 24; *Zohar* 1:46b, 108b; 3:298b; Ginzberg, *Legends*, 5:204–5, n. 91.

777. *YHVH scattered them...* Both heavenly powers and the rebels below.

778. **they were all speaking the holy tongue** See JT *Megillah* 1:11, 71b; *Tanḥuma* (Buber), *Noah* 28; *Targum Yerushalmi*, Genesis 11:1; Ibn Ezra, ad loc.

779. **enunciation is essential...** The pronunciation of Hebrew words stimulates heavenly powers to actualize the speaker's intention. See *Zohar* 3:112b.

780. **the powers above know and recognize only the holy tongue** See BT *Shabbat* 12b: "Rabbi Yoḥanan said, 'If one petitions for his needs in Aramaic, the ministering angels do not attend to him, for they do not know Aramaic.'"

See *Zohar* 1:9b, 74b (*ST*), 88b–89a (*ST*).

781. *Blessed be the name of the blessed Holy One...* The verse actually reads: *Blessed be the name of God....*

782. **Because the blessed Holy One brought secrets...** Despite the fact that humanity would misuse the secrets, God still generously revealed them.

783. **rungs** Various levels of reality, including the demonic.

784. **he returned to the presence of his Lord** Repenting sincerely.

some was revealed, though not as before. Later, through that book of his,[785] he discovered wisdoms; but then people appeared and provoked Him.[786]

"He gave wisdom to Noah, who thereby served the blessed Holy One. After-ward what is written? *He drank of the wine and became drunk, and exposed himself* (Genesis 9:21), as has been explained.[787]

"He gave wisdom to Abraham, who thereby served the blessed Holy One. Afterward Ishmael issued from him, who provoked the blessed Holy One. Sim-ilarly Isaac, from whom issued Esau.[788] Jacob married two sisters.[789]

"He gave wisdom to Moses. What is written of him? *Throughout My house he is faithful* (Numbers 12:7). There was none as faithful as Moses: he performed on all those rungs, yet his heart did not stray into desiring any of them;[790] rather, he stood firm in supernal faith fittingly.

"He gave supernal wisdom to King Solomon. Afterward what is written of him? *Proverbs of Solomon* (Proverbs 1:1). *An oracle. The man spoke:* 'לאיתיאל (*Le-Iti'el*), *To Ithiel, to Ithiel* ואכל (*ve-Ukhal*), *and Ucal*' (ibid. 30:1). Solomon said, 'אתי אל (*Itti El*), *God is with me.* Wisdom is His. ואוכל (*Ve-ukhal*), *And I can*, do what I desire!' Later, *YHVH stirred up* שטן (*satan*), *an adversary, against Solomon* (1 Kings 11:14).[791]

785. **that book of his** According to BT *Bava Metsi'a* 85b–86a, Rabbi Yehudah the Prince once saw *The Book of Adam*, which contained the genealogy of the entire human race. See Genesis 5:1; *Bereshit Rabbah* 24:1; BT *Sanhedrin* 38b. This book is not to be confused with the Apocryphal *Book of Adam*, known in various versions, though the Apocryphal book may have influenced the *Zohar*'s depiction of the *Book of Adam*. According to various medieval traditions, the angel Raziel transmitted a magical book to Adam. Later, probably in the seventeenth century, *Sefer Razi'el* was compiled in its present form, comprising ancient magical, mystical, and cosmological teachings.

Adam's book is referred to frequently in the *Zohar*. See 1:17b, 37b, 55a–b, 58b, 72b, 90b; 2:70a–b, 131a, 143b, 180a, 181a, 197a; 3:10a, 68b; *ZH* 37b; Ginzberg, *Legends*, 5:117–18, n. 110; Liebes, *Peraqim*, 85–87; Wineman, *Mystic Tales from the Zohar*, 35–54.

786. **then people appeared and provoked Him** They misused the wisdom contained in the book, employing it selfishly for magi-cal purposes.

787. *He drank of the wine and became drunk…* See above, pages 433–34.

788. **Ishmael issued from him…Esau** Abraham and Isaac were tainted by engen-dering Ishmael and Esau. See *Sifrei*, Deuter-onomy 31; *Bereshit Rabbah* 68:11.

789. **Jacob married two sisters** Leah and Rachel. Such an act is explicitly forbid-den in Leviticus 18:18; see BT *Pesaḥim* 119b; *Zohar* 1:168a. Elsewhere the *Zohar* offers mystical justification for this act. See 1:153b; 2:126b; Moses de León, *Sefer ha-Rimmon*, 351–55; idem, *She'elot u-Tshuvot*, 40–41.

790. **his heart did not stray…** Moses explored all aspects of both the divine and the demonic realms, yet he was not seduced by any evil power.

791. *The man spoke:* 'לאיתיאל (*Le-Iti'el*), *To Ithiel…*' In Deuteronomy 17:17, the king is commanded not to *have many wives lest his heart turn astray.* King Solomon dis-obeyed this command, offering the follow-ing rationalization, according to *Shemot Rabbah* 6:1: "*The man spoke:* 'לאיתיאל (*Le-Iti'el*), *To Ithiel.* The only reason that the blessed Holy One decreed *he shall not have*

446

"Come and see: With fragments of wisdom discovered by these people from wisdom of the ancients, they antagonized the blessed Holy One, built a tower, and perpetrated all they did—until they were scattered over the face of the earth, lacking the wisdom to accomplish anything. But in the time to come the blessed Holy One will arouse wisdom in the world, with which He will be served, as is written: *I will put My spirit within you and cause you*—not like the ancients who ruined the world with it, but rather: *cause you to follow My laws and carefully observe My rules* (Ezekiel 36:27)."

Rabbi Yose and Rabbi Ḥiyya were walking on the way. Rabbi Yose said to Rabbi Ḥiyya, "Let us open with Torah and say a word!"[792]

Rabbi Yose opened, saying, "*For YHVH your God walks about amid your camp to save you and deliver your enemies to you. Your camps are to be holy, so that He not see among you anything indecent and turn away from you* (Deuteronomy 23:15). *For YHVH your God* מתהלך (*mithallekh*), *walks about.* The verse should read מהלך (*mehallekh*), *walks.* But as is said: *walking about in the garden in the breeze of the day* (Genesis 3:8).[793] This is the tree from which Adam ate.[794] *Mithallekh*—female; *mehallekh*—male.[795] This is who walked in front of Israel when they were walking in the desert, as is written: *And YHVH walks before them by day* (Exodus 13:21).[796] This is who walks in front of a

447

---

many wives was *lest his heart turn astray. Le-Iti'el!* [Solomon] said, '*Itti El, God is with me, ve-ukhal, and I will be able* [to withstand the temptation].' But what is written of him? *In Solomon's old age, his wives turned away his heart* [*after other gods*] (1 Kings 11:4)."

792. **Let us open with Torah and say a word!** While walking on the way, one should be engaged in words of Torah. See BT *Ta'anit* 10b: "Rabbi Il'ai son of Berekhiah said, 'Two disciples of the wise who are walking on the way and are not engaged in words of Torah deserve to be burned.'"

On the importance of engaging in Torah while on a journey, see Deuteronomy 6:7; BT *Eruvin* 54a; *Zohar* 1:7a, 58b, 69b–70a, 87a, 115b.

793. **The verse should read** מהלך (*mehallekh*), *walks...* The reflexive form of the verb (*mithallekh*) is unusual in this context. See *Bereshit Rabbah* 19:7: "*They heard the sound of YHVH Elohim walking about in the garden in the breeze of the day....* Rabbi

Abba son of Kahana said, 'The verse does not read מהלך (*mehallekh*), *walking,* but rather מתהלך (*mithallekh*), *walking about,* leaping up. The essence of *Shekhinah* was in the lower realms. As soon as Adam sinned, it withdrew to the first heaven.'"

See Naḥmanides on Genesis 3:8; Gikatilla, *Sha'arei Orah,* 15–17; *Zohar* 1:52a; *ZḤ* 18d (*MhN*).

794. **tree from which Adam ate** The Tree of Knowledge of Good and Evil, symbolizing *Shekhinah.*

795. **Mithallekh—female; mehallekh—male** Though grammatically both words are masculine, מתהלך (*mithallekh*), *walks about,* includes the letter ת (*tav*), often a feminine marker. For Rabbi Yose, apparently, this letter implies the divine feminine, *Shekhinah.* The simpler verbal form, מהלך (*mehallekh*), *walks,* lacks this letter and so implies the masculine, *Tif'eret.*

796. **This is who walked in front of Israel...And YHVH...** Implying *Shekhinah.*

person when he is walking on the way, as is written: *Righteousness goes before him, and he sets out on his way* (Psalms 85:14).[797] This is who walks in front of a person when he is virtuous. Why? *To save you and deliver your enemies to you*—so that one is saved on the way, not overpowered by the other.[798] So one should guard himself against his sins and purify himself. What is written? *Your camps are to be holy.* Why קדוש (qadosh), *holy*? The verse should read קדושים (qedoshim), *holy.*[799] However, *Your camps are to be qadosh, holy*— smooth members of the body, composing, arraying the body. So, *Your camps are to be qadosh.*[800]

"*So that He not see among you anything indecent. What is anything indecent?* Indecency of indecencies, despised by the blessed Holy One more than anything.[801] Since the verse states: *So that He not see among you* ערות (ervat), *indecent,* why דבר (davar), *anything*? Because this signifies the wicked of the world who befoul and defile themselves with the word issuing from their

448

Though the name *YHVH* usually symbolizes *Tif'eret,* when *Shekhinah* is fully united with Him, She shares this name. See *Zohar* 2:215a; 3:9b, 166a.

Alternatively, the conjunction *and* signifies *Shekhinah.* See *Bereshit Rabbah* 51:2: "Rabbi El'azar said, 'Wherever it is said: *And YHVH,* this implies: He and His Court.'" In Kabbalah this court symbolizes *Shekhinah,* who derives from the *sefirah* of *Din* ("Judgment") and pronounces the divine decree, so the phrase *And YHVH* encompasses "He [*Tif'eret,* known as *YHVH*] and His Court [*Shekhinah*]."

See JT *Berakhot* 9:5, 14b; Rashi on Exodus 12:29; *Zohar* 1:15b, 64b, 107b; 2:37b, 44b; 3:149a. The hermeneutical significance of *and* was championed by Rabbi Akiva. See BT *Yevamot* 68b; *Sanhedrin* 51b.

797. **This is who walks in front of a person...Righteousness...** See BT *Berakhot* 14a: "Rav Idi son of Avin said in the name of Rabbi Yitshak son of Ishyan, 'Whoever prays and then sets out on the way, the blessed Holy One fulfills his desires, as is said: *Righteousness goes before him, and he sets out on his way.*'" In the Talmudic passage, *righteousness* (or: *justice*) implies justification by prayer, which guarantees a successful journey. Here in the *Zohar, Righteousness* is a name of *Shekhinah,* who symbolizes divine

justice and accompanies the worthy on the way. See *Zohar* 1:49a–50a, 58b.

798. **the other** The demonic, or another.

799. **Why** קדוש (qadosh), *holy*? **The verse should read** קדושים (qedoshim), *holy* Rabbi Yose reads the word מחניך (mahanekha) as a plural, meaning *camps,* though it is normally understood as singular: *camp.* See *Minhat Shai,* ad loc. The plural would require a plural adjective: *qedoshim,* rather than the singular: *qadosh.*

800. *Your camps are to be qadosh, holy*— **smooth members of the body...** The plural, *camps,* refers to the numerous limbs, which together comprise the single body, described by the singular adjective: *qadosh.* See *Zohar* 3:75b.

"Smooth members" renders two senses of one term, שייפי (shaifei). Deriving from a root meaning "to smooth, rub, slip," the word signifies "limbs" in the *Zohar,* perhaps based on the Talmudic expression (BT *Sotah* 7b) על איבריה לשפא (al eivreih le-shafa), "each limb entered its socket"—"slipping" into place—or "...the chest."

See *Arukh,* s.v. *shaf;* Rashi, ad loc., and on Job 33:21, citing *Hullin* 42b; *Zohar* 3:170a.

801. **Indecency of indecencies...** Illicit sexual behavior, or the verbal indecency described in the following lines.

mouths. This is *ervat davar, indecency of word.*[802] Why to such an extreme?[803] Because He is walking in front of you, and if you act like this, He will immediately *turn away from you,* no longer walking with you but turning away. As for us, look, we are walking on the way, so let us engage in words of Torah! For Torah crowns a person's head, so *Shekhinah* never departs from him."[804]

Rabbi Ḥiyya opened, saying, "YHVH *said, 'Look, they are one people with one language for them all . . .'* (Genesis 11:6). Come and see what is written: *When they journeyed* מקדם (*mi-qedem*), *from the east* (ibid., 2). What is *mi-qedem*? מקדמונו (*Mi-Qadmono*) From Primordial One, of the world.[805] *They found [a valley in the land of Shinar]* (ibid.). The verse should read *They saw.* Why *they found*?[806] They found a find there from mysteries of wisdom of the ancients, deposited there by victims of the Flood,[807] with which they tried to perpetrate their deed, rebelling against the blessed Holy One. They vocalized and perpetrated [76b] the act.[808]

"See what is written: *Look, they are one people with one language for them all.* 'Since they share a single mind, a single will, and speak the holy tongue, *now nothing that they scheme to do will be barred to them!* (ibid., 6). No one can thwart their act! What will I do? I will derange the rungs above[809] and their language below, so their action will be thwarted.' Now since they shared a single will and mind, and spoke the holy tongue, it is written: *Nothing that they scheme to do will be barred to them*—supernal Judgment is powerless against

449

802. *ervat davar . . .* Foul language. Because דבר (*davar*) means both "thing" and "word," this phrase can be rendered as *anything indecent* or *indecency of word.* See JT *Terumot* 1:5, 40d; *Vayiqra Rabbah* 24:7.

803. **Why to such an extreme?** Why is obscenity considered so repulsive?

804. *Shekhinah* **never departs from him** See M *Avot* 3:6: "Rabbi Ḥalafta of Kefar Ḥananya says, 'Ten who are sitting engaged in Torah, *Shekhinah* abides among them. . . . Even five . . . ; even three . . . ; even two . . . ; even one. . . .'"

805. מקדמונו (*Mi-Qadmono*), **From Primordial One, of the world** See *Bereshit Rabbah* 38:7: "*When they journeyed* מקדם (*mi-qedem*), *from the east. . . .* Rabbi El'azar son of Rabbi Shim'on said, 'They removed themselves מקדמונו (*mi-qadmono*), from the Primordial One, of the world, saying, "We

desire neither Him nor His divinity."'" See above, page 440.

806. **Why *they found*?** One finds only something lost or abandoned.

807. **deposited there by victims of the Flood** Rabbi Ḥiyya is apparently playing with the words שנער (*shin'ar*) and אתנער (*itne'ar*), "deposited." See a similar play on words in *Eikhah Rabbah, Petiḥta* 23; BT *Shabbat* 113b. Cf. above, page 447: "With fragments of wisdom discovered by these people from wisdom of the ancients . . ."

808. **They vocalized and perpetrated the act** The power of their words, spoken in unison in Hebrew, effected the construction of the Tower. See above, page 445.

809. **rungs above** The heavenly powers invoked by their words. See above, page 445; *Eikhah Rabbah* 2:5.

them. All the more so, we Companions who engage in Torah, sharing a single mind and will!"[810]

Rabbi Yose said, "From here we learn that quarrelers do not endure. For as long as these inhabitants of the world shared a single will and mind, even though they rebelled against the blessed Holy One, supernal Judgment could not prevail against them. As soon as they differed, immediately *YHVH scattered them from there over the face of all the earth* (ibid., 8)."[811]

Rabbi Ḥiyya said, "By implication, all depends on the word of the mouth.[812] For as soon as it was scrambled, immediately *YHVH scattered them from there.* But of the time to come, what is written? *Then I will transform the language of the peoples into a pure one, so they may all call upon the name of YHVH and serve Him shoulder to shoulder* (Zephaniah 3:9). Similarly, *YHVH will be king over all the earth. On that day YHVH will be one and His name one* (Zechariah 14:9)."[813]

810. **All the more so, we Companions...** By engaging intimately in Torah, we will be protected and can accomplish whatever we wish. See *Zohar* 2:190b.

811. **as long as these inhabitants of the world shared a single will...** See *Sifrei*, Numbers 42: "Rabbi El'azar son of Rabbi El'azar ha-Kappar says, 'Great is peace, for even idolators who live peacefully cannot be harmed by Satan, as it were...; but as soon as they differ,... *now they bear their* *guilt* (Hosea 10:2).'"
See *Bereshit Rabbah* 38:6; *Tanḥuma, Tsav* 7; *Zohar* 1:200b.

812. **all depends on the word of the mouth** See *Tanḥuma, Metsora* 2: "All depends upon the tongue."

813. **Then I will transform the language...** See *Yalqut Shim'oni*, Zephaniah, 567; Rashi and Ibn Ezra on Deuteronomy 6:4; Radak on Zephaniah 3:9.

REFERENCE MATTER

add.	addendum
Add.	Additional
Arukh	Nathan ben Yehiel of Rome, *Sefer he-Arukh*
Battei Midrashot	Shlomo Aharon Wertheimer, ed., *Battei Midrashot*
B.C.E.	before the Common Era
Beit ha-Midrash	Adolph Jellinek, ed., *Beit ha-Midrash*
BT	Babylonian Talmud
C9	MS Add. 1023, University Library, Cambridge
C12	MS Dd. 4.2, 1, University Library, Cambridge
C13	MS Dd. 10.14, 4, University Library, Cambridge
ca.	*circa*, approximately
C.E.	Common Era
chap.	chapter
Cr	Cremona edition of *Sefer ha-Zohar*
ed.	editor (pl. eds.); edition; edited by
esp.	especially
DE	*Derekh Emet*, in *Sefer ha-Zohar*, ed. Reuven Margaliot
DE (emendations)	Joseph Ḥamiz, ed., *Derekh Emet*
diss.	dissertation
frag.	fragmentary
Galante	Abraham Galante, in *Or ha-Ḥammah*, ed. Abraham Azulai
Hash	*Hashmatot*
Ḥayyat	Judah Ḥayyat, *Minḥat Yehudah*
Heikh	*Heikhalot*
intro	introduction
IR	*Idra Rabba*
IZ	*Idra Zuta*
JQR	*Jewish Quarterly Review*
JT	Jerusalem Talmud
KP	Shim'on Lavi, *Ketem Paz*
L2	MS 762, British Museum, London
L27	MS Gaster 747, British Museum, London
L32	MS Gaster 773, British Museum, London
M	Mishnah; Mantua edition of *Sefer ha-Zohar*
M7	MS Hebr. 217, Bayerische Staatsbibliothek, Munich
Ma'arikh	Menaḥem ben Judah de Lonzano, *Sefer ha-Ma'arikh*

Mat	*Matnitin*
Matt, *Zohar*	Daniel Chanan Matt, trans. and ed., *Zohar: The Book of Enlightenment*
MhN	*Midrash ha-Ne'lam*
MM	Shalom Buzaglo, *Miqdash Melekh*
MmD	Daniel Frisch, *Peirush Matoq mi-Devash*
Mopsik	Charles Mopsik, trans. and ed., *Le Zohar*
MS (pl. MSS)	manuscript(s)
Ms1	MS Guenzburg 83, Russian State Library, Moscow
Ms3	MS Guenzburg 487, Russian State Library, Moscow
n. (pl. nn.)	note(s)
N23	MS 1761, Jewish Theological Seminary, New York
n.d.	no date
Nefesh David	David Luria, *Nefesh David*
NJV	New Jewish Version: *JPS Hebrew-English Tanakh*
NO	Ḥayyim Joseph David Azulai, *Nitsotsei Orot*
n.p.	no publisher
NZ	Reuven Margaliot, *Nitsotsei Zohar*
O2	MS 1564, Bodleian Library, Oxford
O16	MS 2433, Bodleian Library, Oxford
OH	Abraham Azulai, ed., *Or ha-Ḥammah*
OL	Abraham Azulai, *Or ha-Levanah*
OY	Moses Cordovero, *Or Yaqar*
P1	MS héb. 778, Bibliothèque nationale, Paris
P2	MS héb. 779, Bibliothèque nationale, Paris
P4	MS héb. 781, Bibliothèque nationale, Paris
par.	paragraph
Pereq Shirah	Malachi Beit-Arié, ed., *Pereq Shirah*
Piq	*Piqqudin*
pl.	plural
Pr6	MS Perreau 15/A, Biblioteca Palatina, Parma
QhM	*Qav ha-Middah*
R1	MS 2971, Biblioteca Casanatense, Rome
RM	*Ra'aya Meheimna*
RR	*Raza de-Razin*
Scholem	Gershom Scholem, *Sefer ha-Zohar shel Gershom Scholem*
SdTs	*Sifra di-Tsni'uta*
ShS	*Shir ha-Shirim*
SO	*Sitrei Otiyyot*
Soncino	Harry Sperling et al., trans., *The Zohar* (Soncino Press)
ST	*Sitrei Torah*
Sullam	Yehudah Ashlag, *Sefer ha-Zohar...im...ha-Sullam*
T1	MS Friedberg 5-015, University of Toronto Library
Tiq	*Tiqqunim* (in *Zohar Ḥadash*)
Tos	*Tosefta*
trans.	translator(s); translated by
TZ	*Tiqqunei ha-Zohar*
V5	MS ebr. 206, Biblioteca Apostolica, Vatican
V6	MS ebr. 207, Biblioteca Apostolica, Vatican
V7	MS ebr. 208, Biblioteca Apostolica, Vatican

V16	MS Neofiti 23, Biblioteca Apostolica, Vatican
Vital	Ḥayyim Vital, in *Or ha-Ḥammah,* ed. Abraham Azulai
YN	Yechiel Bar-Lev, *Bei'ur Yedid Nefesh*
ZḤ	*Zohar Ḥadash*
Zohorei Ya'bets	Jacob Emden, *Zohorei Ya'bets*

Transliteration of Hebrew and Aramaic

א	alef	ʾ[1]	ל	lamed	l
ב	bet	b	מ	mem	m
ב	vet	v	נ	nun	n
ג	gimel	g	ס	samekh	s
ד	dalet	d	ע	ayin	ʾ[2]
ה	he	h	פ	pe	p
ו	vav	v	פ	phe	f[3]
ז	zayin	z	צ	tsadi	ts
ח	ḥet	ḥ	ק	qof	q
ט	tet	t	ר	resh	r
י	yod	y, i	שׁ	shin	sh
כ	kaf	k	שׂ	sin	s
כ	khaf	kh	ת	tav	t

The English equivalent letter is doubled when a strong *dagesh* in Hebrew or Aramaic characterizes a verbal conjugation or indicates an assimilated letter, e.g., *dibber, yitten*. The English letter is not doubled when preceded by a hyphenated prefix, e.g., *ha-sefer, la-melekh, mi-tokh*.

Proper names that appear in roman type do not follow the above schema. Biblical names are rendered according to the *JPS Hebrew-English Tanakh*. Rabbinic names are rendered according to common convention, e.g., Akiva, Resh Lakish. Medieval names are Anglicized, e.g., Moses de León, Joseph Gikatilla. Authors' names in the Bibliography follow library listings or the *Encyclopaedia Judaica*.

1. *Alef* is not transliterated at the beginning or end of a word nor after a hyphenated prefix. Elsewhere it is transliterated only when accompanied by a vowel, e.g., *Shemu'el*.
2. *Ayin* is not transliterated at the beginning of a word, nor after a hyphenated prefix, nor, unless accompanied by a vowel, at the end of a word.
3. Occasionally transliterated as *ph* to compare or contrast it to the letter *pe*.

alef   The first letter of the Hebrew alphabet; the beginning of divine and human speech.

amidah   "Standing"; the central prayer, recited three times daily.

amora, pl. *amora'im*   "Speaker, interpreter"; a teacher living in the centuries following the compilation of the Mishnah (ca. 200 C.E.) and whose opinions are recorded in subsequent rabbinic literature.

apophatic   Referring to knowledge of God obtained by way of negation.

Ashkenaz   Germany (mainly the Rhineland) and northern France.

Ayin   "Nothingness"; the creative "no-thingness" of God, out of which all being emanates.

Binah   "Understanding"; the third *sefirah;* the Divine Mother who gives birth to the seven lower *sefirot.*

blessed Holy One   Common rabbinic name for God. In the *Zohar* it often designates *Tif'eret.*

Din   "Judgment"; the fifth *sefirah;* the left arm of the divine body, balancing *Ḥesed.* The roots of evil lie here; also called *Gevurah.*

Eikhah   The Book of Lamentations.

Ein Sof   "There is no end"; that which is boundless; the Infinite. The ultimate reality of God beyond all specific qualities of the *sefirot;* the God beyond God.

Elohim   "God, gods"; a biblical name for God. In the *Zohar* it has various sefirotic associations: *Binah, Gevurah, Shekhinah.*

Gedullah   "Greatness"; the fourth *sefirah;* the outpouring of God's great goodness; also called *Ḥesed.*

Geihinnom   "Valley of Hinnom"; Hell.

Gevurah   "Power"; the fifth *sefirah;* also called *Din.*

gimatriyya   Derived from the Greek *geometria* ("measuring the earth"); a method of interpretation based on the numerical value of Hebrew letters.

halakhah   "Practice, law," from the root הלך (*hlkh*), "to walk": the way that one should follow.

Haqdamat Sefer ha-Zohar   "Introduction to the *Zohar*"; not an introduction per se but a typical collection of passages, apparently intended to introduce the reader to the atmosphere of the book. *Zohar* 1:1a–14b.

Hashmatot   "Omissions"; additions printed at the end of each of the three standard Aramaic volumes of the *Zohar,* drawn from the Cremona edition and *Zohar Ḥadash.*

ḥasid, pl. *ḥasidim*   "Pious one," devotee, saint, lover of God.

Heikhalot "Palaces"; descriptions of the heavenly palaces in *Zohar* 1:38a–45b; 2:244b–268b.

Ḥesed "Loving-kindness, love, grace"; the fourth *sefirah;* the right arm of the divine body, balancing *Din;* also called *Gedullah.*

Hod "Splendor"; the eighth *sefirah;* the left leg of the divine body; source of prophecy along with *Netsaḥ.*

Ḥokhmah "Wisdom"; the second *sefirah;* the primordial point of emanation.

Holy Ancient One The most ancient manifestation of *Ein Sof* through *Keter,* Its crown.

idra "Threshing place," assembly.

Idra Rabba "The Great Assembly"; a description of the gathering of Rabbi Shim'on and the Companions at the threshing house, where profound mysteries of divine being are expounded. *Zohar* 3:127b–145a.

Idra Zuta "The Small Assembly"; a description of the last gathering of Rabbi Shim'on and the Companions, the master's final teachings, and his ecstatic death. *Zohar* 3:287b–296b.

Israel Often, the people of Israel.

Kabbalah Hebrew, קבלה (*qabbalah*), "receiving, that which is received, tradition"; originally referring to tradition in general (or to post-Mosaic Scripture), but from the thirteenth century onward, specifically to the esoteric teachings of Judaism.

Keter "Crown"; the first sefirah; coeternal with *Ein Sof;* also called *Ratson* ("Will") and *Ayin* ("Nothingness").

Lilith A demoness who harms babies and seduces men; married to Samael.

Malkhut "Kingdom"; the tenth *sefirah,* ruling the lower worlds; also called *Shekhinah.*

Matnitin "Our Mishnah"; short pieces scattered throughout the *Zohar,* most of which appear as utterances of a heavenly voice urging the Companions to arouse themselves and open their hearts to the mysteries. Some of them contain principles of kabbalistic teaching in a condensed form, constituting a kind of mystical Mishnah, expounded in the main section of the *Zohar.*

menorah Candelabrum of seven branches; a feature of the wilderness Tabernacle and of the Temple in Jerusalem.

midrash, pl. midrashim Homiletical or legal interpretation of the Bible.

Midrash ha-Ne'lam "The Concealed Midrash, the Esoteric Midrash"; an early stratum of the *Zohar.* Its language is a mixture of Hebrew and Aramaic. *Midrash ha-Ne'lam* on the Torah pertains to several portions of Genesis, the beginning of Exodus, and several other portions; it is printed partly alongside the main text of the *Zohar* and partly in *Zohar Ḥadash. Midrash ha-Ne'lam* on Song of Songs, Ruth, and Lamentations is printed in *Zohar Ḥadash.* The subject matter of *Midrash ha-Ne'lam* is mostly Creation, the soul, and the world to come; its style is often allegorical.

mishkan "Dwelling"; God's dwelling place during Israel's forty years in the wilderness; the tabernacle constructed by Moses and the Children of Israel.

Mishnah Collection of oral teachings compiled near the beginning of the third century by Rabbi Yehudah ha-Nasi; the earliest codification of Jewish Oral Law; the core of the Talmud.

mitsvah, pl. mitsvot "Commandment"; one of the 613 commandments of the Torah or one of various rabbinic precepts; religious duty; by extension, good deed.

Mizraḥi "Eastern"; referring to Jews of Middle Eastern or North African origin.

Netsaḥ "Endurance"; the seventh *sefirah;* the right leg of the divine body; source of prophecy along with *Hod.*

Oral Torah   The rabbinic interpretation of the Written Torah (the Five Books of Moses); in Kabbalah, a symbol of *Shekhinah.*

Other Side   Aramaic, סטרא אחרא (*Sitra Aḥra*); the demonic realm, shadow of the divine.

parashah   "Portion"; portion of the Torah read on a particular Sabbath, named after its opening word (or phrase) or a key word (or phrase) in the opening sentence.

Piqqudin   "Commandments"; kabbalistic interpretations of the commandments scattered throughout the *Zohar* (to be distinguished from *Ra'aya Meheimna*).

Qav ha-Middah   "The Standard of Measure"; a detailed description of the process of emanation delivered by Rabbi Shim'on. *Zohar Ḥadash* 56d–58d.

Ra'aya Meheimna   "The Faithful Shepherd"; a separate composition on the kabbalistic meaning of the commandments, printed piecemeal in the *Zohar.* Here Moses, the Faithful Shepherd, appears to Rabbi Shim'on and the Companions, revealing secrets.

Raḥamim   "Compassion"; the sixth *sefirah,* harmonizing the polar opposites, *Ḥesed* and *Din;* also called *Tif'eret.*

Rav Metivta   "Head of the Academy"; an account of a visionary journey of Rabbi Shim'on and the Companions to the Garden of Eden, where they hear mysteries concerning the life to come from one of the heads of the heavenly academy. *Zohar* 3:161b–174a.

Raza de-Razin   "The Secret of Secrets"; a separate section dealing with physiognomy and chiromancy (*Zohar* 2:70a–75a, *Zohar Ḥadash* 35b–37c). A second version is incorporated into the main body of the *Zohar* (2:70a–78a).

Rosh Hashanah   The Jewish New Year, celebrated on the first two days of the Hebrew month Tishrei.

Rut   The Book of Ruth.

Samael   Prince of demons, married to Lilith; identical with Satan.

Sava   "The Elder."

Sava de-Mishpatim   "The Old Man of [Torah portion] *Mishpatim*"; an account of the Companions' encounter with a donkey-driver who turns out to be a master of wisdom. *Zohar* 2:94b–114a.

Sefer ha-Zohar   "The Book of Radiance."

sefirah, pl. *sefirot*   Literally, "counting," number, numerical entity; in Kabbalah, one of the ten aspects of divine personality, nine of which emanate from *Ein Sof* and the first *sefirah, Keter.* See the diagram on page xi.

Shaddai   An obscure divine name, which may originally have meant "[God] of the mountain." In Kabbalah it often denotes *Shekhinah.*

Shekhinah   "Presence," divine immanence; the tenth and last *sefirah;* female partner of *Tif'eret;* also called *Malkhut.*

Shema   Literally, "hear"; central prayer recited morning and evening, comprising Deuteronomy 6:4–9; 11:13–21; and Numbers 15:37–41. The opening verse is: *Hear O Israel! YHVH our God, YHVH is one!*

Shir ha-Shirim   The Book of Song of Songs.

Sifra di-Tsni'uta   "Book of Concealment"; an anonymous, highly condensed commentary on the beginning of the Torah in short, obscure sentences, divided into five chapters. Its subject is the mysteries of divine being. *Zohar* 2:176b–179a.

Sitrei Otiyyot   "Secrets of the Letters"; a discourse by Rabbi Shim'on focusing on the letters of the divine name *YHVH* and how they symbolize the process of emanation. *Zohar Ḥadash* 1b–7b.

461

Sitrei Torah "Secrets of Torah"; interpretations of certain verses of Genesis, printed in separate columns parallel to the main body of the *Zohar,* and in *Zohar Ḥadash.* It includes allegorical explanations of the mysteries of the soul.

Talmud Each of the two compilations of Jewish law, legend, ethics, and theology comprising the Mishnah and its vast commentary (the Gemara) by rabbis of the third through fifth centuries. The Jerusalem Talmud was compiled ca. 400 C.E.; the Babylonian Talmud, about one hundred years later.

tanna, pl. *tanna'im* "One who repeats, teacher"; an authority cited in the Mishnah or belonging to the Mishnaic period (first two centuries of the Common Era); an Amoraic scholar whose task was to memorize and recite tannaitic texts.

Targum "Translation"; an Aramaic translation of the Torah or the Bible.

tav The last letter of the Hebrew alphabet.

tefillin "Phylacteries"; two black leather boxes containing passages from the Torah (Exodus 13:1–10, 11–16; Deuteronomy 6:4–9; 11:13–21) written on parchment. They are bound by black leather straps on the left arm and on the head, and are prescribed for men to wear during weekday morning prayer. Each of the biblical passages indicates that the Children of Israel should place a sign upon their hand and a frontlet (or reminder) between their eyes.

teshuvah "Returning," returning to God, repentance.

Tif'eret "Beauty, glory"; the sixth *sefirah,* harmonizing the polar opposites, Ḥesed and *Din;* male partner of *Shekhinah;* the torso of the divine body; also called *Raḥamim.*

Tiqqunei ha-Zohar "Embellishments on the *Zohar*"; an independent book whose setting is similar to *Ra'aya Meheimna.* It comprises a commentary on the beginning of Genesis, each *tiqqun* opening with a new interpretation of the word בראשית (*be-reshit*), "in the beginning."

Tiqqunim "Embellishments"; additional material in the genre of *Tiqqunei ha-Zohar,* printed in *Zohar Ḥadash* 93c–122b.

Torah "Instruction, teaching"; the Five Books of Moses (Genesis through Deuteronomy); by extension, the entire corpus of Jewish religious literature.

Tosefta "Addenda"; in rabbinic literature, a collection of laws parallel to and contemporary with the Mishnah. In the *Zohar, Tosefta* is similar to *Matnitin.*

Tsaddiq "Righteous One"; a name for *Yesod,* the ninth *sefirah.*

Written Torah The Five Books of Moses (Genesis through Deuteronomy); in Kabbalah, a symbol of *Tif'eret.*

Yah A contracted form of the divine name *YHVH.*

Yanuqa "The Child"; the story of a wonder child who confounds and amazes the Companions. *Zohar* 3:186a–192a.

Yesod "Foundation"; the ninth *sefirah,* who channels the flow of emanation to *Shekhinah;* the phallus of the divine body; also called *Tsaddiq.*

YHVH The ineffable name of God, deriving from the root הוה (*hvh*), "to be." In the *Zohar* it often symbolizes *Tif'eret.*

Yom Kippur The Day of Atonement, observed on the tenth of the Hebrew month Tishrei.

zohar "Radiance, splendor."

Zohar Ḥadash "New Zohar"; a collection of Zoharic texts not included in the early editions of the *Zohar.* It was first printed in Salonika in 1597. The title is misleading since *Zohar Ḥadash* contains much of *Midrash ha-Ne'lam,* an early stratum of the *Zohar.*

462

This bibliography includes works cited and utilized by the translator, except for standard rabbinic texts and most reference works. Readers seeking further resources on the *Zohar* can consult *The Library of Gershom Scholem on Jewish Mysticism: Catalogue,* edited by Joseph Dan, Esther Liebes, and Shmuel Reem.

1. MANUSCRIPTS OF THE ZOHAR[1]

Cambridge, University Library. Heb. Add. 1023; Dd. 4.2, 1; Dd. 10.14, 4.
London, British Museum. 762; Gaster 747, 773.
Moscow, Guenzburg Collection, Russian State Library. 83, 487.
Munich, Bayerische Staatsbibliothek. Cod. Hebr. 217.
New York, Jewish Theological Seminary. 1761.
Oxford, Bodleian Library. 1564, 2433.
Paris, Bibliothèque nationale. Héb. 778, 779, 781.
Parma, Biblioteca Palatina. Perreau 15/A.
Rome, Biblioteca Casanatense. 2971.
Toronto, Friedberg Collection, University of Toronto Library. 5-015.
Vatican, Biblioteca Apostolica. Ebr. 206, 207, 208; Neofiti 23.

2. EDITIONS OF THE ZOHAR

A. Zohar on the Torah

Sefer ha-Zohar. 3 vols. Mantua: Meir ben Efraim and Jacob ben Naftali, 1558–60.
Sefer ha-Zohar. Cremona: Vincenzo Conti, 1559–60.
Sefer ha-Zohar. 3 vols. Lublin: Zevi Jaffe, 1623.
Sefer ha-Zohar. 3 vols. Sulzbach: Moses Bloch, 1684.
Sefer ha-Zohar. 3 vols. Amsterdam: Solomon Proops, 1715.
Sefer ha-Zohar. 3 vols. Constantinople: Jonah ben Jacob, 1736.
Sefer ha-Zohar. 3 vols. Vilna: Romm, 1882.
Sefer ha-Zohar. Edited by Reuven Margaliot. 4th ed. 3 vols. Jerusalem: Mossad Harav Kook, 1964.

1. For a list of eighty-four *Zohar* manuscripts, see Rubin, "Mif'al ha-Zohar," 172–73.

B. Zohar Ḥadash

Tappuḥei Zahav. Thiengen: Joseph ben Naftali, 1559. *Midrash ha-Ne'lam* on Ruth.
Midrash ha-Ne'lam al Megillat Rut. Venice: Abraham ben Solomon Alon, 1566.
   Reprint, Jerusalem: Daniel Abrams, 1992.
Zohar u-Midrash ha-Ne'lam... Salonika: Joseph Abraham Bat Sheva, 1597.
Zohar Ḥadash u-Midrash ha-Ne'lam... Cracow: Isaac ben Aaron, 1603.
Zohar Ḥadash u-Midrash ha-Ne'lam... Venice: Gerolamo Bragadini, 1658.
Zohar Ḥadash. Edited by Reuven Margaliot. Jerusalem: Mossad Harav Kook, 1953.
   Reprint, 1978.

C. Tiqqunei ha-Zohar

Tiqqunei ha-Zohar. Mantua: Meir of Padua and Jacob of Gazolo, 1558.
Tiqqunei ha-Zohar. Edited by Reuven Margaliot. Jerusalem: Mossad Harav Kook, 1948.
   Reprint, 1978.

3. TRANSLATIONS OF THE *ZOHAR*

A. Hebrew

Ashlag, Yehudah, trans. and ed., completed by Yehudah Zevi Brandwein. *Sefer
   ha-Zohar...im...ha-Sullam.* 22 vols. Jerusalem: Ḥevrah Lehotsa'at Hazohar,
   1945–58.
Bar-Lev, Yechiel, trans. and ed. *Sefer ha-Zohar...im Bei'ur Yedid Nefesh.* 14 vols.
   Petaḥ Tikvah: n.p., 1992–97.
Edri, Yehudah, trans. and ed. *Sefer ha-Zohar...meturgam bilshon ha-qodesh.* 10 vols.
   Jerusalem: Yerid Hasefarim, 1998.
Frisch, Daniel, trans. and ed. *Sefer ha-Zohar...Peirush Matoq mi-Devash.* 15 vols.
   Jerusalem: Mekhon Da'at Yosef, 1993–99.
Lachower, Fischel, and Isaiah Tishby, trans. and eds. *Mishnat ha-Zohar.* Vol. 1. 3d ed.
   Jerusalem: Mosad Bialik, 1971. An anthology.
Tishby, Isaiah, trans. and ed. *Mishnat ha-Zohar.* Vol. 2. Jerusalem: Mosad Bialik, 1961.
   An anthology.
Zeitlin, Hillel, trans. and ed. "Haqdamat Sefer ha-Zohar, Meturgemet u-Mvo'eret."
   Meẓudah 1 (1943): 36–82.

B. English

Berg, Michael, ed. *The Zohar by Rabbi Shimon bar Yochai with the Sulam commentary
   of Rabbi Yehuda Ashlag...* 23 vols. Tel Aviv: Yeshivat Kol Yehudah, 1999–2003. The
   English translation is based on the Hebrew translation by Yehudah Ashlag.
Berg, Philip S. *The Essential Zohar: The Source of Kabbalistic Wisdom.* New York: Bell
   Tower, 2002. Selections.
Blumenthal, David R. *Understanding Jewish Mysticism: A Source Reader.* New York:
   Ktav, 1978. Selections.
Brody, Seth, trans. and ed. *Rabbi Ezra ben Solomon of Gerona: Peirush Shir ha-Shirim
   (Commentary on the Song of Songs) and Other Kabbalistic Commentaries,* 147–206.
   Kalamazoo: Medieval Institute Publications, 1999. Translation of *Midrash ha-
   Ne'lam* on Lamentations.
Englander, Lawrence A., trans. and ed., with Herbert W. Basser. *The Mystical Study of
   Ruth: Midrash ha-Ne'elam of the Zohar to the Book of Ruth.* Atlanta: Scholars Press,
   1993.

Giller, Pinchas. *Reading the Zohar: The Sacred Text of the Kabbalah,* 159–73. New York: Oxford University Press, 2001. Translation of *Sifra di-Tsni'uta* and *Zohar* 2:122b–123b.

Lachower, Fischel, and Isaiah Tishby, Hebrew trans. and eds. *The Wisdom of the Zohar: An Anthology of Texts.* Translated by David Goldstein. Vols. 1 and 2. London: Littman Library of Jewish Civilization, 1989.

Mathers, Samuel Liddell MacGregor. *Kabbala Denudata: The Kabbalah Unveiled.* London: G. Redway, 1887. Translated from *Kabbala Denudata,* by Christian Knorr von Rosenroth.

Matt, Daniel Chanan, trans. and ed. *Zohar: The Book of Enlightenment.* Mahwah, N.J.: Paulist Press, 1983. An anthology.

_____, trans. and ed. *Zohar: Annotated and Explained.* Woodstock, Vt.: Skylight Paths, 2002. An anthology.

Miller, Moshe, trans. and ed. *Zohar: Selections Translated and Annotated by Moshe Miller.* Morristown: Fiftieth Gate Publications, 2000.

Rosenberg, David. *Dreams of Being Eaten Alive: The Literary Core of the Kabbalah.* New York: Harmony Books, 2000. Selections.

Rosenberg, Roy A., trans. and ed. *The Anatomy of God: The Book of Concealment, The Greater Holy Assembly and The Lesser Holy Assembly of the Zohar, with The Assembly of the Tabernacle.* New York: Ktav, 1973.

Sassoon, George, trans., and Rodney Dale, ed. *The Kabbalah Decoded: A new translation of the 'Ancient of Days' texts of the Zohar.* London: Duckworth, 1978. Translation of *Idra Rabba, Idra Zuta, Sifra di-Tsni'uta,* and *Zohar* 2:122b–123b.

Scholem, Gershom G., ed., with the special assistance of Sherry Abel. *Zohar: The Book of Splendor—Basic Readings from the Kabbalah.* New York: Schocken, 1949. Reprint, 1971. An anthology.

Sperling, Harry, Maurice Simon, and Paul P. Levertoff, trans. *The Zohar.* 5 vols. London: Soncino Press, 1931–34.

Tishby, Isaiah, Hebrew trans. and ed. *The Wisdom of the Zohar: An Anthology of Texts.* Translated by David Goldstein. Vol. 3. London: Littman Library of Jewish Civilization, 1989.

Wald, Stephen G. *The Doctrine of the Divine Name: An Introduction to Classical Kabbalistic Theology.* Atlanta: Scholars Press, 1988. Translation of *Sitrei Otiyyot.*

Wineman, Aryeh, trans. and ed. *Mystic Tales from the Zohar.* Philadelphia: Jewish Publication Society, 1997.

C. French

Mopsik, Charles, trans. and ed. *Le Zohar.* 4 vols. Lagrasse: Verdier, 1981–96.

_____. *Le Zohar: Cantique des Cantiques.* Lagrasse: Verdier, 1999.

_____. *Le Zohar: Lamentations.* Lagrasse: Verdier, 2000.

_____. *Le Zohar: Le livre de Ruth.* Lagrasse: Verdier, 1987.

D. German

Müller, Ernst, trans. and ed. *Der Sohar, das heilige Buch der Kabbala.* Vienna: H. Glanz, 1932. An anthology.

Scholem, Gershom G., trans. and ed. *Die Geheimnisse der Schöpfung: Ein Kapitel aus dem Sohar.* Berlin: Schocken, 1935. Translation of *Zohar* 1:15a–22a.

E. Latin

Knorr von Rosenroth, Christian. *Kabbala Denudata.* 4 vols. Sulzbach, 1677–84; Frankfurt am Main, 1684. Translation of *Sifra di-Tsni'uta, Idra Rabba,* and *Idra Zuta.*

4. COMMENTARIES ON THE *ZOHAR*

Ashlag, Yehudah, trans. and ed., completed by Yehudah Zevi Brandwein. *Sefer ha-Zohar . . . im . . . ha-Sullam.* 22 vols. Jerusalem: Ḥevrah Lehotsa'at Hazohar, 1945–58.

Azulai, Abraham, ed. *Or ha-Ḥammah.* 4 vols. Peremyshlyany: Zupnik, Knoller and Wolf, 1896–98. Reprint, 4 vols. in 3, Bene-Berak: Yahadut, 1973.

_____. *Or ha-Levanah.* Peremyshlyany: Zupnik and Knoller, 1899. Reprint, Jerusalem: Sha'arei Ziv, n.d.

Azulai, Ḥayyim Joseph David. "Nitsotsei Orot." In *Sefer ha-Zohar,* edited by Reuven Margaliot. 4th ed. 3 vols. Jerusalem: Mossad Harav Kook, 1964.

Bar-Lev, Yechiel, trans. and ed. *Sefer ha-Zohar . . . im Bei'ur Yedid Nefesh.* 14 vols. Petaḥ Tikvah: n.p., 1992–97.

Buzaglo, Shalom. *Hadrat Melekh.* Amsterdam: Gerard Johann Yonson, 1776. Reprint, Bene-Berak: Bet Hasofer, 1974.

_____. *Hadrat Melekh . . . Penei Melekh . . . Hod Melekh . . . Kevod Melekh.* London: Moses ben Hirts, 1770–73. Reprint, Bene-Berak: Bet Hasofer, 1974.

_____. *Miqdash Melekh ha-Shalem.* 5 vols. Jerusalem: Benei Yissakhar, 1995–2000.

Cordovero, Moses. *Or Yaqar.* 21 vols. Jerusalem: Achuzat Israel, 1962–95.

"Derekh Emet." In *Sefer ha-Zohar,* edited by Reuven Margaliot. 4th ed. 3 vols. Jerusalem: Mossad Harav Kook, 1964.

Elijah ben Solomon of Vilna. *Yahel Or.* Vilna: Romm, 1882. Reprint, Jerusalem: n.p., 1972.

Emden, Jacob. *Zohorei Ya'bets.* Edited by Abraham Bick. Jerusalem: Mossad Harav Kook, 1975.

Frisch, Daniel, trans. and ed. *Sefer ha-Zohar . . . Peirush Matoq mi-Devash.* 15 vols. Jerusalem: Mekhon Da'at Yosef, 1993–99.

Galante, Abraham. *Zohorei Ḥammah.* 2 vols. Vol. 1, Munkacs: P. Bleier, 1881. Vol. 2, Peremyshlyany: Zupnik and Knoller, 1882. An abridgment by Abraham Azulai of Galante's unpublished *Yareaḥ Yaqar,* incorporated into Azulai's *Or ha-Ḥammah.*

Horowitz, Zevi Hirsch. *Aspaqlaryah ha-Me'irah.* Fürth: Itzik ve-Yatmei Ḥayyim, 1776. Reprint, Jerusalem: Mekhon Sha'arei Ziv, 1983.

Lavi, Shim'on. *Ketem Paz.* 2 vols. Leghorn: Eli'ezer Sedon, 1795. 1 vol. Djerba: Jacob Haddad, 1940. Reprint, 2 vols. Jerusalem: Ahavat Shalom, 1981. The first vol. of the Jerusalem edition is a reprint of the Djerba edition; the second vol. is a reprint of the second vol. of the Leghorn edition.

Luria, David. "Nefesh David." Addendum to *Yahel Or,* by Elijah ben Solomon of Vilna. Vilna: Romm, 1882. Reprint, addendum to *Sefer Kitvei ha-Ga'on R. David Luria (Pirqei de-Rabbi Eli'ezer).* Jerusalem: n.p., 1990.

Margaliot, Reuven. "Nitsotsei Zohar." In *Sefer ha-Zohar,* edited by Reuven Margaliot. 4th ed. 3 vols. Jerusalem: Mossad Harav Kook, 1964.

Scholem, Gershom. *Sefer ha-Zohar shel Gershom Scholem* [*Gershom Scholem's Annotated Zohar*]. 6 vols. Jerusalem: Magnes Press, 1992.

Vital, Ḥayyim. "Haggahot Maharḥu." In *Sefer ha-Zohar,* edited by Reuven Margaliot. 4th ed. 3 vols. Jerusalem: Mossad Harav Kook, 1964.

Zacuto, Moses ben Mordecai. *Peirush ha-Remez la-Zohar ha-Qadosh.* Moshav Bitḥah: Kol Bitḥah, 1998.

5. LEXICONS OF THE *ZOHAR*

Baer, Issachar. *Imrei Binah.* Prague: Moshe Katz, 1611.

Huss, Boaz, ed. "Bei'ur ha-Millim ha-Zarot she-be-Sefer ha-Zohar." *Kabbalah* 1 (1996): 167–204.

Isaiah ben Eli'ezer Ḥayyim. *Yesha Yah.* Venice: Giovanni Vendramin, 1637.

Liebes, Yehuda. *Peraqim be-Millon Sefer ha-Zohar.* Jerusalem: Hebrew University, 1982.

Lonzano, Menaḥem ben Judah de. *Sefer ha-Ma'arikh.* Printed with *Sefer he-Arukh* by Nathan ben Yeḥiel of Rome, edited by Shemuel Schlesinger. Tel Aviv: Yetsu Sifrei Kodesh, n.d.

Luria, David. "Va-Ye'esof David." Addendum to *Qadmut Sefer ha-Zohar* by David Luria, 73–82. Warsaw: Meir Yeḥiel Halter, 1887.

Neuhausen, Simon A. *Nirdefei Zohar.* Baltimore: Neuhausen, 1923.

6. OTHER PRIMARY SOURCES

Abudarham, David ben Joseph. *Abudarham ha-Shalem.* Edited by Abraham J. Wertheimer. 2d ed. Jerusalem: Hateḥiyah, 1963.

Abulafia, Todros ben Joseph. *Otsar ha-Kavod ha-Shalem.* Warsaw, 1879. Reprint: Jerusalem: Makor, 1970.

_____. *Sha'ar ha-Razim.* Edited by Michal Kushnir-Oron. Jerusalem: Mosad Bialik, 1989.

Alfa Beita de-Ven Sira.[2] Edited by Moritz Steinschneider. Berlin: A. Friedlaender, 1858.

Alfonso el Sabio. *Cantigas de Santa Maria.* Edited by Walter Mettman. Vigo: Ediciòns Xerais de Galicia, 1981.

Al-Nakawa, Israel ben Joseph. *Menorat ha-Ma'or.* Edited by Hyman G. Enelow. 4 vols. New York: Bloch Publishing Company, 1929–32.

Anav, Zedekiah ben Abraham. *Shibbolei ha-Leqet ha-Shalem.* Edited by Solomon Buber. Vilna: Romm, 1886.

Angelino, Joseph [David ben Judah he-Ḥasid, pseud.]. *Livnat ha-Sappir.* Jerusalem: Azriel, 1913. Reprint, Jerusalem: Makor, 1971.

Arama, Isaac ben Moses. *Aqedat Yitsḥaq.* Pressburg: Victor Kittseer, 1849.

Azriel ben Menaḥem of Gerona. *Peirush ha-Aggadot le-Rabbi Azri'el.* Edited by Isaiah Tishby. 2d ed. Jerusalem: Magnes Press, 1982.

Azulai, Ḥayyim Joseph David. *Devash le-Fi.* Jerusalem: Yahadut, 1986.

Baḥya ben Asher. *Bei'ur al ha-Torah.* Edited by Chaim D. Chavel. 3 vols. Jerusalem: Mossad Harav Kook, 1971–72.

Bar Ḥiyya, Abraham. *Hegyon ha-Nefesh.* Leipzig: Freiman, 1860.

Beit-Arié, Malachi, ed. "Pereq Shirah: Mevo'ot u-Mahadurah Biqqortit." 2 vols. Ph.D. diss., Hebrew University, 1966.

Cordovero, Moses. *Pardes Rimmonim.* Munkacs: Kahana and Fried, 1906. Reprint, Jerusalem: Mordechai Etyah, 1962.

David ben Judah he-Ḥasid. *The Book of Mirrors: Sefer Mar'ot ha-Zove'ot.* Edited by Daniel Chanan Matt. Chico, Calif.: Scholars Press, 1982.

Eilenburg, Issachar Ber. *Be'er Sheva.* Warsaw: Nathan Schriftgiesser, 1890.

Eisenstein, Judah D., ed. *Otsar Midrashim.* 2 vols. New York: Eisenstein, 1915.

El'azar ben Judah of Worms. *Ḥokhmat ha-Nefesh.* Lemberg: A. N. Süs, 1876.

467

2.   References to *Alfa Beita de-Ven Sira* are cited according to Yassif, *Sippurei Ben Sira bi-Ymei ha-Beinayim.*

_____. *Peirushei Siddur ha-Tefillah la-Roqeaḥ.* Edited by Moshe Hershler and Yehudah Alter Hershler. 2 vols. Jerusalem: Mekhon Harav Hershler, 1994.

Ezra ben Solomon of Gerona. *Le Commentaire d'Ezra de Gérone sur le Cantique des Cantiques.* Translated and edited by Georges Vajda. Paris: Aubier-Montaigne, 1969.

_____. "Peirush le-Shir ha-Shirim." In *Kitvei Ramban,* edited by Chaim D. Chavel, 2:471–518. Jerusalem: Mossad Harav Kook, 1964.

_____. *Rabbi Ezra ben Solomon of Gerona: Peirush Shir ha-Shirim (Commentary on the Song of Songs) and Other Kabbalistic Commentaries, 7–145.* Translated and edited by Seth Brody. Kalamazoo: Medieval Institute Publications, 1999.

Faraday, Michael. *A Course of Six Lectures on the Chemical History of a Candle.* Edited by William Crookes. London: Griffin, Bohn and Co., 1861.

Fox, Everett, trans. and ed. *The Five Books of Moses.* New York: Schocken, 1995.

Friedlander, Gerald, trans. and ed. *Pirke de Rabbi Eliezer.* London, 1916. Reprint, New York: Sepher-Hermon Press, 1981.

Friedman, Richard Elliott. *Commentary on the Torah with a New English Translation.* San Francisco: HarperSanFrancisco, 2001.

Gikatilla, Joseph. *Ginnat Egoz.* Jerusalem: Yeshivat Haḥayyim Vehashalom, 1989.

_____. *Sha'arei Orah.* Warsaw: Orgelbrand, 1883. Reprint, Jerusalem: Mordechai Etyah, 1960.

_____. *Sha'arei Tsedeq.* Cracow: Fischer and Deutscher, 1881.

Halevi, Judah. *Sefer ha-Kuzari.* Translated by Yehuda Even Shmuel. Tel Aviv: Dvir, 1972.

Ḥayyat, Judah. "Minḥat Yehudah." Mantua: Meir ben Efraim, 1558. Reprint, Jerusalem: Makor, 1963. Commentary on *Ma'arekhet ha-Elohut.*

Hume, Robert E., ed. *The Thirteen Principal Upanishads.* New York: Oxford University Press, 1971.

Ibn Akhnin, Joseph. *Peirush Shir ha-Shirim.* Edited by Abraham S. Halkin. Jerusalem: Mekitzei Nirdamim, 1964.

Ibn Ezra, Abraham [pseud.]. *Sefer ha-Atsamim.* Edited by Menasheh Grossberg. London: Eliyahu Zev Rabinovitch, 1901.

Ibn Gabbai, Meir. *Avodat ha-Qodesh.* Warsaw: Y. Unterhendler, 1883. Reprint, Jerusalem: Lewin-Epstein, 1973.

_____. *Tola'at Ya'aqov.* Warsaw: Yitzḥak Goldman, 1876. Reprint, Jerusalem: Mekor Ḥayyim, 1967.

Ibn Latif, Isaac. "Iggeret ha-Teshuvah." *Kovez al Yad* 1 (1885): 33–70.

Isaac ben Samuel of Acre. "Peirusho . . . le-. . . . Sefer Yetsirah." Edited by Gershom Scholem. *Kiryat Sefer* 31 (1956): 379–96.

Isaac the Blind. "Peirush Sefer Yetsirah." Appendix to Gershom Scholem, *Ha-Qabbalah be-Provans,* edited by Rivka Schatz. Jerusalem: Academon, 1970.

Jacob ben Sheshet. "Ha-Emunah ve-ha-Bittaḥon." In *Kitvei Ramban,* edited by Chaim D. Chavel, 2:339–448. Jerusalem: Mossad Harav Kook, 1964.

_____. *Meshiv Devarim Nekhoḥim.* Edited by Georges Vajda. Jerusalem: Israel Academy of Sciences and Humanities, 1968.

Jellinek, Adolph, ed. *Beit ha-Midrash.* 3d ed. 6 vols. in 2. Jerusalem: Wahrmann Books, 1967.

JPS Hebrew-English Tanakh. Philadelphia: Jewish Publication Society, 1999.

Judah ben Barzillai. *Peirush Sefer Yetsirah.* Edited by S. J. Halberstam. Berlin: M'kize Nirdamim, 1885.

Judah ben Samuel he-Ḥasid. *Sefer Ḥasidim.* Edited by Reuven Margaliot. Jerusalem: Mossad Harav Kook, 1957.

_____. *Sefer Ḥasidim.* Edited by Jehuda Wistinetzki. Berlin: Itzkowski, 1891. Reprint, Jerusalem: Vagshel, 1998.

Kaplan, Aryeh, trans. and ed. *Sefer Yetzirah: The Book of Creation*. York Beach, Maine: Samuel Weiser, 1990.

Kasher, Menaḥem M. *Ḥumash Torah Shelemah*. 2d ed. 12 vols. Jerusalem: Beth Torah Shelemah, 1992.

Landau, Jacob Baruch. *Ha-Agur ha-Shalem*. Edited by Moshe Hershler. Jerusalem: Moznayim, 1960.

Lazar, Moshe, ed. *The Ladino Five Scrolls (Abraham Asa's Versions of the Hebrew and Aramaic Texts)*. Culver City, Calif.: Labyrinthos, 1992.

Lerner, Myron Bialik. "Aggadat Rut u-Midrash Rut Rabbah." 3 vols. Ph.D. diss., Hebrew University, 1971.

Lewin, Benjamin M., ed. *Otsar ha-Geonim*. 13 vols. Jerusalem: Mossad Harav Kook, 1928–62.

Ma'arekhet ha-Elohut. Mantua: Meir ben Efraim, 1558. Reprint, Jerusalem: Makor, 1963.

Matt, Daniel C., trans. and ed. *The Essential Kabbalah: The Heart of Jewish Mysticism*. San Francisco: HarperSanFrancisco, 1995.

Moses ben Shem Tov de León. *The Book of the Pomegranate: Moses de León's Sefer ha-Rimmon*. Edited by Elliot R. Wolfson. Atlanta: Scholars Press, 1988.

———. Commentary on the Ten *Sefirot* (untitled fragment). MS Hebr. 47, Bayerische Staatsbibliothek, Munich.

———. *Mishkan ha-Edut*. MS Or. Quat. 833, Staatsbibliothek, Berlin.

———. "Or Zaru'a." Edited by Alexander Altmann. *Kovez al Yad*, n.s., 9 (1980): 219–93.

———. *Orḥot Ḥayyim (Tsavva'at Rabbi Eli'ezer)*. Edited by Gershon Henikh. Warsaw: Meir Halter, 1891. Reprint, Bene-Berak: Agudat Ḥasidei Radzyn, 1990.

———. *Peirush ha-Merkavah*. Edited by Asi-Farber Ginat. Edited for publication by Daniel Abrams. Los Angeles: Cherub Press, 1998.

———. "Seder Gan Eden." In *Beit ha-Midrash*, edited by Adolph Jellinek, 3:131–40, 194–98. Jerusalem: Wahrmann Books, 1967.

———. "Sefer ha-Mishqal: Text and Study." Edited by Jochanan H. A. Wijnhoven. Ph.D. diss., Brandeis University, 1964. Supersedes an earlier, corrupt edition: *Ha-Nefesh ha-Ḥakhamah*. Basle: Konrad Waldkirch, 1608.

———. "Sefer Maskiyyot Kesef." Edited by Jochanan H. A. Wijnhoven. M.A. diss., Brandeis University, 1961.

———. "She'elot u-Tshuvot be-Inyenei Qabbalah." In *Ḥiqrei Qabbalah u-Shluḥoteha*, edited by Isaiah Tishby, 1:36–75. Jerusalem: Magnes Press, 1982.

———. *Sheqel ha-Qodesh*. Edited by A. W. Greenup. London, 1911. Reprint, Jerusalem: n.p., 1969.

———. *Sheqel ha-Qodesh*. Edited by Charles Mopsik. Los Angeles: Cherub Press, 1996. Cited in the Commentary according to both this edition and, in parentheses, Greenup's edition.

———. "Shushan Edut." Edited by Gershom Scholem. *Kovez al Yad*, n.s., 8 (1976): 325–70.

———. "Sod Eser Sefirot Belimah." Edited by Gershom Scholem. *Kovez al Yad*, n.s., 8 (1976): 371–84.

———. "Sod Ḥag ha-Shavu'ot." In *Qovets Sifrei Qabbalah*. MS Schocken 14, Schocken Library, Jerusalem.

Naḥmanides, Moses. *Kitvei Ramban*. Edited by Chaim D. Chavel. 2 vols. Jerusalem: Mossad Harav Kook, 1964.

———. "Peirush Sefer Yetsirah." Edited by Gershom Scholem. *Kiryat Sefer* 6 (1929–30): 385–419.

Nissim ben Jacob. *Ḥibbur Yafeh me-ha-Yeshu'ah.* Translated and edited by Ḥayyim Z. Hirschberg. Jerusalem: Mossad Harav Kook, 1954.

"Pirqei Rabbi Eli'ezer." Edited by Michael Higger. *Ḥoreb* 8 (1944): 82–119; 9 (1946): 94–166; 10 (1948): 185–294.

Pirqei Rabbi Eli'ezer. Commentary by David Luria; edited by Samuel ben Eli'ezer Luria. Warsaw: Bomberg, 1852. Reprint, New York: Om, 1946.

Recanati, Menaḥem. *Peirush al ha-Torah (Levushei Or Yeqarot).* Lemberg: Karl Budweiser, 1880–81. Reprint, Jerusalem: Mordechai Etyah, 1961.

"Re'uyyot Yeḥezqel." Edited by Ithamar Gruenwald. *Temirin* 1 (1972): 101–39.

Robinson, James M., ed. *The Nag Hammadi Library in English.* 3d ed. Leiden: E. J. Brill, 1988.

Sahula, Isaac ben Solomon Abi. *Meshal ha-Qadmoni.* Tel Aviv: Maḥbarot Lesifrut, 1953.

Schäfer, Peter, ed. *Synopse zur Hekhalot-Literatur.* Tübingen: J. C. B. Mohr, 1981.

Scholem, Gerhard, trans. and ed. *Das Buch Bahir.* Leipzig: W. Drugulin, 1923. Reprint, Darmstadt: Wissenschaftliche Buchgesellschaft, 1970.

Scholem, Gershom, ed. "Havdalah de-R. Aqiva." *Tarbiz* 50 (1981): 243–81.

Sefer ha-Bahir. Edited by Daniel Abrams. Los Angeles: Cherub Press, 1994. Cited in the Commentary according to both this edition and, in parentheses, Margaliot's edition.

Sefer ha-Bahir. Edited by Reuven Margaliot. Jerusalem: Mossad Harav Kook, 1951. Reprint, 1978.

Sefer ha-Peli'ah. Peremyshlyany: Zupnik, Knoller, and Hammerschmidt, 1883. Reprint, Israel: Books Export Enterprises, n.d.

Sefer ha-Temunah. Lemberg: Rahatin, 1892. Reprint, Israel: Books Export Enterprises, n.d.

Sefer ha-Yashar. Edited by Joseph Dan. Jerusalem: Mosad Bialik, 1986.

Sefer Razi'el ha-Mal'akh. Amsterdam: Moses M. Coutinho, 1701.

Sefer Yetsirah. Jerusalem: Lewin-Epstein, 1965.

Sha'arei Teshuvah (Teshuvot ha-Ge'onim). Edited by Wolf Leiter. Pittsburgh: Maimonides Institute, 1946. Reprint, Jerusalem: H. Vagshel, n.d.

Shoshan Sodot. Edited by Moses ben Jacob of Kiev. Petaḥ Tikvah: Or Haganuz, 1995.

Shpielman, Mordechai ben Tsvi Hirsh. *Tif'eret Tsevi.* 3 vols. Brooklyn, N.Y., 1981–89.

Simḥah ben Samuel of Vitry. *Maḥazor Vitri.* Edited by Shim'on Hurwitz. Nüremberg: J. Bulka, 1923.

Teshuvot ha-Ge'onim. Edited by Jacob Musaphia. Lyck: M'kize Nirdamim, 1864.

Teshuvot ha-Ge'onim (Sha'arei Teshuvah). Livorno: Eliyahu ben Amozeg, 1869. Reprint, Jerusalem: H. Vagshel, n.d.

Vital, Ḥayyim. *Sha'ar ha-Kavvanot.* 2 vols. Jerusalem: n.p., 1988.

Yassif, Eli. *Sippurei Ben Sira bi-Ymei ha-Beinayim.* Jerusalem: Magnes Press, 1984.

Wertheimer, Shlomo Aharon, ed. *Battei Midrashot.* 2d ed., revised by Abraham J. Wertheimer. 2 vols. Jerusalem: Ketav Vasepher, 1980.

Zacuto, Abraham. *Sefer Yuḥasin ha-Shalem.* Edited by Zevi H. Filipowski. 2d ed., revised by Abraham H. Freimann. Frankfurt am Main: Wahrmann, 1925.

7. OTHER SECONDARY SOURCES

Aaron Selig ben Moses. *Ammudei Sheva.* Cracow: Menaḥem Naḥum Meisels, 1635.

Abrams, Daniel. "Critical and Post-Critical Textual Scholarship of Jewish Mystical Literature." *Kabbalah* 1 (1996): 17–71.

———. "Eimatai Ḥubberah ha-Haqdamah le-Sefer ha-Zohar?" *Asufot* 8 (1994): 211–26.

_____ . "Knowing the Maiden without Eyes: Reading the Sexual Reconstruction of the Jewish Mystic in a Zoharic Parable." *Da'at* 50–52 (2003): lix–lxxxiii.

Altmann, Alexander. "The Gnostic Background of the Rabbinic Adam Legends." *Jewish Quarterly Review* 35 (1945): 371–91.

_____ . *Studies in Religious Philosophy and Mysticism.* Ithaca: Cornell University Press, 1969.

Amado Lévy-Valensi, Eliane. *Le Moïse de Freud ou la référence occultée.* Monaco: Éditions du Rocher, 1984.

_____ . *La Poétique du Zohar.* Paris: Éditions de L'Éclat, 1996.

Anidjar, Gil. "Jewish Mysticism Alterable and Unalterable: On *Orienting* Kabbalah Studies and the 'Zohar of Christian Spain.'" *Jewish Social Studies,* n.s., 3 (1996): 89–157.

_____ . *"Our Place in al-Andalus": Kabbalah, Philosophy, Literature in Arab Jewish Letters.* Stanford: Stanford University Press, 2002.

Assaf, Simha. "Le-Fulmus al Hadpasat Sifrei Qabbalah." *Sinai* 5 (1939): 360–68.

Assis, Yom Tov. "Sexual Behavior in Mediaeval Hispano-Jewish Society." In *Jewish History: Essays in Honour of Chimen Abramsky,* edited by Ada Rapoport-Albert and Steven J. Zipperstein, 25–60. London: Peter Halban, 1988.

Avida, Yehuda. "Ever Mahaziq Ever." *Sinai* 29 (1951): 401–2.

Bacher, Wilhelm. "Le baisement des mains dans le Zohar." *Revue des études juives* 22 (1891): 137–38; 23 (1891): 133–34.

_____ . "Derash et haggada dans le Zohar." *Revue des études juives* 23 (1891): 312–13.

_____ . "L'exégèse biblique dans le Zohar." *Revue des études juives* 22 (1891): 33–46, 219–29.

_____ . "Judaeo-Christian Polemics in the Zohar." *Jewish Quarterly Review* 3 (1891): 781–84.

_____ . "Das Merkwort PRDS in der Jüdischen Bibelexegese." *Zeitschrift für die alttestamentliche Wissenschaft* 13 (1893): 294–305.

Baer, Issachar. *Yesh Sakhar.* Prague: Gershom Katz, 1609.

Baer, Yitzhak. "Ha-Reqa ha-Histori shel ha-Ra'aya Meheimna." *Zion* 5 (1940): 1–44.

_____ . *A History of the Jews in Christian Spain.* 2 vols. Translated by Louis Schoffman. Philadelphia: Jewish Publication Society, 1978.

_____ . "Todros ben Yehudah ha-Levi u-Zmano." *Zion* 2 (1937): 19–55.

Basilea, Solomon Aviad Sar-Shalom. *Emunat Hakhamim.* Mantua: S. Benedetto, 1730.

Bedini, Silvio A. "The Compartmented Cylindrical Clepsydra." *Technology and Culture* 3 (1962): 115–41.

Beit-Arié, Malachi. "Transmission of Texts by Scribes and Copyists: Unconscious and Critical Interferences." *Bulletin of the John Rylands University Library of Manchester* 75:3 (1993): 33–51.

Belkin, Samuel. "Ha-Midrash ha-Ne'lam u-Mqorotav ba-Midrashim ha-Aleksandroniyyim ha-Qedumim." *Sura* 3 (1957–58): 25–92.

Benamozegh, Elijah ben Abraham. *Ta'am Le-Shad.* Livorno: Eliyahu ben Amozeg Vehavero, 1863.

Benayahu, Meir. *Ha-Defus ha-Ivri bi-Qrimona.* Jerusalem: Mekhon Ben-Zvi and Mossad Harav Kook, 1971.

_____ . *Ma'amadot u-Moshavot.* Jerusalem: Yad Harav Nissim, 1985.

_____ . "Vikkuah ha-Qabbalah im ha-Halakhah." *Da'at* 5 (1980): 61–115.

Benin, Stephen D. "The Mutability of an Immutable God: Exegesis and Individual Capacity in the *Zohar* and Several Christian Sources." In *Sefer ha-Zohar ve-Doro* (*Mehqerei Yerushalayim be-Mahashevet Yisra'el* 8 [1989]), edited by Joseph Dan, 67–86 (English section). Jerusalem: Hebrew University, 1989.

Bension, Ariel. *The Zohar in Moslem and Christian Spain*. London: Routledge, 1932.

Birnbaum, Solomon A. *The Hebrew Scripts*. Leiden: E. J. Brill, 1971.

Bronsnick, Naḥum M. "Le-Hora'ato shel ha-Shoresh 'Bsm.'" *Sinai* 63 (1968): 81–85.

Burns, Robert I., ed. *Emperor of Culture: Alfonso X the Learned of Castile and His Thirteenth-Century Renaissance*. Philadelphia: University of Pennsylvania Press, 1990.

Chavel, Chaim D. "Sefer ha-Zohar ke-Maqor Ḥashuv le-Feirush ha-Ramban al ha-Torah." *Sinai* 43 (1958): 337–64.

Cohen-Alloro, Dorit. "Ha-Magyah ve-ha-Kishshuf be-Sefer ha-Zohar." Ph.D. diss., Hebrew University, 1989.

_____. *Sod ha-Malbush u-Mar'eh ha-Mal'akh be-Sefer ha-Zohar*. Jerusalem: Hebrew University, 1987.

Corbin, Henry. *The Man of Light in Iranian Sufism*. Translated by Nancy Pearson. Boulder: Shambhala, 1978.

Corominas, Joan, with the collaboration of José A. Pascual. *Diccionario Crítico Etimológico Castellano e Hispánico*. 6 vols. Madrid: Editorial Gredos, 1980–91.

Dan, Joseph. *Gershom Scholem and the Mystical Dimension of Jewish History*. New York: New York University Press, 1987.

_____, ed. *Sefer ha-Zohar ve-Doro* (*Meḥqerei Yerushalayim be-Maḥashevet Yisra'el* 8 [1989]). Jerusalem: Hebrew University, 1989.

Dan, Joseph, Esther Liebes, and Shmuel Reem, eds. *The Library of Gershom Scholem on Jewish Mysticism: Catalogue*. 2 vols., esp. 1:174–232. Jerusalem: Jewish National and University Library, 1999.

Delmedigo, Elijah. *Beḥinat ha-Dat*. Edited by Isacco S. Reggio. Vienna: Anton Edlen van Schmid, 1833.

Delmedigo, Joseph Solomon. *Matsref la-Ḥokhmah*. Odessa: M. A. Belinson, 1864.

Drover, C. B. "A Medieval Monastic Water-Clock." *Antiquarian Horology* 1 (1954): 54–58, 63.

Eisler, Robert. *Weltenmantel und Himmelszelt*. Munich: C. H. Beck'sche, 1910.

Eliade, Mircea, ed. *The Encyclopedia of Religion*. 16 vols. New York: Macmillan, 1987.

Elqayam, Avraham. "Ha-Zohar ha-Qadosh shel Shabbetai Tsevi." *Kabbalah* 3 (1998): 345–87.

Emden, Jacob. *Mitpaḥat Sefarim*. Edited by Reuben Rappaport. Lemberg: Michal Wolf, 1870. Reprint: Jerusalem: Sifriyat Mekorot, 1970.

Farber, Asi. "Iqvotav shel Sefer ha-Zohar be-Khitvei R. Yosef Gikatilla." *Alei Sefer* 9 (1981): 70–83.

_____. "Li-Mqorot Torato ha-Qabbalit ha-Muqdemet shel R. Mosheh de León." *Meḥqerei Yerushalayim be-Maḥashevet Yisra'el* 3 (1984): 67–96.

_____. "Tefisat ha-Merkavah be-Torat ha-Sod be-Me'ah ha-Shelosh-Esreh: 'Sod ha-Egoz' ve-Toledotav." 2 vols. Ph.D. diss., Hebrew University, 1986.

Farber-Ginat, Asi. "Qelippah Qodemet li-Pri." In *Ha-Mitos ba-Yahadut. Eshel Beer-Sheva*, vol. 4, edited by Ḥaviva Pedaya, 118–42. Beer-Sheva: Ben-Gurion University of the Negev Press, 1996.

Fine, Lawrence. "Kabbalistic Texts." In *Back to the Sources: Reading the Classic Jewish Texts*, edited by Barry Holtz, 305–59. New York: Summit Books, 1984.

Finesinger, Sol. "The Custom of Looking at the Fingernails at the Outgoing of the Sabbath." *Hebrew Union College Annual* 12–13 (1937–38): 347–65.

Finkel, Joshua. "The Alexandrian Tradition and the *Midrash ha-Ne'elam*." In *The Leo Jung Jubilee Volume*, edited by Menaḥem Kasher, 77–103. New York: Jewish Center, 1962.

Fishbane, Eitan. "Tears of Disclosure: The Role of Weeping in Zoharic Narrative." *Journal of Jewish Thought and Philosophy* 11 (2002): 25–47.

472

Fishbane, Michael. *The Exegetical Imagination: On Jewish Thought and Theology.* Cambridge: Harvard University Press, 1998.

Fluegel, Maurice. "Philosophy and Qabbala: The Zohar, Copernicus and Modern Astronomy." *The Menorah* 29 (1900): 77–84.

Franck, Adolphe. *The Kabbalah, or, The Religious Philosophy of the Hebrews.* Translated by Isaac Sossnitz. New York: Kabbalah Publishing Company, 1926.

Friedman, Aryeh Lev. *Tsidqat ha-Tsaddiq.* Jerusalem: Sifrai, 1944.

Frisch, Daniel. *Otsar ha-Zohar ha-Shalem.* 4 vols. Jerusalem: n.p., 1976–77.

Gaster, Moses. "A Gnostic Fragment from the Zohar." *The Quest* 14 (1923): 452–69.

Giller, Pinchas. *The Enlightened Will Shine: Symbolization and Theurgy in the Later Strata of the Zohar.* Albany: State University of New York Press, 1993.

———. "Love and Upheaval in the *Zohar's Sabba de-Mishpatim.*" *Journal of Jewish Thought and Philosophy* 7 (1997): 31–60.

———. *Reading the Zohar: The Sacred Text of the Kabbalah.* New York: Oxford University Press, 2001.

Ginsburg, Elliot K. "The Image of the Divine and Person in Zoharic Kabbalah." In *In Search of the Divine: Some Unexpected Consequences of Interfaith Dialogue,* edited by Larry D. Shinn, 61–94. New York: Paragon House, 1987.

———. *The Sabbath in the Classical Kabbalah.* Albany: State University of New York Press, 1989.

———. "Tiqsei ha-Havdalah ba-Qabbalah ha-Zoharit." In *Sefer ha-Zohar ve-Doro (Mehqerei Yerushalayim be-Mahashevet Yisra'el* 8 [1989]), edited by Joseph Dan, 183–216. Jerusalem: Hebrew University, 1989.

Ginzberg, Louis. *Legends of the Jews.* 7 vols. Translated by Henrietta Szold and Paul Radin. Philadelphia: Jewish Publication Society, 1909–38.

Goldberg, Harvey E. "The Zohar in Southern Morocco: A Study in the Ethnography of Texts." *History of Religion* 29 (1990): 233–58.

Goldreich, Amos. "Beirurim bi-R'iyyato ha-Atsmit shel Ba'al Tiqqunei ha-Zohar." In *Massu'ot,* edited by Michal Oron and Amos Goldreich, 459–96. Jerusalem: Mosad Bialik, 1994.

———. "'La'az' Ibberi bi-Fragment bilti Yadu'a shel Ba'al Tiqqunei ha-Zohar." In *Sefer ha-Zohar ve-Doro (Mehqerei Yerushalayim be-Mahashevet Yisra'el* 8 [1989]), edited by Joseph Dan, 89–121. Jerusalem: Hebrew University, 1989.

———. "Sefer ha-Gevul le-R. David ben Yehudah he-Hasid: Darkhei Ibbud shel Tekst Zohari Dor Ehad Aharei Hofa'at ha-Zohar." M.A. diss., Tel Aviv University, 1972.

Goldschmidt, Ernst P. *Medieval Texts and Their First Appearance in Print.* London: Oxford University Press, 1943.

Gottlieb, Efraim. *Mehqarim be-Sifrut ha-Qabbalah.* Edited by Joseph Hacker. Tel Aviv: Tel Aviv University, 1976.

———. *Ha-Qabbalah be-Khitvei Rabbenu Bahya ben Asher.* Jerusalem: Kiryath Sepher, 1970.

Graetz, Heinrich. *Geschichte der Juden von den ältesten Zeiten bis auf die Gegenwart.* 4th ed. Vol. 7, appendix 12. Leipzig: O. Leiner, 1905.

Green, Arthur. "Bride, Spouse, Daughter: Images of the Feminine in Classical Jewish Sources." In *On Being a Jewish Feminist: A Reader,* edited by Susannah Heschel, 248–60. New York: Schocken, 1983.

———. *A Guide to the Zohar.* Stanford: Stanford University Press, 2004.

———. *Keter: The Crown of God in Early Jewish Mysticism.* Princeton: Princeton University Press, 1997.

———. "*Shekhinah,* the Virgin Mary, and the Song of Songs: Reflections on a Kabbalistic Symbol in Its Historical Context." *AJS Review* 26 (2002): 1–52.

473

_____. "The *Ẓaddiq* as *Axis Mundi* in Later Judaism." In *Essential Papers on Kabbalah*, edited by Lawrence Fine, 291–314. New York: New York University Press, 1995.

_____. "The Zohar: Jewish Mysticism in Medieval Spain." In *Essential Papers on Kabbalah*, edited by Lawrence Fine, 27–66. New York: New York University Press, 1995.

Greenberg, Moshe. *Ezekiel 1–20*. Anchor Bible, vol. 22. Garden City, N.Y.: Doubleday, 1983.

Gross, Moshe D. "Le-Qadmuto shel ha-Zohar ha-Qadosh." *Sinai* 41 (1957): 244–47.

Grözinger, Karl E. "Masoret ve-Ḥiddush bi-Tfisat ha-Shir ba-Zohar." In *Sefer ha-Zohar ve-Doro (Meḥqerei Yerushalayim be-Maḥashevet Yisra'el* 8 [1989]), edited by Joseph Dan, 347–55. Jerusalem: Hebrew University, 1989.

Gruenwald, Ithamar. "Ha-Metsi'ut ha-Midrashit: Mi-Derashot Ḥazal li-Drashot ha-Mequbbalim." In *Sefer ha-Zohar ve-Doro (Meḥqerei Yerushalayim be-Maḥashevet Yisra'el* 8 [1989]), edited by Joseph Dan, 255–98. Jerusalem: Hebrew University, 1989.

Guttmann, Julius. *Philosophies of Judaism*. Translated by David W. Silverman. New York: Schocken, 1973.

Hacker, Joseph. "Iggeret Ḥadashah min ha-Pulmus al Hadpasat ha-Zohar be-Italyah." In *Massu'ot*, edited by Michal Oron and Amos Goldreich, 120–30. Jerusalem: Mosad Bialik, 1994.

Hallamish, Moshe. *Ha-Qabbalah ba-Tefillah ba-Halakhah u-va-Minhag*. Ramat Gan: Bar-Ilan University, 2000.

Ḥamiẓ, Joseph ben Judah, ed. *Derekh Emet*. Venice, 1658.

Havlin, Shlomo Z. "Sefer Torah she-Katav le-Atsmo Rabbenu Nissim mi-Gerondi." *Alei Sefer* 12 (1986): 13–19.

Hecker, Joel. "Each Man Ate an Angel's Meal: Eating and Embodiment in the *Zohar*." Ph.D. diss., New York University, 1996.

_____. "Mystical Eating and Food Practices in the *Zohar*." In *Judaism in Practice: From the Middle Ages through the Early Modern Period*, edited by Lawrence Fine, 353–63. New York: New York University Press, 2001.

Heide, Albert van der. "PARDES: Methodological reflections on the theory of the Four Senses." *Journal of Jewish Studies* 34 (1983): 147–59.

Hellner-Eshed, Melila. "'Im Ta'iru ve-Im Te'oreru et ha-Ahavah': Sefat ha-Hit'orerut be-Sefer ha-Zohar." *Kabbalah* 5 (2000): 327–52.

_____. "*Ve-Nahar Yotse me-Eden*": Al Sefat ha-Ḥavayah ha-Mistit ba-Zohar. Tel Aviv: Am Oved-Alma, forthcoming.

_____. "'Ve-Nahar Yotse me-Eden': Pesuqei Hit'orerut ba-Zohar." *Kabbalah* 2 (1997): 287–310.

_____. "Nefesh ha-Qanna be-Sefer ha-Zohar." *Ellu va-Ellu* 4 (1997): 98–116.

Heschel, Abraham J. *Torah min ha-Shamayim ba-Aspaqlaryah shel ha-Dorot*. 3 vols. London: Soncino, 1962–65; Jerusalem: Jewish Theological Seminary of America, 1990.

Hill, Donald R. *Arabic Water-Clocks*. Aleppo, Syria: Institute for the History of Arabic Science, 1981.

Horodezky, Samuel A. *Ha-Mistorin be-Yisra'el*. Vol. 2, bk. 2, *Ginzei Seter*. Tel Aviv: N. Tverski, 1952.

Ḥoshen, Moshe and Dalyah. "Le-Veirur Mispar Leshonot be-Sefer ha-Zohar." *Sinai* 110 (1992): 274–77.

Hubka, Thomas C. "Beit ha-Keneset be-Gwozdiec, Sha'ar ha-Shamayim: Hashpa'at Sefer ha-Zohar al ha-Omanut ve-ha-Adrikhalut." In *Ha-Mitos ba-Yahadut. Eshel Beer-Sheva*, vol. 4, edited by Ḥaviva Pedaya, 263–316. Beer-Sheva: Ben-Gurion University of the Negev Press, 1996.

_____. "The *Zohar* and the Polish Synagogue: The Practical Influence of a Sacred Text." *Journal of Jewish Thought and Philosophy* 9 (2000): 173–210.

Huss, Boaz. *Al Adnei Faz: Ha-Qabbalah shel R. Shim'on Ibn Lavi.* Jerusalem: Magnes Press, 1990.

_____. "The Anthological Interpretation: The Emergence of Anthologies of Zohar Commentaries in the Seventeenth Century." *Prooftexts* 19 (1999): 1–19.

_____. "Ḥakham Adif mi-Navi: R. Shim'on bar Yoḥai u-Mosheh Rabbenu ba-Zohar." *Kabbalah* 4 (1999): 103–39.

_____. "Hofa'ato shel Sefer ha-Zohar." *Tarbiz* 70 (2001): 507–42.

_____. "Maqom Qadosh, Zeman Qadosh, Sefer Qadosh: Hashpa'at Sefer ha-Zohar al Minhagei ha-Aliyyah la-Regel le-Meiron va-Ḥagigot Lag ba-Omer." *Kabbalah* 7 (2002): 237–56.

_____. "*Sefer ha-Zohar* as a Canonical, Sacred and Holy Text: Changing Perspectives of the Book of Splendor between the Thirteenth and Eighteenth Centuries." *Journal of Jewish Thought and Philosophy* 7 (1998): 257–307.

_____. "Ha-Shabbeta'ut ve-Toledot Hitqabbelut Sefer ha-Zohar." In *Ha-Ḥalom ve-Shivro: Ha-Tenu'ah ha-Shabbeta'it u-Shluḥoteha.* Vol. 1 (*Meḥqerei Yerushalayim be-Maḥashevet Yisra'el* 16 [2001]), edited by Rachel Elior, 53–71. Jerusalem: Hebrew University, 2001.

Idel, Moshe. *Absorbing Perfections: Kabbalah and Interpretation.* New Haven: Yale University Press, 2002.

_____. "Erets ha-Sodot: Divrei Teguvah le-Yehudah Liebes." In *Tsiyyon ve-Tsiyyonut be-qerev Yehudei Sefarad ve-ha-Mizraḥ,* edited by W. Zeev Harvey et al., 45–49. Jerusalem: Misgav Yerushalayim, 2002.

_____. *Golem: Jewish Magical and Mystical Traditions on the Artificial Anthropoid.* Albany: State University of New York Press, 1990.

_____. "Infinities of Torah in Kabbalah." In *Midrash and Literature,* edited by Geoffrey H. Hartman and Sanford Budick, 141–57. New Haven: Yale University Press, 1986.

_____. "Kabbalah and Elites in Thirteenth-Century Spain." *Mediterranean Historical Review* 9 (1994): 5–19.

_____. *Kabbalah: New Perspectives.* New Haven: Yale University Press, 1988.

_____. "The Kabbalah's 'Window of Opportunities,' 1270–1290." In *Me'ah She'arim: Studies in Medieval Spiritual Life in Memory of Isadore Twersky,* edited by Ezra Fleischer et al., 171–208. Jerusalem: Magnes Press, 2001.

_____. "Le-Gilguleha shel Tekhniqah Qedumah shel Ḥazon Nevu'i bi-Ymei ha-Beinayim." *Sinai* 86 (1979): 1–7.

_____. "Ha-Maḥashavah ha-Ra'ah shel ha-El." *Tarbiz* 49 (1980): 356–64.

_____. "Major Currents in Italian Kabbalah between 1560–1660." *Italia Judaica* 2 (1986): 243–62.

_____. "Olam ha-Mal'akhim bi-Dmut Adam." *Meḥqerei Yerushalayim be-Maḥashevet Yisra'el* 3 (1984): 1–66.

_____. "Orienting, Orientalizing or Disorienting the Study of Kabbalah: 'An Almost Absolutely Unique' Case of Occidentalism." *Kabbalah* 2 (1997): 13–47.

_____. "PaRDeS: Some Reflections on Kabbalistic Hermeneutics." In *Death, Ecstasy, and Other Worldly Journeys,* edited by John J. Collins and Michael Fishbane, 249–68. Albany: State University of New York Press, 1995.

_____. "Qeta lo Yadu'a mi-Midrash ha-Ne'lam." In *Sefer ha-Zohar ve-Doro* (*Meḥqerei Yerushalayim be-Maḥashevet Yisra'el* 8 [1989]), edited by Joseph Dan, 73–87. Jerusalem: Hebrew University, 1989.

_____. *R. Menaḥem Recanati ha-Mequbbal.* Vol 1. Jerusalem: Schocken, 1998.

475

_____ . "Ha-Sefirot she-me-al ha-Sefirot." *Tarbiz* 51 (1982): 239–80.

_____ . "Sexual Metaphors and Praxis in the Kabbalah." In *The Jewish Family: Metaphor and Memory,* edited by David Kraemer, 197–223. New York: Oxford University Press, 1989.

_____ . "Targumo shel R. David ben Yehudah he-Ḥasid le-Sefer ha-Zohar u-Feirushav la-Alfa Beita." *Alei Sefer* 8 (1980): 60–73; 9 (1981): 84–98; 10 (1982): 25–35.

_____ . "Tefisat ha-Torah be-Sifrut ha-Heikhalot ve-Gilguleha ba-Qabbalah." *Meḥqerei Yerushalayim be-Maḥashevet Yisra'el* 1 (1981): 23–84.

_____ . "We Have No Kabbalistic Tradition on This." In *Rabbi Moses Naḥmanides (Ramban): Explorations in His Religious and Literary Virtuosity,* edited by Isadore Twersky, 51–73. Cambridge: Harvard University Press, 1983.

_____ . "Zohar." In *The Encyclopedia of Religion,* edited by Mircea Eliade, 15: 578–79. New York: Macmillan, 1987.

_____ . "The Zohar as Exegesis." In *Mysticism and Sacred Scripture,* ed. Steven T. Katz, 87–100. New York: Oxford University Press, 2000.

Jaynes, Julian. *The Origin of Consciousness in the Breakdown of the Bicameral Mind.* Boston: Houghton Mifflin, 1976.

Jellinek, Adolph. *Beiträge zur Geschichte der Kabbala.* 2 vols. Leipzig: C. L. Fritzsche, 1852.

_____ . *Moses ben Schem-Tob de Leon und sein Verhältniss zum Sohar.* Leipzig: Heinrich Hunger, 1851.

Joël, David H. *Midrash ha-Zohar: Die Religionsphilosophie des Sohar und ihr Verhältniss zur allgemeinen jüdischen Theologie.* Leipzig: C. L. Fritzsche, 1849.

Jung, Carl G. *Collected Works.* 21 vols. Edited by Gerhard Adler, Michael Fordham, and Herbert Read. Translated by R. F. C. Hull. Princeton: Princeton University Press, 1970–79.

Kaddari, Menaḥem Z. *Diqduq ha-Lashon ha-Aramit shel ha-Zohar.* Jerusalem: Kiryath Sepher, 1971.

_____ . "Inyanim Milloniyyim min 'Ha-Midrash ha-Ne'lam.'" *Leshonenu* 22 (1958): 178–80.

_____ . "Qetav ha-Yad ha-Rishon shel ha-Zohar." *Tarbiz* 27 (1958): 265–77.

Kaminka, Aharon. "Le-Qadmut Sefer ha-Zohar." *Sinai* 7 (1940): 116–19.

_____ . "Ha-Ra'yonot ha-Sodiyyim shel R. Shim'on bar Yoḥai." In *Sefer Klausner,* edited by Naphtali H. Tur-Sinai et al., 171–80. Tel Aviv: Amanut, 1937.

Karppe, Salomon. *Études sur les origines et la nature du Zohar.* Paris: F. Alcan, 1901.

Kasher, Menaḥem M. "Ha-Zohar." In *Sinai Jubilee Volume,* edited by Yehudah Lev Hakohen Maimon, 40–56. Jerusalem: Mossad Harav Kook, 1958.

Katz, Jacob. *Halakhah ve-Qabbalah.* Jerusalem: Magnes Press, 1984.

Kiener, Ronald C. "From *Ba'al ha-Zohar* to Prophet to Ecstatic: The Vicissitudes of Abulafia in Contemporary Scholarship." In *Gershom Scholem's 'Major Trends in Jewish Mysticism': 50 Years After,* edited by Peter Schäfer and Joseph Dan, 145–59. Tübingen: J. C. B. Mohr, 1994.

_____ . "The Image of Islam in the *Zohar*." In *Sefer ha-Zohar ve-Doro* (*Meḥqerei Yerushalayim be-Maḥashevet Yisra'el* 8 [1989]), edited by Joseph Dan, 43–65 (English section). Jerusalem: Hebrew University, 1989.

Kunitz, Moses. *Sefer Ben Yoḥai.* Vienna: Georg Holzinger, 1815.

Kupfer, Ephraim. "Te'udot Ḥadashot be-Inyan ha-Pulmus bi-Dvar Hadpasat Sefer ha-Zohar." *Michael* 1 (1973): 302–18.

Lachower, Yeruḥam Fishel. "Be-Sha'ar ha-Migdal." In *Al Gevul ha-Yashan ve-he-Ḥadash.* Jerusalem: Mosad Bialik, 1951.

476

Landauer, Meyer H. "Vorläufiger Bericht über meine Entdeckung in Ansehung des Sohar." *Literaturblatt des Orients* 6 (1845): 322–750 passim.

Langer, Mordecai G. *Die Erotik der Kabbala*. Prague: Josef Flesch, 1923.

Lerner, Myron B. "Ma'aseh ha-Tanna ve-ha-Met." *Asufot* 2 (1988): 29–70.

———. "Meḥqerei Talmud." *Sinai* 59 (1966): 15–22.

Libowitz, Nehemiah S. "Halatsot ve-Divrei Biqqoret be-Sefer ha-Zohar." *Ha-Ẓofeh le-Ḥokhmat Yisrael* 11 (1927): 36–45.

Libowitz, Yehoshua. "Hitnahagut ha-Rofe ha-Idei'ali 'Qartena Asya' kimto'ar be-Sefer ha-Zohar." *Korot* 8 (1982): 111–21.

Lieberman, Saul. *Tosefta ki-Fshutah: A Comprehensive Commentary on the Tosefta*. 10 vols. New York: Jewish Theological Seminary of America, 1955–88.

Liebes, Yehuda. "Golem be-Gimatriyya Ḥokhmah." *Kiryat Sefer* 63 (1991): 1305–22.

———. "Keitsad Nitḥabber Sefer ha-Zohar." In *Sefer ha-Zohar ve-Doro* (*Meḥqerei Yerushalayim be-Maḥashevet Yisra'el* 8 [1989]), edited by Joseph Dan, 1–71. Jerusalem: Hebrew University, 1989.

———. "Ha-Mashiaḥ shel ha-Zohar: Lidmuto ha-Meshiḥit shel R. Shim'on bar Yoḥai." In *Ha-Ra'yon ha-Meshiḥi be-Yisra'el,* edited by Shmuel Reem, 87–236. Jerusalem: Israel Academy of Sciences and Humanities, 1982.

———. "Myth vs. Symbol in the Zohar and in Lurianic Kabbalah." In *Essential Papers on Kabbalah,* edited by Lawrence Fine, 212–42. New York: New York University Press, 1995.

———. "Sefer Sheqel ha-Qodesh le-R. Mosheh de León..." *Kabbalah* 2 (1997): 271–85.

———. "Sefer Tsaddiq Yesod Olam: Mitos Shabbeta'i." *Da'at* 1 (1978): 73–120.

———. "Sefer Yetsirah etsel R. Shelomoh ibn Gabirol u-Feirush ha-Shir 'Ahavtikh.'" *Meḥqerei Yerushalayim be-Maḥashevet Yisra'el* 6:3–4 (1987): 73–123.

———. "Shimmushan shel Millim be-Sefer ha-Zohar." In *R. Efraim Gottlieb Z"l: Hartsa'ah le-Zikhro...,* 17–19. Jerusalem: Hebrew University, 1974.

———. *Studies in Jewish Myth and Jewish Messianism*. Translated by Batya Stein. Albany: State University of New York Press, 1993.

———. *Studies in the Zohar*. Translated by Arnold Schwartz, Stephanie Nakache, and Penina Peli. Albany: State University of New York Press, 1993.

———. "'Terein Urzilin de-Ayyalta': Derashato ha-Sodit shel ha-Ari lifnei Mitato." In *Qabbalat ha-Ari* (*Meḥqerei Yerushalayim be-Maḥashevet Yisra'el* 10 [1992]), edited by Rachel Elior and Yehuda Liebes, 113–69. Jerusalem: Hebrew University, 1992.

———. *Torat ha-Yetsirah shel Sefer Yetsirah*. Tel Aviv: Schocken, 2000.

———. "Ziqqat ha-Zohar le-Erets Yisra'el." In *Tsiyyon ve-Tsiyyonut be-qerev Yehudei Sefarad ve-ha-Mizraḥ,* edited by W. Zeev Harvey et al., 31–44. Jerusalem: Misgav Yerushalayim, 2002.

———. "Ha-Zohar ke-Renesans." *Da'at* 46 (2001): 5–11.

———. "Ha-Zohar ke-Sefer Halakhah." *Tarbiz* 64 (1995): 581–605.

———. "Zohar ve-Eros." *Alpayim* 9 (1994): 67–119.

Löw, Immanuel. *Die Flora der Juden*. 4 vols. in 5. Vienna: R. Löwit, 1924–34. Reprint, 4 vols., Hildesheim: Georg Olms, 1967.

Luria, David. *Qadmut Sefer ha-Zohar*. Warsaw: Meir Yeḥiel Halter, 1887.

Luzzatto, Samuel David. *Vikkuaḥ al Ḥokhmat ha-Qabbalah ve-al Qadmut Sefer ha-Zohar...* Gorizia: Y. Zeitz, 1852.

Maimon, Yehudah L. "Nitsotsei Or ve-Zohar." *Sinai* 19 (1946): 169–95.

Marcus, Jacob. *The Jew in the Medieval World: A Source Book, 315–1791*. Cincinnati: Sinai Press, 1938.

Margaliot, Reuven. *Mal'akhei Elyon*. Jerusalem: Mossad Harav Kook, 1964.

477

———. "Ha-Rambam ve-ha-Zohar." *Sinai* 32 (1952–53): 263–74; 33 (1953): 9–15, 128–35, 219–24, 349–54; 34 (1953–54): 227–30, 386–95.

———. *Sha'arei Zohar*. Jerusalem: Mossad Harav Kook, 1978.

———. "She'elot be-Viqqoret ha-Zohar mi-tokh Yedi'otav al Erets Yisra'el." *Sinai* 9 (1941): 237–40.

Margalit, David. "Al 'Sod ha-Sodot' ha-Meyuḥas le-Aristo ve-'Raza de-Razin' asher ba-Zohar." *Korot* 5–6 (1955): 3–10.

Matt, Daniel C. *"Ayin*: The Concept of Nothingness in Jewish Mysticism." In *Essential Papers on Kabbalah*, edited by Lawrence Fine, 67–108. New York: New York University Press, 1995.

———. "Matnita di-Lan: Tekhniqah shel Ḥiddush be-Sefer ha-Zohar." In *Sefer ha-Zohar ve-Doro (Meḥqerei Yerushalayim be-Maḥashevet Yisra'el* 8 [1989]), edited by Joseph Dan, 123–45. Jerusalem: Hebrew University, 1989.

———. "The Mystic and the *Miẓwot*." In *Jewish Spirituality: From the Bible through the Middle Ages*, edited by Arthur Green, 367–404. New York: Crossroad, 1986.

———. "New-Ancient Words: The Aura of Secrecy in the *Zohar*." In *Gershom Scholem's 'Major Trends in Jewish Mysticism': 50 Years After*, edited by Peter Schäfer and Joseph Dan, 181–207. Tübingen: J. C. B. Mohr, 1994.

Matt, Hershel J. *Walking Humbly with God: The Life and Writings of Rabbi Hershel Jonah Matt*. Edited by Daniel C. Matt. Hoboken: Ktav, 1993.

Meged, Matti. *Ha-Or ha-Neḥshakh: Arakhim Estetiyyim be-Sefer ha-Zohar*. Tel Aviv: Sifriyat Hapoalim, 1980.

Meroz, Ronit. "'Va-Ani lo Hayiti Sham?': Quvlanotav shel Rashbi al pi Sippur Zohari lo Yadu'a." *Tarbiz* 71 (2002): 163–93.

———. "Mirkevet Yeḥezqel: Peirush Zohari bilti Yadu'a." *Te'udah* 16–17 (2001): 567–616.

———. "Mivnehu ha-Meqori shel Sefer ha-Zohar." *Proceedings of the Twelfth World Congress of Jewish Studies*. Forthcoming.

———. "The Path of Silence: An Unknown Story from a *Zohar* Manuscript." Forthcoming.

———. *Ha-Peninah, ha-Dag, ve-ha-Matstsah: Ha-Biyyografyah ha-Ruḥanit shel Rashbi, o Mivnehu ha-Qadum shel Sefer ha-Zohar*. Jerusalem: Mosad Bialik, forthcoming.

———. "Zoharic Narratives and Their Adaptations." *Hispania Judaica Bulletin* 3 (2000): 3–63.

Meshi-Zahav, Menaḥem Mendel. *Qovets Sifrei Setam*. Jerusalem: Mekhon ha-Talmud ha-Yisre'eli ha-Shalem, 1970.

Milgrom, Jacob. *Leviticus*. Anchor Bible, vols. 3–3B. New York: Doubleday, 1991–2000.

Milikowsky, Chaim. "Further on Editing Rabbinic Texts," *Jewish Quarterly Review* 90 (1999): 137–49.

Milzahagi, Eliakim. *Zohorei Ravyah*. MS Heb. 121, 4°, Jewish National and University Library, Jerusalem.

Modena, Leone. *Ari Nohem*. Edited by Nehemiah S. Libowitz. Jerusalem: Darom, 1929.

Mopsik, Charles. "Les autres dieux dans le Zohar." In *Colloque des intellectuels juifs de langue française*. Paris: Denoël, 1985.

———. "La controverse d'amour dans le Zohar: Moment critique de l'émanation et modèle idéal." In *La controverse et ses formes*, edited by Alain Le Boulluec, 71–97. Paris: Le Cerf, 1995.

———. "Le corpus zoharique, ses titres et ses amplifications." In *La formation des canons scripturaires*, edited by Michel Tardieu, 75–105. Paris: Le Cerf, 1993.

———. "Le judéo-araméen tardif, langue de la Cabale théosophique." *Cahiers du Judaïsme* 6 (1999–2000): 4–14.

_____. "Moïse de León, le *Sheqel ha-Qodesh* et la rédaction du *Zohar:* Une réponse à Yehuda Liebes." *Kabbalah* 3 (1998): 177–218.

_____. "Pensée, voix et parole dans le 'Zohar.'" *Revue de l'histoire des religions*, 213 (1996): 385–414.

Myer, Isaac. *Qabbalah: The Philosophical Writings of Solomon ben Yehudah ibn Gebirol, or Avicebron, and their connection with the Hebrew Qabbalah and Sepher ha-Zohar.* Philadelphia: Isaac Myer, 1888.

Nathan ben Yehiel of Rome. *Arukh ha-Shalem.* 9 vols. Edited by Alexander Kohut, with *Tosefot he-Arukh ha-Shalem,* by Samuel Krauss. New York: Pardes, 1955.

_____. *Sefer he-Arukh.* Edited by Shemuel Schlesinger. Tel Aviv: Yetsu Sifrei Kodesh, n.d.

Neubauer, Adolf. "The Bahir and the Zohar." *Jewish Quarterly Review* 4 (1892): 357–68.

Neuhausen, Simon A. *Sifriyyah shel Ma'lah.* Berehovo: Samuel Klein, 1937.

_____. *Zohorei Zohar.* St. Louis: Dat Veda'at, 1929.

Neumann, Erich. *The Origins and History of Consciousness.* Princeton: Princeton University Press, 1970.

Neumark, David. *Toledot ha-Filosofyah be-Yisra'el.* Vol. 1. New York: A. I. Shtibel, 1921.

Noy, Dov. "Histakkelut ba-Tsippornayim bi-Sh'at ha-Havdalah." *Mahanayim* 85–86 (1963): 166–73.

Oron, Michal. "'Kol ha-Neshamah Tehallel Yah': Bittui Allegori li-Tfisat ha-Mavet be-Sefer ha-Zohar." *Dappim le-Mehqar be-Sifrut* 4 (1988): 35–38.

_____. "Me-Omanut ha-Derush shel Ba'al ha-Zohar." In *Sefer ha-Zohar ve-Doro (Mehqerei Yerushalayim be-Mahashevet Yisra'el* 8 [1989]), edited by Joseph Dan, 299–310. Jerusalem: Hebrew University, 1989.

_____. "Sheloshah Peirushim le-Ma'aseh Vereshit u-Mashma'utam be-Heqer Sefer ha-Zohar." *Da'at* 50–52 (2003): 183–99.

_____. "Simeni kha-Hotam al Libbekha: Iyyunim ba-Poetiqah shel Ba'al ha-Zohar be-Farashat Sava de-Mishpatim." In *Massu'ot,* edited by Michal Oron and Amos Goldreich, 1–24. Jerusalem: Mosad Bialik, 1994.

_____. "Sippur ha-Otiyyot u-Mqorotav: Iyyun be-Midrash ha-Zohar al Otiyyot ha-Alef Beit." *Mehqerei Yerushalayim be-Mahashevet Yisra'el* 3 (1984): 97–109.

Oron, Michal, and Amos Goldreich, eds. *Massu'ot: Mehqarim be-Sifrut ha-Qabbalah ... Muqdashim le-Zikhro shel Prof. Efraim Gottlieb Z"l.* Jerusalem: Mosad Bialik, 1994.

Pachter, Mordechai. "Bein Lailah le-Voqer." In *Sefer ha-Zohar ve-Doro (Mehqerei Yerushalayim be-Mahashevet Yisra'el* 8 [1989]), edited by Joseph Dan, 311–46. Jerusalem: Hebrew University, 1989.

Patai, Raphael. *The Hebrew Goddess.* 3d ed. Detroit: Wayne State University Press, 1990.

Penkower, Jordan S. "Iyyun Mehuddash be-Sefer Masoret ha-Masoret le-Eliyyahu Bahur: Ihur ha-Niqqud u-Viqqoret Sefer ha-Zohar." *Italyah* 8 (1989): 7–73.

Peretz, Eliyahu. *Ma'alot ha-Zohar: Mafteah Shemot ha-Sefirot.* Jerusalem: Academon, 1987.

Pines, Shlomo. "Ve-Qara el ha-Ayin ve-Nivqa." *Tarbiz* 50 (1981): 339–47.

Pope, Marvin H. *Song of Songs.* Anchor Bible, vol. 7c. Garden City, N.Y.: Doubleday, 1977.

Preis, Karl. "Die Medizin im Sohar." *Monatsschrift für Geschichte und Wissenschaft des Judentums* 72 (1928): 167–84.

Pushinski, Shalom. "Le-Heqer Sefat ha-Zohar." *Yavneh* 2 (1940): 140–47.

Rabin, Ya'akov. "Ha-Refu'ah be-Sefer ha-Zohar uv-Sifrei Qabbalah Aherim." *Harofe Haivri* 31 (1958): 103–13.

Rapoport, Solomon Judah. *Nahalat Yehudah.* Lemberg: n.p., 1873.

Roth, Norman. "Jewish Collaborators in Alfonso's Scientific Work." In *Emperor of Culture: Alfonso X the Learned of Castile and His Thirteenth-Century Renaissance,* edited by Robert I. Burns, 59–71. Philadelphia: University of Pennsylvania Press, 1990.

Rubin, Zvia. "Mif'al ha-Zohar: Mattarot ve-Hessegim." In *Asuppat Kiryat Sefer* (*Musaf le-Kherekh* 68), edited by Yehoshua Rosenberg, 167–74. Jerusalem: Jewish National and University Library, 1998.

———. *Ha-Muva'ot mi-Sefer ha-Zohar be-Feirush al ha-Torah le-R. Menaḥem Recanati.* Jerusalem: Academon, 1992.

Sack, Bracha. *Be-Sha'arei ha-Qabbalah shel Rabbi Mosheh Cordovero.* Beer-Sheva: Ben-Gurion University of the Negev Press, 1995.

———. "Erets ve-Erets Yisra'el ba-Zohar." In *Sefer ha-Zohar ve-Doro* (*Meḥqerei Yerushalayim be-Maḥashevet Yisra'el* 8 [1989]), edited by Joseph Dan, 239–53. Jerusalem: Hebrew University, 1989.

Sandler, Perez. "Li-V'ayat 'Pardes' ve-ha-Shitah ha-Merubba'at." In *Sefer Auerbach,* edited by Arthur Biram, 222–35. Jerusalem: Haḥevrah Leḥeker Hamikra Beyisra'el, 1955.

Sarna, Nahum M. *The JPS Torah Commentary: Genesis.* Philadelphia: Jewish Publication Society, 1989.

Schatz-Uffenheimer, Rivka. "Simlei ha-Yam be-Qabbalat Sefer ha-Zohar." In *Ha-Yam ba-Miqra,* edited by Malachi Pereg, 29–42. Haifa: Ḥevel Yami Leyisrael, 1971.

Schimmel, Annemarie. *Mystical Dimensions of Islam.* Chapel Hill: University of North Carolina Press, 1975.

Scholem, Gershom G. *Alchemie und Kabbala.* Frankfurt am Main: Suhrkamp Verlag, 1984.

———. *Bibliographia Kabbalistica.* Berlin: Schocken, 1933.

———. "Colours and Their Symbolism in Jewish Tradition and Mysticism." *Diogenes* 108 (1979): 84–111; 109 (1980): 64–76.

———. *Devarim be-Go.* Edited by Avraham Shapira. 2d ed. 2 vols. Tel Aviv: Am Oved, 1976.

———. "Ha-Im Ḥibber R. Mosheh de León et Sefer ha-Zohar?" *Madda'ei ha-Yahadut* 1 (1926): 16–29.

———. "Hakkarat Panim ve-Sidrei Sirtutin." In *Sefer Assaf,* edited by Umberto Cassuto et al., 459–95. Jerusalem: Mossad Harav Kook, 1953.

———. "He'arot ve-Tsiyyunim al Sefer ha-Zohar." 2 vols. MS, Scholem Collection, Jewish National and University Library, Jerusalem.

———. "Iqvotav shel Gevirol be-Qabbalah." In *Me'assef Soferei Erets Yisra'el,* edited by Aaron Kabak and Eliezer Steinman, 160–78. Tel Aviv: Agudat Hasoferim, 1940.

———. *Jewish Gnosticism, Merkabah Mysticism, and Talmudic Tradition.* New York: Jewish Theological Seminary of America, 1965.

———. *Kabbalah.* Jerusalem: Keter, 1974.

———. *Le-Ḥeqer Qabbalat R. Yitsḥaq ben Ya'aqov ha-Kohen.* Jerusalem: Tarbiz, 1934.

———. "Le-Ḥeqer Torat ha-Gilgul ba-Qabbalah be-Me'ah ha-Shelosh-Esreh." *Tarbiz* 16 (1945): 135–50.

———. "Levush ha-Neshamot ve-'Ḥaluqa de-Rabbanan." *Tarbiz* 24 (1955): 290–306.

———. *Major Trends in Jewish Mysticism.* 3d ed. New York: Schocken, 1967.

———. *Meḥqerei Qabbalah.* Vol. 1. Edited by Joseph Ben-Shlomo and Moshe Idel. Tel Aviv: Am Oved, 1998.

———. "Meqorotav shel 'Ma'aseh Rabbi Gedi'el ha-Tinoq' be-Sifrut ha-Qabbalah." In *Le-Agnon Shai,* edited by Dov Sadan and Ephraim E. Urbach, 289–305. Jerusalem: Hava'ad hatsiburi leyovel hashiv'im shel Shai Agnon, 1959.

_____. *The Messianic Idea in Judaism.* New York: Schocken, 1971.

_____. "The Name of God and the Linguistic Theory of the Kabbalah." *Diogenes* 79 (1972): 59–80; 80 (1972): 164–94.

_____. *On the Kabbalah and Its Symbolism.* Translated by Ralph Manheim. New York: Schocken, 1969.

_____. *On the Mystical Shape of the Godhead: Basic Concepts in the Kabbalah.* Translated by Joachim Neugroschel, edited by Jonathan Chipman. New York: Schocken, 1991.

_____. *Origins of the Kabbalah.* Edited by R. J. Zwi Werblowsky, translated by Allan Arkush. Philadelphia: Jewish Publication Society; Princeton: Princeton University Press, 1987.

_____. "Parashah Ḥadashah min ha-Midrash ha-Ne'lam she-ba-Zohar." In *Sefer ha-Yovel li-Khvod Levi Ginzberg,* 425–46. New York: American Academy for Jewish Research, 1945.

_____. "Peraqim Ḥadashim me-Inyenei Ashmedai ve-Lilit." *Tarbiz* 19 (1948): 160–75.

_____. *Peraqim le-Toledot Sifrut ha-Qabbalah.* Jerusalem: Azriel, 1931.

_____. *Ha-Qabbalah be-Provans.* Edited by Rivka Schatz. Jerusalem: Academon, 1970.

_____. "Qabbalot R. Ya'aqov ve-R. Yitsḥaq benei R. Ya'aqov ha-Kohen." *Madda'ei ha-Yahadut* 2 (1927): 163–293.

_____. "Seridei Sifro shel R. Shem Tov ibn Ga'on al Yesodot Torat ha-Sefirot." *Kiryat Sefer* 8 (1931–32): 397–408, 534–42; 9 (1932–33): 126–33.

_____. "She'elot be-Viqqoret ha-Zohar mi-tokh Yedi'otav al Erets Yisra'el." *Zion (Me'assef)* 1 (1926): 40–55.

_____. "Sippur bilti Yadu'a al Metsi'at Sefer ha-Zohar." *Kiryat Sefer* 1 (1924–25): 166.

_____. "Teshuvot ha-Meyuḥasot le-R. Yosef Gikatilla." In *Festschrift Dr. Jakob Freimann,* 163–70. Berlin: Viktoria, 1937.

_____. "Te'udah Ḥadashah le-Toledot Reshit ha-Qabbalah." In *Sefer Bialik,* edited by Jacob Fichman, 141–62. Tel Aviv: Amanut, 1934.

_____. "Ha-Tsitat ha-Rishon min ha-Midrash ha-Ne'lam." *Tarbiz* 3 (1932): 181–83.

_____. *Über einige Grundbegriffe des Judentums.* Frankfurt am Main: Suhrkamp, 1970.

_____. "Eine unbekannte mystische Schrift des Mose de Leon." *Monatsschrift für Geschichte und Wissenschaft des Judentums* 71 (1927): 109–23.

_____. "Vulliauds Uebersetzung des Sifra di-Zeniutha aus dem Sohar und andere neuere Literatur zur Geschichte der Kabbala." *Monatsschrift für Geschichte und Wissenschaft des Judentums* 75 (1931): 347–62, 444–55.

_____. "The Zohar, Translated by Harry Sperling and Maurice Simon." *The Jewish Review* 1 (1933): 82–88.

Secret, François. *Le Zóhar chez les kabbalistes chrétiens de la Renaissance.* Paris: Durlacher, 1958.

Sed-Rajna, Gabrielle. "Manuscrits du *Tiqquney ha-Zohar.*" *Revue des études juives* 129 (1970): 161–78.

Segal, Eliezer. "The Exegetical Craft of the *Zohar:* Toward an Appreciation." *AJS Review* 17 (1992): 31–49.

Shiloah, Amnon, and Ruth Tene. *Nose'ei Musiqah ba-Zohar.* Jerusalem: Magnes Press, 1977.

Silver, Abba H. *A History of Messianic Speculation in Israel.* New York: Macmillan, 1927.

Speiser, Ephraim A. *Genesis.* Anchor Bible, vol. 1. 3d ed. Garden City, N.Y.: Doubleday, 1981.

Stahl, Abraham. "Qeri'ah Pulḥanit shel Sefer ha-Zohar." *Pe'amim* 5 (1980): 77–86.

———. "Ritualistic Reading among Oriental Jews." *Anthropological Quarterly* 52 (1979): 115–20.

Steinschneider, Moritz. *Polemische und apologetische Literatur in arabischer Sprache.* Leipzig: F. A. Brockhaus, 1877.

Stern, Ignaz. "Versuch einer umständlichen Analyse des Sohar." *Ben Chananja* 1–5 (1858–62).

Stern, Samuel M. "Rationalists and Kabbalists in Medieval Allegory." *Journal of Jewish Studies* 6 (1955): 73–86.

Stroumsa, Gedaliahu A. G. *Another Seed: Studies in Gnostic Mythology.* Leiden: E. J. Brill, 1984.

———. "The Early Christian Fish Symbol Reconsidered." In *Messiah and Christos: Studies in the Jewish Origins of Christianity, Presented to David Flusser on the Occasion of His Seventy-Fifth Birthday,* edited by Ithamar Gruenwald, Shaul Shaked, and Gedaliahu G. Stroumsa, 199–205. Tübingen: J. C. B. Mohr, 1992.

Talmage, Frank. "Apples of Gold: The Inner Meaning of Sacred Texts in Medieval Judaism." In *Jewish Spirituality: From the Bible through the Middle Ages,* edited by Arthur Green, 313–55. New York: Crossroad, 1986.

———. "Ha-Munaḥ 'Haggadah' be-Mashal ha-Ahuvah ba-Heikhal be-Sefer ha-Zohar." *Meḥqerei Yerushalayim be-Maḥashevet Yisra'el* 4 (1985): 271–73.

Tamar, David. "Al Hadpasat ha-Zohar." *Oẓar Yehudei Sefarad* 2 (1959): 82–83.

Ta-Shma, Israel M. "Li-Mqorotav ha-Sifrutiyyim shel Sefer ha-Zohar." *Tarbiz* 60 (1991): 663–65.

———. *Minhag Ashkenaz ha-Qadmon: Ḥeqer ve-Iyyun.* 2d ed. Jerusalem: Magnes Press, 1994.

———. *Ha-Nigleh she-ba-Nistar.* 2d ed. Tel Aviv: Hakibbutz Hameuchad, 2001.

———. "The 'Open' Book in Medieval Hebrew Literature: The Problem of Authorized Editions." *Bulletin of the John Rylands University Library of Manchester* 75:3 (1993): 17–24.

———. "Rabbi Yosef Karo bein Ashkenaz li-Sfarad: Le-Ḥeqer Hitpashshetut Sefer ha-Zohar." *Tarbiz* 59 (1990): 153–70.

Tene, Naomi. "Darkhei Itstsuv ha-Sippur be-Sefer ha-Zohar." Ph.D. diss., Bar-Ilan University, 1992.

Tishby, Isaiah. *Ḥiqrei Qabbalah u-Shluḥoteha.* Vol. 1. Jerusalem: Magnes Press, 1982.

Trachtenberg, Joshua. *The Devil and the Jews: The Medieval Conception of the Jews and Its Relation to Modern Antisemitism.* New Haven: Yale University Press, 1943.

———. *Jewish Magic and Superstition: A Study in Folk Religion.* New York: Atheneum, 1974.

Tur-Sinai, N. H. *Ha-Lashon ve-ha-Sefer.* 3 vols. Jerusalem: Mosad Bialik, 1948–56.

Urbach, Ephraim E. *The Sages: Their Concepts and Beliefs.* 2d ed. 2 vols. Translated by Israel Abrahams. Jerusalem: Magnes Press, 1979.

Van Winden, J. C. M. "'Terra Autem Stupida Quadam Erat Admiratione': Reflexions on a remarkable translation of Genesis 1:2a." In *Studies in Gnosticism and Hellenistic Religions presented to Gilles Quispel on the Occasion of his 65th Brithday,* edited by R. Van den Broek and M. J. Vermaseren, 458–66. Leiden: E. J. Brill, 1981.

Verman, Mark. *The Books of Contemplation: Medieval Jewish Mystical Sources.* Albany: State University of New York Press, 1992.

———. "The Development of *Yiḥudim* in Spanish Kabbalah." In *Sefer ha-Zohar ve-Doro (Meḥqerei Yerushalayim be-Maḥashevet Yisra'el* 8 [1989]), edited by Joseph Dan, 25–41 (English section). Jerusalem: Hebrew University, 1989.

Waite, Arthur E. *The Holy Kabbalah.* London: Williams & Norgate, 1929. Reprint, New Hyde Park, N.Y.: University Books, 1960.

Weiss, Joseph. "A Contemporary Poem on the Appearance of the *Zohar*." *Journal of Jewish Studies* 8 (1957): 219–21.

Werblowsky, R. J. Zwi. "Gott als das Nichts im 'Sohar.'" In *Sein und Nichts in der abendländischen Mystik,* edited by Walter Strolz, 73–81. Freiburg: Herder, 1984.

_____. "Philo and the Zohar." *Journal of Jewish Studies* 10 (1959): 25–44, 113–35.

Wijnhoven, Jochanan H. A. "Yaḥasam shel Shenei Ḥibburim me-et R. Mosheh de León le-Sefer ha-Zohar." *Proceedings of the Fourth World Congress of Jewish Studies* 2 (1967–69): 313–15.

_____. "The *Zohar* and the Proselyte." In *Texts and Responses: Studies Presented to Nahum N. Glatzer,* edited by Michael A. Fishbane and Paul R. Mendes-Flohr, 120–40. Leiden: E. J. Brill, 1975.

Wildmann, Isaac Eisik (Ḥaver). *Magen ve-Tsinnah.* Johannisberg: n.p., 1855.

Wilhelm, Ya'akov D. "Sidrei Tiqqunim." In *Alei Ayin: Minḥat Devarim li-Shlomo Zalman Schocken,* 125–46. Tel Aviv: Ha'aretz, 1952.

Wolfson, Elliot R. *Along the Path: Studies in Kabbalistic Myth, Symbolism, and Hermeneutics.* Albany: State University of New York Press, 1995.

_____. "Beautiful Maiden Without Eyes: *Peshat* and *Sod* in Zoharic Hermeneutics." In *The Midrashic Imagination,* edited by Michael Fishbane, 155–203. Albany: State University of New York Press, 1993.

_____. "Biblical Accentuation in a Mystical Key: Kabbalistic Interpretations of the *Te'amim*." *Journal of Jewish Music and Liturgy* 11 (1988–89): 1–16; 12 (1989–90): 1–13.

_____. *Circle in the Square: Studies in the Use of Gender in Kabbalistic Symbolism.* Albany: State University of New York Press, 1995.

_____. "Circumcision and the Divine Name: A Study in the Transmission of Esoteric Doctrine." *Jewish Quarterly Review* 78 (1987): 77–112.

_____. "Coronation of the Sabbath Bride: Kabbalistic Myth and the Ritual of Androgynisation." *Journal of Jewish Thought and Philosophy* 6 (1997): 301–44.

_____. "Dimmui Antropomorfi ve-ha-Simboliqah shel ha-Otiyyot be-Sefer ha-Zohar." In *Sefer ha-Zohar ve-Doro (Meḥqerei Yerushalayim be-Maḥashevet Yisra'el* 8 [1989]), edited by Joseph Dan, 147–81. Jerusalem: Hebrew University, 1989.

_____. "Eunuchs Who Keep the Sabbath: Becoming Male and the Ascetic Ideal in Thirteenth-Century Jewish Mysticism." In *Becoming Male in the Middle Ages,* edited by Jeffrey J. Cohen and Bonnie Wheeler, 151–85. New York: Garland Publishing, 1997.

_____. "Fore/giveness On the Way: Nesting in the Womb of Response." *Graven Images* 4 (1998): 153–69.

_____. "Forms of Visionary Ascent as Ecstatic Experience in Zoharic Literature." In *Gershom Scholem's 'Major Trends in Jewish Mysticism': 50 Years After,* edited by Peter Schäfer and Joseph Dan, 209–35. Tübingen: J. C. B. Mohr, 1994.

_____. "Hai Gaon's Letter and Commentary on *Aleynu:* Further Evidence of R. Moses de León's Pseudepigraphic Activity." *Jewish Quarterly Review* 81 (1991): 365–410.

_____. "The Hermeneutics of Visionary Experience: Revelation and Interpretation in the *Zohar*." *Religion* 18 (1988): 311–45.

_____. "Left Contained in the Right: A Study in Zoharic Hermeneutics." *AJS Review* 11 (1986): 27–52.

_____. "Letter Symbolism and Merkavah Imagery in the *Zohar*." In *Alei Shefer: Studies in the Literature of Jewish Thought Presented to Rabbi Dr. Alexandre Safran,* edited by Moshe Hallamish, 195–236. Ramat Gan: Bar-Ilan University, 1990.

_____. "Light Through Darkness: The Ideal of Human Perfection in the *Zohar*." *Harvard Theological Review* 81 (1988): 73–95.

_____. "Occultation of the Feminine and the Body of Secrecy in Medieval Kabbalah."
In *Rending the Veil: Concealment and Revelation of Secrets in the History of
Religions,* edited by Elliot R. Wolfson, 113–54. New York: Seven Bridges Press, 1999.

_____. "Ontology, Alterity, and Ethics in Kabbalistic Anthropology." *Exemplaria* 12
(2000): 129–55.

_____. "Re/membering the Covenant: Memory, Forgetfulness, and History in the
Zohar." In *Jewish History and Memory: Essays in Honor of Yosef Hayim Yerushalmi,*
edited by Elisheva Carlebach, John M. Efron, and David N. Myers, 214–46.
Hanover, N.H.: University Press of New England, 1998.

_____. *Through a Speculum That Shines: Vision and Imagination in Medieval Jewish
Mysticism.* Princeton: Princeton University Press, 1994.

_____. "Woman—The Feminine as Other in Theosophic Kabbalah: Some
Philosophical Observations on the Divine Androgyne." In *The Other in Jewish
Thought and History: Constructions of Jewish Culture and Identity,* edited by
Laurence. J. Silberstein and Robert. L. Cohn, 166–204. New York: New York
University Press, 1994.

Wolfson, Harry A. *Philo: Foundations of Religious Philosophy in Judaism, Christianity,
and Islam.* 2 vols. Cambridge: Harvard University Press, 1947.

Zeitlin, Hillel. *Al Gevul Shenei Olamot.* Tel Aviv: Yavneh, 1965.

_____. *Be-Fardes ha-Ḥasidut ve-ha-Qabbalah.* Tel Aviv: Yavneh, 1982.

Zlotnik (Avida), Yehuda Leib. *Midrash ha-Melitsah ha-Ivrit.* Jerusalem: Darom, 1938.

Index of Sources

This index includes sources that are quoted (rather than merely cited or alluded to) by either the *Zohar* or the translator. Biblical passages appear mostly in the text of the *Zohar* itself; other listed works appear almost exclusively in the notes.

BIBLICAL LITERATURE

Tanakh (Hebrew Bible)

Genesis

1:1	9, 17–19, 25, 29, 49–51, 62, 68, 77, 107–17, 170–78, 180, 185, 190, 191, 279, 282, 316
1:2	62, 79, 114, 118–21, 181, 182, 187, 247, 287, 315
1:3	122–28, 184, 192, 193, 194, 241–45
1:4	125, 162, 184, 187, 195, 204, 242, 243
1:5	125, 188, 195, 198, 243
1:6	124, 127–37, 198, 199, 201, 244
1:6–8	135
1:7	131, 134, 244
1:8	202
1:9	82, 83, 137–40, 203
1:9–10	202, 245, 253
1:9–10, 11	135
1:10	83, 203, 204
1:10, 12	83, 147
1:11	84, 141–47, 154, 202, 204, 205, 245–46, 253, 362
1:11–12	30
1:12	2, 3, 247
1:14	84, 148–52, 207, 210, 247
1:14–15	84, 160
1:15	85, 152, 160, 169, 210

1:16	152–54, 158, 187, 208, 212, 415, 436
1:17	154, 212
1:17–18	157
1:20	3, 86, 87, 88, 89, 90, 212, 213, 214, 330
1:21	91, 92, 213
1:24	92, 94, 213, 246
1:26	3, 216
1:27	13, 94, 96, 99, 111, 152, 186, 217, 236, 253, 267, 314
1:28	88, 262, 315, 385, 418
1:29	99, 100
1:31	100, 269, 270, 349
1:36	94
2:1	255–57
2:1–3	33
2:2	31, 258
2:2–3	101, 258, 340
2:3	101, 132, 156, 259, 260, 261, 262
2:4	19, 20, 122, 246, 313, 333
2:5	218, 247
2:6	219
2:7	213, 271
2:8	221, 235, 241
2:9	220
2:10	186, 213, 223, 224, 340, 342, 440

Genesis, continued

2:13	312–13
2:15	326
2:16	222
2:16–17	222, 226
2:17	222, 304, 311
2:18	217
2:20	217, 249, 250
2:21	217, 219, 251
2:22	217, 267, 272, 279–80
2:23	273, 280
2:24	252, 273
2:26	253
2:31	253, 254
3:1	225, 225–26, 273, 288
3:3	223, 304
3:4	212
3:5	225
3:6	85, 86, 227–28, 273–74
3:7	227, 229, 296
3:8	290, 447
3:10	290
3:12	349, 443
3:14	431, 435
3:17	229, 247, 331, 414, 417
3:19	228
3:21	230, 437
3:23	298, 326
3:24	79, 149, 297–301, 330
4:1	301–4, 308
4:2	308
4:3	304
4:3–4	303
4:4–5	304–5
4:5	231
4:7	231, 233, 305
4:8	231, 305
4:10	304
4:14	63, 231, 306
4:15	231, 306
4:16	306
4:22	309
4:25	307
4:26	192–93, 318
5:1	130, 235, 236, 310–13, 417
5:2	144, 236, 313–19
5:3	150, 231, 234, 240, 307, 308, 315, 317
5:4	238
5:24	90, 313, 320–21, 334, 429
5:29	241, 331, 343

6:1	363
6:1–9	193
6:2	64, 150, 233, 234, 309, 330, 363, 365
6:3	239, 240, 328–30
6:4	234, 309, 330
6:5	321–23
6:5–13	193
6:6	323–28
6:7	330–32
6:8	333, 341
6:9	339–50, 362, 370, 395, 407
6:10	357–58
6:11	347, 348, 355, 391, 392
6:12	321, 350–52, 399
6:13	225, 304, 329, 383, 392
6:14	365
6:17	382, 383, 386–88
6:17–18	397
6:18	388–92, 398
7:1	392–96, 416
7:3	341
7:4	354–57, 397, 400
7:5	381
7:6	381
7:7	392, 400–402, 406
7:11	366
7:17	402, 403–5
7:23	319, 388, 396, 404, 405–6
8:1	377, 406–9
8:2	356
8:15–16	416
8:20	334, 410
8:21	332, 412, 414, 417
8:22	241
9:1	416–18, 419
9:1–2	419
9:2	95, 417, 418
9:6	417, 428
9:7	419, 420
9:8, 12–13	420–22
9:13	139, 423
9:16	423, 428
9:18	429–32
9:19	432
9:20	332, 341, 362, 433–37
9:21	433, 434, 446
9:22	358, 431
9:25	431, 434, 435
10:9	437–38
11:1	438–41

11:2	440, 449
11:4	441–43
11:5	348, 442
11:6	445, 449
11:8	445, 450
11:10	429, 443
12:6	431
13:3	274
15:16	354
16:5	392
17:1	80, 342
17:4	382
17:14	316
17:21	389
18:1	162
18:30, 32	395
18:32	395
19:24	376
21:1	232
21:6	72
21:7	72
21:8	72
22:3	426–27
23	327
24:63	162
24:67	277, 278
25:8	241
25:26	344
26:19	346
27:1	120
27:11	380–81
27:27	227
27:28	105
28:9	310
28:11	272, 273
28:12	423
28:13	426
28:17	75
28:18	424, 427
28:22	424–25
29:23, 25	131
29:30	272
30:13	271
32:4	381
32:25	224
32:26	163
32:31	49, 60
32:32	162, 163
32:35	162
35:16	139
36:8–9	381

37:2	166
38:7	322, 333, 355–56
38:9	322, 356
40:16	225
49:3	231–32
49:20	260
49:24	422

Exodus

2:2	193
2:4	34
2:13	322
2:19	41
3:5	56
3:14	111, 113
5:1, 3	66
5:21	442, 443
6:5	409
9:25	431
11:3	60
11:5	263
12:22	365, 366, 396, 407, 419
13:1–10	97
13:11–16	97
13:14–15	98
13:19	166
13:21	84, 447
14:15	397–98
14:19	351
14:19–21	48, 127, 312
14:20	326, 353
14:31	291
15:2	291
15:11	14
15:17	45
16:4	168
17:9	42
19:18	178, 412
20:8	15, 34, 260, 266
20:15	178, 291
20:22	271
21:5	281
23:17	9, 428
24:7	3, 370
24:10	138
24:18	5, 200, 385
25:27	189
25:31	438
26:28	7
26:33	200, 202
30:7	125

Exodus, continued

30:13	207
30:32	156
31:2	10
31:14	35
31:16	317
31:17	181
32:8	8, 397
32:10	396
32:11	397
32:13	398
32:14	324, 397
32:16	240, 292
32:30	397
32:32	397
33:4	291, 293
33:5	291, 293, 369, 370
33:6	291, 293, 370
33:7	292, 295
33:11	296
33:20	46, 384
33:23	159
34:6	71
34:22	59
34:28	21
34:30	193, 291
35:35	61
40:17	218

Leviticus

1:3	411
1:17	411, 412
10:1	434
10:1–2	434
11:29	157
11:43	301, 358
11:44	302, 358
12:2	177, 246
13:46	377
16:3	426
16:21	378
18:2	383
18:20	55
18:25	355
19:30	30, 31, 33
19:35	207
20:10	54
22:20	381
24:11	234
24:16	234
25:8–55	258

26:12	347
26:25	391
27:30	100

Numbers

1:51	190
6:1–3	190
6:5	307
6:24–26	121
10:2	439
10:35–36	165
12:7	165, 446
12:8	41
14:10	138
15:20	185–86
16:9	131
16:14	225
16:15	129
16:21	132
16:22	126
16:33	129, 130, 132
17:7	138
18:21	100
19:11	300
19:14	156, 378
20:11	42
20:13	386
24:1	243
24:2	401
24:3	401
24:9	401
25:12	391
25:13	391
26:9	129
27:20	164
28:7	413
28:15	153, 415, 437
29:35	375
30:14	165
35:5	61

Deuteronomy

3:11	72
4:4	249
4:7	191
4:9	103
4:11	79
4:24	202, 282
4:32	5, 114
4:39	84
5:4	169
5:12	33, 260, 266

5:19	279
5:20	79
6:4	74, 81, 82, 113, 140, 322
6:4–9	98
6:5	81
7:9	261
10:8	131
10:12	335
10:17	145
10:19	92
11:13–15	98
11:13–21	98, 99
11:16–17	98
14:4–5	156
14:26	122
16:3	203
16:21	270
17:17	446
18:1–2	368
20:19	223, 231, 305
22:16	272
22:23	285
23:4–5	93
23:9	92
23:11	310
23:15	447
25:3	354
27:9	424
28:3	105
28:10	96, 97
30:19	6
32:4	294
32:17	34
32:18	326
33:1	41, 295
33:10	412
33:2	96
34:10	65

Joshua
1:8	74
3:11	9, 125, 280
3:16	135
9:23	435
10:13	66

Judges
2:12	197
5:2	197
5:7	197, 198
5:11	196–98
13:16	46
13:22	46

1 Samuel
2:27–36	164
2:35	324
3:1	163
4:8	68
6:10–12	421
15:29	163–64
17:4	196
20:31	175
22:20	368
25:29	384

2 Samuel
6:19	136
7:14	261, 302, 306, 307
7:23	159, 251
11–12	54
11:1	56
11:8	56
11:10	276
12:3	55
12:5	56
12:7	56
12:9	55
12:13	56, 435, 436
15:25	259
23:3	66
23:15	346
23:19	42
23:20	38, 39, 40, 43
23:21	41, 42, 60
23:23	42

1 Kings
2:12	427
2:26	368
6:7	438
11:4	447
11:14	446
18:12	250
18:30	389
18:31	390
18:38	285
19:9	91
19:10	91, 390
19:11	119, 121
19:12	119
19:11–12	119, 121

2 Kings
2:11	147
2:23–24	48
4:8	408–9

2 Kings, continued

4:13	409
4:16	47
4:34	47
11:12	90
23:4	271

Isaiah

3:10	185, 345
3:10–11	304
3:18–24	52
5:18	28, 323
6:1	138, 344
6:3	141, 326, 353, 421
6:6	249–50
6:13	110
8:14	278
8:16	23
9:6	216
10:15	191
10:23	15
10:30	366, 367
11:15	288
14:3	265
17:11	221
21:2	343
22:17–19	104
24:5	351–52
24:21	405
25:1	432
25:5	3
25:8	212, 301, 415–16
25:9	344
27:1	213, 251
27:13	98
29:1	39
29:15	400
30:26	212, 416
33:18	36
33:20	292
33:21	209
34:6	299
34:11	287
34:14	209
38:2	73
38:11	383
40:12	140–41, 183
40:17	66
40:26	5–11, 19, 177, 179
40:31	87
41:2	242
41:8	72

43:16	176, 267
44:6	66
44:9	67
45:8	134, 177, 199, 246, 287, 346, 356
45:14	206
46:3	93
46:4	133, 215, 325
48:13	179
49:3	75, 433
50:1	298
51:16	25, 27
54:9	397, 429
54:10	203, 204
54:13	376
55:1	86, 252
55:3	51
55:8	330
57:1	314, 395
57:2	364
57:19	34
57:20	441
58:13	32
59:17	307
59:20	104
60:21	205, 221, 339, 405
62:6	215
63:7	44
63:11	397, 398
63:12	396
63:13	398
64:3	26, 38, 255, 337, 386
66:22	26, 281
66:23	360
66:24	89

Jeremiah

1:1	368
2:22	355, 366, 435
3:1	222, 226, 343
7:28	314
7:31–32	360
10:6	67
10:7	65, 67
10:10	439
10:11	62, 306
10:12	206
13:17	324
23:24	400
27:13	204
30:9	429
31:2	34

31:20   93
31:38   108
33:25   196, 315, 339, 390

Ezekiel
1:1   39
1:4   79
1:5–26   142
1:10   143, 144, 156, 421
1:14   160
1:15–21   142
1:22   117, 160, 199
1:24   420, 421
1:26   420, 423
1:28   46, 138–39, 421, 422
3:12   65, 421
3:19   399
9:3–4   12
9:4   428
9:6   398, 428
10:14   143, 148
18:20   327
20:6   270
27:17   260
32:23   362
34:25   341
34:31   156, 378
36:27   447
37:12–13   404
37:14   404
43:15–16   39
46:1   443

Hosea
1:2   28
3:5   429
6:7   316
10:2   450

Amos
4:12   424
9:11   429

Jonah
2:1   408
3:10   350

Micah
3:4   231
6:7   73
7:15   23
7:18   419

Habakkuk
3:2   47, 49

Zephaniah
2:3   396
3:9   450

Zechariah
1:16   137
2:5   79
9:9   36
13:2   301, 310, 415, 437
14:9   140, 172, 212, 450

Malachi
3:12   93
3:19   299
3:21   337
3:23   259

Psalms
5:5   290, 321, 355
5:8   74
7:12   53
8:1, 4   9
8:4, 10   7
8:5   27, 133, 215, 325
8:6   18, 97, 167, 230, 258, 265,
           281, 324
8:9   90, 250
9:6   402
9:9   206
9:18   360
11:7   13, 293
11:10   77
16:11   164
17:15   426
18:11   201
18:31   150–51
19:2   53, 57, 59
19:3   58
19:4   58
19:5   58
19:6   53, 59
19:7   59
19:8   59
19:11   422
22:1   22
23:4   323
24:1   393
24:2   394
25:8   15

Psalms, continued

25:14	239, 432
26:2	57
29:3	120, 188
29:5	46
29:10	319
29:11	96
30:13	420
31:6	74, 229
31:20	15, 44, 45, 192, 243, 255, 256
32:1	14, 418
33:6	7, 28, 207, 256
34:8–9	62
34:19	71
35:15	268
36:7	378
36:8	327
39:3	228
39:5	363, 384
41:2	117
42:5	9
42:8	134, 177, 199, 245–46, 287, 346, 356
46:9	332, 333, 342
51:5	435
51:12	87
57:6	403
57:12	312
60:14	326
62:13	419
63:12	173
65:2	228
66:5	332, 342–43
68:18	144
69:29	359, 405
73:26	336
75:7	69
77:20	176, 189
83:19	50, 172
85:14	275, 334, 448
86:11	335
89:3	71
89:10	408
89:15	344–45
89:53	337
90:1	41, 165
90:17	54, 57, 132
91:11	88
92:1	345
92:3	229
92:5	311
94:17	54, 57, 360
97:11	2, 194, 242
98:2	420
99:6	165
100:2	294
101:7	201
103:20	87
104:2	117, 171, 193
104:3	207
104:11	174, 220
104:13	207
104:14	10, 142
104:16	172, 190, 220
104:20	214
104:25	134, 362
104:26	214
104:35	319
106:23	398
106:48	210
110:1	280, 365
111:8	219
111:10	49, 173
112:5	344
116:9	26
116:13	2
118:19	232, 305
118:19–20	50
118:22	155, 426
119:120	360–61
122:3	6
124:5	372
127:4	37
135:4	381
139:12	188
139:17	236, 311
140:14	337
144:15	267
145:7	44
145:9	185, 344
145:14	14

Proverbs

1:1	446
1:7	77
2:17	223
3:18	51, 74, 240, 371
3:19	256
4:18	176, 336, 361
4:19	337
5:5	223
5:8	434

492

5:15	345
5:19	22
6:17	28
7:5	434
7:26	28
8:21	25, 36
8:30	29, 256, 359
10:1	348
10:6	314
10:22	416
10:25	166, 198, 362, 422
11:10	353
16:28	28, 212
18:10	237
19:23	78, 323
22:3	406, 407
22:6	238
23:25	415
24:3	116, 170, 173, 200
25:4	182
25:5, 4	328
28:14	81, 82
30:1	446
30:30	367
31:15	136, 158
31:21	41
31:29	273

Job

3:19	209
4:11	367
5:24	276
10:11	156
12:22	183, 195
14:11	39, 394
21:14	357
26:6	361
26:14	188
28:3	364
28:7	18, 97, 176
28:25	201, 202
28:27	29
33:23	88
33:24	88
38:15	2, 45, 81, 148, 159, 184, 192, 242, 255, 337, 386, 416
38:29	174, 179
38:37	202
40:15	143

Song of Songs

1:2	413
1:5	272
1:6	155
1:7	153–54
1:8	154
1:11	4
1:12	180, 320
2:1	172
2:2	1
2:6	173, 270, 274
2:12	3–4
2:16	375
2:17	174
3:6	68, 143
3:7	234, 235
3:9	170–71
3:11	175, 440
4:3	68
4:12	199, 223, 367
4:13	367
6:2	320
6:11	151
7:6	96

Ruth

2:11–12	92
2:19	95

Lamentations

1:8	271
1:10	351
2:9	15
2:13	6
2:15	6
2:17	351, 352
3:23	133, 146, 147, 286

Ecclesiastes

1:7	147, 172, 178, 203
2:8	151
3:11	117, 171
3:21	301, 302
5:5	54, 57
7:14	57
8:14	320
10:3	334
10:20	214

Esther

5:12	225

Daniel

2:20	445
4:13	95
4:22	95
4:24	95

Daniel, continued
   4:26–27 95
   4:28–29 95
   4:32 67, 78, 331
   6:19 323–24
   7:9 25–26, 76
   7:10 88
   9:21 250
   12:2 405
   12:3 109, 114
   12:13 304, 364, 265

Nehemiah
   9:6 113, 233

1 Chronicles
   11:23 60, 61
   16:27 324
   16:33 47
   17:21 96
   21:16 351
   29:11 190

494

2 Chronicles
   20:21 325

New Testament
1 Corinthians
   13:12 209, 244, 268, 272, 291, 384
Revelation
   1:8 112, 175, 233, 280, 344
   9:11 361
   21:2 52

Pseudepigrapha
3 Enoch
   9:1–2 160
   12:5 160

Targum
  Targum Onqelos
    on Genesis 25:27 439
  Targum Yerushalmi (frag.)
    on Genesis 1:1 17

RABBINIC LITERATURE

Mishnah

Avot
   2:10 371
   3:2 43, 412–13
   3:4 409
   3:6 425, 449
   3:14 29
   3:18 248
   4:4 388, 400
   5:1 109, 122, 180
   5:6 101, 132, 139, 156, 262, 420
   5:7 202
   5:16 80
   5:17 129

Berakhot
   2:2 74
   9:5 81

Eduyyot
   2:10 361, 402

Ḥagigah
   2:1 139, 179, 422

Ketubbot
   4:11 268
   5:6 102, 276

Sanhedrin
   7:1 79
   10:1 205, 337, 339, 405
   10:3 402–3, 405

Shabbat
   19:6 91, 197, 205

Shevu'ot
   4:13 103

Sotah
   9:12 314, 354, 413–14
   9:15 80

Uqtsin
   3:12 36

Zevaḥim
   5:4 68

Tosefta

Ḥagigah
   2:6 215

Babylonian Talmud

Arakhin
   16b 399

Avodah Zarah

3b	26
4a	398
5a	236, 310–11, 349
8a	410
20b	80
24b	420–21
72b	374

Bava Batra

16a	71, 224, 225, 250–51, 288–89, 303, 304, 323, 329, 364, 414
25a	217, 280
58a	273
60a	401
74b	213, 251, 314
89b	78
116a	89, 262, 385–86
121b	7, 250

Bava Metsi'a

84a	224
84b	163
85a–b	21
85b	22
85b–86a	130, 333–34, 446
87a	72

Bava Qamma

55a	184
60a–b	365, 396, 407, 419
82a	86, 252
92b	157
93a	392

Beitsah

16a	264
27a	29

Berakhot

3b	70, 425
4b	28, 74, 90, 214, 250
5a	229
6a	96, 97, 310
6b	31
7b	332–33, 343
8a	27, 136
10a	385
10b	398
11b	84–85
13b	82, 83
14a	275, 335, 448

15b	123, 279, 439
17a	26, 60
18a–b	38, 39, 43
19a	56
26b	74, 162, 427
27b	29
28b	18, 46, 363–64
29b	275, 334–35
31b	165
32a	397
33b	335
34b	26, 38, 255, 337, 386
43b	328
51a	2, 300–301
52b	103
53b	70
55a	61
57b	3, 229, 264, 286, 300
58a	107
59a	23
60b	69
61a	217, 268, 269
61b	80
64a	49, 266

Eruvin

13b	129
18b	52, 150, 302, 308
19a	136, 361
54b	29

Ḥagigah

5b	324
11b	5
12a	2, 45, 61, 79, 81, 120, 121, 148, 159, 184, 192, 226–27, 242–43, 255, 286–87, 297, 386, 416
12b	198, 210, 310, 359, 394
13b	65, 79, 160, 238–39
14a	133, 146, 286
14b	201, 222
15a	37, 201, 328
15a–b	7
16a	38, 139, 263, 309–10, 322, 328, 350, 403, 422

Ḥullin

60b	84, 152, 153, 187, 208, 212, 247, 415, 436
91b	426

495

Ketubbot

17a	18
62b	102, 276
111a	404
111b	282

Makkot

10b	300, 302, 358

Megillah

10b	125, 324, 326, 353
13b	102
27a	423
28b	425
29a	403, 429

Menaḥot

29b	246
43b	239

Mo'ed Qatan

16b	66, 370, 436
28a	381

Nedarim

62a	259

Niddah

13a	321, 355, 404
13b	322, 404
17a	273
24b	357
30b	193
73a	255

Pesaḥim

7a	107
54a	128
56a	322
112a	29, 102, 310
117a	393, 418
119a	60

Qiddushin

30b	130–31
40b	294
70b	226
71a	433
72a	70

Rosh ha-Shanah

11a	232
16a	372
16b	235

17a	361–62
21b	18, 167, 258, 265, 281

Sanhedrin

37b	306
38a	218
38b	133, 215, 221, 223, 316, 325
56a	420
58b	322
65b	228
89b	73
92a–b	87
94b	367
96a	40
97a	281
99b	10, 27
105a	401
107a	55, 435
108a	392, 399
108b	356, 389
110b	339–40

Shabbat

12b	62, 445
30b	276
32b	54
33b	77, 395
55a	327, 386
55b	297, 327–28
56a	55
88a	254, 370
88b	24, 25, 27, 257, 268, 301
104a	216, 300, 301, 321, 358
113b	195
114a	256
119b	4, 256, 360
128a	386
137b	196, 316, 339, 390
145b–146a	229–30, 234, 247, 289, 294, 303, 308, 369, 414–15
151b	95, 150, 418
152a	34, 116, 170, 276, 342

Shevu'ot

36a	103

Sotah

7b	138, 373, 448
9a	354
14a	230
17a	275
22a	28

Sukkah

5b	143, 148
29a	248
49a	181, 316
52a	28, 136–37, 323–24
52b	323
53a–b	183

Ta'anit

8b	27, 120, 377
10a	350, 444
10b	410, 447
25b	287
27b	334

Yevamot

49b	209, 244, 268, 272, 291, 384
60b–61a	156, 378
61a	157
62b	276, 314
63b	89, 144, 314

Yoma

4a	385
20a	372–73
21b	40, 142, 282, 406
35b	422

39a	301–2, 321, 358
54a	143, 200–201
75a	299, 330

Minor Tractates

Avot de-Rabbi Natan, A

16	289

Derekh Erets Rabbah

2, 56a	22

Kallah Rabbati

2	321–22, 333, 355, 356, 399, 403–4

Jerusalem Talmud

Eruvin

5:1, 22b	60

Sanhedrin

10:2, 29a	183

Shevi'it

9:5, 39a	409

Ta'anit

4:4, 68b	148, 208, 247

RABBINIC LITERATURE: MIDRASH

Aggadat Olam Qatan

—	41

Bemidbar Rabbah

12:12	218
13:16	25, 257, 301
14:12	231, 240, 311, 315
19:18	327, 384
22:8	69

Bereshit Rabbah

1:1	29, 256, 359
1:3	133
1:4	4, 186
1:10	176
1:15	118, 182
3:2	123, 184, 242
3:6	192
4:2	124, 136, 199
4:5	202
4:6	131, 135, 202, 245, 253

5:1	137
5:8	83
5:9	229
8:1	94, 186, 187, 217, 236, 253, 267, 314
8:2	11
8:3	216
8:10	230
9:2	117, 171
9:5	254
9:7	269, 349
9:10	100, 254
10:2	182
10:6	211
11:5	104, 360
12:6	297
12:9	19, 20
12:15	333
13:3	267, 376, 392
13:13	134, 177, 199, 245, 287, 346, 356

Bereshit Rabbah, continued

14:9	70, 300
15:1	221, 235, 241
15:6	136, 220
16:5	326
16:6	222, 226, 343
17:5	258
17:6	219
18:1	217, 268
19:2	225
19:4	225
19:5	228
19:7	290, 298, 447
20:2	212
20:5	435
20:11	150, 261, 302, 306–7
20:12	230
21:5	110
21:9	149, 299, 330
22:2	221
22:5	303
24:1	400
25:1	320
25:3	241
26:6	427
30:3	340
30:9	395
32:2	293
32:6	402, 406
33:6	350
34:9	410
36:4	434
38:7	440, 449
38:8	442
38:9	348–49, 443
41:3	194
47:6	155, 235, 346
48:8	54
51:2	232, 376, 448
53:10	72
55:4–5	73
60:16	277
68:12	423
77:3	162, 225
79:6	313
82:2	423
85:7	5
87:7	422

Eikhah Rabbah

1:33	326
2:5	319

Mekhilta

Shirata 3	169, 291
Amaleq (Yitro) 1	59–60
Baḥodesh 3	11
Baḥodesh 7	266

Mekhilta de-Rashbi

Exodus 19:11	169

Midrash ha-Gadol

Genesis 3:24	297
Genesis 7:20	357

Midrash Mishlei

1:1	21
31:14	249, 394

Midrash Tehillim

8:7	90, 250
30:4	419
90:5	165
92:3	345
92:5	103
104:4	193

Pesiqta de-Rav Kahana

4:4	257
5:3	291–92
11:20	30, 352
23:1	232

Pesiqta Rabbati

20	27

Pirqei de-Rabbi Eli'ezer

3	116, 171
9	183, 278
11	94, 417
12	216
13	224, 374
18	129–30
20	312–13, 384
21	223, 230, 231, 234, 303, 305, 308
22	234, 357, 388
23	356, 433
24	437
29	90
34	404
46	72–73, 372
51	443

Qohelet Rabbah

on 1:7	21
on 4:1	149
on 9:10	20

Rut Zuta
1:20   31
4:11   31

Seder Eliyyahu Rabbah
1   297

Shemot Rabbah
6:1   446–47
15:22   200
15:26   368, 427, 437
21:4   238
21:5   405–6
35:1   192
47:4   315–16

Shir ha-Shirim Rabbah
on 1:1 115, 170, 438
on 3:7 94, 417–18
on 3:8 290
on 4:5 102
on 4:11 52
on 8:6 240, 292, 296

Sifra
Vayiqra, dibbura dindavah
2:12, 4a   384
6:9, 7c   411
Behuqqotai
3:3, 111b   347

Sifrei
Numbers
42   450
115   283
Deuteronomy
1   415
338   192
357   240

Tanḥuma
Bereshit 9   306
Bereshit 11   241, 331–32
Noaḥ 5   342
Noaḥ 9   406
Vayishlaḥ 8   225, 409
Va'era 14   331
Ki Tissa 33   104, 264, 3
Vayaqhel 6   134, 318–19, 400
Pequdei 1   6
Pequdei 3   355
Vayiqra 8   4, 44, 189, 210, 255,
                265, 336, 339, 408
Metsora 2   450

Tanḥuma (Buber)
Intro 77b   253
Bereshit 17   101, 132, 156, 262
Bereshit 26   261, 302, 306
Noaḥ 5   400
Noaḥ 18   399
Bo 16   307
Vayaqhel 7   117, 171
Tazri'a 2   213
Metsora 17   266
Naso 24   194
Shelaḥ, add. 1 291, 293, 369–70

Vayiqra Rabbah
2:9   92
6:5   352
7:2   71
7:3   410
12:1   434
16:4   52
22:10   142
24:1   233

499

EARLY JEWISH MYSTICAL LITERATURE

Alfa Beita de-Rabbi Aqiva, Version 2
—   215

Pereq Shirah
2:57   69

Seder Rabbah di-Vreshit
17   183, 278–79

Sefer Yetsirah
1:1–2   172, 177
2:2   396
2:2, 4–5   206, 307
2:4   155
2:6   109, 122, 201
4:12   201

MEDIEVAL JEWISH SOURCES

Azriel of Gerona, *Peirush ha-Aggadot*
39   6

Bahir
17 (25)   123, 184, 242
80 (111)   121, 147
97 (147)   192

Donnolo, Shabbetai, *Sefer Ḥakhmoni*
1:10   256

Gikatilla, Joseph, *Sha'arei Orah*
166   282

Ibn Gabirol, Solomon, *Keter Malkhut*
9:101   109

Ibn Latif, Isaac, *Iggeret ha-Teshuvah*
25   169

Lavi, Shim'on, *Ketem Paz*
1:22d   90, 130, 206, 258, 430
1:91a   123, 174, 179

Maimonides, Moses
Guide of the Perplexed
1:2   63
1:59   107–8
2:30   79, 119, 188
Mishneh Torah, Hilkhot Yesodei ha-Torah
1:1   82
3:2   151

Ma'yan Ḥokhmah
—   22

Moses de León
Mishkan ha-Edut
63b   221
Orḥot Ḥayyim
par. 10   69
Sefer ha-Mishqal
44   156
Sheqel ha-Qodesh
11 (13)   164

Rashi
Song of Songs
7:6   97

Sefer Ḥasidim, ed. Margaliot
par. 371   69
par. 522   37
par. 992   69

Sefer Ḥasidim, ed. Wistinetzki
par. 798   69
par. 1066 69
par. 1945 37

POSTBIBLICAL CHRISTIAN SOURCES

Clement of Alexandria, *Excerpts from Theodotus*
78:2   5, 180

Dionysius, *Mystical Theology*
1:1   107

Gospel of Truth
22:27–29 179, 269, 379

Gregory of Nyssa, *Life of Moses*
2:163   107

OTHER

Dante, *Inferno*
3   362

Faraday, Michael, *Chemical History of a Candle*
—   284

בראשית

בריש הורמנותא דמלכא גליף גליפו בטהירו עלאה בוצינא
דקרדינותא כפיק גו סתים דסתימו מריפא דאין סוף
קוטרא בגולמא כעין בעזקא לא חוור ולא אוכם לא סומק ולא ירוק ולא גוון כלל כד
מדיד משיח עביד גוומין לאכסר' לגו בגו בוציב'כפיק חד כביעו דמכיה אנטבעו גוומין
לתתא סתים גו סתימין מרזא דאין סוף פקע בקע ולא בקע אוירא דיליה לא אתיידע
כלל עד דמגו דמחיקו דבקיעותיה כהיר נקודה חדא סתימא עלאה כתר ההוא נקודה
לא אתיידע כלל ובגין כך אקרי ראשית מאמר קדמאה דכלא

והמשכילים יוהירו כזהר הרקיע ונמ'דיקי הרבים ככבים לעולם
ועד **זהר** סתים' דסתמין בטם אוירא דיליה
דמטי ולא מטי מטי כהאי נקודה וכדין אתפשט האי ראשית ועביד ליה
יקרא להיכליה להונכחתא תמן זרע זרעא לאולדא לתועלתא דעלמא ורזא דא זרע
קדם מנכתה **זהר** דזרע זרע' ליקרו'כהאי זרע'דמשי'דארגוון טב דאתחפי
לגו ועביד ליה היכלא דחיהו תונכחתא דוליה ותועלתא דכלא
בהאי ראשית ברא ההוא סתימא דלא אתיידע להיכלא דא היכלא דא אקרי אלדים
ורזא דא כראשי'ברא אלדי' זהר דמכיה כלהו מחארנן אתבריאו ברזא דאתפטטותא
דנקודיה דזהר סתים דא ז'ר בהאי ברא כתיב ברא לית תונסא דכתיב וכרא אלדים
את האדם כבלמו **זהר** דא בראשית קדמאה דכלא

אריך טמא
קדים גליף בליפ כסטרנו אלדים גליפ בליפא בעיטרא אטל
היכלא טמיר ונכיו טריאותא דרזא דראשי'ית אטל ראט דכפיק מראטטית וכל